EXECUTIVE OFFICE OF THE PRESIDENT
OFFICE OF MANAGEMENT AND BUDGET

North
American
Industry
Classification
System

United States, 2007

Published and for sale by:
CLAITOR'S PUBLISHING DIVISION
P.O. Box 261333, Baton Rouge, LA 70826-1333
800-274-1403 (In LA 225-344-0476)
Fax: 225-344-0480
Internet address:
e mail: claitors@claitors.com
World Wide Web: http://www.claitors.com

*We acknowledge the input and assistance of the U.S. Census Bureau, since much of the
following is extracted from their web site at http://www.census.gov

Foreword

The Instituto Nacional de Estadística, Geografía e Informática (INEGI) of Mexico, Statistics Canada, and the United States Office of Management and Budget, through its Economic Classification Policy Committee, have jointly updated the system of classification of economic activities that makes the industrial statistics produced in the three countries comparable. The North American Industry Classification System (NAICS) revision for 2007 is scheduled to go into effect for reference year 2007 in Canada and the United States, and 2009 in Mexico. NAICS was originally developed to provide a consistent framework for the collection, analysis and dissemination of industrial statistics used by government policy analysts, by academics and researchers, by the business community, and by the public. Revisions for 2007 were made to account for our rapidly changing economies.

Classifications serve as a lens through which to view the data they classify. NAICS is the first industry classification system that was developed in accordance with a single principle of aggregation, the principle that producing units that use similar production processes should be grouped together. NAICS also reflects, in a much more explicit way, the enormous changes in technology and in the growth and diversification of services that have marked recent decades. Though NAICS differs from other industry classification systems, the three countries continue to strive to create industries that do not cross two-digit boundaries of the United Nations' International Standard Industrial Classification of All Economic Activities (ISIC). The 2007 revisions of NAICS and ISIC are expected to increase comparability beyond previous levels.

The actual classification reveals only the tip of the work carried out by dedicated staff from INEGI, Statistics Canada, and U.S. statistical agencies. It is through their efforts, painstaking analysis, and spirit of accommodation that NAICS has emerged as a harmonized international classification of economic activities in North America.

Preface

Statistics Canada, Mexico's Instituto Nacional de Estadística, Geografía e Informática (INEGI), and the Economic Classification Policy Committee (ECPC) of the United States, acting on behalf of the Office of Management and Budget, created a common classification system that replaced the existing classification of each country, the Standard Industrial Classification (1980) of Canada, the Mexican Classification of Activities and Products (1994), and the Standard Industrial Classification (1987) of the United States.

The North American Industry Classification System (NAICS) is unique among industry classifications in that it is constructed within a single conceptual framework. Economic units that have similar production processes are classified in the same industry, and the lines drawn between industries demarcate, to the extent practicable, differences in production processes. This supply-based, or production-oriented, economic concept was adopted for NAICS because an industry classification system is a framework for collecting and publishing information on both inputs and outputs, for statistical uses that require that inputs and outputs be used together and be classified consistently. Examples of such uses include measuring productivity, unit labor costs, and the capital intensity of production, estimating employment-output relationships, constructing input-output tables, and other uses that imply the analysis of production relationships in the economy. The classification concept for NAICS will produce data that facilitate such analyses.

In the design of NAICS, attention was given to developing production-oriented classifications for (a) new and emerging industries, (b) service industries in general, and (c) industries engaged in the production of advanced technologies. These special emphases are embodied in the particular features of NAICS, discussed below. These same areas of special emphasis account for many of the differences between the structure of NAICS and the structures of industry classification systems in use elsewhere. NAICS provides enhanced industry comparability among the three North American Free Trade Agreement (NAFTA) trading partners, while also increasing compatibility with the two-digit level of the International Standard Industrial Classification (ISIC Rev.4) of the United Nations.

NAICS divides the economy into 20 sectors. Industries within these sectors are grouped according to the production criterion. Though the goods/services distinction is not explicitly reflected in the structure of NAICS, four sectors are largely goods-producing and 16 are entirely services-producing industries.

A key feature of NAICS is the Information sector that groups industries that primarily create and disseminate a product subject to copyright. The NAICS Information sector brings together those activities that transform information into a commodity that is produced and distributed, and activities that provide the means for distributing those products, other than through traditional wholesale-retail distribution channels. Industries included in this sector are telecommunications; broadcasting; newspaper, book, and periodical publishing; motion picture and sound recording industries; libraries; and other information services.

Another feature of NAICS is a sector for Professional, Scientific, and Technical Services, that comprises establishments engaged in activities where human capital is the major input. The industries within this sector are each defined by the expertise and training of the service provider. The sector includes such industries as offices of lawyers, engineering services, architectural services, advertising agencies, and interior design services.

A sector for Arts, Entertainment, and Recreation greatly expands the number of industries providing services in these three areas.

Another key sector, Health Care and Social Assistance, recognizes the merging of the boundaries of health care and social assistance. The industries in this sector are arranged in an order that reflects the range and extent of health care and social assistance provided. Some important industries are family planning centers, outpatient mental health and substance abuse centers, and community care facilities for the elderly.

In the Manufacturing sector, an important subsector, Computer and Electronic Product Manufacturing, brings together industries producing electronic products and their components. The manufacturers of computers, communications equipment, and semiconductors, for example, are grouped into the same subsector because of the inherent technological similarities of their production processes, and the likelihood that these technologies will continue to converge in the future. The reproduction of packaged software is placed in this sector, rather than in the services sector, because the reproduction of packaged software is a manufacturing process, and the product moves through the wholesale and retail distribution systems like any other manufactured product. NAICS acknowledges the importance of these electronic industries, their rapid growth over the past several years and the likelihood that these industries will, in the future, become even more important in the economies of the three North American countries.

This NAICS structure reflects the levels at which data comparability was agreed upon by the three statistical agencies. The boundaries of all the sectors of NAICS have been delineated. In most sectors, NAICS provides for comparability at the industry (five-digit) level. However, for real estate, utilities, finance and insurance, and for three of the four subsectors in other services (except public administration), three-country comparability will occur either at the industry group (four-digit) or subsector (three-digit) levels. For these sectors, differences in the economies of the three countries prevent full comparability at the NAICS industry level. For retail trade, wholesale trade, and public administration, the three countries' statistical agencies have agreed, at this time, only on the boundaries of the sector (two-digit level). Below the agreed upon level of comparability, each country may add additional detailed industries, as necessary to meet national needs, provided that this additional detail aggregates to the NAICS level.

The United States has adopted the revised classification in their statistical programs for reference years beginning in 2007. Agencies may adopt the 2007 NAICS earlier at their discretion.

Acknowledgments

This revision of the North American Industry Classification System (NAICS) was an immense undertaking requiring the time, energy, creativity, and cooperation of numerous people and organizations throughout the three countries. The work that has been accomplished is a testament to the individual and collective willingness of many persons and organizations both inside and outside government to contribute to the development of NAICS. Within the United States, NAICS was revised under the guidance of the Office of Management and Budget by the Economic Classification Policy Committee (ECPC). Members of the ECPC were **Dennis Fixler** and **Kenneth Johnson (retired)**, Bureau of Economic Analysis, U.S. Department of Commerce; **Thomas L. Mesenbourg**, and **John B. Murphy (Chair)**, Bureau of the Census, U.S. Department of Commerce; and **George S. Werking (retired)**, Bureau of Labor Statistics, U.S. Department of Labor; and ex officio, **Paul Bugg**, Office of Management and Budget.

The ECPC designated representatives from the three major agencies to coordinate the maintenance and upkeep of the system within the United States, and with Canada and Mexico. Designees from these agencies are **Wanda K. Dougherty**, Bureau of the Census; **David Talan**, Bureau of Labor Statistics; and **Jeffrey H. Lowe**, Bureau of Economic Analysis.

In addition to the parties listed above, OMB would like to acknowledge the dedicated staff of the Economic Classifications Development Branch at the Bureau of the Census. This staff was responsible for researching, summarizing, and making preliminary recommendations to the ECPC for comments received from the public on 2007 NAICS revisions; for preparing documents summarizing the ECPC position for use in negotiations with Canada and Mexico; and for preparing all of the manuscript files for the published manual. It was their hard work and dedication that resulted in this complete documentation of 2007 NAICS United States.

Contents

CONTENTS

EXPLANATION OF SYMBOLS

In NAICS United States Structure

Symbol	Explanation
US	United States industry only.
CAN	United States and Canadian industries are comparable.
MEX	United States and Mexican industries are comparable.
[Blank]	[No superscript symbol] Canadian, Mexican, and United States industries are comparable.

In Part I, Titles and Descriptions

Symbol	Explanation
US	United States industry only.
CAN	United States and Canadian industries are comparable.
MEX	United States and Mexican industries are comparable.
[Blank]	[No superscript symbol] Canadian, Mexican, and United States industries are comparable.

In Appendix A

Symbol	Explanation
US	United States industry only.
CAN	United States and Canadian industries are comparable.
MEX	United States and Mexican industries are comparable.
[Blank]	[No superscript symbol] Canadian, Mexican, and United States industries are comparable.
*	Part of 2002 NAICS United States industry

In Appendix B

Symbol	Explanation
pt	Part of 2007 NAICS United States industry

Introduction

Background

In 1937, the Central Statistical Board established an Interdepartmental Committee on Industrial Classification "to develop a plan of classification of various types of statistical data by industries and to promote the general adoption of such classification as the standard classification of the Federal Government.[1]" The List of Industries for manufacturing was first available in 1938, with the List of Industries for nonmanufacturing following in 1939. These Lists of Industries became the first Standard Industrial Classification (SIC) for the United States.

. The SIC was developed for use in the classification of establishments by type of activity in which they are primarily engaged; for purposes of facilitating the collection, tabulation, presentation, and analysis of data relating to establishments; and for promoting uniformity and comparability in the presentation of statistical data collected by various agencies of the United States Government, State agencies, trade associations, and private research organizations. The SIC covered the entire field of economic activities by defining industries in accordance with the composition and structure of the economy.

Since the inception of the SIC in the 1930s, the system has been periodically revised to reflect the economy's changing industrial composition and organization. The last revision of the SIC was in 1987.

Rapid changes in both the U.S. and world economies brought the SIC under increasing criticism. In 1991, an International Conference on the Classification of Economic Activities was convened in Williamsburg, Virginia, to provide a forum for responding to such criticism and to explore new approaches to classifying economic activity. In July 1992, the Office of Management and Budget (OMB) established the Economic Classification Policy Committee (ECPC) and charged it with a "fresh slate" examination of economic classifications for statistical purposes. The ECPC prepared a number of issue papers regarding classification, consulted with outside users, and ultimately joined with Mexico's Instituto Nacional de Estadística, Geografía e Informática (INEGI) and Statistics Canada to develop the North American Industry Classification System (NAICS), that replaced the 1987 U.S. SIC and the classification systems of Canada (1980 SIC) and Mexico (1994 Mexican Classification of Activities and Products (CMAP)).

The dynamic nature of world economies continues to affect classification systems. The creators of NAICS agreed that the classification system should be reviewed every five years, and revised as appropriate to reflect the changing economies of the three countries. The U.S. statistical programs implemented NAICS for the first time in 1997. NAICS was revised in 2002. This 2007 NAICS

---

[1] Pearce, Esther, History of the Standard Industrial Classification, Executive Office of the President, Office of Statistical Standards, U.S. Bureau of the Budget, Washington, DC, July 1957 (mimeograph).

revision was undertaken to achieve one main goal—to modify or create industries to reflect new, emerging, or changing activities and technologies. To that end, the Telecommunications subsector and other areas in the Information sector have been revised to reflect the ever-changing activities of these industries. In addition, in the United States, new industries were created for research and development in biotechnology and executive search services.

The impact of NAICS on various countries has brought about a renewed effort for additional convergence with the many industry classifications used throughout the world. Future revisions of NAICS will continue to strive for greater global comparability.

Purpose of NAICS

NAICS is an industry classification system that groups establishments into industries based on the similarity of their production processes. It is a comprehensive system covering all economic activities. There are 20 sectors and 1,175 industries in 2007 NAICS United States.

NAICS was initially developed and subsequently revised by Mexico's INEGI, Statistics Canada, and the U.S. ECPC (the latter acting on behalf of OMB) to provide common industry definitions for Canada, Mexico, and the United States that will facilitate economic analyses of the economies of the three North American countries. The statistical agencies in the three countries produce information on inputs and outputs, industrial performance, productivity, unit labor costs, and employment. NAICS, which is based on a production-oriented concept, ensures maximum usefulness of industrial statistics for these and similar purposes.

NAICS United States is used by U.S. statistical agencies to facilitate the collection, tabulation, presentation, and analysis of data relating to establishments; and to provide uniformity and comparability in the presentation of statistical data describing the U.S. economy. NAICS United States is designed for statistical purposes. Although the classification also may be used for various administrative, regulatory, and taxation purposes, the requirements of government agencies that use it for nonstatistical purposes played no role in its development or subsequent revision.

Development of NAICS as a Replacement for the U.S. SIC

The U.S. ECPC established by OMB in 1992 was chaired by the Bureau of Economic Analysis, U.S. Department of Commerce, with representatives from the Bureau of the Census, U.S. Department of Commerce, and the Bureau of Labor Statistics, U.S. Department of Labor. The ECPC was asked to examine economic classifications for statistical purposes and to determine the desirability of developing a new industry classification system for the United States based on a single economic concept. On March 31, 1993, OMB published a **Federal Register** notice

(58FR16990-17004) announcing the intention to revise the SIC for 1997, the establishment of the ECPC, and the process for revising the SIC.

In July 1994, the OMB announced plans to develop a new industry classification system in cooperation with Mexico's INEGI and Statistics Canada. The new system—NAICS—replaced the U.S. SIC. The concepts of the new system and the principles upon which NAICS was to be developed were announced in a July 26, 1994 **Federal Register** notice (59FR38092-38096) and were as follows:

1. NAICS will be erected on a production-oriented or supply-based conceptual framework. This means that producing units that use identical or similar production processes will be grouped together in NAICS.

2. The system will give special attention to developing production-oriented classifications for (a) new and emerging industries, (b) service industries in general, and (c) industries engaged in the production of advanced technologies.

3. Time series continuity will be maintained to the extent possible. However, changes in the economy and proposals from data users must be considered. In addition, adjustments will be required for sectors where the United States, Canada, and Mexico have incompatible industry classification definitions in order to produce a common industry system for all three North American countries.

4. The system will strive for compatibility with the two-digit level of the International Standard Industrial Classification of All Economic Activities (ISIC, Rev. 3) of the United Nations.

The structure of NAICS was developed in a series of meetings among the three countries. Public proposals for individual industries from all three countries were considered for acceptance if the proposed industry was based on the production-oriented concept of the system. In the United States, public comments also were solicited as groups of subsectors of NAICS were completed and agreed upon by the three countries. The ECPC published the proposed industries for those subsectors in a series of five successive **Federal Register** notices, in 1995 and 1996, asking for comments from interested data users.

Revision of NAICS for 2007

OMB published a notification of potential revision to NAICS for 2007 in a December 27, 2002 **Federal Register** notice (FR 67 79500-79506). This notice solicited comments on: 1) the relative priority to be assigned to each of the four underlying principles of NAICS; 2) three potential goals for NAICS revision and their relative importance; and 3) new and emerging industries for consideration in potential revisions to NAICS for 2007.

After considering all proposals from the public, consulting with a number of U.S. data users and industry groups, and undertaking extensive discussions with Statistics Canada and Mexico's Instituto Nacional de Estadística, Geografía e

Informática (INEGI), the ECPC formulated a set of recommendations for revisions to NAICS for 2007. OMB published a solicitation of public comments on these recommendations in a March 11, 2005 **Federal Register** notice (FR 70 12390-12399). After reviewing comments to that notice and conducting further consultation with data users and industry groups, OMB decided to adopt the ECPC recommendations presented in the March 11, 2005 notice, with the exception of treatment of real estate investment trusts (REITs). In the final decision, NAICS 525930, Real Estate Investment Trusts, was deleted from the classification and portions reclassified as follows: 1) Equity REITs were classified in the Real Estate Subsector in NAICS Industry Group 5311, Lessors of Real Estate, under individual national industries based on the content of the portfolio of real estate operated by a particular REIT; and (2) Mortgage REITs remained classified in the Finance Sector but were moved from NAICS 525930 to NAICS 525990, Other Financial Vehicles. In addition, OMB decided to accept a recommendation from the public to revise the title of Industry 561422 from 'Telemarketing Bureaus' to 'Telemarketing Bureaus and Other Contact Centers.' OMB published a notice of final decisions regarding NAICS revisions for 2007 in a May 16, 2006 Federal Register notice (FR 71 28532-28533).

Conceptual Framework

NAICS is erected on a production-oriented or supply-based conceptual framework that groups establishments into industries according to similarity in the processes used to produce goods or services. A production-oriented industry classification system ensures that statistical agencies in the three countries can produce information on inputs and outputs, industrial performance, productivity, unit labor costs, employment, and other statistics and structural changes occurring in each of the three economies.

When an industry is defined on a production-oriented concept, producing units within the industry's boundaries share a basic production process; they use closely similar technology. In the language of economics, producing units within an industry share the same production functions; producing units in different industries have different production functions. The boundaries between industries thus demarcate, in principle, differences in production processes and production technologies.

The reasoning behind the three countries' decision to base NAICS on a production-oriented concept is summarized as follows: An industry is a grouping of economic activities. Though it inevitably groups the products of the economic activities that are included in the industry definition, it is not solely a grouping of products; put another way, an industry groups producing units. Accordingly, an industry classification system provides a framework for collecting data on inputs and outputs together.

The uses of economic data that require that data on inputs and outputs be used together and be collected on the same basis, include production analyses, productivity measurement, and studying input usage and input intensities. The North American statistical agencies developed NAICS using a production-oriented concept as the framework for two reasons: (1) an industry classification system groups producing units, not products or services; and (2) groupings of producing units permit the collection of data on inputs and outputs on a comparable basis, which is required for production-oriented analysis, but do not facilitate a comprehensive collection of data on the total output of any particular good or service, which is required for market-oriented analysis. Thus, the efficient organizing concept of an industry classification system is production-oriented rather than market-oriented.

Structure of NAICS

The structure of NAICS is hierarchical. The first two digits of the structure designate the NAICS sectors that represent general categories of economic activities.

NAICS classifies all economic activities into 20 sectors. The NAICS sectors, their two-digit codes, and the distinguishing activities of each are:

11 Agriculture, Forestry, Fishing and Hunting—Activities of this sector are growing crops, raising animals, harvesting timber, and harvesting fish and other animals from farms, ranches, or the animals' natural habitats.

21 Mining, Quarrying, and Oil and Gas Extraction—Activities of this sector are extracting naturally occurring mineral solids, such as coal and ore; liquid minerals, such as crude petroleum; and gases, such as natural gas; and beneficiating (e.g., crushing, screening, washing, and flotation) and other preparation at the mine site, or as part of mining activity.

22 Utilities—Activities of this sector are generating, transmitting, and/or distributing electricity, gas, steam, and water and removing sewage through a permanent infrastructure of lines, mains, and pipe.

23 Construction—Activities of this sector are erecting buildings and other structures (including additions); heavy construction other than buildings; and alterations, reconstruction, installation, and maintenance and repairs.

31-33 Manufacturing—Activities of this sector are the mechanical, physical, or chemical transformation of material, substances, or components into new products.

42 Wholesale Trade—Activities of this sector are selling or arranging for the purchase or sale of goods for resale; capital or durable nonconsumer goods; and raw and intermediate materials and supplies used in production, and providing services incidental to the sale of the merchandise.

44-45 Retail Trade—Activities of this sector are retailing merchandise generally in small quantities to the general public and providing services incidental to the sale of the merchandise.

48-49 Transportation and Warehousing—Activities of this sector are providing transportation of passengers and cargo, warehousing and storing goods, scenic and sightseeing transportation, and supporting these activities.

51 Information—Activities of this sector are distributing information and cultural products, providing the means to transmit or distribute these products as data or communications, and processing data.

52 Finance and Insurance—Activities of this sector involve the creation, liquidation, or change in ownership of financial assets (financial transactions) and/or facilitating financial transactions.

53 Real Estate and Rental and Leasing—Activities of this sector are renting, leasing, or otherwise allowing the use of tangible or intangible assets (except copyrighted works), and providing related services.

54 Professional, Scientific, and Technical Services—Activities of this sector are performing professional, scientific, and technical services for the operations of other organizations.

55 Management of Companies and Enterprises—Activities of this sector are the holding of securities of companies and enterprises, for the purpose of owning controlling interest or influencing their management decisions, or administering, overseeing, and managing other establishments of the same company or enterprise and normally undertaking the strategic or organizational planning and decision making of the company or enterprise.

56 Administrative and Support and Waste Management and Remediation Services—Activities of this sector are performing routine support activities for the day-to-day operations of other organizations.

61 Educational Services—Activities of this sector are providing instruction and training in a wide variety of subjects.

62 Health Care and Social Assistance—Activities of this sector are providing health care and social assistance for individuals.

71 Arts, Entertainment, and Recreation—Activities of this sector are operating or providing services to meet varied cultural, entertainment, and recreational interests of their patrons.

72 Accommodation and Food Services—Activities of this sector are providing customers with lodging and/or preparing meals, snacks, and beverages for immediate consumption.

81 Other Services (except Public Administration)—Activities of this sector are providing services not elsewhere specified, including repairs, religious activities, grantmaking, advocacy, laundry, personal care, death care, and other personal services.

92 Public Administration—Activities of this sector are administration, management, and oversight of public programs by Federal, State, and local governments.

NAICS uses a six-digit coding system to identify particular industries and their placement in this hierarchical structure of the classification system. The first two digits of the code designate the sector, the third designates the subsector, the fourth digit designates the industry group, the fifth digit designates the NAICS industry, and the sixth digit designates the national industry. A zero as the sixth digit generally indicates that the NAICS industry and the U.S. industry are the same.

The subsectors, industry groups, and NAICS industries, in accord with the conceptual principle of NAICS, are production-oriented combinations of establishments. However, the production distinctions become more narrowly defined as one moves down the hierarchy.

NAICS agreements permit each country to designate detailed industries, below the level of a NAICS industry, to meet national needs. The United States has such industry detail in many places in the classification system to recognize large, important U.S. industries that cannot be recognized in the other countries because of size, specialization, or organization of the industry.

Typically the level at which comparable data will be available for Canada, Mexico, and the United States is the five-digit NAICS industry; for some sectors (or subsectors or industry groups) however, the three countries agreed upon the boundaries at a higher level of detail rather than the detailed industry structure (five-digit). Agreement was reached at the sector level for utilities; wholesale trade; retail trade; and public administration and at the subsector level for finance; personal and laundry services; religious, grantmaking, civic, and professional and similar organizations; and waste management and remediation services. For insurance and real estate, the three countries agreed on comparability at the industry group level.

Differences in the economies of the three countries or time constraints necessitated establishing comparability at a higher level of detail for the sectors noted above. For each of these sectors, except wholesale trade and public administration, Canada and the United States have agreed upon an industry structure and hierarchy to ensure comparability of statistics between those two countries. Canada and the United States also have established the same national detail (six-digit) industries where possible, adopting the same codes to describe comparable industries. For this reason, the numbers of the U.S. industries may not be consecutive. In a few cases, it was necessary for the United States to use all of the numbers available to establish its six-digit detail so that the same six-digit codes do not necessarily represent comparable industries in the U.S. and Canada.

NAICS with U.S. detail will be known as NAICS United States (denoted by "US" in Appendix A and a superscript "US" at the end of the title in Part I) while Canada and Mexico will produce six-digit detail and will publish that detail as NAICS Canada and NAICS (SCIAN in Spanish) Mexico.

Definition of an Establishment

NAICS is a classification system for establishments. The establishment as a statistical unit is defined as the smallest operating entity for which records provide information on the cost of resources—materials, labor, and capital—employed to produce the units of output. The output may be sold to other establishments and receipts or sales recorded, or the output may be provided without explicit charge, that is, the good or service may be "sold" within the company itself.

The establishment, in NAICS United States, is generally a single physical location, where business is conducted or where services or industrial operations are performed (for example, a factory, mill, store, hotel, movie theater, mine, farm, airline terminal, sales office, warehouse, or central administrative office). There are cases where records identify distinct and separate economic activities performed at a single physical location (e.g., shops in a hotel). These retailing activities, operated out of the same physical location as the hotel, are identified as separate establishments and classified in retail trade while the hotel is classified in accommodations. In such cases, each activity is treated as a separate establishment provided: (1) no one industry description in the classification includes such combined activities; (2) separate reports can be prepared on the number of employees, their wages and salaries, sales or receipts, and expenses; and (3) employment and output are significant for both activities.

Exceptions to the single location exist for physically dispersed operations, such as construction, transportation, and telecommunications. For these activities the individual sites, projects, fields, networks, lines, or systems of such dispersed activities are not normally considered to be establishments. The establishment is represented by those relatively permanent main or branch offices, terminals, stations, and so forth, that are either (1) directly responsible for supervising such activities, or (2) the base from which personnel operate to carry out these activities.

Although an establishment may be identical with the enterprise (company), the two terms should not be confused. An enterprise (company) may consist of more than one establishment. Such multiunit enterprises may have establishments in more than one industry in NAICS. If such enterprises have a separate establishment primarily engaged in providing headquarters services, these establishments are classified in NAICS Sector 55, Management of Companies and Enterprises.

Although all establishments have output, they may or may not have receipts. In large enterprises it is not unusual for establishments to exist that solely serve other establishments of the same enterprise (auxiliary establishments). In such cases, these units often do not collect receipts from the establishments they serve. This type of support (captive) activity is found throughout the economy and involves goods producing activities as well as services. Units that carry out support activities for the enterprise to which they belong are classified, to the extent feasible, according to the NAICS code related to their own activity. This means that warehouses providing storage facilities for their own enterprise will be classified as a warehouse. For certain analytical purposes, an alternative code may be assigned corresponding to the activity of the enterprise that they support.

Determining an Establishment's Industry Classification

An establishment is classified to an industry when its primary activity meets the definition for that industry. Because establishments may perform more than one activity, it is necessary to determine procedures for identifying the primary activity of the establishment.

In most cases, if an establishment is engaged in more than one activity, the industry code is assigned based on the establishment's principal product or group of products produced or distributed, or services rendered. Ideally, the principal good or service should be determined by its relative share of current production costs and capital investment at the establishment. In practice, however, it is often necessary to use other variables such as revenue, shipments, or employment as proxies for measuring significance.

There are two types of combined activities that are given special attention in NAICS. They are vertical integration and joint production. These combined activities have an economic basis and occur in both goods-producing and services-producing sectors. In some cases, there are efficiencies to be gained from combining certain activities in the same establishment. Some of these combinations occur so commonly or frequently that their combination can be treated as a third activity in its own right and explicitly classified in a specific industry.

One approach to classifying these activities would be to use the primary activity rule, that is, whichever activity is largest. However, the fundamental principle of NAICS is that establishments that employ the same production process should be classified in the same industry. If the premise that the combined activities correspond to a distinct third activity is accepted, then using the primary activity rule would place establishments performing the same combination of activities in different industries, thereby violating the production principle of NAICS. A second reason for NAICS recognizing combined activities is to improve the stability of establishment classification, both over time and among the various agencies that implement the classification. An establishment should remain classified in the same industry unless its production process changes, and different agencies should code the same establishment or type of establishment in the same way. A consistent treatment of establishments with combined activities is more likely if they are classified to a single industry.

Vertical integration involves consecutive stages of fabrication or production processes in which the output of one step is the input of the next. In general, establishments will be classified based on the final process in a vertically integrated production environment, unless specifically identified as classified in another industry. For example, paper may be produced either by establishments that first produce pulp and then consume that pulp to produce paper or by those establishments producing paper from purchased pulp. NAICS specifically specifies that both of these types of paper-producing processes should be classified in NAICS 32212, Paper Mills, the industry, or the final step in paper manufacturing, rather than in NAICS 32211, Pulp Mills. In other cases, NAICS specifies that vertically integrated establishments be classified in the industry representing the first stage of the manufacturing process. For example, steel mills that make steel and also perform other activities such as producing steel castings are classified in NAICS 33111, Iron and Steel Mills and Ferroalloy Manufacturing, the first stage of the manufacturing process.

The joint production of goods or services represents the second type of combined activities. For example, automobile dealers both sell and repair autos; automotive parts dealers may both sell parts and repair automobiles; and musical instrument stores may both sell and rent instruments. In the manufacturing sector, establishments may make two different products such as women's dresses and women's suits, activities that are classified in two different NAICS United States detailed industries. In general, receipts/sales and revenue data are used as a proxy to determine primary activity for these establishments. The assumption is that the activity generating the most receipts is also the activity using the most resources and most indicative of the production process.

In some cases, however, these combined activities have been assigned to a specific NAICS industry. Most of these activities involve either the sale and repair of goods or the sale and rental of goods in the same establishment. For example, establishments that both sell automobile parts and repair automobiles are classified in NAICS 44131, Automotive Parts and Accessories Stores, and those music stores that both sell and rent musical instruments are classified in NAICS 45114, Musical Instrument and Supplies Stores. In other cases, specific industries have been identified for these combined activities, such as NAICS 44711, Gasoline Stations with Convenience Stores.

Classification rules related to the agreement to permit individual country detail at the six-digit level for NAICS sometimes results in less comparable NAICS industries at the five-digit level and above. For example in NAICS, the assignment of the industry code is at the most detailed level of the classification (the six-digit U.S. detail code), except for agriculture. That is, if the value of an establishment's production consists of 30 percent from computers, 30 percent from computer storage devices, and 40 percent from semiconductors and related devices, it will be classified in U.S. detail industry 334413, Semiconductor and Related Device Manufacturing, that will be aggregated to NAICS 33441, Semiconductor and Other Electronic Component Manufacturing, the level that comparable information is shown for all three countries. If the classification for the above example were at the five-digit NAICS level, that establishment would be classified in NAICS 33411, Computer and Peripheral Equipment Manufacturing. There would then be more comparable information at the NAICS level, but it would be impossible to classify this establishment to a U.S. detail six-digit industry.

In agriculture, however, NAICS coding begins at the top of the structure and continues down to the most detailed level (the six-digit U.S. detail code). The existence of a 50 percent rule in agriculture and the presence of combination industries based on families of related agricultural products with none accounting for 50 percent or more of production require a top down coding procedure rather than coding at the most detailed level first as is done in the balance of the classification.

Use of Reporting Units Other than Establishments

NAICS is based on the economic principle that establishments should be grouped together based on their production processes. The NAICS definition of the establishment ensures that, at some level, "establishments": (1) identify the most refined (generally smallest) individual entity possible; (2) can provide the information needed when surveying economic activity; and (3) when aggregated, approximate the statistical universe of economic activity. Each economic survey program, in practice, will need to determine whether the establishment is the most appropriate reporting unit to meet the three criteria listed above with respect to the program's objectives. If not, an alternative reporting unit may have to be identified.

For example, an economic survey of employment or wage data may choose the establishment—generally a physical location—as the reporting unit. Physical locations generally have records for the number of employees and their wages readily available. Therefore, it is reasonable to expect that separate wage and employment data would be available to each switching station in a multiunit telecommunications carrier enterprise and the physical location is a logical choice for the reporting unit.

If the economic survey collects output data, the individual switching stations would not have the total number of telephone calls or a complete accounting of inputs and outputs of the multiunit telecommunications carrier. If a telephone call is routed through three different switching stations and the price is determined at a fourth location, all of the related locations would need to be merged into an alternative reporting unit to measure the volume and value of the output. In this case, the physical location would not be an appropriate reporting unit. The level of aggregation of physical units required to create reporting units will vary greatly depending on the business activity being studied. To efficiently define reporting units, statistical surveys need to evaluate the characteristics of the activities being studied and the organizational structure of the entities producing goods or services. In some cases, the physical location is appropriate, sometimes units will need to be grouped based on homogeneous production characteristics or geographical groupings, and in other cases, the enterprise (company) may form the most appropriate reporting unit.

The practical variation in reporting unit definitions affects comparability of data. A count of units defined as physical locations will be different from a count of units defined based on the need for complete input and output records in the telecommunications industries. It is critical that each data provider clearly identify the reporting unit definition used when presenting summary statistics. The analysis of statistical data from a variety of sources requires the transparency of clearly defined reporting units.

While the reporting unit definition can vary, NAICS is a classification system for establishments, and is based on grouping establishments with similar production function characteristics.

Comparison of NAICS to the International Standard Industrial Classification of All Economic Activities (ISIC)

Recognizing the need for international comparability of economic statistics, the United Nations (UN) first adopted an International Standard Industrial Classification system in 1948. Revisions to the ISIC structure and codes were adopted by the UN's Statistical Commission in 1958, 1968, 1989 with an additional update in 2002.[2] A fourth revision will be released for 2007.

Similar to NAICS, ISIC was designed primarily to provide classifications for grouping activities (rather than enterprises or firms), and the primary focus for the ISIC classification system is the kind of activity in which establishments or other statistical entities are engaged. The main criteria employed in delineating divisions and groups (the two- and three-digit categories, respectively) of ISIC are: (a) the character of the goods and services produced; (b) the uses to which the goods and services are put; and (c) the inputs, the process, and the technology of production.

The third classification criterion of the ISIC is the conceptual foundation of NAICS, and thus, NAICS is aligned more closely with ISIC than was the 1987 SIC system. However, there are differences between the NAICS and ISIC classification schemes. Most important, perhaps, is the single (production process) conceptual framework of NAICS. As noted elsewhere, this is unique among industry classifications.

ISIC Rev. 4 groups economic activity into 21 broad Sections, 88 Divisions, 238 Groups, and 420 Classes. In the coding system, Sections are distinguished by the letters A through U and the Divisions, Groups, and Classes are identified as the two-digit, three-digit, and four-digit groupings, respectively. As was the case with NAICS, the most recent revision of ISIC also focused on improvements to the detail in services sections.

In the development and subsequent revision of NAICS industries, the statistical agencies of the three countries strove to create industries that did not cross ISIC two-digit boundaries. The latest revisions of the NAICS and ISIC are expected to increase comparability beyond previous levels. While the final ISIC Rev. 4 manual was not available at the time of this writing, continuing efforts are underway to list in concordance form the differences between the latest versions of NAICS and ISIC.

---

[2] International Standard Industrial Classification of all Economic Activities, Statistical Papers, Series M, No. 4, United Nations, Lake Success, 1948, International Standard Industrial Classification of All Economic Activities, Statistical Papers, Series M, No. 4, Rev. 1, United Nations, New York, 1958, International Standard Industrial Classification of All Economic Activities, Statistical Papers, Series M, No. 4, Rev. 2, United Nations, New York, 1968. International Standard Industrial Classification of All Economic Activities, Statistical Papers, Series M, No. 4., Rev. 3, United Nations, New York, 1990. International Standard Industrial Classification of All Economic Activities, Statistical Papers, Series M., No. 4, Rev. 3.1, United Nations, New York, 2002.

2007 NAICS United States Structure

The following page contains a summary table of the 2007 NAICS United States structure. This table shows the counts of subsectors, industry groups, industries, and United States detail industries for each of the NAICS sectors.

Following the summary table is a complete listing of the 2007 NAICS United States structure. This list displays the codes and official full titles for the sectors, subsectors, industry groups, industries, and United States detail industries. It also indicates the comparability of the codes with NAICS Canada and NAICS Mexico.

Part II of this manual contains a list of short titles that are recommended for use when space limitations preclude the use of the full titles for the dissemination of data classified to NAICS.

2007 NAICS United States Structure

Sector	Name	Sub-sectors (3-digit)	Industry Groups (4-digit)	NAICS Industries (5-digit)	6-digit Industries		
					U.S. Detail	Same as 5-digit	Total
11	Agriculture, Forestry, Fishing and Hunting	5	19	42	32	32	64
21	Mining, Quarrying, and Oil and Gas Extraction	3	5	10	28	1	29
22	Utilities	1	3	6	6	4	10
23	Construction	3	10	28	4	27	31
31-33	Manufacturing	21	86	184	407	65	472
42	Wholesale Trade	3	19	71	0	71	71
44-45	Retail Trade	12	27	61	24	51	75
48-49	Transportation and Warehousing	11	29	42	25	32	57
51	Information	6	12	27	10	22	32
52	Finance and Insurance	5	11	31	15	26	41
53	Real Estate and Rental and Leasing	3	8	19	9	15	24
54	Professional, Scientific, and Technical Services	1	9	35	19	29	48
55	Management of Companies and Enterprises	1	1	1	3	0	3
56	Administrative and Support and Waste Management and Remediation Services	2	11	29	25	19	44
61	Educational Services	1	7	12	7	10	17
62	Health Care and Social Assistance	4	18	30	16	23	39
71	Arts, Entertainment, and Recreation	3	9	23	3	22	25
72	Accommodation and Food Services	2	7	11	7	8	15
81	Other Services (except Public Administration)	4	14	30	30	19	49
92	Public Administration	8	8	29	0	29	29
	Total	99	313	721	670	505	1175

11   Agriculture, Forestry, Fishing and Hunting

111   Crop Production

1111   Oilseed and Grain Farming

11111	Soybean Farming
111110	Soybean Farming
11112	Oilseed (except Soybean) Farming
111120	Oilseed (except Soybean) Farming[CAN]
11113	Dry Pea and Bean Farming
111130	Dry Pea and Bean Farming[CAN]
11114	Wheat Farming
111140	Wheat Farming
11115	Corn Farming
111150	Corn Farming[CAN]
11116	Rice Farming
111160	Rice Farming
11119	Other Grain Farming
111191	Oilseed and Grain Combination Farming[US]
111199	All Other Grain Farming[US]

1112   Vegetable and Melon Farming

11121	Vegetable and Melon Farming
111211	Potato Farming[CAN]
111219	Other Vegetable (except Potato) and Melon Farming[CAN]

1113   Fruit and Tree Nut Farming

11131	Orange Groves
111310	Orange Groves
11132	Citrus (except Orange) Groves
111320	Citrus (except Orange) Groves[CAN]
11133	Noncitrus Fruit and Tree Nut Farming
111331	Apple Orchards[US]
111332	Grape Vineyards[US]
111333	Strawberry Farming[US]
111334	Berry (except Strawberry) Farming[US]
111335	Tree Nut Farming[US]
111336	Fruit and Tree Nut Combination Farming[US]
111339	Other Noncitrus Fruit Farming[US]

1114   Greenhouse, Nursery, and Floriculture Production

11141	Food Crops Grown Under Cover
111411	Mushroom Production[CAN]
111419	Other Food Crops Grown Under Cover[CAN]
11142	Nursery and Floriculture Production

115 Support Activities for Agriculture and Forestry

1151 Support Activities for Crop Production

- 11511   Support Activities for Crop Production
- 115111   Cotton Ginning[US]
- 115112   Soil Preparation, Planting, and Cultivating[US]
- 115113   Crop Harvesting, Primarily by Machine[US]
- 115114   Postharvest Crop Activities (except Cotton Ginning)[US]
- 115115   Farm Labor Contractors and Crew Leaders[US]
- 115116   Farm Management Services[US]

1152 Support Activities for Animal Production

- 11521   Support Activities for Animal Production
- 115210   Support Activities for Animal Production

1153 Support Activities for Forestry

- 11531   Support Activities for Forestry
- 115310   Support Activities for Forestry

21   Mining, Quarrying, and Oil and Gas Extraction

211 Oil and Gas Extraction

2111   Oil and Gas Extraction

- 21111   Oil and Gas Extraction
- 211111   Crude Petroleum and Natural Gas Extraction[US]
- 211112   Natural Gas Liquid Extraction[US]

212 Mining (except Oil and Gas)

2121   Coal Mining

- 21211   Coal Mining
- 212111   Bituminous Coal and Lignite Surface Mining[US]
- 212112   Bituminous Coal Underground Mining[US]
- 212113   Anthracite Mining[US]

2122   Metal Ore Mining

- 21221   Iron Ore Mining
- 212210   Iron Ore Mining
- 21222   Gold Ore and Silver Ore Mining
- 212221   Gold Ore Mining[MEX]
- 212222   Silver Ore Mining[MEX]
- 21223   Copper, Nickel, Lead, and Zinc Mining
- 212231   Lead Ore and Zinc Ore Mining[CAN]
- 212234   Copper Ore and Nickel Ore Mining[US]
- 21229   Other Metal Ore Mining

212291   Uranium-Radium-Vanadium Ore Mining[CAN]
212299   All Other Metal Ore Mining[CAN]

2123   Nonmetallic Mineral Mining and Quarrying

21231   Stone Mining and Quarrying
212311   Dimension Stone Mining and Quarrying[US]
212312   Crushed and Broken Limestone Mining and Quarrying[US]
212313   Crushed and Broken Granite Mining and Quarrying[US]
212319   Other Crushed and Broken Stone Mining and Quarrying[US]
21232   Sand, Gravel, Clay, and Ceramic and Refractory Minerals Mining and Quarrying
212321   Construction Sand and Gravel Mining[MEX]
212322   Industrial Sand Mining[US]
212324   Kaolin and Ball Clay Mining[US]
212325   Clay and Ceramic and Refractory Minerals Mining[US]
21239   Other Nonmetallic Mineral Mining and Quarrying
212391   Potash, Soda, and Borate Mineral Mining[US]
212392   Phosphate Rock Mining[US]
212393   Other Chemical and Fertilizer Mineral Mining[US]
212399   All Other Nonmetallic Mineral Mining[US]

213 Support Activities for Mining

2131   Support Activities for Mining

21311   Support Activities for Mining
213111   Drilling Oil and Gas Wells
213112   Support Activities for Oil and Gas Operations[US]
213113   Support Activities for Coal Mining[US]
213114   Support Activities for Metal Mining[US]
213115   Support Activities for Nonmetallic Minerals (except Fuels) Mining[US]

22   Utilities

221 Utilities[CAN]

2211   Electric Power Generation, Transmission and Distribution

22111   Electric Power Generation[CAN]
221111   Hydroelectric Power Generation[CAN]
221112   Fossil Fuel Electric Power Generation[CAN]
221113   Nuclear Electric Power Generation[CAN]
221119   Other Electric Power Generation[CAN]

22112	Electric Power Transmission, Control, and Distribution[CAN]
221121	Electric Bulk Power Transmission and Control[CAN]
221122	Electric Power Distribution[CAN]

2212 Natural Gas Distribution[CAN]

| 22121 | Natural Gas Distribution[CAN] |
| 221210 | Natural Gas Distribution[CAN] |

2213 Water, Sewage and Other Systems[CAN]

22131	Water Supply and Irrigation Systems[CAN]
221310	Water Supply and Irrigation Systems[CAN]
22132	Sewage Treatment Facilities[CAN]
221320	Sewage Treatment Facilities[CAN]
22133	Steam and Air-Conditioning Supply[CAN]
221330	Steam and Air-Conditioning Supply[CAN]

23 Construction

236 Construction of Buildings

2361 Residential Building Construction

23611	Residential Building Construction
236115	New Single-Family Housing Construction (except Operative Builders)[US]
236116	New Multifamily Housing Construction (except Operative Builders)[US]
236117	New Housing Operative Builders [US]
236118	Residential Remodelers [US]

2362 Nonresidential Building Construction

23621	Industrial Building Construction
236210	Industrial Building Construction[CAN]
23622	Commercial and Institutional Building Construction
236220	Commercial and Institutional Building Construction[CAN]

237 Heavy and Civil Engineering Construction

2371 Utility System Construction

23711	Water and Sewer Line and Related Structures Construction
237110	Water and Sewer Line and Related Structures Construction[CAN]
23712	Oil and Gas Pipeline and Related Structures Construction

237120	Oil and Gas Pipeline and Related Structures Construction[CAN]
23713	Power and Communication Line and Related Structures Construction
237130	Power and Communication Line and Related Structures Construction[CAN]

2372　Land Subdivision

23721	Land Subdivision
237210	Land Subdivision[CAN]

2373　Highway, Street, and Bridge Construction

23731	Highway, Street, and Bridge Construction
237310	Highway, Street, and Bridge Construction[CAN]

2379　Other Heavy and Civil Engineering Construction

23799	Other Heavy and Civil Engineering Construction
237990	Other Heavy and Civil Engineering Construction[CAN]

238　Specialty Trade Contractors

2381　Foundation, Structure, and Building Exterior Contractors

23811	Poured Concrete Foundation and Structure Contractors[CAN]
238110	Poured Concrete Foundation and Structure Contractors[CAN]
23812	Structural Steel and Precast Concrete Contractors
238120	Structural Steel and Precast Concrete Contractors[CAN]
23813	Framing Contractors[CAN]
238130	Framing Contractors[CAN]
23814	Masonry Contractors[CAN]
238140	Masonry Contractors[CAN]
23815	Glass and Glazing Contractors[CAN]
238150	Glass and Glazing Contractors[CAN]
23816	Roofing Contractors[CAN]
238160	Roofing Contractors[CAN]
23817	Siding Contractors[CAN]
238170	Siding Contractors[CAN]
23819	Other Foundation, Structure, and Building Exterior Contractors[CAN]
238190	Other Foundation, Structure, and Building Exterior Contractors[CAN]

2382 Building Equipment Contractors

23821	Electrical Contractors and Other Wiring Installation Contractors
238210	Electrical Contractors and Other Wiring Installation Contractors
23822	Plumbing, Heating, and Air-Conditioning Contractors
238220	Plumbing, Heating, and Air-Conditioning Contractors[CAN]
23829	Other Building Equipment Contractors
238290	Other Building Equipment Contractors[MEX]

2383 Building Finishing Contractors

23831	Drywall and Insulation Contractors
238310	Drywall and Insulation Contractors[CAN]
23832	Painting and Wall Covering Contractors
238320	Painting and Wall Covering Contractors
23833	Flooring Contractors
238330	Flooring Contractors
23834	Tile and Terrazzo Contractors
238340	Tile and Terrazzo Contractors
23835	Finish Carpentry Contractors
238350	Finish Carpentry Contractors
23839	Other Building Finishing Contractors
238390	Other Building Finishing Contractors

2389 Other Specialty Trade Contractors

23891	Site Preparation Contractors
238910	Site Preparation Contractors
23899	All Other Specialty Trade Contractors
238990	All Other Specialty Trade Contractors

31-33 Manufacturing

311 Food Manufacturing

3111 Animal Food Manufacturing

31111	Animal Food Manufacturing
311111	Dog and Cat Food Manufacturing[CAN]
311119	Other Animal Food Manufacturing[CAN]

3112 Grain and Oilseed Milling

31121	Flour Milling and Malt Manufacturing
311211	Flour Milling[CAN]
311212	Rice Milling[US]
311213	Malt Manufacturing[US]

31122	Starch and Vegetable Fats and Oils Manufacturing
311221	Wet Corn Milling[CAN]
311222	Soybean Processing[US]
311223	Other Oilseed Processing[US]
311225	Fats and Oils Refining and Blending[CAN]
31123	Breakfast Cereal Manufacturing
311230	Breakfast Cereal Manufacturing

3113 Sugar and Confectionery Product Manufacturing

31131	Sugar Manufacturing
311311	Sugarcane Mills[US]
311312	Cane Sugar Refining[US]
311313	Beet Sugar Manufacturing[US]
31132	Chocolate and Confectionery Manufacturing from Cacao Beans
311320	Chocolate and Confectionery Manufacturing from Cacao Beans
31133	Confectionery Manufacturing from Purchased Chocolate
311330	Confectionery Manufacturing from Purchased Chocolate
31134	Nonchocolate Confectionery Manufacturing
311340	Nonchocolate Confectionery Manufacturing

3114 Fruit and Vegetable Preserving and Specialty Food Manufacturing

31141	Frozen Food Manufacturing
311411	Frozen Fruit, Juice, and Vegetable Manufacturing[MEX]
311412	Frozen Specialty Food Manufacturing[MEX]
31142	Fruit and Vegetable Canning, Pickling, and Drying
311421	Fruit and Vegetable Canning[US]
311422	Specialty Canning[US]
311423	Dried and Dehydrated Food Manufacturing[US]

3115 Dairy Product Manufacturing

31151	Dairy Product (except Frozen) Manufacturing
311511	Fluid Milk Manufacturing[CAN]
311512	Creamery Butter Manufacturing[US]
311513	Cheese Manufacturing[US]
311514	Dry, Condensed, and Evaporated Dairy Product Manufacturing[US]
31152	Ice Cream and Frozen Dessert Manufacturing
311520	Ice Cream and Frozen Dessert Manufacturing

3116   Animal Slaughtering and Processing

31161	Animal Slaughtering and Processing
311611	Animal (except Poultry) Slaughtering[CAN]
311612	Meat Processed from Carcasses[US]
311613	Rendering and Meat Byproduct Processing[US]
311615	Poultry Processing[CAN]

3117   Seafood Product Preparation and Packaging

31171	Seafood Product Preparation and Packaging
311711	Seafood Canning[US]
311712	Fresh and Frozen Seafood Processing[US]

3118   Bakeries and Tortilla Manufacturing

31181	Bread and Bakery Product Manufacturing
311811	Retail Bakeries[CAN]
311812	Commercial Bakeries[US]
311813	Frozen Cakes, Pies, and Other Pastries Manufacturing[US]
31182	Cookie, Cracker, and Pasta Manufacturing
311821	Cookie and Cracker Manufacturing[CAN]
311822	Flour Mixes and Dough Manufacturing from Purchased Flour[CAN]
311823	Dry Pasta Manufacturing[CAN]
31183	Tortilla Manufacturing
311830	Tortilla Manufacturing

3119   Other Food Manufacturing

31191	Snack Food Manufacturing
311911	Roasted Nuts and Peanut Butter Manufacturing[CAN]
311919	Other Snack Food Manufacturing[CAN]
31192	Coffee and Tea Manufacturing
311920	Coffee and Tea Manufacturing[CAN]
31193	Flavoring Syrup and Concentrate Manufacturing
311930	Flavoring Syrup and Concentrate Manufacturing
31194	Seasoning and Dressing Manufacturing
311941	Mayonnaise, Dressing, and Other Prepared Sauce Manufacturing[US]
311942	Spice and Extract Manufacturing[US]
31199	All Other Food Manufacturing
311991	Perishable Prepared Food Manufacturing[US]
311999	All Other Miscellaneous Food Manufacturing[US]

312   Beverage and Tobacco Product Manufacturing

3121   Beverage Manufacturing

31211	Soft Drink and Ice Manufacturing
312111	Soft Drink Manufacturing[MEX]

312112   Bottled Water Manufacturing[MEX]
312113   Ice Manufacturing[MEX]
31212   Breweries
312120   Breweries
31213   Wineries
312130   Wineries[CAN]
31214   Distilleries
312140   Distilleries[CAN]

3122   Tobacco Manufacturing

31221   Tobacco Stemming and Redrying
312210   Tobacco Stemming and Redrying
31222   Tobacco Product Manufacturing
312221   Cigarette Manufacturing[MEX]
312229   Other Tobacco Product Manufacturing[US]

313   Textile Mills

3131   Fiber, Yarn, and Thread Mills

31311   Fiber, Yarn, and Thread Mills
313111   Yarn Spinning Mills[US]
313112   Yarn Texturizing, Throwing, and Twisting Mills[US]
313113   Thread Mills[MEX]

3132   Fabric Mills

31321   Broadwoven Fabric Mills

313210   Broadwoven Fabric Mills
31322   Narrow Fabric Mills and Schiffli Machine Embroidery
313221   Narrow Fabric Mills[US]
313222   Schiffli Machine Embroidery[US]
31323   Nonwoven Fabric Mills
313230   Nonwoven Fabric Mills
31324   Knit Fabric Mills
313241   Weft Knit Fabric Mills[US]
313249   Other Knit Fabric and Lace Mills[US]

3133   Textile and Fabric Finishing and Fabric Coating Mills

31331   Textile and Fabric Finishing Mills
313311   Broadwoven Fabric Finishing Mills[US]
313312   Textile and Fabric Finishing (except Broadwoven Fabric) Mills[US]
31332   Fabric Coating Mills
313320   Fabric Coating Mills

314 Textile Product Mills

3141   Textile Furnishings Mills

31411	Carpet and Rug Mills
314110	Carpet and Rug Mills
31412	Curtain and Linen Mills
314121	Curtain and Drapery Mills[US]
314129	Other Household Textile Product Mills[US]

3149   Other Textile Product Mills

31491	Textile Bag and Canvas Mills
314911	Textile Bag Mills[US]
314912	Canvas and Related Product Mills[US]
31499	All Other Textile Product Mills
314991	Rope, Cordage, and Twine Mills[US]
314992	Tire Cord and Tire Fabric Mills[US]
314999	All Other Miscellaneous Textile Product Mills[US]

315 Apparel Manufacturing

3151   Apparel Knitting Mills

31511	Hosiery and Sock Mills
315111	Sheer Hosiery Mills[US]
315119	Other Hosiery and Sock Mills[US]
31519	Other Apparel Knitting Mills
315191	Outerwear Knitting Mills[US]
315192	Underwear and Nightwear Knitting Mills[US]

3152   Cut and Sew Apparel Manufacturing

31521	Cut and Sew Apparel Contractors[CAN]
315211	Men's and Boys' Cut and Sew Apparel Contractors[US]
315212	Women's, Girls', and Infants' Cut and Sew Apparel Contractors[US]
31522	Men's and Boys' Cut and Sew Apparel Manufacturing[CAN]
315221	Men's and Boys' Cut and Sew Underwear and Nightwear Manufacturing[CAN]
315222	Men's and Boys' Cut and Sew Suit, Coat, and Overcoat Manufacturing[CAN]
315223	Men's and Boys' Cut and Sew Shirt (except Work Shirt) Manufacturing[US]
315224	Men's and Boys' Cut and Sew Trouser, Slack, and Jean Manufacturing[US]
315225	Men's and Boys' Cut and Sew Work Clothing Manufacturing[US]

315228   Men's and Boys' Cut and Sew Other Outerwear Manufacturing[US]

31523   Women's and Girls' Cut and Sew Apparel Manufacturing[CAN]

315231   Women's and Girls' Cut and Sew Lingerie, Loungewear, and Nightwear Manufacturing[CAN]

315232   Women's and Girls' Cut and Sew Blouse and Shirt Manufacturing[CAN]

315233   Women's and Girls' Cut and Sew Dress Manufacturing[CAN]

315234   Women's and Girls' Cut and Sew Suit, Coat, Tailored Jacket, and Skirt Manufacturing[CAN]

315239   Women's and Girls' Cut and Sew Other Outerwear Manufacturing[CAN]

31529   Other Cut and Sew Apparel Manufacturing[CAN]

315291   Infants' Cut and Sew Apparel Manufacturing[CAN]

315292   Fur and Leather Apparel Manufacturing[CAN]

315299   All Other Cut and Sew Apparel Manufacturing[CAN]

3159 Apparel Accessories and Other Apparel Manufacturing

31599   Apparel Accessories and Other Apparel Manufacturing

315991   Hat, Cap, and Millinery Manufacturing[MEX]

315992   Glove and Mitten Manufacturing[US]

315993   Men's and Boys' Neckwear Manufacturing[US]

315999   Other Apparel Accessories and Other Apparel Manufacturing[US]

316 Leather and Allied Product Manufacturing

3161 Leather and Hide Tanning and Finishing

31611   Leather and Hide Tanning and Finishing

316110   Leather and Hide Tanning and Finishing

3162 Footwear Manufacturing

31621   Footwear Manufacturing

316211   Rubber and Plastics Footwear Manufacturing[US]

316212   House Slipper Manufacturing[US]

316213   Men's Footwear (except Athletic) Manufacturing[US]

316214   Women's Footwear (except Athletic) Manufacturing[US]

316219   Other Footwear Manufacturing[US]

3169 Other Leather and Allied Product Manufacturing

31699   Other Leather and Allied Product Manufacturing

316991   Luggage Manufacturing[US]

316992   Women's Handbag and Purse Manufacturing[US]
316993   Personal Leather Good (except Women's Handbag and Purse) Manufacturing[US]
316999   All Other Leather Good and Allied Product Manufacturing[US]

321 Wood Product Manufacturing

3211 Sawmills and Wood Preservation

32111   Sawmills and Wood Preservation
321113   Sawmills[US]
321114   Wood Preservation[CAN]

3212 Veneer, Plywood, and Engineered Wood Product Manufacturing

32121   Veneer, Plywood, and Engineered Wood Product Manufacturing
321211   Hardwood Veneer and Plywood Manufacturing[CAN]
321212   Softwood Veneer and Plywood Manufacturing[CAN]
321213   Engineered Wood Member (except Truss) Manufacturing[US]
321214   Truss Manufacturing[US]
321219   Reconstituted Wood Product Manufacturing[US]

3219 Other Wood Product Manufacturing

32191   Millwork
321911   Wood Window and Door Manufacturing[CAN]
321912   Cut Stock, Resawing Lumber, and Planing[US]
321918   Other Millwork (including Flooring)[US]
32192   Wood Container and Pallet Manufacturing
321920   Wood Container and Pallet Manufacturing
32199   All Other Wood Product Manufacturing
321991   Manufactured Home (Mobile Home) Manufacturing[CAN]
321992   Prefabricated Wood Building Manufacturing[CAN]
321999   All Other Miscellaneous Wood Product Manufacturing[CAN]

322 Paper Manufacturing

3221 Pulp, Paper, and Paperboard Mills

32211   Pulp Mills
322110   Pulp Mills[MEX]
32212   Paper Mills
322121   Paper (except Newsprint) Mills[CAN]
322122   Newsprint Mills[CAN]

32213   Paperboard Mills
322130   Paperboard Mills^{CAN}

3222   Converted Paper Product Manufacturing

32221   Paperboard Container Manufacturing
322211   Corrugated and Solid Fiber Box Manufacturing^{CAN}
322212   Folding Paperboard Box Manufacturing^{CAN}
322213   Setup Paperboard Box Manufacturing^{US}
322214   Fiber Can, Tube, Drum, and Similar Products Manufacturing^{US}
322215   Nonfolding Sanitary Food Container Manufacturing^{US}
32222   Paper Bag and Coated and Treated Paper Manufacturing
322221   Coated and Laminated Packaging Paper Manufacturing^{US}
322222   Coated and Laminated Paper Manufacturing^{US}
322223   Coated Paper Bag and Pouch Manufacturing^{US}
322224   Uncoated Paper and Multiwall Bag Manufacturing^{US}
322225   Laminated Aluminum Foil Manufacturing for Flexible Packaging Uses^{US}
322226   Surface-Coated Paperboard Manufacturing^{US}
32223   Stationery Product Manufacturing
322231   Die-Cut Paper and Paperboard Office Supplies Manufacturing^{US}
322232   Envelope Manufacturing^{US}
322233   Stationery, Tablet, and Related Product Manufacturing^{US}
32229   Other Converted Paper Product Manufacturing
322291   Sanitary Paper Product Manufacturing^{CAN}
322299   All Other Converted Paper Product Manufacturing^{CAN}

323 Printing and Related Support Activities

3231   Printing and Related Support Activities

32311   Printing
323110   Commercial Lithographic Printing^{US}
323111   Commercial Gravure Printing^{US}
323112   Commercial Flexographic Printing^{US}
323113   Commercial Screen Printing^{CAN}
323114   Quick Printing^{CAN}
323115   Digital Printing^{CAN}
323116   Manifold Business Forms Printing^{CAN}
323117   Books Printing^{US}

32592	Explosives Manufacturing
325920	Explosives Manufacturing
32599	All Other Chemical Product and Preparation Manufacturing
325991	Custom Compounding of Purchased Resins[CAN]
325992	Photographic Film, Paper, Plate, and Chemical Manufacturing[MEX]
325998	All Other Miscellaneous Chemical Product and Preparation Manufacturing[US]

326 Plastics and Rubber Products Manufacturing

3261 Plastics Product Manufacturing

32611	Plastics Packaging Materials and Unlaminated Film and Sheet Manufacturing
326111	Plastics Bag and Pouch Manufacturing[CAN]
326112	Plastics Packaging Film and Sheet (including Laminated) Manufacturing[US]
326113	Unlaminated Plastics Film and Sheet (except Packaging) Manufacturing[US]
32612	Plastics Pipe, Pipe Fitting, and Unlaminated Profile Shape Manufacturing
326121	Unlaminated Plastics Profile Shape Manufacturing[CAN]
326122	Plastics Pipe and Pipe Fitting Manufacturing[CAN]
32613	Laminated Plastics Plate, Sheet (except Packaging), and Shape Manufacturing
326130	Laminated Plastics Plate, Sheet (except Packaging), and Shape Manufacturing
32614	Polystyrene Foam Product Manufacturing
326140	Polystyrene Foam Product Manufacturing
32615	Urethane and Other Foam Product (except Polystyrene) Manufacturing
326150	Urethane and Other Foam Product (except Polystyrene) Manufacturing
32616	Plastics Bottle Manufacturing
326160	Plastics Bottle Manufacturing
32619	Other Plastics Product Manufacturing
326191	Plastics Plumbing Fixture Manufacturing[CAN]
326192	Resilient Floor Covering Manufacturing[US]
326199	All Other Plastics Product Manufacturing[US]

3262 Rubber Product Manufacturing

32621 Tire Manufacturing

| 326211 | Tire Manufacturing (except Retreading)[MEX] |
| 326212 | Tire Retreading[MEX] |

32622	Rubber and Plastics Hoses and Belting Manufacturing
326220	Rubber and Plastics Hoses and Belting Manufacturing
32629	Other Rubber Product Manufacturing
326291	Rubber Product Manufacturing for Mechanical Use[US]
326299	All Other Rubber Product Manufacturing[US]

327 Nonmetallic Mineral Product Manufacturing

3271 Clay Product and Refractory Manufacturing

32711	Pottery, Ceramics, and Plumbing Fixture Manufacturing
327111	Vitreous China Plumbing Fixture and China and Earthenware Bathroom Accessories Manufacturing[US]
327112	Vitreous China, Fine Earthenware, and Other Pottery Product Manufacturing[US]
327113	Porcelain Electrical Supply Manufacturing[US]
32712	Clay Building Material and Refractories Manufacturing
327121	Brick and Structural Clay Tile Manufacturing[US]
327122	Ceramic Wall and Floor Tile Manufacturing[US]
327123	Other Structural Clay Product Manufacturing[US]
327124	Clay Refractory Manufacturing[US]
327125	Nonclay Refractory Manufacturing[US]

3272 Glass and Glass Product Manufacturing

32721	Glass and Glass Product Manufacturing
327211	Flat Glass Manufacturing[MEX]
327212	Other Pressed and Blown Glass and Glassware Manufacturing[US]
327213	Glass Container Manufacturing[US]
327215	Glass Product Manufacturing Made of Purchased Glass[CAN]

3273 Cement and Concrete Product Manufacturing

32731	Cement Manufacturing
327310	Cement Manufacturing
32732	Ready-Mix Concrete Manufacturing
327320	Ready-Mix Concrete Manufacturing
32733	Concrete Pipe, Brick, and Block Manufacturing
327331	Concrete Block and Brick Manufacturing[US]
327332	Concrete Pipe Manufacturing[US]
32739	Other Concrete Product Manufacturing
327390	Other Concrete Product Manufacturing[CAN]

3274 Lime and Gypsum Product Manufacturing

32741   Lime Manufacturing
327410   Lime Manufacturing
32742   Gypsum Product Manufacturing
327420   Gypsum Product Manufacturing

3279 Other Nonmetallic Mineral Product Manufacturing

32791   Abrasive Product Manufacturing
327910   Abrasive Product Manufacturing
32799   All Other Nonmetallic Mineral Product
        Manufacturing
327991   Cut Stone and Stone Product Manufacturing[US]
327992   Ground or Treated Mineral and Earth
        Manufacturing[US]
327993   Mineral Wool Manufacturing[US]
327999   All Other Miscellaneous Nonmetallic Mineral
        Product Manufacturing[US]

331 Primary Metal Manufacturing

3311 Iron and Steel Mills and Ferroalloy Manufacturing

33111   Iron and Steel Mills and Ferroalloy
        Manufacturing
331111   Iron and Steel Mills[US]
331112   Electrometallurgical Ferroalloy Product
        Manufacturing[US]

3312 Steel Product Manufacturing from Purchased Steel

33121   Iron and Steel Pipe and Tube Manufacturing from
        Purchased Steel
331210   Iron and Steel Pipe and Tube Manufacturing from
        Purchased Steel
33122   Rolling and Drawing of Purchased Steel
331221   Rolled Steel Shape Manufacturing[CAN]
331222   Steel Wire Drawing[CAN]

3313 Alumina and Aluminum Production and Processing

33131   Alumina and Aluminum Production and
        Processing
331311   Alumina Refining[US]
331312   Primary Aluminum Production[US]
331314   Secondary Smelting and Alloying of Aluminum[US]
331315   Aluminum Sheet, Plate, and Foil Manufacturing[US]
331316   Aluminum Extruded Product Manufacturing[US]
331319   Other Aluminum Rolling and Drawing[US]

3314 Nonferrous Metal (except Aluminum) Production and Processing

33141   Nonferrous Metal (except Aluminum) Smelting and Refining

331411   Primary Smelting and Refining of Copper[MEX]

331419   Primary Smelting and Refining of Nonferrous Metal (except Copper and Aluminum)[US]

33142   Copper Rolling, Drawing, Extruding, and Alloying

331421   Copper Rolling, Drawing, and Extruding[US]

331422   Copper Wire (except Mechanical) Drawing[US]

331423   Secondary Smelting, Refining, and Alloying of Copper[US]

33149   Nonferrous Metal (except Copper and Aluminum) Rolling, Drawing, Extruding, and Alloying

331491   Nonferrous Metal (except Copper and Aluminum) Rolling, Drawing, and Extruding[US]

331492   Secondary Smelting, Refining, and Alloying of Nonferrous Metal (except Copper and Aluminum)[US]

3315 Foundries

33151   Ferrous Metal Foundries

331511   Iron Foundries[CAN]

331512   Steel Investment Foundries[US]

331513   Steel Foundries (except Investment)[US]

33152   Nonferrous Metal Foundries

331521   Aluminum Die-Casting Foundries[US]

331522   Nonferrous (except Aluminum) Die-Casting Foundries[US]

331524   Aluminum Foundries (except Die-Casting)[US]

331525   Copper Foundries (except Die-Casting)[US]

331528   Other Nonferrous Foundries (except Die-Casting)[US]

332 Fabricated Metal Product Manufacturing

3321 Forging and Stamping

33211   Forging and Stamping

332111   Iron and Steel Forging[US]

332112   Nonferrous Forging[US]

332114   Custom Roll Forming[US]

332115   Crown and Closure Manufacturing[US]

332116   Metal Stamping[US]

332117   Powder Metallurgy Part Manufacturing[US]

3322   Cutlery and Handtool Manufacturing

33221   Cutlery and Handtool Manufacturing

332211   Cutlery and Flatware (except Precious) Manufacturing[US]

332212   Hand and Edge Tool Manufacturing[US]

332213   Saw Blade and Handsaw Manufacturing[US]

332214   Kitchen Utensil, Pot, and Pan Manufacturing[US]

3323   Architectural and Structural Metals Manufacturing

33231   Plate Work and Fabricated Structural Product Manufacturing

332311   Prefabricated Metal Building and Component Manufacturing[CAN]

332312   Fabricated Structural Metal Manufacturing[US]

332313   Plate Work Manufacturing[US]

33232   Ornamental and Architectural Metal Products Manufacturing

332321   Metal Window and Door Manufacturing[CAN]

332322   Sheet Metal Work Manufacturing[US]

332323   Ornamental and Architectural Metal Work Manufacturing[US]

3324   Boiler, Tank, and Shipping Container Manufacturing

33241   Power Boiler and Heat Exchanger Manufacturing

332410   Power Boiler and Heat Exchanger Manufacturing

33242   Metal Tank (Heavy Gauge) Manufacturing

332420   Metal Tank (Heavy Gauge) Manufacturing

33243   Metal Can, Box, and Other Metal Container (Light Gauge) Manufacturing

332431   Metal Can Manufacturing[CAN]

332439   Other Metal Container Manufacturing[CAN]

3325   Hardware Manufacturing

33251   Hardware Manufacturing

332510   Hardware Manufacturing

3326   Spring and Wire Product Manufacturing

33261   Spring and Wire Product Manufacturing

332611   Spring (Heavy Gauge) Manufacturing[CAN]

332612   Spring (Light Gauge) Manufacturing[US]

332618   Other Fabricated Wire Product Manufacturing[US]

3327   Machine Shops; Turned Product; and Screw, Nut, and Bolt Manufacturing

33271   Machine Shops

332710   Machine Shops

33272   Turned Product and Screw, Nut, and Bolt Manufacturing

332721   Precision Turned Product Manufacturing[US]

332722   Bolt, Nut, Screw, Rivet, and Washer Manufacturing[US]

3328 Coating, Engraving, Heat Treating, and Allied Activities

33281   Coating, Engraving, Heat Treating, and Allied Activities

332811   Metal Heat Treating[US]

332812   Metal Coating, Engraving (except Jewelry and Silverware), and Allied Services to Manufacturers[US]

332813   Electroplating, Plating, Polishing, Anodizing, and Coloring[US]

3329 Other Fabricated Metal Product Manufacturing

33291   Metal Valve Manufacturing

332911   Industrial Valve Manufacturing[US]

332912   Fluid Power Valve and Hose Fitting Manufacturing[US]

332913   Plumbing Fixture Fitting and Trim Manufacturing[US]

332919   Other Metal Valve and Pipe Fitting Manufacturing[US]

33299   All Other Fabricated Metal Product Manufacturing

332991   Ball and Roller Bearing Manufacturing

332992   Small Arms Ammunition Manufacturing[US]

332993   Ammunition (except Small Arms) Manufacturing[US]

332994   Small Arms Manufacturing[US]

332995   Other Ordnance and Accessories Manufacturing[US]

332996   Fabricated Pipe and Pipe Fitting Manufacturing[US]

332997   Industrial Pattern Manufacturing[US]

332998   Enameled Iron and Metal Sanitary Ware Manufacturing[US]

332999   All Other Miscellaneous Fabricated Metal Product Manufacturing[US]

333 Machinery Manufacturing

3331 Agriculture, Construction, and Mining Machinery Manufacturing

33311   Agricultural Implement Manufacturing

333111   Farm Machinery and Equipment Manufacturing[US]

333112	Lawn and Garden Tractor and Home Lawn and Garden Equipment Manufacturing[US]
33312	Construction Machinery Manufacturing
333120	Construction Machinery Manufacturing
33313	Mining and Oil and Gas Field Machinery Manufacturing
333131	Mining Machinery and Equipment Manufacturing[US]
333132	Oil and Gas Field Machinery and Equipment Manufacturing[US]

3332   Industrial Machinery Manufacturing

33321	Sawmill and Woodworking Machinery Manufacturing
333210	Sawmill and Woodworking Machinery Manufacturing
33322	Plastics and Rubber Industry Machinery Manufacturing
333220	Plastics and Rubber Industry Machinery Manufacturing
33329	Other Industrial Machinery Manufacturing
333291	Paper Industry Machinery Manufacturing[CAN]
333292	Textile Machinery Manufacturing[MEX]
333293	Printing Machinery and Equipment Manufacturing[MEX]
333294	Food Product Machinery Manufacturing[US]
333295	Semiconductor Machinery Manufacturing[US]
333298	All Other Industrial Machinery Manufacturing[US]

3333   Commercial and Service Industry Machinery Manufacturing

33331	Commercial and Service Industry Machinery Manufacturing
333311	Automatic Vending Machine Manufacturing[US]
333312	Commercial Laundry, Drycleaning, and Pressing Machine Manufacturing[US]
333313	Office Machinery Manufacturing[US]
333314	Optical Instrument and Lens Manufacturing[US]
333315	Photographic and Photocopying Equipment Manufacturing[US]
333319	Other Commercial and Service Industry Machinery Manufacturing[US]

3334   Ventilation, Heating, Air-Conditioning, and Commercial Refrigeration Equipment Manufacturing

| 33341 | Ventilation, Heating, Air-Conditioning, and Commercial Refrigeration Equipment Manufacturing |
| 333411 | Air Purification Equipment Manufacturing[US] |

333412   Industrial and Commercial Fan and Blower
            Manufacturing^{US}

333414   Heating Equipment (except Warm Air Furnaces)
            Manufacturing^{US}

333415   Air-Conditioning and Warm Air Heating
            Equipment and Commercial and Industrial
            Refrigeration Equipment Manufacturing^{US}

3335   Metalworking Machinery Manufacturing

33351   Metalworking Machinery Manufacturing

333511   Industrial Mold Manufacturing^{CAN}

333512   Machine Tool (Metal Cutting Types)
            Manufacturing^{US}

333513   Machine Tool (Metal Forming Types)
            Manufacturing^{US}

333514   Special Die and Tool, Die Set, Jig, and Fixture
            Manufacturing^{US}

333515   Cutting Tool and Machine Tool Accessory
            Manufacturing^{US}

333516   Rolling Mill Machinery and Equipment
            Manufacturing^{US}

333518   Other Metalworking Machinery Manufacturing^{US}

**3336   Engine, Turbine, and Power Transmission Equipment
Manufacturing**

33361   Engine, Turbine, and Power Transmission
            Equipment Manufacturing

333611   Turbine and Turbine Generator Set Units
            Manufacturing^{CAN}

333612   Speed Changer, Industrial High-Speed Drive, and
            Gear Manufacturing^{US}

333613   Mechanical Power Transmission Equipment
            Manufacturing^{US}

333618   Other Engine Equipment Manufacturing^{US}

3339   Other General Purpose Machinery Manufacturing

33391   Pump and Compressor Manufacturing

333911   Pump and Pumping Equipment Manufacturing^{US}

333912   Air and Gas Compressor Manufacturing^{US}

333913   Measuring and Dispensing Pump Manufacturing^{US}

33392   Material Handling Equipment Manufacturing

333921   Elevator and Moving Stairway Manufacturing^{US}

333922   Conveyor and Conveying Equipment
            Manufacturing^{US}

333923   Overhead Traveling Crane, Hoist, and Monorail
            System Manufacturing^{US}

333924   Industrial Truck, Tractor, Trailer, and Stacker
Machinery Manufacturing[US]

33399   All Other General Purpose Machinery
Manufacturing

333991   Power-Driven Handtool Manufacturing[US]

333992   Welding and Soldering Equipment
Manufacturing[US]

333993   Packaging Machinery Manufacturing[US]

333994   Industrial Process Furnace and Oven
Manufacturing[US]

333995   Fluid Power Cylinder and Actuator
Manufacturing[US]

333996   Fluid Power Pump and Motor Manufacturing[US]

333997   Scale and Balance Manufacturing[US]

333999   All Other Miscellaneous General Purpose
Machinery Manufacturing[US]

334 Computer and Electronic Product Manufacturing

3341 Computer and Peripheral Equipment Manufacturing

33411   Computer and Peripheral Equipment
Manufacturing

334111   Electronic Computer Manufacturing[US]

334112   Computer Storage Device Manufacturing[US]

334113   Computer Terminal Manufacturing[US]

334119   Other Computer Peripheral Equipment
Manufacturing[US]

3342 Communications Equipment Manufacturing

33421   Telephone Apparatus Manufacturing

334210   Telephone Apparatus Manufacturing

33422   Radio and Television Broadcasting and Wireless
Communications Equipment Manufacturing

334220   Radio and Television Broadcasting and Wireless
Communications Equipment Manufacturing

33429   Other Communications Equipment Manufacturing

334290   Other Communications Equipment Manufacturing

3343 Audio and Video Equipment Manufacturing

33431   Audio and Video Equipment Manufacturing

334310   Audio and Video Equipment Manufacturing

3344 Semiconductor and Other Electronic Component Manufacturing

33441   Semiconductor and Other Electronic Component
Manufacturing

334411   Electron Tube Manufacturing[US]

334412   Bare Printed Circuit Board Manufacturing[US]
334413   Semiconductor and Related Device Manufacturing[US]
334414   Electronic Capacitor Manufacturing[US]
334415   Electronic Resistor Manufacturing[US]
334416   Electronic Coil, Transformer, and Other Inductor Manufacturing[US]
334417   Electronic Connector Manufacturing[US]
334418   Printed Circuit Assembly (Electronic Assembly) Manufacturing[US]
334419   Other Electronic Component Manufacturing[US]

3345   Navigational, Measuring, Electromedical, and Control Instruments Manufacturing

33451   Navigational, Measuring, Electromedical, and Control Instruments Manufacturing
334510   Electromedical and Electrotherapeutic Apparatus Manufacturing[US]
334511   Search, Detection, Navigation, Guidance, Aeronautical, and Nautical System and Instrument Manufacturing[CAN]
334512   Automatic Environmental Control Manufacturing for Residential, Commercial, and Appliance Use[US]
334513   Instruments and Related Products Manufacturing for Measuring, Displaying, and Controlling Industrial Process Variables[US]
334514   Totalizing Fluid Meter and Counting Device Manufacturing[US]
334515   Instrument Manufacturing for Measuring and Testing Electricity and Electrical Signals[US]
334516   Analytical Laboratory Instrument Manufacturing[US]
334517   Irradiation Apparatus Manufacturing[US]
334518   Watch, Clock, and Part Manufacturing[US]
334519   Other Measuring and Controlling Device Manufacturing[US]

3346   Manufacturing and Reproducing Magnetic and Optical Media

33461   Manufacturing and Reproducing Magnetic and Optical Media
334611   Software Reproducing[US]
334612   Prerecorded Compact Disc (except Software), Tape, and Record Reproducing[US]
334613   Magnetic and Optical Recording Media Manufacturing[US]

335 Electrical Equipment, Appliance, and Component Manufacturing

3351 Electric Lighting Equipment Manufacturing

33511	Electric Lamp Bulb and Part Manufacturing
335110	Electric Lamp Bulb and Part Manufacturing
33512	Lighting Fixture Manufacturing
335121	Residential Electric Lighting Fixture Manufacturing[US]
335122	Commercial, Industrial, and Institutional Electric Lighting Fixture Manufacturing[US]
335129	Other Lighting Equipment Manufacturing[US]

3352 Household Appliance Manufacturing

33521	Small Electrical Appliance Manufacturing
335211	Electric Housewares and Household Fan Manufacturing[US]
335212	Household Vacuum Cleaner Manufacturing[US]
33522	Major Appliance Manufacturing
335221	Household Cooking Appliance Manufacturing[US]
335222	Household Refrigerator and Home Freezer Manufacturing[US]
335224	Household Laundry Equipment Manufacturing[US]
335228	Other Major Household Appliance Manufacturing[US]

3353 Electrical Equipment Manufacturing

33531	Electrical Equipment Manufacturing
335311	Power, Distribution, and Specialty Transformer Manufacturing[CAN]
335312	Motor and Generator Manufacturing[CAN]
335313	Switchgear and Switchboard Apparatus Manufacturing[US]
335314	Relay and Industrial Control Manufacturing[US]

3359 Other Electrical Equipment and Component Manufacturing

33591	Battery Manufacturing
335911	Storage Battery Manufacturing[US]
335912	Primary Battery Manufacturing[US]
33592	Communication and Energy Wire and Cable Manufacturing
335921	Fiber Optic Cable Manufacturing[US]
335929	Other Communication and Energy Wire Manufacturing[US]
33593	Wiring Device Manufacturing

335931 Current-Carrying Wiring Device Manufacturing[US]
335932 Noncurrent-Carrying Wiring Device Manufacturing[US]
33599 All Other Electrical Equipment and Component Manufacturing
335991 Carbon and Graphite Product Manufacturing[MEX]
335999 All Other Miscellaneous Electrical Equipment and Component Manufacturing[MEX]

336 Transportation Equipment Manufacturing

3361 Motor Vehicle Manufacturing

33611 Automobile and Light Duty Motor Vehicle Manufacturing
336111 Automobile Manufacturing[US]
336112 Light Truck and Utility Vehicle Manufacturing[US]
33612 Heavy Duty Truck Manufacturing
336120 Heavy Duty Truck Manufacturing

3362 Motor Vehicle Body and Trailer Manufacturing

33621 Motor Vehicle Body and Trailer Manufacturing
336211 Motor Vehicle Body Manufacturing[CAN]
336212 Truck Trailer Manufacturing[CAN]
336213 Motor Home Manufacturing[US]
336214 Travel Trailer and Camper Manufacturing[US]

3363 Motor Vehicle Parts Manufacturing

33631 Motor Vehicle Gasoline Engine and Engine Parts Manufacturing
336311 Carburetor, Piston, Piston Ring, and Valve Manufacturing[US]
336312 Gasoline Engine and Engine Parts Manufacturing[US]
33632 Motor Vehicle Electrical and Electronic Equipment Manufacturing
336321 Vehicular Lighting Equipment Manufacturing[US]
336322 Other Motor Vehicle Electrical and Electronic Equipment Manufacturing[US]
33633 Motor Vehicle Steering and Suspension Components (except Spring) Manufacturing
336330 Motor Vehicle Steering and Suspension Components (except Spring) Manufacturing
33634 Motor Vehicle Brake System Manufacturing
336340 Motor Vehicle Brake System Manufacturing
33635 Motor Vehicle Transmission and Power Train Parts Manufacturing

336350	Motor Vehicle Transmission and Power Train Parts Manufacturing
33636	Motor Vehicle Seating and Interior Trim Manufacturing
336360	Motor Vehicle Seating and Interior Trim Manufacturing
33637	Motor Vehicle Metal Stamping
336370	Motor Vehicle Metal Stamping
33639	Other Motor Vehicle Parts Manufacturing
336391	Motor Vehicle Air-Conditioning Manufacturing[US]
336399	All Other Motor Vehicle Parts Manufacturing[US]

3364 Aerospace Product and Parts Manufacturing

33641	Aerospace Product and Parts Manufacturing
336411	Aircraft Manufacturing[US]
336412	Aircraft Engine and Engine Parts Manufacturing[US]
336413	Other Aircraft Parts and Auxiliary Equipment Manufacturing[US]
336414	Guided Missile and Space Vehicle Manufacturing[US]
336415	Guided Missile and Space Vehicle Propulsion Unit and Propulsion Unit Parts Manufacturing[US]
336419	Other Guided Missile and Space Vehicle Parts and Auxiliary Equipment Manufacturing[US]

3365 Railroad Rolling Stock Manufacturing

| 33651 | Railroad Rolling Stock Manufacturing |
| 336510 | Railroad Rolling Stock Manufacturing |

3366 Ship and Boat Building

33661	Ship and Boat Building
336611	Ship Building and Repairing[CAN]
336612	Boat Building[CAN]

3369 Other Transportation Equipment Manufacturing

33699	Other Transportation Equipment Manufacturing
336991	Motorcycle, Bicycle, and Parts Manufacturing[US]
336992	Military Armored Vehicle, Tank, and Tank Component Manufacturing[US]
336999	All Other Transportation Equipment Manufacturing[US]

337 Furniture and Related Product Manufacturing

3371 Household and Institutional Furniture and Kitchen Cabinet Manufacturing

33711	Wood Kitchen Cabinet and Countertop Manufacturing
337110	Wood Kitchen Cabinet and Countertop Manufacturing
33712	Household and Institutional Furniture Manufacturing
337121	Upholstered Household Furniture Manufacturing[CAN]
337122	Nonupholstered Wood Household Furniture Manufacturing[US]
337124	Metal Household Furniture Manufacturing[US]
337125	Household Furniture (except Wood and Metal) Manufacturing[US]
337127	Institutional Furniture Manufacturing[CAN]
337129	Wood Television, Radio, and Sewing Machine Cabinet Manufacturing[US]

3372 Office Furniture (including Fixtures) Manufacturing

33721	Office Furniture (including Fixtures) Manufacturing
337211	Wood Office Furniture Manufacturing[US]
337212	Custom Architectural Woodwork and Millwork Manufacturing[US]
337214	Office Furniture (except Wood) Manufacturing[CAN]
337215	Showcase, Partition, Shelving, and Locker Manufacturing[CAN]

3379 Other Furniture Related Product Manufacturing

33791	Mattress Manufacturing
337910	Mattress Manufacturing
33792	Blind and Shade Manufacturing
337920	Blind and Shade Manufacturing

339 Miscellaneous Manufacturing

3391 Medical Equipment and Supplies Manufacturing

33911	Medical Equipment and Supplies Manufacturing
339112	Surgical and Medical Instrument Manufacturing[US]
339113	Surgical Appliance and Supplies Manufacturing[US]
339114	Dental Equipment and Supplies Manufacturing[US]
339115	Ophthalmic Goods Manufacturing[US]
339116	Dental Laboratories[US]

3399 Other Miscellaneous Manufacturing

33991	Jewelry and Silverware Manufacturing
339911	Jewelry (except Costume) Manufacturing[US]
339912	Silverware and Hollowware Manufacturing[US]

339913	Jewelers' Material and Lapidary Work Manufacturing[US]
339914	Costume Jewelry and Novelty Manufacturing[US]
33992	Sporting and Athletic Goods Manufacturing
339920	Sporting and Athletic Goods Manufacturing
33993	Doll, Toy, and Game Manufacturing
339931	Doll and Stuffed Toy Manufacturing[US]
339932	Game, Toy, and Children's Vehicle Manufacturing[US]
33994	Office Supplies (except Paper) Manufacturing
339941	Pen and Mechanical Pencil Manufacturing[US]
339942	Lead Pencil and Art Good Manufacturing[US]
339943	Marking Device Manufacturing[US]
339944	Carbon Paper and Inked Ribbon Manufacturing[US]
33995	Sign Manufacturing
339950	Sign Manufacturing
33999	All Other Miscellaneous Manufacturing
339991	Gasket, Packing, and Sealing Device Manufacturing[US]
339992	Musical Instrument Manufacturing[US]
339993	Fastener, Button, Needle, and Pin Manufacturing[US]
339994	Broom, Brush, and Mop Manufacturing[US]
339995	Burial Casket Manufacturing[MEX]
339999	All Other Miscellaneous Manufacturing[US]

42   Wholesale Trade

423 Merchant Wholesalers, Durable Goods[US]

4231 Motor Vehicle and Motor Vehicle Parts and Supplies Merchant Wholesalers[US]

42311	Automobile and Other Motor Vehicle Merchant Wholesalers[US]
423110	Automobile and Other Motor Vehicle Merchant Wholesalers[US]
42312	Motor Vehicle Supplies and New Parts Merchant Wholesalers[US]
423120	Motor Vehicle Supplies and New Parts Merchant Wholesalers[US]
42313	Tire and Tube Merchant Wholesalers[US]
423130	Tire and Tube Merchant Wholesalers[US]
42314	Motor Vehicle Parts (Used) Merchant Wholesalers[US]
423140	Motor Vehicle Parts (Used) Merchant Wholesalers[US]

4232 **Furniture and Home Furnishing Merchant Wholesalers**US

42321	Furniture Merchant WholesalersUS
423210	Furniture Merchant WholesalersUS
42322	Home Furnishing Merchant WholesalersUS
423220	Home Furnishing Merchant WholesalersUS

4233 **Lumber and Other Construction Materials Merchant Wholesalers**US

42331	Lumber, Plywood, Millwork, and Wood Panel Merchant WholesalersUS
423310	Lumber, Plywood, Millwork, and Wood Panel Merchant WholesalersUS
42332	Brick, Stone, and Related Construction Material Merchant WholesalersUS
423320	Brick, Stone, and Related Construction Material Merchant WholesalersUS
42333	Roofing, Siding, and Insulation Material Merchant WholesalersUS
423330	Roofing, Siding, and Insulation Material Merchant WholesalersUS
42339	Other Construction Material Merchant WholesalersUS
423390	Other Construction Material Merchant WholesalersUS

4234 **Professional and Commercial Equipment and Supplies Merchant Wholesalers**US

42341	Photographic Equipment and Supplies Merchant WholesalersUS
423410	Photographic Equipment and Supplies Merchant WholesalersUS
42342	Office Equipment Merchant WholesalersUS
423420	Office Equipment Merchant WholesalersUS
42343	Computer and Computer Peripheral Equipment and Software Merchant WholesalersUS
423430	Computer and Computer Peripheral Equipment and Software Merchant WholesalersUS
42344	Other Commercial Equipment Merchant WholesalersUS
423440	Other Commercial Equipment Merchant WholesalersUS
42345	Medical, Dental, and Hospital Equipment and Supplies Merchant WholesalersUS
423450	Medical, Dental, and Hospital Equipment and Supplies Merchant WholesalersUS

42346   Ophthalmic Goods Merchant Wholesalers[US]
423460   Ophthalmic Goods Merchant Wholesalers[US]
42349   Other Professional Equipment and Supplies Merchant Wholesalers[US]
423490   Other Professional Equipment and Supplies Merchant Wholesalers[US]

4235 Metal and Mineral (except Petroleum) Merchant Wholesalers[US]

42351   Metal Service Centers and Other Metal Merchant Wholesalers[US]
423510   Metal Service Centers and Other Metal Merchant Wholesalers[US]
42352   Coal and Other Mineral and Ore Merchant Wholesalers[US]
423520   Coal and Other Mineral and Ore Merchant Wholesalers[US]

4236 Electrical and Electronic Goods Merchant Wholesalers[US]

42361   Electrical Apparatus and Equipment, Wiring Supplies, and Related Equipment Merchant Wholesalers[US]
423610   Electrical Apparatus and Equipment, Wiring Supplies, and Related Equipment Merchant Wholesalers[US]
42362   Electrical and Electronic Appliance, Television, and Radio Set Merchant Wholesalers[US]
423620   Electrical and Electronic Appliance, Television, and Radio Set Merchant Wholesalers[US]
42369   Other Electronic Parts and Equipment Merchant Wholesalers[US]
423690   Other Electronic Parts and Equipment Merchant Wholesalers[US]

4237 Hardware, and Plumbing and Heating Equipment and Supplies Merchant Wholesalers[US]

42371   Hardware Merchant Wholesalers[US]
423710   Hardware Merchant Wholesalers[US]
42372   Plumbing and Heating Equipment and Supplies (Hydronics) Merchant Wholesalers[US]
423720   Plumbing and Heating Equipment and Supplies (Hydronics) Merchant Wholesalers[US]
42373   Warm Air Heating and Air-Conditioning Equipment and Supplies Merchant Wholesalers[US]
423730   Warm Air Heating and Air-Conditioning Equipment and Supplies Merchant Wholesalers[US]

| 42374 | Refrigeration Equipment and Supplies Merchant WholesalersUS |
| 423740 | Refrigeration Equipment and Supplies Merchant WholesalersUS |

4238   Machinery, Equipment, and Supplies Merchant WholesalersUS

42381	Construction and Mining (except Oil Well) Machinery and Equipment Merchant WholesalersUS
423810	Construction and Mining (except Oil Well) Machinery and Equipment Merchant WholesalersUS
42382	Farm and Garden Machinery and Equipment Merchant WholesalersUS
423820	Farm and Garden Machinery and Equipment Merchant WholesalersUS
42383	Industrial Machinery and Equipment Merchant WholesalersUS
423830	Industrial Machinery and Equipment Merchant WholesalersUS
42384	Industrial Supplies Merchant WholesalersUS
423840	Industrial Supplies Merchant WholesalersUS
42385	Service Establishment Equipment and Supplies Merchant WholesalersUS
423850	Service Establishment Equipment and Supplies Merchant WholesalersUS
42386	Transportation Equipment and Supplies (except Motor Vehicle) Merchant WholesalersUS
423860	Transportation Equipment and Supplies (except Motor Vehicle) Merchant WholesalersUS

4239   Miscellaneous Durable Goods Merchant WholesalersUS

42391	Sporting and Recreational Goods and Supplies Merchant WholesalersUS
423910	Sporting and Recreational Goods and Supplies Merchant WholesalersUS
42392	Toy and Hobby Goods and Supplies Merchant WholesalersUS
423920	Toy and Hobby Goods and Supplies Merchant WholesalersUS
42393	Recyclable Material Merchant WholesalersUS
423930	Recyclable Material Merchant WholesalersUS
42394	Jewelry, Watch, Precious Stone, and Precious Metal Merchant WholesalersUS
423940	Jewelry, Watch, Precious Stone, and Precious Metal Merchant WholesalersUS

| 42399 | Other Miscellaneous Durable Goods Merchant Wholesalers[US] |
| 423990 | Other Miscellaneous Durable Goods Merchant Wholesalers[US] |

424 Merchant Wholesalers, Nondurable Goods[US]

4241 Paper and Paper Product Merchant Wholesalers[US]

42411	Printing and Writing Paper Merchant Wholesalers[US]
424110	Printing and Writing Paper Merchant Wholesalers[US]
42412	Stationery and Office Supplies Merchant Wholesalers[US]
424120	Stationery and Office Supplies Merchant Wholesalers[US]
42413	Industrial and Personal Service Paper Merchant Wholesalers[US]
424130	Industrial and Personal Service Paper Merchant Wholesalers[US]

4242 Drugs and Druggists' Sundries Merchant Wholesalers[US]

| 42421 | Drugs and Druggists' Sundries Merchant Wholesalers[US] |
| 424210 | Drugs and Druggists' Sundries Merchant Wholesalers[US] |

4243 Apparel, Piece Goods, and Notions Merchant Wholesalers[US]

42431	Piece Goods, Notions, and Other Dry Goods Merchant Wholesalers[US]
424310	Piece Goods, Notions, and Other Dry Goods Merchant Wholesalers[US]
42432	Men's and Boys' Clothing and Furnishings Merchant Wholesalers[US]
424320	Men's and Boys' Clothing and Furnishings Merchant Wholesalers[US]
42433	Women's, Children's, and Infants' Clothing and Accessories Merchant Wholesalers[US]
424330	Women's, Children's, and Infants' Clothing and Accessories Merchant Wholesalers[US]
42434	Footwear Merchant Wholesalers[US]
424340	Footwear Merchant Wholesalers[US]

4244 Grocery and Related Product Merchant Wholesalers[US]

| 42441 | General Line Grocery Merchant Wholesalers[US] |
| 424410 | General Line Grocery Merchant Wholesalers[US] |

42442	Packaged Frozen Food Merchant Wholesalers[US]
424420	Packaged Frozen Food Merchant Wholesalers[US]
42443	Dairy Product (except Dried or Canned) Merchant Wholesalers[US]
424430	Dairy Product (except Dried or Canned) Merchant Wholesalers[US]
42444	Poultry and Poultry Product Merchant Wholesalers[US]
424440	Poultry and Poultry Product Merchant Wholesalers[US]
42445	Confectionery Merchant Wholesalers[US]
424450	Confectionery Merchant Wholesalers[US]
42446	Fish and Seafood Merchant Wholesalers[US]
424460	Fish and Seafood Merchant Wholesalers[US]
42447	Meat and Meat Product Merchant Wholesalers[US]
424470	Meat and Meat Product Merchant Wholesalers[US]
42448	Fresh Fruit and Vegetable Merchant Wholesalers[US]
424480	Fresh Fruit and Vegetable Merchant Wholesalers[US]
42449	Other Grocery and Related Products Merchant Wholesalers[US]
424490	Other Grocery and Related Products Merchant Wholesalers[US]

4245 Farm Product Raw Material Merchant Wholesalers[US]

42451	Grain and Field Bean Merchant Wholesalers[US]
424510	Grain and Field Bean Merchant Wholesalers[US]
42452	Livestock Merchant Wholesalers[US]
424520	Livestock Merchant Wholesalers[US]
42459	Other Farm Product Raw Material Merchant Wholesalers[US]
424590	Other Farm Product Raw Material Merchant Wholesalers[US]

4246 Chemical and Allied Products Merchant Wholesalers[US]

42461	Plastics Materials and Basic Forms and Shapes Merchant Wholesalers[US]
424610	Plastics Materials and Basic Forms and Shapes Merchant Wholesalers[US]
42469	Other Chemical and Allied Products Merchant Wholesalers[US]
424690	Other Chemical and Allied Products Merchant Wholesalers[US]

4247   Petroleum and Petroleum Products Merchant Wholesalers[US]

42471	Petroleum Bulk Stations and Terminals[US]
424710	Petroleum Bulk Stations and Terminals[US]
42472	Petroleum and Petroleum Products Merchant Wholesalers (except Bulk Stations and Terminals)[US]
424720	Petroleum and Petroleum Products Merchant Wholesalers (except Bulk Stations and Terminals)[US]

4248   Beer, Wine, and Distilled Alcoholic Beverage Merchant Wholesalers[US]

42481	Beer and Ale Merchant Wholesalers[US]
424810	Beer and Ale Merchant Wholesalers[US]
42482	Wine and Distilled Alcoholic Beverage Merchant Wholesalers[US]
424820	Wine and Distilled Alcoholic Beverage Merchant Wholesalers[US]

4249   Miscellaneous Nondurable Goods Merchant Wholesalers[US]

42491	Farm Supplies Merchant Wholesalers[US]
424910	Farm Supplies Merchant Wholesalers[US]
42492	Book, Periodical, and Newspaper Merchant Wholesalers[US]
424920	Book, Periodical, and Newspaper Merchant Wholesalers[US]
42493	Flower, Nursery Stock, and Florists' Supplies Merchant Wholesalers[US]
424930	Flower, Nursery Stock, and Florists' Supplies Merchant Wholesalers[US]
42494	Tobacco and Tobacco Product Merchant Wholesalers[US]
424940	Tobacco and Tobacco Product Merchant Wholesalers[US]
42495	Paint, Varnish, and Supplies Merchant Wholesalers[US]
424950	Paint, Varnish, and Supplies Merchant Wholesalers[US]
42499	Other Miscellaneous Nondurable Goods Merchant Wholesalers[US]
424990	Other Miscellaneous Nondurable Goods Merchant Wholesalers[US]

425 Wholesale Electronic Markets and Agents and Brokers[CAN]

4251 Wholesale Electronic Markets and Agents and Brokers[CAN]

42511	Business to Business Electronic Markets[CAN]
425110	Business to Business Electronic Markets[CAN]
42512	Wholesale Trade Agents and Brokers[CAN]
425120	Wholesale Trade Agents and Brokers[CAN]

44-45 Retail Trade

441 Motor Vehicle and Parts Dealers[CAN]

4411 Automobile Dealers[CAN]

44111	New Car Dealers[CAN]
441110	New Car Dealers[CAN]
44112	Used Car Dealers[CAN]
441120	Used Car Dealers[CAN]

4412 Other Motor Vehicle Dealers[CAN]

44121	Recreational Vehicle Dealers[CAN]
441210	Recreational Vehicle Dealers[CAN]
44122	Motorcycle, Boat, and Other Motor Vehicle Dealers[CAN]
441221	Motorcycle, ATV, and Personal Watercraft Dealers[US]
441222	Boat Dealers[US]
441229	All Other Motor Vehicle Dealers[US]

4413 Automotive Parts, Accessories, and Tire Stores[CAN]

44131	Automotive Parts and Accessories Stores[CAN]
441310	Automotive Parts and Accessories Stores[CAN]
44132	Tire Dealers[CAN]
441320	Tire Dealers[CAN]

442 Furniture and Home Furnishings Stores[CAN]

4421 Furniture Stores[CAN]

44211	Furniture Stores[CAN]
442110	Furniture Stores[CAN]

4422 Home Furnishings Stores[CAN]

44221	Floor Covering Stores[CAN]
442210	Floor Covering Stores[CAN]
44229	Other Home Furnishings Stores[CAN]
442291	Window Treatment Stores[CAN]
442299	All Other Home Furnishings Stores[US]

443 Electronics and Appliance Stores[CAN]

4431 Electronics and Appliance Stores[CAN]

44311	Appliance, Television, and Other Electronics Stores [CAN]
443111	Household Appliance Stores[US]
443112	Radio, Television, and Other Electronics Stores[US]
44312	Computer and Software Stores[CAN]
443120	Computer and Software Stores[CAN]
44313	Camera and Photographic Supplies Stores[CAN]
443130	Camera and Photographic Supplies Stores[CAN]

444 Building Material and Garden Equipment and Supplies Dealers[CAN]

4441 Building Material and Supplies Dealers[CAN]

44411	Home Centers[CAN]
444110	Home Centers[CAN]
44412	Paint and Wallpaper Stores[CAN]
444120	Paint and Wallpaper Stores[CAN]
44413	Hardware Stores[CAN]
444130	Hardware Stores[CAN]
44419	Other Building Material Dealers[CAN]
444190	Other Building Material Dealers[CAN]

4442 Lawn and Garden Equipment and Supplies Stores[CAN]

44421	Outdoor Power Equipment Stores[CAN]
444210	Outdoor Power Equipment Stores[CAN]
44422	Nursery, Garden Center, and Farm Supply Stores[CAN]
444220	Nursery, Garden Center, and Farm Supply Stores[CAN]

445 Food and Beverage Stores[CAN]

4451 Grocery Stores[CAN]

44511	Supermarkets and Other Grocery (except Convenience) Stores[CAN]
445110	Supermarkets and Other Grocery (except Convenience) Stores[CAN]
44512	Convenience Stores[CAN]
445120	Convenience Stores[CAN]

4452 Specialty Food Stores[CAN]

44521	Meat Markets[CAN]
445210	Meat Markets[CAN]
44522	Fish and Seafood Markets[CAN]

445220	Fish and Seafood Markets[CAN]
44523	Fruit and Vegetable Markets[CAN]
445230	Fruit and Vegetable Markets[CAN]
44529	Other Specialty Food Stores[CAN]
445291	Baked Goods Stores[CAN]
445292	Confectionery and Nut Stores[CAN]
445299	All Other Specialty Food Stores[CAN]

4453 Beer, Wine, and Liquor Stores[CAN]

44531	Beer, Wine, and Liquor Stores[CAN]
445310	Beer, Wine, and Liquor Stores[CAN]

446 Health and Personal Care Stores[CAN]

4461 Health and Personal Care Stores[CAN]

44611	Pharmacies and Drug Stores[CAN]
446110	Pharmacies and Drug Stores[CAN]
44612	Cosmetics, Beauty Supplies, and Perfume Stores[CAN]
446120	Cosmetics, Beauty Supplies, and Perfume Stores[CAN]
44613	Optical Goods Stores[CAN]
446130	Optical Goods Stores[CAN]
44619	Other Health and Personal Care Stores[CAN]
446191	Food (Health) Supplement Stores[CAN]
446199	All Other Health and Personal Care Stores[CAN]

447 Gasoline Stations[CAN]

4471 Gasoline Stations[CAN]

44711	Gasoline Stations with Convenience Stores[CAN]
447110	Gasoline Stations with Convenience Stores[CAN]
44719	Other Gasoline Stations[CAN]
447190	Other Gasoline Stations[CAN]

448 Clothing and Clothing Accessories Stores[CAN]

4481 Clothing Stores[CAN]

44811	Men's Clothing Stores[CAN]
448110	Men's Clothing Stores[CAN]
44812	Women's Clothing Stores[CAN]
448120	Women's Clothing Stores[CAN]
44813	Children's and Infants' Clothing Stores[CAN]
448130	Children's and Infants' Clothing Stores[CAN]
44814	Family Clothing Stores[CAN]
448140	Family Clothing Stores[CAN]
44815	Clothing Accessories Stores[CAN]
448150	Clothing Accessories Stores[CAN]

    44819   Other Clothing Stores[CAN]
    448190   Other Clothing Stores[US]

4482 Shoe Stores[CAN]

    44821   Shoe Stores[CAN]
    448210   Shoe Stores[CAN]

4483 Jewelry, Luggage, and Leather Goods Stores[CAN]

    44831   Jewelry Stores[CAN]
    448310   Jewelry Stores[CAN]
    44832   Luggage and Leather Goods Stores[CAN]
    448320   Luggage and Leather Goods Stores[CAN]

451 Sporting Goods, Hobby, Book, and Music Stores[CAN]

4511 Sporting Goods, Hobby, and Musical Instrument Stores[CAN]

    45111   Sporting Goods Stores[CAN]
    451110   Sporting Goods Stores[CAN]
    45112   Hobby, Toy, and Game Stores[CAN]
    451120   Hobby, Toy, and Game Stores[CAN]
    45113   Sewing, Needlework, and Piece Goods Stores[CAN]
    451130   Sewing, Needlework, and Piece Goods Stores[CAN]
    45114   Musical Instrument and Supplies Stores[CAN]
    451140   Musical Instrument and Supplies Stores[CAN]

4512 Book, Periodical, and Music Stores[CAN]

    45121   Book Stores and News Dealers[CAN]
    451211   Book Stores[US]
    451212   News Dealers and Newsstands[US]
    45122   Prerecorded Tape, Compact Disc, and Record Stores[CAN]
    451220   Prerecorded Tape, Compact Disc, and Record Stores[CAN]

452 General Merchandise Stores[CAN]

4521 Department Stores[CAN]

    45211   Department Stores[CAN]
    452111   Department Stores (except Discount Department Stores)[US]
    452112   Discount Department Stores[US]

4529 Other General Merchandise Stores[CAN]

    45291   Warehouse Clubs and Supercenters[CAN]
    452910   Warehouse Clubs and Supercenters[CAN]
    45299   All Other General Merchandise Stores[CAN]
    452990   All Other General Merchandise Stores[US]

453 Miscellaneous Store Retailers^{CAN}

4531   Florists^{CAN}

45311	Florists^{CAN}
453110	Florists^{CAN}

4532   Office Supplies, Stationery, and Gift Stores^{CAN}

45321   Office Supplies and Stationery Stores^{CAN}
453210   Office Supplies and Stationery Stores^{CAN}
45322   Gift, Novelty, and Souvenir Stores^{CAN}
453220   Gift, Novelty, and Souvenir Stores^{CAN}

4533   Used Merchandise Stores^{CAN}

45331   Used Merchandise Stores^{CAN}
453310   Used Merchandise Stores^{CAN}

4539   Other Miscellaneous Store Retailers^{CAN}

45391   Pet and Pet Supplies Stores^{CAN}
453910   Pet and Pet Supplies Stores^{CAN}
45392   Art Dealers^{CAN}
453920   Art Dealers^{CAN}
45393   Manufactured (Mobile) Home Dealers^{CAN}
453930   Manufactured (Mobile) Home Dealers^{CAN}
45399   All Other Miscellaneous Store Retailers^{CAN}
453991   Tobacco Stores^{US}
453998   All Other Miscellaneous Store Retailers (except Tobacco Stores)^{US}

454 Nonstore Retailers^{CAN}

4541   Electronic Shopping and Mail-Order Houses^{CAN}

45411   Electronic Shopping and Mail-Order Houses^{CAN}
454111   Electronic Shopping^{CAN}
454112   Electronic Auctions^{CAN}
454113   Mail-Order Houses^{CAN}

4542   Vending Machine Operators^{CAN}

45421   Vending Machine Operators^{CAN}
454210   Vending Machine Operators^{CAN}

4543   Direct Selling Establishments^{CAN}

45431   Fuel Dealers^{CAN}
454311   Heating Oil Dealers^{CAN}
454312   Liquefied Petroleum Gas (Bottled Gas) Dealers^{CAN}
454319   Other Fuel Dealers^{CAN}
45439   Other Direct Selling Establishments^{CAN}
454390   Other Direct Selling Establishments^{CAN}

48-49 Transportation and Warehousing

481 Air Transportation

4811 Scheduled Air Transportation

48111   Scheduled Air Transportation
481111   Scheduled Passenger Air Transportation[US]
481112   Scheduled Freight Air Transportation[US]

4812 Nonscheduled Air Transportation

48121   Nonscheduled Air Transportation
481211   Nonscheduled Chartered Passenger Air
             Transportation[US]
481212   Nonscheduled Chartered Freight Air
             Transportation[US]
481219   Other Nonscheduled Air Transportation[US]

482 Rail Transportation

4821 Rail Transportation

48211   Rail Transportation
482111   Line-Haul Railroads[US]
482112   Short Line Railroads[CAN]

483 Water Transportation

4831 Deep Sea, Coastal, and Great Lakes Water Transportation

48311   Deep Sea, Coastal, and Great Lakes Water
             Transportation
483111   Deep Sea Freight Transportation[US]
483112   Deep Sea Passenger Transportation[US]
483113   Coastal and Great Lakes Freight Transportation[US]
483114   Coastal and Great Lakes Passenger
             Transportation[US]

4832 Inland Water Transportation

48321   Inland Water Transportation
483211   Inland Water Freight Transportation[US]
483212   Inland Water Passenger Transportation[US]

484 Truck Transportation

4841 General Freight Trucking

48411   General Freight Trucking, Local
484110   General Freight Trucking, Local[CAN]
48412   General Freight Trucking, Long-Distance

484121	General Freight Trucking, Long-Distance, Truckload[CAN]
484122	General Freight Trucking, Long-Distance, Less Than Truckload[CAN]

4842   Specialized Freight Trucking

48421	Used Household and Office Goods Moving
484210	Used Household and Office Goods Moving
48422	Specialized Freight (except Used Goods) Trucking, Local
484220	Specialized Freight (except Used Goods) Trucking, Local[US]
48423	Specialized Freight (except Used Goods) Trucking, Long-Distance
484230	Specialized Freight (except Used Goods) Trucking, Long-Distance[US]

485 Transit and Ground Passenger Transportation

4851   Urban Transit Systems

48511	Urban Transit Systems
485111	Mixed Mode Transit Systems[US]
485112	Commuter Rail Systems[US]
485113	Bus and Other Motor Vehicle Transit Systems[US]
485119	Other Urban Transit Systems[US]

4852   Interurban and Rural Bus Transportation

48521	Interurban and Rural Bus Transportation
485210	Interurban and Rural Bus Transportation

4853   Taxi and Limousine Service

48531	Taxi Service
485310	Taxi Service[CAN]
48532	Limousine Service
485320	Limousine Service

4854   School and Employee Bus Transportation

48541	School and Employee Bus Transportation
485410	School and Employee Bus Transportation

4855   Charter Bus Industry

48551	Charter Bus Industry
485510	Charter Bus Industry

4859   Other Transit and Ground Passenger Transportation

48599	Other Transit and Ground Passenger Transportation
485991	Special Needs Transportation[US]

485999   All Other Transit and Ground Passenger Transportation[US]

486 Pipeline Transportation

4861 Pipeline Transportation of Crude Oil

48611   Pipeline Transportation of Crude Oil
486110   Pipeline Transportation of Crude Oil

4862 Pipeline Transportation of Natural Gas

48621   Pipeline Transportation of Natural Gas
486210   Pipeline Transportation of Natural Gas

4869 Other Pipeline Transportation

48691   Pipeline Transportation of Refined Petroleum Products
486910   Pipeline Transportation of Refined Petroleum Products
48699   All Other Pipeline Transportation
486990   All Other Pipeline Transportation

487 Scenic and Sightseeing Transportation

4871 Scenic and Sightseeing Transportation, Land

48711   Scenic and Sightseeing Transportation, Land
487110   Scenic and Sightseeing Transportation, Land

4872 Scenic and Sightseeing Transportation, Water

48721   Scenic and Sightseeing Transportation, Water
487210   Scenic and Sightseeing Transportation, Water

4879 Scenic and Sightseeing Transportation, Other

48799   Scenic and Sightseeing Transportation, Other
487990   Scenic and Sightseeing Transportation, Other

488 Support Activities for Transportation

4881 Support Activities for Air Transportation

48811   Airport Operations
488111   Air Traffic Control
488119   Other Airport Operations[CAN]
48819   Other Support Activities for Air Transportation
488190   Other Support Activities for Air Transportation

4882 Support Activities for Rail Transportation

48821   Support Activities for Rail Transportation
488210   Support Activities for Rail Transportation

4883 Support Activities for Water Transportation

48831 Port and Harbor Operations
488310 Port and Harbor Operations
48832 Marine Cargo Handling
488320 Marine Cargo Handling
48833 Navigational Services to Shipping
488330 Navigational Services to Shipping[MEX]
48839 Other Support Activities for Water Transportation
488390 Other Support Activities for Water Transportation

4884 Support Activities for Road Transportation

48841 Motor Vehicle Towing
488410 Motor Vehicle Towing
48849 Other Support Activities for Road Transportation
488490 Other Support Activities for Road
    Transportation[CAN]

4885 Freight Transportation Arrangement

48851 Freight Transportation Arrangement
488510 Freight Transportation Arrangement[US]

4889 Other Support Activities for Transportation

48899 Other Support Activities for Transportation
488991 Packing and Crating[US]
488999 All Other Support Activities for Transportation[US]

491 Postal Service

4911 Postal Service

49111 Postal Service
491110 Postal Service

492 Couriers and Messengers

4921 Couriers and Express Delivery Services

49211 Couriers and Express Delivery Services
492110 Couriers and Express Delivery Services

4922 Local Messengers and Local Delivery

49221 Local Messengers and Local Delivery
492210 Local Messengers and Local Delivery

493 Warehousing and Storage

4931 Warehousing and Storage

49311 General Warehousing and Storage
493110 General Warehousing and Storage[CAN]
49312 Refrigerated Warehousing and Storage
493120 Refrigerated Warehousing and Storage

49313	Farm Product Warehousing and Storage
493130	Farm Product Warehousing and Storage
49319	Other Warehousing and Storage
493190	Other Warehousing and Storage

51   Information

511   Publishing Industries (except Internet)

5111   Newspaper, Periodical, Book, and Directory Publishers

51111	Newspaper Publishers
511110	Newspaper Publishers[CAN]
51112	Periodical Publishers
511120	Periodical Publishers[CAN]
51113	Book Publishers
511130	Book Publishers[CAN]
51114	Directory and Mailing List Publishers
511140	Directory and Mailing List Publishers[CAN]
51119	Other Publishers
511191	Greeting Card Publishers[US]
511199	All Other Publishers[US]

5112   Software Publishers

| 51121 | Software Publishers |
| 511210 | Software Publishers |

512 Motion Picture and Sound Recording Industries

5121   Motion Picture and Video Industries

51211	Motion Picture and Video Production
512110	Motion Picture and Video Production[CAN]
51212	Motion Picture and Video Distribution
512120	Motion Picture and Video Distribution
51213	Motion Picture and Video Exhibition
512131	Motion Picture Theaters (except Drive-Ins)[US]
512132	Drive-In Motion Picture Theaters[US]
51219	Postproduction Services and Other Motion Picture and Video Industries
512191	Teleproduction and Other Postproduction Services[US]
512199	Other Motion Picture and Video Industries[US]

5122   Sound Recording Industries

51221	Record Production
512210	Record Production
51222	Integrated Record Production/Distribution
512220	Integrated Record Production/Distribution
51223	Music Publishers

512230	Music Publishers
51224	Sound Recording Studios
512240	Sound Recording Studios
51229	Other Sound Recording Industries
512290	Other Sound Recording Industries

515 Broadcasting (except Internet)

5151 Radio and Television Broadcasting

51511	Radio Broadcasting
515111	Radio Networks[UC]
515112	Radio Stations[US]
51512	Television Broadcasting
515120	Television Broadcasting

5152 Cable and Other Subscription Programming

51521	Cable and Other Subscription Programming
515210	Cable and Other Subscription Programming

517 Telecommunications

5171 Wired Telecommunications Carriers

51711	Wired Telecommunications Carriers
517110	Wired Telecommunications Carriers[US]

5172 Wireless Telecommunications Carriers (except Satellite)

51721	Wireless Telecommunications Carriers (except Satellite)
517210	Wireless Telecommunications Carriers (except Satellite)

5174 Satellite Telecommunications

51741	Satellite Telecommunications
517410	Satellite Telecommunications

5179 Other Telecommunications

51791	Other Telecommunications
517911	Telecommunications Resellers[US]
517919	All Other Telecommunications[US]

518 Data Processing, Hosting, and Related Services

5182 Data Processing, Hosting, and Related Services

51821	Data Processing, Hosting, and Related Services
518210	Data Processing, Hosting, and Related Services

519 Other Information Services

5191 Other Information Services

51911   News Syndicates
519110   News Syndicates
51912   Libraries and Archives
519120   Libraries and Archives[US]
51913   Internet Publishing and Broadcasting and Web
     Search Portals
519130   Internet Publishing and Broadcasting and Web
     Search Portals
51919   All Other Information Services
519190   All Other Information Services

52   Finance and Insurance

521 Monetary Authorities - Central Bank

5211 Monetary Authorities - Central Bank

52111   Monetary Authorities - Central Bank
521110   Monetary Authorities - Central Bank

522 Credit Intermediation and Related Activities

5221 Depository Credit Intermediation[CAN]

52211   Commercial Banking[US]
522110   Commercial Banking[US]
52212   Savings Institutions[US]
522120   Savings Institutions[US]
52213   Credit Unions[CAN]
522130   Credit Unions[CAN]
52219   Other Depository Credit Intermediation[CAN]
522190   Other Depository Credit Intermediation[CAN]

5222 Nondepository Credit Intermediation[CAN]

52221   Credit Card Issuing[CAN]
522210   Credit Card Issuing[CAN]
52222   Sales Financing[CAN]
522220   Sales Financing[CAN]
52229   Other Nondepository Credit Intermediation[CAN]
522291   Consumer Lending[CAN]
522292   Real Estate Credit[US]
522293   International Trade Financing[US]
522294   Secondary Market Financing[US]
522298   All Other Nondepository Credit Intermediation[US]

5223 Activities Related to Credit Intermediation[CAN]

52231   Mortgage and Nonmortgage Loan Brokers[CAN]

522310   Mortgage and Nonmortgage Loan Brokers[CAN]

52232   Financial Transactions Processing, Reserve, and Clearinghouse Activities[CAN]

522320   Financial Transactions Processing, Reserve, and Clearinghouse Activities[US]

52239   Other Activities Related to Credit Intermediation[CAN]

522390   Other Activities Related to Credit Intermediation[CAN]

523 Securities, Commodity Contracts, and Other Financial Investments and Related Activities

5231 Securities and Commodity Contracts Intermediation and Brokerage

52311   Investment Banking and Securities Dealing[CAN]

523110   Investment Banking and Securities Dealing[CAN]

52312   Securities Brokerage[CAN]

523120   Securities Brokerage[CAN]

52313   Commodity Contracts Dealing[CAN]

523130   Commodity Contracts Dealing[CAN]

52314   Commodity Contracts Brokerage[CAN]

523140   Commodity Contracts Brokerage[CAN]

5232 Securities and Commodity Exchanges

52321   Securities and Commodity Exchanges

523210   Securities and Commodity Exchanges

5239 Other Financial Investment Activities

52391   Miscellaneous Intermediation[CAN]

523910   Miscellaneous Intermediation[CAN]

52392   Portfolio Management[CAN]

523920   Portfolio Management[CAN]

52393   Investment Advice[CAN]

523930   Investment Advice[CAN]

52399   All Other Financial Investment Activities[CAN]

523991   Trust, Fiduciary, and Custody Activities[US]

523999   Miscellaneous Financial Investment Activities[US]

524 Insurance Carriers and Related Activities

5241 Insurance Carriers

52411   Direct Life, Health, and Medical Insurance Carriers[CAN]

524113   Direct Life Insurance Carriers[US]

524114   Direct Health and Medical Insurance Carriers[US]

52412	Direct Insurance (except Life, Health, and Medical) Carriers[CAN]
524126	Direct Property and Casualty Insurance Carriers[US]
524127	Direct Title Insurance Carriers[US]
524128	Other Direct Insurance (except Life, Health, and Medical) Carriers[US]
52413	Reinsurance Carriers[CAN]
524130	Reinsurance Carriers[US]

5242   Agencies, Brokerages, and Other Insurance Related Activities

52421	Insurance Agencies and Brokerages[CAN]
524210	Insurance Agencies and Brokerages[CAN]
52429	Other Insurance Related Activities[CAN]
524291	Claims Adjusting[CAN]
524292	Third Party Administration of Insurance and Pension Funds[US]
524298	All Other Insurance Related Activities[US]

525 Funds, Trusts, and Other Financial Vehicles[US]

5251   Insurance and Employee Benefit Funds[US]

52511	Pension Funds[US]
525110	Pension Funds[US]
52512	Health and Welfare Funds[US]
525120	Health and Welfare Funds[US]
52519	Other Insurance Funds[US]
525190	Other Insurance Funds[US]

5259   Other Investment Pools and Funds[US]

52591	Open-End Investment Funds[US]
525910	Open-End Investment Funds[US]
52592	Trusts, Estates, and Agency Accounts[US]
525920	Trusts, Estates, and Agency Accounts[US]
52599	Other Financial Vehicles[US]
525990	Other Financial Vehicles[US]

53   Real Estate and Rental and Leasing

531 Real Estate

5311   Lessors of Real Estate

53111	Lessors of Residential Buildings and Dwellings[CAN]
531110	Lessors of Residential Buildings and Dwellings[US]
53112	Lessors of Nonresidential Buildings (except Miniwarehouses)[CAN]

531120   Lessors of Nonresidential Buildings (except Miniwarehouses)[CAN]

53113   Lessors of Miniwarehouses and Self-Storage Units[CAN]

531130   Lessors of Miniwarehouses and Self-Storage Units[CAN]

53119   Lessors of Other Real Estate Property[CAN]

531190   Lessors of Other Real Estate Property[CAN]

5312   Offices of Real Estate Agents and Brokers

53121   Offices of Real Estate Agents and Brokers

531210   Offices of Real Estate Agents and Brokers

5313   Activities Related to Real Estate

53131   Real Estate Property Managers[CAN]

531311   Residential Property Managers[US]

531312   Nonresidential Property Managers[US]

53132   Offices of Real Estate Appraisers[CAN]

531320   Offices of Real Estate Appraisers[CAN]

53139   Other Activities Related to Real Estate[CAN]

531390   Other Activities Related to Real Estate[CAN]

532   Rental and Leasing Services

5321   Automotive Equipment Rental and Leasing

53211   Passenger Car Rental and Leasing

532111   Passenger Car Rental[CAN]

532112   Passenger Car Leasing[CAN]

53212   Truck, Utility Trailer, and RV (Recreational Vehicle) Rental and Leasing

532120   Truck, Utility Trailer, and RV (Recreational Vehicle) Rental and Leasing[CAN]

5322   Consumer Goods Rental

53221   Consumer Electronics and Appliances Rental

532210   Consumer Electronics and Appliances Rental

53222   Formal Wear and Costume Rental

532220   Formal Wear and Costume Rental

53223   Video Tape and Disc Rental

532230   Video Tape and Disc Rental

53229   Other Consumer Goods Rental

532291   Home Health Equipment Rental[US]

532292   Recreational Goods Rental[US]

532299   All Other Consumer Goods Rental[US]

5323   General Rental Centers

    53231   General Rental Centers
    532310   General Rental Centers

5324   Commercial and Industrial Machinery and Equipment Rental and Leasing

    53241   Construction, Transportation, Mining, and Forestry Machinery and Equipment Rental and Leasing
    532411   Commercial Air, Rail, and Water Transportation Equipment Rental and Leasing[US]
    532412   Construction, Mining, and Forestry Machinery and Equipment Rental and Leasing[US]
    53242   Office Machinery and Equipment Rental and Leasing
    532420   Office Machinery and Equipment Rental and Leasing
    53249   Other Commercial and Industrial Machinery and Equipment Rental and Leasing
    532490   Other Commercial and Industrial Machinery and Equipment Rental and Leasing[CAN]

533 Lessors of Nonfinancial Intangible Assets (except Copyrighted Works)

5331   Lessors of Nonfinancial Intangible Assets (except Copyrighted Works)

    53311   Lessors of Nonfinancial Intangible Assets (except Copyrighted Works)
    533110   Lessors of Nonfinancial Intangible Assets (except Copyrighted Works)

54   Professional, Scientific, and Technical Services

541 Professional, Scientific, and Technical Services

5411   Legal Services

    54111   Offices of Lawyers
    541110   Offices of Lawyers
    54112   Offices of Notaries
    541120   Offices of Notaries
    54119   Other Legal Services
    541191   Title Abstract and Settlement Offices[US]
    541199   All Other Legal Services[US]

5412 Accounting, Tax Preparation, Bookkeeping, and Payroll Services

54121	Accounting, Tax Preparation, Bookkeeping, and Payroll Services
541211	Offices of Certified Public Accountants[US]
541213	Tax Preparation Services[CAN]
541214	Payroll Services[US]
541219	Other Accounting Services[US]

5413 Architectural, Engineering, and Related Services

54131	Architectural Services
541310	Architectural Services
54132	Landscape Architectural Services
541320	Landscape Architectural Services
54133	Engineering Services
541330	Engineering Services
54134	Drafting Services
541340	Drafting Services
54135	Building Inspection Services
541350	Building Inspection Services
54136	Geophysical Surveying and Mapping Services
541360	Geophysical Surveying and Mapping Services
54137	Surveying and Mapping (except Geophysical) Services
541370	Surveying and Mapping (except Geophysical) Services
54138	Testing Laboratories
541380	Testing Laboratories

5414 Specialized Design Services

54141	Interior Design Services
541410	Interior Design Services
54142	Industrial Design Services
541420	Industrial Design Services
54143	Graphic Design Services
541430	Graphic Design Services
54149	Other Specialized Design Services
541490	Other Specialized Design Services

5415 Computer Systems Design and Related Services

54151	Computer Systems Design and Related Services
541511	Custom Computer Programming Services[US]
541512	Computer Systems Design Services[US]
541513	Computer Facilities Management Services[US]
541519	Other Computer Related Services[US]

5416   Management, Scientific, and Technical Consulting Services

54161   Management Consulting Services

541611   Administrative Management and General Management Consulting Services[CAN]

541612   Human Resources Consulting Services[CAN]

541613   Marketing Consulting Services[US]

541614   Process, Physical Distribution, and Logistics Consulting Services[US]

541618   Other Management Consulting Services[US]

54162   Environmental Consulting Services

541620   Environmental Consulting Services

54169   Other Scientific and Technical Consulting Services

541690   Other Scientific and Technical Consulting Services

5417   Scientific Research and Development Services

54171   Research and Development in the Physical, Engineering, and Life Sciences

541711   Research and Development in Biotechnology[US]

541712   Research and Development in the Physical, Engineering, and Life Sciences (except Biotechnology)[US]

54172   Research and Development in the Social Sciences and Humanities

541720   Research and Development in the Social Sciences and Humanities[CAN]

5418   Advertising, Public Relations, and Related Services

54181   Advertising Agencies

541810   Advertising Agencies

54182   Public Relations Agencies

541820   Public Relations Agencies

54183   Media Buying Agencies

541830   Media Buying Agencies

54184   Media Representatives

541840   Media Representatives

54185   Display Advertising

541850   Display Advertising

54186   Direct Mail Advertising

541860   Direct Mail Advertising

54187   Advertising Material Distribution Services

541870   Advertising Material Distribution Services

54189   Other Services Related to Advertising

541890   Other Services Related to Advertising[MEX]

5419	**Other Professional, Scientific, and Technical Services**
54191	Marketing Research and Public Opinion Polling
541910	Marketing Research and Public Opinion Polling
54192	Photographic Services
541921	Photography Studios, Portrait[US]
541922	Commercial Photography[US]
54193	Translation and Interpretation Services
541930	Translation and Interpretation Services
54194	Veterinary Services
541940	Veterinary Services[CAN]
54199	All Other Professional, Scientific, and Technical Services
541990	All Other Professional, Scientific, and Technical Services

55 Management of Companies and Enterprises

551 Management of Companies and Enterprises

5511	**Management of Companies and Enterprises**
55111	Management of Companies and Enterprises
551111	Offices of Bank Holding Companies[US]
551112	Offices of Other Holding Companies[US]
551114	Corporate, Subsidiary, and Regional Managing Offices[CAN]

56 Administrative and Support and Waste Management and Remediation Services

561 Administrative and Support Services

5611	**Office Administrative Services**
56111	Office Administrative Services
561110	Office Administrative Services
5612	**Facilities Support Services**
56121	Facilities Support Services
561210	Facilities Support Services
5613	**Employment Services**
56131	Employment Placement Agencies and Executive Search Services
561311	Employment Placement Agencies[US]
561312	Executive Search Services[US]
56132	Temporary Help Services
561320	Temporary Help Services
56133	Professional Employer Organizations
561330	Professional Employer Organizations

5614   Business Support Services

56141	Document Preparation Services
561410	Document Preparation Services
56142	Telephone Call Centers
561421	Telephone Answering Services[US]
561422	Telemarketing Bureaus and other Contact Centers[MEX]
56143	Business Service Centers
561431	Private Mail Centers[US]
561439	Other Business Service Centers (including Copy Shops)[US]
56144	Collection Agencies
561440	Collection Agencies
56145	Credit Bureaus
561450	Credit Bureaus
56149	Other Business Support Services
561491	Repossession Services[US]
561492	Court Reporting and Stenotype Services[US]
561499	All Other Business Support Services[US]

5615   Travel Arrangement and Reservation Services

56151	Travel Agencies
561510	Travel Agencies
56152	Tour Operators
561520	Tour Operators
56159	Other Travel Arrangement and Reservation Services
561591	Convention and Visitors Bureaus[US]
561599	All Other Travel Arrangement and Reservation Services[US]

5616   Investigation and Security Services

56161	Investigation, Guard, and Armored Car Services
561611	Investigation Services[CAN]
561612	Security Guards and Patrol Services[CAN]
561613	Armored Car Services[CAN]
56162	Security Systems Services
561621	Security Systems Services (except Locksmiths)[CAN]
561622	Locksmiths[CAN]

5617   Services to Buildings and Dwellings

56171	Exterminating and Pest Control Services
561710	Exterminating and Pest Control Services
56172	Janitorial Services
561720	Janitorial Services[MEX]
56173	Landscaping Services

561730   Landscaping Services
56174   Carpet and Upholstery Cleaning Services
561740   Carpet and Upholstery Cleaning Services
56179   Other Services to Buildings and Dwellings
561790   Other Services to Buildings and Dwellings[MEX]

5619 Other Support Services

56191   Packaging and Labeling Services
561910   Packaging and Labeling Services
56192   Convention and Trade Show Organizers
561920   Convention and Trade Show Organizers
56199   All Other Support Services
561990   All Other Support Services

562 Waste Management and Remediation Services

5621 Waste Collection[CAN]

56211   Waste Collection[CAN]
562111   Solid Waste Collection[US]
562112   Hazardous Waste Collection[US]
562119   Other Waste Collection[US]

5622 Waste Treatment and Disposal[CAN]

56221   Waste Treatment and Disposal[CAN]
562211   Hazardous Waste Treatment and Disposal[US]
562212   Solid Waste Landfill[US]
562213   Solid Waste Combustors and Incinerators[US]
562219   Other Nonhazardous Waste Treatment and Disposal[US]

5629 Remediation and Other Waste Management Services[CAN]

56291   Remediation Services[CAN]
562910   Remediation Services[CAN]
56292   Materials Recovery Facilities[CAN]
562920   Materials Recovery Facilities[CAN]
56299   All Other Waste Management Services[CAN]
562991   Septic Tank and Related Services[US]
562998   All Other Miscellaneous Waste Management Services[US]

61 Educational Services

611 Educational Services

6111 Elementary and Secondary Schools

61111   Elementary and Secondary Schools[CAN]
611110   Elementary and Secondary Schools[CAN]

6112   Junior Colleges

61121   Junior Colleges
611210   Junior Colleges[CAN]

6113   Colleges, Universities, and Professional Schools

61131   Colleges, Universities, and Professional Schools
611310   Colleges, Universities, and Professional
            Schools[CAN]

6114   Business Schools and Computer and Management Training

61141   Business and Secretarial Schools
611410   Business and Secretarial Schools[CAN]
61142   Computer Training
611420   Computer Training[CAN]
61143   Professional and Management Development
            Training
611430   Professional and Management Development
            Training[CAN]

6115   Technical and Trade Schools

61151   Technical and Trade Schools
611511   Cosmetology and Barber Schools[US]
611512   Flight Training[US]
611513   Apprenticeship Training[US]
611519   Other Technical and Trade Schools[US]

6116   Other Schools and Instruction

61161   Fine Arts Schools
611610   Fine Arts Schools[CAN]
61162   Sports and Recreation Instruction
611620   Sports and Recreation Instruction[CAN]
61163   Language Schools
611630   Language Schools[CAN]
61169   All Other Schools and Instruction
611691   Exam Preparation and Tutoring[US]
611692   Automobile Driving Schools[US]
611699   All Other Miscellaneous Schools and
            Instruction[US]

6117   Educational Support Services

61171   Educational Support Services
611710   Educational Support Services

62   Health Care and Social Assistance

621 Ambulatory Health Care Services

6211   Offices of Physicians

62111	Offices of Physicians
621111	Offices of Physicians (except Mental Health Specialists)[US]
621112	Offices of Physicians, Mental Health Specialists[US]

6212   Offices of Dentists

62121	Offices of Dentists
621210	Offices of Dentists[CAN]

6213   Offices of Other Health Practitioners

62131	Offices of Chiropractors
621310	Offices of Chiropractors[CAN]
62132	Offices of Optometrists
621320	Offices of Optometrists
62133	Offices of Mental Health Practitioners (except Physicians)
621330	Offices of Mental Health Practitioners (except Physicians)[CAN]
62134	Offices of Physical, Occupational and Speech Therapists, and Audiologists
621340	Offices of Physical, Occupational and Speech Therapists, and Audiologists[CAN]
62139	Offices of All Other Health Practitioners
621391	Offices of Podiatrists[US]
621399	Offices of All Other Miscellaneous Health Practitioners[US]

6214   Outpatient Care Centers

62141	Family Planning Centers
621410	Family Planning Centers[CAN]
62142	Outpatient Mental Health and Substance Abuse Centers
621420	Outpatient Mental Health and Substance Abuse Centers[CAN]
62149	Other Outpatient Care Centers
621491	HMO Medical Centers[US]
621492	Kidney Dialysis Centers[US]
621493	Freestanding Ambulatory Surgical and Emergency Centers[US]
621498	All Other Outpatient Care Centers[US]

6215 Medical and Diagnostic Laboratories

62151   Medical and Diagnostic Laboratories
621511   Medical Laboratories[US]
621512   Diagnostic Imaging Centers[US]

6216 Home Health Care Services

62161   Home Health Care Services
621610   Home Health Care Services

6219 Other Ambulatory Health Care Services

62191   Ambulance Services
621910   Ambulance Services[MEX]
62199   All Other Ambulatory Health Care Services
621991   Blood and Organ Banks[US]
621999   All Other Miscellaneous Ambulatory Health Care Services[US]

622 Hospitals

6221 General Medical and Surgical Hospitals

62211   General Medical and Surgical Hospitals
622110   General Medical and Surgical Hospitals[US]

6222 Psychiatric and Substance Abuse Hospitals

62221   Psychiatric and Substance Abuse Hospitals
622210   Psychiatric and Substance Abuse Hospitals[CAN]

6223 Specialty (except Psychiatric and Substance Abuse) Hospitals

62231   Specialty (except Psychiatric and Substance Abuse) Hospitals
622310   Specialty (except Psychiatric and Substance Abuse) Hospitals[CAN]

623 Nursing and Residential Care Facilities

6231 Nursing Care Facilities

62311   Nursing Care Facilities
623110   Nursing Care Facilities[CAN]

6232 Residential Mental Retardation, Mental Health and Substance Abuse Facilities

62321   Residential Mental Retardation Facilities
623210   Residential Mental Retardation Facilities[CAN]
62322   Residential Mental Health and Substance Abuse Facilities
623220   Residential Mental Health and Substance Abuse Facilities[US]

6233 Community Care Facilities for the Elderly

    62331   Community Care Facilities for the Elderly

    623311   Continuing Care Retirement Communities[US]

    623312   Homes for the Elderly[US]

6239 Other Residential Care Facilities

    62399   Other Residential Care Facilities

    623990   Other Residential Care Facilities[US]

624 Social Assistance

6241 Individual and Family Services

    62411   Child and Youth Services

    624110   Child and Youth Services[CAN]

    62412   Services for the Elderly and Persons with Disabilities

    624120   Services for the Elderly and Persons with Disabilities[CAN]

    62419   Other Individual and Family Services

    624190   Other Individual and Family Services[CAN]

6242 Community Food and Housing, and Emergency and Other Relief Services

    62421   Community Food Services

    624210   Community Food Services[CAN]

    62422   Community Housing Services

    624221   Temporary Shelters[US]

    624229   Other Community Housing Services[US]

    62423   Emergency and Other Relief Services

    624230   Emergency and Other Relief Services[CAN]

6243 Vocational Rehabilitation Services

    62431   Vocational Rehabilitation Services

    624310   Vocational Rehabilitation Services[CAN]

6244 Child Day Care Services

    62441   Child Day Care Services

    624410   Child Day Care Services[CAN]

71   Arts, Entertainment, and Recreation

711 Performing Arts, Spectator Sports, and Related Industries

7111 Performing Arts Companies

    71111   Theater Companies and Dinner Theaters

    711110   Theater Companies and Dinner Theaters[US]

    71112   Dance Companies

711120   Dance Companies[CAN]
71113   Musical Groups and Artists
711130   Musical Groups and Artists[CAN]
71119   Other Performing Arts Companies
711190   Other Performing Arts Companies[CAN]

7112   Spectator Sports

71121   Spectator Sports
711211   Sports Teams and Clubs[CAN]
711212   Racetracks[US]
711219   Other Spectator Sports[US]

7113   Promoters of Performing Arts, Sports, and Similar Events

71131   Promoters of Performing Arts, Sports, and Similar Events with Facilities
711310   Promoters of Performing Arts, Sports, and Similar Events with Facilities[US]
71132   Promoters of Performing Arts, Sports, and Similar Events without Facilities
711320   Promoters of Performing Arts, Sports, and Similar Events without Facilities[MEX]

7114   Agents and Managers for Artists, Athletes, Entertainers, and Other Public Figures

71141   Agents and Managers for Artists, Athletes, Entertainers, and Other Public Figures
711410   Agents and Managers for Artists, Athletes, Entertainers, and Other Public Figures

7115   Independent Artists, Writers, and Performers

71151   Independent Artists, Writers, and Performers
711510   Independent Artists, Writers, and Performers

712 Museums, Historical Sites, and Similar Institutions

7121   Museums, Historical Sites, and Similar Institutions

71211   Museums
712110   Museums[US]
71212   Historical Sites
712120   Historical Sites
71213   Zoos and Botanical Gardens
712130   Zoos and Botanical Gardens[CAN]
71219   Nature Parks and Other Similar Institutions
712190   Nature Parks and Other Similar Institutions

713 Amusement, Gambling, and Recreation Industries

7131 Amusement Parks and Arcades

71311	Amusement and Theme Parks
713110	Amusement and Theme Parks[CAN]
71312	Amusement Arcades
713120	Amusement Arcades

7132 Gambling Industries

71321	Casinos (except Casino Hotels)
713210	Casinos (except Casino Hotels)
71329	Other Gambling Industries
713290	Other Gambling Industries[US]

7139 Other Amusement and Recreation Industries

71391	Golf Courses and Country Clubs
713910	Golf Courses and Country Clubs
71392	Skiing Facilities
713920	Skiing Facilities
71393	Marinas
713930	Marinas
71394	Fitness and Recreational Sports Centers
713940	Fitness and Recreational Sports Centers[CAN]
71395	Bowling Centers
713950	Bowling Centers
71399	All Other Amusement and Recreation Industries
713990	All Other Amusement and Recreation Industries[CAN]

72 Accommodation and Food Services

721 Accommodation

7211 Traveler Accommodation

72111	Hotels (except Casino Hotels) and Motels
721110	Hotels (except Casino Hotels) and Motels[US]
72112	Casino Hotels
721120	Casino Hotels
72119	Other Traveler Accommodation
721191	Bed-and-Breakfast Inns[CAN]
721199	All Other Traveler Accommodation[US]

7212 RV (Recreational Vehicle) Parks and Recreational Camps

72121	RV (Recreational Vehicle) Parks and Recreational Camps
721211	RV (Recreational Vehicle) Parks and Campgrounds[CAN]

721214   Recreational and Vacation Camps (except Campgrounds)[US]

7213   Rooming and Boarding Houses

72131   Rooming and Boarding Houses
721310   Rooming and Boarding Houses[CAN]

722 Food Services and Drinking Places

7221   Full-Service Restaurants

72211   Full-Service Restaurants
722110   Full-Service Restaurants[CAN]

7222   Limited-Service Eating Places

72221   Limited-Service Eating Places
722211   Limited-Service Restaurants[US]
722212   Cafeterias, Grill Buffets, and Buffets[US]
722213   Snack and Nonalcoholic Beverage Bars[US]

7223   Special Food Services

72231   Food Service Contractors
722310   Food Service Contractors
72232   Caterers
722320   Caterers
72233   Mobile Food Services
722330   Mobile Food Services

7224   Drinking Places (Alcoholic Beverages)

72241   Drinking Places (Alcoholic Beverages)
722410   Drinking Places (Alcoholic Beverages)[CAN]

81   Other Services (except Public Administration)

811 Repair and Maintenance

8111   Automotive Repair and Maintenance

81111   Automotive Mechanical and Electrical Repair and Maintenance
811111   General Automotive Repair[CAN]
811112   Automotive Exhaust System Repair[CAN]
811113   Automotive Transmission Repair[US]
811118   Other Automotive Mechanical and Electrical Repair and Maintenance[US]
81112   Automotive Body, Paint, Interior, and Glass Repair
811121   Automotive Body, Paint, and Interior Repair and Maintenance[CAN]
811122   Automotive Glass Replacement Shops[CAN]

81119   Other Automotive Repair and Maintenance
811191   Automotive Oil Change and Lubrication Shops[US]
811192   Car Washes[CAN]
811198   All Other Automotive Repair and Maintenance[US]

8112 **Electronic and Precision Equipment Repair and Maintenance**

81121   Electronic and Precision Equipment Repair and Maintenance
811211   Consumer Electronics Repair and Maintenance[MEX]
811212   Computer and Office Machine Repair and Maintenance[US]
811213   Communication Equipment Repair and Maintenance[US]
811219   Other Electronic and Precision Equipment Repair and Maintenance[US]

8113 **Commercial and Industrial Machinery and Equipment (except Automotive and Electronic) Repair and Maintenance**

81131   Commercial and Industrial Machinery and Equipment (except Automotive and Electronic) Repair and Maintenance
811310   Commercial and Industrial Machinery and Equipment (except Automotive and Electronic) Repair and Maintenance[CAN]

8114 **Personal and Household Goods Repair and Maintenance**

81141   Home and Garden Equipment and Appliance Repair and Maintenance
811411   Home and Garden Equipment Repair and Maintenance[CAN]
811412   Appliance Repair and Maintenance[CAN]
81142   Reupholstery and Furniture Repair
811420   Reupholstery and Furniture Repair
81143   Footwear and Leather Goods Repair
811430   Footwear and Leather Goods Repair
81149   Other Personal and Household Goods Repair and Maintenance
811490   Other Personal and Household Goods Repair and Maintenance[CAN]

812 Personal and Laundry Services

8121 **Personal Care Services**[CAN]

81211   Hair, Nail, and Skin Care Services[CAN]
812111   Barber Shops[US]

812112	Beauty Salons[US]
812113	Nail Salons[US]
81219	Other Personal Care Services[CAN]
812191	Diet and Weight Reducing Centers[US]
812199	Other Personal Care Services[US]

8122 Death Care Services[CAN]

81221	Funeral Homes and Funeral Services[CAN]
812210	Funeral Homes and Funeral Services[CAN]
81222	Cemeteries and Crematories[CAN]
812220	Cemeteries and Crematories[CAN]

8123 Drycleaning and Laundry Services[CAN]

81231	Coin-Operated Laundries and Drycleaners[CAN]
812310	Coin-Operated Laundries and Drycleaners[CAN]
81232	Drycleaning and Laundry Services (except Coin-Operated)[CAN]
812320	Drycleaning and Laundry Services (except Coin-Operated)[CAN]
81233	Linen and Uniform Supply[CAN]
812331	Linen Supply[US]
812332	Industrial Launderers[US]

8129 Other Personal Services[CAN]

81291	Pet Care (except Veterinary) Services[CAN]
812910	Pet Care (except Veterinary) Services[CAN]
81292	Photofinishing[CAN]
812921	Photofinishing Laboratories (except One-Hour)[CAN]
812922	One-Hour Photofinishing[CAN]
81293	Parking Lots and Garages[CAN]
812930	Parking Lots and Garages[CAN]
81299	All Other Personal Services[CAN]
812990	All Other Personal Services[CAN]

813 Religious, Grantmaking, Civic, Professional, and Similar Organizations

8131 Religious Organizations[CAN]

81311	Religious Organizations[CAN]
813110	Religious Organizations[CAN]

8132 Grantmaking and Giving Services[CAN]

81321	Grantmaking and Giving Services[CAN]
813211	Grantmaking Foundations[US]
813212	Voluntary Health Organizations[US]
813219	Other Grantmaking and Giving Services[US]

8133 Social Advocacy Organizations[CAN]

81331   Social Advocacy Organizations[CAN]
813311   Human Rights Organizations[US]
813312   Environment, Conservation and Wildlife Organizations[US]
813319   Other Social Advocacy Organizations[US]

8134 Civic and Social Organizations[CAN]

81341   Civic and Social Organizations[CAN]
813410   Civic and Social Organizations[CAN]

8139 Business, Professional, Labor, Political, and Similar Organizations[CAN]

81391   Business Associations[CAN]
813910   Business Associations[CAN]
81392   Professional Organizations[CAN]
813920   Professional Organizations[CAN]
81393   Labor Unions and Similar Labor Organizations[CAN]
813930   Labor Unions and Similar Labor Organizations[CAN]
81394   Political Organizations[CAN]
813940   Political Organizations[CAN]
81399   Other Similar Organizations (except Business, Professional, Labor, and Political Organizations)[CAN]
813990   Other Similar Organizations (except Business, Professional, Labor, and Political Organizations)[CAN]

814 Private Households

8141 Private Households

81411   Private Households
814110   Private Households

92 Public Administration

921 Executive, Legislative, and Other General Government Support[US]

9211 Executive, Legislative, and Other General Government Support[US]

92111   Executive Offices[US]
921110   Executive Offices[US]
92112   Legislative Bodies[US]
921120   Legislative Bodies[US]
92113   Public Finance Activities[US]
921130   Public Finance Activities[US]

92114	Executive and Legislative Offices, Combined[US]
921140	Executive and Legislative Offices, Combined[US]
92115	American Indian and Alaska Native Tribal Governments[US]
921150	American Indian and Alaska Native Tribal Governments[US]
92119	Other General Government Support[US]
921190	Other General Government Support[US]

922 Justice, Public Order, and Safety Activities[US]

9221 Justice, Public Order, and Safety Activities[US]

92211	Courts[US]
922110	Courts[US]
92212	Police Protection[US]
922120	Police Protection[US]
92213	Legal Counsel and Prosecution[US]
922130	Legal Counsel and Prosecution[US]
92214	Correctional Institutions[US]
922140	Correctional Institutions[US]
92215	Parole Offices and Probation Offices[US]
922150	Parole Offices and Probation Offices[US]
92216	Fire Protection[US]
922160	Fire Protection[US]
92219	Other Justice, Public Order, and Safety Activities[US]
922190	Other Justice, Public Order, and Safety Activities[US]

923 Administration of Human Resource Programs[US]

9231 Administration of Human Resource Programs[US]

92311	Administration of Education Programs[US]
923110	Administration of Education Programs[US]
92312	Administration of Public Health Programs[US]
923120	Administration of Public Health Programs[US]
92313	Administration of Human Resource Programs (except Education, Public Health, and Veterans' Affairs Programs)[US]
923130	Administration of Human Resource Programs (except Education, Public Health, and Veterans' Affairs Programs)[US]
92314	Administration of Veterans' Affairs[US]
923140	Administration of Veterans' Affairs[US]

924 Administration of Environmental Quality Programs^{US}

9241 Administration of Environmental Quality Programs^{US}

92411	Administration of Air and Water Resource and Solid Waste Management Programs^{US}
924110	Administration of Air and Water Resource and Solid Waste Management Programs^{US}
92412	Administration of Conservation Programs^{US}
924120	Administration of Conservation Programs^{US}

925 Administration of Housing Programs, Urban Planning, and Community Development^{US}

9251 Administration of Housing Programs, Urban Planning, and Community Development^{US}

92511	Administration of Housing Programs^{US}
925110	Administration of Housing Programs^{US}
92512	Administration of Urban Planning and Community and Rural Development^{US}
925120	Administration of Urban Planning and Community and Rural Development^{US}

926 Administration of Economic Programs^{US}

9261 Administration of Economic Programs^{US}

92611	Administration of General Economic Programs^{US}
926110	Administration of General Economic Programs^{US}
92612	Regulation and Administration of Transportation Programs^{US}
926120	Regulation and Administration of Transportation Programs^{US}
92613	Regulation and Administration of Communications, Electric, Gas, and other Utilities^{US}
926130	Regulation and Administration of Communications, Electric, Gas, and Other Utilities^{US}
92614	Regulation of Agricultural Marketing and Commodities^{US}
926140	Regulation of Agricultural Marketing and Commodities^{US}
92615	Regulation, Licensing, and Inspection of Miscellaneous Commercial Sectors^{US}
926150	Regulation, Licensing, and Inspection of Miscellaneous Commercial Sectors^{US}

927 Space Research and Technology[US]

9271 Space Research and Technology[US]

92711	Space Research and Technology[US]
927110	Space Research and Technology[US]

928 National Security and International Affairs[US]

9281 National Security and International Affairs[US]

92811	National Security[US]
928110	National Security[US]
92812	International Affairs[US]
928120	International Affairs[US]

Frequently Asked Questions About Economic Classifications

1. What is the purpose of an industry classification system?
   - An industry classification system facilitates the collection, tabulation, presentation, and analysis of data relating to establishments and ensures that data about the U.S. economy published by U.S. statistical agencies are uniform and comparable. NAICS ensures that such data are uniform and comparable among Canada, Mexico, and the United States.

2. What is an establishment?
   - An establishment is generally a single, physical location at which economic activity occurs (e.g., store, factory, farm, etc.). An enterprise, on the other hand, may consist of more than one location performing the same or different types of economic activities. Each establishment of that enterprise is assigned a NAICS code, based on its own primary activity.

3. How can I determine the correct NAICS code for my business?
   - To determine the correct NAICS code for your establishment, first identify the primary business activity. Then refer either to: 1) the NAICS United States Structure near the beginning of the manual to search the titles from the 2-digit level down through the 6-digit, more detailed level, to find the appropriate code; or 2) the Alphabetic Index at the back of the book to search alphabetically for the primary activity and its corresponding code. Next, turn to the industry description of the specified code in Part I of the manual, read the full description of the industry (including the narrative, cross-references, and illustrative examples), and determine if that description fits the activities of your establishment. Electronic references are available at http://www.census.gov/naics.

4. Who assigns NAICS codes to businesses and how?
   - There is no central government agency with the role of assigning, monitoring, or approving NAICS codes for establishments. Different agencies maintain their own lists of business establishments to meet their own programmatic needs. These different agencies use their own methods for assigning NAICS codes to the establishments on their lists. Statistical agencies assign one NAICS code to each establishment based on its primary activity. For example, the Social Security Administration assigns a NAICS code to new businesses based on information provided on their application for an Employer Identification Number. The Census Bureau generally assigns NAICS codes to businesses on its list of establishments based on information provided by the business on a survey or census report form. The Bureau of Labor Statistics initially assigns NAICS codes based on business activity information provided on an application for unemployment insurance.

5. How do I apply for a NAICS code?
   - A business does not 'apply' for a NAICS code. As explained above, statistical agencies generally assign NAICS codes based on information provided by a business on an application form, an administrative report, or on a survey or census report form.

6. How can I get a new NAICS code created for my type of business?
   - Every 5 years NAICS is reviewed for potential revisions, so that the classification system can keep pace with the changing economy. This is the only time that new NAICS codes can be considered. The Office of Management and Budget (OMB), through its Economic Classification Policy Committee (ECPC), will solicit public comments regarding changes to NAICS through a notice published in the Federal Register. The notice will provide details of the format in which comments should be submitted, how and to whom they should be submitted, and the deadline for submission. Generally, the comment period will close 90 days after publication of the notice. During that time, suggestions for new and emerging industries can be submitted to the ECPC. The next scheduled review of NAICS will be for a potential 2012 revision. OMB will publish a Federal Register notice soliciting comments for that revision in early 2008.

7. What is the relationship between NAICS and the Small Business Administration's (SBA) size standards?
   NAICS categories do not distinguish between small and large business, or between for-profit and non-profit. The Small Business Administration (SBA) develops size standards for each NAICS category. To find more information about the SBA size standards, or when the SBA will update their size standards to reflect 2007 NAICS revisions, visit the SBA Web site at www.sba.gov/size/indexsize.html. You may also contact SBA's Office of Size Standards on 202-205-6618 or via email to sizestandards@sba.gov.

8. How do the NAICS codes affect federal procurement and regulatory activities, such as those carried out by the Environmental Protection Agency, OSHA, the Department of Defense, and the General Services Administration?
   - NAICS was developed specifically for the collection and publication of statistical data to foster the comparability of economic estimates for Canada, Mexico, and the United States. The NAICS categories and definitions were not developed to meet the needs of procurement and/or regulatory applications. However, other federal agencies and other organizations have adopted NAICS for procurement and regulatory purposes even though it does not entirely fit their specific needs. For questions regarding these agencies' use of the NAICS system, contact the specific agency. The next section of this manual contains a directory of selected federal agencies that use NAICS.

For answers to other NAICS questions, you may visit the NAICS Web site at http://www.census.gov/naics.

[INTENTIONALLY LEFT BLANK]

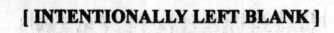

[INTENTIONALLY LEFT BLANK]

[INTENTIONALLY LEFT BLANK]

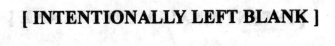
[INTENTIONALLY LEFT BLANK]

[INTENTIONALLY LEFT BLANK]

[INTENTIONALLY LEFT BLANK]

Part I

Titles and Descriptions of Industries

Sector 11—Agriculture, Forestry, Fishing and Hunting

The Sector as a Whole

The Agriculture, Forestry, Fishing and Hunting sector comprises establishments primarily engaged in growing crops, raising animals, harvesting timber, and harvesting fish and other animals from a farm, ranch, or their natural habitats.

The establishments in this sector are often described as farms, ranches, dairies, greenhouses, nurseries, orchards, or hatcheries. A farm may consist of a single tract of land or a number of separate tracts which may be held under different tenures. For example, one tract may be owned by the farm operator and another rented. It may be operated by the operator alone or with the assistance of members of the household or hired employees, or it may be operated by a partnership, corporation, or other type of organization. When a landowner has one or more tenants, renters, croppers, or managers, the land operated by each is considered a farm.

The sector distinguishes two basic activities: agricultural production and agricultural support activities. Agricultural production includes establishments performing the complete farm or ranch operation, such as farm owner-operators, tenant farm operators, and sharecroppers. Agricultural support activities include establishments that perform one or more activities associated with farm operation, such as soil preparation, planting, harvesting, and management, on a contract or fee basis.

Excluded from the Agriculture, Forestry, Hunting and Fishing sector are establishments primarily engaged in agricultural research and establishments primarily engaged in administering programs for regulating and conserving land, mineral, wildlife, and forest use. These establishments are classified in Industry 54171, Research and Development in the Physical, Engineering, and Life Sciences; and Industry 92412, Administration of Conservation Programs, respectively.

111 Crop Production

Industries in the Crop Production subsector grow crops mainly for food and fiber. The subsector comprises establishments, such as farms, orchards, groves, greenhouses, and nurseries, primarily engaged in growing crops, plants, vines, or trees and their seeds.

The industries in this subsector are grouped by similarity of production activity, including biological and physiological characteristics and economic requirements, the length of growing season, degree of crop rotation, extent of input specialization, labor requirements, and capital demands. The production process is typically completed when the raw product or commodity grown reaches the "farm gate" for market, that is, at the point of first sale or price determination.

US—United States industry only. CAN—United States and Canadian industries are comparable. MEX—United States and Mexican industries are comparable. Blank—Canadian, Mexican, and United States industries are comparable.

Establishments are classified to the crop production subsector when crop production (i.e., value of crops for market) accounts for one-half or more of the establishment's total agricultural production. Within the subsector, establishments are classified to a specific industry when a product or industry family of products (i.e., oilseed and grain farming, vegetable and melon farming, fruit and tree nut farming) account for one-half or more of the establishment's agricultural production. Establishments with one-half or more crop production with no one product or family of products of an industry accounting for one-half of the establishment's agricultural production are treated as general combination crop farming and are classified in Industry 11199, All Other Crop Farming.

Industries in the Crop Production subsector include establishments that own, operate, and manage and those that operate and manage. Those that manage only are classified in Subsector 115, Support Activities for Agriculture and Forestry.

1111 Oilseed and Grain Farming

This industry group comprises establishments primarily engaged in (1) growing oilseed and/or grain crops and/or (2) producing oilseed and grain seeds. These crops have an annual life cycle and are typically grown in open fields.

11111 Soybean Farming
See industry description for 111110 below.

111110 Soybean Farming

This industry comprises establishments primarily engaged in growing soybeans and/or producing soybean seeds.

Cross-References.

Establishments engaged in growing soybeans in combination with grain(s) with the soybeans or grain(s) not accounting for one-half of the establishment's agricultural production (value of crops for market) are classified in U.S. Industry 111191, Oilseed and Grain Combination Farming.

11112 Oilseed (except Soybean) Farming
See industry description for 111120 below.

111120 Oilseed (except Soybean) Farming^{CAN}

This industry comprises establishments primarily engaged in growing fibrous oilseed producing plants and/or producing oilseed seeds, such as sunflower, safflower, flax, rape, canola, and sesame.

US—United States industry only. CAN—United States and Canadian industries are comparable. MEX—United States and Mexican industries are comparable. Blank—Canadian, Mexican, and United States industries are comparable.

Cross-References. Establishments primarily engaged in—

- Growing soybeans—are classified in Industry 111110, Soybean Farming; and

- Growing oilseed(s) in combination with grain(s) with no one oilseed (or family of oilseeds) or grain(s) (or family of grains) accounting for one-half of the establishment's agricultural production (value of crops for market)— are classified in U.S. Industry 111191, Oilseed and Grain Combination Farming.

11113 Dry Pea and Bean Farming

See industry description for 111130 below.

111130 Dry Pea and Bean Farming^{CAN}

This industry comprises establishments primarily engaged in growing dry peas, beans, and/or lentils.

Cross-References.

Establishments primarily engaged in growing fresh green beans and peas are classified in U.S. Industry 111219, Other Vegetable (except Potato) and Melon Farming.

11114 Wheat Farming

See industry description for 111140 below.

111140 Wheat Farming

This industry comprises establishments primarily engaged in growing wheat and/or producing wheat seeds.

Cross-References.

Establishments growing wheat in combination with oilseed(s) with the wheat or oilseed(s) not accounting for one-half of the establishment's agricultural production (value of crops for market) are classified in U.S. Industry 111191, Oilseed and Grain Combination Farming.

11115 Corn Farming

See industry description for 111150 below.

111150 Corn Farming^{CAN}

This industry comprises establishments primarily engaged in growing corn (except sweet corn) and/or producing corn seeds.

Cross-References. Establishments primarily engaged in—

- Growing sweet corn—are classified in U.S. Industry 111219, Other Vegetable (except Potato) and Melon Farming; and

- Growing corn in combination with oilseed(s) with the corn or oilseed(s) not accounting for one-half of the establishment's production (value of crops for market)—are classified in U.S. Industry 111191, Oilseed and Grain Combination Farming.

11116 Rice Farming
See industry description for 111160 below.

111160 Rice Farming

This industry comprises establishments primarily engaged in growing rice (except wild rice) and/or producing rice seeds.

Cross-References. Establishments primarily engaged in—

- Growing wild rice—are classified in U.S. Industry 111199, All Other Grain Farming; and

- Growing rice in combination with oilseed(s) with the rice or oilseed(s) not accounting for one-half of the establishment's agricultural production (value of crops for market)—are classified in U.S. Industry 111191, Oilseed and Grain Combination Farming.

11119 Other Grain Farming

This industry comprises establishments primarily engaged in (1) growing grain(s) and/or producing grain seeds (except wheat, corn, and rice) or (2) growing a combination of grain(s) and oilseed(s) with no one grain (or family of grains) or oilseed (or family of oilseeds) accounting for one-half of the establishment's agriculture production (value of crops for market). Combination grain(s) and oilseed(s) establishments may produce oilseed(s) and grain(s) seeds and/or grow oilseed(s) and grain(s).

US—United States industry only. CAN—United States and Canadian industries are comparable. MEX—United States and Mexican industries are comparable. Blank—Canadian, Mexican, and United States industries are comparable.

Illustrative Examples:

Barley farming
Rye farming
Milo farming
Sorghum farming

Oat farming
Wild rice farming
Oilseed and grain combination farming

Cross-References. Establishments primarily engaged in—

- Growing wheat—are classified in Industry 11114, Wheat Farming;

- Growing corn (except sweet corn)—are classified in Industry 11115, Corn Farming;

- Growing sweet corn—are classified in Industry 11121, Vegetable and Melon Farming; and

- Growing rice (except wild rice)—are classified in Industry 11116, Rice Farming.

111191 Oilseed and Grain Combination Farming[US]

This U.S. industry comprises establishments engaged in growing a combination of oilseed(s) and grain(s) with no one oilseed (or family of oilseeds) or grain (or family of grains) accounting for one-half of the establishment's agricultural production (value of crops for market). These establishments may produce oilseed(s) and grain(s) seeds and/cr grow oilseed(s) and grain(s).

Cross-References.

Establishments engaged in growing one grain (or family of grains) or oilseed (or family of oilseeds) accounting for one-half of the establishment's agriculture production (value of crops for market) are classified in Industry Group 1111, Oilseed and Grain Farming accordingly by the prominent grain(s) or oilseed(s) grown.

111199 All Other Grain Farming[US]

This U.S. industry comprises establishments primarily engaged in growing grains and/or producing grain(s) seeds (except wheat, corn, rice, and oilseed(s) and grain(s) combinations).

Illustrative Examples:

Barley farming
Sorghum farming
Oat farming

Wild rice farming
Rye farming

US—United States industry only. CAN—United States and Canadian industries are comparable. MEX—United States and Mexican industries are comparable. Blank—Canadian, Mexican, and United States industries are comparable.

Cross-References. Establishments primarily engaged in—

- Growing wheat—are classified in Industry 111140, Wheat Farming;
- Growing corn—are classified in Industry 111150, Corn Farming;
- Growing rice (except wild rice)—are classified in Industry 111160, Rice Farming;
- Growing sweet corn—are classified in U.S. Industry 111219, Other Vegetable (except Potato) and Melon Farming; and
- Growing a combination of grain(s) and oilseed(s) with no one grain (or family of grains) or oilseed (or family of oilseeds) accounting for one-half of the establishment's agricultural production (value of crops for market)— are classified in U.S. Industry 111191, Oilseed and Grain Combination Farming.

1112 Vegetable and Melon Farming

This industry group comprises establishments primarily engaged in growing root and tuber crops (except sugar beets and peanuts) or edible plants and/or producing root and tuber or edible plant seeds. The crops included in this group have an annual growth cycle and are grown in open fields. Climate and cultural practices limit producing areas but often permit the growing of a combination of crops in a year.

11121 Vegetable and Melon Farming

This industry comprises establishments primarily engaged in one or more of the following: (1) growing vegetable and/or melon crops; (2) producing vegetable and melon seeds; and (3) growing vegetable and/or melon bedding plants.

Cross-References. Establishments primarily engaged in—

- Growing sugar beets—are classified in Industry 11199, All Other Crop Farming;
- Growing vegetables and melons under glass or protective cover—are classified in Industry 11141, Food Crops Grown Under Cover;
- Growing dry peas and beans—are classified in Industry 11113, Dry Pea and Bean Farming;
- Growing corn (except sweet corn)—are classified in Industry 11115, Corn Farming;
- Canning, pickling, and/or drying (artificially) vegetables—are classified in Industry 31142, Fruit and Vegetable Canning, Pickling, and Drying; and

- Growing fruit on trees and other fruit-bearing plants (except melons)—are classified in Industry Group 1113, Fruit and Tree Nut Farming.

111211 Potato Farming^{CAN}

This U.S. industry comprises establishments primarily engaged in growing potatoes and/or producing seed potatoes.

Cross-References.

Establishments primarily engaged in canning or drying potatoes are classified in Industry 31142, Fruit and Vegetable Canning, Pickling, and Drying.

111219 Other Vegetable (except Potato) and Melon Farming^{CAN}

This U.S. industry comprises establishments primarily engaged in one or more of the following: (1) growing melons and/or vegetables (except potatoes; dry peas; dry beans; field, silage, or seed corn; and sugar beets); (2) producing vegetable and/or melon seeds; and (3) growing vegetable and/or melon bedding plants.

Illustrative Examples:

Carrot farming
Squash farming
Green bean farming
Tomato farming
Melon farming (e.g., cantaloupe, casaba, honeydew, watermelon)

Vegetable (except potato) farming
Pepper farming (e.g., bell, chili, green, red, sweet peppers)
Watermelon farming

Cross-References. Establishments primarily engaged in—

- Growing potatoes, including sweet potatoes and yams—are classified in U.S. Industry 111211, Potato Farming;

- Growing sugar beets—are classified in U.S. Industry 111991, Sugar Beet Farming;

- Growing vegetables and melons under glass or protective cover—are classified in U.S. Industry 111419, Other Food Crops Grown Under Cover;

- Growing dry peas and beans—are classified in Industry 111130, Dry Pea and Bean Farming;

- Growing corn (except sweet corn)—are classified in Industry 111150, Corn Farming;

- Canning, pickling, and/or drying (artificially) vegetables—are classified in Industry 31142, Fruit and Vegetable Canning, Pickling, and Drying; and

- Growing fruit on trees and other fruit-bearing plants (except melons)—are classified in Industry Group 1113, Fruit and Tree Nut Farming.

1113 Fruit and Tree Nut Farming

This industry group comprises establishments primarily engaged in growing fruit and/or tree nut crops. The crops included in this industry group are generally not grown from seeds and have a perennial life cycle.

11131 Orange Groves
See industry description for 111310 below.

111310 Orange Groves

This industry comprises establishments primarily engaged in growing oranges.

11132 Citrus (except Orange) Groves
See industry description for 111320 below.

111320 Citrus (except Orange) Groves[CAN]

This industry comprises establishments primarily engaged in growing citrus fruits (except oranges).

Illustrative Examples:

Citrus groves (except oranges)   Tangelo groves
Mandarin groves   Lemon groves
Grapefruit groves   Tangerine groves

Cross-References.

Establishments primarily engaged in growing oranges are classified in Industry 111310, Orange Groves.

11133 Noncitrus Fruit and Tree Nut Farming

This industry comprises establishments primarily engaged in one or more of the following: (1) growing noncitrus fruits (e.g., apples, grapes, berries, peaches);

US—United States industry only. CAN—United States and Canadian industries are comparable. MEX—United States and Mexican industries are comparable. Blank—Canadian, Mexican, and United States industries are comparable.

(2) growing tree nuts (e.g., pecans, almonds, pistachios); or (3) growing a combination of fruit(s) and tree nut(s) with no one fruit (or family of fruit) or family of tree nuts accounting for one-half of the establishment's agriculture production (value of crops for market).

Cross-References. Establishments primarily engaged in—

- Harvesting berries or nuts from native and noncultivated plants—are classified in Industry 11321, Forest Nurseries and Gathering of Forest Products; and

- Canning and/or drying (artificially) fruit—are classified in Industry 31142, Fruit and Vegetable Canning, Pickling, and Drying.

111331 Apple Orchards^{US}

This U.S. industry comprises establishments primarily engaged in growing apples.

Cross-References.

Establishments engaged in growing apples in combination with tree nut(s) with the apples or family of tree nuts not accounting for one-half of the establishment's agriculture production (i.e., value of crops for market) are classified in U.S. Industry 111336, Fruit and Tree Nut Combination Farming.

111332 Grape Vineyards^{US}

This U.S. industry comprises establishments primarily engaged in growing grapes and/or growing grapes to sun dry into raisins.

Cross-References. Establishments primarily engaged in—

- Drying grapes artificially—are classified in U.S. Industry 311423, Dried and Dehydrated Food Manufacturing; and

- Growing grapes in combination with tree nut(s) with the grapes or family of tree nuts not accounting for one-half of the establishment's agriculture production (i.e., value of crops for market)—are classified in U.S. Industry 111336, Fruit and Tree Nut Combination Farming.

111333 Strawberry Farming^{US}

This U.S. industry comprises establishments primarily engaged in growing strawberries.

US—United States industry only. CAN—United States and Canadian industries are comparable. MEX—United States and Mexican industries are comparable. Blank—Canadian, Mexican, and United States industries are comparable.

Cross-References.

Establishments engaged in growing strawberries in combination with tree nut(s) with the strawberries or family of tree nuts not accounting for one-half of the establishment's agriculture production (i.e., value of crops for market) are classified in U.S. Industry 111336, Fruit and Tree Nut Combination Farming.

111334 Berry (except Strawberry) Farming^{US}

This U.S. industry comprises establishments primarily engaged in growing berries.

Illustrative Examples:

Berry (except strawberries) farming	Currant farming
Cranberry farming	Blueberry farming
Blackberry farming	Raspberry farming

Cross-References. Establishments primarily engaged in—

- Growing strawberries—are classified in U.S. Industry 111333, Strawberry Farming;
- Harvesting berries from native and noncultivated bushes or vines—are classified in Industry 113210, Forest Nurseries and Gathering of Forest Products; and
- Growing berries in combination with tree nut(s) with the berries or family of tree nuts not accounting for one-half of the establishment's agriculture production (i.e., value of crops for market)—are classified in U.S. Industry 111336, Fruit and Tree Nut Combination Farming.

111335 Tree Nut Farming^{US}

This U.S. industry comprises establishments primarily engaged in growing tree nuts.

Illustrative Examples:

Almond farming	Macadamia farming
Pistachio farming	Walnut farming
Filbert farming	Pecan farming
Tree nut farming	

Cross-References. Establishments primarily engaged in—

- Growing coconut and coffee—are classified in U.S. Industry 111339, Other Noncitrus Fruit Farming; and

---

US—United States industry only. CAN—United States and Canadian industries are comparable. MEX—United States and Mexican industries are comparable. Blank—Canadian, Mexican, and United States industries are comparable.

- Growing tree nut(s) in combination with fruit(s) with no one fruit (or family of fruit or of tree nuts) accounting for one-half of the establishment's agriculture production (i.e., value of crops for market)—are classified in U.S. Industry 111336, Fruit and Tree Nut Combination Farming.

111336 Fruit and Tree Nut Combination Farming[US]

This U.S. industry comprises establishments primarily engaged in growing a combination of fruit(s) and tree nut(s) with no one fruit (or family of fruit) or family of tree nuts accounting for one-half of the establishment's agriculture production (i.e., value of crops for market).

Cross-References.

Establishments engaged in growing fruit(s) or the family of tree nut(s) accounting for one-half of the establishment's agriculture production (i.e., value of crops for market) are classified in Industry Group 1113, Fruit and Tree Nut Farming accordingly by the prominent fruit(s) or tree nut(s) grown.

111339 Other Noncitrus Fruit Farming[US]

This U.S. industry comprises establishments primarily engaged in growing noncitrus fruits (except apples, grapes, berries, and fruit(s) and tree nut(s) combinations).

Illustrative Examples:

Apricot farming	Peach farming
Fig farming	Coffee farming
Banana farming	Pineapple farming
Noncitrus fruit farming	Date farming
Cherry farming	Prune farming

Cross-References. Establishments primarily engaged in—

- Growing apples—are classified in U.S. Industry 111331, Apple Orchards;

- Growing grapes including sun drying of grapes into raisins—are classified in U.S. Industry 111332, Grape Vineyards;

- Growing strawberries—are classified in U.S. Industry 111333, Strawberry Farming;

- Growing berries (except strawberries)—are classified in U.S. Industry 111334, Berry (except Strawberry) Farming;

- Drying fruit artificially—are classified in U.S. Industry 311423, Dried and Dehydrated Food Manufacturing; and
- Growing noncitrus fruit(s) in combination with tree nut(s) with no one fruit (or family of fruits) or family of tree nuts accounting for one-half of the establishment's agriculture production (i.e., value of crops for market)—are classified in U.S. Industry 111336, Fruit and Tree Nut Combination Farming.

1114 Greenhouse, Nursery, and Floriculture Production

This industry group comprises establishments primarily engaged in growing crops of any kind under cover and/or growing nursery stock and flowers. "Under cover" is generally defined as greenhouses, cold frames, cloth houses, and lath houses. The crops grown are removed at various stages of maturity and have annual and perennial life cycles. The nursery stock includes short rotation woody crops that have growth cycles of 10 years or less.

11141 Food Crops Grown Under Cover

This industry comprises establishments primarily engaged in growing food crops (e.g., fruits, melons, tomatoes) under glass or protective cover.

Cross-References.

Establishments primarily engaged in growing vegetable and melon bedding plants are classified in Industry 11121, Vegetable and Melon Farming.

111411 Mushroom Production^{CAN}

This U.S. industry comprises establishments primarily engaged in growing mushrooms under cover in mines underground, or in other controlled environments.

111419 Other Food Crops Grown Under Cover^{CAN}

This U.S. industry comprises establishments primarily engaged in growing food crops (except mushrooms) under glass or protective cover.

Illustrative Examples:

Alfalfa sprout farming, grown under cover	Fruit farming, grown under cover
	Vegetable farming, grown under cover
Melon farming, grown under cover	Hydroponic crop farming

US—United States industry only. CAN—United States and Canadian industries are comparable. MEX—United States and Mexican industries are comparable. Blank—Canadian, Mexican, and United States industries are comparable.

http://www.census.gov/naics

Cross-References.

Establishments primarily engaged in growing mushrooms under cover are classified in U.S. Industry 111411, Mushroom Production.

11142 Nursery and Floriculture Production

This industry comprises establishments primarily engaged in (1) growing nursery and floriculture products (e.g., nursery stock, shrubbery, cut flowers, flower seeds, foliage plants) under cover or in open fields and/or (2) growing short rotation woody trees with a growing and harvesting cycle of 10 years or less for pulp or tree stock (e.g., cut Christmas trees, cottonwoods).

Cross-References. Establishments primarily engaged in—

- Growing vegetable and melon bedding plants—are classified in Industry 11121, Vegetable and Melon Farming;

- Operating timber tracts (i.e., growing cycle greater than 10 years)—are classified in Industry 11311, Timber Tract Operations; and

- Retailing nursery, tree stock, and floriculture products primarily purchased from others—are classified in Industry 44422, Nursery, Garden Center, and Farm Supply Stores.

111421 Nursery and Tree Production[CAN]

This U.S. industry comprises establishments primarily engaged in (1) growing nursery products, nursery stock, shrubbery, bulbs, fruit stock, sod, and so forth, under cover or in open fields and/or (2) growing short rotation woody trees with a growth and harvest cycle of 10 years or less for pulp or tree stock.

Cross-References. Establishments primarily engaged in—

- Growing vegetable and melon bedding plants—are classified in Industry 11121, Vegetable and Melon Farming;

- Operating timber tracts (i.e., growing cycle greater than 10 years)—are classified in Industry 113110, Timber Tract Operations; and

- Retailing nursery, tree stock, and floriculture products primarily purchased from others—are classified in Industry 444220, Nursery, Garden Center, and Farm Supply Stores.

US—United States industry only. CAN—United States and Canadian industries are comparable. MEX—United States and Mexican industries are comparable. Blank—Canadian, Mexican, and United States industries are comparable.

111422 Floriculture Production^{CAN}

This U.S. industry comprises establishments primarily engaged in growing and/ or producing floriculture products (e.g., cut flowers and roses, cut cultivated greens, potted flowering and foliage plants, and flower seeds) under cover and in open fields.

Cross-References.

Establishments primarily engaged in retailing floriculture products primarily purchased from others are classified in Industry 444220, Nursery, Garden Center, and Farm Supply Stores.

1119 Other Crop Farming

This industry group comprises establishments primarily engaged in (1) growing crops (except oilseed and/or grain; vegetable and/or melon; fruit and tree nut; and greenhouse, nursery, and/or floriculture products). These establishments grow crops, such as tobacco, cotton, sugarcane, hay, sugar beets, peanuts, agave, herbs and spices, and hay and grass seeds; or (2) growing a combination of crops (except a combination of oilseed(s) and grain(s) and a combination of fruit(s) and tree nut(s)).

11191 Tobacco Farming
See industry description for 111910 below.

111910 Tobacco Farming

This industry comprises establishments primarily engaged in growing tobacco.

11192 Cotton Farming
See industry description for 111920 below.

111920 Cotton Farming

This industry comprises establishments primarily engaged in growing cotton.

Cross-References.

Establishments primarily engaged in ginning cotton are classified in U.S. Industry 115111, Cotton Ginning.

11193 Sugarcane Farming
See industry description for 111930 below.

US—United States industry only. CAN—United States and Canadian industries are comparable. MEX—United States and Mexican industries are comparable. Blank—Canadian, Mexican, and United States industries are comparable.

111930 Sugarcane Farming

This industry comprises establishments primarily engaged in growing sugarcane.

11194 Hay Farming
See industry description for 111940 below.

111940 Hay Farming^{CAN}

This industry comprises establishments primarily engaged in growing hay, alfalfa, clover, and/or mixed hay.

Cross-References. Establishments primarily engaged in—

- Growing grain hay—are classified in Industry Group 1111, Oilseed and Grain Farming; and
- Growing grass and hay seeds—are classified in U.S. Industry 111998, All Other Miscellaneous Crop Farming.

11199 All Other Crop Farming

This industry comprises establishments primarily engaged in (1) growing crops (except oilseeds and/or grains; vegetables and/or melons; fruits and/or tree nuts; greenhouse, nursery and/or floriculture products; tobacco; cotton; sugarcane; or hay) or (2) growing a combination of crops (except a combination of oilseed(s) and grain(s); and a combination of fruit(s) and tree nut(s)) with no one crop or family of crops accounting for one-half of the establishment's agricultural production (i.e., value of crops for market).

Illustrative Examples:

Agave farming	Sugar beet farming
Spice farming	Grass seed farming
General combination crop farming	Tea farming
(except oilseed and grain; vegetables	Hay seed farming
and melons; fruit and nut	Maple sap gathering
combinations)	Peanut farming

Cross-References. Establishments primarily engaged in—

- Growing oilseeds and/or wheat, corn, rice, or other grains—are classified in Industry Group 1111, Oilseed and Grain Farming;
- Growing vegetables and/or melons—are classified in Industry Group 1112, Vegetable and Melon Farming;

- Growing fruits and/or tree nuts—are classified in Industry Group 1113, Fruit and Tree Nut Farming;

- Growing greenhouse, nursery, and/or floriculture products—are classified in Industry Group 1114, Greenhouse, Nursery, and Floriculture Production;

- Growing tobacco—are classified in Industry 11191, Tobacco Farming;

- Growing cotton—are classified in Industry 11192, Cotton Farming;

- Growing sugarcane—are classified in Industry 11193, Sugarcane Farming;

- Growing hay—are classified in Industry 11194, Hay Farming; and

- Growing algae, seaweed, or other aquatic plants—are classified in Industry 11251, Aquaculture.

111991 Sugar Beet Farming[US]

This U.S. industry comprises establishments primarily engaged in growing sugar beets.

Cross-References.

Establishments primarily engaged in growing beets (except sugar beets) are classified in U.S. Industry 111219, Other Vegetable (except Potato) and Melon Farming.

111992 Peanut Farming[MEX]

This U.S. industry comprises establishments primarily engaged in growing peanuts.

111998 All Other Miscellaneous Crop Farming[US]

This U.S. industry comprises establishments primarily engaged in one of the following: (1) growing crops (except oilseeds and/or grains; vegetables and/or melons; fruits and/or tree nuts; greenhouse, nursery and/or floriculture products; tobacco; cotton; sugarcane; hay; sugar beets; or peanuts); (2) growing a combination of crops (except a combination of oilseed(s) and grain(s); and a combination of fruit(s) and tree nut(s)) with no one crop or family of crop(s) accounting for one-half of the establishment's agricultural production (i.e., value of crops for market); or (3) gathering tea or maple sap.

US—United States industry only. CAN—United States and Canadian industries are comparable. MEX—United States and Mexican industries are comparable. Blank—Canadian, Mexican, and United States industries are comparable.

Illustrative Examples:

Agave farming	Spice farming
Mint farming	Hay seed farming
General combination crop farming	Grass seed farming
(except oilseed and grain; vegetables	Hop farming
and melons; fruit and tree nut	
combinations)	

Cross-References. Establishments primarily engaged in—

- Growing oilseeds and/or wheat, corn, rice, or other grains—are classified in Industry Group 1111, Oilseed and Grain Farming;

- Growing vegetables and/or melons—are classified in Industry Group 1112, Vegetable and Melon Farming;

- Growing fruits and/or tree nuts—are classified in Industry Group 1113, Fruit and Tree Nut Farming;

- Growing greenhouse, nursery and/or floriculture products—are classified in Industry Group 1114, Greenhouse, Nursery, and Floriculture Production;

- Growing tobacco—are classified in Industry 111910, Tobacco Farming;

- Growing cotton—are classified in Industry 111920, Cotton Farming;

- Growing sugarcane—are classified in Industry 111930, Sugarcane Farming;

- Growing hay—are classified in Industry 111940, Hay Farming;

- Growing sugar beets—are classified in U.S. Industry 111991, Sugar Beet Farming;

- Growing peanuts—are classified in U.S. Industry 111992, Peanut Farming; and

- Growing algae, seaweed, or other aquatic plants—are classified in U.S. Industry 112519, Other Aquaculture.

112 Animal Production

Industries in the Animal Production subsector raise or fatten animals for the sale of animals or animal products. The subsector comprises establishments, such as ranches, farms, and feedlots primarily engaged in keeping, grazing, breeding, or feeding animals. These animals are kept for the products they produce or for eventual sale. The animals are generally raised in various environments, from total confinement or captivity to feeding on an open range pasture. Establishments primarily engaged in the farm raising and production of aquatic animals or plants in controlled or selected aquatic environments are included in this subsector.

US—United States industry only. CAN—United States and Canadian industries are comparable. MEX—United States and Mexican industries are comparable. Blank—Canadian, Mexican, and United States industries are comparable.

The industries in this subsector are grouped by important factors, such as suitable grazing or pasture land, specialized buildings, type of equipment, and the amount and types of labor required. Establishments are classified to the Animal Production subsector when animal production (i.e., value of animals for market) accounts for one-half or more of the establishment's total agricultural production. Establishments with one-half or more animal production with no one animal product or family of animal products of an industry accounting for one-half of the establishment's agricultural production are treated as combination animal farming classified to Industry 11299, All Other Animal Production.

1121 Cattle Ranching and Farming

This industry group comprises establishments primarily engaged in raising cattle, milking dairy cattle, or feeding cattle for fattening.

11211 Beef Cattle Ranching and Farming, including Feedlots

This industry comprises establishments primarily engaged in raising cattle (including cattle for dairy herd replacements), or feeding cattle for fattening.

Cross-References. Establishments primarily engaged in—

- Milking dairy cattle—are classified in Industry 11212, Dairy Cattle and Milk Production; and
- Operating stockyards for transportation and not buying, selling, or auctioning livestock—are classified in Industry 48899, Other Support Activities for Transportation.

112111 Beef Cattle Ranching and Farming^{US}

This U.S. industry comprises establishments primarily engaged in raising cattle (including cattle for dairy herd replacements).

Cross-References.

Establishments primarily engaged in milking dairy cattle are classified in Industry 112120, Dairy Cattle and Milk Production.

112112 Cattle Feedlots^{US}

This U.S. industry comprises establishments primarily engaged in feeding cattle for fattening.

US—United States industry only. CAN—United States and Canadian industries are comparable. MEX—United States and Mexican industries are comparable. Blank—Canadian, Mexican, and United States industries are comparable.

http://www.census.gov/naics

Cross-References.

Establishments primarily engaged in operating stockyards for transportation and not buying, selling, or auctioning livestock are classified in U.S. Industry 488999, All Other Support Activities for Transportation.

11212 Dairy Cattle and Milk Production
See industry description for 112120 below.

112120 Dairy Cattle and Milk Production

This industry comprises establishments primarily engaged in milking dairy cattle.

Cross-References. Establishments primarily engaged in—

- Raising dairy herd replacements—are classified in U.S. Industry 112111, Beef Cattle Ranching and Farming; and

- Milking goats—are classified in Industry 112420, Goat Farming.

11213 Dual-Purpose Cattle Ranching and Farming[MEX]
See industry description for 112130 below.

112130 Dual-Purpose Cattle Ranching and Farming[US]

This industry comprises establishments primarily engaged in raising cattle for both milking and meat production.

Cross-References. Establishments primarily engaged in—

- Milking dairy cattle—are classified in Industry 112120, Dairy Cattle and Milk Production;

- Raising cattle or feeding cattle for fattening—are classified in Industry 11211, Beef Cattle Ranching and Farming, including Feedlots; and

- Operating stockyards for transportation and not buying, selling, or auctioning livestock—are classified in U.S. Industry 488999, All Other Support Activities for Transportation.

1122 Hog and Pig Farming

11221 Hog and Pig Farming
See industry description for 112210 below.

US—United States industry only. CAN—United States and Canadian industries are comparable. MEX—United States and Mexican industries are comparable. Blank—Canadian, Mexican, and United States industries are comparable.

112210 Hog and Pig Farming[CAN]

This industry comprises establishments primarily engaged in raising hogs and pigs. These establishments may include farming activities, such as breeding, farrowing, and the raising of weanling pigs, feeder pigs, or market size hogs.

Cross-References.

Establishments primarily engaged in operating stockyards for transportation and not buying, selling, or auctioning livestock are classified in U.S. Industry 488999, All Other Support Activities for Transportation.

1123 Poultry and Egg Production

This industry group comprises establishments primarily engaged in breeding, hatching, and raising poultry for meat or egg production.

11231 Chicken Egg Production
See industry description for 112310 below.

112310 Chicken Egg Production[CAN]

This industry comprises establishments primarily engaged in raising chickens for egg production. The eggs produced may be for use as table eggs or hatching eggs.

Cross-References.

Establishments primarily engaged in raising chickens for the production of meat are classified in Industry 112320, Broilers and Other Meat Type Chicken Production.

11232 Broilers and Other Meat Type Chicken Production
See industry description for 112320 below.

112320 Broilers and Other Meat Type Chicken Production

This industry comprises establishments primarily engaged in raising broilers, fryers, roasters, and other meat type chickens.

Cross-References.

Establishments primarily engaged in raising chickens for egg production are classified in Industry 112310, Chicken Egg Production.

US—United States industry only. CAN—United States and Canadian industries are comparable. MEX—United States and Mexican industries are comparable. Blank—Canadian, Mexican, and United States industries are comparable.

11233 Turkey Production

See industry description for 112330 below.

112330 Turkey Production

This industry comprises establishments primarily engaged in raising turkeys for meat or egg production.

11234 Poultry Hatcheries

See industry description for 112340 below.

112340 Poultry Hatcheries

This industry comprises establishments primarily engaged in hatching poultry of any kind.

11239 Other Poultry Production

See industry description for 112390 below.

112390 Other Poultry Production[MEX]

This industry comprises establishments primarily engaged in raising poultry (except chickens for meat or egg production and turkeys).

Illustrative Examples:

Duck production	Pheasant production
Ostrich production	Geese production
Emu production	Quail production

Cross-References. Establishments primarily engaged in—

- Raising aviary birds, such as parakeets, canaries, and love birds—are classified in Industry 112990, All Other Animal Production;

- Raising chickens for egg production—are classified in Industry 112310, Chicken Egg Production;

- Raising broilers and other meat type chickens—are classified in Industry 112320, Broilers and Other Meat Type Chicken Production;

- Raising turkeys—are classified in Industry 112330, Turkey Production; and

- Raising swans, peacocks, flamingos or other "adornment birds"—are classified in Industry 112990, All Other Animal Production.

US—United States industry only. CAN—United States and Canadian industries are comparable. MEX—United States and Mexican industries are comparable. Blank—Canadian, Mexican, and United States industries are comparable.

1124 Sheep and Goat Farming

This industry group comprises establishments primarily engaged in raising sheep, lambs, and goats, or feeding lambs for fattening.

11241 Sheep Farming

See industry description for 112410 below.

112410 Sheep Farming

This industry comprises establishments primarily engaged in raising sheep and lambs, or feeding lambs for fattening. The sheep or lambs may be raised for sale or wool production.

Cross-References.

Establishments primarily engaged in operating stockyards for transportation and not buying, selling, or auctioning livestock are classified in U.S. Industry 488999, All Other Support Activities for Transportation.

11242 Goat Farming

See industry description for 112420 below.

112420 Goat Farming

This industry comprises establishments primarily engaged in raising goats.

1125 Aquaculture

11251 Aquaculture

This industry comprises establishments primarily engaged in the farm raising and production of aquatic animals or plants in controlled or selected aquatic environments. These establishments use some form of intervention in the rearing process to enhance production, such as holding in captivity, regular stocking, feeding, and protecting from predators, pests, and disease.

Cross-References.

Establishments primarily engaged in the catching or taking of fish and other aquatic animals from their natural habitat are classified in Industry 11411, Fishing.

US—United States industry only. CAN—United States and Canadian industries are comparable. MEX—United States and Mexican industries are comparable. Blank—Canadian, Mexican, and United States industries are comparable.

112511 Finfish Farming and Fish Hatcheries[US]

This U.S. industry comprises establishments primarily engaged in (1) farm raising finfish (e.g., catfish, trout, goldfish, tropical fish, minnows) and/or (2) hatching fish of any kind.

Cross-References.
Establishments primarily engaged in the catching or taking of finfish from their natural habitat are classified in U.S. Industry 114111, Finfish Fishing.

112512 Shellfish Farming[US]

This U.S. industry comprises establishments primarily engaged in farm raising shellfish (e.g., crayfish, shrimp, oysters, clams, mollusks).

Cross-References.
Establishments primarily engaged in the catching or taking of shellfish from their natural habitat are classified in U.S. Industry 114112, Shellfish Fishing.

112519 Other Aquaculture[US]

This U.S. industry comprises establishments primarily engaged in (1) farm raising of aquatic animals (except finfish and shellfish) and/or (2) farm raising of aquatic plants. Alligator, algae, frog, seaweed, or turtle production is included in this industry.

Cross-References. Establishments primarily engaged in—
- Miscellaneous fishing activities, such as catching or taking of terrapins, turtles, and frogs in their natural habitat—are classified in U.S. Industry 114119, Other Marine Fishing;
- Farm raising finfish—are classified in U.S. Industry 112511, Finfish Farming and Fish Hatcheries;
- Farm raising shellfish—are classified in U.S. Industry 112512, Shellfish Farming; and
- Growing hydroponic crops—are classified in Industry 111419, Other Food Crops Grown Under Cover.

1129 Other Animal Production

This industry group comprises establishments primarily engaged in raising animals and insects (except cattle, hogs and pigs, poultry, sheep and goats, aquaculture)

US—United States industry only. CAN—United States and Canadian industries are comparable. MEX—United States and Mexican industries are comparable. Blank—Canadian, Mexican, and United States industries are comparable.

for sale or product production. These establishments are primarily engaged in raising one of the following: bees, horses and other equines, rabbits and other fur-bearing animals, and so forth, and producing products, such as honey and other bee products. Establishments primarily engaged in raising a combination of animals with no one animal or family of animals accounting for one-half of the establishment's agricultural production (i.e., value of animals for market) are included in this industry group.

11291 Apiculture

See industry description for 112910 below.

112910 Apiculture

This industry comprises establishments primarily engaged in raising bees. These establishments may collect and gather honey; and/or sell queen bees, packages of bees, royal jelly, bees' wax, propolis, venom, and/or other bee products.

11292 Horses and Other Equine Production

See industry description for 112920 below.

112920 Horses and Other Equine Production

This industry comprises establishments primarily engaged in raising horses, mules, donkeys, and other equines. ·

Cross-References.

- Establishments primarily engaged in equine boarding are classified in Industry 115210, Support Activities for Animal Production; and

- Equine owners entering horses in racing or other spectator sporting events are classified in U.S. Industry 711219, Other Spectator Sports.

11293 Fur-Bearing Animal and Rabbit Production

See industry description for 112930 below.

112930 Fur-Bearing Animal and Rabbit Production

This industry comprises establishments primarily engaged in raising fur-bearing animals including rabbits. These animals may be raised for sale or for their pelt production.

US—United States industry only. CAN—United States and Canadian industries are comparable. MEX—United States and Mexican industries are comparable. Blank—Canadian, Mexican, and United States industries are comparable.

Cross-References.

Establishments primarily engaged in the trapping or hunting of wild fur-bearing animals are classified in Industry 114210, Hunting and Trapping.

11299 All Other Animal Production

See industry description for 112990 below.

112990 All Other Animal Production[US]

This industry comprises establishments primarily engaged in: (1) raising animals (except cattle, hogs and pigs, poultry, sheep and goats, aquaculture, apiculture, horses and other equines; and fur-bearing animals including rabbits); or (2) raising a combination of animals, with no one animal or family of animals accounting for one-half of the establishment's agricultural production (i.e., value of animals for market) are included in this industry.

Illustrative Examples:

Bird production (e.g., canaries, parakeets, parrots)
Laboratory animal production (e.g., rats, mice, guinea pigs)
Combination animal farming (except dairy, poultry)

Llama production
Companion animals production (e.g., cats, dogs)
Worm production
Deer production

Cross-References. Establishments primarily engaged in—

- Raising cattle, dairy cattle or feeding cattle for fattening—are classified in Industry Group 1121, Cattle Ranching and Farming;

- Raising hogs and pigs—are classified in Industry Group 1122, Hog and Pig Farming;

- Raising poultry and raising poultry for egg production—are classified in Industry Group 1123, Poultry and Egg Production;

- Raising sheep and goats—are classified in Industry Group 1124, Sheep and Goat Farming;

- Animal aquaculture—are classified in Industry 11251, Aquaculture;

- Raising bees—are classified in Industry 112910, Apiculture;

- Raising horses and other equines—are classified in Industry 112920, Horses and Other Equine Production; and

- Raising fur-bearing animals including rabbits—are classified in Industry 112930, Fur-Bearing Animal and Rabbit Production.

---

113 Forestry and Logging

Industries in the Forestry and Logging subsector grow and harvest timber on a long production cycle (i.e., of 10 years or more). Long production cycles use different production processes than short production cycles, which require more horticultural interventions prior to harvest, resulting in processes more similar to those found in the Crop Production subsector. Consequently, Christmas tree production and other production involving production cycles of less than 10 years, are classified in the Crop Production subsector.

Industries in this subsector specialize in different stages of the production cycle. Reforestation requires production of seedlings in specialized nurseries. Timber production requires natural forest or suitable areas of land that are available for a long duration. The maturation time for timber depends upon the species of tree, the climatic conditions of the region, and the intended purpose of the timber. The harvesting of timber (except when done on an extremely small scale) requires specialized machinery unique to the industry. Establishments gathering forest products, such as gums, barks, balsam needles, rhizomes, fibers, Spanish moss, and ginseng and truffles, are also included in this subsector.

1131 Timber Tract Operations

11311 Timber Tract Operations
See industry description for 113110 below.

113110 Timber Tract Operations

This industry comprises establishments primarily engaged in the operation of timber tracts for the purpose of selling standing timber.

Cross-References. Establishments primarily engaged in—

- Acting as lessors of land with trees as real estate property—are classified in Industry 53119, Lessors of Other Real Estate Property;
- Growing short rotation woody trees (i.e., growing and harvesting cycle is 10 years or less)—are classified in U.S. Industry 111421, Nursery and Tree Production; and
- Cutting timber—are classified in Industry 113310, Logging.

1132 Forest Nurseries and Gathering of Forest Products

11321 Forest Nurseries and Gathering of Forest Products
See industry description for 113210 below.

113210 Forest Nurseries and Gathering of Forest Products[CAN]

This industry comprises establishments primarily engaged in (1) growing trees for reforestation and/or (2) gathering forest products, such as gums, barks, balsam needles, rhizomes, fibers, Spanish moss, ginseng, and truffles.

Cross-References. Establishments primarily engaged in—

* Gathering tea and maple sap—are classified in U.S. Industry 111998, All Other Miscellaneous Crop Farming; and

* Processing maple syrup into other products—are classified in Industry 31199, All Other Food Manufacturing.

1133 Logging

11331 Logging

See industry description for 113310 below.

113310 Logging[MEX]

This industry comprises establishments primarily engaged in one or more of the following: (1) cutting timber; (2) cutting and transporting timber; and (3) producing wood chips in the field.

Cross-References.

Establishments primarily engaged in trucking timber are classified in Industry 484220, Specialized Freight (except Used Goods) Trucking, Local.

114 Fishing, Hunting and Trapping

Industries in the Fishing, Hunting, and Trapping subsector harvest fish and other wild animals from their natural habitats and are dependent upon a continued supply of the natural resource. The harvesting of fish is the predominant economic activity of this subsector and it usually requires specialized vessels that, by the nature of their size, configuration and equipment, are not suitable for any other type of production, such as transportation.

Hunting and trapping activities utilize a wide variety of production processes and are classified in the same subsector as fishing because the availability of

US—United States industry only. CAN—United States and Canadian industries are comparable. MEX—United States and Mexican industries are comparable. Blank—Canadian, Mexican, and United States industries are comparable.

resources and the constraints imposed, such as conservation requirements and proper habitat maintenance, are similar.

1141 Fishing

11411 Fishing

This industry comprises establishments primarily engaged in the commercial catching or taking of finfish, shellfish, or miscellaneous marine products from a natural habitat, such as the catching of bluefish, eels, salmon, tuna, clams, crabs, lobsters, mussels, oysters, shrimp, frogs, sea urchins, and turtles.

Cross-References. Establishments primarily engaged in—

- Farm raising finfish, shellfish or other marine animals and plants—are classified in Industry 11251, Aquaculture; and

- Gathering and processing seafood into canned seafood products—are classified in Industry 31171, Seafood Product Preparation and Packaging.

114111 Finfish Fishing[US]

This U.S. industry comprises establishments primarily engaged in the commercial catching or taking of finfish (e.g., bluefish, salmon, trout, tuna) from their natural habitat.

Cross-References. Establishments primarily engaged in—

- Farm raising finfish—are classified in U.S. Industry 112511, Finfish Farming and Fish Hatcheries; and

- Gathering and processing (known as "floating factory ships") seafood into canned seafood products—are classified in U.S. Industry 311711, Seafood Canning.

114112 Shellfish Fishing[US]

This U.S. industry comprises establishments primarily engaged in the commercial catching or taking of shellfish (e.g., clams, crabs, lobsters, mussels, oysters, sea urchins, shrimp) from their natural habitat.

Cross-References.

Establishments primarily engaged in farm raising shellfish are classified in U.S. Industry 112512, Shellfish Farming.

US—United States industry only. CAN—United States and Canadian industries are comparable. MEX—United States and Mexican industries are comparable. Blank—Canadian, Mexican, and United States industries are comparable.

114119 Other Marine Fishing[US]

This U.S. industry comprises establishments primarily engaged in the commercial catching or taking of marine animals (except finfish and shellfish).

Cross-References. Establishments primarily engaged in—

- Animal or plant aquaculture (except finfish and shellfish)—are classified in U.S. Industry 112519, Other Aquaculture;
- The commercial catching or taking of finfish from their natural habitat—are classified in U.S. Industry 114111, Finfish Fishing; and
- The commercial catching or taking of shellfish from their natural habitat—are classified in U.S. Industry 114112, Shellfish Fishing.

1142 Hunting and Trapping

11421 Hunting and Trapping
See industry description for 114210 below.

114210 Hunting and Trapping

This industry comprises establishments primarily engaged in one or more of the following: (1) commercial hunting and trapping; (2) operating commercial game preserves, such as game retreats; and (3) operating hunting preserves.

Cross-References. Establishments primarily engaged in—

- Operating nature preserves—are classified in Industry 712190, Nature Parks and Other Similar Institutions; and
- Farm raising rabbits and other fur-bearing animals—are classified in Industry 112930, Fur-Bearing Animal and Rabbit Production.

115 Support Activities for Agriculture and Forestry

Industries in the Support Activities for Agriculture and Forestry subsector provide support services that are an essential part of agricultural and forestry production. These support activities may be performed by the agriculture or forestry producing establishment or conducted independently as an alternative source of inputs required for the production process for a given crop, animal, or forestry

---

US—United States industry only. CAN—United States and Canadian industries are comparable. MEX—United States and Mexican industries are comparable. Blank—Canadian, Mexican, and United States industries are comparable.

industry. Establishments that primarily perform these activities independent of the agriculture or forestry producing establishment are in this subsector.

1151 Support Activities for Crop Production

11511 Support Activities for Crop Production

This industry comprises establishments primarily engaged in providing support activities for growing crops.

Illustrative Examples:

Aerial dusting or spraying (i.e., using
  specialized or dedicated aircraft)
Farm management services
Cotton ginning

Planting crops
Cultivating services
Vineyard cultivation services

Cross-References. Establishments primarily engaged in—

* Performing crop production that are generally known as farms, orchards, groves, or vineyards (including sharecroppers and tenant farms)—are classified in the appropriate crop industry within Subsector 111, Crop Production;

* Providing support activities for forestry—are classified in Industry 11531, Support Activities for Forestry;

* Landscaping and horticultural services, such as lawn and maintenance care and ornamental shrub and tree services—are classified in Industry 56173, Landscaping Services;

* Land clearing, land leveling, and earth moving for terracing, ponds, and irrigation—are classified in Industry 23891, Site Preparation Contractors;

* Artificially drying and dehydrating fruits and vegetables—are classified in Industry 31142, Fruit and Vegetable Canning, Pickling, and Drying;

* Stemming and redrying tobacco—are classified in Industry 31221, Tobacco Stemming and Redrying;

* Providing water for irrigation—are classified in Industry 22131, Water Supply and Irrigation Systems; and

* Buying farm products, such as fruits or vegetables, for resale to other wholesalers or retailers, and preparing them for market or further processing—are classified in Industry 42448, Fresh Fruit and Vegetable Merchant Wholesalers.

115111 Cotton Ginning[US]

This U.S. industry comprises establishments primarily engaged in ginning cotton.

115112 Soil Preparation, Planting, and Cultivating[US]

This U.S. industry comprises establishments primarily engaged in performing a soil preparation activity or crop production service, such as plowing, fertilizing, seed bed preparation, planting, cultivating, and crop protecting services.

Cross-References. Establishments primarily engaged in—

- Land clearing, land leveling, and earth moving for terracing, ponds, and irrigation—are classified in Industry 238910, Site Preparation Contractors; and

- Providing water for irrigation—are classified in Industry 221310, Water Supply and Irrigation Systems.

115113 Crop Harvesting, Primarily by Machine[US]

This U.S. industry comprises establishments primarily engaged in mechanical harvesting, picking, and combining of crops, and related activities. The machinery used is provided by the servicing establishment.

Cross-References. Establishments primarily engaged in—

- Providing personnel for manual harvesting—are classified in U.S. Industry 115115, Farm Labor Contractors and Crew Leaders; and

- Providing farm management services (i.e., on a contract or fee basis) and arranging or contracting crop mechanical or manual harvesting operations for the farm(s) it manages—are classified in U.S. Industry 115116, Farm Management Services.

115114 Postharvest Crop Activities (except Cotton Ginning)[US]

This U.S. industry comprises establishments primarily engaged in performing services on crops, subsequent to their harvest, with the intent of preparing them for market or further processing. These establishments provide postharvest activities, such as crop cleaning, sun drying, shelling, fumigating, curing, sorting, grading, packing, and cooling.

US—United States industry only. CAN—United States and Canadian industries are comparable. MEX—United States and Mexican industries are comparable. Blank—Canadian, Mexican, and United States industries are comparable.

Cross-References. Establishments primarily engaged in—

- Ginning cotton—are classified in U.S. Industry 115111, Cotton Ginning;
- Custom grain grinding for animal feed—are classified in U.S. Industry 311119, Other Animal Food Manufacturing;
- Artificially drying and dehydrating fruits and vegetables—are classified in U.S. Industry 311423, Dried and Dehydrated Food Manufacturing;
- Stemming and redrying tobacco—are classified in Industry 312210, Tobacco Stemming and Redrying;
- Buying farm products for resale to other wholesalers or retailers and preparing them for market or further processing—are classified in Industry 424480, Fresh Fruit and Vegetable Merchant Wholesalers; and
- Providing farm management services (i.e., on a contract or fee basis) and arranging or contracting postharvesting crop activities for the farm(s) it manages—are classified in U.S. Industry 115116, Farm Management Services.

115115 Farm Labor Contractors and Crew Leaders[US]

This U.S. industry comprises establishments primarily engaged in supplying labor for agricultural production or harvesting.

Cross-References. Establishments primarily engaged in—

- Providing machine harvesting—are classified in U.S. Industry 115113, Crop Harvesting, Primarily by Machine; and
- Providing farm management services (i.e., on a contract or fee basis) and arranging or contracting farm labor for the farm(s) it manages—are classified in U.S. Industry 115116, Farm Management Services.

115116 Farm Management Services[US]

This U.S. industry comprises establishments primarily engaged in providing farm management services on a contract or fee basis usually to citrus groves, orchards, or vineyards. These establishments always provide management and may arrange or contract for the partial or the complete operations of the farm establishment(s) it manages. Operational activities may include cultivating, harvesting, and/or other specialized agricultural support activities.

Cross-References.

Establishments primarily engaged in crop production that are generally known as farms, orchards, groves, or vineyards (including share croppers and tenant farms), are classified in the appropriate crop industry within Subsector 111, Crop Production.

1152 Support Activities for Animal Production

11521 Support Activities for Animal Production
See industry description for 115210 below.

115210 Support Activities for Animal Production

This industry comprises establishments primarily engaged in performing support activities related to raising livestock (e.g., cattle, goats, hogs, horses, poultry, sheep). These establishments may perform one or more of the following: (1) breeding services for animals, including companion animals (e.g., cats, dogs, pet birds); (2) pedigree record services; (3) boarding horses; (4) dairy herd improvement activities; (5) livestock spraying; and (6) sheep dipping and shearing.

1153 Support Activities for Forestry

11531 Support Activities for Forestry
See industry description for 115310 below.

115310 Support Activities for Forestry

This industry comprises establishments primarily engaged in performing particular support activities related to timber production, wood technology, forestry economics and marketing, and forest protection. These establishments may provide support activities for forestry, such as estimating timber, forest firefighting, forest pest control, and consulting on wood attributes and reforestation.

Cross-References.

Establishments primarily engaged in the public administration and conservation of forest lands are classified in Industry 924120, Administration of Conservation Programs.

US—United States industry only. CAN—United States and Canadian industries are comparable. MEX—United States and Mexican industries are comparable. Blank—Canadian, Mexican, and United States industries are comparable.

Sector 21—Mining, Quarrying, and Oil and Gas Extraction

The Sector as a Whole

The Mining, Quarrying, and Oil and Gas Extraction sector comprises establishments that extract naturally occurring mineral solids, such as coal and ores; liquid minerals, such as crude petroleum; and gases, such as natural gas. The term mining is used in the broad sense to include quarrying, well operations, beneficiating (e.g., crushing, screening, washing, and flotation), and other preparation customarily performed at the mine site, or as a part of mining activity.

The Mining, Quarrying, and Oil and Gas Extraction sector distinguishes two basic activities: mine operation and mining support activities. Mine operation includes establishments operating mines, quarries, or oil and gas wells on their own account or for others on a contract or fee basis. Mining support activities include establishments that perform exploration (except geophysical surveying) and/or other mining services on a contract or fee basis (except mine site preparation and construction of oil/gas pipelines).

Establishments in the Mining, Quarrying, and Oil and Gas Extraction sector are grouped and classified according to the natural resource mined or to be mined. Industries include establishments that develop the mine site, extract the natural resources, and/or those that beneficiate (i.e., prepare) the mineral mined. Beneficiation is the process whereby the extracted material is reduced to particles that can be separated into mineral and waste, the former suitable for further processing or direct use. The operations that take place in beneficiation are primarily mechanical, such as grinding, washing, magnetic separation, and centrifugal separation. In contrast, manufacturing operations primarily use chemical and electrochemical processes, such as electrolysis and distillation. However, some treatments, such as heat treatments, take place in both the beneficiation and the manufacturing (i.e., smelting/refining) stages. The range of preparation activities varies by mineral and the purity of any given ore deposit. While some minerals, such as petroleum and natural gas, require little or no preparation, others are washed and screened, while yet others, such as gold and silver, can be transformed into bullion before leaving the mine site.

Mining, beneficiating, and manufacturing activities often occur in a single location. Separate receipts will be collected for these activities whenever possible. When receipts cannot be broken out between mining and manufacturing, establishments that mine or quarry nonmetallic minerals, and then beneficiate the nonmetallic minerals into more finished manufactured products are classified based on the primary activity of the establishment. A mine that manufactures a small amount of finished products will be classified in Sector 21, Mining, Quarrying, and Oil

---

US—United States industry only. CAN—United States and Canadian industries are comparable. MEX—United States and Mexican industries are comparable. Blank—Canadian, Mexican, and United States industries are comparable.

and Gas Extraction. An establishment that mines whose primary output is a more finished manufactured product will be classified in Sector 31-33, Manufacturing.

211 Oil and Gas Extraction

Industries in the Oil and Gas Extraction subsector operate and/or develop oil and gas field properties. Such activities may include exploration for crude petroleum and natural gas; drilling, completing, and equipping wells; operating separators, emulsion breakers, desilting equipment, and field gathering lines for crude petroleum and natural gas; and all other activities in the preparation of oil and gas up to the point of shipment from the producing property. This subsector includes the production of crude petroleum, the mining and extraction of oil from oil shale and oil sands, and the production of natural gas, sulfur recovery from natural gas, and recovery of hydrocarbon liquids.

Establishments in this subsector include those that operate oil and gas wells on their own account or for others on a contract or fee basis. Establishments primarily engaged in providing support services, on a fee or contract basis, required for the drilling or operation of oil and gas wells (except geophysical surveying and mapping, mine site preparation, and construction of oil/gas pipelines) are classified in Subsector 213, Support Activities for Mining.

2111 Oil and Gas Extraction

21111 Oil and Gas Extraction

This industry comprises establishments primarily engaged in operating and/or developing oil and gas field properties and establishments primarily engaged in recovering liquid hydrocarbons from oil and gas field gases. Such activities may include exploration for crude petroleum and natural gas; drilling, completing, and equipping wells; operation of separators, emulsion breakers, desilting equipment, and field gathering lines for crude petroleum and natural gas; and all other activities in the preparation of oil and gas up to the point of shipment from the producing property. This industry includes the production of crude petroleum, the mining and extraction of oil from oil shale and oil sands, the production of natural gas, sulfur recovery from natural gas, and the recovery of hydrocarbon liquids from oil and gas field gases. Establishments in this industry operate oil and gas wells on their own account or for others on a contract or fee basis.

Cross-References. Establishments primarily engaged in—

- Performing oil field services for operators on a contract or fee basis—are classified in Industry 21311, Support Activities for Mining;

US—United States industry only. CAN—United States and Canadian industries are comparable. MEX—United States and Mexican industries are comparable. Blank—Canadian, Mexican, and United States industries are comparable.

- Manufacturing acyclic and cyclic hydrocarbons from refined petroleum or liquid hydrocarbons—are classified in Industry 32511, Petrochemical Manufacturing;
- Refining crude petroleum into refined petroleum and liquid hydrocarbons— are classified in Industry 32411, Petroleum Refineries; and
- Recovering helium from natural gas—are classified in Industry 32512, Industrial Gas Manufacturing.

211111 Crude Petroleum and Natural Gas Extraction[US]

This U.S. industry comprises establishments primarily engaged in (1) the exploration, development and/or the production of petroleum or natural gas from wells in which the hydrocarbons will initially flow or can be produced using normal pumping techniques or (2) the production of crude petroleum from surface shales or tar sands or from reservoirs in which the hydrocarbons are semisolids. Establishments in this industry operate oil and gas wells on their own account or for others on a contract or fee basis.

Cross-References. Establishments primarily engaged in—

- Performing oil field services for operators on a contract or fee basis—are classified in Industry 21311, Support Activities for Mining;
- Refining crude petroleum into refined petroleum and liquid hydrocarbons— are classified in Industry 324110, Petroleum Refineries; and
- Recovering helium from natural gas—are classified in Industry 325120, Industrial Gas Manufacturing.

211112 Natural Gas Liquid Extraction[US]

This U.S. industry comprises establishments primarily engaged in the recovery of liquid hydrocarbons from oil and gas field gases. Establishments primarily engaged in sulfur recovery from natural gas are included in this industry.

Cross-References. Establishments primarily engaged in—

- Manufacturing acyclic and cyclic hydrocarbons from refined petroleum or converting refined petroleum into liquid hydrocarbons (petrochemicals) and/ or recovering liquid hydrocarbons—are classified in Industry 325110, Petrochemical Manufacturing;
- Refining crude petroleum into refined petroleum and liquid hydrocarbons— are classified in Industry 324110, Petroleum Refineries; and
- Recovering helium from natural gas—are classified in Industry 325120, Industrial Gas Manufacturing.

US—United States industry only. CAN—United States and Canadian industries are comparable. MEX—United States and Mexican industries are comparable. Blank—Canadian, Mexican, and United States industries are comparable.

212 Mining (except Oil and Gas)

Industries in the Mining (except Oil and Gas) subsector primarily engage in mining, mine site development, and beneficiating (i.e., preparing) metallic minerals and nonmetallic minerals, including coal. The term "mining" is used in the broad sense to include ore extraction, quarrying, and beneficiating (e.g., crushing, screening, washing, sizing, concentrating, and flotation), customarily done at the mine site.

Beneficiation is the process whereby the extracted material is reduced to particles which can be separated into mineral and waste, the former suitable for further processing or direct use. The operations that take place in beneficiation are primarily mechanical, such as grinding, washing, magnetic separation, centrifugal separation, and so on. In contrast, manufacturing operations primarily use chemical and electro-chemical processes, such as electrolysis, distillation, and so on. However some treatments, such as heat treatments, take place in both stages: the beneficiation and the manufacturing (i.e., smelting/refining) stages. The range of preparation activities varies by mineral and the purity of any given ore deposit. While some minerals, such as petroleum and natural gas, require little or no preparation, others are washed and screened, while yet others, such as gold and silver, can be transformed into bullion before leaving the mine site.

Establishments in the Mining (except Oil and Gas) subsector include those that have complete responsibility for operating mines and quarries (except oil and gas wells) and those that operate mines and quarries (except oil and gas wells) for others on a contract or fee basis. Establishments primarily engaged in providing support services, on a contract or fee basis, required for the mining and quarrying of minerals are classified in Subsector 213, Support Activities for Mining.

2121 Coal Mining

21211 Coal Mining

This industry comprises establishments primarily engaged in one or more of the following: (1) mining bituminous coal, anthracite, and lignite by underground mining, auger mining, strip mining, culm bank mining, and other surface mining; (2) developing coal mine sites; and (3) beneficiating (i.e., preparing) coal (e.g., cleaning, washing, screening, and sizing coal).

Cross-References. Establishments primarily engaged in—

- Manufacturing coke oven products in coke oven establishments—are classified in Industry 32419, Other Petroleum and Coal Products Manufacturing; and

---

US—United States industry only. CAN—United States and Canadian industries are comparable. MEX—United States and Mexican industries are comparable. Blank—Canadian, Mexican, and United States industries are comparable.

- Manufacturing coal products in steel mills—are classified in Industry 33111, Iron and Steel Mills and Ferroalloy Manufacturing.

212111 Bituminous Coal and Lignite Surface Mining^{US}

This U.S. industry comprises establishments primarily engaged in one or more of the following: (1) surface mining of bituminous coal and lignite; (2) developing bituminous coal and lignite surface mine sites; (3) surface mining and beneficiating (e.g., cleaning, washing, screening, and sizing coal) of bituminous coal; or (4) beneficiating (e.g., cleaning, washing, screening, and sizing coal), but not mining, bituminous coal.

Cross-References. Establishments primarily engaged in—
- Manufacturing coke oven products in coke oven establishments—are classified in U.S. Industry 324199, All Other Petroleum and Coal Products Manufacturing;
- Underground mining of bituminous coal—are classified in U.S. Industry 212112, Bituminous Coal Underground Mining; and
- Mining and/or beneficiating anthracite coal—are classified in U.S. Industry 212113, Anthracite Mining.

212112 Bituminous Coal Underground Mining^{US}

This U.S. industry comprises establishments primarily engaged in one or more of the following: (1) underground mining of bituminous coal; (2) developing bituminous coal underground mine sites; and (3) underground mining and beneficiating of bituminous coal (e.g., cleaning, washing, screening, and sizing coal).

Cross-References. Establishments primarily engaged in—
- Manufacturing coke oven products in coke oven establishments—are classified in U.S. Industry 324199, All Other Petroleum and Coal Products Manufacturing;
- Surface mining and/or beneficiating of bituminous coal or lignite—are classified in U.S. Industry 212111, Bituminous Coal and Lignite Surface Mining; and
- Mining and/or beneficiating anthracite coal—are classified in U.S. Industry 212113, Anthracite Mining.

212113 Anthracite Mining^{US}

This U.S. industry comprises establishments primarily engaged in one or more of the following: (1) mining anthracite coal; (2) developing anthracite coal mine sites; and (3) beneficiating anthracite coal (e.g., cleaning, washing, screening, and sizing coal).

Cross-References. Establishments primarily engaged in—

- Manufacturing coke oven products in coke oven establishments—are classified in U.S. Industry 324199, All Other Petroleum and Coal Products Manufacturing;
- Surface mining and/or beneficiating bituminous coal or lignite—are classified in U.S. Industry 212111, Bituminous Coal and Lignite Surface Mining; and
- Underground mining of bituminous coal—are classified in U.S. Industry 212112, Bituminous Coal Underground Mining.

2122 Metal Ore Mining

This industry group comprises establishments primarily engaged in developing mine sites or mining metallic minerals, and establishments primarily engaged in ore dressing and beneficiating (i.e., preparing) operations, such as crushing, grinding, washing, drying, sintering, concentrating, calcining, and leaching. Beneficiating may be performed at mills operated in conjunction with the mines served or at mills, such as custom mills, operated separately.

21221 Iron Ore Mining
See industry description for 212210 below.

212210 Iron Ore Mining

This industry comprises establishments primarily engaged in (1) developing mine sites, mining, and/or beneficiating (i.e., preparing) iron ores and manganiferous ores valued chiefly for their iron content and/or (2) producing sinter iron ore (except iron ore produced in iron and steel mills) and other iron ore agglomerates.

Cross-References.

Establishments primarily engaged in manufacturing pig iron ore are classified in U.S. Industry 331111, Iron and Steel Mills.

21222 Gold Ore and Silver Ore Mining

This industry comprises establishments primarily engaged in developing the mine site, mining, and/or beneficiating (i.e., preparing) ores valued chiefly for their

---

US—United States industry only. CAN—United States and Canadian industries are comparable. MEX—United States and Mexican industries are comparable. Blank—Canadian, Mexican, and United States industries are comparable.

gold and or silver content. Establishments primarily engaged in the transformation of the gold and silver into bullion or dore bar in combination with mining activities are included in this industry.

Cross-References.

Establishments primarily engaged in manufacturing gold or silver bullion or dore bar without mining are classified in Industry 33141, Nonferrous Metal (except Aluminum) Smelting and Refining.

212221 Gold Ore Mining[MEX]

This U.S. industry comprises establishments primarily engaged in developing the mine site, mining, and/or beneficiating (i.e., preparing) ores valued chiefly for their gold content. Establishments primarily engaged in transformation of the gold into bullion or dore bar in combination with mining activities are included in this industry.

Cross-References.

Establishments primarily engaged in manufacturing gold bullion or dore bar without mining are classified in U.S. Industry 331419, Primary Smelting and Refining of Nonferrous Metal (except Copper and Aluminum).

212222 Silver Ore Mining[MEX]

This U.S. industry comprises establishments primarily engaged in developing the mine site, mining, and/or beneficiating (i.e., preparing) ores valued chiefly for their silver content. Establishments primarily engaged in transformation of the silver into bullion or dore bar in combination with mining activities are included in this industry.

Cross-References.

Establishments primarily engaged in manufacturing silver bullion or dore bar without mining are classified in U.S. Industry 331419, Primary Smelting and Refining of Nonferrous Metal (except Copper and Aluminum).

21223 Copper, Nickel, Lead, and Zinc Mining

This industry comprises establishments primarily engaged in developing the mine site, mining, and/or beneficiating (i.e., preparing) ores valued chiefly for their copper, nickel, lead, or zinc content. Beneficiating includes the transformation of ores into concentrates.

US—United States industry only. CAN—United States and Canadian industries are comparable. MEX—United States and Mexican industries are comparable. Blank—Canadian, Mexican, and United States industries are comparable.

Cross-References. Establishments primarily engaged in—

- Refining copper concentrates—are classified in Industry 33141, Nonferrous Metal (except Aluminum) Smelting and Refining; and

- Developing the mine site, mining, and/or beneficiating iron and manganiferous ores valued for their iron content—are classified in Industry 21221, Iron Ore Mining.

212231   Lead Ore and Zinc Ore Mining[CAN]

This U.S. industry comprises establishments primarily engaged in developing the mine site, mining, and/or beneficiating (i.e., preparing) lead ores, zinc ores, or lead-zinc ores.

212234   Copper Ore and Nickel Ore Mining[US]

This U.S. industry comprises establishments primarily engaged in: (1) developing the mine site, mining, and/or beneficiating (i.e., preparing) copper and/or nickel ores; and (2) recovering copper concentrates by the precipitation, leaching, or electrowinning of copper ore.

Cross-References.

Establishments primarily engaged in refining copper concentrates are classified in U.S. Industry 331411, Primary Smelting and Refining of Copper.

21229   Other Metal Ore Mining

This industry comprises establishments primarily engaged in developing the mine site, mining, and/or beneficiating (i.e., preparing) metal ores (except iron and manganiferous ores valued for their iron content, gold ore, silver ore, copper, nickel, lead, and zinc ore).

Illustrative Examples:

Antimony ores mining and/or beneficiating

Tantalum ores mining and/or beneficiating

Columbite ores mining and/or beneficiating

Tungsten ores mining and/or beneficiating

Ilmenite ores mining and/or beneficiating

Uranium-radium-vanadium ores mining and/or beneficiating

Molybdenum ores mining and/or beneficiating

Cross-References. Establishments primarily engaged in—

- Developing the mine site, mining, and/or beneficiating iron and manganiferous ores valued chiefly for their iron content—are classified in Industry 21221, Iron Ore Mining;

- Developing the mine site, mining, and/or beneficiating ores valued chiefly for their gold or silver content—are classified in Industry 21222, Gold Ore and Silver Ore Mining;

- Developing the mine site, mining, and/or beneficiating ores valued chiefly for their copper, nickel, lead, or zinc content—are classified in Industry 21223, Copper, Nickel, Lead, and Zinc Mining; and

- Enriching uranium—are classified in Industry 32518, Other Basic Inorganic Chemical Manufacturing.

212291 Uranium-Radium-Vanadium Ore Mining[CAN]

This U.S. industry comprises establishments primarily engaged in developing the mine site, mining, and/or beneficiating (i.e., preparing) uranium-radium-vanadium ores.

Cross-References.

Establishments primarily engaged in enriching uranium are classified in U.S. Industry 325188, All Other Basic Inorganic Chemical Manufacturing.

212299 All Other Metal Ore Mining[CAN]

This U.S. industry comprises establishments primarily engaged in developing the mine site, mining, and/or beneficiating (i.e., preparing) metal ores (except iron and manganiferous ores valued for their iron content, gold ore, silver ore, copper, nickel, lead, zinc, and uranium-radium-vanadium ore).

Illustrative Examples:

Antimony ores mining and/or
  beneficiating
Rare-earth metal ores mining and/or
  beneficiating
Columbite ores mining and/or
  beneficiating
Tantalum ores mining and/or
  beneficiating

Ilmenite ores mining and/or
  beneficiating
Tungsten ores mining and/or
  beneficiating
Molybdenum ores mining and/or
  beneficiating

US—United States industry only. CAN—United States and Canadian industries are comparable. MEX—United States and Mexican industries are comparable. Blank—Canadian, Mexican, and United States industries are comparable.

Cross-References. Establishments primarily engaged in—

- Developing the mine site, mining, and/or beneficiating iron and manganiferous ores valued for their iron content—are classified in Industry 212210, Iron Ore Mining;

- Developing the mine site, mining, and/or beneficiating ores valued chiefly for their gold or silver content—are classified in Industry 21222, Gold Ore and Silver Ore Mining;

- Developing the mine site, mining, and/or beneficiating ores valued chiefly for their copper, nickel, lead, or zinc content—are classified in Industry 21223, Copper, Nickel, Lead, and Zinc Mining; and

- Developing the mine site, mining, and/or beneficiating uranium-radium-vanadium ores—are classified in U.S. Industry 212291, Uranium-Radium-Vanadium Ore Mining.

2123 Nonmetallic Mineral Mining and Quarrying

This industry group comprises establishments primarily engaged in developing mine sites, or in mining or quarrying nonmetallic minerals (except fuels). Also included are certain well and brine operations, and preparation plants primarily engaged in beneficiating (e.g., crushing, grinding, washing, and concentrating) nonmetallic minerals.

Beneficiation is the process whereby the extracted material is reduced to particles which can be separated into mineral and waste, the former suitable for further processing or direct use. The operations that take place in beneficiation are primarily mechanical, such as grinding, washing, magnetic separation, and centrifugal separation. In contrast, manufacturing operations primarily use chemical and electrochemical processes, such as electrolysis and distillation. However, some treatments, such as heat treatments, take place in both the beneficiation and the manufacturing (i.e., smelting/refining) stages. The range of preparation activities varies by mineral and the purity of any given ore deposit. While some minerals, such as petroleum and natural gas, require little or no preparation, others are washed and screened, while yet others, such as gold and silver, can be transformed into bullion before leaving the mine site.

21231 Stone Mining and Quarrying

This industry comprises (1) establishments primarily engaged in developing the mine site, mining or quarrying dimension stone (i.e., rough blocks and/or slabs of stone), or mining and quarrying crushed and broken stone and/or (2) preparation plants primarily engaged in beneficiating stone (e.g., crushing, grinding, washing, screening, pulverizing, and sizing).

US—United States industry only. CAN—United States and Canadian industries are comparable. MEX—United States and Mexican industries are comparable. Blank—Canadian, Mexican, and United States industries are comparable.

Cross-References. Establishments primarily engaged in—

- Producing lime—are classified in Industry 32741, Lime Manufacturing; and
- Quarrying and dressing dimension stone—are classified in Industry 32799, All Other Nonmetallic Mineral Product Manufacturing.

212311 Dimension Stone Mining and Quarrying[US]

This U.S. industry comprises establishments primarily engaged in developing the mine site and/or mining or quarrying dimension stone (i.e., rough blocks and/ or slabs of stone).

Cross-References.

Establishments primarily engaged in dressing dimension stone and manufacturing stone products are classified in U.S. Industry 327991, Cut Stone and Stone Product Manufacturing.

212312 Crushed and Broken Limestone Mining and Quarrying[US]

This U.S. industry comprises (1) establishments primarily engaged in developing the mine site, mining or quarrying crushed and broken limestone (including related rocks, such as dolomite, cement rock, marl, travertine, and calcareous tufa); and (2) preparation plants primarily engaged in beneficiating limestone (e.g., grinding or pulverizing).

Cross-References. Establishments primarily engaged in—

- Producing lime—are classified in Industry 327410, Lime Manufacturing; and
- Mining or quarrying bituminous limestone—are classified in U.S. Industry 212319, Other Crushed and Broken Stone Mining and Quarrying.

212313 Crushed and Broken Granite Mining and Quarrying[US]

This U.S. industry comprises: (1) establishments primarily engaged in developing the mine site, and/or mining or quarrying crushed and broken granite (including related rocks, such as gneiss, syenite, and diorite); and (2) preparation plants primarily engaged in beneficiating granite (e.g., grinding or pulverizing).

212319 Other Crushed and Broken Stone Mining and Quarrying US

This U.S. industry comprises: (1) establishments primarily engaged in developing the mine site and/or mining or quarrying crushed and broken stone (except

US—United States industry only. CAN—United States and Canadian industries are comparable. MEX—United States and Mexican industries are comparable. Blank—Canadian, Mexican, and United States industries are comparable.

limestone and granite); (2) preparation plants primarily engaged in beneficiating (e.g., grinding and pulverizing) stone (except limestone and granite); and (3) establishments primarily engaged in mining or quarrying bituminous limestone and bituminous sandstone.

Illustrative Examples:

Bituminous limestone mining and/or beneficiating	Bituminous sandstone mining and/or beneficiating
Marble crushed and broken stone mining and/or beneficiating	Sandstone crushed and broken stone mining and/or beneficiating

Cross-References. Establishments primarily engaged in—

- Mining or quarrying crushed and broken limestone—are classified in U.S. Industry 212312, Crushed and Broken Limestone Mining and Quarrying; and

- Mining or quarrying crushed and broken granite—are classified in U.S. Industry 212313, Crushed and Broken Granite Mining and Quarrying.

21232 Sand, Gravel, Clay, and Ceramic and Refractory Minerals Mining and Quarrying

This industry comprises (1) establishments primarily engaged in developing the mine site and/or mining, quarrying, dredging for sand and gravel, or mining clay, (e.g., china clay, paper clay and slip clay) and (2) preparation plants primarily engaged in beneficiating (e.g., washing, screening, and grinding) sand and gravel, clay, and ceramic and refractory minerals.

Cross-References. Establishments primarily engaged in—

- Calcining, dead burning, or otherwise processing (i.e., beyond basic preparation) clay or refractory minerals—are classified in Industry 32799, All Other Nonmetallic Mineral Product Manufacturing;

- Shaping, molding, baking, burning, or hardening nonclay ceramics, clay and nonclay refractories, and structural clay products—are classified in Industry 32712, Clay Building Material and Refractories Manufacturing; and

- Shaping, molding, glazing, and firing pottery, ceramics, and plumbing fixtures—are classified in Industry 32711, Pottery, Ceramics, and Plumbing Fixture Manufacturing.

212321 Construction Sand and Gravel Mining[MEX]

This U.S. industry comprises establishments primarily engaged in one or more of the following: (1) operating commercial grade (i.e., construction) sand and gravel pits; (2) dredging for commercial grade sand and gravel; and (3) washing, screening, or otherwise preparing commercial grade sand and gravel.

Cross-References.

Establishments primarily engaged in mining industrial grade sand are classified in U.S. Industry 212322, Industrial Sand Mining.

212322 Industrial Sand Mining[US]

This U.S. industry comprises establishments primarily engaged in one or more of the following: (1) operating industrial grade sand pits; (2) dredging for industrial grade sand; and (3) washing, screening, or otherwise preparing industrial grade sand.

Cross-References.

Establishments primarily engaged in mining commercial (i.e., construction) grade gravel are classified in U.S. Industry 212321, Construction Sand and Gravel Mining.

212324 Kaolin and Ball Clay Mining[US]

This U.S. industry comprises (1) establishments primarily engaged in developing the mine site and/or mining kaolin or ball clay (e.g., china clay, paper clay, and slip clay) and (2) establishments primarily engaged in beneficiating (i.e., preparing) kaolin or ball clay.

Cross-References.

Establishments primarily engaged in calcining, dead burning, or otherwise processing (i.e., beyond basic preparation) kaolin and ball clay are classified in U.S. Industry 327992, Ground or Treated Mineral and Earth Manufacturing.

212325 Clay and Ceramic and Refractory Minerals Mining[US]

This U.S. industry comprises establishments primarily engaged in one or more of the following: (1) mining clay (except kaolin and ball), ceramic, or refractory minerals; (2) developing the mine site for clay, ceramic, or refractory minerals; and (3) beneficiating (i.e., preparing) clay (except kaolin and ball), ceramic, or refractory minerals.

US—United States industry only. CAN—United States and Canadian industries are comparable. MEX—United States and Mexican industries are comparable. Blank—Canadian, Mexican, and United States industries are comparable.

Illustrative Examples:

Bentonite mining and/or beneficiating
Fuller's earth mining and/or beneficiating
Common clay mining and/or beneficiating
Magnesite mining and/or beneficiating
Feldspar mining and/or beneficiating

Nepheline syenite mining and/or beneficiating
Fire clay mining and/or beneficiating
Shale (except oil shale) mining and/or beneficiating

Cross-References. Establishments primarily engaged in—

- Shaping, molding, baking, burning, or hardening clay and nonclay refractories, and structural clay products—are classified in Industry 32712, Clay Building Material and Refractories Manufacturing;

- Developing the mine site, mining, and/or beneficiating kaolin or ball clay—are classified in U.S. Industry 212324, Kaolin and Ball Clay Mining; and

- Shaping, molding, glazing, and firing pottery, ceramics, and plumbing fixtures—are classified in Industry 32711, Pottery, Ceramics, and Plumbing Fixture Manufacturing.

21239 Other Nonmetallic Mineral Mining and Quarrying

This industry comprises establishments primarily engaged in developing the mine site, mining, and/or milling or otherwise beneficiating (i.e., preparing) nonmetallic minerals (except coal, stone, sand, gravel, clay, ceramic, and refractory minerals).

Illustrative Examples:

Barite mining and/or beneficiating
Phosphate rock mining and/or beneficiating
Borate, natural, mining and/or beneficiating

Potash mining and/or beneficiating
Peat mining and/or beneficiating
Rock salt mining and/or beneficiating

Cross-References. Establishments primarily engaged in—

- Mining or quarrying dimension stone—are classified in Industry 21231, Stone Mining and Quarrying;

- Mining or quarrying sand, gravel, clay and ceramic and refractory minerals—are classified in Industry 21232, Sand, Gravel, Clay, and Ceramic and Refractory Minerals Mining and Quarrying;

- Calcining, dead burning, or otherwise processing (i.e., beyond basic preparation) minerals, such as talc, mica, feldspar, barite, and soapstone—are classified in Industry 32799, All Other Nonmetallic Mineral Product Manufacturing;

US—United States industry only. CAN—United States and Canadian industries are comparable. MEX—United States and Mexican industries are comparable. Blank—Canadian, Mexican, and United States industries are comparable.

- Manufacturing boron compounds and potassium salts—are classified in Industry 32518, Other Basic Inorganic Chemical Manufacturing;

- Manufacturing table salt—are classified in Industry 31194, Seasoning and Dressing Manufacturing;

- Manufacturing salt (except table salt)—are classified in Industry 32599, All Other Chemical Product and Preparation Manufacturing; and

- Manufacturing phosphoric acid, superphosphates, or other phosphatic fertilizer materials—are classified in Industry 32531, Fertilizer Manufacturing.

212391 Potash, Soda, and Borate Mineral Mining[US]

This U.S. industry comprises establishments primarily engaged in developing the mine site, mining and/or milling, or otherwise beneficiating (i.e., preparing) natural potassium, sodium, or boron compounds. Drylake brine operations are included in this industry, as well as establishments engaged in producing the specified minerals from underground and open pit mines.

Cross-References. Establishments primarily engaged in—

- Manufacturing boron compounds and potassium salts—are classified in U.S. Industry 325188, All Other Basic Inorganic Chemical Manufacturing;

- Manufacturing sodium carbonate—are classified in U.S. Industry 325181, Alkalies and Chlorine Manufacturing; and

- Manufacturing table salt—are classified in U.S. Industry 311942, Spice and Extract Manufacturing.

212392 Phosphate Rock Mining[US]

This U.S. industry comprises establishments primarily engaged in developing the mine site, mining, milling, and/or drying or otherwise beneficiating (i.e., preparing) phosphate rock.

Cross-References.

Establishments primarily engaged in manufacturing phosphoric acid, superphosphates, or other phosphatic fertilizer materials are classified in U.S. Industry 325312, Phosphatic Fertilizer Manufacturing.

212393 Other Chemical and Fertilizer Mineral Mining[US]

This U.S. industry comprises establishments primarily engaged in developing the mine site, mining, milling, and/or drying or otherwise beneficiating (i.e., preparing) chemical or fertilizer mineral raw materials (except potash, soda, boron, and phosphate rock).

Illustrative Examples:

Barite mining and/or beneficiating
Rock salt mining and/or beneficiating
Celestite mining and/or beneficiating

Sulfur mining and/or beneficiating
Fluorspar mining and/or beneficiating

Cross-References. Establishments primarily engaged in—

- Mining and/or milling or otherwise beneficiating natural potassium, sodium, or boron compounds—are classified in U.S. Industry 212391, Potash, Soda, and Borate Mineral Mining;

- Manufacturing industrial salt—are classified in U.S. Industry 325998, All Other Miscellaneous Chemical Product and Preparation Manufacturing;

- Mining, milling, drying, and/or sintering or otherwise beneficiating phosphate rock—are classified in U.S. Industry 212392, Phosphate Rock Mining; and

- Manufacturing table salt—are classified in U.S. Industry 311942, Spice and Extract Manufacturing.

212399 All Other Nonmetallic Mineral Mining[US]

This U.S. industry comprises establishments primarily engaged in developing the mine site, mining and/or milling or otherwise beneficiating (i.e., preparing) nonmetallic minerals (except stone, sand, gravel, clay, ceramic, refractory minerals, chemical and fertilizer minerals).

Illustrative Examples:

Gypsum mining and/or beneficiating
Soapstone mining and/or beneficiating
Mica mining and/or beneficiating

Talc mining and/or beneficiating
Pyrophyllite mining and/or beneficiating

Cross-References. Establishments primarily engaged in—

- Mining or quarrying stone—are classified in Industry 21231, Stone Mining and Quarrying;

- Mining, quarrying, or beneficiating sand, gravel, clay, and ceramic and refractory minerals—are classified in Industry 21232, Sand, Gravel, Clay, and Ceramic and Refractory Minerals Mining and Quarrying;

- Mining, quarrying or beneficiating natural potash, soda, and borate—are classified in U.S. Industry 212391, Potash, Soda, and Borate Mineral Mining; and

- Mining and/or milling or otherwise beneficiating phosphate rock—are classified in U.S. Industry 212392, Phosphate Rock Mining.

213 Support Activities for Mining

Industries in the Support Activities for Mining subsector group establishments primarily providing support services, on a contract or fee basis, required for the mining and quarrying of minerals and for the extraction of oil and gas. Establishments performing exploration (except geophysical surveying and mapping) for minerals, on a contract or fee basis, are included in this subsector. Exploration includes traditional prospecting methods, such as taking core samples and making geological observations at prospective sites.

The activities performed on a contract or fee basis by establishments in the Support Activities for Mining subsector are also often performed in-house by mining operators. These activities include: taking core samples, making geological observations at prospective sites, excavating slush pits and cellars, and such oil and gas operations as spudding in, drilling in, redrilling, directional drilling, well surveying; running, cutting, and pulling casings, tubes and rods; cementing wells, shooting wells; perforating well casings; acidizing and chemically treating wells; and cleaning out, bailing, and swabbing wells.

2131 Support Activities for Mining

21311 Support Activities for Mining

This industry comprises establishments primarily engaged in providing support services, on a contract or fee basis, required for the mining and quarrying of minerals and for the extraction of oil and gas. Drilling, taking core samples, and making geological observations at prospective sites (except geophysical surveying and mapping) for minerals, on a contract or fee basis, are included in this industry.

Cross-References. Establishments primarily engaged in—

- Performing geophysical surveying and mapping services for minerals (i.e., coal, metal ores, oil and gas, and nonmetallic minerals) on a contract or fee basis—are classified in Industry 54136, Geophysical Surveying and Mapping Services;

- Mining, quarrying, and/or beneficiating on a contract or fee basis—are classified in Subsector 212, Mining (except Oil and Gas) based on the mineral mined; and

- Operating oil and gas field properties on a contract or fee basis—are classified in Subsector 211, Oil and Gas Extraction, based on the activity.

US—United States industry only. CAN—United States and Canadian industries are comparable. MEX—United States and Mexican industries are comparable. Blank—Canadian, Mexican, and United States industries are comparable.

213111 Drilling Oil and Gas Wells

This U.S. industry comprises establishments primarily engaged in drilling oil and gas wells for others on a contract or fee basis. This industry includes contractors that specialize in spudding in, drilling in, redrilling, and directional drilling.

Cross-References. Establishments primarily engaged in—

- Performing exploration (except geophysical surveying and mapping) services for oil and gas on a contract or fee basis—are classified in U.S. Industry 213112, Support Activities for Oil and Gas Operations; and

- Performing geophysical surveying and mapping services for oil and gas on a contract or fee basis—are classified in Industry 541360, Geophysical Surveying and Mapping Services.

213112 Support Activities for Oil and Gas Operations[US]

This U.S. industry comprises establishments primarily engaged in performing support activities on a contract or fee basis for oil and gas operations (except site preparation and related construction activities). Services included are exploration (except geophysical surveying and mapping); excavating slush pits and cellars, well surveying; running, cutting, and pulling casings, tubes, and rods; cementing wells, shooting wells; perforating well casings; acidizing and chemically treating wells; and cleaning out, bailing, and swabbing wells.

Cross-References. Establishments primarily engaged in—

- Contract drilling for oil and gas—are classified in U.S. Industry 213111, Drilling Oil and Gas Wells;

- Operating oil and gas field properties on a contract or fee basis—are classified in Industry 21111, Oil and Gas Extraction;

- Performing geophysical surveying and mapping services for oil and gas on a contract or fee basis—are classified in Industry 541360, Geophysical Surveying and Mapping Services;

- Oil and gas pipeline and related structures construction—are classified in Industry 237120, Oil and Gas Pipeline and Related Structures Construction; and

- Site preparation and related construction activities on a contract or fee basis—are classified in Industry 238910, Site Preparation Contractors.

US—United States industry only. CAN—United States and Canadian industries are comparable. MEX—United States and Mexican industries are comparable. Blank—Canadian, Mexican, and United States industries are comparable.

213113 Support Activities for Coal Mining^{US}

This U.S. industry comprises establishments primarily engaged in providing support activities for coal mining (except site preparation and related construction activities) on a contract or fee basis. Exploration for coal is included in this industry. Exploration includes traditional prospecting methods, such as taking core samples and making geological observations at prospective sites.

Cross-References. Establishments primarily engaged in—

- ‣ Performing geophysical surveying and mapping services for coal on a contract or fee basis—are classified in Industry 541360, Geophysical Surveying and Mapping Services;
- Operating coal mines or quarries on a contract or fee basis—are classified in Industry 21211, Coal Mining, based on the type of coal mined; and
- Site preparation and related construction activities on a contract or fee basis—are classified in Industry 238910, Site Preparation Contractors.

213114 Support Activities for Metal Mining^{US}

This U.S. industry comprises establishments primarily engaged in providing support activities (except site preparation and related construction activities) on a contract or fee basis for the mining and quarrying of metallic minerals and for the extraction of metal ores. Exploration for minerals is included in this industry. Exploration (except geophysical surveying and mapping services) includes traditional prospecting methods, such as taking core samples and making geological observations at prospective sites.

Cross-References. Establishments primarily engaged in—

- Performing geophysical surveying and mapping services for metallic minerals on a contract or fee basis—are classified in Industry 541360, Geophysical Surveying and Mapping Services;
- Operating metallic mineral mines or quarries on a contract or fee basis— are classified in Industry Group 2122, Metal Ore Mining, based on the type of ore mined; and
- Site preparation and related construction activities on a contract or fee basis—are classified in Industry 238910, Site Preparation Contractors.

213115 Support Activities for Nonmetallic Minerals (except Fuels) Mining^{US}

This U.S. industry comprises establishments primarily engaged in providing support activities, on a fee or contract basis, for the mining and quarrying of

---

nonmetallic minerals (except fuel) and for the extraction of nonmetallic minerals (except site preparation and related construction activities). Exploration for minerals is included in this industry. Exploration (except geophysical surveying and mapping services) includes traditional prospecting methods, such as taking core samples and making geological observations at prospective sites.

Cross-References. Establishments primarily engaged in—

- Performing geophysical surveying and mapping services for nonmetallic minerals on a contract or fee basis—are classified in Industry 541360, Geophysical Surveying and Mapping Services;

- Operating nonmetallic mineral mines or quarries on a contract or fee basis— are classified in Industry Group 2123, Nonmetallic Mineral Mining and Quarrying, based on the type of mineral mined or quarried; and

- Site preparation and related construction activities—are classified in Industry 238910, Site Preparation Contractors.

US—United States industry only. CAN—United States and Canadian industries are comparable. MEX—United States and Mexican industries are comparable. Blank—Canadian, Mexican, and United States industries are comparable.

Sector 22—Utilities

The Sector as a Whole

The Utilities sector comprises establishments engaged in the provision of the following utility services: electric power, natural gas, steam supply, water supply, and sewage removal. Within this sector, the specific activities associated with the utility services provided vary by utility: electric power includes generation, transmission, and distribution; natural gas includes distribution; steam supply includes provision and/or distribution; water supply includes treatment and distribution; and sewage removal includes collection, treatment, and disposal of waste through sewer systems and sewage treatment facilities.

Excluded from this sector are establishments primarily engaged in waste management services classified in Subsector 562, Waste Management and Remediation Services. These establishments also collect, treat, and dispose of waste materials; however, they do not use sewer systems or sewage treatment facilities.

221 Utilities^{CAN}

Industries in the Utilities subsector provide electric power, natural gas, steam supply, water supply, and sewage removal through a permanent infrastructure of lines, mains, and pipes. Establishments are grouped together based on the utility service provided and the particular system or facilities required to perform the service.

2211 Electric Power Generation, Transmission and Distribution

This industry group comprises establishments primarily engaged in generating, transmitting, and/or distributing electric power. Establishments in this industry group may perform one or more of the following activities: (1) operate generation facilities that produce electric energy; (2) operate transmission systems that convey the electricity from the generation facility to the distribution system; and (3) operate distribution systems that convey electric power received from the generation facility or the transmission system to the final consumer.

22111 Electric Power Generation^{CAN}

This industry comprises establishments primarily engaged in operating electric power generation facilities. These facilities convert other forms of energy, such as water power (i.e., hydroelectric), fossil fuels, nuclear power, and solar power,

---

US—United States industry only. CAN—United States and Canadian industries are comparable. MEX—United States and Mexican industries are comparable. Blank—Canadian, Mexican, and United States industries are comparable.

into electrical energy. The establishments in this industry produce electric energy and provide electricity to transmission systems or to electric power distribution systems.

Cross-References.

Establishments primarily engaged in operating trash incinerators that also generate electricity are classified in Industry 56221, Waste Treatment and Disposal.

221111 Hydroelectric Power Generation^{CAN}

This U.S. industry comprises establishments primarily engaged in operating hydroelectric power generation facilities. These facilities use water power to drive a turbine and produce electric energy. The electric energy produced in these establishments is provided to electric power transmission systems or to electric power distribution systems.

221112 Fossil Fuel Electric Power Generation^{CAN}

This U.S. industry comprises establishments primarily engaged in operating fossil fuel powered electric power generation facilities. These facilities use fossil fuels, such as coal, oil, or gas, in internal combustion or combustion turbine conventional steam process to produce electric energy. The electric energy produced in these establishments is provided to electric power transmission systems or to electric power distribution systems.

221113 Nuclear Electric Power Generation^{CAN}

This U.S. industry comprises establishments primarily engaged in operating nuclear electric power generation facilities. These facilities use nuclear power to produce electric energy. The electric energy produced in these establishments is provided to electric power transmission systems or to electric power distribution systems.

221119 Other Electric Power Generation^{CAN}

This U.S. industry comprises establishments primarily engaged in operating electric power generation facilities (except hydroelectric, fossil fuel, nuclear). These facilities convert other forms of energy, such as solar, wind, or tidal power, into electrical energy. The electric energy produced in these establishments is provided to electric power transmission systems or to electric power distribution systems.

US—United States industry only. CAN—United States and Canadian industries are comparable. MEX—United States and Mexican industries are comparable. Blank—Canadian, Mexican, and United States industries are comparable.

Cross-References. Establishments primarily engaged in—

- Operating trash disposal incinerators that also generate electricity—are classified in U.S. Industry 562213, Solid Waste Combustors and Incinerators;

- Operating hydroelectric power generation facilities—are classified in U.S. Industry 221111, Hydroelectric Power Generation;

- Operating fossil fuel powered electric power generation facilities—are classified in U.S. Industry 221112, Fossil Fuel Electric Power Generation; and

- Operating nuclear electric power generation facilities—are classified in U.S. Industry 221113, Nuclear Electric Power Generation.

22112 Electric Power Transmission, Control, and Distribution[CAN]

This industry comprises establishments primarily engaged in operating electric power transmission systems, controlling (i.e., regulating voltages) the transmission of electricity, and/or distributing electricity. The transmission system includes lines and transformer stations. These establishments arrange, facilitate, or coordinate the transmission of electricity from the generating source to the distribution centers, other electric utilities, or final consumers. The distribution system consists of lines, poles, meters, and wiring that deliver the electricity to final consumers.

Cross-References.

Establishments primarily engaged in generating electric energy are classified in Industry 22111, Electric Power Generation.

221121 Electric Bulk Power Transmission and Control[CAN]

This U.S. industry comprises establishments primarily engaged in operating electric power transmission systems and/or controlling (i.e., regulatory voltage) the transmission of electricity from the generating source to distribution centers or other electric utilities. The transmission system includes lines and transformer stations.

Cross-References. Establishments primarily engaged in—

- Generating electric energy—are classified in Industry 22111, Electric Power Generation; and

- Distributing electricity to final consumers—are classified in U.S. Industry 221122, Electric Power Distribution.

US—United States industry only. CAN—United States and Canadian industries are comparable. MEX—United States and Mexican industries are comparable. Blank—Canadian, Mexican, and United States industries are comparable.

221122 Electric Power Distribution[CAN]

This U.S. industry comprises electric power establishments primarily engaged in either (1) operating electric power distribution systems (i.e., consisting of lines, poles, meters, and wiring) or (2) operating as electric power brokers or agents that arrange the sale of electricity via power distribution systems operated by others.

Cross-References. Establishments primarily engaged in—

- Generating electric energy—are classified in Industry 22111, Electric Power Generation; and

- Transmitting electricity between generating sources or distribution centers— are classified in U.S. Industry 221121, Electric Bulk Power Transmission and Control.

2212 Natural Gas Distribution[CAN]

22121 Natural Gas Distribution[CAN]
See industry description for 221210 below.

221210 Natural Gas Distribution[CAN]

This industry comprises: (1) establishments primarily engaged in operating gas distribution systems (e.g., mains, meters); (2) establishments known as gas marketers that buy gas from the well and sell it to a distribution system; (3) establishments known as gas brokers or agents that arrange the sale of gas over gas distribution systems operated by others; and (4) establishments primarily engaged in transmitting and distributing gas to final consumers.

Cross-References. Establishments primarily engaged in—

- Pipeline transportation of natural gas from process plants to local distribution systems—are classified in Industry 486210, Pipeline Transportation of Natural Gas; and

- Retailing liquefied petroleum (LP) gas via direct selling—are classified in U.S. Industry 454312, Liquefied Petroleum Gas (Bottled Gas) Dealers.

2213 Water, Sewage and Other Systems[CAN]

22131 Water Supply and Irrigation Systems[CAN]
See industry description for 221310 below.

US—United States industry only. CAN—United States and Canadian industries are comparable. MEX—United States and Mexican industries are comparable. Blank—Canadian, Mexican, and United States industries are comparable.

http://www.census.gov/naics

221310 Water Supply and Irrigation Systems^{CAN}

This industry comprises establishments primarily engaged in operating water treatment plants and/or operating water supply systems. The water supply system may include pumping stations, aqueducts, and/or distribution mains. The water may be used for drinking, irrigation, or other uses.

22132 Sewage Treatment Facilities^{CAN}
See industry description for 221320 below.

221320 Sewage Treatment Facilities^{CAN}

This industry comprises establishments primarily engaged in operating sewer systems or sewage treatment facilities that collect, treat, and dispose of waste.

Cross-References. Establishments primarily engaged in—

- Operating waste treatment or disposal facilities (except sewer systems or sewage treatment facilities)—are classified in Industry 56221, Waste Treatment and Disposal;
- Pumping (i.e., cleaning) septic tanks and cesspools—are classified in U.S. Industry 562991, Septic Tank and Related Services; and
- Cleaning and rodding sewers and catch basins— are classified in U.S. Industry 562998, All Other Miscellaneous Waste Management Services.

22133 Steam and Air-Conditioning Supply^{CAN}
See industry description for 221330 below.

221330 Steam and Air-Conditioning Supply^{CAN}

This industry comprises establishments primarily engaged in providing steam, heated air, or cooled air. The steam distribution may be through mains.

Sector 23—Construction

The Sector as a Whole

The construction sector comprises establishments primarily engaged in the construction of buildings or engineering projects (e.g., highways and utility systems). Establishments primarily engaged in the preparation of sites for new construction and establishments primarily engaged in subdividing land for sale as building sites also are included in this sector.

Construction work done may include new work, additions, alterations, or maintenance and repairs. Activities of these establishments generally are managed at a fixed place of business, but they usually perform construction activities at multiple project sites. Production responsibilities for establishments in this sector are usually specified in (1) contracts with the owners of construction projects (prime contracts) or (2) contracts with other construction establishments (subcontracts).

Establishments primarily engaged in contracts that include responsibility for all aspects of individual construction projects are commonly known as general contractors, but also may be known as design-builders, construction managers, turnkey contractors, or (in cases where two or more establishments jointly secure a general contract) joint-venture contractors. Construction managers that provide oversight and scheduling only (i.e., agency) as well as construction managers that are responsible for the entire project (i.e., at risk) are included as general contractor type establishments. Establishments of the "general contractor type" frequently arrange construction of separate parts of their projects through subcontracts with other construction establishments.

Establishments primarily engaged in activities to produce a specific component (e.g., masonry, painting, and electrical work) of a construction project are commonly known as specialty trade contractors. Activities of specialty trade contractors are usually subcontracted from other construction establishments, but especially in remodeling and repair construction, the work may be done directly for the owner of the property.

Establishments primarily engaged in activities to construct buildings to be sold on sites that they own are known as operative builders, but also may be known as speculative builders or merchant builders. Operative builders produce buildings in a manner similar to general contractors, but their production processes also include site acquisition and securing of financial backing. Operative builders are most often associated with the construction of residential buildings. Like general contractors, they may subcontract all or part of the actual construction work on their buildings.

There are substantial differences in the types of equipment, work force skills, and other inputs required by establishments in this sector. To highlight these differences and variations in the underlying production functions, this sector is divided into three subsectors.

US—United States industry only. CAN—United States and Canadian industries are comparable. MEX—United States and Mexican industries are comparable. Blank—Canadian, Mexican, and United States industries are comparable.

Subsector 236, Construction of Buildings, comprises establishments of the general contractor type and operative builders involved in the construction of buildings. Subsector 237, Heavy and Civil Engineering Construction, comprises establishments involved in the construction of engineering projects. Subsector 238, Specialty Trade Contractors, comprises establishments engaged in specialty trade activities generally needed in the construction of all types of buildings.

Force account construction is construction work performed by an enterprise primarily engaged in some business other than construction for its own account and use, using employees of the enterprise. This activity is not included in the construction sector unless the construction work performed is the primary activity of a separate establishment of the enterprise. The installation and the ongoing repair and maintenance of telecommunications and utility networks is excluded from construction when the establishments performing the work are not independent contractors. Although a growing proportion of this work is subcontracted to independent contractors in the Construction Sector, the operating units of telecommunications and utility companies performing this work are included with the telecommunications or utility activities.

236 Construction of Buildings

The Construction of Buildings subsector comprises establishments primarily responsible for the construction of buildings. The work performed may include new work, additions, alterations, or maintenance and repairs. The on-site assembly of precut, panelized, and prefabricated buildings and construction of temporary buildings are included in this subsector. Part or all of the production work for which the establishments in this subsector have responsibility may be subcontracted to other construction establishments—usually specialty trade contractors.

Establishments in this subsector are classified based on the types of buildings they construct. This classification reflects variations in the requirements of the underlying production processes.

2361 Residential Building Construction

23611 Residential Building Construction

This Industry comprises establishments primarily responsible for the construction or remodeling and renovation of single-family and multifamily residential buildings. Included in this industry are residential housing general contractors (i.e., new construction, remodeling, or renovating existing residential structures), operative builders and remodelers of residential structures, residential project construction management firms, and residential design-build firms.

US—United States industry only. CAN—United States and Canadian industries are comparable. MEX—United States and Mexican industries are comparable. Blank—Canadian, Mexican, and United States industries are comparable.

Cross-References. Establishments primarily engaged in—

- Performing specialized construction work on houses and other residential buildings, generally on a subcontract basis—are classified in Subsector 238, Specialty Trade Contractors;

- Performing manufactured (mobile) home setup and tie-down work—are classified in Industry 23899, All Other Specialty Trade Contractors; and

- Constructing and leasing residential buildings on their own account—are classified in Industry 53111, Lessors of Residential Buildings and Dwellings.

236115 New Single-Family Housing Construction (except Operative Builders)[US]

This U.S. industry comprises general contractor establishments primarily responsible for the entire construction of new single-family housing, such as single-family detached houses and town houses or row houses where each housing unit (1) is separated from its neighbors by a ground-to-roof wall and (2) has no housing units constructed above or below. This industry includes general contractors responsible for the on-site assembly of modular and prefabricated houses. Single-family housing design-build firms and single-family construction management firms acting as general contractors are included in this industry.

Cross-References. Establishments primarily engaged in—

- Building single-family houses on their own account for sale as speculative builders or merchant builders—are classified in U.S. Industry 236117, New Housing Operative Builders;

- Remodeling or repairing existing houses and other residential buildings— are classified in U.S. Industry 236118, Residential Remodelers;

- Performing manufactured (mobile) home setup and tie-down work—are classified in Industry 238990, All Other Specialty Trade Contractors;

- Performing specialized construction work on houses and other residential buildings, generally on a subcontract basis—are classified in Subsector 238, Specialty Trade Contractors; and

- Constructing and leasing residential buildings on their own account—are classified in Industry 531110, Lessors of Residential Buildings and Dwellings.

236116 New Multifamily Housing Construction (except Operative Builders)[US]

This U.S. industry comprises general contractor establishments responsible for the construction of new multifamily residential housing units (e.g., high-rise, garden, town house apartments, and condominiums where each unit is not separated from its neighbors by a ground-to-roof wall). Multifamily design-build firms and multifamily housing construction management firms acting as general contractors are included in this industry.

Cross-References. Establishments primarily engaged in—

- Building multifamily buildings on their own account for sale as speculative builders or merchant builders—are classified in U.S. Industry 236117, New Housing Operative Builders;
- Remodeling or repairing existing multifamily housing and other residential buildings—are classified in U.S. Industry 236118, Residential Remodelers;
- Performing specialized construction work on multifamily housing and other residential buildings, generally on a subcontract basis—are classified in Subsector 238, Specialty Trade Contractors; and
- Constructing and leasing residential buildings on their own account—are classified in Industry 531110, Lessors of Residential Buildings and Dwellings.

236117 New Housing Operative Builders[US]

This U.S. industry comprises establishments primarily engaged in building new homes on land that is owned or controlled by the builder rather than the homebuyer or investor. The land is included with the sale of the home. Establishments in this industry build single and/or multifamily homes. These establishments are often referred to as merchant builders, but are also known as production or for-sale builders.

Cross-References. Establishments primarily engaged in—

- Building single-family houses for others as general contractors—are classified in U.S. Industry 236115, New Single-Family Housing Construction (except Operative Builders);
- Building multifamily residential buildings for others as general contractors—are classified in U.S. Industry 236116, New Multifamily Housing Construction (except Operative Builders);
- Remodeling or repairing existing houses and other residential buildings, either for others or on own account for sale—are classified in U.S. Industry 236118, Residential Remodelers;
- Performing specialized construction work on houses or other residential buildings, generally on a subcontract basis—are classified in Subsector 238, Specialty Trade Contractors; and

---

US—United States industry only. CAN—United States and Canadian industries are comparable. MEX—United States and Mexican industries are comparable. Blank—Canadian, Mexican, and United States industries are comparable.

- Constructing and leasing residential buildings on their own account—are classified in Industry 531110, Lessors of Residential Buildings and Dwellings.

236118 Residential Remodelers^{US}

This U.S. industry comprises establishments primarily responsible for the remodeling construction (including additions, alterations, reconstruction, maintenance, and repair work) of houses and other residential buildings, single-family, and multifamily. Included in this industry are remodeling general contractors, operative remodelers, remodeling design-build firms, and remodeling project construction management firms.

Cross-References. Establishments primarily engaged in—

- Building single-family houses for others as general contractors—are classified in U.S. Industry 236115, New Single-Family Housing Construction (except Operative Builders);
- Building multifamily buildings for others as general contractors—are classified in U.S. Industry 236116, New Multifamily Housing Construction (except Operative Builders);
- Building houses or other residential buildings, on their own account for sale as speculative builders or merchant builders—are classified in U.S. Industry 236117, New Housing Operative Builders;
- Remodeling nonresidential buildings—are classified in Industry Group 2362, Nonresidential Building Construction, based on the type of structure being remodeled;
- Performing specialized construction work on houses or other residential buildings generally on a subcontract basis—are classified in Subsector 238, Specialty Trade Contractors; and
- Constructing and leasing residential buildings on their own account—are classified in Industry 531110, Lessors of Residential Buildings and Dwellings.

2362 Nonresidential Building Construction

This industry group comprises establishments primarily responsible for the construction (including new work, additions, alterations, maintenance, and repairs) of nonresidential buildings. This industry group includes nonresidential general contractors, nonresidential operative builders, nonresidential design-build firms, and nonresidential project construction management firms.

US—United States industry only. CAN—United States and Canadian industries are comparable. MEX—United States and Mexican industries are comparable. Blank—Canadian, Mexican, and United States industries are comparable.

23621 Industrial Building Construction
See industry description for 236210 below.

236210 Industrial Building Construction^{CAN}

This industry comprises establishments primarily responsible for the construction (including new work, additions, alterations, maintenance, and repairs) of industrial buildings (except warehouses). The construction of selected additional structures, whose production processes are similar to those for industrial buildings (e.g., incinerators, cement plants, blast furnaces, and similar nonbuilding structures), is included in this industry. Included in this industry are industrial building general contractors, industrial building operative builders, industrial building design-build firms, and industrial building construction management firms.

Illustrative Examples:

Assembly plant construction
Furnace, industrial plant, construction
Cannery construction
Mine loading and discharging station
    construction
Cement plant construction
Paper or pulp mill construction
Chemical plant (except petrochemical)
    construction

Pharmaceutical manufacturing plant
    construction
Factory construction
Steel mill construction
Food processing plant construction
Waste disposal plant (except sewage
    treatment) construction

Cross-References. Establishments primarily engaged in—

- Constructing oil refineries and petrochemical plants—are classified in Industry 237120, Oil and Gas Pipeline and Related Structures Construction;

- Constructing water treatment plants, sewage treatment plants, and pumping stations for water and sewer systems—are classified in Industry 237110, Water and Sewer Line and Related Structures Construction;

- Constructing power generation plants (except hydroelectric)—are classified in Industry 237130, Power and Communication Line and Related Structures Construction;

- Constructing industrial warehouses—are classified in Industry 236220, Commercial and Institutional Building Construction; and

- Performing specialized construction work on industrial buildings, generally on a subcontract basis—are classified in Subsector 238, Specialty Trade Contractors.

23622 Commercial and Institutional Building Construction
See industry description for 236220 below.

US—United States industry only. CAN—United States and Canadian industries are comparable. MEX—United States and Mexican industries are comparable. Blank—Canadian, Mexican, and United States industries are comparable.

236220 Commercial and Institutional Building Construction^{CAN}

This industry comprises establishments primarily responsible for the construction (including new work, additions, alterations, maintenance, and repairs) of commercial and institutional buildings and related structures, such as stadiums, grain elevators, and indoor swimming facilities. This industry includes establishments responsible for the on-site assembly of modular or prefabricated commercial and institutional buildings. Included in this industry are commercial and institutional building general contractors, commercial and institutional building operative builders, commercial and institutional building design-build firms, and commercial and institutional building project construction management firms.

Illustrative Examples:

Airport building construction
Office building construction
Arena construction
Parking garage construction
Barrack construction
Prison construction
Farm building construction
Radio and television broadcast studio
   construction
Fire station construction
Religious building (e.g., church,
   synagogue, mosque, temple)
   construction

Grain elevator construction
Restaurant construction
Hospital construction
School building construction
Hotel construction
Shopping mall construction
Indoor swimming facility construction
Warehouse construction (e.g.,
   commercial, industrial, manufacturing,
   private)

Cross-References. Establishments primarily engaged in—

- Constructing structures that are integral parts of utility systems (e.g., storage tanks, pumping stations) or are used to produce products for these systems (e.g., power plants, refineries)—are classified in Industry Group 2371, Utility System Construction, based on type of construction project;

- Performing specialized construction work on commercial and institutional buildings, generally on a subcontract basis—are classified in Subsector 238, Specialty Trade Contractors; and

- Constructing buildings on their own account for rent or lease—are classified in Industry Group 5311, Lessors of Real Estate.

237 Heavy and Civil Engineering Construction

The Heavy and Civil Engineering Construction subsector comprises establishments whose primary activity is the construction of entire engineering projects

US—United States industry only. CAN—United States and Canadian industries are comparable. MEX—United States and Mexican industries are comparable. Blank—Canadian, Mexican, and United States industries are comparable.

(e.g., highways and dams), and specialty trade contractors, whose primary activity is the production of a specific component for such projects. Specialty trade contractors in Heavy and Civil Engineering Construction generally are performing activities that are specific to heavy and civil engineering construction projects and are not normally performed on buildings. The work performed may include new work, additions, alterations, or maintenance and repairs.

Specialty trade activities are classified in this subsector if the skills and equipment present are specific to heavy or civil engineering construction projects. For example, specialized equipment is needed to paint lines on highways. This equipment is not normally used in building applications so the activity is classified in this subsector. Traffic signal installation, while specific to highways, uses much of the same skills and equipment that are needed for electrical work in building projects and is therefore classified in Subsector 238, Specialty Trade Contractors.

Construction projects involving water resources (e.g., dredging and land drainage) and projects involving open space improvement (e.g., parks and trails) are included in this subsector. Establishments whose primary activity is the subdivision of land into individual building lots usually perform various additional site-improvement activities (e.g., road building and utility line installation), and are included in this subsector.

Establishments in this subsector are classified based on the types of structures that they construct. This classification reflects variations in the requirements of the underlying production processes.

2371 Utility System Construction

This industry group comprises establishments primarily engaged in the construction of distribution lines and related buildings and structures for utilities (i.e., water, sewer, petroleum, gas, power, and communication). All structures (including buildings) that are integral parts of utility systems (e.g., storage tanks, pumping stations, power plants, and refineries) are included in this industry group.

23711 Water and Sewer Line and Related Structures Construction
See industry description for 237110 below.

237110 Water and Sewer Line and Related Structures Construction[CAN]

This industry comprises establishments primarily engaged in the construction of water and sewer lines, mains, pumping stations, treatment plants, and storage tanks. The work performed may include new work, reconstruction, rehabilitation, and repairs. Specialty trade contractors are included in this group if they are

US—United States industry only. CAN—United States and Canadian industries are comparable. MEX—United States and Mexican industries are comparable. Blank—Canadian, Mexican, and United States industries are comparable.

engaged in activities primarily related to water, sewer line, and related structures construction. All structures (including buildings) that are integral parts of water and sewer networks (e.g., storage tanks, pumping stations, water treatment plants, and sewage treatment plants) are included in this industry.

Illustrative Examples:

Distribution line, sewer and water, construction

Sewer main, pipe, and connection, construction

Fire hydrant installation

Storm sewer construction

Irrigation systems construction

Water main and line construction

Pumping station, water and sewage system, construction

Water system storage tank and tower construction

Reservoir construction

Water treatment plant construction

Sewage disposal plant construction

Water well drilling, digging, boring, or sinking (except water intake wells in oil and gas fields)

Cross-References.

Establishments primarily engaged in constructing marine facilities (e.g., ports), flood control structures, dams, or hydroelectric power generation facilities are classified in Industry 237990, Other Heavy and Civil Engineering Construction.

23712 Oil and Gas Pipeline and Related Structures Construction
See industry description for 237120 below.

237120 Oil and Gas Pipeline and Related Structures Construction[CAN]

This industry comprises establishments primarily engaged in the construction of oil and gas lines, mains, refineries, and storage tanks. The work performed may include new work, reconstruction, rehabilitation, and repairs. Specialty trade contractors are included in this group if they are engaged in activities primarily related to oil and gas pipeline and related structures construction. All structures (including buildings) that are integral parts of oil and gas networks (e.g., storage tanks, pumping stations, and refineries) are included in this industry.

Illustrative Examples:

Distribution line, gas and oil, construction

Oil refinery construction

Gas main construction

Petrochemical plant construction

Gathering line, gas and oil field, construction

Pumping station, gas and oil transmission, construction

Natural gas pipeline construction

Storage tank, natural gas or oil, tank farm or field, construction

Natural gas processing plant construction

US—United States industry only. CAN—United States and Canadian industries are comparable. MEX—United States and Mexican industries are comparable. Blank—Canadian, Mexican, and United States industries are comparable.

Cross-References.

Establishments primarily engaged in building chemical plants (except petro-chemical) and similar process or batch facilities are classified in Industry 236210, Industrial Building Construction.

23713 Power and Communication Line and Related Structures Construction

See industry description for 237130 below.

237130 Power and Communication Line and Related Structures Construction[CAN]

This industry comprises establishments primarily engaged in the construction of power lines and towers, power plants, and radio, television, and telecommunications transmitting/receiving towers. The work performed may include new work, recon-struction, rehabilitation, and repairs. Specialty trade contractors are included in this group if they are engaged in activities primarily related to power and communi-cation line and related structures construction. All structures (including buildings) that are integral parts of power and communication networks (e.g., transmitting towers, substations, and power plants) are included.

Illustrative Examples:

Alternative energy (e.g., geothermal, ocean wave, solar, wind) structure construction
Power line stringing
Cellular phone tower construction
Radio transmitting tower construction
Co-generation plant construction
Satellite receiving station construction
Communication tower construction
Telephone line stringing

Electric light and power plant (except hydroelectric) construction
Transformer station and substation, electric power, construction
Electric power transmission line and tower construction
Underground cable (e.g., cable television, electricity, telephone) laying
Nuclear power plant construction

Cross-References. Establishments primarily engaged in—

- Constructing hydroelectric generating facilities—are classified in Industry 237990, Other Heavy and Civil Engineering Construction;

- Constructing broadcast studios and similar nonresidential buildings—are classified in Industry 236220, Commercial and Institutional Building Con-struction;

- Performing electrical work within buildings—are classified in Industry 238210, Electrical Contractors and Other Wiring Installation Contractors;

US—United States industry only. CAN—United States and Canadian industries are comparable. MEX—United States and Mexican industries are comparable. Blank—Canadian, Mexican, and United States industries are comparable.

- Line slashing or cutting (except maintenance)—are classified in Industry 238910, Site Preparation Contractors;

- Installing and maintaining communication transmission lines performed by telecommunications companies—are classified in Subsector 517, Telecommunications;

- Locating underground utility lines prior to digging—are classified in Industry 561990, All Other Support Services; and

- Tree and brush trimming for overhead utility lines—are classified in Industry 561730, Landscaping Services.

2372 Land Subdivision

23721 Land Subdivision
See industry description for 237210 below.

237210 Land Subdivision^{CAN}

This industry comprises establishments primarily engaged in servicing land and subdividing real property into lots, for subsequent sale to builders. Servicing of land may include excavation work for the installation of roads and utility lines. The extent of work may vary from project to project. Land subdivision precedes building activity and the subsequent building is often residential, but may also be commercial tracts and industrial parks. These establishments may do all the work themselves or subcontract the work to others. Establishments that perform only the legal subdivision of land are not included in this industry.

Cross-References. Establishments primarily engaged in—

- Constructing buildings, for sale, on lots they subdivide—are classified based on the type of construction project, in Industry Group 2361, Residential Building Construction, or Industry Group 2362, Nonresidential Building Construction;

- Installing roads on a subcontract basis for land subdividers—are classified in Industry 237310, Highway, Street, and Bridge Construction;

- Installing utilities on a subcontract basis for land subdividers—are classified in Industry Group 2371, Utility System Construction;

- Preparing land owned by others for building construction—are classified in Industry 238910, Site Preparation Contractors;

- Constructing buildings, for rent or own use, on lots they subdivide—are classified in Industry Group 5311, Lessors of Real Estate; and

---

US—United States industry only. CAN—United States and Canadian industries are comparable. MEX—United States and Mexican industries are comparable. Blank—Canadian, Mexican, and United States industries are comparable.

- Legal subdivision of land without land preparation—are classified elsewhere in the classification system based on the primary activity of the establishment.

2373 Highway, Street, and Bridge Construction

23731 Highway, Street, and Bridge Construction
See industry description for 237310 below.

237310 Highway, Street, and Bridge Construction[CAN]

This industry comprises establishments primarily engaged in the construction of highways (including elevated), streets, roads, airport runways, public sidewalks, or bridges. The work performed may include new work, reconstruction, rehabilitation, and repairs. Specialty trade contractors are included in this group if they are engaged in activities primarily related to highway, street, and bridge construction (e.g., installing guardrails on highways).

Illustrative Examples:

Airport runway construction
Highway line painting
Causeway construction
Painting traffic lanes or parking lot lines
Culverts, highway, road, and street, construction
Pothole filling, highway, road, street, or bridge

Elevated highway construction
Resurfacing, highway, road, street, or bridge
Guardrail construction
Sign erection, highway, road, street, or bridge

Cross-References. Establishments primarily engaged in—

- Constructing tunnels—are classified in Industry 237990, Other Heavy and Civil Engineering Construction;

- Highway lighting and signal installation—are classified in Industry 238210, Electrical Contractors and Other Wiring Installation Contractors;

- Painting bridges—are classified in Industry 238320, Painting and Wall Covering Contractors; and

- Constructing parking lots, private driveways, sidewalks, or erecting billboards—are classified in Industry 238990, All Other Specialty Trade Contractors.

US—United States industry only. CAN—United States and Canadian industries are comparable. MEX—United States and Mexican industries are comparable. Blank—Canadian, Mexican, and United States industries are comparable.

2379 Other Heavy and Civil Engineering Construction

23799 Other Heavy and Civil Engineering Construction
See industry description for 237990 below.

237990 Other Heavy and Civil Engineering Construction^{CAN}

This industry comprises establishments primarily engaged in heavy and engineering construction projects (excluding highway, street, bridge, and distribution line construction). The work performed may include new work, reconstruction, rehabilitation, and repairs. Specialty trade contractors are included in this group if they are engaged in activities primarily related to engineering construction projects (excluding highway, street, bridge, distribution line, oil and gas structure, and utilities building and structure construction). Construction projects involving water resources (e.g., dredging and land drainage), development of marine facilities, and projects involving open space improvement (e.g., parks and trails) are included in this industry.

Illustrative Examples:

Channel construction
Land drainage contractors
Dam construction
Marine construction
Dock construction
Microtunneling contractors
Dredging (e.g., canal, channel, ditch, waterway)
Nuclear waste disposal site construction
Earth retention system construction
Park ground and recreational open space improvement construction

Flood control project construction
Railroad construction
Golf course construction
Subway construction
Horizontal drilling (e.g., cable, pipeline, sewer installation)
Trenching, underwater
Hydroelectric generating station construction
Tunnel construction

Cross-References. Establishments primarily engaged in—

- Constructing water mains, sewers, and related structures—are classified in Industry 237110, Water and Sewer Line and Related Structures Construction;

- Constructing oil and gas pipelines and related structures—are classified in Industry 237120, Oil and Gas Pipeline and Related Structures Construction;

- Constructing power and communication transmission lines and related structures—are classified in Industry 237130, Power and Communication Line and Related Structures Construction;

US—United States industry only. CAN—United States and Canadian industries are comparable. MEX—United States and Mexican industries are comparable. Blank—Canadian, Mexican, and United States industries are comparable.

- Constructing highways, streets, and bridges—are classified in Industry 237310, Highway, Street, and Bridge Construction; and

- Trenching (except underwater)—are classified in U.S. Industry 238910, Site Preparation Contractors.

238 Specialty Trade Contractors

The Specialty Trade Contractors subsector comprises establishments whose primary activity is performing specific activities (e.g., pouring concrete, site preparation, plumbing, painting, and electrical work) involved in building construction or other activities that are similar for all types of construction, but that are not responsible for the entire project. The work performed may include new work, additions, alterations, maintenance, and repairs. The production work performed by establishments in this subsector is usually subcontracted from establishments of the general contractor type or operative builders, but especially in remodeling and repair construction, work also may be done directly for the owner of the property. Specialty trade contractors usually perform most of their work at the construction site, although they may have shops where they perform prefabrication and other work. Establishments primarily engaged in preparing sites for new construction are also included in this subsector.

There are substantial differences in types of equipment, work force skills, and other inputs required by specialty trade contractors. Establishments in this subsector are classified based on the underlying production function for the specialty trade in which they specialize. Throughout the Specialty Trade Contractors subsector, establishments commonly provide both the parts and labor required to complete work. For example, electrical contractors supply the current-carrying and noncurrent-carrying wiring devices that are required to install a circuit. Plumbing, Heating, and Air-Conditioning contractors also supply the parts required to complete a contract.

Establishments that specialize in activities primarily related to heavy and civil engineering construction that are not normally performed on buildings, such as the painting of lines on highways are classified in Subsector 237, Heavy and Civil Engineering Construction.

Establishments that are primarily engaged in selling construction materials are classified in Sector 42, Wholesale Trade, or Sector 44-45, Retail Trade, based on the characteristics of the selling unit.

2381 Foundation, Structure, and Building Exterior Contractors

This industry group comprises establishments primarily engaged in the specialty trades needed to complete the basic structure (i.e., foundation, frame, and shell)

US—United States industry only. CAN—United States and Canadian industries are comparable. MEX—United States and Mexican industries are comparable. Blank—Canadian, Mexican, and United States industries are comparable.

of buildings. The work performed may include new work, additions, alterations, maintenance, and repairs.

23811 Poured Concrete Foundation and Structure Contractors[CAN]

See industry description for 238110 below.

238110 Poured Concrete Foundation and Structure Contractors[CAN]

This industry comprises establishments primarily engaged in pouring and finishing concrete foundations and structural elements. This industry also includes establishments performing grout and shotcrete work. The work performed may include new work, additions, alterations, maintenance, and repairs.

Illustrative Examples:

Concrete pouring and finishing	Concrete work (except paving)
Gunite contractors	Shotcrete contractors
Concrete pumping (i.e., placement)	Footing and foundation concrete
Mud-jacking contractors	contractors

Cross-References. Establishments primarily engaged in—

- Constructing or paving streets, highways, and public sidewalks—are classified in Industry 237310, Highway, Street, and Bridge Construction;

- Concrete sealing, coating, waterproofing, or dampproofing—are classified in Industry 238390, Other Building Finishing Contractors; and

- Paving residential driveways, commercial parking lots, and other private parking areas—are classified in Industry 238990, All Other Specialty Trade Contractors.

23812 Structural Steel and Precast Concrete Contractors

See industry description for 238120 below.

238120 Structural Steel and Precast Concrete Contractors[CAN]

This industry comprises establishments primarily engaged in: (1) erecting and assembling structural parts made from steel or precast concrete (e.g., steel beams, structural steel components, and similar products of precast concrete); and/or (2) assembling and installing other steel construction products (e.g., steel rods, bars, rebar, mesh, and cages) to reinforce poured-in-place concrete. The work performed may include new work, additions, alterations, maintenance, and repairs.

US—United States industry only. CAN—United States and Canadian industries are comparable. MEX—United States and Mexican industries are comparable. Blank—Canadian, Mexican, and United States industries are comparable.

Illustrative Examples:

Concrete product (e.g., structural precast, structural prestressed) installation

Rebar contractors

Erecting structural steel

Reinforcing steel contractors

Placing and tying reinforcing rod at a construction site

Structural steel contractors

Precast concrete panel, slab, or form installation

Cross-References.

Establishments primarily engaged in pouring concrete at the construction site for building foundations or structural elements are classified in Industry 238110, Poured Concrete Foundation and Structure Contractors.

23813 Framing Contractors^{CAN}
See industry description for 238130 below.

238130 Framing Contractors^{CAN}

This industry comprises establishments primarily engaged in structural framing and sheathing using materials other than structural steel or concrete. The work performed may include new work, additions, alterations, maintenance, and repairs.

Illustrative Examples:

Building framing (except structural steel)

Post frame contractors

Foundation, building, wood, contractors

Steel framing contractors

Framing contractors

Wood frame component (e.g., truss) fabrication on site

Cross-References. Establishments primarily engaged in—

• Finish carpentry—are classified in Industry 238350, Finish Carpentry Contractors; and

• Installing structural steel, precast concrete framing, or structural elements— are classified in Industry 238120, Structural Steel and Precast Concrete Contractors.

23814 Masonry Contractors^{CAN}
See industry description for 238140 below.

238140 Masonry Contractors^{CAN}

This industry comprises establishments primarily engaged in masonry work, stone setting, brick laying, and other stone work. The work performed may include new work, additions, alterations, maintenance, and repairs.

US—United States industry only. CAN—United States and Canadian industries are comparable. MEX—United States and Mexican industries are comparable. Blank—Canadian, Mexican, and United States industries are comparable.

Illustrative Examples:

Block laying
Marble, granite, and slate, exterior,
   contractors
Brick laying
Masonry pointing, cleaning, or caulking

Concrete block laying
Stucco contractors
Foundation (e.g., brick, block, stone),
   building, contractors

Cross-References. Establishments primarily engaged in—

- Erecting the basic structure of buildings by pouring concrete—are classified in Industry 238110, Poured Concrete Foundation and Structure Contractors;

- Interior marble, granite, and slate work—are classified in Industry 238340, Tile and Terrazzo Contractors; and

- Laying precast stones or bricks for patios, sidewalks, and driveways; or paving residential driveways, commercial parking lots and other private parking areas—are classified in Industry 238990, All Other Specialty Trade Contractors.

23815 Glass and Glazing Contractors[CAN]

See industry description for 238150 below.

238150 Glass and Glazing Contractors[CAN]

This industry comprises establishments primarily engaged in installing glass panes in prepared openings (i.e., glazing work) and other glass work for buildings. The work performed may include new work, additions, alterations, maintenance, and repairs.

Illustrative Examples:

Decorative glass and mirror installation
Glazing contractors
Glass cladding installation
Stained glass installation
Glass coating and tinting (except
   automotive) contractors

Window pane or sheet installation
Glass installation (except automotive)
   contractors

Cross-References. Establishments primarily engaged in—

- Installing prefabricated window units—are classified in Industry 238350, Finish Carpentry Contractors; and

- The replacement, repair, and/or tinting of automotive glass—are classified in U.S. Industry 811122, Automotive Glass Replacement Shops.

23816 Roofing Contractors^{CAN}

See industry description for 238160 below.

238160 Roofing Contractors^{CAN}

This industry comprises establishments primarily engaged in roofing. This industry also includes establishments treating roofs (i.e., spraying, painting, or coating) and installing skylights. The work performed may include new work, additions, alterations, maintenance, and repairs.

Illustrative Examples:

Painting, spraying, or coating, roof
Sheet metal roofing installation

Shake and shingle, roof, installation
Skylight installation

Cross-References. Establishments primarily engaged in—

- Installing roof trusses and sheathing attached to trusses—are classified in Industry 238130, Framing Contractors; and

- Installing downspouts, gutters, fascia, and soffits—are classified in Industry 238170, Siding Contractors.

23817 Siding Contractors^{CAN}

See industry description for 238170 below.

238170 Siding Contractors^{CAN}

This industry comprises establishments primarily engaged in installing siding of wood, aluminum, vinyl, or other exterior finish material (except brick, stone, stucco, or curtain wall). This industry also includes establishments installing gutters and downspouts. The work performed may include new work, additions, alterations, maintenance, and repairs.

Illustrative Examples:

Downspout, gutter, and gutter guard
installation
Siding (e.g., vinyl, wood, aluminum)
installation

Fascia and soffit installation

Cross-References. Establishments primarily engaged in—

- Installing brick, stone, or stucco building exterior finish materials—are classified in Industry 238140, Masonry Contractors;

US—United States industry only. CAN—United States and Canadian industries are comparable. MEX—United States and Mexican industries are comparable. Blank—Canadian, Mexican, and United States industries are comparable.

- Installing curtain wall—are classified in Industry 238190, Other Foundation, Structure, and Building Exterior Contractors; and

- Installing sheet metal duct work—are classified in Industry 238220, Plumbing, Heating, and Air-Conditioning Contractors.

23819 Other Foundation, Structure, and Building Exterior Contractors[CAN]

See industry description for 238190 below.

238190 Other Foundation, Structure, and Building Exterior Contractors[CAN]

This industry comprises establishments primarily engaged in building foundation and structure trades work (except poured concrete, structural steel, precast concrete, framing, masonry, glass, and glazing, roofing, and siding). The work performed may include new work, additions, alterations, maintenance, and repairs.

Illustrative Examples:

Curtain wall, metal, installation
Forms for poured concrete, erecting, and dismantling
Decorative steel and wrought iron work installation

Ornamental metal work installation
Fire escape installation
Welding, on site, contractors

Cross-References. Establishments primarily engaged in—

- Poured concrete foundation and structure work—are classified in Industry 238110, Poured Concrete Foundation and Structure Contractors;

- Installation of structural steel or precast concrete building components—are classified in Industry 238120, Structural Steel and Precast Concrete Contractors;

- Framing buildings—are classified in Industry 238130, Framing Contractors;

- Masonry work—are classified in Industry 238140, Masonry Contractors;

- Glass and glazing work—are classified in Industry 238150, Glass and Glazing Contractors;

- Installing or repairing roofs—are classified in Industry 238160, Roofing Contractors; and

- Installing siding—are classified in Industry 238170, Siding Contractors.

2382 Building Equipment Contractors

This industry group comprises establishments primarily engaged in installing or servicing equipment that forms part of a building mechanical system (e.g., electricity, water, heating, and cooling). The work performed may include new work, additions, alterations, maintenance, and repairs. Contractors installing specialized building equipment, such as elevators, escalators, service station equipment, and central vacuum cleaning systems are also included.

23821 Electrical Contractors and Other Wiring Installation Contractors
See industry description for 238210 below.

238210 Electrical Contractors and Other Wiring Installation Contractors

This industry comprises establishments primarily engaged in installing and servicing electrical wiring and equipment. Contractors included in this industry may include both the parts and labor when performing work. These contractors may perform new work, additions, alterations, maintenance, and repairs.

Illustrative Examples:

Airport runway lighting contractors
Fiber optic cable (except transmission line) contractors
Alarm system (e.g., fire, burglar), electric, installation only
Highway, street, and bridge lighting and electrical signal installation
Audio equipment (except automotive) installation contractors
Home automation system installation
Cable splicing, electrical or fiber optic
Lighting system installation
Cable television hookup contractors
Telecommunications equipment and wiring (except transmission line) installation contractors
Computer and network cable installation
Traffic signal installation
Environmental control system installation

Cross-References. Establishments primarily engaged in—

- Installing and maintaining telecommunications lines by telecommunications companies—are classified in Subsector 517, Telecommunications;

- Constructing power and communication transmission lines—are classified in Industry 237130, Power and Communication Line and Related Structures Construction; and

- Burglar and fire alarm installation combined with sales, maintenance, or monitoring services—are classified in U.S. Industry 561621, Security Systems Services (except Locksmiths).

US—United States industry only. CAN—United States and Canadian industries are comparable. MEX—United States and Mexican industries are comparable. Blank—Canadian, Mexican, and United States industries are comparable.

23822 Plumbing, Heating, and Air-Conditioning Contractors
See industry description for 238220 below.

238220 Plumbing, Heating, and Air-Conditioning Contractors[CAN]

This industry comprises establishments primarily engaged in installing and servicing plumbing, heating, and air-conditioning equipment. Contractors in this industry may provide both parts and labor when performing work. The work performed may include new work, additions, alterations, maintenance, and repairs.

Illustrative Examples:

Cooling tower installation

Heating, ventilation, and air-conditioning (HVAC) contractors

Duct work (e.g., cooling, dust collection, exhaust, heating, ventilation) installation

Lawn sprinkler system installation

Fire sprinkler system installation

Mechanical contractors

Fireplace, natural gas, installation

Refrigeration system (e.g., commercial, industrial, scientific) installation

Furnace installation

Sewer hook-up and connection, building

Cross-References. Establishments primarily engaged in—

- Installing electrical controls for HVAC systems—are classified in Industry 238210, Electrical Contractors and Other Wiring Installation Contractors;

- Duct cleaning—are classified in Industry 561790, Other Services to Buildings and Dwellings; and

- Installing septic tanks—are classified in Industry 238910, Site Preparation Contractors.

23829 Other Building Equipment Contractors
See industry description for 238290 below.

238290 Other Building Equipment Contractors[MEX]

This industry comprises establishments primarily engaged in installing or servicing building equipment (except electrical, plumbing, heating, cooling, or ventilation equipment). The repair and maintenance of miscellaneous building equipment is included in this industry. The work performed may include new work, additions, alterations, maintenance, and repairs.

Illustrative Examples:

Automated and revolving door installation

Dismantling large-scale machinery and equipment

US—United States industry only. CAN—United States and Canadian industries are comparable. MEX—United States and Mexican industries are comparable. Blank—Canadian, Mexican, and United States industries are comparable.

Lightning protection equipment (e.g.,
lightning rod) installation
Boiler and pipe insulation installation
Machine rigging
Commercial-type door installation
Millwrights
Conveyor system installation
Overhead door, commercial- or
industrial-type, installation

Revolving door installation
Elevator installation
Satellite dish, household-type,
installation
Escalator installation
Vacuum cleaning system, built-in,
installation
Gasoline pump, service station,
installation

Cross-References. Establishments primarily engaged in—

- Manufacturing of industrial equipment with incidental installation—are classified in Sector 31-33, Manufacturing; and
- Repair and maintenance of commercial refrigeration equipment or production equipment—are classified in Industry 811310, Commercial and Industrial Machinery and Equipment (except Automotive and Electronic) Repair and Maintenance.

2383 Building Finishing Contractors

This industry group comprises establishments primarily engaged in the specialty trades needed to finish buildings. The work performed may include new work, additions, alterations, maintenance, and repairs.

23831 Drywall and Insulation Contractors
See industry description for 238310 below.

238310 Drywall and Insulation Contractors^{CAN}

This industry comprises establishments primarily engaged in drywall, plaster work, and building insulation work. Plaster work includes applying plain or ornamental plaster, and installation of lath to receive plaster. The work performed may include new work, additions, alterations, maintenance, and repairs.

Illustrative Examples:

Acoustical ceiling tile and panel
installation
Lathing contractors
Drop ceiling installation
Plastering (i.e., ornamental, plain)
contractors
Drywall contractors

Soundproofing contractors
Fresco (i.e., decorative plaster finishing)
contractors
Taping and finishing drywall
Gypsum board installation
Wall cavity and attic space insulation
installation

US—United States industry only. CAN—United States and Canadian industries are comparable.
MEX—United States and Mexican industries are comparable. Blank—Canadian, Mexican, and United
States industries are comparable.

Cross-References. Establishments primarily engaged in—

- Applying stucco—are classified in Industry 238140, Masonry Contractors; and

- Insulating pipes and boilers—are classified in Industry 238290, Other Building Equipment Contractors.

23832 Painting and Wall Covering Contractors
See industry description for 238320 below.

238320 Painting and Wall Covering Contractors

This industry comprises establishments primarily engaged in interior or exterior painting or interior wall covering. The work performed may include new work, additions, alterations, maintenance, and repairs.

Illustrative Examples:

Bridge painting
Paperhanging or removal contractors
House painting
Ship painting contractors

Paint and wallpaper stripping
Wallpaper hanging and removal contractors

Cross-References. Establishments primarily engaged in—

- Painting lines on highways, streets, and parking lots—are classified in Industry 237310, Highway, Street, and Bridge Construction;

- Roof painting—are classified in Industry 238160, Roofing Contractors; and

- Installing wood paneling—are classified in Industry 238350, Finish Carpentry Contractors.

23833 Flooring Contractors
See industry description for 238330 below.

238330 Flooring Contractors

This industry comprises establishments primarily engaged in the installation of resilient floor tile, carpeting, linoleum, and hardwood flooring. The work performed may include new work, additions, alterations, maintenance, and repairs.

US—United States industry only. CAN—United States and Canadian industries are comparable. MEX—United States and Mexican industries are comparable. Blank—Canadian. Mexican. and United States industries are comparable.

Illustrative Examples:

Carpet, installation only
Resilient floor tile or sheet (e.g., linoleum, rubber, vinyl), installation only
Floor laying, scraping, finishing, and refinishing

Resurfacing hardwood flooring
Hardwood flooring, installation only
Vinyl flooring contractors

Cross-References. Establishments primarily engaged in—

- Laying concrete flooring—are classified in Industry 238110, Poured Concrete Foundation and Structure Contractors;

- Installing stone or ceramic floor tile—are classified in Industry 238340, Tile and Terrazzo Contractors; and

- Selling and installing carpet and other flooring products as retail establishments—are classified in Sector 44-45, Retail Trade.

23834   Tile and Terrazzo Contractors
See industry description for 238340 below.

238340   Tile and Terrazzo Contractors

This industry comprises establishments primarily engaged in setting and installing ceramic tile, stone (interior only), and mosaic and/or mixing marble particles and cement to make terrazzo at the job site. The work performed may include new work, additions, alterations, maintenance, and repairs.

Illustrative Examples:

Ceramic tile installation
Mosaic work
Mantel, marble or stone, installation
Stone flooring installation

Marble, granite, and slate, interior installation contractors
Tile (except resilient) laying and setting

Cross-References. Establishments primarily engaged in—

- Exterior marble, granite, and slate work—are classified in Industry 238140, Masonry Contractors;

- Manufacturing precast terrazzo products—are classified in Industry 327390, Other Concrete Product Manufacturing; and

- Installing, without selling resilient floor tile—are classified in Industry 238330, Flooring Contractors.

23835 Finish Carpentry Contractors

See industry description for 238350 below.

238350 Finish Carpentry Contractors

This industry comprises establishments primarily engaged in finish carpentry work. The work performed may include new work, additions, alterations, maintenance, and repairs.

Illustrative Examples:

Built-in wood cabinets constructed on site

Molding or trim, wood or plastic, installation

Counter top, residential-type, installation

Paneling installation

Door and window frame construction

Prefabricated kitchen and bath cabinet, residential-type, installation

Garage door, residential-type, installation

Ship joinery contractors

Millwork installation

Window and door, residential-type, of any material, prefabricated, installation

Cross-References. Establishments primarily engaged in—

- Installing skylights—are classified in Industry 238160, Roofing Contractors;

- Framing—are classified in Industry 238130, Framing Contractors; and

- Building custom kitchen and bath cabinets (except free standing) in a shop— are classified in Industry 337110, Wood Kitchen Cabinet and Countertop Manufacturing.

23839 Other Building Finishing Contractors

See industry description for 238390 below.

238390 Other Building Finishing Contractors

This industry comprises establishments primarily engaged in building finishing trade work (except drywall, plaster, and insulation work; painting and wall covering work; flooring work; tile and terrazzo work; and finish carpentry work). The work performed may include new work, additions, alterations, maintenance, and repairs.

Illustrative Examples:

Bath tub refinishing on site

Fabricating metal cabinets or countertops on site

Countertop and cabinet, metal (except residential-type), installation

Waterproofing contractors

Closet organizer system installation
Modular furniture system attachment and
installation
Concrete coating, glazing, or sealing
Trade show exhibit installation and
dismantling

Drapery fixture (e.g., hardware, rods,
tracks) installation
Window shade and blind installation

Cross-References. Establishments primarily engaged in—

* Installing drywall, plaster, or insulation—are classified in Industry 238310, Drywall and Insulation Contractors;

* Installing or removing paint or wall coverings—are classified in Industry 238320, Painting and Wall Covering Contractors;

* Installing or repairing wood floors, resilient flooring, and carpet—are classified in Industry 238330, Flooring Contractors;

* Setting tile or performing terrazzo work—are classified in Industry 238340, Tile and Terrazzo Contractors; and

* Finish carpentry—are classified in Industry 238350, Finish Carpentry Contractors.

2389 Other Specialty Trade Contractors

23891 Site Preparation Contractors
See industry description for 238910 below.

238910 Site Preparation Contractors

This industry comprises establishments primarily engaged in site preparation activities, such as excavating and grading, demolition of buildings and other structures, and septic system installation. Earth moving and land clearing for all types of sites (e.g., building, nonbuilding, mining) is included in this industry. Establishments primarily engaged in construction equipment rental with operator (except cranes) are also included.

Illustrative Examples:

Blasting, building demolition
Foundation digging (i.e., excavation)
Concrete breaking and cutting for
demolition
Foundation drilling contractors
Cutting new rights of way
Grading construction sites

Septic system contractors
Dirt moving for construction
Trenching (except underwater)
Equipment rental (except crane),
construction, with operator
Underground tank (except hazardous)
removal

US—United States industry only. CAN—United States and Canadian industries are comparable. MEX—United States and Mexican industries are comparable. Blank—Canadian, Mexican, and United States industries are comparable.

Demolition, building and structure
Line slashing or cutting (except
  maintenance)
Dewatering contractors

Excavating, earthmoving, or land
  clearing contractors
Wrecking, building or other structure

Cross-References. Establishments primarily engaged in—

- Earth retention or underwater trenching—are classified in Industry 237990, Other Heavy and Civil Engineering Construction;

- Crane rental with operator—are classified in Industry 238990, All Other Specialty Trade Contractors;

- Overburden removal as an activity prior to mineral removal from quarries or open pit mines—are classified in Sector 21, Mining, Quarrying, and Oil and Gas Extraction;

- Drilling oil and gas field water intake wells—are classified in U.S. Industry 213111, Drilling Oil and Gas Wells;

- Dismantling tanks in oil fields—are classified in U.S. Industry 213112, Support Activities for Oil and Gas Operations;

- Construction equipment rental without an operator—are classified in U.S. Industry 532412, Construction, Mining, and Forestry Machinery and Equipment Rental and Leasing;

- Tree and brush trimming for overhead utility lines—are classified in Industry 561730, Landscaping Services; and

- Nuclear power plant decommissioning and environmental remediation work, such as the removal of underground steel tanks for hazardous materials— are classified in Industry 562910, Remediation Services.

23899 All Other Specialty Trade Contractors

See industry description for 238990 below.

238990 All Other Specialty Trade Contractors

This industry comprises establishments primarily engaged in specialized trades (except foundation, structure, and building exterior contractors; building equipment contractors; building finishing contractors; and site preparation contractors). The specialty trade work performed includes new work, additions, alterations, maintenance, and repairs.

US—United States industry only. CAN—United States and Canadian industries are comparable. MEX—United States and Mexican industries are comparable. Blank—Canadian, Mexican, and United States industries are comparable.

Illustrative Examples:

Billboard erection

Outdoor swimming pool construction

Cleaning building interiors during and immediately after construction

Paver, brick (e.g., driveway, patio, sidewalk), installation

Crane rental with operator

Paving, residential and commercial driveway and parking lot

Driveway paving or sealing

Sandblasting building exteriors

Fence installation

Scaffold erecting and dismantling

Interlocking brick and block installation

Steeplejack work

Manufactured (mobile) home, set up and tie-down

Cross-References. Establishments primarily engaged in—

- Foundation, structure, and building exterior work—are classified in Industry Group 2381, Foundation, Structure, and Building Exterior Contractors;

- Installing, repairing, or maintaining building mechanical systems—are classified in Industry Group 2382, Building Equipment Contractors;

- Finishing buildings—are classified in Industry Group 2383, Building Finishing Contractors;

- Paving public highways, streets, and roads—are classified in Industry 237310, Highway, Street, and Bridge Construction;

- Construction equipment rental with an operator (except cranes) or preparing land for building construction—are classified in Industry 238910, Site Preparation Contractors;

- Construction equipment rental without an operator—are classified in U.S. Industry 532412, Construction, Mining, and Forestry Machinery and Equipment Rental and Leasing;

- Radon testing—are classified in Industry 541380, Testing Laboratories;

- Power washing and other building exterior cleaning (except sandblasting)—are classified in Industry 561790, Other Services to Buildings and Dwellings; and

- Environmental remediation work, such as asbestos abatement—are classified in Industry 562910, Remediation Services.

Sector 31-33—Manufacturing

The Sector as a Whole

The Manufacturing sector comprises establishments engaged in the mechanical, physical, or chemical transformation of materials, substances, or components into new products. The assembling of component parts of manufactured products is considered manufacturing, except in cases where the activity is appropriately classified in Sector 23, Construction.

Establishments in the Manufacturing sector are often described as plants, factories, or mills and characteristically use power-driven machines and materials-handling equipment. However, establishments that transform materials or substances into new products by hand or in the worker's home and those engaged in selling to the general public products made on the same premises from which they are sold, such as bakeries, candy stores, and custom tailors, may also be included in this sector. Manufacturing establishments may process materials or may contract with other establishments to process their materials for them. Both types of establishments are included in manufacturing.

The materials, substances, or components transformed by manufacturing establishments are raw materials that are products of agriculture, forestry, fishing, mining, or quarrying as well as products of other manufacturing establishments. The materials used may be purchased directly from producers, obtained through customary trade channels, or secured without recourse to the market by transferring the product from one establishment to another, under the same ownership.

The new product of a manufacturing establishment may be finished in the sense that it is ready for utilization or consumption, or it may be semifinished to become an input for an establishment engaged in further manufacturing. For example, the product of the alumina refinery is the input used in the primary production of aluminum; primary aluminum is the input to an aluminum wire drawing plant; and aluminum wire is the input for a fabricated wire product manufacturing establishment.

The subsectors in the Manufacturing sector generally reflect distinct production processes related to material inputs, production equipment, and employee skills. In the machinery area, where assembling is a key activity, parts and accessories for manufactured products are classified in the industry of the finished manufactured item when they are made for separate sale. For example, a replacement refrigerator door would be classified with refrigerators and an attachment for a piece of metal working machinery would be classified with metal working machinery. However, components, input from other manufacturing establishments, are classified based on the production function of the component manufacturer. For example, electronic components are classified in Subsector 334, Computer and Electronic Product Manufacturing and stampings are classified in Subsector 332, Fabricated Metal Product Manufacturing.

US—United States industry only. CAN—United States and Canadian industries are comparable. MEX—United States and Mexican industries are comparable. Blank—Canadian, Mexican, and United States industries are comparable.

Manufacturing establishments often perform one or more activities that are classified outside the Manufacturing sector of NAICS. For instance, almost all manufacturing has some captive research and development or administrative operations, such as accounting, payroll, or management. These captive services are treated the same as captive manufacturing activities. When the services are provided by separate establishments, they are classified to the NAICS sector where such services are primary, not in manufacturing.

The boundaries of manufacturing and the other sectors of the classification system can be somewhat blurry. The establishments in the manufacturing sector are engaged in the transformation of materials into new products. Their output is a new product. However, the definition of what constitutes a new product can be somewhat subjective. As clarification, the following activities are considered manufacturing in NAICS:

Milk bottling and pasteurizing;

Water bottling and processing;

Fresh fish packaging (oyster shucking, fish filleting);

Apparel jobbing (assigning of materials to contract factories or shops for fabrication or other contract operations) as well as contracting on materials owned by others;

Printing and related activities;

Ready-mixed concrete production;

Leather converting;

Grinding of lenses to prescription;

Wood preserving;

Electroplating, plating, metal heat treating, and polishing for the trade;

Lapidary work for the trade;

Fabricating signs and advertising displays;

Rebuilding or remanufacturing machinery (i.e., automotive parts)

Ship repair and renovation;

Machine shops; and

Tire retreading.

Conversely, there are activities that are sometimes considered manufacturing, but which for NAICS are classified in another sector (i.e., not classified as manufacturing). They include:

1. Logging, classified in Sector 11, Agriculture, Forestry, Fishing and Hunting, is considered a harvesting operation;

2. The beneficiating of ores and other minerals, classified in Sector 21, Mining, Quarrying, and Oil and Gas Extraction, is considered part of the activity of mining;

3. The construction of structures and fabricating operations performed at the site of construction by contractors, is classified in Sector 23, Construction;

4. Establishments engaged in breaking of bulk and redistribution in smaller lots, including packaging, repackaging, or bottling products, such as liquors or chemicals; the customized assembly of computers; sorting of scrap; mixing paints to customer order; and cutting metals to customer order, classified in Sector 42, Wholesale Trade or Sector 44-45, Retail Trade, produce a modified version of the same product, not a new product; and

---

US—United States industry only. CAN—United States and Canadian industries are comparable. MEX—United States and Mexican industries are comparable. Blank—Canadian, Mexican, and United States industries are comparable.

5. Publishing and the combined activity of publishing and printing, classified in Sector 51, Information, perform the transformation of information into a product whereas the value of the product to the consumer lies in the information content, not in the format in which it is distributed (i.e., the book or software diskette).

311 Food Manufacturing

Industries in the Food Manufacturing subsector transform livestock and agricultural products into products for intermediate or final consumption. The industry groups are distinguished by the raw materials (generally of animal or vegetable origin) processed into food products.

The food products manufactured in these establishments are typically sold to wholesalers or retailers for distribution to consumers, but establishments primarily engaged in retailing bakery and candy products made on the premises not for immediate consumption are included.

Establishments primarily engaged in manufacturing beverages are classified in Subsector 312, Beverage and Tobacco Product Manufacturing.

3111 Animal Food Manufacturing

31111 Animal Food Manufacturing

This industry comprises establishments primarily engaged in manufacturing food and feed for animals from ingredients, such as grains, oilseed mill products, and meat products.

Cross-References. Establishments primarily engaged in—

- Slaughtering animals for feed—are classified in Industry 31161, Animal Slaughtering and Processing; and

- Manufacturing vitamins and minerals for animals—are classified in Industry 32541, Pharmaceutical and Medicine Manufacturing.

311111 Dog and Cat Food Manufacturing[CAN]

This U.S. industry comprises establishments primarily engaged in manufacturing dog and cat food from ingredients, such as grains, oilseed mill products, and meat products.

Cross-References. Establishments primarily engaged in—

- Manufacturing food for animals (except dog and cat)—are classified in U.S. Industry 311119, Other Animal Food Manufacturing;

US—United States industry only. CAN—United States and Canadian industries are comparable. MEX—United States and Mexican industries are comparable. Blank—Canadian, Mexican, and United States industries are comparable.

- Slaughtering animals for feed—are classified in Industry 31161, Animal Slaughtering and Processing; and

- Manufacturing vitamins and minerals for dogs and cats—are classified in Industry 32541, Pharmaceutical and Medicine Manufacturing.

311119 Other Animal Food Manufacturing^{CAN}

This U.S. industry comprises establishments primarily engaged in manufacturing animal food (except dog and cat) from ingredients, such as grains, oilseed mill products, and meat products.

Cross-References. Establishments primarily engaged in—

- Manufacturing dog and cat foods—are classified in U.S. Industry 311111, Dog and Cat Food Manufacturing;

- Slaughtering animals for feed—are classified in Industry 31161, Animal Slaughtering and Processing; and

- Manufacturing vitamins and minerals for animals—are classified in Industry 32541, Pharmaceutical and Medicine Manufacturing.

3112 Grain and Oilseed Milling

31121 Flour Milling and Malt Manufacturing

This industry comprises establishments primarily engaged in one or more of the following: (1) milling flour or meal from grains or vegetables; (2) preparing flour mixes or doughs from flour milled in the same establishment; (3) milling, cleaning, and polishing rice; and (4) manufacturing malt from barley, rye, or other grains.

Cross-References. Establishments primarily engaged in—

- Preparing breakfast cereals from flour milled in the same establishment— are classified in Industry 31123, Breakfast Cereal Manufacturing;

- Crushing soybeans or wet milling corn and vegetables—are classified in Industry 31122, Starch and Vegetable Fats and Oils Manufacturing;

- Manufacturing prepared flour mixes or doughs from flour ground elsewhere—are classified in Industry 31182, Cookie, Cracker, and Pasta Manufacturing;

- Brewing malt beverages—are classified in Industry 31212, Breweries;

US—United States industry only. CAN—United States and Canadian industries are comparable. MEX—United States and Mexican industries are comparable. Blank—Canadian, Mexican, and United States industries are comparable.

- Mixing purchased dried and dehydrated ingredients with purchased rice—are classified in Industry 31199, All Other Food Manufacturing;

- Drying and/or dehydrating ingredients and packaging them with purchased rice—are classified in Industry 31142, Fruit and Vegetable Canning, Pickling, and Drying; and

- Manufacturing malt extract and syrups—are classified in Industry 31194, Seasoning and Dressing Manufacturing.

311211 Flour Milling[CAN]

This U.S. industry comprises establishments primarily engaged in (1) milling flour or meal from grains (except rice) or vegetables and/or (2) milling flour and preparing flour mixes or doughs.

Cross-References. Establishments primarily engaged in—

- Preparing breakfast cereals from flour milled in the same establishment—are classified in Industry 311230, Breakfast Cereal Manufacturing;

- Manufacturing prepared flour mixes or doughs from flour ground elsewhere—are classified in U.S. Industry 311822, Flour Mixes and Dough Manufacturing from Purchased Flour;

- Milling rice or cleaning and polishing rice—are classified in U.S. Industry 311212, Rice Milling;

- Wet milling corn and vegetables—are classified in U.S. Industry 311221, Wet Corn Milling; and

- Crushing soybean and extracting soybean oil—are classified in U.S. Industry 311222, Soybean Processing.

311212 Rice Milling[US]

This U.S. industry comprises establishments primarily engaged in one of the following: (1) milling rice; (2) cleaning and polishing rice; or (3) milling, cleaning, and polishing rice. The establishments in this industry may package the rice they mill with other ingredients.

Cross-References. Establishments primarily engaged in—

- Drying and/or dehydrating ingredients and packaging them with purchased rice—are classified in U.S. Industry 311423, Dried and Dehydrated Food Manufacturing; and

---

US—United States industry only. CAN—United States and Canadian industries are comparable. MEX—United States and Mexican industries are comparable. Blank—Canadian, Mexican, and United States industries are comparable.

- Mixing purchased dried and/or dehydrated ingredients with purchased rice—are classified in U.S. Industry 311999, All Other Miscellaneous Food Manufacturing.

311213 Malt Manufacturing[US]

This U.S. industry comprises establishments primarily engaged in manufacturing malt from barley, rye, or other grains.

Cross-References. Establishments primarily engaged in—

- Brewing malt beverages—are classified in Industry 312120, Breweries; and

- Manufacturing malt extract and syrups—are classified in U.S. Industry 311942, Spice and Extract Manufacturing.

31122 Starch and Vegetable Fats and Oils Manufacturing

This industry comprises establishments primarily engaged in one or more of the following: (1) wet milling corn and vegetables; (2) crushing oilseeds and tree nuts; (3) refining and/or blending vegetable oils; (4) manufacturing shortening and margarine; and (5) blending purchased animal fats with vegetable fats.

Cross-References. Establishments primarily engaged in—

- Manufacturing table syrups from corn syrup and starch base dessert powders—are classified in Industry 31199, All Other Food Manufacturing;

- Reducing maple sap to maple syrup—are classified in Industry 11199, All Other Crop Farming;

- Milling flour or meal from grains and vegetables—are classified in Industry 31121, Flour Milling and Malt Manufacturing;

- Wet milling corn to produce nonpotable ethyl alcohol—are classified in Industry 32519, Other Basic Organic Chemical Manufacturing;

- Rendering or refining animal fats and oils—are classified in Industry 31161, Animal Slaughtering and Processing; and

- Manufacturing laundry starches—are classified in Industry 32561, Soap and Cleaning Compound Manufacturing.

311221 Wet Corn Milling[CAN]

This U.S. industry comprises establishments primarily engaged in wet milling corn and other vegetables (except to make ethyl alcohol). Examples of products

---

US—United States industry only. CAN—United States and Canadian industries are comparable. MEX—United States and Mexican industries are comparable. Blank—Canadian, Mexican, and United States industries are comparable.

made in these establishments are corn sweeteners, such as glucose, dextrose, and fructose; corn oil; and starches (except laundry).

Cross-References. Establishments primarily engaged in—

- Refining and/or blending corn oil from purchased oils—are classified in U.S. Industry 311225, Fats and Oils Refining and Blending;
- Manufacturing sweetening syrups from corn syrup and starch base dessert powders—are classified in U.S. Industry 311999, All Other Miscellaneous Food Manufacturing;
- Reducing maple sap to maple syrup—are classified in U.S. Industry 111998, All Other Miscellaneous Crop Farming;
- Milling (except wet milling) corn—are classified in U.S. Industry 311211, Flour Milling;
- Wet milling corn to produce nonpotable ethyl alcohol—are classified in U.S. Industry 325193, Ethyl Alcohol Manufacturing; and
- Manufacturing laundry starches—are classified in U.S. Industry 325612, Polish and Other Sanitation Good Manufacturing.

311222 Soybean Processing[US]

This U.S. industry comprises establishments engaged in crushing soybeans. Examples of products produced in these establishments are soybean oil, soybean cake and meal, and soybean protein isolates and concentrates.

Cross-References. Establishments primarily engaged in—

- Refining and/or blending soybean oil from purchased oil—are classified in U.S. Industry 311225, Fats and Oils Refining and Blending;
- Wet milling corn and other vegetables—are classified in U.S. Industry 311221, Wet Corn Milling; and
- Crushing oilseeds (except soybeans) and tree nuts—are classified in U.S. Industry 311223, Other Oilseed Processing.

311223 Other Oilseed Processing[US]

This U.S. industry comprises establishments engaged in crushing oilseeds (except soybeans) and tree nuts, such as cottonseeds, linseeds, peanuts, and sunflower seeds.

US—United States industry only. CAN—United States and Canadian industries are comparable. MEX—United States and Mexican industries are comparable. Blank—Canadian, Mexican, and United States industries are comparable.

Cross-References. Establishments primarily engaged in—

- Wet milling corn and other vegetables—are classified in U.S. Industry 311221, Wet Corn Milling;
- Crushing soybeans—are classified in U.S. Industry 311222, Soybean Processing; and
- Refining and/or blending vegetable, oilseed, and tree nut oils from purchased oils—are classified in U.S. Industry 311225, Fats and Oils Refining and Blending.

311225 Fats and Oils Refining and Blending^{CAN}

This U.S. industry comprises establishments primarily engaged in one or more of the following: (1) manufacturing shortening and margarine from purchased fats and oils; (2) refining and/or blending vegetable, oilseed, and tree nut oils from purchased oils; and (3) blending purchased animal fats with purchased vegetable fats.

Cross-References. Establishments primarily engaged in—

- Refining and/or blending soybean oil in soybean crushing mills—are classified in U.S. Industry 311222, Soybean Processing;
- Refining and/or blending corn oil made by wet corn milling—are classified in U.S. Industry 311221, Wet Corn Milling;
- Refining and/or blending oilseeds (except soybeans) and tree nuts in crushing mills—are classified in U.S. Industry 311223, Other Oilseed Processing; and
- Rendering or refining animal fats and oils—are classified in Industry 31161, Animal Slaughtering and Processing.

31123 Breakfast Cereal Manufacturing
See industry description for 311230 below.

311230 Breakfast Cereal Manufacturing

This industry comprises establishments primarily engaged in manufacturing breakfast cereal foods.

Cross-References. Establishments primarily engaged in—

- Manufacturing nonchocolate-coated granola bars and other types of breakfast bars—are classified in Industry 311340, Nonchocolate Confectionery Manufacturing;

- Manufacturing chocolate-coated granola bars from purchased chocolate—are classified in Industry 311330, Confectionery Manufacturing from Purchased Chocolate;
- Manufacturing chocolate-coated granola bars from cacao beans—are classified in Industry 311320, Chocolate and Confectionery Manufacturing from Cacao Beans; and
- Manufacturing coffee substitutes from grain—are classified in Industry 311920, Coffee and Tea Manufacturing.

3113 Sugar and Confectionery Product Manufacturing

This industry group comprises (1) establishments that process agricultural inputs, such as sugarcane, beet, and cacao, to give rise to a new product (sugar or chocolate), and (2) those that begin with sugar and chocolate and process these further.

31131 Sugar Manufacturing

This industry comprises establishments primarily engaged in manufacturing raw sugar, liquid sugar, and refined sugar from sugarcane, raw cane sugar and sugar beets.

Cross-References. Establishments primarily engaged in—

- Manufacturing corn sweeteners by wet milling corn—are classified in Industry 31122, Starch and Vegetable Fats and Oils Manufacturing;
- Manufacturing table syrups from corn syrup and starch base dessert powders—are classified in Industry 31199, All Other Food Manufacturing;
- Reducing maple sap to maple syrup—are classified in Industry 11199, All Other Crop Farming; and
- Manufacturing synthetic sweeteners (i.e., sweetening agents), such as saccharin and sugar substitutes (i.e., synthetic sweetener blended with other ingredients)—are classified in Subsector 325, Chemical Manufacturing.

311311 Sugarcane Mills[US]

This U.S. industry comprises establishments primarily engaged in processing sugarcane.

Cross-References. Establishments primarily engaged in—

- Manufacturing refined cane sugar from raw cane sugar—are classified in U.S. Industry 311312, Cane Sugar Refining;

US—United States industry only. CAN—United States and Canadian industries are comparable. MEX—United States and Mexican industries are comparable. Blank—Canadian, Mexican, and United States industries are comparable.

- Manufacturing beet sugar—are classified in U.S. Industry 311313, Beet Sugar Manufacturing;

- Manufacturing corn sweeteners by wet milling corn—are classified in U.S. Industry 311221, Wet Corn Milling;

- Manufacturing table syrups from corn syrup—are classified in U.S. Industry 311999, All Other Miscellaneous Food Manufacturing; and

- Manufacturing synthetic sweeteners (i.e., sweetening agents), such as saccharin and sugar substitutes (i.e., synthetic sweetener blended with other ingredients)—are classified in Subsector 325, Chemical Manufacturing.

311312 Cane Sugar Refining[US]

This U.S. industry comprises establishments primarily engaged in refining cane sugar from raw cane sugar.

Cross-References. Establishments primarily engaged in—

- Processing and refining sugarcane—are classified in U.S. Industry 311311, Sugarcane Mills;

- Manufacturing beet sugar—are classified in U.S. Industry 311313, Beet Sugar Manufacturing;

- Manufacturing corn sweeteners by wet milling corn—are classified in U.S. Industry 311221, Wet Corn Milling;

- Reducing maple sap to maple syrup—are classified in U.S. Industry 111998, All Other Miscellaneous Crop Farming;

- Manufacturing table syrups from corn syrup—are classified in U.S. Industry 311999, All Other Miscellaneous Food Manufacturing; and

- Manufacturing synthetic sweeteners (i.e., sweetening agents), such as saccharin and sugar substitutes (i.e., synthetic sweetener blended with other ingredients)—are classified in Subsector 325, Chemical Manufacturing.

311313 Beet Sugar Manufacturing[US]

This U.S. industry comprises establishments primarily engaged in manufacturing refined beet sugar from sugar beets.

Cross-References. Establishments primarily engaged in—

- Manufacturing raw cane sugar and/or refined cane sugar from sugarcane—are classified in U.S. Industry 311311, Sugarcane Mills;

US—United States industry only. CAN—United States and Canadian industries are comparable. MEX—United States and Mexican industries are comparable. Blank—Canadian, Mexican. and United States industries are comparable.

- Manufacturing refined cane sugar from raw cane sugar—are classified in U.S. Industry 311312, Cane Sugar Refining;

- Manufacturing corn sweeteners by wet milling corn—are classified in U.S. Industry 311221, Wet Corn Milling;

- Manufacturing table syrups from corn syrup—are classified in U.S. Industry 311999, All Other Miscellaneous Food Manufacturing;

- Reducing maple sap to maple syrup—are classified in U.S. Industry 111998, All Other Miscellaneous Crop Farming; and

- Manufacturing synthetic sweeteners (i.e., sweetening agents), such as saccharin and sugar substitutes (i.e., synthetic sweetener blended with other ingredients)—are classified in Subsector 325, Chemical Manufacturing.

31132 Chocolate and Confectionery Manufacturing from Cacao Beans
See industry description for 311320 below.

311320 Chocolate and Confectionery Manufacturing from Cacao Beans

This industry comprises establishments primarily engaged in shelling, roasting, and grinding cacao beans and making chocolate cacao products and chocolate confectioneries.

Cross-References. Establishments primarily engaged in—

- Manufacturing, not for immediate consumption, chocolate confectioneries from chocolate made elsewhere—are classified in Industry 311330, Confectionery Manufacturing from Purchased Chocolate;

- Manufacturing, not for immediate consumption, nonchocolate candies—are classified in Industry 311340, Nonchocolate Confectionery Manufacturing;

- Preparing and selling confectioneries for immediate consumption—are classified in U.S. Industry 722213, Snack and Nonalcoholic Beverage Bars; and

- Retailing confectioneries not for immediate consumption made elsewhere— are classified in U.S. Industry 445292, Confectionery and Nut Stores.

31133 Confectionery Manufacturing from Purchased Chocolate
See industry description for 311330 below.

311330 Confectionery Manufacturing from Purchased Chocolate

This industry comprises establishments primarily engaged in manufacturing chocolate confectioneries from chocolate produced elsewhere. Included in this

---

US—United States industry only. CAN—United States and Canadian industries are comparable. MEX—United States and Mexican industries are comparable. Blank—Canadian, Mexican, and United States industries are comparable.

industry are establishments primarily engaged in retailing chocolate confectionery products not for immediate consumption made on the premises from chocolate made elsewhere.

Cross-References. Establishments primarily engaged in—

- Manufacturing chocolate confectioneries from cacao beans—are classified in Industry 311320, Chocolate and Confectionery Manufacturing from Cacao Beans;
- Manufacturing nonchocolate confectioneries—are classified in Industry 311340, Nonchocolate Confectionery Manufacturing;
- Retailing confectioneries not for immediate consumption made elsewhere— are classified in U.S. Industry 445292, Confectionery and Nut Stores; and
- Preparing and selling confectioneries for immediate consumption—are classified in U.S. Industry 722213, Snack and Nonalcoholic Beverage Bars.

31134 Nonchocolate Confectionery Manufacturing
See industry description for 311340 below.

311340 Nonchocolate Confectionery Manufacturing

This industry comprises establishments primarily engaged in manufacturing nonchocolate confectioneries. Included in this industry are establishments primary engaged in retailing nonchocolate confectionery products not for immediate consumption made on the premises.

Cross-References. Establishments primarily engaged in—

- Manufacturing chocolate confectioneries from cacao beans—are classified in Industry 311320, Chocolate and Confectionery Manufacturing from Cacao Beans;
- Manufacturing chocolate confectioneries from chocolate made elsewhere— are classified in Industry 311330, Confectionery Manufacturing from Purchased Chocolate;
- Retailing confectioneries not for immediate consumption made elsewhere— are classified in U.S. Industry 445292, Confectionery and Nut Stores;
- Preparing and selling confectioneries for immediate consumption—are classified in U.S. Industry 722213, Snack and Nonalcoholic Beverage Bars; and
- Roasting, salting, drying, cooking, or canning nuts and seeds—are classified in U.S. Industry 311911, Roasted Nuts and Peanut Butter Manufacturing.

3114 Fruit and Vegetable Preserving and Specialty Food Manufacturing

This industry group includes (1) establishments that freeze food and (2) those that use preservation processes, such as pickling, canning, and dehydrating. Both types begin their production process with inputs of vegetable or animal origin.

31141 Frozen Food Manufacturing

This industry comprises establishments primarily engaged in manufacturing frozen fruit, frozen juices, frozen vegetables, and frozen specialty foods (except seafood), such as frozen dinners, entrees, and side dishes; frozen pizza; frozen whipped toppings; and frozen waffles, pancakes, and french toast.

Cross-References. Establishments primarily engaged in—

- Manufacturing frozen dairy specialties—are classified in Industry 31152, Ice Cream and Frozen Dessert Manufacturing;

- Manufacturing frozen bakery products—are classified in Industry 31181, Bread and Bakery Product Manufacturing;

- Manufacturing frozen seafood products—are classified in Industry 31171, Seafood Product Preparation and Packaging; and

- Manufacturing frozen meat products—are classified in Industry 31161, Animal Slaughtering and Processing.

311411 Frozen Fruit, Juice, and Vegetable Manufacturing^MEX

This U.S. industry comprises establishments primarily engaged in manufacturing frozen fruits; frozen vegetables; and frozen fruit juices, ades, drinks, cocktail mixes and concentrates.

Cross-References.

Establishments primarily engaged in manufacturing frozen specialty foods are classified in U.S. Industry 311412, Frozen Specialty Food Manufacturing.

311412 Frozen Specialty Food Manufacturing^MEX

This U.S. industry comprises establishments primarily engaged in manufacturing frozen specialty foods (except seafood), such as frozen dinners, entrees, and side dishes; frozen pizza; frozen whipped topping; and frozen waffles, pancakes, and french toast.

Cross-References. Establishments primarily engaged in—

- Manufacturing frozen dairy specialties—are classified in Industry 311520, Ice Cream and Frozen Dessert Manufacturing;

- Manufacturing frozen bakery products—are classified in U.S. Industry 311813, Frozen Cakes, Pies, and Other Pastries Manufacturing;

- Manufacturing frozen fruits, frozen fruit juices, and frozen vegetables— are classified in U.S. Industry 311411, Frozen Fruit, Juice, and Vegetable Manufacturing;

- Manufacturing frozen meat products—are classified in Industry 31161, Animal Slaughtering and Processing; and

- Manufacturing frozen seafood products—are classified in U.S. Industry 311712, Fresh and Frozen Seafood Processing.

31142 Fruit and Vegetable Canning, Pickling, and Drying

This industry comprises establishments primarily engaged in manufacturing canned, pickled, and dried fruits, vegetables, and specialty foods. Establishments in this industry may package the dried or dehydrated ingredients they make with other purchased ingredients. Examples of products made by these establishments are canned juices; canned baby foods; canned soups (except seafood); canned dry beans; canned tomato-based sauces, such as catsup, salsa, chili, spaghetti, barbeque, and tomato paste, pickles, relishes, jams and jellies, dried soup mixes and bullions, and sauerkraut.

Cross-References. Establishments primarily engaged in—

- Manufacturing canned dairy products—are classified in Industry 31151, Dairy Product (except Frozen) Manufacturing;

- Manufacturing canned seafood soups and seafood products—are classified in Industry 31171, Seafood Product Preparation and Packaging;

- Manufacturing canned meat products—are classified in Industry 31161, Animal Slaughtering and Processing;

- Milling rice and packaging it with other ingredients or manufacturing vegetable flours and meals—are classified in Industry 31121, Flour Milling and Malt Manufacturing;

- Manufacturing dry pasta and packaging it with other ingredients—are classified in Industry 31182, Cookie, Cracker, and Pasta Manufacturing;

- Mixing purchased dried and/or dehydrated potatoes, rice, and pasta and packaging them with other purchased ingredients; mixing purchased dried

---

US—United States industry only. CAN—United States and Canadian industries are comparable. MEX—United States and Mexican industries are comparable. Blank—Canadian, Mexican, and United States industries are comparable.

and/or dehydrated ingredients for soup mixes and bouillon; and manufacturing canned puddings—are classified in Industry 31199, All Other Food Manufacturing;

- Manufacturing dry salad dressing and dry sauce mixes—are classified in Industry 31194, Seasoning and Dressing Manufacturing; and

- Manufacturing canned fruit and vegetable drinks, cocktails, and ades—are classified in Industry 31211, Soft Drink and Ice Manufacturing.

311421 Fruit and Vegetable Canning[US]

This U.S. industry comprises establishments primarily engaged in manufacturing canned, pickled, and brined fruits and vegetables. Examples of products made in these establishments are canned juices; canned jams and jellies; canned tomato-based sauces, such as catsup, salsa, chili, spaghetti, barbeque, and tomato paste; pickles, relishes, and sauerkraut.

Cross-References. Establishments primarily engaged in—

- Manufacturing canned baby foods, canned soups (except seafood), and canned specialty foods (except seafood)—are classified in U.S. Industry 311422, Specialty Canning;

- Manufacturing canned seafood soups and canned seafood products—are classified in U.S. Industry 311711, Seafood Canning;

- Manufacturing canned meat products—are classified in Industry 31161, Animal Slaughtering and Processing; and

- Manufacturing canned fruit and vegetable drinks, cocktails, and ades—are classified in U.S. Industry 312111, Soft Drink Manufacturing.

311422 Specialty Canning[US]

This U.S. industry comprises establishments primarily engaged in manufacturing canned specialty foods. Examples of products made in these establishments are canned baby food, canned baked beans, canned soups (except seafood), canned spaghetti, and other canned nationality foods.

Cross-References. Establishments primarily engaged in—

- Manufacturing canned dairy products—are classified in U.S. Industry 311514, Dry, Condensed, and Evaporated Dairy Product Manufacturing;

- Manufacturing canned fruits, canned vegetables, and canned juices—are classified in U.S. Industry 311421, Fruit and Vegetable Canning;

- Manufacturing canned seafood soups and canned seafood products—are classified in U.S. Industry 311711, Seafood Canning;

- Manufacturing canned meat products—are classified in Industry 31161, Animal Slaughtering and Processing; and

- Manufacturing canned puddings—are classified in U.S. Industry 311999, All Other Miscellaneous Food Manufacturing.

311423 Dried and Dehydrated Food Manufacturing[US]

This U.S. industry comprises establishments primarily engaged in (1) drying (including freeze-dried) and/or dehydrating fruits, vegetables, and soup mixes and bouillon and/or (2) drying and/or dehydrating ingredients and packaging them with other purchased ingredients, such as rice and dry pasta.

Cross-References. Establishments primarily engaged in—

- Milling rice and packaging it with other ingredients—are classified in U.S. Industry 311212, Rice Milling;

- Manufacturing dry pasta and packaging it with other ingredients—are classified in U.S. Industry 311823, Dry Pasta Manufacturing;

- Manufacturing vegetable flours and meals—are classified in U.S. Industry 311211, Flour Milling;

- Mixing purchased dried and/or dehydrated potatoes, rice, and dry pasta, and packaging them with other purchased ingredients, and mixing purchased dried and/or dehydrated ingredients for soup mixes and bouillon—are classified in U.S. Industry 311999, All Other Miscellaneous Food Manufacturing; and

- Manufacturing dry salad dressing and dry sauce mixes—are classified in U.S. Industry 311942, Spice and Extract Manufacturing.

3115 Dairy Product Manufacturing

This industry group comprises establishments that manufacture dairy products from raw milk, processed milk, and dairy substitutes.

31151 Dairy Product (except Frozen) Manufacturing

This industry comprises establishments primarily engaged in one or more of the following: (1) manufacturing dairy products (except frozen) from raw milk and/or processed milk products; (2) manufacturing dairy substitutes (except frozen)

---

from soybeans and other nondairy substances; and (3) manufacturing dry, condensed, concentrated, and evaporated dairy and dairy substitute products.

Cross-References. Establishments primarily engaged in—

- Manufacturing cheese-based salad dressings—are classified in Industry 31194, Seasoning and Dressing Manufacturing;
- Manufacturing margarine or margarine-butter blends—are classified in Industry 31122, Starch and Vegetable Fats and Oils Manufacturing;
- Manufacturing frozen whipped toppings—are classified in Industry 31141, Frozen Food Manufacturing; and
- Manufacturing ice cream, frozen yogurt, and other frozen dairy desserts—are classified in Industry 31152, Ice Cream and Frozen Dessert Manufacturing.

311511 Fluid Milk Manufacturing^{CAN}

This U.S. industry comprises establishments primarily engaged in (1) manufacturing processed milk products, such as pasteurized milk or cream and sour cream and/or (2) manufacturing fluid milk dairy substitutes from soybeans and other nondairy substances.

Cross-References. Establishments primarily engaged in—

- Manufacturing dry mix whipped toppings, canned milk, and ultra high temperature milk—are classified in U.S. Industry 311514, Dry, Condensed, and Evaporated Dairy Product Manufacturing;
- Manufacturing frozen whipped toppings—are classified in U.S. Industry 311412, Frozen Specialty Food Manufacturing; and
- Manufacturing ice cream and frozen yogurt and other frozen desserts—are classified in Industry 311520, Ice Cream and Frozen Dessert Manufacturing.

311512 Creamery Butter Manufacturing^{US}

This U.S. industry comprises establishments primarily engaged in manufacturing creamery butter from milk and/or processed milk products.

Cross-References.

Establishments primarily engaged in manufacturing margarine or margarine-butter blends are classified in U.S. Industry 311225, Fats and Oils Refining and Blending.

US—United States industry only. CAN—United States and Canadian industries are comparable. MEX—United States and Mexican industries are comparable. Blank—Canadian, Mexican, and United States industries are comparable.

311513 Cheese Manufacturing[US]

This U.S. industry comprises establishments primarily engaged in (1) manufacturing cheese products (except cottage cheese) from raw milk and/or processed milk products and/or (2) manufacturing cheese substitutes from soybean and other nondairy substances.

Cross-References. Establishments primarily engaged in—

- Manufacturing cheese-based salad dressings—are classified in U.S. Industry 311941, Mayonnaise, Dressing, and Other Prepared Sauce Manufacturing; and

- Manufacturing cottage cheese—are classified in U.S. Industry 311511, Fluid Milk Manufacturing.

311514 Dry, Condensed, and Evaporated Dairy Product Manufacturing[US]

This U.S. industry comprises establishments primarily engaged in manufacturing dry, condensed, and evaporated milk and dairy substitute products.

Cross-References. Establishments primarily engaged in—

- Manufacturing fluid milk products—are classified in U.S. Industry 311511, Fluid Milk Manufacturing;

- Manufacturing creamery butter—are classified in U.S. Industry 311512, Creamery Butter Manufacturing; and

- Manufacturing cheese products—are classified in U.S. Industry 311513, Cheese Manufacturing.

31152 Ice Cream and Frozen Dessert Manufacturing
See industry description for 311520 below.

311520 Ice Cream and Frozen Dessert Manufacturing

This industry comprises establishments primarily engaged in manufacturing ice cream, frozen yogurts, frozen ices, sherbets, frozen tofu, and other frozen desserts (except bakery products).

Cross-References. Establishments primarily engaged in—

- Manufacturing frozen bakery products—are classified in U.S. Industry 311813, Frozen Cakes, Pies, and Other Pastries Manufacturing; and

---

US—United States industry only. CAN—United States and Canadian industries are comparable. MEX—United States and Mexican industries are comparable. Blank—Canadian, Mexican, and United States industries are comparable.

- Manufacturing ice cream and ice milk mixes—are classified in U.S. Industry 311514, Dry, Condensed, and Evaporated Dairy Product Manufacturing.

3116 Animal Slaughtering and Processing

31161 Animal Slaughtering and Processing

This industry comprises establishments primarily engaged in one or more of the following: (1) slaughtering animals; (2) preparing processed meats and meat byproducts; and (3) rendering and/or refining animal fat, bones, and meat scraps. This industry includes establishments primarily engaged in assembly cutting and packing of meats (i.e., boxed meats) from purchased carcasses.

Cross-References. Establishments primarily engaged in—

- Manufacturing canned meat for baby food—are classified in Industry 31142, Fruit and Vegetable Canning, Pickling, and Drying;
- Manufacturing meat-based animal feeds from carcasses—are classified in Industry 31111, Animal Food Manufacturing;
- Blending purchased animal fats with vegetable fats—are classified in Industry 31122, Starch and Vegetable Fats and Oils Manufacturing;
- Manufacturing canned and frozen specialty foods containing meat, such as nationality foods (e.g., enchiladas, pizza, egg rolls) and frozen dinners— are classified in Industry Group 3114, Fruit and Vegetable Preserving and Specialty Food Manufacturing;
- Drying, freezing, or breaking eggs—are classified in Industry 31199, All Other Food Manufacturing; and
- Cutting meat (except boxed meat)—are classified in Industry 42447, Meat and Meat Product Merchant Wholesalers.

311611 Animal (except Poultry) Slaughtering[CAN]

This U.S. industry comprises establishments primarily engaged in slaughtering animals (except poultry and small game). Establishments that slaughter and prepare meats are included in this industry.

Cross-References. Establishments primarily engaged in—

- Processing meat and meat byproducts (except poultry and small game) from purchased meats—are classified in U.S. Industry 311612, Meat Processed from Carcasses;

- Slaughtering and/or processing poultry and small game—are classified in U.S. Industry 311615, Poultry Processing;

- Rendering lard and other animal fats and oils, animal fat, bones, and meat scraps—are classified in U.S. Industry 311613, Rendering and Meat Byproduct Processing; and

- Manufacturing canned and frozen specialty foods containing meat, such as nationality foods (e.g., enchiladas, egg rolls, pizza) and frozen dinners—are classified in Industry Group 3114, Fruit and Vegetable Preserving and Specialty Food Manufacturing.

311612 Meat Processed from Carcasses[US]

This U.S. industry comprises establishments primarily engaged in processing or preserving meat and meat byproducts (except poultry and small game) from purchased meats. This industry includes establishments primarily engaged in assembly cutting and packing of meats (i.e., boxed meats) from purchased meats.

Cross-References. Establishments primarily engaged in—

- Slaughtering animals (except poultry and small game)—are classified in U.S. Industry 311611, Animal (except Poultry) Slaughtering;

- Slaughtering poultry and small game—are classified in U.S. Industry 311615, Poultry Processing;

- Rendering animal fat, bones, and meat scraps—are classified in U.S. Industry 311613, Rendering and Meat Byproduct Processing;

- Manufacturing canned meats for baby food—are classified in U.S. Industry 311422, Specialty Canning;

- Manufacturing meat-based animal feeds from carcasses—are classified in Industry 31111, Animal Food Manufacturing;

- Manufacturing canned and frozen specialty foods containing meat, such as nationality foods (e.g., enchiladas, egg rolls, pizza) and frozen dinners—are classified in Industry Group 3114, Fruit and Vegetable Preserving and Specialty Food Manufacturing; and

- Cutting meat (except boxed meat)—are classified in U.S. Industry 424470, Meat and Meat Product Merchant Wholesalers.

311613 Rendering and Meat Byproduct Processing[US]

This U.S. industry comprises establishments primarily engaged in rendering animal fat, bones, and meat scraps.

US—United States industry only. CAN—United States and Canadian industries are comparable. MEX—United States and Mexican industries are comparable. Blank—Canadian, Mexican, and United States industries are comparable.

Cross-References.

Establishments primarily engaged in blending purchased animal fats with vegetable fats are classified in U.S. Industry 311225, Fats and Oils Refining and Blending.

311615 Poultry Processing^{CAN}

This U.S. industry comprises establishments primarily engaged in (1) slaughtering poultry and small game and/or (2) preparing processed poultry and small game meat and meat byproducts.

Cross-References. Establishments primarily engaged in—

- Slaughtering animals (except poultry and small game) and/or preparing meats—are classified in U.S. Industry 311611, Animal (except Poultry) Slaughtering;

- Preparing meat and meat byproducts (except poultry and small game) from purchased meats—are classified in U.S. Industry 311612, Meat Processed from Carcasses;

- Rendering animal fat, bones, and meat scraps—are classified in U.S. Industry 311613, Rendering and Meat Byproduct Processing;

- Canning poultry and small game for baby food—are classified in U.S. Industry 311422, Specialty Canning;

- Producing meat-based animal feeds from carcasses—are classified in Industry 31111, Animal Food Manufacturing;

- Manufacturing canned and frozen meat products, such as nationality foods (e.g., enchiladas, egg rolls, pizza) and frozen dinners—are classified in Industry Group 3114, Fruit and Vegetable Preserving and Specialty Food Manufacturing; and

- Drying, freezing, and breaking eggs—arc classified in U.S. Industry 311999, All Other Miscellaneous Food Manufacturing.

3117 Seafood Product Preparation and Packaging

31171 Seafood Product Preparation and Packaging

This industry comprises establishments primarily engaged in one or more of the following: (1) canning seafood (including soup); (2) smoking, salting, and drying seafood; (3) eviscerating fresh fish by removing heads, fins, scales, bones, and entrails; (4) shucking and packing fresh shellfish; (5) processing marine fats and oils; and (6) freezing seafood. Establishments known as "floating factory

---

US—United States industry only. CAN—United States and Canadian industries are comparable. MEX—United States and Mexican industries are comparable. Blank—Canadian, Mexican, and United States industries are comparable.

ships" that are engaged in the gathering and processing of seafood into canned seafood products are included in this industry.

311711 Seafood Canning[US]

This U.S. industry comprises establishments primarily engaged in (1) canning seafood (including soup) and marine fats and oils and/or (2) smoking, salting, and drying seafood. Establishments known as "floating factory ships" that are engaged in the gathering and processing of seafood into canned seafood products are included in this industry.

Cross-References.

Establishments primarily engaged in preparing fresh and frozen seafood and marine fats and oils are classified in U.S. Industry 311712, Fresh and Frozen Seafood Processing.

311712 Fresh and Frozen Seafood Processing[US]

This U.S. industry comprises establishments primarily engaged in one or more of the following: (1) eviscerating fresh fish by removing heads, fins, scales, bones, and entrails; (2) shucking and packing fresh shellfish; (3) manufacturing frozen seafood; and (4) processing fresh and frozen marine fats and oils.

Cross-References.

Establishments primarily engaged in canning and curing seafood are classified in U.S. Industry 311711, Seafood Canning.

3118 Bakeries and Tortilla Manufacturing

31181 Bread and Bakery Product Manufacturing

This industry comprises establishments primarily engaged in manufacturing fresh and frozen bread and other bakery products.

Cross-References. Establishments primarily engaged in—

- Manufacturing cookies and crackers—are classified in Industry 31182, Cookie, Cracker, and Pasta Manufacturing;
- Preparing and selling bakery products (e.g., cookies, pretzels) for immediate consumption—are classified in Industry 72221, Limited-Service Eating Places;

US—United States industry only. CAN—United States and Canadian industries are comparable. MEX—United States and Mexican industries are comparable. Blank—Canadian, Mexican, and United States industries are comparable.

- Retailing bakery products not for immediate consumption made elsewhere—are classified in Industry 44529, Other Specialty Food Stores; and

- Manufacturing pretzels (except soft)—are classified in Industry 31191, Snack Food Manufacturing.

311811 Retail Bakeries[CAN]

This U.S. industry comprises establishments primarily engaged in retailing bread and other bakery products not for immediate consumption made on the premises from flour, not from prepared dough.

Cross-References. Establishments primarily engaged in—

- Retailing bakery products not for immediate consumption made elsewhere—are classified in U.S. Industry 445291, Baked Goods Stores;

- Preparing and selling bakery products (e.g., cookies, pretzels) for immediate consumption—are classified in U.S. Industry 722213, Snack and Nonalcoholic Beverage Bars;

- Manufacturing fresh or frozen breads and other fresh bakery (except cookies and crackers) products—are classified in U.S. Industry 311812, Commercial Bakeries; and

- Manufacturing cookies and crackers—are classified in U.S. Industry 311821, Cookie and Cracker Manufacturing.

311812 Commercial Bakeries[US]

This U.S. industry comprises establishments primarily engaged in manufacturing fresh and frozen bread and bread-type rolls and other fresh bakery (except cookies and crackers) products.

Cross-References. Establishments primarily engaged in—

- Retailing bread and other bakery products not for immediate consumption made on the premises from flour, not from prepared dough—are classified in U.S. Industry 311811, Retail Bakeries;

- Manufacturing frozen bakery products (except bread)—are classified in U.S. Industry 311813, Frozen Cakes, Pies, and Other Pastries Manufacturing;

- Preparing and selling bakery products (e.g., cookies, pretzels) for immediate consumption—are classified in U.S. Industry 722213, Snack and Nonalcoholic Beverage Bars;

- Retailing bakery products not for immediate consumption made elsewhere—are classified in U.S. Industry 445291, Baked Goods Stores;

- Manufacturing cookies and crackers—are classified in U.S. Industry 311821, Cookie and Cracker Manufacturing; and

- Manufacturing pretzels (except soft)—are classified in U.S. Industry 311919, Other Snack Food Manufacturing.

311813 Frozen Cakes, Pies, and Other Pastries Manufacturing[US]

This U.S. industry comprises establishments primarily engaged in manufacturing frozen bakery products (except bread), such as cakes, pies, and doughnuts.

Cross-References. Establishments primarily engaged in—

- Manufacturing frozen breads—are classified in U.S. Industry 311812, Commercial Bakeries;

- Retailing bakery products not for immediate consumption made on the premises from flour, not from prepared dough—are classified in U.S. Industry 311811, Retail Bakeries;

- Preparing and selling bakery products (e.g., cookies, pretzels) for immediate consumption—are classified in U.S. Industry 722213, Snack and Nonalcoholic Beverage Bars;

- Manufacturing cookies and crackers—are classified in U.S. Industry 311821, Cookie and Cracker Manufacturing; and

- Retailing bakery products not for immediate consumption made elsewhere—are classified in U.S. Industry 445291, Baked Goods Stores.

31182 Cookie, Cracker, and Pasta Manufacturing

This industry comprises establishments primarily engaged in one of the following: (1) manufacturing cookies and crackers; (2) preparing flour and dough mixes and dough from flour ground elsewhere; and (3) manufacturing dry pasta. The establishments in this industry may package the dry pasta they manufacture with other ingredients.

Cross-References. Establishments primarily engaged in—

- Preparing and selling bakery products (e.g., cookies, pretzels) for immediate consumption—are classified in Industry 72221, Limited-Service Eating Places;

- Retailing bakery products not for immediate consumption made elsewhere—are classified in Industry 44529, Other Specialty Food Stores;

- Manufacturing bakery products (e.g., bread, cookies, pies)—are classified in Industry 31181, Bread and Bakery Product Manufacturing;

- Milling flour and preparing flour mixes or doughs—are classified in Industry 31121, Flour Milling and Malt Manufacturing;

- Manufacturing canned pasta specialties—are classified in Industry 31142, Fruit and Vegetable Canning, Pickling, and Drying;

- Manufacturing fresh pasta—are classified in Industry 31199, All Other Food Manufacturing;

- Manufacturing pretzels (except soft)—are classified in Industry 31191, Snack Food Manufacturing;

- Mixing purchased dried and/or dehydrated ingredients with purchased dry pasta—are classified in Industry 31199, All Other Food Manufacturing; and

- Drying and/or dehydrating ingredients and packaging them with purchased dry pasta—are classified in Industry 31142, Fruit and Vegetable Canning, Pickling, and Drying.

311821 Cookie and Cracker Manufacturing[CAN]

This U.S. industry comprises establishments primarily engaged in manufacturing cookies, crackers, and other products, such as ice cream cones.

Cross-References. Establishments primarily engaged in—

- Preparing and selling bakery products (e.g., cookies, pretzels) for immediate consumption—are classified in U.S. Industry 722213, Snack and Nonalcoholic Beverage Bars;

- Retailing bakery products not for immediate consumption made elsewhere—are classified in U.S. Industry 445291, Baked Goods Stores;

- Manufacturing bakery products (e.g., breads, cookies, pies)—are classified in Industry 31181, Bread and Bakery Product Manufacturing; and

- Manufacturing pretzels (except soft)—are classified in U.S. Industry 311919, Other Snack Food Manufacturing.

311822 Flour Mixes and Dough Manufacturing from Purchased Flour[CAN]

This U.S. industry comprises establishments primarily engaged in manufacturing prepared flour mixes or dough mixes from flour ground elsewhere.

US—United States industry only. CAN—United States and Canadian industries are comparable. MEX—United States and Mexican industries are comparable. Blank—Canadian, Mexican, and United States industries are comparable.

Cross-References

Establishments primarily engaged in milling flour and preparing flour mixes or doughs are classified in U.S. Industry 311211, Flour Milling.

311823 Dry Pasta Manufacturing^{CAN}

This U.S. industry comprises establishments primarily engaged in manufacturing dry pasta. The establishments in this industry may package the dry pasta they manufacture with other ingredients.

Cross-References. Establishments primarily engaged in—

- Manufacturing fresh pasta—are classified in U.S. Industry 311991, Perishable Prepared Food Manufacturing;

- Manufacturing pasta specialties—are classified in Industry Group 3114, Fruit and Vegetable Preserving and Specialty Food Manufacturing;

- Mixing purchased dried and/or dehydrated ingredients with purchased dry pasta—are classified in U.S. Industry 311999, All Other Miscellaneous Food Manufacturing; and

- Drying and/or dehydrating ingredients packaged with purchased dry pasta—are classified in U.S. Industry 311423, Dried and Dehydrated Food Manufacturing.

31183 Tortilla Manufacturing

See industry description for 311830 below.

311830 Tortilla Manufacturing

This industry comprises establishments primarily engaged in manufacturing tortillas.

Cross-References. Establishments primarily engaged in—

- Manufacturing canned nationality foods using tortillas—are classified in U.S. Industry 311422, Specialty Canning;

- Manufacturing frozen nationality foods using tortillas—are classified in U.S. Industry 311412, Frozen Specialty Food Manufacturing; and

- Manufacturing tortilla chips—are classified in U.S. Industry 311919, Other Snack Food Manufacturing.

US—United States industry only. CAN—United States and Canadian industries are comparable. MEX—United States and Mexican industries are comparable. Blank—Canadian, Mexican, and United States industries are comparable.

3119 Other Food Manufacturing

This industry group comprises establishments primarily engaged in manufacturing food (except animal food; grain and oilseed milling; sugar and confectionery products; preserved fruit, vegetable, and specialty foods; dairy products; meat products; seafood products; and bakeries and tortillas). The industry group includes industries with different production processes, such as snack food manufacturing; coffee and tea manufacturing; concentrate, syrup, condiment, and spice manufacturing; and, in general, an entire range of other miscellaneous food product manufacturing.

31191 Snack Food Manufacturing

This industry comprises establishments primarily engaged in one or more of the following: (1) salting, roasting, drying, cooking, or canning nuts; (2) processing grains or seeds into snacks; (3) manufacturing peanut butter; and (4) manufacturing potato chips, corn chips, popped popcorn, pretzels (except soft), pork rinds, and similar snacks.

Cross-References. Establishments primarily engaged in—

- Manufacturing crackers—are classified in Industry 31182, Cookie, Cracker, and Pasta Manufacturing;

- Manufacturing unpopped popcorn—are classified in Industry 31199, All Other Food Manufacturing;

- Manufacturing chocolate or candy-coated nuts and candy-covered popcorn—are classified in Industry Group 3113, Sugar and Confectionery Product Manufacturing; and

- Manufacturing soft pretzels—are classified in Industry 31181, Bread and Bakery Product Manufacturing.

311911 Roasted Nuts and Peanut Butter Manufacturing^{CAN}

This U.S. industry comprises establishments primarily engaged in one or more of the following: (1) salting, roasting, drying, cooking, or canning nuts; (2) processing grains or seeds into snacks; and (3) manufacturing peanut butter.

Cross-References.

Establishments primarily engaged in manufacturing chocolate or candy-coated nuts and candy-covered popcorn are classified in Industry Group 3113, Sugar and Confectionery Product Manufacturing.

US—United States industry only. CAN—United States and Canadian industries are comparable. MEX—United States and Mexican industries are comparable. Blank—Canadian, Mexican, and United States industries are comparable.

311919 Other Snack Food Manufacturing^{CAN}

This U.S. industry comprises establishments primarily engaged in manufacturing snack foods (except roasted nuts and peanut butter).

Illustrative Examples:

Corn chips and related corn snacks
manufacturing
Potato chips manufacturing
Popped popcorn (except candy-covered)
manufacturing

Pretzels (except soft) manufacturing
Pork rinds manufacturing
Tortilla chips manufacturing

Cross-References. Establishments primarily engaged in—

- Manufacturing cookies and crackers—are classified in U.S. Industry 311821, Cookie and Cracker Manufacturing;

- Manufacturing candy covered popcorn and nonchocolate granola bars—are classified in Industry 311340, Nonchocolate Confectionery Manufacturing;

- Salting, roasting, drying, cooking, or canning nuts and seeds—are classified in U.S. Industry 311911, Roasted Nuts and Peanut Butter Manufacturing;

- Manufacturing unpopped popcorn—are classified in U.S. Industry 311999, All Other Miscellaneous Food Manufacturing; and

- Manufacturing soft pretzels—are classified in U.S. Industry 311812, Commercial Bakeries.

31192 Coffee and Tea Manufacturing
See industry description for 311920 below.

311920 Coffee and Tea Manufacturing^{CAN}

This industry comprises establishments primarily engaged in one or more of the following: (1) roasting coffee; (2) manufacturing coffee and tea concentrates (including instant and freeze-dried); (3) blending tea; (4) manufacturing herbal tea; and (5) manufacturing coffee extracts, flavorings, and syrups.

Cross-References.

Establishments primarily engaged in bottling and canning iced tea are classified in U.S. Industry 312111, Soft Drink Manufacturing.

31193 Flavoring Syrup and Concentrate Manufacturing
See industry description for 311930 below.

311930 Flavoring Syrup and Concentrate Manufacturing

This industry comprises establishments primarily engaged in manufacturing flavoring syrup drink concentrates and related products for soda fountain use or for the manufacture of soft drinks.

Cross-References. Establishments primarily engaged in—

- Manufacturing chocolate syrup—are classified in Industry 311320, Chocolate and Confectionery Manufacturing from Cacao Beans;
- Manufacturing flavoring extracts (except coffee and meat) and natural food colorings—are classified in U.S. Industry 311942, Spice and Extract Manufacturing;
- Manufacturing coffee extracts—are classified in Industry 311920, Coffee and Tea Manufacturing;
- Manufacturing meat extracts—are classified in Industry 31161, Animal Slaughtering and Processing;
- Manufacturing powdered drink mixes (except coffee, tea, chocolate, or milk-based) and table syrup from corn syrup—are classified in U.S. Industry 311999, All Other Miscellaneous Food Manufacturing;
- Reducing maple sap to maple syrup—are classified in U.S. Industry 111998, All Other Miscellaneous Crop Farming; and
- Manufacturing natural nonfood colorings—are classified in U.S. Industry 325199, All Other Basic Organic Chemical Manufacturing.

31194 Seasoning and Dressing Manufacturing

This industry comprises establishments primarily engaged in one or more of the following: (1) manufacturing dressings and sauces, such as mayonnaise, salad dressing, vinegar, mustard, horseradish, soy sauce, tarter sauce, Worcestershire sauce, and other prepared sauces (except tomato-based and gravies); (2) manufacturing spices, table salt, seasoning, and flavoring extracts (except coffee and meat), and natural food colorings; and (3) manufacturing dry mix food preparations, such as salad dressing mixes, gravy and sauce mixes, frosting mixes, and other dry mix preparations.

Cross-References. Establishments primarily engaged in—

- Manufacturing catsup and other tomato-based sauces—are classified in Industry 31142, Fruit and Vegetable Canning, Pickling, and Drying;

US—United States industry only. CAN—United States and Canadian industries are comparable. MEX—United States and Mexican industries are comparable. Blank—Canadian, Mexican, and United States industries are comparable.

- Mixing purchased dried and/or dehydrated potato, rice, and pasta and packaging them with other purchased ingredients, and manufacturing prepared frosting—are classified in Industry 31199, All Other Food Manufacturing;

- Drying and/or dehydrating ingredients for dry soup mixes and bouillon—are classified in Industry 31142, Fruit and Vegetable Canning, Pickling, and Drying;

- Mixing purchased dried and/or dehydrated ingredients for dry soup mixes and bouillon—are classified in Industry 31199, All Other Food Manufacturing;

- Manufacturing industrial salts—are classified in Industry 32599, All Other Chemical Product and Preparation Manufacturing;

- Manufacturing flavoring syrups (except coffee-based syrups)—are classified in Industry 31193, Flavoring Syrup and Concentrate Manufacturing;

- Manufacturing synthetic food colorings—are classified in Industry 32513, Synthetic Dye and Pigment Manufacturing;

- Manufacturing natural organic colorings for nonfood uses—are classified in Industry 32519, Other Basic Organic Chemical Manufacturing;

- Manufacturing coffee extracts—are classified in Industry 31192, Coffee and Tea Manufacturing;

- Manufacturing meat extracts—are classified in Industry 31161, Animal Slaughtering and Processing; and

- Manufacturing gravies—are classified in Industry 31199, All Other Food Manufacturing.

311941 Mayonnaise, Dressing, and Other Prepared Sauce Manufacturing[US]

This U.S. industry comprises establishments primarily engaged in manufacturing mayonnaise, salad dressing, vinegar, mustard, horseradish, soy sauce, tarter sauce, Worcestershire sauce, and other prepared sauces (except tomato-based and gravy).

Cross-References. Establishments primarily engaged in—

- Manufacturing catsup and similar tomato-based sauces—are classified in U.S. Industry 311421, Fruit and Vegetable Canning;

- Manufacturing dry salad dressing and dry sauce mixes—are classified in U.S. Industry 311942, Spice and Extract Manufacturing; and

- Manufacturing gravies—are classified in U.S. Industry 311999, All Other Miscellaneous Food Manufacturing.

311942 Spice and Extract Manufacturing[US]

This U.S. industry comprises establishments primarily engaged in (1) manufacturing spices, table salt, seasonings, flavoring extracts (except coffee and meat), and natural food colorings and/or (2) manufacturing dry mix food preparations, such as salad dressing mixes, gravy and sauce mixes, frosting mixes, and other dry mix preparations.

Cross-References. Establishments primarily engaged in—

- Manufacturing catsup and other tomato-based sauces—are classified in U.S. Industry 311421, Fruit and Vegetable Canning;

- Manufacturing mayonnaise, dressings, and prepared nontomato-based sauces—are classified in U.S. Industry 311941, Mayonnaise, Dressing, and Other Prepared Sauce Manufacturing;

- Manufacturing industrial salts—are classified in U.S. Industry 325998, All Other Miscellaneous Chemical Product and Preparation Manufacturing;

- Drying and/or dehydrating ingredients for dry soup mixes and bouillon—are classified in U.S. Industry 311423, Dried and Dehydrated Food Manufacturing;

- Mixing purchased dried and/or dehydrated ingredients for dry soup mixes and bouillon—are classified in U.S. Industry 311999, All Other Miscellaneous Food Manufacturing;

- Manufacturing flavoring syrups (except coffee-based syrups)—are classified in Industry 311930, Flavoring Syrup and Concentrate Manufacturing;

- Mixing purchased dried and/or dehydrated potato, rice, and pasta and packaging them with other purchased ingredients, and manufacturing prepared frosting—are classified in U.S. Industry 311999, All Other Miscellaneous Food Manufacturing;

- Manufacturing coffee extracts and/or coffee-based syrups—are classified in Industry 311920, Coffee and Tea Manufacturing;

- Manufacturing meat extracts—are classified in Industry 31161, Animal Slaughtering and Processing;

- Manufacturing synthetic food colorings—are classified in U.S. Industry 325132, Synthetic Organic Dye and Pigment Manufacturing; and

- Manufacturing natural organic colorings for nonfood uses—are classified in U.S. Industry 325199, All Other Basic Organic Chemical Manufacturing.

31199 All Other Food Manufacturing

This industry comprises establishments primarily engaged in manufacturing food (except animal food; grain and oilseed milling; sugar and confectionery products; preserved fruits, vegetables, and specialties; dairy products; meat products; seafood products; bakeries and tortillas; snack foods; coffee and tea; flavoring syrups and concentrates; seasonings; and dressings). Included in this industry are establishments primarily engaged in mixing purchased dried and/or dehydrated ingredients including those mixing purchased dried and/or dehydrated ingredients for soup mixes and bouillon.

Illustrative Examples:

Baking powder manufacturing
Fresh pizza manufacturing
Cut or peeled fresh vegetables
  manufacturing
Honey processing
Dessert puddings manufacturing
Popcorn (except popped) manufacturing

Egg substitutes manufacturing
Powdered drink mixes (except chocolate,
  coffee, tea, or milk based)
  manufacturing
Fresh pasta manufacturing
Sweetening syrups (except pure maple)
  manufacturing

Cross-References. Establishments primarily engaged in—

- Manufacturing animal foods—are classified in Industry Group 3111, Animal Food Manufacturing;

- Milling grain and oilseed—are classified in Industry Group 3112, Grain and Oilseed Milling;

- Manufacturing sugar and confectionery products—are classified in Industry Group 3113, Sugar and Confectionery Product Manufacturing;

- Preserving fruit, vegetables, and specialty foods—are classified in Industry Group 3114, Fruit and Vegetable Preserving and Specialty Food Manufacturing;

- Manufacturing dairy products—are classified in Industry Group 3115, Dairy Product Manufacturing;

- Manufacturing meat products—are classified in Industry Group 3116, Animal Slaughtering and Processing;

- Manufacturing seafood products—are classified in Industry Group 3117, Seafood Product Preparation and Packaging;

- Manufacturing bakery and tortilla products—are classified in Industry Group 3118, Bakeries and Tortilla Manufacturing;

- Manufacturing snack foods—are classified in Industry 31191, Snack Food Manufacturing;

- Manufacturing coffee and tea—are classified in Industry 31192, Coffee and Tea Manufacturing;

- Manufacturing flavoring syrups and concentrates (except coffee-based)—are classified in Industry 31193, Flavoring Syrup and Concentrate Manufacturing;

- Manufacturing seasonings and dressings—are classified in Industry 31194, Seasoning and Dressing Manufacturing;

- Milling rice and packaging it with other ingredients—are classified in Industry 31121, Flour Milling and Malt Manufacturing;

- Manufacturing dry pasta and packaging it with other ingredients—are classified in Industry 31182, Cookie, Cracker, and Pasta Manufacturing; and

- Drying and/or dehydrating ingredients and packaging them with other purchased ingredients—are classified in Industry 31142, Fruit and Vegetable Canning, Pickling, and Drying.

311991 Perishable Prepared Food Manufacturing[US]

This U.S. industry comprises establishments primarily engaged in manufacturing perishable prepared foods, such as salads, sandwiches, prepared meals, fresh pizza, fresh pasta, and peeled or cut vegetables.

311999 All Other Miscellaneous Food Manufacturing[US]

This U.S. industry comprises establishments primarily engaged in manufacturing food (except animal food; grain and oilseed milling; sugar and confectionery products; preserved fruits, vegetables, and specialties; dairy products; meat products; seafood products; bakeries and tortillas; snack foods; coffee and tea; flavoring syrups and concentrates; seasonings and dressings; and perishable prepared food). Included in this industry are establishments primarily engaged in mixing purchased dried and/or dehydrated ingredients including those mixing purchased dried and/or dehydrated ingredients for soup mixes and bouillon.

Illustrative Examples:

Baking powder manufacturing	Egg substitutes manufacturing
Popcorn (except popped) manufacturing	Sweetening syrups (except pure maple)
Cake frosting, prepared, manufacturing	manufacturing
Powdered drink mixes (except chocolate,	Gelatin dessert preparations
coffee, tea, or milk based)	manufacturing
˙manufacturing	Yeast manufacturing
Dessert puddings manufacturing	Honey processing

US—United States industry only. CAN—United States and Canadian industries are comparable. MEX—United States and Mexican industries are comparable. Blank—Canadian, Mexican, and United States industries are comparable.

Cross-References. Establishments primarily engaged in—

- Manufacturing animal foods—are classified in Industry Group 3111, Animal Food Manufacturing;

- Milling grain and oilseed—are classified in Industry Group 3112, Grain and Oilseed Milling;

- Manufacturing sugar and confectionery products—are classified in Industry Group 3113, Sugar and Confectionery Product Manufacturing;

- Preserving fruit, vegetable, and specialty foods—are classified in Industry Group 3114, Fruit and Vegetable Preserving and Specialty Food Manufacturing;

- Manufacturing dairy products—are classified in Industry Group 3115, Dairy Product Manufacturing;

- Manufacturing meat products—are classified in Industry Group 3116, Animal Slaughtering and Processing;

- Manufacturing seafood products—are classified in Industry Group 3117, Seafood Product Preparation and Packaging;

- Manufacturing bakery and tortilla products—are classified in Industry Group 3118, Bakeries and Tortilla Manufacturing;

- Manufacturing snack foods—are classified in Industry 31191, Snack Food Manufacturing;

- Manufacturing coffee and tea—are classified in Industry 31192, Coffee and Tea Manufacturing;

- Manufacturing flavoring syrups and concentrates (except coffee-based)—are classified in Industry 31193, Flavoring Syrup and Concentrate Manufacturing;

- Manufacturing seasonings and dressings—are classified in Industry 31194, Seasoning and Dressing Manufacturing;

- Manufacturing perishable prepared foods—are classified in U.S. Industry 311991, Perishable Prepared Food Manufacturing;

- Milling rice and packaging it with other ingredients—are classified in U.S. Industry 311212, Rice Milling;

- Manufacturing dry pasta and packaging it with ingredients—are classified in U.S. Industry 311823, Dry Pasta Manufacturing; and

- Drying and/or dehydrating ingredients and packaging them with other purchased ingredients—are classified in U.S. Industry 311423, Dried and Dehydrated Food Manufacturing.

US—United States industry only. CAN—United States and Canadian industries are comparable. MEX—United States and Mexican industries are comparable. Blank—Canadian, Mexican, and United States industries are comparable.

312 Beverage and Tobacco Product Manufacturing

Industries in the Beverage and Tobacco Product Manufacturing subsector manufacture beverages and tobacco products. The industry group, Beverage Manufacturing, includes three types of establishments: (1) those that manufacture nonalcoholic beverages; (2) those that manufacture alcoholic beverages through the fermentation process; and (3) those that produce distilled alcoholic beverages. Ice manufacturing, while not a beverage, is included with nonalcoholic beverage manufacturing because it uses the same production process as water purification.

In the case of activities related to the manufacture of beverages, the structure follows the defined production processes. Brandy, a distilled beverage, was not placed under distillery product manufacturing, but rather under the NAICS class for winery product manufacturing since the production process used in the manufacturing of alcoholic grape-based beverages produces both wines (fermented beverage) and brandies (distilled beverage).

The industry group, Tobacco Manufacturing, includes two types of establishments: (1) those engaged in redrying and stemming tobacco and, (2) those that manufacture tobacco products, such as cigarettes and cigars.

3121 Beverage Manufacturing

31211 Soft Drink and Ice Manufacturing

This industry comprises establishments primarily engaged in one or more of the following: (1) manufacturing soft drinks; (2) manufacturing ice; and (3) purifying and bottling water.

Cross-References. Establishments primarily engaged in—

- • Canning fruit and vegetable juices—are classified in Industry 31142, Fruit and Vegetable Canning, Pickling, and Drying;

- • Manufacturing soft drink bases—are classified in Industry 31193, Flavoring Syrup and Concentrate Manufacturing;

- • Manufacturing nonalcoholic cider—are classified in Industry 31194, Seasoning and Dressing Manufacturing;

- • Manufacturing dry ice—are classified in Industry 32512, Industrial Gas Manufacturing;

- • Manufacturing milk-based drinks—are classified in Industry 31151, Dairy Product (except Frozen) Manufacturing;

- • Manufacturing nonalcoholic beers—are classified in Industry 31212, Breweries;

- Manufacturing nonalcoholic wines—are classified in Industry 31213, Wineries; and

- Bottling purchased purified water—are classified in Industry 42449, Other Grocery and Related Products Merchant Wholesalers.

312111 Soft Drink Manufacturing^{MEX}

This U.S. industry comprises establishments primarily engaged in manufacturing soft drinks and artificially carbonated waters.

Cross-References. Establishments primarily engaged in—

- Canning fruit and vegetable juices—are classified in U.S. Industry 311421, Fruit and Vegetable Canning;

- Manufacturing fruit syrups for flavoring—are classified in Industry 31193, Flavoring Syrup and Concentrate Manufacturing;

- Manufacturing nonalcoholic cider—are classified in U.S. Industry 311941, Mayonnaise, Dressing, and Other Prepared Sauce Manufacturing;

- Purifying and bottling water (except artificially carbonated and flavored water)—are classified in U.S. Industry 312112, Bottled Water Manufacturing;

- Manufacturing milk-based drinks—are classified in U.S. Industry 311511, Fluid Milk Manufacturing;

- Manufacturing nonalcoholic beers—are classified in Industry 312120, Breweries; and

- Manufacturing nonalcoholic wines—are classified in Industry 312130, Wineries.

312112 Bottled Water Manufacturing^{MEX}

This U.S. industry comprises establishments primarily engaged in purifying and bottling water (including naturally carbonated).

Cross-References. Establishments primarily engaged in—

- Manufacturing artificially carbonated waters—are classified in U.S. Industry 312111, Soft Drink Manufacturing; and

- Bottling purchased purified water—are classified in Industry 424490, Other Grocery and Related Products Merchant Wholesalers.

US—United States industry only. CAN—United States and Canadian industries are comparable. MEX—United States and Mexican industries are comparable. Blank—Canadian, Mexican, and United States industries are comparable.

312113 Ice Manufacturing^MEX

This U.S. industry comprises establishments primarily engaged in manufacturing ice.

Cross-References.

Establishments primarily. engaged in manufacturing dry ice are classified in Industry 325120, Industrial Gas Manufacturing.

31212 Breweries
See industry description for 312120 below.

312120 Breweries

This industry comprises establishments primarily engaged in brewing beer, ale, malt liquors, and nonalcoholic beer.

Cross-References. Establishments primarily engaged in—

- Bottling purchased malt beverages—are classified in Industry 424810, Beer and Ale Merchant Wholesalers; and

- Manufacturing malt—are classified in U.S. Industry 311213, Malt Manufacturing.

31213 Wineries
See industry description for 312130 below.

312130 Wineries^CAN

This industry comprises establishments primarily engaged in one or more of the following: (1) growing grapes and manufacturing wines and brandies; (2) manufacturing wines and brandies from grapes and other fruits grown elsewhere; and (3) blending wines and brandies.

Cross-References.

Establishments primarily engaged in bottling purchased wines are classified in Industry 424820, Wine and Distilled Alcoholic Beverage Merchant Wholesalers.

31214 Distilleries
See industry description for 312140 below.

US—United States industry only. CAN—United States and Canadian industries are comparable. MEX—United States and Mexican industries are comparable. Blank—Canadian, Mexican, and United States industries are comparable.

312140 Distilleries^{CAN}

This industry comprises establishments primarily engaged in one or more of the following: (1) distilling potable liquors (except brandies); (2) distilling and blending liquors; and (3) blending and mixing liquors and other ingredients.

Cross-References. Establishments primarily engaged in—

- Manufacturing nonpotable ethyl alcohol—are classified in U.S. Industry 325193, Ethyl Alcohol Manufacturing;

- Bottling liquors made elsewhere—are classified in Industry 424820, Wine and Distilled Alcoholic Beverage Merchant Wholesalers; and

- Manufacturing brandies—are classified in Industry 312130, Wineries.

3122 Tobacco Manufacturing

31221 Tobacco Stemming and Redrying
See industry description for 312210 below.

312210 Tobacco Stemming and Redrying

This industry comprises establishments primarily engaged in the stemming and redrying of tobacco.

Cross-References. Establishments primarily engaged in—

- Reconstituting tobacco—are classified in U.S. Industry 312229, Other Tobacco Product Manufacturing;

- Selling leaf tobacco as merchant wholesalers that also engage in stemming tobacco—are classified in Industry 424940, Tobacco and Tobacco Product Merchant Wholesalers; and

- Selling leaf tobacco as agents or brokers that also engage in stemming tobacco—are classified in Industry 425120, Wholesale Trade Agents and Brokers.

31222 Tobacco Product Manufacturing

This industry comprises establishments primarily engaged in manufacturing cigarettes, cigars, smoking and chewing tobacco, and reconstituted tobacco.

US—United States industry only. CAN—United States and Canadian industries are comparable. MEX—United States and Mexican industries are comparable. Blank—Canadian, Mexican, and United States industries are comparable.

Cross-References.

Establishments primarily engaged in stemming and redrying tobacco are classified in Industry 31221, Tobacco Stemming and Redrying.

312221 Cigarette Manufacturing[MEX]

This U.S. industry comprises establishments primarily engaged in manufacturing cigarettes.

Cross-References.

Establishments primarily engaged in manufacturing cigars, smoking tobacco, chewing tobacco, and reconstituted tobacco are classified in U.S. Industry 312229, Other Tobacco Product Manufacturing.

312229 Other Tobacco Product Manufacturing[US]

This U.S. industry comprises establishments primarily engaged in manufacturing tobacco products (except cigarettes).

Illustrative Examples:

Chewing tobacco manufacturing   Snuff manufacturing
Reconstituting tobacco   Prepared pipe tobacco manufacturing
Cigar manufacturing

Cross-References. Establishments primarily engaged in—

- Manufacturing cigarettes—are classified in U.S. Industry 312221, Cigarette Manufacturing; and

- Stemming and redrying tobacco—are classified in Industry 312210, Tobacco Stemming and Redrying.

313 Textile Mills

Industries in the Textile Mills subsector group establishments that transform a basic fiber (natural or synthetic) into a product, such as yarn or fabric that is further manufactured into usable items, such as apparel, sheets, towels, and textile bags for individual or industrial consumption. The further manufacturing may be performed in the same establishment and classified in this subsector, or it may be performed at a separate establishment and be classified elsewhere in manufacturing.

The main processes in this subsector include preparation and spinning of fiber, knitting or weaving of fabric, and the finishing of the textile. The NAICS structure

US—United States industry only. CAN—United States and Canadian industries are comparable. MEX—United States and Mexican industries are comparable. Blank—Canadian, Mexican, and United States industries are comparable.

follows and captures this process flow. Major industries in this flow, such as preparation of fibers, weaving of fabric, knitting of fabric, and fiber and fabric finishing, are uniquely identified. Texturizing, throwing, twisting, and winding of yarn contains aspects of both fiber preparation and fiber finishing and is classified with preparation of fibers rather than with finishing of fiber.

NAICS separates the manufacturing of primary textiles and the manufacturing of textile products (except apparel) when the textile product is produced from purchased primary textiles, such as fabric. The manufacturing of textile products (except apparel) from purchased fabric is classified in Subsector 314, Textile Product Mills, and apparel from purchased fabric is classified in Subsector 315, Apparel Manufacturing.

Excluded from this subsector are establishments that weave or knit fabric and make garments. These establishments are included in Subsector 315, Apparel Manufacturing.

3131 Fiber, Yarn, and Thread Mills

31311 Fiber, Yarn, and Thread Mills

This industry comprises establishments primarily engaged in one or more of the following: (1) spinning yarn; (2) manufacturing thread of any fiber; (3) texturizing, throwing, twisting, and winding purchased yarn or manmade fiber filaments; and (4) producing hemp yarn and further processing into rope or bags.

Cross-References.

Establishments primarily engaged in manufacturing artificial and synthetic fibers and filaments and texturizing these filaments are classified in Industry 32522, Artificial and Synthetic Fibers and Filaments Manufacturing.

313111 Yarn Spinning Mills[US]

This U.S. industry comprises establishments primarily engaged in spinning yarn from any fiber and/or producing hemp yarn and further processing into rope or bags.

313112 Yarn Texturizing, Throwing, and Twisting Mills[US]

This U.S. industry comprises establishments primarily engaged in texturizing, throwing, twisting, spooling, or winding purchased yarns or manmade fiber filaments.

US—United States industry only. CAN—United States and Canadian industries are comparable. MEX—United States and Mexican industries are comparable. Blank—Canadian, Mexican, and United States industries are comparable.

Cross-References.

Establishments primarily engaged in manufacturing artificial and synthetic fiber and filament and texturizing these fibers and filaments are classified in Industry 32522, Artificial and Synthetic Fibers and Filaments Manufacturing.

313113 Thread Mills[MEX]

This U.S. industry comprises establishments primarily engaged in manufacturing thread (e.g., sewing, hand-knitting, crochet) of all fibers.

3132 Fabric Mills

31321 Broadwoven Fabric Mills
See industry description for 313210 below.

313210 Broadwoven Fabric Mills

This industry comprises establishments primarily engaged in weaving broadwoven fabrics and felts (except tire fabrics and rugs). Establishments in this industry may weave only, weave and finish, or weave, finish, and further fabricate fabric products.

Cross-References. Establishments primarily engaged in—

* Weaving widths specifically constructed for cutting to narrow widths—are classified in U.S. Industry 313221, Narrow Fabric Mills;
* Weaving or tufting carpet and rugs—are classified in Industry 314110, Carpet and Rug Mills; and
* Making tire cord and tire fabrics—are classified in U.S. Industry 314992, Tire Cord and Tire Fabric Mills.

31322 Narrow Fabric Mills and Schiffli Machine Embroidery

This industry comprises establishments primarily engaged in one or more of the following: (1) weaving or braiding narrow fabrics; (2) manufacturing Schiffli machine embroideries; and (3) making fabric-covered elastic yarn and thread.

313221 Narrow Fabric Mills[US]

This U.S. industry comprises establishments primarily engaged in (1) weaving or braiding narrow fabrics in their final form or initially made in wider widths

---

that are specially constructed for narrower widths and/or (2) making fabric-covered elastic yarn and thread. Establishments in this industry may weave only; weave and finish; or weave, finish, and further fabricate fabric products.

313222 Schiffli Machine Embroidery[US]

This U.S. industry comprises establishments primarily engaged in manufacturing Schiffli machine embroideries.

31323 Nonwoven Fabric Mills
See industry description for 313230 below.

313230 Nonwoven Fabric Mills

This industry comprises establishments primarily engaged in manufacturing nonwoven fabrics and felts. Processes used include bonding and/or interlocking fibers by mechanical, chemical, thermal, or solvent means, or by combinations thereof.

31324 Knit Fabric Mills

This industry comprises establishments primarily engaged in one of the following: (1) knitting weft (i.e., circular) and warp (i.e., flat) fabric; (2) knitting and finishing weft and warp fabric; (3) manufacturing lace; or (4) manufacturing, dyeing, and finishing lace and lace goods. Establishments in this industry may knit only; knit and finish; or knit, finish, and further fabricate fabric products (except apparel).

Cross-References.

Establishments primarily engaged in knitting apparel are classified in Industry Group 3151, Apparel Knitting Mills.

313241 Weft Knit Fabric Mills[US]

This U.S. industry comprises establishments primarily engaged in knitting weft (i.e., circular) fabric or knitting and finishing weft fabric. Establishments in this industry may knit only; knit and finish; or knit, finish, and further fabricate fabric products (except apparel).

Cross-References.

Establishments primarily engaged in knitting apparel are classified in Industry Group 3151, Apparel Knitting Mills.

US—United States industry only. CAN—United States and Canadian industries are comparable. MEX—United States and Mexican industries are comparable. Blank—Canadian, Mexican, and United States industries are comparable.

313249 Other Knit Fabric and Lace Mills^{US}

This U.S. industry comprises establishments primarily engaged in one of the following: (1) knitting warp (i.e., flat) fabric; (2) knitting and finishing warp fabric; (3) manufacturing lace; or (4) manufacturing, dyeing, or finishing lace and lace goods. Establishments in this industry may knit only; knit and finish; or knit, finish, and further fabricate fabric products (except apparel).

Cross-References.

Establishments primarily engaged in knitting apparel are classified in Industry Group 3151, Apparel Knitting Mills.

3133 Textile and Fabric Finishing and Fabric Coating Mills

31331 Textile and Fabric Finishing Mills

This industry comprises (1) establishments primarily engaged in finishing of textiles, fabrics, and apparel, and (2) establishments of converters who buy fabric goods in the grey, have them finished on contract, and sell at wholesale. Finishing operations include: bleaching, dyeing, printing (e.g., roller, screen, flock, plisse), stonewashing, and other mechanical finishing, such as preshrinking, shrinking, sponging, calendering, mercerizing, and napping; as well as cleaning, scouring, and the preparation of natural fibers and raw stock.

Cross-References. Establishments primarily engaged in—

- Coating or impregnating fabrics—are classified in Industry 31332, Fabric Coating Mills;
- Knitting or knitting and finishing fabric—are classified in Industry 31324, Knit Fabric Mills;
- Manufacturing and finishing apparel—are classified in Subsector 315, Apparel Manufacturing;
- Weaving and finishing fabrics—are classified in Industry Group 3132, Fabric Mills;
- Manufacturing and finishing rugs and carpets—are classified in Industry 31411, Carpet and Rug Mills; and
- Printing on apparel—are classified in Industry 32311, Printing.

313311 Broadwoven Fabric Finishing Mills^{US}

This U.S. industry comprises (1) establishments primarily engaged in finishing broadwoven fabrics, and (2) establishments of converters who buy broadwoven

---

US—United States industry only. CAN—United States and Canadian industries are comparable. MEX—United States and Mexican industries are comparable. Blank—Canadian, Mexican, and United States industries are comparable.

fabrics in the grey, have them finished on contract, and sell at wholesale. Finishing operations include bleaching, dyeing, printing (roller, screen, flock, plisse), and other mechanical finishing, such as preshrinking, shrinking, sponging, calendering, mercerizing and napping.

Cross-References. Establishments primarily engaged in—

- Coating or impregnating fabrics—are classified in Industry 313320, Fabric Coating Mills; and

- Weaving and finishing broadwoven fabrics—are classified in Industry 313210, Broadwoven Fabric Mills.

313312 Textile and Fabric Finishing (except Broadwoven Fabric) Mills[US]

This U.S. industry comprises (1) establishments primarily engaged in dyeing, bleaching, printing, and other finishing of textiles, apparel, and fabrics (except broadwoven) and (2) establishments of converters who buy fabrics (except broadwoven) in the grey, have them finished on contract, and sell at wholesale. Finishing operations include bleaching, dyeing, printing (e.g., roller, screen, flock, plisse), stonewashing, and other mechanical finishing, such as preshrinking, shrinking, sponging, calendering, mercerizing and napping; as well as cleaning, scouring, and the preparation of natural fibers and raw stock.

Cross-References. Establishments primarily engaged in—

- Knitting and finishing fabric—are classified in Industry 31324, Knit Fabric Mills;

- Finishing broadwoven fabric—are classified in U.S. Industry 313311, Broadwoven Fabric Finishing Mills;

- Weaving and finishing narrow woven fabric—are classified in U.S. Industry 313221, Narrow Fabric Mills;

- Manufacturing and finishing apparel—are classified in Subsector 315, Apparel Manufacturing;

- Coating or impregnating fabrics—are classified in Industry 313320, Fabric Coating Mills; and

- Printing on apparel—are classified in Industry 32311, Printing.

31332 Fabric Coating Mills
See industry description for 313320 below.

US—United States industry only. CAN—United States and Canadian industries are comparable. MEX—United States and Mexican industries are comparable. Blank—Canadian, Mexican, and United States industries are comparable.

313320 Fabric Coating Mills

This industry comprises establishments primarily engaged in coating, laminating, varnishing, waxing, and rubberizing textiles and apparel.

Cross-References.

Establishments primarily engaged in dyeing and finishing textiles are classified in Industry 31331, Textile and Fabric Finishing Mills.

314 Textile Product Mills

Industries in the Textile Product Mills subsector group establishments that make textile products (except apparel). With a few exceptions, processes used in these industries are generally cut and sew (i.e., purchasing fabric and cutting and sewing to make nonapparel textile products, such as sheets and towels).

3141 Textile Furnishings Mills

31411 Carpet and Rug Mills
See industry description for 314110 below.

314110 Carpet and Rug Mills

This industry comprises establishments primarily engaged in (1) manufacturing woven, tufted, and other carpets and rugs, such as art squares, floor mattings, needlepunch carpeting, and door mats and mattings, from textile materials or from twisted paper, grasses, reeds, sisal, jute, or rags and/or (2) finishing carpets and rugs.

31412 Curtain and Linen Mills

This industry comprises establishments primarily engaged in manufacturing household textile products, such as curtains, draperies, linens, bedspreads, sheets, tablecloths, towels, and shower curtains, from purchased materials.

Cross-References. Establishments primarily engaged in—

- Weaving broadwoven fabrics—are classified in Industry 31321, Broadwoven Fabric Mills;
- Manufacturing lace curtains on lace machines—are classified in Industry 31324, Knit Fabric Mills;

- Manufacturing textile blanket, wardrobe, and laundry bags—are classified in Industry 31491, Textile Bag and Canvas Mills; and

- Manufacturing mops—are classified in Industry 33999, All Other Miscellaneous Manufacturing.

314121 Curtain and Drapery Mills^{US}

This U.S. industry comprises establishments primarily engaged in manufacturing window curtains and draperies from purchased fabrics or sheet goods. The curtains and draperies may be made on a stock or custom basis for sale to individual retail customers.

Cross-References.

Establishments primarily engaged in manufacturing lace curtains on lace machines are classified in U.S. Industry 313249, Other Knit Fabric and Lace Mills.

314129 Other Household Textile Product Mills^{US}

This U.S. industry comprises establishments primarily engaged in manufacturing household textile products (except window curtains and draperies), such as bedspreads, sheets, tablecloths, towels, and shower curtains, from purchased materials.

Cross-References. Establishments primarily engaged in—

- Weaving fabrics—are classified in Industry 313210, Broadwoven Fabric Mills;

- Manufacturing blanket, laundry, and wardrobe bags—are classified in U.S. Industry 314911, Textile Bag Mills;

- Manufacturing mops—are classified in U.S. Industry 339994, Broom, Brush, and Mop Manufacturing; and

- Manufacturing window curtains and draperies—are classified in U.S. Industry 314121, Curtain and Drapery Mills.

3149 Other Textile Product Mills

This industry group comprises establishments primarily engaged in making textile products (except carpets and rugs, curtains and draperies, and other household textile products) from purchased materials.

US—United States industry only. CAN—United States and Canadian industries are comparable. MEX—United States and Mexican industries are comparable. Blank—Canadian, Mexican, and United States industries are comparable.

31491 Textile Bag and Canvas Mills

This industry comprises establishments primarily engaged in manufacturing textile bags, awnings, tents, and related products from purchased textile fabrics.

Cross-References. Establishments primarily engaged in—

- Manufacturing plastic bags—are classified in Industry 32611, Plastics Packaging Materials and Unlaminated Film and Sheet Manufacturing;
- Manufacturing canvas blinds and shades—are classified in Industry 33792, Blind and Shade Manufacturing;
- Manufacturing luggage—are classified in Industry 31699, Other Leather and Allied Product Manufacturing; and
- Manufacturing women's handbags and purses of leather or other material (except precious metal)—are classified in Industry 31699, Other Leather and Allied Product Manufacturing.

314911 Textile Bag Mills[US]

This U.S. industry comprises establishments primarily engaged in manufacturing bags from purchased textile fabrics or yarns.

Illustrative Examples:

Canvas bags manufacturing
Seed bags made from purchased woven
  or knitted materials
Laundry bags made from purchased
  woven or knitted materials

Textile bags made from purchased
  woven or knitted materials

Cross-References. Establishments primarily engaged in—

- Manufacturing plastics bags—are classified in U.S. Industry 326111, Plastics Bag and Pouch Manufacturing;
- Manufacturing luggage—are classified in U.S. Industry 316991, Luggage Manufacturing; and
- Manufacturing women's handbags and purses of leather or other material, except precious metal—are classified in U.S. Industry 316992, Women's Handbag and Purse Manufacturing.

314912 Canvas and Related Product Mills[US]

This U.S. industry comprises establishments primarily engaged in manufacturing canvas and canvas-like products, such as awnings, sails, tarpaulins, and tents, from purchased fabrics.

US—United States industry only. CAN—United States and Canadian industries are comparable. MEX—United States and Mexican industries are comparable. Blank—Canadian, Mexican, and United States industries are comparable.

Cross-References. Establishments primarily engaged in—

- Manufacturing canvas blinds and shades—are classified in Industry 337920, Blind and Shade Manufacturing; and
- Manufacturing canvas bags—are classified in U.S. Industry 314911, Textile Bag Mills.

31499 All Other Textile Product Mills

This industry comprises establishments primarily engaged in manufacturing nonapparel textile products (except carpet, rugs, curtains, linens, bags, and canvas products) from purchased materials. This industry includes establishments primarily engaged in decorative stitching such as embroidery or other art needlework on textile products, including apparel.

Illustrative Examples:

Batts and batting (except nonwoven fabrics) manufacturing
Fishing nets made from purchased materials
Carpet cutting and binding
Sleeping bags manufacturing
Diapers (except disposable) made from purchased fabric
Textile fire hoses made from purchased materials
Dust cloths made from purchased fabric
Embroidering on textile products for the trade
Weatherstripping made from purchased textiles

Cross-References. Establishments primarily engaged in—

- Manufacturing yarns and thread—are classified in Industry 31311, Fiber, Yarn, and Thread Mills;
- Manufacturing carpets and rugs—are classified in Industry 31411, Carpet and Rug Mills;
- Manufacturing apparel—are classified in Subsector 315, Apparel Manufacturing;
- Manufacturing curtains and linens—are classified in Industry 31412, Curtain and Linen Mills; and
- Manufacturing textile bags and canvas products—are classified in Industry 31491, Textile Bag and Canvas Mills.

314991 Rope, Cordage, and Twine Mills[US]

This U.S. industry comprises establishments primarily engaged in manufacturing rope, cable, cordage, twine, and related products from all materials (e.g., abaca, sisal, henequen, hemp, cotton, paper, jute, flax, manmade fibers including glass).

US—United States industry only. CAN—United States and Canadian industries are comparable. MEX—United States and Mexican industries are comparable. Blank—Canadian, Mexican, and United States industries are comparable.

Cross-References.

Establishments primarily engaged in spinning yarns and filaments are classified in U.S. Industry 313111, Yarn Spinning Mills.

314992 Tire Cord and Tire Fabric Mills[US]

This U.S. industry comprises establishments primarily engaged in manufacturing cord and fabric of polyester, rayon, cotton, glass, steel, or other materials for use in reinforcing rubber tires, industrial belting, and similar uses.

314999 All Other Miscellaneous Textile Product Mills[US]

This U.S. industry comprises establishments primarily engaged in manufacturing textile products (except carpets and rugs; curtains and linens; textile bags and canvas products; rope, cordage, and twine; and tire cords and tire fabrics) from purchased materials. These establishments may further embellish the textile products they manufacture with decorative stitching. Establishments primarily engaged in adding decorative stitching such as embroidery or other art needlework on textile products, including apparel, on a contract or fee basis for the trade, are included in this industry.

Illustrative Examples:

Batts and batting (except nonwoven fabrics) manufacturing
Embroidering on textile products or apparel for the trade
Carpet cutting and binding
Sleeping bags manufacturing

Diapers (except disposable) made from purchased materials
Textile fire hoses made from purchased materials
Dust cloths made from purchased fabric

Cross-References. Establishments primarily engaged in—

- Manufacturing yarns and thread—are classified in Industry 31311, Fiber, Yarn, and Thread Mills;

- Manufacturing carpets and rugs—are classified in Industry 314110, Carpet and Rug Mills;

- Manufacturing curtains and linens—are classified in Industry 31412, Curtain and Linen Mills;

- Manufacturing textile bags and canvas products—are classified in Industry 31491, Textile Bag and Canvas Mills;

- Manufacturing rope, cordage, and twine—are classified in U.S. Industry 314991, Rope, Cordage, and Twine Mills; and

---

US—United States industry only. CAN—United States and Canadian industries are comparable. MEX—United States and Mexican industries are comparable. Blank—Canadian, Mexican, and United States industries are comparable.

- Manufacturing tire cords and tire fabrics—are classified in U.S. Industry 314992, Tire Cord and Tire Fabric Mills.

315 Apparel Manufacturing

Industries in the Apparel Manufacturing subsector group establishments with two distinct manufacturing processes: (1) cut and sew (i.e., purchasing fabric and cutting and sewing to make a garment), and (2) the manufacture of garments in establishments that first knit fabric and then cut and sew the fabric into a garment. The Apparel Manufacturing subsector includes a diverse range of establishments manufacturing full lines of ready-to-wear apparel and custom apparel: apparel contractors, performing cutting or sewing operations on materials owned by others; jobbers performing entrepreneurial functions involved in apparel manufacture; and tailors, manufacturing custom garments for individual clients are all included. Knitting, when done alone, is classified in the Textile Mills subsector, but when knitting is combined with the production of complete garments, the activity is classified in Apparel Manufacturing.

3151 Apparel Knitting Mills

This industry group comprises establishments primarily engaged in knitting apparel or knitting fabric and then manufacturing apparel. This industry group includes jobbers performing entrepreneurial functions involved in knitting apparel and accessories. Knitting fabric, without manufacturing apparel, is classified in Subsector 313, Textile Mills.

31511 Hosiery and Sock Mills

This industry comprises establishments primarily engaged in knitting or knitting and finishing hosiery and socks.

Cross-References. Establishments primarily engaged in—

- Manufacturing orthopedic hosiery—are classified in Industry 33911, Medical Equipment and Supplies Manufacturing;

- Manufacturing slipper socks from purchased socks—are classified in Industry 31621, Footwear Manufacturing; and

- Finishing apparel products only—are classified in Industry 31331, Textile and Fabric Finishing Mills.

US—United States industry only. CAN—United States and Canadian industries are comparable. MEX—United States and Mexican industries are comparable. Blank—Canadian, Mexican, and United States industries are comparable.

315111 Sheer Hosiery Mills[US]

This U.S. industry comprises establishments primarily engaged in knitting or knitting and finishing women's, misses', and girls' full-length and knee-length sheer hosiery (except socks).

Cross-References. Establishments primarily engaged in—

- Knitting or knitting and finishing socks—are classified in U.S. Industry 315119, Other Hosiery and Sock Mills;

- Finishing apparel products only—are classified in U.S. Industry 313312, Textile and Fabric Finishing (except Broadwoven Fabric) Mills; and

- Manufacturing orthopedic hosiery—are classified in U.S. Industry 339113, Surgical Appliance and Supplies Manufacturing.

315119 Other Hosiery and Sock Mills[US]

This U.S. industry comprises establishments primarily engaged in knitting or knitting and finishing hosiery (except women's, misses', and girls' full-length and knee-length sheer hosiery).

Cross-References. Establishments primarily engaged in—

- Knitting or knitting and finishing women's, misses', and girls' full-length and knee-length sheer hosiery—are classified in U.S. Industry 315111, Sheer Hosiery Mills;

- Manufacturing orthopedic hosiery—are classified in U.S. Industry 339113, Surgical Appliance and Supplies Manufacturing;

- Finishing apparel products only—are classified in U.S. Industry 313312, Textile and Fabric Finishing (except Broadwoven Fabric) Mills; and

- Manufacturing slipper socks from purchased socks—are classified in U.S. Industry 316212, House Slipper Manufacturing.

31519 Other Apparel Knitting Mills

This industry comprises establishments primarily engaged in one of the following: (1) knitting underwear, outerwear, and/or nightwear; (2) knitting fabric and manufacturing underwear, outerwear, and/or nightwear; or (3) knitting, manufacturing, and finishing knit underwear, outerwear, and/or nightwear.

US—United States industry only. CAN—United States and Canadian industries are comparable. MEX—United States and Mexican industries are comparable. Blank—Canadian, Mexican, and United States industries are comparable.

Cross-References. Establishments primarily engaged in—

- Manufacturing outerwear, underwear, and nightwear from purchased fabric—are classified in Industry Group 3152, Cut and Sew Apparel Manufacturing; and

- Finishing apparel products only—are classified in Industry 31331, Textile and Fabric Finishing Mills.

315191 Outerwear Knitting Mills^{US}

This U.S. industry comprises establishments primarily engaged in one or more of the following: (1) knitting outerwear; (2) knitting fabric and manufacturing outerwear; and (3) knitting, manufacturing, and finishing knit outerwear. Examples of products made in knit outerwear mills are shirts, shorts, sweat suits, sweaters, gloves, and pants.

Cross-References. Establishments primarily engaged in—

- Manufacturing outerwear from purchased fabric—are classified in Industry Group 3152, Cut and Sew Apparel Manufacturing;

- Finishing apparel products only—are classified in U.S. Industry 313312, Textile and Fabric Finishing (except Broadwoven Fabric) Mills; and

- Knitting underwear and nightwear, knitting fabric and manufacturing underwear and nightwear, or knitting, manufacturing, and finishing knit underwear and nightwear—are classified in U.S. Industry 315192, Underwear and Nightwear Knitting Mills.

315192 Underwear and Nightwear Knitting Mills^{US}

This U.S. industry comprises establishments primarily engaged in one of the following: (1) knitting underwear and nightwear; (2) knitting fabric and manufacturing underwear and nightwear; or (3) knitting, manufacturing, and finishing knit underwear and nightwear. Examples of products produced in underwear and nightwear knitting mills are briefs, underwear T-shirts, pajamas, nightshirts, foundation garments, and panties.

Cross-References. Establishments primarily engaged in—

- Manufacturing underwear and nightwear from purchased fabric—are classified in Industry Group 3152, Cut and Sew Apparel Manufacturing; and

- Finishing apparel products only—are classified in U.S. Industry 313312, Textile and Fabric Finishing (except Broadwoven Fabric) Mills.

US—United States industry only. CAN—United States and Canadian industries are comparable. MEX—United States and Mexican industries are comparable. Blank—Canadian, Mexican, and United States industries are comparable.

3152 Cut and Sew Apparel Manufacturing

This industry group comprises establishments primarily engaged in manufacturing cut and sew apparel from woven fabric or purchased knit fabric. Included in this industry group is a diverse range of establishments manufacturing full lines of ready-to-wear apparel and custom apparel: apparel contractors, performing cutting or sewing operations on materials owned by others; jobbers performing entrepreneurial functions involved in apparel manufacture; and tailors, manufacturing custom garments for individual clients. Establishments weaving or knitting fabric, without manufacturing apparel, are classified in Subsector 313, Textile Mills.

31521 Cut and Sew Apparel Contractors^{CAN}

This industry comprises establishments commonly referred to as contractors primarily engaged in (1) cutting materials owned by others for apparel and accessories and/or (2) sewing materials owned by others for apparel and accessories.

Cross-References. Establishments primarily engaged in—

- Manufacturing men's and boys' apparel from purchased fabric—are classified in Industry 31522, Men's and Boys' Cut and Sew Apparel Manufacturing;

- Manufacturing women's and girls' apparel from purchased fabric—are classified in Industry 31523, Women's and Girls' Cut and Sew Apparel Manufacturing;

- Manufacturing infants' apparel and all other cut and sew apparel from purchased fabric—are classified in Industry 31529, Other Cut and Sew Apparel Manufacturing; and

- Manufacturing apparel accessories from purchased fabric—are classified in Industry 31599, Apparel Accessories and Other Apparel Manufacturing.

315211 Men's and Boys' Cut and Sew Apparel Contractors^{US}

This U.S. industry comprises establishments commonly referred to as contractors primarily engaged in (1) cutting materials owned by others for men's and boys' apparel and/or (2) sewing materials owned by others for men's and boys' apparel.

Cross-References. Establishments primarily engaged in—

- Manufacturing men's and boys' apparel from purchased fabric—are classified in Industry 31522, Men's and Boys' Cut and Sew Apparel Manufacturing;

US—United States industry only. CAN—United States and Canadian industries are comparable. MEX—United States and Mexican industries are comparable. Blank—Canadian, Mexican, and United States industries are comparable.

- Manufacturing infants' apparel from purchased fabric—are classified in U.S. Industry 315291, Infants' Cut and Sew Apparel Manufacturing;
- Manufacturing men's and boys' apparel accessories from purchased fabric—are classified in Industry 31599, Apparel Accessories and Other Apparel Manufacturing; and
- Embroidering men's and boys' apparel on a contract or fee basis for the trade—are classified in Industry 314999, All Other Miscellaneous Textile Product Mills.

315212 Women's, Girls', and Infants' Cut and Sew Apparel Contractors[US]

This U.S. industry comprises establishments commonly referred to as contractors primarily engaged in (1) cutting materials owned by others for women's, girls', and infants' apparel and accessories and/or (2) sewing materials owned by others for women's, girls', and infants' apparel and accessories.

Cross-References. Establishments primarily engaged in—

- Manufacturing women's and girls' apparel from purchased fabric—are classified in Industry 31523, Women's and Girls' Cut and Sew Apparel Manufacturing;
- Manufacturing infants' apparel from purchased fabric—are classified in U.S. Industry 315291, Infants' Cut and Sew Apparel Manufacturing;
- Manufacturing women's, girls', and infants' apparel accessories from purchased fabric—are classified in Industry 31599, Apparel Accessories and Other Apparel Manufacturing; and
- Embroidering women's, girls', and infants' apparel on a contract or fee basis for the trade—are classified in Industry 314999, All Other Miscellaneous Textile Product Mills.

31522 Men's and Boys' Cut and Sew Apparel Manufacturing[CAN]

This industry comprises establishments primarily engaged in manufacturing men's and boys' cut and sew apparel from purchased fabric. Men's and boys' clothing jobbers, who perform entrepreneurial functions involved in apparel manufacture, including buying raw materials, designing and preparing samples, arranging for apparel to be made from their materials, and marketing finished apparel, are included.

US—United States industry only. CAN—United States and Canadian industries are comparable. MEX—United States and Mexican industries are comparable. Blank—Canadian, Mexican, and United States industries are comparable.

Cross-References. Establishments primarily engaged in—

- Cutting and/or sewing materials owned by others for men's and boys' apparel—are classified in Industry 31521, Cut and Sew Apparel Contractors;

- Knitting men's and boys' apparel or knitting fabric and manufacturing men's and boys' apparel—are classified in Industry Group 3151, Apparel Knitting Mills; and

- Manufacturing fur or leather apparel and team athletic uniforms—are classified in Industry 31529, Other Cut and Sew Apparel Manufacturing.

315221 Men's and Boys' Cut and Sew Underwear and Nightwear Manufacturing[CAN]

This U.S. industry comprises establishments primarily engaged in manufacturing men's and boys' underwear and nightwear from purchased fabric. Men's and boys' underwear and nightwear jobbers, who perform entrepreneurial functions involved in apparel manufacture, including buying raw materials, designing and preparing samples, arranging for apparel to be made from their materials, and marketing finished apparel, are included. Examples of products made by these establishments are briefs, bathrobes, underwear T-shirts and shorts, nightshirts, and pajamas.

Cross-References. Establishments primarily engaged in—

- Knitting men's and boys' underwear and nightwear and/or knitting and manufacturing men's and boys' underwear and nightwear—are classified in U.S. Industry 315192, Underwear and Nightwear Knitting Mills; and

- Cutting and/or sewing materials owned by others for men's and boys' underwear and nightwear—are classified in U.S. Industry 315211, Men's and Boys' Cut and Sew Apparel Contractors.

315222 Men's and Boys' Cut and Sew Suit, Coat, and Overcoat Manufacturing[CAN]

This U.S. industry comprises establishments primarily engaged in manufacturing men's and boys' suits, overcoats, sport coats, tuxedos, dress uniforms, and other tailored apparel (except fur and leather) from purchased fabric. Men's and boys' suit, coat, and overcoat jobbers, who perform entrepreneurial functions involved in apparel manufacture, including buying raw materials, designing and preparing samples, arranging for apparel to be made from their materials, and marketing finished apparel, are included.

US—United States industry only. CAN—United States and Canadian industries are comparable. MEX—United States and Mexican industries are comparable. Blank—Canadian, Mexican, and United States industries are comparable.

Cross-References. Establishments primarily engaged in—

- Manufacturing men's and boys' nontailored coats and jackets such as down coats and windbreakers made from purchased fabric—are classified in U.S. Industry 315228, Men's and Boys' Cut and Sew Other Outerwear Manufacturing;

- Manufacturing fur and leather apparel—are classified in U.S. Industry 315292, Fur and Leather Apparel Manufacturing;

- Manufacturing men's and boys' washable service apparel from purchased fabric—are classified in U.S. Industry 315225, Men's and Boys' Cut and Sew Work Clothing Manufacturing;

- Manufacturing men's and boys' team athletic uniforms from purchased fabric—are classified in U.S. Industry 315299, All Other Cut and Sew Apparel Manufacturing; and

- Cutting and/or sewing materials owned by others for men's and boys' suits, coats, and overcoats—are classified in U.S. Industry 315211, Men's and Boys' Cut and Sew Apparel Contractors.

315223 Men's and Boys' Cut and Sew Shirt (except Work Shirt) Manufacturing[US]

This U.S. industry comprises establishments primarily engaged in manufacturing men's and boys' outerwear shirts from purchased fabric. Men's and boys' shirt (except work shirt) jobbers, who perform entrepreneurial functions involved in apparel manufacture, including buying raw materials, designing and preparing samples, arranging for apparel to be made from their materials, and marketing finished apparel, are included. Unisex outerwear shirts, such as T-shirts and sweatshirts that are sized without specific reference to gender (i.e., adult S, M, L, XL) are included in this industry.

Cross-References. Establishments primarily engaged in—

- Manufacturing men's and boys' work shirts from purchased fabric—are classified in U.S. Industry 315225, Men's and Boys' Cut and Sew Work Clothing Manufacturing;

- Manufacturing men's and boys' underwear T-shirts and underwear tank tops from purchased fabric—are classified in U.S. Industry 315221, Men's and Boys' Cut and Sew Underwear and Nightwear Manufacturing;

- Cutting and/or sewing materials owned by others for men's and boys' shirts—are classified in U.S. Industry 315211, Men's and Boys' Cut and Sew Apparel Contractors; and

---

US—United States industry only. CAN—United States and Canadian industries are comparable. MEX—United States and Mexican industries are comparable. Blank—Canadian, Mexican, and United States industries are comparable.

- Knitting men's and boys' outerwear shirts or knitting fabric and manufacturing men's and boys' outerwear shirts—are classified in U.S. Industry 315191, Outerwear Knitting Mills.

315224 Men's and Boys' Cut and Sew Trouser, Slack, and Jean Manufacturing[US]

This U.S. industry comprises establishments primarily engaged in manufacturing men's and boys' jeans, dungarees, and other separate trousers and slacks (except work pants) from purchased fabric. Men's and boys' trouser, slack, and jean jobbers, who perform entrepreneurial functions involved in apparel manufacture, including buying raw materials, designing and preparing samples, arranging for apparel to be made from their materials, and marketing finished apparel, are included.

Cross-References. Establishments primarily engaged in—

- Manufacturing men's and boys' work pants from purchased fabric—are classified in U.S. Industry 315225, Men's and Boys' Cut and Sew Work Clothing Manufacturing;
- Manufacturing fur and leather apparel—are classified in U.S. Industry 315292, Fur and Leather Apparel Manufacturing;
- Manufacturing men's and boys' sweatpants and shorts from purchased fabric—are classified in U.S. Industry 315228, Men's and Boys' Cut and Sew Other Outerwear Manufacturing; and
- Cutting and/or sewing materials owned by others for men's and boys' separate trousers, slacks, and jeans—are classified in U.S. Industry 315211, Men's and Boys' Cut and Sew Apparel Contractors.

315225 Men's and Boys' Cut and Sew Work Clothing Manufacturing[US]

This U.S. industry comprises establishments primarily engaged in manufacturing men's and boys' work shirts, work pants (excluding jeans and dungarees), other work clothing, and washable service apparel from purchased fabric. Men's and boys' work clothing jobbers, who perform entrepreneurial functions involved in apparel manufacture, including buying raw materials, designing and preparing samples, arranging for apparel to be made from their materials, and marketing finished apparel, are included. Examples of products made by these establishments are washable service apparel, laboratory coats, work shirts, work pants (except jeans and dungarees), and hospital apparel.

US—United States industry only. CAN—United States and Canadian industries are comparable. MEX—United States and Mexican industries are comparable. Blank—Canadian, Mexican, and United States industries are comparable.

Cross-References. Establishments primarily engaged in—

- Manufacturing men's and boys' separate trousers, slacks, and pants, including jeans and dungarees from purchased fabric—are classified in U.S. Industry 315224, Men's and Boys' Cut and Sew Trouser, Slack, and Jean Manufacturing; and

- Cutting and/or sewing materials owned by others for men's and boys' work clothing—are classified in U.S. Industry 315211, Men's and Boys' Cut and Sew Apparel Contractors.

315228 Men's and Boys' Cut and Sew Other Outerwear Manufacturing[US]

This U.S. industry comprises establishments primarily engaged in manufacturing men's and boys' cut and sew outerwear from purchased fabric (except underwear, nightwear, shirts, suits, overcoats and tailored coats, separate trousers and slacks, and work clothing). Men's and boys' other outerwear jobbers, who perform entrepreneurial functions involved in apparel manufacture, including buying raw materials, designing and preparing samples, arranging for apparel to be made from their materials, and marketing finished apparel, are included. Unisex sweatpants and similar garments that are sized without specific reference to gender (i.e., adult S, M, L, XL) are also included in this industry. Examples of products made by these establishments are athletic clothing (except athletic uniforms), bathing suits, down coats, outerwear shorts, windbreakers and jackets, and jogging suits.

Cross-References. Establishments primarily engaged in—

- Manufacturing men's and boys' athletic uniforms from purchased fabric—are classified in U.S. Industry 315299, All Other Cut and Sew Apparel Manufacturing;

- Manufacturing leather and fur apparel—are classified in U.S. Industry 315292, Fur and Leather Apparel Manufacturing;

- Knitting men's and boys' apparel or knitting fabric and manufacturing men's and boys' apparel—are classified in Industry Group 3151, Apparel Knitting Mills;

- Cutting and/or sewing materials owned by others for men's and boys' apparel—are classified in U.S. Industry 315211, Men's and Boys' Cut and Sew Apparel Contractors;

- Manufacturing men's and boys' underwear and nightwear from purchased fabric—are classified in U.S. Industry 315221, Men's and Boys' Cut and Sew Underwear and Nightwear Manufacturing;

US—United States industry only. CAN—United States and Canadian industries are comparable. MEX—United States and Mexican industries are comparable. Blank—Canadian, Mexican, and United States industries are comparable.

- Manufacturing men's and boys' tailored suits, coats, and overcoats from purchased fabric—are classified in U.S. Industry 315222, Men's and Boys' Cut and Sew Suit, Coat, and Overcoat Manufacturing;

- Manufacturing men's and boys' outerwear shirts (except work shirts) from purchased fabric—are classified in U.S. Industry 315223, Men's and Boys' Cut and Sew Shirt (except Work Shirt) Manufacturing;

- Manufacturing men's and boys' separate pants, trousers, and slacks from purchased fabric—are classified in U.S. Industry 315224, Men's and Boys' Cut and Sew Trouser, Slack, and Jean Manufacturing; and

- Manufacturing men's and boys' work clothing from purchased fabric—are classified in U.S. Industry 315225, Men's and Boys' Cut and Sew Work Clothing Manufacturing.

31523 Women's and Girls' Cut and Sew Apparel Manufacturing[CAN]

This industry comprises establishments primarily engaged in manufacturing women's and girls' apparel from purchased fabric. Women's and girls' clothing jobbers, who perform entrepreneurial functions involved in apparel manufacture, including buying raw materials, designing and preparing samples, arranging for apparel to be made from their materials, and marketing finished apparel, are included.

Cross-References. Establishments primarily engaged in—

- Knitting women's and girls' apparel or knitting fabric and manufacturing women's and girls' apparel—are classified in Industry Group 3151, Apparel Knitting Mills;

- Manufacturing unisex outerwear garments, such as T-shirts, sweatshirts, and sweatpants that are sized without reference to specific gender (i.e., adult S, M, L, XL)—are classified in Industry 31522, Men's and Boys' Cut and Sew Apparel Manufacturing;

- Cutting and/or sewing materials owned by others for women's and girls' apparel—are classified in Industry 31521, Cut and Sew Apparel Contractors; and

- Manufacturing fur or leather apparel and team athletic uniforms—are classified in Industry 31529, Other Cut and Sew Apparel Manufacturing.

315231 Women's and Girls' Cut and Sew Lingerie, Loungewear, and Nightwear Manufacturing[CAN]

This U.S. industry comprises establishments primarily engaged in manufacturing women's and girls' bras, girdles, and other underwear; lingerie; loungewear; and nightwear from purchased fabric. Women's and girls' lingerie, loungewear, and nightwear jobbers, who perform entrepreneurial functions involved in apparel manufacture, including buying raw materials, designing and preparing samples, arranging for apparel to be made from their materials, and marketing finished apparel, are included. Examples of products made by these establishments are bathrobes, foundation garments, nightgowns, pajamas, panties, and slips.

Cross-References. Establishments primarily engaged in—

- Knitting women's and girls' underwear, nightwear, and lingerie or knitting fabric and manufacturing women's and girls' underwear, nightwear, and lingerie—are classified in U.S. Industry 315192, Underwear and Nightwear Knitting Mills; and

- Cutting and/or sewing materials owned by others for women's and girls' underwear, nightwear, and lingerie—are classified in U.S. Industry 315212, Women's, Girls', and Infants' Cut and Sew Apparel Contractors.

315232 Women's and Girls' Cut and Sew Blouse and Shirt Manufacturing[CAN]

This U.S. industry comprises establishments primarily engaged in manufacturing women's and girls' blouses and shirts from purchased fabric. Women's and girls' blouse and shirt jobbers, who perform entrepreneurial functions involved in apparel manufacture, including buying raw materials, designing and preparing samples, arranging for apparel to be made from their materials, and marketing finished apparel, are included.

Cross-References. Establishments primarily engaged in—

- Knitting women's and girls' blouses, shirts, and tops or knitting fabric and manufacturing women's and girls' blouses, shirts, and tops—are classified in U.S. Industry 315191, Outerwear Knitting Mills;

- Manufacturing unisex outerwear shirts, such as T-shirts and sweatshirts that are sized without specific reference to gender (i.e., adult S, M, L, XL)— are classified in U.S. Industry 315223, Men's and Boys' Cut and Sew Shirt (except Work Shirt) Manufacturing; and

- Cutting and/or sewing materials owned by others for women's and girls' shirts and blouses—are classified in U.S. Industry 315212, Women's, Girls', and Infants' Cut and Sew Apparel Contractors.

315233 Women's and Girls' Cut and Sew Dress Manufacturing[CAN]

This U.S. industry comprises establishments primarily engaged in manufacturing women's and girls' dresses from purchased fabric. Women's and girls' dress

US—United States industry only. CAN—United States and Canadian industries are comparable. MEX—United States and Mexican industries are comparable. Blank—Canadian, Mexican, and United States industries are comparable.

http://www.census.gov/naics

jobbers, who perform entrepreneurial functions involved in apparel manufacture, including buying raw materials, designing and preparing samples, arranging for apparel to be made from their materials, and marketing finished apparel, are included.

Cross-References. Establishments primarily engaged in—

- Knitting women's and girls' dresses or knitting fabric and manufacturing women's and girls' dresses—are classified in U.S. Industry 315191, Outerwear Knitting Mills; and

- Cutting and/or sewing materials owned by others for women's and girls' dresses—are classified in U.S. Industry 315212, Women's, Girls', and Infants' Cut and Sew Apparel Contractors.

315234 Women's and Girls' Cut and Sew Suit, Coat, Tailored Jacket, and Skirt Manufacturing[CAN]

This U.S. industry comprises establishments primarily engaged in manufacturing women's and girls' suits, pantsuits, skirts, tailored jackets, vests, raincoats, and other tailored coats, (except fur and leather coats) from purchased fabric. Women's and girls' suit, coat, tailored jacket, and skirt jobbers, who perform entrepreneurial functions involved in apparel manufacture, including buying raw materials, designing and preparing samples, arranging for apparel to be made from their materials, and marketing finished apparel, are included.

Cross-References. Establishments primarily engaged in—

- Manufacturing women's and girls' team athletic uniforms from purchased fabric—are classified in U.S. Industry 315299, All Other Cut and Sew Apparel Manufacturing;

- Manufacturing women's and girls' separate slacks, jeans, pants, and nontailored coats and jackets, such as down coats and windbreakers from purchased fabric—are classified in U.S. Industry 315239, Women's and Girls' Cut and Sew Other Outerwear Manufacturing;

- Manufacturing fur and leather apparel—are classified in U.S. Industry 315292, Fur and Leather Apparel Manufacturing;

- Knitting women's and girls' tailored skirts, suits, vests, and coats or knitting fabric and manufacturing women's and girls' tailored skirts, suits, vests, and coats—are classified in U.S. Industry 315191, Outerwear Knitting Mills; and

- Cutting and/or sewing materials owned by others for women's and girls' suits, coats, tailored jackets, and skirts—are classified in U.S. Industry 315212, Women's, Girls', and Infants' Cut and Sew Apparel Contractors.

US—United States industry only. CAN—United States and Canadian industries are comparable. MEX—United States and Mexican industries are comparable. Blank—Canadian, Mexican, and United States industries are comparable.

315239 Women's and Girls' Cut and Sew Other Outerwear Manufacturing[CAN]

This U.S. industry comprises establishments primarily engaged in manufacturing women's and girls' cut and sew apparel from purchased fabric (except underwear, lingerie, nightwear, blouses, shirts, dresses, suits, tailored coats, tailored jackets, and skirts). Women's and girls' other outerwear clothing jobbers, who perform entrepreneurial functions involved in apparel manufacture, including buying raw materials, designing and preparing samples, arranging for apparel to be made from their materials, and marketing finished apparel, are included. Examples of products made by these establishments are bathing suits, down coats, sweaters, jogging suits, outerwear pants and shorts, and windbreakers.

Cross-References. Establishments primarily engaged in—

- Manufacturing women's and girls' team athletic uniforms from purchased fabric—are classified in U.S. Industry 315299, All Other Cut and Sew Apparel Manufacturing;

- Knitting women's and girls' apparel or knitting fabric and manufacturing women's and girls' apparel—are classified in U.S. Industry 315191, Outerwear Knitting Mills;

- Manufacturing women's and girls' fur and leather apparel—are classified in U.S. Industry 315292, Fur and Leather Apparel Manufacturing;

- Cutting and/or sewing materials owned by others for women's and girls' apparel—are classified in U.S. Industry 315212, Women's, Girls', and Infants' Cut and Sew Apparel Contractors;

- Manufacturing women's and girls' lingerie, loungewear, and nightwear from purchased fabric—are classified in U.S. Industry 315231, Women's and Girls' Cut and Sew Lingerie, Loungewear, and Nightwear Manufacturing;

- Manufacturing women's and girls' blouses and outerwear shirts from purchased fabric—are classified in U.S. Industry 315232, Women's and Girls' Cut and Sew Blouse and Shirt Manufacturing;

- Manufacturing unisex sweatpants and similar outerwear garments that are sized without specific reference to gender (i.e., adult S, M, L, XL)—are classified in U.S. Industry 315228, Men's and Boys' Cut and Sew Other Outerwear Manufacturing;

- Manufacturing women's and girls' dresses from purchased fabric—are classified in U.S. Industry 315233, Women's and Girls' Cut and Sew Dress Manufacturing; and

---

US—United States industry only. CAN—United States and Canadian industries are comparable. MEX—United States and Mexican industries are comparable. Blank—Canadian, Mexican, and United States industries are comparable.

- Manufacturing women's and girls' suits, skirts, and tailored coats and jackets from purchased fabric—are classified in U.S. Industry 315234, Women's and Girls' Cut and Sew Suit, Coat, Tailored Jacket, and Skirt Manufacturing.

31529 Other Cut and Sew Apparel Manufacturing[CAN]

This industry comprises establishments primarily engaged in manufacturing cut and sew apparel from purchased fabric (except men's, boys', women's, and girls' apparel). This industry includes establishments manufacturing apparel, such as fur apparel, leather apparel, infants' apparel, costumes, and clerical vestments.

Cross-References. Establishments primarily engaged in—

- Manufacturing men's and boys' apparel from purchased fabric—are classified in Industry 31522, Men's and Boys' Cut and Sew Apparel Manufacturing;
- Manufacturing women's and girls' apparel from purchased fabric—are classified in Industry 31523, Women's and Girls' Cut and Sew Apparel Manufacturing;
- Knitting apparel or knitting fabric and manufacturing apparel—are classified in Industry Group 3151, Apparel Knitting Mills;
- Cutting and/or sewing materials owned by others for apparel—are classified in Industry 31521, Cut and Sew Apparel Contractors;
- Manufacturing fur and leather mittens and gloves—are classified in Industry 31599, Apparel Accessories and Other Apparel Manufacturing; and
- Dyeing and dressing furs—are classified in Industry 31611, Leather and Hide Tanning and Finishing.

315291 Infants' Cut and Sew Apparel Manufacturing[CAN]

This U.S. industry comprises establishments primarily engaged in manufacturing infants' dresses, blouses, shirts, and all other infants' wear from purchased fabric. Infants' clothing jobbers, who perform entrepreneurial functions involved in apparel manufacture, including buying raw materials, designing and preparing samples, arranging for apparel to be made from their materials, and marketing finished apparel, are included. For the purposes of classification, the term ''infants' apparel'' includes apparel for young children of an age not exceeding 24 months.

Cross-References. Establishments primarily engaged in—

- Knitting infants' apparel or knitting fabric and manufacturing infants' apparel—are classified in U.S. Industry 315191, Outerwear Knitting Mills; and

---

US—United States industry only. CAN—United States and Canadian industries are comparable. MEX—United States and Mexican industries are comparable. Blank—Canadian, Mexican, and United States industries are comparable.

- Cutting and/or sewing materials owned by others for infants' apparel—are classified in U.S. Industry 315212, Women's, Girls', and Infants' Cut and Sew Apparel Contractors.

315292 Fur and Leather Apparel Manufacturing[CAN]

This U.S. industry comprises establishments primarily engaged in manufacturing cut and sew fur and leather apparel, and sheep-lined clothing. Fur and leather apparel jobbers, who perform entrepreneurial functions involved in apparel manufacture, including buying raw materials, designing and preparing samples, arranging for apparel to be made from their materials, and marketing finished apparel, are included.

Cross-References. Establishments primarily engaged in—

- Cutting and/or sewing materials owned by others for apparel—are classified in Industry 31521, Cut and Sew Apparel Contractors;
- Dyeing and dressing furs—are classified in Industry 316110, Leather and Hide Tanning and Finishing; and
- Manufacturing fur and leather mittens and gloves—are classified in U.S. Industry 315992, Glove and Mitten Manufacturing.

315299 All Other Cut and Sew Apparel Manufacturing[CAN]

This U.S. industry comprises establishments primarily engaged in manufacturing cut and sew apparel from purchased fabric (except cut and sew apparel contractors; men's and boys' cut and sew underwear, nightwear, suits, coats, shirts, trousers, work clothing, and other outerwear; women's and girls' lingerie, blouses, shirts, dresses, suits, coats, and other outerwear; infants' apparel; and fur and leather apparel). Clothing jobbers for these products, who perform entrepreneurial functions involved in apparel manufacture, including buying raw materials, designing and preparing samples, arranging for apparel to be made from their materials, and marketing finished apparel, are included. Examples of products made by these establishments are team athletic uniforms, band uniforms, academic caps and gowns, clerical vestments, and costumes.

Cross-References. Establishments primarily engaged in—

- Cutting and/or sewing materials owned by others for apparel—are classified in Industry 31521, Cut and Sew Apparel Contractors;
- Knitting apparel or knitting fabric and manufacturing apparel—are classified in Industry Group 3151, Apparel Knitting Mills;

- Manufacturing men's and boys' underwear and nightwear from purchased fabric—are classified in U.S. Industry 315221, Men's and Boys' Cut and Sew Underwear and Nightwear Manufacturing;

- Manufacturing men's and boys' suits, coats, and overcoats from purchased fabric—are classified in U.S. Industry 315222, Men's and Boys' Cut and Sew Suit, Coat, and Overcoat Manufacturing;

- Manufacturing men's and boys' shirts (except work shirts) from purchased fabric—are classified in U.S. Industry 315223, Men's and Boys' Cut and Sew Shirt (except Work Shirt) Manufacturing;

- Manufacturing men's and boys' pants, slacks, trousers, and jeans from purchased fabric—are classified in U.S. Industry 315224, Men's and Boys' Cut and Sew Trouser, Slack, and Jean Manufacturing;

- Manufacturing men's and boys' work clothing from purchased fabric—are classified in U.S. Industry 315225, Men's and Boys' Cut and Sew Work Clothing Manufacturing;

- Manufacturing other men's and boys' outerwear from purchased fabric—are classified in U.S. Industry 315228, Men's and Boys' Cut and Sew Other Outerwear Manufacturing;

- Manufacturing women's and girls' lingerie and nightwear from purchased fabric—are classified in U.S. Industry 315231, Women's and Girls' Cut and Sew Lingerie, Loungewear, and Nightwear Manufacturing;

- Manufacturing women's and girls' blouses and shirts from purchased fabric—are classified in U.S. Industry 315232, Women's and Girls' Cut and Sew Blouse and Shirt Manufacturing;

- Manufacturing women's and girls' dresses from purchased fabric—are classified in U.S. Industry 315233, Women's and Girls' Cut and Sew Dress Manufacturing;

- Manufacturing women's and girls' suits, tailored coats and jackets, and skirts from purchased fabric—are classified in U.S. Industry 315234, Women's and Girls' Cut and Sew Suit, Coat, Tailored Jacket, and Skirt Manufacturing;

- Manufacturing other women's and girls' outerwear from purchased fabric—are classified in U.S. Industry 315239, Women's and Girls' Cut and Sew Other Outerwear Manufacturing;

- Manufacturing infants' apparel from purchased fabric—are classified in U.S. Industry 315291, Infants' Cut and Sew Apparel Manufacturing; and

- Manufacturing fur and leather apparel—are classified in U.S. Industry 315292, Fur and Leather Apparel Manufacturing.

US—United States industry only. CAN—United States and Canadian industries are comparable. MEX—United States and Mexican industries are comparable. Blank—Canadian, Mexican, and United States industries are comparable.

3159 Apparel Accessories and Other Apparel Manufacturing

This industry group comprises establishments primarily engaged in manufacturing apparel accessories and other apparel (except apparel knitting mills, apparel contractors, men's and boys' cut and sew apparel, women's and girls' cut and sew apparel, infants' cut and sew apparel, fur and leather apparel, and all other cut and sew apparel). This industry group includes jobbers performing entrepreneurial functions involved in manufacturing apparel accessories.

31599 Apparel Accessories and Other Apparel Manufacturing

This industry comprises establishments primarily engaged in manufacturing apparel and accessories (except apparel knitting mills, cut and sew apparel contractors, men's and boys' cut and sew apparel, women's and girls' cut and sew apparel, and other cut and sew apparel). Jobbers, who perform entrepreneurial functions involved in apparel accessories manufacture, including buying raw materials, designing and preparing samples, arranging for apparel accessories to be made from their materials, and marketing finished apparel accessories, are included. Examples of products made by these establishments are belts, caps, gloves (except medical, sporting, safety), hats, and neckties.

Cross-References. Establishments primarily engaged in—

- Cutting and/or sewing materials owned by others for apparel accessories— are classified in Industry 31521, Cut and Sew Apparel Contractors;
- Manufacturing paper hats and caps—are classified in Industry 32229, Other Converted Paper Product Manufacturing;
- Manufacturing plastics or rubber hats and caps (except bathing caps)—are classified in Subsector 326, Plastics and Rubber Products Manufacturing;
- Manufacturing athletic gloves, such as boxing gloves, baseball gloves, golf gloves, batting gloves, and racquetball gloves—are classified in Industry 33992, Sporting and Athletic Goods Manufacturing;
- Manufacturing metal fabric, metal mesh, or rubber gloves—are classified in Industry 33911, Medical Equipment and Supplies Manufacturing;
- Knitting apparel, mittens, gloves, hats, and caps or knitting fabric and manufacturing apparel, mittens, gloves, hats, and caps—are classified in Industry Group 3151, Apparel Knitting Mills;
- Cutting and/or sewing materials owned by others for apparel—are classified in Industry 31521, Cut and Sew Apparel Contractors;
- Manufacturing men's and boys' underwear and outerwear from purchased fabric—are classified in Industry 31522, Men's and Boys' Cut and Sew Apparel Manufacturing;

US—United States industry only. CAN—United States and Canadian industries are comparable. MEX—United States and Mexican industries are comparable. Blank—Canadian, Mexican, and United States industries are comparable.

- Manufacturing women's and girls' underwear and outerwear from purchased fabric—are classified in Industry 31523, Women's and Girls' Cut and Sew Apparel Manufacturing; and

- Manufacturing other apparel from purchased fabric and manufacturing fur and leather apparel, hats, and caps—are classified in Industry 31529, Other Cut and Sew Apparel Manufacturing.

315991 Hat, Cap, and Millinery Manufacturing^{MEX}

This U.S. industry comprises establishments primarily engaged in manufacturing cut and sew hats, caps, millinery, and hat bodies from purchased fabric. Jobbers, who perform entrepreneurial functions involved in hat, cap, and millinery manufacture, including buying raw materials, designing and preparing samples, arranging for hats, caps, and millinery to be made from their materials, and marketing finished hats, caps, and millinery, are included.

Cross-References. Establishments primarily engaged in—

- Cutting and/or sewing materials owned by others for hats, caps, and millinery—are classified in Industry 31521, Cut and Sew Apparel Contractors;

- Manufacturing paper hats and caps—are classified in U.S. Industry 322299, All Other Converted Paper Product Manufacturing;

- Manufacturing plastics or rubber hats and caps (except bathing caps)—are classified in Subsector 326, Plastics and Rubber Products Manufacturing; and

- Manufacturing fur and leather hats and caps—are classified in U.S. Industry 315292, Fur and Leather Apparel Manufacturing.

315992 Glove and Mitten Manufacturing^{US}

This U.S. industry comprises establishments primarily engaged in manufacturing cut and sew gloves (except rubber, metal, and athletic gloves) and mittens from purchased fabric, fur, leather, or from combinations of fabric, fur, or leather. Jobbers, who perform entrepreneurial functions involved in glove and mitten manufacture, including buying raw materials, designing and preparing samples, arranging for gloves and mittens to be made from their materials, and marketing finished gloves and mittens, are included.

Cross-References. Establishments primarily engaged in—

- Cutting and/or sewing materials owned by others for gloves and mittens— are classified in Industry 31521, Cut and Sew Apparel Contractors;

US—United States industry only. CAN—United States and Canadian industries are comparable. MEX—United States and Mexican industries are comparable. Blank—Canadian, Mexican, and United States industries are comparable.

- Knitting mittens and gloves or knitting fabric and manufacturing mittens and gloves—are classified in U.S. Industry 315191, Outerwear Knitting Mills;
- Manufacturing athletic gloves, such as boxing gloves, baseball gloves, golf gloves, batting gloves, and racquetball gloves—are classified in Industry 339920, Sporting and Athletic Goods Manufacturing; and
- Manufacturing metal fabric, metal mesh, or rubber gloves—are classified in U.S. Industry 339113, Surgical Appliance and Supplies Manufacturing.

315993 Men's and Boys' Neckwear Manufacturing[US]

This U.S. industry comprises establishments primarily engaged in manufacturing men's and boys' cut and sew neckties, scarves, and mufflers from purchased fabric, leather, or from combinations of leather and fabric. Men's and boys' neckwear jobbers, who perform entrepreneurial functions involved in neckwear manufacture, including buying raw materials, designing and preparing samples, arranging for neckwear to be made from their materials, and marketing finished neckwear, are included.

Cross-References.

Establishments primarily engaged in cutting and/or sewing materials owned by others for men's and boys' neckwear are classified in U.S. Industry 315211, Men's and Boys' Cut and Sew Apparel Contractors.

315999 Other Apparel Accessories and Other Apparel Manufacturing[US]

This U.S. industry comprises establishments primarily engaged in manufacturing apparel and apparel accessories (except apparel knitting mills; cut and sew apparel contractors; cut and sew apparel; hats and caps; mittens and gloves; and men's and boys' neckwear). Jobbers for these products, who perform entrepreneurial functions involved in other apparel and accessory manufacture, including buying raw materials, designing and preparing samples, arranging for other apparel and accessories to be made from their materials, and marketing finished other apparel and accessories, are included. Examples of products made by these establishments are apparel trimmings and findings, belts, women's scarves, and suspenders.

Cross-References. Establishments primarily engaged in—

- Knitting apparel or knitting fabric and manufacturing apparel—are classified in Industry Group 3151, Apparel Knitting Mills;
- Cutting and/or sewing materials owned by others for apparel—are classified in Industry 31521, Cut and Sew Apparel Contractors;

US—United States industry only. CAN—United States and Canadian industries are comparable. MEX—United States and Mexican industries are comparable. Blank—Canadian, Mexican, and United States industries are comparable.

- Manufacturing men's and boys' cut and sew underwear and outerwear from purchased fabric—are classified in Industry 31522, Men's and Boys' Cut and Sew Apparel Manufacturing;

- Manufacturing women's and girls' cut and sew underwear and outerwear from purchased fabric—are classified in Industry 31523, Women's and Girls' Cut and Sew Apparel Manufacturing;

- Manufacturing infants' cut and sew apparel from purchased fabric—are classified in U.S. Industry 315291, Infants' Cut and Sew Apparel Manufacturing;

- Manufacturing fur and leather apparel—are classified in U.S. Industry 315292, Fur and Leather Apparel Manufacturing;

- Manufacturing hats, caps, and millinery—are classified in U.S. Industry 315991, Hat, Cap, and Millinery Manufacturing;

- Manufacturing gloves and mittens—are classified in U.S. Industry 315992, Glove and Mitten Manufacturing; and

- Manufacturing men's and boys' neckwear—are classified in U.S. Industry 315993, Men's and Boys' Neckwear Manufacturing.

316 Leather and Allied Product Manufacturing

Establishments in the Leather and Allied Product Manufacturing subsector transform hides into leather by tanning or curing and fabricating the leather into products for final consumption. It also includes the manufacture of similar products from other materials, including products (except apparel) made from "leather substitutes," such as rubber, plastics, or textiles. Rubber footwear, textile luggage, and plastics purses or wallets are examples of "leather substitute" products included in this group. The products made from leather substitutes are included in this subsector because they are made in similar ways leather products are made (e.g., luggage). They are made in the same establishments, so it is not practical to separate them.

The inclusion of leather making in this subsector is partly because leather tanning is a relatively small industry that has few close neighbors as a production process, partly because leather is an input to some of the other products classified in this subsector and partly for historical reasons.

3161 Leather and Hide Tanning and Finishing

31611 Leather and Hide Tanning and Finishing
See industry description for 316110 below.

US—United States industry only. CAN—United States and Canadian industries are comparable. MEX—United States and Mexican industries are comparable. Blank—Canadian, Mexican, and United States industries are comparable.

316110 Leather and Hide Tanning and Finishing

This industry comprises establishments primarily engaged in one or more of the following: (1) tanning, currying, and finishing hides and skins; (2) having others process hides and skins on a contract basis; and (3) dyeing or dressing furs.

3162 Footwear Manufacturing

31621 Footwear Manufacturing

This industry comprises establishments primarily engaged in manufacturing footwear (except orthopedic extension footwear).

Cross-References.

Establishments primarily engaged in manufacturing orthopedic extension footwear are classified in Industry 33911, Medical Equipment and Supplies Manufacturing.

316211 Rubber and Plastics Footwear Manufacturing[US]

This U.S. industry comprises establishments primarily engaged in manufacturing rubber and plastics footwear with vulcanized rubber or plastics soles, molded or cemented to rubber, plastics, or fabric uppers, and rubber and plastics protective footwear.

Cross-References. Establishments primarily engaged in—

- Manufacturing house slippers with fabric uppers and rubber or plastics soles—are classified in U.S. Industry 316212, House Slipper Manufacturing;
- Manufacturing men's footwear (except athletic) with leather or vinyl uppers, regardless of sole material—are classified in U.S. Industry 316213, Men's Footwear (except Athletic) Manufacturing;
- Manufacturing women's footwear (except athletic) with leather or vinyl uppers, regardless of sole material—are classified in U.S. Industry 316214, Women's Footwear (except Athletic) Manufacturing; and
- Manufacturing youths' children's and infants' footwear and athletic footwear with leather or vinyl uppers, regardless of sole material—are classified in U.S. Industry 316219, Other Footwear Manufacturing.

316212 House Slipper Manufacturing^{US}

This U.S. industry comprises establishments primarily engaged in manufacturing house slippers and slipper socks, regardless of material.

316213 Men's Footwear (except Athletic) Manufacturing^{US}

This U.S. industry comprises establishments primarily engaged in manufacturing men's footwear designed primarily for dress, street, and work. This industry includes men's shoes with rubber or plastics soles and leather or vinyl uppers.

Cross-References. Establishments primarily engaged in—

- Manufacturing men's footwear with fabric uppers and rubber or plastics soles—are classified in U.S. Industry 316211, Rubber and Plastics Footwear Manufacturing;
- Manufacturing orthopedic extension footwear—are classified in U.S. Industry 339113, Surgical Appliance and Supplies Manufacturing; and
- Manufacturing men's leather or vinyl upper athletic footwear and youths' and boys' footwear—are classified in U.S. Industry 316219, Other Footwear Manufacturing.

316214 Women's Footwear (except Athletic) Manufacturing^{US}

This U.S. industry comprises establishments primarily engaged in manufacturing women's footwear designed for dress, street, and work. This industry includes women's shoes with rubber or plastics soles and leather or vinyl uppers.

Cross-References. Establishments primarily engaged in—

- Manufacturing women's footwear with fabric uppers and rubber or plastics soles and rubber or plastics sandals—are classified in U.S. Industry 316211, Rubber and Plastics Footwear Manufacturing;
- Manufacturing orthopedic extension footwear—are classified in U.S. Industry 339113, Surgical Appliance and Supplies Manufacturing; and
- Manufacturing women's leather or vinyl upper athletic footwear and youths' and girls' footwear—are classified in U.S. Industry 316219, Other Footwear Manufacturing.

316219 Other Footwear Manufacturing^{US}

This U.S. industry comprises establishments primarily engaged in manufacturing other footwear (except rubber and plastics footwear; house slippers; men's footwear (except athletic); and women's footwear (except athletic)).

US—United States industry only. CAN—United States and Canadian industries are comparable. MEX—United States and Mexican industries are comparable. Blank—Canadian, Mexican, and United States industries are comparable.

Illustrative Examples:

Athletic shoes (except rubber-soled, fabric upper) manufacturing
Cleated athletic shoes manufacturing
Ballet slippers manufacturing
Infants' shoes (except plastics and rubber footwear) manufacturing

Children's shoes (except plastics and rubber footwear and orthopedic extension shoes) manufacturing

Cross-References. Establishments primarily engaged in—

- Manufacturing rubber and plastics footwear with fabric uppers—are classified in U.S. Industry 316211, Rubber and Plastics Footwear Manufacturing;

- Manufacturing house slippers—are classified in U.S. Industry 316212, House Slipper Manufacturing;

- Manufacturing men's footwear (except athletic)—are classified in U.S. Industry 316213, Men's Footwear (except Athletic) Manufacturing;

- Manufacturing orthopedic extension footwear—are classified in Industry 339113, Surgical Appliance and Supplies Manufacturing; and

- Manufacturing women's footwear (except athletic)—are classified in U.S. Industry 316214, Women's Footwear (except Athletic) Manufacturing.

3169 Other Leather and Allied Product Manufacturing

31699 Other Leather and Allied Product Manufacturing

This industry comprises establishments primarily engaged in manufacturing leather products (except footwear and apparel) from purchased leather or leather substitutes (e.g., fabric, plastics).

Illustrative Examples:

Billfolds, all materials, manufacturing
Shoe soles, leather, manufacturing
Boot and shoe cut stock and findings, leather, manufacturing
Toilet kits and cases (except metal) manufacturing
Dog furnishings (e.g., collars, leashes, harnesses, muzzles), manufacturing

Watchbands (except metal) manufacturing
Luggage, all materials, manufacturing
Welders' jackets, leggings, and sleeves, leather, manufacturing
Purses, women's, all materials (except metal), manufacturing

Cross-References. Establishments primarily engaged in—

- Manufacturing leather apparel—are classified in Industry 31529, Other Cut and Sew Apparel Manufacturing;

US—United States industry only. CAN—United States and Canadian industries are comparable. MEX—United States and Mexican industries are comparable. Blank—Canadian, Mexican, and United States industries are comparable.

http://www.census.gov/naics

- Manufacturing leather gloves, mittens, belts, and apparel accessories—are classified in Industry 31599, Apparel Accessories and Other Apparel Manufacturing;

- Manufacturing footwear—are classified in Industry 31621, Footwear Manufacturing;

- Manufacturing nonleather soles—are classified elsewhere based on the primary input material;

- Manufacturing small articles made of metal carried on or about the person made of metal—are classified in Industry 33991, Jewelry and Silverware Manufacturing; and

- Manufacturing leather gaskets—are classified in Industry 33999, All Other Miscellaneous Manufacturing.

316991 Luggage Manufacturing^{US}

This U.S. industry comprises establishments primarily engaged in manufacturing luggage of any material.

316992 Women's Handbag and Purse Manufacturing^{US}

This U.S. industry comprises establishments primarily engaged in manufacturing women's handbags and purses of any material (except precious metal).

Cross-References.

Establishments primarily engaged in manufacturing precious metal handbags and purses are classified in U.S. Industry 339911, Jewelry (except Costume) Manufacturing.

316993 Personal Leather Good (except Women's Handbag and Purse) Manufacturing^{US}

This U.S. industry comprises establishments primarily engaged in manufacturing personal leather goods (i.e., small articles of any material (except metal) normally carried on or about the person or in a handbag). Examples of personal leather goods made by these establishments are billfolds, coin purses, key cases, toilet kits, and watchbands (except metal).

Cross-References. Establishments primarily engaged in—

- Manufacturing personal goods of precious metal—are classified in U.S. Industry 339911, Jewelry (except Costume) Manufacturing; and

- Manufacturing personal goods of metal (except precious)—are classified in U.S. Industry 339914, Costume Jewelry and Noveity Manufacturing.

316999 All Other Leather Good and Allied Product Manufacturing[US]

This U.S. industry comprises establishments primarily engaged in manufacturing leather goods (except footwear, luggage, handbags, purses, and personal leather goods).

Illustrative Examples:

Boot and shoe cut stock and findings, leather, manufacturing
Shoe soles, leather, manufacturing
Dog furnishings (e.g., collars, leashes, harnesses, muzzles) manufacturing

Welders' jackets, leggings, and sleeves, leather, manufacturing
Leather belting for machinery (e.g., flat, solid, twisted, built-up) manufacturing

Cross-References. Establishments primarily engaged in—

- Manufacturing leather gloves or mittens—are classified in U.S. Industry 315992, Glove and Mitten Manufacturing;

- Manufacturing leather apparel belts—are classified in U.S. Industry 315999, Other Apparel Accessories and Other Apparel Manufacturing;

- Manufacturing footwear—are classified in Industry 31621, Footwear Manufacturing;

- Manufacturing luggage of any material—are classified in U.S. Industry 316991, Luggage Manufacturing;

- Manufacturing handbags and purses—are classified in U.S. Industry 316992, Women's Handbag and Purse Manufacturing;

- Manufacturing personal leather goods, such as wallets and key cases, of all materials (except metal)—are classified in U.S. Industry 316993, Personal Leather Good (except Women's Handbag and Purse) Manufacturing;

- Manufacturing nonleather soles—are classified elsewhere based on the primary input material;

- Manufacturing leather apparel—are classified in U.S. Industry 315292, Fur and Leather Apparel Manufacturing; and

- Manufacturing leather gaskets—are classified in U.S. Industry 339991, Gasket, Packing, and Sealing Device Manufacturing.

US—United States industry only. CAN—United States and Canadian industries are comparable. MEX—United States and Mexican industries are comparable. Blank—Canadian, Mexican, and United States industries are comparable.

321 Wood Product Manufacturing

Industries in the Wood Product Manufacturing subsector manufacture wood products, such as lumber, plywood, veneers, wood containers, wood flooring, wood trusses, manufactured homes (i.e., mobile homes), and prefabricated wood buildings. The production processes of the Wood Product Manufacturing subsector include sawing, planing, shaping, laminating, and assembling of wood products starting from logs that are cut into bolts, or lumber that then may be further cut, or shaped by lathes or other shaping tools. The lumber or other transformed wood shapes may also be subsequently planed or smoothed, and assembled into finished products, such as wood containers. The Wood Product Manufacturing subsector includes establishments that make wood products from logs and bolts that are sawed and shaped, and establishments that purchase sawed lumber and make wood products. With the exception of sawmills and wood preservation establishments, the establishments are grouped into industries mainly based on the specific products manufactured.

3211 Sawmills and Wood Preservation

This industry group comprises establishments whose primary production process begins with logs or bolts that are transformed into boards, dimension lumber, beams, timbers, poles, ties, shingles, shakes, siding, and wood chips. Establishments that cut and treat round wood and/or treat wood products made in other establishments to prevent rotting by impregnation with creosote or other chemical compounds are also included in this industry group.

32111 Sawmills and Wood Preservation

This industry comprises establishments primarily engaged in one or more of the following: (1) sawing dimension lumber, boards, beams, timber, poles, ties, shingles, shakes, siding, and wood chips from logs or bolts; (2) sawing round wood poles, pilings, and posts and treating them with preservatives; and (3) treating wood sawed, planed, or shaped in other establishments with creosote or other preservatives to prevent decay and to protect against fire and insects. Sawmills may plane the rough lumber that they make with a planing machine to achieve smoothness and uniformity of size.

Cross-References. Establishments primarily engaged in—

- Operating portable chipper mills in the field—are classified in Industry 11331, Logging;

- Manufacturing wood products (except round wood poles, pilings, and posts) and treating them with preservatives—are classified elsewhere in Subsector 321, Wood Product Manufacturing, based on the related production process;
- Manufacturing veneer from logs and bolts or manufacturing engineered lumber and structural members other than solid wood—are classified in Industry 32121, Veneer, Plywood, and Engineered Wood Product Manufacturing; and
- Planing purchased lumber or manufacturing cut stock or dimension stock (i.e., shapes) from logs or bolts—are classified in Industry 32191, Millwork.

321113 Sawmills[US]

This U.S. industry comprises establishments primarily engaged in sawing dimension lumber, boards, beams, timbers, poles, ties, shingles, shakes, siding, and wood chips from logs or bolts. Sawmills may plane the rough lumber that they make with a planing machine to achieve smoothness and uniformity of size.

Cross-References. Establishments primarily engaged in—

- Planing purchased lumber or manufacturing cut stock or dimension stock (i.e., shapes) from logs or bolts—are classified in Industry 32191, Millwork;
- Manufacturing veneer from logs or bolts—are classified in Industry 32121, Veneer, Plywood, and Engineered Wood Product Manufacturing; and
- Operating portable chipper mills in the field—are classified in U.S. Industry 113310, Logging.

321114 Wood Preservation[CAN]

This U.S. industry comprises establishments primarily engaged in (1) treating wood sawed, planed, or shaped in other establishments with creosote or other preservatives, such as alkaline copper quat, copper azole, and sodium borates, to prevent decay and to protect against fire and insects and/or (2) sawing round wood poles, pilings, and posts and treating them with preservatives.

Cross-References.

Establishments primarily engaged in manufacturing wood products (except round wood poles, pilings, and posts) and treating them with preservatives are classified elsewhere in Subsector 321, Wood Product Manufacturing, based on the related production process.

3212 Veneer, Plywood, and Engineered Wood Product Manufacturing

---

US—United States industry only. CAN—United States and Canadian industries are comparable. MEX—United States and Mexican industries are comparable. Blank—Canadian, Mexican, and United States industries are comparable.

32121 Veneer, Plywood, and Engineered Wood Product Manufacturing

This industry comprises establishments primarily engaged in one or more of the following: (1) manufacturing veneer and/or plywood; (2) manufacturing engineered wood members; and (3) manufacturing reconstituted wood products. This industry includes manufacturing plywood from veneer made in the same establishment or from veneer made in other establishments, and manufacturing plywood faced with nonwood materials, such as plastics or metal.

Illustrative Examples:

Fabricated structural wood members
   manufacturing
Plywood manufacturing
Laminated structural wood members
   manufacturing
Reconstituted wood sheets and boards
   manufacturing
Medium density fiberboard (MDF)
   manufacturing

Roof trusses, wood, manufacturing
Oriented strandboard (OSB)
   manufacturing
Veneer mills
Particleboard manufacturing
Waferboard manufacturing

Cross-References. Establishments primarily engaged in—

- Manufacturing veneer and further processing that veneer into wood containers or wood container parts in the same establishment—are classified in Industry 32192, Wood Container and Pallet Manufacturing;

- Manufacturing prefabricated wood buildings or wood sections, and panels for buildings—are classified in Industry 32199, All Other Wood Product Manufacturing; and

- Manufacturing solid wood structural members, such as dimension lumber and timber from logs or bolts in sawmills—are classified in Industry 32111, Sawmills and Wood Preservation.

321211 Hardwood Veneer and Plywood Manufacturing[CAN]

This U.S. industry comprises establishments primarily engaged in manufacturing hardwood veneer and/or hardwood plywood.

Cross-References. Establishments primarily engaged in—

- Manufacturing veneer and further processing that veneer into wood containers or wood container parts—are classified in Industry 321920, Wood Container and Pallet Manufacturing;

US—United States industry only. CAN—United States and Canadian industries are comparable. MEX—United States and Mexican industries are comparable. Blank—Canadian, Mexican, and United States industries are comparable.

- Manufacturing softwood veneer and softwood plywood—are classified in U.S. Industry 321212, Softwood Veneer and Plywood Manufacturing; and
- Manufacturing reconstituted wood sheets and boards—are classified in U.S. Industry 321219, Reconstituted Wood Product Manufacturing.

321212 Softwood Veneer and Plywood Manufacturing^{CAN}

This U.S. industry comprises establishments primarily engaged in manufacturing softwood veneer and/or softwood plywood.

Cross-References. Establishments primarily engaged in—

- Manufacturing veneer and further processing that veneer into wood containers or wood container parts—are classified in Industry 321920, Wood Container and Pallet Manufacturing;
- Manufacturing hardwood veneer and hardwood plywood—are classified in U.S. Industry 321211, Hardwood Veneer and Plywood Manufacturing; and
- Manufacturing reconstituted wood sheets and boards—are classified in U.S. Industry 321219, Reconstituted Wood Product Manufacturing.

321213 Engineered Wood Member (except Truss) Manufacturing^{US}

This U.S. industry comprises establishments primarily engaged in manufacturing fabricated or laminated wood arches and/or other fabricated or laminated wood structural members.

Illustrative Examples:

Finger joint lumber manufacturing	Timbers, structural, glue laminated or
Parallel strand lumber	pre-engineered wood, manufacturing
manufacturing	Laminated veneer lumber (LVL)
I-joists, wood, fabricating	manufacturing

Cross-References. Establishments primarily engaged in—

- Manufacturing prefabricated wood buildings, or wood sections, and panels for buildings—are classified in U.S. Industry 321992, Prefabricated Wood Building Manufacturing;
- Manufacturing wood trusses—are classified in U.S. Industry 321214, Truss Manufacturing; and
- Manufacturing solid wood structural members, such as dimension lumber and timber from logs or bolts—are classified in U.S. Industry 321113, Sawmills.

US—United States industry only. CAN—United States and Canadian industries are comparable. MEX—United States and Mexican industries are comparable. Blank—Canadian, Mexican, and United States industries are comparable.

321214 Truss Manufacturing[US]

This U.S. industry comprises establishments primarily engaged in manufacturing laminated or fabricated wood roof and floor trusses.

Cross-References.

Establishments primarily engaged in manufacturing wood I-joists are classified in U.S. Industry 321213, Engineered Wood Member (except Truss) Manufacturing.

321219 Reconstituted Wood Product Manufacturing[US]

This U.S. industry comprises establishments primarily engaged in manufacturing reconstituted wood sheets and boards.

Illustrative Examples:

Medium density fiberboard (MDF)
  manufacturing
Reconstituted wood sheets and boards
  manufacturing

Oriented strandboard (OSB)
  manufacturing
Waferboard manufacturing
Particleboard manufacturing

Cross-References. Establishments primarily engaged in—

- Manufacturing softwood plywood—are classified in U.S. Industry 321212, Softwood Veneer and Plywood Manufacturing; and

- Manufacturing hardwood plywood—are classified in U.S. Industry 321211, Hardwood Veneer and Plywood Manufacturing.

3219 Other Wood Product Manufacturing

This industry group comprises establishments primarily engaged in manufacturing wood products (except establishments operating sawmills and wood preservation facilities; and establishments manufacturing veneer, plywood, or engineered wood products).

32191 Millwork

This industry comprises establishments primarily engaged in manufacturing hardwood and softwood cut stock and dimension stock (i.e., shapes); wood windows and wood doors; and other millwork including wood flooring. Dimension stock or cut stock is defined as lumber and worked wood products cut or shaped to specialized sizes. These establishments generally use woodworking machinery, such as jointers, planers, lathes, and routers to shape wood.

US—United States industry only. CAN—United States and Canadian industries are comparable. MEX—United States and Mexican industries are comparable. Blank—Canadian, Mexican, and United States industries are comparable.

Cross-References. Establishments primarily engaged in—

- Manufacturing dimension lumber, boards, beams, timbers, poles, ties, shingles, shakes, siding, and wood chips from logs and bolts—are classified in Industry 32111, Sawmills and Wood Preservation;
- Fabricating millwork at the construction site—are classified in Industry 23835, Finish Carpentry Contractors; and
- Manufacturing wood furniture frames and finished wood furniture parts—are classified in Industry 33721, Office Furniture (including Fixtures) Manufacturing.

321911 Wood Window and Door Manufacturing[CAN]

This U.S. industry comprises establishments primarily engaged in manufacturing window and door units, sash, window and door frames, and doors from wood or wood clad with metal or plastics.

Cross-References.

Establishments primarily engaged in fabricating wood windows or wood doors at the construction site are classified in Industry 238350, Finish Carpentry Contractors.

321912 Cut Stock, Resawing Lumber, and Planing[US]

This U.S. industry comprises establishments primarily engaged in one or more of the following: (1) manufacturing dimension lumber from purchased lumber; (2) manufacturing dimension stock (i.e., shapes) or cut stock; (3) resawing the output of sawmills; and (4) planing purchased lumber. These establishments generally use woodworking machinery, such as jointers, planers, lathes, and routers to shape wood.

Cross-References. Establishments primarily engaged in—

- Manufacturing dimension lumber, boards, beams, timbers, poles, ties, shingles, shakes, siding, and wood chips from logs or bolts—are classified in U.S. Industry 321113, Sawmills;
- Manufacturing wood stairwork, wood molding, wood trim, and other millwork—are classified in U.S. Industry 321918, Other Millwork (including Flooring); and
- Manufacturing wood furniture frames and finished wood furniture parts—are classified in U.S. Industry 337215, Showcase, Partition, Shelving, and Locker Manufacturing.

US—United States industry only. CAN—United States and Canadian industries are comparable. MEX—United States and Mexican industries are comparable. Blank—Canadian, Mexican, and United States industries are comparable.

321918 Other Millwork (including Flooring)[US]

This U.S. industry comprises establishments primarily engaged in manufacturing millwork (except wood windows, wood doors, and cut stock).

Illustrative Examples:

Clear and finger joint wood moldings
 manufacturing
Stairwork (e.g., newel posts, railings,
 stairs, staircases), wood, manufacturing
Decorative wood moldings (e.g., base,
 chair rail, crown, shoe) manufacturing
Wood flooring manufacturing
Ornamental woodwork (e.g., cornices,
 mantel) manufacturing
Wood shutters manufacturing
Planing mills, millwork

Cross-References. Establishments primarily engaged in—

- Manufacturing wood windows and doors—are classified in U.S. Industry 321911, Wood Window and Door Manufacturing; and

- Manufacturing cut stock, resawing lumber, and/or planing purchased lumber—are classified in U.S. Industry 321912, Cut Stock, Resawing Lumber, and Planing.

32192 Wood Container and Pallet Manufacturing
See industry description for 321920 below.

321920 Wood Container and Pallet Manufacturing

This industry comprises establishments primarily engaged in manufacturing wood pallets, wood box shook, wood boxes, other wood containers, and wood parts for pallets and containers.

Cross-References.

Establishments primarily engaged in manufacturing wood burial caskets are classified in U.S. Industry 339995, Burial Casket Manufacturing.

32199 All Other Wood Product Manufacturing

This industry comprises establishments primarily engaged in manufacturing wood products (except establishments operating sawmills and wood preservation facilities; and establishments manufacturing veneer, plywood, engineered wood products, millwork, wood containers, or pallets).

Illustrative Examples:

Mobile home manufacturing
Sections, prefabricated wood building, manufacturing
Panels, prefabricated wood building, manufacturing

Wood dowels manufacturing
Prefabricated wood buildings
Wood handles (e.g., broom, handtool, mop), manufacturing

Cross-References. Establishments primarily engaged in—

- Operating sawmills or preserving wood—are classified in Industry 32111, Sawmills and ꞌWood Preservation;

- Manufacturing veneer, plywood, and engineered wood products—are classified in Industry 32121, Veneer, Plywood, and Engineered Wood Product Manufacturing;

- Manufacturing millwork—are classified in Industry 32191, Millwork;

- Manufacturing wood containers, pallets, and wood container parts—are classified in Industry 32192, Wood Container and Pallet Manufacturing;

- Manufacturing travel trailers with self-contained facilities for storage of water and waste—are classified in Industry 33621, Motor Vehicle Body and Trailer Manufacturing; and

- Fabricating of wood buildings or wood sections and panels for buildings at the construction site—are classified in Sector 23, Construction.

321991 Manufactured Home (Mobile Home) Manufacturing[CAN]

This U.S. industry comprises establishments primarily engaged in making manufactured homes (i.e., mobile homes) and nonresidential mobile buildings. Manufactured homes are designed to accept permanent water, sewer, and utility connections and although equipped with wheels, they are not intended for regular highway movement.

Cross-References. Establishments primarily engaged in—

- Manufacturing prefabricated wood buildings not equipped with wheels—are classified in U.S. Industry 321992, Prefabricated Wood Building Manufacturing; and

- Manufacturing travel trailers with self-contained facilities for storage of water and waste—are classified in U.S. Industry 336214, Travel Trailer and Camper Manufacturing.

US—United States industry only. CAN—United States and Canadian industries are comparable. MEX—United States and Mexican industries are comparable. Blank—Canadian, Mexican, and United States industries are comparable.

321992 Prefabricated Wood Building Manufacturing^{CAN}

This U.S. industry comprises establishments primarily engaged in manufacturing prefabricated wood buildings and wood sections and panels for prefabricated wood buildings.

Cross-References. Establishments primarily engaged in—

- Fabricating wood buildings or wood sections and panels for buildings at the construction site—are classified in Sector 23, Construction; and

- Making manufactured homes (i.e., mobile homes)—are classified in U.S. Industry 321991, Manufactured Home (Mobile Home) Manufacturing.

321999 All Other Miscellaneous Wood Product Manufacturing^{CAN}

This U.S. industry comprises establishments primarily engaged in manufacturing wood products (except establishments operating sawmills and preservation facilities; establishments manufacturing veneer, engineered wood products, millwork, wood containers, pallets, and wood container parts; and establishments making manufactured homes (i.e., mobile homes) and prefabricated buildings and components).

Illustrative Examples:

Cork products (except gaskets) manufacturing	Shoe trees manufacturing
Wood handles (e.g., broom, handtool, mop), manufacturing	Wood stepladders manufacturing
	Wood dowels manufacturing
Kiln drying lumber	Wood toilet seats manufacturing
Wood kitchenware manufacturing	Wood extension ladders manufacturing
	Wood toothpicks manufacturing

Cross-References. Establishments primarily engaged in—

- Operating sawmills and preserving wood—are classified in Industry 32111, Sawmills and Wood Preservation;

- Manufacturing veneer and engineered wood products—are classified in Industry 32121, Veneer, Plywood, and Engineered Wood Product Manufacturing;

- Manufacturing millwork—are classified in Industry 32191, Millwork;

- Manufacturing boxes, box shook, wood containers, pallets, and wood parts for containers—are classified in Industry 321920, Wood Container and Pallet Manufacturing;

US—United States industry only. CAN—United States and Canadian industries are comparable. MEX—United States and Mexican industries are comparable. Blank—Canadian, Mexican, and United States industries are comparable.

- Making manufactured homes (i.e., mobile homes)—are classified in U.S. Industry 321991, Manufactured Home (Mobile Home) Manufacturing; and

- Manufacturing prefabricated wood buildings or wood sections and panels for buildings—are classified in U.S. Industry 321992, Prefabricated Wood Building Manufacturing.

322 Paper Manufacturing

Industries in the Paper Manufacturing subsector make pulp, paper, or converted paper products. The manufacturing of these products is grouped together because they constitute a series of vertically connected processes. More than one is often carried out in a single establishment. There are essentially three activities. The manufacturing of pulp involves separating the cellulose fibers from other impurities in wood or used paper. The manufacturing of paper involves matting these fibers into a sheet. Converted paper products are made from paper and other materials by various cutting and shaping techniques and includes coating and laminating activities.

The Paper Manufacturing subsector is subdivided into two industry groups, the first for the manufacturing of pulp and paper and the second for the manufacturing of converted paper products. Paper making is treated as the core activity of the subsector. Therefore, any establishment that makes paper (including paperboard), either alone or in combination with pulp manufacturing or paper converting, is classified as a paper or paperboard mill. Establishments that make pulp without making paper are classified as pulp mills. Pulp mills, paper mills and paperboard mills comprise the first industry group.

Establishments that make products from purchased paper and other materials make up the second industry group, Converted Paper Product Manufacturing. This general activity is then subdivided based, for the most part, on process distinctions. Paperboard container manufacturing uses corrugating, cutting, and shaping machinery to form paperboard into containers. Paper bag and coated and treated paper manufacturing establishments cut and coat paper and foil. Stationery product manufacturing establishments make a variety of paper products used for writing, filing, and similar applications. Other converted paper product manufacturing includes, in particular, the conversion of sanitary paper stock into such things as tissue paper and disposable diapers.

An important process used in the Paper Bag and Coated and Treated Paper Manufacturing industry is lamination, often combined with coating. Lamination and coating makes a composite material with improved properties of strength, impermeability, and so on. The laminated materials may be paper, metal foil, or plastics film. While paper is often one of the components, it is not always. Lamination of plastics film to plastics film is classified in the NAICS Subsector 326, Plastics and Rubber Products Manufacturing, because establishments that do this

---

US—United States industry only. CAN—United States and Canadian industries are comparable. MEX—United States and Mexican industries are comparable. Blank—Canadian, Mexican, and United States industries are comparable.

often first make the film. The same situation holds with respect to bags. The manufacturing of bags from plastics only, whether or not laminated, is classified in Subsector 326, Plastics and Rubber Products Manufacturing, but all other bag manufacturing is classified in this subsector.

Excluded from this subsector are photosensitive papers. These papers are chemically treated and are classified in Industry 32599, All Other Chemical Product and Preparation Manufacturing.

3221 Pulp, Paper, and Paperboard Mills

This industry group comprises establishments primarily engaged in manufacturing pulp, paper, or paperboard.

32211 Pulp Mills
See industry description for 322110 below.

322110 Pulp Mills^{MEX}

This industry comprises establishments primarily engaged in manufacturing pulp without manufacturing paper or paperboard. The pulp is made by separating the cellulose fibers from the other impurities in wood or other materials, such as used or recycled rags, linters, scrap paper, and straw.

Cross-References. Establishments primarily engaged in—

- Manufacturing both pulp and paper—are classified in Industry 32212, Paper Mills; and

- Manufacturing both pulp and paperboard—are classified in Industry 322130, Paperboard Mills.

32212 Paper Mills

This industry comprises establishments primarily engaged in manufacturing paper from pulp. These establishments may manufacture or purchase pulp. In addition, the establishments may convert the paper they make. The activity of making paper classifies an establishment into this industry regardless of the output.

Cross-References. Establishments primarily engaged in—

- Manufacturing pulp without manufacturing paper—are classified in Industry 32211, Pulp Mills;

US—United States industry only. CAN—United States and Canadian industries are comparable. MEX—United States and Mexican industries are comparable. Blank—Canadian, Mexican, and United States industries are comparable.

- Manufacturing paperboard—are classified in Industry 32213, Paperboard Mills;

- Converting paper without manufacturing paper—are classified in Industry Group 3222, Converted Paper Product Manufacturing; and

- Manufacturing photographic sensitized paper—are classified in Industry 32599, All Other Chemical Product and Preparation Manufacturing.

322121 Paper (except Newsprint) Mills[CAN]

This U.S. industry comprises establishments primarily engaged in manufacturing paper (except newsprint and uncoated groundwood paper) from pulp. These establishments may manufacture or purchase pulp. In addition, the establishments may also convert the paper they make.

Cross-References. Establishments primarily engaged in—

- Manufacturing newsprint and uncoated groundwood paper—are classified in U.S. Industry 322122, Newsprint Mills;

- Converting paper without manufacturing paper—are classified in Industry Group 3222, Converted Paper Product Manufacturing;

- Manufacturing paperboard—are classified in Industry 322130, Paperboard Mills;

- Manufacturing pulp without manufacturing paper—are classified in Industry 322110, Pulp Mills; and

- Manufacturing photographic sensitized paper from purchased paper—are classified in U.S. Industry 325992, Photographic Film, Paper, Plate, and Chemical Manufacturing.

322122 Newsprint Mills[CAN]

This U.S. industry comprises establishments primarily engaged in manufacturing newsprint and uncoated groundwood paper from pulp. These establishments may manufacture or purchase pulp. In addition, the establishments may also convert the paper they make.

Cross-References. Establishments primarily engaged in—

- Manufacturing paper (except newsprint and uncoated groundwood)—are classified in U.S. Industry 322121, Paper (except Newsprint) Mills;

- Converting paper without manufacturing paper—are classified in Industry Group 3222, Converted Paper Product Manufacturing;

US—United States industry only. CAN—United States and Canadian industries are comparable. MEX—United States and Mexican industries are comparable. Blank—Canadian, Mexican, and United States industries are comparable.

- Manufacturing paperboard—are classified in Industry 322130, Paperboard Mills; and

- Manufacturing pulp without manufacturing paper—are classified in Industry 322110, Pulp Mills.

32213 Paperboard Mills

See industry description for 322130 below.

322130 Paperboard Mills^{CAN}

This industry comprises establishments primarily engaged in manufacturing paperboard from pulp. These establishments may manufacture or purchase pulp. In addition, the establishments may also convert the paperboard they make.

Cross-References. Establishments primarily engaged in—

- Manufacturing pulp without manufacturing paperboard—are classified in Industry 322110, Pulp Mills;

- Converting paperboard without manufacturing paperboard—are classified in Industry Group 3222, Converted Paper Product Manufacturing; and

- Manufacturing insulation board and other reconstituted wood fiberboard— are classified in U.S. Industry 321219, Reconstituted Wood Product Manufacturing.

3222 Converted Paper Product Manufacturing

This industry group comprises establishments primarily engaged in converting paper or paperboard without manufacturing paper or paperboard.

32221 Paperboard Container Manufacturing

This industry comprises establishments primarily engaged in converting paperboard into containers without manufacturing paperboard. These establishments use corrugating, cutting, and shaping machinery to form paperboard into containers. Products made by these establishments include boxes, corrugated sheets, pads, pallets, paper dishes, and fiber drums, and reels.

Cross-References. Establishments primarily engaged in—

- Manufacturing similar items of plastics materials—are classified in Industry Group 3261, Plastics Product Manufacturing;

US—United States industry only. CAN—United States and Canadian industries are comparable. MEX—United States and Mexican industries are comparable. Blank—Canadian, Mexican, and United States industries are comparable.

- Manufacturing paperboard and converting paperboard into containers—are classified in Industry 32213, Paperboard Mills;
- Manufacturing egg cartons, food trays, and other food containers from molded pulp—are classified in Industry 32229, Other Converted Paper Product Manufacturing;
- Manufacturing paper and converting paper into containers—are classified in Industry 32212, Paper Mills; and
- Manufacturing paper bags without manufacturing paper—are classified in Industry 32222, Paper Bag and Coated and Treated Paper Manufacturing.

322211 Corrugated and Solid Fiber Box Manufacturing[CAN]

This U.S. industry comprises establishments primarily engaged in laminating purchased paper or paperboard into corrugated or solid fiber boxes and related products, such as pads, partitions, pallets, and corrugated paper without manufacturing paperboard. These boxes are generally used for shipping.

Cross-References. Establishments primarily engaged in—

- Manufacturing setup paperboard boxes (except corrugated or laminated solid fiber boxes)—are classified in U.S. Industry 322213, Setup Paperboard Box Manufacturing;
- Manufacturing folding paperboard boxes (except corrugated or laminated solid fiber boxes)—are classified in U.S. Industry 322212, Folding Paperboard Box Manufacturing; and
- Manufacturing paperboard and converting paperboard into boxes—are classified in Industry 322130, Paperboard Mills.

322212 Folding Paperboard Box Manufacturing[CAN]

This U.S. industry comprises establishments primarily engaged in converting paperboard (except corrugated) into folding paperboard boxes without manufacturing paper and paperboard.

Cross-References. Establishments primarily engaged in—

- Manufacturing setup paperboard boxes (except corrugated)—are classified in U.S. Industry 322213, Setup Paperboard Box Manufacturing;
- Manufacturing corrugated and solid fiber boxes—are classified in U.S. Industry 322211, Corrugated and Solid Fiber Box Manufacturing;

- Manufacturing paperboard and converting paperboard into containers—are classified in Industry 322130, Paperboard Mills;

- Manufacturing paper and converting paper into containers—are classified in Industry 32212, Paper Mills;

- Manufacturing milk cartons—are classified in U.S. Industry 322215, Nonfolding Sanitary Food Container Manufacturing; and

- Manufacturing paper bags—are classified in Industry 32222, Paper Bag and Coated and Treated Paper Manufacturing.

322213 Setup Paperboard Box Manufacturing^{US}

This U.S. industry comprises establishments primarily engaged in converting paperboard into setup paperboard boxes (i.e., rigid-sided boxes not shipped flat) without manufacturing paperboard.

Cross-References. Establishments primarily engaged in—

- Manufacturing folding paperboard boxes (except corrugated)—are classified in U.S. Industry 322212, Folding Paperboard Box Manufacturing;

- Manufacturing corrugated and solid fiber boxes—are classified in U.S. Industry 322211, Corrugated and Solid Fiber Box Manufacturing; and

- Manufacturing paperboard and converting paperboard into containers—are classified in Industry 322130, Paperboard Mills.

322214 Fiber Can, Tube, Drum, and Similar Products Manufacturing^{US}

This U.S. industry comprises establishments primarily engaged in converting paperboard into fiber cans, tubes, drums, and similar products without manufacturing paperboard.

Cross-References.

Establishments primarily engaged in manufacturing paperboard and converting paperboard into containers are classified in Industry 322130, Paperboard Mills.

322215 Nonfolding Sanitary Food Container Manufacturing^{US}

This U.S. industry comprises establishments primarily engaged in converting sanitary foodboard into food containers (except folding).

US—United States industry only. CAN—United States and Canadian industries are comparable. MEX—United States and Mexican industries are comparable. Blank—Canadian, Mexican, and United States industries are comparable.

Cross-References. Establishments primarily engaged in—

- Manufacturing sanitary food containers of solely plastics materials—are classified in Industry Group 3261, Plastics Product Manufacturing;
- Manufacturing egg cartons, food trays, and other food containers from molded pulp—are classified in U.S. Industry 322299, All Other Converted Paper Product Manufacturing; and
- Manufacturing folding sanitary cartons—are classified in U.S. Industry 322212, Folding Paperboard Box Manufacturing.

32222 Paper Bag and Coated and Treated Paper Manufacturing

This industry comprises establishments primarily engaged in one or more of the following: (1) cutting and coating paper and paperboard; (2) cutting and laminating paper, paperboard, and other flexible materials (except plastics film to plastics film); (3) manufacturing bags, multiwall bags, sacks of paper, metal foil, coated paper, laminates, or coated combinations of paper and foil with plastics film; (4) manufacturing laminated aluminum and other converted metal foils from purchased foils; and (5) surface coating paper or paperboard.

Cross-References. Establishments primarily engaged in—

- Manufacturing paper from pulp—are classified in Industry 32212, Paper Mills;
- Manufacturing photographic sensitized paper—are classified in Industry 32599, All Other Chemical Product and Preparation Manufacturing;
- Manufacturing textile bags—are classified in Industry 31491, Textile Bag and Canvas Mills;
- Manufacturing single and multiwall plastics bags or plastics laminated bags—are classified in Industry 32611, Plastics Packaging Materials and Unlaminated Film and Sheet Manufacturing;
- Making aluminum and aluminum foil—are classified in Industry 33131, Alumina and Aluminum Production and Processing; and
- Cutting purchased aluminum foil into smaller lengths and widths—are classified in Industry 33299, All Other Fabricated Metal Product Manufacturing.

322221 Coated and Laminated Packaging Paper Manufacturing[US]

This U.S. industry comprises establishments primarily engaged in performing one or more of the following activities associated with the manufacture of paper

---

US—United States industry only. CAN—United States and Canadian industries are comparable. MEX—United States and Mexican industries are comparable. Blank—Canadian, Mexican, and United States industries are comparable.

packaging materials: (1) cutting and coating paper; and (2) cutting and laminating paper with other flexible packaging materials (except foil to paper laminates). The products manufactured by establishments in this industry are made from purchased sheet materials and may be printed in the same establishment.

Cross-References. Establishments primarily engaged in—

- Manufacturing coated or laminated paper for nonpackaging purposes—are classified in U.S. Industry 322222, Coated and Laminated Paper Manufacturing;

- Manufacturing plastics to plastics packaging laminations—are classified in U.S. Industry 326112, Plastics Packaging Film and Sheet (including Laminated) Manufacturing;

- Printing on purchased packaging materials—are classified in Industry Group 3231, Printing and Related Support Activities, based on printing process used;

- Manufacturing foil to paper packaging laminations or laminating aluminum foil for flexible packaging uses—are classified in U.S. Industry 322225, Laminated Aluminum Foil Manufacturing for Flexible Packaging Uses;

- Manufacturing unsupported plastic film—are classified in U.S. Industry 326113, Unsupported Plastics Film and Sheet (except Packaging) Manufacturing;

- Making aluminum and aluminum foil—are classified in Industry 33131, Alumina and Aluminum Production and Processing;

- Cutting purchased aluminum foil into smaller lengths and widths—are classified in U.S. Industry 332999, All Other Miscellaneous Fabricated Metal Product Manufacturing; and

- Manufacturing paper from pulp—are classified in Industry 32212, Paper Mills.

322222 Coated and Laminated Paper Manufacturing[US]

This U.S. industry comprises establishments primarily engaged in performing one or more of the following activities associated with making products designed for purposes other than packaging: (1) cutting and coating paper; (2) cutting and laminating paper and other flexible materials (except plastics film to plastics film); and (3) laminating aluminum and other metal foils for nonpackaging uses from purchased foils. The products made in this industry are made from purchased sheet materials and may be printed in the same establishment.

US—United States industry only. CAN—United States and Canadian industries are comparable. MEX—United States and Mexican industries are comparable. Blank—Canadian, Mexican, and United States industries are comparable.

Illustrative Examples:

Book paper made by coating purchased paper

Tapes, pressure sensitive (e.g., cellophane, masking), made from purchased paper or other structures

Gift wrap, laminated, made from purchased paper

Wallpaper made from purchased paper or other materials

Gummed paper products (e.g., labels sheets, tapes) made from purchased paper

Cross-References. Establishments primarily engaged in—

- Manufacturing coated and laminated paper for packaging uses—are classified in U.S. Industry 322221, Coated and Laminated Packaging Paper Manufacturing;

- Manufacturing photographic sensitized paper—are classified in U.S. Industry 325992, Photographic Film, Paper, Plate, and Chemical Manufacturing;

- Making aluminum and aluminum foil—are classified in Industry 33131, Alumina and Aluminum Production and Processing;

- Cutting purchased aluminum foil into smaller lengths and widths—are classified in U.S. Industry 332999, All Other Miscellaneous Fabricated Metal Product Manufacturing; and

- Manufacturing laminated aluminum foil for flexible packaging uses—are classified in U.S. Industry 322225, Laminated Aluminum Foil Manufacturing for Flexible Packaging Uses.

322223 Coated Paper Bag and Pouch Manufacturing[US]

This U.S. Industry comprises establishments primarily engaged in manufacturing: (1) bags or pouches of coated paper; (2) bags or pouches of metal foil; and/or (3) bags or pouches of paper laminated with plastics and/or foil. The products manufactured by establishments in this industry are made from purchased roll stock and may be printed in the same establishment.

Cross-References. Establishments primarily engaged in—

- Manufacturing uncoated paper bags and multiwall bags and sacks—are classified in U.S. Industry 322224, Uncoated Paper and Multiwall Bag Manufacturing;

- Manufacturing textile bags—are classified in U.S. Industry 314911, Textile Bag Mills;

- Manufacturing single and multiwall plastics bags—are classified in U.S. Industry 326111, Plastics Bag and Pouch Manufacturing; and

---

US—United States industry only. CAN—United States and Canadian industries are comparable. MEX—United States and Mexican industries are comparable. Blank—Canadian, Mexican, and United States industries are comparable.

- Printing on purchased packaging materials—are classified in Industry Group 3231, Printing and Related Support Activities, based on printing process used.

322224 Uncoated Paper and Multiwall Bag Manufacturing[US]

This U.S. industry comprises establishments primarily engaged in manufacturing uncoated paper bags or multiwall bags and sacks.

Cross-References. Establishments primarily engaged in—

- Manufacturing single wall and multiwall bags from plastics unsupported film—are classified in U.S. Industry 326111, Plastics Bag and Pouch Manufacturing;

- Manufacturing bags of coated paper, of metal foil, or of laminated or coated combinations of plastics, foil, and paper bags—are classified in U.S. Industry 322223, Coated Paper Bag and Pouch Manufacturing; and

- Manufacturing textile bags—are classified in U.S. Industry 314911, Textile Bag Mills.

322225 Laminated Aluminum Foil Manufacturing for Flexible Packaging Uses[US]

This U.S. industry comprises establishments primarily engaged in laminating aluminum and other metal foil into products with flexible packaging uses or gift wrap and other packaging wrap applications.

Cross-References. Establishments primarily engaged in—

- Manufacturing plain aluminum foil—are classified in U.S. Industry 331315, Aluminum Sheet, Plate, and Foil Manufacturing;

- Manufacturing laminated aluminum bags and liners—are classified in U.S. Industry 322223, Coated Paper Bag and Pouch Manufacturing;

- Manufacturing converted aluminum and other metal foils for nonpackaging uses from purchased foils—are classified in U.S. Industry 322222, Coated and Laminated Paper Manufacturing; and

- Manufacturing cookware, dinnerware, and other semirigid metal containers—are classified in U.S. Industry 332999, All Other Miscellaneous Fabricated Metal Product Manufacturing.

US—United States industry only. CAN—United States and Canadian industries are comparable. MEX—United States and Mexican industries are comparable. Blank—Canadian, Mexican, and United States industries are comparable.

322226 Surface-Coated Paperboard Manufacturing[US]

This U.S. industry comprises establishments primarily engaged in laminating, lining, or surface coating purchased paperboard to make other paperboard products.

32223 Stationery Product Manufacturing

This industry comprises establishments primarily engaged in converting paper or paperboard into products used for writing, filing, art work, and similar applications.

Illustrative Examples:

Die-cut paper products for office use made from purchased paper or paperboard

Tablets (e.g., memo, note, writing) made from purchased paper

Envelopes (i.e., mailing, stationery) made from any material

Tapes (e.g., adding machines, calculator, cash register) made from purchased paper

Stationery made from purchased paper

Cross-References.

Establishments primarily engaged in manufacturing die-cut paper and paperboard products other than office supplies are classified in U.S. Industry 322299, All Other Converted Paper Product Manufacturing.

322231 Die-Cut Paper and Paperboard Office Supplies Manufacturing[US]

This U.S. industry comprises establishments primarily engaged in converting paper rollstock or paperboard into die-cut paper or paperboard office supplies. For the purpose of this industry, office supplies are defined as office products, such as filing folders, index cards, rolls for adding machines, file separators and dividers, tabulating cards, and other paper and paperboard office supplies.

Cross-References. Establishments primarily engaged in—

- Manufacturing die-cut paper and paperboard products (except office supplies)—are classified in U.S. Industry 322299, All Other Converted Paper Product Manufacturing; and

- Manufacturing paper and paperboard products used for writing and similar applications (e.g., looseleaf fillers, notebooks, pads, stationery, tablets)—are classified in U.S. Industry 322233, Stationery, Tablet, and Related Product Manufacturing.

US—United States industry only. CAN—United States and Canadian industries are comparable. MEX—United States and Mexican industries are comparable. Blank—Canadian, Mexican, and United States industries are comparable.

322232 Envelope Manufacturing[US]

This U.S. industry comprises establishments primarily engaged in manufacturing envelopes for mailing or stationery of any material including combinations.

Cross-References.

Establishments primarily engaged in manufacturing stationery are classified in U.S. Industry 322233, Stationery, Tablet, and Related Product Manufacturing.

322233 Stationery, Tablet, and Related Product Manufacturing[US]

This U.S. industry comprises establishments primarily engaged in converting paper and paperboard into products used for writing and similar applications (e.g., looseleaf fillers, notebooks, pads, stationery, tablets).

Cross-References. Establishments primarily engaged in—

- Manufacturing envelopes—are classified in U.S. Industry 322232, Envelope Manufacturing; and

- Manufacturing die-cut paper and paperboard office supplies—are classified in U.S. Industry 322231, Die-Cut Paper and Paperboard Office Supplies Manufacturing.

32229 Other Converted Paper Product Manufacturing

This industry comprises establishments primarily engaged in (1) converting paper and paperboard into products (except containers, bags, coated and treated paper and paperboard, and stationery products), or (2) converting pulp into pulp products, such as disposable diapers, or molded pulp egg cartons, food trays, and dishes. Processes used include laminating or lining purchased paper or paperboard.

Illustrative Examples:

Crepe paper made from purchased paper
Paper novelties made from purchased paper
Die-cut paper products (except for office use) made from purchased paper or paperboard

Sanitary products made from purchased sanitary paper stock
Molded pulp products (e.g., egg cartons, food containers, food trays) manufacturing

Cross-References. Establishments primarily engaged in—

- Manufacturing pulp from wood or from other materials—are classified in Industry 32211, Pulp Mills;

US—United States industry only. CAN—United States and Canadian industries are comparable. MEX—United States and Mexican industries are comparable. Blank—Canadian, Mexican, and United States industries are comparable.

- Manufacturing paper from pulp or making pulp and manufacturing paper—are classified in Industry 32212, Paper Mills;

- Manufacturing paperboard from pulp or making pulp and manufacturing paperboard—are classified in Industry 32213, Paperboard Mills;

- Manufacturing paperboard containers—are classified in Industry 32221, Paperboard Container Manufacturing;

- Manufacturing bags of coated, laminated, or uncoated paper, of metal foil, or combinations thereof—are classified in Industry 32222, Paper Bag and Coated and Treated Paper Manufacturing; and

- Manufacturing stationery and other related office supplies—are classified in Industry 32223, Stationery Product Manufacturing.

322291 Sanitary Paper Product Manufacturing^{CAN}

This U.S. industry comprises establishments primarily engaged in converting purchased sanitary paper stock or wadding into sanitary paper products, such as facial tissues, handkerchiefs, table napkins, toilet paper, towels, disposable diapers, sanitary napkins, and tampons.

322299 All Other Converted Paper Product Manufacturing^{CAN}

This U.S. industry comprises establishments primarily engaged in converting paper or paperboard into products (except containers, bags, coated and treated paper, stationery products, and sanitary paper products) or converting pulp into pulp products, such as egg cartons, food trays, and other food containers from molded pulp.

Illustrative Examples:

Crepe paper made from purchased paper

Molded pulp products (e.g., egg cartons, food containers, food trays) manufacturing

Die-cut paper products (except for office use) made from purchased paper or paperboard

Paper novelties made from purchased paper

Cross-References. Establishments primarily engaged in—

- Manufacturing pulp from wood or from other materials—are classified in Industry 322110, Pulp Mills;

- Manufacturing paper from pulp or making pulp and manufacturing paper—are classified in Industry 32212, Paper Mills;

US—United States industry only. CAN—United States and Canadian industries are comparable. MEX—United States and Mexican industries are comparable. Blank—Canadian, Mexican, and United States industries are comparable.

- Manufacturing paperboard from pulp or making pulp and manufacturing paperboard—are classified in Industry 322130, Paperboard Mills;

- Manufacturing paperboard containers—are classified in Industry 32221, Paperboard Container Manufacturing;

- Manufacturing bags of coated, laminated, or uncoated paper, of metal foil, or combinations thereof—are classified in Industry 32222, Paper Bag and Coated and Treated Paper Manufacturing; and

- Manufacturing stationery and other related office supplies—are classified in Industry 32223, Stationery Product Manufacturing.

323 Printing and Related Support Activities

Industries in the Printing and Related Support Activities subsector print products, such as newspapers, books, labels, business cards, stationery, business forms, and other materials, and perform support activities, such as data imaging, platemaking services, and bookbinding. The support activities included here are an integral part of the printing industry, and a product (a printing plate, a bound book, or a computer disk or file) that is an integral part of the printing industry is almost always provided by these operations.

Processes used in printing include a variety of methods used to transfer an image from a plate, screen, film, or computer file to some medium, such as paper, plastics, metal, textile articles, or wood. The most prominent of these methods is to transfer the image from a plate or screen to the medium (lithographic, gravure, screen, and flexographic printing). A rapidly growing new technology uses a computer file to directly "drive" the printing mechanism to create the image and new electrostatic and other types of equipment (digital or nonimpact printing).

In contrast to many other classification systems that locate publishing of printed materials in manufacturing, NAICS classifies the publishing of printed products in Subsector 511, Publishing Industries (except Internet). Though printing and publishing are often carried out by the same enterprise (a newspaper, for example), it is less and less the case that these distinct activities are carried out in the same establishment. When publishing and printing are done in the same establishment, the establishment is classified in Sector 51, Information, in the appropriate NAICS industry even if the receipts for printing exceed those for publishing.

This subsector includes printing on clothing because the production process for that activity is printing, not clothing manufacturing. For instance, the printing of T-shirts is included in this subsector. In contrast, printing on fabric (or grey goods) is not included. This activity is part of the process of finishing the fabric and is included in the NAICS Textile Mills subsector in Industry 31331, Textile and Fabric Finishing Mills.

US—United States industry only. CAN—United States and Canadian industries are comparable. MEX—United States and Mexican industries are comparable. Blank—Canadian, Mexican, and United States industries are comparable.

3231 Printing and Related Support Activities

32311 Printing

This industry comprises establishments primarily engaged in printing on apparel and textile products, paper, metal, glass, plastics, and other materials, except fabric (grey goods). The printing processes employed include, but are not limited to, lithographic, gravure, screen, flexographic, digital, and letterpress. Establishments in this industry do not manufacture the stock that they print, but may perform postprinting activities, such as folding, cutting, or laminating the materials they print, and mailing.

Cross-References. Establishments primarily engaged in—

- Providing photocopying service on nondigital photocopy equipment without performing traditional printing activities—are classified in Industry 56143, Business Service Centers;

- Printing on grey goods—are classified in Industry 31331, Textile and Fabric Finishing Mills;

- Printing and publishing, known as publishers—are classified in Subsector 511, Publishing Industries (except Internet); and

- Performing prepress or postpress services without performing traditional printing activities—are classified in Industry 32312, Support Activities for Printing.

323110 Commercial Lithographic Printing[US]

This U.S. industry comprises establishments primarily engaged in lithographic (i.e., offset) printing without publishing (except books, grey goods, and manifold business forms). This industry includes establishments engaged in lithographic printing on purchased stock materials, such as stationery, letterhead, invitations, labels, and similar items, on a job order basis.

Cross-References. Establishments primarily engaged in—

- Quick printing—are classified in U.S. Industry 323114, Quick Printing;

- Printing on grey goods—are classified in Industry 31331, Textile and Fabric Finishing Mills;

- Printing books and pamphlets—are classified in U.S. Industry 323117, Books Printing;

- Printing manifold business forms including checkbooks—are classified in U.S. Industry 323116, Manifold Business Forms Printing;

US—United States industry only. CAN—United States and Canadian industries are comparable. MEX—United States and Mexican industries are comparable. Blank—Canadian, Mexican, and United States industries are comparable.

- Manufacturing printed stationery, invitations, labels, and similar items—are classified in Subsector 322, Paper Manufacturing; and

- Printing and publishing, known as publishers—are classified in Subsector 511, Publishing Industries (except Internet).

323111 Commercial Gravure Printing[US]

This U.S. industry comprises establishments primarily engaged in gravure printing without publishing (except books, grey goods, and manifold business forms). This industry includes establishments engaged in gravure printing on purchased stock materials, such as stationery, letterhead, invitations, labels, and similar items, on a job order basis.

Cross-References. Establishments primarily engaged in—

- Printing on grey goods—are classified in Industry 31331, Textile and Fabric Finishing Mills;

- Printing books and pamphlets—are classified in U.S. Industry 323117, Books Printing;

- Printing manifold business forms including checkbooks—are classified in U.S. Industry 323116, Manifold Business Forms Printing;

- Manufacturing printed stationery, invitations, labels, and similar items—are classified in Subsector 322, Paper Manufacturing; and

- Printing and publishing, known as publishers—are classified in Subsector 511, Publishing Industries (except Internet).

323112 Commercial Flexographic Printing[US]

This U.S. industry comprises establishments primarily engaged in flexographic printing without publishing (except books, grey goods, and manifold business forms). This industry includes establishments engaged in flexographic printing on purchased stock materials, such as stationery, invitations, labels, and similar items, on a job order basis.

Cross-References. Establishments primarily engaged in—

- Printing on grey goods—are classified in Industry 31331, Textile and Fabric Finishing Mills;

- Printing books and pamphlets—are classified in U.S. Industry 323117, Books Printing;

US—United States industry only. CAN—United States and Canadian industries are comparable. MEX—United States and Mexican industries are comparable. Blank—Canadian, Mexican, and United States industries are comparable.

- Printing manifold business forms including checkbooks—are classified in U.S. Industry 323116, Manifold Business Forms Printing;

- Manufacturing printed stationery, invitations, labels, and similar items—are classified elsewhere in Subsector 322, Paper Manufacturing; and

- Printing and publishing, known as publishers—are classified in Subsector 511, Publishing Industries (except Internet).

323113 Commercial Screen Printing^{CAN}

This U.S. industry comprises establishments primarily engaged in screen printing without publishing (except books, grey goods, and manifold business forms). This industry includes establishments engaged in screen printing on purchased stock materials, such as stationery, invitations, labels, and similar items, on a job order basis. Establishments primarily engaged in printing on apparel and textile products, such as T-shirts, caps, jackets, towels, and napkins, are included in this industry.

Cross-References. Establishments primarily engaged in—

- Printing on grey goods—are classified in Industry 31331, Textile and Fabric Finishing Mills;

- Printing books and pamphlets—are classified in U.S. Industry 323117, Books Printing;

- Printing manifold business forms including checkbooks—are classified in U.S. Industry 323116, Manifold Business Forms Printing;

- Manufacturing printed stationery, invitations, labels, and similar items—are classified in Subsector 322, Paper Manufacturing; and

- Printing and publishing, known as publishers—are classified in Subsector 511, Publishing Industries (except Internet).

323114 Quick Printing^{CAN}

This U.S. industry comprises establishments primarily engaged in traditional printing activities, such as short-run offset printing or prepress services, in combination with providing document photocopying service. Prepress services include receiving documents in electronic format and directly duplicating from the electronic file and formatting, colorizing, and otherwise modifying the original document to improve presentation. These establishments, known as quick printers, generally provide short-run printing and copying with fast turnaround times.

US—United States industry only. CAN—United States and Canadian industries are comparable. MEX—United States and Mexican industries are comparable. Blank—Canadian, Mexican, and United States industries are comparable.

Cross-References. Establishments primarily engaged in—

- Providing photocopying service on nondigital photocopy equipment without performing traditional printing activities—are classified in U.S. Industry 561439, Other Business Service Centers (including Copy Shops);
- Printing with lithographic equipment known as commercial lithographic printers—are classified in U.S. Industry 323110, Commercial Lithographic Printing; and
- Digital printing on graphical material—are classified in U.S. Industry 323115, Digital Printing.

323115 Digital Printing^{CAN}

This U.S. industry comprises establishments primarily engaged in printing graphical materials using digital printing equipment. Establishments known as digital printers typically provide sophisticated prepress services including using scanners to input images and computers to manipulate and format the graphic images prior to printing.

Cross-References.

Establishments primarily engaged in printing with "up front" computer files on conventional-type printing equipment are classified to books, manifold business forms, or based on the type of printing equipment (e.g., lithographic, flexographic, screen) being used.

323116 Manifold Business Forms Printing^{CAN}

This U.S. industry comprises establishments primarily engaged in printing special forms, including checkbooks, for use in the operation of a business. The forms may be in single and multiple sets, including carbonized, interleaved with carbon, or otherwise processed for multiple reproduction.

Cross-References.

Establishments primarily engaged in manufacturing single layered continuous computer paper and similar products are classified in U.S. Industry 322231, Die-Cut Paper and Paperboard Office Supplies Manufacturing.

323117 Books Printing^{US}

This U.S. industry comprises establishments primarily engaged in printing or printing and binding books and pamphlets without publishing.

US—United States industry only. CAN—United States and Canadian industries are comparable. MEX—United States and Mexican industries are comparable. Blank—Canadian, Mexican, and United States industries are comparable.

Cross-References. Establishments primarily engaged in—

- Printing and publishing, known as book publishers—are classified in Subsector 511, Publishing Industries (except Internet); and

- Binding books without printing in the same establishment—are classified in U.S. Industry 323121, Tradebinding and Related Work.

323118 Blankbook, Looseleaf Binders, and Devices Manufacturing[US]

This U.S. industry comprises establishments primarily engaged in manufacturing blankbooks, looseleaf devices, and binders. Establishments in this industry may print or print and bind.

Cross-References. Establishments primarily engaged in—

- Checkbook printing—are classified in U.S. Industry 323116, Manifold Business Forms Printing; and

- Binding books without printing in the same establishment—are classified in U.S. Industry 323121, Tradebinding and Related Work.

323119 Other Commercial Printing[US]

This U.S. industry comprises establishments primarily engaged in commercial printing (except lithographic, gravure, screen, or flexographic printing) without publishing (except books, grey goods, and manifold business forms). Printing processes included in this industry are letterpress printing and engraving printing. This industry includes establishments engaged in commercial printing on purchased stock materials, such as stationery, invitations, labels, and similar items, on a job order basis.

Cross-References. Establishments primarily engaged in—

- Lithographic, gravure, screen, or flexographic printing on purchased stock materials (except books, grey goods, and manifold business forms)—are classified in Industry 32311, Printing, by printing process employed;

- Printing on grey goods—are classified in Industry 31331, Textile and Fabric Finishing Mills;

- Quick printing—are classified in U.S. Industry 323114, Quick Printing;

- Digital printing on graphical materials—are classified in U.S. Industry 323115, Digital Printing;

- Printing books and pamphlets—are classified in U.S. Industry 323117, Books Printing;

- Printing manifold business forms, including checkbooks—are classified in U.S. Industry 323116, Manifold Business Forms Printing;
- Manufacturing printed stationery, invitations, labels, and similar items— are classified in Subsector 322, Paper Manufacturing; and
- Printing and publishing, known as book publishers—are classified in Subsector 511, Publishing Industries (except Internet).

32312 Support Activities for Printing

This industry comprises establishments primarily engaged in performing prepress (e.g., platemaking, typesetting) and postpress services (e.g., book binding) in support of printing activities.

Cross-References. Establishments primarily engaged in—

- Engraving of the type done on metal—are classified in Industry 33281, Coating, Engraving, Heat Treating, and Allied Activities;
- Manufacturing photosensitive plates for printing—are classified in Industry 32599, All Other Chemical Product and Preparation Manufacturing;
- Manufacturing blank plates for printing—are classified in Industry 33329, Other Industrial Machinery Manufacturing; and
- Printing books or printing and binding books—are classified in Industry 32311, Printing.

323121 Tradebinding and Related Work[US]

This U.S. industry comprises establishments primarily engaged in one or more of the following: (1) tradebinding; (2) sample mounting; and (3) postpress services (e.g., book or paper bronzing, die-cutting, edging, embossing, folding, gilding, gluing, indexing).

Cross-References.

Establishments primarily engaged in printing books or printing and binding books are classified in U.S. Industry 323117, Books Printing.

323122 Prepress Services[US]

This U.S. industry comprises (1) establishments primarily engaged in prepress services, such as imagesetting or typesetting, for printers and (2) establishments primarily engaged in preparing film or plates for printing purposes.

US—United States industry only. CAN—United States and Canadian industries are comparable. MEX—United States and Mexican industries are comparable. Blank—Canadian, Mexican, and United States industries are comparable.

Cross-References. Establishments primarily engaged in—

- Engraving of the type done on metal—are classified in U.S. Industry 332812, Metal Coating, Engraving (except Jewelry and Silverware), and Allied Services to Manufacturers;
- Manufacturing blank plates (except photosensitive plates) for printing—are classified in U.S. Industry 333293, Printing Machinery and Equipment Manufacturing; and
- Manufacturing photosensitive plates for printing—are classified in U.S. Industry 325992, Photographic Film, Paper, Plate, and Chemical Manufacturing.

324 Petroleum and Coal Products Manufacturing

The Petroleum and Coal Products Manufacturing subsector is based on the transformation of crude petroleum and coal into usable products. The dominant process is petroleum refining that involves the separation of crude petroleum into component products through such techniques as cracking and distillation.

In addition, this subsector includes establishments that primarily further process refined petroleum and coal products and produce products, such as asphalt coatings and petroleum lubricating oils. However, establishments that manufacture petrochemicals from refined petroleum are classified in Industry 32511, Petrochemical Manufacturing.

3241 Petroleum and Coal Products Manufacturing

32411 Petroleum Refineries
See industry description for 324110 below.

324110 Petroleum Refineries

This industry comprises establishments primarily engaged in refining crude petroleum into refined petroleum. Petroleum refining involves one or more of the following activities: (1) fractionation; (2) straight distillation of crude oil; and (3) cracking.

Cross-References. Establishments primarily engaged in—

- Manufacturing asphalt paving, roofing, and saturated materials from refined petroleum—are classified in Industry 32412, Asphalt Paving, Roofing, and Saturated Materials Manufacturing;

US—United States industry only. CAN—United States and Canadian industries are comparable. MEX—United States and Mexican industries are comparable. Blank—Canadian, Mexican, and United States industries are comparable.

- Manufacturing paper mats and felts and saturating them with asphalt or tar into rolls and sheets—are classified in U.S. Industry 322121, Paper (except Newsprint) Mills;

- Blending or compounding refined petroleum to make lubricating oils and greases and/or re-refining used petroleum lubricating oils—are classified in U.S. Industry 324191, Petroleum Lubricating Oil and Grease Manufacturing;

- Manufacturing synthetic lubricating oils and greases—are classified in U.S. Industry 325998, All Other Miscellaneous Chemical Product and Preparation Manufacturing;

- Recovering natural gasoline and/or liquid hydrocarbons from oil and gas field gases—are classified in Industry 21111, Oil and Gas Extraction;

- Manufacturing acyclic and cyclic aromatic hydrocarbons (i.e., petrochemicals) from refined petroleum or liquid hydrocarbons—are classified in Industry 325110, Petrochemical Manufacturing;

- Manufacturing cyclic and acyclic chemicals (except petrochemicals)—are classified in Industry 32519, Other Basic Organic Chemical Manufacturing;

- Manufacturing coke oven products in steel mills—are classified in U.S. Industry 331111, Iron and Steel Mills; and

- Manufacturing coke oven products in coke oven establishments—are classified in U.S. Industry, 324199, All Other Petroleum and Coal Products Manufacturing.

32412 Asphalt Paving, Roofing, and Saturated Materials Manufacturing

This industry comprises establishments primarily engaged in (1) manufacturing asphalt and tar paving mixtures and blocks and roofing cements and coatings from purchased asphaltic materials and/or (2) saturating purchased mats and felts with asphalt or tar from purchased asphaltic materials.

Cross-References. Establishments primarily engaged in—

- Refining crude petroleum and manufacturing asphalt and tar paving, roofing, and saturated materials—are classified in Industry 32411, Petroleum Refineries; and

- Manufacturing paper mats and felts and saturating them with asphalt or tar—are classified in Industry 32212, Paper Mills.

324121 Asphalt Paving Mixture and Block Manufacturing[CAN]

This U.S. industry comprises establishments primarily engaged in manufacturing asphalt and tar paving mixtures and blocks from purchased asphaltic materials.

US—United States industry only. CAN—United States and Canadian industries are comparable. MEX—United States and Mexican industries are comparable. Blank—Canadian, Mexican, and United States industries are comparable.

Cross-References.

Establishments primarily engaged in refining crude petroleum and manufacturing asphalt and tar paving mixtures and blocks are classified in Industry 324110, Petroleum Refineries.

324122 Asphalt Shingle and Coating Materials Manufacturing[CAN]

This U.S. industry comprises establishments primarily engaged in (1) saturating purchased mats and felts with asphalt or tar from purchased asphaltic materials and (2) manufacturing asphalt and tar and roofing cements and coatings from purchased asphaltic materials.

Cross-References. Establishments primarily engaged in—

- Refining crude petroleum and saturating purchased mats and felts with asphalt or tar into rolls and sheets and/or refining crude petroleum and manufacturing asphalt and tar roofing cements and coatings—are classified in Industry 324110, Petroleum Refineries; and

- Manufacturing paper mats and felts and saturating them with asphalt or tar into rolls and sheets—are classified in U.S. Industry 322121, Paper (except Newsprint) Mills.

32419 Other Petroleum and Coal Products Manufacturing

This industry comprises establishments primarily engaged in manufacturing petroleum products (except asphalt paving, roofing and saturated materials) from refined petroleum or coal products made in coke ovens not integrated with a steel mill.

Illustrative Examples:

Coke oven products (e.g., coke, gases, tars) made in coke oven establishments

Petroleum brake fluids made from refined petroleum

Petroleum briquettes made from refined petroleum

Petroleum jelly made from refined petroleum

Petroleum lubricating oils and greases made from refined petroleum

Petroleum waxes made from refined petroleum

Re-refined used petroleum lubricating oils

Cross-References. Establishments primarily engaged in—

- Manufacturing petroleum products by refining crude petroleum—are classified in Industry 32411, Petroleum Refineries;

- Manufacturing asphalt and tar paving, roofing, and saturated materials from refined petroleum—are classified in Industry 32412, Asphalt Paving, Roofing, and Saturated Materials Manufacturing;

- Manufacturing coke oven products in steel mills—are classified in Industry 33111, Iron and Steel Mills and Ferroalloy Manufacturing;

- Manufacturing acyclic and cyclic aromatic hydrocarbons (i.e., petrochemicals) from refined petroleum or liquid hydrocarbons—are classified in Industry 32511, Petrochemical Manufacturing;

- Manufacturing cyclic and acyclic organic chemicals (except petrochemicals)—are classified in Industry 32519, Other Basic Organic Chemical Manufacturing; and

- Manufacturing synthetic lubricating oils and greases--are classified in Industry 32599, All Other Chemical Product and Preparation Manufacturing.

324191 Petroleum Lubricating Oil and Grease Manufacturing[MEX]

This U.S. industry comprises establishments primarily engaged in blending or compounding refined petroleum to make lubricating oils and greases and/or re-refining used petroleum lubricating oils.

Cross-References. Establishments primarily engaged in—

- Refining crude petroleum and manufacturing lubricating oils and greases—are classified in Industry 324110, Petroleum Refineries; and

- Manufacturing synthetic lubricating oils and greases—are classified in U.S. Industry 325998, All Other Miscellaneous Chemical Product and Preparation Manufacturing.

324199 All Other Petroleum and Coal Products Manufacturing[MEX]

This U.S. industry comprises establishments primarily engaged in manufacturing petroleum products (except asphalt paving, roofing, and saturated materials and lubricating oils and greases) from refined petroleum and coal products made in coke ovens not integrated with a steel mill.

Illustrative Examples:

Coke oven products (e.g., coke, gases, tars) made in coke oven establishments

Petroleum briquettes made from refined petroleum

Petroleum jelly made from refined petroleum

Petroleum waxes made from refined petroleum

Cross-References. Establishments primarily engaged in—

- Manufacturing petroleum products by refining crude petroleum—are classified in Industry 324110, Petroleum Refineries;

- Manufacturing asphalt paving and roofing materials from refined petroleum—are classified in Industry 32412, Asphalt Paving, Roofing, and Saturated Materials Manufacturing;

- Blending and compounding petroleum lubricating oils and greases and/or re-refining used petroleum lubrication oils and greases—are classified in U.S. Industry 324191, Petroleum Lubricating Oil and Grease Manufacturing;

- Manufacturing coke oven products in steel mills—are classified in U.S. Industry 331111, Iron and Steel Mills;

- Manufacturing acyclic and cyclic aromatic hydrocarbons (i.e., petrochemicals) from refined petroleum or liquid hydrocarbons—are classified in Industry 325110, Petrochemical Manufacturing; and

- Manufacturing cyclic and acyclic organic chemicals (except petrochemicals)—are classified in Industry 32519, Other Basic Organic Chemical Manufacturing.

325 Chemical Manufacturing

The Chemical Manufacturing subsector is based on the transformation of organic and inorganic raw materials by a chemical process and the formulation of products. This subsector distinguishes the production of basic chemicals that comprise the first industry group from the production of intermediate and end products produced by further processing of basic chemicals that make up the remaining industry groups.

This subsector does not include all industries transforming raw materials by a chemical process. It is common for some chemical processing to occur during mining operations. These beneficiating operations, such as copper concentrating, are classified in Sector 21, Mining, Quarrying, and Oil and Gas Extraction. Furthermore, the refining of crude petroleum is included in Subsector 324, Petroleum and Coal Products Manufacturing. In addition, the manufacturing of aluminum oxide is included in Subsector 331, Primary Metal Manufacturing; and beverage distilleries are classified in Subsector 312, Beverage and Tobacco Product Manufacturing. As in the case of these two activities, the grouping of industries into subsectors may take into account the association of the activities performed with other activities in the subsector.

US—United States industry only. CAN—United States and Canadian industries are comparable. MEX—United States and Mexican industries are comparable. Blank—Canadian, Mexican, and United States industries are comparable.

3251 Basic Chemical Manufacturing

This industry group comprises establishments primarily engaged in manufacturing chemicals using basic processes, such as thermal cracking and distillation. Chemicals manufactured in this industry group are usually separate chemical elements or separate chemically-defined compounds.

32511 Petrochemical Manufacturing
See industry description for 325110 below.

325110 Petrochemical Manufacturing

This industry comprises establishments primarily engaged in (1) manufacturing acyclic (i.e., aliphatic) hydrocarbons such as ethylene, propylene, and butylene made from refined petroleum or liquid hydrocarbons and/or (2) manufacturing cyclic aromatic hydrocarbons such as benzene, toluene, styrene, xylene, ethyl benzene, and cumene made from refined petroleum or liquid hydrocarbons.

Cross-References. Establishments primarily engaged in—

- Manufacturing petrochemicals by refining crude petroleum—are classified in Industry 324110, Petroleum Refineries;
- Manufacturing acetylene—are classified in Industry 325120, Industrial Gas Manufacturing;
- Manufacturing basic organic chemicals (except petrochemicals)—are classified in Industry 32519, Other Basic Organic Chemical Manufacturing; and
- Recovering liquid hydrocarbons from oil and gas field gases—are classified in Industry 21111, Oil and Gas Extraction.

32512 Industrial Gas Manufacturing
See industry description for 325120 below.

325120 Industrial Gas Manufacturing

This industry comprises establishments primarily engaged in manufacturing industrial organic and inorganic gases in compressed, liquid, and solid forms.

Cross-References. Establishments primarily engaged in—

- Manufacturing chlorine gas—are classified in U.S. Industry 325181, Alkalies and Chlorine Manufacturing; and

---

US—United States industry only. CAN—United States and Canadian industries are comparable. MEX—United States and Mexican industries are comparable. Blank—Canadian, Mexican, and United States industries are comparable.

- Manufacturing ethane and butane gases made from refined petroleum or liquid hydrocarbons—are classified in Industry 325110, Petrochemical Manufacturing.

32513 Synthetic Dye and Pigment Manufacturing

This industry comprises establishments primarily engaged in manufacturing synthetic organic and inorganic dyes and pigments, such as lakes and toners (except electrostatic and photographic).

Cross-References. Establishments primarily engaged in—

- Manufacturing wood byproducts used as dying materials—are classified in Industry 32519, Other Basic Organic Chemical Manufacturing;
- Manufacturing carbon, bone, and lamp black—are classified in Industry 32518, Other Basic Inorganic Chemical Manufacturing;
- Manufacturing electrostatic and photographic toners—are classified in Industry 32599, All Other Chemical Product and Preparation Manufacturing;
- Manufacturing natural food colorings—are classified in Industry 31193, Flavoring Syrup and Concentrate Manufacturing; and
- Manufacturing natural organic colorings for nonfood uses—are classified in Industry 32519, Other Basic Organic Chemical Manufacturing.

325131 Inorganic Dye and Pigment Manufacturing[US]

This U.S. industry comprises establishments primarily engaged in manufacturing inorganic dyes and pigments.

Cross-References. Establishments primarily engaged in—

- Manufacturing wood byproducts used as dyeing materials—are classified in U.S. Industry 325191, Gum and Wood Chemical Manufacturing;
- Manufacturing organic synthetic dyes and pigments—are classified in U.S. Industry 325132, Synthetic Organic Dye and Pigment Manufacturing;
- Manufacturing carbon, bone, and lamp black—are classified in U.S. Industry 325182, Carbon Black Manufacturing; and
- Manufacturing natural food colorings—are classified in Industry 311930, Flavoring Syrup and Concentrate Manufacturing.

US—United States industry only. CAN—United States and Canadian industries are comparable. MEX—United States and Mexican industries are comparable. Blank—Canadian, Mexican, and United States industries are comparable.

325132 Synthetic Organic Dye and Pigment Manufacturing[US]

This U.S. industry comprises establishments primarily engaged in manufacturing synthetic organic dyes and pigments, such as lakes and toners (except electrostatic and photographic).

Cross-References. Establishments primarily engaged in—

- Manufacturing wood byproducts used as dyeing materials—are classified in U.S. Industry 325191, Gum and Wood Chemical Manufacturing;

- Manufacturing inorganic dyes and pigments—are classified in U.S. Industry 325131, Inorganic Dye and Pigment Manufacturing;

- Manufacturing electrostatic and photographic toners—are classified in U.S. Industry 325992, Photographic Film, Paper, Plate, and Chemical Manufacturing;

- Manufacturing natural food colorings—are classified in Industry 311930, Flavoring Syrup and Concentrate Manufacturing; and

- Manufacturing natural organic colorings for nonfood uses (except wood byproducts)—are classified in U.S. Industry 325199, All Other Basic Organic Chemical Manufacturing.

32518 Other Basic Inorganic Chemical Manufacturing

This industry comprises establishments primarily engaged in manufacturing basic inorganic chemicals (except industrial gases and synthetic dyes and pigments).

Illustrative Examples:

Alkalies manufacturing
Hydrochloric acid manufacturing
Aluminum compounds, not specified
  elsewhere by process, manufacturing
Potassium inorganic compounds, not
  specified elsewhere by process,
  manufacturing

Carbides (e.g., baron, calcium, silium,
  tungsten) manufacturing
Radioactive isotopes manufacturing
Carbon black manufacturing
Sulfides and sulfites manufacturing
Chlorine manufacturing
Sulfuric acid manufacturing

Cross-References. Establishments primarily engaged in—

- Manufacturing industrial gases—are classified in Industry 32512, Industrial Gas Manufacturing;

- Manufacturing inorganic dyes and pigments—are classified in Industry 32513, Synthetic Dye and Pigment Manufacturing;

US—United States industry only. CAN—United States and Canadian industries are comparable. MEX—United States and Mexican industries are comparable. Blank—Canadian, Mexican, and United States industries are comparable.

- Manufacturing household bleaches—are classified in Industry 32561, Soap and Cleaning Compound Manufacturing;
- Mining and/or beneficiating alkalies—are classified in Industry 21239, Other Nonmetallic Mineral Mining and Quarrying;
- Manufacturing chlorine preparations (e.g., for swimming pools)—are classified in Industry 32599, All Other Chemical Product and Preparation Manufacturing;
- Manufacturing nitrogenous and phosphoric fertilizers and fertilizer materials—are classified in Industry 32531, Fertilizer Manufacturing;
- Manufacturing aluminum oxide (alumina)—are classified in Industry 33131, Alumina and Aluminum Production and Processing;
- Manufacturing inorganic insecticidal, herbicidal, fungicidal and pesticidal preparations—are classified in Industry 32532, Pesticide and Other Agricultural Chemical Manufacturing; and
- Manufacturing photographic chemicals—are classified in Industry 32599, All Other Chemical Product and Preparation Manufacturing.

325181 Alkalies and Chlorine Manufacturing^{CAN}

This U.S. industry comprises establishments primarily engaged in manufacturing chlorine, sodium hydroxide (i.e., caustic soda), and other alkalies often using an electrolysis process.

Cross-References. Establishments primarily engaged in—

- Mining and beneficiating alkalies—are classified in U.S. Industry 212391, Potash, Soda, and Borate Mineral Mining;
- Manufacturing chlorine preparations (e.g., for swimming pools)—are classified in U.S. Industry 325998, All Other Miscellaneous Chemical Product and Preparation Manufacturing;
- Manufacturing industrial bleaches—are classified in U.S. Industry 325188, All Other Basic Inorganic Chemical Manufacturing; and
- Manufacturing household bleaches—are classified in U.S. Industry 325612, Polish and Other Sanitation Good Manufacturing.

325182 Carbon Black Manufacturing^{US}

This U.S. industry comprises establishments primarily engaged in manufacturing carbon black, bone black, and lamp black.

US—United States industry only. CAN—United States and Canadian industries are comparable. MEX—United States and Mexican industries are comparable. Blank—Canadian, Mexican, and United States industries are comparable.

Cross-References.

Establishments primarily engaged in manufacturing pigments are classified in Industry 32513, Synthetic Dye and Pigment Manufacturing.

325188 All Other Basic Inorganic Chemical Manufacturing[US]

This U.S. industry comprises establishments primarily engaged in manufacturing basic inorganic chemicals (except industrial gases, inorganic dyes and pigments, alkalies and chlorine, and carbon black).

Illustrative Examples:

Aluminum compounds, not specified
  elsewhere by process, manufacturing
Potassium inorganic compounds, not
  specified elsewhere by process,
  manufacturing
Carbides (e.g., baron, calcium, silicon,
  tungsten) manufacturing

Sodium inorganic compounds, not
  specified elsewhere by process,
  manufacturing
Fluorine manufacturing
Sulfides and sulfites manufacturing
Hydrochloric acid manufacturing
Sulfuric acid manufacturing

Cross-References. Establishments primarily engaged in—

- Manufacturing industrial gases—are classified in Industry 325120, Industrial Gas Manufacturing;

- Manufacturing inorganic dyes and pigments—are classified in U.S. Industry 325131, Inorganic Dye and Pigment Manufacturing;

- Manufacturing alkalies and chlorine—are classified in U.S. Industry 325181, Alkalies and Chlorine Manufacturing;

- Manufacturing carbon black—are classified in U.S. Industry 325182, Carbon Black Manufacturing;

- Manufacturing household bleaches—are classified in U.S. Industry 325612, Polish and Other Sanitation Good Manufacturing;

- Manufacturing nitrogenous and phosphoric fertilizers and fertilizer material—are classified in Industry 32531, Fertilizer Manufacturing;

- Manufacturing aluminum oxide (i.e., alumina)—are classified in U.S. Industry 331311, Alumina Refining;

- Manufacturing inorganic insecticidal, herbicidal, fungicidal, and pesticidal preparations—are classified in Industry 325320, Pesticide and Other Agricultural Chemical Manufacturing; and

- Manufacturing photographic chemicals—are classified in U.S. Industry 325992, Photographic Film, Paper, Plate, and Chemical Manufacturing.

US—United States industry only. CAN—United States and Canadian industries are comparable. MEX—United States and Mexican industries are comparable. Blank—Canadian, Mexican, and United States industries are comparable.

32519 Other Basic Organic Chemical Manufacturing

This industry comprises establishments primarily engaged in manufacturing basic organic chemicals (except petrochemicals, industrial gases, and synthetic dyes and pigments).

Illustrative Examples:

Carbon organic compounds, not specified elsewhere by process, manufacturing

Organo-inorganic compound manufacturing

Cyclic intermediates made from refined petroleum or natural gas

Plasticizers (i.e., basic synthetic chemical) manufacturing

Enzyme proteins (i.e., basic synthetic chemicals) (except pharmaceutical use) manufacturing

Silicone (except resins) manufacturing

Fatty acids (e.g., margaric, oleic, stearic) manufacturing

Synthetic sweeteners (i.e., sweetening agents) manufacturing

Gum and wood chemicals manufacturing

Cross-References. Establishments primarily engaged in—

- Manufacturing petrochemicals from refined petroleum or liquid hydrocarbons—are classified in Industry 32511, Petrochemical Manufacturing;

- Manufacturing petrochemicals by refining crude petroleum—are classified in Industry 32411, Petroleum Refineries;

- Manufacturing organic industrial gases—are classified in Industry 32512, Industrial Gas Manufacturing;

- Manufacturing synthetic organic dyes and pigments—are classified in Industry 32513, Synthetic Dye and Pigment Manufacturing;

- Manufacturing natural glycerin—are classified in Industry 32561, Soap and Cleaning Compound Manufacturing;

- Manufacturing activated charcoal—are classified in Industry 32599, All Other Chemical Product and Preparation Manufacturing;

- Manufacturing organic insecticidal, herbicidal, fungicidal, and pesticidal preparations—are classified in Industry 32532, Pesticide and Other Agricultural Chemical Manufacturing;

- Manufacturing elastomers—are classified in Industry 32521, Resin and Synthetic Rubber Manufacturing;

- Manufacturing urea—are classified in Industry 32531, Fertilizer Manufacturing;

- Manufacturing coal tar crudes in integrated steel mills with coke ovens— are classified in Industry 33111, Iron and Steel Mills and Ferroalloy Manufacturing;

US—United States industry only. CAN—United States and Canadian industries are comparable. MEX—United States and Mexican industries are comparable. Blank—Canadian, Mexican, and United States industries are comparable.

- Manufacturing coal tar crudes in coke ovens not integrated with steel mills and fuel briquettes from refined petroleum—are classified in Industry 32419, Other Petroleum and Coal Products Manufacturing; and

- Manufacturing natural food colorings—are classified in Industry 31194, Seasoning and Dressing Manufacturing.

325191 Gum and Wood Chemical Manufacturing[US]

This U.S. industry comprises establishments primarily engaged in (1) distilling wood or gum into products, such as tall oil and wood distillates, and (2) manufacturing wood or gum chemicals, such as naval stores, natural tanning materials, charcoal briquettes, and charcoal (except activated).

Cross-References. Establishments primarily engaged in—

- Manufacturing activated charcoal—are classified in U.S. Industry 325998, All Other Miscellaneous Chemical Product and Preparation Manufacturing; and

- Manufacturing fuel briquettes from refined petroleum—are classified in U.S. Industry 324199, All Other Petroleum and Coal Products Manufacturing.

325192 Cyclic Crude and Intermediate Manufacturing[US]

This U.S. industry comprises establishments primarily engaged in (1) distilling coal tars and/or (2) manufacturing cyclic crudes or cyclic intermediates (i.e., hydrocarbons, except aromatic petrochemicals) from refined petroleum or natural gas.

Cross-References. Establishments primarily engaged in—

- Manufacturing cyclic chemicals (except aromatic and intermediates)—are classified in U.S. Industry 325199, All Other Basic Organic Chemical Manufacturing;

- Manufacturing aromatic petrochemicals from refined petroleum or natural gas—are classified in Industry 325110, Petrochemical Manufacturing;

- Manufacturing aromatic petrochemicals by refining crude petroleum—are classified in Industry 324110, Petroleum Refineries;

- Distilling wood products—are classified in U.S. Industry 325191, Gum and Wood Chemical Manufacturing;

- Manufacturing coal tar crudes in steel mills with coke ovens—are classified in U.S. Industry 331111, Iron and Steel Mills; and

---

US—United States industry only. CAN—United States and Canadian industries are comparable. MEX—United States and Mexican industries are comparable. Blank—Canadian, Mexican, and United States industries are comparable.

- Manufacturing coal tar crudes in coke oven establishments and fuel briquettes from refined petroleum—are classified in U.S. Industry 324199, All Other Petroleum and Coal Products Manufacturing.

325193 Ethyl Alcohol Manufacturing[US]

This U.S. industry comprises establishments primarily engaged in manufacturing nonpotable ethyl alcohol.

Cross-References. Establishments primarily engaged in—

- Distilling liquors (except brandy)—are classified in Industry 312140, Distilleries; and
- Manufacturing brandies—are classified in Industry 312130, Wineries.

325199 All Other Basic Organic Chemical Manufacturing[US]

This U.S. industry comprises establishments primarily engaged in manufacturing basic organic chemical products (except aromatic petrochemicals, industrial gases, synthetic organic dyes and pigments, gum and wood chemicals, cyclic crudes and intermediates, and ethyl alcohol).

Illustrative Examples:

Calcium organic compounds, not specified elsewhere by process, manufacturing

Organo-inorganic compound manufacturing

Carbon organic compounds, not specified elsewhere by process, manufacturing

Plasticizers (i.e., basic synthetic chemical) manufacturing

Enzyme proteins (i.e., basic synthetic chemicals) (except pharmaceutical use) manufacturing

Silicone (except resins) manufacturing

Fatty acids (e.g., margaric, oleic, stearic) manufacturing

Synthetic sweeteners (i.e., sweetening agents) manufacturing

Cross-References. Establishments primarily engaged in—

- Manufacturing aromatic petrochemicals from refined petroleum or natural gas—are classified in Industry 325110, Petrochemical Manufacturing;
- Manufacturing aromatic petrochemicals by refining crude petroleum—are classified in Industry 324110, Petroleum Refineries;
- Manufacturing organic industrial gases—are classified in Industry 325120, Industrial Gas Manufacturing;
- Manufacturing synthetic organic dyes and pigments—are classified in U.S. Industry 325132, Synthetic Organic Dye and Pigment Manufacturing;

US—United States industry only. CAN—United States and Canadian industries are comparable. MEX—United States and Mexican industries are comparable. Blank—Canadian, Mexican, and United States industries are comparable.

- Manufacturing ethyl alcohol—are classified in U.S. Industry 325193, Ethyl Alcohol Manufacturing;

- Manufacturing organic insecticidal, herbicidal, fungicidal, and pesticidal preparations—are classified in Industry 325320, Pesticide and Other Agricultural Chemical Manufacturing;

- Manufacturing elastomers—are classified in Industry 32521, Resin and Synthetic Rubber Manufacturing;

- Manufacturing urea—are classified in U.S. Industry 325311, Nitrogenous Fertilizer Manufacturing;

- Manufacturing natural glycerin—are classified in U.S. Industry 325611, Soap and Other Detergent Manufacturing; and

- Manufacturing natural food colorings—are classified in U.S. Industry 311942, Spice and Extract Manufacturing.

3252 Resin, Synthetic Rubber, and Artificial Synthetic Fibers and Filaments Manufacturing

32521 Resin and Synthetic Rubber Manufacturing

This industry comprises establishments primarily engaged in one or more of the following: (1) manufacturing synthetic resins, plastics materials, and nonvulcanizable elastomers and mixing and blending resins on a custom basis; (2) manufacturing noncustomized synthetic resins; and (3) manufacturing synthetic rubber.

Cross-References. Establishments primarily engaged in—

- Manufacturing plastics resins and converting resins into plastics products—are classified in Industry Group 3261, Plastics Product Manufacturing;

- Processing natural, synthetic, or reclaimed rubber into intermediate or final products—are classified in Industry Group 3262, Rubber Product Manufacturing;

- Custom compounding resins made elsewhere—are classified in Industry ·32599, All Other Chemical Product and Preparation Manufacturing; and

- Manufacturing resin adhesives—are classified in Industry 32552, Adhesive Manufacturing.

325211 Plastics Material and Resin Manufacturing[US]

This U.S. industry comprises establishments primarily engaged in (1) manufacturing resins, plastics materials, and nonvulcanizable thermoplastic elastomers

---

US—United States industry only. CAN—United States and Canadian industries are comparable. MEX—United States and Mexican industries are comparable. Blank—Canadian, Mexican, and United States industries are comparable.

and mixing and blending resins on a custom basis and/or (2) manufacturing non-customized synthetic resins.

Cross-References. Establishments primarily engaged in—

- Manufacturing plastics resins and converting the resins into plastics products—are classified in 3261, Plastics Product Manufacturing;
- Custom compounding resins made elsewhere—are classified in U.S. Industry 325991, Custom Compounding of Purchased Resins; and
- Manufacturing plastics adhesives—are classified in Industry 325520, Adhesive Manufacturing.

325212 Synthetic Rubber Manufacturing[MEX]

This U.S. industry consists of establishments primarily engaged in manufacturing synthetic rubber.

Cross-References. Establishments primarily engaged in—

- Processing natural, synthetic, or reclaimed rubber into intermediate or final products (except adhesives)—are classified in Industry Group 3262, Rubber Product Manufacturing; and
- Manufacturing rubber adhesives—are classified in Industry 325520, Adhesive Manufacturing.

32522 Artificial and Synthetic Fibers and Filaments Manufacturing

This industry comprises establishments primarily engaged in (1) manufacturing cellulosic (i.e., rayon and acetate) and noncellulosic (i.e., nylon, polyolefin, and polyester) fibers and filaments in the form of monofilament, filament yarn, staple, or tow or (2) manufacturing and texturing cellulosic and noncellulosic fibers and filaments.

Cross-References. Establishments primarily engaged in—

- Texturizing cellulosic and noncellulosic fiber and filament made elsewhere—are classified in Industry 31311, Fiber, Yarn, and Thread Mills; and
- Manufacturing textile glass fibers—are classified in Industry 32721, Glass and Glass Product Manufacturing.

325221 Cellulosic Organic Fiber Manufacturing[US]

This U.S. industry comprises establishments primarily engaged in (1) manufacturing cellulosic (i.e., rayon and acetate) fibers and filaments in the form of

---

US—United States industry only. CAN—United States and Canadian industries are comparable. MEX—United States and Mexican industries are comparable. Blank—Canadian, Mexican, and United States industries are comparable.

monofilament, filament yarn, staple, or tow or (2) manufacturing and texturizing cellulosic fibers and filaments.

Cross-References. Establishments primarily engaged in—

- Texturizing cellulosic fibers and filaments made elsewhere—are classified in U.S. Industry 313112, Yarn Texturizing, Throwing, and Twisting Mills; and

- Manufacturing noncellulosic fibers and filaments—are classified in U.S. Industry 325222, Noncellulosic Organic Fiber Manufacturing.

325222 Noncellulosic Organic Fiber Manufacturing[US]

This U.S. industry consists of establishments primarily engaged in (1) manufacturing noncellulosic (i.e., nylon, polyolefin, and polyester) fibers and filaments in the form of monofilament, filament yarn, staple, or tow, or (2) manufacturing and texturizing noncellulosic fibers and filaments.

Cross-References. Establishments primarily engaged in—

- Texturizing noncellulosic fibers—are classified in U.S. Industry 313112, Yarn Texturizing, Throwing, and Twisting Mills;

- Manufacturing cellulose fibers—are classified in U.S. Industry 325221, Cellulosic Organic Fiber Manufacturing; and

- Manufacturing textile glass fibers—are classified in U.S. Industry 327212, Other Pressed and Blown Glass and Glassware Manufacturing.

3253 Pesticide, Fertilizer, and Other Agricultural Chemical Manufacturing

32531 Fertilizer Manufacturing

This industry comprises establishments primarily engaged in one or more of the following: (1) manufacturing nitrogenous or phosphatic fertilizer materials; (2) manufacturing fertilizers from sewage or animal waste; (3) manufacturing nitrogenous or phosphatic materials and mixing with other ingredients into fertilizers; and (4) mixing ingredients made elsewhere into fertilizers.

325311 Nitrogenous Fertilizer Manufacturing[US]

This U.S. industry comprises establishments primarily engaged in one or more of the following: (1) manufacturing nitrogenous fertilizer materials and mixing

---

US—United States industry only. CAN—United States and Canadian industries are comparable. MEX—United States and Mexican industries are comparable. Blank—Canadian, Mexican, and United States industries are comparable.

ingredients into fertilizers; (2) manufacturing fertilizers from sewage or animal waste; and (3) manufacturing nitrogenous materials and mixing them into fertilizers.

Cross-References.

Establishments primarily engaged in mixing ingredients made elsewhere into nitrogenous fertilizers are classified in U.S. Industry 325314, Fertilizer (Mixing Only) Manufacturing.

325312 Phosphatic Fertilizer Manufacturing[US]

This U.S. industry comprises establishments primarily engaged in (1) manufacturing phosphatic fertilizer materials or (2) manufacturing phosphatic materials and mixing them into fertilizers.

Cross-References.

Establishments primarily engaged in mixing ingredients made elsewhere into phosphatic fertilizers are classified in U.S. Industry 325314, Fertilizer (Mixing Only) Manufacturing.

325314 Fertilizer (Mixing Only) Manufacturing[CAN]

This U.S. industry comprises establishments primarily engaged in mixing ingredients made elsewhere into fertilizers.

Cross-References. Establishments primarily engaged in—

- Manufacturing nitrogenous fertilizer materials or fertilizer materials from sewage or animal waste and mixing these ingredients into nitrogenous fertilizers—are classified in U.S. Industry 325311, Nitrogenous Fertilizer Manufacturing; and
- Manufacturing phosphatic fertilizer materials and mixing ingredients into fertilizers—are classified in U.S. Industry 325312, Phosphatic Fertilizer Manufacturing.

32532 Pesticide and Other Agricultural Chemical Manufacturing
See industry description for 325320 below.

325320 Pesticide and Other Agricultural Chemical Manufacturing

This industry comprises establishments primarily engaged in the formulation and preparation of agricultural and household pest control chemicals (except fertilizers).

US—United States industry only. CAN—United States and Canadian industries are comparable. MEX—United States and Mexican industries are comparable. Blank—Canadian, Mexican, and United States industries are comparable.

Cross-References. Establishments primarily engaged in—

- Manufacturing basic chemicals requiring further processing before use as agriculture chemicals—are classified in Industry Group 3251, Basic Chemical Manufacturing;

- Manufacturing fertilizers—are classified in Industry 32531, Fertilizer Manufacturing; and

- Manufacturing agricultural lime products—are classified in Industry 327410, Lime Manufacturing.

3254 Pharmaceutical and Medicine Manufacturing

32541 Pharmaceutical and Medicine Manufacturing

This industry comprises establishments primarily engaged in one or more of the following: (1) manufacturing biological and medicinal products; (2) processing (i.e., grading, grinding, and milling) botanical drugs and herbs; (3) isolating active medicinal principals from botanical drugs and herbs; and (4) manufacturing pharmaceutical products intended for internal and external consumption in such forms as ampoules, tablets, capsules, vials, ointments, powders, solutions, and suspensions.

325411 Medicinal and Botanical Manufacturing[US]

This U.S. industry comprises establishments primarily engaged in (1) manufacturing uncompounded medicinal chemicals and their derivatives (i.e., generally for use by pharmaceutical preparation manufacturers) and/or (2) grading, grinding, and milling uncompounded botanicals.

Cross-References. Establishments primarily engaged in—

- Manufacturing packaged compounded medicinals and botanicals—are classified in U.S. Industry 325412, Pharmaceutical Preparation Manufacturing; and

- Manufacturing vaccines, toxoids, blood fractions, and culture media of plant or animal origin (except for diagnostic use)—are classified in U.S. Industry 325414, Biological Product (except Diagnostic) Manufacturing.

325412 Pharmaceutical Preparation Manufacturing[US]

This U.S. industry comprises establishments primarily engaged in manufacturing in-vivo diagnostic substances and pharmaceutical preparations (except biological)

---

intended for internal and external consumption in dose forms, such as ampoules, tablets, capsules, vials, ointments, powders, solutions, and suspensions.

Cross-References. Establishments primarily engaged in—

- Manufacturing uncompounded medicinal chemicals and their derivatives— are classified in U.S. Industry 325411, Medicinal and Botanical Manufacturing;
- Manufacturing in-vitro diagnostic substances—are classified in U.S. Industry 325413, In-Vitro Diagnostic Substance Manufacturing; and
- Manufacturing vaccines, toxoids, blood fractions, and culture media of plant or animal origin (except for diagnostic use)—are classified in U.S. Industry 325414, Biological Product (except Diagnostic) Manufacturing.

325413 In-Vitro Diagnostic Substance Manufacturing[US]

This U.S. industry comprises establishments primarily engaged in manufacturing in-vitro (i.e., not taken internally) diagnostic substances, such as chemical, biological, or radioactive substances. The substances are used for diagnostic tests that are performed in test tubes, petri dishes, machines, and other diagnostic test-type devices.

Cross-References.

Establishments primarily engaged in manufacturing in-vivo diagnostic substances are classified in U.S. Industry 325412, Pharmaceutical Preparation Manufacturing.

325414 Biological Product (except Diagnostic) Manufacturing[US]

This U.S. industry comprises establishments primarily engaged in manufacturing vaccines, toxoids, blood fractions, and culture media of plant or animal origin (except diagnostic).

Cross-References. Establishments primarily engaged in—

- Manufacturing in-vitro diagnostic substances—are classified in U.S. Industry 325413, In-Vitro Diagnostic Substance Manufacturing; and
- Manufacturing pharmaceutical preparations, (except biological and in-vivo diagnostic substances)—are classified in U.S. Industry 325412, Pharmaceutical Preparation Manufacturing.

US—United States industry only. CAN—United States and Canadian industries are comparable. MEX—United States and Mexican industries are comparable. Blank—Canadian, Mexican, and United States industries are comparable.

3255 Paint, Coating, and Adhesive Manufacturing

32551 Paint and Coating Manufacturing
See industry description for 325510 below.

325510 Paint and Coating Manufacturing

This industry comprises establishments primarily engaged in (1) mixing pigments, solvents, and binders into paints and other coatings, such as stains, varnishes, lacquers, enamels, shellacs, and water repellant coatings for concrete and masonry, and/or (2) manufacturing allied paint products, such as putties, paint and varnish removers, paint brush cleaners, and frit.

Cross-References. Establishments primarily engaged in—

- Manufacturing creosote—are classified in Industry 32519, Other Basic Organic Chemical Manufacturing;
- Manufacturing caulking compounds and sealants—are classified in Industry 325520, Adhesive Manufacturing;
- Manufacturing artists' paints—are classified in U.S. Industry 339942, Lead Pencil and Art Good Manufacturing; and
- Manufacturing turpentine—are classified in U.S. Industry 325191, Gum and Wood Chemical Manufacturing.

32552 Adhesive Manufacturing
See industry description for 325520 below.

325520 Adhesive Manufacturing

This industry comprises establishments primarily engaged in manufacturing adhesives, glues, and caulking compounds.

Cross-References. Establishments primarily engaged in—

- Manufacturing asphalt and tar roofing cements from purchased asphaltic materials—are classified in U.S. Industry 324122, Asphalt Shingle and Coating Materials Manufacturing; and
- Manufacturing gypsum based caulking compounds—are classified in Industry 327420, Gypsum Product Manufacturing.

US—United States industry only. CAN—United States and Canadian industries are comparable. MEX—United States and Mexican industries are comparable. Blank—Canadian, Mexican, and United States industries are comparable.

3256 Soap, Cleaning Compound, and Toilet Preparation Manufacturing

32561 Soap and Cleaning Compound Manufacturing

This industry comprises establishments primarily engaged in manufacturing and packaging soap and other cleaning compounds, surface active agents, and textile and leather finishing agents used to reduce tension or speed the drying process.

Cross-References. Establishments primarily engaged in—

* Manufacturing synthetic glycerin—are classified in Industry 32519, Other Basic Organic Chemical Manufacturing;

* Manufacturing industrial bleaches—are classified in Industry 32518, Other Basic Inorganic Chemical Manufacturing; and

* Manufacturing shampoos and shaving preparations—are classified in Industry 32562, Toilet Preparation Manufacturing.

325611 Soap and Other Detergent Manufacturing[US]

This U.S. industry comprises establishments primarily engaged in manufacturing and packaging soaps and other detergents, such as laundry detergents; dishwashing detergents; toothpaste gels, and tooth powders; and natural glycerin.

Cross-References. Establishments primarily engaged in—

* Manufacturing synthetic glycerin—are classified in U.S. Industry 325199, All Other Basic Organic Chemical Manufacturing; and

* Manufacturing shampoos and shaving preparations—are classified in Industry 325620, Toilet Preparation Manufacturing.

325612 Polish and Other Sanitation Good Manufacturing[US]

This U.S. industry comprises establishments primarily engaged in manufacturing and packaging polishes and specialty cleaning preparations.

Cross-References.

Establishments primarily engaged in manufacturing chlorine dioxide (i.e., industrial bleaching agent) are classified in U.S. Industry 325188, All Other Basic Inorganic Chemical Manufacturing.

US—United States industry only. CAN—United States and Canadian industries are comparable. MEX—United States and Mexican industries are comparable. Blank—Canadian, Mexican, and United States industries are comparable.

325613 Surface Active Agent Manufacturing[US]

This U.S. industry comprises establishments primarily engaged in (1) manufacturing bulk surface active agents for use as wetting agents, emulsifiers, and penetrants, and/or (2) manufacturing textiles and leather finishing agents used to reduce tension or speed the drying process.

32562 Toilet Preparation Manufacturing
See industry description for 325620 below.

325620 Toilet Preparation Manufacturing

This industry comprises establishments primarily engaged in preparing, blending, compounding, and packaging toilet preparations, such as perfumes, shaving preparations, hair preparations, face creams, lotions (including sunscreens), and other cosmetic preparations.

Cross-References.
Establishments primarily engaged in manufacturing toothpaste are classified in U.S. Industry 325611, Soap and Other Detergent Manufacturing.

3259 Other Chemical Product and Preparation Manufacturing

This industry group comprises establishments primarily engaged in manufacturing chemical products (except basic chemicals; resins, synthetic rubber, cellulosic and noncellulosic fibers and filaments; pesticides, fertilizers, and other agricultural chemicals; pharmaceuticals and medicines; paints, coatings, and adhesives; soaps and cleaning compounds; and toilet preparations).

32591 Printing Ink Manufacturing
See industry description for 325910 below.

325910 Printing Ink Manufacturing

This industry comprises establishments primarily engaged in manufacturing printing and inkjet inks and inkjet cartridges.

Cross-References. Establishments primarily engaged in—

- Recycling inkjet cartridges—are classified in U.S. Industry 811212, Computer and Office Machine Repair and Maintenance;

US—United States industry only. CAN—United States and Canadian industries are comparable. MEX—United States and Mexican industries are comparable. Blank—Canadian, Mexican, and United States industries are comparable.

- Manufacturing writing, drawing, and stamping ink—are classified in U.S. Industry 325998, All Other Miscellaneous Chemical Product and Preparation Manufacturing; and

- Manufacturing toners and toner cartridges for photocopiers, fax machines, computer printers, and similar office machines—are classified in U.S. Industry 325992, Photographic Film, Paper, Plate, and Chemical Manufacturing.

32592 Explosives Manufacturing

See industry description for 325920 below.

325920 Explosives Manufacturing

This industry comprises establishments primarily engaged in manufacturing explosives.

Cross-References. Establishments primarily engaged in—

- Manufacturing ammunition, ammunition detonators, and percussion caps—are classified in U.S. Industry 332992, Small Arms Ammunition Manufacturing; and

- Manufacturing pyrotechnics—are classified in U.S. Industry 325998, All Other Miscellaneous Chemical Product and Preparation Manufacturing.

32599 All Other Chemical Product and Preparation Manufacturing

This industry comprises establishments primarily engaged in manufacturing chemical products (except basic chemicals, resins, and synthetic rubber; cellulosic and noncellulosic fibers and filaments; pesticides, fertilizers, and other agricultural chemicals; pharmaceuticals and medicines; paints, coatings, and adhesives; and soaps, cleaning compounds, and toilet preparations; printing inks; and explosives).

Illustrative Examples:

Activated carbon and charcoal manufacturing
Photographic chemicals manufacturing
Antifreeze preparations manufacturing
Pyrotechnics (e.g., flares, flashlight bombs, signals) manufacturing
Custom compounding (i.e., blending and mixing) of purchased plastics resins

Sugar substitutes (i.e., synthetic sweeteners blended with other ingredients) made from purchased synthetic sweeteners
Industrial salt manufacturing
Swimming pool chemical preparations manufacturing
Matches and matchbook manufacturing
Writing inks and fluids manufacturing

Cross-References. Establishments primarily engaged in—

- Manufacturing basic chemicals—are classified in Industry Group 3251, Basic Chemical Manufacturing;

- Manufacturing resins, synthetic rubber, and artificial synthetic fibers and filaments—are classified in Industry Group 3252, Resin, Synthetic Rubber, and Artificial Synthetic Fibers and Filaments Manufacturing;

- Manufacturing pesticides, fertilizers, and other agricultural chemicals—are classified in Industry Group 3253, Pesticide, Fertilizer, and Other Agricultural Chemical Manufacturing;

- Manufacturing pharmaceuticals and medicine including medicinal vegetable gelatin (i.e., agar-agar)—are classified in Industry Group 3254, Pharmaceutical and Medicine Manufacturing;

- Manufacturing paints, coatings, and adhesives—are classified in Industry Group 3255, Paint, Coating, and Adhesive Manufacturing;

- Manufacturing soaps and cleaning compounds—are classified in Industry Group 3256, Soap, Cleaning Compound, and Toilet Preparation Manufacturing;

- Manufacturing printing and inkjet inks—are classified in Industry 32591, Printing Ink Manufacturing;

- Manufacturing explosives—are classified in Industry 32592, Explosives Manufacturing;

- Manufacturing photographic paper stock (i.e., unsensitized) and paper mats, mounts, easels, and folders for photographic use—are classified in Subsector 322, Paper Manufacturing;

- Manufacturing dessert gelatins—are classified in Industry 31199, All Other Food Manufacturing; and

- Manufacturing medicinal gelatins—are classified in Industry 32541, Pharmaceutical and Medicine Manufacturing.

325991 Custom Compounding of Purchased Resins^{CAN}

This industry comprises establishments primarily engaged in (1) custom mixing and blending plastics resins made elsewhere or (2) reformulating plastics resins from recycled plastics products.

Cross-References.

Establishments primarily engaged in manufacturing synthetic resins and custom mixing and blending resins are classified in U.S. Industry 325211, Plastics Material and Resin Manufacturing.

US—United States industry only. CAN—United States and Canadian industries are comparable. MEX—United States and Mexican industries are comparable. Blank—Canadian, Mexican, and United States industries are comparable.

325992 Photographic Film, Paper, Plate, and Chemical Manufacturing[MEX]

This U.S. industry comprises establishments primarily engaged in manufacturing sensitized film, sensitized paper, sensitized cloth, sensitized plates, toners (i.e., for photocopiers, laser printers, and similar electrostatic printing devices), toner cartridges, and photographic chemicals.

Cross-References.

Establishments primarily engaged in manufacturing photographic paper stock (i.e., unsensitized) and paper mats, mounts, easels, and folders for photographic use are classified in Subsector 322, Paper Manufacturing.

325998 All Other Miscellaneous Chemical Product and Preparation Manufacturing[US]

This U.S. industry comprises establishments primarily engaged in manufacturing chemical products (except basic chemicals, resins, synthetic rubber; cellulosic and noncellulosic fiber and filaments; pesticides, fertilizers, and other agricultural chemicals; pharmaceuticals and medicines; paints, coatings and adhesives; soap, cleaning compounds, and toilet preparations; printing inks; explosives; custom compounding of purchased resins; and photographic films, papers, plates, and chemicals).

Illustrative Examples:

Activated carbon and charcoal
  manufacturing
Pyrotechnics (e.g., flares, flashlight
  bombs, signals) manufacturing
Antifreeze preparations manufacturing
Sugar substitutes (i.e., synthetic
  sweeteners blended with other
  ingredients) made from purchased
  synthetic sweeteners manufacturing

Industrial salt manufacturing
Swimming pool chemical preparations
  manufacturing
Lighter fluids (e.g., charcoal, cigarette)
  manufacturing
Writing inks manufacturing
Matches and matchbook manufacturing

Cross-References. Establishments primarily engaged in—

- Manufacturing basic chemicals—are classified in Industry Group 3251, Basic Chemical Manufacturing;

- Manufacturing resins, synthetic rubber, and artificial synthetic fibers and filaments—are classified in Industry Group 3252, Resin, Synthetic Rubber, and Artificial Synthetic Fibers and Filaments Manufacturing;

US—United States industry only. CAN—United States and Canadian industries are comparable. MEX—United States and Mexican industries are comparable. Blank—Canadian, Mexican, and United States industries are comparable.

- Manufacturing pesticides, fertilizers, and other agricultural chemicals—are classified in Industry Group 3253, Pesticide, Fertilizer, and Other Agricultural Chemical Manufacturing;

- Manufacturing pharmaceuticals and medicines including medicinal vegetable gelatin (i.e., agar-agar)—are classified in Industry Group 3254, Pharmaceutical and Medicine Manufacturing;

- Manufacturing paints, coatings, and adhesives—are classified in Industry Group 3255, Paint, Coating, and Adhesive Manufacturing;

- Manufacturing soaps and cleaning compounds—are classified in Industry Group 3256, Soap, Cleaning Compound, and Toilet Preparation Manufacturing;

- Manufacturing printing and inkjet inks—are classified in Industry 325910, Printing Ink Manufacturing;

- Manufacturing explosives—are classified in Industry 325920, Explosives Manufacturing;

- Custom compounding purchased plastics resins—are classified in U.S. Industry 325991, Custom Compounding of Purchased Resins;

- Manufacturing photographic films, papers, plates, and chemicals—are classified in U.S. Industry 325992, Photographic Film, Paper, Plate, and Chemical Manufacturing; and

- Manufacturing dessert gelatin—are classified in U.S. Industry 311999, All Other Miscellaneous Food Manufacturing.

326 Plastics and Rubber Products Manufacturing

Industries in the Plastics and Rubber Products Manufacturing subsector make goods by processing plastics materials and raw rubber. The core technology employed by establishments in this subsector is that of plastics or rubber product production. Plastics and rubber are combined in the same subsector because plastics are increasingly being used as a substitute for rubber; however the subsector is generally restricted to the production of products made of just one material, either solely plastics or rubber.

Many manufacturing activities use plastics or rubber, for example the manufacture of footwear, or furniture. Typically, the production process of these products involves more than one material. In these cases, technologies that allow disparate materials to be formed and combined are of central importance in describing the manufacturing activity. In NAICS, such activities (the footwear and furniture manufacturing) are not classified in the Plastics and Rubber Products Manufacturing subsector because the core technologies for these activities are diverse and involve multiple materials.

US—United States industry only. CAN—United States and Canadian industries are comparable. MEX—United States and Mexican industries are comparable. Blank—Canadian, Mexican, and United States industries are comparable.

Within the Plastics and Rubber Products Manufacturing subsector, a distinction is made between plastics and rubber products at the industry group level, although it is not a rigid distinction, as can be seen from the definition of Industry 32622, Rubber and Plastics Hoses and Belting Manufacturing. As materials technology progresses, plastics are increasingly being used as a substitute for rubber; and eventually, the distinction may disappear as a basis for establishment classification.

In keeping with the core technology focus of plastics, lamination of plastics film to plastics film as well as the production of bags from plastics only is classified in this subsector. Lamination and bag production involving plastics and materials other than plastics are classified in the NAICS Subsector 322, Paper Manufacturing.

3261 Plastics Product Manufacturing

This industry group comprises establishments primarily engaged in processing new or spent (i.e., recycled) plastics resins into intermediate or final products, using such processes as compression molding; extrusion molding; injection molding; blow molding; and casting. Within most of these industries, the production process is such that a wide variety of products can be made.

32611 Plastics Packaging Materials and Unlaminated Film and Sheet Manufacturing

This industry comprises establishments primarily engaged in (1) converting plastics resins into unsupported plastics film and sheet and/or (2) forming, coating or laminating plastics film and sheet into plastics bags.

Cross-References. Establishments primarily engaged in—

- Laminating plastics sheet (except for packaging)—are classified in Industry 32613, Laminated Plastics Plate, Sheet (except Packaging), and Shape Manufacturing;

- Manufacturing plastics blister and bubble packaging—are classified in Industry 32619, Other Plastics Product Manufacturing; and

- Coating or laminating combinations of plastics, foils and paper (except plastics film to plastics film) into film, sheet or bags—are classified in Industry 32222, Paper Bag and Coated and Treated Paper Manufacturing.

326111 Plastics Bag and Pouch Manufacturing[CAN]

This U.S. Industry comprises establishments primarily engaged in: (1) converting plastics resins into plastics bags or pouches; and/or (2) forming, coating, or laminating plastics film or sheet into single web or multi-web plastics bags or pouches. Establishments in this industry may print on the bags or pouches they manufacture.

Cross-References. Establishments primarily engaged in—

- Manufacturing laminated or coated combinations of plastics, foils, and paper (except plastics film to plastics film) materials into single wall bags—are classified in U.S. Industry 322223, Coated Paper Bag and Pouch Manufacturing;

- Manufacturing laminated or coated combinations of plastics, foils, and paper (except plastics film to plastics film) into multiwalled bags—are classified in U.S. Industry 322224, Uncoated Paper and Multiwall Bag Manufacturing; and

- Printing on purchased packaging materials—are classified in Industry Group 3231, Printing and Related Support Activities, based on the printing process used.

326112 Plastics Packaging Film and Sheet (including Laminated) Manufacturing[US]

This U.S. industry comprises establishments primarily engaged in converting plastics resins into plastics packaging (flexible) film and packaging sheet.

Cross-References. Establishments primarily engaged in—

- Converting plastics resins into plastics film and unlaminated sheet (except packaging)—are classified in U.S. Industry 326113, Unlaminated Plastics Film and Sheet (except Packaging) Manufacturing;

- Laminating or coating packaging combinations of plastics, foils, and paper (except plastics film to plastics film) film and sheet—are classified in U.S. Industry 322221, Coated and Laminated Packaging Paper Manufacturing;

- Laminating or coating combinations of plastics, foils, and paper (except plastics film to plastics film) nonpackaging film and sheet—are classified in U.S. Industry 322222, Coated and Laminated Paper Manufacturing;

- Laminating plastics sheet (except for packaging)—are classified in Industry 326130, Laminated Plastics Plate, Sheet (except Packaging), and Shape Manufacturing; and

- Manufacturing plastics bags—are classified in U.S. Industry 326111, Plastics Bag and Pouch Manufacturing.

326113 Unlaminated Plastics Film and Sheet (except Packaging) Manufacturing[US]

This U.S. industry comprises establishments primarily engaged in converting plastics resins into plastics film and unlaminated sheet (except packaging).

Cross-References. Establishments primarily engaged in—

- Converting plastics resins into plastics packaging film and unlaminated packaging sheet—are classified in U.S. Industry 326112, Plastics Packaging Film and Sheet (including Laminated) Manufacturing;

- Laminating plastics sheet (except for packaging)—are classified in Industry 326130, Laminated Plastics Plate, Sheet (except Packaging), and Shape Manufacturing;

- Laminating or coating a combination of plastics, foils, and paper (except plastics film to plastics film) nonpackaging film and sheet—are classified in U.S. Industry 322222, Coated and Laminated Paper Manufacturing; and

- Manufacturing plastics bags—are classified in U.S. Industry 326111, Plastics Bag and Pouch Manufacturing.

32612 Plastics Pipe, Pipe Fitting, and Unlaminated Profile Shape Manufacturing

This industry comprises establishments primarily engaged in manufacturing plastics pipes and pipe fittings, and plastics profile shapes such as rod, tube, and sausage casings.

Cross-References. Establishments primarily engaged in—

- Manufacturing plastics hose—are classified in Industry 32622, Rubber and Plastics Hoses and Belting Manufacturing;

- Manufacturing noncurrent carrying plastics conduit—are classified in Industry 33593, Wiring Device Manufacturing;

- Manufacturing plastics plumbing fixtures—are classified in Industry 32619, Other Plastics Product Manufacturing; and

- Manufacturing plastics film, plastics unlaminated sheet, and plastics bags—are classified in Industry 32611, Plastics Packaging Materials and Unlaminated Film and Sheet Manufacturing.

US—United States industry only. CAN—United States and Canadian industries are comparable. MEX—United States and Mexican industries are comparable. Blank—Canadian, Mexican, and United States industries are comparable.

326121 Unlaminated Plastics Profile Shape Manufacturing^{CAN}

This U.S. industry comprises establishments primarily engaged in converting plastics resins into nonrigid plastics profile shapes (except film, sheet, and bags), such as rod, tube, and sausage casings.

Cross-References. Establishments primarily engaged in—

- Manufacturing plastics film, plastics unlaminated sheet, and plastics bags— are classified in Industry 32611, Plastics Packaging Materials and Unlaminated Film and Sheet Manufacturing; and

- Manufacturing plastics hoses—are classified in Industry 326220, Rubber and Plastics Hoses and Belting Manufacturing.

326122 Plastics Pipe and Pipe Fitting Manufacturing^{CAN}

This U.S. industry comprises establishments primarily engaged in converting plastics resins into rigid plastics pipes and pipe fittings.

Cross-References. Establishments primarily engaged in—

- Manufacturing plastics hose—are classified in Industry 326220, Rubber and Plastics Hoses and Belting Manufacturing;

- Manufacturing noncurrent-carrying plastics conduit—are classified in U.S. Industry 335932, Noncurrent-Carrying Wiring Device Manufacturing; and

- Manufacturing plastics plumbing fixtures—are classified in U.S. Industry 326191, Plastics Plumbing Fixture Manufacturing.

32613 Laminated Plastics Plate, Sheet (except Packaging), and Shape Manufacturing

See industry description for 326130 below.

326130 Laminated Plastics Plate, Sheet (except Packaging), and Shape Manufacturing

This industry comprises establishments primarily engaged in laminating plastics profile shapes such as plate, sheet (except packaging), and rod. The lamination process generally involves bonding or impregnating profiles with plastics resins and compressing them under heat.

Cross-References. Establishments primarily engaged in—

- Manufacturing plastics film, plastics unlaminated sheet, and plastics bags— are classified in Industry 32611, Plastics Packaging Materials and Unlaminated Film and Sheet Manufacturing; and

- Coating or laminating nonplastics film, sheet, or bags with plastics—are classified in Industry 32222, Paper Bag and Coated and Treated Paper Manufacturing.

32614 Polystyrene Foam Product Manufacturing
See industry description for 326140 below.

326140 Polystyrene Foam Product Manufacturing

This industry comprises establishments primarily engaged in manufacturing polystyrene foam products.

Cross-References.

Establishments primarily engaged in manufacturing plastics foam products (except polystyrene) are classified in Industry 326150, Urethane and Other Foam Product (except Polystyrene) Manufacturing.

32615 Urethane and Other Foam Product (except Polystyrene) Manufacturing
See industry description for 326150 below.

326150 Urethane and Other Foam Product (except Polystyrene) Manufacturing

This industry comprises establishments primarily engaged in manufacturing plastics foam products (except polystyrene).

Cross-References.

Establishments primarily engaged in manufacturing polystyrene foam products are classified in Industry 326140, Polystyrene Foam Product Manufacturing.

32616 Plastics Bottle Manufacturing
See industry description for 32616 below.

US—United States industry only. CAN—United States and Canadian industries are comparable. MEX—United States and Mexican industries are comparable. Blank—Canadian, Mexican, and United States industries are comparable.

http://www.census.gov/naics

326160 Plastics Bottle Manufacturing

This industry comprises establishments primarily engaged in manufacturing plastics bottles.

Cross-References.

Establishments primarily engaged in manufacturing plastics containers (except bottles) are classified in U.S. Industry 326199, All Other Plastics Product Manufacturing.

32619 Other Plastics Product Manufacturing

This industry comprises establishments primarily engaged in manufacturing resilient floor covering and other plastics products (except film, sheet, bags, profile shapes, pipes, pipe fittings, laminates, foam products, and bottles).

Illustrative Examples:

Inflatable plastics swimming pool rafts and similar flotation devices manufacturing

Plastics hardware manufacturing

Plastics bowls and bowl covers manufacturing

Plastics or fiberglass plumbing fixtures (e.g., toilets, shower stalls, urinals) manufacturing

Plastics cups (except foam) manufacturing

Plastics siding manufacturing

Plastics dinnerware (except foam) manufacturing

Plastics trash containers manufacturing

Plastics gloves manufacturing

Resilient floor coverings (e.g., sheet, tiles) manufacturing

Cross-References. Establishments primarily engaged in—

- Manufacturing plastics film, plastics unlaminated sheet, and plastics bags— are classified in Industry 32611, Plastics Packaging Materials and Unlaminated Film and Sheet Manufacturing;

- Manufacturing plastics pipes, pipe fittings, and plastics profile shapes (except films, sheet, bags)—are classified in Industry 32612, Plastics Pipe, Pipe Fitting, and Unlaminated Profile Shape Manufacturing;

- Laminating plastics profile shapes, such as plate, sheet, and rod—are classified in Industry 32613, Laminated Plastics Plate, Sheet (except Packaging), and Shape Manufacturing;

- Manufacturing polystyrene foam products—are classified in Industry 32614, Polystyrene Foam Product Manufacturing;

- Manufacturing foam products (except polystyrene)—are classified in Industry 32615, Urethane and Other Foam Product (except Polystyrene) Manufacturing;

- Manufacturing plastics bottles—are classified in Industry 32616, Plastics Bottle Manufacturing;

- Manufacturing plastics furniture parts—are classified in Industry 33721, Office Furniture (including Fixtures) Manufacturing;

- Assembling plastics components into plumbing fixture fittings, such as faucets—are classified in Industry 33291, Metal Valve Manufacturing; and

- Manufacturing rubber floor mats and rubber treads—are classified in Industry 32629, Other Rubber Product Manufacturing.

326191 Plastics Plumbing Fixture Manufacturing[CAN]

This U.S. industry comprises establishments primarily engaged in manufacturing plastics or fiberglass plumbing fixtures. Examples of products made by these establishments are plastics or fiberglass bathtubs, hot tubs, portable toilets, and shower stalls.

Cross-References. Establishments primarily engaged in—

- Assembling plastics components into plumbing fixture fittings, such as faucets—are classified in U.S. Industry 332913, Plumbing Fixture Fitting and Trim Manufacturing; and

- Manufacturing plastics pipe and pipe fittings—are classified in U.S. Industry 326122, Plastics Pipe and Pipe Fitting Manufacturing.

326192 Resilient Floor Covering Manufacturing[US]

This U.S. industry comprises establishments primarily engaged in manufacturing resilient floor coverings for permanent installation.

Cross-References.

Establishments primarily engaged in manufacturing rubber floor mats and rubber treads are classified in U.S. Industry 326299, All Other Rubber Product Manufacturing.

326199 All Other Plastics Product Manufacturing[US]

This U.S. industry comprises establishments primarily engaged in manufacturing plastics products (except film, sheet, bags, profile shapes, pipes, pipe fittings, laminates, foam products, bottles, plumbing fixtures, and resilient floor coverings).

US—United States industry only. CAN—United States and Canadian industries are comparable. MEX—United States and Mexican industries are comparable. Blank—Canadian, Mexican, and United States industries are comparable.

Illustrative Examples:

Plastics air mattresses manufacturing
Plastics gloves manufacturing
Plastics bowls and bowl covers
  manufacturing
Plastics hardware manufacturing
Plastics clothes hangers manufacturing
Plastics siding manufacturing

Plastics cups (except foam)
  manufacturing
Plastics trash containers manufacturing
Plastics dinnerware (except foam)
  manufacturing
Inflatable plastics swimming pool rafts
  and similar flotation devices manufacturing

Cross-References. Establishments primarily engaged in—

- Manufacturing plastics film, plastics unlaminated sheet, and plastics bags— are classified in Industry 32611, Plastics Packaging Materials and Unlaminated Film and Sheet Manufacturing;

- Manufacturing plastics pipes, pipe fittings, and plastics profile shapes (except film, sheet, bags)—are classified in Industry 32612, Plastics Pipe, Pipe Fitting, and Unlaminated Profile Shape Manufacturing;

- Laminating plastics profile shapes, such as plate, sheet, and rod—are classified in Industry 326130, Laminated Plastics Plate, Sheet (except Packaging), and Shape Manufacturing;

- Manufacturing polystyrene foam products—are classified in Industry 326140, Polystyrene Foam Product Manufacturing;

- Manufacturing foam (except polystyrene) products—are classified in Industry 326150, Urethane and Other Foam Product (except Polystyrene) Manufacturing;

- Manufacturing plastics bottles—are classified in Industry 326160, Plastics Bottle Manufacturing;

- Manufacturing heavy-duty inflatable plastics boats—are classified in Industry 336612, Boat Building;

- Manufacturing plastics furniture parts and components—are classified in U.S. Industry 337215, Showcase, Partition, Shelving, and Locker Manufacturing;

- Manufacturing plastics plumbing fixtures—are classified in U.S. Industry 326191, Plastics Plumbing Fixture Manufacturing;

- Manufacturing resilient floor coverings—are classified in U.S. Industry 326192, Resilient Floor Covering Manufacturing; and

- Assembling plastics components into plumbing fixtures fittings such as faucets—are classified in U.S. Industry 332913, Plumbing Fixture Fitting and Trim Manufacturing.

US—United States industry only. CAN—United States and Canadian industries are comparable. MEX—United States and Mexican industries are comparable. Blank—Canadian, Mexican, and United States industries are comparable.

3262 Rubber Product Manufacturing

This industry group comprises establishments primarily engaged in processing natural, synthetic, or reclaimed rubber materials into intermediate or final products using processes, such as vulcanizing, cementing, molding, extruding, and lathe-cutting.

32621 Tire Manufacturing

This industry comprises establishments primarily engaged in manufacturing tires and inner tubes from natural and synthetic rubber and retreading or rebuilding tires.

Cross-References. Establishments primarily engaged in—

- Repairing tires, such as plugging—are classified in Industry 81119, Other Automotive Repair and Maintenance; and

- Retailing tires—are classified in Industry 44132, Tire Dealers.

326211 Tire Manufacturing (except Retreading)^{MEX}

This U.S. industry comprises establishments primarily engaged in manufacturing tires and inner tubes from natural and synthetic rubber.

Cross-References.

Establishments primarily engaged in retreading or rebuilding tires are classified in U.S. Industry 326212, Tire Retreading.

326212 Tire Retreading^{MEX}

This U.S. industry comprises establishments primarily engaged in retreading or rebuilding tires.

Cross-References. Establishments primarily engaged in—

- Repairing tires, such as plugging—are classified in U.S. Industry 811198, All Other Automotive Repair and Maintenance;

- Retailing tires—are classified in Industry 441320, Tire Dealers; and

- Manufacturing tires and inner tubes from natural and synthetic rubber—are classified in U.S. Industry 326211, Tire Manufacturing (except Retreading).

US—United States industry only. CAN—United States and Canadian industries are comparable. MEX--United States and Mexican industries are comparable. Blank—Canadian, Mexican, and United States industries are comparable.

32622 Rubber and Plastics Hoses and Belting Manufacturing
See industry description for 326220 below.

326220 Rubber and Plastics Hoses and Belting Manufacturing

This industry comprises establishments primarily engaged in manufacturing rubber hose and/or plastics (reinforced) hose and belting from natural and synthetic rubber and/or plastics resins. Establishments manufacturing garden hoses from purchased hose are included in this industry.

Cross-References. Establishments primarily engaged in—

- Manufacturing rubber tubing—are classified in U.S. Industry 326299, All Other Rubber Product Manufacturing;

- Manufacturing plastics tubing—are classified in U.S. Industry 326121, Unlaminated Plastics Profile Shape Manufacturing;

- Manufacturing extruded, lathe-cut, molded rubber goods (except tubing) for mechanical applications—are classified in U.S. Industry 326291, Rubber Product Manufacturing for Mechanical Use; and

- Manufacturing fluid power hose assemblies—are classified in U.S. Industry 332912, Fluid Power Valve and Hose Fitting Manufacturing.

32629 Other Rubber Product Manufacturing

This industry comprises establishments primarily engaged in manufacturing rubber products (except tires, hoses, and belting) from natural and synthetic rubber.

Illustrative Examples:

Birth control devices (e.g., diaphragms, prophylactics) manufacturing	Mechanical rubber goods (i.e., molded, extruded, lathe-cut) manufacturing
Rubber floor mats (e.g., door, bath) manufacturing	Rubber tubing manufacturing
Latex foam rubber manufacturing	Reclaiming rubber from waste and scrap
Rubber hair care products (e.g., combs, curlers) manufacturing	Rubber bands manufacturing
	Rubber balloons manufacturing

Cross-References. Establishments primarily engaged in—

- Manufacturing tires and inner tubes—are classified in Industry 32621, Tire Manufacturing;

- Manufacturing rubber hoses and belting—are classified in Industry 32622, Rubber and Plastics Hoses and Belting Manufacturing;

- Rubberizing fabric—are classified in Industry 31332, Fabric Coating Mills;
- Manufacturing rubber gaskets, packing, and sealing devices—are classified in Industry 33999, All Other Miscellaneous Manufacturing;
- Manufacturing rubber gloves—are classified in Industry 33911, Medical Equipment and Supplies Manufacturing;
- Manufacturing rubber clothing accessories (e.g., bathing caps)—are classified in Industry 31599, Apparel Accessories and Other Apparel Manufacturing; and
- Manufacturing rubber toys—are classified in Industry 33993, Doll, Toy, and Game Manufacturing.

326291 Rubber Product Manufacturing for Mechanical Use[US]

This U.S. industry comprises establishments primarily engaged in manufacturing rubber goods (except tubing) for mechanical applications, using the processes of molding, extruding or lathe-cutting. Products of this industry are generally parts for motor vehicles, machinery, and equipment.

Cross-References.

Establishments primarily engaged in manufacturing rubber tubing from natural and synthetic rubber or in manufacturing rubber products for mechanical applications using processes other than molding, extruding or lathe-cutting are classified in U.S. Industry 326299, All Other Rubber Product Manufacturing.

326299 All Other Rubber Product Manufacturing[US]

This U.S. industry comprises establishments primarily engaged in manufacturing rubber products (except tires; hoses and belting; and molded, extruded, and lathe-cut rubber goods for mechanical applications (except rubber tubing)) from natural and synthetic rubber. Establishments manufacturing rubber tubing made from natural and synthetic rubber, regardless of process used, are included in this industry.

Illustrative Examples:

Birth control devices (i.e., diaphragms, prophylactics) manufacturing
Rubber floor mats (e.g., door, bath) manufacturing
Latex foam rubber manufacturing
Rubber hair care products (e.g., combs, curlers) manufacturing

Reclaiming rubber from waste and scrap
Rubber tubing manufacturing
Rubber balloons manufacturing
Rubber bands manufacturing

US—United States industry only. CAN—United States and Canadian industries are comparable. MEX—United States and Mexican industries are comparable. Blank—Canadian, Mexican, and United States industries are comparable.

Cross-References. Establishments primarily engaged in—

- Manufacturing tires, inner tubes, and tire rebuilding—are classified in Industry 32621, Tire Manufacturing;

- Manufacturing rubber hoses and belting—are classified in Industry 326220, Rubber and Plastics Hoses and Belting Manufacturing;

- Manufacturing heavy-duty inflatable rubber boats—are classified in U.S. Industry 336612, Boat Building;

- Molding, extruding, and lathe-cutting rubber to manufacture rubber goods (except tubing) for mechanical applications—are classified in Industry 326291, Rubber Product Manufacturing for Mechanical Use;

- Rubberizing fabrics—are classified in Industry 313320, Fabric Coating Mills;

- Manufacturing rubber gaskets, packing, and sealing devices—are classified in U.S. Industry 339991, Gasket, Packing, and Sealing Device Manufacturing;

- Manufacturing rubber toys—are classified in Industry 33993, Doll, Toy, and Game Manufacturing;

- Manufacturing rubber gloves—are classified in U.S. Industry 339113, Surgical Appliance and Supplies Manufacturing; and

- Manufacturing rubber clothing accessories (e.g., bathing caps)—are classified in U.S. Industry 315999, Other Apparel Accessories and Other Apparel Manufacturing.

327 Nonmetallic Mineral Product Manufacturing

The Nonmetallic Mineral Product Manufacturing subsector transforms mined or quarried nonmetallic minerals, such as sand, gravel, stone, clay, and refractory materials, into products for intermediate or final consumption. Processes used include grinding, mixing, cutting, shaping, and honing. Heat often is used in the process and chemicals are frequently mixed to change the composition, purity, and chemical properties for the intended product. For example, glass is produced by heating silica sand to the melting point (sometimes combined with cullet or recycled glass) and then drawn, floated, or blow molded to the desired shape or thickness. Refractory materials are heated and then formed into bricks or other shapes for use in industrial applications.

The Nonmetallic Mineral Product Manufacturing subsector includes establishments that manufacture products, such as bricks, refractories, ceramic products, and glass and glass products, such as plate glass and containers. Also included are cement and concrete products, lime, gypsum and other nonmetallic mineral products including abrasive products, ceramic plumbing fixtures, statuary, cut stone products, and mineral wool. The products are used in a wide range of activities from construction and heavy and light manufacturing to articles for personal use.

Mining, beneficiating, and manufacturing activities often occur in a single location. Separate receipts will be collected for these activities whenever possible. When receipts cannot be broken out between mining and manufacturing, establishments that mine or quarry nonmetallic minerals, beneficiate the nonmetallic minerals and further process the nonmetallic minerals into a more finished manufactured product are classified based on the primary activity of the establishment. A mine that manufactures a small amount of finished products will be classified in Sector 21, Mining, Quarrying, and Oil and Gas Extraction. An establishment that mines whose primary output is a more finished manufactured product will be classified in the Manufacturing Sector.

Excluded from the Nonmetallic Mineral Product Manufacturing subsector are establishments that primarily beneficiate mined nonmetallic minerals. Beneficiation is the process whereby the extracted material is reduced to particles that can be separated into mineral and waste, the former suitable for further processing or direct use. Beneficiation establishments are included in Sector 21, Mining, Quarrying, and Oil and Gas Extraction.

3271 Clay Product and Refractory Manufacturing

32711 Pottery, Ceramics, and Plumbing Fixture Manufacturing

This industry comprises establishments primarily engaged in shaping, molding, glazing, and firing pottery, ceramics, and plumbing fixtures made entirely or partly of clay or other ceramic materials.

Cross-References. Establishments primarily engaged in—

- Manufacturing ferrite microwave devices and electronic components—are classified in Subsector 334, Computer and Electronic Product Manufacturing;

- Manufacturing enameled iron and steel plumbing fixtures—are classified in Industry 33299, All Other Fabricated Metal Product Manufacturing;

- Manufacturing metal bathroom accessories—are classified in Subsector 332, Fabricated Metal Product Manufacturing;

- Manufacturing plastic bathroom accessories, cultured marble, and other plastic plumbing fixtures—are classified in Industry 32619, Other Plastics Product Manufacturing; and

- Manufacturing clay building materials, such as ceramic tile, bricks, and clay roofing tiles, and refractories—are classified in Industry 32712, Clay Building Material and Refractories Manufacturing.

US—United States industry only. CAN—United States and Canadian industries are comparable. MEX—United States and Mexican industries are comparable. Blank—Canadian, Mexican, and United States industries are comparable.

327111 Vitreous China Plumbing Fixture and China and Earthenware Bathroom Accessories Manufacturing[US]

This U.S. industry comprises establishments primarily engaged in manufacturing vitreous china plumbing fixtures and china and earthenware bathroom accessories, such as faucet handles, towel bars, and soap dishes.

Cross-References. Establishments primarily engaged in—

- Manufacturing enameled iron and steel plumbing fixtures—are classified in U.S. Industry 332998, Enameled Iron and Metal Sanitary Ware Manufacturing;
- Manufacturing metal bathroom accessories—are classified in Subsector 332, Fabricated Metal Product Manufacturing;
- Manufacturing plastics bathroom accessories—are classified in U.S. Industry 326199, All Other Plastics Product Manufacturing;
- Manufacturing cultured marble and other plastics plumbing fixtures—are classified in U.S. Industry 326191, Plastics Plumbing Fixture Manufacturing; and
- Manufacturing china and earthenware products (except bathroom fixtures and accessories)—are classified in U.S. Industry 327112, Vitreous China, Fine Earthenware, and Other Pottery Product Manufacturing.

327112 Vitreous China, Fine Earthenware, and Other Pottery Product Manufacturing[US]

This U.S. industry comprises establishments primarily engaged in manufacturing table and kitchen articles, art and ornamental items, and similar vitreous china, fine earthenware, stoneware, coarse earthenware, and pottery products.

Illustrative Examples:

Chemical stoneware (i.e., pottery products) manufacturing
Earthenware table and kitchen articles, coarse, manufacturing
Clay and ceramic statuary manufacturing
Florists' articles, red earthenware, manufacturing

Cooking ware (e.g., stoneware, coarse earthenware, pottery) manufacturing
Vases, pottery (e.g., china, earthenware, stoneware), manufacturing

Cross-References. Establishments primarily engaged in—

- Manufacturing vitreous china plumbing fixtures—are classified in U.S. Industry 327111, Vitreous China Plumbing Fixture and China and Earthenware Bathroom Accessories Manufacturing;

- Manufacturing porcelain and ceramic electrical products, such as insulators—are classified in U.S. Industry 327113, Porcelain Electrical Supply Manufacturing; and
- Manufacturing clay building materials, such as ceramic tile, bricks, and clay roofing tiles, and refractories—are classified in Industry 32712, Clay Building Material and Refractories Manufacturing.

327113 Porcelain Electrical Supply Manufacturing[US]

This U.S. industry comprises establishments primarily engaged in manufacturing porcelain electrical insulators, molded porcelain parts for electrical devices, ferrite or ceramic magnets, and electronic and electrical supplies from nonmetallic minerals, such as clay and ceramic materials.

Cross-References.

Establishments primarily engaged in manufacturing ferrite microwave devices and electronic components are classified in Subsector 334, Computer and Electronic Product Manufacturing.

32712 Clay Building Material and Refractories Manufacturing

This industry comprises establishments primarily engaged in shaping, molding, baking, burning, or hardening clay refractories, nonclay refractories, ceramic tile, structural clay tile, brick, and other structural clay building materials.

Cross-References. Establishments primarily engaged in—

- Manufacturing glass blocks—are classified in Industry 32721, Glass and Glass Product Manufacturing;
- Manufacturing concrete brick and block—are classified in Industry 32733, Concrete Pipe, Brick, and Block Manufacturing; and
- Manufacturing resilient flooring—are classified in Industry 32619, Other Plastics Product Manufacturing.

327121 Brick and Structural Clay Tile Manufacturing[US]

This U.S. industry comprises establishments primarily engaged in manufacturing brick and structural clay tiles.

Cross-References. Establishments primarily engaged in—

- Manufacturing clay fire brick (i.e., refractories)—are classified in U.S. Industry 327124, Clay Refractory Manufacturing;

US—United States industry only. CAN—United States and Canadian industries are comparable. MEX—United States and Mexican industries are comparable. Blank—Canadian, Mexican, and United States industries are comparable.

- Manufacturing nonclay fire brick (i.e., refractories)—are classified in U.S. Industry 327125, Nonclay Refractory Manufacturing;

- Manufacturing glass brick—are classified in Industry 32721, Glass and Glass Product Manufacturing;

- Manufacturing concrete bricks—are classified in U.S. Industry 327331, Concrete Block and Brick Manufacturing; and

- Manufacturing adobe bricks or clay roofing tiles—are classified in U.S. Industry 327123, Other Structural Clay Product Manufacturing.

327122 Ceramic Wall and Floor Tile Manufacturing[US]

This U.S. industry comprises establishments primarily engaged in manufacturing ceramic wall and floor tiles.

Cross-References. Establishments primarily engaged in—

- Manufacturing structural clay tiles—are classified in U.S. Industry 327121, Brick and Structural Clay Tile Manufacturing;

- Manufacturing clay drain tiles—are classified in U.S. Industry 327123, Other Structural Clay Product Manufacturing; and

- Manufacturing resilient flooring and asphalt floor tiles—are classified in U.S. Industry 326192, Resilient Floor Covering Manufacturing.

327123 Other Structural Clay Product Manufacturing[US]

This U.S. industry comprises establishments primarily engaged in manufacturing clay sewer pipe, drain tile, flue lining tile, architectural terra-cotta, and other structural clay products.

Cross-References. Establishments primarily engaged in—

- Manufacturing bricks and structural clay tiles—are classified in U.S. Industry 327121, Brick and Structural Clay Tile Manufacturing;

- Manufacturing ceramic floor and wall tiles—are classified in U.S. Industry 327122, Ceramic Wall and Floor Tile Manufacturing;

- Manufacturing clay refractories—are classified in U.S. Industry 327124, Clay Refractory Manufacturing; and

- Manufacturing nonclay refractories—are classified in U.S. Industry 327125, Nonclay Refractory Manufacturing.

327124 Clay Refractory Manufacturing[US]

This U.S. industry comprises establishments primarily engaged in manufacturing clay refractory, mortar, brick, block, tile, and fabricated clay refractories, such as melting pots. A refractory is a material that will retain its shape and chemical identity when subjected to high temperatures and is used in applications that require extreme resistance to heat, such as furnace linings.

Cross-References.

Establishments primarily engaged in manufacturing nonclay refractories are classified in U.S. Industry 327125, Nonclay Refractory Manufacturing.

327125 Nonclay Refractory Manufacturing[US]

This U.S. industry comprises establishments primarily engaged in manufacturing nonclay refractory, mortar, brick, block, tile, and fabricated nonclay refractories, such as graphite, magnesite, silica, or alumina crucibles. A refractory is a material that will retain its shape and chemical identity when subjected to high temperatures and is used in applications that require extreme resistance to heat, such as furnace linings.

Cross-References.

Establishments primarily engaged in manufacturing clay refractories are classified in U.S. Industry 327124, Clay Refractory Manufacturing.

3272 Glass and Glass Product Manufacturing

32721 Glass and Glass Product Manufacturing

This industry comprises establishments primarily engaged in manufacturing glass and/or glass products. Establishments in this industry may manufacture glass and/or glass products by melting silica sand or cullet, or purchasing glass.

Cross-References. Establishments primarily engaged in—

- Manufacturing glass wool (i.e., fiberglass) insulation products—are classified in Industry 32799, All Other Nonmetallic Mineral Product Manufacturing;

- Manufacturing optical lenses (except ophthalmic), such as magnifying, photographic, and projection lenses—are classified in Industry 33331, Commercial and Service Industry Machinery Manufacturing;

US—United States industry only. CAN—United States and Canadian industries are comparable. MEX—United States and Mexican industries are comparable. Blank—Canadian, Mexican, and United States industries are comparable.

- Grinding ophthalmic (i.e., eyeglass) lenses for the trade—are classified in Industry 33911, Medical Equipment and Supplies Manufacturing; and

- Manufacturing fiber optic cable from purchased fiber optic strand—are classified in Industry 33592, Communication and Energy Wire and Cable Manufacturing.

327211 Flat Glass Manufacturing[MEX]

This U.S. industry comprises establishments primarily engaged in (1) manufacturing flat glass by melting silica sand or cullet or (2) manufacturing both flat glass and laminated glass by melting silica sand or cullet.

Cross-References.

Establishments primarily engaged in manufacturing laminated glass from purchased flat glass are classified in U.S. Industry 327215, Glass Product Manufacturing Made of Purchased Glass.

327212 Other Pressed and Blown Glass and Glassware Manufacturing[US]

This U.S. industry comprises establishments primarily engaged in manufacturing glass by melting silica sand or cullet and making pressed, blown, or shaped glass or glassware (except glass packaging containers).

Cross-References. Establishments primarily engaged in—

- Manufacturing flat glass—are classified in U.S. Industry 327211, Flat Glass Manufacturing;

- Manufacturing glass packaging containers in glassmaking operations—are classified in U.S. Industry 327213, Glass Container Manufacturing;

- Manufacturing glass wool (i.e., fiberglass) insulation—are classified in U.S. Industry 327993, Mineral Wool Manufacturing;

- Manufacturing glassware from purchased glass—are classified in U.S. Industry 327215, Glass Product Manufacturing Made of Purchased Glass; and

- Manufacturing fiber optic cable from purchased fiber optic strand—are classified in U.S. Industry 335921, Fiber Optic Cable Manufacturing.

327213 Glass Container Manufacturing[US]

This U.S. industry comprises establishments primarily engaged in manufacturing glass packaging containers.

US—United States industry only. CAN—United States and Canadian industries are comparable. MEX—United States and Mexican industries are comparable. Blank—Canadian, Mexican, and United States industries are comparable.

327215 Glass Product Manufacturing Made of Purchased Glass[CAN]

This U.S. industry comprises establishments primarily engaged in coating, laminating, tempering, or shaping purchased glass.

Cross-References. Establishments primarily engaged in—

- Manufacturing optical lenses (except ophthalmic), such as magnifying, photographic, and projection lenses—are classified in U.S. Industry 333314, Optical Instrument and Lens Manufacturing;

- Manufacturing ophthalmic (i.e., eyeglass) lenses—are classified in U.S. Industry 339115, Ophthalmic Goods Manufacturing; and

- Manufacturing fiber optic cable from purchased fiber optic strand—are classified in U.S. Industry 335921, Fiber Optic Cable Manufacturing.

3273 Cement and Concrete Product Manufacturing

32731 Cement Manufacturing

See industry description for 327310 below.

327310 Cement Manufacturing

This industry comprises establishments primarily engaged in manufacturing portland, natural, masonry, pozzolanic, and other hydraulic cements. Cement manufacturing establishments may calcine earths or mine, quarry, manufacture, or purchase lime.

Cross-References. Establishments primarily engaged in—

- Mining or quarrying limestone—are classified in U.S. Industry 212312, Crushed and Broken Limestone Mining and Quarrying;

- Manufacturing lime—are classified in Industry 327410, Lime Manufacturing;

- Manufacturing ready-mix concrete—are classified in Industry 327320, Ready-Mix Concrete Manufacturing; and

- Manufacturing dry mix concrete—are classified in U.S. Industry 327999, All Other Miscellaneous Nonmetallic Mineral Product Manufacturing.

32732 Ready-Mix Concrete Manufacturing

See industry description for 327320 below.

US—United States industry only. CAN—United States and Canadian industries are comparable. MEX—United States and Mexican industries are comparable. Blank—Canadian, Mexican, and United States industries are comparable.

http://www.census.gov/naics

327320 Ready-Mix Concrete Manufacturing

This industry comprises establishments, such as batch plants or mix plants, primarily engaged in manufacturing concrete delivered to a purchaser in a plastic and unhardened state. Ready-mix concrete manufacturing establishments may mine, quarry, or purchase sand and gravel.

Cross-References. Establishments primarily engaged in—

- Operating sand or gravel pits—are classified in U.S. Industry 212321, Construction Sand and Gravel Mining; and

- Manufacturing dry mix concrete—are classified in U.S. Industry 327999, All Other Miscellaneous Nonmetallic Mineral Product Manufacturing.

32733 Concrete Pipe, Brick, and Block Manufacturing

This industry comprises establishments primarily engaged in manufacturing concrete pipe, brick, and block.

Cross-References.

Establishments primarily engaged in manufacturing concrete products (except brick, block, and pipe) are classified in Industry 32739, Other Concrete Product Manufacturing.

327331 Concrete Block and Brick Manufacturing[US]

This U.S. industry comprises establishments primarily engaged in manufacturing concrete block and brick.

327332 Concrete Pipe Manufacturing[US]

This U.S. industry comprises establishments primarily engaged in manufacturing concrete pipe.

32739 Other Concrete Product Manufacturing
See industry description for 327390 below.

327390 Other Concrete Product Manufacturing[CAN]

This industry comprises establishments primarily engaged in manufacturing concrete products (except block, brick, and pipe).

US—United States industry only. CAN—United States and Canadian industries are comparable. MEX—United States and Mexican industries are comparable. Blank—Canadian, Mexican, and United States industries are comparable.

Cross-References. Establishments primarily engaged in—

- Manufacturing concrete brick and block—are classified in U.S. Industry 327331, Concrete Block and Brick Manufacturing; and
- Manufacturing concrete pipe—are classified in U.S. Industry 327332, Concrete Pipe Manufacturing.

3274 Lime and Gypsum Product Manufacturing

32741 Lime Manufacturing
See industry description for 327410 below.

327410 Lime Manufacturing

This industry comprises establishments primarily engaged in manufacturing lime from calcitic limestone, dolomitic limestone, or other calcareous materials, such as coral, chalk, and shells. Lime manufacturing establishments may mine, quarry, collect, or purchase the sources of calcium carbonate.

Cross-References.

Establishments primarily engaged in manufacturing dolomite refractories are classified in U.S. Industry 327125, Nonclay Refractory Manufacturing.

32742 Gypsum Product Manufacturing
See industry description for 327420 below.

327420 Gypsum Product Manufacturing

This industry comprises establishments primarily engaged in manufacturing gypsum products, such as wallboard, plaster, plasterboard, molding, ornamental moldings, statuary, and architectural plaster work. Gypsum product manufacturing establishments may mine, quarry, or purchase gypsum.

Cross-References.

Establishments primarily engaged in operating gypsum mines or quarries are classified in U.S. Industry 212399, All Other Nonmetallic Mineral Mining.

3279 Other Nonmetallic Mineral Product Manufacturing

The Other Nonmetallic Mineral Product Manufacturing industry group comprises establishments manufacturing nonmetallic mineral products (except clay products, refractory products, glass products, cement and concrete products, lime, and gypsum products).

32791 Abrasive Product Manufacturing
See industry description for 327910 below.

327910 Abrasive Product Manufacturing

This industry comprises establishments primarily engaged in manufacturing abrasive grinding wheels of natural or synthetic materials, abrasive-coated products, and other abrasive products.

Illustrative Examples:

Aluminum oxide (fused) abrasives
  manufacturing
Sandpaper manufacturing
Buffing and polishing wheels, abrasive
  and nonabrasive, manufacturing

Silicon carbide abrasives manufacturing
Diamond dressing wheels manufacturing
Whetstones manufacturing

Cross-References. Establishments primarily engaged in—

- Mining and cutting grindstones, pulpstones, and whetstones—are classified in U.S. Industry 212399, All Other Nonmetallic Mineral Mining;

- Manufacturing plastic scouring pads—are classified in U.S. Industry 326199, All Other Plastics Product Manufacturing; and

- Manufacturing metallic scouring sponges and soap impregnated scouring pads—are classified in U.S. Industry 332999, All Other Miscellaneous Fabricated Metal Product Manufacturing.

32799 All Other Nonmetallic Mineral Product Manufacturing

This industry comprises establishments primarily engaged in manufacturing nonmetallic mineral products (except pottery, ceramics, and plumbing fixtures; clay building materials and refractories; glass and glass products; cement; ready-mix concrete; concrete products; lime; gypsum products; and abrasive products).

Cross-References. Establishments primarily engaged in—

- Manufacturing pottery, ceramics, and plumbing fixtures—are classified in Industry 32711, Pottery, Ceramics, and Plumbing Fixture Manufacturing;

- Mining or quarrying stone, earth, or other nonmetallic minerals—are classified in Industry Group 2123, Nonmetallic Mineral Mining and Quarrying;

US—United States industry only. CAN—United States and Canadian industries are comparable. MEX—United States and Mexican industries are comparable. Blank—Canadian, Mexican, and United States industries are comparable.

- Buying and selling semifinished monuments and tombstones with no work other than polishing, lettering, or shaping to custom order—are classified in Sector 42, Wholesale Trade or Sector 44-45, Retail Trade;

- Manufacturing clay building materials and refractories—are classified in Industry 32712, Clay Building Material and Refractories Manufacturing;

- Manufacturing glass and glass products—are classified in Industry 32721, Glass and Glass Product Manufacturing;

- Manufacturing cement—are classified in Industry 32731, Cement Manufacturing;

- Mixing and delivering ready-mix concrete—are classified in Industry 32732, Ready-Mix Concrete Manufacturing;

- Manufacturing concrete pipe, brick, and block—are classified in Industry 32733, Concrete Pipe, Brick, and Block Manufacturing;

- Manufacturing concrete products (except pipe, brick, and block)—are classified in Industry 32739, Other Concrete Product Manufacturing;

- Manufacturing lime—are classified in Industry 32741, Lime Manufacturing;

- Manufacturing gypsum products—are classified in Industry 32742, Gypsum Product Manufacturing;

- Manufacturing abrasive products—are classified in Industry 32791, Abrasive Product Manufacturing; and

- Manufacturing metallic scouring pads and steel wool—are classified in Industry 33299, All Other Fabricated Metal Product Manufacturing.

327991 Cut Stone and Stone Product Manufacturing[US]

This U.S. industry comprises establishments primarily engaged in cutting, shaping, and finishing granite, marble, limestone, slate, and other stone for building and miscellaneous uses. Stone product manufacturing establishments may mine, quarry, or purchase stone.

Cross-References. Establishments primarily engaged in—

- Mining or quarrying stone—are classified in Industry Group 2123, Nonmetallic Mineral Mining and Quarrying; and

- Buying and selling semifinished monuments and tombstones with no work other than polishing, lettering, or shaping to custom order—are classified in Sector 42, Wholesale Trade or Sector 44-45, Retail Trade.

US—United States industry only. CAN—United States and Canadian industries are comparable. MEX—United States and Mexican industries are comparable. Blank—Canadian, Mexican, and United States industries are comparable.

327992 Ground or Treated Mineral and Earth Manufacturing[US]

This U.S. industry comprises establishments primarily engaged in calcining, dead burning, or otherwise processing beyond beneficiation, clays, ceramic and refractory minerals, barite, and miscellaneous nonmetallic minerals.

Cross-References.

Establishments primarily engaged in crushing, grinding, pulverizing, washing, screening, sizing, or otherwise beneficiating mined clays, ceramics and refractory, and other miscellaneous nonmetallic minerals are classified in Industry Group 2123, Nonmetallic Mineral Mining and Quarrying.

327993 Mineral Wool Manufacturing[US]

This U.S. industry comprises establishments primarily engaged in manufacturing mineral wool and mineral wool (i.e., fiberglass) insulation products made of such siliceous materials as rock, slag, and glass or combinations thereof.

Cross-References.

Establishments primarily engaged in manufacturing metallic scouring pads and steel wool are classified in U.S. Industry 332999, All Other Miscellaneous Fabricated Metal Product Manufacturing.

327999 All Other Miscellaneous Nonmetallic Mineral Product Manufacturing[US]

This U.S. industry comprises establishments primarily engaged in manufacturing nonmetallic mineral products (except pottery, ceramics, and plumbing fixtures; clay building materials and refractories; glass and glass products; cement; ready-mix concrete; concrete products; lime; gypsum products; abrasive products; cut stone and stone products; ground and treated minerals and earth; and mineral wool).

Illustrative Examples:

Dry mix concrete manufacturing
Stucco and stucco products
  manufacturing

Mica products manufacturing
Synthetic stones, for gem stones and
  industrial use, manufacturing

Cross-References. Establishments primarily engaged in—

- Manufacturing pottery, ceramics, and plumbing fixtures—are classified in Industry 32711, Pottery, Ceramics, and Plumbing Fixture Manufacturing;

US—United States industry only. CAN—United States and Canadian industries are comparable. MEX—United States and Mexican industries are comparable. Blank—Canadian, Mexican, and United States industries are comparable.

- Manufacturing clay building materials and refractories—are classified in Industry 32712, Clay Building Material and Refractories Manufacturing;

- Manufacturing glass and glass products—are classified in Industry 32721, Glass and Glass Product Manufacturing;

- Manufacturing cement—are classified in Industry 327310, Cement Manufacturing;

- Mixing and delivering ready-mix concrete—are classified in Industry 327320, Ready-Mix Concrete Manufacturing;

- Manufacturing concrete pipe, brick, and block—are classified in Industry 32733, Concrete Pipe, Brick, and Block Manufacturing;

- Manufacturing concrete products (except pipe, brick, and block)—are classified in Industry 327390, Other Concrete Product Manufacturing;

- Manufacturing lime—are classified in Industry 327410, Lime Manufacturing;

- Manufacturing gypsum products—are classified in Industry 327420, Gypsum Product Manufacturing;

- Manufacturing abrasives and abrasive products—are classified in Industry 327910, Abrasive Product Manufacturing;

- Manufacturing cut stone and stone products—are classified in U.S. Industry 327991, Cut Stone and Stone Product Manufacturing;

- Manufacturing ground and treated minerals and earth (i.e., not at the mine site)—are classified in U.S. Industry 327992, Ground or Treated Mineral and Earth Manufacturing; and

- Manufacturing mineral wool and fiberglass insulation products—are classified in U.S. Industry 327993, Mineral Wool Manufacturing.

331 Primary Metal Manufacturing

Industries in the Primary Metal Manufacturing subsector smelt and/or refine ferrous and nonferrous metals from ore, pig or scrap, using electrometallurgical and other process metallurgical techniques. Establishments in this subsector also manufacture metal alloys and superalloys by introducing other chemical elements to pure metals. The output of smelting and refining, usually in ingot form, is used in rolling, drawing, and extruding operations to make sheet, strip, bar, rod, or wire, and in molten form to make castings and other basic metal products.

Primary manufacturing of ferrous and nonferrous metals begins with ore or concentrate as the primary input. Establishments manufacturing primary metals from ore and/or concentrate remain classified in the primary smelting, primary

---

refining, or iron and steel mill industries regardless of the form of their output. Establishments primarily engaged in secondary smelting and/or secondary refining recover ferrous and nonferrous metals from scrap and/or dross. The output of the secondary smelting and/or secondary refining industries is limited to shapes, such as ingot or billet, that will be further processed. Recovery of metals from scrap often occurs in establishments that are primarily engaged in activities, such as rolling, drawing, extruding, or similar processes.

Excluded from the Primary Metal Manufacturing subsector are establishments primarily engaged in manufacturing ferrous and nonferrous forgings (except ferrous forgings made in steel mills) and stampings. Although forging, stamping, and casting are all methods used to make metal shapes, forging and stamping do not use molten metals and are included in Subsector 332, Fabricated Metal Product Manufacturing. Establishments primarily engaged in operating coke ovens are classified in Industry 32419, Other Petroleum and Coal Products Manufacturing.

3311 Iron and Steel Mills and Ferroalloy Manufacturing

33111 Iron and Steel Mills and Ferroalloy Manufacturing

This industry comprises establishments primarily engaged in one or more of the following: (1) direct reduction of iron ore; (2) manufacturing pig iron in molten or solid form; (3) converting pig iron into steel; (4) manufacturing ferroalloys; (5) making steel; (6) making steel and manufacturing shapes (e.g., bar, plate, rod, sheet, strip, wire); and (7) making steel and forming pipe and tube.

Cross-References. Establishments primarily engaged in—

- Manufacturing nonferrous superalloys, such as cobalt or nickel-based super-alloys—are classified in Industry 33149, Nonferrous Metal (except Copper and Aluminum) Rolling, Drawing, Extruding, and Alloying; and

- Operating coke ovens—are classified in Industry 32419, Other Petroleum and Coal Products Manufacturing.

331111 Iron and Steel Mills[US]

This U.S. industry comprises establishments primarily engaged in one or more of the following: (1) direct reduction of iron ore; (2) manufacturing pig iron in molten or solid form; (3) converting pig iron into steel; (4) making steel; (5) making steel and manufacturing shapes (e.g., bar, plate, rod, sheet, strip, wire); and (6) making steel and forming tube and pipe.

US—United States industry only. CAN—United States and Canadian industries are comparable. MEX—United States and Mexican industries are comparable. Blank—Canadian, Mexican, and United States industries are comparable.

Cross-References. Establishments primarily engaged in—

- Operating coke ovens—are classified in Industry 324199, All Other Petroleum and Coal Products Manufacturing;

- Manufacturing ferroalloys (i.e., alloying elements used to improve, strengthen, or otherwise alter the characteristics of steel)—are classified in U.S. Industry 331112, Electrometallurgical Ferroalloy Product Manufacturing;

- Manufacturing concrete reinforcing bar by rolling and drawing steel from purchased steel—are classified in U.S. Industry 331221, Rolled Steel Shape Manufacturing; and

- Manufacturing fabricated structural metal products from concrete reinforcing bars and fabricated bar joists—are classified in U.S. Industry 332312, Fabricated Structural Metal Manufacturing.

331112 Electrometallurgical Ferroalloy Product Manufacturing[US]

This U.S. industry comprises establishments primarily engaged in manufacturing electrometallurgical ferroalloys. Ferroalloys add critical elements, such as silicon and manganese for carbon steel and chromium, vanadium, tungsten, titanium, and molybdenum for low- and high-alloy metals. Ferroalloys include iron-rich alloys and more pure forms of elements added during the steel manufacturing process that alter or improve the characteristics of the metal being made.

Cross-References. Establishments primarily engaged in—

- Manufacturing electrometallurgical steel and iron-based superalloys—are classified in U.S. Industry 331111, Iron and Steel Mills; and

- Manufacturing nonferrous superalloys, such as cobalt or nickel-based superalloys—are classified in U.S. Industry 331492, Secondary Smelting, Refining, and Alloying of Nonferrous Metal (except Copper and Aluminum).

3312 Steel Product Manufacturing from Purchased Steel

This industry group comprises establishments primarily engaged in manufacturing iron and steel tube and pipe, drawing steel wire, and rolling or drawing shapes from purchased iron or steel.

33121 Iron and Steel Pipe and Tube Manufacturing from Purchased Steel

See industry description for 331210 below.

331210 Iron and Steel Pipe and Tube Manufacturing from Purchased Steel

This industry comprises establishments primarily engaged in manufacturing welded, riveted, or seamless pipe and tube from purchased iron or steel.

Cross-References.

Establishments primarily engaged in making steel and further processing the steel into steel pipe and tube are classified in U.S. Industry 331111, Iron and Steel Mills.

33122 Rolling and Drawing of Purchased Steel

This industry comprises establishments primarily engaged in rolling and/or drawing steel shapes, such as plate, sheet, strip, rod, and bar, from purchased steel.

Cross-References. Establishments primarily engaged in—

- Making steel and rolling and/or drawing steel—are classified in Industry 33111, Iron and Steel Mills and Ferroalloy Manufacturing; and

- Manufacturing wire products from purchased wire—are classified in Industry 33261, Spring and Wire Product Manufacturing.

331221 Rolled Steel Shape Manufacturing[CAN]

This U.S. industry comprises establishments primarily engaged in rolling or drawing shapes (except wire), such as plate, sheet, strip, rod, and bar, from purchased steel.

Cross-References. Establishments primarily engaged in—

- Making steel and rolling or drawing steel shapes—are classified in U.S. Industry 331111, Iron and Steel Mills;

- Manufacturing concrete reinforcing bars in an iron and steel mill—are classified in U.S. Industry 331111, Iron and Steel Mills;

- Drawing wire from purchased steel—are classified in U.S. Industry 331222, Steel Wire Drawing; and

- Manufacturing fabricated structural metal products from concrete reinforcing bars and fabricated bar joists—are classified in U.S. Industry 332312, Fabricated Structural Metal Manufacturing.

US—United States industry only. CAN—United States and Canadian industries are comparable. MEX—United States and Mexican industries are comparable. Blank—Canadian, Mexican, and United States industries are comparable.

331222 Steel Wire Drawing^{CAN}

This U.S. industry comprises establishments primarily engaged in drawing wire from purchased steel.

Cross-References. Establishments primarily engaged in—

- Making steel and drawing steel wire—are classified in U.S. Industry 331111, Iron and Steel Mills; and

- Manufacturing wire products, such as nails, spikes, and paper clips, from purchased steel wire—are classified in Industry 33261, Spring and Wire Product Manufacturing.

3313 Alumina and Aluminum Production and Processing

33131 Alumina and Aluminum Production and Processing

This industry comprises establishments primarily engaged in one or more of the following: (1) refining alumina; (2) making (i.e., the primary production) aluminum from alumina; (3) recovering aluminum from scrap or dross; (4) alloying purchased aluminum; and (5) manufacturing aluminum primary forms (e.g., bar, foil, pipe, plate, rod, sheet, tube, wire).

Cross-References. Establishments primarily engaged in—

- Manufacturing aluminum oxide abrasives and refractories—are classified in Subsector 327, Nonmetallic Mineral Product Manufacturing;

- Sorting and breaking up scrap aluminum metal without also smelting or refining—are classified in Sector 42, Wholesale Trade; and

- Operating facilities where commingled recyclable materials, such as paper, plastics, used beverage cans, and metals are sorted into distinct categories without also smelting or refining—are classified in Industry 56292, Materials Recovery Facilities.

331311 Alumina Refining^{US}

This U.S. industry comprises establishments primarily engaged in refining alumina (i.e., aluminum oxide) generally from bauxite.

Cross-References. Establishments primarily engaged in—

- Manufacturing aluminum oxide abrasives and refractories—are classified in Subsector 327, Nonmetallic Mineral Product Manufacturing; and

---

US—United States industry only. CAN—United States and Canadian industries are comparable. MEX—United States and Mexican industries are comparable. Blank—Canadian, Mexican, and United States industries are comparable.

- Making aluminum from alumina—are classified in U.S. Industry 331312, Primary Aluminum Production.

331312 Primary Aluminum Production[US]

This U.S. industry comprises establishments primarily engaged in (1) making aluminum from alumina and/or (2) making aluminum from alumina and rolling, drawing, extruding, or casting the aluminum they make into primary forms (e.g., bar, billet, ingot, plate, rod, sheet, strip). Establishments in this industry may make primary aluminum or aluminum-based alloys from alumina.

Cross-References. Establishments primarily engaged in—

- Refining alumina—are classified in U.S. Industry 331311, Alumina Refining; and

- Recovering aluminum from scrap or alloying purchased aluminum—are classified in U.S. Industry 331314, Secondary Smelting and Alloying of Aluminum.

331314 Secondary Smelting and Alloying of Aluminum[US]

This U.S. industry comprises establishments primarily engaged in (1) recovering aluminum and aluminum alloys from scrap and/or dross (i.e., secondary smelting) and making billet or ingot (except by rolling) and/or (2) manufacturing alloys, powder, paste, or flake from purchased aluminum.

Cross-References. Establishments primarily engaged in—

- Making aluminum and/or aluminum alloys from alumina—are classified in U.S. Industry 331312, Primary Aluminum Production;

- Refining alumina—are classified in U.S. Industry 331311, Alumina Refining;

- Manufacturing aluminum sheet, plate, and foil from purchased aluminum or by recovering aluminum from scrap and flat rolling or continuous casting—are classified in U.S. Industry 331315, Aluminum Sheet, Plate, and Foil Manufacturing;

- Manufacturing aluminum extruded products from purchased aluminum or by recovering aluminum from scrap and extruding—are classified in U.S. Industry 331316, Aluminum Extruded Product Manufacturing;

- Manufacturing rolled ingot or billet from purchased aluminum or by recovering aluminum from scrap and rolling or drawing—are classified in U.S. Industry 331319, Other Aluminum Rolling and Drawing;

- Sorting and breaking up scrap metal without also smelting or refining—are classified in Industry 423930, Recyclable Material Merchant Wholesalers; and

- Operating facilities where commingled recyclable materials, such as paper, plastics, used beverage cans, and metals, are sorted into distinct categories without also smelting or refining—are classified in Industry 562920, Materials Recovery Facilities.

331315 Aluminum Sheet, Plate, and Foil Manufacturing[US]

This U.S. industry comprises establishments primarily engaged in (1) flat rolling or continuous casting sheet, plate, foil and welded tube from purchased aluminum; and/or (2) recovering aluminum from scrap and flat rolling or continuous casting sheet, plate, foil, and welded tube in integrated mills.

Cross-References.

Establishments primarily engaged in making aluminum from alumina and flat rolling or continuous casting aluminum sheet, plate, foil, and welded tube are classified in U.S. Industry 331312, Primary Aluminum Production.

331316 Aluminum Extruded Product Manufacturing[US]

This U.S. industry comprises establishments primarily engaged in (1) extruding aluminum bar, pipe, and tube blooms or extruding or drawing tube from purchased aluminum; and/or (2) recovering aluminum from scrap and extruding bar, pipe, and tube blooms or drawing tube in integrated mills.

Cross-References.

Establishments primarily engaged in making aluminum from alumina and extruding aluminum bar, pipe, tube or tube blooms are classified in U.S. Industry 331312, Primary Aluminum Production.

331319 Other Aluminum Rolling and Drawing[US]

This U.S. Industry comprises establishments primarily engaged in (1) rolling, drawing, or extruding shapes (except flat rolled sheet, plate, foil, and welded tube; extruded rod, bar, pipe, and tube blooms; and drawn or extruded tube) from purchased aluminum and/or (2) recovering aluminum from scrap and rolling, drawing or extruding shapes (except flat rolled sheet, plate, foil, and welded tube; extruded rod, bar, pipe, and tube blooms; and drawn or extruded tube) in integrated mills.

US—United States industry only. CAN—United States and Canadian industries are comparable. MEX—United States and Mexican industries are comparable. Blank—Canadian, Mexican, and United States industries are comparable.

Cross-References. Establishments primarily engaged in—

- Flat rolling sheet, plate, foil, and welded tube from either purchased aluminum or by recovering aluminum from scrap and flat rolling or continuous casting—are classified in U.S. Industry 331315, Aluminum Sheet, Plate, and Foil Manufacturing;

- Extruding rod, bar, pipe, tube and tube blooms or drawing tube from purchased aluminum or by recovering aluminum from scrap and extruding—are classified in U.S. Industry 331316, Aluminum Extruded Product Manufacturing; and

- Making aluminum from alumina and making aluminum shapes—are classified in U.S. Industry 331312, Primary Aluminum Production.

3314 Nonferrous Metal (except Aluminum) Production and Processing

33141 Nonferrous Metal (except Aluminum) Smelting and Refining

This industry comprises establishments primarily engaged in (1) smelting ores into nonferrous metals and/or (2) the primary refining of nonferrous metals (except aluminum) using electrolytic or other processes.

Cross-References. Establishments primarily engaged in—

- Making aluminum from alumina or recovery of aluminum from scrap—are classified in Industry 33131, Alumina and Aluminum Production and Processing;

- Recovering copper or copper alloys from scrap or dross and/or alloying, rolling, drawing, and extruding purchased copper—are classified in Industry 33142, Copper Rolling, Drawing, Extruding, and Alloying;

- Recovering nonferrous metals (except copper and aluminum) from scrap and/or alloying, rolling, drawing, and extruding purchased nonferrous metals (except copper and aluminum)—are classified in Industry 33149, Nonferrous Metal (except Copper and Aluminum) Rolling, Drawing, Extruding, and Alloying;

- Mining and making copper and other nonferrous concentrates (including gold and silver bullion) using processes, such as solvent extraction or electrowinning—are classified in Industry Group 2122, Metal Ore Mining;

- Sorting and breaking up scrap metal without also smelting or refining—are classified in Sector 42, Wholesale Trade; and

- Operating facilities where commingled recyclable materials, such as paper, plastics, used beverage cans, and metals, are sorted into distinct categories

without also smelting or refining—are classified in Industry 56292, Materials Recovery Facilities.

331411 Primary Smelting and Refining of Copper[MEX]

This U.S. industry comprises establishments primarily engaged in (1) smelting copper ore and/or (2) the primary refining of copper by electrolytic methods or other processes. Establishments in this industry make primary copper and copper-based alloys, such as brass and bronze, from ore or concentrates.

Cross-References. Establishments primarily engaged in—

- Recovering copper or copper alloys from scrap and making primary forms and/or alloying purchased copper—are classified in U.S. Industry 331423, Secondary Smelting, Refining, and Alloying of Copper;

- Mining and making copper concentrates by processes, such as solvent extraction or electrowinning—are classified in U.S. Industry 212234, Copper Ore and Nickel Ore Mining;

- Drawing copper wire (except mechanical) from purchased copper or recovering copper from scrap and drawing wire (except mechanical)—are classified in U.S. Industry 331422, Copper Wire (except Mechanical) Drawing; and

- Rolling, drawing, or extruding copper shapes (except communication and energy wire) from purchased copper or recovering copper from scrap and rolling, drawing, and extruding copper shapes—are classified in U.S. Industry 331421, Copper Rolling, Drawing, and Extruding.

331419 Primary Smelting and Refining of Nonferrous Metal (except Copper and Aluminum)[US]

This U.S. industry comprises establishments primarily engaged in (1) making (i.e., the primary production) nonferrous metals by smelting ore and/or (2) the primary refining of nonferrous metals by electrolytic methods or other processes.

Cross-References. Establishments primarily engaged in—

- Recovering nonferrous metals (except copper and aluminum) from scrap and making primary forms and/or alloying purchased nonferrous metals (except copper and aluminum)—are classified in U.S. Industry 331492, Secondary Smelting, Refining, and Alloying of Nonferrous Metal (except Copper and Aluminum);

- Making aluminum from alumina—are classified in U.S. Industry 331312, Primary Aluminum Production;

US—United States industry only. CAN—United States and Canadian industries are comparable. MEX—United States and Mexican industries are comparable. Blank—Canadian, Mexican, and United States industries are comparable.

- Primary smelting and primary refining of copper—are classified in U.S. Industry 331411, Primary Smelting and Refining of Copper;

- Mining and making copper and other nonferrous concentrates (including gold and silver bullion), by processes, such as solvent extraction or electrowinning—are classified in Industry Group 2122, Metal Ore Mining; and

- Rolling, drawing, and/or extruding nonferrous metal shapes (except copper and aluminum) from purchased nonferrous metals (except copper and aluminum) or by recovering nonferrous metals (except copper and aluminum) and rolling, drawing, or extruding—are classified in U.S. Industry 331491, Nonferrous Metal (except Copper and Aluminum) Rolling, Drawing, and Extruding.

33142 Copper Rolling, Drawing, Extruding, and Alloying

This industry comprises establishments primarily engaged in one or more of the following: (1) recovering copper or copper alloys from scraps; (2) alloying purchased copper; (3) rolling, drawing, or extruding shapes, (e.g., bar, plate, sheet, strip, tube, wire) from purchased copper; and (4) recovering copper or copper alloys from scrap and rolling, drawing, or extruding shapes (e.g., bar, plate, sheet, strip, tube, wire).

Cross-References. Establishments primarily engaged in—

- Smelting copper ore, primary copper refining, and/or rolling, drawing, or extruding primary copper made in the same establishment—are classified in Industry 33141, Nonferrous Metal (except Aluminum) Smelting and Refining;

- Manufacturing wire products from purchased wire—are classified in Industry 33261, Spring and Wire Product Manufacturing;

- Insulating purchased copper wire—are classified in Industry 33592, Communication and Energy Wire and Cable Manufacturing;

- Sorting and breaking up scrap metal without also smelting or refining—are classified in Sector 42, Wholesale Trade;

- Operating facilities where commingled recyclable materials, such as paper, plastics, used beverage cans, and metals, are sorted into distinct categories without also smelting or refining—are classified in Industry 56292, Materials Recovery Facilities;

- Die-casting purchased copper—are classified in Industry 33152, Nonferrous Metal Foundries; and

- Recovering nonferrous metals (except copper and aluminum) from scrap, and/or rolling, drawing, extruding, or alloying purchased nonferrous metals (except copper and aluminum)—are classified in Industry 33149, Nonferrous Metal (except Copper and Aluminum) Rolling, Drawing, Extruding, and Alloying.

331421 Copper Rolling, Drawing, and Extruding[US]

This U.S. industry comprises establishments primarily engaged in (1) rolling, drawing, and/or extruding shapes (e.g., bar, plate, sheet, strip, tube (except bare or insulated copper communication or energy wire), from purchased copper; and/or (2) recovering copper from scrap and rolling, drawing, and/or extruding shapes (e.g., bar, plate, sheet, strip, tube (except bare or insulated copper communication or energy wire in integrated mills)).

Cross-References. Establishments primarily engaged in—
- Recovering copper or copper alloys from scrap and making primary forms and/or alloying purchased copper—are classified in.U.S. Industry 331423, Secondary Smelting, Refining, and Alloying of Copper;
- Drawing copper wire (except mechanical) from purchased copper or recovering copper from scrap and drawing copper wire (except mechanical)—are classified in U.S. Industry 331422, Copper Wire (except Mechanical) Drawing;
- Die-casting purchased copper—are classified in U.S. Industry 331522, Nonferrous (except Aluminum) Die-Casting Foundries;
- Making primary copper and rolling, drawing, and/or extruding copper shapes (e.g., bar, plate, rod, sheet, strip)—are classified in U.S. Industry 331411, Primary Smelting and Refining of Copper; and
- Rolling, drawing, or extruding shapes from purchased nonferrous metal (except copper and aluminum) or recovering nonferrous metals (except copper and aluminum) from scrap and rolling, drawing, or extruding—are classified in U.S. Industry 331491, Nonferrous Metal (except Copper and Aluminum) Rolling, Drawing, and Extruding.

331422 Copper Wire (except Mechanical) Drawing[US]

This U.S. industry comprises establishments primarily engaged in drawing or drawing and insulating communication and energy wire and cable from purchased copper or in integrated secondary smelting and wire drawing plants.

Cross-References. Establishments primarily engaged in—
- Manufacturing copper mechanical wire from purchased copper or by recovering copper from scrap and drawing or extruding—are classified in U.S. Industry 331421, Copper Rolling, Drawing, and Extruding;

- Insulating purchased copper wire—are classified in U.S. Industry 335929, Other Communication and Energy Wire Manufacturing;

- Making primary copper and drawing copper wire—are classified in U.S. Industry 331411, Primary Smelting and Refining of Copper; and

- Manufacturing wire products from purchased copper wire—are classified in Industry 33261, Spring and Wire Product Manufacturing.

331423 Secondary Smelting, Refining, and Alloying of Copper[US]

This U.S. industry comprises establishments primarily engaged in (1) recovering copper and copper alloys from scrap and/or (2) alloying purchased copper. Establishments in this industry make primary forms, such as ingot, wire bar, cake, and slab from copper or copper alloys, such as brass and bronze.

Cross-References. Establishments primarily engaged in—

- Sorting and breaking up scrap metal without also smelting or refining—are classified in Industry 423930, Recyclable Material Merchant Wholesalers;

- Operating facilities where commingled recyclable materials, such as paper, plastics, used beverage cans, and metals, are sorted into distinct categories without also smelting or refining—are classified in Industry 562920, Materials Recovery Facilities;

- Smelting copper ore and/or the primary refining of copper—are classified in U.S. Industry 331411, Primary Smelting and Refining of Copper;

- Recovering copper and copper alloys from scrap and rolling, drawing, or extruding shapes—are classified in U.S. Industry 331421, Copper Rolling, Drawing, and Extruding;

- Recovering copper and copper alloys from scrap and drawing wire (except mechanical)—are classified in U.S. Industry 331422, Copper Wire (except Mechanical) Drawing; and

- Recovering nonferrous metals (except copper, aluminum) from scrap and making primary forms and/or alloying purchased nonferrous metals (except copper and aluminum)—are classified in U.S. Industry 331492, Secondary Smelting, Refining, and Alloying of Nonferrous Metal (except Copper and Aluminum).

33149 Nonferrous Metal (except Copper and Aluminum) Rolling, Drawing, Extruding, and Alloying

This industry comprises establishments primarily engaged in one or more of the following: (1) recovering nonferrous metals (except copper and aluminum)

US—United States industry only. CAN—United States and Canadian industries are comparable. MEX—United States and Mexican industries are comparable. Blank—Canadian, Mexican, and United States industries are comparable.

and nonferrous metal alloys from scrap; (2) alloying purchased nonferrous metals (except copper and aluminum); (3) rolling, drawing, and extruding shapes from purchased nonferrous metals (except copper and aluminum); and (4) recovering nonferrous metals from scrap (except copper and aluminum) and rolling, drawing, or extruding shapes in integrated facilities.

Cross-References. Establishments primarily engaged in—

- Rolling, drawing, and/or extruding aluminum or secondary smelting and alloying of aluminum—are classified in Industry 33131, Alumina and Aluminum Production and Processing;

- Recovering copper and copper alloys from scrap, alloying purchased copper, rolling, drawing, or extruding shapes from purchased copper, and recovering copper or copper alloys from scrap and rolling, drawing, or extruding shapes in integrated mills—are classified in Industry 33142, Copper Rolling, Drawing, Extruding, and Alloying;

- Insulating purchased nonferrous wire—are classified in Industry 33592, Communication and Energy Wire and Cable Manufacturing;

- Making primary nonferrous metals and rolling, drawing, or extruding nonferrous metal shapes—are classified in Industry 33141, Nonferrous Metal (except Aluminum) Smelting and Refining;

- Manufacturing products from purchased wire—are classified in Industry 33261, Spring and Wire Product Manufacturing;

- Sorting and breaking up scrap metal without also smelting or refining—are classified in Sector 42, Wholesale Trade; and

- Operating facilities where commingled recyclable materials, such as paper, plastics, used beverage cans, and metals, are sorted into distinct categories without also smelting or refining—are classified in Industry 56292, Materials Recovery Facilities.

331491 Nonferrous Metal (except Copper and Aluminum) Rolling, Drawing, and Extruding[US]

This U.S. industry comprises establishments primarily engaged in (1) rolling, drawing, or extruding shapes (e.g., bar, plate, sheet, strip, tube) from purchased nonferrous metals) and/or (2) recovering nonferrous metals from scrap and rolling, drawing, and/or extruding shapes (e.g., bar, plate, sheet, strip, tube) in integrated mills.

US—United States industry only. CAN—United States and Canadian industries are comparable. MEX—United States and Mexican industries are comparable. Blank—Canadian, Mexican, and United States industries are comparable.

Cross-References. Establishments primarily engaged in—

- Rolling, drawing, and/or extruding shapes from purchased copper or recovering copper from scrap and rolling, drawing, or extruding shapes—are classified in U.S. Industry 331421, Copper Rolling, Drawing, and Extruding;

- Recovering nonferrous metals (except copper and aluminum) from scrap and making primary forms and/or alloying purchased nonferrous metals—are classified in U.S. Industry 331492, Secondary Smelting, Refining, and Alloying of Nonferrous Metal (except Copper and Aluminum);

- Rolling, drawing, and/or extruding aluminum—are classified in Industry 33131, Alumina and Aluminum Production and Processing;

- Making primary nonferrous metals and rolling, drawing, or extruding nonferrous metal shapes—are classified in U.S. Industry 331419, Primary Smelting and Refining of Nonferrous Metal (except Copper and Aluminum); and

- Insulating purchased nonferrous wire—are classified in U.S. Industry 335929, Other Communication and Energy Wire Manufacturing.

331492 Secondary Smelting, Refining, and Alloying of Nonferrous Metal (except Copper and Aluminum)[US]

This U.S. industry comprises establishments primarily engaged in (1) alloying purchased nonferrous metals and/or (2) recovering nonferrous metals from scrap. Establishments in this industry make primary forms (e.g., bar, billet, bloom, cake, ingot, slab, slug, wire) using smelting or refining processes.

Cross-References. Establishments primarily engaged in—

- Recovering aluminum and aluminum alloys from scrap and/or alloying purchased aluminum—are classified in U.S. Industry 331314, Secondary Smelting and Alloying of Aluminum;

- Sorting and breaking up scrap metal without also smelting or refining—are classified in Industry 423930, Recyclable Material Merchant Wholesalers;

- Recovering nonferrous metals from scrap and rolling, drawing, or extruding shapes in integrated facilities—are classified in U.S. Industry 331491, Nonferrous Metal (except Copper and Aluminum) Rolling, Drawing, and Extruding;

- Operating facilities where commingled recyclable materials, such as paper, plastics, used beverage cans, and metals, are sorted into distinct categories without also smelting or refining—are classified in Industry 562920, Materials Recovery Facilities; and

---

- Recovering copper and copper alloys from scrap and making primary forms; and/or alloying purchased copper—are classified in U.S. Industry 331423, Secondary Smelting, Refining, and Alloying of Copper.

3315 Foundries

This industry group comprises establishments primarily engaged in pouring molten metal into molds or dies to form castings. Establishments making castings and further manufacturing, such as machining or assembling, a specific manufactured product are classified in the industry of the finished product. Foundries may perform operations, such as cleaning and deburring, on the castings they manufacture. More involved processes, such as tapping, threading, milling, or machining to tight tolerances, that transform castings into more finished products are classified elsewhere in the manufacturing sector based on the product being made.

Establishments in this industry group make castings from purchased metals or in integrated secondary smelting and casting facilities. When the production of primary metals is combined with making castings, the establishment is classified in 331 with the primary metal being made.

33151 Ferrous Metal Foundries

This industry comprises establishments primarily engaged in pouring molten iron and steel into molds of a desired shape to make castings. Establishments in this industry purchase iron and steel made in other establishments.

Cross-References.

Establishments primarily engaged in manufacturing iron or steel castings and further manufacturing them into finished products are classified based on the specific finished product.

331511 Iron Foundries^{CAN}

This U.S. industry comprises establishments primarily engaged in pouring molten pig iron or iron alloys into molds to manufacture castings, (e.g., cast iron manhole covers, cast iron pipe, cast iron skillets). Establishments in this industry purchase iron made in other establishments.

Cross-References.

Establishments primarily engaged in manufacturing iron castings and further manufacturing them into finished products are classified based on the specific finished product.

US—United States industry only. CAN—United States and Canadian industries are comparable. MEX—United States and Mexican industries are comparable. Blank—Canadian, Mexican, and United States industries are comparable.

331512 Steel Investment Foundries[US]

This U.S. industry comprises establishments primarily engaged in manufacturing steel investment castings. Investment molds are formed by covering a wax shape with a refractory slurry. After the refractory slurry hardens, the wax is melted, leaving a seamless mold. Investment molds provide highly detailed, consistent castings. Establishments in this industry purchase steel made in other establishments.

Cross-References. Establishments primarily engaged in—

- Manufacturing steel castings (except steel investment castings)—are classified in U.S. Industry 331513, Steel Foundries (except Investment); and
- Manufacturing steel investment castings and further manufacturing them into finished products—are classified based on the specific finished product.

331513 Steel Foundries (except Investment)[US]

This U.S. industry comprises establishments primarily engaged in manufacturing steel castings (except steel investment castings). Establishments in this industry purchase steel made in other establishments.

Cross-References. Establishments primarily engaged in—

- Manufacturing steel investment castings—are classified in U.S. Industry 331512, Steel Investment Foundries; and
- Manufacturing steel castings and further manufacturing them into finished products—are classified based on the specific finished product.

33152 Nonferrous Metal Foundries

This industry comprises establishments primarily engaged in pouring and/or introducing molten nonferrous metal, under high pressure, into metal molds or dies to manufacture castings. Establishments in this industry purchase nonferrous metals made in other establishments.

Cross-References. Establishments primarily engaged in—

- Manufacturing iron or steel castings—are classified in Industry 33151, Ferrous Metal Foundries; and
- Manufacturing nonferrous metal castings and further manufacturing them into finished products—are classified based on the specific finished product.

331521 Aluminum Die-Casting Foundries[US]

This U.S. industry comprises establishments primarily engaged in introducing molten aluminum, under high pressure, into molds or dies to make aluminum die-castings. Establishments in this industry purchase aluminum made in other establishments.

Cross-References. Establishments primarily engaged in—

- Pouring molten aluminum into molds to manufacture aluminum castings— are classified in U.S. Industry 331524, Aluminum Foundries (except Die-Casting); and

- Manufacturing aluminum die-castings and further manufacturing them into finished products—are classified based on the specific finished product.

331522 Nonferrous (except Aluminum) Die-Casting Foundries[US]

This U.S. industry comprises establishments primarily engaged in introducing molten nonferrous metal (except aluminum), under high pressure, into molds to make nonferrous metal die-castings. Establishments in this industry purchase nonferrous metals made in other establishments.

Cross-References. Establishments primarily engaged in—

- Manufacturing aluminum die-castings—are classified in U.S. Industry 331521, Aluminum Die-Casting Foundries;

- Pouring molten aluminum into molds to manufacture aluminum castings— are classified in U.S. Industry 331524, Aluminum Foundries (except Die-Casting);

- Pouring molten copper into molds to manufacture copper castings—are classified in U.S. Industry 331525, Copper Foundries (except Die-Casting);

- Pouring molten nonferrous metal (except copper and aluminum) into molds to manufacture nonferrous (except copper and aluminum) castings—are classified in U.S. Industry 331528, Other Nonferrous Foundries (except Die-Casting); and

- Manufacturing nonferrous die-castings and further manufacturing them into finished products—are classified based on the specific finished product.

331524 Aluminum Foundries (except Die-Casting)[US]

This U.S. industry comprises establishments primarily engaged in pouring molten aluminum into molds to manufacture aluminum castings. Establishments in this industry purchase aluminum made in other establishments.

US—United States industry only. CAN—United States and Canadian industries are comparable. MEX—United States and Mexican industries are comparable. Blank—Canadian, Mexican, and United States industries are comparable.

Cross-References. Establishments primarily engaged in—

- Manufacturing aluminum die-castings—are classified in U.S. Industry 331521, Aluminum Die-Casting Foundries; and

- Manufacturing aluminum or aluminum alloy castings and further manufacturing them into finished products—are classified based on the specific finished product.

331525 Copper Foundries (except Die-Casting)[US]

This U.S. industry comprises establishments primarily engaged in pouring molten copper into molds to manufacture copper castings. Establishments in this industry purchase copper made in other establishments.

Cross-References. Establishments primarily engaged in—

- Manufacturing copper die-castings—are classified in U.S. Industry 331522, Nonferrous (except Aluminum) Die-Casting Foundries; and

- Manufacturing copper castings and further manufacturing them into finished products—are classified based on the specific finished product.

331528 Other Nonferrous Foundries (except Die-Casting)[US]

This U.S. industry comprises establishments primarily engaged in pouring molten nonferrous metals (except aluminum and copper) into molds to manufacture nonferrous castings (except aluminum die-castings, nonferrous (except aluminum) die-castings, aluminum castings, and copper castings). Establishments in this industry purchase nonferrous metals, such as nickel, lead, and zinc, made in other establishments.

Cross-References. Establishments primarily engaged in—

- Manufacturing aluminum die-castings—are classified in U.S. Industry 331521, Aluminum Die-Casting Foundries;

- Manufacturing nonferrous (except aluminum) die-castings—are classified in U.S. Industry 331522, Nonferrous (except Aluminum) Die-Casting Foundries;

- Pouring molten aluminum into molds to manufacture aluminum castings—are classified in U.S. Industry 331524, Aluminum Foundries (except Die-Casting);

- Manufacturing copper castings—are classified in U.S. Industry 331525, Copper Foundries (except Die-Casting); and

- Manufacturing nonferrous castings and further manufacturing them into finished products—are classified based on the specific finished product.

332 Fabricated Metal Product Manufacturing

Industries in the Fabricated Metal Product Manufacturing subsector transform metal into intermediate or end products, other than machinery, computers and electronics, and metal furniture, or treat metals and metal formed products fabricated elsewhere. Important fabricated metal processes are forging, stamping, bending, forming, and machining, used to shape individual pieces of metal; and other processes, such as welding and assembling, used to join separate parts together. Establishments in this subsector may use one of these processes or a combination of these processes.

The NAICS structure for this subsector distinguishes the forging and stamping processes in a single industry. The remaining industries in the subsector group establishments based on similar combinations of processes used to make products.

The manufacturing performed in the Fabricated Metal Product Manufacturing subsector begins with manufactured metal shapes. The establishments in this subsector further fabricate the purchased metal shapes into a product. For instance, the Spring and Wire Product Manufacturing industry starts with wire and fabricates such items.

Within manufacturing there are other establishments that make the same products made by this subsector; only these establishments begin production further back in the production process. These establishments have a more integrated operation. For instance, one establishment may manufacture steel, draw it into wire, and make wire products in the same establishment. Such operations are classified in the Primary Metal Manufacturing subsector.

3321 Forging and Stamping

33211 Forging and Stamping

This industry comprises establishments primarily engaged in one or more of the following: (1) manufacturing forgings from purchased metals; (2) manufacturing metal custom roll forming products; (3) manufacturing metal stamped and spun products (except automotive, cans, coins); and (4) manufacturing powder metallurgy products. Establishments making metal forgings, metal stampings, and metal spun products and further manufacturing (e.g., machining, assembling) a specific manufactured product are classified in the industry of the finished product. Metal forging, metal stamping, and metal spun products establishments may perform surface finishing operations, such as cleaning and deburring, on the products they manufacture.

Cross-References. Establishments primarily engaged in—

- Manufacturing metal forgings in integrated primary metal establishments— are classified in Subsector 331, Primary Metal Manufacturing;
- Stamping automotive stampings—are classified in Industry 33637, Motor Vehicle Metal Stamping;
- Manufacturing and installing rolled formed seamless gutters at construction sites—are classified in Industry 23839, Other Building Finishing Contractors; and
- Stamping coins—are classified in Industry 33991, Jewelry and Silverware Manufacturing.

332111 Iron and Steel Forging[US]

This U.S. industry comprises establishments primarily engaged in manufacturing iron and steel forgings from purchased iron and steel by hammering mill shapes. Establishments making iron and steel forgings and further manufacturing (e.g., machining, assembling) a specific manufactured product are classified in the industry of the finished product. Iron and steel forging establishments may perform surface finishing operations, such as cleaning and deburring, on the forgings they manufacture.

Cross-References. Establishments primarily engaged in—

- Manufacturing iron and steel forgings in integrated iron and steel mills— are classified in U.S. Industry 331111, Iron and Steel Mills; and
- Manufacturing nonferrous forgings—are classified in U.S. Industry 332112, Nonferrous Forging.

332112 Nonferrous Forging[US]

This U.S. industry comprises establishments primarily engaged in manufacturing nonferrous forgings from purchased nonferrous metals by hammering mill shapes. Establishments making nonferrous forgings and further manufacturing (e.g., machining, assembling) a specific manufactured product are classified in the industry of the finished product. Nonferrous forging establishments may perform surface finishing operations, such as cleaning and deburring, on the forgings they manufacture.

Cross-References. Establishments primarily engaged in—

- Manufacturing iron and steel forgings—are classified in U.S. Industry 332111, Iron and Steel Forging; and

---

US—United States industry only. CAN—United States and Canadian industries are comparable. MEX—United States and Mexican industries are comparable. Blank—Canadian, Mexican, and United States industries are comparable.

- Manufacturing nonferrous forgings in integrated primary or secondary non-ferrous metal production facilities—are classified in Subsector 331, Primary Metal Manufacturing.

332114   Custom Roll Forming[US]

This U.S. industry comprises establishments primarily engaged in custom roll forming metal products by use of rotary motion of rolls with various contours to bend or shape the products.

Cross-References.

Establishments primarily engaged in manufacturing and installing rolled formed seamless gutters at construction sites are classified in Industry 238390, Other Building Finishing Contractors.

332115   Crown and Closure Manufacturing[US]

This U.S. industry comprises establishments primarily engaged in stamping metal crowns and closures, such as bottle caps and home canning lids and rings.

332116   Metal Stamping[US]

This U.S. industry comprises establishments primarily engaged in manufacturing unfinished metal stampings and spinning unfinished metal products (except crowns, cans, closures, automotive, and coins). Establishments making metal stampings and metal spun products and further manufacturing (e.g., machining, assembling) a specific product are classified in the industry of the finished product. Metal stamping and metal spun products establishments may perform surface finishing operations, such as cleaning and deburring, on the products they manufacture.

Cross-References. Establishments primarily engaged in—

- Stamping automotive stampings—are classified in Industry 336370, Motor Vehicle Metal Stamping;
- Stamping metal crowns and closures—are classified in U.S. Industry 332115, Crown and Closure Manufacturing;
- Manufacturing metal cans—are classified in U.S. Industry 332431, Metal Can Manufacturing; and
- Stamping coins—are classified in U.S. Industry 339911, Jewelry (except Costume) Manufacturing.

US—United States industry only. CAN—United States and Canadian industries are comparable. MEX—United States and Mexican industries are comparable. Blank—Canadian, Mexican, and United States industries are comparable.

332117 Powder Metallurgy Part Manufacturing[US]

This U.S. industry comprises establishments primarily engaged in manufacturing powder metallurgy products using any of the various powder metallurgy processing techniques, such as pressing and sintering or metal injection molding. Establishments in this industry generally make a wide range of parts on a job or order basis.

3322 Cutlery and Handtool Manufacturing

33221 Cutlery and Handtool Manufacturing

This industry comprises establishments primarily engaged in one or more of the following: (1) manufacturing nonprecious and precious plated metal cutlery and flatware; (2) manufacturing nonpowered hand and edge tools; (3) manufacturing nonpowered handsaws; (4) manufacturing saw blades, all types (including those for sawing machines); and (5) manufacturing metal kitchen utensils (except cutting-type) and pots and pans (except those manufactured by casting (e.g., cast iron skillets) or stamped without further fabrication).

Cross-References. Establishments primarily engaged in—

- Manufacturing precious (except precious plated) metal cutlery and flatware—are classified in Industry 33991, Jewelry and Silverware Manufacturing;
- Manufacturing electric razors and hair clippers for use on humans—are classified in Industry 33521, Small Electrical Appliance Manufacturing;
- Manufacturing power hedge shears and trimmers and electric hair clippers for use on animals—are classified in Industry 33311, Agricultural Implement Manufacturing;
- Manufacturing metal cutting dies, attachments, and accessories for machine tools—are classified in Industry 33351, Metalworking Machinery Manufacturing;
- Manufacturing handheld power-driven handtools—are classified in Industry 33399, All Other General Purpose Machinery Manufacturing; and
- Manufacturing finished cast iron kitchen utensils (i.e., cast iron skillets) and castings for kitchen utensils, pots, and pans—are classified in Industry Group 3315, Foundries.

332211 Cutlery and Flatware (except Precious) Manufacturing[US]

This U.S. industry comprises establishments primarily engaged in manufacturing nonprecious and precious plated metal cutlery and flatware.

US—United States industry only. CAN—United States and Canadian industries are comparable. MEX—United States and Mexican industries are comparable. Blank—Canadian, Mexican, and United States industries are comparable.

Cross-References. Establishments primarily engaged in—

- Manufacturing precious (except precious plated) metal cutlery and flatware—are classified in U.S. Industry 339912, Silverware and Hollowware Manufacturing;
- Manufacturing electric razors and hair clippers for use on humans and housewares—are classified in U.S. Industry 335211, Electric Housewares and Household Fan Manufacturing;
- Manufacturing power hedge shears and trimmers—are classified in U.S. Industry 333112, Lawn and Garden Tractor and Home Lawn and Garden Equipment Manufacturing; and
- Manufacturing nonelectric hair clippers for use on animals—are classified in U.S. Industry 332212, Hand and Edge Tool Manufacturing.

332212 Hand and Edge Tool Manufacturing[US]

This industry comprises establishments primarily engaged in manufacturing nonpowered hand and edge tools (except saws).

Cross-References. Establishments primarily engaged in—

- Manufacturing saw blades and handsaws—are classified in U.S. Industry 332213, Saw Blade and Handsaw Manufacturing;
- Manufacturing metal cutting dies, attachments, and accessories for machine tools—are classified in Industry 33351, Metalworking Machinery Manufacturing;
- Manufacturing handheld power-driven handtools—are classified in U.S. Industry 333991, Power-Driven Handtool Manufacturing;
- Manufacturing electric razors and hair clippers for use on humans—are classified in U.S. Industry 335211, Electric Housewares and Household Fan Manufacturing;
- Manufacturing electric hair clippers for use on animals—are classified in U.S. Industry 333111, Farm Machinery and Equipment Manufacturing; and
- Manufacturing nonelectric household-type scissors and shears—are classified in U.S. Industry 332211, Cutlery and Flatware (except Precious) Manufacturing.

332213 Saw Blade and Handsaw Manufacturing[US]

This U.S. industry comprises establishments primarily engaged in (1) manufacturing nonpowered handsaws and/or (2) manufacturing saw blades, all types (including those for power sawing machines).

Cross-References.

Establishments primarily engaged in manufacturing handheld powered saws are classified in U.S. Industry 333991, Power-Driven Handtool Manufacturing.

332214 Kitchen Utensil, Pot, and Pan Manufacturing[US]

This U.S. industry comprises establishments primarily engaged in manufacturing metal kitchen utensils (except cutting-type), pots, and pans (except those manufactured by casting (e.g., cast iron skillets) or stamped without further fabrication).

Cross-References. Establishments primarily engaged in—

- Manufacturing finished cast metal kitchen utensils or castings for kitchen utensils—are classified in Industry Group 3315, Foundries;
- Manufacturing stampings for kitchen utensils, pots, and pans—are classified in U.S. Industry 332116, Metal Stamping; and
- Manufacturing metal cutting-type kitchen utensils—are classified in U.S. Industry 332211, Cutlery and Flatware (except Precious) Manufacturing.

3323 Architectural and Structural Metals Manufacturing

33231 Plate Work and Fabricated Structural Product Manufacturing

This industry comprises establishments primarily engaged in manufacturing one or more of the following: (1) prefabricated metal buildings, panels and sections; (2) structural metal products; and (3) metal plate work products.

Cross-References. Establishments primarily engaged in—

- Making manufactured homes (i.e., mobile homes) and prefabricated wood buildings—are classified in Industry 32199, All Other Wood Product Manufacturing;
- Constructing buildings, bridges, and other heavy construction projects on site—are classified in Sector 23, Construction;
- Building ships, boats, and barges—are classified in Industry 33661, Ship and Boat Building;
- Manufacturing power boilers and heat exchangers—are classified in Industry 33241, Power Boiler and Heat Exchanger Manufacturing;
- Manufacturing heavy gauge tanks—are classified in Industry 33242, Metal Tank (Heavy Gauge) Manufacturing;

- Manufacturing metal plate cooling towers—are classified in Industry 33341, Ventilation, Heating, Air-Conditioning, and Commercial Refrigeration Equipment Manufacturing; and

- Manufacturing metal windows, doors, and studs—are classified in Industry 33232, Ornamental and Architectural Metal Products Manufacturing.

332311 Prefabricated Metal Building and Component Manufacturing^{CAN}

This U.S. industry comprises establishments primarily engaged in manufacturing prefabricated metal buildings, panels, and sections.

Cross-References. Establishments primarily engaged in—

- Making manufactured homes (i.e., mobile homes) and prefabricated wood buildings—are classified in Industry 32199, All Other Wood Product Manufacturing;

- Constructing prefabricated buildings on site—are classified in Subsector 236, Construction of Buildings; and

- Manufacturing metal windows and doors—are classified in U.S. Industry 332321, Metal Window and Door Manufacturing.

332312 Fabricated Structural Metal Manufacturing^{US}

This U.S. industry comprises establishments primarily engaged in fabricating structural metal products, such as assemblies of concrete reinforcing bars and fabricated bar joists.

Cross-References. Establishments primarily engaged in—

- Manufacturing concrete reinforcing bars in an iron and steel mill—are classified in U.S. Industry 331111, Iron and Steel Mills;

- Manufacturing metal windows and doors—are classified in U.S. Industry 332321, Metal Window and Door Manufacturing;

- Manufacturing metal studs—are classified in U.S. Industry 332322, Sheet Metal Work Manufacturing;

- Constructing buildings, bridges, and other heavy construction projects on site—are classified in Sector 23, Construction;

- Manufacturing concrete reinforcing bar by rolling and drawing steel from purchased steel—are classified in U.S. Industry 331221, Rolled Steel Shape Manufacturing;

- Building ships, boats, and barges—are classified in Industry 33661, **Ship and Boat Building**; and

- Prefabricating metal buildings, panels, and sections—are classified in U.S. Industry 332311, Prefabricated Metal Building and Component Manufacturing.

332313 Plate Work Manufacturing[US]

This industry comprises establishments primarily engaged in manufacturing fabricated metal plate work by cutting, punching, bending, shaping, and welding purchased metal plate.

Cross-References. Establishments primarily engaged in—

- Manufacturing power boilers and heat exchangers—are classified in Industry 332410, Power Boiler and Heat Exchanger Manufacturing;

- Manufacturing heavy gauge tanks—are classified in Industry 332420, **Metal Tank (Heavy Gauge) Manufacturing**; and

- Manufacturing metal plate cooling towers—are classified in U.S. Industry 333415, Air-Conditioning and Warm Air Heating Equipment and Commercial and Industrial Refrigeration Equipment Manufacturing.

33232 Ornamental and Architectural Metal Products Manufacturing

This industry comprises establishments primarily engaged in manufacturing one or more of the following: (1) metal framed windows (i.e., typically using purchased glass) and metal doors; (2) sheet metal work; and (3) ornamental and architectural metal products.

Cross-References. Establishments primarily engaged in—

- Manufacturing metal covered (i.e., clad) wood windows and doors—are classified in Industry 32191, Millwork;

- Manufacturing bins, cans, vats, and light tanks of sheet metal—are classified in Industry 33243, Metal Can, Box, and Other Metal Container (Light Gauge) Manufacturing;

- Manufacturing prefabricated metal buildings, panels, and sections—are classified in Industry 33231, Plate Work and Fabricated Structural Product Manufacturing;

- Fabricating sheet metal work on site—are classified in Subsector 238, Specialty Trade Contractors;

- Manufacturing metal stampings (except automotive, coins) and custom roll forming products—are classified in Industry 33211, Forging and Stamping;
- Manufacturing automotive stampings—are classified in Industry 33637, Motor Vehicle Metal Stamping; and
- Stamping coins—are classified in Industry 33991, Jewelry and Silverware Manufacturing.

332321 Metal Window and Door Manufacturing^{CAN}

This U.S. industry comprises establishments primarily engaged in manufacturing metal framed windows (i.e., typically using purchased glass) and metal doors. Examples of products made by these establishments are metal door frames; metal framed window and door screens; and metal molding and trim (except automotive).

Cross-References. Establishments primarily engaged in—

- Manufacturing wood or metal covered (i.e., clad) wood framed windows and doors—are classified in U.S. Industry 321911, Wood Window and Door Manufacturing; and
- Manufacturing metal automotive molding and trim—are classified in Industry 336370, Motor Vehicle Metal Stamping.

332322 Sheet Metal Work Manufacturing^{US}

This U.S. industry comprises establishments primarily engaged in manufacturing sheet metal work (except stampings).

Cross-References. Establishments primarily engaged in—

- Manufacturing sheet metal bins, vats, and light tanks of sheet metal—are classified in U.S. Industry 332439, Other Metal Container Manufacturing;
- Manufacturing metal cans, lids, and ends—are classified in U.S. Industry 332431, Metal Can Manufacturing;
- Fabricating sheet metal work on site—are classified in Subsector 238, Specialty Trade Contractors;
- Manufacturing metal stampings (except automotive, coins) and custom roll forming products—are classified in Industry 33211, Forging and Stamping;
- Manufacturing automotive stampings—are classified in Industry 336370, Motor Vehicle Metal Stamping; and
- Stamping coins—are classified in U.S. Industry 339911, Jewelry (except Costume) Manufacturing.

US—United States industry only. CAN—United States and Canadian industries are comparable. MEX—United States and Mexican industries are comparable. Blank—Canadian, Mexican, and United States industries are comparable.

332323 Ornamental and Architectural Metal Work Manufacturing[US]

This U.S. industry comprises establishments primarily engaged in manufacturing ornamental and architectural metal work, such as staircases, metal open steel flooring, fire escapes, railings, and scaffolding.

Cross-References.

Establishments primarily engaged in manufacturing prefabricated metal buildings, panels, and sections are classified in U.S. Industry 332311, Prefabricated Metal Building and Component Manufacturing.

3324 Boiler, Tank, and Shipping Container Manufacturing

33241 Power Boiler and Heat Exchanger Manufacturing
See industry description for 332410 below.

332410 Power Boiler and Heat Exchanger Manufacturing

This industry comprises establishments primarily engaged in manufacturing power boilers and heat exchangers. Establishments in this industry may perform installation in addition to manufacturing power boilers and heat exchangers.

Cross-References. Establishments primarily engaged in—

- Manufacturing heavy gauge metal tanks—are classified in Industry 332420, Metal Tank (Heavy Gauge) Manufacturing;
- Manufacturing steam or hot water low pressure heating boilers—are classified in U.S. Industry 333414, Heating Equipment (except Warm Air Furnaces) Manufacturing; and
- Installing power boilers and heat exchanges without manufacturing—are classified in Industry 238220, Plumbing, Heating, and Air-Conditioning Contractors.

33242 Metal Tank (Heavy Gauge) Manufacturing
See industry description for 332420 below.

332420 Metal Tank (Heavy Gauge) Manufacturing

This industry comprises establishments primarily engaged in cutting, forming, and joining heavy gauge metal to manufacture tanks, vessels, and other containers.

US—United States industry only. CAN—United States and Canadian industries are comparable. MEX—United States and Mexican industries are comparable. Blank—Canadian, Mexican, and United States industries are comparable.

Cross-References. Establishments primarily engaged in—

- Manufacturing power boilers—are classified in Industry 332410, Power Boiler and Heat Exchanger Manufacturing;
- Manufacturing light gauge metal containers—are classified in Industry 33243, Metal Can, Box, and Other Metal Container (Light Gauge) Manufacturing; and
- Installing heavy gauge metal tanks without manufacturing—are classified in Industry 238120, Structural Steel and Precast Concrete Contractors.

33243 Metal Can, Box, and Other Metal Container (Light Gauge) Manufacturing

This industry comprises establishments primarily engaged in forming light gauge metal containers.

Cross-References. Establishments primarily engaged in—

- Manufacturing foil containers—are classified in Industry 33299, All Other Fabricated Metal Product Manufacturing;
- Reconditioning barrels and drums—are classified in Industry 81131, Commercial and Industrial Machinery and Equipment (except Automotive and Electronic) Repair and Maintenance; and
- Manufacturing heavy gauge metal containers—are classified in Industry 33242, Metal Tank (Heavy Gauge) Manufacturing.

332431 Metal Can Manufacturing[CAN]

This U.S. industry comprises establishments primarily engaged in manufacturing metal cans, lids, and ends.

Cross-References. Establishments primarily engaged in—

- Manufacturing foil containers—are classified in U.S. Industry 332999, All Other Miscellaneous Fabricated Metal Product Manufacturing; and
- Manufacturing light gauge metal containers (except cans)—are classified in U.S. Industry 332439, Other Metal Container Manufacturing.

332439 Other Metal Container Manufacturing[CAN]

This U.S. industry comprises establishments primarily engaged in manufacturing metal (light gauge) containers (except cans).

US—United States industry only. CAN—United States and Canadian industries are comparable. MEX—United States and Mexican industries are comparable. Blank—Canadian, Mexican, and United States industries are comparable.

Illustrative Examples:

Light gauge metal bins manufacturing
Light gauge metal tool boxes
  manufacturing
Light gauge metal drums manufacturing
Light gauge metal vats manufacturing
Light gauge metal garbage cans
  manufacturing

Metal air cargo containers manufacturing
Light gauge metal lunch boxes
  manufacturing
Metal barrels manufacturing
Light gauge metal mailboxes
  manufacturing
Vacuum bottles and jugs manufacturing

Cross-References. Establishments primarily engaged in—

- Manufacturing foil containers—are classified in U.S. Industry 332999, All Other Miscellaneous Fabricated Metal Product Manufacturing;

- Manufacturing metal cans—are classified in U.S. Industry 332431, Metal Can Manufacturing;

- Reconditioning barrels and drums—are classified in Industry 811310, Commercial and Industrial Machinery and Equipment (except Automotive and Electronic) Repair and Maintenance; and

- Manufacturing heavy gauge metal containers—are classified in Industry 332420, Metal Tank (Heavy Gauge) Manufacturing.

3325 Hardware Manufacturing

33251 Hardware Manufacturing
See industry description for 332510 below.

332510 Hardware Manufacturing

This industry comprises establishments primarily engaged in manufacturing metal hardware, such as metal hinges, metal handles, keys, and locks (except coin-operated, time locks).

Cross-References. Establishments primarily engaged in—

- Manufacturing bolts, nuts, screws, rivets, washers, hose clamps, and turnbuckles—are classified in U.S. Industry 332722, Bolt, Nut, Screw, Rivet, and Washer Manufacturing;

- Manufacturing nails and spikes from wire drawn elsewhere—are classified in U.S. Industry 332618, Other Fabricated Wire Product Manufacturing;

- Manufacturing metal furniture parts (except hardware)—are classified in U.S. Industry 337215, Showcase, Partition, Shelving, and Locker Manufacturing;

- Drawing wire and manufacturing nails and spikes—are classified in Subsector 331, Primary Metal Manufacturing;
- Manufacturing pole line and transmission hardware—are classified in U.S. Industry 335932, Noncurrent-Carrying Wiring Device Manufacturing;
- Manufacturing coin-operated locking mechanisms—are classified in U.S. Industry 333311, Automatic Vending Machine Manufacturing;
- Manufacturing time locks—are classified in U.S. Industry 334518, Watch, Clock, and Part Manufacturing;
- Manufacturing fireplace fixtures and equipment, traps, handcuffs and leg irons, ladder jacks, and other like metal products—are classified in U.S. Industry 332999, All Other Miscellaneous Fabricated Metal Product Manufacturing;
- Manufacturing fire hose nozzles and couplings—are classified in U.S. Industry 332919, Other Metal Valve and Pipe Fitting Manufacturing; and
- Manufacturing luggage and utility racks—are classified in U.S. Industry 336399, All Other Motor Vehicle Parts Manufacturing.

3326 Spring and Wire Product Manufacturing

33261 Spring and Wire Product Manufacturing

This industry comprises establishments primarily engaged in (1) manufacturing steel springs by forming, such as cutting, bending, and heat winding, metal rod or strip stock and/or (2) manufacturing wire springs and fabricated wire products from wire drawn elsewhere (except watch and clock springs).

Cross-References. Establishments primarily engaged in—

- Manufacturing watch and clock springs from purchased wire—are classified in Industry 33451, Navigational, Measuring, Electromedical, and Control Instruments Manufacturing;
- Drawing wire and manufacturing wire products—are classified in Subsector 331, Primary Metal Manufacturing; and
- Manufacturing nonferrous insulated wire from wire drawn elsewhere—are classified in Industry 33592, Communication and Energy Wire and Cable Manufacturing.

332611 Spring (Heavy Gauge) Manufacturing^{CAN}

This U.S. industry comprises establishments primarily engaged in manufacturing heavy gauge springs by forming, such as cutting, bending, and heat winding, rod or strip stock.

US—United States industry only. CAN—United States and Canadian industries are comparable. MEX—United States and Mexican industries are comparable. Blank—Canadian, Mexican, and United States industries are comparable.

Cross-References. Establishments primarily engaged in—

- Manufacturing light gauge springs from purchased wire or strip—are classified in U.S. Industry 332612, Spring (Light Gauge) Manufacturing; and

- Drawing wire and manufacturing wire spring—are classified in Subsector 331, Primary Metal Manufacturing.

332612 Spring (Light Gauge) Manufacturing[US]

This U.S. industry comprises establishments primarily engaged in manufacturing light gauge springs from purchased wire or strip.

Cross-References. Establishments primarily engaged in —

- Manufacturing watch and clock springs—are classified in U.S. Industry 334518, Watch, Clock, and Part Manufacturing;

- Manufacturing heavy gauge springs—are classified in U.S. Industry 332611, Spring (Heavy Gauge) Manufacturing; and

- Drawing wire and manufacturing wire springs—are classified in Subsector 331, Primary Metal Manufacturing.

332618 Other Fabricated Wire Product Manufacturing[US]

This U.S. industry comprises establishments primarily engaged in manufacturing fabricated wire products (except springs) made from purchased wire.

Illustrative Examples:

Barbed wire made from purchased wire
Noninsulated wire cable made from purchased wire
Chain link fencing and fence gates made from purchased wire
Paper clips made from purchased wire

Metal baskets made from purchased wire
Woven wire cloth made from purchased wire
Nails, brads, and staples made from purchased wire

Cross-References. Establishments primarily engaged in—

- Drawing wire and manufacturing wire products—are classified in Subsector 331, Primary Metal Manufacturing;

- Manufacturing heavy gauge springs—are classified in U.S. Industry 332611, Spring (Heavy Gauge) Manufacturing;

- Manufacturing light gauge springs from purchased wire or strip—are classified in U.S. Industry 332612, Spring (Light Gauge) Manufacturing; and

- Insulating nonferrous wire from wire drawn elsewhere—are classified in U.S. Industry 335929, Other Communication and Energy Wire Manufacturing.

3327 Machine Shops; Turned Product; and Screw, Nut, and Bolt Manufacturing

33271 Machine Shops
See industry description for 332710 below.

332710 Machine Shops

This industry comprises establishments known as machine shops primarily engaged in machining metal and plastic parts and parts of other composite materials on a job or order basis. Generally machine shop jobs are low volume using machine tools, such as lathes (including computer numerically controlled); automatic screw machines; and machines for boring, grinding, and milling.

Cross-References. Establishments primarily engaged in—
- Repairing industrial machinery and equipment—are classified in Industry 811310, Commercial and Industrial Machinery and Equipment (except Automotive and Electronic) Repair and Maintenance; and
- Manufacturing parts (except on a job or order basis) for machinery and equipment—are generally classified in the same manufacturing industry that makes complete machinery and equipment.

33272 Turned Product and Screw, Nut, and Bolt Manufacturing

This industry comprises establishments primarily engaged in (1) machining precision turned products or (2) manufacturing metal bolts, nuts, screws, rivets, and other industrial fasteners. Included in this industry are establishments primarily engaged in manufacturing parts for machinery and equipment on a customized basis.

Cross-References.

Establishments primarily engaged in manufacturing plastics fasteners are classified in Industry 32619, Other Plastics Product Manufacturing.

332721 Precision Turned Product Manufacturing[US]

This U.S. industry comprises establishments known as precision turned manufacturers primarily engaged in machining precision products of all materials on a job or order basis. Generally precision turned product jobs are large volume using machines, such as automatic screw machines, rotary transfer machines, computer numerically controlled (CNC) lathes, or turning centers.

Cross-References.

Establishments primarily engaged in manufacturing metal bolts, nuts, screws, rivets, washers, and other industrial fasteners on machines, such as headers, threaders, and nut forming machines, are classified in U.S. Industry 332722, Bolt, Nut, Screw, Rivet, and Washer Manufacturing.

332722 Bolt, Nut, Screw, Rivet, and Washer Manufacturing[US]

This U.S. industry comprises establishments primarily engaged in manufacturing metal bolts, nuts, screws, rivets, and washers, and other industrial fasteners using machines, such as headers, threaders, and nut forming machines.

Cross-References. Establishments primarily engaged in—

- Manufacturing precision turned products—are classified in U.S. Industry 332721, Precision Turned Product Manufacturing; and

- Manufacturing plastics fasteners—are classified in U.S. Industry 326199, All Other Plastics Product Manufacturing.

3328 Coating, Engraving, Heat Treating, and Allied Activities

33281 Coating, Engraving, Heat Treating, and Allied Activities

This industry comprises establishments primarily engaged in one or more of the following: (1) heat treating metals and metal products; (2) enameling, lacquering, and varnishing metals and metal products; (3) hot dip galvanizing metals and metal products; (4) engraving, chasing, or etching metals and metal products (except jewelry; personal goods carried on or about the person, such as compacts and cigarette cases; precious metal products (except precious plated flatware and other plated ware); and printing plates); (5) powder coating metals and metal products; (6) electroplating, plating, anodizing, coloring, and finishing metals and metal products; and (7) providing other metal surfacing services for the trade. Establishments in this industry coat, engrave, and heat treat metals and metal formed products fabricated elsewhere.

Cross-References. Establishments primarily engaged in—

- Engraving, chasing or etching jewelry, metal personal goods, or precious (except precious plated) metal flatware and other plated ware—are classified in Industry 33991, Jewelry and Silverware Manufacturing;

US—United States industry only. CAN—United States and Canadian industries are comparable. MEX—United States and Mexican industries are comparable. Blank—Canadian, Mexican, and United States industries are comparable.

- Engraving, chasing or etching printing plates—are classified in Industry 32312, Support Activities for Printing; and
- Both fabricating and coating, engraving, and heat treating metals and metal products—are classified in manufacturing according to the product made.

332811   Metal Heat Treating^{US}

This U.S. industry comprises establishments primarily engaged in heat treating, such as annealing, tempering, and brazing, metals and metal products for the trade.

Cross-References.

Establishments primarily engaged in both fabricating and heat treating metal products are classified in the Manufacturing sector according to the product made.

332812   Metal Coating, Engraving (except Jewelry and Silverware), and Allied Services to Manufacturers^{US}

This U.S. industry comprises establishments primarily engaged in one or more of the following: (1) enameling, lacquering, and varnishing metals and metal products; (2) hot dip galvanizing metals and metal products; (3) engraving, chasing, or etching metals and metal products (except jewelry; personal goods carried on or about the person, such as compacts and cigarette cases; precious metal products (except precious plated flatware and other plated ware); and printing plates); (4) powder coating metals and metal products; and (5) providing other metal surfacing services for the trade. Included in this industry are establishments that perform these processes on other materials, such as plastics, in addition to metals.

Cross-References. Establishments primarily engaged in—

- Both fabricating and coating and engraving products—are classified in the Manufacturing sector according to the product made;
- Engraving, chasing or etching jewelry, metal personal goods, or precious metal products (except precious plated metal flatware and other plated ware)—are classified in Industry 33991, Jewelry and Silverware Manufacturing; and
- Engraving, chasing or etching printing plates—are classified in U.S. Industry 323122, Prepress Services.

332813   Electroplating, Plating, Polishing, Anodizing, and Coloring^{US}

This U.S. industry comprises establishments primarily engaged in electroplating, plating, anodizing, coloring, buffing, polishing, cleaning, and sandblasting metals

---

and metal products for the trade. Included in this industry are establishments that perform these processes on other materials, such as plastics, in addition to metals.

Cross-References.

Establishments primarily engaged in both fabricating and electroplating, plating, polishing, anodizing, and coloring products are classified in the Manufacturing sector according to the product made.

3329 Other Fabricated Metal Product Manufacturing

This industry group comprises establishments primarily engaged in manufacturing fabricated metal products (except forgings and stampings, cutlery and handtools, architectural and structural metals, boilers, tanks, shipping containers, hardware, spring and wire products, machine shop products, turned products, screws, and nuts and bolts).

33291 Metal Valve Manufacturing

This industry comprises establishments primarily engaged in manufacturing one or more of the following metal valves: (1) industrial valves; (2) fluid power valves and hose fittings; (3) plumbing fixture fittings and trim; and (4) other metal valves and pipe fittings.

Cross-References. Establishments primarily engaged in—

- Manufacturing fluid power cylinders and pumps—are classified in Industry 33399, All Other General Purpose Machinery Manufacturing;

- Manufacturing intake and exhaust valves for internal combustion engines— are classified in Industry 33631, Motor Vehicle Gasoline Engine and Engine Parts Manufacturing;

- Manufacturing metal shower rods and metal couplings from purchased metal pipe—are classified in Industry 33299, All Other Fabricated Metal Product Manufacturing;

- Manufacturing plastics aerosol spray nozzles—are classified in Industry 32619, Other Plastics Product Manufacturing;

- Casting iron pipe fittings and couplings without machining—are classified in Industry 33151, Ferrous Metal Foundries; and

- Manufacturing plastics pipe fittings and couplings—are classified in Industry 32612, Plastics Pipe, Pipe Fitting, and Unlaminated Profile Shape Manufacturing.

US—United States industry only. CAN—United States and Canadian industries are comparable. MEX—United States and Mexican industries are comparable. Blank—Canadian, Mexican, and United States industries are comparable.

http://www.census.gov/naics

332911   Industrial Valve Manufacturing[US]

This U.S. industry comprises establishments primarily engaged in manufacturing industrial valves and valves for water works and municipal water systems.

Illustrative Examples:

Complete fire hydrants manufacturing
Industrial-type globe valves
    manufacturing
Industrial-type ball valves manufacturing
Industrial-type plug valves
    manufacturing
Industrial-type butterfly valves
    manufacturing

Industrial-type solenoid valves (except
    fluid power) manufacturing
Industrial-type check valves
    manufacturing
Industrial-type steam traps manufacturing
Industrial-type gate valves manufacturing
Valves for nuclear applications
    manufacturing

Cross-References. Establishments primarily engaged in—

- Manufacturing fluid power valves—are classified in U.S. Industry 332912, Fluid Power Valve and Hose Fitting Manufacturing; and

- Manufacturing plumbing and heating valves—are classified in U.S. Industry 332919, Other Metal Valve and Pipe Fitting Manufacturing.

332912   Fluid Power Valve and Hose Fitting Manufacturing[US]

This U.S. industry comprises establishments primarily engaged in manufacturing fluid power valves and hose fittings.

Illustrative Examples:

Fluid power aircraft subassemblies
Hydraulic and pneumatic hose and tube
    fittings

Hose assemblies for fluid power systems
Hydraulic and pneumatic valves

Cross-References. Establishments primarily engaged in—

- Manufacturing fluid power cylinders—are classified in U.S. Industry 333995, Fluid Power Cylinder and Actuator Manufacturing;

- Manufacturing fluid power pumps—are classified in U.S. Industry 333996, Fluid Power Pump and Motor Manufacturing;

- Manufacturing intake and exhaust valves for internal combustion engines— are classified in U.S. Industry 336311, Carburetor, Piston, Piston Ring, and Valve Manufacturing;

- Manufacturing industrial-type valves—are classified in U.S. Industry 332911, Industrial Valve Manufacturing; and

---

US—United States industry only. CAN—United States and Canadian industries are comparable. MEX—United States and Mexican industries are comparable. Blank—Canadian, Mexican, and United States industries are comparable.

http://www.census.gov/naics

- Manufacturing plumbing and heating valves—are classified in U.S. Industry 332919, Other Metal Valve and Pipe Fitting Manufacturing.

332913 Plumbing Fixture Fitting and Trim Manufacturing[US]

This U.S. industry comprises establishments primarily engaged in manufacturing metal and plastics plumbing fixture fittings and trim, such as faucets, flush valves, and shower heads.

Cross-References. Establishments primarily engaged in—

- Manufacturing metal shower rods—are classified in U.S. Industry 332999, All Other Miscellaneous Fabricated Metal Product Manufacturing; and

- Manufacturing fire hose nozzles, lawn hose nozzles, water traps, and couplings—are classified in U.S. Industry 332919,Other Metal Valve and Pipe Fitting Manufacturing.

332919 Other Metal Valve and Pipe Fitting Manufacturing[US]

This U.S. industry comprises establishments primarily engaged in manufacturing metal valves (except industrial valves, fluid power valves, fluid power hose fittings, and plumbing fixture fittings and trim).

Illustrative Examples:

Aerosol valves manufacturing
Metal hose couplings (except fluid power) manufacturing
Firefighting nozzles manufacturing
Metal pipe flanges and flange unions manufacturing

Lawn hose nozzles manufacturing
Plumbing and heating in-line valves (e.g., check, cutoff, stop) manufacturing
Lawn sprinklers manufacturing
Water traps manufacturing

Cross-References. Establishments primarily engaged in—

- Manufacturing fluid power valves and hose fittings—are classified in U.S. Industry 332912, Fluid Power Valve and Hose Fitting Manufacturing;

- Manufacturing industrial valves—are classified in U.S. Industry 332911, Industrial Valve Manufacturing;

- Manufacturing plastics aerosol spray nozzles—are classified in U.S. Industry 326199, All Other Plastics Product Manufacturing;

- Casting iron pipe fittings and couplings without machining—are classified in U.S. Industry 331511, Iron Foundries;

- Manufacturing metal couplings from purchased metal pipe—are classified in U.S. Industry 332996, Fabricated Pipe and Pipe Fitting Manufacturing; and

- Manufacturing plastics pipe fittings and couplings—are classified in U.S. Industry 326122, Plastics Pipe and Pipe Fitting Manufacturing.

33299 All Other Fabricated Metal Product Manufacturing

This industry comprises establishments primarily engaged in manufacturing fabricated metal products (except forgings and stampings, cutlery and handtools, architectural and structural metal products, boilers, tanks, shipping containers, hardware, spring and wire products, machine shop products, turned products, screws, nuts and bolts, and metal valves).

Illustrative Examples:

Ammunition manufacturing
Industrial pattern manufacturing
Ball and roller bearing manufacturing
Metal safes manufacturing
Enameled iron and metal sanitary ware
  manufacturing
Portable metal ladder manufacturing

Fabricated pipe and pipe fittings made
  from purchased metal pipe
Small arms and other ordnance
  manufacturing
Foil container (except bags)
  manufacturing
Steel wool manufacturing

Cross-References. Establishments primarily engaged in—

- Manufacturing forgings, stampings, and powder metallurgy parts—are classified in Industry 33211, Forging and Stamping;

- Manufacturing cutlery and handtools—are classified in Industry 33221, Cutlery and Handtool Manufacturing;

- Manufacturing architectural and structural metals—are classified in Industry Group 3323, Architectural and Structural Metals Manufacturing;

- Manufacturing boilers, tanks, and shipping containers—are classified in Industry Group 3324, Boiler, Tank, and Shipping Container Manufacturing;

- Manufacturing hardware and safe and vault locks—are classified in Industry 33251, Hardware Manufacturing;

- Manufacturing spring and wire products—are classified in Industry 33261, Spring and Wire Product Manufacturing;

- Manufacturing machine shop products, turned products, screws, and nuts and bolts—are classified in Industry Group 3327, Machine Shops; Turned Product; and Screw, Nut, and Bolt Manufacturing;

- Coating, engraving, heat treating and allied activities—are classified in Industry 33281, Coating, Engraving, Heat Treating, and Allied Activities;

- Manufacturing plain bearings—are classified in Industry 33361, Engine, Turbine, and Power Transmission Equipment Manufacturing;

- Manufacturing military tanks—are classified in Industry 33699, Other Transportation Equipment Manufacturing;

- Manufacturing guided missiles—are classified in Industry 33641, Aerospace Product and Parts Manufacturing;

- Manufacturing cast iron pipe and fittings—are classified in Industry 33151, Ferrous Metal Foundries;

- Manufacturing pipe system fittings (except cast iron couplings and couplings made from purchased pipe) and metal aerosol spray nozzles—are classified in Industry 33291, Metal Valve Manufacturing;

- Manufacturing welded and seamless steel pipes from purchased steel— are classified in Industry 33121, Iron and Steel Pipe and Tube Manufacturing from Purchased Steel;

- Manufacturing plastics plumbing fixtures and plastics portable chemical toilets—are classified in Industry 32619, Other Plastics Product Manufacturing;

- Manufacturing vitreous and semivitreous pottery sanitary ware—are classified in Industry 32711, Pottery, Ceramics, and Plumbing Fixture Manufacturing;

- Manufacturing blasting caps, detonating caps, and safety fuses—are classified in Industry 32592, Explosives Manufacturing;

- Manufacturing fireworks—are classified in Industry 32599, All Other Chemical Product and Preparation Manufacturing;

- Manufacturing metal furniture frames—are classified in Industry 33721, Office Furniture (including Fixtures) Manufacturing;

- Manufacturing metal mechanically refrigerated drinking fountains—are classified in Industry 33341, Ventilation, Heating, Air-Conditioning, and Commercial Refrigeration Equipment Manufacturing;

- Manufacturing metal foil bags—are classified in Industry 32222, Paper Bag and Coated and Treated Paper Manufacturing;

- Manufacturing aluminum foil—are classified in Industry 33131, Alumina and Aluminum Production and Processing;

- Manufacturing metal foil (except aluminum)—are classified in Industry Group 3314, Nonferrous Metal (except Aluminum) Production and Processing; and

- Manufacturing metal burial vaults—are classified in Industry 33999, All Other Miscellaneous Manufacturing.

US—United States industry only. CAN—United States and Canadian industries are comparable. MEX—United States and Mexican industries are comparable. Blank—Canadian, Mexican, and United States industries are comparable.

332991 Ball and Roller Bearing Manufacturing

This U.S. industry comprises establishments primarily engaged in manufacturing ball and roller bearings of all materials.

Cross-References.

Establishments primarily engaged in manufacturing plain bearings are classified in U.S. Industry 333613, Mechanical Power Transmission Equipment Manufacturing.

332992 Small Arms Ammunition Manufacturing[US]

This U.S. industry comprises establishments primarily engaged in manufacturing small arms ammunition.

Cross-References. Establishments primarily engaged in—

- Manufacturing ammunition (except small arms)—are classified in U.S. Industry 332993, Ammunition (except Small Arms) Manufacturing;
- Manufacturing blasting and detonating caps and safety fuses—are classified in Industry 325920, Explosives Manufacturing; and
- Manufacturing fireworks—are classified in U.S. Industry 325998, All Other Miscellaneous Chemical Product and Preparation Manufacturing.

332993 Ammunition (except Small Arms) Manufacturing[US]

This U.S. industry comprises establishments primarily engaged in manufacturing ammunition (except small arms). Examples of products made by these establishments are bombs, depth charges, rockets (except guided missiles), grenades, mines, and torpedoes.

Cross-References. Establishments primarily engaged in—

- Manufacturing small arms ammunition—are classified in U.S. Industry 332992, Small Arms Ammunition Manufacturing;
- Manufacturing blasting and detonating caps and safety fuses—are classified in Industry 325920, Explosives Manufacturing;
- Manufacturing fireworks—are classified in U.S. Industry 325998, All Other Miscellaneous Chemical Product and Preparation Manufacturing; and
- Manufacturing guided missiles—are classified in U.S. Industry 336414, Guided Missile and Space Vehicle Manufacturing.

US—United States industry only. CAN—United States and Canadian industries are comparable. MEX—United States and Mexican industries are comparable. Blank—Canadian, Mexican, and United States industries are comparable.

332994 Small Arms Manufacturing[US]

This U.S. industry comprises establishments primarily engaged in manufacturing small firearms that are carried and fired by the individual.

Cross-References.

Establishments primarily engaged in manufacturing firearms (except small) are classified in U.S. Industry 332995, Other Ordnance and Accessories Manufacturing.

332995 Other Ordnance and Accessories Manufacturing[US]

This U.S. industry comprises establishments primarily engaged in manufacturing ordnance (except small arms) and accessories.

Cross-References. Establishments primarily engaged in—

- Manufacturing small arms—are classified in U.S. Industry 332994, Small Arms Manufacturing;

- Manufacturing military tanks—are classified in U.S. Industry 336992, Military Armored Vehicle, Tank, and Tank Component Manufacturing; and

- Manufacturing guided missiles—are classified in U.S. Industry 336414, Guided Missile and Space Vehicle Manufacturing.

332996 Fabricated Pipe and Pipe Fitting Manufacturing[US]

This U.S. industry comprises establishments primarily engaged in fabricating, such as cutting, threading, and bending metal pipes and pipe fittings made from purchased metal pipe.

Cross-References. Establishments primarily engaged in—

- Manufacturing cast iron pipe and fittings—are classified in U.S. Industry 331511, Iron Foundries;

- Manufacturing pipe system fittings (except cast iron couplings)—are classified in U.S. Industry 332919, Other Metal Valve and Pipe Fitting Manufacturing; and

- Manufacturing welded and seamless steel pipes from purchased steel—are classified in Industry 331210, Iron and Steel Pipe and Tube Manufacturing from Purchased Steel.

US—United States industry only. CAN—United States and Canadian industries are comparable. MEX—United States and Mexican industries are comparable. Blank—Canadian, Mexican, and United States industries are comparable.

332997 Industrial Pattern Manufacturing^{US}

This U.S. industry comprises establishments primarily engaged in manufacturing industrial patterns.

332998 Enameled Iron and Metal Sanitary Ware Manufacturing^{US}

This U.S. industry comprises establishments primarily engaged in manufacturing enameled iron and metal sanitary ware.

Cross-References. Establishments primarily engaged in—

* Manufacturing plastics plumbing fixtures—are classified in U.S. Industry 326191, Plastics Plumbing Fixture Manufacturing;

* Manufacturing vitreous and semivitreous pottery sanitary ware—are classified in U.S. Industry 327111, Vitreous China Plumbing Fixture and China and Earthenware Bathroom Accessories Manufacturing;

* Manufacturing plastics portable chemical toilets—are classified in U.S. Industry 326199, All Other Plastics Product Manufacturing; and

* Manufacturing metal mechanically refrigerated drinking fountains—are classified in U.S. Industry 333415, Air-Conditioning and Warm Air Heating Equipment and Commercial and Industrial Refrigeration Equipment Manufacturing.

332999 All Other Miscellaneous Fabricated Metal Product Manufacturing^{US}

This U.S. industry comprises establishments primarily engaged in manufacturing fabricated metal products (except forgings and stampings, cutlery and handtools, architectural and structural metals, boilers, tanks, shipping containers, hardware, spring and wire products, machine shop products, turned products, screws, nuts and bolts, metal valves, ball and roller bearings, ammunition, small arms and other ordnances, fabricated pipes and pipe fittings, industrial patterns, and enameled iron and metal sanitary ware).

Illustrative Examples:

Foil containers (except bags) manufacturing	Permanent metallic magnets manufacturing
Metal safes manufacturing	Metal pallets manufacturing
Metal hair curlers manufacturing	Portable metal ladders manufacturing
Metal vaults (except burial) manufacturing	Metal pipe hangers and supports manufacturing
Metal ironing boards manufacturing	Steel wool manufacturing

Cross-References. Establishments primarily engaged in—

- Manufacturing forgings and stampings—are classified in Industry 33211, Forging and Stamping;

- Manufacturing cutlery and handtools—are classified in Industry 33221, Cutlery and Handtool Manufacturing;

- Manufacturing architectural and structural metals—are classified in Industry Group 3323, Architectural and Structural Metals Manufacturing;

- Manufacturing boilers, tanks, and shipping containers—are classified in Industry Group 3324, Boiler, Tank, and Shipping Container Manufacturing;

- Manufacturing hardware and safe and vault locks—are classified in Industry 332510, Hardware Manufacturing;

- Manufacturing spring and wire products—are classified in Industry 33261, Spring and Wire Product Manufacturing;

- Manufacturing machine shop products, turned products, screws, and nut and bolt—are classified in Industry Group 3327, Machine Shops; Turned Product; and Screw, Nut, and Bolt Manufacturing;

- Coating, engraving, heat treating and allied activities—are classified in Industry 33281, Coating, Engraving, Heat Treating, and Allied Activities;

- Manufacturing ball and roller bearings—are classified in U.S. Industry 332991, Ball and Roller Bearing Manufacturing;

- Manufacturing small arms ammunition—are classified in U.S. Industry 332992, Small Arms Ammunition Manufacturing;

- Manufacturing ammunition (except small arms)—are classified in U.S. Industry 332993, Ammunition (except Small Arms) Manufacturing;

- Manufacturing small firearms that are carried and fired by the individual— are classified in U.S. Industry 332994, Small Arms Manufacturing;

- Manufacturing ordnance (except small) and accessories—are classified in U.S. Industry 332995, Other Ordnance and Accessories Manufacturing;

- Manufacturing metal pipes and pipe fittings from metal pipe produced elsewhere—are classified in U.S. Industry 332996, Fabricated Pipe and Pipe Fitting Manufacturing;

- Manufacturing cast iron pipe and fittings—are classified in U.S. Industry 331511, Iron Foundries;

- Manufacturing welded and seamless steel pipes from purchased steel—are classified in Industry 331210, Iron and Steel Pipe and Tube Manufacturing from Purchased Steel;

- Manufacturing metal furniture frames—are classified in U.S. Industry 337215, Showcase, Partition, Shelving, and Locker Manufacturing;

US—United States industry only. CAN—United States and Canadian industries are comparable. MEX—United States and Mexican industries are comparable. Blank—Canadian, Mexican, and United States industries are comparable.

- Manufacturing powder metallurgy parts—are classified in U.S. Industry 332117, Powder Metallurgy Part Manufacturing;

- Manufacturing metal boxes—are classified in U.S. Industry 332439, Other Metal Container Manufacturing;

- Manufacturing metal nozzles, hose couplings, and aerosol valves—are classified in U.S. Industry 332919, Other Metal Valve and Pipe Fitting Manufacturing;

- Manufacturing metal foil bags—are classified in U.S. Industry 322223, Coated Paper Bag and Pouch Manufacturing;

- Manufacturing aluminum foil—are classified in Industry 33131, Alumina and Aluminum Production and Processing;

- Manufacturing metal foil (except aluminum)—are classified in Industry Group 3314, Nonferrous Metal (except Aluminum) Production and Processing; and

- Manufacturing metal burial vaults—are classified in U.S. Industry 339995, Burial Casket Manufacturing.

333 Machinery Manufacturing

Industries in the Machinery Manufacturing subsector create end products that apply mechanical force, for example, the application of gears and levers, to perform work. Some important processes for the manufacture of machinery are forging, stamping, bending, forming, and machining that are used to shape individual pieces of metal. Processes, such as welding and assembling are used to join separate parts together. Although these processes are similar to those used in metal fabricating establishments, machinery manufacturing is different because it typically employs multiple metal forming processes in manufacturing the various parts of the machine. Moreover, complex assembly operations are an inherent part of the production process.

In general, design considerations are very important in machinery production. Establishments specialize in making machinery designed for particular applications. Thus, design is considered to be part of the production process for the purpose of implementing NAICS. The NAICS structure reflects this by defining industries and industry groups that make machinery for different applications. A broad distinction exists between machinery that is generally used in a variety of industrial applications (i.e., general purpose machinery) and machinery that is designed to be used in a particular industry (i.e., special purpose machinery). Three industry groups consist of special purpose machinery—Agricultural, Construction, and Mining Machinery Manufacturing; Industrial Machinery Manufacturing; and Commercial and Service Industry Machinery Manufacturing. The other industry groups make general-purpose machinery: Ventilation, Heating, Air Conditioning, and Commercial Refrigeration Equipment Manufacturing; Metalworking Machinery Manufacturing; Engine, Turbine, and Power Transmission Equipment Manufacturing; and Other General Purpose Machinery Manufacturing.

3331 Agriculture, Construction, and Mining Machinery Manufacturing

33311 Agricultural Implement Manufacturing

This industry comprises establishments primarily engaged in manufacturing farm machinery and equipment, powered mowing equipment and other powered home lawn and garden equipment.

Illustrative Examples:

Combines (i.e., harvester-threshers) manufacturing
Milking machines manufacturing
Cotton ginning machinery manufacturing
Planting machines, farm-type, manufacturing
Tractors and attachments, lawn and garden-type and farm-type, manufacturing

Poultry brooders, feeders, and waterers manufacturing
Plows, farm-type, manufacturing
Fertilizing machinery, farm-type, manufacturing
Powered lawnmowers manufacturing
Haying machines manufacturing
Snowblowers and throwers, residential-type, manufacturing

Cross-References. Establishments primarily engaged in—

* Manufacturing agricultural handtools and nonpowered lawnmowers—are classified in Industry 33221, Cutlery and Handtool Manufacturing;

* Manufacturing farm conveyors—are classified in Industry 33392, Material Handling Equipment Manufacturing; and

* Manufacturing forestry machinery and equipment, such as brush, limb and log chippers; log splitters; and equipment—are classified in Industry 33312, Construction Machinery Manufacturing.

333111 Farm Machinery and Equipment Manufacturing[US]

This U.S. industry comprises establishments primarily engaged in manufacturing agricultural and farm machinery and equipment, and other turf and grounds care equipment, including planting, harvesting, and grass mowing equipment (except lawn and garden-type).

US—United States industry only. CAN—United States and Canadian industries are comparable. MEX—United States and Mexican industries are comparable. Blank—Canadian, Mexican, and United States industries are comparable.

Illustrative Examples:

Combines (i.e., harvester-threshers) manufacturing

Plows, farm-type, manufacturing

Cotton ginning machinery manufacturing

Tractors and attachments, farm-type, manufacturing

Feed processing equipment, farm-type, manufacturing

Haying machines manufacturing

Fertilizing machinery, farm-type, manufacturing

Milking machines manufacturing

Planting machines, farm-type, manufacturing

Poultry brooders, feeders, and waterers manufacturing

Cross-References. Establishments primarily engaged in—

- Manufacturing farm conveyors—are classified in U.S. Industry 333922, Conveyor and Conveying Equipment Manufacturing;

- Manufacturing tractors and lawnmowers for home lawn and garden care— are classified in U.S. Industry 333112, Lawn and Garden Tractor and Home Lawn and Garden Equipment Manufacturing; and

- Manufacturing construction-type tractors—are classified in Industry 333120, Construction Machinery Manufacturing.

333112 Lawn and Garden Tractor and Home Lawn and Garden Equipment Manufacturing[US]

This U.S. industry comprises establishments primarily engaged in manufacturing powered lawnmowers, lawn and garden tractors, and other home lawn and garden equipment, such as tillers, shredders, yard vacuums, and leaf blowers.

Cross-References. Establishments primarily engaged in—

- Manufacturing commercial mowing and other turf and grounds care equipment—are classified in U.S. Industry 333111, Farm Machinery and Equipment Manufacturing; and

- Manufacturing nonpowered lawn and garden shears, edgers, pruners, and lawnmowers—are classified in U.S. Industry 332212, Hand and Edge Tool Manufacturing.

33312 Construction Machinery Manufacturing
See industry description for 333120 below.

333120 Construction Machinery Manufacturing

This industry comprises establishments primarily engaged in manufacturing construction machinery, surface mining machinery, and logging equipment.

US—United States industry only. CAN—United States and Canadian industries are comparable. MEX—United States and Mexican industries are comparable. Blank—Canadian, Mexican, and United States industries are comparable.

Illustrative Examples:

Backhoes manufacturing

Pile-driving equipment manufacturing

Bulldozers manufacturing

Portable crushing, pulverizing, and
screening machinery manufacturing

Construction and surface mining-type
rock drill bits manufacturing

Powered post hole diggers manufacturing

Construction-type tractors and
attachments manufacturing

Road graders manufacturing

Off-highway trucks manufacturing

Surface mining machinery (except
drilling) manufacturing

Cross-References. Establishments primarily engaged in—

- Manufacturing drilling and underground mining machinery and equipment—are classified in Industry 33313, Mining and Oil and Gas Field Machinery Manufacturing;

- Manufacturing industrial plant overhead traveling cranes, hoists, truck-type cranes and hoists, winches, aerial work platforms, and automotive wrecker hoists—are classified in Industry 33392, Material Handling Equipment Manufacturing; and

- Manufacturing rail layers, ballast distributors and other railroad track-laying equipment—are classified in Industry 336510, Railroad Rolling Stock Manufacturing.

33313 Mining and Oil and Gas Field Machinery Manufacturing

This industry comprises establishments primarily engaged in manufacturing oil and gas field and underground mining machinery and equipment.

Illustrative Examples:

Coal breakers, cutters, and pulverizers
manufacturing

Oil and gas field-type derricks
manufacturing

Core drills, underground mining-type,
manufacturing

Oil and gas field-type drilling machinery
and equipment (except offshore floating
platforms) manufacturing

Mineral processing and beneficiating
machinery manufacturing

Stationary rock crushing machinery
manufacturing

Mining cars manufacturing

Water well drilling machinery
manufacturing

Cross-References. Establishments primarily engaged in—

- Manufacturing offshore oil and gas well drilling and production floating platforms—are classified in Industry 33661, Ship and Boat Building;

- Manufacturing surface mining machinery and equipment—are classified in Industry 33312, Construction Machinery Manufacturing;

- Manufacturing coal and ore conveyors—are classified in Industry 33392, Material Handling Equipment Manufacturing;

- Manufacturing underground mining locomotives—are classified in Industry 33651, Railroad Rolling Stock Manufacturing; and

- Manufacturing pumps and pumping equipment—are classified in Industry 33391, Pump and Compressor Manufacturing.

333131 Mining Machinery and Equipment Manufacturing[US]

This U.S. industry comprises establishments primarily engaged in (1) manufacturing underground mining machinery and equipment, such as coal breakers, mining cars, core drills, coal cutters, rock drills and (2) manufacturing mineral beneficiating machinery and equipment used in surface or underground mines.

Cross-References. Establishments primarily engaged in—

- Manufacturing surface mining machinery and equipment—are classified in Industry 333120, Construction Machinery Manufacturing;

- Manufacturing well-drilling machinery—are classified in U.S. Industry 333132, Oil and Gas Field Machinery and Equipment Manufacturing;

- Manufacturing coal and ore conveyors—are classified in U.S. Industry 333922, Conveyor and Conveying Equipment Manufacturing; and

- Manufacturing underground mining locomotives—are classified in Industry 336510, Railroad Rolling Stock Manufacturing.

333132 Oil and Gas Field Machinery and Equipment Manufacturing[US]

This U.S. industry comprises establishments primarily engaged in (1) manufacturing oil and gas field machinery and equipment, such as oil and gas field drilling machinery and equipment; oil and gas field production machinery and equipment; and oil and gas field derricks and (2) manufacturing water well drilling machinery.

Cross-References. Establishments primarily engaged in—

- Manufacturing offshore oil and gas well drilling and production floating platforms—are classified in U.S. Industry 336611, Ship Building and Repairing;

- Manufacturing underground mining drills—are classified in U.S. Industry 333131, Mining Machinery and Equipment Manufacturing; and

---

US—United States industry only. CAN—United States and Canadian industries are comparable. MEX—United States and Mexican industries are comparable. Blank—Canadian, Mexican, and United States industries are comparable.

- Manufacturing pumps and pumping equipment—are classified in U.S. Industry 333911, Pump and Pumping Equipment Manufacturing.

3332 Industrial Machinery Manufacturing

33321 Sawmill and Woodworking Machinery Manufacturing
See industry description for 333210 below.

333210 Sawmill and Woodworking Machinery Manufacturing

This industry comprises establishments primarily engaged in manufacturing sawmill and woodworking machinery (except handheld), such as circular and band sawing equipment, planing machinery, and sanding machinery.

Cross-References. Establishments primarily engaged in—

- Manufacturing planes, axes, drawknives, and handsaws—are classified in Industry 33221, Cutlery and Handtool Manufacturing; and
- Manufacturing power-driven handtools—are classified in U.S. Industry 333991, Power-Driven Handtool Manufacturing.

33322 Plastics and Rubber Industry Machinery Manufacturing
See industry description for 333220 below.

333220 Plastics and Rubber Industry Machinery Manufacturing

This industry comprises establishments primarily engaged in manufacturing plastics and rubber products making machinery, such as plastics compression, extrusion and injection molding machinery and equipment, and tire building and recapping machinery and equipment.

Cross-References.

Establishments primarily engaged in manufacturing industrial metal molds for plastics and rubber products making machinery are classified in U.S. Industry 333511, Industrial Mold Manufacturing.

33329 Other Industrial Machinery Manufacturing

This industry comprises establishments primarily engaged in manufacturing industrial machinery (except agricultural and farm-type, construction, mining, sawmill and woodworking, and plastics and rubber products making machinery).

US—United States industry only. CAN—United States and Canadian industries are comparable. MEX—United States and Mexican industries are comparable. Blank—Canadian, Mexican, and United States industries are comparable.

Illustrative Examples:

Bakery ovens manufacturing

Printing presses (except textile) manufacturing

Chemical processing machinery and equipment manufacturing

Semiconductor making machinery manufacturing

Glass making machinery (e.g., blowing, forming, molding) manufacturing

Sewing machines (including household-type) manufacturing

Paper making machinery manufacturing

Tannery machinery manufacturing

Petroleum refinery machinery manufacturing

Textile making machinery manufacturing

Cross-References. Establishments primarily engaged in—

- Manufacturing agricultural and farm-type, construction, and mining machinery—are classified in Industry Group 3331, Agriculture, Construction, and Mining Machinery Manufacturing;

- Manufacturing sawmill and woodworking machinery—are classified in Industry 33321, Sawmill and Woodworking Machinery Manufacturing;

- Manufacturing plastics and rubber products making machinery—are classified in Industry 33322, Plastics and Rubber Industry Machinery Manufacturing;

- Manufacturing food and beverage packaging machinery—are classified in Industry 33399, All Other General Purpose Machinery Manufacturing;

- Manufacturing commercial and industrial refrigeration and freezer equipment—are classified in Industry 33341, Ventilation, Heating, Air-Conditioning, and Commercial Refrigeration Equipment Manufacturing;

- Manufacturing commercial-type cooking and food warming equipment, automotive maintenance equipment (except mechanics' handtools) and photocopiers—are classified in Industry 33331, Commercial and Service Industry Machinery Manufacturing; and

- Manufacturing mechanics' handtools—are classified in Industry 33221, Cutlery and Handtool Manufacturing.

333291 Paper Industry Machinery Manufacturing[CAN]

This U.S. industry comprises establishments primarily engaged in manufacturing paper industry machinery for making paper and paper products, such as pulp making machinery, paper and paperboard making machinery, and paper and paperboard converting machinery.

Cross-References.

Establishments primarily engaged in manufacturing printing machinery are classified in U.S. Industry 333293, Printing Machinery and Equipment Manufacturing.

US—United States industry only. CAN—United States and Canadian industries are comparable. MEX—United States and Mexican industries are comparable. Blank—Canadian, Mexican, and United States industries are comparable.

333292 Textile Machinery Manufacturing^{MEX}

This U.S. industry comprises establishments primarily engaged in manufacturing textile machinery for making thread, yarn, and fiber.

Illustrative Examples:

Drawing machinery for textiles manufacturing

Spinning machinery for textiles manufacturing

Extruding machinery for yarn manufacturing

Textile making machinery (except sewing machines) manufacturing

Finishing machinery for textiles manufacturing

Texturizing machinery for textiles manufacturing

Knitting machinery manufacturing

Weaving machinery manufacturing

Cross-References.

Establishments primarily engaged in manufacturing sewing machines are classified in U.S. Industry 333298, All Other Industrial Machinery Manufacturing.

333293 Printing Machinery and Equipment Manufacturing^{MEX}

This U.S. industry comprises establishments primarily engaged in manufacturing printing and bookbinding machinery and equipment, such as printing presses, typesetting machinery, and bindery machinery.

Cross-References. Establishments primarily engaged in—

- Manufacturing textile printing machinery—are classified in U.S. Industry 333292, Textile Machinery Manufacturing; and

- Manufacturing photocopiers—are classified in U.S. Industry 333315, Photographic and Photocopying Equipment Manufacturing.

333294 Food Product Machinery Manufacturing^{US}

This U.S. industry comprises establishments primarily engaged in manufacturing food and beverage manufacturing-type machinery and equipment, such as dairy product plant machinery and equipment (e.g., homogenizers, pasteurizers, ice cream freezers), bakery machinery and equipment (e.g., dough mixers, bake ovens, pastry rolling machines), meat and poultry processing and preparation machinery, and other commercial food products machinery (e.g., slicers, choppers, and mixers).

Cross-References. Establishments primarily engaged in—

- Manufacturing food and beverage packaging machinery—are classified in U.S. Industry 333993, Packaging Machinery Manufacturing;

- Manufacturing commercial and industrial refrigeration and freezer equipment—are classified in U.S. Industry 333415, Air-Conditioning and Warm Air Heating Equipment and Commercial and Industrial Refrigeration Equipment Manufacturing; and

- Manufacturing commercial-type cooking and food warming equipment—are classified in U.S. Industry 333319, Other Commercial and Service Industry Machinery Manufacturing.

333295 Semiconductor Machinery Manufacturing[US]

This U.S. industry comprises establishments primarily engaged in manufacturing wafer processing equipment, semiconductor assembly and packaging equipment, and other semiconductor making machinery.

Cross-References. Establishments primarily engaged in—

- Manufacturing printed circuit board manufacturing machinery—are classified in U.S. Industry 333298, All Other Industrial Machinery Manufacturing; and

- Manufacturing semiconductor testing instruments—are classified in U.S. Industry 334515, Instrument Manufacturing for Measuring and Testing Electricity and Electrical Signals.

333298 All Other Industrial Machinery Manufacturing[US]

This U.S. industry comprises establishments primarily engaged in manufacturing industrial machinery (except agricultural and farm-type, construction and mining machinery, sawmill and woodworking machinery, plastics and rubber making machinery, paper and paperboard making machinery, textile machinery, printing machinery and equipment, food manufacturing-type machinery, and semiconductor making machinery).

Illustrative Examples:

Chemical processing machinery and equipment manufacturing

Petroleum refining machinery manufacturing

Cigarette making machinery manufacturing

Glass making machinery (e.g., blowing, forming, molding) manufacturing

Tannery machinery manufacturing

Laboratory distilling equipment manufacturing

Sewing machines (including household-type) manufacturing

Circuit board making machinery manufacturing

Shoe making and repairing machinery manufacturing

Wire and cable insulating machinery manufacturing

Light bulb and tube (i.e., electric lamp) machinery manufacturing

Cross-References. Establishments primarily engaged in—

- Manufacturing agricultural and farm-type, construction, and mining machinery—are classified in Industry Group 3331, Agriculture, Construction, and Mining Machinery Manufacturing;

- Manufacturing sawmill and woodworking machinery—are classified in Industry 333210, Sawmill and Woodworking Machinery Manufacturing;

- Manufacturing plastics and rubber products making machinery—are classified in Industry 333220, Plastics and Rubber Industry Machinery Manufacturing;

- Manufacturing paper and paperboard making machinery—are classified in U.S. Industry 333291, Paper Industry Machinery Manufacturing;

- Manufacturing textile machinery—are classified in U.S. Industry 333292, Textile Machinery Manufacturing;

- Manufacturing printing and bookbinding machinery and equipment—are classified in U.S. Industry 333293, Printing Machinery and Equipment Manufacturing;

- Manufacturing food and beverage manufacturing-type machinery—are classified in U.S. Industry 333294, Food Product Machinery Manufacturing;

- Manufacturing semiconductor making machinery—are classified in U.S. Industry 333295, Semiconductor Machinery Manufacturing;

- Manufacturing automotive maintenance equipment (except mechanics' handtools)—are classified in U.S. Industry 333319, Other Commercial and Service Industry Machinery Manufacturing; and

- Manufacturing mechanics' handtools—are classified in U.S. Industry 332212, Hand and Edge Tool Manufacturing.

3333 Commercial and Service Industry Machinery Manufacturing

33331 Commercial and Service Industry Machinery Manufacturing

This industry comprises establishments primarily engaged in manufacturing commercial and service machinery, such as automatic vending machinery, commercial laundry and dry-cleaning machinery, office machinery, photographic and photocopying machinery, optical instruments and machinery, automotive maintenance equipment (except mechanic's handtools), industrial vacuum cleaners, and commercial-type cooking equipment.

Cross-References. Establishments primarily engaged in—

- Manufacturing household-type appliances—are classified in Industry Group 3352, Household Appliance Manufacturing;

- Manufacturing computer and peripheral equipment (including point-of-sale terminals and automatic teller machines (ATMs))—are classified in Industry 33411, Computer and Peripheral Equipment Manufacturing;

- Manufacturing facsimile equipment—are classified in Industry 33421, Telephone Apparatus Manufacturing;

- Manufacturing timeclocks, timestamps, and electron and proton microscopes—are classified in Industry 33451, Navigational, Measuring, Electromedical, and Control Instruments Manufacturing;

- Manufacturing pencil sharpeners and staplers—are classified in Industry 33994, Office Supplies (except Paper) Manufacturing;

- Manufacturing sensitized film, paper, cloth, and plates, and prepared photographic chemicals—are classified in Industry 32599, All Other Chemical Product and Preparation Manufacturing;

- Manufacturing ophthalmic focus lenses—are classified in Industry 33911, Medical Equipment and Supplies Manufacturing;

- Manufacturing television, video, and digital cameras—are classified in Subsector 334, Computer and Electronic Product Manufacturing;

- Manufacturing coin-operated arcade games—are classified in Industry 33999, All Other Miscellaneous Manufacturing;

- Manufacturing mechanics' handtools—are classified in Industry 33221, Cutlery and Handtool Manufacturing;

- Manufacturing molded plastics lens blanks—are classified in Industry 32619, Other Plastics Product Manufacturing; and

- Manufacturing molded glass lens blanks—are classified in Industry 32721, Glass and Glass Product Manufacturing.

333311 Automatic Vending Machine Manufacturing[US]

This U.S. industry comprises establishments primarily engaged in (1) manufacturing coin, token, currency or magnetic card operated vending machines and/

US—United States industry only. CAN—United States and Canadian industries are comparable. MEX—United States and Mexican industries are comparable. Blank—Canadian, Mexican, and United States industries are comparable.

http://www.census.gov/naics

or (2) manufacturing coin-operated mechanisms for machines, such as vending machines, lockers, and laundry machines.

Cross-References.

Establishments primarily engaged in manufacturing coin-operated arcade games are classified in U.S. Industry 339999, All Other Miscellaneous Manufacturing.

333312 Commercial Laundry, Drycleaning, and Pressing Machine Manufacturing[US]

This U.S. industry comprises establishments primarily engaged in manufacturing commercial and industrial laundry and drycleaning equipment and pressing machines.

Cross-References.

Establishments primarily engaged in manufacturing household-type laundry equipment are classified in U.S. Industry 335224, Household Laundry Equipment Manufacturing.

333313 Office Machinery Manufacturing[US]

This U.S. industry comprises establishments primarily engaged in manufacturing office machinery (except computers and photocopying equipment), such as mail-handling machinery and equipment, calculators, typewriters, and dedicated word processing equipment.

Cross-References. Establishments primarily engaged in—

- Manufacturing computers and peripheral (including point-of-sale terminals and automatic teller machines (ATMs)) equipment—are classified in Industry 33411, Computer and Peripheral Equipment Manufacturing;

- Manufacturing photocopy equipment—are classified in U.S. Industry 333315, Photographic and Photocopying Equipment Manufacturing;

- Manufacturing facsimile equipment—are classified in Industry 334210, Telephone Apparatus Manufacturing;

- Manufacturing timeclocks and timestamps—are classified in U.S. Industry 334518, Watch, Clock, and Part Manufacturing; and

- Manufacturing pencil sharpeners, staplers, staple removers, hand paper punches, cutters, trimmers, and other hand office equipment—are classified in U.S. Industry 339942, Lead Pencil and Art Good Manufacturing.

US—United States industry only. CAN—United States and Canadian industries are comparable. MEX—United States and Mexican industries are comparable. Blank—Canadian, Mexican, and United States industries are comparable.

333314 Optical Instrument and Lens Manufacturing[US]

This U.S. industry comprises establishments primarily engaged in one or more of the following: (1) manufacturing optical instruments and lens, such as binoculars, microscopes (except electron, proton), telescopes, prisms, and lenses (except ophthalmic); (2) coating or polishing lenses (except ophthalmic); and (3) mounting lenses (except ophthalmic).

Cross-References. Establishments primarily engaged in—

- Manufacturing ophthalmic focus lenses—are classified in U.S. Industry 339115, Ophthalmic Goods Manufacturing;

- Manufacturing electron and proton microscopes—are classified in U.S. Industry 334516, Analytical Laboratory Instrument Manufacturing;

- Manufacturing molded plastics lens blanks—are classified in U.S. Industry 326199, All Other Plastics Product Manufacturing; and

- Manufacturing molded glass lens blanks—are classified in U.S. Industry 327212, Other Pressed and Blown Glass and Glassware Manufacturing.

333315 Photographic and Photocopying Equipment Manufacturing[US]

This U.S. industry comprises establishments primarily engaged in manufacturing photographic and photocopying equipment, such as cameras (except television, video and digital) projectors, film developing equipment, photocopying equipment, and microfilm equipment.

Cross-References. Establishments primarily engaged in—

- Manufacturing sensitized film, paper, cloth, and plates, and prepared photographic chemicals—are classified in U.S. Industry 325992, Photographic Film, Paper, Plate, and Chemical Manufacturing;

- Manufacturing photographic lenses—are classified in U.S. Industry 333314, Optical Instrument and Lens Manufacturing; and

- Manufacturing television, video, and digital cameras—are classified in Subsector 334, Computer and Electronic Product Manufacturing.

333319 Other Commercial and Service Industry Machinery Manufacturing[US]

This U.S. industry comprises establishments primarily engaged in manufacturing commercial and service industry equipment (except automatic vending machines, commercial laundry, drycleaning and pressing machines, office machinery, optical instruments and lenses, and photographic and photocopying equipment).

US—United States industry only. CAN—United States and Canadian industries are comparable. MEX—United States and Mexican industries are comparable. Blank—Canadian, Mexican, and United States industries are comparable.

http://www.census.gov/naics

Illustrative Examples:

Carnival and amusement park rides
    manufacturing
Mechanical carpet sweepers
    manufacturing
Carwashing machinery manufacturing
Motor vehicle alignment equipment
    manufacturing
Commercial-type coffee makers and urns
    manufacturing
Power washer cleaning equipment
    manufacturing

Commercial-type cooking equipment
    (i.e., fryers, microwave ovens, ovens,
    ranges) manufacturing
Teaching machines (e.g., flight
    simulators) manufacturing
Industrial and commercial-type vacuum
    cleaners manufacturing
Water treatment equipment
    manufacturing

Cross-References. Establishments primarily engaged in—

- Manufacturing automatic vending machines—are classified in U.S. Industry 333311, Automatic Vending Machine Manufacturing;

- Manufacturing commercial laundry drycleaning and pressing machines— are classified in U.S. Industry 333312, Commercial Laundry, Drycleaning, and Pressing Machine Manufacturing;

- Manufacturing office machinery—are classified in U.S. Industry 333313, Office Machinery Manufacturing;

- Manufacturing optical instruments and lenses—are classified in U.S. Industry 333314, Optical Instrument and Lens Manufacturing;

- Manufacturing photographic and photocopying equipment—are classified in U.S. Industry 333315, Photographic and Photocopying Equipment Manufacturing;

- Manufacturing household-type appliances—are classified in Industry Group 3352, Household Appliance Manufacturing; and

- Manufacturing mechanics' handtools—are classified in U.S. Industry 332212, Hand and Edge Tool Manufacturing.

3334 Ventilation, Heating, Air-Conditioning, and Commercial Refrigeration Equipment Manufacturing

33341 Ventilation, Heating, Air-Conditioning, and Commercial Refrigeration Equipment Manufacturing

This industry comprises establishments primarily engaged in manufacturing ventilating, heating, air-conditioning, and commercial and industrial refrigeration and freezer equipment.

Illustrative Examples:

Air-conditioner filters manufacturing
Heating boilers manufacturing
Air-conditioning and warm air heating
combination units manufacturing
Industrial and commercial-type fans
manufacturing
Attic fans manufacturing
Refrigerated counter and display cases
manufacturing

Dust and fume collecting equipment
manufacturing
Refrigerated drinking fountains
manufacturing
Gas fireplaces manufacturing
Space heaters (except portable electric)
manufacturing

Cross-References. Establishments primarily engaged in—

- Manufacturing household-type fans (except attic), portable electric space heaters, humidifiers, dehumidifiers, and air purification equipment—are classified in Industry 33521, Small Electrical Appliance Manufacturing;

- Manufacturing household-type appliances, such as cooking stoves, ranges, refrigerators, and freezers—are classified in Industry 33522, Major Appliance Manufacturing;

- Manufacturing commercial-type cooking equipment—are classified in Industry 33329, Other Industrial Machinery Manufacturing;

- Manufacturing industrial, power, and marine boilers—are classified in Industry 33241, Power Boiler and Heat Exchanger Manufacturing;

- Manufacturing industrial process furnaces and ovens—are classified in Industry 33399, All Other General Purpose Machinery Manufacturing; and

- Manufacturing motor vehicle air-conditioning systems and compressors—are classified in Industry 33639, Other Motor Vehicle Parts Manufacturing.

333411 Air Purification Equipment Manufacturing[US]

This U.S. industry comprises establishments primarily engaged in manufacturing stationary air purification equipment, such as industrial dust and fume collection equipment, electrostatic precipitation equipment, warm air furnace filters, air washers, and other dust collection equipment.

Cross-References. Establishments primarily engaged in—

- Manufacturing air-conditioning units (except motor vehicle)—are classified in U.S. Industry 333415, Air-Conditioning and Warm Air Heating Equipment and Commercial and Industrial Refrigeration Equipment Manufacturing;

US—United States industry only. CAN—United States and Canadian industries are comparable. MEX—United States and Mexican industries are comparable. Blank—Canadian, Mexican, and United States industries are comparable.

- Manufacturing motor vehicle air-conditioning systems and compressors—are classified in U.S. Industry 336391, Motor Vehicle Air-Conditioning Manufacturing;

- Manufacturing household-type fans (except attic) and portable air purification equipment—are classified in U.S. Industry 335211, Electric Housewares and Household Fan Manufacturing; and

- Manufacturing industrial and commercial blowers, industrial and commercial exhaust and ventilating fans, and attic fans—are classified in U.S. Industry 333412, Industrial and Commercial Fan and Blower Manufacturing.

333412 Industrial and Commercial Fan and Blower Manufacturing[US]

This U.S. industry comprises establishments primarily engaged in manufacturing attic fans and industrial and commercial fans and blowers, such as commercial exhaust fans and commercial ventilating fans.

Cross-References. Establishments primarily engaged in—

- Manufacturing air-conditioning units (except motor vehicle)—are classified in U.S. Industry 333415, Air-Conditioning and Warm Air Heating Equipment and Commercial and Industrial Refrigeration Equipment Manufacturing;

- Manufacturing motor vehicle air-conditioning systems and compressors—are classified in U.S. Industry 336391, Motor Vehicle Air-Conditioning Manufacturing;

- Manufacturing household-type fans (except attic) and portable air purification equipment—are classified in U.S. Industry 335211, Electric Housewares and Household Fan Manufacturing; and

- Manufacturing stationary air purification equipment—are classified in U.S. Industry 333411, Air Purification Equipment Manufacturing.

333414 Heating Equipment (except Warm Air Furnaces) Manufacturing[US]

This U.S. industry comprises establishments primarily engaged in manufacturing heating equipment (except electric and warm air furnaces), such as heating boilers, heating stoves, floor and wall furnaces, and wall and baseboard heating units.

US—United States industry only. CAN—United States and Canadian industries are comparable. MEX—United States and Mexican industries are comparable. Blank—Canadian, Mexican, and United States industries are comparable.

Cross-References. Establishments primarily engaged in—

- Manufacturing warm air furnaces—are classified in U.S. Industry 333415, Air-Conditioning and Warm Air Heating Equipment and Commercial and Industrial Refrigeration Equipment Manufacturing;
- Manufacturing electric space heaters—are classified in U.S. Industry 335211, Electric Housewares and Household Fan Manufacturing;
- Manufacturing household-type cooking stoves and ranges—are classified in U.S. Industry 335221, Household Cooking Appliance Manufacturing;
- Manufacturing industrial, power, and marine boilers—are classified in Industry 332410, Power Boiler and Heat Exchanger Manufacturing;
- Manufacturing industrial process furnaces and ovens—are classified in U.S. Industry 333994, Industrial Process Furnace and Oven Manufacturing; and
- Manufacturing commercial-type cooking equipment—are classified in U.S. Industry 333319, Other Commercial and Service Industry Machinery Manufacturing.

333415 Air-Conditioning and Warm Air Heating Equipment and Commercial and Industrial Refrigeration Equipment Manufacturing^{US}

This U.S. industry comprises establishments primarily engaged in (1) manufacturing air-conditioning (except motor vehicle) and warm air furnace equipment and/or (2) manufacturing commercial and industrial refrigeration and freezer equipment.

Illustrative Examples:

Air-conditioning and warm air heating combination units manufacturing
Humidifying equipment (except portable) manufacturing
Air-conditioning compressors (except motor vehicle) manufacturing
Refrigerated counter and display cases manufacturing
Air-conditioning condensers and condensing units manufacturing

Refrigerated drinking fountains manufacturing
Dehumidifiers (except portable electric) manufacturing
Snow making machinery manufacturing
Heat pumps manufacturing
Soda fountain cooling and dispensing equipment manufacturing

Cross-References. Establishments primarily engaged in—

- Manufacturing motor vehicle air-conditioning systems and compressors— are classified in U.S. Industry 336391, Motor Vehicle Air-Conditioning Manufacturing;

US—United States industry only. CAN—United States and Canadian industries are comparable. MEX—United States and Mexican industries are comparable. Blank—Canadian, Mexican, and United States industries are comparable.

- Manufacturing household-type refrigerators and freezers—are classified in U.S. Industry 335222, Household Refrigerator and Home Freezer Manufacturing;

- Manufacturing portable electric space heaters, humidifiers, and dehumidifiers—are classified in U.S. Industry 335211, Electric Housewares and Household Fan Manufacturing;

- Manufacturing heating boilers, heating stoves, floor and wall mount furnaces, and electric wall and baseboard heating units—are classified in U.S. Industry 333414, Heating Equipment (except Warm Air Furnaces) Manufacturing; and

- Manufacturing furnace air filters—are classified in U.S. Industry 333411, Air Purification Equipment Manufacturing.

3335 Metalworking Machinery Manufacturing

33351 Metalworking Machinery Manufacturing

This industry comprises establishments primarily engaged in manufacturing metalworking machinery, such as metal cutting and metal forming machine tools; cutting tools; and accessories for metalworking machinery; special dies, tools, jigs, and fixtures; industrial molds; rolling mill machinery; assembly machinery; coil handling, conversion, or straightening equipment; and wire drawing and fabricating machines.

Cross-References. Establishments primarily engaged in—

- Manufacturing handtools (except power-driven), cutting dies (except metal cutting), sawblades, and handsaws—are classified in Industry 33221, Cutlery and Handtool Manufacturing;

- Manufacturing casting molds for heavy steel ingots—are classified in Industry 33151, Ferrous Metal Foundries; and

- Manufacturing power-driven handtools and welding and soldering equipment—are classified in Industry 33399, All Other General Purpose Machinery Manufacturing.

333511 Industrial Mold Manufacturing^{CAN}

This U.S. industry comprises establishments primarily engaged in manufacturing industrial molds for casting metals or forming other materials, such as plastics, glass, or rubber.

US—United States industry only. CAN—United States and Canadian industries are comparable. MEX—United States and Mexican industries are comparable. Blank—Canadian, Mexican, and United States industries are comparable.

Cross-References.

Establishments primarily engaged in manufacturing casting molds for steel ingots are classified in U.S. Industry 331511, Iron Foundries.

333512 Machine Tool (Metal Cutting Types) Manufacturing[US]

This U.S. industry comprises establishments primarily engaged in manufacturing metal cutting machine tools (except handtools).

Illustrative Examples:

Home workshop metal cutting machine tools (except handtools, welding equipment) manufacturing

Metalworking grinding machines manufacturing

Metalworking boring machines manufacturing

Metalworking lathes manufacturing

Metalworking buffing and polishing machines manufacturing

Metalworking milling machines manufacturing

Metalworking drilling machines manufacturing

Cross-References. Establishments primarily engaged in—

- Manufacturing welding and soldering equipment—are classified in U.S. Industry 333992, Welding and Soldering Equipment Manufacturing;

- Manufacturing metal-forming machine tools--are classified in U.S. Industry 333513, Machine Tool (Metal Forming Types) Manufacturing;

- Manufacturing power-driven metal cutting handtools—are classified in U.S. Industry 333991, Power-Driven Handtool Manufacturing; and

- Manufacturing accessories and attachments for metal cutting machine tools—are classified in U.S. Industry 333515, Cutting Tool and Machine Tool Accessory Manufacturing.

333513 Machine Tool (Metal Forming Types) Manufacturing[US]

This U.S. industry comprises establishments primarily engaged in manufacturing metal forming machine tools (except handtools), such as punching, sheering, bending, forming, pressing, forging and die-casting machines.

Cross-References. Establishments primarily engaged in—

- Manufacturing welding and soldering equipment—are classified in U.S. Industry 333992, Welding and Soldering Equipment Manufacturing;

- Manufacturing metal-cutting machine tools—are classified in U.S. Industry 333512, Machine Tool (Metal Cutting Types) Manufacturing;

- Manufacturing power-driven handtools—are classified in U.S. Industry 333991, Power-Driven Handtool Manufacturing;
- Manufacturing rolling mill machinery and equipment—are classified in U.S. Industry 333516, Rolling Mill Machinery and Equipment Manufacturing; and
- Manufacturing accessories and attachments for metal forming machine tools—are classified in U.S. Industry 333515, Cutting Tool and Machine Tool Accessory Manufacturing.

333514 Special Die and Tool, Die Set, Jig, and Fixture Manufacturing[US]

This U.S. industry comprises establishments, known as tool and die shops, primarily engaged in manufacturing special tools and fixtures, such as cutting dies and jigs.

Cross-References. Establishments primarily engaged in—

- Manufacturing molds for die-casting and foundry casting; and metal molds for plaster working, rubber working, plastics working, and glass working machinery—are classified in U.S. Industry 333511, Industrial Mold Manufacturing;
- Manufacturing molds for heavy steel ingots—are classified in U.S. Industry 331511, Iron Foundries; and
- Manufacturing cutting dies for materials other than metal—are classified in U.S. Industry 332212, Hand and Edge Tool Manufacturing.

333515 Cutting Tool and Machine Tool Accessory Manufacturing[US]

This U.S. industry comprises establishments primarily engaged in manufacturing accessories and attachments for metal cutting and metal forming machine tools.

Illustrative Examples:

Knives and bits for metalworking lathes, planers, and shapers manufacturing
Metalworking drill bits manufacturing

Measuring attachments (e.g., sine bars) for machine tool manufacturing
Taps and dies (i.e., machine tool accessories) manufacturing

Cross-References. Establishments primarily engaged in—

- Manufacturing accessories and attachments for cutting and forming machines (except metal cutting, metal forming machinery)—are classified in U.S. Industry 332212, Hand and Edge Tool Manufacturing; and

• Manufacturing saw blades and handsaws—are classified in U.S. Industry 332213, Saw Blade and Handsaw Manufacturing.

333516 Rolling Mill Machinery and Equipment Manufacturing^{US}

This U.S. industry comprises establishments primarily engaged in manufacturing rolling mill machinery and equipment for metal production.

333518 Other Metalworking Machinery Manufacturing^{US}

This U.S. industry comprises establishments primarily engaged in manufacturing metal working machinery (except industrial molds; metal cutting machine tools; metal forming machine tools; special dies and tools, die sets, jigs, and fixtures; cutting tools and machine tool accessories; and rolling mill machinery and equipment).

Illustrative Examples:

Assembly machines manufacturing
Metalworking coil winding and cutting
  machinery manufacturing
Cradle assemblies machinery (i.e., wire
  making equipment) manufacturing

Wire drawing and fabricating machinery
  and equipment (except dies)
  manufacturing

Cross-References. Establishments primarily engaged in—

• Manufacturing industrial molds—are classified in U.S. Industry 333511, Industrial Mold Manufacturing;

• Manufacturing metal cutting machinery—are classified in U.S. Industry 333512, Machine Tool (Metal Cutting Types) Manufacturing;

• Manufacturing metal forming machinery—are classified in U.S. Industry 333513, Machine Tool (Metal Forming Types) Manufacturing;

• Manufacturing special dies and tools, die sets, jigs, and fixtures—are classified in U.S. Industry 333514, Special Die and Tool, Die Set, Jig, and Fixture Manufacturing;

• Manufacturing cutting tools and machine tool accessories—are classified in U.S. Industry 333515, Cutting Tool and Machine Tool Accessory Manufacturing; and

• Manufacturing rolling mill machinery—are classified in U.S. Industry 333516, Rolling Mill Machinery and Equipment Manufacturing.

3336 Engine, Turbine, and Power Transmission Equipment Manufacturing

---

US—United States industry only. CAN—United States and Canadian industries are comparable. MEX—United States and Mexican industries are comparable. Blank—Canadian, Mexican, and United States industries are comparable.

33361 Engine, Turbine, and Power Transmission Equipment Manufacturing

This industry comprises establishments primarily engaged in manufacturing turbines, power transmission equipment, and internal combustion engines (except automotive gasoline and aircraft).

Illustrative Examples:

Clutches and brakes (except electromagnetic industrial controls, motor vehicle) manufacturing
Power transmission pulleys manufacturing
Diesel and semidiesel engines manufacturing
Speed changers (i.e., power transmission equipment) manufacturing
Electric outboard motors manufacturing

Speed reducers (i.e., power transmission equipment) manufacturing
Plain bearings (except internal combustion engine) manufacturing
Turbine generator set units manufacturing
Plain bushings (except internal combustion engine) manufacturing
Universal joints (except aircraft, motor vehicle) manufacturing

Cross-References. Establishments primarily engaged in—

- Manufacturing motor vehicle power transmission equipment—are classified in Industry 33635, Motor Vehicle Transmission and Power Train Parts Manufacturing;

- Manufacturing aircraft engines and aircraft power transmission equipment— are classified in Industry 33641, Aerospace Product and Parts Manufacturing;

- Manufacturing ball and roller bearings—are classified in Industry 33299, All Other Fabricated Metal Product Manufacturing;

- Manufacturing gasoline automotive engines—are classified in Industry 33631, Motor Vehicle Gasoline Engine and Engine Parts Manufacturing; and

- Manufacturing electric power transmission, electric power distribution equipment, generators, or prime mover generator sets (except turbines)— are classified in Industry 33531, Electrical Equipment Manufacturing.

333611 Turbine and Turbine Generator Set Units Manufacturing[CAN]

This U.S. industry comprises establishments primarily engaged in manufacturing turbines (except aircraft); and complete turbine generator set units, such as steam, hydraulic, gas, and wind.

US—United States industry only. CAN—United States and Canadian industries are comparable. MEX—United States and Mexican industries are comparable. Blank—Canadian, Mexican, and United States industries are comparable.

Cross-References. Establishments primarily engaged in—

- Manufacturing aircraft turbines—are classified in U.S. Industry 336412, Aircraft Engine and Engine Parts Manufacturing; and

- Manufacturing generators or prime mover generator sets (except turbines)— are classified in U.S. Industry 335312, Motor and Generator Manufacturing.

333612 Speed Changer, Industrial High-Speed Drive, and Gear Manufacturing^{US}

This U.S. industry comprises establishments primarily engaged in manufacturing gears, speed changers, and industrial high-speed drives (except hydrostatic).

Cross-References. Establishments primarily engaged in—

- Manufacturing motor vehicle power transmission equipment—are classified in Industry 336350, Motor Vehicle Transmission and Power Train Parts Manufacturing;

- Manufacturing aircraft power transmission equipment—are classified in U.S. Industry 336413, Other Aircraft Parts and Auxiliary Equipment Manufacturing; and

- Manufacturing industrial hydrostatic transmissions—are classified in U.S. Industry 333996, Fluid Power Pump and Motor Manufacturing.

333613 Mechanical Power Transmission Equipment Manufacturing^{US}

This U.S. industry comprises establishments primarily engaged in manufacturing mechanical power transmission equipment (except motor vehicle and aircraft), such as plain bearings, clutches (except motor vehicle and electromagnetic industrial control), couplings, joints, and drive chains.

Cross-References. Establishments primarily engaged in—

- Manufacturing motor vehicle power transmission equipment—are classified in Industry 336350, Motor Vehicle Transmission and Power Train Parts Manufacturing;

- Manufacturing aircraft power transmission equipment—are classified in U.S. Industry 336413, Other Aircraft Parts and Auxiliary Equipment Manufacturing;

- Manufacturing ball and roller bearings—are classified in U.S. Industry 332991, Ball and Roller Bearing Manufacturing; and

- Manufacturing gears, speed changers, and industrial high-speed drives (except hydrostatic)—are classified in U.S. Industry 333612, Speed Changer, Industrial High-Speed Drive, and Gear Manufacturing.

333618 Other Engine Equipment Manufacturing[US]

This U.S. industry comprises establishments primarily engaged in manufacturing internal combustion engines (except automotive gasoline and aircraft).

Cross-References. Establishments primarily engaged in—

- Manufacturing gasoline motor vehicle engines and motor vehicle transmissions—are classified in Industry Group 3363, Motor Vehicle Parts Manufacturing;
- Manufacturing gasoline aircraft engines and aircraft transmissions—are classified in Industry 33641, Aerospace Product and Parts Manufacturing;
- Manufacturing turbine and turbine generator sets units—are classified in U.S. Industry 333611, Turbine and Turbine Generator Set Units Manufacturing;
- Manufacturing speed changers and industrial high-speed drivers and gears—are classified in U.S. Industry 333612, Speed Changer, Industrial High-Speed Drive, and Gear Manufacturing; and
- Manufacturing mechanical power transmission equipment (except motor vehicle and aircraft)—are classified in U.S. Industry 333613, Mechanical Power Transmission Equipment Manufacturing.

3339 Other General Purpose Machinery Manufacturing

33391 Pump and Compressor Manufacturing

This industry comprises establishments primarily engaged in manufacturing pumps and compressors, such as general purpose air and gas compressors, nonagricultural spraying and dusting equipment, general purpose pumps and pumping equipment (except fluid power pumps and motors), and measuring and dispensing pumps.

Cross-References. Establishments primarily engaged in—

- Manufacturing fluid power pumps and motors and handheld pneumatic spray guns—are classified in Industry 33399, All Other General Purpose Machinery Manufacturing;

- Manufacturing agricultural spraying and dusting equipment—are classified in Industry 33311, Agricultural Implement Manufacturing;

- Manufacturing laboratory vacuum pumps—are classified in Industry 33911, Medical Equipment and Supplies Manufacturing;

- Manufacturing pumps and air-conditioning systems and compressors for motor vehicles—are classified in Industry Group 3363, Motor Vehicle Parts Manufacturing; and

- Manufacturing air-conditioning systems and compressors (except motor vehicle)—are classified in Industry 33341, Ventilation, Heating, Air-Conditioning, and Commercial Refrigeration Equipment Manufacturing.

333911 Pump and Pumping Equipment Manufacturing^{US}

This U.S. industry comprises establishments primarily engaged in manufacturing general purpose pumps and pumping equipment (except fluid power pumps and motors), such as reciprocating pumps, turbine pumps, centrifugal pumps, rotary pumps, diaphragm pumps, domestic water system pumps, oil well and oil field pumps and sump pumps.

Cross-References. Establishments primarily engaged in—

- Manufacturing fluid power pumps and motors—are classified in U.S. Industry 333996, Fluid Power Pump and Motor Manufacturing;

- Manufacturing measuring and dispensing pumps—are classified in U.S. Industry 333913, Measuring and Dispensing Pump Manufacturing;

- Manufacturing vacuum pumps (except laboratory)—are classified in U.S. Industry 333912, Air and Gas Compressor Manufacturing;

- Manufacturing laboratory vacuum pumps—are classified in U.S. Industry 339113, Surgical Appliance and Supplies Manufacturing; and

- Manufacturing fluid pumps for motor vehicles, such as oil pumps, water pumps, and power steering pumps—are classified in Industry Group 3363, Motor Vehicle Parts Manufacturing.

333912 Air and Gas Compressor Manufacturing^{US}

This U.S. industry comprises establishments primarily engaged in manufacturing general purpose air and gas compressors, such as reciprocating compressors, centrifugal compressors, vacuum pumps (except laboratory), and nonagricultural spraying and dusting compressors and spray gun units.

US—United States industry only. CAN—United States and Canadian industries are comparable. MEX—United States and Mexican industries are comparable. Blank—Canadian, Mexican, and United States industries are comparable.

Cross-References. Establishments primarily engaged in—

- Manufacturing refrigeration and air-conditioning (except motor vehicle) systems and compressors—are classified in U.S. Industry 333415, Air-Conditioning and Warm Air Heating Equipment and Commercial and Industrial Refrigeration Equipment Manufacturing;
- Manufacturing motor vehicle air-conditioning systems and compressors— are classified in U.S. Industry 336391, Motor Vehicle Air-Conditioning Manufacturing;
- Manufacturing fluid power pumps and motors—are classified in U.S. Industry 333996, Fluid Power Pump and Motor Manufacturing;
- Manufacturing agricultural spraying and dusting equipment—are classified in U.S. Industry 333111, Farm Machinery and Equipment Manufacturing;
- Manufacturing laboratory vacuum pumps—are classified in U.S. Industry 339113, Surgical Appliance and Supplies Manufacturing; and
- Manufacturing handheld pneumatic spray guns—are classified in U.S. Industry 333991, Power-Driven Handtool Manufacturing.

333913 Measuring and Dispensing Pump Manufacturing[US]

This U.S. industry comprises establishments primarily engaged in manufacturing measuring and dispensing pumps, such as gasoline pumps and lubricating oil measuring and dispensing pumps.

Cross-References.

Establishments primarily engaged in manufacturing pumps and pumping equipment for general industrial use are classified in U.S. Industry 333911, Pump and Pumping Equipment Manufacturing.

33392 Material Handling Equipment Manufacturing

This industry comprises establishments primarily engaged in manufacturing material handling equipment, such as elevators and moving stairs; conveyors and conveying equipment; overhead traveling cranes, hoists, and monorail systems; and industrial trucks, tractors, trailers, and stacker machinery.

Cross-References. Establishments primarily engaged in—

- Manufacturing motor vehicle-type trailers—are classified in Industry 33621, Motor Vehicle Body and Trailer Manufacturing;

US—United States industry only. CAN—United States and Canadian industries are comparable. MEX—United States and Mexican industries are comparable. Blank—Canadian, Mexican, and United States industries are comparable.

http://www.census.gov/naics

- Manufacturing farm-type tractors—are classified in Industry 33311, Agricultural Implement Manufacturing;

- Manufacturing construction-type tractors and cranes—are classified in Industry 33312, Construction Machinery Manufacturing; and

- Manufacturing power transmission pulleys—are classified in Industry 33361, Engine, Turbine, and Power Transmission Equipment Manufacturing.

333921 Elevator and Moving Stairway Manufacturing^{US}

This U.S. industry comprises establishments primarily engaged in manufacturing elevators and moving stairways.

Illustrative Examples:

Automobile lifts (i.e., garage-type, service station) manufacturing
Moving walkways manufacturing

Escalators manufacturing
Passenger and freight elevators manufacturing

Cross-References.

Establishments primarily engaged in manufacturing commercial conveyor systems and equipment are classified in U.S. Industry 333922, Conveyor and Conveying Equipment Manufacturing.

333922 Conveyor and Conveying Equipment Manufacturing^{US}

This U.S. industry comprises establishments primarily engaged in manufacturing conveyors and conveying equipment, such as gravity conveyors, trolley conveyors, tow conveyors, pneumatic tube conveyors, carousel conveyors, farm conveyors, and belt conveyors.

Cross-References. Establishments primarily engaged in—

- Manufacturing passenger or freight elevators, dumbwaiters, and moving stairways—are classified in U.S. Industry 333921, Elevator and Moving Stairway Manufacturing; and

- Manufacturing overhead traveling cranes and monorail systems—are classified in U.S. Industry 333923, Overhead Traveling Crane, Hoist, and Monorail System Manufacturing.

333923 Overhead Traveling Crane, Hoist, and Monorail System Manufacturing[US]

This U.S. industry comprises establishments primarily engaged in manufacturing overhead traveling cranes, hoists, and monorail systems.

Illustrative Examples:

Aerial work platforms manufacturing
Metal pulleys (except power transmission) manufacturing
Automobile wrecker (i.e., tow truck) hoists manufacturing

Winches manufacturing
Block and tackle manufacturing

Cross-References. Establishments primarily engaged in—

- Manufacturing construction-type cranes—are classified in Industry 333120, Construction Machinery Manufacturing;

- Manufacturing aircraft loading hoists—are classified in U.S. Industry 333924, Industrial Truck, Tractor, Trailer, and Stacker Machinery Manufacturing; and

- Manufacturing power transmission pulleys—are classified in U.S. Industry 333613, Mechanical Power Transmission Equipment Manufacturing.

333924 Industrial Truck, Tractor, Trailer, and Stacker Machinery Manufacturing[US]

This U.S. industry comprises establishments primarily engaged in manufacturing industrial trucks, tractors, trailers, and stackers (i.e., truck-type) such as forklifts, pallet loaders and unloaders, and portable loading docks.

Cross-References. Establishments primarily engaged in—

- Manufacturing motor vehicle-type trailers—are classified in Industry 33621, Motor Vehicle Body and Trailer Manufacturing;

- Manufacturing farm-type tractors—are classified in U.S. Industry 333111, Farm Machinery and Equipment Manufacturing; and

- Manufacturing construction-type tractors—are classified in Industry 333120, Construction Machinery Manufacturing.

33399 All Other General Purpose Machinery Manufacturing

This industry comprises establishments primarily engaged in manufacturing general purpose machinery (except ventilation, heating, air-conditioning, and commercial refrigeration equipment; metal working machinery; engines, turbines, and power transmission equipment; pumps and compressors; and material handling equipment).

Illustrative Examples:

Automatic fire sprinkler systems manufacturing
Industrial-type furnaces manufacturing
Bridge and gate lifting machinery manufacturing
Packaging machinery manufacturing
Fluid power cylinders manufacturing

Power-driven handtools manufacturing
Fluid power pumps manufacturing
Scales manufacturing
Hydraulic and pneumatic jacks manufacturing
Welding equipment manufacturing

Cross-References. Establishments primarily engaged in—

- Manufacturing ventilating, heating, air-conditioning (except motor vehicle), commercial refrigeration, and furnace filters—are classified in Industry 33341, Ventilation, Heating, Air-Conditioning, and Commercial Refrigeration Equipment Manufacturing;

- Manufacturing metalworking machinery—are classified in Industry Group 3335, Metalworking Machinery Manufacturing;

- Manufacturing engine, turbine, and power transmission equipment—are classified in Industry Group 3336, Engine, Turbine, and Power Transmission Equipment Manufacturing;

- Manufacturing pumps and compressors—are classified in Industry 33391, Pump and Compressor Manufacturing;

- Manufacturing material handling equipment—are classified in Industry 33392, Material Handling Equipment Manufacturing;

- Manufacturing motor vehicle air-conditioning systems and compressors, engine filters, and pumps—are classified in Industry Group 3363, Motor Vehicle Parts Manufacturing;

- Manufacturing metal cutting and metal forming machinery—are classified in Industry 33351, Metalworking Machinery Manufacturing;

- Manufacturing power driven heavy construction and mining hand operated tools, such as tampers and augers—are classified in Industries 33312, Construction Machinery Manufacturing and 33313, Mining and Oil and Gas Field Machinery Manufacturing;

- Manufacturing bakery ovens and industrial kilns, such as cement, wood, and chemical—are classified in Industry 33329, Other Industrial Machinery Manufacturing;

US—United States industry only. CAN—United States and Canadian industries are comparable. MEX—United States and Mexican industries are comparable. Blank—Canadian, Mexican, and United States industries are comparable.

- Manufacturing mechanical jacks, handheld soldering irons, countersink bits, drill bits, router bits, milling cutters, and other machine tools for woodcutting—are classified in Industry 33221, Cutlery and Handtool Manufacturing;

- Manufacturing carnival amusement park equipment, automotive maintenance equipment, and coin-operated vending machines—are classified in Industry 33331, Commercial and Service Industry Machinery Manufacturing; and

- Manufacturing transformers for arc-welding—are classified in Industry 33531, Electrical Equipment Manufacturing.

333991 Power-Driven Handtool Manufacturing[US]

This U.S. industry comprises establishments primarily engaged in manufacturing power-driven (e.g., battery, corded, pneumatic) handtools, such as drills, screwguns, circular saws, chain saws, staplers, and nailers.

Cross-References. Establishments primarily engaged in—

- Manufacturing metal cutting-type and metal forming-type machines (including home workshop)—are classified in Industry 33351, Metalworking Machinery Manufacturing;

- Manufacturing countersink bits, drill bits, router bits, milling cutters, and other machine tools for woodcutting—are classified in U.S. Industry 332212, Hand and Edge Tool Manufacturing;

- Manufacturing power-driven heavy construction or mining hand operated tools, such as tampers, jackhammers, and augers—are classified in U.S. Industry 333120, Construction Machinery Manufacturing and U.S. Industry 33313, Mining and Oil and Gas Field Machinery Manufacturing; and

- Manufacturing powered home lawn and garden equipment—are classified in U.S. Industry 333112, Lawn and Garden Tractor and Home Lawn and Garden Equipment Manufacturing.

333992 Welding and Soldering Equipment Manufacturing[US]

This U.S. industry comprises establishments primarily engaged in manufacturing welding and soldering equipment and accessories (except transformers), such as arc, resistance, gas, plasma, laser, electron beam, and ultrasonic welding equipment; welding electrodes; coated or cored welding wire; and soldering equipment (except handheld).

US—United States industry only. CAN—United States and Canadian industries are comparable. MEX—United States and Mexican industries are comparable. Blank—Canadian, Mexican, and United States industries are comparable.

Cross-References. Establishments primarily engaged in—

- Manufacturing handheld soldering irons—are classified in U.S. Industry 332212, Hand and Edge Tool Manufacturing; and

- Manufacturing transformers for arc-welding—are classified in U.S. Industry 335311, Power, Distribution, and Specialty Transformer Manufacturing.

333993 Packaging Machinery Manufacturing^{US}

This U.S. industry comprises establishments primarily engaged in manufacturing packaging machinery, such as wrapping, bottling, canning, and labeling machinery.

333994 Industrial Process Furnace and Oven Manufacturing^{US}

This U.S. Industry comprises establishments primarily engaged in manufacturing industrial process ovens, induction and dielectric heating equipment, and kilns (except cement, chemical, wood). Included in this industry are establishments manufacturing laboratory furnaces and ovens.

Cross-References. Establishments primarily engaged in—

- Manufacturing bakery ovens—are classified in U.S. Industry 333294, Food Product Machinery Manufacturing;

- Manufacturing cement, wood, and chemical kilns—are classified in U.S. Industry 333298, All Other Industrial Machinery Manufacturing; and

- Manufacturing cremating ovens—are classified in U.S. Industry 333999, All Other Miscellaneous General Purpose Machinery Manufacturing.

333995 Fluid Power Cylinder and Actuator Manufacturing^{US}

This U.S. industry comprises establishments primarily engaged in manufacturing fluid power (i.e., hydraulic and pneumatic) cylinders and actuators.

333996 Fluid Power Pump and Motor Manufacturing^{US}

This U.S. industry comprises establishments primarily engaged in manufacturing fluid power (i.e., hydraulic and pneumatic) pumps and motors.

Cross-References. Establishments primarily engaged in—

- Manufacturing fluid pumps for motor vehicles, such as oil pumps, water pumps, and power steering pumps—are classified in Industry Group 3363, Motor Vehicle Parts Manufacturing;

US—United States industry only. CAN—United States and Canadian industries are comparable. MEX—United States and Mexican industries are comparable. Blank—Canadian, Mexican, and United States industries are comparable.

- Manufacturing general purpose pumps (except fluid power)—are classified in U.S. Industry 333911, Pump and Pumping Equipment Manufacturing; and

- Manufacturing air compressors—are classified in U.S. Industry 333912, Air and Gas Compressor Manufacturing.

333997 Scale and Balance Manufacturing[US]

This U.S. industry comprises establishments primarily engaged in manufacturing scales and balances, including those used in laboratories.

333999 All Other Miscellaneous General Purpose Machinery Manufacturing[US]

This U.S. industry comprises establishments primarily engaged in manufacturing general purpose machinery (except ventilating, heating, air-conditioning, and commercial refrigeration equipment; metal working machinery; engines, turbines, and power transmission equipment; pumps and compressors; material handling equipment; power-driven handtools; welding and soldering equipment; packaging machinery; industrial process furnaces and ovens; fluid power cylinders and actuators; fluid power pumps and motors; and scales and balances).

Illustrative Examples:

Automatic fire sprinkler systems manufacturing
General purpose-type sieves and screening equipment manufacturing
Baling machinery (e.g., paper, scrap metal) manufacturing
Hydraulic and pneumatic jacks manufacturing

Bridge and gate lifting machinery manufacturing
Industrial and general line filters (except internal combustion engine, warm air furnace) manufacturing
Cremating ovens manufacturing
Centrifuges, industrial- and laboratory-type, manufacturing

Cross-References. Establishments primarily engaged in—

- Manufacturing ventilating, heating, air-conditioning (except motor vehicle), and commercial refrigeration—are classified in Industry 33341, Ventilation, Heating, Air-Conditioning, and Commercial Refrigeration Equipment Manufacturing;

- Manufacturing motor vehicle air-conditioning systems and compressors—are classified in U.S. Industry 336391, Motor Vehicle Air-Conditioning Manufacturing;

- Manufacturing material handling equipment—are classified in Industry 33392, Material Handling Equipment Manufacturing;

- Manufacturing power-driven handtools—are classified in U.S. Industry 333991, Power-Driven Handtool Manufacturing;

- Manufacturing welding and soldering equipment (except handheld soldering irons)—are classified in U.S. Industry 333992, Welding and Soldering Equipment Manufacturing;

- Manufacturing packaging machinery—are classified in U.S. Industry 333993, Packaging Machinery Manufacturing;

- Manufacturing bakery ovens and cement, wood, and chemical kilns—are classified in U.S. Industry 333298, All Other Industrial Machinery Manufacturing;

- Manufacturing industrial process furnaces and ovens (except bakery)—are classified in U.S. Industry 333994, Industrial Process Furnace and Oven Manufacturing;

- Manufacturing fluid power cylinders and actuators—are classified in U.S. Industry 333995, Fluid Power Cylinder and Actuator Manufacturing;

- Manufacturing fluid power pumps and motors—are classified in U.S. Industry 333996, Fluid Power Pump and Motor Manufacturing;

- Manufacturing scales and balances—are classified in U.S. Industry 333997, Scale and Balance Manufacturing;

- Manufacturing carnival and amusement park equipment, automotive maintenance equipment and coin-operated vending machines—are classified in Industry 33331, Commercial and Service Industry Machinery Manufacturing;

- Manufacturing motor vehicle engine filters and pumps—are classified in Industry Group 3363, Motor Vehicle Parts Manufacturing; and

- Manufacturing mechanical jacks—are classified in U.S. Industry 332212, Hand and Edge Tool Manufacturing.

334 Computer and Electronic Product Manufacturing

Industries in the Computer and Electronic Product Manufacturing subsector group establishments that manufacture computers, computer peripherals, communications equipment, and similar electronic products, and establishments that manufacture components for such products. The Computer and Electronic Product Manufacturing industries have been combined in the hierarchy of NAICS because of the economic significance they have attained. Their rapid growth suggests that they will become even more important to the economies of all three North American countries in the future, and in addition their manufacturing processes are fundamentally different from the manufacturing processes of other machinery and equipment.

US—United States industry only. CAN—United States and Canadian industries are comparable. MEX—United States and Mexican industries are comparable. Blank—Canadian, Mexican, and United States industries are comparable.

The design and use of integrated circuits and the application of highly specialized miniaturization technologies are common elements in the production technologies of the computer and electronic subsector. Convergence of technology motivates this NAICS subsector. Digitalization of sound recording, for example, causes both the medium (the compact disc) and the equipment to resemble the technologies for recording, storing, transmitting, and manipulating data. Communications technology and equipment have been converging with computer technology. When technologically-related components are in the same sector, it makes it easier to adjust the classification for future changes, without needing to redefine its basic structure. The creation of the Computer and Electronic Product Manufacturing subsector assists in delineating new and emerging industries because the activities that will serve as the probable sources of new industries, such as computer manufacturing and communications equipment manufacturing, or computers and audio equipment, are brought together. As new activities emerge, they are less likely therefore, to cross the subsector boundaries of the classification.

3341 Computer and Peripheral Equipment Manufacturing

33411 Computer and Peripheral Equipment Manufacturing

This industry comprises establishments primarily engaged in manufacturing and/or assembling electronic computers, such as mainframes, personal computers, workstations, laptops, and computer servers; and computer peripheral equipment, such as storage devices, printers, monitors, input/output devices and terminals. Computers can be analog, digital, or hybrid. Digital computers, the most common type, are devices that do all of the following: (1) store the processing program or programs and the data immediately necessary for the execution of the program; (2) can be freely programmed in accordance with the requirements of the user; (3) perform arithmetical computations specified by the user; and (4) execute, without human intervention, a processing program that requires the computer to modify its execution by logical decision during the processing run. Analog computers are capable of simulating mathematical models and comprise at least analog, control, and programming elements.

Cross-References. Establishments primarily engaged in—

- Manufacturing digital telecommunications switches, local area network and wide area network communications equipment, such as bridges, routers, and gateways—are classified in Industry 33421, Telephone Apparatus Manufacturing;

- Manufacturing blank magnetic and optical recording media—are classified in Industry 33461, Manufacturing and Reproducing Magnetic and Optical Media;

- Manufacturing machinery or equipment that incorporate electronic computers for operation or control purposes and embedded control applications—are classified in the Manufacturing sector based on the classification of the complete machinery or equipment;

- Manufacturing external audio speakers for computer use—are classified in Industry 33431, Audio and Video Equipment Manufacturing;

- Manufacturing internal loaded printed circuit board devices, such as sound, video, controller, and network interface cards; internal and external computer modems; and semiconductor storage devices—are classified in Industry 33441, Semiconductor and Other Electronic Component Manufacturing; and

- Manufacturing other parts, such as casings, stampings, cable sets, and switches, for computers, storage devices and other peripheral equipment—are classified in the Manufacturing sector based on their associated production processes.

334111 Electronic Computer Manufacturing^{US}

This U.S. industry comprises establishments primarily engaged in manufacturing and/or assembling electronic computers, such as mainframes, personal computers, workstations, laptops, and computer servers. Computers can be analog, digital, or hybrid. Digital computers, the most common type, are devices that do all of the following: (1) store the processing program or programs and the data immediately necessary for the execution of the program; (2) can be freely programmed in accordance with the requirements of the user; (3) perform arithmetical computations specified by the user; and (4) execute, without human intervention, a processing program that requires the computer to modify its execution by logical decision during the processing run. Analog computers are capable of simulating mathematical models and contain at least analog, control, and programming elements. The manufacture of computers includes the assembly or integration of processors, coprocessors, memory, storage, and input/output devices into a user-programmable final product.

Cross-References. Establishments primarily engaged in—

- Manufacturing digital telecommunications switches, local area network and wide area network communication equipment, such as bridges, routers, and gateways—are classified in Industry 334210, Telephone Apparatus Manufacturing;

- Manufacturing blank magnetic and optical recording media—are classified in U.S. Industry 334613, Magnetic and Optical Recording Media Manufacturing;

- Manufacturing machinery or equipment that incorporates electronic computers for operation or control purposes and embedded control applications—

are classified in the Manufacturing sector based on the classification of the complete machinery or equipment;

- Manufacturing internal, loaded, printed circuit board devices, such as sound, video, controller, and network interface cards; internal and external computer modems; and solid state storage devices for computers—are classified in Industry 33441, Semiconductor and Other Electronic Component Manufacturing;

- Manufacturing other parts, such as casings, stampings, cable sets, and switches, for computers—are classified in the Manufacturing sector based on their associated production processes; and

- Retailing computers with on-site assembly—are classified in Industry 443120, Computer and Software Stores.

334112 Computer Storage Device Manufacturing[US]

This U.S. industry comprises establishments primarily engaged in manufacturing computer storage devices that allow the storage and retrieval of data from a phase change, magnetic, optical, or magnetic/optical media. Examples of products made by these establishments are CD-ROM drives, floppy disk drives, hard disk drives, and tape storage and backup units.

Cross-References. Establishments primarily engaged in—

- Manufacturing blank magnetic and optical recording media—are classified in U.S. Industry 334613, Magnetic and Optical Recording Media Manufacturing;

- Manufacturing semiconductor storage devices, such as memory chips—are classified in U.S. Industry 334413, Semiconductor and Related Device Manufacturing;

- Manufacturing drive controller cards, internal or external to the storage device—are classified in U.S. Industry 334418, Printed Circuit Assembly (Electronic Assembly) Manufacturing; and

- Manufacturing other parts, such as casings, stampings, cable sets, and switches, for computer storage devices—are classified in the Manufacturing sector based on their associated production processes.

334113 Computer Terminal Manufacturing[US]

This U.S. industry comprises establishments primarily engaged in manufacturing computer terminals. Computer terminals are input/output devices that connect with a central computer for processing.

US—United States industry only. CAN—United States and Canadian industries are comparable. MEX—United States and Mexican industries are comparable. Blank—Canadian, Mexican, and United States industries are comparable.

Cross-References. Establishments primarily engaged in—

- Manufacturing point-of-sale terminals, funds transfer, automatic teller machines, and monitors—are classified in U.S. Industry 334119, Other Computer Peripheral Equipment Manufacturing;

- Manufacturing internal loaded printed circuit board devices, such as sound, video, controller, and network interface cards for computer terminals—are classified in U.S. Industry 334418, Printed Circuit Assembly (Electronic Assembly) Manufacturing; and

- Manufacturing other parts, such as casings, stampings, cable sets, and switches, for computer terminals—are classified in the Manufacturing sector based on their associated production processes.

334119 Other Computer Peripheral Equipment Manufacturing[US]

This U.S. industry comprises establishments primarily engaged in manufacturing computer peripheral equipment (except storage devices and computer terminals).

Illustrative Examples:

Automatic teller machines (ATM) manufacturing
Optical readers and scanners manufacturing
Joystick devices manufacturing
Plotters, computer, manufacturing
Keyboards, computer peripheral equipment, manufacturing

Point-of-sale terminals, manufacturing
Monitors, computer peripheral equipment, manufacturing
Printers, computer, manufacturing
Mouse devices, computer peripheral equipment, manufacturing

Cross-References. Establishments primarily engaged in—

- Manufacturing local area network and wide area network communications equipment, such as bridges, routers, and gateways—are classified in Industry 334210, Telephone Apparatus Manufacturing;

- Manufacturing computer storage devices—are classified in U.S. Industry 334112, Computer Storage Device Manufacturing;

- Manufacturing computer terminals—are classified in U.S. Industry 334113, Computer Terminal Manufacturing;

- Manufacturing external audio speakers for computer use—are classified in Industry 334310, Audio and Video Equipment Manufacturing;

- Manufacturing internal, loaded, printed circuit board devices, such as sound, video, controller, and network interface cards; and internal and external computer modems used as computer peripherals—are classified in U.S.

Industry 334418, Printed Circuit Assembly (Electronic Assembly) Manufacturing; and

- Manufacturing other parts, such as casings, stampings, cable sets, and switches, for computer peripheral equipment—are classified in the Manufacturing sector based on their associated production processes.

3342 Communications Equipment Manufacturing

33421 Telephone Apparatus Manufacturing
See industry description for 334210 below.

334210 Telephone Apparatus Manufacturing

This industry comprises establishments primarily engaged in manufacturing wire telephone and data communications equipment. These products may be standalone or board-level components of a larger system. Examples of products made by these establishments are central office switching equipment, cordless telephones (except cellular), PBX equipment, telephones, telephone answering machines, LAN modems, multi-user modems, and other data communications equipment, such as bridges, routers, and gateways.

Cross-References. Establishments primarily engaged in—

- Manufacturing internal and external computer modems, single-user fax/modems and electronic components used in telephone apparatus—are classified in Industry 33441, Semiconductor and Other Electronic 'Component Manufacturing; and
- Manufacturing cellular telephones—are classified in Industry 334220, Radio and Television Broadcasting and Wireless Communications Equipment Manufacturing.

33422 Radio and Television Broadcasting and Wireless Communications Equipment Manufacturing
See industry description for 334220 below.

334220 Radio and Television Broadcasting and Wireless Communications Equipment Manufacturing

This industry comprises establishments primarily engaged in manufacturing radio and television broadcast and wireless communications equipment. Examples of products made by these establishments are: transmitting and receiving antennas,

---

US—United States industry only. CAN—United States and Canadian industries are comparable. MEX—United States and Mexican industries are comparable. Blank—Canadian. Mexican. and United States industries are comparable.

cable television equipment, GPS equipment, pagers, cellular phones, mobile communications equipment, and radio and television studio and broadcasting equipment.

Cross-References. Establishments primarily engaged in—

- Manufacturing household-type audio and video equipment, such as televisions and radio sets—are classified in Industry 334310, Audio and Video Equipment Manufacturing;

- Manufacturing wired and nonwired intercommunications equipment (i.e., intercoms)—are classified in Industry 334290, Other Communications Equipment Manufacturing; and

- Manufacturing equipment for measuring and testing communications signals—are classified in Industry 334515, Instrument Manufacturing for Measuring and Testing Electricity and Electrical Signals.

33429　Other Communications Equipment Manufacturing

See industry description for 334290 below.

334290　Other Communications Equipment Manufacturing

This industry comprises establishments primarily engaged in manufacturing communications equipment (except telephone apparatus, and radio and television broadcast, and wireless communications equipment).

Illustrative Examples:

Fire detection and alarm systems
　manufacturing
Signals (e.g., highway, pedestrian,
　railway, traffic) manufacturing

Intercom systems and equipment
　manufacturing

Cross-References. Establishments primarily engaged in—

- Manufacturing telephone apparatus—are classified in Industry 334210, Telephone Apparatus Manufacturing;

- Manufacturing radio and television broadcast and wireless communications equipment—are classified in Industry 334220, Radio and Television Broadcasting and Wireless Communications Equipment Manufacturing; and

- Manufacturing automobile audio and related equipment—are classified in Industry 334310, Audio and Video Equipment Manufacturing.

US—United States industry only. CAN—United States and Canadian industries are comparable. MEX—United States and Mexican industries are comparable. Blank—Canadian, Mexican, and United States industries are comparable.

http://www.census.gov/naics

3343 Audio and Video Equipment Manufacturing

33431 Audio and Video Equipment Manufacturing
See industry description for 334310 below.

334310 Audio and Video Equipment Manufacturing

This industry comprises establishments primarily engaged in manufacturing electronic audio and video equipment for home entertainment, motor vehicles, and public address and musical instrument amplification. Examples of products made by these establishments are video cassette recorders, televisions, stereo equipment, speaker systems, household-type video cameras, jukeboxes, and amplifiers for musical instruments and public address systems.

Cross-References. Establishments primarily engaged in—

- Manufacturing telephone answering machines—are classified in Industry 334210, Telephone Apparatus Manufacturing;
- Manufacturing photographic (i.e., still and motion picture) equipment— are classified in U.S. Industry 333315, Photographic and Photocopying Equipment Manufacturing;
- Manufacturing phonograph needles and cartridges—are classified in Industry 33441, Semiconductor and Other Electronic Component Manufacturing;
- Manufacturing auto theft alarms—are classified in Industry 334290, Other Communications Equipment Manufacturing; and
- Manufacturing mobile radios, such as citizens band and FM transceivers for household or motor vehicle uses; studio and broadcast video cameras; and cable decoders and satellite television equipment—are classified in Industry 334220, Radio and Television Broadcasting and Wireless Communications Equipment Manufacturing.

3344 Semiconductor and Other Electronic Component Manufacturing

33441 Semiconductor and Other Electronic Component Manufacturing

This industry comprises establishments primarily engaged in manufacturing semiconductors and other components for electronic applications. Examples of products made by these establishments are capacitors, resistors, microprocessors,

---

bare and loaded printed circuit boards, electron tubes, electronic connectors, and computer modems.

Cross-References. Establishments primarily engaged in—

- Manufacturing X-ray tubes—are classified in Industry 33451, Navigational, Measuring, Electromedical, and Control Instruments Manufacturing;

- Manufacturing glass blanks for electron tubes—are classified in Industry 32721, Glass and Glass Product Manufacturing;

- Manufacturing telephone system components or modules—are classified in Industry 33421, Telephone Apparatus Manufacturing;

- Manufacturing finished products that incorporate loaded printed circuit boards—are classified in the Manufacturing sector based on the production process of making the final product;

- Manufacturing communications antennas—are classified in Industry 33422, Radio and Television Broadcasting and Wireless Communications Equipment Manufacturing; and

- Manufacturing coils, switches, transformers, connectors, capacitors, rheostats, and similar devices for electrical applications—are classified in Subsector 335, Electrical Equipment, Appliance, and Component Manufacturing.

334411 Electron Tube Manufacturing[US]

This U.S. industry comprises establishments primarily engaged in manufacturing electron tubes and parts (except glass blanks). Examples of products made by these establishments are cathode ray tubes (i.e., picture tubes), klystron tubes, magnetron tubes, and traveling wave tubes.

Cross-References. Establishments primarily engaged in—

- Manufacturing X-ray tubes—are classified in U.S. Industry 334517, Irradiation Apparatus Manufacturing; and

- Manufacturing glass blanks for electron tubes—are classified in Industry 32721, Glass and Glass Product Manufacturing.

334412 Bare Printed Circuit Board Manufacturing[US]

This U.S. industry comprises establishments primarily engaged in manufacturing bare (i.e., rigid or flexible) printed circuit boards without mounted electronic components. These establishments print, perforate, plate, screen, etch, or photoprint interconnecting pathways for electric current on laminates.

US—United States industry only. CAN—United States and Canadian industries are comparable. MEX—United States and Mexican industries are comparable. Blank—Canadian, Mexican, and United States industries are comparable.

Cross-References. Establishments primarily engaged in—

- Loading components onto printed circuit boards, or whose output is loaded printed circuit boards—are classified in U.S. Industry 334418, Printed Circuit Assembly (Electronic Assembly) Manufacturing; and

- Manufacturing printed circuit laminates—are classified in U.S. Industry 334419, Other Electronic Component Manufacturing.

334413 Semiconductor and Related Device Manufacturing[US]

This U.S. industry comprises establishments primarily engaged in manufacturing semiconductors and related solid state devices. Examples of products made by these establishments are integrated circuits, memory chips, microprocessors, diodes, transistors, solar cells and other optoelectronic devices.

334414 Electronic Capacitor Manufacturing[US]

This U.S. industry comprises establishments primarily engaged in manufacturing electronic fixed and variable capacitors and condensers.

Cross-References.

Establishments primarily engaged in manufacturing electrical capacitors for power generation and distribution, heavy industrial equipment, induction heating and melting, and similar industrial applications are classified in U.S. Industry 335999, All Other Miscellaneous Electrical Equipment and Component Manufacturing.

334415 Electronic Resistor Manufacturing[US]

This U.S. industry comprises establishments primarily engaged in manufacturing electronic resistors, such as fixed and variable resistors, resistor networks, thermistors, and varistors.

Cross-References.

Establishments primarily engaged in manufacturing electronic rheostats are classified in U.S. Industry 334419, Other Electronic Component Manufacturing.

334416 Electronic Coil, Transformer, and Other Inductor Manufacturing[US]

This U.S. industry comprises establishments primarily engaged in manufacturing electronic inductors, such as coils and transformers.

US—United States industry only. CAN—United States and Canadian industries are comparable. MEX—United States and Mexican industries are comparable. Blank—Canadian, Mexican, and United States industries are comparable.

Cross-References.

Establishments primarily engaged in manufacturing electrical transformers used in the generation, storage, transmission, transformation, distribution, and utilization of electrical energy are classified in U.S. Industry 335311, Power, Distribution, and Specialty Transformer Manufacturing.

334417 Electronic Connector Manufacturing[US]

This U.S. industry comprises establishments primarily engaged in manufacturing electronic connectors, such as coaxial, cylindrical, rack and panel, pin and sleeve, printed circuit and fiber optic.

Cross-References.

Establishments primarily engaged in manufacturing electrical connectors, such as plugs, bus bars, twist on wire connectors and terminals, are classified in U.S. Industry 335931, Current-Carrying Wiring Device Manufacturing.

334418 Printed Circuit Assembly (Electronic Assembly) Manufacturing[US]

This U.S. industry comprises establishments primarily engaged in loading components onto printed circuit boards or who manufacture and ship loaded printed circuit boards. Also known as printed circuit assemblies, electronics assemblies, or modules, these products are printed circuit boards that have some or all of the semiconductor and electronic components inserted or mounted and are inputs to a wide variety of electronic systems and devices.

Cross-References. Establishments primarily engaged in—

- Manufacturing printed circuit laminates—are classified in U.S. Industry 334419, Other Electronic Component Manufacturing;
- Manufacturing bare printed circuit boards—are classified in U.S. Industry 334412, Bare Printed Circuit Board Manufacturing;
- Manufacturing telephone system components or modules—are classified in Industry 334210, Telephone Apparatus Manufacturing; and
- Manufacturing finished products that incorporate loaded printed circuit boards—are classified in the Manufacturing sector based on the production process of making the final product.

334419 Other Electronic Component Manufacturing[US]

This U.S. industry comprises establishments primarily engaged in manufacturing electronic components (except electron tubes; bare printed circuit boards; semicon-

US—United States industry only. CAN—United States and Canadian industries are comparable. MEX—United States and Mexican industries are comparable. Blank—Canadian, Mexican, and United States industries are comparable.

ductors and related devices; electronic capacitors; electronic resistors; coils, transformers and other inductors; connectors; and loaded printed circuit boards).

Illustrative Examples:

Crystals and crystal assemblies,
electronic, manufacturing
Printed circuit laminates manufacturing
LCD (liquid crystal display) unit screens
manufacturing
Switches for electronic applications
manufacturing
Microwave components manufacturing
Transducers (except pressure)
manufacturing
Piezolelectric devices manufacturing

Cross-References. Establishments primarily engaged in—

- Manufacturing electron tubes—are classified in U.S. Industry 334411, Electron Tube Manufacturing;

- Manufacturing bare printed circuit boards—are classified in U.S. Industry 334412, Bare Printed Circuit Board Manufacturing;

- Manufacturing semiconductors, photonic integrated circuits, and/or silicon wave guides—are classified in U.S. Industry 334413, Semiconductor and Related Device Manufacturing;

- Manufacturing electronic capacitors—are classified in U.S. Industry 334414, Electronic Capacitor Manufacturing;

- Manufacturing electronic resistors—are classified in U.S. Industry 334415, Electronic Resistor Manufacturing;

- Manufacturing electronic inductors—are classified in U.S. Industry 334416, Electronic Coil, Transformer, and Other Inductor Manufacturing;

- Manufacturing electronic connectors—are classified in U.S. Industry 334417, Electronic Connector Manufacturing;

- Loading components onto printed circuit boards or whose output is loaded printed circuit boards—are classified in U.S. Industry 334418, Printed Circuit Assembly (Electronic Assembly) Manufacturing; and

- Manufacturing communications antennas—are classified in Industry 334220, Radio and Television Broadcasting and Wireless Communications Equipment Manufacturing.

3345 Navigational, Measuring, Electromedical, and Control Instruments Manufacturing

US—United States industry only. CAN—United States and Canadian industries are comparable. MEX—United States and Mexican industries are comparable. Blank—Canadian, Mexican, and United States industries are comparable.

33451 Navigational, Measuring, Electromedical, and Control Instruments Manufacturing

This industry comprises establishments primarily engaged in manufacturing navigational, measuring, electromedical, and control instruments. Examples of products made by these establishments are aeronautical instruments, appliance regulators and controls (except switches), laboratory analytical instruments, navigation and guidance systems, and physical properties testing equipment.

Cross-References. Establishments primarily engaged in—

- Manufacturing global positioning system (GPS) equipment—are classified in Industry 33422, Radio and Television Broadcasting and Wireless Communications Equipment Manufacturing;

- Manufacturing motor control switches and relays (including timing relays)—are classified in Industry 33531, Electrical Equipment Manufacturing;

- Manufacturing switches for appliances—are classified in Industry 33593, Wiring Device Manufacturing;

- Manufacturing optical instruments—are classified in Industry 33331, Commercial and Service Industry Machinery Manufacturing;

- Manufacturing glass watch and clock crystals—are classified in Industry 32721, Glass and Glass Product Manufacturing;

- Manufacturing plastics watch and clock crystals—are classified in Industry 32619, Other Plastics Product Manufacturing; and

- Manufacturing medical thermometers and other nonelectrical medical apparatus—are classified in Industry Group 3391, Medical Equipment and Supplies Manufacturing.

334510 Electromedical and Electrotherapeutic Apparatus Manufacturing[US]

This U.S. industry comprises establishments primarily engaged in manufacturing electromedical and electrotherapeutic apparatus, such as magnetic resonance imaging equipment, medical ultrasound equipment, pacemakers, hearing aids, electrocardiographs, and electromedical endoscopic equipment.

Cross-References. Establishments primarily engaged in—

- Manufacturing medical irradiation apparatus—are classified in U.S. Industry 334517, Irradiation Apparatus Manufacturing; and

- Manufacturing nonelectrical medical and therapeutic apparatus—are classified in Industry Group 3391, Medical Equipment and Supplies Manufacturing.

334511 Search, Detection, Navigation, Guidance, Aeronautical, and Nautical System and Instrument Manufacturing[CAN]

This U.S. industry comprises establishments primarily engaged in manufacturing search, detection, navigation, guidance, aeronautical, and nautical systems and instruments. Examples of products made by these establishments are aircraft instruments (except engine), flight recorders, navigational instruments and systems, radar systems and equipment, and sonar systems and equipment.

Cross-References. Establishments primarily engaged in—

- Manufacturing global positioning system (GPS) equipment—are classified in Industry 334220, Radio and Television Broadcasting and Wireless Communications Equipment Manufacturing; and

- Manufacturing aircraft engine instruments and meteorological systems and equipment—are classified in U.S. Industry 334519, Other Measuring and Controlling Device Manufacturing.

334512 Automatic Environmental Control Manufacturing for Residential, Commercial, and Appliance Use[US]

This U.S. industry comprises establishments primarily engaged in manufacturing automatic controls and regulators for applications, such as heating, air-conditioning, refrigeration and appliances.

Cross-References. Establishments primarily engaged in—

- Manufacturing industrial process controls—are classified in U.S. Industry 334513, Instruments and Related Products Manufacturing for Measuring, Displaying, and Controlling Industrial Process Variables;

- Manufacturing motor control switches and relays—are classified in U.S. Industry 335314, Relay and Industrial Control Manufacturing;

- Manufacturing switches for appliances—are classified in U.S. Industry 335931, Current-Carrying Wiring Device Manufacturing; and

---

- Manufacturing appliance timers—are classified in U.S. Industry 334518, Watch, Clock, and Part Manufacturing.

334513   Instruments and Related Products Manufacturing for Measuring, Displaying, and Controlling Industrial Process Variables[US]

This U.S. industry comprises establishments primarily engaged in manufacturing instruments and related devices for measuring, displaying, indicating, recording, transmitting, and controlling industrial process variables. These instruments measure, display or control (monitor, analyze, and so forth) industrial process variables, such as temperature, humidity, pressure, vacuum, combustion, flow, level, viscosity, density, acidity, concentration, and rotation.

Cross-References. Establishments primarily engaged in—

- Manufacturing instruments for measuring or testing of electricity and electrical signals—are classified in U.S. Industry 334515, Instrument Manufacturing for Measuring and Testing Electricity and Electrical Signals;

- Manufacturing medical thermometers—are classified in U.S. Industry 339112, Surgical and Medical Instrument Manufacturing;

- Manufacturing glass hydrometers and thermometers for other nonmedical uses—are classified in U.S. Industry 334519, Other Measuring and Controlling Device Manufacturing;

- Manufacturing instruments and instrumentation systems for laboratory analysis of samples—are classified in U.S. Industry 334516, Analytical Laboratory Instrument Manufacturing; and

- Manufacturing optical alignment and display instruments, optical comparators, and optical test and inspection equipment—are classified in U.S. Industry 333314, Optical Instrument and Lens Manufacturing.

334514   Totalizing Fluid Meter and Counting Device Manufacturing[US]

This U.S. industry comprises establishments primarily engaged in manufacturing totalizing (i.e., registering) fluid meters and counting devices. Examples of products made by these establishments are gas consumption meters, water consumption meters, parking meters, taxi meters, motor vehicle gauges, and fare collection equipment.

US—United States industry only. CAN—United States and Canadian industries are comparable. MEX—United States and Mexican industries are comparable. Blank—Canadian, Mexican, and United States industries are comparable.

Cross-References. Establishments primarily engaged in—

- Manufacturing integrating meters and counters for measuring the characteristics of electricity and electrical signals—are classified in U.S. Industry 334515, Instrument Manufacturing for Measuring and Testing Electricity and Electrical Signals; and

- Manufacturing instruments and devices that measure, display, or control (i.e., monitor or analyze) related industrial process variables—are classified in U.S. Industry 334513, Instruments and Related Products Manufacturing for Measuring, Displaying, and Controlling Industrial Process Variables.

334515 Instrument Manufacturing for Measuring and Testing Electricity and Electrical Signals[US]

This U.S. industry comprises establishments primarily engaged in manufacturing instruments for measuring and testing the characteristics of electricity and electrical signals. Examples of products made by these establishments are circuit and continuity testers, voltmeters, ohm meters, wattmeters, multimeters, and semiconductor test equipment.

Cross-References.

Establishments primarily engaged in manufacturing electronic monitoring, evaluating, and other electronic support equipment for navigational, radar, and sonar systems are classified in U.S. Industry 334511, Search, Detection, Navigation, Guidance, Aeronautical, and Nautical System and Instrument Manufacturing.

334516 Analytical Laboratory Instrument Manufacturing[US]

This U.S. industry comprises establishments primarily engaged in manufacturing instruments and instrumentation systems for laboratory analysis of the chemical or physical composition or concentration of samples of solid, fluid, gaseous, or composite material.

Cross-References. Establishments primarily engaged in—

- Manufacturing instruments for monitoring and analyzing continuous samples from medical patients—are classified in U.S. Industry 334510, Electro-medical and Electrotherapeutic Apparatus Manufacturing; and

- Manufacturing instruments and related devices that measure, display, or control (i.e., monitor or analyze) industrial process variables—are classified in U.S. Industry 334513, Instruments and Related Products Manufacturing for Measuring, Displaying, and Controlling Industrial Process Variables.

334517 Irradiation Apparatus Manufacturing[US]

This U.S. industry comprises establishments primarily engaged in manufacturing irradiation apparatus and tubes for applications, such as medical diagnostic, medical therapeutic, industrial, research and scientific evaluation. Irradiation can take the form of beta-rays, gamma-rays, X-rays, or other ionizing radiation.

334518 Watch, Clock, and Part Manufacturing[US]

This U.S. industry comprises establishments primarily engaged in manufacturing and/or assembling: clocks; watches; timing mechanisms for clockwork operated devices; time clocks; time and date recording devices; and clock and watch parts (except crystals), such as springs, jewels, and modules.

Cross-References. Establishments primarily engaged in—

- Manufacturing glass watch and clock crystals—are classified in Industry 32721, Glass and Glass Product Manufacturing;

- Manufacturing plastics watch and clock crystals—are classified in U.S. Industry 326199, All Other Plastics Product Manufacturing; and

- Manufacturing timing relays—are classified in U.S. Industry 335314, Relay and Industrial Control Manufacturing.

334519 Other Measuring and Controlling Device Manufacturing[US]

This U.S. industry comprises establishments primarily engaged in manufacturing measuring and controlling devices (except search, detection, navigation, guidance, aeronautical, and nautical instruments and systems; automatic environmental controls for residential, commercial, and appliance use; instruments for measurement, display, and control of industrial process variables; totalizing fluid meters and counting devices; instruments for measuring and testing electricity and electrical signals; analytical laboratory instruments; watches, clocks, and parts; irradiation equipment; and electromedical and electrotherapeutic apparatus).

Illustrative Examples:

Aircraft engine instruments manufacturing
Polygraph machines manufacturing
Automotive emissions testing equipment manufacturing
Radiation detection and monitoring instruments manufacturing

Meteorological instruments manufacturing
Surveying instruments manufacturing
Physical properties testing and inspection equipment manufacturing
Thermometers, liquid-in-glass and bimetal types (except medical), manufacturing

---

US—United States industry only. CAN—United States and Canadian industries are comparable. MEX—United States and Mexican industries are comparable. Blank—Canadian, Mexican, and United States industries are comparable.

Cross-References. Establishments primarily engaged in—

- Manufacturing medical thermometers—are classified in U.S. Industry 339112, Surgical and Medical Instrument Manufacturing;

- Manufacturing search, detection, navigation, guidance, aeronautical, and nautical systems and instruments—are classified in U.S. Industry 334511, Search, Detection, Navigation, Guidance, Aeronautical, and Nautical System and Instrument Manufacturing;

- Manufacturing automatic controls and regulators for applications, such as heating, air-conditioning, refrigeration and appliances—are classified in U.S. Industry 334512, Automatic Environmental Control Manufacturing for Residential, Commercial, and Appliance Use;

- Manufacturing instruments and related devices that measure, display, or control (i.e., monitor or analyze) industrial process variables—are classified in U.S. Industry 334513, Instruments and Related Products Manufacturing for Measuring, Displaying, and Controlling Industrial Process Variables;

- Manufacturing totalizing (i.e., registering) fluid meters and counting devices, including motor vehicle gauges—are classified in U.S. Industry 334514, Totalizing Fluid Meter and Counting Device Manufacturing;

- Manufacturing instruments for measuring and testing the characteristics of electricity and electrical signals—are classified in U.S. Industry 334515, Instrument Manufacturing for Measuring and Testing Electricity and Electrical Signals;

- Manufacturing instruments for laboratory analysis of the physical composition or concentration of samples of solid, fluid, gaseous, or composite materials—are classified in U.S. Industry 334516, Analytical Laboratory Instrument Manufacturing;

- Manufacturing and/or assembling watches, clocks, or parts—are classified in U.S. Industry 334518, Watch, Clock, and Part Manufacturing;

- Manufacturing X-ray apparatus, tubes, or related irradiation apparatus—are classified in U.S. Industry 334517, Irradiation Apparatus Manufacturing; and

- Manufacturing electromedical and electrotherapeutic apparatus—are classified in U.S. Industry 334510, Electromedical and Electrotherapeutic Apparatus Manufacturing.

3346 Manufacturing and Reproducing Magnetic and Optical Media

33461 Manufacturing and Reproducing Magnetic and Optical Media

This industry comprises establishments primarily engaged in (1) manufacturing optical and magnetic media, such as blank audio tape, blank video tape, and blank

---

diskettes and/or (2) mass duplicating (i.e., making copies) audio, video, software, and other data on magnetic, optical, and similar media.

Cross-References. Establishments primarily engaged in—

- Designing, developing, and publishing prepackaged software—are classified in Industry 51121, Software Publishers; and

- Audio, motion picture and/or video production and/or distribution—are classified in Subsector 512, Motion Picture and Sound Recording Industries.

334611 Software Reproducing[US]

This U.S. industry comprises establishments primarily engaged in mass reproducing computer software. These establishments do not generally develop any software. They mass reproduce data and programs on magnetic or optical media, such as CD-ROMs, diskettes, tapes, or cartridges. This industry includes establishments that mass reproduce game cartridges.

Cross-References.

Establishments primarily engaged in designing, developing, and publishing prepackaged software are classified in Industry 511210, Software Publishers.

334612 Prerecorded Compact Disc (except Software), Tape, and Record Reproducing[US]

This U.S. industry comprises establishments primarily engaged in mass reproducing audio and video material on magnetic or optical media. Examples of products mass reproduced by these establishments are prerecorded audio compact discs, audio and video cassettes, and digital video discs (DVDs).

Cross-References. Establishments primarily engaged in—

- Designing, developing, and publishing prepackaged software—are classified in Industry 511210, Software Publishers;

- Audio, motion picture and/or video production and/or distribution—are classified in Subsector 512, Motion Picture and Sound Recording Industries; and

- Manufacturing blank audio and video tape, blank diskettes, and blank optical discs—are classified in U.S. Industry 334613, Magnetic and Optical Recording Media Manufacturing.

US—United States industry only. CAN—United States and Canadian industries are comparable. MEX—United States and Mexican industries are comparable. Blank—Canadian, Mexican, and United States industries are comparable.

334613 Magnetic and Optical Recording Media Manufacturing[US]

This U.S. industry comprises establishments primarily engaged in manufacturing magnetic and optical recording media, such as blank magnetic tape, blank diskettes, blank optical discs, hard drive media, and blank magnetic tape cassettes.

Cross-References. Establishments primarily engaged in—

- Mass reproducing computer software—are classified in U.S. Industry 334611, Software Reproducing; and

- Mass reproducing audio and video material—are classified in U.S. Industry 334612, Prerecorded Compact Disc (except Software), Tape, and Record Reproducing.

335 Electrical Equipment, Appliance, and Component Manufacturing

Industries in the Electrical Equipment, Appliance, and Component Manufacturing subsector manufacture products that generate, distribute and use electrical power. Electric Lighting Equipment Manufacturing establishments produce electric lamp bulbs, lighting fixtures, and parts. Household Appliance Manufacturing establishments make both small and major electrical appliances and parts. Electrical Equipment Manufacturing establishments make goods, such as electric motors, generators, transformers, and switchgear apparatus. Other Electrical Equipment and Component Manufacturing establishments make devices for storing electrical power (e.g., batteries), for transmitting electricity (e.g., insulated wire), and wiring devices (e.g., electrical outlets, fuse boxes, and light switches).

3351 Electric Lighting Equipment Manufacturing

33511 Electric Lamp Bulb and Part Manufacturing
See industry description for 335110 below.

335110 Electric Lamp Bulb and Part Manufacturing

This industry comprises establishments primarily engaged in manufacturing electric light bulbs and tubes, and parts and components (except glass blanks for electric light bulbs).

Cross-References. Establishments primarily engaged in—

- Manufacturing glass blanks for electric light bulbs—are classified in U.S. Industry 327212, Other Pressed and Blown Glass and Glassware Manufacturing;

US—United States industry only. CAN—United States and Canadian industries are comparable. MEX —United States and Mexican industries are comparable. Blank—Canadian, Mexican, and United States industries are comparable.

- Manufacturing vehicular lighting fixtures—are classified in U.S. Industry 336321, Vehicular Lighting Equipment Manufacturing;

- Manufacturing light emitting diodes (LEDs)—are classified in U.S. Industry 334413, Semiconductor and Related Device Manufacturing; and

- Manufacturing other lighting fixtures (except vehicular)—are classified in Industry 33512, Lighting Fixture Manufacturing.

33512 Lighting Fixture Manufacturing

This industry comprises establishments primarily engaged in manufacturing electric lighting fixtures (except vehicular), nonelectric lighting equipment, lamp shades (except glass and plastics), and lighting fixture components (except current-carrying wiring devices).

Cross-References. Establishments primarily engaged in—

- Manufacturing vehicular lighting fixtures—are classified in Industry 33632, Motor Vehicle Electrical and Electronic Equipment Manufacturing;

- Manufacturing electric light bulbs, tubes, and parts—are classified in Industry 33511, Electric Lamp Bulb and Part Manufacturing;

- Manufacturing current-carrying wiring devices for lighting fixtures—are classified in Industry 33593, Wiring Device Manufacturing;

- Manufacturing ceiling fans or bath fans with integrated lighting fixtures—are classified in Industry 33521, Small Electrical Appliance Manufacturing;

- Manufacturing plastics lamp shades—are classified in Industry 32619, Other Plastics Product Manufacturing;

- Manufacturing glassware and glass parts for lighting fixtures—are classified in Industry 32721, Glass and Glass Product Manufacturing; and

- Manufacturing signaling devices that incorporate electric light bulbs, such as traffic and railway signals—are classified in Industry 33429, Other Communications Equipment Manufacturing.

335121 Residential Electric Lighting Fixture Manufacturing[US]

This U.S. industry comprises establishments primarily engaged in manufacturing fixed or portable residential electric lighting fixtures and lamp shades of metal, paper, or textiles. Residential electric lighting fixtures include those for use both inside and outside the residence.

US—United States industry only. CAN—United States and Canadian industries are comparable. MEX—United States and Mexican industries are comparable. Blank—Canadian, Mexican, and United States industries are comparable.

Illustrative Examples:

Ceiling lighting fixtures, residential, manufacturing	Chandeliers, residential, manufacturing
Table lamps (i.e., lighting fixtures) manufacturing	

Cross-References. Establishments primarily engaged in—

- Manufacturing glassware for residential lighting fixtures—are classified in Industry 32721, Glass and Glass Product Manufacturing;

- Manufacturing plastics lamp shades—are classified in U.S. Industry 326199, All Other Plastics Product Manufacturing;

- Manufacturing electric light bulbs, tubes, and parts—are classified in Industry 335110, Electric Lamp Bulb and Part Manufacturing;

- Manufacturing ceiling fans or bath fans with integrated lighting fixtures—are classified in U.S. Industry 335211, Electric Housewares and Household Fan Manufacturing;

- Manufacturing current-carrying wiring devices for lighting fixtures—are classified in U.S. Industry 335931, Current-Carrying Wiring Device Manufacturing;

- Manufacturing commercial, industrial, and institutional electric lighting fixtures—are classified in U.S. Industry 335122, Commercial, Industrial, and Institutional Electric Lighting Fixture Manufacturing; and

- Manufacturing other lighting fixtures, such as street lights, flashlights, and nonelectric lighting fixtures—are classified in U.S. Industry 335129, Other Lighting Equipment Manufacturing.

335122 Commercial, Industrial, and Institutional Electric Lighting Fixture Manufacturing[US]

This U.S. industry comprises establishments primarily engaged in manufacturing commercial, industrial, and institutional electric lighting fixtures.

Cross-References. Establishments primarily engaged in—

- Manufacturing glassware for commercial, industrial, and institutional electric lighting fixtures—are classified in Industry 32721, Glass and Glass Product Manufacturing;

- Manufacturing residential electric lighting fixtures—are classified in U.S. Industry 335121, Residential Electric Lighting Fixture Manufacturing;

US—United States industry only. CAN—United States and Canadian industries are comparable. MEX—United States and Mexican industries are comparable. Blank—Canadian, Mexican, and United States industries are comparable.

- Manufacturing current-carrying wiring devices for lighting fixtures—are classified in U.S. Industry 335931, Current-Carrying Wiring Device Manufacturing;

- Manufacturing vehicular lighting fixtures—are classified in U.S. Industry 336321, Vehicular Lighting Equipment Manufacturing;

- Manufacturing electric light bulbs, tubes, and parts—are classified in Industry 335110, Electric Lamp Bulb and Part Manufacturing; and

- Manufacturing other lighting fixtures, such as street lights, flashlights, and nonelectric lighting equipment—are classified in U.S. Industry 335129, Other Lighting Equipment Manufacturing.

335129 Other Lighting Equipment Manufacturing[US]

This U.S. industry comprises establishments primarily engaged in manufacturing electric lighting fixtures (except residential, commercial, industrial, institutional, and vehicular electric lighting fixtures) and nonelectric lighting equipment.

Illustrative Examples:

Christmas tree lighting sets, electric, manufacturing
Lanterns (e.g., carbide, electric, gas, gasoline, kerosene) manufacturing
Fireplace logs, electric, manufacturing
Spotlights (except vehicular) manufacturing

Flashlights manufacturing
Street lighting fixtures (except traffic signals) manufacturing
Insect lamps, electric, manufacturing

Cross-References. Establishments primarily engaged in—

- Manufacturing glassware for lighting fixtures—are classified in Industry 32721, Glass and Glass Product Manufacturing;

- Manufacturing electric light bulbs, tubes, and parts—are classified in Industry 335110, Electric Lamp Bulb and Part Manufacturing;

- Manufacturing current-carrying wiring devices for lighting fixtures—are classified in U.S. Industry 335931, Current-Carrying Wiring Device Manufacturing;

- Manufacturing residential electric lighting fixtures—are classified in U.S. Industry 335121, Residential Electric Lighting Fixture Manufacturing;

- Manufacturing commercial, industrial, and institutional electric lighting fixtures—are classified in U.S. Industry 335122, Commercial, Industrial, and Institutional Electric Lighting Fixture Manufacturing;

- Manufacturing vehicular lighting fixtures—are classified in U.S. Industry 336321, Vehicular Lighting Equipment Manufacturing; and

- Manufacturing signaling devices that incorporate electric light bulbs, such as traffic and railway signals—are classified in Industry 334290, Other Communications Equipment Manufacturing.

3352 Household Appliance Manufacturing

33521 Small Electrical Appliance Manufacturing

This industry comprises establishments primarily engaged in manufacturing small electric appliances and electric housewares, household-type fans, household-type vacuum cleaners, and other electric household-type floor care machines.

Cross-References. Establishments primarily engaged in—

- Manufacturing room air-conditioners, attic fans, wall and baseboard heating units for permanent installation, and commercial ventilation and exhaust fans—are classified in Industry 33341, Ventilation, Heating, Air-Conditioning, and Commercial Refrigeration Equipment Manufacturing;

- Manufacturing commercial, industrial, and institutional vacuum cleaners, and mechanical carpet sweepers—are classified in Industry 33331, Commercial and Service Industry Machinery Manufacturing;

- Manufacturing major household-type appliances, such as washing machines, dryers, stoves, and hot water heaters—are classified in Industry 33522, Major Appliance Manufacturing; and

- Installing central vacuum cleaning systems—are classified in Industry 23829, Other Building Equipment Contractors.

335211 Electric Housewares and Household Fan Manufacturing[US]

This U.S. industry comprises establishments primarily engaged in manufacturing small electric appliances and electric housewares for heating, cooking, and other purposes, and electric household-type fans (except attic fans).

Illustrative Examples:

Bath fans, residential, manufacturing
Portable electric space heaters
  manufacturing

Portable humidifiers and dehumidifiers
  manufacturing
Electronic blankets manufacturing

US—United States industry only. CAN—United States and Canadian industries are comparable. MEX—United States and Mexican industries are comparable. Blank—Canadian, Mexican, and United States industries are comparable.

Ceiling fans, residential,
manufacturing
Portable hair dryers, electric,
manufacturing
Curling irons, household-type electric,
manufacturing

Scissors, electric, manufacturing
Portable cooking appliances (except
microwave, convection ovens),
household-type electric, manufacturing
Ventilating and exhaust fans (except attic
fans), household-type, manufacturing

Cross-References. Establishments primarily engaged in—

- Manufacturing attic fans—are classified in U.S. Industry 333412, Industrial and Commercial Fan and Blower Manufacturing;

- Manufacturing wall and baseboard heating units for permanent installation—are classified in U.S. Industry 333414, Heating Equipment (except Warm Air Furnaces) Manufacturing;

- **Manufacturing room air-conditioners—are classified in U.S. Industry 333415,** Air-Conditioning and Warm Air Heating Equipment and Commercial and Industrial Refrigeration Equipment Manufacturing; and

- Manufacturing microwave and convection ovens—are classified in U.S. Industry 335221, Household Cooking Appliance Manufacturing.

335212 Household Vacuum Cleaner Manufacturing[US]

This U.S. industry comprises establishments primarily engaged in manufacturing electric vacuum cleaners, electric floor waxing machines, and other electric floor care machines typically for household use.

Cross-References. Establishments primarily engaged in—

- Manufacturing electric vacuum cleaners for commercial, industrial, and institutional uses, and mechanical carpet sweepers—are classified in U.S. Industry 333319, Other Commercial and Service Industry Machinery Manufacturing; and

- Installing central vacuum cleaning systems—are classified in Industry 238290, Other Building Equipment Contractors.

33522 Major Appliance Manufacturing

This industry comprises establishments primarily engaged in manufacturing household-type cooking appliances, household-type laundry equipment, household-type refrigerators, upright and chest freezers, and other electrical and nonelectrical major household-type appliances, such as dishwashers, water heaters, and garbage disposal units.

Cross-References. Establishments primarily engaged in—

- Manufacturing small electric appliances and electric housewares, such as hot plates, griddles, toasters, and electric irons—are classified in Industry 33521, Small Electrical Appliance Manufacturing;

- Manufacturing commercial and industrial refrigerators and freezers—are classified in Industry 33341, Ventilation, Heating, Air-Conditioning, and Commercial Refrigeration Equipment Manufacturing;

- Manufacturing commercial-type cooking equipment and commercial-type laundry, drycleaning, and pressing equipment—are classified in Industry 33331, Commercial and Service Industry Machinery Manufacturing; and

- Manufacturing household-type sewing machines—are classified in Industry 33329, Other Industrial Machinery Manufacturing.

335221 Household Cooking Appliance Manufacturing^{US}

This U.S. industry comprises establishments primarily engaged in manufacturing household-type electric and nonelectric cooking equipment (except small electric appliances and electric housewares).

Cross-References. Establishments primarily engaged in—

- Manufacturing small electric appliances and electric housewares used for cooking, such as electric skillets, electric hot plates, electric griddles, toasters, and percolators—are classified in U.S. Industry 335211, Electric Housewares and Household Fan Manufacturing; and

- Manufacturing commercial-type cooking equipment—are classified in U.S. Industry 333319, Other Commercial and Service Industry Machinery Manufacturing.

335222 Household Refrigerator and Home Freezer Manufacturing^{US}

This U.S. industry comprises establishments primarily engaged in manufacturing household-type refrigerators and upright and chest freezers.

Cross-References.

Establishments primarily engaged in manufacturing commercial and industrial refrigeration equipment, such as refrigerators and freezers, are classified in U.S. Industry 333415, Air-Conditioning and Warm Air Heating Equipment and Commercial and Industrial Refrigeration Equipment Manufacturing.

US—United States industry only. CAN—United States and Canadian industries are comparable. MEX—United States and Mexican industries are comparable. Blank—Canadian, Mexican, and United States industries are comparable.

335224 Household Laundry Equipment Manufacturing^{US}

This U.S. industry comprises establishments primarily engaged in manufacturing household-type laundry equipment.

Cross-References. Establishments primarily engaged in—

- Manufacturing portable electric irons—are classified in U.S. Industry 335211, Electric Housewares and Household Fan Manufacturing; and

- Manufacturing commercial-type laundry and drycleaning equipment—are classified in U.S. Industry 333312, Commercial Laundry, Drycleaning, and Pressing Machine Manufacturing.

335228 Other Major Household Appliance Manufacturing^{US}

This U.S. industry comprises establishments primarily engaged in manufacturing electric and nonelectric major household-type appliances (except cooking equipment, refrigerators, upright and chest freezers, and household-type laundry equipment.

Illustrative Examples:

Dishwashers, household-type, manufacturing	Garbage disposal units, household-type, manufacturing
Hot water heaters (including nonelectric), household-type, manufacturing	Trash and garbage compactors, household-type, manufacturing

Cross-References. Establishments primarily engaged in—

- Manufacturing household-type cooking equipment—are classified in U.S. Industry 335221, Household Cooking Appliance Manufacturing;

- Manufacturing household-type sewing machines—are classified in U.S. Industry 333298, All Other Industrial Machinery Manufacturing;

- Manufacturing household-type refrigerators and upright and chest freezers—are classified in U.S. Industry 335222, Household Refrigerator and Home Freezer Manufacturing; and

- Manufacturing small electric appliances—are classified in U.S. Industry 335211, Electric Housewares and Household Fan Manufacturing.

3353 Electrical Equipment Manufacturing

33531 Electrical Equipment Manufacturing

This industry comprises establishments primarily engaged in manufacturing power, distribution, and specialty transformers; electric motors, generators, and motor generator sets; switchgear and switchboard apparatus; relays; and industrial controls.

Cross-References. Establishments primarily engaged in—

- Manufacturing turbine generator set units and electric outboard motors—are classified in Industry 33361, Engine, Turbine, and Power Transmission Equipment Manufacturing;

- Manufacturing electronic component-type transformers and switches—are classified in Industry 33441, Semiconductor and Other Electronic Component Manufacturing;

- Manufacturing environmental controls and industrial process control instruments—are classified in Industry 33451, Navigational, Measuring, Electromedical, and Control Instruments Manufacturing;

- Manufacturing switches for electrical circuits, such as pushbutton and snap switches—are classified in Industry 33593, Wiring Device Manufacturing;

- Manufacturing complete welding and soldering equipment—are classified in Industry 33399, All Other General Purpose Machinery Manufacturing; and

- Manufacturing starting motors and generators for internal combustion engines—are classified in Industry 33632, Motor Vehicle Electrical and Electronic Equipment Manufacturing.

335311 Power, Distribution, and Specialty Transformer Manufacturing[CAN]

This U.S. industry comprises establishments primarily engaged in manufacturing power, distribution, and specialty transformers (except electronic components). Industrial-type and consumer-type transformers in this industry vary (e.g., step up or step down) voltage but do not convert alternating to direct or direct to alternating current.

Illustrative Examples:

Distribution transformers, electric, manufacturing

Fluorescent ballasts (i.e., transformers) manufacturing

US—United States industry only. CAN—United States and Canadian industries are comparable. MEX—United States and Mexican industries are comparable. Blank—Canadian, Mexican, and United States industries are comparable.

Substation transformers, electric power distribution, manufacturing	Transmission and distribution voltage regulators manufacturing

Cross-References.

Establishments primarily engaged in manufacturing electronic component-type transformers are classified in U.S. Industry 334416, Electronic Coil, Transformer, and Other Inductor Manufacturing.

335312 Motor and Generator Manufacturing[CAN]

This U.S. industry comprises establishments primarily engaged in manufacturing electric motors (except internal combustion engine starting motors), power generators (except battery charging alternators for internal combustion engines), and motor generator sets (except turbine generator set units). This industry includes establishments rewinding armatures on a factory basis.

Cross-References. Establishments primarily engaged in—

- Manufacturing electric outboard motors—are classified in U.S. Industry 333618, Other Engine Equipment Manufacturing;

- Manufacturing gas, steam, or hydraulic turbine generator set units—are classified in U.S. Industry 333611, Turbine and Turbine Generator Set Units Manufacturing;

- Manufacturing starting motors and battery charging alternators for internal combustion engines—are classified in U.S. Industry 336322, Other Motor Vehicle Electrical and Electronic Equipment Manufacturing;

- Rewinding armatures, not on a factory basis—are classified in Industry 811310, Commercial and Industrial Machinery and Equipment (except Automotive and Electronic) Repair and Maintenance; and

- Manufacturing complete welding and soldering equipment—are classified in U.S. Industry 333992, Welding and Soldering Equipment Manufacturing.

335313 Switchgear and Switchboard Apparatus Manufacturing[US]

This U.S. industry comprises establishments primarily engaged in manufacturing switchgear and switchboard apparatus.

Illustrative Examples:

Circuit breakers, power, manufacturing	Duct for electrical switchboard apparatus manufacturing
Fuses, electric, manufacturing	

Control panels, electric power
distribution, manufacturing
Power switching equipment
manufacturing

Switches, electric power (except
pushbutton, snap, solenoid, tumbler),
manufacturing

Cross-References. Establishments primarily engaged in—

- Manufacturing relays—are classified in U.S. Industry 335314, Relay and Industrial Control Manufacturing;
- Manufacturing switches for electronic applications—are classified in U.S. Industry 334419, Other Electronic Component Manufacturing; and
- Manufacturing snap, pushbutton, and similar switches for electrical circuits—are classified in U.S. Industry 335931, Current-Carrying Wiring Device Manufacturing.

335314 Relay and Industrial Control Manufacturing[US]

This U.S. industry comprises establishments primarily engaged in manufacturing relays, motor starters and controllers, and other industrial controls and control accessories.

Cross-References. Establishments primarily engaged in—

- Manufacturing environmental and appliance control equipment—are classified in U.S. Industry 334512, Automatic Environmental Control Manufacturing for Residential, Commercial, and Appliance Use; and
- Manufacturing instruments for controlling industrial process variables—are classified in U.S. Industry 334513, Instruments and Related Products Manufacturing for Measuring, Displaying, and Controlling Industrial Process Variables.

3359 Other Electrical Equipment and Component Manufacturing

This industry group comprises establishments manufacturing electrical equipment and components (except electric lighting equipment, household-type appliances, transformers, switchgear, relays, motors, and generators).

33591 Battery Manufacturing

This industry comprises establishments primarily engaged in manufacturing primary and storage batteries.

US—United States industry only. CAN—United States and Canadian industries are comparable. MEX—United States and Mexican industries are comparable. Blank—Canadian, Mexican, and United States industries are comparable.

335911 Storage Battery Manufacturing[US]

This U.S. industry comprises establishments primarily engaged in manufacturing storage batteries.

Illustrative Examples:

Lead acid storage batteries
manufacturing

Rechargeable nickel cadmium (NICAD) batteries manufacturing

Cross-References.

Establishments primarily engaged in manufacturing primary batteries are classified in U.S. Industry 335912, Primary Battery Manufacturing.

335912 Primary Battery Manufacturing[US]

This U.S. industry comprises establishments primarily engaged in manufacturing wet or dry primary batteries.

Illustrative Examples:

Disposable flashlight batteries
manufacturing
Lithium batteries, primary,
manufacturing

Dry cells, primary (e.g., AAA, AA, C, D, 9V), manufacturing
Watch batteries manufacturing

Cross-References.

Establishments primarily engaged in manufacturing storage batteries are classified in U.S. Industry 335911, Storage Battery Manufacturing.

33592 Communication and Energy Wire and Cable Manufacturing

This industry comprises establishments insulating fiber-optic cable, and manufacturing insulated nonferrous wire and cable from nonferrous wire drawn in other establishments.

Cross-References. Establishments primarily engaged in—

- Drawing nonferrous wire—are classified in Subsector 331, Primary Metal Manufacturing;

- Manufacturing cable sets consisting of insulated wire and various connectors for electronic applications—are classified in Industry 33441, Semiconductor and Other Electronic Component Manufacturing;

US—United States industry only. CAN—United States and Canadian industries are comparable. MEX—United States and Mexican industries are comparable. Blank—Canadian, Mexican, and United States industries are comparable.

- Manufacturing extension cords, appliance cords, and similar electrical cord sets from purchased, insulated wire or cable—are classified in Industry 33599, All Other Electrical Equipment and Component Manufacturing; and

- Manufacturing unsheathed fiber-optic materials—are classified in Industry 32721, Glass and Glass Product Manufacturing.

335921 Fiber Optic Cable Manufacturing[US]

This U.S. industry comprises establishments primarily engaged in manufacturing insulated fiber-optic cable from purchased fiber-optic strand.

Cross-References. Establishments primarily engaged in—

- Manufacturing unsheathed fiber-optic materials—are classified in Industry 32721, Glass and Glass Product Manufacturing; and

- Manufacturing insulated nonferrous wire and cable from purchased wire— are classified in U.S. Industry 335929, Other Communication and Energy Wire Manufacturing.

335929 Other Communication and Energy Wire Manufacturing[US]

This U.S. industry comprises establishments primarily engaged in manufacturing insulated wire and cable of nonferrous metals from purchased wire.

Cross-References. Establishments primarily engaged in—

- Manufacturing cable sets consisting of insulated wire and various connectors for electronic applications—are classified in U.S. Industry 334419, Other Electronic Component Manufacturing;

- Manufacturing extension cords, appliance cords, and similar electrical cord sets from purchased insulated wire—are classified in U.S. Industry 335999, All Other Miscellaneous Electrical Equipment and Component Manufacturing;

- Drawing and insulating copper wire in the same establishment—are classified in U.S. Industry 331422, Copper Wire (except Mechanical) Drawing;

- Drawing and insulating aluminum wire in the same establishment—are classified in U.S. Industry 331319, Other Aluminum Rolling and Drawing; and

- Drawing nonferrous wire (except copper and aluminum)—are classified in U.S. Industry 331491, Nonferrous Metal (except Copper and Aluminum) Rolling, Drawing, and Extruding.

US—United States industry only. CAN—United States and Canadian industries are comparable. MEX—United States and Mexican industries are comparable. Blank—Canadian, Mexican, and United States industries are comparable.

33593 Wiring Device Manufacturing

This industry comprises establishments primarily engaged in manufacturing current-carrying wiring devices and noncurrent-carrying wiring devices for wiring electrical circuits.

Cross-References. Establishments primarily engaged in—

- Manufacturing ceramic and glass insulators—are classified in Subsector 327, Nonmetallic Mineral Product Manufacturing; and

- Manufacturing electronic component-type connectors, sockets, and switches—are classified in Industry 33441, Semiconductor and Other Electronic Component Manufacturing.

335931 Current-Carrying Wiring Device Manufacturing[US]

This U.S. industry comprises establishments primarily engaged in manufacturing current-carrying wiring devices.

Illustrative Examples:

Bus bars, electrical conductors (except switchgear-type), manufacturing	Receptacles (i.e., outlets), electrical, manufacturing
Lightning arrestors and coils manufacturing	Lamp holders manufacturing
GFCI (ground fault circuit interrupters) manufacturing	Switches for electrical wiring (e.g., pressure, pushbutton, snap, tumbler) manufacturing

Cross-References. Establishments primarily engaged in—

- Manufacturing electronic component-type connectors—are classified in U.S. Industry 334417, Electronic Connector Manufacturing;

- Manufacturing noncurrent-carrying wiring devices—are classified in U.S. Industry 335932, Noncurrent-Carrying Wiring Device Manufacturing; and

- Manufacturing electronic component-type sockets and switches—are classified in U.S. Industry 334419, Other Electronic Component Manufacturing.

335932 Noncurrent-Carrying Wiring Device Manufacturing[US]

This U.S. industry comprises establishments primarily engaged in manufacturing noncurrent-carrying wiring devices.

Illustrative Examples:

Boxes, electrical wiring (e.g., junction, outlet, switch), manufacturing	Conduits and fittings, electrical, manufacturing

Face plates (i.e., outlet or switch covers) manufacturing

Transmission pole and line hardware manufacturing

Cross-References. Establishments primarily engaged in—

- Manufacturing porcelain and ceramic insulators—are classified in U.S. Industry 327113, Porcelain Electrical Supply Manufacturing;

- Manufacturing current-carrying wiring devices—are classified in U.S. Industry 335931, Current-Carrying Wiring Device Manufacturing; and

- Manufacturing glass insulators—are classified in Industry 32721, Glass and Glass Product Manufacturing.

33599 All Other Electrical Equipment and Component Manufacturing

This industry comprises establishments primarily engaged in manufacturing electrical equipment (except electric lighting equipment, household-type appliances, transformers, motors, generators, switchgear, relays, industrial controls, batteries, communication and energy wire and cable, and wiring devices).

Illustrative Examples:

Carbon and graphite electrodes and brushes manufacturing
Surge suppressors manufacturing

Extension cords made from purchased insulated wire

Cross-References. Establishments primarily engaged in—

- Manufacturing lighting equipment—are classified in Industry Group 3351, Electric Lighting Equipment Manufacturing;

- Manufacturing household-type appliances—are classified in Industry Group 3352, Household Appliance Manufacturing;

- Manufacturing transformers, motors, generators, switchgear, relays, and industrial controls—are classified in Industry 33531, Electrical Equipment Manufacturing;

- Manufacturing batteries—are classified in Industry 33591, Battery Manufacturing;

- Manufacturing communication and energy wire—are classified in Industry 33592, Communication and Energy Wire and Cable Manufacturing;

- Manufacturing current-carrying and noncurrent-carrying wiring devices— are classified in Industry 33593, Wiring Device Manufacturing;

- Manufacturing carbon or graphite gaskets—are classified in Industry 33999, All Other Miscellaneous Manufacturing;

- Manufacturing electronic component-type rectifiers, voltage regulating integrated circuits, power converting integrated circuits, electronic capacitors, electronic resistors, and similar devices—are classified in Industry 33441, Semiconductor and Other Electronic Component Manufacturing; and

- Manufacturing equipment incorporating lasers—are classified in various subsectors of manufacturing based on the associated production process of the finished equipment.

335991 Carbon and Graphite Product Manufacturing[MEX]

This U.S. industry comprises establishments primarily engaged in manufacturing carbon, graphite, and metal-graphite brushes and brush stock; carbon or graphite electrodes for thermal and electrolytic uses; carbon and graphite fibers; and other carbon, graphite, and metal-graphite products.

Cross-References.

Establishments primarily engaged in manufacturing carbon or graphite gaskets are classified in U.S. Industry 339991, Gasket, Packing, and Sealing Device Manufacturing.

335999 All Other Miscellaneous Electrical Equipment and Component Manufacturing[MEX]

This U.S. industry comprises establishments primarily engaged in manufacturing industrial and commercial electric apparatus and other equipment (except lighting equipment, household appliances, transformers, motors, generators, switchgear, relays, industrial controls, batteries, communication and energy wire and cable, wiring devices, and carbon and graphite products). This industry includes power converters (i.e., AC to DC and DC to AC), power supplies, surge suppressors, and similar equipment for industrial-type and consumer-type equipment.

Illustrative Examples:

Appliance cords made from purchased insulated wire	Door opening and closing devices, electrical, manufacturing
Extension cords made from purchased insulated wire	Surge suppressers manufacturing
Battery chargers, solid-state, manufacturing	Electric bells manufacturing
Inverters manufacturing	Uninterruptible power supplies (UPS) manufacturing

Cross-References. Establishments primarily engaged in—

- Manufacturing lighting equipment—are classified in Industry Group 3351, Electric Lighting Equipment Manufacturing;

US—United States industry only. CAN—United States and Canadian industries are comparable. MEX—United States and Mexican industries are comparable. Blank—Canadian, Mexican, and United States industries are comparable.

- Manufacturing household-type appliances—are classified in Industry Group 3352, Household Appliance Manufacturing;

- Manufacturing transformers, motors, generators, switchgear, relays, and industrial controls—are classified in Industry 33531, Electrical Equipment Manufacturing;

- Manufacturing primary and storage batteries—are classified in Industry 33591, Battery Manufacturing;

- Manufacturing communication and energy wire and cable from purchased wire or fiber-optic strand—are classified in Industry 33592, Communication and Energy Wire and Cable Manufacturing;

- Manufacturing current-carrying and noncurrent-carrying wiring devices—are classified in Industry 33593, Wiring Device Manufacturing;

- Manufacturing electronic component-type rectifiers (except semiconductor)—are classified in U.S. Industry 334419, Other Electronic Component Manufacturing;

- Manufacturing semiconductor rectifiers, voltage regulating integrated circuits, power converting integrated circuits, and similar semiconductor devices—are classified in U.S. Industry 334413, Semiconductor and Related Device Manufacturing;

- Manufacturing electronic component-type capacitors and condensers—are classified in U.S. Industry 334414, Electronic Capacitor Manufacturing;

- Manufacturing carbon and graphite products—are classified in U.S. Industry 335991, Carbon and Graphite Product Manufacturing; and

- Manufacturing equipment incorporating lasers—are classified in various manufacturing subsectors based on the associated production process of the finished equipment.

336 Transportation Equipment Manufacturing

Industries in the Transportation Equipment Manufacturing subsector produce equipment for transporting people and goods. Transportation equipment is a type of machinery. An entire subsector is devoted to this activity because of the significance of its economic size in all three North American countries.

Establishments in this subsector utilize production processes similar to those of other machinery manufacturing establishments—bending, forming, welding, machining, and assembling metal or plastic parts into components and finished products. However, the assembly of components and subassemblies and their further assembly into finished vehicles tends to be a more common production process in this subsector than in the Machinery Manufacturing subsector.

US—United States industry only. CAN—United States and Canadian industries are comparable. MEX—United States and Mexican industries are comparable. Blank—Canadian, Mexican, and United States industries are comparable.

NAICS has industry groups for the manufacture of equipment for each mode of transport—road, rail, air and water. Parts for motor vehicles warrant a separate industry group because of their importance and because parts manufacture requires less assembly, and the establishments that manufacture only parts are not as vertically integrated as those that make complete vehicles.

Land use motor vehicle equipment not designed for highway operation (e.g., agricultural equipment, construction equipment, and materials handling equipment) is classified in the appropriate NAICS subsector based on the type and use of the equipment.

3361 Motor Vehicle Manufacturing

33611 Automobile and Light Duty Motor Vehicle Manufacturing

This industry comprises establishments primarily engaged in (1) manufacturing complete automobile and light duty motor vehicles (i.e., body and chassis or unibody) or (2) manufacturing chassis only.

Cross-References.

Establishments primarily engaged in manufacturing car, truck, and bus bodies and assembling vehicles on a purchased chassis and manufacturing kit cars for highway use are classified in Industry 33621, Motor Vehicle Body and Trailer Manufacturing.

336111 Automobile Manufacturing[US]

This U.S. industry comprises establishments primarily engaged in (1) manufacturing complete automobiles (i.e., body and chassis or unibody) or (2) manufacturing automobile chassis only.

Cross-References.

Establishments primarily engaged in manufacturing car bodies and assembling vehicles on a purchased chassis and manufacturing kit cars for highway use are classified in U.S. Industry 336211, Motor Vehicle Body Manufacturing.

336112 Light Truck and Utility Vehicle Manufacturing[US]

This U.S. industry comprises establishments primarily engaged in (1) manufacturing complete light trucks and utility vehicles (i.e., body and chassis) or (2) manufacturing light truck and utility vehicle chassis only. Vehicles made include light duty vans, pick-up trucks, minivans, and sport utility vehicles.

US—United States industry only. CAN—United States and Canadian industries are comparable. MEX—United States and Mexican industries are comparable. Blank—Canadian, Mexican, and United States industries are comparable.

Cross-References.

Establishments primarily engaged in manufacturing truck and bus bodies and assembling vehicles on a purchased chassis are classified in U.S. Industry 336211, Motor Vehicle Body Manufacturing.

33612 Heavy Duty Truck Manufacturing
See industry description for 336120 below.

336120 Heavy Duty Truck Manufacturing

This industry comprises establishments primarily engaged in (1) manufacturing heavy duty truck chassis and assembling complete heavy duty trucks, buses, heavy duty motor homes, and other special purpose heavy duty motor vehicles for highway use or (2) manufacturing heavy duty truck chassis only.

Cross-References. Establishments primarily engaged in—

- Manufacturing truck and bus bodies and assembling vehicles on a purchased chassis—are classified in U.S. Industry 336211, Motor Vehicle Body Manufacturing;

- Manufacturing motor homes on purchased chassis—are classified in U.S. Industry 336213, Motor Home Manufacturing;

- Manufacturing vans, minivans, and light trucks—are classified in U.S. Industry 336112, Light Truck and Utility Vehicle Manufacturing;

- Manufacturing military armored vehicles—are classified in U.S. Industry 336992, Military Armored Vehicle, Tank, and Tank Component Manufacturing; and

- Manufacturing off highway construction equipment—are classified in Industry 333120, Construction Machinery Manufacturing.

3362 Motor Vehicle Body and Trailer Manufacturing

33621 Motor Vehicle Body and Trailer Manufacturing

This industry comprises establishments primarily engaged in (1) manufacturing motor vehicle bodies and cabs or (2) manufacturing truck, automobile and utility trailers, truck trailer chassis, detachable trailer bodies, and detachable trailer chassis. The products made may be sold separately or may be assembled on purchased chassis and sold as complete vehicles.

US—United States industry only. CAN—United States and Canadian industries are comparable. MEX—United States and Mexican industries are comparable. Blank—Canadian, Mexican, and United States industries are comparable.

Motor homes are units where the motor and the living quarters are contained in the same integrated unit, while travel trailers are designed to be towed by a motor unit, such as an automobile or a light truck.

Illustrative Examples:

Bodies and cabs, truck, manufacturing	Semitrailer manufacturing
Pickup canopies, caps, or covers manufacturing	Motor homes, self-contained, assembling on purchased chassis
Camper unit, slide-in, for pick-up trucks, manufacturing	Travel trailers, recreational, manufacturing

Cross-References. Establishments primarily engaged in—

- Making manufactured homes (i.e., mobile homes)—are classified in Industry 32199, All Other Wood Product Manufacturing;

- Customizing automotive vehicle and trailer interiors (i.e., van conversions) on an individual basis—are classified in Industry 81112, Automotive Body, Paint, Interior, and Glass Repair;

- Manufacturing light duty motor home chassis and assembling complete motor homes—are classified in Industry 33611, Automobile and Light Duty Motor Vehicle Manufacturing; and

- Manufacturing heavy duty truck chassis and assembling heavy duty trucks, buses, motor homes, and other special purpose heavy duty motor vehicles for highway use—are classified in Industry 33612, Heavy Duty Truck Manufacturing.

336211 Motor Vehicle Body Manufacturing^{CAN}

This U.S. industry comprises establishments primarily engaged in manufacturing truck and bus bodies and cabs and automobile bodies. The products made may be sold separately or may be assembled on purchased chassis and sold as complete vehicles.

Cross-References.

Establishments primarily engaged in manufacturing heavy duty chassis and assembling heavy duty trucks, buses, motor homes, and other special purpose heavy duty motor vehicles for highway use are classified in Industry 336120, Heavy Duty Truck Manufacturing.

336212 Truck Trailer Manufacturing^{CAN}

This U.S. industry comprises establishments primarily engaged in manufacturing truck trailers, truck trailer chassis, cargo container chassis, detachable trailer bodies, and detachable trailer chassis for sale separately.

US—United States industry only. CAN—United States and Canadian industries are comparable. MEX—United States and Mexican industries are comparable. Blank—Canadian, Mexican, and United States industries are comparable.

http://www.census.gov/naics

Cross-References.

Establishments primarily engaged in manufacturing utility trailers, light-truck trailers, and travel trailers are classified in U.S. Industry 336214, Travel Trailer and Camper Manufacturing.

336213 Motor Home Manufacturing[US]

This U.S. industry comprises establishments primarily engaged in (1) manufacturing motor homes on purchased chassis and/or (2) manufacturing conversion vans on an assembly line basis. Motor homes are units where the motor and the living quarters are integrated in the same unit.

Cross-References. Establishments primarily engaged in—

- Manufacturing light duty motor homes chassis and assembling complete motor homes—are classified in U.S. Industry 336112, Light Truck and Utility Vehicle Manufacturing;

- Customizing automotive vehicle and trailer interiors (i.e., van conversions) on an individual basis—are classified in U.S. Industry 811121, Automotive Body, Paint, and Interior Repair and Maintenance; and

- Producing manufactured homes (i.e., mobile homes)—are classified in U.S. Industry 321991, Manufactured Home (Mobile Home) Manufacturing.

336214 Travel Trailer and Camper Manufacturing[US]

This U.S. industry comprises establishments primarily engaged in one or more of the following: (1) manufacturing travel trailers and campers designed to attach to motor vehicles; (2) manufacturing pickup coaches (i.e., campers) and caps (i.e., covers) for mounting on pickup trucks; and (3) manufacturing automobile, utility and light-truck trailers. Travel trailers do not have their own motor but are designed to be towed by a motor unit, such as an automobile or a light truck.

Illustrative Examples:

Automobile transporter trailers, single car, manufacturing
Travel trailers, recreational, manufacturing
Camping trailers and chassis manufacturing

Utility trailers manufacturing
Horse trailers (except fifth wheel type) manufacturing

Cross-References.

Establishments primarily engaged in making manufactured homes (i.e., mobile homes) designed to accept permanent water, sewer, and utility connections and equipped with wheels, but not intended for regular highway use, are classified in U.S. Industry 321991, Manufactured Home (Mobile Home) Manufacturing.

3363 Motor Vehicle Parts Manufacturing

33631 Motor Vehicle Gasoline Engine and Engine Parts Manufacturing

This industry comprises establishments primarily engaged in manufacturing and/ or rebuilding motor vehicle gasoline engines, and engine parts, whether or not for vehicular use.

Illustrative Examples:

Carburetors, all types, manufacturing

Pistons and piston rings
  manufacturing

Crankshaft assemblies, automotive and
  truck gasoline engine, manufacturing

Pumps (e.g., fuel, oil, water), mechanical
  automotive and truck gasoline engine
  (except power steering), manufacturing

Cylinder heads, automotive and truck
  gasoline engine, manufacturing

Timing gears and chains, automotive and
  truck gasoline engine, manufacturing

Fuel injection systems and parts,
  automotive and truck gasoline engine,
  manufacturing

Valves, engine, intake and exhaust,
  manufacturing

Manifolds (i.e., intake and exhaust),
  automotive and truck gasoline engine,
  manufacturing

Cross-References. Establishments primarily engaged in—

- Manufacturing wiring harnesses and other vehicular electrical and electronic equipment—are classified in Industry 33632, Motor Vehicle Electrical and Electronic Equipment Manufacturing;

- Manufacturing transmission and power train equipment—are classified in Industry 33635, Motor Vehicle Transmission and Power Train Parts Manufacturing;

- Manufacturing radiators—are classified in Industry 33639, Other Motor Vehicle Parts Manufacturing;

- Manufacturing steering and suspension components—are classified in Industry 33633, Motor Vehicle Steering and Suspension Components (except Spring) Manufacturing;

- Manufacturing parts for machine repair and equipment parts (except electric) on a job or shop basis—are classified in Industry 33271, Machine Shops;

- Manufacturing rubber and plastic belts and hoses without fittings—are classified in Industry 32622, Rubber and Plastics Hoses and Belting Manufacturing; and

---

- Manufacturing stationary and diesel engines—are classified in Industry 33361, Engine, Turbine, and Power Transmission Equipment Manufacturing.

336311 Carburetor, Piston, Piston Ring, and Valve Manufacturing[US]

This U.S. industry comprises establishments primarily engaged in manufacturing and/or rebuilding carburetors, pistons, piston rings, and engine intake and exhaust valves.

Cross-References.

Establishments primarily engaged in manufacturing parts for machine repair and equipment parts (except electric) on a job or shop basis are classified in Industry 332710, Machine Shops.

336312 Gasoline Engine and Engine Parts Manufacturing[US]

This U.S. industry comprises establishments primarily engaged in manufacturing and/or rebuilding gasoline motor vehicle engines and gasoline motor vehicle engine parts, excluding carburetors, pistons, piston rings, and valves.

Illustrative Examples:

Crankshaft assemblies, automotive and truck gasoline engine, manufacturing

Positive crankcase ventilation (PCV) valves, engine, manufacturing

Flywheels and ring gears, automotive and truck gasoline engine, manufacturing

Pumps (e.g., fuel, oil, water), mechanical, automotive and truck gasoline engine (except power steering), manufacturing

Fuel injection systems and parts, automotive and truck gasoline engine, manufacturing

Timing gears and chains, automotive and truck gasoline engine, manufacturing

Manifolds (i.e., intake and exhaust), automotive and truck gasoline engine, manufacturing

Cross-References. Establishments primarily engaged in—

- Manufacturing carburetors, pistons, piston rings, and valves—are classified in U.S. Industry 336311, Carburetor, Piston, Piston Ring, and Valve Manufacturing;

- Manufacturing wiring harnesses and other vehicular electrical and electronic equipment—are classified in U.S. Industry 336322, Other Motor Vehicle Electrical and Electronic Equipment Manufacturing;

US—United States industry only. CAN—United States and Canadian industries are comparable. MEX—United States and Mexican industries are comparable. Blank—Canadian, Mexican, and United States industries are comparable.

- Manufacturing transmission and power train equipment—are classified in Industry 336350, Motor Vehicle Transmission and Power Train Parts Manufacturing;

- Manufacturing radiators—are classified in U.S. Industry 336399, All Other Motor Vehicle Parts Manufacturing;

- Manufacturing steering and suspension components—are classified in Industry 336330, Motor Vehicle Steering and Suspension Components (except Spring) Manufacturing;

- Manufacturing rubber and plastic belts and hoses without fittings—are classified in Industry 326220, Rubber and Plastics Hoses and Belting Manufacturing; and

- Manufacturing stationary and diesel engines—are classified in U.S. Industry 333618, Other Engine Equipment Manufacturing.

33632 Motor Vehicle Electrical and Electronic Equipment Manufacturing

This industry comprises establishments primarily engaged in (1) manufacturing vehicular lighting and/or (2) manufacturing and/or rebuilding motor vehicle electrical and electronic equipment. The products made can be used for all types of transportation equipment (i.e., aircraft, automobiles, trains, ships).

Illustrative Examples:

Alternators and generators for internal combustion engines manufacturing
Generators for internal combustion engines manufacturing
Automotive lighting fixtures manufacturing
Ignition wiring harness for internal combustion engines manufacturing
Coils, ignition, internal combustion engines, manufacturing
Instrument control panels (i.e., assembling purchased gauges), automotive, truck, and bus, manufacturing

Distributors for internal combustion engines manufacturing
Spark plugs for internal combustion engines manufacturing
Electrical ignition cable sets for internal combustion engines manufacturing
Windshield washer pumps, automotive, truck, and bus, manufacturing

Cross-References. Establishments primarily engaged in—

- Manufacturing automotive lamps—are classified in Industry 33511, Electric Lamp Bulb and Part Manufacturing;

- Manufacturing batteries—are classified in Industry 33591, Battery Manufacturing;
- Manufacturing electric motors for motor vehicles (including electric vehicles)—are classified in Industry 33531, Electrical Equipment Manufacturing;
- Manufacturing railway traffic control signals and passenger car alarms—are classified in Industry 33429, Other Communications Equipment Manufacturing; and
- Manufacturing car stereos—are classified in Industry 33431, Audio and Video Equipment Manufacturing.

336321 Vehicular Lighting Equipment Manufacturing[US]

This U.S. industry comprises establishments primarily engaged in manufacturing vehicular lighting fixtures.

Cross-References.

Establishments primarily engaged in manufacturing automotive lamps (i.e., bulbs) are classified in Industry 335110, Electric Lamp Bulb and Part Manufacturing.

336322 Other Motor Vehicle Electrical and Electronic Equipment Manufacturing[US]

This U.S. industry comprises establishments primarily engaged in manufacturing and/or rebuilding electrical and electronic equipment for motor vehicles and internal combustion engines.

Illustrative Examples:

Alternators and generators for internal combustion engines manufacturing

Ignition wiring harness for internal combustion engines manufacturing

Coils, ignition, internal combustion engines, manufacturing

Instrument control panel (i.e., assembling purchased gauges), automotive, truck, and bus, manufacturing

Distributors for internal combustion engines manufacturing

Spark plugs for internal combustion engines manufacturing

Electrical ignition cable sets for internal combustion engines manufacturing

Windshield washer pumps, automotive, truck, and bus, manufacturing

Generators for internal combustion engines manufacturing

Cross-References. Establishments primarily engaged in—

- Manufacturing vehicular lighting equipment—are classified in U.S. **Industry 336321, Vehicular Lighting Equipment Manufacturing;**

- Manufacturing automotive lamps—are classified in **Industry 335110, Electric Lamp Bulb and Part Manufacturing;**

- Manufacturing batteries—are classified in U.S. **Industry 335911, Storage Battery Manufacturing;**

- Manufacturing electric motors for electric vehicles—are classified in U.S. **Industry 335312, Motor and Generator Manufacturing;**

- Manufacturing railway traffic control signals and passenger car alarms— are classified in **Industry 334290, Other Communications Equipment Manufacturing; and**

- Manufacturing car stereos—are classified in **Industry 334310, Audio and Video Equipment Manufacturing.**

33633 Motor Vehicle Steering and Suspension Components (except Spring) Manufacturing
See industry description for 336330 below.

336330 Motor Vehicle Steering and Suspension Components (except Spring) Manufacturing

This industry comprises establishments primarily engaged in manufacturing and/ or rebuilding motor vehicle steering mechanisms and suspension components (except springs).

Illustrative Examples:

Rack and pinion steering assemblies manufacturing

Steering wheels, automotive, truck, and bus, manufacturing

Shock absorbers, automotive, truck, and bus, manufacturing

Struts, automotive, truck, and bus, manufacturing

Steering columns, automotive, truck, and bus, manufacturing

Cross-References.

Establishments primarily engaged in manufacturing springs are classified in Industry 33261, Spring and Wire Product Manufacturing.

33634 Motor Vehicle Brake System Manufacturing
See industry description for 336340 below.

US—United States industry only. CAN—United States and Canadian industries are comparable. MEX—United States and Mexican industries are comparable. Blank—Canadian, Mexican, and United States industries are comparable.

336340 Motor Vehicle Brake System Manufacturing

This industry comprises establishments primarily engaged in manufacturing and/or rebuilding motor vehicle brake systems and related components.

Illustrative Examples:

Brake cylinders, master and wheel, automotive, truck, and bus, manufacturing

Brake pads and shoes, automotive, truck, and bus, manufacturing

Brake drums, automotive, truck, and bus, manufacturing

Calipers, brake, automotive, truck, and bus, manufacturing

Brake hose assemblies manufacturing

Cross-References.

Establishments primarily engaged in manufacturing rubber and plastics belts and hoses without fittings are classified in Industry 326220, Rubber and Plastics Hoses and Belting Manufacturing.

33635 Motor Vehicle Transmission and Power Train Parts Manufacturing
See industry description for 336350 below.

336350 Motor Vehicle Transmission and Power Train Parts Manufacturing

This industry comprises establishments primarily engaged in manufacturing and/or rebuilding motor vehicle transmissions and power train parts.

Illustrative Examples:

Automatic transmissions, automotive, truck, and bus, manufacturing

Differential and rear axle assemblies, automotive, truck, and bus, manufacturing

Axle bearings, automotive, truck, and bus, manufacturing

Torque converters, automotive, truck, and bus, manufacturing

Constant velocity joints, automotive, truck, and bus, manufacturing

Universal joints, automotive, truck, and bus, manufacturing

33636 Motor Vehicle Seating and Interior Trim Manufacturing
See industry description for 336360 below.

336360 Motor Vehicle Seating and Interior Trim Manufacturing

This industry comprises establishments primarily engaged in manufacturing motor vehicle seating, seats, seat frames, seat belts, and interior trimmings.

US—United States industry only. CAN—United States and Canadian industries are comparable. MEX—United States and Mexican industries are comparable. Blank—Canadian, Mexican, and United States industries are comparable.

Cross-References.

Establishments primarily engaged in manufacturing convertible tops for vehicles and those manufacturing air bags are classified in U.S. Industry 336399, **All Other** Motor Vehicle Parts Manufacturing.

33637   Motor Vehicle Metal Stamping

See industry description for 336370 below.

336370   Motor Vehicle Metal Stamping

This industry comprises establishments primarily engaged in manufacturing motor vehicle stampings, such as fenders, tops, body parts, trim, and molding.

Cross-References. Establishments primarily engaged in—

- Manufacturing stampings and further processing the stampings—are classified according to the process of the specific product made; and

- Manufacturing stampings (except motor vehicle)—are classified in U.S. Industry 332116, Metal Stamping.

33639   Other Motor Vehicle Parts Manufacturing

This industry comprises establishments primarily engaged in manufacturing and/ or rebuilding motor vehicle parts and accessories (except motor vehicle gasoline engines and engine parts, motor vehicle electrical and electronic equipment, motor vehicle steering and suspension components, motor vehicle brake systems, motor vehicle transmissions and power train parts, motor vehicle seating and interior trim, and motor vehicle stampings).

Illustrative Examples:

Air bag assemblies manufacturing
Mufflers and resonators, motor vehicle, manufacturing
Air-conditioners, motor vehicle, manufacturing
Radiators and cores manufacturing

Catalytic converters, engine exhaust, automotive, truck, and bus, manufacturing
Wheels (i.e., rims), automotive, truck, and bus, manufacturing

Cross-References. Establishments primarily engaged in—

- Manufacturing motor vehicle gasoline engines and engine parts—are classified in Industry 33631, Motor Vehicle Gasoline Engine and Engine Parts Manufacturing;

- Manufacturing motor vehicle electrical and electronic equipment—are classified in Industry 33632, Motor Vehicle Electrical and Electronic Equipment Manufacturing;

- Manufacturing motor vehicle steering and suspension components—are classified in Industry 33633, Motor Vehicle Steering and Suspension Components (except Spring) Manufacturing;

- Manufacturing motor vehicle brake systems—are classified in Industry 33634, Motor Vehicle Brake System Manufacturing;

- Manufacturing motor vehicle transmissions and power train parts—are classified in Industry 33635, Motor Vehicle Transmission and Power Train Parts Manufacturing;

- Manufacturing motor vehicle seating and interior trim—are classified in Industry 33636, Motor Vehicle Seating and Interior Trim Manufacturing;

- Manufacturing motor vehicle stampings—are classified in Industry 33637, Motor Vehicle Metal Stamping; and

- Manufacturing air-conditioning systems and compressors (except motor vehicle air-conditioning systems)—are classified in Industry 33341, Ventilation, Heating, Air-Conditioning, and Commercial Refrigeration Equipment Manufacturing.

336391 Motor Vehicle Air-Conditioning Manufacturing[US]

This U.S. industry comprises establishments primarily engaged in manufacturing air-conditioning systems and compressors for motor vehicles, such as automobiles, trucks, buses, aircraft, farm machinery, construction machinery, and other related vehicles.

Cross-References.

Establishments primarily engaged in manufacturing air-conditioning systems and compressors (except motor vehicle air-conditioning systems) are classified in U.S. Industry 333415, Air-Conditioning and Warm Air Heating Equipment and Commercial and Industrial Refrigeration Equipment Manufacturing.

336399 All Other Motor Vehicle Parts Manufacturing[US]

This U.S. industry comprises establishments primarily engaged in manufacturing and/or rebuilding motor vehicle parts and accessories (except motor vehicle gasoline engines and engine parts, motor vehicle electrical and electronic equipment, motor vehicle steering and suspension components, motor vehicle brake systems,

---

US—United States industry only. CAN—United States and Canadian industries are comparable. MEX—United States and Mexican industries are comparable. Blank—Canadian, Mexican, and United States industries are comparable.

motor vehicle transmissions and power train parts, motor vehicle seating and interior trim, motor vehicle stampings, and motor vehicle air-conditioning systems and compressors).

Illustrative Examples:

Air bag assemblies manufacturing

Mufflers and resonators, motor vehicle, manufacturing

Air-filters, automotive, truck, and bus, manufacturing

Radiators and cores manufacturing

Catalytic converters, engine exhaust, automotive, truck, and bus, manufacturing

Wheels (i.e., rims), automotive, truck, and bus, manufacturing

Cross-References. Establishments primarily engaged in—

- Manufacturing motor vehicle gasoline engines and engine parts—are classified in Industry 33631, Motor Vehicle Gasoline Engine and Engine Parts Manufacturing;

- Manufacturing motor vehicle electrical and electronic equipment—are classified in Industry 33632, Motor Vehicle Electrical and Electronic Equipment Manufacturing;

- Manufacturing motor vehicle steering and suspension components—are classified in Industry 336330, Motor Vehicle Steering and Suspension Components (except Spring) Manufacturing;

- Manufacturing motor vehicle brake systems—are classified in Industry 336340, Motor Vehicle Brake System Manufacturing;

- Manufacturing motor vehicle transmissions and power train parts—are classified in Industry 336350, Motor Vehicle Transmission and Power Train Parts Manufacturing;

- Manufacturing motor vehicle seating and interior trim—are classified in Industry 336360, Motor Vehicle Seating and Interior Trim Manufacturing;

- Manufacturing motor vehicle stampings—are classified in Industry 336370, Motor Vehicle Metal Stamping; and

- Manufacturing motor vehicle air-conditioning systems and compressors—are classified in U.S. Industry 336391, Motor Vehicle Air-Conditioning Manufacturing.

3364   Aerospace Product and Parts Manufacturing

33641   Aerospace Product and Parts Manufacturing

This industry comprises establishments primarily engaged in one or more of the following: (1) manufacturing complete aircraft, missiles, or space vehicles;

(2) manufacturing aerospace engines, propulsion units, auxiliary equipment or parts; (3) developing and making prototypes of aerospace products; (4) aircraft conversion (i.e., major modifications to systems); and (5) complete aircraft or propulsion systems overhaul and rebuilding (i.e., periodic restoration of aircraft to original design specifications).

Cross-References.

- Establishments primarily engaged in manufacturing space satellites are classified in Industry 33422, Radio and Television Broadcasting and Wireless Communications Equipment Manufacturing;

- Establishments primarily engaged in the repair of aircraft or aircraft engines (except overhauling, conversion, and rebuilding) are classified in Industry 48819, Other Support Activities for Air Transportation;

- Research and development establishments primarily engaged in aerospace R&D (except prototype production) are classified in Industry 54171, Research and Development in the Physical, Engineering, and Life Sciences;

- Establishments primarily engaged in manufacturing aircraft engine intake and exhaust valves, pistons, or engine filters are classified in Industry 33631, Motor Vehicle Gasoline Engine and Engine Parts Manufacturing;

- Establishments primarily engaged in manufacturing of aircraft seating are classified in Industry 33636, Motor Vehicle Seating and Interior Trim Manufacturing;

- Establishments primarily engaged in manufacturing aeronautical, navigational, and guidance systems and instruments are classified in Industry 33451, Navigational, Measuring, Electromedical, and Control Instruments Manufacturing;

- Establishment primarily engaged in manufacturing aircraft engine electrical (aeronautical electrical) equipment or aircraft lighting fixtures are classified in Industry 33632, Motor Vehicle Electrical and Electronic Equipment Manufacturing; and

- Establishments primarily engaged in manufacturing of aircraft fluid power subassemblies are classified in Industry 33291, Metal Valve Manufacturing.

336411 Aircraft Manufacturing[US]

This U.S. industry comprises establishments primarily engaged in one or more of the following: (1) manufacturing or assembling complete aircraft; (2) developing and making aircraft prototypes; (3) aircraft conversion (i.e., major modifications to systems); and (4) complete aircraft overhaul and rebuilding (i.e., periodic restoration of aircraft to original design specifications).

US—United States industry only. CAN—United States and Canadian industries are comparable. MEX—United States and Mexican industries are comparable. Blank—Canadian, Mexican, and United States industries are comparable.

Cross-References.

- Establishments primarily engaged in manufacturing guided missiles and space vehicles are classified in U.S. Industry 336414, Guided Missile and Space Vehicle Manufacturing;

- Establishments primarily engaged in the repair of aircraft (except overhauling, conversion, and rebuilding) are classified in Industry 488190, Other Support Activities for Air Transportation; and

- Research and development establishments primarily engaged in aircraft R&D (except prototype production) are classified in Industry 541712, Research and Development in the Physical, Engineering, and Life Sciences (except Biotechnology).

336412 Aircraft Engine and Engine Parts Manufacturing[US]

This U.S. industry comprises establishments primarily engaged in one or more of the following: (1) manufacturing aircraft engines and engine parts; (2) developing and making prototypes of aircraft engines and engine parts; (3) aircraft propulsion system conversion (i.e., major modifications to systems); and (4) aircraft propulsion systems overhaul and rebuilding (i.e., periodic restoration of aircraft propulsion system to original design specifications).

Cross-References.

- Establishments primarily engaged in manufacturing guided missile and space vehicle propulsion units and parts are classified in U.S. Industry 336415, Guided Missile and Space Vehicle Propulsion Unit and Propulsion Unit Parts Manufacturing;

- Establishments primarily engaged in manufacturing aircraft intake and exhaust valves and pistons are classified in U.S. Industry 336311, Carburetor, Piston, Piston Ring, and Valve Manufacturing;

- Establishments primarily engaged in manufacturing aircraft internal combustion engine filters are classified in U.S. Industry 336312, Gasoline Engine and Engine Parts Manufacturing;

- Establishments primarily engaged in the repair of aircraft engines (except overhauling, conversion, and rebuilding) are classified in Industry 488190, Other Support Activities for Air Transportation;

- Research and development establishments primarily engaged in aircraft engine and engine parts R&D (except prototype production) are classified in Industry 541712, Research and Development in the Physical, Engineering, and Life Sciences (except Biotechnology); and

---

- Establishments primarily engaged in manufacturing aeronautical instruments are classified in U.S. Industry 334511, Search, Detection, Navigation, Guidance, Aeronautical, and Nautical System and Instrument Manufacturing.

336413 Other Aircraft Parts and Auxiliary Equipment Manufacturing[US]

This U.S. industry comprises establishment primarily engaged in (1) manufacturing aircraft parts or auxiliary equipment (except engines and aircraft fluid power subassemblies) and/or (2) developing and making prototypes of aircraft parts and auxiliary equipment. Auxiliary equipment includes such items as crop dusting apparatus, armament racks, inflight refueling equipment, and external fuel tanks.

Cross-References.

- Establishments primarily engaged in manufacturing aircraft engines and engine parts are classified in U.S. Industry 336412, Aircraft Engine and Engine Parts Manufacturing;
- Establishments primarily engaged in manufacturing aeronautical instruments are classified in U.S. Industry 334511, Search, Detection, Navigation, Guidance, Aeronautical, and Nautical System and Instrument Manufacturing;
- Establishments primarily engaged in manufacturing aircraft lighting fixtures are classified in U.S. Industry 336321, Vehicular Lighting Equipment Manufacturing;
- Establishments primarily engaged in manufacturing aircraft engine electrical (aeronautical electrical) equipment are classified in U.S. Industry 336322, Other Motor Vehicle Electrical and Electronic Equipment Manufacturing;
- Establishments primarily engaged in manufacturing guided missile and space vehicle parts and auxiliary equipment are classified in U.S. Industry 336419, Other Guided Missile and Space Vehicle Parts and Auxiliary Equipment Manufacturing;
- Establishments primarily engaged in manufacturing of aircraft fluid power subassemblies are classified in U.S. Industry 332912, Fluid Power Valve and Hose Fitting Manufacturing;
- Establishments primarily engaged in manufacturing of aircraft seating are classified in Industry 336360, Motor Vehicle Seating and Interior Trim Manufacturing; and

US—United States industry only. CAN—United States and Canadian industries are comparable. MEX—United States and Mexican industries are comparable. Blank—Canadian, Mexican, and United States industries are comparable.

- Research and development establishments primarily engaged in aircraft parts and auxiliary equipment R&D (except prototype production) are classified in Industry 541712, Research and Development in the Physical, Engineering, and Life Sciences (except Biotechnology).

336414 Guided Missile and Space Vehicle Manufacturing[US]

This U.S. industry comprises establishments primarily engaged in (1) manufacturing complete guided missiles and space vehicles and/or (2) developing and making prototypes of guided missiles or space vehicles.

Cross-References.

- Establishments primarily engaged in manufacturing space satellites are classified in Industry 334220, Radio and Television Broadcasting and Wireless Communications Equipment Manufacturing; and
- Research and development establishments primarily engaged in guided missile and space vehicle R&D (except prototype production) are classified in Industry 541712, Research and Development in the Physical, Engineering, and Life Sciences (except Biotechnology).

336415 Guided Missile and Space Vehicle Propulsion Unit and Propulsion Unit Parts Manufacturing[US]

This U.S. industry comprises establishments primarily engaged in (1) manufacturing guided missile and/or space vehicle propulsion units and propulsion unit parts and/or (2) developing and making prototypes of guided missile and space vehicle propulsion units and propulsion unit parts.

Cross-References.

Research and development establishments primarily engaged in guided missile and space propulsion unit and propulsion unit parts R&D (except prototype production) are classified in Industry 541712, Research and Development in the Physical, Engineering, and Life Sciences (except Biotechnology).

336419 Other Guided Missile and Space Vehicle Parts and Auxiliary Equipment Manufacturing[US]

This U.S. Industry comprises establishments primarily engaged in (1) manufacturing guided missile and space vehicle parts and auxiliary equipment (except guided missile and space vehicle propulsion units and propulsion unit parts) and/

US—United States industry only. CAN—United States and Canadian industries are comparable. MEX—United States and Mexican industries are comparable. Blank—Canadian, Mexican, and United States industries are comparable.

http://www.census.gov/nalcs

or (2) developing and making prototypes of guided missile and space vehicle parts and auxiliary equipment.

Cross-References.

- Establishments primarily engaged in manufacturing navigational and guidance systems are classified in U.S. Industry 334511, Search, Detection, Navigation, Guidance, Aeronautical, and Nautical System and Instrument Manufacturing;

- Establishments primarily engaged in manufacturing guided missile and space vehicle propulsion units and propulsion unit parts are classified in U.S. Industry 336415, Guided Missile and Space Vehicle Propulsion Unit and Propulsion Unit Parts Manufacturing; and

- Research and development establishments primarily engaged in guided missile and space vehicle parts and auxiliary equipment R&D (except prototype production) are classified in Industry 541712, Research and Development in the Physical, Engineering, and Life Sciences (except Biotechnology).

3365 Railroad Rolling Stock Manufacturing

33651 Railroad Rolling Stock Manufacturing
See industry description for 336510 below.

336510 Railroad Rolling Stock Manufacturing

This industry comprises establishments primarily engaged in one or more of the following: (1) manufacturing and/or rebuilding locomotives, locomotive frames and parts; (2) manufacturing railroad, street, and rapid transit cars and car equipment for operation on rails for freight and passenger service; and (3) manufacturing rail layers, ballast distributors, rail tamping equipment and other railway track maintenance equipment.

Cross-References.

- Establishments primarily engaged in manufacturing mining rail cars are classified in U.S. Industry 333131, Mining Machinery and Equipment Manufacturing;

- Establishments primarily engaged in manufacturing locomotive fuel lubricating or cooling medium pumps are classified in U.S. Industry 333911, Pump and Pumping Equipment Manufacturing;

- Repair establishments of railroad and local transit companies primarily engaged in repairing railroad and transit cars are classified in Industry 488210, Support Activities for Rail Transportation; and

- Establishments not owned by railroad or local transit companies engaged in repairing railroad cars and locomotive engines are classified in Industry 811310, Commercial and Industrial Machinery and Equipment (except Automotive and Electronic) Repair and Maintenance.

3366 Ship and Boat Building

33661 Ship and Boat Building

This industry comprises establishments primarily engaged in operating shipyards or boat yards (i.e., ship or boat manufacturing facilities). Shipyards are fixed facilities with drydocks and fabrication equipment capable of building a ship, defined as watercraft typically suitable or intended for other than personal or recreational use. Boats are defined as watercraft typically suitable or intended for personal use. Activities of shipyards include the construction of ships, their repair, conversion and alteration, the production of prefabricated ship and barge sections, and specialized services, such as ship scaling.

Illustrative Examples:

Barge building	Rigid inflatable boats (RIBs)
Inflatable rubber boats, heavy-duty,	manufacturing
manufacturing	Drilling and production platforms,
Boat yards (i.e., boat manufacturing	floating, oil and gas, building
facilities)	Rowboats manufacturing
Passenger ship building	Inflatable plastic boats, heavy-duty,
Cargo ship building	manufacturing

Cross-References. Establishments primarily engaged in—

- Manufacturing inflatable rubber swimming pool rafts and similar flotation devices—are classified in Industry 32629, Other Rubber Product Manufacturing;

- Manufacturing inflatable plastic swimming pool rafts and similar flotation devices—are classified in Industry 32619, Other Plastics Product Manufacturing;

- Fabricating structural assemblies or components for ships, or subcontractors engaged in ship painting, joinery, carpentry work, and electrical wiring installation—are classified based on the production process used; and

- Ship repairs performed in floating drydocks—are classified in Industry 48839, Other Support Activities for Water Transportation.

US—United States industry only. CAN—United States and Canadian industries are comparable. MEX—United States and Mexican industries are comparable. Blank—Canadian, Mexican, and United States industries are comparable.

336611 Ship Building and Repairing^{CAN}

This U.S. industry comprises establishments primarily engaged in operating a shipyard. Shipyards are fixed facilities with drydocks and fabrication equipment capable of building a ship, defined as watercraft typically suitable or intended for other than personal or recreational use. Activities of shipyards include the construction of ships, their repair, conversion and alteration, the production of prefabricated ship and barge sections, and specialized services, such as ship scaling.

Illustrative Examples:

Barge building
Passenger ship building
Cargo ship building

Submarine building
Drilling and production platforms, floating, oil and gas, building

Cross-References. Establishments primarily engaged in—

- Fabricating structural assemblies or components for ships, or subcontractors engaged in ship painting, joinery, carpentry work, and electrical wiring installation—are classified based on the production process used; and

- Ship repairs performed in floating drydocks—are classified in Industry 488390, Other Support Activities for Water Transportation.

336612 Boat Building^{CAN}

This U.S. industry comprises establishments primarily engaged in building boats. Boats are defined as watercraft not built in shipyards and typically of the type suitable or intended for personal use. Included in this industry are establishments that manufacture heavy-duty inflatable rubber or inflatable plastic boats (RIBs).

Illustrative Examples:

Dinghy (except inflatable rubber) manufacturing
Rigid inflatable boats (RIBs) manufacturing
Inflatable plastic boats, heavy-duty, manufacturing
Rowboats manufacturing

Inflatable rubber boats, heavy-duty, manufacturing
Sailboat building, not done in shipyards
Motorboats, inboard or outboard, building
Yacht building, not done in shipyards

Cross-References. Establishments primarily engaged in—

- Ship building or ship repairs performed in a shipyard—are classified in U.S. Industry 336611, Ship Building and Repairing;

- Manufacturing inflatable rubber swimming pool rafts and similar flotation devices—are classified in Industry 326299, All Other Rubber Product Manufacturing; and

- Manufacturing inflatable plastic swimming pool rafts and similar flotation devices—are classified in Industry 326199, All Other Plastics Product Manufacturing.

3369 Other Transportation Equipment Manufacturing

This industry group comprises establishments primarily engaged in manufacturing transportation equipment (except motor vehicles and parts, aerospace products and parts, railroad rolling stock, ship building, and boat manufacturing).

33699 Other Transportation Equipment Manufacturing

This industry comprises establishments primarily engaged in manufacturing motorcycles, bicycles, metal tricycles, complete military armored vehicles, tanks, self-propelled weapons, vehicles pulled by draft animals, and other transportation equipment (except motor vehicles, boats, ships, railroad rolling stock, and aerospace products), including parts thereof.

Cross-References. Establishments primarily engaged in—

- Manufacturing ships and boats—are classified in Industry 33661, Ship and Boat Building;

- Manufacturing aerospace products and parts—are classified in Industry 33641, Aerospace Product and Parts Manufacturing;

- Manufacturing motor vehicle parts—are classified in Industry Group 3363, Motor Vehicle Parts Manufacturing;

- Manufacturing children's vehicles (except bicycles and metal tricycles)—are classified in Industry 33993, Doll, Toy, and Game Manufacturing;

- Manufacturing railroad rolling stock—are classified in Industry 33651, Railroad Rolling Stock Manufacturing; and

- Manufacturing motor vehicles—are classified in Industry Group 3361, Motor Vehicle Manufacturing.

336991 Motorcycle, Bicycle, and Parts Manufacturing[US]

This U.S. industry comprises establishments primarily engaged in manufacturing motorcycles, bicycles, tricycles and similar equipment, and parts.

US—United States industry only. CAN—United States and Canadian industries are comparable. MEX—United States and Mexican industries are comparable. Blank—Canadian, Mexican, and United States industries are comparable.

Cross-References. Establishments primarily engaged in—

- Manufacturing children's vehicles (except bicycles and metal tricycles)—are classified in U.S. Industry 339932, Game, Toy, and Children's Vehicle Manufacturing; and

- Manufacturing golf carts and other similar personnel carriers—are classified in U.S. Industry 336999, All Other Transportation Equipment Manufacturing.

336992 Military Armored Vehicle, Tank, and Tank Component Manufacturing[US]

This U.S. industry comprises establishments primarily engaged in manufacturing complete military armored vehicles, combat tanks, specialized components for combat tanks, and self-propelled weapons.

Cross-References.

Establishments primarily engaged in manufacturing nonarmored military universal carriers are classified in U.S. Industry 336112, Light Truck and Utility Vehicle Manufacturing.

336999 All Other Transportation Equipment Manufacturing[US]

This U.S. industry comprises establishments primarily engaged in manufacturing transportation equipment (except motor vehicles, motor vehicle parts, boats, ships, railroad rolling stock, aerospace products, motorcycles, bicycles, armored vehicles and tanks).

Illustrative Examples:

All-terrain vehicles (ATVs), wheeled or tracked, manufacturing
Golf carts and similar motorized passenger carriers manufacturing
Animal-drawn vehicles and parts manufacturing
Race cars manufacturing
Gocarts (except children's) manufacturing
Snowmobiles and parts manufacturing

Cross-References. Establishments primarily engaged in—

- Manufacturing motorcycles, bicycles and parts—are classified in U.S. Industry 336991, Motorcycle, Bicycle, and Parts Manufacturing;

- Manufacturing military armored vehicles, tanks, and tank components—are classified in U.S. Industry 336992, Military Armored Vehicle, Tank, and Tank Component Manufacturing;

US—United States industry only. CAN—United States and Canadian industries are comparable. MEX—United States and Mexican industries are comparable. Blank—Canadian, Mexican, and United States industries are comparable.

- Manufacturing ships and boats—are classified in Industry 33661, Ship and Boat Building;

- Manufacturing aerospace products and parts—are classified in Industry 33641, Aerospace Product and Parts Manufacturing;

- Manufacturing motor vehicle parts—are classified in Industry Group 3363, Motor Vehicle Parts Manufacturing;

- Manufacturing railroad rolling stock—are classified in Industry 336510, Railroad Rolling Stock Manufacturing; and

- Manufacturing motor vehicles—are classified in Industry Group 3361, Motor Vehicle Manufacturing.

337 Furniture and Related Product Manufacturing

Industries in the Furniture and Related Product Manufacturing subsector make furniture and related articles, such as mattresses, window blinds, cabinets, and fixtures. The processes used in the manufacture of furniture include the cutting, bending, molding, laminating, and assembly of such materials as wood, metal, glass, plastics, and rattan. However, the production process for furniture is not solely bending metal, cutting and shaping wood, or extruding and molding plastics. Design and fashion trends play an important part in the production of furniture. The integrated design of the article for both esthetic and functional qualities is also a major part of the process of manufacturing furniture. Design services may be performed by the furniture establishment's work force or may be purchased from industrial designers.

Furniture may be made of any material, but the most common ones used in North America are metal and wood. Furniture manufacturing establishments may specialize in making articles primarily from one material. Some of the equipment required to make a wooden table, for example, is different from that used to make a metal one. However, furniture is usually made from several materials. A wooden table might have metal brackets, and a wooden chair a fabric or plastics seat. Therefore, in NAICS, furniture initially is classified based on the type of furniture (application for which it is designed) rather than the material used. For example, an upholstered sofa is treated as household furniture, although it may also be used in hotels or offices.

When classifying furniture according to the component material from which it is made, furniture made from more than one material is classified based on the material used in the frame, or if there is no frame, the predominant component material. Upholstered household furniture (excluding kitchen and dining room chairs with upholstered seats) is classified without regard to the frame material. Kitchen or dining room chairs with upholstered seats are classified according to the frame material.

Furniture may be made on a stock or custom basis and may be shipped assembled or unassembled (i.e., knockdown). The manufacture of furniture parts and frames is included in this subsector.

Some of the processes used in furniture manufacturing are similar to processes that are used in other segments of manufacturing. For example, cutting and assembly occurs in the production of wood trusses that are classified in Subsector 321, Wood Product Manufacturing. However, the multiple processes that distinguish wood furniture manufacturing from wood product manufacturing warrant inclusion of wooden furniture manufacturing in the Furniture and Related Product Manufacturing subsector. Metal furniture manufacturing uses techniques that are also employed in the manufacturing of roll-formed products classified in Subsector 332, Fabricated Metal Product Manufacturing. The molding process for plastics furniture is similar to the molding of other plastics products. However, plastics furniture producing establishments tend to specialize in furniture.

NAICS attempts to keep furniture manufacturing together, but there are two notable exceptions: seating for transportation equipment and specialized hospital furniture (e.g., hospital beds and operating tables). These exceptions are related to the fact that some of the aspects of the production process for these products, primarily the design, are highly integrated with the other manufactured goods, namely motor vehicles and health equipment.

3371 Household and Institutional Furniture and Kitchen Cabinet Manufacturing

This industry group comprises establishments manufacturing household-type furniture, such as living room, kitchen and bedroom furniture and institutional (i.e., public building) furniture, such as furniture for schools, theaters, and churches.

33711 Wood Kitchen Cabinet and Countertop Manufacturing
See industry description for 337110 below.

337110 Wood Kitchen Cabinet and Countertop Manufacturing

This industry comprises establishments primarily engaged in manufacturing wood or plastics laminated on wood kitchen cabinets, bathroom vanities, and countertops (except freestanding). The cabinets and counters may be made on a stock or custom basis.

Cross-References. Establishments primarily engaged in—

* Manufacturing metal kitchen and bathroom cabinets (except freestanding)—are classified in U.S. Industry 337124, Metal Household Furniture Manufacturing;

US—United States industry only. CAN—United States and Canadian industries are comparable. MEX—United States and Mexican industries are comparable. Blank—Canadian, Mexican, and United States industries are comparable.

- Manufacturing plastics countertops—are classified in U.S. Industry 326199, All Other Plastics Product Manufacturing;

- Manufacturing stone countertops—are classified in U.S. Industry 327991, Cut Stone and Stone Product Manufacturing; and

- Manufacturing wood or plastics laminated on wood countertops (except kitchen and bathroom)—are classified in U.S. Industry 337215, Showcase, Partition, Shelving, and Locker Manufacturing.

33712 Household and Institutional Furniture Manufacturing

This industry comprises establishments primarily engaged in manufacturing household-type and public building furniture (i.e., library, school, theater, and church furniture). This industry includes establishments that manufacture general purpose hospital, laboratory and/or dental furniture (e.g., stools, tables, benches). The furniture may be made on a stock or custom basis and may be assembled or unassembled (i.e., knockdown).

Cross-References. Establishments primarily engaged in—

- Manufacturing specialized hospital and/or dental furniture (e.g., hospital beds, operating tables, dental chairs)—are classified in Industry 33911, Medical Equipment and Supplies Manufacturing;

- Manufacturing wood or plastics laminated on wood kitchen cabinets, bathroom vanities, and countertops (except freestanding)—are classified in Industry 33711, Wood Kitchen Cabinet and Countertop Manufacturing;

- Manufacturing office-type furniture and/or office or store fixtures—are classified in Industry 33721, Office Furniture (including Fixtures) Manufacturing; and

- Repairing or refinishing furniture—are classified in Industry 81142, Reupholstery and Furniture Repair.

337121 Upholstered Household Furniture Manufacturing[CAN]

This U.S. industry comprises establishments primarily engaged in manufacturing upholstered household-type furniture. The furniture may be made on a stock or custom basis.

Cross-References. Establishments primarily engaged in—

- Reupholstering furniture or upholstering frames to individual order—are classified in Industry 811420, Reupholstery and Furniture Repair;

- Manufacturing wood kitchen and dining room chairs with upholstered seats or backs—are classified in U. S. Industry 337122, Nonupholstered Wood Household Furniture Manufacturing;

- Manufacturing metal kitchen and dining room chairs with upholstered seats or backs—are classified in U.S. Industry 337124, Metal Household Furniture Manufacturing; and

- Manufacturing kitchen and dining room chairs (except wood and metal) with upholstered seats or backs—are classified in U.S. Industry 337125, Household Furniture (except Wood and Metal) Manufacturing.

337122 Nonupholstered Wood Household Furniture Manufacturing[US]

This U.S. industry comprises establishments primarily engaged in manufacturing nonupholstered wood household-type furniture and freestanding cabinets (except television, radio, and sewing machine cabinets). The furniture may be made on a stock or custom basis and may be assembled or unassembled (i.e., knockdown).

Cross-References. Establishments primarily engaged in—

- Manufacturing reed, rattan, plastics and similar furniture—are classified in U.S. Industry 337125, Household Furniture (except Wood and Metal) Manufacturing;

- Manufacturing wood or plastics laminated on wood kitchen cabinets, bathroom vanities, and countertops (except freestanding)—are classified in Industry 337110, Wood Kitchen Cabinet and Countertop Manufacturing;

- Manufacturing wood television, stereo, loudspeaker, and sewing machine cabinets (i.e., housings)—are classified in U.S. Industry 337129, Wood Television, Radio, and Sewing Machine Cabinet Manufacturing; and

- Repairing or refinishing furniture—are classified in Industry 811420, Reupholstery and Furniture Repair.

337124 Metal Household Furniture Manufacturing[US]

This U.S. industry comprises establishments primarily engaged in manufacturing metal household-type furniture and freestanding cabinets. The furniture may be made on a stock or custom basis and may be assembled or unassembled (i.e., knockdown).

Cross-References.

Establishments primarily engaged in manufacturing specialized metal hospital furniture including beds are classified in Industry 33911, Medical Equipment and Supplies Manufacturing.

337125 Household Furniture (except Wood and Metal) Manufacturing[US]

This U.S. industry comprises establishments primarily engaged in manufacturing household-type furniture of materials other than wood or metal, such as plastics, reed, rattan, wicker, and fiberglass. The furniture may be made on a stock or custom basis and may be assembled or unassembled (i.e., knockdown).

Cross-References. Establishments primarily engaged in—

* Manufacturing concrete, ceramic, or stone furniture—are classified in Subsector 327, Nonmetallic Mineral Product Manufacturing, according to the materials used;

* Manufacturing upholstered household-type furniture—are classified in U.S. Industry 337121, Upholstered Household Furniture Manufacturing;

* Manufacturing metal household-type furniture—are classified in U.S. Industry 337124, Metal Household Furniture Manufacturing; and

* Manufacturing nonupholstered wood household-type furniture—are classified in U.S. Industry 337122, Nonupholstered Wood Household Furniture Manufacturing.

337127 Institutional Furniture Manufacturing[CAN]

This U.S. industry comprises establishments primarily engaged in manufacturing institutional-type furniture (e.g., library, school, theater, and church furniture). Included in this industry are establishments primarily engaged in manufacturing general purpose hospital, laboratory, and dental furniture (e.g., tables, stools, and benches). The furniture may be made on a stock or custom basis and may be assembled or unassembled (i.e., knockdown).

Cross-References. Establishments primarily engaged in—

* Manufacturing specialized hospital furniture (e.g., hospital beds, operating tables)—are classified in U.S. Industry 339113, Surgical Appliance and Supplies Manufacturing;

* Manufacturing specialized dental furniture (e.g., dental chairs)—are classified in U.S. Industry 339114, Dental Equipment and Supplies Manufacturing;

US—United States industry only. CAN—United States and Canadian industries are comparable. MEX—United States and Mexican industries are comparable. Blank—Canadian, Mexican, and United States industries are comparable.

- Manufacturing wood kitchen cabinets, wood bathroom vanities, and countertops designed for permanent installation—are classified in Industry 337110, Wood Kitchen Cabinet and Countertop Manufacturing;

- Manufacturing office-type furniture and/or office or store fixtures—are classified in Industry 33721, Office Furniture (including Fixtures) Manufacturing; and

- Repairing or refinishing furniture—are classified in Industry 811420, Reupholstery and Furniture Repair.

337129 Wood Television, Radio, and Sewing Machine Cabinet Manufacturing^{US}

This U.S. industry comprises establishments primarily engaged in manufacturing wood cabinets used as housings by television, stereo, loudspeaker, and sewing machine manufacturers.

Cross-References. Establishments primarily engaged in—

- Manufacturing plastics housings used by television, stereo, loudspeaker, and sewing machine manufacturers—are classified in U.S. Industry 326199, All Other Plastics Product Manufacturing;

- Manufacturing metal housings used by television, stereo, loudspeaker, and sewing machine manufacturers—are classified in U.S. Industry 332322, Sheet Metal Work Manufacturing;

- Manufacturing freestanding wood household-type cabinets (e.g., entertainment centers, stands) for consumer electronics—are classified in U.S. Industry 337122, Nonupholstered Wood Household Furniture Manufacturing;

- Manufacturing freestanding metal household-type cabinets (e.g., entertainment centers, stands) for consumer electronics—are classified in U.S. Industry 337124, Metal Household Furniture Manufacturing; and

- Manufacturing freestanding household-type cabinets (e.g., entertainment centers, stands) (except wood and metal) for consumer electronics—are classified in U.S. Industry 337125, Household Furniture (except Wood and Metal) Manufacturing.

3372 Office Furniture (including Fixtures) Manufacturing

33721 Office Furniture (including Fixtures) Manufacturing

This industry comprises establishments primarily engaged in manufacturing office furniture and/or office and store fixtures. The furniture may be made on a stock or custom basis and may be assembled or unassembled (i.e., knockdown).

US—United States industry only. CAN—United States and Canadian industries are comparable. MEX—United States and Mexican industries are comparable. Blank—Canadian, Mexican, and United States industries are comparable.

Cross-References. Establishments primarily engaged in—

- Manufacturing millwork on a factory basis—are classified in Industry 32191, Millwork;

- Manufacturing household-type and institutional-type furniture—are classified in Industry 33712, Household and Institutional Furniture Manufacturing;

- Manufacturing refrigerated cabinets, showcases, and display cases—are classified in Industry 33341, Ventilation, Heating, Air-Conditioning, and Commercial Refrigeration Equipment Manufacturing; and

- Manufacturing metal safes and vaults—are classified in Industry 33299, All Other Fabricated Metal Product Manufacturing.

337211 Wood Office Furniture Manufacturing[US]

This U.S. industry comprises establishments primarily engaged in manufacturing wood office-type furniture. The furniture may be made on a stock or custom basis and may be assembled or unassembled (i.e., knockdown).

337212 Custom Architectural Woodwork and Millwork Manufacturing[US]

This U.S. industry comprises establishments primarily engaged in manufacturing custom designed interiors consisting of architectural woodwork and fixtures utilizing wood, wood products, and plastics laminates. All of the industry output is made to individual order on a job shop basis and requires skilled craftsmen as a labor input. A job might include custom manufacturing of display fixtures, gondolas, wall shelving units, entrance and window architectural detail, sales and reception counters, wall paneling, and matching furniture.

Cross-References. Establishments primarily engaged in—

- Manufacturing millwork on a factory basis—are classified in U.S. Industry 321918, Other Millwork (including Flooring);

- Manufacturing wood office-type furniture on a stock or custom basis—are classified in U.S. Industry 337211, Wood Office Furniture Manufacturing; and

- Manufacturing wood office-type furniture and store fixtures on a stock basis—are classified in U.S. Industry 337215, Showcase, Partition, Shelving, and Locker Manufacturing.

US—United States industry only. CAN—United States and Canadian industries are comparable. MEX—United States and Mexican industries are comparable. Blank—Canadian, Mexican, and United States industries are comparable.

337214 Office Furniture (except Wood) Manufacturing^{CAN}

This U.S. industry comprises establishments primarily engaged in manufacturing nonwood office-type furniture. The furniture may be made on a stock or custom basis and may be assembled or unassembled (i.e., knockdown).

337215 Showcase, Partition, Shelving, and Locker Manufacturing^{CAN}

This U.S. industry comprises establishments primarily engaged in manufacturing wood and nonwood office and store fixtures, shelving, lockers, frames, partitions, and related fabricated products of wood and nonwood materials, including plastics laminated fixture tops. The products are made on a stock or custom basis and may be assembled or unassembled (i.e., knockdown). Establishments exclusively making furniture parts (e.g., frames) are included in this industry.

Cross-References. Establishments primarily engaged in—

- Manufacturing refrigerated cabinets, showcases, and display cases—are classified in U.S. Industry 333415, Air-Conditioning and Warm Air Heating Equipment and Commercial and Industrial Refrigeration Equipment Manufacturing;
- Manufacturing metal safes and vaults—are classified in U.S. Industry 332999, All Other Miscellaneous Fabricated Metal Product Manufacturing; and
- Manufacturing wood or plastics laminated kitchen and bathroom countertops—are classified in Industry 337110, Wood Kitchen Cabinet and Countertop Manufacturing.

3379 Other Furniture Related Product Manufacturing

This industry group comprises establishments manufacturing furniture related products, such as mattresses, blinds, and shades.

33791 Mattress Manufacturing
See industry description for 337910 below.

337910 Mattress Manufacturing

This industry comprises establishments primarily engaged in manufacturing innerspring, box spring, and noninnerspring mattresses, including mattresses for waterbeds.

US—United States industry only. CAN—United States and Canadian industries are comparable. MEX—United States and Mexican industries are comparable. Blank—Canadian, Mexican, and United States industries are comparable.

Cross-References. Establishments primarily engaged in—

- Manufacturing individual wire springs—are classified in Industry 33261, Spring and Wire Product Manufacturing; and

- Manufacturing inflatable mattresses—are classified in Subsector 326, Plastics and Rubber Products Manufacturing.

33792 Blind and Shade Manufacturing

See industry description for 337920 below.

337920 Blind and Shade Manufacturing

This industry comprises establishments primarily engaged in manufacturing one or more of the following: venetian blinds, other window blinds, shades; curtain and drapery rods, poles; and/or curtain and drapery fixtures. The blinds and shades may be made on a stock or custom basis and may be made of any material.

Cross-References. Establishments primarily engaged in—

- Manufacturing canvas awnings—are classified in U.S. Industry 314912, Canvas and Related Product Mills; and

- Manufacturing curtains and draperies—are classified in U.S. Industry 314121, Curtain and Drapery Mills.

339 Miscellaneous Manufacturing

Industries in the Miscellaneous Manufacturing subsector make a wide range of products that cannot readily be classified in specific NAICS subsectors in manufacturing. Processes used by these establishments vary significantly, both among and within industries. For example, a variety of manufacturing processes are used in manufacturing sporting and athletic goods that include products such as tennis racquets and golf balls. The processes for these products differ from each other, and the processes differ significantly from the fabrication processes used in making dolls or toys, the melting and shaping of precious metals to make jewelry, and the bending, forming, and assembly used in making medical products.

The industries in this subsector are defined by what is made rather than how it is made. Although individual establishments might be appropriately classified elsewhere in the NAICS structure, for historical continuity, these product-based industries were maintained. In most cases, no one process or material predominates for an industry.

US—United States industry only. CAN—United States and Canadian industries are comparable. MEX—United States and Mexican industries are comparable. Blank—Canadian, Mexican, and United States industries are comparable.

Establishments in this subsector manufacture products as diverse as medical equipment and supplies, jewelry, sporting goods, toys, and office supplies.

3391 Medical Equipment and Supplies Manufacturing

33911 Medical Equipment and Supplies Manufacturing

This industry comprises establishments primarily engaged in manufacturing medical equipment and supplies. Examples of products made by these establishments are surgical and medical instruments, surgical appliances and supplies, dental equipment and supplies, orthodontic goods, ophthalmic goods, dentures, and orthodontic appliances.

Cross-References. Establishments primarily engaged in—

- Manufacturing laboratory instruments, X-ray apparatus, electromedical apparatus (including electronic hearing aids), and thermometers (except medical)—are classified in Industry 33451, Navigational, Measuring, Electromedical, and Control Instruments Manufacturing;

- Manufacturing molded glass lens blanks—are classified in Industry 32721, Glass and Glass Product Manufacturing;

- Manufacturing molded plastics lens blanks—are classified in Industry 32619, Other Plastics Product Manufacturing;

- Retailing and grinding prescription eyeglasses—are classified in Industry 44613, Optical Goods Stores;

- Manufacturing sporting goods helmets and protective equipment—are classified in Industry 33992, Sporting and Athletic Goods Manufacturing;

- Manufacturing general purpose hospital, laboratory and/or dental furniture (e.g., stools, tables, benches)—are classified in Industry 33712, Household and Institutional Furniture Manufacturing;

- Manufacturing laboratory scales and balances, laboratory furnaces and ovens, and/or laboratory centrifuges—are classified in Industry 33399, All Other General Purpose Machinery Manufacturing;

- Manufacturing laboratory distilling equipment—are classified in Industry 33329, Other Industrial Machinery Manufacturing; and

- Manufacturing laboratory freezers—are classified in Industry 33341, Ventilation, Heating, Air-Conditioning, and Commercial Refrigeration Equipment Manufacturing.

339112 Surgical and Medical Instrument Manufacturing[US]

This U.S. industry comprises establishments primarily engaged in manufacturing medical, surgical, ophthalmic, and veterinary instruments and apparatus (except electrotherapeutic, electromedical and irradiation apparatus). Examples of products made by these establishments are syringes, hypodermic needles, anesthesia apparatus, blood transfusion equipment, catheters, surgical clamps, and medical thermometers.

Cross-References. Establishments primarily engaged in—

- Manufacturing electromedical and electrotherapeutic apparatus—are classified in U.S. Industry 334510, Electromedical and Electrotherapeutic Apparatus Manufacturing;

- Manufacturing irradiation apparatus—are classified in U.S. Industry 334517, Irradiation Apparatus Manufacturing;

- Manufacturing surgical and orthopedic appliances or specialized hospital furniture (except dental) (e.g., hospital beds, operating tables)—are classified in U.S. Industry 339113, Surgical Appliance and Supplies Manufacturing;

- Manufacturing dental equipment, dental supplies, dental laboratory apparatus, and dental laboratory furniture—are classified in U.S. Industry 339114, Dental Equipment and Supplies Manufacturing;

- Manufacturing general purpose hospital, laboratory and/or dental furniture (e.g., stools, tables, benches)—are classified in U.S. Industry 337127, Institutional Furniture Manufacturing;

- Manufacturing thermometers (except medical)—are classified in U.S. Industry 334519, Other Measuring and Controlling Device Manufacturing; and

- Manufacturing ophthalmic goods—are classified in U.S. Industry 339115, Ophthalmic Goods Manufacturing.

339113 Surgical Appliance and Supplies Manufacturing[US]

This U.S. industry comprises establishments primarily engaged in manufacturing surgical appliances and supplies. Examples of products made by these establishments are orthopedic devices, prosthetic appliances, surgical dressings, crutches, surgical sutures, personal industrial safety devices (except protective eyewear), hospital beds, and operating room tables.

Cross-References. Establishments primarily engaged in—

- Manufacturing dental equipment, dental supplies, dental laboratory apparatus, and specialized dental laboratory furniture (e.g. dental chairs)—are

---

US—United States industry only. CAN—United States and Canadian industries are comparable. MEX—United States and Mexican industries are comparable. Blank—Canadian, Mexican, and United States industries are comparable.

classified in U.S. Industry 339114, Dental Equipment and Supplies Manufacturing;

- Manufacturing general purpose hospital, laboratory and/or dental furniture (e.g., stools, tables, benches)—are classified in U.S. Industry 337127, Institutional Furniture Manufacturing;

- Manufacturing electronic hearing aids—are classified in U.S. Industry 334510, Electromedical and Electrotherapeutic Apparatus Manufacturing;

- Manufacturing industrial protective eyewear—are classified in U.S. Industry 339115, Ophthalmic Goods Manufacturing; and

- Manufacturing sporting goods helmets and protective equipment—are classified in Industry 339920, Sporting and Athletic Goods Manufacturing.

339114 Dental Equipment and Supplies Manufacturing[US]

This U.S. industry comprises establishments primarily engaged in manufacturing dental equipment and supplies used by dental laboratories and offices of dentists, such as dental chairs, dental instrument delivery systems, dental hand instruments, and dental impression material and dental cements.

Cross-References.

Establishments primarily engaged in manufacturing dentures, crowns, bridges, and orthodontic appliances customized for individual application are classified in U.S. Industry 339116, Dental Laboratories.

339115 Ophthalmic Goods Manufacturing[US]

This U.S. industry comprises establishments primarily engaged in manufacturing ophthalmic goods. Examples of products made by these establishments are prescription eyeglasses (except manufactured in a retail setting), contact lenses, sunglasses, eyeglass frames, and reading glasses made to standard powers, and protective eyewear.

Cross-References. Establishments primarily engaged in—

- Manufacturing molded glass lens blanks—are classified in U.S. Industry 327212, Other Pressed and Blown Glass and Glassware Manufacturing;

- Manufacturing molded plastics lens blanks—are classified in U.S. Industry 326199, All Other Plastics Product Manufacturing; and

- Retailing and grinding prescription eyeglasses—are classified in Industry 446130, Optical Goods Stores.

US—United States industry only. CAN—United States and Canadian industries are comparable. MEX—United States and Mexican industries are comparable. Blank—Canadian, Mexican, and United States industries are comparable.

339116 Dental Laboratories[US]

This U.S. industry comprises establishments primarily engaged in manufacturing dentures, crowns, bridges, and orthodontic appliances customized for individual application.

Cross-References.

Establishments primarily engaged in manufacturing dental equipment and supplies are classified in U.S. Industry 339114, Dental Equipment and Supplies Manufacturing.

3399 Other Miscellaneous Manufacturing

33991 Jewelry and Silverware Manufacturing

This industry comprises establishments primarily engaged in one or more of the following: (1) manufacturing, engraving, chasing, or etching jewelry; (2) manufacturing metal personal goods (i.e., small articles carried on or about the person, such as compacts or cigarette cases); (3) manufacturing, engraving, chasing, or etching precious metal solid, precious metal clad, or pewter cutlery and flatware; (4) manufacturing, engraving, chasing, or etching personal metal goods (i.e., small articles carried on or about the person, such as compacts or cigarette cases); (5) stamping coins; (6) manufacturing unassembled jewelry parts and stock shop products, such as sheet, wire, and tubing; (7) cutting, slabbing, tumbling, carving, engraving, polishing, or faceting precious or semiprecious stones and gems; (8) recutting, repolishing, and setting gem stones; and (9) drilling, sawing, and peeling cultured and costume pearls.

Cross-References. Establishments primarily engaged in—

- Manufacturing nonprecious and precious plated metal cutlery and flatware— are classified in Industry 33221, Cutlery and Handtool Manufacturing;

- Manufacturing nonprecious plated ware (except cutlery, flatware)—are classified in Industry 33299, All Other Fabricated Metal Product Manufacturing;

- Engraving, chasing, or etching nonprecious and precious plated metal flatware and other plated ware and plated jewelry—are classified in Industry 33281, Coating, Engraving, Heat Treating, and Allied Activities;

- Manufacturing synthetic stones or gem stones—are classified in Industry 32799, All Other Nonmetallic Mineral Product Manufacturing; and

- Manufacturing personal goods (except metal) carried on or about the person, such as compacts and cigarette cases—are classified in Industry 31699, Other Leather and Allied Product Manufacturing.

US—United States industry only. CAN—United States and Canadian industries are comparable. MEX—United States and Mexican industries are comparable. Blank—Canadian, Mexican, and United States industries are comparable.

339911 Jewelry (except Costume) Manufacturing[US]

This U.S. industry comprises establishments primarily engaged in one or more of the following: (1) manufacturing, engraving, chasing, or etching precious metal solid or precious metal clad jewelry; (2) manufacturing, engraving, chasing, or etching personal goods (i.e., small articles carried on or about the person, such as compacts or cigarette cases) made of precious solid or clad metal; and (3) stamping coins.

Cross-References. Establishments primarily engaged in—

- Manufacturing, engraving, chasing, or etching costume jewelry and nonprecious metal personal goods—are classified in U.S. Industry 339914, Costume Jewelry and Novelty Manufacturing;

- Manufacturing jewelers' materials or performing lapidary work—are classified in U.S. Industry 339913, Jewelers' Material and Lapidary Work Manufacturing; and

- Plating jewelry—are classified in U.S. Industry 332813, Electroplating, Plating, Polishing, Anodizing, and Coloring.

339912 Silverware and Hollowware Manufacturing[US]

This U.S. industry comprises establishments primarily engaged in manufacturing, engraving, chasing, or etching precious metal solid, precious metal clad, or pewter flatware and other hollowware.

Cross-References. Establishments primarily engaged in—

- Manufacturing nonprecious and precious plated metal cutlery and flatware—are classified in U.S. Industry 332211, Cutlery and Flatware (except Precious) Manufacturing;

- Manufacturing nonprecious metal plated ware (except cutlery and flatware)—are classified in U.S. Industry 332999, All Other Miscellaneous Fabricated Metal Product Manufacturing;

- Engraving, chasing, or etching nonprecious and precious plated metal cutlery, flatware and other plated ware—are classified in U.S. Industry 332812, Metal Coating, Engraving (except Jewelry and Silverware), and Allied Services to Manufacturers; and

- Manufacturing, engraving, chasing, or etching precious (except precious plated) metal jewelry and personal goods—are classified in U.S. Industry 339911, Jewelry (except Costume) Manufacturing.

339913 Jewelers' Material and Lapidary Work Manufacturing[US]

This U.S. industry comprises establishments primarily engaged in one or more of the following: (1) manufacturing unassembled jewelry parts and stock shop products, such as sheet, wire, and tubing; (2) cutting, slabbing, tumbling, carving, engraving, polishing or faceting precious or semiprecious stones and gems; (3) recutting, repolishing, and setting gem stones; and (4) drilling, sawing, and peeling cultured pearls.

Cross-References. Establishments primarily engaged in—

- Manufacturing synthetic stones—are classified in U.S. Industry 327999, All Other Miscellaneous Nonmetallic Mineral Product Manufacturing; and

- Manufacturing costume pearls—are classified in U.S. Industry 339914, Costume Jewelry and Novelty Manufacturing.

339914 Costume Jewelry and Novelty Manufacturing[US]

This U.S. industry comprises establishments primarily engaged in (1) manufacturing, engraving, chasing, and etching costume jewelry; and/or (2) manufacturing, engraving, chasing, or etching nonprecious metal personal goods (i.e., small articles carried on or about the person, such as compacts or cigarette cases). This industry includes establishments primarily engaged in manufacturing precious plated jewelry and precious plated personal goods.

Cross-References. Establishments primarily engaged in—

- Manufacturing, engraving, chasing, or etching precious (except precious plated) metal jewelry and novelties—are classified in U.S. Industry 339911, Jewelry (except Costume) Manufacturing;

- Manufacturing personal goods (except metal) carried on or about the person, such as compacts and cigarette cases—are classified in U.S. Industry 316993, Personal Leather Good (except Women's Handbag and Purse); and

- Manufacturing synthetic stones—are classified in U.S. Industry 327999, All Other Miscellaneous Nonmetallic Mineral Product Manufacturing.

33992 Sporting and Athletic Goods Manufacturing
See industry description for 339920 below.

339920 Sporting and Athletic Goods Manufacturing

This industry comprises establishments primarily engaged in manufacturing sporting and athletic goods (except apparel and footwear).

US—United States industry only. CAN—United States and Canadian industries are comparable. MEX—United States and Mexican industries are comparable. Blank—Canadian, Mexican, and United States industries are comparable.

Cross-References. Establishments primarily engaged in—

- Manufacturing athletic apparel—are classified in Subsector 315, Apparel Manufacturing;
- Manufacturing athletic footwear—are classified in U.S. Industry 316219, Other Footwear Manufacturing; and
- Manufacturing small arms and small arms ammunition—are classified in Industry 33299, All Other Fabricated Metal Product Manufacturing.

33993 Doll, Toy, and Game Manufacturing

This industry comprises establishments primarily engaged in manufacturing dolls, toys, and games, such as complete dolls, doll parts, doll clothes, action figures, toys, games (including electronic), hobby kits, and children's vehicles (except metal bicycles and tricycles).

Cross-References. Establishments primarily engaged in—

- Manufacturing bicycles and metal tricycles—are classified in Industry 33699, Other Transportation Equipment Manufacturing;
- Manufacturing sporting and athletic goods—are classified in Industry 33992, Sporting and Athletic Goods Manufacturing;
- Manufacturing coin-operated game machines—are classified in Industry 33999, All Other Miscellaneous Manufacturing; and
- Manufacturing electronic video game cartridges and reproducing video game software—are classified in Industry 33461, Manufacturing and Reproducing Magnetic and Optical Media.

339931 Doll and Stuffed Toy Manufacturing[US]

This U.S. industry comprises establishments primarily engaged in manufacturing complete dolls, doll parts, and doll clothes, action figures, and stuffed toys.

Cross-References.

Establishments primarily engaged in manufacturing toys (except stuffed) are classified in U.S. Industry 339932, Game, Toy, and Children's Vehicle Manufacturing.

339932 Game, Toy, and Children's Vehicle Manufacturing[US]

This U.S. industry comprises establishments primarily engaged in manufacturing games (including electronic), toys, and children's vehicles (except bicycles and metal tricycles).

US—United States industry only. CAN—United States and Canadian industries are comparable. MEX—United States and Mexican industries are comparable. Blank—Canadian, Mexican, and United States industries are comparable.

Cross-References. Establishments primarily engaged in—

- Manufacturing dolls and stuffed toys—are classified in U.S. Industry 339931, Doll and Stuffed Toy Manufacturing;

- Manufacturing metal tricycles and bicycles—are classified in U.S. Industry 336991, Motorcycle, Bicycle, and Parts Manufacturing;

- Manufacturing sporting and athletic goods—are classified in Industry 339920, Sporting and Athletic Goods Manufacturing;

- Manufacturing coin-operated game machines—are classified in U.S. Industry 339999, All Other Miscellaneous Manufacturing; and

- Mass reproducing electronic video game cartridges—are classified in U.S. Industry 334611, Software Reproducing.

33994 Office Supplies (except Paper) Manufacturing

This industry comprises establishments primarily engaged in manufacturing office supplies. Examples of products made by these establishments are pens, pencils, felt tip markers, crayons, chalk, pencil sharpeners, staplers, hand operated stamps, modeling clay, and inked ribbons.

Cross-References. Establishments primarily engaged in—

- Manufacturing writing, drawing, and india inks—are classified in Industry 32599, All Other Chemical Product and Preparation Manufacturing;

- Manufacturing drafting tables and boards—are classified in Industry 33712, Household and Institutional Furniture Manufacturing;

- Manufacturing rubber erasers—are classified in Industry 32629, Other Rubber Product Manufacturing;

- Manufacturing paper office supplies—are classified in Subsector 322, Paper Manufacturing;

- Manufacturing manifold business forms, blankbooks, and looseleaf binders—are classified in Industry 32311, Printing; and

- Manufacturing inkjet cartridges—are classified in Industry 32591, Printing Ink Manufacturing.

339941 Pen and Mechanical Pencil Manufacturing[US]

This U.S. industry comprises establishments primarily engaged in manufacturing pens, ballpoint pen refills and cartridges, mechanical pencils, and felt tipped markers.

US—United States industry only. CAN—United States and Canadian industries are comparable. MEX—United States and Mexican industries are comparable. Blank—Canadian, Mexican, and United States industries are comparable.

Cross-References. Establishments primarily engaged in—

- Manufacturing nonmechanical pencils and pencil leads—are classified in U.S. Industry 339942, Lead Pencil and Art Good Manufacturing;
- Manufacturing writing, drawing, and india inks—are classified in U.S. Industry 325998, All Other Miscellaneous Chemical Product and Preparation Manufacturing; and
- Manufacturing rubber erasers—are classified in U.S. Industry 326299, All Other Rubber Product Manufacturing.

339942 Lead Pencil and Art Good Manufacturing[US]

This U.S. industry comprises establishments primarily engaged in manufacturing nonmechanical pencils, and art goods. Examples of products made by these establishments are pencil leads, crayons, chalk, framed blackboards, pencil sharpeners, staplers, artists' palettes and paints, and modeling clay.

Cross-References. Establishments primarily engaged in—

- Manufacturing mechanical pencils—are classified in U.S. Industry 339941, Pen and Mechanical Pencil Manufacturing;
- Manufacturing writing, drawing, and india inks—are classified in U.S. Industry 325998, All Other Miscellaneous Chemical Product and Preparation Manufacturing;
- Manufacturing rubber erasers—are classified in U.S. Industry 326299, All Other Rubber Product Manufacturing;
- Manufacturing paper office supplies—are classified in Subsector 322, Paper Manufacturing;
- Printing manifold business forms and manufacturing blankbooks and loose-leaf binders and devices—are classified in Industry 32311, Printing; and
- Manufacturing drafting tables and boards—are classified in U.S. Industry 337127, Institutional Furniture Manufacturing.

339943 Marking Device Manufacturing[US]

This U.S. industry comprises establishments primarily engaged in manufacturing marking devices, such as hand operated stamps, embossing stamps, stamp pads, and stencils.

Cross-References.

Establishments primarily engaged in manufacturing felt tipped markers are classified in U.S. Industry 339941, Pen and Mechanical Pencil Manufacturing.

US—United States industry only. CAN—United States and Canadian industries are comparable. MEX—United States and Mexican industries are comparable. Blank—Canadian, Mexican, and United States industries are comparable.

339944 Carbon Paper and Inked Ribbon Manufacturing[US]

This U.S. industry comprises establishments primarily engaged in manufacturing carbon paper and inked ribbons.

Cross-References.

Establishments primarily engaged in manufacturing inkjet cartridges are classified in Industry 325910, Printing Ink Manufacturing.

33995 Sign Manufacturing
See industry description for 339950 below.

339950 Sign Manufacturing

This industry comprises establishments primarily engaged in manufacturing signs and related displays of all materials (except printing paper and paperboard signs, notices, displays).

Cross-References. Establishments primarily engaged in—

- Printing advertising specialties or printing paper and paperboard signs, notices, and displays—are classified in Industry 32311, Printing;

- Manufacturing and printing advertising specialties—are classified in the manufacturing sector according to products manufactured;

- Manufacturing die-cut paperboard displays—are classified in U.S. Industry 322299, All Other Converted Paper Product Manufacturing; and

- Sign lettering and painting—are classified in Industry 541890, Other Services Related to Advertising.

33999 All Other Miscellaneous Manufacturing

This industry comprises establishments primarily engaged in miscellaneous manufacturing (except medical equipment and supplies, jewelry and flatware, sporting and athletic goods, dolls, toys, games, office supplies (except paper), and signs).

Illustrative Examples:

Artificial Christmas trees manufacturing	Coin-operated amusement machines
Floor and dust mops manufacturing	(except jukebox) manufacturing
Burial caskets and cases manufacturing	Portable fire extinguishers manufacturing

---

US—United States industry only. CAN—United States and Canadian industries are comparable. MEX—United States and Mexican industries are comparable. Blank—Canadian, Mexican, and United States industries are comparable.

Gasket, packing, and sealing devices
  manufacturing
Candles manufacturing
Musical instruments (except toy)
  manufacturing

Fasteners, buttons, needles, and pins
  (except precious metals or precious and
  semiprecious stones and gems)
  manufacturing
Umbrellas manufacturing

Cross-References. Establishments primarily engaged in—

- Manufacturing medical equipment and supplies—are classified in Industry Group 3391, Medical Equipment and Supplies Manufacturing;

- Manufacturing jewelry and flatware—are classified in Industry 33991, Jewelry and Silverware Manufacturing;

- Manufacturing sporting and athletic goods—are classified in Industry 33992, Sporting and Athletic Goods Manufacturing;

- Manufacturing dolls, toys, and games—are classified in Industry 33993, Doll, Toy, and Game Manufacturing;

- Manufacturing office supplies (except paper)—are classified in Industry 33994, Office Supplies (except Paper) Manufacturing;

- Manufacturing signs—are classified in Industry 33995, Sign Manufacturing;

- Manufacturing concrete burial vaults—are classified in Industry 32739, Other Concrete Product Manufacturing;

- Manufacturing Christmas tree glass ornaments and glass lamp shades—are classified in Industry 32721, Glass and Glass Product Manufacturing;

- Manufacturing Christmas tree lighting sets—are classified in Industry 33512, Lighting Fixture Manufacturing;

- Manufacturing beauty and barber chairs—are classified in Industry 33712, Household and Institutional Furniture Manufacturing;

- Manufacturing burnt wood articles—are classified in Industry 32199, All Other Wood Product Manufacturing;

- Dressing and bleaching furs—are classified in Industry 31611, Leather and Hide Tanning and Finishing;

- Manufacturing paper, textile, and metal lamp shades—are classified in Industry 33512, Lighting Fixture Manufacturing;

- Manufacturing plastics lamp shades—are classified in Industry 32619, Other Plastics Product Manufacturing;

- Manufacturing matches—are classified in Industry 32599, All Other Chemical Product and Preparation Manufacturing;

- Manufacturing metal products, such as metal combs and hair curlers—are classified in Industry 33299, All Other Fabricated Metal Product Manufacturing;

- Manufacturing plastics products, such as plastics combs and hair curlers—are classified in Industry 32619, Other Plastics Product Manufacturing; and

- Manufacturing electric hair clippers for use on humans—are classified in Industry 33521, Small Electrical Appliance Manufacturing.

339991 Gasket, Packing, and Sealing Device Manufacturing[US]

This U.S. industry comprises establishments primarily engaged in manufacturing gaskets, packing, and sealing devices of all materials.

339992 Musical Instrument Manufacturing[US]

This U.S. industry comprises establishments primarily engaged in manufacturing musical instruments (except toys).

Cross-References.

Establishments primarily engaged in manufacturing toy musical instruments are classified in U.S. Industry 339932, Game, Toy, and Children's Vehicle Manufacturing.

339993 Fastener, Button, Needle, and Pin Manufacturing[US]

This U.S. industry comprises establishments primarily engaged in manufacturing fasteners, buttons, needles, pins, and buckles (except precious metals or precious and semiprecious stones and gems).

Cross-References. Establishments primarily engaged in—

- Manufacturing buttons, pins, and buckles made of precious metals or precious and semiprecious stones and gems—are classified in U.S. Industry 339911, Jewelry (except Costume) Manufacturing;

- Manufacturing hypodermic and suture needles—are classified in U.S. Industry 339112, Surgical and Medical Instrument Manufacturing; and

- Manufacturing phonograph and styli needles—are classified in U.S. Industry 334419, Other Electronic Component Manufacturing.

339994 Broom, Brush, and Mop Manufacturing[US]

This U.S. industry comprises establishments primarily engaged in manufacturing brooms, mops, and brushes.

US—United States industry only. CAN—United States and Canadian industries are comparable. MEX—United States and Mexican industries are comparable. Blank—Canadian, Mexican, and United States industries are comparable.

339995 Burial Casket Manufacturing^{MEX}

This U.S. industry comprises establishments primarily engaged in manufacturing burial caskets, cases, and vaults (except concrete).

Cross-References.

Establishments primarily engaged in manufacturing concrete burial vaults are classified in Industry 327390, Other Concrete Product Manufacturing.

339999 All Other Miscellaneous Manufacturing^{US}

This U.S. industry comprises establishments primarily engaged in miscellaneous manufacturing (except medical equipment and supplies, jewelry and flatware, sporting and athletic goods, dolls, toys, games, office supplies (except paper), musical instruments, fasteners, buttons, needles, pins, brooms, brushes, mops, and burial caskets).

Illustrative Examples:

Artificial Christmas trees manufacturing
Hair pieces (e.g., wigs, toupees, wiglets) manufacturing
Candles manufacturing
Portable fire extinguishers manufacturing
Christmas tree ornaments (except glass and electric) manufacturing

Potpourri manufacturing
Cigarette lighters (except precious metal) manufacturing
Tobacco pipes manufacturing
Coin-operated amusement machines (except jukebox) manufacturing
Umbrellas manufacturing

Cross-References. Establishments primarily engaged in—

- Manufacturing medical equipment and supplies—are classified in Industry Group 3391, Medical Equipment and Supplies Manufacturing;

- Manufacturing jewelry and flatware—are classified in Industry 33991, Jewelry and Silverware Manufacturing;

- Manufacturing sporting and athletic goods—are classified in Industry 339920, Sporting and Athletic Goods Manufacturing;

- Manufacturing dolls, toys, and games—are classified in Industry 33993, Doll, Toy, and Game Manufacturing;

- Manufacturing office supplies (except paper)—are classified in Industry 33994, Office Supplies (except Paper) Manufacturing;

- Manufacturing signs—are classified in Industry 33995, Sign Manufacturing;

- Manufacturing gasket, packing, and sealing devices—are classified in U.S. Industry 339991, Gasket, Packing, and Sealing Device Manufacturing;

- Manufacturing musical instruments—are classified in U.S. Industry 339992, Musical Instrument Manufacturing;

- Manufacturing fasteners, buttons, needles, and pins—are classified in U.S. Industry 339993, Fastener, Button, Needle, and Pin Manufacturing;

- Manufacturing brooms, brushes, and mops—are classified in U.S. Industry 339994, Broom, Brush, and Mop Manufacturing;

- Manufacturing burial caskets—are classified in U.S. Industry 339995, Burial Casket Manufacturing;

- Manufacturing Christmas tree glass ornaments and glass lamp shades—are classified in U.S. Industry 327215, Glass Product Manufacturing Made of Purchased Glass;

- Manufacturing Christmas tree lighting sets—are classified in U.S. Industry 335129, Other Lighting Equipment Manufacturing;

- Manufacturing beauty and barber chairs—are classified in U.S. Industry 337127, Institutional Furniture Manufacturing;

- Manufacturing burnt wood articles—are classified in U.S. Industry 321999, All Other Miscellaneous Wood Product Manufacturing;

- Dressing and bleaching furs—are classified in Industry 316110, Leather and Hide Tanning and Finishing;

- Manufacturing paper, textile, and metal lamp shades—are classified in U.S. Industry 335121, Residential Electric Lighting Fixture Manufacturing;

- Manufacturing plastics lamp shades—are classified in U.S. Industry 326199, All Other Plastics Product Manufacturing;

- Manufacturing matches—are classified in U.S. Industry 325998, All Other Miscellaneous Chemical Product and Preparation Manufacturing;

- Manufacturing metal products, such as metal combs and hair curlers—are classified in U.S. Industry 332999, All Other Miscellaneous Fabricated Metal Product Manufacturing;

- Manufacturing plastics products, such as plastics combs and hair curlers—are classified in U.S. Industry 326199, All Other Plastics Product Manufacturing; and

- Manufacturing electric hair clippers for use on humans—are classified in U.S. Industry 335211, Electric Housewares and Household Fan Manufacturing.

US—United States industry only. CAN—United States and Canadian industries are comparable. MEX—United States and Mexican industries are comparable. Blank—Canadian, Mexican, and United States industries are comparable.

Sector 42—Wholesale Trade

The Sector as a Whole

The Wholesale Trade sector comprises establishments engaged in wholesaling merchandise, generally without transformation, and rendering services incidental to the sale of merchandise. The merchandise described in this sector includes the outputs of agriculture, mining, manufacturing, and certain information industries, such as publishing.

The wholesaling process is an intermediate step in the distribution of merchandise. Wholesalers are organized to sell or arrange the purchase or sale of (a) goods for resale (i.e., goods sold to other wholesalers or retailers), (b) capital or durable nonconsumer goods, and (c) raw and intermediate materials and supplies used in production.

Wholesalers sell merchandise to other businesses and normally operate from a warehouse or office. These warehouses and offices are characterized by having little or no display of merchandise. In addition, neither the design nor the location of the premises is intended to solicit walk-in traffic. Wholesalers do not normally use advertising directed to the general public. Customers are generally reached initially via telephone, in-person marketing, or by specialized advertising that may include Internet and other electronic means. Follow-up orders are either vendor-initiated or client-initiated, generally based on previous sales, and typically exhibit strong ties between sellers and buyers. In fact, transactions are often conducted between wholesalers and clients that have long-standing business relationships.

This sector comprises two main types of wholesalers: merchant wholesalers that sell goods on their own account and business to business electronic markets, agents, and brokers that arrange sales and purchases for others generally for a commission or fee.

(1) Establishments that sell goods on their own account are known as wholesale merchants, distributors, jobbers, drop shippers, and import/export merchants. Also included as wholesale merchants are sales offices and sales branches (but not retail stores) maintained by manufacturing, refining, or mining enterprises apart from their plants or mines for the purpose of marketing their products. Merchant wholesale establishments typically maintain their own warehouse, where they receive and handle goods for their customers. Goods are generally sold without transformation, but may include integral functions, such as sorting, packaging, labeling, and other marketing services.

(2) Establishments arranging for the purchase or sale of goods owned by others or purchasing goods, generally on a commission basis are known as business to business electronic markets, agents and brokers, commission merchants, import/export agents and brokers, auction companies, and manufacturers' representatives. These establishments operate from offices and generally do not own or handle the goods they sell.

US—United States industry only. CAN—United States and Canadian industries are comparable. MEX—United States and Mexican industries are comparable. Blank—Canadian, Mexican, and United States industries are comparable.

Some wholesale establishments may be connected with a single manufacturer and promote and sell the particular manufacturers' products to a wide range of other wholesalers or retailers. Other wholesalers may be connected to a retail chain, or limited number of retail chains, and only provide a variety of products needed by that particular retail operation(s). These wholesalers may obtain the products from a wide range of manufacturers. Still other wholesalers may not take title to the goods, but act as agents and brokers for a commission.

Although, in general, wholesaling normally denotes sales in large volumes, durable nonconsumer goods may be sold in single units. Sales of capital or durable nonconsumer goods used in the production of goods and services, such as farm machinery, medium and heavy duty trucks, and industrial machinery, are always included in wholesale trade.

423 Merchant Wholesalers, Durable Goods[US]

Industries in the Merchant Wholesalers, Durable Goods subsector sell capital or durable goods to other businesses. Merchant wholesalers generally take title to the goods that they sell; in other words, they buy and sell goods on their own account. Durable goods are new or used items generally with a normal life expectancy of three years or more. Durable goods merchant wholesale trade establishments are engaged in wholesaling products, such as motor vehicles, furniture, construction materials, machinery and equipment (including household-type appliances), metals and minerals (except petroleum), sporting goods, toys and hobby goods, recyclable materials, and parts.

Business-to-business electronic markets, agents, and brokers primarily engaged in wholesaling durable goods, generally on a commission or fee basis, are classified in Subsector 425, Wholesale Electronic Markets and Agents and Brokers.

4231 Motor Vehicle and Motor Vehicle Parts and Supplies Merchant Wholesalers[US]

This industry group comprises establishments primarily engaged in the merchant wholesale distribution of automobiles and other motor vehicles, motor vehicle supplies, tires, and new and used parts.

42311 Automobile and Other Motor Vehicle Merchant Wholesalers[US]
See industry description for 423110 below.

423110 Automobile and Other Motor Vehicle Merchant Wholesalers[US]

This industry comprises establishments primarily engaged in the merchant wholesale distribution of new and used passenger automobiles, trucks, trailers, and other motor vehicles, such as motorcycles, motor homes, and snowmobiles.

42312 Motor Vehicle Supplies and New Parts Merchant Wholesalers[US]

See industry description for 423120 below.

423120 Motor Vehicle Supplies and New Parts Merchant Wholesalers[US]

This industry comprises establishments primarily engaged in the merchant wholesale distribution of motor vehicle supplies, accessories, tools, and equipment; and new motor vehicle parts (except new tires and tubes).

Cross-References. Establishments primarily engaged in—

- Merchant wholesale distribution of new and/or used tires and tubes—are classified in Industry 423130, Tire and Tube Merchant Wholesalers;

- Merchant wholesale distribution of automotive chemicals (except lubricating oils and greases)—are classified in Industry 424690, Other Chemical and Allied Products Merchant Wholesalers;

- Merchant wholesale distribution of lubricating oils and greases—are classified in Industry 424720, Petroleum and Petroleum Products Merchant Wholesalers (except Bulk Stations and Terminals); and

- Merchant wholesale distribution of used motor vehicle parts—are classified in Industry 423140, Motor Vehicle Parts (Used) Merchant Wholesalers.

42313 Tire and Tube Merchant Wholesalers[US]

See industry description for 423130 below.

423130 Tire and Tube Merchant Wholesalers[US]

This industry comprises establishments primarily engaged in the merchant wholesale distribution of new and/or used tires and tubes for passenger and commercial vehicles.

Cross-References. Establishments primarily engaged in—

- Merchant wholesale distribution of other new automobile parts and accessories—are classified in Industry 423120, Motor Vehicle Supplies and New Parts Merchant Wholesalers; and

- Merchant wholesale distribution of other used automobile parts and accessories—are classified in Industry 423140, Motor Vehicle Parts (Used) Merchant Wholesalers.

US—United States industry only. CAN—United States and Canadian industries are comparable. MEX—United States and Mexican industries are comparable. Blank—Canadian, Mexican, and United States industries are comparable.

42314 Motor Vehicle Parts (Used) Merchant Wholesalers^{US}

See industry description for 423140 below.

423140 Motor Vehicle Parts (Used) Merchant Wholesalers^{US}

This industry comprises establishments primarily engaged in the merchant wholesale distribution of used motor vehicle parts (except used tires and tubes) and establishments primarily engaged in dismantling motor vehicles for the purpose of selling the parts.

Cross-References. Establishments primarily engaged in—

- Dismantling motor vehicles for the purpose of selling scrap—are classified in Industry 423930, Recyclable Material Merchant Wholesalers; and

- Merchant wholesale distribution of new and/or used tires and tubes—are classified in Industry 423130, Tire and Tube Merchant Wholesalers.

4232 Furniture and Home Furnishing Merchant Wholesalers^{US}

42321 Furniture Merchant Wholesalers^{US}

See industry description for 423210 below.

423210 Furniture Merchant Wholesalers^{US}

This industry comprises establishments primarily engaged in the merchant wholesale distribution of furniture (except hospital beds, medical furniture, and drafting tables).

Illustrative Examples:

Household-type furniture merchant wholesalers	Public building furniture merchant wholesalers
Outdoor furniture merchant wholesalers	Office furniture merchant wholesalers
Mattresses merchant wholesalers	Religious furniture merchant wholesalers

Cross-References. Establishments primarily engaged in—

- Merchant wholesale distribution of partitions, shelving, lockers, and store fixtures—are classified in Industry 423440, Other Commercial Equipment Merchant Wholesalers;

- Merchant wholesale distribution of hospital beds and medical furniture—are classified in Industry 423450, Medical, Dental, and Hospital Equipment and Supplies Merchant Wholesalers; and

---

US—United States industry only. CAN—United States and Canadian industries are comparable. MEX—United States and Mexican industries are comparable. Blank—Canadian, Mexican, and United States industries are comparable.

- Merchant wholesale distribution of drafting tables—are classified in Industry 423490, Other Professional Equipment and Supplies Merchant Wholesalers.

42322 Home Furnishing Merchant Wholesalers^{US}
See industry description for 423220 below.

423220 Home Furnishing Merchant Wholesalers^{US}

This industry comprises establishments primarily engaged in the merchant wholesale distribution of home furnishings and/or housewares.

Illustrative Examples:

Carpet merchant wholesalers
Glassware merchant wholesalers
Chinaware merchant wholesalers
Household-type cooking utensil
  merchant wholesalers
Curtain merchant wholesalers
Lamp merchant wholesalers

Drapery merchant wholesalers
Linen (e.g., bath, bed, table) merchant
  wholesalers
Floor covering merchant wholesalers
Window blind and shade merchant
  wholesalers

Cross-References. Establishments primarily engaged in—

- Merchant wholesale distribution of electrical household-type goods—are classified in Industry 423620, Electrical and Electronic Appliance, Television, and Radio Set Merchant Wholesalers; and
- Merchant wholesale distribution of precious metal flatware—are classified in Industry 423940, Jewelry, Watch, Precious Stone, and Precious Metal Merchant Wholesalers.

4233 Lumber and Other Construction Materials Merchant Wholesalers^{US}

42331 Lumber, Plywood, Millwork, and Wood Panel Merchant Wholesalers^{US}
See industry description for 423310 below.

423310 Lumber, Plywood, Millwork, and Wood Panel Merchant Wholesalers^{US}

This industry comprises establishments primarily engaged in the merchant wholesale distribution of lumber; plywood; reconstituted wood fiber products;

US—United States industry only. CAN—United States and Canadian industries are comparable. MEX—United States and Mexican industries are comparable. Blank—Canadian, Mexican, and United States industries are comparable.

wood fencing; doors and windows and their frames (all materials); wood roofing and siding; and/or other wood or metal millwork.

Cross-References. Establishments primarily engaged in—

- Merchant wholesale distribution of nonwood roofing and siding materials— are classified in Industry 423330, Roofing, Siding, and Insulation Material Merchant Wholesalers; and

- Merchant wholesale distribution of timber and timber products, such as railroad ties, logs, firewood, and pulpwood—are classified in Industry 423990, Other Miscellaneous Durable Goods Merchant Wholesalers.

42332 Brick, Stone, and Related Construction Material Merchant Wholesalers^{US}

See industry description for 423320 below.

423320 Brick, Stone, and Related Construction Material Merchant Wholesalers^{US}

This industry comprises establishments primarily engaged in the merchant wholesale distribution of stone, cement, lime, construction sand, and gravel; brick; asphalt and concrete mixtures; and/or concrete, stone, and structural clay products.

Cross-References. Establishments primarily engaged in—

- Merchant wholesale distribution of refractory brick and other refractory products—are classified in Industry 423840, Industrial Supplies Merchant Wholesalers; and

- Selling ready-mix concrete—are classified in Industry 327320, Ready-Mix Concrete Manufacturing.

42333 Roofing, Siding, and Insulation Material Merchant Wholesalers^{US}

See industry description for 423330 below.

423330 Roofing, Siding, and Insulation Material Merchant Wholesalers^{US}

This industry comprises establishments primarily engaged in the merchant wholesale distribution of nonwood roofing and nonwood siding and insulation materials.

Cross-References.

Establishments primarily engaged in the merchant wholesale distribution of wood roofing and wood siding are classified in Industry 423310, Lumber, Plywood, Millwork, and Wood Panel Merchant Wholesalers.

42339 Other Construction Material Merchant Wholesalers[US]
See industry description for 423390 below.

423390 Other Construction Material Merchant Wholesalers[US]

This industry comprises (1) establishments primarily engaged in the merchant wholesale distribution of manufactured homes (i.e., mobile homes) and/or prefabricated buildings and (2) establishments primarily engaged in the merchant wholesale distribution of construction materials (except lumber, plywood, millwork, wood panels, brick, stone, roofing, siding, electrical and wiring supplies, and insulation materials).

Illustrative Examples:

Flat glass merchant wholesalers
Prefabricated buildings (except wood)
  merchant wholesalers
Ornamental ironwork merchant
  wholesalers

Wire fencing and fencing accessories
  merchant wholesalers
Plate glass merchant wholesalers

Cross-References. Establishments primarily engaged in—

- Merchant wholesale distribution of products of the primary metals industries—are classified in Industry 423510, Metal Service Centers and Other Metal Merchant Wholesalers;

- Merchant wholesale distribution of lumber; plywood; reconstituted wood fiber products; wood fencing; doors, windows, and their frames; wood roofing and wood siding; and other wood or metal millwork—are classified in Industry 423310, Lumber, Plywood, Millwork, and Wood Panel Merchant Wholesalers;

- Merchant wholesale distribution of stone, cement, lime, construction sand and gravel; brick; asphalt and concrete mixtures (except ready-mix concrete); and/or concrete, stone, and structural clay products—are classified in Industry 423320, Brick, Stone, and Related Construction Material Merchant Wholesalers;

- Merchant wholesale distribution of nonwood roofing, nonwood siding and insulation materials—are classified in Industry 423330, Roofing, Siding, and Insulation Material Merchant Wholesalers;

- Merchant wholesale distribution of electrical supplies and wiring supplies—are classified in Industry 423610, Electrical Apparatus and Equipment, Wiring Supplies, and Related Equipment Merchant Wholesalers; and

- Selling ready-mix concrete—are classified in Industry 327320, Ready-Mix Concrete Manufacturing.

4234 Professional and Commercial Equipment and Supplies Merchant Wholesalers[US]

This industry group comprises establishments primarily engaged in the merchant wholesale distribution of photographic equipment and supplies; office, computer, and computer peripheral equipment; and medical, dental, hospital, ophthalmic, and other commercial and professional equipment and supplies.

42341 Photographic Equipment and Supplies Merchant Wholesalers[US]

See industry description for 423410 below.

423410 Photographic Equipment and Supplies Merchant Wholesalers[US]

This industry comprises establishments primarily engaged in the merchant wholesale distribution of photographic equipment and supplies (except office equipment).

Illustrative Examples:

Photofinishing equipment merchant wholesalers

Television cameras merchant wholesalers

Photographic camera equipment and supplies merchant wholesalers

Video cameras (except household-type) merchant wholesalers

Photographic film merchant wholesalers

Cross-References. Establishments primarily engaged in—

- Merchant wholesale distribution of household-type video cameras—are classified in Industry 423620, Electrical and Electronic Appliance, Television, and Radio Set Merchant Wholesalers; and

- Merchant wholesale distribution of office equipment, such as photocopy and microfilm equipment—are classified in Industry 423420, Office Equipment Merchant Wholesalers.

42342 Office Equipment Merchant Wholesalers[US]
See industry description for 423420 below.

423420 Office Equipment Merchant Wholesalers[US]

This industry comprises establishments primarily engaged in the merchant wholesale distribution of office machines and related equipment (except computers and computer peripheral equipment).

Illustrative Examples:

Accounting machines\merchant
 wholesalers
Mailing machine merchant wholesalers
Calculator and calculating machines
 merchant wholesalers

Microfilm equipment and supplies
 merchant wholesalers
Cash register merchant wholesalers
Security safe merchant wholesalers
Copying machine merchant wholesalers

Cross-References. Establishments primarily engaged in—

* Merchant wholesale distribution of office furniture—are classified in Industry 423210, Furniture Merchant Wholesalers;

* Merchant wholesale distribution of computers and computer peripheral equipment—are classified in Industry 423430, Computer and Computer Peripheral Equipment and Software Merchant Wholesalers; and

* Merchant wholesale distribution of office supplies—are classified in Industry 424120, Stationery and Office Supplies Merchant Wholesalers.

42343 Computer and Computer Peripheral Equipment and Software Merchant Wholesalers[US]
See industry description for 423430 below.

423430 Computer and Computer Peripheral Equipment and Software Merchant Wholesalers[US]

This industry comprises establishments primarily engaged in the merchant wholesale distribution of computers, computer peripheral equipment, loaded computer boards, and/or computer software.

Cross-References. Establishments primarily engaged in—

* Merchant wholesale distribution of modems and other electronic communications equipment—are classified in Industry 423690, Other Electronic Parts and Equipment Merchant Wholesalers; and

- Selling, planning, and designing computer systems that integrate computer hardware, software, and communication technologies—are classified in U.S. Industry 541512, Computer Systems Design Services.

42344 Other Commercial Equipment Merchant Wholesalers[US]
See industry description for 423440 below.

423440 Other Commercial Equipment Merchant Wholesalers[US]

This industry comprises establishments primarily engaged in the merchant wholesale distribution of commercial and related machines and equipment (except photographic equipment and supplies; office equipment; and computers and computer peripheral equipment and software) generally used in restaurants and stores.

Illustrative Examples:

Balances and scales (except laboratory) merchant wholesalers

Commercial shelving merchant wholesalers

Coin-operated merchandising machine merchant wholesalers

Electrical sign merchant wholesalers

Commercial chinaware merchant wholesalers

Partitions merchant wholesalers

Commercial cooking equipment merchant wholesalers

Store fixture (except refrigerated) merchant wholesalers

Cross-References. Establishments primarily engaged in—

- Merchant wholesale distribution of photographic equipment and supplies—are classified in Industry 423410, Photographic Equipment and Supplies Merchant Wholesalers;

- Merchant wholesale distribution of office machines and related equipment—are classified in Industry 423420, Office Equipment Merchant Wholesalers;

- Merchant wholesale distribution of computers, computer peripheral equipment, and computer software—are classified in Industry 423430, Computer and Computer Peripheral Equipment and Software Merchant Wholesalers;

- Merchant wholesale distribution of laboratory scales and balances (except medical and dental)—are classified in Industry 423490, Other Professional Equipment and Supplies Merchant Wholesalers; and

- Merchant wholesale distribution of refrigerated store fixtures—are classified in Industry 423740, Refrigeration Equipment and Supplies Merchant Wholesalers.

42345 Medical, Dental, and Hospital Equipment and Supplies Merchant Wholesalers[US]
See industry description for 423450 below.

US—United States industry only. CAN—United States and Canadian industries are comparable. MEX—United States and Mexican industries are comparable. Blank—Canadian, Mexican, and United States industries are comparable.

423450 Medical, Dental, and Hospital Equipment and Supplies Merchant Wholesalers^{US}

This industry comprises establishments primarily engaged in the merchant wholesale distribution of professional medical equipment, instruments, and supplies (except ophthalmic equipment and instruments and goods used by ophthalmologists, optometrists, and opticians).

Illustrative Examples:

Dental equipment and supplies merchant wholesalers

Medical dressings merchant wholesalers

Electromedical equipment merchant wholesalers

Patient monitoring equipment merchant wholesalers

Hospital beds merchant wholesalers

Prosthetic appliance and supplies merchant wholesalers

Hospital furniture merchant wholesalers

Surgical instrument and apparatus merchant wholesalers

Medical and dental X-ray machine merchant wholesalers

Cross-References.

Establishments primarily engaged in the merchant wholesale distribution of professional equipment, instruments and/or goods sold, prescribed, or used by ophthalmologists, optometrists, and opticians are classified in Industry 423460, Ophthalmic Goods Merchant Wholesalers.

42346 Ophthalmic Goods Merchant Wholesalers^{US}
See industry description for 423460 below.

423460 Ophthalmic Goods Merchant Wholesalers^{US}

This industry comprises establishments primarily engaged in the merchant wholesale distribution of professional equipment, instruments, and/or goods sold, prescribed, or used by ophthalmologists, optometrists, and opticians.

Illustrative Examples:

Binocular merchant wholesalers

Optometric equipment and supplies merchant wholesalers

Ophthalmic frame merchant wholesalers

Sunglasses merchant wholesalers

Ophthalmic lenses merchant wholesalers

42349 Other Professional Equipment and Supplies Merchant Wholesalers^{US}
See industry description for 423490 below.

US—United States industry only. CAN—United States and Canadian industries are comparable. MEX—United States and Mexican industries are comparable. Blank—Canadian, Mexican, and United States industries are comparable.

423490 Other Professional Equipment and Supplies Merchant Wholesalers[US]

This industry comprises establishments primarily engaged in the merchant wholesale distribution of professional equipment and supplies (except ophthalmic goods and medical, dental, and hospital equipment and supplies).

Illustrative Examples:

Church supplies (except silverware, plated ware) merchant wholesalers

School equipment and supplies (except books, furniture) merchant wholesalers

Drafting tables and instruments merchant wholesalers

Scientific instruments merchant wholesalers

Laboratory equipment (except medical, dental) merchant wholesalers

Surveying equipment and supplies merchant wholesalers

Cross-References. Establishments primarily engaged in—

- Merchant wholesale distribution of professional equipment, instruments, and/or goods sold, prescribed, or used by ophthalmologists, optometrists, and opticians, such as ophthalmic frames and lenses, and sunglasses—are classified in Industry 423460, Ophthalmic Goods Merchant Wholesalers;

- Merchant wholesale distribution of medical professional equipment, instruments, and supplies used by medical and dental practitioners (except ophthalmic equipment, instruments, and goods used by ophthalmologists, optometrists, and opticians) and medical facilities—are classified in Industry 423450, Medical, Dental, and Hospital Equipment and Supplies Merchant Wholesalers;

- Merchant wholesale distribution of silverware and plated flatware—are classified in Industry 423940, Jewelry, Watch, Precious Stone, and Precious Metal Merchant Wholesalers;

- Merchant wholesale distribution of books—are classified in Industry 424920, Book, Periodical, and Newspaper Merchant Wholesalers; and

- Merchant wholesale distribution of school furniture—are classified in Industry 423210, Furniture Merchant Wholesalers.

4235 Metal and Mineral (except Petroleum) Merchant Wholesalers[US]

42351 Metal Service Centers and Other Metal Merchant Wholesalers[US]

See industry description for 423510 below.

423510 Metal Service Centers and Other Metal Merchant Wholesalers[US]

This industry comprises establishments primarily engaged in the merchant wholesale distribution of products of the primary metals industries. Service centers maintain inventory and may perform functions, such as sawing, shearing, bending, leveling, cleaning, or edging, on a custom basis as part of sales transactions.

Illustrative Examples:

Cast iron pipe merchant wholesalers
Metal rod merchant wholesalers
Metal bars (except precious) merchant wholesalers
Metal sheet merchant wholesalers
Metal ingots (except precious) merchant wholesalers

Metal spike merchant wholesalers
Metal pipe merchant wholesalers
Nail merchant wholesalers
Metal plate merchant wholesalers
Noninsulated wire merchant wholesalers

Cross-References. Establishments primarily engaged in—

- Merchant wholesale distribution of gold, silver, and platinum—are classified in Industry 423940, Jewelry, Watch, Precious Stone, and Precious Metal Merchant Wholesalers;

- Merchant wholesale distribution of automotive, industrial, and other recyclable metal scrap—are classified in Industry 423930, Recyclable Material Merchant Wholesalers; and

- Merchant wholesale distribution of insulated wire—are classified in Industry 423610, Electrical Apparatus and Equipment, Wiring Supplies, and Related Equipment Merchant Wholesalers.

42352 Coal and Other Mineral and Ore Merchant Wholesalers[US]
See industry description for 423520 below.

423520 Coal and Other Mineral and Ore Merchant Wholesalers[US]

This industry comprises establishments primarily engaged in the merchant wholesale distribution of coal, coke, metal ores, and/or nonmetallic minerals (except precious and semiprecious stones and minerals used in construction, such as sand and gravel).

Cross-References. Establishments primarily engaged in—

- Merchant wholesale distribution of nonmetallic minerals used in construction, such as sand and gravel—are classified in Industry 423320, Brick, Stone, and Related Construction Material Merchant Wholesalers;

- Merchant wholesale distribution of crude petroleum—are classified in Industry Group 4247, Petroleum and Petroleum Products Merchant Wholesalers; and

- Merchant wholesale distribution of precious and semiprecious stones and metals—are classified in Industry 423940, Jewelry, Watch, Precious Stone, and Precious Metal Merchant Wholesalers.

4236 Electrical and Electronic Goods Merchant Wholesalers^{US}

42361 Electrical Apparatus and Equipment, Wiring Supplies, and Related Equipment Merchant Wholesalers^{US}
See industry description for 423610 below.

423610 Electrical Apparatus and Equipment, Wiring Supplies, and Related Equipment Merchant Wholesalers^{US}

This industry comprises establishments primarily engaged in the merchant wholesale distribution of electrical construction materials; wiring supplies; electric light fixtures; light bulbs; and/or electrical power equipment for the generation, transmission, distribution, or control of electric energy.

42362 Electrical and Electronic Appliance, Television, and Radio Set Merchant Wholesalers^{US}
See industry description for 423620 below.

423620 Electrical and Electronic Appliance, Television, and Radio Set Merchant Wholesalers^{US}

This industry comprises establishments primarily engaged in the merchant wholesale distribution of household-type electrical appliances, room air-conditioners, gas and electric clothes dryers, and/or household-type audio or video equipment.

Illustrative Examples:

Electric water heater merchant wholesalers

Household-type sewing machine merchant wholesalers

Household-type radio (including automotive) merchant wholesalers

Household-type video camera merchant wholesalers

Household-type refrigerator merchant wholesalers

Television set merchant wholesalers

US—United States industry only. CAN—United States and Canadian industries are comparable. MEX—United States and Mexican industries are comparable. Blank—Canadian, Mexican, and United States industries are comparable.

Cross-References. Establishments primarily engaged in—

- Merchant wholesale distribution of gas household-type appliances (except gas clothes dryers)—are classified in Industry 423720, Plumbing and Heating Equipment and Supplies (Hydronics) Merchant Wholesalers; and

- Merchant wholesale distribution of nonhousehold-type video cameras—are classified in Industry 423410, Photographic Equipment and Supplies Merchant Wholesalers.

42369 Other Electronic Parts and Equipment Merchant Wholesalers^{US}

See industry description for 423690 below.

423690 Other Electronic Parts and Equipment Merchant Wholesalers^{US}

This industry comprises establishments primarily engaged in the merchant wholesale distribution of electronic parts and equipment (except electrical apparatus and equipment, wiring supplies, and construction materials; electrical and electronic appliances; and television and radio sets).

Illustrative Examples:

Blank audio or video tape merchant wholesalers

Communications equipment merchant wholesalers

Blank compact disc (CD) merchant wholesalers

Radar equipment merchant wholesalers

Blank digital video disc (DVD) merchant wholesalers

Telegraph equipment merchant wholesalers

Blank diskette merchant wholesalers

Telephone equipment merchant wholesalers

Broadcasting equipment merchant wholesalers

Unloaded computer board merchant wholesalers

Cross-References. Establishments primarily engaged in—

- Merchant wholesale distribution of household-type electrical appliances, and television and radio sets—are classified in Industry 423620, Electrical and Electronic Appliance, Television, and Radio Set Merchant Wholesalers;

- Merchant wholesale distribution of computers, computer peripheral equipment, and loaded computer boards—are classified in Industry 423430, Computer and Computer Peripheral Equipment and Software Merchant Wholesalers; and

- Merchant wholesale distribution of electrical construction materials, wiring supplies, electric light fixtures, light bulbs, and/or electrical power equip-

US—United States industry only. CAN—United States and Canadian industries are comparable. MEX—United States and Mexican industries are comparable. Blank—Canadian, Mexican, and United States industries are comparable.

ment for generation, transmission, distribution, or control of electric energy—are classified in Industry 423610, Electrical Apparatus and Equipment, Wiring Supplies, and Related Equipment Merchant Wholesalers.

4237 Hardware, and Plumbing and Heating Equipment and Supplies Merchant Wholesalers^{US}

42371 Hardware Merchant Wholesalers^{US}
See industry description for 423710 below.

423710 Hardware Merchant Wholesalers^{US}

This industry comprises establishments primarily engaged in the merchant wholesale distribution of hardware, knives, or handtools.

Illustrative Examples:

Brads merchant wholesalers
Knives (except disposable plastics) merchant wholesalers
Cutlery merchant wholesalers
Power handtools (e.g., drills, saws, sanders) merchant wholesalers

Fasteners (e.g., bolts, nuts, rivets, screws) merchant wholesalers
Staples merchant wholesalers
Handtools (except motor vehicle, machinists' precision) merchant wholesalers
Tacks merchant wholesalers

Cross-References. Establishments primarily engaged in—

- Merchant wholesale distribution of nails, noninsulated wire, and screening—are classified in Industry 423510, Metal Service Centers and Other Metal Merchant Wholesalers;
- Merchant wholesale distribution of motor vehicle handtools and equipment—are classified in Industry 423120, Motor Vehicle Supplies and New Parts Merchant Wholesalers;
- Merchant wholesale distribution of machinists' precision handtools—are classified in Industry 423830, Industrial Machinery and Equipment Merchant Wholesalers; and
- Merchant wholesale distribution of disposable plastics knives and eating utensils—are classified in Industry 424130, Industrial and Personal Service Paper Merchant Wholesalers.

42372 Plumbing and Heating Equipment and Supplies (Hydronics) Merchant Wholesalers^{US}
See industry description for 423720 below.

US—United States industry only. CAN—United States and Canadian industries are comparable. MEX—United States and Mexican industries are comparable. Blank—Canadian, Mexican, and United States industries are comparable.

423720 Plumbing and Heating Equipment and Supplies (Hydronics) Merchant Wholesalers^{US}

This industry comprises establishments primarily engaged in the merchant wholesale distribution of plumbing equipment, hydronic heating equipment, household-type gas appliances (except gas clothes dryers), and/or supplies.

Cross-References. Establishments primarily engaged in—

- Selling and installing plumbing, heating and air conditioning equipment— are classified in Industry 238220, Plumbing, Heating, and Air-Conditioning Contractors;

- Merchant wholesale distribution of warm air heating and air-conditioning equipment—are classified in Industry 423730, Warm Air Heating and Air-Conditioning Equipment and Supplies Merchant Wholesalers; and

- Merchant wholesale distribution of household-type electrical appliances, room air-conditioners, gas clothes dryers, and/or household-type audio or video equipment—are classified in Industry 423620, Electrical and Electronic Appliance, Television, and Radio Set Merchant Wholesalers.

42373 Warm Air Heating and Air-Conditioning Equipment and Supplies Merchant Wholesalers^{US}
See industry description for 423730 below.

423730 Warm Air Heating and Air-Conditioning Equipment and Supplies Merchant Wholesalers^{US}

This industry comprises establishments primarily engaged in the merchant wholesale distribution of warm air heating and air-conditioning equipment and supplies.

Illustrative Examples:

Air pollution control equipment and supplies merchant wholesalers
Nonportable electric baseboard heaters merchant wholesalers
Air-conditioning equipment (except room units) merchant wholesalers

Warm-air central heating equipment merchant wholesalers
Automotive air-conditioners merchant wholesalers

Cross-References. Establishments primarily engaged in—

- Merchant wholesale distribution of household-type electrical appliances and

US—United States industry only. CAN—United States and Canadian industries are comparable. MEX—United States and Mexican industries are comparable. Blank—Canadian, Mexican, and United States industries are comparable.

http://www.census.gov/naics

room air-conditioners—are classified in Industry 423620, Electrical and Electronic Appliance, Television, and Radio Set Merchant Wholesalers;

- Merchant wholesale distribution of hydronic heating equipment—are classified in Industry 423720, Plumbing and Heating Equipment and Supplies (Hydronics) Merchant Wholesalers; and

- Selling and installing warm air heating and air-conditioning equipment— are classified in Industry 238220, Plumbing, Heating, and Air-Conditioning Contractors.

42374 Refrigeration Equipment and Supplies Merchant Wholesalers[US]

See industry description for 423740 below.

423740 Refrigeration Equipment and Supplies Merchant Wholesalers[US]

This industry comprises establishments primarily engaged in the merchant wholesale distribution of refrigeration equipment (except household-type refrigerators, freezers, and air-conditioners).

Illustrative Examples:

Cold storage machinery merchant wholesalers

Refrigerated display cases merchant wholesalers

Commercial refrigerators merchant wholesalers

Water coolers merchant wholesalers

Cross-References. Establishments primarily engaged in—

- Merchant wholesale distribution of household-type refrigerators, freezers, and room air-conditioners—are classified in Industry 423620, Electrical and Electronic Appliance, Television, and Radio Set Merchant Wholesalers; and

- Merchant wholesale distribution of air-conditioning equipment (except room units)—are classified in Industry 423730, Warm Air Heating and Air-Conditioning Equipment and Supplies Merchant Wholesalers.

4238 Machinery, Equipment, and Supplies Merchant Wholesalers[US]

This industry group comprises establishments primarily engaged in the merchant wholesale distribution of construction, mining, farm, garden, industrial, service establishment, and transportation machinery, equipment and supplies.

US—United States industry only. CAN—United States and Canadian industries are comparable. MEX—United States and Mexican industries are comparable. Blank—Canadian, Mexican, and United States industries are comparable.

42381 Construction and Mining (except Oil Well) Machinery and Equipment Merchant Wholesalers^{US}
See industry description for 423810 below.

423810 Construction and Mining (except Oil Well) Machinery and Equipment Merchant Wholesalers^{US}

This industry comprises establishments primarily engaged in the merchant wholesale distribution of specialized machinery, equipment, and related parts generally used in construction, mining (except oil well), and logging activities.

Illustrative Examples:

Excavating machinery and equipment merchant wholesalers

Road construction and maintenance machinery merchant wholesalers

Forestry machinery and equipment merchant wholesalers

Scaffolding merchant wholesalers

Mining cranes merchant wholesalers

Cross-References.

Establishments primarily engaged in the merchant wholesale distribution of oil well machinery and equipment are classified in Industry 423830, Industrial Machinery and Equipment Merchant Wholesalers.

42382 Farm and Garden Machinery and Equipment Merchant Wholesalers^{US}
See industry description for 423820 below.

423820 Farm and Garden Machinery and Equipment Merchant Wholesalers^{US}

This industry comprises establishments primarily engaged in the merchant wholesale distribution of specialized machinery, equipment, and related parts generally used in agricultural, farm, and lawn and garden activities.

Illustrative Examples:

Animal feeders merchant wholesalers

Milking machinery and equipment merchant wholesalers

Harvesting machinery and equipment merchant wholesalers

Planting machinery and equipment merchant wholesalers

Lawnmowers merchant wholesalers

42383 Industrial Machinery and Equipment Merchant Wholesalers^{US}
See industry description for 423830 below.

423830 Industrial Machinery and Equipment Merchant Wholesalers^{US}

This industry comprises establishments primarily engaged in the merchant wholesale distribution of specialized machinery, equipment, and related parts generally used in manufacturing, oil well, and warehousing activities.

Illustrative Examples:

Fluid power transmission equipment merchant wholesalers

Metalworking machinery and equipment merchant wholesalers

Food-processing machinery and equipment merchant wholesalers

Oil well machinery and equipment merchant wholesalers

Materials handling machinery and equipment merchant wholesalers

Cross-References. Establishments primarily engaged in—

- Merchant wholesale distribution of specialized machinery, equipment, and related parts generally used in construction, mining (except oil well), and logging activities—are classified in Industry 423810, Construction and Mining (except Oil Well) Machinery and Equipment Merchant Wholesalers; and

- Merchant wholesale distribution of supplies used in machinery and equipment generally used in manufacturing, oil well, and warehousing activities— are classified in Industry 423840, Industrial Supplies Merchant Wholesalers.

42384 Industrial Supplies Merchant Wholesalers^{US}
See industry description for 423840 below.

423840 Industrial Supplies Merchant Wholesalers^{US}

This industry comprises establishments primarily engaged in the merchant wholesale distribution of supplies for machinery and equipment generally used in manufacturing, oil well, and warehousing activities.

Illustrative Examples:

Industrial containers merchant wholesalers

Refractory materials (e.g., brick, blocks, shapes) merchant wholesalers

Industrial diamonds merchant wholesalers

Welding supplies (except welding gases) merchant wholesalers

Printing inks merchant wholesalers

US—United States industry only. CAN—United States and Canadian industries are comparable. MEX—United States and Mexican industries are comparable. Blank—Canadian, Mexican, and United States industries are comparable.

Cross-References. Establishments primarily engaged in—

- Merchant wholesale distribution of hydraulic and pneumatic (fluid power) pumps, motors, pistons, and valves—are classified in Industry 423830, Industrial Machinery and Equipment Merchant Wholesalers; and

- Merchant wholesale distribution of welding gases—are classified in Industry 424690, Other Chemical and Allied Products Merchant Wholesalers.

42385 Service Establishment Equipment and Supplies Merchant Wholesalers[US]

See industry description for 423850 below.

423850 Service Establishment Equipment and Supplies Merchant Wholesalers[US]

This industry comprises establishments primarily engaged in the merchant wholesale distribution of specialized equipment and supplies of the type used by service establishments (except specialized equipment and supplies used in offices, stores, hotels, restaurants, schools, health and medical facilities, photographic facilities, and specialized equipment used in transportation and construction activities).

Illustrative Examples:

Amusement park equipment merchant wholesalers

Janitorial equipment and supplies merchant wholesalers

Beauty parlor equipment and supplies merchant wholesalers

Undertakers' equipment and supplies merchant wholesalers

Car wash equipment and supplies merchant wholesalers

Upholsterers' equipment and supplies (except fabrics) merchant wholesalers

Drycleaning equipment and supplies merchant wholesalers

Cross-References. Establishments primarily engaged in—

- Merchant wholesale distribution of janitorial and automotive chemicals—are classified in Industry 424690, Other Chemical and Allied Products Merchant Wholesalers;

- Merchant wholesale distribution of piece goods, fabrics, knitting yarns (except industrial), thread and other notions—are classified in Industry 424310, Piece Goods, Notions, and Other Dry Goods Merchant Wholesalers; and

- Merchant wholesale distribution of industrial yarns—are classified in Industry 424990, Other Miscellaneous Nondurable Goods Merchant Wholesalers.

US—United States industry only. CAN—United States and Canadian industries are comparable. MEX—United States and Mexican industries are comparable. Blank—Canadian, Mexican, and United States industries are comparable.

42386 Transportation Equipment and Supplies (except Motor Vehicle) Merchant Wholesalers[US]

See industry description for 423860 below.

423860 Transportation Equipment and Supplies (except Motor Vehicle) Merchant Wholesalers[US]

This industry comprises establishments primarily engaged in the merchant wholesale distribution of transportation equipment and supplies (except marine pleasure craft and motor vehicles).

Illustrative Examples:

Aircraft merchant wholesalers
Railroad cars merchant wholesalers

Motorized passenger golf carts merchant wholesalers
Ships merchant wholesalers

Cross-References. Establishments primarily engaged in—

* Merchant wholesale distribution of motor vehicles and motor vehicle parts—are classified in Industry Group 4231, Motor Vehicle and Motor Vehicle Parts and Supplies Merchant Wholesalers; and
* Merchant wholesale distribution of marine pleasure craft—are classified in Industry 423910, Sporting and Recreational Goods and Supplies Merchant Wholesalers.

4239 Miscellaneous Durable Goods Merchant Wholesalers[US]

This industry group comprises establishments primarily engaged in the merchant wholesale distribution of sporting, recreational, toy, hobby, and jewelry goods and supplies, and precious stones and metals.

42391 Sporting and Recreational Goods and Supplies Merchant Wholesalers[US]

See industry description for 423910 below.

423910 Sporting and Recreational Goods and Supplies Merchant Wholesalers[US]

This industry comprises establishments primarily engaged in the merchant wholesale distribution of sporting goods and accessories; billiard and pool supplies; sporting firearms and ammunition; and/or marine pleasure craft, equipment, and supplies.

US—United States industry only. CAN—United States and Canadian industries are comparable. MEX—United States and Mexican industries are comparable. Blank—Canadian, Mexican, and United States industries are comparable.

Cross-References. Establishments primarily engaged in—

- Merchant wholesale distribution of motor vehicles and trailers—are classified in Industry 423110, Automobile and Other Motor Vehicle Merchant Wholesalers;

- Merchant wholesale distribution of motorized passenger golf carts—are classified in Industry 423860, Transportation Equipment and Supplies (except Motor Vehicle) Merchant Wholesalers; and

- Merchant wholesale distribution of athletic apparel and athletic footwear—are classified in Industry Group 4243, Apparel, Piece Goods, and Notions Merchant Wholesalers.

42392 Toy and Hobby Goods and Supplies Merchant Wholesalers[US]

See industry description for 423920 below.

423920 Toy and Hobby Goods and Supplies Merchant Wholesalers[US]

This industry comprises establishments primarily engaged in the merchant wholesale distribution of games, toys, fireworks, playing cards, hobby goods and supplies, and/or related goods.

42393 Recyclable Material Merchant Wholesalers[US]

See industry description for 423930 below.

423930 Recyclable Material Merchant Wholesalers[US]

This industry comprises establishments primarily engaged in the merchant wholesale distribution of automotive scrap, industrial scrap, and other recyclable materials. Included in this industry are auto wreckers primarily engaged in dismantling motor vehicles for the purpose of wholesaling scrap.

Cross-References. Establishments primarily engaged in—

- Dismantling motor vehicles for the purpose of selling used parts—are classified in Industry 423140, Motor Vehicle Parts (Used) Merchant Wholesalers; and

- Operating facilities where commingled recyclable materials, such as paper, plastics, used beverage cans, and metals are sorted into distinct categories—are classified in Industry 562920, Materials Recovery Facilities.

US—United States industry only. CAN—United States and Canadian industries are comparable. MEX—United States and Mexican industries are comparable. Blank—Canadian, Mexican, and United States industries are comparable.

42394 Jewelry, Watch, Precious Stone, and Precious Metal Merchant Wholesalers[US]

See industry description for 423940 below.

423940 Jewelry, Watch, Precious Stone, and Precious Metal Merchant Wholesalers[US]

This industry comprises establishments primarily engaged in the merchant wholesale distribution of jewelry, precious and semiprecious stones, precious metals and metal flatware, costume jewelry, watches, clocks, silverware, and/or jewelers' findings.

Cross-References. Establishments primarily engaged in—

- Merchant wholesale distribution of precious metal ores or concentrates—are classified in Industry 423520, Coal and Other Mineral and Ore Merchant Wholesalers; and

- Merchant wholesale distribution of nonprecious flatware—are classified in Industry 423220, Home Furnishing Merchant Wholesalers.

42399 Other Miscellaneous Durable Goods Merchant Wholesalers[US]

See industry description for 423990 below.

423990 Other Miscellaneous Durable Goods Merchant Wholesalers[US]

This industry comprises establishments primarily engaged in the merchant wholesale distribution of durable goods (except motor vehicle and motor vehicle parts and supplies; furniture and home furnishings; lumber and other construction materials; professional and commercial equipment and supplies; metals and minerals (except petroleum); electrical goods; hardware, and plumbing and heating equipment and supplies; machinery, equipment and supplies; sporting and recreational goods and supplies; toy and hobby goods and supplies; recyclable materials; and jewelry, watches, precious stones and precious metals).

Illustrative Examples:

Musical instruments merchant wholesalers

Prerecorded audio and video tapes and discs merchant wholesalers

Phonograph records merchant wholesalers

Prerecorded compact discs (CDs) and digital video discs (DVDs) merchant wholesalers

Prerecorded audio and video cassettes merchant wholesalers

Timber and timber products (except lumber) merchant wholesalers

---

Cross-References. Establishments primarily engaged in—

- Merchant wholesale distribution of automobiles and other motor vehicles, motor vehicle supplies, tires, and new and used parts—are classified in Industry Group 4231, Motor Vehicle and Motor Vehicle Parts and Supplies Merchant Wholesalers;

- Merchant wholesale distribution of furniture and home furnishings—are classified in Industry Group 4232, Furniture and Home Furnishing Merchant Wholesalers;

- Merchant wholesale distribution of lumber, plywood, millwork, wood panels, brick, stone, roofing, siding, and other nonelectrical construction materials—are classified in Industry Group 4233, Lumber and Other Construction Materials Merchant Wholesalers;

- Merchant wholesale distribution of photographic; office; computer and computer peripheral; medical, dental, hospital, ophthalmic; and other commercial and professional equipment and supplies—are classified in Industry Group 4234, Professional and Commercial Equipment and Supplies Merchant Wholesalers;

- Merchant wholesale distribution of coal and other minerals and ores and semifinished metal products—are classified in Industry Group 4235, Metal and Mineral (except Petroleum) Merchant Wholesalers;

- Merchant wholesale distribution of electrical goods—are classified in Industry Group 4236, Electrical and Electronic Goods Merchant Wholesalers;

- Merchant wholesale distribution of hardware; and plumbing, heating, air conditioning, and refrigeration equipment and supplies—are classified in Industry Group 4237, Hardware, and Plumbing and Heating Equipment and Supplies Merchant Wholesalers;

- Merchant wholesale distribution of construction, mining, farm, garden, industrial, service establishment, and transportation machinery, equipment and supplies—are classified in Industry Group 4238, Machinery, Equipment, and Supplies Merchant Wholesalers;

- Merchant wholesale distribution of sporting goods and accessories; billiard and pool supplies; sporting firearms and ammunition; and/or marine pleasure craft, equipment, and supplies—are classified in Industry 423910, Sporting and Recreational Goods and Supplies Merchant Wholesalers;

- Merchant wholesale distribution of toys, fireworks, playing cards, hobby goods and supplies and/or related goods—are classified in Industry 423920, Toy and Hobby Goods and Supplies Merchant Wholesalers;

- Merchant wholesale distribution of automotive, industrial, and other recyclable materials—are classified in Industry 423930, Recyclable Material Merchant Wholesalers; and

- Merchant wholesale distribution of jewelry, precious and semiprecious stones, precious metals and metal flatware, costume jewelry, watches, clocks, silverware, and/or jewelers' findings—are classified in Industry 423940, Jewelry, Watch, Precious Stone, and Precious Metal Merchant Wholesalers.

424 Merchant Wholesalers, Nondurable Goods[US]

Industries in the Merchant Wholesalers, Nondurable Goods subsector sell nondurable goods to other businesses. Nondurable goods are items generally with a normal life expectancy of less than three years. Nondurable goods merchant wholesale trade establishments are engaged in wholesaling products, such as paper and paper products, chemicals and chemical products, drugs, textiles and textile products, apparel, footwear, groceries, farm products, petroleum and petroleum products, alcoholic beverages, books, magazines, newspapers, flowers and nursery stock, and tobacco products.

The detailed industries within the subsector are organized in the classification structure based on the products sold.

Business to business electronic markets, agents, and brokers primarily engaged in wholesaling nondurable goods, generally on a commission or fee basis, are classified in Subsector 425, Wholesale Electronic Markets and Agents and Brokers.

4241 Paper and Paper Product Merchant Wholesalers[US]

42411 Printing and Writing Paper Merchant Wholesalers[US]
See industry description for 424110 below.

424110 Printing and Writing Paper Merchant Wholesalers[US]

This industry comprises establishments primarily engaged in the merchant wholesale distribution of bulk printing and/or writing paper generally on rolls for further processing.

Illustrative Examples:

Bulk envelope paper merchant wholesalers

Bulk paper (e.g., fine, printing, writing) merchant wholesalers

Bulk groundwood paper merchant wholesalers

Cross-References.

Establishments primarily engaged in the merchant wholesale distribution of stationery are classified in Industry 424120, Stationery and Office Supplies Merchant Wholesalers.

US—United States industry only. CAN—United States and Canadian industries are comparable. MEX—United States and Mexican industries are comparable. Blank—Canadian, Mexican, and United States industries are comparable.

42412 Stationery and Office Supplies Merchant Wholesalers^{US}

See industry description for 424120 below.

424120 Stationery and Office Supplies Merchant Wholesalers^{US}

This industry comprises establishments primarily engaged in the merchant wholesale distribution of stationery, office supplies, and/or gift wrap.

Illustrative Examples:

Computer paper supplies merchant
  wholesalers
Photocopy supplies merchant wholesalers
Envelope merchant wholesalers
Social stationery merchant wholesalers

File cards and folders merchant
  wholesalers
Typewriter paper merchant wholesalers
Greeting cards merchant wholesalers
Writing pens merchant wholesalers
Pencils merchant wholesalers

Cross-References.

Establishments primarily engaged in the merchant wholesale distribution of bulk printing and/or writing paper are classified in Industry 424110, Printing and Writing Paper Merchant Wholesalers.

42413 Industrial and Personal Service Paper Merchant Wholesalers^{US}

See industry description for 424130 below.

424130 Industrial and Personal Service Paper Merchant Wholesalers^{US}

This industry comprises establishments primarily engaged in the merchant wholesale distribution of kraft wrapping and other coarse paper, paperboard, converted paper (except stationery and office supplies), and/or related disposable plastics products.

Illustrative Examples:

Disposable plastics eating utensils
  merchant wholesalers
Paper napkins merchant wholesalers
Paper and disposable plastics dishes
  merchant wholesalers
Paperboard and disposable plastics boxes
  merchant wholesalers

Paper and disposable plastics shipping
  supplies merchant wholesalers
Plastics bags merchant wholesalers
Paper bags merchant wholesalers
Sanitary paper products merchant
  wholesalers

US—United States industry only. CAN—United States and Canadian industries are comparable.
MEX—United States and Mexican industries are comparable. Blank—Canadian, Mexican, and United States industries are comparable.

Cross-References.

Establishments primarily engaged in the merchant wholesale distribution of stationery, office supplies, and/or gift wrap are classified in Industry 424120, Stationery and Office Supplies Merchant Wholesalers.

4242 Drugs and Druggists' Sundries Merchant Wholesalers^{US}

42421 Drugs and Druggists' Sundries Merchant Wholesalers^{US}
See industry description for 424210 below.

424210 Drugs and Druggists' Sundries Merchant Wholesalers^{US}

This industry comprises establishments primarily engaged in the merchant wholesale distribution of biological and medical products; botanical drugs and herbs; and pharmaceutical products intended for internal and external consumption in such forms as ampoules, tablets, capsules, vials, ointments, powders, solutions, and suspensions.

Illustrative Examples:

Antibiotics merchant wholesalers
Endocrine substances merchant
  wholesalers
Blood derivatives merchant wholesalers
In-vitro and in-vivo diagnostics merchant
  wholesalers

Botanicals merchant wholesalers
Vaccines merchant wholesalers
Cosmetics merchant wholesalers
Vitamins merchant wholesalers

Cross-References.

Establishments primarily engaged in the merchant wholesale distribution of surgical, dental, and hospital equipment are classified in Industry 423450, Medical, Dental, and Hospital Equipment and Supplies Merchant Wholesalers.

4243 Apparel, Piece Goods, and Notions Merchant Wholesalers^{US}

42431 Piece Goods, Notions, and Other Dry Goods Merchant Wholesalers^{US}
See industry description for 424310 below.

424310 Piece Goods, Notions, and Other Dry Goods Merchant Wholesalers^{US}

This industry comprises establishments primarily engaged in the merchant wholesale distribution of piece goods, fabrics, knitting yarns (except industrial), ·thread and other notions, and/or hair accessories.

US—United States industry only. CAN—United States and Canadian industries are comparable. MEX—United States and Mexican industries are comparable. Blank—Canadian, Mexican, and United States industries are comparable.

Cross-References.

- Establishments primarily engaged as converters who buy fabric goods in the grey, have them finished on a contract basis, and sell at wholesale are classified in Industry 31331, Textile and Fabric Finishing Mills.

- Establishments primarily engaged in merchant wholesale distribution of industrial yarns are classified in Industry 424990, Other Miscellaneous Nondurable Goods Merchant Wholesalers.

42432 Men's and Boys' Clothing and Furnishings Merchant Wholesalers^{US}

See industry description for 424320 below.

424320 Men's and Boys' Clothing and Furnishings Merchant Wholesalers^{US}

This industry comprises establishments primarily engaged in the merchant wholesale distribution of men's and/or boys' clothing and furnishings.

Illustrative Examples:

Men's and boys' hosiery merchant wholesalers

Men's and boys' suits merchant wholesalers

Men's and boys' nightwear merchant wholesalers

Men's and boys' underwear merchant wholesalers

Men's and boys' sportswear merchant wholesalers

Men's and boys' work clothing merchant wholesalers

Cross-References.

Establishments primarily engaged in the merchant wholesale distribution of unisex clothing and men's fur clothing are classified in Industry 424330, Women's, Children's, and Infants' Clothing and Accessories Merchant Wholesalers.

42433 Women's, Children's, and Infants' Clothing and Accessories Merchant Wholesalers^{US}

See industry description for 424330 below.

424330 Women's, Children's, and Infants' Clothing and Accessories Merchant Wholesalers^{US}

This industry comprises establishments primarily engaged in the merchant wholesale distribution of (1) women's, children's, infants', and/or unisex clothing and accessories and/or (2) fur clothing.

US—United States industry only. CAN—United States and Canadian industries are comparable. MEX—United States and Mexican industries are comparable. Blank—Canadian, Mexican, and United States industries are comparable.

Illustrative Examples:

Dresses merchant wholesalers
Millinery merchant wholesalers
Fur clothing merchant wholesalers

Women's, children's, and infants'
hosiery merchant wholesalers
Lingerie merchant wholesalers

42434 Footwear Merchant Wholesalers[US]
See industry description for 424340 below.

424340 Footwear Merchant Wholesalers[US]

This industry comprises establishments primarily engaged in the merchant wholesale distribution of footwear (including athletic) of leather, rubber, and other materials.

4244 Grocery and Related Product Merchant Wholesalers[US]

42441 General Line Grocery Merchant Wholesalers[US]
See industry description for 424410 below.

424410 General Line Grocery Merchant Wholesalers[US]

This industry comprises establishments primarily engaged in the merchant wholesale distribution of a general line (wide range) of groceries.

Cross-References.

Establishments primarily engaged in the merchant wholesale distribution of a specialized line of groceries are classified elsewhere in Sector 42, Wholesale Trade, according to the product sold.

42442 Packaged Frozen Food Merchant Wholesalers[US]
See industry description for 424420 below.

424420 Packaged Frozen Food Merchant Wholesalers[US]

This industry comprises establishments primarily engaged in the merchant wholesale distribution of packaged frozen foods (except dairy products).

Illustrative Examples:

Frozen bakery products merchant
wholesalers

Packaged frozen meats merchant
wholesalers

US—United States industry only. CAN—United States and Canadian industries are comparable. MEX—United States and Mexican industries are comparable. Blank—Canadian, Mexican, and United States industries are comparable.

Packaged frozen fish merchant
wholesalers
Frozen juices merchant wholesalers

Frozen vegetables merchant wholesalers
Packaged frozen poultry merchant
wholesalers

Cross-References.

Establishments primarily engaged in the merchant wholesale distribution of frozen dairy products are classified in Industry 424430, Dairy Product (except Dried or Canned) Merchant Wholesalers.

42443 Dairy Product (except Dried or Canned) Merchant Wholesalers[US]

See industry description for 424430 below.

424430 Dairy Product (except Dried or Canned) Merchant Wholesalers[US]

This industry comprises establishments primarily engaged in the merchant wholesale distribution of dairy products (except dried or canned).

Illustrative Examples:

Butter merchant wholesalers
Fluid milk (except canned) merchant
wholesalers
Cheese merchant wholesalers

Ice cream and ices merchant wholesalers
Cream merchant wholesalers
Yogurt merchant wholesalers

Cross-References. Establishments primarily engaged in—

- Merchant wholesale distribution of dried or canned dairy products and dairy substitutes—are classified in Industry 424490, Other Grocery and Related Products Merchant Wholesalers; and

- Pasteurizing and bottling milk—are classified in U.S. Industry 311511, Fluid Milk Manufacturing.

42444 Poultry and Poultry Product Merchant Wholesalers[US]

See industry description for 424440 below.

424440 Poultry and Poultry Product Merchant Wholesalers[US]

This industry comprises establishments primarily engaged in the merchant wholesale distribution of poultry and/or poultry products (except canned and packaged frozen).

US—United States industry only. CAN—United States and Canadian industries are comparable. MEX—United States and Mexican industries are comparable. Blank—Canadian, Mexican, and United States industries are comparable.

Cross-References. Establishments primarily engaged in—

- Merchant wholesale distribution of packaged frozen poultry—are classified in Industry 424420, Packaged Frozen Food Merchant Wholesalers;

- Merchant wholesale distribution of canned poultry—are classified in Industry 424490, Other Grocery and Related Products Merchant Wholesalers; and

- Slaughtering and dressing poultry—are classified in U.S. Industry 311615, Poultry Processing.

42445 Confectionery Merchant Wholesalers[US]

See industry description for 424450 below.

424450 Confectionery Merchant Wholesalers[US]

This industry comprises establishments primarily engaged in the merchant wholesale distribution of confectioneries; salted or roasted nuts; popcorn; potato, corn, and similar chips; and/or fountain fruits and syrups.

Cross-References. Establishments primarily engaged in—

- Merchant wholesale distribution of frozen pretzels—are classified in Industry 424420, Packaged Frozen Food Merchant Wholesalers; and

- Merchant wholesale distribution of pretzels (except frozen)—are classified in Industry 424490, Other Grocery and Related Products Merchant Wholesalers.

42446 Fish and Seafood Merchant Wholesalers[US]

See industry description for 424460 below.

424460 Fish and Seafood Merchant Wholesalers[US]

This industry comprises establishments primarily engaged in the merchant wholesale distribution of fish and seafood (except canned or packaged frozen).

Cross-References. Establishments primarily engaged in—

- Merchant wholesale distribution of packaged frozen fish and seafood—are classified in Industry 424420, Packaged Frozen Food Merchant Wholesalers;

- Merchant wholesale distribution of canned fish and seafood—are classified in Industry 424490, Other Grocery and Related Products Merchant Wholesalers; and

---

US—United States industry only. CAN—United States and Canadian industries are comparable. MEX—United States and Mexican industries are comparable. Blank—Canadian, Mexican, and United States industries are comparable.

- Canning, smoking, salting, drying, or freezing seafood and shucking and packing fresh shellfish—are classified in Industry 31171, Seafood Product Preparation and Packaging.

42447 Meat and Meat Product Merchant Wholesalers[US]
See industry description for 424470 below.

424470 Meat and Meat Product Merchant Wholesalers[US]

This industry comprises establishments primarily engaged in the merchant wholesale distribution of meats and meat products (except canned and packaged frozen) and/or lard.

Cross-References. Establishments primarily engaged in—

- Merchant wholesale distribution of packaged frozen meats—are classified in Industry 424420, Packaged Frozen Food Merchant Wholesalers;
- Merchant wholesale distribution of canned meats—are classified in Industry 424490, Other Grocery and Related Products Merchant Wholesalers; and
- Preparing boxed beef—are classified in U.S. Industry 311612, Meat Processed from Carcasses.

42448 Fresh Fruit and Vegetable Merchant Wholesalers[US]
See industry description for 424480 below.

424480 Fresh Fruit and Vegetable Merchant Wholesalers[US]

This industry comprises establishments primarily engaged in the merchant wholesale distribution of fresh fruits and vegetables.

42449 Other Grocery and Related Products Merchant Wholesalers[US]
See industry description for 424490 below.

424490 Other Grocery and Related Products Merchant Wholesalers[US]

This industry comprises establishments primarily engaged in the merchant wholesale distribution of groceries and related products (except a general line of groceries); packaged frozen food; dairy products (except dried and canned); poultry products (except canned); confectioneries; fish and seafood (except canned); meat products (except canned); and fresh fruits and vegetables). Included in this industry are establishments primarily engaged in the bottling and merchant wholesale distribution of spring and mineral waters processed by others.

Illustrative Examples:

Bakery products (except frozen) merchant wholesalers	Canned fruits merchant wholesalers
	Dried milk merchant wholesalers
Canned seafood merchant wholesalers	Canned meats merchant wholesalers
Canned fish merchant wholesalers	Soft drinks merchant wholesalers
Canned vegetables merchant wholesalers	Canned milk merchant wholesalers

Cross-References. Establishments primarily engaged in—

- Merchant wholesale distribution of grains, field beans, livestock, and other farm product raw materials—are classified in Industry Group 4245, Farm Product Raw Material Merchant Wholesalers;

- Merchant wholesale distribution of beer, wine, and distilled alcoholic beverages—are classified in Industry Group 4248, Beer, Wine, and Distilled Alcoholic Beverage Merchant Wholesalers;

- Bottling soft drinks—are classified in Industry 31211, Soft Drink and Ice Manufacturing;

- Merchant wholesale distribution of a general line of groceries—are classified in Industry 424410, General Line Grocery Merchant Wholesalers;

- Merchant wholesale distribution of packaged frozen foods (except dairy)—are classified in Industry 424420, Packaged Frozen Food Merchant Wholesalers;

- Merchant wholesale distribution of dairy products—are classified in Industry 424430, Dairy Product (except Dried or Canned) Merchant Wholesalers;

- Merchant wholesale distribution of poultry and poultry products (except canned and packaged frozen)—are classified in Industry 424440, Poultry and Poultry Product Merchant Wholesalers;

- Merchant wholesale distribution of confectioneries; salted or roasted nuts; popcorn; potato, corn, and similar chips; and/or fountain fruits and syrups—are classified in Industry 424450, Confectionery Merchant Wholesalers;

- Merchant wholesale distribution of fish and seafoods (except canned and packaged frozen)—are classified in Industry 424460, Fish and Seafood Merchant Wholesalers;

- Merchant wholesale distribution of meats (except canned and packaged frozen)—are classified in Industry 424470, Meat and Meat Product Merchant Wholesalers;

US—United States industry only. CAN—United States and Canadian industries are comparable. MEX—United States and Mexican industries are comparable. Blank—Canadian, Mexican, and United States industries are comparable.

http://www.census.gov/naics

- Merchant wholesale distribution of fresh fruits and vegetables—are classified in Industry 424480, Fresh Fruit and Vegetable Merchant Wholesalers;

- Purifying and bottling water—are classified in U.S. Industry 312112, Bottled Water Manufacturing; and

- Roasting coffee—are classified in Industry 311920, Coffee and Tea Manufacturing.

4245 Farm Product Raw Material Merchant Wholesalers^{US}

This industry group comprises establishments primarily engaged in the merchant wholesale distribution of agricultural products (except raw milk, live poultry, and fresh fruit and vegetables), such as grains, field beans, livestock, and other farm product raw materials (excluding seeds).

42451 Grain and Field Bean Merchant Wholesalers^{US}
See industry description for 424510 below.

424510 Grain and Field Bean Merchant Wholesalers^{US}

This industry comprises establishments primarily engaged in the merchant wholesale distribution of grains, such as corn, wheat, oats, barley, and unpolished rice; dry beans; and soybeans and other inedible beans. Included in this industry are establishments primarily engaged in operating country or terminal grain elevators primarily for the purpose of wholesaling.

Cross-References. Establishments primarily engaged in—

- Merchant wholesale distribution of field and garden seeds—are classified in Industry 424910, Farm Supplies Merchant Wholesalers; and

- Operating grain elevators for storage only—are classified in Industry 493130, Farm Product Warehousing and Storage.

42452 Livestock Merchant Wholesalers^{US}
See industry description for 424520 below.

424520 Livestock Merchant Wholesalers^{US}

This industry comprises establishments primarily engaged in the merchant wholesale distribution of livestock (except horses and mules).

US—United States industry only. CAN—United States and Canadian industries are comparable. MEX—United States and Mexican industries are comparable. Blank—Canadian, Mexican, and United States industries are comparable.

Illustrative Examples:

Cattle merchant wholesalers	Goats merchant wholesalers
Hogs merchant wholesalers	Sheep merchant wholesalers

Cross-References.

Establishments primarily engaged in the merchant wholesale distribution of horses and mules are classified in Industry 424590, Other Farm Product Raw Material Merchant Wholesalers.

42459 Other Farm Product Raw Material Merchant Wholesalers[US]

See industry description for 424590 below.

424590 Other Farm Product Raw Material Merchant Wholesalers[US]

This industry comprises establishments primarily engaged in the merchant wholesale distribution of farm products (except grain and field beans, livestock, raw milk, live poultry, and fresh fruits and vegetables).

Illustrative Examples:

Chicks merchant wholesalers	Horses merchant wholesalers
Mules merchant wholesalers	Raw pelts merchant wholesalers
Hides merchant wholesalers	Leaf tobacco merchant wholesalers
Raw cotton merchant wholesalers	

Cross-References. Establishments primarily engaged in—

- Merchant wholesale distribution of raw milk—are classified in Industry 424430, Dairy Product (except Dried or Canned) Merchant Wholesalers;

- Merchant wholesale distribution of live poultry (except chicks)—are classified in Industry 424440, Poultry and Poultry Product Merchant Wholesalers;

- Merchant wholesale distribution of grain, dry beans, and soybeans and other inedible beans—are classified in Industry 424510, Grain and Field Bean Merchant Wholesalers;

- Merchant wholesale distribution of livestock (except horses and mules), such as cattle, hogs, sheep, and goats—are classified in Industry 424520, Livestock Merchant Wholesalers; and

- Merchant wholesale distribution of fresh fruits and vegetables—are classified in Industry 424480, Fresh Fruit and Vegetable Merchant Wholesalers.

4246 Chemical and Allied Products Merchant Wholesalers[US]

This industry group comprises establishments primarily engaged in the merchant wholesale distribution of chemicals, plastics materials and basic forms and shapes, and allied products.

42461 Plastics Materials and Basic Forms and Shapes Merchant Wholesalers[US]
See industry description for 424610 below.

424610 Plastics Materials and Basic Forms and Shapes Merchant Wholesalers[US]

This industry comprises establishments primarily engaged in the merchant wholesale distribution of plastics materials and resins, and unsupported plastics film, sheet, sheeting, rod, tube, and other basic forms and shapes.

42469 Other Chemical and Allied Products Merchant Wholesalers[US]
See industry description for 424690 below.

424690 Other Chemical and Allied Products Merchant Wholesalers[US]

This industry comprises establishments primarily engaged in the merchant wholesale distribution of chemicals and allied products (except agricultural and medicinal chemicals, paints and varnishes, fireworks, and plastics materials and basic forms and shapes).

Illustrative Examples:

Acids merchant wholesalers
Industrial chemicals merchant
  wholesalers
Automotive chemicals (except
  lubricating oils and greases) merchant
  wholesalers

Industrial salts merchant wholesalers
Dyestuffs merchant wholesalers
Rosins merchant wholesalers
Explosives (except ammunition and
  fireworks) merchant wholesalers
Turpentine merchant wholesalers

Cross-References. Establishments primarily engaged in—

- Merchant wholesale distribution of ammunition—are classified in Industry Group 4239, Miscellaneous Durable Goods Merchant Wholesalers;
- Merchant wholesale distribution of biological and medical products; botanical drugs and herbs; and pharmaceutical products intended for internal and

---

external consumption in such forms as ampoules, tablets, capsules, vials, ointments, powders, solutions, and suspensions—are classified in Industry 424210, Drugs and Druggists' Sundries Merchant Wholesalers;

- Merchant wholesale distribution of farm supplies, such as animal feeds, fertilizers, agricultural chemicals, pesticides, seeds and plant bulbs—are classified in Industry 424910, Farm Supplies Merchant Wholesalers;

- Merchant wholesale distribution of paints, and varnishes and similar coatings, pigments, wallpaper, and supplies, such as paint brushes and rollers— are classified in Industry 424950, Paint, Varnish, and Supplies Merchant Wholesalers;

- Merchant wholesale distribution of lubricating oils and greases—are classified in Industry 424720, Petroleum and Petroleum Products Merchant Wholesalers (except Bulk Stations and Terminals);

- Merchant wholesale distribution of fireworks—are classified in Industry 423920, Toy and Hobby Goods and Supplies Merchant Wholesalers; and

- Merchant wholesale distribution of plastics materials and resins, and unsupported plastics film, sheet, sheeting, rod, tube, and other basic forms and shapes—are classified in Industry 424610, Plastics Materials and Basic Forms and Shapes Merchant Wholesalers.

4247 Petroleum and Petroleum Products Merchant Wholesalers[US]

42471 Petroleum Bulk Stations and Terminals[US]

See industry description for 424710 below.

424710 Petroleum Bulk Stations and Terminals[US]

This industry comprises establishments with bulk liquid storage facilities primarily engaged in the merchant wholesale distribution of crude petroleum and petroleum products, including liquefied petroleum gas.

Cross-References.

Establishments primarily engaged in bulk storage of petroleum are classified in Industry 493190, Other Warehousing and Storage.

42472 Petroleum and Petroleum Products Merchant Wholesalers (except Bulk Stations and Terminals)[US]

See industry description for 424720 below.

424720 Petroleum and Petroleum Products Merchant Wholesalers (except Bulk Stations and Terminals)[US]

This industry comprises establishments primarily engaged in the merchant wholesale distribution of petroleum and petroleum products (except from bulk liquid storage facilities).

Illustrative Examples:

Bottled liquid petroleum gas merchant wholesalers

Gasoline merchant wholesalers (except bulk stations, terminals)

Fuel oil merchant wholesalers (except bulk stations, terminals)

Lubricating oil and grease merchant wholesalers (except bulk stations, terminals)

Cross-References.

Establishments primarily engaged in the merchant wholesale distribution of crude petroleum and petroleum products from bulk liquid storage facilities are classified in Industry 424710, Petroleum Bulk Stations and Terminals.

4248 Beer, Wine, and Distilled Alcoholic Beverage Merchant Wholesalers[US]

42481 Beer and Ale Merchant Wholesalers[US]
See industry description for 424810 below.

424810 Beer and Ale Merchant Wholesalers[US]

This industry comprises establishments primarily engaged in the merchant wholesale distribution of beer, ale, porter, and other fermented malt beverages.

42482 Wine and Distilled Alcoholic Beverage Merchant Wholesalers[US]
See industry description for 424820 below.

424820 Wine and Distilled Alcoholic Beverage Merchant Wholesalers[US]

This industry comprises establishments primarily engaged in the merchant wholesale distribution of wine, distilled alcoholic beverages, and/or neutral spirits and ethyl alcohol used in blended wines and distilled liquors.

US—United States industry only. CAN—United States and Canadian industries are comparable. MEX—United States and Mexican industries are comparable. Blank—Canadian, Mexican, and United States industries are comparable.

4249 Miscellaneous Nondurable Goods Merchant Wholesalers^{US}

This industry group comprises establishments primarily engaged in the merchant wholesale distribution of nondurable goods, such as farm supplies; books, periodicals and newspapers; flowers; nursery stock; paints; varnishes; tobacco and tobacco products; and other miscellaneous nondurable goods, such as cut Christmas trees and pet supplies.

42491 Farm Supplies Merchant Wholesalers^{US}
See industry description for 424910 below.

424910 Farm Supplies Merchant Wholesalers^{US}

This industry comprises establishments primarily engaged in the merchant wholesale distribution of farm supplies, such as animal feeds, fertilizers, agricultural chemicals, pesticides, plant seeds, and plant bulbs.

Cross-References. Establishments primarily engaged in—

- Merchant wholesale distribution of pet food—are classified in Industry 424490, Other Grocery and Related Products Merchant Wholesalers;

- Merchant wholesale distribution of grains—are classified in Industry 424510, Grain and Field Bean Merchant Wholesalers;

- Merchant wholesale distribution of pet supplies—are classified in Industry 424990, Other Miscellaneous Nondurable Goods Merchant Wholesalers; and

- Merchant wholesale distribution of nursery stock (except seeds and plant bulbs)—are classified in Industry 424930, Flower, Nursery Stock, and Florists' Supplies Merchant Wholesalers.

42492 Book, Periodical, and Newspaper Merchant Wholesalers^{US}
See industry description for 424920 below.

424920 Book, Periodical, and Newspaper Merchant Wholesalers^{US}

This industry comprises establishments primarily engaged in the merchant wholesale distribution of books, periodicals, and newspapers.

42493 Flower, Nursery Stock, and Florists' Supplies Merchant Wholesalers^{US}
See industry description for 424930 below.

US—United States industry only. CAN—United States and Canadian industries are comparable. MEX—United States and Mexican industries are comparable. Blank—Canadian, Mexican, and United States industries are comparable.

424930 Flower, Nursery Stock, and Florists' Supplies Merchant Wholesalers[US]

This industry comprises establishments primarily engaged in the merchant wholesale distribution of flowers, florists' supplies, and/or nursery stock (except plant seeds and plant bulbs).

Cross-References. Establishments primarily engaged in—

- Merchant wholesale distribution of cut Christmas trees—are classified in Industry 424990, Other Miscellaneous Nondurable Goods Merchant Wholesalers; and
- Merchant wholesale distribution of plant seeds and plant bulbs—are classified in Industry 424910, Farm Supplies Merchant Wholesalers.

42494 Tobacco and Tobacco Product Merchant Wholesalers[US]
See industry description for 424940 below.

424940 Tobacco and Tobacco Product Merchant Wholesalers[US]

This industry comprises establishments primarily engaged in the merchant wholesale distribution of tobacco products, such as cigarettes, snuff, cigars, and pipe tobacco.

Cross-References.

Establishments primarily engaged in the merchant wholesale distribution of leaf tobacco are classified in Industry 424590, Other Farm Product Raw Material Merchant Wholesalers.

42495 Paint, Varnish, and Supplies Merchant Wholesalers[US]
See industry description for 424950 below.

424950 Paint, Varnish, and Supplies Merchant Wholesalers[US]

This industry comprises establishments primarily engaged in the merchant wholesale distribution of paints, varnishes, and similar coatings; pigments; wallpaper; and supplies, such as paint brushes and rollers.

Cross-References.

Establishments primarily engaged in the merchant wholesale distribution of artists' paints are classified in Industry 424990, Other Miscellaneous Nondurable Goods Merchant Wholesalers.

42499   Other Miscellaneous Nondurable Goods Merchant Wholesalers[US]

See industry description for 424990 below.

424990   Other Miscellaneous Nondurable Goods Merchant Wholesalers[US]

This industry comprises establishments primarily engaged in the merchant wholesale distribution of nondurable goods (except printing and writing paper; stationery and office supplies; industrial and personal service paper; drugs and druggists' sundries; apparel, piece goods, and notions; grocery and related products; farm product raw materials; chemical and allied products; petroleum and petroleum products; beer, wine, and distilled alcoholic beverages; farm supplies; books, periodicals and newspapers; flower, nursery stock and florists' supplies; tobacco and tobacco products; and paint, varnishes, wallpaper, and supplies).

Illustrative Examples:

Artists' supplies merchant wholesalers
Pet supplies (except pet food) merchant
  wholesalers
Burlap merchant wholesalers

Statuary goods (except religious)
  merchant wholesalers
Christmas trees merchant wholesalers
Textile bags merchant wholesalers
Industrial yarn merchant wholesalers

Cross-References. Establishments primarily engaged in—

- Distribution of advertising specialties—are classified in Industry 541890, Other Services Related to Advertising;

- Merchant wholesale distribution of farm supplies—are classified in Industry 424910, Farm Supplies Merchant Wholesalers;

- Merchant wholesale distribution of books, periodicals, and newspapers—are classified in Industry 424920, Book, Periodical, and Newspaper Merchant Wholesalers;

- Merchant wholesale distribution of flowers, nursery stock, and florists' supplies—are classified in Industry 424930, Flower, Nursery Stock, and Florists' Supplies Merchant Wholesalers;

- Merchant wholesale distribution of tobacco and its products—are classified in Industry 424940, Tobacco and Tobacco Product Merchant Wholesalers;

- Merchant wholesale distribution of paints, varnishes, and similar coatings; pigments; wallpaper; and supplies—are classified in Industry 424950, Paint, Varnish, and Supplies Merchant Wholesalers;

- Merchant wholesale distribution of bulk printing and/or writing paper— are classified in Industry 424110, Printing and Writing Paper Merchant Wholesalers;

- Merchant wholesale distribution of stationery, office supplies, and/or gift wrap—are classified in Industry 424120, Stationery and Office Supplies Merchant Wholesalers;

- Merchant wholesale distribution of wrapping and other coarse paper, paperboard, converted paper (except stationery and office supplies), and related disposable plastics products—are classified in Industry 424130, Industrial and Personal Service Paper Merchant Wholesalers;

- Merchant wholesale distribution of biological and medical products; botanical drugs and herbs; and pharmaceutical products intended for internal and external consumption—are classified in Industry 424210, Drugs and Druggists' Sundries Merchant Wholesalers;

- Merchant wholesale distribution of clothing and accessories, footwear, piece goods, yard goods, notions, and/or hair accessories—are classified in Industry Group 4243, Apparel, Piece Goods, and Notions Merchant Wholesalers;

- Merchant wholesale distribution of meat, poultry, seafood, confectioneries, fruits and vegetables; and other groceries and related products—are classified in Industry Group 4244, Grocery and Related Product Merchant Wholesalers;

- Merchant wholesale distribution of grains, field beans, livestock, and other farm product raw materials—are classified in Industry Group 4245, Farm Product Raw Material Merchant Wholesalers;

- Merchant wholesale distribution of chemicals; plastics materials and basic forms and shapes; and allied products—are classified in Industry Group 4246, Chemical and Allied Products Merchant Wholesalers;

- Merchant wholesale distribution of petroleum and petroleum products— are classified in Industry Group 4247, Petroleum and Petroleum Products Merchant Wholesalers;

- Merchant wholesale distribution of beer, ale, wine, and distilled alcoholic beverages—are classified in Industry Group 4248, Beer, Wine, and Distilled Alcoholic Beverage Merchant Wholesalers;

- Merchant wholesale distribution of pet foods—are classified in Industry 424490, Other Grocery and Related Products Merchant Wholesalers;

- Merchant wholesale distribution of religious statuary—are classified in Industry 423990, Other Miscellaneous Durable Goods Merchant Wholesalers; and

---

US—United States industry only. CAN—United States and Canadian industries are comparable. MEX—United States and Mexican industries are comparable. Blank—Canadian, Mexican, and United States industries are comparable.

- Merchant wholesale distribution of knitting yarns (except industrial)—are classified in Industry 424310, Piece Goods, Notions, and Other Dry Goods Merchant Wholesalers.

425 Wholesale Electronic Markets and Agents and Brokers[CAN]

Industries in the Wholesale Electronic Markets and Agents and Brokers subsector arrange for the sale of goods owned by others, generally on a fee or commission basis. They act on behalf of the buyers and sellers of goods. This subsector contains agents and brokers as well as business to business electronic markets that facilitate wholesale trade. '

4251 Wholesale Electronic Markets and Agents and Brokers[CAN]

42511 Business to Business Electronic Markets[CAN]
See industry description for 425110 below.

425110 Business to Business Electronic Markets[CAN]

This industry comprises business-to-business electronic markets bringing together buyers and sellers of goods using the Internet or other electronic means and generally receiving a commission or fee for the service. Business-to-business electronic markets for durable and nondurable goods are included in this industry.

Cross-References.

Establishments primarily engaged in bringing together buyers and sellers of goods using the Internet in a business-to-consumer or consumer-to-consumer environment are classified in Industry 45411, Electronic Shopping and Mail-Order Houses.

42512 Wholesale Trade Agents and Brokers[CAN]
See industry description for 425120 below.

425120 Wholesale Trade Agents and Brokers[CAN]

This industry comprises wholesale trade agents and brokers acting on behalf of buyers or sellers in the wholesale distribution of goods. Agents and brokers do not take title to the goods being sold but rather receive a commission or fee for their service. Agents and brokers for all durable and nondurable goods are included in this industry.

US—United States industry only. CAN—United States and Canadian industries are comparable. MEX—United States and Mexican industries are comparable. Blank—Canadian, Mexican, and United States industries are comparable.

Illustrative Examples:

Independent sales representatives   Manufacturers' sales representatives

Cross-References.

Establishments acting in the capacity of agents or brokers that operate using the Internet or other electronic means instead of a sales force are classified in Industry 425110, Business to Business Electronic Markets.

Sector 44-45—Retail Trade

The Sector as a Whole

The Retail Trade sector comprises establishments engaged in retailing merchandise, generally without transformation, and rendering services incidental to the sale of merchandise.

The retailing process is the final step in the distribution of merchandise; retailers are, therefore, organized to sell merchandise in small quantities to the general public. This sector comprises two main types of retailers: store and nonstore retailers.

1. Store retailers operate fixed point-of-sale locations, located and designed to attract a high volume of walk-in customers. In general, retail stores have extensive displays of merchandise and use mass-media advertising to attract customers. They typically sell merchandise to the general public for personal or household consumption, but some also serve business and institutional clients. These include establishments, such as office supply stores, computer and software stores, building materials dealers, plumbing supply stores, and electrical supply stores. Catalog showrooms, gasoline stations, automotive dealers, and mobile home dealers are treated as store retailers.

   In addition to retailing merchandise, some types of store retailers are also engaged in the provision of after-sales services, such as repair and installation. For example, new automobile dealers, electronics and appliance stores, and musical instrument and supplies stores often provide repair services. As a general rule, establishments engaged in retailing merchandise and providing after-sales services are classified in this sector.

   The first eleven subsectors of retail trade are store retailers. The establishments are grouped into industries and industry groups typically based on one or more of the following criteria:

   (a) The merchandise line or lines carried by the store; for example, specialty stores are distinguished from general-line stores.

   (b) The usual trade designation of the establishments. This criterion applies in cases where a store type is well recognized by the industry and the public, but difficult to define strictly in terms of merchandise lines carried; for example, pharmacies, hardware stores, and department stores.

   (c) Capital requirements in terms of display equipment; for example, food stores have equipment requirements not found in other retail industries.

   (d) Human resource requirements in terms of expertise; for example, the staff of an automobile dealer requires knowledge in financing, registering, and licensing issues that are not necessary in other retail industries.

US—United States industry only. CAN—United States and Canadian industries are comparable. MEX—United States and Mexican industries are comparable. Blank—Canadian, Mexican, and United States industries are comparable.

2. Nonstore retailers, like store retailers, are organized to serve the general public, but their retailing methods differ. The establishments of this subsector reach customers and market merchandise with methods, such as the broadcasting of "infomercials," the broadcasting and publishing of direct-response advertising, the publishing of paper and electronic catalogs, door-to-door solicitation, in-home demonstration, selling from portable stalls (street vendors, except food), and distribution through vending machines. Establishments engaged in the direct sale (nonstore) of products, such as home heating oil dealers and home delivery newspaper routes are included here.

The buying of goods for resale is a characteristic of retail trade establishments that particularly distinguishes them from establishments in the agriculture, manufacturing, and construction industries. For example, farms that sell their products at or from the point of production are not classified in retail, but rather in agriculture. Similarly, establishments that both manufacture and sell their products to the general public are not classified in retail, but rather in manufacturing. However, establishments that engage in processing activities incidental to retailing are classified in retail. This includes establishments, such as optical goods stores that do in-store grinding of lenses, and meat and seafood markets.

Wholesalers also engage in the buying of goods for resale, but they are not usually organized to serve the general public. They typically operate from a warehouse or office and neither the design nor the location of these premises is intended to solicit a high volume of walk-in traffic. Wholesalers supply institutional, industrial, wholesale, and retail clients; their operations are, therefore, generally organized to purchase, sell, and deliver merchandise in larger quantities. However, dealers of durable nonconsumer goods, such as farm machinery and heavy duty trucks, are included in wholesale trade even if they often sell these products in single units.

441 Motor Vehicle and Parts Dealers[CAN]

Industries in the Motor Vehicle and Parts Dealers subsector retail motor vehicles and parts from fixed point-of-sale locations. Establishments in this subsector typically operate from a showroom and/or an open lot where the vehicles are on display. The display of vehicles and the related parts require little by way of display equipment. The personnel generally include both the sales and sales support staff familiar with the requirements for registering and financing a vehicle as well as a staff of parts experts and mechanics trained to provide repair and maintenance services for the vehicles. Specific industries have been included in this subsector to identify the type of vehicle being retailed.

Sales of capital or durable nonconsumer goods, such as medium and heavy-duty trucks, are always included in wholesale trade. These goods are virtually never sold through retail methods.

US—United States industry only. CAN—United States and Canadian industries are comparable. MEX—United States and Mexican industries are comparable. Blank—Canadian, Mexican, and United States industries are comparable.

4411 Automobile Dealers^{CAN}

This industry group comprises establishments primarily engaged in retailing new and used automobiles and light trucks, such as sport utility vehicles, and passenger and cargo vans.

44111 New Car Dealers^{CAN}
See industry description for 441110 below.

441110 New Car Dealers^{CAN}

This industry comprises establishments primarily engaged in retailing new automobiles and light trucks, such as sport utility vehicles, and passenger and cargo vans, or retailing these new vehicles in combination with activities, such as repair services, retailing used cars, and selling replacement parts and accessories.

Illustrative Examples:

Automobile dealers, new only, or new and used

Light utility truck dealers, new only, or new and used

Cross-References. Establishments primarily engaged in—

- Retailing used automobiles and light trucks without retailing new automobiles and light trucks are classified in Industry 441120, Used Car Dealers; and

- Providing automotive repair services without retailing new automotive vehicles—are classified in Industry Group 8111, Automotive Repair and Maintenance.

44112 Used Car Dealers^{CAN}
See industry description for 441120 below.

441120 Used Car Dealers^{CAN}

This industry comprises establishments primarily engaged in retailing used automobiles and light trucks, such as sport utility vehicles, and passenger and cargo vans.

Illustrative Examples:

Antique auto dealers
Light truck dealers, used only

Automobile dealers, used only

US—United States industry only. CAN—United States and Canadian industries are comparable. MEX—United States and Mexican industries are comparable. Blank—Canadian, Mexican, and United States industries are comparable.

Cross-References.

Establishments primarily engaged in retailing new automobiles and light trucks are classified in Industry 441110, New Car Dealers.

4412 Other Motor Vehicle Dealers[CAN]

This industry group comprises establishments primarily engaged in retailing new and used vehicles (except automobiles, light trucks, such as sport utility vehicles, and passenger and cargo vans).

44121 Recreational Vehicle Dealers[CAN]
See industry description for 441210 below.

441210 Recreational Vehicle Dealers[CAN]

This industry comprises establishments primarily engaged in retailing new and/or used recreational vehicles commonly referred to as RVs or retailing these new vehicles in combination with activities, such as repair services and selling replacement parts and accessories.

Illustrative Examples:

Motor home dealers
Recreational vehicle parts and
  accessories stores

Recreational vehicle (RV) dealers
Travel trailer dealers

Cross-References. Establishments primarily engaged in—

- Retailing new or used boat trailers and utility trailers—are classified in Industry 44122, Motorcycle, Boat, and Other Motor Vehicle Dealers; and
- Retailing manufactured homes (i.e., mobile homes), parts, and equipment— are classified in Industry 453930, Manufactured (Mobile) Home Dealers.

44122 Motorcycle, Boat, and Other Motor Vehicle Dealers[CAN]

This industry comprises establishments primarily engaged in retailing new and used motorcycles, boats, and other vehicles (except automobiles, light trucks, and recreational vehicles), or retailing these new vehicles in combination with activities, such as repair services and selling replacement parts and accessories.

Illustrative Examples:

Aircraft dealers
Motorcycle dealers
All-terrain vehicle (ATV) dealers

Utility trailer dealers
Boat dealers, new and used

US—United States industry only. CAN—United States and Canadian industries are comparable. MEX—United States and Mexican industries are comparable. Blank—Canadian, Mexican, and United States industries are comparable.

Cross-References. Establishments primarily engaged in—

- Retailing new nonmotorized bicycles, surfboards, or wind sail boards—are classified in Industry 45111, Sporting Goods Stores;
- Retailing used nonmotorized bicycles, surfboards, or wind sail boards—are classified in Industry 45331, Used Merchandise Stores;
- Retailing new or used automobiles and light trucks—are classified in Industry Group 4411, Automobile Dealers;
- Retailing new or used recreational vehicles, such as travel trailers—are classified in Industry 44121, Recreational Vehicle Dealers;
- Providing repair services for vehicles without retailing new vehicles—are classified in the appropriate industry for the repair services; and
- Retailing fuel and marine supplies at a marina—are classified in Industry 71393, Marinas.

441221 Motorcycle, ATV, and Personal Watercraft Dealers[US]

This U.S. industry comprises establishments primarily engaged in retailing new and/or used motorcycles, motor scooters, motorbikes, mopeds, off-road all-terrain vehicles, and personal watercraft, or retailing these new vehicles in combination with repair services and selling replacement parts and accessories.

Illustrative Examples:

All-terrain vehicle (ATV) dealers
Motorcycle parts and accessories dealers
Moped dealers
Personal watercraft dealers
Motorcycle dealers

Cross-References. Establishments primarily engaged in—

- Providing motorcycle repair services without retailing new motorcycles—are classified in Industry 811490, Other Personal and Household Goods Repair and Maintenance;
- Retailing new nonmotorized bicycles—are classified in Industry 451110, Sporting Goods Stores;
- Retailing used nonmotorized bicycles—are classified in Industry 453310, Used Merchandise Stores; and
- Retailing new or used boats—are classified in U.S. Industry 441222, Boat Dealers.

441222 Boat Dealers[US]

This U.S. industry comprises establishments primarily engaged in (1) retailing new and/or used boats or retailing new boats in combination with activities, such as repair services and selling replacement parts and accessories, and/or (2) retailing new and/or used outboard motors, boat trailers, marine supplies, parts, and accessories.

Illustrative Examples:

Boat dealers (e.g., powerboats, rowboats, sailboats)

Outboard motor dealers
Marine supply dealers

Cross-References. Establishments primarily engaged in—

- Retailing new surfboards or wind sail boards—are classified in Industry 451110, Sporting Goods Stores;
- Retailing used surfboards or wind sail boards—are classified in Industry 453310, Used Merchandise Stores;
- Providing boat repair services without retailing new boats—are classified in Industry 811490, Other Personal and Household Goods Repair and Maintenance;
- Retailing new or used personal watercraft—are classified in U.S. Industry 441221, Motorcycle, ATV, and Personal Watercraft Dealers; and
- Operating docking and/or storage facilities for pleasure craft owners—are classified in Industry 713930, Marinas.

441229 All Other Motor Vehicle Dealers[US]

This U.S. industry comprises establishments primarily engaged in retailing new and/or used utility trailers and vehicles (except automobiles, light trucks, recreational vehicles, motorcycles, boats, motor scooters, motorbikes, off-road all-terrain vehicles, and personal watercraft) or retailing these new vehicles in combination with activities, such as repair services and selling replacement parts and accessories.

Illustrative Examples:

Aircraft dealers
Snowmobile dealers

Powered golf cart dealers
Utility trailer dealers

Cross-References. Establishments primarily engaged in—

- Retailing new automobiles and light trucks—are classified in Industry 441110, New Car Dealers;
- Retailing used automobiles and light trucks—are classified in Industry 441120, Used Car Dealers;

- Retailing new or used recreational vehicles, such as travel trailers—are classified in Industry 441210, Recreational Vehicle Dealers;

- Retailing new or used motorcycles, motor scooters, motorbikes, off-road all-terrain vehicles, and personal watercraft—are classified in U.S. Industry 441221, Motorcycle, ATV, and Personal Watercraft Dealers;

- Retailing new or used boats, outboard motors, boat trailers, and marine supplies—are classified in U.S. Industry 441222, Boat Dealers; and

- Providing vehicle repair services without retailing new vehicles—are classified in the appropriate industry for the repair services.

4413 Automotive Parts, Accessories, and Tire Stores^{CAN}

44131 Automotive Parts and Accessories Stores^{CAN}
See industry description for 441310 below.

441310 Automotive Parts and Accessories Stores^{CAN}

This industry comprises one or more of the following: (1) establishments known as automotive supply stores primarily engaged in retailing new, used, and/or rebuilt automotive parts and accessories; (2) automotive supply stores that are primarily engaged in both retailing automotive parts and accessories and repairing automobiles; and (3) establishments primarily engaged in retailing and installing automotive accessories.

Illustrative Examples:

Automotive parts and supply stores	Used automotive parts stores
Truck cap stores	Speed shops
Automotive stereo stores	

Cross-References. Establishments primarily engaged in—

- Retailing automotive parts and accessories via electronic home shopping, mail-order, or direct sale—are classified in Subsector 454, Nonstore Retailers;

- Retailing new or used tires—are classified in Industry 441320, Tire Dealers; and

- Repairing and replacing automotive parts, such as transmissions, mufflers, and brake linings (except establishments known as automotive supply stores)—are classified in Industry 81111, Automotive Mechanical and Electrical Repair and Maintenance.

US—United States industry only. CAN—United States and Canadian industries are comparable. MEX—United States and Mexican industries are comparable. Blank—Canadian, Mexican, and United States industries are comparable.

44132   Tire Dealers^{CAN}

See industry description for 441320 below.

441320   Tire Dealers^{CAN}

This industry comprises establishments primarily engaged in retailing new and/ or used tires and tubes or retailing new tires in combination with automotive repair services.

Cross-References. Establishments primarily engaged in—

- Retailing tires via electronic home shopping, mail-order, or direct sale— are classified in Subsector 454, Nonstore Retailers; and

- Tire retreading or recapping—are classified in U.S. Industry 326212, Tire Retreading.

442   Furniture and Home Furnishings Stores^{CAN}

Industries in the Furniture and Home Furnishings Stores subsector retail new furniture and home furnishings from fixed point-of-sale locations. Establishments in this subsector usually operate from showrooms and have substantial areas for the presentation of their products. Many offer interior decorating services in addition to the sale of products.

4421   Furniture Stores^{CAN}

44211   Furniture Stores^{CAN}

See industry description for 442110 below.

442110   Furniture Stores^{CAN}

This industry comprises establishments primarily engaged in retailing new furniture, such as household furniture (e.g., baby furniture box springs and mattresses) and outdoor furniture; office furniture (except those sold in combination with office supplies and equipment); and/or furniture sold in combination with major appliances, home electronics, home furnishings, or floor coverings.

Cross-References. Establishments primarily engaged in—

- Retailing furniture via electronic home shopping, mail-order, or direct sale— are classified in Subsector 454, Nonstore Retailers;

US—United States industry only. CAN—United States and Canadian industries are comparable. MEX—United States and Mexican industries are comparable. Blank—Canadian, Mexican, and United States industries are comparable.

- Retailing used furniture—are classified in Industry 453310, Used Merchandise Stores;

- Retailing custom furniture made on premises—are classified in Subsector 337, Furniture and Related Product Manufacturing; and

- Retailing new office furniture and a range of new office equipment and supplies—are classified in Industry 453210, Office Supplies and Stationery Stores.

4422 Home Furnishings Stores^{CAN}

This industry group comprises establishments primarily engaged in retailing new home furnishings (except furniture).

44221 Floor Covering Stores^{CAN}
See industry description for 442210 below.

442210 Floor Covering Stores^{CAN}

This industry comprises establishments primarily engaged in retailing new floor coverings, such as rugs and carpets, vinyl floor coverings, and floor tile (except ceramic or wood only); or retailing new floor coverings in combination with installation and repair services.

Cross-References. Establishments primarily engaged in—

- Retailing floor coverings via electronic home shopping, mail-order, or direct sale—are classified in Subsector 454, Nonstore Retailers;

- Installing floor coverings without retailing new floor coverings—are classified in Industry 238330, Flooring Contractors;

- Retailing ceramic floor tile or wood floor coverings only—are classified in Industry 444190, Other Building Material Dealers; and

- Retailing used rugs and carpets—are classified in Industry 453310, Used Merchandise Stores.

44229 Other Home Furnishings Stores^{CAN}

This industry comprises establishments primarily engaged in retailing new home furnishings (except furniture and floor coverings).

US—United States industry only. CAN—United States and Canadian industries are comparable. MEX—United States and Mexican industries are comparable. Blank—Canadian, Mexican, and United States industries are comparable.

Illustrative Examples:

Bath shops   Window treatment stores
Kitchenware stores   Glassware stores
Chinaware stores

Cross-References. Establishments primarily engaged in—

- Retailing home furnishings via electronic home shopping, mail-order, or direct sale—are classified in Subsector 454, Nonstore Retailers;

- Retailing custom curtains and draperies made on premises—are classified in Industry 31412, Curtain and Linen Mills;

- Retailing new mirrored glass, lighting fixtures, and new ceramic floor tile or wood floor coverings only—are classified in Industry 44419, Other Building Material Dealers;

- Retailing new furniture—are classified in Industry 44211, Furniture Stores;

- Retailing new floor coverings (except ceramic or wood only)—are classified in Industry 44221, Floor Covering Stores; and

- Retailing used home furnishings—are classified in Industry 45331, Used Merchandise Stores.

442291 Window Treatment Stores[CAN]

This U.S. industry comprises establishments primarily engaged in retailing new window treatments, such as curtains, drapes, blinds, and shades.

Cross-References. Establishments primarily engaged in—

- Retailing window treatments via electronic home shopping, mail-order, or direct sale—are classified in Subsector 454, Nonstore Retailers; and

- Retailing custom curtains and draperies made on premises—are classified in U.S. Industry 314121, Curtain and Drapery Mills.

442299 All Other Home Furnishings Stores[US]

This U.S. industry comprises establishments primarily engaged in retailing new home furnishings (except floor coverings, furniture, and window treatments).

Illustrative Examples:

Bath shops   Picture frame stores
Kitchenware stores   Glassware stores
Chinaware stores   Wood-burning stove stores

Linen stores   Houseware stores
Electric lamp shops

Cross-References. Establishments primarily engaged in—

- Selling home furnishings via electronic home shopping, mail-order, or direct sale—are classified in Subsector 454, Nonstore Retailers;

- Retailing new mirrored glass or lighting fixtures—are classified in Industry 444190, Other Building Material Dealers;

- Retailing new furniture—are classified in Industry 442110, Furniture Stores;

- Retailing new floor coverings—are classified in Industry 442210, Floor Covering Stores;

- Retailing new window treatments—are classified in U.S. Industry 442291, Window Treatment Stores; and

- Retailing used home furnishings—are classified in Industry 453310, Used Merchandise Stores.

443 Electronics and Appliance Stores[CAN]

Industries in the Electronics and Appliance Stores subsector retail new electronics and appliances from point-of-sale locations. Establishments in this subsector often operate from locations that have special provisions for floor displays requiring special electrical capacity to accommodate the proper demonstration of the products. The staff includes sales personnel knowledgeable in the characteristics and warranties of the line of goods retailed and may also include trained repair persons to handle the maintenance and repair of the electronic equipment and appliances. The classifications within this subsector are made principally on the type of product and knowledge required to operate each type of store.

4431 Electronics and Appliance Stores[CAN]

This industry group comprises establishments primarily engaged in retailing the following new products: household-type appliances, cameras, computers, and other electronic goods.

44311 Appliance, Television, and Other Electronics Stores[CAN]

This industry comprises establishments primarily engaged in one of the following: (1) retailing an array of new household-type appliances and consumer-type electronic products, such as radios, televisions, and computers; (2) specializing in

---

US—United States industry only. CAN—United States and Canadian industries are comparable. MEX—United States and Mexican industries are comparable. Blank—Canadian, Mexican, and United States industries are comparable.

retailing a single line of new consumer-type electronic products (except computers); and (3) retailing these new products in combination with repair services.

Illustrative Examples:

Appliance stores   Consumer electronics stores
Radio and television stores

Cross-References. Establishments primarily engaged in—

- Retailing new electronic products via electronic home shopping, mail-order, or direct sale—are classified in Subsector 454, Nonstore Retailers;
- Retailing new computers, computer peripherals, and prepackaged computer software without retailing other consumer-type electronic products or office equipment, office furniture, and office supplies; or retailing these products in combination with repair services—are classified in Industry 44312, Computer and Software Stores;
- Retailing new computers, computer peripherals, and prepackaged software in combination with retailing new office equipment, office furniture, and office supplies—are classified in Industry 45321, Office Supplies and Stationery Stores;
- Retailing new sewing machines in combination with selling new sewing supplies, fabrics, patterns, yarns, and other needlework accessories—are classified in Industry 45113, Sewing, Needlework, and Piece Goods Stores;
- Retailing new electronic toys—are classified in Industry 45112, Hobby, Toy, and Game Stores;
- Providing television or other electronic equipment repair services without retailing new televisions or electronic equipment—are classified in Industry 81121, Electronic and Precision Equipment Repair and Maintenance;
- Providing household-type appliance repair services without retailing new appliances—are classified in Industry 81141, Home and Garden Equipment and Appliance Repair and Maintenance;
- Retailing used appliance and electronic products—are classified in Industry 45331, Used Merchandise Stores;
- Retailing new still and motion picture cameras—are classified in Industry 44313, Camera and Photographic Supplies Stores; and
- Retailing automotive electronic sound systems—are classified in Industry 44131, Automotive Parts and Accessories Stores.

443111 Household Appliance Stores[US]

This U.S. industry comprises establishments known as appliance stores primarily engaged in retailing an array of new household appliances, such as refrigerators, dishwashers, ovens, irons, coffeemakers, hair dryers, electric razors, room air-conditioners, microwave ovens, sewing machines, and vacuum cleaners, or retailing new appliances in combination with appliance repair services.

Cross-References. Establishments primarily engaged in—

- Retailing household appliances via electronic home shopping, mail-order, or direct sale—are classified in Subsector 454, Nonstore Retailers;
- Retailing new sewing machines in combination with selling new sewing supplies, fabrics, patterns, yarns, and other needlework accessories—are classified in Industry 451130, Sewing, Needlework, and Piece Goods Stores;
- Providing household-type appliance repair services without retailing new appliances—are classified in U.S. Industry 811412, Appliance Repair and Maintenance; and
- Retailing used appliances—are classified in Industry 453310, Used Merchandise Stores.

443112 Radio, Television, and Other Electronics Stores^{US}

This U.S. industry comprises: (1) establishments known as consumer electronics stores primarily engaged in retailing a general line of new consumer-type electronic products; (2) establishments specializing in retailing a single line of consumer-type electronic products (except computers); or (3) establishments primarily engaged in retailing these new electronic products in combination with repair services.

Illustrative Examples:

Consumer electronic stores
Stereo stores (except automotive)

Radio and television stores
Telephone stores (including cellular)

Cross-References. Establishments primarily engaged in—

- Retailing electronic goods via electronic home shopping, mail-order, or direct sale—are classified in Subsector 454, Nonstore Retailers;
- Retailing automotive electronic sound systems—are classified in Industry 441310, Automotive Parts and Accessories Stores;
- Retailing new computers, computer peripherals, and prepackaged computer software without retailing other consumer-type electronic products or office equipment, office furniture and office supplies; or retailing these new computer products in combination with repair services—are classified in Industry 443120, Computer and Software Stores;
- Retailing new computers, computer peripherals, and prepackaged software in combination with retailing new office equipment, office furniture, and

office supplies—are classified in Industry 453210, Office Supplies and Stationery Stores;

- Retailing new still and motion picture cameras—are classified in Industry 443130, Camera and Photographic Supplies Stores;

- Providing television or other electronic equipment repair services without retailing new televisions or electronic products—are classified in Industry 81121, Electronic and Precision Equipment Repair and Maintenance;

- Retailing new electronic toys—are classified in Industry 451120, Hobby, Toy, and Game Stores; and

- Retailing used electronics—are classified in Industry 453310, Used Merchandise Stores.

44312 Computer and Software Stores[CAN]
See industry description for 443120 below.

443120 Computer and Software Stores[CAN]

This industry comprises establishments primarily engaged in retailing new computers, computer peripherals, and prepackaged computer software without retailing other consumer-type electronic products or office equipment, office furniture, and office supplies; or retailing these new products in combination with repair and support services.

Cross-References. Establishments primarily engaged in—

- Retailing computers and software via electronic home shopping, mail-order, or direct sale—are classified in Subsector 454, Nonstore Retailers;

- Retailing new electronic toys, such as dedicated video game consoles and handheld electronic games—are classified in Industry 451120, Hobby, Toy, and Game Stores;

- Providing computer repair services without retailing new computers—are classified in U.S. Industry 811212, Computer and Office Machine Repair and Maintenance;

- Retailing new computers, computer peripherals, and prepackaged software in combination with retailing new office equipment, office furniture, and office supplies—are classified in Industry 453210, Office Supplies and Stationery Stores;

- Retailing a general line of new electronic products or specializing in retailing a single line of consumer-type electronic products (except computers)—are

US—United States industry only. CAN—United States and Canadian industries are comparable. MEX—United States and Mexican industries are comparable. Blank—Canadian, Mexican, and United States industries are comparable.

http://www.census.gov/naics

classified in U.S. Industry 443112, Radio, Television, and Other Electronics Stores; and

- Retailing used computers, computer software, video games, and handheld electronic games—are classified in Industry 453310, Used Merchandise Stores.

44313 Camera and Photographic Supplies Stores^{CAN}

See industry description for 443130 below.

443130 Camera and Photographic Supplies Stores^{CAN}

This industry comprises establishments primarily engaged in either retailing new cameras, photographic equipment, and photographic supplies or retailing new cameras and photographic equipment in combination with activities, such as repair services and film developing.

Cross-References. Establishments primarily engaged in—

- Retailing camera and photographic supplies via electronic home shopping, mail-order, or direct sale—are classified in Subsector 454, Nonstore Retailers;
- Retailing new video cameras—are classified in U.S. Industry 443112, Radio, Television, and Other Electronics Stores;
- One-hour film developing without retailing a range of new photographic equipment and supplies—are classified in U.S. Industry 812922, One-Hour Photofinishing;
- Providing repair services for photographic equipment without retailing new photographic equipment—are classified in U.S. Industry 811211, Consumer Electronics Repair and Maintenance;
- Developing film and/or producing photographic prints, slides, and enlargements (except one-hour photofinishing labs)—are classified in U.S. Industry 812921, Photofinishing Laboratories (except One-Hour); and
- Retailing used cameras and photographic equipment—are classified in Industry 453310, Used Merchandise Stores.

444 Building Material and Garden Equipment and Supplies Dealers^{CAN}

Industries in the Building Material and Garden Equipment and Supplies Dealers subsector retail new building material and garden equipment and supplies from

---

US—United States industry only. CAN—United States and Canadian industries are comparable. MEX—United States and Mexican industries are comparable. Blank—Canadian, Mexican, and United States industries are comparable.

fixed point-of-sale locations. Establishments in this subsector have display equipment designed to handle lumber and related products and garden equipment and supplies that may be kept either indoors or outdoors under covered areas. The staff is usually knowledgeable in the use of the specific products being retailed in the construction, repair, and maintenance of the home and associated grounds.

4441 Building Material and Supplies Dealers[CAN]

This industry group comprises establishments primarily engaged in retailing new building materials and supplies.

44411 Home Centers[CAN]
See industry description for 444110 below.

444110 Home Centers[CAN]

This industry comprises establishments known as home centers primarily engaged in retailing a general line of new home repair and improvement materials and supplies, such as lumber, plumbing goods, electrical goods, tools, housewares, hardware, and lawn and garden supplies, with no one merchandise line predominating. The merchandise lines are normally arranged in separate departments.

44412 Paint and Wallpaper Stores[CAN]
See industry description for 444120 below.

444120 Paint and Wallpaper Stores[CAN]

This industry comprises establishments known as paint and wallpaper stores primarily engaged in retailing paint, wallpaper, and related supplies.

44413 Hardware Stores[CAN]
See industry description for 444130 below.

444130 Hardware Stores[CAN]

This industry comprises establishments known as hardware stores primarily engaged in retailing a general line of new hardware items, such as tools and builders' hardware.

US—United States industry only. CAN—United States and Canadian industries are comparable. MEX—United States and Mexican industries are comparable. Blank—Canadian, Mexican, and United States industries are comparable.

Cross-References. Establishments primarily engaged in—

- Retailing hardware items via electronic home shopping, mail order, or direct sale—are classified in Subsector 454, Nonstore Retailers;

- Retailing a general line of home repair and improvement materials and supplies, known as home centers—are classified in Industry 444110, Home Centers; and

- Retailing used hardware items—are classified in Industry 453310, Used Merchandise Stores.

44419 Other Building Material Dealers[CAN]
See industry description for 444190 below.

444190 Other Building Material Dealers[CAN]

This industry comprises establishments (except those known as home centers, paint and wallpaper stores, and hardware stores) primarily engaged in retailing specialized lines of new building materials, such as lumber, fencing, glass, doors, plumbing fixtures and supplies, electrical supplies, prefabricated buildings and kits, and kitchen and bath cabinets and countertops to be installed.

Illustrative Examples:

Electrical supply stores
Kitchen cabinet (except custom) stores
Fencing dealers
Lumber yards, retail
Floor covering stores, wood or ceramic
  tile only

Plumbing supply stores
Garage door dealers
Prefabricated building dealers
Glass stores

Cross-References. Establishments primarily engaged in—

- Retailing building materials via electronic home shopping, mail-order, or direct sale—are classified in Subsector 454, Nonstore Retailers;

- Retailing used building materials—are classified in Industry 453310, Used Merchandise Stores;

- Providing carpentry/installation services for products—are classified in Industry 238350, Finish Carpentry Contractors;

- Installing plumbing fixtures and supplies—are classified in Industry 238220, Plumbing, Heating, and Air-Conditioning Contractors;

- Installing electrical supplies, such as lighting fixtures and ceiling fans— are classified in Industry 238210, Electrical Contractors and Other Wiring Installation Contractors;

US—United States industry only. CAN—United States and Canadian industries are comparable. MEX—United States and Mexican industries are comparable. Blank—Canadian, Mexican, and United States industries are comparable.

- Making custom furniture (e.g., kitchen cabinets)—are classified in Subsector 337, Furniture and Related Product Manufacturing;
- Retailing a general line of new hardware items, known as hardware stores— are classified in Industry 444130, Hardware Stores;
- Retailing paint and wallpaper, known as paint and wallpaper stores—are classified in Industry 444120, Paint and Wallpaper Stores; and
- Retailing a general line of home repair and improvement materials and supplies, known as home centers—are classified in Industry 444110, Home Centers.

4442 Lawn and Garden Equipment and Supplies Stores^{CAN}

This industry group comprises establishments primarily engaged in retailing new lawn and garden equipment and supplies.

44421 Outdoor Power Equipment Stores^{CAN}
See industry description for 444210 below.

444210 Outdoor Power Equipment Stores^{CAN}

This industry comprises establishments primarily engaged in retailing new outdoor power equipment or retailing new outdoor power equipment in combination with activities, such as repair services and selling replacement parts.

Cross-References. Establishments primarily engaged in—

- Retailing outdoor power equipment via electronic home shopping, mail-order, or direct sale—are classified in Subsector 454, Nonstore Retailers;
- Providing outdoor power equipment repair services without retailing new outdoor power equipment—are classified in U.S. Industry 811411, Home and Garden Equipment Repair and Maintenance; and
- Retailing used outdoor power equipment—are classified in Industry 453310, Used Merchandise Stores.

44422 Nursery, Garden Center, and Farm Supply Stores^{CAN}
See industry description for 444220 below.

444220 Nursery, Garden Center, and Farm Supply Stores^{CAN}

This industry comprises establishments primarily engaged in retailing nursery and garden products, such as trees, shrubs, plants, seeds, bulbs, and sod, that are

US—United States industry only. CAN—United States and Canadian industries are comparable. MEX—United States and Mexican industries are comparable. Blank—Canadian, Mexican, and United States industries are comparable.

predominantly grown elsewhere. These establishments may sell a limited amount of a product they grow themselves. Also included in this industry are establishments primarily engaged in retailing farm supplies, such as animal (non-pet) feed.

Cross-References. Establishments primarily engaged in—

- Retailing nursery and garden products via electronic home shopping, mail-order, or direct sale—are classified in Subsector 454, Nonstore Retailers;

- Providing landscaping services—are classified in Industry 561730, Landscaping Services; and

- Growing and retailing nursery stock—are classified in U.S. Industry 111421, Nursery and Tree Production.

445 Food and Beverage Stores^{CAN}

Industries in the Food and Beverage Stores subsector usually retail food and beverages merchandise from fixed point-of-sale locations. Establishments in this subsector have special equipment (e.g., freezers, refrigerated display cases, refrigerators) for displaying food and beverage goods. They have staff trained in the processing of food products to guarantee the proper storage and sanitary conditions required by regulatory authority.

4451 Grocery Stores^{CAN}

This industry group comprises establishments primarily engaged in retailing a general line of food products.

44511 Supermarkets and Other Grocery (except Convenience) Stores^{CAN}
See industry description for 445110 below.

445110 Supermarkets and Other Grocery (except Convenience) Stores^{CAN}

This industry comprises establishments generally known as supermarkets and grocery stores primarily engaged in retailing a general line of food, such as canned and frozen foods; fresh fruits and vegetables; and fresh and prepared meats, fish, and poultry. Included in this industry are delicatessen-type establishments primarily engaged in retailing a general line of food.

US—United States industry only. CAN—United States and Canadian industries are comparable. MEX—United States and Mexican industries are comparable. Blank—Canadian, Mexican, and United States industries are comparable.

Cross-References. Establishments primarily engaged in—

- Retailing automotive fuels in combination with a convenience store or food mart—are classified in Industry 447110, Gasoline Stations with Convenience Stores;

- Retailing a limited line of goods, known as convenience stores or food marts (except those with fuel pumps)—are classified in Industry 445120, Convenience Stores;

- Retailing frozen food and freezer plans via direct sales to residential customers—are classified in Industry 454390, Other Direct Selling Establishments;

- Providing food services in delicatessen-type establishments—are classified in U.S. Industry 722211, Limited-Service Restaurants; and

- Retailing fresh meat in delicatessen-type establishments—are classified in Industry 445210, Meat Markets.

44512 Convenience Stores[CAN]

See industry description for 445120 below.

445120 Convenience Stores[CAN]

This industry comprises establishments known as convenience stores or food marts (except those with fuel pumps) primarily engaged in retailing a limited line of goods that generally includes milk, bread, soda, and snacks.

Cross-References. Establishments primarily engaged in—

- Retailing a general line of food, known as supermarkets and grocery stores— are classified in Industry 445110, Supermarkets and Other Grocery (except Convenience) Stores; and

- Retailing automotive fuels in combination with a convenience store or food mart—are classified in Industry 447110, Gasoline Stations with Convenience Stores.

4452 Specialty Food Stores[CAN]

This industry group comprises establishments primarily engaged in retailing specialized lines of food.

44521 Meat Markets[CAN]

See industry description for 445210 below.

US—United States industry only. CAN--United States and Canadian industries are comparable. MEX—United States and Mexican industries are comparable. Blank—Canadian, Mexican, and United States industries are comparable.

445210 Meat Markets^{CAN}

This industry comprises establishments primarily engaged in retailing fresh, frozen, or cured meats and poultry. Delicatessen-type establishments primarily engaged in retailing fresh meat are included in this industry.

Illustrative Examples:

Baked ham stores
Meat markets
Butcher shops

Poultry dealers
Frozen meat shops

Cross-References. Establishments primarily engaged in—

- Retailing meat and poultry via electronic home shopping, mail-order, or direct sale—are classified in Subsector 454, Nonstore Retailers;
- Retailing a general line of food, known as supermarkets and grocery stores— are classified in Industry 445110, Supermarkets and Other Grocery (except Convenience) Stores; and
- Providing food services in delicatessen-type establishments—are classified in U.S. Industry 722211, Limited-Service Restaurants.

44522 Fish and Seafood Markets^{CAN}
See industry description for 445220 below.

445220 Fish and Seafood Markets^{CAN}

This industry comprises establishments primarily engaged in retailing fresh, frozen, or cured fish and seafood products.

Cross-References.
Establishments primarily engaged in retailing fish and seafood products via electronic home shopping, mail-order, or direct sale are classified in Subsector 454, Nonstore Retailers.

44523 Fruit and Vegetable Markets^{CAN}
See industry description for 445230 below.

445230 Fruit and Vegetable Markets^{CAN}

This industry comprises establishments primarily engaged in retailing fresh fruits and vegetables.

Cross-References. Establishments primarily engaged in—

- Retailing fruits and vegetables via electronic home shopping, mail-order, or direct sale—are classified in Subsector 454, Nonstore Retailers; and

- Growing and selling vegetables and/or fruits at roadside stands—are classified in Subsector 111, Crop Production.

44529 Other Specialty Food Stores[CAN]

This industry comprises establishments primarily engaged in retailing specialty foods (except meat, fish, seafood, and fruits and vegetables) not for immediate consumption and not made on premises.

Illustrative Examples:

Baked goods stores (except immediate consumption)
Dairy product stores
Coffee and tea (i.e., packaged) stores
Gourmet food stores
Confectionery (i.e., packaged) stores
Nut (i.e., packaged) stores

Cross-References. Establishments primarily engaged in—

- Retailing specialty foods via electronic home shopping, mail-order, or direct sale—are classified in Subsector 454, Nonstore Retailers;

- Retailing baked goods made on the premises, but not for immediate consumption—are classified in Industry 31181, Bread and Bakery Product Manufacturing;

- Retailing fresh, frozen, or cured meats and poultry—are classified in Industry 44521, Meat Markets;

- Retailing fresh, frozen, or cured fish and seafood products—are classified in Industry 44522, Fish and Seafood Markets;

- Retailing fresh fruits and vegetables—are classified in Industry 44523, Fruit and Vegetable Markets;

- Retailing candy and confectionery products not for immediate consumption and not made on premises—are classified in Industry Group 3113, Sugar and Confectionery Product Manufacturing; and

- Selling snack foods (e.g., doughnuts, bagels, ice cream, popcorn) for immediate consumption—are classified in Subsector 722, Food Services and Drinking Places.

445291 Baked Goods Stores[CAN]

This U.S. industry comprises establishments primarily engaged in retailing baked goods not for immediate consumption and not made on the premises.

Cross-References. Establishments primarily engaged in—

- Retailing baked goods via electronic home shopping, mail-order, or direct sale—are classified in Subsector 454, Nonstore Retailers;

- Selling snack foods (e.g., doughnuts, bagels, ice cream, popcorn) for immediate consumption—are classified in U.S. Industry 722213, Snack and Nonalcoholic Beverage Bars; and

- Retailing baked goods made on the premises but not for immediate consumption—are classified in Industry 311811, Retail Bakeries.

445292 Confectionery and Nut Stores[CAN]

This U.S. industry comprises establishments primarily engaged in retailing candy and other confections, nuts, and popcorn not for immediate consumption and not made on the premises.

Cross-References. Establishments primarily engaged in—

- Retailing confectionery goods and nuts via electronic home shopping, mail-order, or direct sale—are classified in Subsector 454, Nonstore Retailers;

- Retailing confectionery goods and nuts made on premises and not packaged for immediate consumption—are classified in Industry Group 3113, Sugar and Confectionery Product Manufacturing;

- Selling snack foods (e.g., doughnuts, bagels, ice cream, popcorn) for immediate consumption—are classified in U.S. Industry 722213, Snack and Nonalcoholic Beverage Bars; and

- Retailing baked goods made on the premises but not for immediate consumption—are classified in Industry 311811, Retail Bakeries.

445299 All Other Specialty Food Stores[CAN]

This U.S. industry comprises establishments primarily engaged in retailing miscellaneous specialty foods (except meat, fish, seafood, fruit and vegetables, confections, nuts, popcorn, and baked goods) not for immediate consumption and not made on the premises.

Illustrative Examples:

Coffee and tea (i.e., packaged) stores	Spice stores
Soft drink (i.e., bottled) stores	Gourmet food stores
Dairy product stores	Water (i.e., bottled) stores.

US—United States industry only. CAN—United States and Canadian industries are comparable. MEX—United States and Mexican industries are comparable. Blank—Canadian, Mexican, and United States industries are comparable.

Cross-References. Establishments primarily engaged in—

- Retailing specialty foods via electronic home shopping, mail-order, or direct sale—are classified in Subsector 454, Nonstore Retailers;

- Selling snack foods (e.g., doughnuts, bagels, ice cream, popcorn) for immediate consumption—are classified in U.S. Industry 722213, Snack and Non-alcoholic Beverage Bars;

- Retailing fresh, frozen, or cured meats and poultry—are classified in Industry 445210, Meat Markets;

- Retailing fresh, frozen, or cured fish and seafood products—are classified in Industry 445220, Fish and Seafood Markets;

- Retailing fresh fruits and vegetables—are classified in Industry 445230, Fruit and Vegetable Markets;

- Retailing candy and other confections, nuts, and popcorn not for immediate consumption and not made on the premises—are classified in U.S. Industry 445292, Confectionery and Nut Stores; and

- Retailing baked goods not for immediate consumption and not made on the premises—are classified in U.S. Industry 445291, Baked Goods Stores.

4453 Beer, Wine, and Liquor Stores[CAN]

44531 Beer, Wine, and Liquor Stores[CAN]
See industry description for 445310 below.

445310 Beer, Wine, and Liquor Stores[CAN]

This industry comprises establishments primarily engaged in retailing packaged alcoholic beverages, such as ale, beer, wine, and liquor.

Cross-References.

Establishments primarily engaged in retailing packaged liquor in combination with providing prepared drinks for immediate consumption on the premises are classified in Industry 722410, Drinking Places (Alcoholic Beverages).

446 Health and Personal Care Stores[CAN]

Industries in the Health and Personal Care Stores subsector retail health and personal care merchandise from fixed point-of-sale locations. Establishments in this subsector are characterized principally by the products they retail, and some

---

US—United States industry only. CAN—United States and Canadian industries are comparable. MEX—United States and Mexican industries are comparable. Blank—Canadian, Mexican, and United States industries are comparable.

health and personal care stores may have specialized staff trained in dealing with the products. Staff may include pharmacists, opticians, and other professionals engaged in retailing, advising customers, and/or fitting the product sold to the customer's needs.

4461 Health and Personal Care Stores^{CAN}

This industry group comprises establishments primarily engaged in retailing health and personal care products.

44611 Pharmacies and Drug Stores^{CAN}
See industry description for 446110 below.

446110 Pharmacies and Drug Stores^{CAN}

This industry comprises establishments known as pharmacies and drug stores engaged in retailing prescription or nonprescription drugs and medicines.

Cross-References. Establishments primarily engaged in—

- Retailing food supplement products, such as vitamins, nutrition supplements, and body enhancing supplements—are classified in U.S. Industry 446191, Food (Health) Supplement Stores; and

- Retailing prescription and nonprescription drugs via electronic home shopping, mail-order, or direct sale—are classified in Subsector 454, Nonstore Retailers.

44612 Cosmetics, Beauty Supplies, and Perfume Stores^{CAN}
See industry description for 446120 below.

446120 Cosmetics, Beauty Supplies, and Perfume Stores^{CAN}

This industry comprises establishments known as cosmetic or perfume stores or beauty supply shops primarily engaged in retailing cosmetics, perfumes, toiletries, and personal grooming products.

Cross-References. Establishments primarily engaged in—

- Providing beauty parlor services—are classified in U.S. Industry 812112, Beauty Salons; and

---

US—United States industry only. CAN—United States and Canadian industries are comparable. MEX—United States and Mexican industries are comparable. Blank—Canadian, Mexican, and United States industries are comparable.

- Retailing perfumes, cosmetics, and beauty supplies via electronic home shopping, mail-order, or direct sale—are classified in Subsector 454, Nonstore Retailers.

44613 Optical Goods Stores^{CAN}

See industry description for 446130 below.

446130 Optical Goods Stores^{CAN}

This industry comprises establishments primarily engaged in one or more of the following: (1) retailing and fitting prescription eyeglasses and contact lenses; (2) retailing prescription eyeglasses in combination with the grinding of lenses to order on the premises; and (3) selling nonprescription eyeglasses. ˙

Cross-References. Establishments primarily engaged in—

- Grinding lenses without retailing lenses—are classified in U.S. Industry 339115, Ophthalmic Goods Manufacturing;

- The private or group practice of optometry, even though glasses and contact lenses are sold at these establishments—are classified in Industry 621320, Offices of Optometrists; and

- Retailing eyeglasses and contact lenses via mail-order—are classified in U.S. Industry 454113, Mail-Order Houses.

44619 Other Health and Personal Care Stores^{CAN}

This industry comprises establishments primarily engaged in retailing health and personal care items (except drugs, medicines, optical goods, perfumes, cosmetics, and beauty supplies).

Illustrative Examples:

Convalescent supply stores	Sick room supply stores
Prosthetic stores	Hearing aid stores
Food (i.e., health) supplement stores	

Cross-References. Establishments primarily engaged in—

- Retailing health and personal care items via electronic home shopping, mail-order, or direct sale—are classified in Subsector 454, Nonstore Retailers;

- Retailing orthopedic shoes—are classified in Industry 44821, Shoe Stores;

- Retailing orthopedic and prosthetic appliances that are made on premises—are classified in Industry 33911, Medical Equipment and Supplies Manufacturing;
- Retailing prescription and nonprescription drugs and medicines—are classified in Industry 44611, Pharmacies and Drug Stores;
- Retailing eyeglasses and contact lenses—are classified in Industry 44613, Optical Goods Stores;
- Retailing perfumes, cosmetics, and beauty supplies—are classified in Industry 44612, Cosmetics, Beauty Supplies, and Perfume Stores; and
- Retailing naturally organic foods, such as fruits and vegetables, dairy products, and cereals and grains—are classified in Subsector 445, Food and Beverage Stores.

446191 Food (Health) Supplement Stores^{CAN}

This U.S. industry comprises establishments primarily engaged in retailing food supplement products, such as vitamins, nutrition supplements, and body enhancing supplements.

Cross-References. Establishments primarily engaged in—
- Retailing food supplement products via electronic home shopping, mail-order, or direct sale—are classified in Subsector 454, Nonstore Retailers;
- Retailing prescription and nonprescription drugs and medicines—are classified in Industry 446110, Pharmacies and Drug Stores; and
- Retailing naturally organic foods, such as fruits and vegetables, dairy products, and cereals and grains—are classified in Subsector 445, Food and Beverage Stores.

446199 All Other Health and Personal Care Stores^{CAN}

This U.S. industry comprises establishments primarily engaged in retailing specialized lines of health and personal care merchandise (except drugs, medicines, optical goods, cosmetics, beauty supplies, perfume, and food supplement products).

Illustrative Examples:

Convalescent supply stores	Hearing aid stores
Prosthetic stores	Sick room supply stores

Cross-References. Establishments primarily engaged in—
- Retailing specialized health and personal care merchandise via electronic home shopping, mail-order, or direct sale—are classified in Subsector 454, Nonstore Retailers;

US—United States industry only. CAN—United States and Canadian industries are comparable. MEX—United States and Mexican industries are comparable. Blank—Canadian, Mexican, and United States industries are comparable.

- Retailing food supplement products—are classified in U.S. Industry 446191, Food (Health) Supplement Stores;

- Retailing prescription or nonprescription drugs and medicines—are classified in Industry 446110, Pharmacies and Drug Stores;

- Retailing eyeglasses and contact lenses—are classified in Industry 446130, Optical Goods Stores;

- Retailing perfumes, cosmetics, and beauty supplies—are classified in Industry 446120, Cosmetics, Beauty Supplies, and Perfume Stores;

- Retailing orthopedic shoes—are classified in Industry 448210, Shoe Stores; and

- Retailing orthopedic and prosthetic appliances that are made on premises—are classified in U.S. Industry 339113, Surgical Appliance and Supplies Manufacturing.

447 Gasoline Stations^{CAN}

Industries in the Gasoline Stations subsector retail automotive fuels (e.g., gasoline, diesel fuel, gasohol) and automotive oils or retail these products in combination with convenience store items. These establishments have specialized equipment for the storage and dispensing of automotive fuels.

4471 Gasoline Stations^{CAN}

44711 Gasoline Stations with Convenience Stores^{CAN}
See industry description for 447110 below.

447110 Gasoline Stations with Convenience Stores^{CAN}

This industry comprises establishments engaged in retailing automotive fuels (e.g., diesel fuel, gasohol, gasoline) in combination with convenience store or food mart items. These establishments can either be in a convenience store (i.e., food mart) setting or a gasoline station setting. These establishments may also provide automotive repair services.

Cross-References. Establishments primarily engaged in—

- Retailing automotive fuels without a convenience store—are classified in Industry 447190, Other Gasoline Stations; and

- Retailing a limited line of goods, known as convenience stores or food marts (except those with fuel pumps)—are classified in Industry 445120, Convenience Stores.

US—United States industry only. CAN—United States and Canadian industries are comparable. MEX—United States and Mexican industries are comparable. Blank—Canadian, Mexican, and United States industries are comparable.

44719 Other Gasoline Stations^{CAN}

See industry description for 447190 below.

447190 Other Gasoline Stations^{CAN}

This industry comprises establishments known as gasoline stations (except those with convenience stores) primarily engaged in one of the following: (1) retailing automotive fuels (e.g., diesel fuel, gasohol, gasoline) or (2) retailing these fuels in combination with activities, such as providing repair services; selling automotive oils, replacement parts, and accessories; and/or providing food services.

Illustrative Examples:

Gasoline stations without convenience stores	Truck stops
	Marine service stations

Cross-References. Establishments primarily engaged in—

- Repairing motor vehicles without retailing automotive fuels—are classified in Industry Group 8111, Automotive Repair and Maintenance; and

- Retailing automotive fuels in combination with a convenience store or food mart—are classified in Industry 447110, Gasoline Stations with Convenience Stores.

448 Clothing and Clothing Accessories Stores^{CAN}

Industries in the Clothing and Clothing Accessories Stores subsector retail new clothing and clothing accessories merchandise from fixed point-of-sale locations. Establishments in this subsector have similar display equipment and staff that is knowledgeable regarding fashion trends and the proper match of styles, colors, and combinations of clothing and accessories to the characteristics and tastes of the customer.

4481 Clothing Stores^{CAN}

This industry group comprises establishments primarily engaged in retailing new clothing.

44811 Men's Clothing Stores^{CAN}

See industry description for 448110 below.

US—United States industry only. CAN—United States and Canadian industries are comparable. MEX—United States and Mexican industries are comparable. Blank—Canadian, Mexican, and United States industries are comparable.

448110 Men's Clothing Stores^{CAN}

This industry comprises establishments primarily engaged in retailing a general line of new men's and boys' clothing. These establishments may provide basic alterations, such as hemming, taking in or letting out seams, or lengthening or shortening sleeves.

Cross-References. Establishments primarily engaged in—

- Retailing men's and boys' clothing via electronic home shopping, mail-order, or direct sale—are classified in Subsector 454, Nonstore Retailers;
- Retailing custom men's clothing made on the premises—are classified in Industry Group 3152, Cut and Sew Apparel Manufacturing;
- Retailing new men's and boys' accessories—are classified in Industry 448150, Clothing Accessories Stores;
- Retailing specialized new apparel, such as raincoats, leather coats, fur apparel, and swimwear—are classified in Industry 448190, Other Clothing Stores;
- Retailing new clothing for all genders and age groups—are classified in Industry 448140, Family Clothing Stores;
- Retailing secondhand clothes—are classified in Industry 453310, Used Merchandise Stores; and
- Providing clothing alterations and repair—are classified in Industry 811490, Other Personal and Household Goods Repair and Maintenance.

44812 Women's Clothing Stores^{CAN}
See industry description for 448120 below.

448120 Women's Clothing Stores^{CAN}

This industry comprises establishments primarily engaged in retailing a general line of new women's, misses' and juniors' clothing, including maternity wear. These establishments may provide basic alterations, such as hemming, taking in or letting out seams, or lengthening or shortening sleeves.

Cross-References. Establishments primarily engaged in—

- Retailing women's clothing via electronic home shopping, mail-order, or direct sale—are classified in Subsector 454, Nonstore Retailers;
- Retailing custom women's clothing made on premises—are classified in Industry Group 3152, Cut and Sew Apparel Manufacturing;

- Retailing new women's accessories—are classified in Industry 448150, Clothing Accessories Stores;

- Retailing new clothing for all genders and age groups—are classified in Industry 448140, Family Clothing Stores;

- Retailing specialized new apparel, such as bridal gowns, raincoats, leather coats, fur apparel, and swimwear—are classified in Industry 448190, Other Clothing Stores;

- Retailing secondhand clothes—are classified in Industry 453310, Used Merchandise Stores; and

- Providing clothing alterations and repair—are classified in Industry 811490, Other Personal and Household Goods Repair and Maintenance.

44813 Children's and Infants' Clothing Stores^{CAN}

See industry description for 448130 below.

448130 Children's and Infants' Clothing Stores^{CAN}

This industry comprises establishments primarily engaged in retailing a general line of new children's and infants' clothing. These establishments may provide basic alterations, such as hemming, taking in or letting out seams, or lengthening or shortening sleeves.

Cross-References. Establishments primarily engaged in—

- Retailing children's and infants' clothing via electronic home shopping, mail-order, or direct sale—are classified in Subsector 454, Nonstore Retailers;

- Retailing new children's and infants' accessories—are classified in Industry 448150, Clothing Accessories Stores;

- Retailing new clothing for all genders or age groups—are classified in Industry 448140, Family Clothing Stores;

- Retailing secondhand clothes—are classified in Industry 453310, Used Merchandise Stores; and

- Providing clothing alterations and repair—are classified in Industry 811490, Other Personal and Household Goods Repair and Maintenance.

44814 Family Clothing Stores^{CAN}

See industry description for 448140 below.

448140 Family Clothing Stores^{CAN}

This industry comprises establishments primarily engaged in retailing a general line of new clothing for men, women, and children, without specializing in sales for an individual gender or age group. These establishments may provide basic alterations, such as hemming, taking in or letting out seams, or lengthening or shortening sleeves.

Cross-References. Establishments primarily engaged in—

- Retailing clothing for all genders via electronic home shopping, mail-order, or direct sale—are classified in Subsector 454, Nonstore Retailers;
- Retailing new men's and boys' clothing—are classified in Industry 448110, Men's Clothing Stores;
- Retailing new women's, misses', and juniors' clothing—are classified in Industry 448120, Women's Clothing Stores;
- Retailing new children's and infants' clothing—are classified in Industry 448130, Children's and Infants' Clothing Stores;
- Retailing specialized new apparel, such as raincoats, bridal gowns, leather coats, fur apparel, and swimwear—are classified in Industry 448190, Other Clothing Stores;
- Providing clothing alterations and repair—are classified in Industry 811490, Other Personal and Household Goods Repair and Maintenance; and
- Retailing secondhand clothes—are classified in Industry 453310, Used Merchandise Stores.

44815 Clothing Accessories Stores^{CAN}
See industry description for 448150 below.

448150 Clothing Accessories Stores^{CAN}

This industry comprises establishments primarily engaged in retailing single or combination lines of new clothing accessories, such as hats and caps, costume jewelry, gloves, handbags, ties, wigs, toupees, and belts.

Illustrative Examples:

Costume jewelry stores	Neckwear stores
Wig and hairpiece stores	

Cross-References. Establishments primarily engaged in—

- Retailing specialized lines of clothing via electronic home shopping, mail-order, or direct sale—are classified in Subsector 454, Nonstore Retailers;

- Retailing precious jewelry and watches—are classified in Industry 448310, Jewelry Stores;

- Retailing used clothing accessories—are classified in Industry 453310, Used Merchandise Stores;

- Retailing luggage, briefcases, trunks, or these products in combination with a general line of leather items (except leather apparel), known as luggage and leather goods stores—are classified in Industry 448320, Luggage and Leather Goods Stores; and

- Retailing leather apparel—are classified in Industry 448190, Other Clothing Stores.

44819 Other Clothing Stores^{CAN}

See industry description for 448190 below.

448190 Other Clothing Stores^{US}

This industry comprises establishments primarily engaged in retailing specialized lines of new clothing (except general lines of men's, women's, children's, infants', and family clothing). These establishments may provide basic alterations, such as hemming, taking in or letting out seams, or lengthening or shortening sleeves.

Illustrative Examples:

Bridal gown (except custom) shops	Fur apparel stores
Leather coat stores	Swimwear stores
Costume shops	Hosiery stores
Lingerie stores	Uniform (except athletic) stores

Cross-References. Establishments primarily engaged in—

- Retailing specialized apparel via electronic home shopping, mail-order, or direct sale—are classified in Subsector 454, Nonstore Retailers;

- Retailing custom apparel and accessories made on the premises—are classified in Subsector 315, Apparel Manufacturing;

- Retailing new men's and boys' clothing—are classified in Industry 448110, Men's Clothing Stores;

- Retailing new women's, misses', and juniors' clothing, including maternity wear—are classified in Industry 448120, Women's Clothing Stores;

- Retailing new children's and infants' clothing—are classified in Industry 448130, Children's and Infants' Clothing Stores;

- Retailing new clothing for all genders or age groups—are classified in Industry 448140, Family Clothing Stores;

- Retailing athletic uniforms—are classified in Industry 451110, Sporting Goods Stores;

- Retailing secondhand clothes—are classified in Industry 453310, Used Merchandise Stores;

- Retailing luggage, briefcases, trunks, or these products in combination with a general line of leather items (except leather apparel), known as luggage and leather goods stores—are classified in Industry 448320, Luggage and Leather Goods Stores; and

- Providing clothing alterations and repair—are classified in Industry 811490, Other Personal and Household Goods Repair and Maintenance.

4482 Shoe Stores^{CAN}

44821 Shoe Stores^{CAN}
See industry description for 448210 below.

448210 Shoe Stores^{CAN}

This industry comprises establishments primarily engaged in retailing all types of new footwear (except hosiery and specialty sports footwear, such as golf shoes, bowling shoes, and spiked shoes). Establishments primarily engaged in retailing new tennis shoes or sneakers are included in this industry.

Cross-References. Establishments primarily engaged in—

- Retailing footwear via electronic home shopping, mail-order, or direct sale— are classified in Subsector 454, Nonstore Retailers;

- Retailing hosiery—are classified in Industry 448190, Other Clothing Stores;

- Retailing new specialty sports footwear (e.g., bowling shoes, golf shoes, spiked shoes)—are classified in Industry 451110, Sporting Goods Stores; and

- Retailing used footwear—are classified in Industry 453310, Used Merchandise Stores.

4483 Jewelry, Luggage, and Leather Goods Stores^{CAN}

This industry group comprises establishments primarily engaged in retailing new jewelry (except costume jewelry); new silver and plated silverware; new

---

watches and clocks; and new luggage with or without a general line of new leather goods and accessories, such as hats, gloves, handbags, ties, and belts.

44831 Jewelry Stores^{CAN}
See industry description for 448310 below.

448310 Jewelry Stores^{CAN}

This industry comprises establishments primarily engaged in retailing one or more of the following items: (1) new jewelry (except costume jewelry); (2) new sterling and plated silverware; and (3) new watches and clocks. Also included are establishments retailing these new products in combination with lapidary work and/or repair services.

Cross-References. Establishments primarily engaged in—

- Retailing new costume jewelry—are classified in Industry 448150, Clothing Accessories Stores;
- Retailing jewelry via electronic home shopping, mail-order, or direct sale— are classified in Subsector 454, Nonstore Retailers;
- Retailing antiques or used jewelry, silverware, and watches and clocks— are classified in Industry 453310, Used Merchandise Stores;
- Providing jewelry or watch and clock repair without retailing new jewelry or watches and clocks—are classified in Industry 811490, Other Personal and Household Goods Repair and Maintenance; and
- Cutting and setting gem stones—are classified in U.S. Industry 339913, Jewelers' Material and Lapidary Work Manufacturing.

44832 Luggage and Leather Goods Stores^{CAN}
See industry description for 448320 below.

448320 Luggage and Leather Goods Stores^{CAN}

This industry comprises establishments known as luggage and leather goods stores primarily engaged in retailing new luggage, briefcases, and trunks, or retailing these new products in combination with a general line of leather items (except leather apparel), such as belts, gloves, and handbags.

Cross-References. Establishments primarily engaged in—

- Retailing luggage and leather goods via electronic home shopping, mail-order, or direct sale—are classified in Subsector 454, Nonstore Retailers;

- Retailing used luggage and leather goods—are classified in Industry 453310, Used Merchandise Stores;

- Retailing single or combination lines of new clothing accessories (e.g., gloves, handbags, or leather belts)—are classified in Industry 448150, Clothing Accessories Stores; and

- Retailing new leather coats—are classified in Industry 448190, Other Clothing Stores.

451 Sporting Goods, Hobby, Book, and Music Stores[CAN]

Industries in the Sporting Goods, Hobby, Book, and Music Stores subsector are engaged in retailing and providing expertise on use of sporting equipment or other specific leisure activities, such as needlework and musical instruments. Book stores are also included in this subsector.

4511 Sporting Goods, Hobby, and Musical Instrument Stores[CAN]

This industry group comprises establishments primarily engaged in retailing new sporting goods, games and toys, and musical instruments.

45111 Sporting Goods Stores[CAN]
See industry description for 451110 below.

451110 Sporting Goods Stores[CAN]

This industry comprises establishments primarily engaged in retailing new sporting goods, such as bicycles and bicycle parts; camping equipment; exercise and fitness equipment; athletic uniforms; specialty sports footwear; and sporting goods, equipment, and accessories.

Illustrative Examples:

Athletic uniform supply stores
Fishing supply stores
Bicycle (except motorized) shops
Golf pro shops
Bowling equipment and supply stores
Saddlery stores

Diving equipment stores
Sporting goods (e.g., scuba, skiing, outdoor) stores
Exercise equipment stores
Sporting gun shops

Cross-References. Establishments primarily engaged in—

- Retailing sporting goods via electronic home shopping, mail order, or direct sale—are classified in Subsector 454, Nonstore Retailers;

US—United States industry only. CAN—United States and Canadian industries are comparable. MEX—United States and Mexican industries are comparable. Blank—Canadian, Mexican, and United States industries are comparable.

- Retailing new or used campers (pickup coaches) and camping trailers—are classified in Industry 441210, Recreational Vehicle Dealers;

- Retailing new or used snowmobiles, motorized bicycles, and motorized golf carts—are classified in Industry 44122, Motorcycle, Boat, and Other Motor Vehicle Dealers;

- Retailing new shoes (except specialty sports footwear, such as golf shoes, bowling shoes, and spiked shoes)—are classified in Industry 448210, Shoe Stores;

- Repairing or servicing sporting goods, without retailing new sporting goods—are classified in Industry 811490, Other Personal and Household Goods Repair and Maintenance; and

- Retailing used sporting goods and used bicycles—are classified in Industry 453310, Used Merchandise Stores.

45112 Hobby, Toy, and Game Stores^{CAN}

See industry description for 451120 below.

451120 Hobby, Toy, and Game Stores^{CAN}

This industry comprises establishments primarily engaged in retailing new toys, games, and hobby and craft supplies (except needlecraft).

Cross-References. Establishments primarily engaged in—

- Retailing toys, games, and hobby and craft supplies via electronic home shopping, mail-order, or direct sale—are classified in Subsector 454, Nonstore Retailers;

- Retailing artists' supplies or collectors' items, such as coins, stamps, autographs, and cards—are classified in U.S. Industry 453998, All Other Miscellaneous Store Retailers (except Tobacco Stores);

- Retailing new computer software (e.g., game software)—are classified in Industry 443120, Computer and Software Stores;

- Retailing used toys, games, and hobby supplies—are classified in Industry 453310, Used Merchandise Stores; and

- Retailing new sewing supplies, fabrics, and needlework accessories—are classified in Industry 451130, Sewing, Needlework, and Piece Goods Stores.

45113 Sewing, Needlework, and Piece Goods Stores^{CAN}

See industry description for 451130 below.

451130 Sewing, Needlework, and Piece Goods Stores[CAN]

This industry comprises establishments primarily engaged in retailing new sewing supplies, fabrics, patterns, yarns, and other needlework accessories or retailing these products in combination with selling new sewing machines.

Illustrative Examples:

Fabric shops
Sewing supply stores

Needlecraft sewing supply stores
Upholstery materials stores

Cross-References. Establishments primarily engaged in—

- Retailing sewing supplies via electronic home shopping, mail-order, or direct sale—are classified in Subsector 454, Nonstore Retailers;

- Retailing new sewing machines only and in combination with retailing other new appliances—are classified in U.S. Industry 443111, Household Appliance Stores; and

- Retailing used sewing, needlework, and piece goods—are classified in Industry 453310, Used Merchandise Stores.

45114 Musical Instrument and Supplies Stores[CAN]
See industry description for 451140 below.

451140 Musical Instrument and Supplies Stores[CAN]

This industry comprises establishments primarily engaged in retailing new musical instruments, sheet music, and related supplies; or retailing these new products in combination with musical instrument repair, rental, or music instruction.

Illustrative Examples:

Musical instrument stores
Sheet music stores

Piano stores

Cross-References. Establishments primarily engaged in—

- Retailing musical instruments, sheet music, and related supplies via electronic home shopping, mail-order, or direct sale—are classified in Subsector 454, Nonstore Retailers;

- Retailing new musical recordings—are classified in Industry 451220, Prerecorded Tape, Compact Disc, and Record Stores; and

- Retailing used musical instruments, sheet music, and related supplies—are classified in Industry 453310, Used Merchandise Stores.

US—United States industry only. CAN—United States and Canadian industries are comparable. MEX—United States and Mexican industries are comparable. Blank—Canadian, Mexican, and United States industries are comparable.

4512 Book, Periodical, and Music Stores[CAN]

This industry group comprises establishments primarily engaged in retailing new books, newspapers, magazines, and prerecorded audio and video media.

45121 Book Stores and News Dealers[CAN]

This industry comprises establishments primarily engaged in retailing new books, newspapers, magazines, and other periodicals.

Cross-References. Establishments primarily engaged in—

- Retailing newspapers, magazines, and other periodicals via electronic home shopping, mail-order, or direct sale—are classified in Subsector 454, Nonstore Retailers;
- Home delivery of newspapers—are classified in Industry 45439, Other Direct Selling Establishments; and
- Retailing used books, newspapers, magazines, and other periodicals—are classified in Industry 45331, Used Merchandise Stores.

451211 Book Stores[US]

This U.S. industry comprises establishments primarily engaged in retailing new books.

Cross-References. Establishments primarily engaged in—

- Retailing books via electronic home shopping, mail-order, or direct sale— are classified in Subsector 454, Nonstore Retailers; and
- Retailing used books—are classified in Industry 453310, Used Merchandise Stores.

451212 News Dealers and Newsstands[US]

This U.S. industry comprises establishments primarily engaged in retailing current newspapers, magazines, and other periodicals.

Cross-References. Establishments primarily engaged in—

- Home delivery of newspapers—are classified in Industry 454390, Other Direct Selling Establishments;

US—United States industry only. CAN—United States and Canadian industries are comparable. MEX—United States and Mexican industries are comparable. Blank—Canadian, Mexican, and United States industries are comparable.

- Retailing newspapers and periodicals by mail-order—are classified in Industry 454113, Mail-Order Houses; and

- Retailing used newspapers, magazines, and other periodicals—are classified in Industry 453310, Used Merchandise Stores.

45122 Prerecorded Tape, Compact Disc, and Record Stores[CAN]
See industry description for 451220 below.

451220 Prerecorded Tape, Compact Disc, and Record Stores[CAN]

This industry comprises establishments primarily engaged in retailing new prerecorded audio and video tapes, compact discs (CDs), digital video discs (DVDs), and phonograph records.

Cross-References. Establishments primarily engaged in—

- Retailing new computer software—are classified in Industry 443120, Computer and Software Stores;

- Retailing prerecorded tapes, compact discs (CDs), digital video discs (DVDs), and records by mail-order—are classified in Industry 454113, Mail-Order Houses;

- Retailing used phonograph records and prerecorded audio and video tapes and discs—are classified in Industry 453310, Used Merchandise Stores; and

- Retailing new audio sound equipment (except automotive)—are classified in U.S. Industry 443112, Radio, Television, and Other Electronics Stores.

452 General Merchandise Stores[CAN]

Industries in the General Merchandise Stores subsector retail new general merchandise from fixed point-of-sale locations. Establishments in this subsector are unique in that they have the equipment and staff capable of retailing a large variety of goods from a single location. This includes a variety of display equipment and staff trained to provide information on many lines of products.

4521 Department Stores[CAN]

45211 Department Stores[CAN]

This industry comprises establishments known as department stores primarily engaged in retailing a wide range of the following new products with no one merchandise line predominating: apparel, furniture, appliances and home furnishings; and selected additional items, such as paint, hardware, toiletries, cosmetics, photographic equipment, jewelry, toys, and sporting goods. Merchandise lines are normally arranged in separate departments.

Cross-References. Establishments primarily engaged in—

- Retailing packaged grocery items in combination with general lines of merchandise with no one merchandise line predominating—are classified in Industry 45291, Warehouse Clubs and Supercenters;

- Retailing apparel without a significant amount of housewares or general merchandise—are classified in Subsector 448, Clothing and Clothing Accessories Stores;

- Retailing general lines of merchandise via electronic home shopping, mail-order, or direct sale—are classified in Subsector 454, Nonstore Retailers; and

- Retailing used merchandise—are classified in Industry 45331, Used Merchandise Stores.

452111 Department Stores (except Discount Department Stores)^{US}

This U.S. industry comprises establishments known as department stores that have separate departments for various merchandise lines, such as apparel, jewelry, home furnishings, and linens, each with separate cash registers and sales associates. Department stores in this industry generally do not have central customer checkout and cash register facilities.

Cross-References. Establishments primarily engaged in—

- Retailing apparel without a significant amount of housewares or general merchandise—are classified in Subsector 448, Clothing and Clothing Accessories Stores;

- Retailing a wide variety of general merchandise in department stores with central customer checkout and cash register facilities—are classified in U.S. Industry 452112, Discount Department Stores; and

- Retailing a wide variety of general merchandise in combination with a general line of perishable groceries, such as fresh meat, vegetable, and dairy products—are classified in Industry 452910, Warehouse Clubs and Supercenters.

452112 Discount Department Stores^{US}

This U.S. industry comprises establishments known as department stores that have central customer checkout areas, generally in the front of the store, and that may have additional cash registers located in one or more individual departments. Department stores in this industry sell a wide range of general merchandise (except fresh, perishable foods).

Cross-References. Establishments primarily engaged in—

- Retailing apparel without a significant amount of housewares or general merchandise—are classified in Subsector 448, Clothing and Clothing Accessories Stores;

- Retailing a wide variety of general merchandise in department stores with separate cash registers and sales associates for each department—are classified in U.S. Industry 452111, Department Stores (except Discount Department Stores); and

- Retailing a wide variety of general merchandise in combination with a general line of perishable groceries, such as fresh meat, vegetable, and dairy products—are classified in Industry 452910, Warehouse Clubs and Supercenters.

4529 Other General Merchandise Stores^{CAN}

This industry group comprises establishments primarily engaged in retailing new goods in general merchandise stores (except department stores).

45291 Warehouse Clubs and Supercenters^{CAN}
See industry description for 452910 below.

452910 Warehouse Clubs and Supercenters^{CAN}

This industry comprises establishments known as warehouse clubs, superstores or supercenters primarily engaged in retailing a general line of groceries in combination with general lines of new merchandise, such as apparel, furniture, and appliances.

Cross-References. Establishments primarily engaged in—

- Retailing general lines of merchandise via electronic home shopping, mail-order, or direct sale—are classified in Subsector 454, Nonstore Retailers;

- Retailing a general line of food, generally known as supermarkets and grocery stores—are classified in Industry 445110, Supermarkets and Other Grocery (except Convenience) Stores;

- Retailing general lines of new merchandise with little grocery item sales—are classified in Industry 452990, All Other General Merchandise Stores;

- Retailing new merchandise in discount department stores—are classified in U.S. Industry 452112, Discount Department Stores;

- Retailing new merchandise in department stores other than discount department stores—are classified in U.S. Industry 452111, Department Stores (except Discount Department Stores); and

- Retailing used merchandise—are classified in Industry 453310, Used Merchandise Stores.

45299 All Other General Merchandise Stores[CAN]

See industry description for 452990 below.

452990 All Other General Merchandise Stores[US]

This industry comprises establishments primarily engaged in retailing new goods in general merchandise stores (except department stores, warehouse clubs, superstores, and supercenters). These establishments retail a general line of new merchandise, such as apparel, automotive parts, dry goods, hardware, groceries, housewares or home furnishings, and other lines in limited amounts, with none of the lines predominating.

Illustrative Examples:

Dollar stores
General stores
General merchandise catalog showrooms
 (except catalog mail-order)

General merchandise trading posts
Home and auto supply stores
Variety stores

Cross-References. Establishments primarily engaged in—

- Retailing general lines of merchandise via electronic home shopping, mail-order, or direct sale—are classified in Subsector 454, Nonstore Retailers;

- Retailing automotive parts—are classified in Industry 441310, Automotive Parts and Accessories Stores;

- Retailing merchandise in department stores—are classified in Industry 45211, Department Stores;

- Retailing merchandise in warehouse clubs, superstores, or supercenters—are classified in Industry 452910, Warehouse Clubs and Supercenters;

- Retailing merchandise in catalog showrooms of mail-order houses—are classified in U.S. Industry 454113, Mail-Order Houses;

- Retailing a general line of new hardware items, known as hardware stores—are classified in Industry 444130, Hardware Stores;

US—United States industry only. CAN—United States and Canadian industries are comparable. MEX—United States and Mexican industries are comparable. Blank—Canadian, Mexican, and United States industries are comparable.

- Retailing a general line of new home repair and improvement materials and supplies, known as home centers—are classified in Industry 444110, Home Centers; and

- Retailing used merchandise—are classified in Industry 453310, Used Merchandise Stores.

453 Miscellaneous Store Retailers[CAN]

Industries in the Miscellaneous Store Retailers subsector retail merchandise from fixed point-of-sale locations (except new or used motor vehicles and parts; new furniture and home furnishings; new appliances and electronic products; new building materials and garden equipment and supplies; food and beverages; health and personal care goods; gasoline; new clothing and accessories; and new sporting goods, hobby goods, books, and music). Establishments in this subsector include stores with unique characteristics like florists, used merchandise stores, and pet and pet supply stores as well as other store retailers.

4531 Florists[CAN]

45311 Florists[CAN]
See industry description for 453110 below.

453110 Florists[CAN]

This industry comprises establishments known as florists primarily engaged in retailing cut flowers, floral arrangements, and potted plants purchased from others. These establishments usually prepare the arrangements they sell.

Cross-References. Establishments primarily engaged in—

- Retailing flowers or nursery stock grown on premises—are classified in Industry 11142, Nursery and Floriculture Production;

- Retailing trees, shrubs, plants, seeds, bulbs, and sod grown elsewhere—are classified in Industry 444220, Nursery, Garden Center, and Farm Supply Stores; and

- Retailing flowers via electronic home shopping, mail-order, or direct sale—are classified in Subsector 454, Nonstore Retailers.

4532 Office Supplies, Stationery, and Gift Stores[CAN]

45321 Office Supplies and Stationery Stores[CAN]
See industry description for 453210 below.

US—United States industry only. CAN—United States and Canadian industries are comparable. MEX—United States and Mexican industries are comparable. Blank—Canadian, Mexican, and United States industries are comparable.

453210 Office Supplies and Stationery Stores^{CAN}

This industry comprises establishments primarily engaged in one or more of the following: (1) retailing new stationery, school supplies, and office supplies; (2) retailing a combination of new office equipment, furniture, and supplies; and (3) retailing new office equipment, furniture, and supplies in combination with selling new computers.

Cross-References. Establishments primarily engaged in—

- Retailing stationery, school supplies, and office supplies via electronic shopping, mail-order, or direct sale—are classified in Subsector 454, Nonstore Retailers;

- Retailing greeting cards—are classified in Industry 453220, Gift, Novelty, and Souvenir Stores;

- Retailing new typewriters—are classified in U.S. Industry 443112, Radio, Television, and Other Electronics Stores;

- Retailing new computers without retailing other consumer-type electronic products or office equipment, furniture, and supplies—are classified in Industry 443120, Computer and Software Stores;

- Printing business forms—are classified in Industry 32311, Printing;

- Retailing new office furniture—are classified in Industry 442110, Furniture Stores; and

- Retailing used office supplies—are classified in Industry 453310, Used Merchandise Stores.

45322 Gift, Novelty, and Souvenir Stores^{CAN}
See industry description for 453220 below.

453220 Gift, Novelty, and Souvenir Stores^{CAN}

This industry comprises establishments primarily engaged in retailing new gifts, novelty merchandise, souvenirs, greeting cards, seasonal and holiday decorations, and curios.

Illustrative Examples:

Balloon shops	Curio shops
Greeting card shops	Souvenir shops
Christmas stores	Gift shops
Novelty shops	

US—United States industry only. CAN—United States and Canadian industries are comparable. MEX—United States and Mexican industries are comparable. Blank—Canadian, Mexican, and United States industries are comparable.

Cross-References. Establishments primarily engaged in—

- Retailing gifts and novelties via electronic home shopping, mail-order, or direct sale—are classified in Subsector 454, Nonstore Retailers;

- Retailing stationery—are classified in Industry 453210, Office Supplies and Stationery Stores; and

- Retailing used curios and novelties—are classified in Industry 453310, Used Merchandise Stores.

4533 Used Merchandise Stores^{CAN}

45331 Used Merchandise Stores^{CAN}
See industry description for 453310 below.

453310 Used Merchandise Stores^{CAN}

This industry comprises establishments primarily engaged in retailing used merchandise, antiques, and secondhand goods (except motor vehicles, such as automobiles, RVs, motorcycles, and boats; motor vehicle parts; tires; and mobile homes).

Illustrative Examples:

Antique shops	Used merchandise thrift shops
Used household-type appliance stores	Used clothing stores
Used book stores	Used sporting goods stores

Cross-References. Establishments primarily engaged in—

- Retailing used merchandise via electronic home shopping, mail-order, or direct sale—are classified in Subsector 454, Nonstore Retailers;

- Operating pawnshops—are classified in U.S. Industry 522298, All Other Nondepository Credit Intermediation;

- Retailing used automobiles—are classified in Industry 441120, Used Car Dealers;

- Retailing used automobile parts (except tires and tubes)—are classified in Industry 441310, Automotive Parts and Accessories Stores;

- Retailing used tires—are classified in Industry 441320, Tire Dealers;

- Retailing used mobile homes—are classified in Industry 453930, Manufactured (Mobile) Home Dealers;

- Retailing used motorcycles—are classified in U.S. Industry 441221, Motorcycle, ATV, and Personal Watercraft Dealers;

- Retailing used recreational vehicles—are classified in Industry 441210, Recreational Vehicle Dealers;

- Retailing used boats—are classified in U.S. Industry 441222, Boat Dealers;

- Retailing used aircraft, snowmobiles, and utility trailers—are classified in U.S. Industry 441229, All Other Motor Vehicle Dealers; and

- Retailing a general line of used merchandise on an auction basis (except electronic auctions)—are classified in U.S. Industry 453998, All Other Miscellaneous Store Retailers (except Tobacco Stores).

4539 Other Miscellaneous Store Retailers[CAN]

This industry group comprises establishments primarily engaged in retailing new miscellaneous specialty store merchandise (except motor vehicle and parts dealers; furniture and home furnishings stores; consumer-type electronics and appliance stores; building material and garden equipment and supplies dealers; food and beverage stores; health and personal care stores; gasoline stations; clothing and clothing accessories stores; sporting goods, hobby, book, and music stores; general merchandise stores; florists; office supplies, stationery, and gift stores; and used merchandise stores).

45391 Pet and Pet Supplies Stores[CAN]
See industry description for 453910 below.

453910 Pet and Pet Supplies Stores[CAN]

This industry comprises establishments primarily engaged in retailing pets, pet foods, and pet supplies.

Cross-References. Establishments primarily engaged in—

- Retailing pets, pet foods, and pet supplies via electronic home shopping, mail-order, or direct sale—are classified in Subsector 454, Nonstore Retailers;

- Providing pet grooming and boarding services—are classified in Industry 812910, Pet Care (except Veterinary) Services; and

- Providing veterinary services—are classified in Industry 541940, Veterinary Services.

45392 Art Dealers[CAN]
See industry description for 453920 below.

US—United States industry only. CAN—United States and Canadian industries are comparable. MEX—United States and Mexican industries are comparable. Blank—Canadian, Mexican, and United States industries are comparable.

453920   Art Dealers^CAN

This industry comprises establishments primarily engaged in retailing original and limited edition art works. Included in this industry are establishments primarily engaged in displaying works of art for retail sale in art galleries.

Cross-References. Establishments primarily engaged in—

- Retailing original and limited edition art works via electronic home shopping, mail-order, or direct sale—are classified in Subsector 454, Nonstore Retailers;

- Retailing art reproductions (except limited editions)—are classified in U.S. Industry 442299, All Other Home Furnishings Stores;

- Retailing artists' supplies—are classified in U.S. Industry 453998, All Other Miscellaneous Store Retailers (except Tobacco Stores); and

- Displaying works of art not for retail sale in art galleries—are classified in Industry 712110, Museums.

45393   Manufactured (Mobile) Home Dealers^CAN
See industry description for 453930 below.

453930   Manufactured (Mobile) Home Dealers^CAN

This industry comprises establishments primarily engaged in retailing new and/ or used manufactured homes (i.e., mobile homes), parts, and equipment.

Cross-References. Establishments primarily engaged in—

- Retailing new or used motor homes, campers, and travel trailers—are classified in Industry 441210, Recreational Vehicle Dealers; and

- Retailing prefabricated buildings and kits without construction—are classified in Industry 444190, Other Building Material Dealers.

45399   All Other Miscellaneous Store Retailers^CAN

This industry comprises establishments primarily engaged in retailing specialized lines of merchandise (except motor vehicle and parts dealers; furniture and home furnishings stores; electronics and appliance stores; building material and garden equipment and supplies dealers; food and beverage stores; health and personal care stores; gasoline stations; clothing and clothing accessories stores; sporting goods, hobby, book, and music stores; general merchandise stores; florists; office

---

supplies, stationery and gift stores; used merchandise stores; pet and pet supplies; art dealers; and manufactured home (i.e., mobile home) dealers). This industry also includes establishments primarily engaged in retailing a general line of new and used merchandise on an auction basis (except electronic auctions).

Illustrative Examples:

Art supply stores
Swimming pool supply stores, new
Cemetery memorial (e.g., markers, headstones, vaults) dealers

Tobacco stores
Cigar stores

Cross-References. Establishments primarily engaged in—

- Retailing merchandise via electronic home shopping, mail-order, or direct sale—are classified in Subsector 454, Nonstore Retailers;

- Auctioning on the location of others as independent auctioneers—are classified in Industry 56199, All Other Support Services;

- Retailing pets and pet supplies—are classified in Industry 45391, Pet and Pet Supplies Stores;

- Retailing original and limited edition art works—are classified in Industry 45392, Art Dealers;

- Retailing manufactured homes (i.e., mobile homes)—are classified in Industry 45393, Manufactured (Mobile) Home Dealers;

- Retailing new books—are classified in Industry 45121, Book Stores and News Dealers;

- Retailing new jewelry (except costume jewelry)—are classified in Industry 44831, Jewelry Stores;

- Retailing new costume jewelry—are classified in Industry 44815, Clothing Accessories Stores;

- Operating pawnshops-are classified in Industry 52229, Other Nondepository Credit Intermediation; and

- Retailing used merchandise (except automobiles, RVs, mobile homes, motorcycles, boats, motor vehicle parts, tires, aircraft, snowmobiles, and utility trailers)—are classified in Industry 45331, Used Merchandise Stores.

453991 Tobacco Stores[US]

This U.S. industry comprises establishments primarily engaged in retailing cigarettes, cigars, tobacco, pipes, and other smokers' supplies.

US—United States industry only. CAN—United States and Canadian industries are comparable. MEX—United States and Mexican industries are comparable. Blank—Canadian, Mexican, and United States industries are comparable.

Illustrative Examples:

Cigar stores

Smokers' supply stores

Cigarette stands (i.e., permanent)

Tobacco stores

Cross-References.

Establishments primarily engaged in retailing tobacco products and supplies via electronic home shopping, mail-order, or direct sale are classified in Subsector 454, Nonstore Retailers.

453998 All Other Miscellaneous Store Retailers (except Tobacco Stores)[US]

This U.S. industry comprises establishments primarily engaged in retailing specialized lines of merchandise (except motor vehicle and parts dealers; furniture and home furnishings stores; electronics and appliance stores; building material and garden equipment and supplies dealers; food and beverage stores; health and personal care stores; gasoline stations; clothing and clothing accessories stores; sporting goods, hobby, book and music stores; general merchandise stores; florists; office supplies, stationery and gift stores; used merchandise stores; pet and pet supplies stores; art dealers; manufactured home (i.e., mobile homes) dealers; and tobacco stores). This industry also includes establishments primarily engaged in retailing a general line of new and used merchandise on an auction basis (except electronic auctions).

Illustrative Examples:

Art supply stores

General merchandise auction houses

Candle shops

Home security equipment stores

Cemetery memorial (e.g., headstones, markers, vaults) dealers

Hot tub stores

Collectors' items (e.g., autograph, coin, card, stamp) shops

Swimming pool supply stores

Fireworks shops (permanent location)

Trophy (e.g., awards and plaques) shops

Flower shops, artificial or dried

Cross-References. Establishments primarily engaged in—

- Retailing specialized lines of merchandise via electronic home shopping, mail-order, or direct sale—are classified in Subsector 454, Nonstore Retailers;

- Retailing merchandise via electronic auctions—are classified in Industry 454112, Electronic Auctions;

- Auctioning (i.e., on the location of others as independent auctioneers)— are classified in Industry 561990, All Other Support Services;

- Retailing pets and pet supplies—are classified in Industry 453910, Pet and Pet Supplies Stores;

- Retailing original and limited edition art works—are classified in Industry 453920, Art Dealers;

- Retailing manufactured homes (i.e., mobile homes)—are classified in Industry 453930, Manufactured (Mobile) Home Dealers;

- Retailing cigarettes, cigars, tobacco, pipes, and other smokers' supplies—are classified in U.S. Industry 453991, Tobacco Stores;

- Retailing antiques—are classified in Industry 453310, Used Merchandise Stores;

- Retailing new books—are classified in Industry 451211, Book Stores;

- Retailing new jewelry (except costume jewelry)—are classified in Industry 448310, Jewelry Stores; and

- Retailing new costume jewelry—are classified in Industry 448150, Clothing Accessories Stores.

454 Nonstore Retailers^{CAN}

Industries in the Nonstore Retailers subsector retail merchandise using methods, such as the broadcasting of infomercials, the broadcasting and publishing of direct response advertising, the publishing of paper and electronic catalogs, door-to-door solicitation, in-home demonstration, selling from portable stalls and distribution through vending machines. Establishments in this subsector include mail-order houses, vending machine operators, home delivery sales, door-to-door sales, party plan sales, electronic shopping, and sales through portable stalls (e.g., street vendors, except food). Establishments engaged in the direct sale (i.e., nonstore) of products, such as home heating oil dealers and newspaper delivery service providers are included in this subsector.

4541 Electronic Shopping and Mail-Order Houses^{CAN}

45411 Electronic Shopping and Mail-Order Houses^{CAN}

This industry comprises establishments primarily engaged in retailing all types of merchandise using non-store means, such as catalogs, toll free telephone numbers, or electronic media, such as interactive television or computer. Included in this industry are establishments primarily engaged in retailing from catalog showrooms of mail-order houses.

Illustrative Examples:

Catalog (i.e., order-taking) offices of mail-order houses

Internet auction sites, retail

Collectors' items, mail-order houses

Mail-order book clubs (not publishing)

Computer software, mail-order houses

Mail-order houses

Home shopping television orders

Web retailers

Cross-References. Establishments primarily engaged in—

- Store retailing or a combination of store retailing and non-store retailing in the same establishment—are classified in Sector 44-45, Retail Trade, based on the classification of the store portion of the activity;

- Facilitating business to business electronic sales of new and used merchandise on an auction basis using the Internet—are classified in Industry 42511, Business to Business Electronic Markets; and

- Providing telemarketing (e.g., telephone marketing) services for others— are classified in Industry 56142, Telephone Call Centers.

454111 Electronic Shopping^{CAN}

This U.S. Industry comprises establishments engaged in retailing all types of merchandise using the Internet.

Cross-References. Establishments primarily engaged in—

- Store retailing or a combination of store retailing and Internet retailing in the same establishment—are classified in Sector 44-45, Retail Trade, based on the classification of the store portion of the activity; and

- Retailing all types of merchandise using catalogs or television to generate clients and display merchandise—are classified in U.S. Industry 454113, Mail-Order Houses.

454112 Electronic Auctions^{CAN}

This U.S. Industry comprises establishments engaged in providing sites for and facilitating consumer-to-consumer or business-to-consumer trade in new and used goods, on an auction basis, using the Internet. Establishments in this industry provide the electronic location for retail auctions, but do not take title to the goods being sold.

Cross-References. Establishments primarily engaged in—

- Retailing a general line of new and used merchandise on an auction basis from physical auction sites—are classified in U.S. Industry 453998, All Other Miscellaneous Store Retailers (except Tobacco Stores);

US—United States industry only. CAN—United States and Canadian industries are comparable. MEX—United States and Mexican industries are comparable. Blank—Canadian, Mexican, and United States industries are comparable.

- Facilitating business to business sales of new and used merchandise on an auction basis using the Internet—are classified in Industry 425110, Business to Business Electronic Markets; and

- A combination of Internet auction and auction house sales in the same establishment—are classified in Sector 44-45, Retail Trade, based on the classification of the auction house portion of the activity.

454113 Mail-Order Houses^{CAN}

This U.S. industry comprises establishments primarily engaged in retailing all types of merchandise using mail catalogs or television to generate clients and display merchandise. Included in this industry are establishments primarily engaged in retailing from catalog showrooms of mail-order houses as well as establishments providing a combination of Internet and mail-order sales.

Illustrative Examples:

Catalog (i.e., order-taking) offices of mail-order houses	Mail-order book clubs (not publishing)
Home shopping television orders	Computer software, mail-order houses
Collectors' items, mail-order houses	Mail-order houses

Cross-References. Establishments primarily engaged in—

- Providing telemarketing (e.g., telephone marketing) services for others— are classified in U.S. Industry 561422, Telemarketing Bureaus and Other Contact Centers; and

- Retailing merchandise using store and nonstore methods at the same establishment—are classified in Store retail activities based on the store portion of the activity.

4542 Vending Machine Operators^{CAN}

45421 Vending Machine Operators^{CAN}
See industry description for 454210 below.

454210 Vending Machine Operators^{CAN}

This industry comprises establishments primarily engaged in retailing merchandise through vending machines that they service.

US—United States industry only. CAN—United States and Canadian industries are comparable. MEX—United States and Mexican industries are comparable. Blank—Canadian, Mexican, and United States industries are comparable.

Cross-References. Establishments primarily engaged in—

- Selling insurance policies through vending machines—are classified in Subsector 524, Insurance Carriers and Related Activities;
- Supplying and servicing coin-operated photobooths, restrooms, and lockers—are classified in Industry 812990, All Other Personal Services; and
- Supplying and servicing coin-operated amusement and gambling devices in places of business operated by others—are classified in Subsector 713, Amusement, Gambling, and Recreation Industries.

4543 Direct Selling Establishments[CAN]

This industry group comprises establishments primarily engaged in nonstore retailing (except electronic, mail-order, or vending machine sales). These establishments typically go to the customers' location rather than the customer coming to them (e.g., door-to-door sales, home parties). Examples of establishments in this industry are home delivery newspaper routes; home delivery of heating oil, liquefied petroleum (LP) gas, and other fuels; locker meat provisioners; frozen food and freezer plan providers; coffee-break services providers; and bottled water or water softener services.

45431 Fuel Dealers[CAN]

This industry comprises establishments primarily engaged in retailing heating oil, liquefied petroleum (LP) gas, and other fuels via direct selling.

Cross-References. Establishments primarily engaged in—

- Providing oil burner repair services—are classified in Industry 81141, Home and Garden Equipment and Appliance Repair and Maintenance; and
- Installing oil burners—are classified in Industry 23822, Plumbing, Heating, and Air-Conditioning Contractors.

454311 Heating Oil Dealers[CAN]

This U.S. industry comprises establishments primarily engaged in retailing heating oil via direct selling.

Cross-References. Establishments primarily engaged in—

- Providing oil burner repair services—are classified in U.S. Industry 811411, Home and Garden Equipment Repair and Maintenance; and

---

US—United States industry only. CAN—United States and Canadian industries are comparable. MEX—United States and Mexican industries are comparable. Blank—Canadian, Mexican, and United States industries are comparable.

- Installing oil burners—are classified in Industry 238220, Plumbing, Heating, and Air-Conditioning Contractors.

454312 Liquefied Petroleum Gas (Bottled Gas) Dealers^{CAN}

This U.S. industry comprises establishments primarily engaged in retailing liquefied petroleum (LP) gas via direct selling.

454319 Other Fuel Dealers^{CAN}

This U.S. industry comprises establishments primarily engaged in retailing fuels (except liquefied petroleum gas and heating oil) via direct selling.

45439 Other Direct Selling Establishments^{CAN}
See industry description for 454390 below.

454390 Other Direct Selling Establishments^{CAN}

This industry comprises establishments primarily engaged in retailing merchandise (except food for immediate consumption and fuel) via direct sale to the customer by means, such as in-house sales (i.e., party plan merchandising), truck or wagon sales, and portable stalls (i.e., street vendors).

Illustrative Examples:

Direct selling bottled water providers	Direct selling locker meat provisioners
Direct selling home delivery newspaper routes	Direct selling frozen food and freezer plan providers
Direct selling coffee-break service providers	Direct selling party plan merchandisers

Cross-References. Establishments primarily engaged in—

- Preparing and selling meals and snacks for immediate consumption from motorized vehicles or nonmotorized carts, catering a route—are classified in Industry 722330, Mobile Food Services;
- Retailing heating oil via direct sale—are classified in U.S. Industry 454311, Heating Oil Dealers;
- Retailing liquefied petroleum (LP) gas via direct sale—are classified in U.S. Industry 454312, Liquefied Petroleum Gas (Bottled Gas) Dealers; and
- Retailing other fuels, such as coal or wood, via direct sale—are classified in U.S. Industry 454319, Other Fuel Dealers.

US—United States industry only. CAN—United States and Canadian industries are comparable. MEX—United States and Mexican industries are comparable. Blank—Canadian, Mexican, and United States industries are comparable.

Sector 48-49—Transportation and Warehousing

The Sector as a Whole

The Transportation and Warehousing sector includes industries providing transportation of passengers and cargo, warehousing and storage for goods, scenic and sightseeing transportation, and support activities related to modes of transportation. Establishments in these industries use transportation equipment or transportation related facilities as a productive asset. The type of equipment depends on the mode of transportation. The modes of transportation are air, rail, water, road, and pipeline.

The Transportation and Warehousing sector distinguishes three basic types of activities: subsectors for each mode of transportation, a subsector for warehousing and storage, and a subsector for establishments providing support activities for transportation. In addition, there are subsectors for establishments that provide passenger transportation for scenic and sightseeing purposes, postal services, and courier services.

A separate subsector for support activities is established in the sector because, first, support activities for transportation are inherently multimodal, such as freight transportation arrangement, or have multimodal aspects. Secondly, there are production process similarities among the support activity industries.

One of the support activities identified in the support activity subsector is the routine repair and maintenance of transportation equipment (e.g., aircraft at an airport, railroad rolling stock at a railroad terminal, or ships at a harbor or port facility). Such establishments do not perform complete overhauling or rebuilding of transportation equipment (i.e., periodic restoration of transportation equipment to original design specifications) or transportation equipment conversion (i.e., major modification to systems). An establishment that primarily performs factory (or shipyard) overhauls, rebuilding, or conversions of aircraft, railroad rolling stock, or a ship is classified in Subsector 336, Transportation Equipment Manufacturing according to the type of equipment.

Many of the establishments in this sector often operate on networks, with physical facilities, labor forces, and equipment spread over an extensive geographic area.

Warehousing establishments in this sector are distinguished from merchant wholesaling in that the warehouse establishments do not sell the goods.

Excluded from this sector are establishments primarily engaged in providing travel agent services that support transportation and other establishments, such as hotels, businesses, and government agencies. These establishments are classified in Sector 56, Administrative and Support and Waste Management and Remediation Services. Also, establishments primarily engaged in providing rental and leasing of transportation equipment without operator are classified in Subsector 532, Rental and Leasing Services.

US—United States industry only. CAN—United States and Canadian industries are comparable. MEX—United States and Mexican industries are comparable. Blank—Canadian, Mexican, and United States industries are comparable.

481 Air Transportation

Industries in the Air Transportation subsector provide air transportation of passengers and/or cargo using aircraft, such as airplanes and helicopters. The subsector distinguishes scheduled from nonscheduled air transportation. Scheduled air carriers fly regular routes on regular schedules and operate even if flights are only partially loaded. Nonscheduled carriers often operate during nonpeak time slots at busy airports. These establishments have more flexibility with respect to choice of airport, hours of operation, load factors, and similar operational characteristics. Nonscheduled carriers provide chartered air transportation of passengers, cargo, or specialty flying services. Specialty flying services establishments use general-purpose aircraft to provide a variety of specialized flying services.

Scenic and sightseeing air transportation and air courier services are not included in this subsector but are included in Subsector 487, Scenic and Sightseeing Transportation and in Subsector 492, Couriers and Messengers. Although these activities may use aircraft, they are different from the activities included in air transportation. Air sightseeing does not usually involve place-to-place transportation; the passenger's flight (e.g., balloon ride, aerial sightseeing) typically starts and ends at the same location. Courier services (individual package or cargo delivery) include more than air transportation; road transportation is usually required to deliver the cargo to the intended recipient.

4811 Scheduled Air Transportation

48111 Scheduled Air Transportation

This industry comprises establishments primarily engaged in providing air transportation of passengers and/or cargo over regular routes and on regular schedules. Establishments in this industry operate flights even if partially loaded. Establishments primarily engaged in providing scheduled air transportation of mail on a contract basis are included in this industry.

Illustrative Examples:

Air commuter carriers, scheduled
Scheduled air passenger carriers
Scheduled air cargo carriers (except
  air couriers)

Scheduled helicopter passenger
  carriers

Cross-References. Establishments primarily engaged in—

- Providing air courier services—are classified in Industry 49211, Couriers and Express Delivery Services;

US—United States industry only. CAN—United States and Canadian industries are comparable. MEX—United States and Mexican industries are comparable. Blank—Canadian, Mexican, and United States industries are comparable.

- Providing air transportation of passengers, cargo, or specialty flying services with no regular routes and regular schedules—are classified in Industry 48121, Nonscheduled Air Transportation; and

- Providing helicopter rides for scenic and sightseeing transportation—are classified in Industry 48799, Scenic and Sightseeing Transportation, Other.

481111 Scheduled Passenger Air Transportation[US]

This U.S. industry comprises establishments primarily engaged in providing air transportation of passengers or passengers and freight over regular routes and on regular schedules. Establishments in this industry operate flights even if partially loaded. Scheduled air passenger carriers including commuter and helicopter carriers (except scenic and sightseeing) are included in this industry.

Cross-References. Establishments primarily engaged in—

- Providing air transportation of passengers or passengers and cargo with no regular routes and regular schedules—are classified in U.S. Industry 481211, Nonscheduled Chartered Passenger Air Transportation;

- Providing helicopter rides for scenic and sightseeing transportation—are classified in Industry 487990, Scenic and Sightseeing Transportation, Other; and

- Providing air transportation of cargo (without transporting passengers) over regular routes and on regular schedules—are classified in U.S. Industry 481112, Scheduled Freight Air Transportation.

481112 Scheduled Freight Air Transportation[US]

This U.S. industry comprises establishments primarily engaged in providing air transportation of cargo without transporting passengers over regular routes and on regular schedules. Establishments in this industry operate flights even if partially loaded. Establishments primarily engaged in providing scheduled air transportation of mail on a contract basis are included in this industry.

Cross-References. Establishments primarily engaged in—

- Providing air courier services—are classified in Industry 492110, Couriers and Express Delivery Services;

- Providing air transportation of cargo with no regular routes and regular schedules—are classified in U.S. Industry 481212, Nonscheduled Chartered Freight Air Transportation; and

- Providing air transportation of passengers or passengers and cargo over regular routes and on regular schedules—are classified in U.S. Industry 481111, Scheduled Passenger Air Transportation.

4812 Nonscheduled Air Transportation

48121 Nonscheduled Air Transportation

This industry comprises establishments primarily engaged in (1) providing air transportation of passengers and/or cargo with no regular routes and regular schedules or (2) providing specialty flying services with no regular routes and regular schedules using general purpose aircraft. These establishments have more flexibility with respect to choice of airports, hours of operation, load factors, and similar operational characteristics.

Illustrative Examples:

Air taxi services	Aircraft charter services
Nonscheduled air freight transportation services	Nonscheduled air passenger transportation services

Cross-References. Establishments primarily engaged in—

- Crop dusting using specialized aircraft—are classified in Industry 11511, Support Activities for Crop Production;

- Fighting forest fires using specialized water bombers—are classified in Industry 11531, Support Activities for Forestry;

- Providing air transportation of passengers and/or cargo over regular routes and on regular schedules—are classified in Industry 48111, Scheduled Air Transportation;

- Providing specialized air sightseeing services—are classified in Industry 48799, Scenic and Sightseeing Transportation, Other;

- Aerial gathering of geophysical data—are classified in Industry 54136, Geophysical Surveying and Mapping Services;

- Providing aerial and/or other surveying and mapping services—are classified in Industry 54137, Surveying and Mapping (except Geophysical) Services;

- Providing air ambulance services using specialized equipment—are classified in Industry 62191, Ambulance Services;

- Operating specialized flying schools, including all training for commercial pilots—are classified in Industry 61151, Technical and Trade Schools;

US—United States industry only. CAN—United States and Canadian industries are comparable. MEX—United States and Mexican industries are comparable. Blank—Canadian, Mexican, and United States industries are comparable.

- Operating recreation aviation clubs—are classified in Industry 71399, All Other Amusement and Recreation Industries;

- Operating advocacy aviation clubs—are classified in Industry 81331, Social Advocacy Organizations; and

- Providing air courier services—are classified in Industry 49211, Couriers and Express Delivery Services.

481211 Nonscheduled Chartered Passenger Air Transportation[US]

This U.S. industry comprises establishments primarily engaged in providing air transportation of passengers or passengers and cargo with no regular routes and regular schedules.

Cross-References. Establishments primarily engaged in—

- Providing specialty air transportation or flying services with no regular routes and regular schedules using general purpose aircraft—are classified in U.S. Industry 481219, Other Nonscheduled Air Transportation;

- Providing specialized air sightseeing services—are classified in Industry 487990, Scenic and Sightseeing Transportation, Other;

- Providing air transportation of passengers or passengers and cargo over regular routes and on regular schedules—are classified in U.S. Industry 481111, Scheduled Passenger Air Transportation; and

- Providing air transportation of cargo (without transporting passengers) with no regular routes and schedules—are classified in U.S. Industry 481212, Nonscheduled Chartered Freight Air Transportation.

481212 Nonscheduled Chartered Freight Air Transportation[US]

This U.S. industry comprises establishments primarily engaged in providing air transportation of cargo without transporting passengers with no regular routes and regular schedules.

Cross-References. Establishments primarily engaged in—

- Providing specialty air transportation or flying services with no regular routes and regular schedules using general purpose aircraft—are classified in U.S. Industry 481219, Other Nonscheduled Air Transportation;

- Providing air courier services—are classified in Industry 492110, Couriers and Express Delivery Services;

US—United States industry only. CAN—United States and Canadian industries are comparable. MEX—United States and Mexican industries are comparable. Blank—Canadian, Mexican, and United States industries are comparable.

- Providing air transportation of cargo without transporting passengers over regular routes and on regular schedules—are classified in U.S. Industry 481112, Scheduled Freight Air Transportation; and

- Providing air transportation of cargo and passengers with no regular routes and schedules—are classified in U.S. Industry 481211, Nonscheduled Chartered Passenger Air Transportation.

481219 Other Nonscheduled Air Transportation[US]

This U.S. industry comprises establishments primarily engaged in providing air transportation with no regular routes and regular schedules (except nonscheduled chartered passenger and/or cargo air transportation). These establishments provide a variety of specialty air transportation or flying services based on individual customer needs using general purpose aircraft.

Illustrative Examples:

Aircraft charter services (i.e., general purpose aircraft used for a variety of specialty air and flying services)

Aviation clubs providing a variety of air transportation activities to the general public

Cross-References. Establishments primarily engaged in—

- Providing air transportation of passengers or passengers and cargo with no regular routes and regular schedules—are classified in U.S. Industry 481211, Nonscheduled Chartered Passenger Air Transportation;

- Providing air transportation of cargo without transporting passengers with no regular routes and regular schedules—are classified in U.S. Industry 481212, Nonscheduled Chartered Freight Air Transportation;

- Crop dusting using specialized aircraft—are classified in U.S. Industry 115112, Soil Preparation, Planting, and Cultivating;

- Fighting forest fires using specialized water bombers—are classified in Industry 115310, Support Activities for Forestry;

- Providing specialized air sightseeing services—are classified in Industry 487990, Scenic and Sightseeing Transportation, Other;

- Operating specialized flying schools, including all training for commercial pilots—are classified in U.S. Industry 611512, Flight Training;

- Providing specialized air ambulance services using specialized equipment—are classified in Industry 621910, Ambulance Services;

- Operating recreation aviation clubs—are classified in Industry 713990, All Other Amusement and Recreation Industries;

US—United States industry only. CAN—United States and Canadian industries are comparable. MEX—United States and Mexican industries are comparable. Blank—Canadian, Mexican, and United States industries are comparable.

- Operating advocacy aviation clubs—are classified in U.S. Industry 813319, Other Social Advocacy Organizations;

- Aerial gathering of geophysical data for surveying and mapping—are classified in Industry 541360, Geophysical Surveying and Mapping Services; and

- Providing aerial and/or other surveying and mapping services—are classified in Industry 541370, Surveying and Mapping (except Geophysical) Services.

482 Rail Transportation

Industries in the Rail Transportation subsector provide rail transportation of passengers and/or cargo using railroad rolling stock. The railroads in this subsector primarily either operate on networks, with physical facilities, labor force, and equipment spread over an extensive geographic area, or operate over a short distance on a local rail line.

Scenic and sightseeing rail transportation and street railroads, commuter rail, and rapid transit are not included in this subsector but are included in Subsector 487, Scenic and Sightseeing Transportation, and Subsector 485, Transit and Ground Passenger Transportation, respectively. Although these activities use railroad rolling stock, they are different from the activities included in rail transportation. Sightseeing and scenic railroads do not usually involve place-to-place transportation; the passenger's trip typically starts and ends at the same location. Commuter railroads operate in a manner more consistent with local and urban transit and are often part of integrated transit systems.

4821 Rail Transportation

48211 Rail Transportation

This industry comprises establishments primarily engaged in operating railroads (except street railroads, commuter rail, urban rapid transit, and scenic and sightseeing trains). Line-haul railroads and short line railroads are included in this industry.

Cross-References. Establishments primarily engaged in—

- Operating street railroads, commuter rail, and urban rapid transit systems—are classified in Industry Group 4851, Urban Transit Systems;

- Operating scenic and sightseeing trains—are classified in Industry 48711, Scenic and Sightseeing Transportation, Land; and

- Operating switching and terminal facilities as separate establishments—are classified in Industry 48821, Support Activities for Rail Transportation.

US—United States industry only. CAN—United States and Canadian industries are comparable. MEX—United States and Mexican industries are comparable. Blank—Canadian, Mexican, and United States industries are comparable.

482111   Line-Haul Railroads[US]

This U.S. industry comprises establishments known as line-haul railroads primarily engaged in operating railroads for the transport of passengers and/or cargo over a long distance within a rail network. These establishments provide for the intercity movement of trains between the terminals and stations on main and branch lines of a line-haul rail network (except for local switching services).

Cross-References. Establishments primarily engaged in—

- Operating switching and terminal facilities as separate establishments—are classified in Industry 488210, Support Activities for Rail Transportation;

- Operating railroads over a short distance on local rail lines—are classified in U.S. Industry 482112, Short Line Railroads; and

- Operating commuter rail systems—are classified in U.S. Industry 485112, Commuter Rail Systems.

482112   Short Line Railroads[CAN]

This U.S. industry comprises establishments known as short line railroads primarily engaged in operating railroads for the transport of cargo over a short distance on local rail lines not part of a rail network.

Cross-References. Establishments primarily engaged in—

- Operating street railroads, commuter rail, and urban rapid transit systems—are classified in Industry Group 4851, Urban Transit Systems;

- Operating scenic and sightseeing trains—are classified in Industry 487110, Scenic and Sightseeing Transportation, Land;

- Operating switching and terminal facilities as separate establishments—are classified in Industry 488210, Support Activities for Rail Transportation; and

- Operating railroads for the transport of passengers and/or cargo over a long distance—are classified in U.S. Industry 482111, Line-Haul Railroads.

483 Water Transportation

Industries in the Water Transportation subsector provide water transportation of passengers and cargo using watercraft, such as ships, barges, and boats.

The subsector is composed of two industry groups: (1) one for deep sea, coastal, and Great Lakes; and (2) one for inland water transportation. This split typically reflects the difference in equipment used.

US—United States industry only. CAN—United States and Canadian industries are comparable. MEX—United States and Mexican industries are comparable. Blank—Canadian, Mexican, and United States industries are comparable.

Scenic and sightseeing water transportation services are not included in this subsector but are included in Subsector 487, Scenic and Sightseeing Transportation. Although these activities use watercraft, they are different from the activities included in water transportation. Water sightseeing does not usually involve place-to-place transportation; the passenger's trip starts and ends at the same location.

4831 Deep Sea, Coastal and Great Lakes Water Transportation

48311 Deep Sea, Coastal, and Great Lakes Water Transportation

This industry comprises establishments primarily engaged in providing deep sea, coastal, Great Lakes, and St. Lawrence Seaway water transportation. Marine transportation establishments using the facilities of the St. Lawrence Seaway Authority Commission are considered to be using the Great Lakes Water Transportation System.

Cross-References. Establishments primarily engaged in—

- Providing inland water transportation on lakes, rivers, or intracoastal waterways (except on the Great Lakes System)—are classified in Industry 48321, Inland Water Transportation;
- Providing scenic and sightseeing water transportation, such as harbor cruises—are classified in Industry 48721, Scenic and Sightseeing Transportation, Water; and
- Operating floating casinos (i.e., gambling cruises, river boat gambling casinos)—are classified in Industry 71321, Casinos (except Casino Hotels).

483111 Deep Sea Freight Transportation[US]

This U.S. industry comprises establishments primarily engaged in providing deep sea transportation of cargo to or from foreign ports.

Cross-References.

Establishments primarily engaged in providing deep sea transportation of cargo to and from domestic ports are classified in U.S. Industry 483113, Coastal and Great Lakes Freight Transportation.

483112 Deep Sea Passenger Transportation[US]

This U.S. industry comprises establishments primarily engaged in providing deep sea transportation of passengers to or from foreign ports.

US—United States industry only. CAN—United States and Canadian industries are comparable. MEX—United States and Mexican industries are comparable. Blank—Canadian, Mexican, and United States industries are comparable.

Cross-References. Establishments primarily engaged in—

- Providing deep sea transportation of passengers to and from domestic ports—are classified in U.S. Industry 483114, Coastal and Great Lakes Passenger Transportation; and

- Operating floating casinos (i.e., gambling cruises)—are classified in Industry 713210, Casinos (except Casino Hotels).

483113 Coastal and Great Lakes Freight Transportation[US]

This U.S. industry comprises establishments primarily engaged in providing water transportation of cargo in coastal waters, on the Great Lakes System, or deep seas between ports of the United States, Puerto Rico, and United States island possessions or protectorates. Marine transportation establishments using the facilities of the St. Lawrence Seaway Authority Commission are considered to be using the Great Lakes Water Transportation System. Establishments primarily engaged in providing coastal and/or Great Lakes barge transportation services are included in this industry.

Cross-References. Establishments primarily engaged in—

- Providing deep sea transportation of cargo to or from foreign ports—are classified in U.S. Industry 483111, Deep Sea Freight Transportation; and

- Providing inland water transportation of cargo on lakes, rivers, or intra-coastal waterways (except on the Great Lakes System)—are classified in U.S. Industry 483211, Inland Water Freight Transportation.

483114 Coastal and Great Lakes Passenger Transportation[US]

This U.S. industry comprises establishments primarily engaged in providing water transportation of passengers in coastal waters, the Great Lakes System, or deep seas between ports of the United States, Puerto Rico, and United States island possessions and protectorates. Marine transportation establishments using the facilities of the St. Lawrence Seaway Authority Commission are considered to be using the Great Lakes Water Transportation System.

Cross-References. Establishments primarily engaged in—

- Providing inland water transportation of passengers on lakes, rivers or intracoastal waterways (except on the Great Lakes System)—are classified in U.S. Industry 483212, Inland Water Passenger Transportation;

- Providing scenic and sightseeing water transportation, such as harbor cruises—are classified in Industry 487210, Scenic and Sightseeing Transportation, Water; and

---

US—United States industry only. CAN—United States and Canadian industries are comparable. MEX—United States and Mexican industries are comparable. Blank—Canadian, Mexican, and United States industries are comparable.

- Operating floating casinos (i.e., gambling cruises)—are classified in Industry 713210, Casinos (except Casino Hotels).

4832 Inland Water Transportation

48321 Inland Water Transportation

This industry comprises establishments primarily engaged in providing inland water transportation of passengers and/or cargo on lakes, rivers, or intracoastal waterways (except on the Great Lakes System).

Cross-References. Establishments primarily engaged in—

- Providing water transportation in deep sea, coastal, or on the Great Lakes System—are classified in Industry Group 4831, Deep Sea, Coastal, and Great Lakes Water Transportation;

- Providing scenic and sightseeing water transportation, such as harbor cruises—are classified in Industry 48721, Scenic and Sightseeing Transportation, Water; and

- Operating floating casinos (i.e., gambling cruises, river boat gambling casinos)—are classified in Industry 71321, Casinos (except Casino Hotels).

483211 Inland Water Freight Transportation[US]

This U.S. industry comprises establishments primarily engaged in providing inland water transportation of cargo on lakes, rivers, or intracoastal waterways (except on the Great Lakes System).

Cross-References. Establishments primarily engaged in—

- Providing deep sea transportation of cargo to and from foreign ports—are classified in U.S. Industry 483111, Deep Sea Freight Transportation; and

- Providing water transportation of cargo in coastal waters or on the Great Lakes System—are classified in U.S. Industry 483113, Coastal and Great Lakes Freight Transportation.

483212 Inland Water Passenger Transportation[US]

This U.S. industry comprises establishments primarily engaged in providing inland water transportation of passengers on lakes, rivers, or intracoastal waterways (except on the Great Lakes System).

US—United States industry only. CAN—United States and Canadian industries are comparable. MEX—United States and Mexican industries are comparable. Blank—Canadian, Mexican, and United States industries are comparable.

Cross-References. Establishments primarily engaged in—

- Providing deep sea transportation of passengers to and from foreign ports—are classified in U.S. Industry 483112, Deep Sea Passenger Transportation;

- Operating cruise ships or ferries in coastal waters or on the Great Lakes System—are classified in U.S. Industry 483114, Coastal and Great Lakes Passenger Transportation; and

- Providing scenic and sightseeing water transportation, such as harbor cruises—are classified in Industry 487210, Scenic and Sightseeing Transportation, Water.

484 Truck Transportation

Industries in the Truck Transportation subsector provide over-the-road transportation of cargo using motor vehicles, such as trucks and tractor trailers. The subsector is subdivided into general freight trucking and specialized freight trucking. This distinction reflects differences in equipment used, type of load carried, scheduling, terminal, and other networking services. General freight transportation establishments handle a wide variety of general commodities, generally palletized, and transported in a container or van trailer. Specialized freight transportation is the transportation of cargo that, because of size, weight, shape, or other inherent characteristics require specialized equipment for transportation.

Each of these industry groups is further subdivided based on distance traveled. Local trucking establishments primarily carry goods within a single metropolitan area and its adjacent nonurban areas. Long distance trucking establishments carry goods between metropolitan areas.

The Specialized Freight Trucking industry group includes a separate industry for Used Household and Office Goods Moving. The household and office goods movers are separated because of the substantial network of establishments that has developed to deal with local and long-distance moving and the associated storage. In this area, the same establishment provides both local and long-distance services, while other specialized freight establishments generally limit their services to either local or long-distance hauling.

4841 General Freight Trucking

This industry group comprises establishments primarily engaged in providing general freight trucking. General freight establishments handle a wide variety of commodities, generally palletized, and transported in a container or van trailer. The establishments of this industry group provide a combination of the following network activities: local pickup, local sorting and terminal operations, line-haul, destination sorting and terminal operations, and local delivery.

US—United States industry only. CAN—United States and Canadian industries are comparable. MEX—United States and Mexican industries are comparable. Blank—Canadian, Mexican, and United States industries are comparable.

48411 General Freight Trucking, Local

See industry description for 484110 below.

484110 General Freight Trucking, Local[CAN]

This industry comprises establishments primarily engaged in providing local general freight trucking. General freight establishments handle a wide variety of commodities, generally palletized and transported in a container or van trailer. Local general freight trucking establishments usually provide trucking within a metropolitan area which may cross state lines. Generally the trips are same-day return.

Cross-References. Establishments primarily engaged in—

- Operating independent trucking terminals—are classified in Industry 488490, Other Support Activities for Road Transportation; and

- Providing general freight long-distance trucking including all North American international travel—are classified in Industry 48412, General Freight Trucking, Long-Distance.

48412 General Freight Trucking, Long-Distance

This industry comprises establishments primarily engaged in providing long-distance general freight trucking. General freight establishments handle a wide variety of commodities, generally palletized and transported in a container or van trailer. Long-distance general freight trucking establishments usually provide trucking between metropolitan areas which may cross North American country borders. Included in this industry are establishments operating as truckload (TL) or less than truckload (LTL) carriers.

Cross-References. Establishments primarily engaged in—

- Providing courier services—are classified in Industry 49211, Couriers and Express Delivery Services;

- Providing warehousing services of general freight—are classified in Industry 49311, General Warehousing and Storage;

- Providing specialized freight trucking—are classified in Industry Group 4842, Specialized Freight Trucking;

- Operating independent trucking terminals—are classified in Industry 48849, Other Support Activities for Road Transportation; and

- Providing local general freight trucking services—are classified in Industry 48411, General Freight Trucking, Local.

US—United States industry only. CAN—United States and Canadian industries are comparable. MEX—United States and Mexican industries are comparable. Blank—Canadian, Mexican, and United States industries are comparable.

484121 General Freight Trucking, Long-Distance, Truckload[CAN]

This U.S. industry comprises establishments primarily engaged in providing long-distance general freight truckload (TL) trucking. These long-distance general freight truckload carrier establishments provide full truck movement of freight from origin to destination. The shipment of freight on a truck is characterized as a full single load not combined with other shipments.

Cross-References. Establishments primarily engaged in—

- Providing general freight long-distance, less than truckload trucking—are classified in U.S. Industry 484122, General Freight Trucking, Long-Distance, Less Than Truckload;

- Providing specialized freight trucking—are classified in Industry Group 4842, Specialized Freight Trucking;

- Operating independent trucking terminals—are classified in Industry 488490, Other Support Activities for Road Transportation; and

- Providing local general freight trucking services—are classified in Industry 484110, General Freight Trucking, Local.

484122 General Freight Trucking, Long-Distance, Less Than Truckload[CAN]

This U.S. industry comprises establishments primarily engaged in providing long-distance, general freight, less than truckload (LTL) trucking. LTL carriage is characterized as multiple shipments combined onto a single truck for multiple deliveries within a network. These establishments are generally characterized by the following network activities: local pickup, local sorting and terminal operations, line-haul, destination sorting and terminal operations, and local delivery.

Cross-References. Establishments primarily engaged in—

- Providing courier services—are classified in Industry 492110, Couriers and Express Delivery Services;

- Providing warehousing services of general freight—are classified in Industry 493110, General Warehousing and Storage;

- Providing specialized freight trucking—are classified in Industry Group 4842, Specialized Freight Trucking;

- Operating independent trucking terminals—are classified in Industry 488490, Other Support Activities for Road Transportation;

US—United States industry only. CAN—United States and Canadian industries are comparable. MEX—United States and Mexican industries are comparable. Blank—Canadian, Mexican, and United States industries are comparable.

- Providing general freight long-distance truckload trucking—are classified in U.S. Industry 484121, General Freight Trucking, Long-Distance, Truckload; and

- Providing local general freight trucking services—are classified in Industry 484110, General Freight Trucking, Local.

4842 Specialized Freight Trucking

This industry group comprises establishments primarily engaged in providing local or long-distance specialized freight trucking. The establishments of this industry are primarily engaged in the transportation of freight which, because of size, weight, shape, or other inherent characteristics, requires specialized equipment, such as flatbeds, tankers, or refrigerated trailers. This industry includes the transportation of used household, institutional, and commercial furniture and equipment.

48421 Used Household and Office Goods Moving

See industry description for 484210 below.

484210 Used Household and Office Goods Moving

This industry comprises establishments primarily engaged in providing local or long-distance trucking of used household, used institutional, or used commercial furniture and equipment. Incidental packing and storage activities are often provided by these establishments.

48422 Specialized Freight (except Used Goods) Trucking, Local

See industry description for 484220 below.

484220 Specialized Freight (except Used Goods) Trucking, Local[US]

This industry comprises establishments primarily engaged in providing local, specialized trucking. Local trucking establishments provide trucking within a metropolitan area that may cross state lines. Generally the trips are same-day return.

Illustrative Examples:

Local agricultural products trucking
Local dump trucking (e.g., gravel, sand, top-soil)

Local boat hauling
Local livestock trucking
Local bulk liquids trucking

US—United States industry only. CAN—United States and Canadian industries are comparable. MEX—United States and Mexican industries are comparable. Blank—Canadian, Mexican, and United States industries are comparable.

Cross-References. Establishments primarily engaged in—

- Providing long-distance specialized freight (except used goods) trucking including all North American international travel—are classified in Industry 48423, Specialized Freight (except Used Goods) Trucking, Long-Distance;

- Providing local general freight trucking—are classified in U.S. Industry 484110, General Freight Trucking, Local;

- Providing trucking of used household and office goods—are classified in Industry 484210, Used Household and Office Goods Moving; and

- Providing waste collection—are classified in Industry Group 5621, Waste Collection.

48423 Specialized Freight (except Used Goods) Trucking, Long-Distance

See industry description for 484230 below.

484230 Specialized Freight (except Used Goods) Trucking, Long-Distance[US]

This industry comprises establishments primarily engaged in providing long-distance specialized trucking. These establishments provide trucking between metropolitan areas that may cross North American country borders.

Illustrative Examples:

Long-distance automobile carrier trucking
Long-distance refrigerated product trucking

Long-distance bulk liquid trucking
Long-distance trucking of waste
Long-distance hazardous material trucking

Cross-References. Establishments primarily engaged in—

- Providing local specialized freight trucking (except used goods)—are classified in Industry 484220, Specialized Freight (except Used Goods) Trucking, Local;

- Providing long-distance general freight trucking including all North American international travel—are classified in Industry 48412, General Freight Trucking, Long-Distance;

- Providing trucking of used household and office goods—are classified in Industry 484210, Used Household and Office Goods Moving; and

- Collecting and/or hauling hazardous waste, nonhazardous waste, and/or recyclable materials within a local area—are classified in Industry 56211, Waste Collection.

US—United States industry only. CAN—United States and Canadian industries are comparable. MEX—United States and Mexican industries are comparable. Blank—Canadian, Mexican, and United States industries are comparable.

485 Transit and Ground Passenger Transportation

Industries in the Transit and Ground Passenger Transportation subsector include a variety of passenger transportation activities, such as urban transit systems; chartered bus, school bus, and interurban bus transportation; and taxis. These activities are distinguished based primarily on such production process factors as vehicle types, routes, and schedules.

In this subsector, the principal splits identify scheduled transportation as separate from nonscheduled transportation. The scheduled transportation industry groups are Urban Transit Systems, Interurban and Rural Bus Transportation, and School and Employee Bus Transportation. The nonscheduled industry groups are the Charter Bus Industry and Taxi and Limousine Service. The Other Transit and Ground Passenger Transportation industry group includes both scheduled and nonscheduled transportation.

Scenic and sightseeing ground transportation services are not included in this subsector but are included in Subsector 487, Scenic and Sightseeing Transportation. Sightseeing does not usually involve place-to-place transportation; the passenger's trip starts and ends at the same location.

4851 Urban Transit Systems

48511 Urban Transit Systems

This industry comprises establishments primarily engaged in operating local and suburban passenger transit systems over regular routes and on regular schedules within a metropolitan area and its adjacent nonurban areas. Such transportation systems involve the use of one or more modes of transport including light rail, commuter rail, subways, and streetcars, as well as buses and other motor vehicles.

Cross-References. Establishments primarily engaged in—

- Providing scenic and sightseeing transportation—are classified in Industry 48711, Scenic and Sightseeing Transportation, Land;
- Providing support services to transit and ground transportation—are classified in Industry Group 4884, Support Activities for Road Transportation; and
- Providing interurban and rural bus transportation—are classified in Industry 48521, Interurban and Rural Bus Transportation.

485111 Mixed Mode Transit Systems[US]

This U.S. industry comprises establishments primarily engaged in operating local and suburban ground passenger transit systems using more than one mode

---

US—United States industry only. CAN—United States and Canadian industries are comparable. MEX—United States and Mexican industries are comparable. Blank—Canadian, Mexican, and United States industries are comparable.

of transport over regular routes and on regular schedules within a metropolitan area and its adjacent nonurban areas.

Cross-References. Establishments primarily engaged in—

- Operating local and suburban passenger transit systems using only one mode of transportation—are classified according to the mode of transport; and

- Providing support services to transit and ground passenger transportation— are classified in Industry Group 4884, Support Activities for Road Transportation.

485112 Commuter Rail Systems[US]

This U.S. industry comprises establishments primarily engaged in operating local and suburban commuter rail systems over regular routes and on a regular schedule within a metropolitan area and its adjacent nonurban areas. Commuter rail is usually characterized by reduced fares, multiple ride, and commutation tickets and mostly used by passengers during the morning and evening peak periods.

Cross-References. Establishments primarily engaged in—

- Operating local and suburban mass passenger transit systems using both commuter rail and another mode of transport—are classified in U.S. Industry 485111, Mixed Mode Transit Systems;

- Operating a subway system—are classified in U.S. Industry 485119, Other Urban Transit Systems; and

- Providing scenic and sightseeing transportation on land—are classified in Industry 487110, Scenic and Sightseeing Transportation, Land.

485113 Bus and Other Motor Vehicle Transit Systems[US]

This U.S. industry comprises establishments primarily engaged in operating local and suburban passenger transportation systems using buses or other motor vehicles over regular routes and on regular schedules within a metropolitan area and its adjacent nonurban areas.

Cross-References. Establishments primarily engaged in—

- Operating local and suburban passenger transportation systems using both a bus or other motor vehicle and another mode of transport—are classified in U.S. Industry 485111, Mixed Mode Transit Systems;

- Providing interurban and rural bus transportation—are classified in Industry 485210, Interurban and Rural Bus Transportation; and

US—United States industry only. CAN—United States and Canadian industries are comparable. MEX—United States and Mexican industries are comparable. Blank—Canadian, Mexican, and United States industries are comparable.

http://www.census.gov/naics

- Providing scenic and sightseeing transportation using buses or other motor vehicles—are classified in Industry 487110, Scenic and Sightseeing Transportation, Land.

485119 Other Urban Transit Systems[US]

This U.S. industry comprises establishments primarily engaged in operating local and suburban ground passenger transit systems (except mixed mode transit systems, commuter rail systems, and buses and other motor vehicles) over regular routes and on regular schedules within a metropolitan area and its adjacent nonurban areas.

Illustrative Examples:

Commuter cable car systems
(i.e., stand-alone)
Light rail systems (i.e., stand-alone)
Commuter tramway systems
(i.e., stand-alone)

Monorail transit systems
(i.e., stand-alone)
Commuter trolley systems
(i.e., stand-alone)

Cross-References. Establishments primarily engaged in—

- Operating local and suburban ground passenger transit systems using more than one mode of transport—are classified in U.S. Industry 485111, Mixed Mode Transit Systems;

- Providing local and suburban passenger transportation using commuter rail systems—are classified in U.S. Industry 485112, Commuter Rail Systems; and

- Operating local and suburban bus transit systems—are classified in U.S. Industry 485113, Bus and Other Motor Vehicle Transit Systems.

4852 Interurban and Rural Bus Transportation

48521 Interurban and Rural Bus Transportation

See industry description for 485210 below.

485210 Interurban and Rural Bus Transportation

This industry comprises establishments primarily engaged in providing bus passenger transportation over regular routes and on regular schedules, principally outside a single metropolitan area and its adjacent nonurban areas.

US—United States industry only. CAN—United States and Canadian industries are comparable. MEX—United States and Mexican industries are comparable. Blank—Canadian, Mexican, and United States industries are comparable.

Cross-References. Establishments primarily engaged in—

- Providing scenic and sightseeing transportation using buses—are classified in Industry 487110, Scenic and Sightseeing Transportation, Land;
- Providing buses for charter—are classified in Industry 485510, Charter Bus Industry;
- Operating local and suburban bus transit systems—are classified in U.S. Industry 485113, Bus and Other Motor Vehicle Transit Systems; and
- Operating independent bus terminals—are classified in Industry 488490, Other Support Activities for Road Transportation.

4853 Taxi and Limousine Service

48531 Taxi Service
See industry description for 485310 below.

485310 Taxi Service^{CAN}

This industry comprises establishments primarily engaged in providing passenger transportation by automobile or van, not operated over regular routes and on regular schedules. Establishments of taxicab owner/operators, taxicab fleet operators, or taxicab organizations are included in this industry.

Cross-References. Establishments primarily engaged in—

- Providing special needs transportation services (except to and from school or work) for the infirm, elderly, or handicapped—are classified in U.S. Industry 485991, Special Needs Transportation;
- Providing limousine services—are classified in Industry 485320, Limousine Service; and
- Providing scheduled shuttle services between hotels, airports, or other destination points—are classified in U.S. Industry 485999, All Other Transit and Ground Passenger Transportation.

48532 Limousine Service
See industry description for 485320 below.

485320 Limousine Service

This industry comprises establishments primarily engaged in providing an array of specialty and luxury passenger transportation services via limousine or luxury

---

sedans generally on a reserved basis. These establishments do not operate over regular routes and on regular schedules.

Cross-References. Establishments primarily engaged in—

- Providing taxi services—are classified in Industry 485310, Taxi Service; and
- Providing scheduled shuttle services between hotels, airports, or other destination points—are classified in U.S. Industry 485999, All Other Transit and Ground Passenger Transportation.

4854 School and Employee Bus Transportation

48541 School and Employee Bus Transportation
See industry description for 485410 below.

485410 School and Employee Bus Transportation

This industry comprises establishments primarily engaged in providing buses and other motor vehicles to transport pupils to and from school or employees to and from work.

Cross-References. Establishments primarily engaged in—

- Operating local and suburban bus transit systems—are classified in U.S. Industry 485113, Bus and Other Motor Vehicle Transit Systems;
- Providing interurban and rural bus transportation—are classified in Industry 485210, Interurban and Rural Bus Transportation; and
- Providing buses for charter—are classified in Industry 485510, Charter Bus Industry.

4855 Charter Bus Industry

48551 Charter Bus Industry
See industry description for 485510 below.

485510 Charter Bus Industry

This industry comprises establishments primarily engaged in providing buses for charter. These establishments provide bus services to meet customers' road transportation needs and generally do not operate over fixed routes and on regular schedules.

Cross-References. Establishments primarily engaged in—

- Providing scenic and local sightseeing transportation using buses—are classified in Industry 487110, Scenic and Sightseeing Transportation, Land; and
- Providing interurban and rural bus transportation—are classified in Industry 485210, Interurban and Rural Bus Transportation.

4859 Other Transit and Ground Passenger Transportation

48599 Other Transit and Ground Passenger Transportation

This industry comprises establishments primarily engaged in providing other transit and ground passenger transportation (except urban transit systems, interurban and rural bus transportation, taxi services, school and employee bus transportation, charter bus services, and limousine services (except shuttle services)). Shuttle services (except employee bus) and special needs transportation services are included in this industry. Shuttle services establishments generally travel within a metropolitan area and its adjacent nonurban areas on regular routes, on regular schedules and provide services between hotels, airports, or other destination points. Special Needs Transportation establishments provide passenger transportation to the infirm, elderly, or handicapped. These establishments may use specially equipped vehicles to provide passenger transportation.

Cross-References. Establishments primarily engaged in—

- Providing school or employee bus transportation for the infirm, elderly, or handicapped—are classified in Industry 48541, School and Employee Bus Transportation;
- Providing ambulance services for emergency and medical purposes—are classified in Industry 62191, Ambulance Services;
- Operating urban transit systems—are classified in Industry Group 4851, Urban Transit Systems;
- Providing interurban and rural bus transportation—are classified in Industry 48521, Interurban and Rural Bus Transportation;
- Providing taxi services and/or limousine services (except shuttle services)—are classified in Industry Group 4853, Taxi and Limousine Service; and
- Providing buses for charter—are classified in Industry 48551, Charter Bus Industry.

485991 Special Needs Transportation[US]

This U.S. industry comprises establishments primarily engaged in providing special needs transportation (except to and from school or work) to the infirm,

---

US—United States industry only. CAN—United States and Canadian industries are comparable. MEX—United States and Mexican industries are comparable. Blank—Canadian, Mexican, and United States industries are comparable.

elderly, or handicapped. These establishments may use specially equipped vehicles to provide passenger transportation.

Cross-References. Establishments primarily engaged in—

- Providing school or employee bus transportation for the infirm, elderly, or handicapped—are classified in Industry 485410, School and Employee Bus Transportation; and

- Providing ambulance services for emergency and medical purposes—are classified in Industry 62191, Ambulance Services.

485999 All Other Transit and Ground Passenger Transportation[US]

This U.S. industry comprises establishments primarily engaged in providing ground passenger transportation (except urban transit systems; interurban and rural bus transportation, taxi and/or limousine services (except shuttle services), school and employee bus transportation, charter bus services, and special needs transportation). Establishments primarily engaged in operating shuttle services and vanpools are included in this industry. Shuttle services establishments generally provide travel on regular routes and on regular schedules between hotels, airports, or other destination points.

Cross-References. Establishments primarily engaged in—

- Operating urban transit systems—are classified in Industry Group 4851, Urban Transit Systems;

- Providing interurban and rural bus transportation—are classified in Industry 485210, Interurban and Rural Bus Transportation;

- Providing taxi and/or limousine services (except shuttle services)—are classified in Industry Group 4853, Taxi and Limousine Service;

- Providing school and employee bus transportation (including for the infirm, elderly, or handicapped)—are classified in Industry 485410, School and Employee Bus Transportation;

- Providing buses for charter—are classified in Industry 485510, Charter Bus Industry;

- Providing special needs transportation (except to and from school or work) for the infirm, elderly, or handicapped—are classified in Industry 485991, Special Needs Transportation; and

- Providing ambulance services for emergency and medical purposes—are classified in Industry 621910, Ambulance Services.

US—United States industry only. CAN—United States and Canadian industries are comparable. MEX—United States and Mexican industries are comparable. Blank—Canadian, Mexican, and United States industries are comparable.

486 Pipeline Transportation

Industries in the Pipeline Transportation subsector use transmission pipelines to transport products, such as crude oil, natural gas, refined petroleum products, and slurry. Industries are identified based on the products transported (i.e., pipeline transportation of crude oil, natural gas, refined petroleum products, and other products).

The Pipeline Transportation of Natural Gas industry includes the storage of natural gas because the storage is usually done by the pipeline establishment and because a pipeline is inherently a network in which all the nodes are interdependent.

4861 Pipeline Transportation of Crude Oil

48611 Pipeline Transportation of Crude Oil
See industry description for 486110 below.

486110 Pipeline Transportation of Crude Oil

This industry comprises establishments primarily engaged in the pipeline transportation of crude oil.

Cross-References. Establishments primarily engaged in—

- Providing the pipeline transportation of natural gas—are classified in Industry 486210, Pipeline Transportation of Natural Gas; and
- Providing the pipeline transportation of refined petroleum products—are classified in Industry 486910, Pipeline Transportation of Refined Petroleum Products.

4862 Pipeline Transportation of Natural Gas

48621 Pipeline Transportation of Natural Gas
See industry description for 486210 below.

486210 Pipeline Transportation of Natural Gas

This industry comprises establishments primarily engaged in the pipeline transportation of natural gas from processing plants to local distribution systems.

Cross-References.

Establishments primarily engaged in providing natural gas to the end consumer are classified in Industry 221210, Natural Gas Distribution.

US—United States industry only. CAN—United States and Canadian industries are comparable. MEX—United States and Mexican industries are comparable. Blank—Canadian, Mexican, and United States industries are comparable.

4869 Other Pipeline Transportation

This industry group comprises establishments primarily engaged in the pipeline transportation of products (except crude oil and natural gas).

48691 Pipeline Transportation of Refined Petroleum Products
See industry description for 486910 below.

486910 Pipeline Transportation of Refined Petroleum Products

This industry comprises establishments primarily engaged in the pipeline transportation of refined petroleum products.

48699 All Other Pipeline Transportation
See industry description for 486990 below.

486990 All Other Pipeline Transportation

This industry comprises establishments primarily engaged in the pipeline transportation of products except crude oil, natural gas, and refined petroleum products.

Cross-References. Establishments primarily engaged in—

- Providing pipeline transportation of crude oil—are classified in Industry 486110, Pipeline Transportation of Crude Oil;
- Providing pipeline transportation of natural gas—are classified in Industry 486210, Pipeline Transportation of Natural Gas;
- Providing pipeline transportation of refined petroleum products—are classified in Industry 486910, Pipeline Transportation of Refined Petroleum Products; and
- Operating water distribution systems—are classified in Industry 221310, Water Supply and Irrigation Systems.

487 Scenic and Sightseeing Transportation

Industries in the Scenic and Sightseeing Transportation subsector utilize transportation equipment to provide recreation and entertainment. These activities have a production process distinct from passenger transportation carried out for the purpose of other types of for-hire transportation. This process does not emphasize efficient transportation; in fact, such activities often use obsolete vehicles, such

---

US—United States industry only. CAN—United States and Canadian industries are comparable. MEX—United States and Mexican industries are comparable. Blank—Canadian, Mexican, and United States industries are comparable.

as steam trains, to provide some extra ambience. The activity is local in nature, usually involving a same-day return to the point of departure.

The Scenic and Sightseeing Transportation subsector is separated into three industries based on the mode: land, water, and other.

Activities that are recreational in nature and involve participation by the customer, such as white-water rafting, are generally excluded from this subsector, unless they impose an impact on part of the transportation system. Charter boat fishing, for example, is included in the Scenic and Sightseeing Transportation, Water industry.

4871 Scenic and Sightseeing Transportation, Land

48711 Scenic and Sightseeing Transportation, Land
See industry description for 487110 below.

487110 Scenic and Sightseeing Transportation, Land

This industry comprises establishments primarily engaged in providing scenic and sightseeing transportation on land, such as sightseeing buses and trolleys, steam train excursions, and horse-drawn sightseeing rides. The services provided are usually local and involve same-day return to place of origin.

Cross-References. Establishments primarily engaged in—

- Operating aerial trams or aerial cable cars—are classified in Industry 487990, Scenic and Sightseeing Transportation, Other;

- Providing sporting services, such as pack trains—are classified in Industry 713990, All Other Amusement and Recreation Industries;

- Providing intercity and rural bus transportation—are classified in Industry 485210, Interurban and Rural Bus Transportation;

- Providing buses for charter—are classified in Industry 485510, Charter Bus Industry;

- Operating local and suburban passenger transit systems—are classified in Industry 48511, Urban Transit Systems; and

- Providing passenger travel arrangements and tours—are classified in Industry Group 5615, Travel Arrangement and Reservation Services.

4872 Scenic and Sightseeing Transportation, Water

48721 Scenic and Sightseeing Transportation, Water
See industry description for 487210 below.

US—United States industry only. CAN—United States and Canadian industries are comparable. MEX—United States and Mexican industries are comparable. Blank—Canadian, Mexican, and United States industries are comparable.

487210 Scenic and Sightseeing Transportation, Water

This industry comprises establishments primarily engaged in providing scenic and sightseeing transportation on water. The services provided are usually local and involve same-day return to place of origin.

Illustrative Examples:

Airboat (i.e., swamp buggy) operation
Excursion boat operation
Charter fishing boat services

Harbor sightseeing tours
Dinner cruises

Cross-References. Establishments primarily engaged in—

- Providing recreation services, such as fishing guides, white-water rafting, parasailing, and water skiing—are classified in Industry 713990, All Other Amusement and Recreation Industries;

- Providing water taxi services—are classified in Industry 48321, Inland Water Transportation;

- Providing water transportation of passengers—are classified in Subsector 483, Water Transportation;

- Operating floating casinos (i.e., gambling cruises or river boat casinos)—are classified in Industry 713210, Casinos (except Casino Hotels); and

- Providing boat rental without operators—are classified in U.S. Industry 532292, Recreational Goods Rental.

4879 Scenic and Sightseeing Transportation, Other

48799 Scenic and Sightseeing Transportation, Other
See industry description for 487990 below.

487990 Scenic and Sightseeing Transportation, Other

This industry comprises establishments primarily engaged in providing scenic and sightseeing transportation (except on land and water). The services provided are usually local and involve same-day return to place of departure.

Illustrative Examples:

Aerial cable cars, scenic and sightseeing
operation
Helicopter rides, scenic and sightseeing
operation
Aerial tramways, scenic and sightseeing
operation

Hot air balloon rides, scenic and
sightseeing operation
Glider excursions

Cross-References. Establishments primarily engaged in—

- Providing recreational activities, such as hang gliding—are classified in Industry 713990, All Other Amusement and Recreation Industries; and

- Providing scheduled or nonscheduled air transportation of passengers or specialty flying services—are classified in Subsector 481, Air Transportation.

488 Support Activities for Transportation

Industries in the Support Activities for Transportation subsector provide services which support transportation. These services may be provided to transportation carrier establishments or to the general public. This subsector includes a wide array of establishments, including air traffic control services, marine cargo handling, and motor vehicle towing.

The Support Activities for Transportation subsector includes services to transportation but is separated by type of mode serviced. The Support Activities for Rail Transportation industry includes services to the rail industry (e.g., railroad switching and terminal establishments).

Ship repair and maintenance not done in a shipyard are included in Other Support Activities for Water Transportation. An example would be floating drydock services in a harbor.

Excluded from this subsector are establishments primarily engaged in providing factory conversion and overhaul of transportation equipment, which are classified in Subsector 336, Transportation Equipment Manufacturing. Also, establishments primarily engaged in providing rental and leasing of transportation equipment without operator are classified in Subsector 532, Rental and Leasing Services.

4881 Support Activities for Air Transportation

This industry group comprises establishments primarily engaged in providing services to the air transportation industry. These services include airport operation, servicing, repairing (except factory conversion and overhaul of aircraft), maintaining and storing aircraft, and ferrying aircraft.

48811 Airport Operations

This industry comprises establishments primarily engaged in (1) operating international, national, or civil airports or public flying fields or (2) supporting airport operations (except special food services contractors), such as rental of hangar space, air traffic control services, baggage handling services, and cargo handling services.

US—United States industry only. CAN—United States and Canadian industries are comparable. MEX—United States and Mexican industries are comparable. Blank—Canadian, Mexican, and United States industries are comparable.

Cross-References. Establishments primarily engaged in—

- Providing factory conversion, overhaul, and rebuilding of aircraft—are classified in Industry 33641, Aerospace Product and Parts Manufacturing;
- Wholesaling fuel at airports—are classified in Industry 424720, Petroleum and Petroleum Products Merchant Wholesalers (except Bulk Stations and Terminals);
- Providing airport janitorial services—are classified in Industry 56172, Janitorial Services; and
- Providing food services at airports on a contractual arrangement (i.e., food service contractors)—are classified in Industry 72231, Food Service Contractors.

488111 Air Traffic Control

This U.S. industry comprises establishments primarily engaged in providing air traffic control services to regulate the flow of air traffic.

488119 Other Airport Operations[CAN]

This U.S. industry comprises establishments primarily engaged in (1) operating international, national, or civil airports, or public flying fields or (2) supporting airport operations, such as rental of hangar space, and providing baggage handling and/or cargo handling services.

Cross-References. Establishments primarily engaged in—

- Providing air traffic control services—are classified in U.S. Industry 488111, Air Traffic Control;
- Providing factory conversion, overhaul, and rebuilding of aircraft—are classified in Industry 33641, Aerospace Product and Parts Manufacturing;
- Wholesaling fuel at airports—are classified in Industry 424720, Petroleum and Petroleum Products Merchant Wholesalers (except Bulk Stations and Terminals);
- Providing airport janitorial services—are classified in Industry 561720, Janitorial Services; and
- Providing food services at airports on a contractual arrangement—are classified in Industry 722310, Food Service Contractors.

48819 Other Support Activities for Air Transportation
See industry description for 488190 below.

488190   Other Support Activities for Air Transportation

This industry comprises establishments primarily engaged in providing specialized services for air transportation (except air traffic control and other airport operations).

Illustrative Examples:

Aircraft maintenance and repair services   Aircraft testing services
(except factory conversions, overhauls,
rebuilding)

Cross-References. Establishments primarily engaged in—

- Wholesaling fuel at airports—are classified in Industry 424720, Petroleum and Petroleum Products Merchant Wholesalers (except Bulk Stations and Terminals);
- Providing aircraft janitorial services—are classified in Industry 561720, Janitorial Services;
- Providing air traffic control services—are classified in U.S. Industry 488111, Air Traffic Control;
- Providing airport operations (except air traffic control)—are classified in U.S. Industry 488119, Other Airport Operations;
- Providing factory conversion, overhaul, and rebuilding of aircraft—are classified in Industry 33641, Aerospace Product and Parts Manufacturing; and
- Providing food services to airlines on a contractual arrangement—are classified in Industry 722310, Food Service Contractors.

4832   Support Activities for Rail Transportation

48821   Support Activities for Rail Transportation
See industry description for 488210 below.

488210   Support Activities for Rail Transportation

This industry comprises establishments primarily engaged in providing specialized services for railroad transportation including servicing, routine repairing (except factory conversion, overhaul or rebuilding of rolling stock), and maintaining rail cars; loading and unloading rail cars; and operating independent terminals.

Cross-References. Establishments primarily engaged in—

- Providing railroad car rental—are classified in U.S. Industry 532411, Commercial Air, Rail, and Water Transportation Equipment Rental and Leasing;

- Factory conversion, overhaul, or rebuilding of railroad rolling stock—are classified in Industry 336510, Railroad Rolling Stock Manufacturing; and

- Providing rail car janitorial services—are classified in Industry 561720, Janitorial Services.

4883 Support Activities for Water Transportation

48831 Port and Harbor Operations
See industry description for 488310 below.

488310 Port and Harbor Operations

This industry comprises establishments primarily engaged in operating ports, harbors (including docking and pier facilities), or canals.

Cross-References. Establishments primarily engaged in—

- Providing stevedoring and other marine cargo handling services—are classified in Industry 488320, Marine Cargo Handling;

- Providing navigational services to shipping—are classified in Industry 488330, Navigational Services to Shipping; and

- Operating docking and/or storage facilities and commonly known as marinas—are classified in Industry 713930, Marinas.

48832 Marine Cargo Handling
See industry description for 488320 below.

488320 Marine Cargo Handling

This industry comprises establishments primarily engaged in providing stevedoring and other marine cargo handling services (except warehousing).

Cross-References. Establishments primarily engaged in—

- Preparing freight for transportation—are classified in U.S. Industry 488991, Packing and Crating;

US—United States industry only. CAN—United States and Canadian industries are comparable. MEX—United States and Mexican industries are comparable. Blank—Canadian, Mexican, and United States industries are comparable.

- Operating general merchandise, refrigerated, or other warehousing and storage facilities—are classified in Subsector 493, Warehousing and Storage; and

- Operating docking and pier facilities—are classified in Industry 488310, Port and Harbor Operations.

48833 Navigational Services to Shipping
See industry description for 488330 below.

488330 Navigational Services to Shipping[MEX]

This industry comprises establishments primarily engaged in providing navigational services to shipping. Marine salvage establishments are included in this industry.

Illustrative Examples:

Docking and undocking marine vessel services
Piloting services, water transportation

Marine vessel traffic reporting services
Tugboat services, harbor operation

Cross-References. Establishments primarily engaged in—

- Providing water transportation of barges (except coastal or Great Lakes barge transportation services)—are classified in U.S. Industry 483211, Inland Water Freight Transportation; and

- Providing coastal and/or Great Lakes barge transportation services—are classified in U.S. Industry 483113, Coastal and Great Lakes Freight Transportation.

48839 Other Support Activities for Water Transportation
See industry description for 488390 below.

488390 Other Support Activities for Water Transportation

This industry comprises establishments primarily engaged in providing services to water transportation (except port and harbor operations; marine cargo handling services; and navigational services to shipping).

Illustrative Examples:

Floating drydocks (i.e., maintenance and routine repairs for ships)

Ship scaling services
Marine cargo checkers and surveyors

Cross-References. Establishments primarily engaged in—

- Ship painting—are classified in Industry 238320, Painting and Wall Covering Contractors;
- Providing ship janitorial services—are classified in Industry 561720, Janitorial Services;
- Operating port, harbor, or canal facilities—are classified in Industry 488310, Port and Harbor Operations;
- Providing dredging services—are classified in Industry 237990, Other Heavy and Civil Engineering Construction;
- Providing stevedoring and other marine cargo handling services—are classified in Industry 488320, Marine Cargo Handling;
- Providing navigational services to shipping—are classified in Industry 488330, Navigational Services to Shipping; and
- Providing ship overhauling or repairs in a shipyard—are classified in U.S. Industry 336611, Ship Building and Repairing.

4884 Support Activities for Road Transportation

48841 Motor Vehicle Towing
See industry description for 488410 below.

488410 Motor Vehicle Towing

This industry comprises establishments primarily engaged in towing light or heavy motor vehicles, both local and long distance. These establishments may provide incidental services, such as storage and emergency road repair services.

Cross-References. Establishments primarily engaged in—

- Operating gasoline stations—are classified in Industry Group 4471, Gasoline Stations;
- Providing automotive repair and maintenance—are classified in Industry Group 8111, Automotive Repair and Maintenance; and
- Both retailing automotive parts and accessories, and repairing automobiles and known as automotive supply stores—are classified in Industry 441310, Automotive Parts and Accessories Stores.

48849 Other Support Activities for Road Transportation
See industry description for 488490 below.

US—United States industry only. CAN—United States and Canadian industries are comparable. MEX—United States and Mexican industries are comparable. Blank—Canadian, Mexican, and United States industries are comparable.

488490 Other Support Activities for Road Transportation^{CAN}

This industry comprises establishments primarily engaged in providing services (except motor vehicle towing) to road network users.

Illustrative Examples:

Bridge, tunnel, and highway operations
Pilot car services (i.e., wide load warning services)

Driving services (e.g., automobile, truck delivery)
Truck or weighing station operations

Cross-References. Establishments primarily engaged in—

- Providing automotive repair and maintenance—are classified in Industry Group 8111, Automotive Repair and Maintenance;

- Providing towing services to motor vehicles—are classified in Industry 488410, Motor Vehicle Towing;

- Providing a network for busing in combination with providing terminal services—are classified in Industry 485210, Interurban and Rural Bus Transportation; and

- Providing a network for trucking in combination with providing terminal services—are classified in Subsector 484, Truck Transportation.

4885 Freight Transportation Arrangement

48851 Freight Transportation Arrangement

See industry description for 488510 below.

488510 Freight Transportation Arrangement^{US}

This industry comprises establishments primarily engaged in arranging transportation of freight between shippers and carriers. These establishments are usually known as freight forwarders, marine shipping agents, or customs brokers and offer a combination of services spanning transportation modes.

Cross-References.

Establishments primarily engaged in tariff and freight rate consulting services are classified in U.S. Industry 541614, Process, Physical Distribution, and Logistics Consulting Services.

US—United States industry only. CAN—United States and Canadian industries are comparable. MEX—United States and Mexican industries are comparable. Blank—Canadian, Mexican, and United States industries are comparable.

4889 Other Support Activities for Transportation

48899 Other Support Activities for Transportation

This industry comprises establishments primarily engaged in providing support activities to transportation (except for air transportation; rail transportation; water transportation; road transportation; and freight transportation arrangement).

Illustrative Examples:

Arrangement of vanpools or carpools   Independent pipeline terminal facilities
Stockyards (i.e., not for fattening or
  selling livestock)

Cross-References. Establishments primarily engaged in—

- Providing support activities for air transportation—are classified in Industry Group 4881, Support Activities for Air Transportation;

- Providing support activities for rail transportation—are classified in Industry Group 4882, Support Activities for Rail Transportation;

- Providing support activities for water transportation—are classified in Industry Group 4883, Support Activities for Water Transportation;

- Providing support activities for road transportation—are classified in Industry Group 4884, Support Activities for Road Transportation;

- Arranging transportation of freight between shippers and carriers—are classified in Industry 48851, Freight Transportation Arrangement;

- Providing tariff and freight rate consulting services—are classified in Industry 54161, Management Consulting Services;

- Operating stockyards for fattening livestock—are classified in Subsector 112, Animal Production; and

- Providing packaging and labeling services—are classified in Industry 56191, Packaging and Labeling Services.

488991 Packing and Crating[US]

This U.S. industry comprises establishments primarily engaged in packing, crating, and otherwise preparing goods for transportation.

Cross-References.

Establishments primarily engaged in providing packaging and labeling services are classified in Industry 561910, Packaging and Labeling Services.

488999 All Other Support Activities for Transportation[US]

This U.S. industry comprises establishments primarily engaged in providing support activities to transportation (except for air transportation; rail transportation; water transportation; road transportation; freight transportation arrangement; and packing and crating).

Illustrative Examples:

Arrangement of vanpools or carpools	Independent pipeline terminal facilities
Stockyards (i.e., not for fattening or selling livestock)	

Cross-References. Establishments primarily engaged in—

* Operating stockyards for fattening livestock—are classified in Subsector 112, Animal Production;
* Providing tariff and freight rate consulting services—are classified in U.S. Industry 541614, Process, Physical Distribution, and Logistics Consulting Services;
* Providing packing and crating services for transportation—are classified in U.S. Industry 488991, Packing and Crating;
* Providing support activities for air transportation—are classified in Industry Group 4881, Support Activities for Air Transportation;
* Providing support activities for rail transportation—are classified in Industry 488210, Support Activities for Rail Transportation;
* Providing support activities for water transportation—are classified in Industry Group 4883, Support Activities for Water Transportation;
* Providing support activities for road transportation—are classified in Industry Group 4884, Support Activities for Road Transportation; and
* Arranging transportation of freight between shippers and carriers—are classified in Industry 488510, Freight Transportation Arrangement.

491 Postal Service

The Postal Service subsector includes the activities of the National Post Office and its subcontractors operating under a universal service obligation to provide mail services, and using the infrastructure required to fulfill that obligation. These services include delivering letters and small parcels. These articles can be described as those that can be handled by one person without using special equipment. This allows the collection, pick-up, and delivery operations to be done with limited

US—United States industry only. CAN—United States and Canadian industries are comparable. MEX—United States and Mexican industries are comparable. Blank—Canadian, Mexican, and United States industries are comparable.

http://www.census.gov/naics

labor costs and minimal equipment. Sorting and transportation activities, where necessary, are generally mechanized. The restriction to small parcels distinguishes these establishments from those in the transportation industries. These establishments may also provide express delivery services using the infrastructure established for provision of basic mail services.

The traditional activity of the National Postal Service is described in this subsector. Subcontractors include rural post offices on contract to the Postal Service.

Bulk transportation of mail on contract to the Postal Service is not included here, because it is usually done by transportation establishments that carry other customers' cargo as well. Establishments that provide courier and express delivery services without operating under a universal service obligation are classified in subsector 492, Couriers and Messengers.

4911 Postal Service

49111 Postal Service
See industry description for 491110 below.

491110 Postal Service

This industry comprises establishments primarily engaged in providing mail services under a universal service obligation. Mail services include the carriage of letters, printed matter, or mailable packages, including acceptance, collection, processing, and delivery. Due to the infrastructure requirements of providing mail service under a universal service obligation, postal service establishments often provide parcel and express delivery services in addition to the mail service. Establishments primarily engaged in performing one or more parts of the basic mail service, such as sorting, routing and/or delivery (except bulk transportation of mail) are included in this industry.

Cross-References. Establishments primarily engaged in—

- Providing bulk transportation of mail on a contract basis to and from postal service establishments—are classified in Industry Group 4841, General Freight Trucking;

- Providing services outside of the basic mail service, such as mail presort, mail consolidation, or address bar coding services, on a contract or fee basis—are classified in Industry 561499, All Other Business Support Services;

- Providing courier services—are classified in Industry 492110, Couriers and Express Delivery Services;

US—United States industry only. CAN—United States and Canadian industries are comparable. MEX—United States and Mexican industries are comparable. Blank—Canadian, Mexican, and United States industries are comparable.

- Providing mailbox services along with other business services—are classified in U.S. Industry 561431, Private Mail Centers; and

- Providing local messenger and delivery services—are classified in Industry 492210, Local Messengers and Local Delivery.

492 Couriers and Messengers

Industries in the Couriers and Messengers subsector provide intercity and/or local delivery of parcels and documents (including express delivery services) without operating under a universal service obligation. These articles can be described as those that may be handled by one person without using special equipment. This allows the collection, pick-up, and delivery operations to be done with limited labor costs and minimal equipment. Sorting and transportation activities, where necessary, are generally mechanized. The restriction to small parcels partly distinguishes these establishments from those in the transportation industries. The complete network of courier services establishments also distinguishes these transportation services from local messenger and delivery establishments in this subsector. This includes the establishments that perform intercity transportation as well as establishments that, under contract to them, perform local pick-up and delivery. Messengers, which usually deliver within a metropolitan or single urban area, may use bicycle, foot, small truck, or van.

4921 Couriers and Express Delivery Services

49211 Couriers and Express Delivery Services
See industry description for 492110 below.

492110 Couriers and Express Delivery Services

This industry comprises establishments primarily engaged in providing air, surface, or combined mode courier and express delivery services of parcels, but not operating under a universal service obligation. These parcels can include goods and documents, but the express delivery services are not part of the normal mail service. These services are generally between metropolitan areas or urban centers, but the establishments of this industry form a network that includes local pick-up and delivery to serve their customers' needs.

Illustrative Examples:

Air courier services, except establishments operating under a universal service obligation
Express delivery services, except establishments operating under a universal service obligation

Courier services (i.e., intercity network), except establishments operating under a universal service obligation

---

US—United States industry only. CAN—United States and Canadian industries are comparable. MEX—United States and Mexican industries are comparable. Blank—Canadian, Mexican, and United States industries are comparable.

Cross-References. Establishments primarily engaged in—

- Providing parcel and express delivery services in addition to mail services under a universal service obligation—are classified in Industry 491110, Postal Service;

- Providing messenger and delivery services within a metropolitan area or within an urban center—are classified in Industry 492210, Local Messengers and Local Delivery; and

- Providing the truck transportation of palletized general freight—are classified in Industry Group 4841, General Freight Trucking.

4922 Local Messengers and Local Delivery

49221 Local Messengers and Local Delivery
See industry description for 492210 below.

492210 Local Messengers and Local Delivery

This industry comprises establishments primarily engaged in providing local messenger and delivery services of small items within a single metropolitan area or within an urban center. These establishments generally provide point-to-point pickup and delivery and do not operate as part of an intercity courier network.

Illustrative Examples:

Alcoholic beverages delivery
  services
Letters, documents, or small parcels
  local delivery services

Grocery delivery services (i.e.,
  independent service from grocery store)
Restaurant meals delivery services (i.e.,
  independent service from restaurant)

Cross-References. Establishments primarily engaged in—

- Providing local letter and parcel delivery services as part of an intercity courier network—are classified in Industry 492110, Couriers and Express Delivery Services;

- Operating the National Postal Service or providing postal services on a contract basis (except the bulk transportation of mail)—are classified in Industry 491110, Postal Service; and

- Providing the bulk transportation of mail on a contract basis to and from Postal Service establishments—are classified in Industry Group 4841, General Freight Trucking.

US—United States industry only. CAN—United States and Canadian industries are comparable. MEX—United States and Mexican industries are comparable. Blank—Canadian, Mexican, and United States industries are comparable.

493 Warehousing and Storage

Industries in the Warehousing and Storage subsector are primarily engaged in operating warehousing and storage facilities for general merchandise, refrigerated goods, and other warehouse products. These establishments provide facilities to store goods. They do not sell the goods they handle. These establishments take responsibility for storing the goods and keeping them secure. They may also provide a range of services, often referred to as logistics services, related to the distribution of goods. Logistics services can include labeling, breaking bulk, inventory control and management, light assembly, order entry and fulfillment, packaging, pick and pack, price marking and ticketing, and transportation arrangement. However, establishments in this industry group always provide warehousing or storage services in addition to any logistic services. Furthermore, the warehousing or storage of goods must be more than incidental to the performance of services, such as price marking.

Bonded warehousing and storage services and warehouses located in free trade zones are included in the industries of this subsector.

4931 Warehousing and Storage

49311 General Warehousing and Storage
See industry description for 493110 below.

493110 General Warehousing and Storage^{CAN}

This industry comprises establishments primarily engaged in operating merchandise warehousing and storage facilities. These establishments generally handle goods in containers, such as boxes, barrels, and/or drums, using equipment, such as forklifts, pallets, and racks. They are not specialized in handling bulk products of any particular type, size, or quantity of goods or products.

Cross-References. Establishments primarily engaged in—

- Renting or leasing space for self storage—are classified in Industry 531130, Lessors of Miniwarehouses and Self-Storage Units; and

- Selling in combination with handling and/or distributing goods to other wholesale or retail establishments—are classified in Sector 42, Wholesale Trade.

49312 Refrigerated Warehousing and Storage
See industry description for 493120 below.

US—United States industry only. CAN—United States and Canadian industries are comparable. MEX—United States and Mexican industries are comparable. Blank—Canadian, Mexican, and United States industries are comparable.

493120 Refrigerated Warehousing and Storage

This industry comprises establishments primarily engaged in operating refrigerated warehousing and storage facilities. Establishments primarily engaged in the storage of furs for the trade are included in this industry. The services provided by these establishments include blast freezing, tempering, and modified atmosphere storage services.

Cross-References.

Establishments primarily engaged in storing furs (except for the trade) and garments are classified in Industry 812320, Drycleaning and Laundry Services (except Coin-Operated).

49313 Farm Product Warehousing and Storage
See industry description for 493130 below.

493130 Farm Product Warehousing and Storage

This industry comprises establishments primarily engaged in operating bulk farm product warehousing and storage facilities (except refrigerated). Grain elevators primarily engaged in storage are included in this industry.

Cross-References. Establishments primarily engaged in—

- Operating refrigerated warehousing and storage facilities—are classified in Industry 493120, Refrigerated Warehousing and Storage; and

- Storing grains and field beans (i.e., grain elevators) as an incidental activity to sales—are classified in Industry 424510, Grain and Field Bean Merchant Wholesalers.

49319 Other Warehousing and Storage
See industry description for 493190 below.

493190 Other Warehousing and Storage

This industry comprises establishments primarily engaged in operating warehousing and storage facilities (except general merchandise, refrigerated, and farm product warehousing and storage).

Illustrative Examples:

Bulk petroleum storage	Document storage and warehousing
Lumber storage terminals	Whiskey warehousing

US—United States industry only. CAN—United States and Canadian industries are comparable. MEX—United States and Mexican industries are comparable. Blank—Canadian, Mexican, and United States industries are comparable.

Cross-References. Establishments primarily engaged in—

- Renting or leasing space for self storage—are classified in Industry 531130, Lessors of Miniwarehouses and Self-Storage Units;

- Storing hazardous materials for treatment and disposal—are classified in U.S. Industry 562211, Hazardous Waste Treatment and Disposal;

- Operating general warehousing and storage facilities—are classified in Industry 493110, General Warehousing and Storage;

- Wholesaling of petroleum bulk—are classified in Industry 424710, Petroleum Bulk Stations and Terminals;

- Operating refrigerated warehousing and storage facilities—are classified in Industry 493120, Refrigerated Warehousing and Storage; and

- Operating farm product warehousing and storage facilities—are classified in Industry 493130, Farm Product Warehousing and Storage.

Sector 51—Information

The Sector as a Whole

The Information sector comprises establishments engaged in the following processes: (a) producing and distributing information and cultural products, (b) providing the means to transmit or distribute these products as well as data or communications, and (c) processing data.

The main components of this sector are the publishing industries, including software publishing, and both traditional publishing and publishing exclusively on the Internet; the motion picture and sound recording industries; the broadcasting industries, including traditional broadcasting and those broadcasting exclusively over the Internet; the telecommunications industries; Web search portals, data processing industries, and the information services industries.

The expressions "information age" and "global information economy" are used with considerable frequency today. The general idea of an "information economy" includes both the notion of industries primarily producing, processing, and distributing information, as well as the idea that every industry is using available information and information technology to reorganize and make themselves more productive.

For the purposes of NAICS, it is the transformation of information into a commodity that is produced and distributed by a number of growing industries that is at issue. The Information sector groups three types of establishments: (1) those engaged in producing and distributing information and cultural products; (2) those that provide the means to transmit or distribute these products as well as data or communications; and (3) those that process data. Cultural products are those that directly express attitudes, opinions, ideas, values, and artistic creativity; provide entertainment; or offer information and analysis concerning the past and present. Included in this definition are popular, mass-produced products as well as cultural products that normally have a more limited audience, such as poetry books, literary magazines, or classical records.

The unique characteristics of information and cultural products, and of the processes involved in their production and distribution, distinguish the Information sector from the goods-producing and service-producing sectors. Some of these characteristics are:

1. Unlike traditional goods, an "information or cultural product," such as a newspaper on-line or television program, does not necessarily have tangible qualities, nor is it necessarily associated with a particular form. A movie can be shown at a movie theater, on a television broadcast, through video-on-demand or rented at a local video store. A sound recording can be aired on radio, embedded in multimedia products, or sold at a record store.

US—United States industry only. CAN—United States and Canadian industries are comparable. MEX—United States and Mexican industries are comparable. Blank—Canadian, Mexican, and United States industries are comparable.

2. Unlike traditional services, the delivery of these products does not require direct contact between the supplier and the consumer.

3. The value of these products to the consumer lies in their informational, educational, cultural, or entertainment content, not in the format in which they are distributed. Most of these products are protected from unlawful reproduction by copyright laws.

4. The intangible property aspect of information and cultural products makes the processes involved in their production and distribution very different from goods and services. Only those possessing the rights to these works are authorized to reproduce, alter, improve, and distribute them. Acquiring and using these rights often involves significant costs. In addition, technology is revolutionizing the distribution of these products. It is possible to distribute them in a physical form, via broadcast, or on-line.

5. Distributors of information and cultural products can easily add value to the products they distribute. For instance, broadcasters add advertising not contained in the original product. This capacity means that unlike traditional distributors, they derive revenue not from sale of the distributed product to the final consumer, but from those who pay for the privilege of adding information to the original product. Similarly, a directory and mailing list publisher can acquire the rights to thousands of previously published newspaper and periodical articles and add new value by providing search and software and organizing the information in a way that facilitates research and retrieval. These products often command a much higher price than the original information.

The distribution modes for information commodities may either eliminate the necessity for traditional manufacture, or reverse the conventional order of manufacture-distribute: A newspaper distributed on-line, for example, can be printed locally or by the final consumer. Similarly, it is anticipated that packaged software, which today is mainly bought through the traditional retail channels, will soon be available mainly on-line. The NAICS Information sector is designed to make such economic changes transparent as they occur, or to facilitate designing surveys that will monitor the new phenomena and provide data to analyze the changes.

Many of the industries in the NAICS Information sector are engaged in producing products protected by copyright law, or in distributing them (other than distribution by traditional wholesale and retail methods). Examples are traditional publishing industries, software and directory and mailing list publishing industries, and film and sound industries. Broadcasting and telecommunications industries and information providers and processors are also included in the Information sector, because their technologies are so closely linked to other industries in the Information sector.

US—United States industry only. CAN—United States and Canadian industries are comparable. MEX—United States and Mexican industries are comparable. Blank—Canadian, Mexican, and United States industries are comparable.

511 Publishing Industries (except Internet)

Industries in the Publishing Industries (except Internet) subsector group establishments engaged in the publishing of newspapers, magazines, other periodicals, and books, as well as directory and mailing list and software publishing. In general, these establishments, which are known as publishers, issue copies of works for which they usually possess copyright. Works may be in one or more formats including traditional print form, CD-ROM, or proprietary electronic networks. Publishers may publish works originally created by others for which they have obtained the rights and/or works that they have created in-house. Software publishing is included here because the activity, creation of a copyrighted product and bringing it to market, is equivalent to the creation process for other types of intellectual products.

In NAICS, publishing—the reporting, writing, editing, and other processes that are required to create an edition of a newspaper—is treated as a major economic activity in its own right, rather than as a subsidiary activity to a manufacturing activity, printing. Thus, publishing is classified in the Information sector; whereas, printing remains in the NAICS Manufacturing sector. In part, the NAICS classification reflects the fact that publishing increasingly takes place in establishments that are physically separate from the associated printing establishments. More crucially, the NAICS classification of book and newspaper publishing is intended to portray their roles in a modern economy, in which they do not resemble manufacturing activities.

Music publishers are not included in the Publishing Industries (except Internet) subsector, but are included in the Motion Picture and Sound Recording Industries subsector. Reproduction of prepackaged software is treated in NAICS as a manufacturing activity; on-line distribution of software products is in the Information sector, and custom design of software to client specifications is included in the Professional, Scientific, and Technical Services sector. These distinctions arise because of the different ways that software is created, reproduced, and distributed.

The Publishing Industries (except Internet) subsector does not include establishments that publish exclusively on the Internet. Establishments publishing exclusively on the Internet are included in Subsector 519, Other Information Service. The Publishing Industries (except Internet) subsector also excludes products, such as manifold business forms. Information is not the essential component of these items. Establishments producing these items are included in Subsector 323, Printing and Related Support Activities.

5111 Newspaper, Periodical, Book, and Directory Publishers

This industry group comprises establishments primarily engaged in publishing newspapers, magazines, other periodicals, books, directories and mailing lists, and other works, such as calendars, greeting cards, and maps. These works are characterized by the intellectual creativity required in their development and are usually protected by copyright. Publishers distribute or arrange for the distribution of these works.

Publishing establishments may create the works in-house, contract for, purchase, or compile works that were originally created by others. These works may be published in one or more formats, such as print and/or electronic form, including proprietary electronic networks. Establishments in this industry may print, reproduce, or offer direct access to the works themselves or may arrange with others to carry out such functions.

Establishments that both print and publish may fill excess capacity with commercial or job printing. However, the publishing activity is still considered to be the primary activity of these establishments.

51111 Newspaper Publishers

See industry description for 511110 below.

511110 Newspaper Publishers[CAN]

This industry comprises establishments known as newspaper publishers. Establishments in this industry carry out operations necessary for producing and distributing newspapers, including gathering news; writing news columns, feature stories, and editorials; and selling and preparing advertisements. These establishments may publish newspapers in print or electronic form.

Cross-References.

• Establishments publishing newspapers exclusively on the Internet are classified in Industry 519130, Internet Publishing and Broadcasting and Web Search Portals;

• Establishments primarily engaged in printing newspapers without publishing are classified in Industry 32311, Printing;

• Establishments, such as trade associations, schools and universities, and social welfare organizations that publish newsletters for distribution to their membership, but that are not commonly known as newspaper publishers, are classified according to their primary activity designation;

• Establishments primarily engaged in supplying the news media with information, such as news, reports, and pictures, are classified in Industry 519110, News Syndicates; and

• Establishments of independent representatives primarily engaged in selling advertising space are classified in Industry 541840, Media Representatives.

US—United States industry only. CAN—United States and Canadian industries are comparable. MEX—United States and Mexican industries are comparable. Blank—Canadian, Mexican. and United States industries are comparable.

51112 Periodical Publishers

See industry description for 511120 below.

511120 Periodical Publishers^{CAN}

This industry comprises establishments known either as magazine publishers or periodical publishers. These establishments carry out the operations necessary for producing and distributing magazines and other periodicals, such as gathering, writing, and editing articles, and selling and preparing advertisements. These establishments may publish magazines and other periodicals in print or electronic form.

Illustrative Examples:

Comic book publishers (except exclusive Internet publishing)
Radio and television guide publishers (except exclusive publishing)
Magazine publishers (except exclusive Internet publishing)

Scholarly journal publishers (except exclusive Internet publishing)
Newsletter publishers (except exclusive Internet publishing)
Trade journal publishers (except exclusive Internet publishing)

Cross-References.

- Establishments publishing periodicals exclusively on the Internet are classified in Industry 519130, Internet Publishing and Broadcasting and Web Search Portals;

- Establishments primarily engaged in printing periodicals without publishing are classified in Industry 32311, Printing;

- Establishments, such as trade associations, schools and universities, and social welfare organizations, that publish magazines and periodicals for distribution to their membership, but that are not commonly known as periodical publishers, are classified according to their primary activity designation;

- Establishments primarily engaged in publishing directories and mailing lists are classified in Industry 511140, Directory and Mailing List Publishers; and

- Establishments of independent representatives primarily engaged in selling advertising space are classified in Industry 541840, Media Representatives.

51113 Book Publishers

See industry description for 511130 below.

US—United States industry only. CAN—United States and Canadian industries are comparable. MEX—United States and Mexican industries are comparable. Blank—Canadian, Mexican, and United States industries are comparable.

511130 Book Publishers[CAN]

This industry comprises establishments known as book publishers. Establishments in this industry carry out design, editing, and marketing activities necessary for producing and distributing books. These establishments may publish books in print, electronic, or audio form.

Illustrative Examples:

Atlas publishers (except exclusive
  Internet publishing)
Religious book publishers (except
  exclusive Internet publishing)
Book publishers (except exclusive
  Internet publishing)
School textbook publishers (except
  exclusive Internet publishing)

Encyclopedia publishers (except
  exclusive Internet publishing)
Technical manual publishers (except
  exclusive Internet publishing)
Map publishers (except exclusive
  Internet publishing)
Travel guide book publishers (except
  exclusive Internet publishing)

Cross-References.

- Establishments publishing books on the Internet exclusively are classified in Industry 519130, Internet Publishing and Broadcasting and Web Search Portals;

- Establishments primarily engaged in printing books without publishing are classified in Industry 32311, Printing;

- Establishments known as music publishers are classified in Industry 512230, Music Publishers;

- Establishments, such as trade associations, schools and universities, and social welfare organizations, that publish books for distribution to their membership, that are not commonly known as book publishers, are classified according to their primary activity designation; and

- Book clubs primarily engaged in direct sales activities without publishing are classified in Industry 454390, Other Direct Selling Establishments.

51114 Directory and Mailing List Publishers

See industry description for 511140 below.

511140 Directory and Mailing List Publishers[CAN]

This industry comprises establishments primarily engaged in publishing directories, mailing lists, and collections or compilations of fact. The products are typically protected in their selection, arrangement and/or presentation. Examples are lists of mailing addresses, telephone directories, directories of businesses, collections or compilations of proprietary drugs or legal case results, compilations of public records, etc. These establishments may publish directories and mailing lists in print or electronic form.

Illustrative Examples:

Business directory publishers (except exclusive Internet publishing)

Mailing list publishers (except exclusive Internet publishing)

Directory publishers (except exclusive Internet publishing)

Telephone directory publishers (except exclusive Internet publishing)

Cross-References. Establishments primarily engaged in—

- Operating web search portals or developing and publishing, exclusively on the Internet, collections or compilations of creative works or facts—are classified in Industry 519130, Internet Publishing and Broadcasting and Web Search Portals;

- Compiling mailing lists in conjunction with providing direct mail advertising services—are classified in Industry 541860, Direct Mail Advertising;

- Printing without publishing directories and mailing lists—are classified in Industry 32311, Printing;

- Publishing computer software—are classified in Industry 511210, Software Publishers;

- Creating and publishing encyclopedias and similar collections of creative works in print and/or electronic media—are classified in Industry 511130, Book Publishers; and

- Creating and publishing collections of creative works that are periodically updated—are classified in Industry 511120, Periodical Publishers.

51119 Other Publishers

This industry comprises establishments known as publishers (except newspaper, magazine, book, directory, mailing list, and music publishers). These establishments may publish works in print or electronic form.

Illustrative Examples:

Art print publishers (except exclusive Internet publishing)

Greeting card publishers (except exclusive Internet publishing)

Calendar publishers (except exclusive Internet publishing)

US—United States industry only. CAN—United States and Canadian industries are comparable. MEX—United States and Mexican industries are comparable. Blank—Canadian, Mexican, and United States industries are comparable.

Cross-References.

- Establishments publishing exclusively on the Internet are classified in Industry 51913, Internet Publishing and Broadcasting and Web Search Portals;

- Establishments known as newspaper publishers are classified in Industry 51111, Newspaper Publishers;

- Establishments known as magazine and other periodical publishers are classified in Industry 51112, Periodical Publishers;

- Establishments known as book publishers are classified in Industry 51113, Book Publishers;

- Establishments primarily engaged in publishing directories and mailing lists are classified in Industry 51114, Directory and Mailing List Publishers;

- Establishments known as music publishers are classified in Industry 51223, Music Publishers; and

- Establishments primarily engaged in manufacturing manifold business forms are classified in Industry 32311, Printing.

511191 Greeting Card Publishers[US]

This U.S. industry comprises establishments primarily engaged in publishing greeting cards.

Cross-References. Establishments primarily engaged in—

- Publishing greeting cards exclusively on the Internet—are classified in Industry 519130, Internet Publishing and Broadcasting and Web Search Portals; and

- Printing greeting cards without publishing—are classified in Industry 32311, Printing.

511199 All Other Publishers[US]

This U.S. industry comprises establishments generally known as publishers (except newspaper, magazine, book, directory, database, music, and greeting card publishers). These establishments may publish works in print or electronic form.

Illustrative Examples:

Art print publishers (except exclusive Internet publishing)

Calendar publishers (except exclusive Internet publishing)

US—United States industry only. CAN—United States and Canadian industries are comparable. MEX—United States and Mexican industries are comparable. Blank—Canadian, Mexican, and United States industries are comparable.

Cross-References.

- Establishments publishing exclusively on the Internet are classified in Industry 519130, Internet Publishing and Broadcasting and Web Search Portals;
- Establishments known as newspaper publishers are classified in Industry 511110, Newspaper Publishers;
- Establishments known as magazine or other periodical publishers are classified in Industry 511120, Periodical Publishers;
- Establishments known as book publishers are classified in Industry 511130, Book Publishers;
- Establishments primarily engaged in publishing directories and mailing lists are classified in Industry 511140, Directory and Mailing List Publishers;
- Establishments primarily engaged in greeting card publishing are classified in U.S. Industry 511191, Greeting Card Publishers;
- Establishments known as music publishers are classified in Industry 512230, Music Publishers;
- Establishments primarily engaged in manufacturing manifold business forms are classified in U.S. Industry 323116, Manifold Business Forms Printing; and
- Establishments primarily engaged in manufacturing day schedulers are classified in U.S. Industry 323118, Blankbook, Looseleaf Binders, and Devices Manufacturing.

5112 Software Publishers

51121 Software Publishers
See industry description for 511210 below.

511210 Software Publishers

This industry comprises establishments primarily engaged in computer software publishing or publishing and reproduction. Establishments in this industry carry out operations necessary for producing and distributing computer software, such as designing, providing documentation, assisting in installation, and providing support services to software purchasers. These establishments may design, develop, and publish, or publish only.

Cross-References. Establishments primarily engaged in—

- Reselling packaged software—are classified in Sector 42, Wholesale Trade or Sector 44-45, Retail Trade;

- Providing access to software for clients from a central host site—are classified in Industry 518210, Data Processing, Hosting, and Related Services;

- Designing software to meet the needs of specific users—are classified in U.S. Industry 541511, Custom Computer Programming Services; and

- Mass duplication of software—are classified in U.S. Industry 334611, Software Reproducing.

512 Motion Picture and Sound Recording Industries

Industries in the Motion Picture and Sound Recording Industries subsector group establishments involved in the production and distribution of motion pictures and sound recordings. While producers and distributors of motion pictures and sound recordings issue works for sale as traditional publishers do, the processes are sufficiently different to warrant placing establishments engaged in these activities in a separate subsector. Production is typically a complex process that involves several distinct types of establishments that are engaged in activities, such as contracting with performers, creating the film or sound content, and providing technical postproduction services. Film distribution is often to exhibitors, such as theaters and broadcasters, rather than through the wholesale and retail distribution chain. When the product is in a mass-produced form, NAICS treats production and distribution as the major economic activity as it does in the Publishing Industries subsector, rather than as a subsidiary activity to the manufacture of such products.

This subsector does not include establishments primarily engaged in the wholesale distribution of videocassettes and sound recordings, such as compact discs and audio tapes; these establishments are included in the Wholesale Trade sector. Reproduction of videocassettes and sound recordings that is carried out separately from establishments engaged in production and distribution is treated in NAICS as a manufacturing activity.

5121 Motion Picture and Video Industries

This industry group comprises establishments primarily engaged in the production and/or distribution of motion pictures, videos, television programs, or commercials; in the exhibition of motion pictures; or in the provision of postproduction and related services.

51211 Motion Picture and Video Production
See industry description for 512110 below.

US—United States industry only. CAN—United States and Canadian industries are comparable. MEX—United States and Mexican industries are comparable. Blank—Canadian, Mexican, and United States industries are comparable.

512110 Motion Picture and Video Production^{CAN}

This industry comprises establishments primarily engaged in producing, or producing and distributing motion pictures, videos, television programs, or television commercials.

Cross-References. Establishments primarily engaged in—

- Producing motion pictures and videos on contract as independent producers—are classified in Industry 711510, Independent Artists, Writers, and Performers;
- Providing teleproduction and other postproduction services—are classified in U.S. Industry 512191, Teleproduction and Other Postproduction Services;
- Providing video taping of weddings, special events, and/or business inventories—are classified in Industry 54192, Photographic Services;
- Providing motion picture laboratory services—are classified in U.S. Industry 512199, Other Motion Picture and Video Industries;
- Providing mass duplication and packaging of video tapes—are classified in U.S. Industry 334612, Prerecorded Compact Disc (except Software), Tape, and Record Reproducing; and
- Acquiring distribution rights and distributing motion pictures and videos—are classified in Industry 512120, Motion Picture and Video Distribution.

51212 Motion Picture and Video Distribution
See industry description for 512120 below.

512120 Motion Picture and Video Distribution

This industry comprises establishments primarily engaged in acquiring distribution rights and distributing film and video productions to motion picture theaters, television networks and stations, and exhibitors.

Cross-References. Establishments primarily engaged in—

- Producing and distributing motion pictures and videos—are classified in Industry 512110, Motion Picture and Video Production;
- Merchant wholesale distribution of blank video cassette tapes and discs—are classified in Industry 423690, Other Electronic Parts and Equipment Merchant Wholesalers;
- Merchant wholesale distribution of prerecorded video cassette tapes and discs—are classified in Industry 423990, Other Miscellaneous Durable Goods Merchant Wholesalers;

US—United States industry only. CAN—United States and Canadian industries are comparable. MEX—United States and Mexican industries are comparable. Blank—Canadian, Mexican, and United States industries are comparable.

- Providing mass duplication and packaging of video tapes—are classified in U.S. Industry 334612, Prerecorded Compact Disc (except Software), Tape, and Record Reproducing;

- Providing motion picture footage (via film libraries) to producers—are classified in U.S. Industry 512199, Other Motion Picture and Video Industries;

- Renting video tapes and discs to the general public—are classified in Industry 532230, Video Tape and Disc Rental; and

- Selling video cassettes and discs to the general public—are classified in Industry 451220, Prerecorded Tape, Compact Disc, and Record Stores.

51213 Motion Picture and Video Exhibition

This industry comprises establishments primarily engaged in operating motion picture theaters and/or exhibiting motion pictures or videos at film festivals, and so forth.

512131 Motion Picture Theaters (except Drive-Ins)[US]

This U.S. industry comprises establishments primarily engaged in operating motion picture theaters (except drive-ins) and/or exhibiting motion pictures or videos at film festivals, and so forth.

512132 Drive-In Motion Picture Theaters[US]

This U.S. industry comprises establishments primarily engaged in operating drive-in motion picture theaters.

51219 Postproduction Services and Other Motion Picture and Video Industries

This industry comprises establishments primarily engaged in providing postproduction services and other services to the motion picture industry, including specialized motion picture or video postproduction services, such as editing, film/tape transfers, titling, subtitling, credits, closed captioning, and computer-produced graphics, animation and special effects, as well as developing and processing motion picture film.

Illustrative Examples:

Motion picture film laboratories	Postproduction facilities
Stock footage film libraries	Teleproduction services

US—United States industry only. CAN—United States and Canadian industries are comparable. MEX—United States and Mexican industries are comparable. Blank—Canadian, Mexican, and United States industries are comparable.

Cross-References. Establishments primarily engaged in—

- Mass duplicating video tapes and film—are classified in Industry 33461, Manufacturing and Reproducing Magnetic and Optical Media;
- Providing audio services for film, television, and video productions—are classified in Industry 51224, Sound Recording Studios;
- Renting wardrobes and costumes for motion picture production—are classified in Industry 53222, Formal Wear and Costume Rental;
- Renting studio equipment—are classified in Industry 53249, Other Commercial and Industrial Machinery and Equipment Rental and Leasing; and
- Casting actors and actresses with production companies—are classified in Industry 56131, Employment Placement Agencies and Executive Search Services.

512191 Teleproduction and Other Postproduction Services[US]

This U.S. industry comprises establishments primarily engaged in providing specialized motion picture or video postproduction services, such as editing, film/tape transfers, subtitling, credits, closed captioning, and animation and special effects.

Cross-References. Establishments primarily engaged in—

- Mass duplicating video tapes and film—are classified in Industry 33461, Manufacturing and Reproducing Magnetic and Optical Media;
- Developing and processing motion picture film—arc classified in U.S. Industry 512199, Other Motion Picture and Video Industries;
- Providing audio services for film, television, and video productions—are classified in Industry 512240, Sound Recording Studios; and
- Acquiring distribution rights and distributing film and video productions to motion picture theaters, television networks and stations, and exhibitors—are classified in Industry 512120, Motion Picture and Video Distribution.

512199 Other Motion Picture and Video Industries[US]

This U.S. industry comprises establishments primarily engaged in providing motion picture and video services (except motion picture and video production, distribution, exhibition, and teleproduction and other postproduction services).

Illustrative Examples:

Motion picture film laboratories   Stock footage film libraries

---

US—United States industry only. CAN—United States and Canadian industries are comparable. MEX—United States and Mexican industries are comparable. Blank—Canadian, Mexican, and United States industries are comparable.

Cross-References. Establishments primarily engaged in—

- Renting wardrobes and costumes for motion picture production—are classified in Industry 532220, Formal Wear and Costume Rental;

- Renting studio equipment—are classified in Industry 532490, Other Commercial and Industrial Machinery and Equipment Rental and Leasing;

- Casting actors and actresses with production companies—are classified in U.S. Industry 561311, Employment Placement Agencies;

- Motion picture and video production—are classified in Industry 512110, Motion Picture and Video Production;

- Motion picture and video distribution—are classified in Industry 512120, Motion Picture and Video Distribution;

- Teleproduction and other postproduction services—are classified in U.S. Industry 512191, Teleproduction and Other Postproduction Services; and

- Motion picture and video exhibition—are classified in Industry 51213, Motion Picture and Video Exhibition.

5122 Sound Recording Industries

This industry group comprises establishments primarily engaged in producing and distributing musical recordings, in publishing music, or in providing sound recording and related services.

51221 Record Production
See industry description for 512210 below.

512210 Record Production

This industry comprises establishments primarily engaged in record production (e.g., tapes, CDs). These establishments contract with artists and arrange and finance the production of original master recordings. Establishments in this industry hold the copyright to the master recording and derive most of their revenues from the sales, leasing, and licensing of master recordings. Establishments in this industry do not have their own duplication or distribution capabilities.

Cross-References. Establishments primarily engaged in—

- Releasing, promoting, and distributing recordings—are classified in Industry 512220, Integrated Record Production/Distribution;

- Promoting and authorizing the use of musical works in various media— are classified in Industry 512230, Music Publishers;

- Mass duplication services—are classified in U.S. Industry 334612, Prerecorded Compact Disc (except Software), Tape, and Record Reproducing;

- Merchant wholesale distribution of blank audio cassettes, tapes, and discs—are classified in Industry 423690, Other Electronic Parts and Equipment Merchant Wholesalers;

- Merchant wholesale distribution of prerecorded audio cassettes, tapes, and discs—are classified in Industry 423990, Other Miscellaneous Durable Goods Merchant Wholesalers;

- Managing the careers of artists—are classified in Industry 711410, Agents and Managers for Artists, Athletes, Entertainers, and Other Public Figures;

- Providing facilities and technical expertise for recording musical performances—are classified in Industry 512240, Sound Recording Studios; and

- Producing albums on contract as independent producers—are classified in Industry 711510, Independent Artists, Writers, and Performers.

51222 Integrated Record Production/Distribution
See industry description for 512220 below.

512220 Integrated Record Production/Distribution

This industry comprises establishments primarily engaged in releasing, promoting, and distributing sound recordings. These establishments manufacture or arrange for the manufacture of recordings, such as audio tapes/cassettes and compact discs, and promote and distribute these products to wholesalers, retailers, or directly to the public. Establishments in this industry produce master recordings themselves, or obtain reproduction and distribution rights to master recordings produced by record production companies or other integrated record companies.

Cross-References. Establishments primarily engaged in—

- Contracting with musical artists, arranging for the production of master recordings, and marketing the reproduction rights—are classified in Industry 512210, Record Production;

- Providing facilities and technical expertise for recording musical performances—are classified in Industry 512240, Sound Recording Studios;

- Mass duplication of recorded products—are classified in U.S. Industry 334612, Prerecorded Compact Disc (except Software), Tape, and Record Reproducing;

- Merchant wholesale distribution of prerecorded audio cassettes, tapes, and discs—are classified in Industry 423990, Other Miscellaneous Durable Goods Merchant Wholesalers; and

---

US—United States industry only. CAN—United States and Canadian industries are comparable. MEX—United States and Mexican industries are comparable. Blank—Canadian, Mexican, and United States industries are comparable.

- Retailing records, tapes, and compact discs without producing recordings—are classified in Sector 44-45, Retail Trade.

51223   Music Publishers

See industry description for 512230 below.

512230   Music Publishers

This industry comprises establishments primarily engaged in acquiring and registering copyrights for musical compositions in accordance with law and promoting and authorizing the use of these compositions in recordings, radio, television, motion pictures, live performances, print, or other media. Establishments in this industry represent the interests of the songwriter or other owners of musical compositions to produce revenues from the use of such works, generally through licensing agreements. These establishments may own the copyright or act as administrator of the music copyrights on behalf of copyright owners. Publishers of music books and sheet music are included in this industry.

Cross-References.

Establishments primarily engaged as independent songwriters who act as their own publishers are classified in Industry 711510, Independent Artists, Writers, and Performers.

51224   Sound Recording Studios

See industry description for 512240 below.

512240   Sound Recording Studios

This industry comprises establishments primarily engaged in providing the facilities and technical expertise for sound recording in a studio. This industry includes establishments that provide audio production and postproduction services to produce master recordings. These establishments may provide audio services for film, television, and video productions.

Cross-References. Establishments primarily engaged in—

- Releasing, promoting, and distributing sound recordings—are classified in Industry 512220, Integrated Record Production/Distribution;
- Providing mass duplication of recorded products—are classified in U.S. Industry 334612, Prerecorded Compact Disc (except Software), Tape, and Record Reproducing; and

---

US—United States industry only. CAN—United States and Canadian industries are comparable. MEX—United States and Mexican industries are comparable. Blank—Canadian, Mexican, and United States industries are comparable.

- Contracting with musical artists, arranging for the production of master recordings, and marketing the reproduction rights—are classified in Industry 512210, Record Production.

51229 Other Sound Recording Industries
See industry description for 512290 below.

512290 Other Sound Recording Industries

This industry comprises establishments primarily engaged in providing sound recording services (except record production, distribution, music publishing, and sound recording in a studio). Establishments in this industry provide services, such as the audio recording of meetings and conferences.

Cross-References. Establishments primarily engaged in—

- Producing records, including contracting with musical artists, arranging and financing the production of master recordings, and marketing the reproduction rights—are classified in Industry 512210, Record Production;

- Releasing, promoting, and distributing sound recordings—are classified in Industry 512220, Integrated Record Production/Distribution;

- Promoting and authorizing the use of musical works in various media—are classified in Industry 512230, Music Publishers;

- Providing facilities and expertise for recording musical performance—are classified in Industry 512240, Sound Recording Studios;

- Providing mass duplication of recorded products—are classified in U.S. Industry 334612, Prerecorded Compact Disc (except Software), Tape, and Record Reproducing; and

- Organizing and promoting the presentation of performing arts productions—are classified in Industry Group 7113, Promoters of Performing Arts, Sports, and Similar Events.

515 Broadcasting (except Internet)

Industries in the Broadcasting (except Internet) subsector include establishments that create content or acquire the right to distribute content and subsequently broadcast the content. The industry groups (Radio and Television Broadcasting and Cable and Other Subscription Programming) are based on differences in the methods of communication and the nature of services provided. The Radio and Television Broadcasting industry group includes establishments that operate broad-

US—United States industry only. CAN—United States and Canadian industries are comparable. MEX—United States and Mexican industries are comparable. Blank—Canadian, Mexican, and United States industries are comparable.

http://www.census.gov/naics

casting studios and facilities for over the air or satellite delivery of radio and television programs of entertainment, news, talk, and the like. These establishments are often engaged in the production and purchase of programs and generating revenues from the sale of air time to advertisers and from donations, subsidies, and/or the sale of programs. The Cable and Other Subscription Programming industry group includes establishments operating studios and facilities for the broadcasting of programs that are typically narrowcast in nature (limited format, such as news, sports, education, and youth-oriented programming) on a subscription or fee basis.

The distribution of cable and other subscription programming is included in Subsector 517, Telecommunications. Establishments that broadcast exclusively on the Internet are included in Subsector 519, Other Information Services.

5151 Radio and Television Broadcasting

This industry group comprises establishments primarily engaged in operating broadcast studios and facilities for over-the-air or satellite delivery of radio and television programs. These establishments are often engaged in the production or purchase of programs or generate revenues from the sale of air time to advertisers, from donations and subsidies, or from the sale of programs.

51511 Radio Broadcasting

This industry comprises establishments primarily engaged in broadcasting audio signals. These establishments operate radio broadcasting studios and facilities for the transmission of aural programming to the public, to affiliates, or to subscribers. The radio programs may include entertainment, news, talk shows, business data, or religious services.

Cross-References. Establishments primarily engaged in—

- Broadcasting exclusively on the Internet—are classified in Industry 51913, Internet Publishing and Broadcasting and Web Search Portals; and

- Producing taped radio programming—are classified in Industry 51229, Other Sound Recording Industries.

515111 Radio Networks[US]

This U.S. industry comprises establishments primarily engaged in assembling and transmitting aural programming to their affiliates or subscribers via over-the-air broadcasts, cable, or satellite. The programming covers a wide variety of material, such as news services, religious programming, weather, sports, or music.

US—United States industry only. CAN—United States and Canadian industries are comparable. MEX—United States and Mexican industries are comparable. Blank—Canadian, Mexican, and United States industries are comparable.

Cross-References. Establishments primarily engaged in—

- Broadcasting exclusively on the Internet—are classified in Industry 519130, Internet Publishing and Broadcasting and Web Search Portals; and
- Producing taped radio programming—are classified in Industry 512290, Other Sound Recording Industries.

515112 Radio Stations[US]

This U.S. industry comprises establishments primarily engaged in broadcasting aural programs by radio to the public. Programming may originate in their own studio, from an affiliated network, or from external sources.

51512 Television Broadcasting
See industry description for 515120 below.

515120 Television Broadcasting

This industry comprises establishments primarily engaged in broadcasting images together with sound. These establishments operate television broadcasting studios and facilities for the programming and transmission of programs to the public. These establishments also produce or transmit visual programming to affiliated broadcast television stations, which in turn broadcast the programs to the public on a predetermined schedule. Programming may originate in their own studio, from an affiliated network, or from external sources.

Cross-References. Establishments primarily engaged in—

- Broadcasting exclusively on the Internet—are classified in Industry 519130, Internet Publishing and Broadcasting and Web Search Portals;
- Producing taped television program materials—are classified in Industry 512110, Motion Picture and Video Production;
- Furnishing cable and other pay television services—are classified in Industry 517110, Wired Telecommunications Carriers; and
- Producing and broadcasting television programs for cable and satellite television systems—are classified in Industry 515210, Cable and Other Subscription Programming.

5152 Cable and Other Subscription Programming

51521 Cable and Other Subscription Programming
See industry description for 515210 below.

515210 Cable and Other Subscription Programming

This industry comprises establishments primarily engaged in operating studios and facilities for the broadcasting of programs on a subscription or fee basis. The broadcast programming is typically narrowcast in nature (e.g., limited format, such as news, sports, education, or youth-oriented). These establishments produce programming in their own facilities or acquire programming from external sources. The programming material is usually delivered to a third party, such as cable systems or direct-to-home satellite systems, for transmission to viewers.

Cross-References. Establishments primarily engaged in—

- Producing taped television program material—are classified in Industry 512110, Motion Picture and Video Production;
- Producing and transmitting television programs to affiliated stations—are classified in Industry 515120, Television Broadcasting;
- Furnishing cable and other pay television services—are classified in Industry 517110, Wired Telecommunications Carriers; and
- Retailing merchandise by electronic media, such as television—are classified in Industry 45411, Electronic Shopping and Mail-Order Houses.

517 Telecommunications

Industries in the Telecommunications subsector group establishments that provide telecommunications and the services related to that activity (e.g., telephony, including Voice over Internet Protocol (VoIP); cable and satellite television distribution services; Internet access; telecommunications reselling services). The Telecommunications subsector is primarily engaged in operating, and/or providing access to facilities for the transmission of voice, data, text, sound, and video. Transmission facilities may be based on a single technology or a combination of technologies. Establishments in the Telecommunications subsector are grouped into four industry groups. The first three are comprised of establishments that operate transmission facilities and infrastructure that they own and/or lease, and provide telecommunications services using those facilities. The distinction among the first three industry groups is the type of infrastructure operated (i.e., wired, wireless, or satellite). The fourth industry group is comprised of establishments that provide support activities, telecommunications reselling services, or many of the same services provided by establishments in the first three industry groups, but do not operate as telecommunications carriers. Establishments primarily engaged as independent contractors in the installation and maintenance of broadcasting and telecommunications systems are classified in Sector 23, Construction. Establishments known as Internet cafes, primarily engaged in offering limited Internet

---

US—United States industry only. CAN—United States and Canadian industries are comparable. MEX—United States and Mexican industries are comparable. Blank—Canadian, Mexican, and United States industries are comparable.

connectivity in combination with other services such as facsimile services, training, rental of on-site personal computers, game rooms, or food services are classified in Subsector 561, Administrative and Support Services, or Subsector 722, Food Services and Drinking Places, depending on the primary activity.

5171 Wired Telecommunications Carriers

51711 Wired Telecommunications Carriers
See industry description for 517110 below.

517110 Wired Telecommunications Carriers[US]

This industry comprises establishments primarily engaged in operating and/or providing access to transmission facilities and infrastructure that they own and/or lease for the transmission of voice, data, text, sound, and video using wired telecommunications networks. Transmission facilities may be based on a single technology or a combination of technologies. Establishments in this industry use the wired telecommunications network facilities that they operate to provide a variety of services, such as wired telephony services, including VoIP services; wired (cable) audio and video programming distribution; and wired broadband Internet services. By exception, establishments providing satellite television distribution services using facilities and infrastructure that they operate are included in this industry.

Illustrative Examples:

Broadband Internet service providers, wired (e.g. cable, DSL)
Local telephone carriers, wired
Cable television distribution services
Long-distance telephone carriers, wired
Closed circuit television (CCTV) services
VoIP service providers, using own operated wired telecommunications infrastructure

Direct-to-home satellite system (DTH) services
Telecommunications carriers, wired
Satellite television distribution systems
Multichannel multipoint distribution services (MMDS)

Cross-References. Establishments primarily engaged in—

- Producing and distributing a channel of television programming for cable or satellite television systems—are classified in Industry 515210, Cable and Other Subscription Programming;
- Operating coin-operated pay telephones—are classified in Industry 812990, All Other Personal Services;

- Operating and maintaining wireless telecommunications networks—are classified in Industry 517210, Wireless Telecommunications Carriers (except Satellite);

- Producing and distributing radio programs for cable or satellite radio systems—are classified in U.S. Industry 515111, Radio Networks;

- Reselling telecommunications services (except satellite telecommunications), without operating a network—are classified in U.S. Industry 517911, Telecommunications Resellers;

- Publishing telephone directories—are classified in Industry 511140, Directory and Mailing List Publishers;

- Reselling satellite telecommunications services—are classified in Industry 517410, Satellite Telecommunications;

- Providing Internet access services via client-supplied telecommunications connections (e.g. dial up ISP's)—are classified in U.S. Industry 517919, All Other Telecommunications;

- Providing voice over Internet protocol (VoIP) services via client-supplied telecommunications connections—are classified in U.S. Industry 517919, All Other Telecommunications;

- Providing limited Internet connectivity at locations known as Internet cafes, in combination with other services such as facsimile services, training, rental of on-site personal computers, games rooms, or food services—are classified in U.S. Industry 561439, Other Business Service Centers (including Copy Shops) or Subsector 722, Food Services and Drinking Places, depending on the primary activity.

5172 Wireless Telecommunications Carriers (except Satellite)

51721 Wireless Telecommunications Carriers (except Satellite)
See industry description for 517210 below.

517210 Wireless Telecommunications Carriers (except Satellite)

This industry comprises establishments engaged in operating and maintaining switching and transmission facilities to provide communications via the airwaves. Establishments in this industry have spectrum licenses and provide services using that spectrum, such as cellular phone services, paging services, wireless Internet access, and wireless video services.

US—United States industry only. CAN—United States and Canadian industries are comparable. MEX—United States and Mexican industries are comparable. Blank—Canadian, Mexican, and United States industries are comparable.

Illustrative Examples:

Cellular telephone services	Paging services, except satellite
Wireless Internet service providers, except satellite	Wireless telephone communications carriers, except satellite

Cross-References. Establishments primarily engaged in—

- Operating and maintaining wired telecommunications networks—are classified in Industry 517110, Wired Telecommunications Carriers;

- Operating and maintaining satellite networks—are classified in Industry 517410, Satellite Telecommunications;

- Providing satellite television distribution services—are classified in Industry 517110, Wired Telecommunications Carriers; and

- Operating as mobile virtual network operations (MVNO)—are classified in U.S. Industry 517911, Telecommunications Resellers.

5174 Satellite Telecommunications

51741 Satellite Telecommunications
See industry description for 517410 below.

517410 Satellite Telecommunications

This industry comprises establishments primarily engaged in providing telecommunications services to other establishments in the telecommunications and broadcasting industries by forwarding and receiving communications signals via a system of satellites or reselling satellite telecommunications.

Cross-References.

Establishments primarily engaged in providing direct-to-home satellite television services to individual households or consumers are classified in Industry 517110, Wired Telecommunications Carriers.

5179 Other Telecommunications

51791 Other Telecommunications

This industry comprises establishments primarily engaged in (1) purchasing access and network capacity from owners and operators of telecommunications networks and reselling wired and wireless telecommunications services (except

---

US—United States industry only. CAN—United States and Canadian industries are comparable. MEX—United States and Mexican industries are comparable. Blank—Canadian, Mexican, and United States industries are comparable.

satellite) to businesses and households; (2) providing specialized telecommunications services, such as satellite tracking, communications telemetry, and radar station operation; (3) providing satellite terminal stations and associated facilities connected with one or more terrestrial systems and capable of transmitting telecommunications to, and receiving telecommunications from, satellite systems; or (4) providing Internet access services or Voice over Internet protocol (VoIP) services via client-supplied telecommunications connections. Establishments in this industry do not operate as telecommunications carriers. Mobile virtual network operators (MVNO) are included in this industry.

517911 Telecommunications Resellers[US]

This U.S. industry comprises establishments engaged in purchasing access and network capacity from owners and operators of telecommunications networks and reselling wired and wireless telecommunications services (except satellite) to businesses and households. Establishments in this industry resell telecommunications; they do not operate transmission facilities and infrastructure. Mobile virtual network operators (MVNOs) are included in this industry.

Cross-References. Establishments primarily engaged in—

- Operating and maintaining wired telecommunications networks—are classified in Industry 517110, Wired Telecommunications Carriers;

- Operating and maintaining wireless telecommunications networks—are classified in Industry 517210, Wireless Telecommunications Carriers (except Satellite); and

- Reselling satellite telecommunications services—are classified in Industry 517410, Satellite Telecommunications.

517919 All Other Telecommunications[US]

This U.S. industry comprises establishments primarily engaged in providing specialized telecommunications services, such as satellite tracking, communications telemetry, and radar station operation. This industry also includes establishments primarily engaged in providing satellite terminal stations and associated facilities connected with one or more terrestrial systems and capable of transmitting telecommunications to, and receiving telecommunications from, satellite systems. Establishments providing Internet services or voice over Internet protocol (VoIP) services via client-supplied telecommunications connections are also included in this industry.

US—United States industry only. CAN—United States and Canadian industries are comparable. MEX—United States and Mexican industries are comparable. Blank—Canadian, Mexican, and United States industries are comparable.

Illustrative Examples:

Dial-up Internet service providers
VoIP service providers, using client-
  supplied telecommunications
  connections

Internet service providers using client-
  supplied telecommunications
  connections (e.g., dial-up ISPs)
Satellite tracking stations

Cross-References. Establishments primarily engaged in—

- Providing wired broadband Internet services via own operated telecommunications infrastructure—are classified in Industry 517110, Wired Telecommunications Carriers;

- Providing wired VoIP services via own operated telecommunications infrastructure—are classified in Industry 517110, Wired Telecommunications Carriers;

- Providing expert advice in the field of information technology or in integrating communication and computer systems—are classified in Industry 54151, Computer Systems Design and Related Services; and

- Providing satellite telecommunications services—are classified in Industry 517410, Satellite Telecommunications.

518 Data Processing, Hosting, and Related Services

Industries in the Data Processing, Hosting, and Related Services subsector group establishments that provide the infrastructure for hosting and/or data processing services.

5182 Data Processing, Hosting, and Related Services

51821 Data Processing, Hosting, and Related Services
See industry description for 518210 below.

518210 Data Processing, Hosting, and Related Services

This industry comprises establishments primarily engaged in providing infrastructure for hosting or data processing services. These establishments may provide specialized hosting activities, such as web hosting, streaming services or application hosting; provide application service provisioning; or may provide general time-share mainframe facilities to clients. Data processing establishments provide complete processing and specialized reports from data supplied by clients or provide automated data processing and data entry services.

US—United States industry only. CAN—United States and Canadian industries are comparable. MEX—United States and Mexican industries are comparable. Blank—Canadian, Mexican, and United States industries are comparable.

Illustrative Examples:

Application hosting
Optical scanning services
Application service providers
Web hosting
Computer data storage services

Video and audio streaming service
Computer input preparation services
Microfilm imaging services
Computer time rental

Cross-References. Establishments primarily engaged in—

- Providing text processing and related document preparation activities—are classified in Industry 561410, Document Preparation Services;

- Providing on-site management and operation of a client's data-processing facilities—are classified in U.S. Industry 541513, Computer Facilities Management Services;

- Providing wired broadband Internet access services using own operated telecommunications infrastructure, in combination with web hosting—are classified in Industry 517110, Wired Telecommunications Carriers;

- Providing Internet access via client-supplied telecommunications connections in combination with web hosting—are classified in U.S. Industry 517919, All Other Telecommunications;

- Operating web search portals—are classified in U.S. Industry 519130, Internet Publishing and Broadcasting and Web Search Portals;

- Providing access to computers and office equipment, as well as other office support services—are classified in Industry 56143, Business Service Centers;

- Processing financial transactions, such as credit card transactions—are classified in Industry 522320, Financial Transactions Processing, Reserve, and Clearinghouse Activities; and

- Providing payroll processing services—are classified in U.S. Industry 541214, Payroll Services.

519 Other Information Services

Industries in the Other Information Services subsector group establishments supplying information, storing and providing access to information, searching and retrieving information, operating Web sites that use search engines to allow for searching information on the Internet, or publishing and/or broadcasting content exclusively on the Internet. The main components of the subsector are news syndicates, libraries, archives, exclusive Internet publishing and/or broadcasting, and Web Search Portals.

US—United States industry only. CAN—United States and Canadian industries are comparable. MEX—United States and Mexican industries are comparable. Blank—Canadian, Mexican, and United States industries are comparable.

5191 Other Information Services

51911 News Syndicates
See industry description for 519110 below.

519110 News Syndicates

This industry comprises establishments primarily engaged in supplying information, such as news reports, articles, pictures, and features, to the news media.

Cross-References.
Independent writers and journalists (including photojournalists) are classified in Industry 711510, Independent Artists, Writers, and Performers.

51912 Libraries and Archives
See industry description for 519120 below.

519120 Libraries and Archives[US]

This industry comprises establishments primarily engaged in providing library or archive services. These establishments are engaged in maintaining collections of documents (e.g., books, journals, newspapers, and music) and facilitating the use of such documents (recorded information regardless of its physical form and characteristics) as are required to meet the informational, research, educational, or recreational needs of their user. These establishments may also acquire, research, store, preserve, and generally make accessible to the public historical documents, photographs, maps, audio material, audiovisual material, and other archival material of historical interest. All or portions of these collections may be accessible electronically.

Cross-References. Establishments primarily engaged in—

- Providing stock footage (via motion picture and video tape libraries) to the media, multimedia, and advertising industries—are classified in U.S. Industry 512199, Other Motion Picture and Video Industries;
- Providing stock music to the media, multimedia, and advertising industries—are classified in Industry 512290, Other Sound Recording Industries;
- Providing stock photos to the media, multimedia, and advertising industries—are classified in Industry 519190, All Other Information Services; and

---

- Distributing film and video productions to motion picture theaters, television networks and stations, and exhibitors—are classified in U.S. Industry 512120, Motion Picture and Video Distribution.

51913　Internet Publishing and Broadcasting and Web Search Portals

See industry description for 519130 below.

519130　Internet Publishing and Broadcasting and Web Search Portals

This industry comprises establishments primarily engaged in 1) publishing and/or broadcasting content on the Internet exclusively or 2) operating Web sites that use a search engine to generate and maintain extensive databases of Internet addresses and content in an easily searchable format (and known as Web search portals). The publishing and broadcasting establishments in this industry do not provide traditional (non-Internet) versions of the content that they publish or broadcast. They provide textual, audio, and/or video content of general or specific interest on the Internet exclusively. Establishments known as Web search portals often provide additional Internet services, such as e-mail, connections to other web sites, auctions, news, and other limited content, and serve as a home base for Internet users.

Illustrative Examples:

Internet book publishers	Internet periodical publishers
Internet sports sites	Internet radio stations
Internet entertainment sites	Internet search portals
Internet video broadcast sites	Web search portals
Internet game sites	Internet search Web sites
Internet news publishers	

Cross-References. Establishments primarily engaged in—

- Providing wired broadband Internet access using own operated telecommunications infrastructure—are classified in U.S. Industry 517110, Wired Telecommunications Carriers;

- Providing both Internet publishing and other print or electronic (e.g., CD-ROM, diskette) editions in the same establishment or using proprietary networks to distribute content—are classified in Subsector 511, Publishing Industries (except Internet) based on the materials produced;

- Providing Internet access via client-supplied telecommunications connections—are classified in U.S. Industry 517919, All Other Telecommunications;

US—United States industry only. CAN—United States and Canadian industries are comparable. MEX—United States and Mexican industries are comparable. Blank—Canadian, Mexican, and United States industries are comparable.

- Providing streaming services on content owned by others—are classified in Industry 518210, Data Processing, Hosting, and Related Services;

- Wholesaling goods on the Internet—are classified in Sector 42, Wholesale Trade;

- Retailing goods on the Internet—are classified in Sector 44-45, Retail Trade; and

- Operating stock brokerages, travel reservation systems, purchasing services, and similar activities using the Internet rather than traditional methods—are classified with the more traditional establishments providing these services.

51919 All Other Information Services

See industry description for 519190 below.

519190 All Other Information Services

This industry comprises establishments primarily engaged in providing other information services (except news syndicates, libraries, archives, Internet publishing and broadcasting, and Web search portals).

Illustrative Examples:

News clipping services   Stock photo agencies
Telephone-based information services

Cross-References. Establishments primarily engaged in—

- Providing wired broadband Internet access services using own operated telecommunications infrastructure—are classified in Industry 517110, Wired Telecommunications Carriers;

- Providing Internet access via client-supplied telecommunications connections—are classified in U.S. Industry 517919, All Other Telecommunications;

- Publishing (except exclusively on the Internet)—are classified in Subsector 511, Publishing Industries (except Internet);

- Publishing or broadcasting exclusively on the Internet—are classified in Industry 519130, Internet Publishing and Broadcasting and Web Search Portals;

- Operating Web search portals—are classified in U.S. Industry 519130, Internet Publishing and Broadcasting and Web Search Portals;

- Operating news syndicates—are classified in Industry 519110, News Syndicates; and

- Operating libraries and archives—are classified in Industry 519120, Libraries and Archives.

Sector 52—Finance and Insurance

The Sector as a Whole

The Finance and Insurance sector comprises establishments primarily engaged in financial transactions (transactions involving the creation, liquidation, or change in ownership of financial assets) and/or in facilitating financial transactions. Three principal types of activities are identified:

1. Raising funds by taking deposits and/or issuing securities and, in the process, incurring liabilities. Establishments engaged in this activity use raised funds to acquire financial assets by making loans and/or purchasing securities. Putting themselves at risk, they channel funds from lenders to borrowers and transform or repackage the funds with respect to maturity, scale, and risk. This activity is known as financial intermediation.

2. Pooling of risk by underwriting insurance and annuities. Establishments engaged in this activity collect fees, insurance premiums, or annuity considerations; build up reserves; invest those reserves; and make contractual payments. Fees are based on the expected incidence of the insured risk and the expected return on investment.

3. Providing specialized services facilitating or supporting financial intermediation, insurance, and employee benefit programs.

In addition, monetary authorities charged with monetary control are included in this sector.

The subsectors, industry groups, and industries within the NAICS Finance and Insurance sector are defined on the basis of their unique production processes. As with all industries, the production processes are distinguished by their use of specialized human resources and specialized physical capital. In addition, the way in which these establishments acquire and allocate financial capital, their source of funds, and the use of those funds provides a third basis for distinguishing characteristics of the production process. For instance, the production process in raising funds through deposit-taking is different from the process of raising funds in bond or money markets. The process of making loans to individuals also requires different production processes than does the creation of investment pools or the underwriting of securities.

Most of the Finance and Insurance subsectors contain one or more industry groups of (1) intermediaries with similar patterns of raising and using funds and (2) establishments engaged in activities that facilitate, or are otherwise related to, that type of financial or insurance intermediation. Industries within this sector are defined in terms of activities for which a production process can be specified, and many of these activities are not exclusive to a particular type of financial institution. To deal with the varied activities taking place within existing financial institutions,

---

the approach is to split these institutions into components performing specialized services. This requires defining the units engaged in providing those services and developing procedures that allow for their delineation. These units are the equivalents for finance and insurance of the establishments defined for other industries.

The output of many financial services, as well as the inputs and the processes by which they are combined, cannot be observed at a single location and can only be defined at a higher level of the organizational structure of the enterprise. Additionally, a number of independent activities that represent separate and distinct production processes may take place at a single location belonging to a multilocation financial firm. Activities are more likely to be homogeneous with respect to production characteristics than are locations, at least in financial services. The classification defines activities broadly enough that it can be used both by those classifying by location and by those employing a more top-down approach to the delineation of the establishment.

Establishments engaged in activities that facilitate, or are otherwise related to, the various types of intermediation have been included in individual subsectors, rather than in a separate subsector dedicated to services alone because these services are performed by intermediaries, as well as by specialist establishments, the extent to which the activity of the intermediaries can be separately identified is not clear.

The Finance and Insurance sector has been defined to encompass establishments primarily engaged in financial transactions; that is, transactions involving the creation, liquidation, change in ownership of financial assets; or in facilitating financial transactions. Financial industries are extensive users of electronic means for facilitating the verification of financial balances, authorizing transactions, transferring funds to and from transactors' accounts, notifying banks (or credit card issuers) of the individual transactions, and providing daily summaries. Since these transaction processing activities are integral to the production of finance and insurance services, establishments that principally provide a financial transaction processing service are classified to this sector, rather than to the data processing industry in the Information sector.

Legal entities that hold portfolios of assets on behalf of others are significant and data on them are required for a variety of purposes. Thus for NAICS, these funds, trusts, and other financial vehicles are the fifth subsector of the Finance and Insurance sector. These entities earn interest, dividends, and other property income, but have little or no employment and no revenue from the sale of services. Separate establishments and employees devoted to the management of funds are classified in Industry Group 5239, Other Financial Investment Activities.

521 Monetary Authorities-Central Bank

The Monetary Authorities-Central Bank subsector groups establishments that engage in performing central banking functions, such as issuing currency, managing the Nation's money supply and international reserves, holding deposits that repre-

---

sent the reserves of other banks and other central banks, and acting as a fiscal agent for the central government.

5211 Monetary Authorities-Central Bank

52111 Monetary Authorities-Central Bank
See industry description for 521110 below.

521110 Monetary Authorities-Central Bank

This industry comprises establishments primarily engaged in performing central banking functions, such as issuing currency, managing the Nation's money supply and international reserves, holding deposits that represent the reserves of other banks and other central banks, and acting as a fiscal agent for the central government.

Cross-References.

Establishments of the Board of Governors of the Federal Reserve System are classified in Industry 921130, Public Finance Activities.

522 Credit Intermediation and Related Activities

Industries in the Credit Intermediation and Related Activities subsector group establishments that (1) lend funds raised from depositors; (2) lend funds raised from credit market borrowing; or (3) facilitate the lending of funds or issuance of credit by engaging in such activities as mortgage and loan brokerage, clearinghouse and reserve services, and check cashing services.

5221 Depository Credit Intermediation[CAN]

This industry group comprises establishments primarily engaged in accepting deposits (or share deposits) and in lending funds from these deposits. Within this group, industries are defined on the basis of differences in the types of deposit liabilities assumed and in the nature of the credit extended.

52211 Commercial Banking[US]
See industry description for 522110 below.

US—United States industry only. CAN—United States and Canadian industries are comparable. MEX—United States and Mexican industries are comparable. Blank—Canadian, Mexican, and United States industries are comparable.

522110 Commercial Banking^{US}

This industry comprises establishments primarily engaged in accepting demand and other deposits and making commercial, industrial, and consumer loans. Commercial banks and branches of foreign banks are included in this industry.

Cross-References.

- Establishments primarily engaged in credit card banking are classified in Industry 522210, Credit Card Issuing;
- Establishments known as industrial banks and primarily engaged in accepting deposits are classified in Industry 522190, Other Depository Credit Intermediation; and
- Establishments of depository institutions primarily engaged in trust activities are classified in U.S. Industry 523991, Trust, Fiduciary, and Custody Activities.

52212 Savings Institutions^{US}

See industry description for 522120 below.

522120 Savings Institutions^{US}

This U.S. industry comprises establishments primarily engaged in accepting time deposits, making mortgage and real estate loans, and investing in high-grade securities. Savings and loan associations and savings banks are included in this industry.

Cross-References.

Establishments primarily engaged in accepting demand and other deposits and making all types of loans are classified in Industry 522110, Commercial Banking.

52213 Credit Unions^{CAN}

See industry description for 522130 below.

522130 Credit Unions^{CAN}

This industry comprises establishments primarily engaged in accepting members' share deposits in cooperatives that are organized to offer consumer loans to their members.

US—United States industry only. CAN—United States and Canadian industries are comparable. MEX—United States and Mexican industries are comparable. Blank—Canadian, Mexican, and United States industries are comparable.

52219 Other Depository Credit Intermediation^{CAN}
See industry description for 522190 below.

522190 Other Depository Credit Intermediation^{CAN}

This industry comprises establishments primarily engaged in accepting deposits and lending funds (except commercial banking, savings institutions, and credit unions). Establishments known as industrial banks or Morris Plans and primarily engaged in accepting deposits, and private banks (i.e., unincorporated banks) are included in this industry.

Cross-References.

- Establishments primarily engaged in accepting demand and other deposits and making all types of loans are classified in Industry 522110, Commercial Banking;
- Establishments primarily engaged in accepting time deposits are classified in Industry 522120, Savings Institutions;
- Establishments primarily engaged in accepting members' share deposits in cooperatives are classified in Industry 522130, Credit Unions; and
- Establishments known as industrial banks and Morris Plans and are primarily engaged in providing nondepository credit are classified in U.S. Industry 522298, All Other Nondepository Credit Intermediation.

5222 Nondepository Credit Intermediation^{CAN}

This industry group comprises establishments, both public (government-sponsored enterprises) and private, primarily engaged in extending credit or lending funds raised by credit market borrowing, such as issuing commercial paper or other debt instruments or by borrowing from other financial intermediaries. Within this group, industries are defined on the basis of the type of credit being extended.

52221 Credit Card Issuing^{CAN}
See industry description for 522210 below.

522210 Credit Card Issuing^{CAN}

This industry comprises establishments primarily engaged in providing credit by issuing credit cards. Credit card issuance provides the funds required to purchase goods and services in return for payment of the full balance or payments on an installment basis. Credit card banks are included in this industry.

US—United States industry only. CAN—United States and Canadian industries are comparable. MEX—United States and Mexican industries are comparable. Blank—Canadian, Mexican, and United States industries are comparable.

Cross-References.

Establishments primarily engaged in issuing cards that contain a stored prepaid value are classified with the industry providing the service represented by the cards, such as transit fare cards, in Subsector 482, Rail Transportation, and long-distance telephone cards in Subsector 517, Telecommunications.

52222 Sales Financing^{CAN}
See industry description for 522220 below.

522220 Sales Financing^{CAN}

This industry comprises establishments primarily engaged in sales financing or sales financing in combination with leasing. Sales financing establishments are primarily engaged in lending money for the purpose of providing collateralized goods through a contractual installment sales agreement, either directly from or through arrangements with dealers.

Cross-References.

Establishments not engaged in sales financing, but primarily engaged in providing leases for equipment and other assets are classified in Subsector 532, Rental and Leasing Services.

52229 Other Nondepository Credit Intermediation^{CAN}

This industry comprises establishments primarily engaged in making cash loans or extending credit through credit instruments (except credit cards and sales finance agreements).

Illustrative Examples:

Consumer finance companies (i.e., unsecured cash loans)	International trade financing
Mortgage companies	Secondary market financing

Cross-References. Establishments primarily engaged in—

- Providing credit sales by issuing credit cards—are classified in Industry 52221, Credit Card Issuing;

- Providing leases for equipment and other assets without sales financing—are classified in Subsector 532, Rental and Leasing Services;

- Accepting deposits and lending funds from these deposits—are classified in Industry Group 5221, Depository Credit Intermediation;

US—United States industry only. CAN—United States and Canadian industries are comparable. MEX—United States and Mexican industries are comparable. Blank—Canadian, Mexican, and United States industries are comparable.

- Arranging loans for others on a commission or fee basis—are classified in Industry 52231, Mortgage and Nonmortgage Loan Brokers; and

- Guaranteeing international trade loans—are classified in Industry 52412, Direct Insurance (except Life, Health, and Medical) Carriers.

522291 Consumer Lending[CAN]

This U.S. industry comprises establishments primarily engaged in making unsecured cash loans to consumers.

Illustrative Examples:

Finance companies (i.e., unsecured cash loans)
Personal credit institutions (i.e., unsecured cash loans)

Loan companies (i.e., consumer, personal, student, small)
Student loans companies

Cross-References. Establishments primarily engaged in—

- Accepting deposits and lending funds from these deposits—arc classified in Industry Group 5221, Depository Credit Intermediation; and

- Arranging loans for others on a commission or fee basis—are classified in Industry 522310, Mortgage and Nonmortgage Loan Brokers.

522292 Real Estate Credit[US]

This U.S. industry comprises establishments primarily engaged in lending funds with real estate as collateral.

Illustrative Examples:

Home equity credit lending
Mortgage companies

Mortgage banking (i.e., nondepository mortgage lending)

Cross-References. Establishments primarily engaged in—

- Servicing loans—are classified in Industry 522390, Other Activities Related to Credit Intcrmediation;

- Arranging loans for others on a commission or fee basis—are classified in Industry 522310, Mortgage and Nonmortgage Loan Brokers; and

- Accepting deposits and lending funds secured by real estate—are classified in Industry Group 5221, Depository Credit Intermediation.

US—United States industry only. CAN—United States and Canadian industries are comparable. MEX—United States and Mexican industries are comparable. Blank—Canadian, Mexican, and United States industries are comparable.

522293 International Trade Financing[US]

This U.S. industry comprises establishments primarily engaged in providing one or more of the following: (1) working capital funds to U.S. exporters; (2) lending funds to foreign buyers of U.S. goods; and/or (3) lending funds to domestic buyers of imported goods.

Illustrative Examples:

Agreement corporations (i.e., international trade financing)
Export-Import banks

Edge Act corporations (i.e., international trade financing)
Trade banks (i.e., international trade financing)

Cross-References. Establishments primarily engaged in—

- Guaranteeing international trade loans—are classified in U.S. Industry 524126, Direct Property and Casualty Insurance Carriers;

- Brokering international trade loans—are classified in Industry 522310, Mortgage and Nonmortgage Loan Brokers; and

- Accepting deposits and lending funds from these deposits—are classified in Industry Group 5221, Depository Credit Intermediation.

522294 Secondary Market Financing[US]

This U.S. industry comprises establishments primarily engaged in buying, pooling, and repackaging loans for sale to others on the secondary market.

Illustrative Examples:

Federal Home Loan Mortgage Corporation (FHLMC)
Government National Mortgage Association (GNMA)

Federal National Mortgage Association (FNMA)
Student Loan Marketing Association (SLMA)

522298 All Other Nondepository Credit Intermediation[US]

This U.S. industry comprises establishments primarily engaged in providing nondepository credit (except credit card issuing, sales financing, consumer lending, real estate credit, international trade financing, and secondary market financing). Examples of types of lending in this industry are: short-term inventory credit, agricultural lending (except real estate and sales financing) and consumer cash lending secured by personal property.

US—United States industry only. CAN—United States and Canadian industries are comparable. MEX—United States and Mexican industries are comparable. Blank—Canadian, Mexican, and United States industries are comparable.

Illustrative Examples:

Commodity Credit Corporation
Morris Plans (i.e., known as),
  nondepository
Factoring accounts receivable

Pawnshops
Industrial banks (i.e., known as),
  nondepository

Cross-References.

- Establishments primarily engaged in providing credit sales funding are classified in Industry 522210, Credit Card Issuing;
- Establishments primarily engaged in sales financing or sales financing in combination with leasing are classified in Industry 522220, Sales Financing;
- Establishments primarily engaged in making unsecured cash loans to consumers are classified in U.S. Industry 522291, Consumer Lending;
- Establishments primarily engaged in lending funds with real estate as collateral are classified in U.S. Industry 522292, Real Estate Credit;
- Establishments primarily engaged in international trade financing are classified in U.S. Industry 522293, International Trade Financing;
- Establishments primarily engaged in buying, pooling, and repackaging loans for sale to others on the secondary market are classified in U.S. Industry 522294, Secondary Market Financing; and
- Establishments known as industrial banks or Morris Plans and are primarily engaged in accepting deposits are classified in Industry 522190, Other Depository Credit Intermediation.

5223 Activities Related to Credit Intermediation[CAN]

This industry group comprises establishments primarily engaged in facilitating credit intermediation by performing activities, such as arranging loans by bringing borrowers and lenders together and clearing checks and credit card transactions.

52231 Mortgage and Nonmortgage Loan Brokers[CAN]
See industry description for 522310 below.

522310 Mortgage and Nonmortgage Loan Brokers[CAN]

This industry comprises establishments primarily engaged in arranging loans by bringing borrowers and lenders together on a commission or fee basis.

Cross-References. Establishments primarily engaged in—

- Lending funds with real estate as collateral—are classified in U.S. Industry 522292, Real Estate Credit; and

---

US—United States industry only. CAN—United States and Canadian industries are comparable. MEX—United States and Mexican industries are comparable. Blank—Canadian, Mexican, and United States industries are comparable.

http://www.census.gov/naics

• Servicing loans—are classified in Industry 522390, Other Activities Related to Credit Intermediation.

52232 Financial Transactions Processing, Reserve, and Clearinghouse Activities[CAN]
See industry description for 522320 below.

522320 Financial Transactions Processing, Reserve, and Clearinghouse Activities[US]

This industry comprises establishments primarily engaged in providing one or more of the following: (1) financial transaction processing (except central bank); (2) reserve and liquidity services (except central bank); and/or (3) check or other financial instrument clearinghouse services (except central bank).

Illustrative Examples:

Automated clearinghouses, bank or check (except central bank)

Credit card processing services

Check clearing services (except central bank)

Electronic funds transfer services

Cross-References.

• Establishments primarily engaged in nonfinancial data and electronic transaction processing are classified in Industry Group 5182, Data Processing, Hosting, and Related Services; and

• Establishments of the central bank primarily engaged in check clearing and other financial transaction processing are classified in Industry 521110, Monetary Authorities-Central Bank.

52239 Other Activities Related to Credit Intermediation[CAN]
See industry description for 522390 below.

522390 Other Activities Related to Credit Intermediation[CAN]

This industry comprises establishments primarily engaged in facilitating credit intermediation (except mortgage and loan brokerage; and financial transactions processing, reserve, and clearinghouse activities).

Illustrative Examples:

Check cashing services

Money order issuance services

Loan servicing

Travelers' check issuance services

Money transmission services

US—United States industry only. CAN—United States and Canadian industries are comparable. MEX—United States and Mexican industries are comparable. Blank—Canadian, Mexican, and United States industries are comparable.

http://www.census.gov/naics

Cross-References. Establishments primarily engaged in—

- Arranging loans for others on a commission or fee basis—are classified in Industry 522310, Mortgage and Nonmortgage Loan Brokers;

- Providing financial transactions processing, reserve, and clearinghouse activities—are classified in Industry 522320, Financial Transactions Processing, Reserve, and Clearinghouse Activities;

- Foreign currency exchange dealing—are classified in Industry 523130, Commodity Contracts Dealing; and

- Providing escrow services (except real estate)—are classified in U.S. Industry 523991, Trust, Fiduciary, and Custody Activities.

523 Securities, Commodity Contracts, and Other Financial Investments and Related Activities

Industries in the Securities, Commodity Contracts, and Other Financial Investments and Related Activities subsector group establishments that are primarily engaged in one of the following: (1) underwriting securities issues and/or making markets for securities and commodities; (2) acting as agents (i.e., brokers) between buyers and sellers of securities and commodities; (3) providing securities and commodity exchange services; and (4) providing other services, such as managing portfolios of assets; providing investment advice; and trust, fiduciary, and custody services.

5231 Securities and Commodity Contracts Intermediation and Brokerage

This industry group comprises establishments primarily engaged in putting capital at risk in the process of underwriting securities issues or in making markets for securities and commodities; and those acting as agents and/or brokers between buyers and sellers of securities and commodities, usually charging a commission.

52311 Investment Banking and Securities Dealing^{CAN}
See industry description for 523110 below.

523110 Investment Banking and Securities Dealing^{CAN}

This industry comprises establishments primarily engaged in underwriting, originating, and/or maintaining markets for issues of securities. Investment bankers act as principals (i.e., investors who buy or sell on their own account) in firm commitment transactions or act as agents in best effort and standby commitments. This industry also includes establishments acting as principals in buying or selling securities generally on a spread basis, such as securities dealers or stock option dealers.

Illustrative Examples:

Bond dealing (i.e., acting as a principal   Stock option dealing
  in dealing securities to investors)   Securities underwriting

Cross-References.

- Establishments primarily engaged in acting as agents (i.e., brokers) in buying or selling securities on a commission or transaction fee basis are classified in Industry 523120, Securities Brokerage; and

- Investment clubs or individual investors primarily engaged in buying or selling financial contracts (e.g., securities) on their own account are classified in Industry 523910, Miscellaneous Intermediation.

52312 Securities Brokerage^{CAN}
See industry description for 523120 below.

523120 Securities Brokerage^{CAN}

This industry comprises establishments primarily engaged in acting as agents (i.e., brokers) between buyers and sellers in buying or selling securities on a commission or transaction fee basis.

Illustrative Examples:

Mutual fund agencies (i.e., brokerages)   Securities brokerages
Stock brokerages

Cross-References.

Establishments primarily engaged in investment banking and securities dealing (i.e., buying or selling securities on their own account) are classified in Industry 523110, Investment Banking and Securities Dealing.

52313 Commodity Contracts Dealing^{CAN}
See industry description for 523130 below.

523130 Commodity Contracts Dealing^{CAN}

This industry comprises establishments primarily engaged in acting as principals (i.e., investors who buy or sell for their own account) in buying or selling spot or

---

futures commodity contracts or options, such as precious metals, foreign currency, oil, or agricultural products, generally on a spread basis.

Cross-References. Establishments primarily engaged in—

- Acting as agents (i.e., brokers) in buying or selling spot or future commodity contracts on a commission or transaction fee basis—are classified in Industry 523140, Commodity Contracts Brokerage; and

- Buying and selling physical commodities for resale to other than the general public—are classified in Sector 42, Wholesale Trade.

52314 Commodity Contracts Brokerage^{CAN}
See industry description for 523140 below.

523140 Commodity Contracts Brokerage^{CAN}

This industry comprises establishments primarily engaged in acting as agents (i.e., brokers) in buying or selling spot or future commodity contracts or options on a commission or transaction fee basis.

Illustrative Examples:

Commodity contracts brokerages
Financial futures brokerages

Commodity futures brokerages

Cross-References. Establishments primarily engaged in—

- Acting as principals in buying or selling spot or futures commodity contracts generally on a spread basis—are classified in Industry 523130, Commodity Contracts Dealing; and

- Buying and selling physical commodities for resale to other than the general public—are classified in Sector 42, Wholesale Trade.

5232 Securities and Commodity Exchanges

52321 Securities and Commodity Exchanges
See industry description for 523210 below.

523210 Securities and Commodity Exchanges

This industry comprises establishments primarily engaged in furnishing physical or electronic marketplaces for the purpose of facilitating the buying and selling of stocks, stock options, bonds, or commodity contracts.

US—United States industry only. CAN—United States and Canadian industries are comparable. MEX—United States and Mexican industries are comparable. Blank—Canadian, Mexican, and United States industries are comparable.

Cross-References.

Establishments primarily engaged in investment banking, and securities dealing, securities brokering, commodity contracts dealing, or commodity contracts brokering are classified in Industry Group 5231, Securities and Commodity Contracts Intermediation and Brokerage.

5239 Other Financial Investment Activities

This industry group, comprises establishments primarily engaged in one of the following: (1) acting as principals in buying or selling financial contracts (except investment bankers, securities dealers, and commodity contracts dealers); (2) acting as agents (i.e., brokers) (except securities brokerages and commodity contracts brokerages) in buying or selling financial contracts; or (3) providing other investment services (except securities and commodity exchanges), such as portfolio management; investment advice; and trust, fiduciary, and custody services.

52391 Miscellaneous Intermediation[CAN]
See industry description for 523910 below.

523910 Miscellaneous Intermediation[CAN]

This industry comprises establishments primarily engaged in acting as principals (except investment bankers, securities dealers, and commodity contracts dealers) in buying or selling of financial contracts generally on a spread basis. Principals are investors that buy or sell for their own account.

Illustrative Examples:

Investment clubs
Tax liens dealing (i.e., acting as a
  principal in dealing tax liens to
  investors)

Mineral royalties or leases dealing (i.e.,
  acting as a principal in dealing royalties
  or leases to investors)
Venture capital companies

Cross-References.

Establishments primarily engaged in investment banking, securities dealing, securities brokering, commodity contracts dealing, or commodity contracts brokering are classified in Industry Group 5231, Securities and Commodity Contracts Intermediation and Brokerage.

52392 Portfolio Management[CAN]
See industry description for 523920 below.

US—United States industry only. CAN—United States and Canadian industries are comparable. MEX—United States and Mexican industries are comparable. Blank—Canadian, Mexican, and United States industries are comparable.

523920 Portfolio Management^{CAN}

This industry comprises establishments primarily engaged in managing the portfolio assets (i.e., funds) of others on a fee or commission basis. Establishments in this industry have the authority to make investment decisions, and they derive fees based on the size and/or overall performance of the portfolio.

Illustrative Examples:

Managing trusts
Pension fund managing

Mutual fund managing
Portfolio fund managing

Cross-References.

Establishments primarily engaged in investment banking, securities dealing, securities brokering, commodity contracts dealing, or commodity contracts brokering are classified in Industry Group 5231, Securities and Commodity Contracts Intermediation and Brokerage.

52393 Investment Advice^{CAN}
See industry description for 523930 below.

523930 Investment Advice^{CAN}

This industry comprises establishments primarily engaged in providing customized investment advice to clients on a fee basis, but do not have the authority to execute trades. Primary activities performed by establishments in this industry are providing financial planning advice and investment counseling to meet the goals and needs of specific clients.

Illustrative Examples:

Financial investment advice services, customized, fees paid by client
Investment advisory services, customized, fees paid by client

Financial planning services, customized, fees paid by client

Cross-References.

- Establishments providing investment advice in conjunction with their primary activity, such as portfolio management, or the sale of stocks, bonds, annuities, and real estate, are classified according to their primary activity; and

- Establishments known as publishers providing generalized investment information to subscribers are classified in Subsector 511, Publishing Industries

---

US—United States industry only. CAN—United States and Canadian industries are comparable. MEX—United States and Mexican industries are comparable. Blank—Canadian, Mexican, and United States industries are comparable.

(except Internet) or Industry 519130, Internet Publishing and Broadcasting and Web Search Portals.

52399 All Other Financial Investment Activities[CAN]

This industry comprises establishments primarily engaged in acting as agents or brokers (except securities brokerages and commodity contracts brokerages) in buying and selling financial contracts providing financial investment activities (except securities and commodity exchanges, portfolio management, and investment advice).

Illustrative Examples:

Bank trust offices	Escrow agencies (except real estate)
Fiduciary agencies (except real estate)	Stock quotation services

Cross-References. Establishments primarily engaged in—

- Investment banking, securities dealing, securities brokerage, commodity contracts dealing, or commodity contracts brokering—are classified in Industry Group 5231, Securities and Commodity Contracts Intermediation and Brokerage;

- Acting as principals (except investment bankers, securities dealers, and commodity contracts dealers) in buying or selling financial contracts (except securities or commodity contracts)—are classified in Industry 52391, Miscellaneous Intermediation;

- Furnishing physical or electronic marketplaces for the purpose of facilitating the buying and selling of securities and commodities—are classified in Industry 52321, Securities and Commodity Exchanges;

- Managing the portfolio assets (i.e., funds) of others—are classified in Industry 52392, Portfolio Management;

- Providing customized investment advice—are classified in Industry 52393, Investment Advice;

- Awarding grants from trust funds—are classified in Industry 81321, Grantmaking and Giving Services;

- Performing real estate escrow or real estate fiduciary activities—are classified in Industry 53139, Other Activities Related to Real Estate; and

- Financial transactions processing, reserve, and clearinghouse activities—are classified in Industry 52232, Financial Transactions Processing, Reserve, and Clearinghouse Activities.

US—United States industry only. CAN—United States and Canadian industries are comparable. MEX—United States and Mexican industries are comparable. Blank—Canadian, Mexican, and United States industries are comparable.

523991 Trust, Fiduciary, and Custody Activities[US]

This U.S. industry comprises establishments primarily engaged in providing trust, fiduciary, and custody services to others, as instructed, on a fee or contract basis, such as bank trust offices and escrow agencies (except real estate).

Cross-References. Establishments primarily engaged in—

- Managing the portfolio assets (i.e., funds) of others—are classified in Industry 523920, Portfolio Management;

- Performing real estate escrow or real estate fiduciary activities—are classified in Industry 531390, Other Activities Related to Real Estate; and

- Awarding grants from trust funds—are classified in Industry 81321, Grantmaking and Giving Services.

523999 Miscellaneous Financial Investment Activities[US]

This U.S. industry comprises establishments primarily engaged in acting as agents and/or brokers (except securities brokerages and commodity contracts brokerages) in buying or selling financial contracts and those providing financial investment services (except securities and commodity exchanges; portfolio management; investment advice; and trust, fiduciary, and custody services) on a fee or commission basis.

Illustrative Examples:

Exchange clearinghouses, commodities or securities	Stock quotation services
	Gas lease brokers' offices

Cross-References. Establishments primarily engaged in—

- Investment banking, securities dealing, securities brokering, commodity contracts dealing, or commodity contracts brokering—are classified in Industry Group 5231, Securities and Commodity Contracts Intermediation and Brokerage;

- Acting as principals (except investment bankers, securities dealers, and commodity contracts dealers) in buying or selling financial contracts—are classified in Industry 523910, Miscellaneous Intermediation;

- Furnishing physical or electronic marketplaces for the purpose of facilitating the buying and selling of securities and commodities—are classified in Industry 523210, Securities and Commodity Exchanges;

- Managing the portfolio assets (i.e., funds) of others—are classified in Industry 523920, Portfolio Management;

- Providing customized investment advice—are classified in Industry 523930, Investment Advice;
- Providing trust, fiduciary, and custody services to others—are classified in U.S. Industry 523991, Trust, Fiduciary, and Custody Activities; and
- Financial transactions processing, reserve, and clearinghouse activities— are classified in Industry 522320, Financial Transactions Processing, Reserve, and Clearinghouse Activities.

524 Insurance Carriers and Related Activities

Industries in the Insurance Carriers and Related Activities subsector group establishments that are primarily engaged in one of the following: (1) underwriting (assuming the risk, assigning premiums, and so forth) annuities and insurance policies or (2) facilitating such underwriting by selling insurance policies, and by providing other insurance and employee-benefit related services.

5241 Insurance Carriers

This industry group comprises establishments primarily engaged in underwriting (assuming the risk, assigning premiums, and so forth) annuities and insurance policies and investing premiums to build up a portfolio of financial assets to be used against future claims. Direct insurance carriers are establishments that are primarily engaged in initially underwriting and assuming the risk of annuities and insurance policies. Reinsurance carriers are establishments that are primarily engaged in assuming all or part of the risk associated with an existing insurance policy (or set of policies) originally underwritten by another insurance carrier.

Industries are defined in terms of the type of risk being insured against, such as death, loss of employment because of age or disability, and/or property damage. Contributions and premiums are set on the basis of actuarial calculations of probable payouts based on risk factors from experience tables and expected investment returns on reserves.

52411 Direct Life, Health, and Medical Insurance Carriers[CAN]

This industry comprises establishments primarily engaged in initially underwriting (i.e., assuming the risk and assigning premiums) annuities and life insurance policies, disability income insurance policies, accidental death and dismemberment insurance policies, and health and medical insurance policies.

Cross-References.

- Establishments primarily engaged in reinsuring life insurance policies are classified in Industry 52413, Reinsurance Carriers;

US—United States industry only. CAN—United States and Canadian industries are comparable. MEX—United States and Mexican industries are comparable. Blank—Canadian, Mexican, and United States industries are comparable.

- Legal entities (i.e., funds, plans, and/or programs) organized to provide insurance and employee benefits exclusively for the sponsor, firm, or its employees or members are classified in Industry Group 5251, Insurance and Employee Benefit Funds; and

- HMO establishments providing health care services are classified in Industry 62149, Other Outpatient Care Centers.

524113 Direct Life Insurance Carriers[US]

This U.S. industry comprises establishments primarily engaged in initially under-writing (i.e., assuming the risk and assigning premiums) annuities and life insurance policies, disability income insurance policies, and accidental death and dismemberment insurance policies.

Cross-References.

- Establishments primarily engaged in reinsuring life insurance policies, disability income insurance policies, and accidental death and dismemberment insurance policies are classified in Industry 524130, Reinsurance Carriers; and

- Legal entities (i.e., funds, plans, and/or programs) organized to provide insurance and employee benefits exclusively for the sponsor, firm, or its employees or members are classified in Industry Group 5251, Insurance and Employee Benefit Funds.

524114 Direct Health and Medical Insurance Carriers[US]

This U.S. industry comprises establishments primarily engaged in initially under-writing (i.e., assuming the risk and assigning premiums) health and medical insurance policies. Group hospitalization plans and HMO establishments (except those providing health care services) that provide health and medical insurance policies without providing health care services are included in this industry.

Cross-References.

- HMO establishments that provide both health care services and underwrite health and medical insurance are classified in U.S. Industry 621491, HMO Medical Centers;

- Establishments primarily engaged in reinsuring health insurance policies are classified in Industry 524130, Reinsurance Carriers; and

- Legal entities (i.e., funds, plans, and/or programs) organized to provide health- and welfare-related employee benefits exclusively for the sponsor's employees or members are classified in Industry 525120, Health and Welfare Funds.

US—United States industry only. CAN—United States and Canadian industries are comparable. MEX—United States and Mexican industries are comparable. Blank—Canadian, Mexican, and United States industries are comparable.

52412 Direct Insurance (except Life, Health, and Medical) Carriers^{CAN}

This industry comprises establishments primarily engaged in initially underwriting (i.e., assuming the risk and assigning premiums) various types of insurance policies (except life, disability income, accidental death and dismemberment, and health and medical insurance policies).

Illustrative Examples:

Automobile insurance carriers, direct
Property and casualty insurance carriers, direct
Bank deposit insurance carriers, direct
Title insurance carriers, real estate, direct

Mortgage guaranty insurance carriers, direct
Warranty insurance carriers (e.g., appliance, automobile, homeowners, product), direct

Cross-References.

- Establishments primarily engaged in reinsuring insurance policies are classified in Industry 524130, Reinsurance Carriers;

- Legal entities (i.e., funds, plans, and/or programs) organized to provide insurance and employee benefits exclusively for the sponsor, firm, or its employees or members are classified in Industry Group 5251, Insurance and Employee Benefit Funds; and

- Establishments primarily engaged in initially underwriting annuities and life insurance policies, disability income insurance policies, accidental death and dismemberment insurance policies, and health and medical insurance policies are classified in Industry 52411, Direct Life, Health, and Medical Insurance Carriers.

524126 Direct Property and Casualty Insurance Carriers^{US}

This U.S. industry comprises establishments primarily engaged in initially underwriting (i.e., assuming the risk and assigning premiums) insurance policies that protect policyholders against losses that may occur as a result of property damage or liability.

Illustrative Examples:

Automobile insurance carriers, direct
Malpractice insurance carriers, direct
Fidelity insurance carriers, direct
Mortgage guaranty insurance carriers, direct

Homeowners insurance carriers, direct
Surety insurance carriers, direct
Liability insurance carriers, direct

US—United States industry only. CAN—United States and Canadian industries are comparable. MEX—United States and Mexican industries are comparable. Blank—Canadian, Mexican, and United States industries are comparable.

Cross-References.

Establishments primarily engaged in reinsuring property and casualty insurance policies are classified in Industry 524130, Reinsurance Carriers.

524127 Direct Title Insurance Carriers[US]

This U.S. industry comprises establishments primarily engaged in initially underwriting (i.e., assuming the risk and assigning premiums) insurance policies to protect the owners of real estate or real estate creditors against loss sustained by reason of any title defect to real property.

Cross-References.

Establishments primarily engaged in reinsuring title insurance policies are classified in Industry 524130, Reinsurance Carriers.

524128 Other Direct Insurance (except Life, Health, and Medical) Carriers[US]

This U.S. industry comprises establishments primarily engaged in initially underwriting (e.g., assuming the risk, assigning premiums) insurance policies (except life, disability income, accidental death and dismemberment, health and medical, property and casualty, and title insurance policies).

Illustrative Examples:

Bank deposit insurance carriers, direct
Product warranty insurance carriers, direct
Deposit or share insurance carriers, direct

Warranty insurance carriers (e.g., appliance, automobile, homeowners, product), direct

Cross-References. Establishments primarily engaged in—

- Reinsuring insurance policies—are classified in Industry 524130, Reinsurance Carriers;

- Initially underwriting annuities and life insurance policies, disability income insurance policies, and accidental death and dismemberment insurance policies—are classified in U.S. Industry 524113, Direct Life Insurance Carriers;

- Initially underwriting health and medical insurance policies—are classified in U.S. Industry 524114, Direct Health and Medical Insurance Carriers;

- Initially underwriting property and casualty insurance policies—are classified in U.S. Industry 524126, Direct Property and Casualty Insurance Carriers; and

- Initially underwriting title insurance policies—are classified in U.S. Industry 524127, Direct Title Insurance Carriers.

52413 Reinsurance Carriers[CAN]

See industry description for 524130 below.

524130 Reinsurance Carriers[US]

This industry comprises establishments primarily engaged in assuming all or part of the risk associated with existing insurance policies originally underwritten by other insurance carriers.

Cross-References. Establishments primarily engaged in—

- Initially underwriting annuities and life insurance policies, disability income insurance policies, accidental death and dismemberment insurance policies, and health and medical insurance policies—are classified in Industry 52411, Direct Life, Health, and Medical Insurance Carriers; and

- Initially underwriting various types of insurance policies (except life, disability income, accidental death and dismemberment, and health and medical insurance policies)—are classified in Industry 52412, Direct Insurance (except Life, Health, and Medical) Carriers.

5242 Agencies, Brokerages, and Other Insurance Related Activities

This industry group comprises establishments primarily engaged in (1) acting as agents (i.e., brokers) in selling annuities and insurance policies or (2) providing other employee benefits and insurance related services, such as claims adjustment and third party administration.

52421 Insurance Agencies and Brokerages[CAN]

See industry description for 524210 below.

524210 Insurance Agencies and Brokerages[CAN]

This industry comprises establishments primarily engaged in acting as agents (i.e., brokers) in selling annuities and insurance policies.

Cross-References.

Establishments primarily engaged in underwriting annuities and insurance policies are classified in Industry Group 5241, Insurance Carriers.

52429 Other Insurance Related Activities^{CAN}

This industry comprises establishments primarily engaged in providing services related to insurance (except insurance agencies and brokerages).

Illustrative Examples:

Claims adjusting
Insurance plan administrative services

Insurance adjusting

Cross-References. Establishments primarily engaged in—

- Managing the portfolio assets (i.e., funds) of others—are classified in Industry 52392, Portfolio Management;
- Acting as agents (i.e., brokers) in selling annuities and insurance policies—are classified in Industry 52421, Insurance Agencies and Brokerages; and
- Providing actuarial consulting services—are classified in Industry 54161, Management Consulting Services.

524291 Claims Adjusting^{CAN}

This industry comprises establishments primarily engaged in investigating, appraising, and settling insurance claims.

524292 Third Party Administration of Insurance and Pension Funds^{US}

This U.S. industry comprises establishments primarily engaged in providing third party administration services of insurance and pension funds, such as claims processing and other administrative services to insurance carriers, employee-benefit plans, and self-insurance funds.

Cross-References. Establishments primarily engaged in—

- Managing the portfolio assets (i.e., funds) of others—are classified in Industry 523920, Portfolio Management; and
- Providing actuarial consulting services—are classified in U.S. Industry 541612, Human Resources Consulting Services.

524298 All Other Insurance Related Activities^{US}

This U.S. industry comprises establishments primarily engaged in providing insurance services on a contract or fee basis (except insurance agencies and brokerages, claims adjusting, and third party administration). Insurance advisory services and insurance ratemaking services are included in this industry.

Cross-References. Establishments primarily engaged in—

- Providing actuarial consulting services—are classified in U.S. Industry 541612, Human Resources Consulting Services;

- Acting as agents (i.e., brokers) in selling annuities and insurance policies—are classified in Industry 524210, Insurance Agencies and Brokerages;

- Insurance claims adjusting—are classified in U.S. Industry 524291, Claims Adjusting; and

- Third party administration services of insurance and pension funds—are classified in U.S. Industry 524292, Third Party Administration of Insurance and Pension Funds.

525 Funds, Trusts, and Other Financial Vehicles[US]

Industries in the Funds, Trusts, and Other Financial Vehicles subsector are comprised of legal entities (i.e., funds, plans, and/or programs) organized to pool securities or other assets on behalf of shareholders or beneficiaries of employee benefit or other trust funds. The portfolios are customized to achieve specific investment characteristics, such as diversification, risk, rate of return, and price volatility. These entities earn interest, dividends, and other investment income, but have little or no employment and no revenue from the sale of services. Establishments with employees devoted to the management of funds are classified in Industry Group 5239, Other Financial Investment Activities.

Establishments primarily engaged in holding the securities of (or other equity interests in) other firms are classified in Sector 55, Management of Companies and Enterprises. Equity Real Estate Investment Trusts (REITs) that are primarily engaged in leasing buildings, dwellings, or other real estate property to others are classified in Subsector 531, Real Estate.

5251 Insurance and Employee Benefit Funds[US]

This industry group comprises legal entities (i.e., funds, plans, and/or programs) organized to provide insurance and employee benefits exclusively for the sponsor, firm, or its employees or members.

52511 Pension Funds[US]

See industry description for 525110 below.

525110 Pension Funds^{US}

This industry comprises legal entities (i.e., funds, plans, and/or programs) organized to provide retirement income benefits exclusively for the sponsor's employees or members.

Illustrative Examples:

Employee benefit plans
Retirement plans

Pension funds and plans

Cross-References. Establishments primarily engaged in—

- Managing portfolios of pension funds—are classified in Industry 523920, Portfolio Management; and

- Initially underwriting annuities—are classified in U.S. Industry 524113, Direct Life Insurance Carriers.

52512 Health and Welfare Funds^{US}
See industry description for 525120 below.

525120 Health and Welfare Funds^{US}

This industry comprises legal entities (i.e., funds, plans, and/or programs) organized to provide medical, surgical, hospital, vacation, training, and other health- and welfare-related employee benefits exclusively for the sponsor's employees or members.

Cross-References. Establishments primarily engaged in—

- Managing portfolios of health and welfare funds—are classified in Industry 523920, Portfolio Management; and

- Third party claims administration of health and welfare plans—are classified in U.S. Industry 524292, Third Party Administration of Insurance and Pension Funds.

52519 Other Insurance Funds^{US}
See industry description for 525190 below.

525190 Other Insurance Funds^{US}

This industry comprises legal entities (i.e., funds (except pension, and health- and welfare-related employee benefit funds)) organized to provide insurance exclusively for the sponsor, firm, or its employees or members. Self-insurance funds (except employee benefit funds) and workers' compensation insurance funds are included in this industry.

Cross-References.

- Legal entities (i.e., funds, plans, and/or programs) organized to provide retirement income benefits exclusively for the sponsor's employees or members are classified in Industry 525110, Pension Funds;

- Legal entities (i.e., funds, plans, and/or programs) organized to provide health- and welfare-related employee benefits exclusively for the sponsor's employees or members are classified in Industry 525120, Health and Welfare Funds;

- Establishments primarily engaged in managing portfolios of insurance funds are classified in Industry 523920, Portfolio Management;

- Establishments primarily engaged in third party claims administration of insurance, and other employee benefit funds are classified in U.S. Industry 524292, Third Party Administration of Insurance and Pension Funds; and

- Establishments primarily engaged in providing insurance on a fee or contract basis are classified in Industry Group 5241, Insurance Carriers.

5259 Other Investment Pools and Funds[US]

This industry group comprises legal entities (i.e., investment pools and/or funds) organized to pool securities or other assets (except insurance and employee-benefit funds) on behalf of shareholders, unitholders, or beneficiaries.

52591 Open-End Investment Funds[US]
See industry description for 525910 below.

525910 Open-End Investment Funds[US]

This industry comprises legal entities (i.e., open-end investment funds) organized to pool assets that consist of securities or other financial instruments. Shares in these pools are offered to the public in an initial offering with additional shares offered continuously and perpetually and redeemed at a specific price determined by the net asset value.

Illustrative Examples:

Investment funds, open-ended   Money market mutual funds, open-ended

---

US—United States industry only. CAN—United States and Canadian industries are comparable. MEX—United States and Mexican industries are comparable. Blank—Canadian, Mexican, and United States industries are comparable.

52592 Trusts, Estates, and Agency Accounts[US]

See industry description for 525920 below.

525920 Trusts, Estates, and Agency Accounts[US]

This industry comprises legal entities, trusts, estates, or agency accounts, administered on behalf of the beneficiaries under the terms of a trust agreement, will, or agency agreement.

Illustrative Examples:

Bankruptcy estates
Private estates (i.e., administering on
  behalf of beneficiaries)

Personal investment trusts
Testamentary trusts

Cross-References. Establishments primarily engaged in—

- Managing portfolios of trusts—are classified in Industry 523920, Portfolio Management;
- Administering personal estates—are classified in U.S. Industry 523991, Trust, Fiduciary, and Custody Activities; and
- Operating businesses of trusts and bankruptcy estates—are classified according to the kind of business operated.

52599 Other Financial Vehicles[US]

See industry description for 525990 below.

525990 Other Financial Vehicles[US]

This industry comprises legal entities (i.e., funds (except insurance and employee benefit funds; open-end investment funds; trusts, estates, and agency accounts)). Included in this industry are mortgage Real Estate Investment Trusts (REITs).

Illustrative Examples:

Closed-end investment funds
Special purpose vehicles
Collateralized Mortgage Obligations
  (CMOs)
Unit investment trust funds

Face-amount certificate funds
Mortgage real estate investment trusts
  (REITs)
Real Estate Mortgage Investment
  Conduits (REMICs)

Cross-References.

- Legal entities (i.e., funds, plans, and programs) that provide insurance and

---

employee benefits exclusively for the sponsor, firm, or its employees or members are classified in Industry Group 5251, Insurance and Employee Benefit Funds;

- Legal entities (i.e., open-end investment funds) organized to pool assets that consist of securities or other financial instruments, where the pools are offered to the public in an initial offering with additional shares offered continuously and perpetually at a specific price determined by the net asset value, are classified in Industry 525910, Open-End Investment Funds;

- Legal entities (i.e., trusts, estates, or agency accounts) administered on behalf of the beneficiaries under the terms of a trust agreement, will, or agency agreement are classified in Industry 525920, Trusts, Estates, and Agency Accounts; and

- Equity Real Estate Investment Trusts (REITs) that are primarily engaged in leasing buildings, dwellings, or other real estate property to others are classified in Industry Group 5311, Lessors of Real Estate based on primary type of real estate property leased.

US—United States industry only. CAN—United States and Canadian industries are comparable. MEX—United States and Mexican industries are comparable. Blank—Canadian, Mexican, and United States industries are comparable.

http://www.census.gov/naics

Sector 53—Real Estate and Rental and Leasing

The Sector as a Whole

The Real Estate and Rental and Leasing sector comprises establishments primarily engaged in renting, leasing, or otherwise allowing the use of tangible or intangible assets, and establishments providing related services. The major portion of this sector comprises establishments that rent, lease, or otherwise allow the use of their own assets by others. The assets may be tangible, as is the case of real estate and equipment, or intangible, as is the case with patents and trademarks.

This sector also includes establishments primarily engaged in managing real estate for others, selling, renting and/or buying real estate for others, and appraising real estate. These activities are closely related to this sector's main activity, and it was felt that from a production basis they would best be included here. In addition, a substantial proportion of property management is self-performed by lessors.

The main components of this sector are the real estate lessors industries (including equity real estate investment trusts (REITs)); equipment lessors industries (including motor vehicles, computers, and consumer goods); and lessors of nonfinancial intangible assets (except copyrighted works).

Excluded from this sector are establishments primarily engaged in renting or leasing equipment with operators. Establishments renting or leasing equipment with operators are classified in various subsectors of NAICS depending on the nature of the services provided (e.g., transportation, construction, agriculture). These activities are excluded from this sector because the client is paying for the expertise and knowledge of the equipment operator, in addition to the rental of the equipment. In many cases, such as the rental of heavy construction equipment, the operator is essential to operate the equipment.

531 Real Estate

Industries in the Real Estate subsector group establishments that are primarily engaged in renting or leasing real estate to others; managing real estate for others; selling, buying, or renting real estate for others; and providing other real estate related services, such as appraisal services.

This subsector includes equity Real Estate Investment Trusts (REITs) that are primarily engaged in leasing buildings, dwellings, or other real estate property to others. Mortgage REITs are classified in Subsector 525, Funds, Trusts, and Other Financial Vehicles.

Establishments primarily engaged in subdividing and developing unimproved real estate and constructing buildings for sale are classified in Subsector 236, Construction of Buildings. Establishments primarily engaged in subdividing and

US—United States industry only. CAN—United States and Canadian industries are comparable. MEX—United States and Mexican industries are comparable. Blank—Canadian, Mexican, and United States industries are comparable.

http://www.census.gov/naics

improving raw land for subsequent sale to builders are classified in Subsector 237, Heavy and Civil Engineering Construction.

5311 Lessors of Real Estate

53111 Lessors of Residential Buildings and Dwellings[CAN]
See industry description for 531110 below.

531110 Lessors of Residential Buildings and Dwellings[US]

This industry comprises establishments primarily engaged in acting as lessors of buildings used as residences or dwellings, such as single-family homes, apartment buildings, and town homes. Included in this industry are owner-lessors and establishments renting real estate and then acting as lessors in subleasing it to others. The establishments in this industry may manage the property themselves or have another establishment manage it for them.

Cross-References.

Establishments primarily engaged in managing residential real estate for others are classified in U.S. Industry 531311, Residential Property Managers.

53112 Lessors of Nonresidential Buildings (except Miniwarehouses)[CAN]
See industry description for 531120 below.

531120 Lessors of Nonresidential Buildings (except Miniwarehouses)[CAN]

This industry comprises establishments primarily engaged in acting as lessors of buildings (except miniwarehouses and self-storage units) that are not used as residences or dwellings. Included in this industry are: (1) owner-lessors of nonresidential buildings; (2) establishments renting real estate and then acting as lessors in subleasing it to others; and (3) establishments providing full service office space, whether on a lease or service contract basis. The establishments in this industry may manage the property themselves or have another establishment manage it for them.

Cross-References. Establishments primarily engaged in—

- Acting as lessors of buildings used as residences or dwellings—are classified in Industry 531110, Lessors of Residential Buildings and Dwellings;

US—United States industry only. CAN—United States and Canadian industries are comparable. MEX—United States and Mexican industries are comparable. Blank—Canadian, Mexican, and United States industries are comparable.

- Renting or leasing space for self-storage—are classified in Industry 531130, Lessors of Miniwarehouses and Self-Storage Units;

- Managing nonresidential real estate for others—are classified in U.S. Industry 531312, Nonresidential Property Managers;

- Providing a range of office support services, such as mailbox rental, other postal and mailing (except direct mail advertising) services, document copying services, facsimile services, word processing services or on-site personal computer rental, that are not providing office space—are classified in Industry 56143, Business Service Centers;

- Managing and operating arenas, stadiums, theaters, or other related facilities and promoting and organizing performing arts productions, sports events, and similar events at those facilities—are classified in Industry 711310, Promoters of Performing Arts, Sports, and Similar Events with Facilities; and

- Operating public and contract general merchandise warehousing and storage facilities—are classified in Industry 493110, General Warehousing and Storage.

53113 Lessors of Miniwarehouses and Self-Storage Units[CAN]

See industry description for 531130 below.

531130 Lessors of Miniwarehouses and Self-Storage Units[CAN]

This industry comprises establishments primarily engaged in renting or leasing space for self-storage. These establishments provide secure space (i.e., rooms, compartments, lockers, containers, or outdoor space) where clients can store and retrieve their goods.

Cross-References. Establishments primarily engaged in—

- Operating public and contract general merchandise warehousing and storage facilities—are classified in Industry 493110, General Warehousing and Storage; and

- Operating coin-operated lockers—are classified in Industry 812990, All Other Personal Services.

53119 Lessors of Other Real Estate Property[CAN]

See industry description for 531190 below.

US—United States industry only. CAN—United States and Canadian industries are comparable. MEX—United States and Mexican industries are comparable. Blank—Canadian, Mexican, and United States industries are comparable.

531190 Lessors of Other Real Estate Property[CAN]

This industry comprises establishments primarily engaged in acting as lessors of real estate (except buildings), such as manufactured home (i.e., mobile home) sites, vacant lots, and grazing land.

Cross-References. Establishments primarily engaged in—

- Acting as lessors of buildings used as residences or dwellings including manufactured (mobile) homes on-site—are classified in Industry 531110, Lessors of Residential Buildings and Dwellings;

- Acting as lessors of buildings (except miniwarehouses and self-storage units) that are not used as residences or dwellings—are classified in Industry 531120, Lessors of Nonresidential Buildings (except Miniwarehouses); and

- Renting or leasing space for self-storage—are classified in Industry 531130, Lessors of Miniwarehouses and Self-Storage Units.

5312 Offices of Real Estate Agents and Brokers

53121 Offices of Real Estate Agents and Brokers
See industry description for 531210 below.

531210 Offices of Real Estate Agents and Brokers

This industry comprises establishments primarily engaged in acting as agents and/or brokers in one or more of the following: (1) selling real estate for others; (2) buying real estate for others; and (3) renting real estate for others.

5313 Activities Related to Real Estate

This industry group comprises establishments primarily engaged in providing real estate services (except lessors of real estate and offices of real estate agents and brokers). Included in this industry group are establishments primarily engaged in activities, such as managing real estate for others and appraising real estate.

53131 Real Estate Property Managers[CAN]

This industry comprises establishments primarily engaged in managing real property for others. Management includes ensuring that various activities associated with the overall operation of the property are performed, such as collecting rents, and overseeing other services (e.g., maintenance, security, trash removal.)

Cross-References.

- • Establishments primarily engaged in acting as lessors of real estate are classified in Industry Group 5311, Lessors of Real Estate; and
- • Establishments formed on behalf of individual condominium owners or homeowners are classified in Industry 81399, Other Similar Organizations (except Business, Professional, Labor, and Political Organizations).

531311 Residential Property Managers[US]

This U.S. industry comprises establishments primarily engaged in managing residential real estate for others.

Cross-References.

- • Establishments primarily engaged in managing nonresidential real estate for others are classified in U.S. Industry 531312, Nonresidential Property Managers;
- • Establishments primarily engaged in acting as lessors of buildings used as residences or dwellings are classified in Industry 531110, Lessors of Residential Buildings and Dwellings; and
- • Establishments formed on behalf of individual residential condominium owners or homeowners are classified in Industry 81399, Other Similar Organizations (except Business, Professional, Labor, and Political Organizations).

531312 Nonresidential Property Managers[US]

This U.S. industry comprises establishments primarily engaged in managing nonresidential real estate for others.

Cross-References.

- • Establishments primarily engaged in managing residential real estate for others are classified in U.S. Industry 531311, Residential Property Managers;
- • Establishments primarily engaged in acting as lessors of buildings (except miniwarehouses and self storage units) that are not used as residences or dwellings are classified in Industry 531120, Lessors of Nonresidential Buildings (except Miniwarehouses);
- • Establishments primarily engaged in renting or leasing space for self-storage are classified in Industry 531130, Lessors of Miniwarehouses and Self-Storage Units; and

---

- Establishments formed on behalf of individual nonresidential condominium owners are classified in Industry 81399, Other Similar Organizations (except Business, Professional, Labor, and Political Organizations).

53132 Offices of Real Estate Appraisers[CAN]

See industry description for 531320 below.

531320 Offices of Real Estate Appraisers[CAN]

This industry comprises establishments primarily engaged in estimating the fair market value of real estate.

53139 Other Activities Related to Real Estate[CAN]

See industry description for 531390 below.

531390 Other Activities Related to Real Estate[CAN]

This industry comprises establishments primarily engaged in performing real estate related services (except lessors of real estate, offices of real estate agents and brokers, real estate property managers, and offices of real estate appraisers).

Illustrative Examples:

Real estate escrow agencies   Real estate fiduciaries' offices
Real estate listing services

Cross-References. Establishments primarily engaged in—

- Acting as lessors of real estate—are classified in Industry Group 5311, Lessors of Real Estate;

- Selling, buying, and/or renting real estate for others—are classified in Industry 531210, Offices of Real Estate Agents and Brokers;

- Managing real estate for others—are classified in Industry 53131, Real Estate Property Managers;

- Estimating fair market value of real estate—are classified in Industry 531320, Offices of Real Estate Appraisers; and

- Researching public land records for ownership of titles and/or conveying real estate titles—are classified in U.S. Industry 541191, Title Abstract and Settlement Offices.

US—United States industry only. CAN—United States and Canadian industries are comparable. MEX—United States and Mexican industries are comparable. Blank—Canadian, Mexican, and United States industries are comparable.

532 Rental and Leasing Services

Industries in the Rental and Leasing Services subsector include establishments that provide a wide array of tangible goods, such as automobiles, computers, consumer goods, and industrial machinery and equipment, to customers in return for a periodic rental or lease payment.

The subsector includes two main types of establishments: (1) those that are engaged in renting consumer goods and equipment and (2) those that are engaged in leasing machinery and equipment often used for business operations. The first type typically operates from a retail-like or store-front facility and maintains inventories of goods that are rented for short periods of time. The latter type typically does not operate from retail-like locations or maintain inventories, and offers longer term leases. These establishments work directly with clients to enable them to acquire the use of equipment on a lease basis, or they work with equipment vendors or dealers to support the marketing of equipment to their customers under lease arrangements. Equipment lessors generally structure lease contracts to meet the specialized needs of their clients and use their remarketing expertise to find other users for previously leased equipment. Establishments that provide operating and capital (i.e., finance) leases are included in this subsector.

Establishments primarily engaged in leasing in combination with providing loans are classified in Sector 52, Finance and Insurance. Establishments primarily engaged in leasing real property are classified in Subsector 531, Real Estate. Those establishments primarily engaged in renting or leasing equipment with operators are classified in various subsectors of NAICS depending on the nature of the services provided (e.g., Transportation, Construction, Agriculture). These activities are excluded from this subsector since the client is paying for the expertise and knowledge of the equipment operator, in addition to the rental of the equipment. In many cases, such as the rental of heavy construction equipment, the operator is essential to operate the equipment. Likewise, since the provision of crop harvesting services includes both the equipment and operator, it is included in the agriculture subsector. The rental or leasing of copyrighted works is classified in Sector 51, Information, and the rental or leasing of assets, such as patents, trademarks, and/ or licensing agreements is classified in Subsector 533, Lessors of Nonfinancial Intangible Assets (except Copyrighted Works).

5321 Automotive Equipment Rental and Leasing

This industry group comprises establishments primarily engaged in renting or leasing the following types of vehicles: passenger cars and trucks without drivers, and utility trailers. These establishments generally operate from a retail-like facility. Some establishments offer only short-term rental, others only longer-term leases, and some provide both types of services.

US—United States industry only. CAN—United States and Canadian industries are comparable. MEX—United States and Mexican industries are comparable. Blank—Canadian, Mexican, and United States industries are comparable.

53211 Passenger Car Rental and Leasing

This industry comprises establishments primarily engaged in renting or leasing passenger cars without drivers.

Cross-References. Establishments primarily engaged in—

- Renting or leasing passenger cars with drivers (e.g., limousines, hearses, taxis)—are classified in Industry Group 4853, Taxi and Limousine Service;
- Retailing passenger cars through sales or lease arrangements—are classified in Industry Group 4411, Automobile Dealers; and
- Leasing passenger cars in combination with providing loans to buyers of such vehicles—are classified in Sector 52, Finance and Insurance.

532111 Passenger Car Rental[CAN]

This industry comprises establishments primarily engaged in renting passenger cars without drivers, generally for short periods of time.

Cross-References. Establishments primarily engaged in—

- Leasing passenger cars without drivers, generally for long periods of time— are classified in U.S. Industry 532112, Passenger Car Leasing; and
- Renting or leasing passenger cars with drivers (e.g., limousines, hearses, taxis)—are classified in Industry Group 4853, Taxi and Limousine Service.

532112 Passenger Car Leasing[CAN]

This industry comprises establishments primarily engaged in leasing passenger cars without drivers, generally for long periods of time.

Cross-References. Establishments primarily engaged in—

- Renting passenger cars without drivers, generally for short periods of time— are classified in U.S. Industry 532111, Passenger Car Rental;
- Renting or leasing passenger cars with drivers (e.g., limousines, hearses, taxis)—are classified in Industry Group 4853, Taxi and Limousine Service;
- Retailing passenger cars through sales or lease arrangements—are classified in Industry Group 4411, Automobile Dealers; and
- Leasing passenger cars in combination with providing loans to buyers of such vehicles—are classified in Sector 52, Finance and Insurance.

US—United States industry only. CAN—United States and Canadian industries are comparable. MEX—United States and Mexican industries are comparable. Blank—Canadian, Mexican, and United States industries are comparable.

53212 Truck, Utility Trailer, and RV (Recreational Vehicle) Rental and Leasing

See industry description for 532120 below.

532120 Truck, Utility Trailer, and RV (Recreational Vehicle) Rental and Leasing[CAN]

This industry comprises establishments primarily engaged in renting or leasing, without drivers, one or more of the following: trucks, truck tractors, buses, semitrailers, utility trailers, or RVs (recreational vehicles).

Cross-References. Establishments primarily engaged in—

* Renting recreational goods, such as pleasure boats, canoes, motorcycles, mopeds, or bicycles—are classified in Industry 53229, Other Consumer Goods Rental;

* Renting or leasing farm tractors, industrial equipment, and industrial trucks, such as forklifts and other materials handling equipment—are classified in Industry 532490, Other Commercial and Industrial Machinery and Equipment Rental and Leasing;

* Renting or leasing mobile home sites—are classified in Industry 53119, Lessors of Other Real Estate Property;

* Retailing vehicles commonly referred to as RVs through sales or lease arrangements—are classified in Industry 44121, Recreational Vehicle Dealers; and

* Leasing trucks, utility trailers, and RVs in combination with providing loans to buyers of such vehicles—are classified in Sector 52, Finance and Insurance.

5322 Consumer Goods Rental

This industry group comprises establishments primarily engaged in renting personal and household-type goods. Establishments classified in this industry group generally provide short-term rental although in some instances, the goods may be leased for longer periods of time. These establishments often operate from a retail-like or store-front facility.

53221 Consumer Electronics and Appliances Rental

See industry description for 532210 below.

532210 Consumer Electronics and Appliances Rental

This industry comprises establishments primarily engaged in renting consumer electronics equipment and appliances, such as televisions, stereos, and refrigerators. Included in this industry are appliance rental centers.

Cross-References. Establishments primarily engaged in—

- Renting or leasing computers—are classified in Industry 532420, Office Machinery and Equipment Rental and Leasing; and
- Renting a range of consumer, commercial, and industrial equipment, such as lawn and garden equipment, home repair tools, and party and banquet equipment—are classified in Industry 532310, General Rental Centers.

53222 Formal Wear and Costume Rental
See industry description for 532220 below.

532220 Formal Wear and Costume Rental

This industry comprises establishments primarily engaged in renting clothing, such as formal wear, costumes (e.g., theatrical), or other clothing (except laundered uniforms and work apparel).

Cross-References.

Establishments primarily engaged in laundering and supplying uniforms and other work apparel are classified in Industry 81233, Linen and Uniform Supply.

53223 Video Tape and Disc Rental
See industry description for 532230 below.

532230 Video Tape and Disc Rental

This industry comprises establishments primarily engaged in renting prerecorded video tapes and discs for home electronic equipment.

Cross-References. Establishments primarily engaged in—

- Theatrical distribution of motion pictures and videos—are classified in Subsector 512, Motion Picture and Sound Recording Industries;
- Renting video recorders and players—are classified in Industry 532210, Consumer Electronics and Appliances Rental; and

---

US—United States industry only. CAN—United States and Canadian industries are comparable. MEX—United States and Mexican industries are comparable. Blank—Canadian, Mexican, and United States industries are comparable.

- Retailing prerecorded video tapes and discs—are classified in Industry 451220, Prerecorded Tape, Compact Disc, and Record Stores.

53229 Other Consumer Goods Rental

This industry comprises establishments primarily engaged in renting consumer goods (except consumer electronics and appliances, formal wear and costumes, and prerecorded video tapes).

Illustrative Examples:

Furniture rental centers   Party rental supply centers
Sporting goods rental

Cross-References. Establishments primarily engaged in—

- Renting consumer electronics and appliances—are classified in Industry 53221, Consumer Electronics and Appliances Rental;

- Renting formal wear and costumes—are classified in Industry 53222, Formal Wear and Costume Rental;

- Renting prerecorded video tapes and discs—are classified in Industry 53223, Video Tape and Disc Rental;

- Renting a general line of products, such as lawn and garden equipment, home repair tools, and party and banquet equipment—are classified in Industry 53231, General Rental Centers;

- Renting medical equipment (except home health equipment), such as electro-medical and electrotherapeutic apparatus—are classified in Industry 53249, Other Commercial and Industrial Machinery and Equipment Rental and Leasing;

- Providing home health care services and home health equipment—are classified in Industry 62161, Home Health Care Services; and

- Retailing and renting musical instruments—are classified in Industry 45114, Musical Instrument and Supplies Stores.

532291 Home Health Equipment Rental[US]

This U.S. industry comprises establishments primarily engaged in renting home-type health and invalid equipment, such as wheel chairs, hospital beds, oxygen tanks, walkers, and crutches.

Cross-References. Establishments primarily engaged in—

- Renting medical equipment (except home health equipment), such as electro-medical and electrotherapeutic apparatus—are classified in Industry 532490,

Other Commercial and Industrial Machinery and Equipment Rental and Leasing; and

- Providing home health care services and home health equipment—are classified in Industry 62161, Home Health Care Services.

532292 Recreational Goods Rental[US]

This U.S. industry comprises establishments primarily engaged in renting recreational goods, such as bicycles, canoes, motorcycles, skis, sailboats, beach chairs, and beach umbrellas.

532299 All Other Consumer Goods Rental[US]

This U.S. industry comprises establishments primarily engaged in renting consumer goods and products (except consumer electronics and appliances; formal wear and costumes; prerecorded video tapes and discs for home electronic equipment; home health furniture and equipment; and recreational goods). Included in this industry are furniture rental centers and party rental supply centers.

Cross-References. Establishments primarily engaged in—

- Renting consumer electronics and appliances—are classified in Industry 532210, Consumer Electronics and Appliances Rental;
- Renting formal wear and costumes—are classified in Industry 532220, Formal Wear and Costume Rental;
- Renting video tapes and discs—are classified in Industry 532230, Video Tape and Disc Rental;
- Renting home health furniture and equipment—are classified in U.S. Industry 532291, Home Health Equipment Rental;
- Renting recreational goods—are classified in U.S. Industry 532292, Recreational Goods Rental;
- Retailing and renting musical instruments—are classified in Industry 451140, Musical Instrument and Supplies Stores; and
- Renting a range of consumer, commercial, and industrial equipment, such as lawn and garden equipment, home repair tools, and party and banquet equipment—are classified in Industry 532310, General Rental Centers.

5323 General Rental Centers

53231 General Rental Centers
See industry description for 532310 below.

US—United States industry only. CAN—United States and Canadian industries are comparable. MEX—United States and Mexican industries are comparable. Blank—Canadian, Mexican, and United States industries are comparable.

532310 General Rental Centers

This industry comprises establishments primarily engaged in renting a range of consumer, commercial, and industrial equipment. Establishments in this industry typically operate from conveniently located facilities where they maintain inventories of goods and equipment that they rent for short periods of time. The type of equipment that establishments in this industry provide often includes, but is not limited to: audio visual equipment, contractors' and builders' tools and equipment, home repair tools, lawn and garden equipment, moving equipment and supplies, and party and banquet equipment and supplies.

Cross-References. Establishments primarily engaged in—

- Renting trucks and trailers without drivers—are classified in Industry 532120, Truck, Utility Trailer, and RV (Recreational Vehicle) Rental and Leasing;

- Renting party and banquet equipment—are classified in Industry 53229, Other Consumer Goods Rental;

- Renting heavy construction equipment without operators—are classified in U.S. Industry 532412, Construction, Mining, and Forestry Machinery and Equipment Rental and Leasing; and

- Renting specialized types of commercial and industrial equipment, such as garden tractors or public address systems—are classified in Industry 532490, Other Commercial and Industrial Machinery and Equipment Rental and Leasing.

5324 Commercial and Industrial Machinery and Equipment Rental and Leasing

This industry group comprises establishments primarily engaged in renting or leasing commercial-type and industrial-type machinery and equipment. The types of establishments included in this industry group are generally involved in providing capital or investment-type equipment that clients use in their business operations. These establishments typically cater to a business clientele and do not generally operate a retail-like or store-front facility.

53241 Construction, Transportation, Mining, and Forestry Machinery and Equipment Rental and Leasing

This industry comprises establishments primarily engaged in renting or leasing one or more of the following without operators: heavy construction, off-highway

---

US—United States industry only. CAN—United States and Canadian industries are comparable. MEX—United States and Mexican industries are comparable. Blank—Canadian, Mexican, and United States industries are comparable.

transportation, mining, and forestry machinery and equipment. Establishments in this industry may rent or lease products, such as aircraft, railroad cars, steamships, tugboats, bulldozers, earthmoving equipment, well-drilling machinery and equipment, or cranes.

Cross-References. Establishments primarily engaged in—

- Renting or leasing automobiles or trucks without operators—are classified in Industry Group 5321, Automotive Equipment Rental and Leasing;
- Renting or leasing air, rail, highway, and water transportation equipment with operators—are classified in Sector 48-49, Transportation and Warehousing, based on their primary activity;
- Renting or leasing heavy construction equipment with operators—are classified in Industry Group 2389, Other Specialty Trade Contractors;
- Renting or leasing heavy equipment for mining with operators—are classified in Industry 21311, Support Activities for Mining;
- Renting or leasing heavy equipment for forestry with operators—are classified in Industry Group 1153, Support Activities for Forestry; and
- Leasing heavy equipment in combination with providing loans to buyers of such equipment—are classified in Sector 52, Finance and Insurance.

532411 Commercial Air, Rail, and Water Transportation Equipment Rental and Leasing^{US}

This U.S. industry comprises establishments primarily engaged in renting or leasing off-highway transportation equipment without operators, such as aircraft, railroad cars, steamships, or tugboats.

Cross-References. Establishments primarily engaged in—

- Renting or leasing air, rail, highway, and water transportation equipment with operators—are classified in Sector 48-49, Transportation and Warehousing, based on their primary activity;
- Renting pleasure boats—are classified in U.S. Industry 532292, Recreational Goods Rental; and
- Renting or leasing automobiles or trucks without drivers—are classified in Industry Group 5321, Automotive Equipment Rental and Leasing.

532412 Construction, Mining, and Forestry Machinery and Equipment Rental and Leasing^{US}

This U.S. industry comprises establishments primarily engaged in renting or leasing heavy equipment without operators that may be used for construction,

---

US—United States industry only. CAN—United States and Canadian industries are comparable. MEX—United States and Mexican industries are comparable. Blank—Canadian, Mexican, and United States industries are comparable.

mining, or forestry, such as bulldozers, earthmoving equipment, well-drilling machinery and equipment, or cranes.

Cross-References. Establishments primarily engaged in—

- Renting or leasing of cranes with operators—are classified in Industry 238990, All Other Specialty Trade Contractors;

- Renting or leasing of construction equipment with operators (except cranes)—are classified in 238910, Site Preparation Contractors;

- Renting or leasing heavy equipment for mining with operators—are classified in Industry 21311, Support Activities for Mining;

- Renting or leasing heavy equipment for forestry with operators—are classified in Industry Group 1153, Support Activities for Forestry; and

- Leasing heavy equipment in combination with providing loans to buyers of such equipment—are classified in Sector 52, Finance and Insurance.

53242 Office Machinery and Equipment Rental and Leasing
See industry description for 532420 below.

532420 Office Machinery and Equipment Rental and Leasing

This industry comprises establishments primarily engaged in renting or leasing office machinery and equipment, such as computers, office furniture, duplicating machines (i.e., copiers), or facsimile machines.

Cross-References. Establishments primarily engaged in—

- Renting or leasing residential furniture—are classified in Industry 53229, Other Consumer Goods Rental; and

- Leasing office machinery and equipment in combination with providing loans to buyers of such equipment—are classified in Sector 52, Finance and Insurance.

53249 Other Commercial and Industrial Machinery and Equipment Rental and Leasing
See industry description for 532490 below.

532490 Other Commercial and Industrial Machinery and Equipment Rental and Leasing[CAN]

This industry comprises establishments primarily engaged in renting or leasing nonconsumer-type machinery and equipment (except heavy construction, transportation, mining, and forestry machinery and equipment without operators; and office machinery and equipment). Establishments in this industry rent or lease products, such as manufacturing equipment; metalworking, telecommunications, motion picture, or theatrical machinery and equipment; institutional (i.e., public building) furniture, such as furniture for schools, theaters, or buildings; or agricultural equipment without operators.

Cross-References. Establishments primarily engaged in—

- Renting or leasing heavy equipment without operators—are classified in Industry 53241, Construction, Transportation, Mining, and Forestry Machinery and Equipment Rental and Leasing;

- Renting or leasing office machinery and equipment—are classified in Industry 532420, Office Machinery and Equipment Rental and Leasing;

- Renting or leasing agricultural machinery and equipment with operators— are classified in Subsector 115, Support Activities for Agriculture and Forestry;

- Renting home furniture or medical equipment for home use—are classified in Industry 53229, Other Consumer Goods Rental; and

- Leasing nonconsumer machinery and equipment in combination with providing loans to buyers of such equipment—are classified in Sector 52, Finance and Insurance.

533 Lessors of Nonfinancial Intangible Assets (except Copyrighted Works)

Industries in the Lessors of Nonfinancial Intangible Assets (except Copyrighted Works) subsector include establishments that are primarily engaged in assigning rights to assets, such as patents, trademarks, brand names, and/or franchise agreements for which a royalty payment or licensing fee is paid to the asset holder. Establishments in this subsector own the patents, trademarks, and/or franchise agreements that they allow others to use or reproduce for a fee and may or may not have created those assets.

Establishments that allow franchisees the use of the franchise name, contingent on the franchisee buying products or services from the franchisor, are classified elsewhere.

Excluded from this subsector are establishments primarily engaged in leasing real property and establishments primarily engaged in leasing tangible assets, such as automobiles, computers, consumer goods, and industrial machinery and equipment. These establishments are classified in Subsector 531, Real Estate and Subsector 532, Rental and Leasing Services, respectively.

US—United States industry only. CAN—United States and Canadian industries are comparable. MEX—United States and Mexican industries are comparable. Blank—Canadian, Mexican, and United States industries are comparable.

5331 Lessors of Nonfinancial Intangible Assets (except Copyrighted Works)

53311 Lessors of Nonfinancial Intangible Assets (except Copyrighted Works)

See industry description for 533110 below.

533110 Lessors of Nonfinancial Intangible Assets (except Copyrighted Works)

This industry comprises establishments primarily engaged in assigning rights to assets, such as patents, trademarks, brand names, and/or franchise agreements for which a royalty payment or licensing fee is paid to the asset holder.

Cross-References.

- Establishments primarily engaged in producing, reproducing, and/or distributing copyrighted works are classified in Sector 51, Information;

- Independent artists, writers, and performers primarily engaged in creating copyrighted works are classified in Industry 711510, Independent Artists, Writers, and Performers;

- Establishments primarily engaged in leasing real property are classified in Subsector 531, Real Estate;

- Establishments primarily engaged in leasing tangible assets, such as automobiles, computers, consumer goods, and industrial machinery and equipment, are classified in Subsector 532, Rental and Leasing Services; and

- Establishments that allow franchisees the use of the franchise name, contingent on the franchisee buying products or services from the franchisor are classified elsewhere.

US—United States industry only. CAN—United States and Canadian industries are comparable. MEX—United States and Mexican industries are comparable. Blank—Canadian, Mexican, and United States industries are comparable.

http://www.census.gov/naics

Sector 54—Professional, Scientific, and Technical Services

The Sector as a Whole

The Professional, Scientific, and Technical Services sector comprises establishments that specialize in performing professional, scientific, and technical activities for others. These activities require a high degree of expertise and training. The establishments in this sector specialize according to expertise and provide these services to clients in a variety of industries and, in some cases, to households. Activities performed include: legal advice and representation; accounting, bookkeeping, and payroll services; architectural, engineering, and specialized design services; computer services; consulting services; research services; advertising services; photographic services; translation and interpretation services; veterinary services; and other professional, scientific, and technical services.

This sector excludes establishments primarily engaged in providing a range of day-to-day office administrative services, such as financial planning, billing and recordkeeping, personnel, and physical distribution and logistics. These establishments are classified in Sector 56, Administrative and Support and Waste Management and Remediation Services.

541 Professional, Scientific, and Technical Services

Industries in the Professional, Scientific, and Technical Services subsector group establishments engaged in processes where human capital is the major input. These establishments make available the knowledge and skills of their employees, often on an assignment basis, where an individual or team is responsible for the delivery of services to the client. The individual industries of this subsector are defined on the basis of the particular expertise and training of the services provider.

The distinguishing feature of the Professional, Scientific, and Technical Services subsector is the fact that most of the industries grouped in it have production processes that are almost wholly dependent on worker skills. In most of these industries, equipment and materials are not of major importance, unlike health care, for example, where "high tech" machines and materials are important collaborating inputs to labor skills in the production of health care. Thus, the establishments classified in this subsector sell expertise. Much of the expertise requires degrees, though not in every case.

5411 Legal Services

54111 Offices of Lawyers
See industry description for 541110 below.

US—United States industry only. CAN—United States and Canadian industries are comparable. MEX—United States and Mexican industries are comparable. Blank—Canadian, Mexican, and United States industries are comparable.

541110 Offices of Lawyers

This industry comprises offices of legal practitioners known as lawyers or attorneys (i.e., counselors-at-law) primarily engaged in the practice of law. Establishments in this industry may provide expertise in a range or in specific areas of law, such as criminal law, corporate law, family and estate law, patent law, real estate law, or tax law.

Cross-References.

Establishments of legal practitioners (except lawyers or attorneys) primarily engaged in providing specialized legal or paralegal services are classified in Industry 54119, Other Legal Services.

54112 Offices of Notaries
See industry description for 541120 below.

541120 Offices of Notaries

This industry comprises establishments (except offices of lawyers and attorneys) primarily engaged in drafting, approving, and executing legal documents, such as real estate transactions, wills, and contracts; and in receiving, indexing, and storing such documents.

Cross-References.

- Establishments of lawyers and attorneys primarily engaged in the practice of law are classified in Industry 541110, Offices of Lawyers; and

- Establishments of notaries public engaged in activities, such as administering oaths and taking affidavits and depositions, witnessing and certifying signatures on documents, but not empowered to draw and approve legal documents and contracts, are classified in U.S. Industry 541199, All Other Legal Services.

54119 Other Legal Services

This industry comprises establishments of legal practitioners (except lawyers and attorneys) primarily engaged in providing specialized legal or paralegal services.

Illustrative Examples:

Notary public services	Patent agent services (i.e., patent filing
Process serving services	and searching services)

US—United States industry only. CAN—United States and Canadian industries are comparable. MEX—United States and Mexican industries are comparable. Blank—Canadian, Mexican, and United States industries are comparable.

Paralegal services
Real estate settlement offices

Real estate title abstract companies

Cross-References.

- Establishments of lawyers and attorneys primarily engaged in the practice of law are classified in Industry 54111, Offices of Lawyers; and

- Establishments (except offices of lawyers, attorneys, and paralegals) primarily engaged in providing arbitration and conciliation services are classified in Industry 54199, All Other Professional, Scientific, and Technical Services.

541191 Title Abstract and Settlement Offices[US]

This U.S. industry comprises establishments (except offices of lawyers and attorneys) primarily engaged in one or more of the following activities: (1) researching public land records to gather information relating to real estate titles; (2) preparing documents necessary for the transfer of the title, financing, and settlement; (3) conducting final real estate settlements and closings; and (4) filing legal and other documents relating to the sale of real estate. Real estate settlement offices, title abstract companies, and title search companies are included in this industry.

Cross-References.

Establishments of lawyers and attorneys primarily engaged in the practice of law are classified in Industry 541110, Offices of Lawyers.

541199 All Other Legal Services[US]

This U.S. industry comprises establishments of legal practitioners (except offices of lawyers and attorneys, settlement offices, and title abstract offices). These establishments are primarily engaged in providing specialized legal or paralegal services.

Illustrative Examples:

Notary public services
Patent agent services (i.e., patent filing
  and searching services)

Paralegal services
Process serving services

Cross-References.

- Establishments of lawyers and attorneys primarily engaged in the practice of law are classified in Industry 541110, Offices of Lawyers;

- Establishments (except offices of lawyers and attorneys) primarily engaged in researching public land records for ownership or title; preparing docu-

---

US—United States industry only. CAN—United States and Canadian industries are comparable. MEX—United States and Mexican industries are comparable. Blank—Canadian, Mexican, and United States industries are comparable.

ments necessary for the transfer of the title, financing, and settlement; conducting final real estate settlements and closings; and/or filing legal and other documents relating to the sale of real estate are classified in U.S. Industry 541191, Title Abstract and Settlement Offices; and

- Establishments (except offices of lawyers, attorneys, and paralegals) primarily engaged in providing arbitration and conciliation services are classified in Industry 541990, All Other Professional, Scientific, and Technical Services.

5412 Accounting, Tax Preparation, Bookkeeping, and Payroll Services

54121 Accounting, Tax Preparation, Bookkeeping, and Payroll Services

This industry comprises establishments primarily engaged in providing services, such as auditing of accounting records, designing accounting systems, preparing financial statements, developing budgets, preparing tax returns, processing payrolls, bookkeeping, and billing.

Illustrative Examples:

Accountants' offices	Bookkeeping services
Payroll processing services	Tax return preparation services

Cross-References.

Establishments providing computer data processing services at their own facility for others are classified in Industry 51821, Data Processing, Hosting, and Related Services.

541211 Offices of Certified Public Accountants[US]

This U.S. industry comprises establishments of accountants that are certified to audit the accounting records of public and private organizations and to attest to compliance with generally accepted accounting practices. Offices of certified public accountants (CPAs) may provide one or more of the following accounting services: (1) auditing financial statements; (2) designing accounting systems; (3) preparing financial statements; (4) developing budgets; and (5) providing advice on matters related to accounting. These establishments may also provide related services, such as bookkeeping, tax return preparation, and payroll processing.

Cross-References. Establishments primarily engaged in—

- Providing tax return preparation services only—are classified in U.S. Industry 541213, Tax Preparation Services;

US—United States industry only. CAN—United States and Canadian industries are comparable. MEX—United States and Mexican industries are comparable. Blank—Canadian, Mexican, and United States industries are comparable.

- Providing payroll processing services only—are classified in U.S. Industry 541214, Payroll Services; and

- Providing accounting, bookkeeping, and billing services—are classified in U.S. Industry 541219, Other Accounting Services.

541213 Tax Preparation Services[CAN]

This U.S. industry comprises establishments (except offices of CPAs) engaged in providing tax return preparation services without also providing accounting, bookkeeping, billing, or payroll processing services. Basic knowledge of tax law and filing requirements is required.

Cross-References.

- Establishments of CPAs are classified in U.S. Industry 541211, Offices of Certified Public Accountants;

- Establishments of non-CPAs providing payroll services along with tax return preparation services are classified in U.S. Industry 541214, Payroll Services;

- Establishments of non-CPAs providing accounting, bookkeeping, or billing services along with tax return preparation services are classified in U.S. Industry 541219, Other Accounting Services; and

- Establishments providing computer data processing services at their own facility for others are classified in Industry 518210, Data Processing, Hosting, and Related Services.

541214 Payroll Services[US]

This U.S. industry comprises establishments (except offices of CPAs) engaged in the following without also providing accounting, bookkeeping, or billing services: (1) collecting information on hours worked, pay rates, deductions, and other payroll-related data from their clients; and (2) using that information to generate paychecks, payroll reports, and tax filings. These establishments may use data processing and tabulating techniques as part of providing their services.

Cross-References.

- Establishments of CPAs are classified in U.S. Industry 541211, Offices of Certified Public Accountants;

- Establishments of non-CPAs providing tax return preparation services only are classified in U.S. Industry 541213, Tax Preparation Services; and

---

US—United States industry only. CAN—United States and Canadian industries are comparable. MEX—United States and Mexican industries are comparable. Blank—Canadian, Mexican, and United States industries are comparable.

- Establishments of non-CPAs providing accounting, bookkeeping, or billing services along with payroll services are classified in U.S. Industry 541219, Other Accounting Services.

541219 Other Accounting Services[US]

This U.S. industry comprises establishments (except offices of CPAs) engaged in providing accounting services (except tax return preparation services only or payroll services only). These establishments may also provide tax return preparation or payroll services. Accountant (except CPA) offices, bookkeeper offices, and billing offices are included in this industry.

Cross-References.

- Establishments of CPAs are classified in U.S. Industry 541211, Offices of Certified Public Accountants;

- Establishments of non-CPAs engaged in providing tax return preparation services only are classified in U.S. Industry 541213, Tax Preparation Services; and

- Establishments of non-CPAs engaged in providing payroll services only are classified in U.S. Industry 541214, Payroll Services.

5413 Architectural, Engineering, and Related Services

54131 Architectural Services
See industry description for 541310 below.

541310 Architectural Services

This industry comprises establishments primarily engaged in planning and designing residential, institutional, leisure, commercial, and industrial buildings and structures by applying knowledge of design, construction procedures, zoning regulations, building codes, and building materials.

Cross-References. Establishments primarily engaged in—

- Planning and designing the development of land areas—are classified in Industry 541320, Landscape Architectural Services; and

- Both the design and construction of buildings, highways, or other structures or in managing construction projects—are classified in Sector 23, Construction, according to the type of project.

US—United States industry only. CAN—United States and Canadian industries are comparable. MEX—United States and Mexican industries are comparable. Blank—Canadian, Mexican, and United States industries are comparable.

54132 Landscape Architectural Services
See industry description for 541320 below.

541320 Landscape Architectural Services

This industry comprises establishments primarily engaged in planning and designing the development of land areas for projects, such as parks and other recreational areas; airports; highways; hospitals; schools; land subdivisions; and commercial, industrial, and residential areas, by applying knowledge of land characteristics, location of buildings and structures, use of land areas, and design of landscape projects.

Illustrative Examples:

Garden planning services
Landscape architects' offices
Golf course or ski area design services

Landscape consulting services
Industrial land use planning services
Landscape design services

Cross-References.

Establishments primarily engaged in providing landscape care and maintenance services and/or installing trees, shrubs, plants, lawns, or gardens along with the design of landscape plans are classified in Industry 561730, Landscaping Services.

54133 Engineering Services
See industry description for 541330 below.

541330 Engineering Services

This industry comprises establishments primarily engaged in applying physical laws and principles of engineering in the design, development, and utilization of machines, materials, instruments, structures, processes, and systems. The assignments undertaken by these establishments may involve any of the following activities: provision of advice, preparation of feasibility studies, preparation of preliminary and final plans and designs, provision of technical services during the construction or installation phase, inspection and evaluation of engineering projects, and related services.

Illustrative Examples:

Civil engineering services
Environmental engineering services
Construction engineering services

Mechanical engineering services
Engineers' offices

US—United States industry only. CAN—United States and Canadian industries are comparable. MEX—United States and Mexican industries are comparable. Blank—Canadian, Mexican, and United States industries are comparable.

Cross-References. Establishments primarily engaged in—

- Planning and designing computer systems that integrate computer hardware, software, and communication technologies—are classified in U.S. Industry 541512, Computer Systems Design Services;

- Performing surveying and mapping services of the surface of the earth, including the sea floor—are classified in Industry 541370, Surveying and Mapping (except Geophysical) Services;

- Gathering, interpreting, and mapping geophysical data—are classified in Industry 541360, Geophysical Surveying and Mapping Services;

- Creating and developing designs and specifications that optimize the use, value, and appearance of products—are classified in Industry 541420, Industrial Design Services;

- Providing advice and assistance to others on environmental issues, such as the control of environmental contamination from pollutants, toxic substances, and hazardous materials—are classified in Industry 541620, Environmental Consulting Services; and

- Both the design and construction of buildings, highways, and other structures or in managing construction projects—are classified in Sector 23, Construction, according to the type of project.

54134 Drafting Services
See industry description for 541340 below.

541340 Drafting Services

This industry comprises establishments primarily engaged in drawing detailed layouts, plans, and illustrations of buildings, structures, systems, or components from engineering and architectural specifications.

54135 Building Inspection Services
See industry description for 541350 below.

541350 Building Inspection Services

This industry comprises establishments primarily engaged in providing building inspection services. These establishments typically evaluate all aspects of the building structure and component systems and prepare a report on the physical condition of the property, generally for buyers or others involved in real estate transactions. Building inspection bureaus and establishments providing home inspection services are included in this industry.

US—United States industry only. CAN—United States and Canadian industries are comparable. MEX—United States and Mexican industries are comparable. Blank—Canadian, Mexican, and United States industries are comparable.

Cross-References. Establishments primarily engaged in—

- Inspecting buildings for termites and other pests—are classified in Industry 561710, Exterminating and Pest Control Services;
- Inspecting buildings for hazardous materials—are classified in Industry 541620, Environmental Consulting Services; and
- Conducting inspections and enforcing public building codes and standards— are classified in Industry 925110, Administration of Housing Programs.

54136 Geophysical Surveying and Mapping Services
See industry description for 541360 below.

541360 Geophysical Surveying and Mapping Services

This industry comprises establishments primarily engaged in gathering, interpreting, and mapping geophysical data. Establishments in this industry often specialize in locating and measuring the extent of subsurface resources, such as oil, gas, and minerals, but they may also conduct surveys for engineering purposes. Establishments in this industry use a variety of surveying techniques depending on the purpose of the survey, including magnetic surveys, gravity surveys, seismic surveys, or electrical and electromagnetic surveys.

Cross-References.

Establishments primarily engaged in taking core samples, drilling test wells, or other mine development activities (except geophysical surveying and mapping) on a contract basis for others are classified in Industry 21311, Support Activities for Mining.

54137 Surveying and Mapping (except Geophysical) Services
See industry description for 541370 below.

541370 Surveying and Mapping (except Geophysical) Services

This industry comprises establishments primarily engaged in performing surveying and mapping services of the surface of the earth, including the sea floor. These services may include surveying and mapping of areas above or below the surface of the earth, such as the creation of view easements or segregating rights in parcels of land by creating underground utility easements.

Illustrative Examples:

Cadastral surveying services	Topographic surveying services
Mapping (except geophysical) services	Geodetic surveying services
Cartographic surveying services	

US—United States industry only. CAN—United States and Canadian industries are comparable. MEX—United States and Mexican industries are comparable. Blank—Canadian, Mexican, and United States industries are comparable.

Cross-References. Establishments primarily engaged in—

- Providing geophysical surveying and mapping services—are classified in Industry 541360, Geophysical Surveying and Mapping Services;
- Publishing atlases and maps, except for exclusive Internet publishing—are classified in U.S. Industry 511130, Book Publishers; and
- Publishing atlases and maps exclusively on the Internet—are classified in U.S. Industry 519130, Internet Publishing and Broadcasting and Web Search Portals.

54138 Testing Laboratories
See industry description for 541380 below.

541380 Testing Laboratories

This industry comprises establishments primarily engaged in performing physical, chemical, and other analytical testing services, such as acoustics or vibration testing, assaying, biological testing (except medical and veterinary), calibration testing, electrical and electronic testing, geotechnical testing, mechanical testing, nondestructive testing, or thermal testing. The testing may occur in a laboratory or on-site.

Cross-References. Establishments primarily engaged in—

- Laboratory testing for the medical profession—are classified in Industry 62151, Medical and Diagnostic Laboratories;
- Veterinary testing services—are classified in Industry 541940, Veterinary Services; and
- Auto emissions testing—are classified in U.S. Industry 811198, All Other Automotive Repair and Maintenance.

5414 Specialized Design Services

This industry group comprises establishments providing specialized design services (except architectural, engineering, and computer systems design).

54141 Interior Design Services
See industry description for 541410 below.

541410 Interior Design Services

This industry comprises establishments primarily engaged in planning, designing, and administering projects in interior spaces to meet the physical and aesthetic needs of people using them, taking into consideration building codes, health and safety regulations, traffic patterns and floor planning, mechanical and electrical needs, and interior fittings and furniture. Interior designers and interior design consultants work in areas, such as hospitality design, health care design, institutional design, commercial and corporate design, and residential design. This industry also includes interior decorating consultants engaged exclusively in providing aesthetic services associated with interior spaces.

54142 Industrial Design Services
See industry description for 541420 below.

541420 Industrial Design Services

This industry comprises establishments primarily engaged in creating and developing designs and specifications that optimize the use, value, and appearance of their products. These services can include the determination of the materials, construction, mechanisms, shape, color, and surface finishes of the product, taking into consideration human characteristics and needs, safety, market appeal, and efficiency in production, distribution, use, and maintenance. Establishments providing automobile or furniture industrial design services or industrial design consulting services are included in this industry.

Cross-References. Establishments primarily engaged in—

- Applying physical laws and principles of engineering in the design, development, and utilization of machines, materials, instruments, structures, processes, and systems—are classified in Industry 541330, Engineering Services; and

- Designing clothing, shoes, or jewelry—are classified in Industry 541490, Other Specialized Design Services.

54143 Graphic Design Services
See industry description for 541430 below.

541430 Graphic Design Services

This industry comprises establishments primarily engaged in planning, designing, and managing the production of visual communication in order to convey specific messages or concepts, clarify complex information, or project visual identities. These services can include the design of printed materials, packaging, advertising, signage systems, and corporate identification (logos). This industry also includes commercial artists engaged exclusively in generating drawings and illustrations requiring technical accuracy or interpretative skills.

Illustrative Examples:

Commercial art studios

Independent commercial or graphic artists

Corporate identification (i.e., logo) design services

Medical art or illustration services

Graphic design consulting services

Cross-References.

- Establishments primarily engaged in creating and/or placing public display advertising material are classified in Industry 541850, Display Advertising; and

- Independent artists primarily engaged in creating and selling visual artwork for noncommercial use and independent cartoonists are classified in Industry 711510, Independent Artists, Writers, and Performers.

54149 Other Specialized Design Services

See industry description for 541490 below.

541490 Other Specialized Design Services

This industry comprises establishments primarily engaged in providing professional design services (except architectural, landscape architecture, engineering, interior, industrial, graphic, and computer system design).

Illustrative Examples:

Costume design services (except independent theatrical costume designers)

Jewelry design services

Fashion design services

Float design services

Shoe design services

Fur design services

Textile design services

Cross-References. Establishments primarily engaged in—

- Providing architectural design services—are classified in Industry 541310, Architectural Services;

- Providing landscape architecture design services—are classified in Industry 541320, Landscape Architectural Services;

- Providing engineering design services—are classified in Industry 541330, Engineering Services;

- Providing interior design services—are classified in Industry 541410, Interior Design Services;

- Providing industrial design services—are classified in Industry 541420, Industrial Design Services;

- Providing graphic design services—are classified in Industry 541430, Graphic Design Services;

- Providing computer systems design services—are classified in U.S. Industry 541512, Computer Systems Design Services; and

- Operating as independent theatrical designers—are classified in Industry 711510, Independent Artists, Writers, and Performers.

5415 Computer Systems Design and Related Services
See industry description for 54151 below.

54151 Computer Systems Design and Related Services

This industry comprises establishments primarily engaged in providing expertise in the field of information technologies through one or more of the following activities: (1) writing, modifying, testing, and supporting software to meet the needs of a particular customer; (2) planning and designing computer systems that integrate computer hardware, software, and communication technologies; (3) onsite management and operation of clients' computer systems and/or data processing facilities; and (4) other professional and technical computer-related advice and services.

Illustrative Examples:

Computer facilities management services
Custom computer programming services
Computer hardware or software
  consulting services

Software installation services
Computer systems integration design
  services

Cross-References. Establishments primarily engaged in—

- Selling computer hardware or software products from retail-like locations and providing supporting services, such as customized assembly of personal computers—are classified in Industry 44312, Computer and Software Stores;

- Merchant wholesaling computer hardware or software products and providing supporting services, such as customized assembly of personal computers—are classified in Industry 423430, Computer and Computer Peripheral Equipment and Software Merchant Wholesalers;

- Publishing packaged software—are classified in Industry 51121, Software Publishers; and

- Providing computer data processing services at their own facility for others—are classified in Industry 518210, Data Processing, Hosting, and Related Services.

541511 Custom Computer Programming Services^{US}

This U.S. industry comprises establishments primarily engaged in writing, modifying, testing, and supporting software to meet the needs of a particular customer.

Cross-References. Establishments primarily engaged in—

- Publishing packaged software—are classified in Industry 511210, Software Publishers; and

- Planning and designing computer systems that integrate computer hardware, software, and communication technologies, even though such establishments may provide custom software as an integral part of their services— are classified in U.S. Industry 541512, Computer Systems Design Services.

541512 Computer Systems Design Services^{US}

This U.S. industry comprises establishments primarily engaged in planning and designing computer systems that integrate computer hardware, software, and communication technologies. The hardware and software components of the system may be provided by this establishment or company as part of integrated services or may be provided by third parties or vendors. These establishments often install the system and train and support users of the system.

Illustrative Examples:

Computer systems integration design consulting services
Local area network (LAN) computer systems integration design services

Information management computer systems integration design services
Office automation computer systems integration design services

Cross-References. Establishments primarily engaged in—

- Selling computer hardware or software products and systems from retail-like locations, and providing supporting services, such as customized assembly of personal computers—are classified in Industry 443120, Computer and Software Stores; and

- Merchant wholesaling computer hardware or software products and providing supporting services, such as customized assembly of personal comput-

US—United States industry only. CAN—United States and Canadian industries are comparable. MEX—United States and Mexican industries are comparable. Blank—Canadian, Mexican, and United States industries are comparable.

http://www.census.gov/naics

ers—are classified in Industry 423430, Computer and Computer Peripheral Equipment and Software Merchant Wholesalers.

541513 Computer Facilities Management Services[US]

This U.S. industry comprises establishments primarily engaged in providing on-site management and operation of clients' computer systems and/or data processing facilities. Establishments providing computer systems or data processing facilities support services are included in this industry.

Cross-References.

Establishments primarily engaged in providing computer data processing services at their own facility for others are classified in Industry 518210, Data Processing, Hosting, and Related Services.

541519 Other Computer Related Services[US]

This U.S. industry comprises establishments primarily engaged in providing computer related services (except custom programming, systems integration design, and facilities management services). Establishments providing computer disaster recovery services or software installation services are included in this industry.

Cross-References. Establishments primarily engaged in—

- Providing custom computer programming services—are classified in U.S. Industry 541511, Custom Computer Programming Services;
- Providing computer systems integration design services—are classified in U.S. Industry 541512, Computer Systems Design Services; and
- Providing computer systems and/or data processing facilities management services—are classified in U.S. Industry 541513, Computer Facilities Management Services.

5416 Management, Scientific, and Technical Consulting Services

54161 Management Consulting Services

This industry comprises establishments primarily engaged in providing advice and assistance to businesses and other organizations on management issues, such as strategic and organizational planning; financial planning and budgeting; marketing objectives and policies; human resource policies, practices, and planning; production scheduling; and control planning.

US—United States industry only. CAN—United States and Canadian industries are comparable. MEX—United States and Mexican industries are comparable. Blank—Canadian, Mexican, and United States industries are comparable.

Illustrative Examples:

Actuarial, benefit, and compensation consulting services	Process, physical distribution, and logistics consulting services
Marketing consulting services	Human resources consulting services
Administrative and general management consulting services	

Cross-References.

- Establishments primarily engaged in providing a range of day-to-day office administrative services, such as financial planning, billing and recordkeeping, personnel, and physical distribution and logistics are classified in Industry 56111, Office Administrative Services;

- Establishments primarily engaged in providing executive search, recruitment, and placement services are classified in Industry 56131, Employment Placement Agencies and Executive Search Services;

- Establishments primarily engaged in administering, overseeing, and managing other establishments of the company or enterprise (except government establishments) are classified in Industry 55111, Management of Companies and Enterprises;

- Government establishments primarily engaged in administering, overseeing, and managing governmental programs are classified in Sector 92, Public Administration;

- Establishments primarily engaged in professional and management development training are classified in Industry 61143, Professional and Management Development Training;

- Establishments primarily engaged in listing employment vacancies and in selecting, referring, and placing applicants in employment are classified in Industry 56131, Employment Placement Agencies and Executive Search Services;

- Establishments primarily engaged in developing and implementing public relations plans are classified in Industry 54182, Public Relations Agencies;

- Establishments primarily engaged in developing and conducting marketing research or public opinion polling are classified in Industry 54191, Marketing Research and Public Opinion Polling;

- Establishments primarily engaged in planning and designing industrial processes and systems are classified in Industry 54133, Engineering Services;

- Establishments primarily engaged in planning and designing computer systems are classified in Industry 54151, Computer Systems Design and Related Services; and

US—United States industry only. CAN—United States and Canadian industries are comparable. MEX—United States and Mexican industries are comparable. Blank—Canadian, Mexican, and United States industries are comparable.

- Establishments primarily engaged in providing financial investment advice services are classified in Industry 52393, Investment Advice.

541611 Administrative Management and General Management Consulting Services[CAN]

This U.S. industry comprises establishments primarily engaged in providing operating advice and assistance to businesses and other organizations on administrative management issues, such as financial planning and budgeting, equity and asset management, records management, office planning, strategic and organizational planning, site selection, new business startup, and business process improvement. This industry also includes establishments of general management consultants that provide a full range of administrative; human resource; marketing; process, physical distribution, and logistics; or other management consulting services to clients.

Illustrative Examples:

Administrative management consulting services
Site selection consulting services
Financial management (except investment advice) consulting services

Strategic planning consulting services
General management consulting services

Cross-References.

- Establishments primarily engaged in providing a range of day-to-day office administrative services, such as financial planning, billing and recordkeeping, personnel, and physical distribution and logistics, are classified in Industry 561110, Office Administrative Services;

- Establishments providing operations consulting services are classified in U.S. Industry 541614, Process, Physical Distribution, and Logistics Consulting Services;

- Establishments primarily engaged in administering, overseeing, and managing other establishments of the company or enterprise (except government establishments) are classified in U.S. Industry 551114, Corporate, Subsidiary, and Regional Managing Offices;

- Government establishments primarily engaged in administering, overseeing, and managing governmental programs are classified in Sector 92, Public Administration; and

- Establishments primarily engaged in providing investment advice are classified in Industry 523930, Investment Advice.

US—United States industry only. CAN—United States and Canadian industries are comparable. MEX—United States and Mexican industries are comparable. Blank—Canadian, Mexican, and United States industries are comparable.

541612 Human Resources Consulting Services^{CAN}

This U.S. industry comprises establishments primarily engaged in providing advice and assistance to businesses and other organizations in one or more of the following areas: (1) human resource and personnel policies, practices, and procedures; (2) employee benefits planning, communication, and administration; (3) compensation systems planning; and (4) wage and salary administration.

Illustrative Examples:

Benefit or compensation consulting services

Employee assessment consulting services

Personnel management consulting services

Human resources consulting services

Cross-References. Establishments primarily engaged in—

- Providing professional and management development training—are classified in Industry 611430, Professional and Management Development Training;

- Listing employment vacancies and in selecting, referring, and placing applicants in employment—are classified in U.S. Industry 561311, Employment Placement Agencies; and

- Providing executive search, recruitment, and placement services—are classified in U.S. Industry 561312, Executive Search Services.

541613 Marketing Consulting Services^{US}

This U.S. industry comprises establishments primarily engaged in providing operating advice and assistance to businesses and other organizations on marketing issues, such as developing marketing objectives and policies, sales forecasting, new product developing and pricing, licensing and franchise planning, and marketing planning and strategy.

Illustrative Examples:

Customer services management consulting services

New product development consulting services

Marketing management consulting services

Sales management consulting services

Cross-References. Establishments primarily engaged in—

- Developing and implementing public relations plans—are classified in Industry 541820, Public Relations Agencies; and

---

- Developing and conducting marketing research or public opinion polling— are classified in Industry 541910, Marketing Research and Public Opinion Polling.

541614 Process, Physical Distribution, and Logistics Consulting Services[US]

This U.S. industry comprises establishments primarily engaged in providing operating advice and assistance to businesses and other organizations in areas, such as: (1) manufacturing operations improvement; (2) productivity improvement; (3) production planning and control; (4) quality assurance and quality control; (5) inventory management; (6) distribution networks; (7) warehouse use, operations, and utilization; (8) transportation and shipment of goods and materials; and (9) materials management and handling.

Illustrative Examples:

Freight rate or tariff rate consulting services

Productivity improvement consulting services

Inventory planning and control management consulting services

Transportation management consulting services

Manufacturing management consulting services

Cross-References. Establishments primarily engaged in—

- Planning and designing industrial processes and systems—are classified in Industry 541330, Engineering Services; and

- Providing computer systems integration design services—are classified in U.S. Industry 541512, Computer Systems Design Services.

541618 Other Management Consulting Services[US]

This U.S. industry comprises establishments primarily engaged in providing management consulting services (except administrative and general management consulting; human resources consulting; marketing consulting; or process, physical distribution, and logistics consulting). Establishments providing telecommunications or utilities management consulting services are included in this industry.

Cross-References. Establishments primarily engaged in—

- Providing administrative and general management consulting services—are classified in U.S. Industry 541611, Administrative Management and General Management Consulting Services;

- Providing human resources consulting services—are classified in U.S. Industry 541612, Human Resources Consulting Services;

- Providing marketing consulting services—are classified in U.S. Industry 541613, Marketing Consulting Services; and

- Providing process, physical distribution, and logistics consulting services— are classified in U.S. Industry 541614, Process, Physical Distribution, and Logistics Consulting Services.

54162 Environmental Consulting Services
See industry description for 541620 below.

541620 Environmental Consulting Services

This industry comprises establishments primarily engaged in providing advice and assistance to businesses and other organizations on environmental issues, such as the control of environmental contamination from pollutants, toxic substances, and hazardous materials. These establishments identify problems (e.g., inspect buildings for hazardous materials), measure and evaluate risks, and recommend solutions. They employ a multidisciplined staff of scientists, engineers, and other technicians with expertise in areas, such as air and water quality, asbestos contamination, remediation, and environmental law. Establishments providing sanitation or site remediation consulting services are included in this industry.

Cross-References. Establishments primarily engaged in—

- Environmental remediation—are classified in Industry 562910, Remediation Services; and

- Providing environmental engineering services—are classified in Industry 541330, Engineering Services.

54169 Other Scientific and Technical Consulting Services
See industry description for 541690 below.

541690 Other Scientific and Technical Consulting Services

This industry comprises establishments primarily engaged in providing advice and assistance to businesses and other organizations on scientific and technical issues (except environmental).

Illustrative Examples:

Agricultural consulting services	Radio consulting services
Motion picture consulting services	Economic consulting services

---

US—United States industry only. CAN—United States and Canadian industries are comparable. MEX—United States and Mexican industries are comparable. Blank—Canadian, Mexican, and United States industries are comparable.

Biological consulting services
Physics consulting services
Chemical consulting services

Safety consulting services
Energy consulting services
Security consulting services

Cross-References.

Establishments primarily engaged in environmental consulting are classified in Industry 541620, Environmental Consulting Services.

5417 Scientific Research and Development Services

This industry group comprises establishments engaged in conducting original investigation undertaken on a systematic basis to gain new knowledge (research) and/or the application of research findings or other scientific knowledge for the creation of new or significantly improved products or processes (experimental development). The industries within this industry group are defined on the basis of the domain of research; that is, on the scientific expertise of the establishment.

54171 Research and Development in the Physical, Engineering, and Life Sciences

This industry comprises establishments primarily engaged in conducting research and experimental development in the physical, engineering, and life sciences, such as agriculture, electronics, environmental, biology, botany, biotechnology, computers, chemistry, food, fisheries, forests, geology, health, mathematics, medicine, oceanography, pharmacy, physics, veterinary, and other allied subjects.

Cross-References. Establishments primarily engaged in—

- Providing veterinary testing services—are classified in Industry 54194, Veterinary Services;

- Providing medical laboratory testing for humans—are classified in Industry 62151, Medical and Diagnostic Laboratories;

- Providing physical, chemical, or other analytical testing services (except medical or veterinary), such as acoustics or vibration testing, calibration testing, electrical and electronic testing, geotechnical testing, mechanical testing, nondestructive testing, or thermal testing—are classified in Industry 54138, Testing Laboratories; and

- Manufacturing vaccines, toxoids, blood fractions, and culture media of plant or animal origin (except diagnostic use) and/or uncompounded medicinal chemicals and their derivatives (i.e., enzyme proteins and antibiotics for pharmaceutical use)—are classified in Industry 32541, Pharmaceutical and Medicine Manufacturing.

US—United States industry only. CAN—United States and Canadian industries are comparable. MEX—United States and Mexican industries are comparable. Blank—Canadian, Mexican, and United States industries are comparable.

http://www.census.gov/naics

541711 Research and Development in Biotechnology[US]

This U.S. industry comprises establishments primarily engaged in conducting biotechnology research and experimental development. Biotechnology research and experimental development involves the study of the use of microorganisms and cellular and biomolecular processes to develop or alter living or non-living materials. This research and development in biotechnology may result in development of new biotechnology processes or in prototypes of new or genetically-altered products that may be reproduced, utilized, or implemented by various industries.

Illustrative Examples:

Recombinant DNA research and experimental development laboratories
DNA technologies (e.g., microarrays) research and experimental development laboratories
Cloning research and experimental development laboratories

Protein engineering research and experimental development laboratories
Nucleic acid chemistry research and experimental development laboratories
Nanobiotechnologies research and experimental development laboratories

Cross-References. Establishments primarily engaged in—

- Conducting research and experimental development in the physical, engineering, and life sciences (except biotechnology)—are classified in U.S. Industry 541712, Research and Development in the Physical, Engineering, and Life Sciences (except Biotechnology);

- Providing veterinary testing services—are classified in Industry 541940, Veterinary Services;

- Providing physical, chemical, or other analytical testing services (except medical or veterinary), such as acoustics or vibration testing, calibration testing, electrical and electronic testing, geotechnical testing, mechanical testing, nondestructive testing, or thermal testing—are classified in Industry 541380, Testing Laboratories;

- Manufacturing vaccines, toxoids, blood fractions, and culture media of plant or animal origin (except diagnostic use)—are classified in U.S. Industry 325414, Biological Product (except Diagnostic) Manufacturing; and

- Manufacturing uncompounded medicinal chemicals and their derivatives (i.e., enzyme proteins and antibiotics for pharmaceutical use)—are classified in U.S. Industry 325411, Medicinal and Botanical Manufacturing.

541712 Research and Development in the Physical, Engineering, and Life Sciences (except Biotechnology)[US]

This U.S. Industry comprises establishments primarily engaged in conducting research and experimental development (except biotechnology research and experi-

---

US—United States industry only. CAN—United States and Canadian industries are comparable. MEX—United States and Mexican industries are comparable. Blank—Canadian, Mexican, and United States industries are comparable.

mental development) in the physical, engineering, and life sciences, such as agriculture, electronics, environmental, biology, botany, computers, chemistry, food, fisheries, forests, geology, health, mathematics, medicine, oceanography, pharmacy, physics, veterinary and other allied subjects.

Cross-References. Establishments primarily engaged in—

- Providing physical, chemical, or other analytical testing services (except medical or veterinary)—are classified in Industry 541380, Testing Laboratories;
- Providing medical laboratory testing for humans—are classified in U.S. Industry 621511, Medical Laboratories;
- Conducting research and experimental development in biotechnology—are classified in U.S. Industry 541711, Research and Development in Biotechnology; and
- Providing veterinary testing services—are classified in Industry 541940, Veterinary Services.

54172 Research and Development in the Social Sciences and Humanities
See industry description for 541720 below.

541720 Research and Development in the Social Sciences and Humanities^{CAN}

This industry comprises establishments primarily engaged in conducting research and analyses in cognitive development, sociology, psychology, language, behavior, economic, and other social science and humanities research.

Cross-References.

Establishments primarily engaged in marketing research are classified in Industry 541910, Marketing Research and Public Opinion Polling.

5418 Advertising, Public Relations, and Related Services

54181 Advertising Agencies
See industry description for 541810 below.

541810 Advertising Agencies

This industry comprises establishments primarily engaged in creating advertising campaigns and placing such advertising in periodicals, newspapers, radio and television, or other media. These establishments are organized to provide a full range of services (i.e., through in-house capabilities or subcontracting), including advice, creative services, account management, production of advertising material, media planning, and buying (i.e., placing advertising).

Cross-References. Establishments primarily engaged in—

- Purchasing advertising space from media outlets and reselling it directly to advertising agencies or individual companies—are classified in Industry 541830, Media Buying Agencies;

- Conceptualizing and producing artwork or graphic designs without providing other advertising agency services—are classified in Industry 541430, Graphic Design Services;

- Creating direct mail advertising campaigns—are classified in Industry 541860, Direct Mail Advertising;

- Providing marketing consulting services—are classified in U.S. Industry 541613, Marketing Consulting Services; and

- Selling media time or space for media owners as independent representatives—are classified in Industry 541840, Media Representatives.

54182 Public Relations Agencies

See industry description for 541820 below.

541820 Public Relations Agencies

This industry comprises establishments primarily engaged in designing and implementing public relations campaigns. These campaigns are designed to promote the interests and image of their clients. Establishments providing lobbying, political consulting, or public relations consulting are included in this industry.

54183 Media Buying Agencies

See industry description for 541830 below.

541830 Media Buying Agencies

This industry comprises establishments primarily engaged in purchasing advertising time or space from media outlets and reselling it to advertising agencies or individual companies directly.

US—United States industry only. CAN—United States and Canadian industries are comparable. MEX—United States and Mexican industries are comparable. Blank—Canadian, Mexican, and United States industries are comparable.

Cross-References. Establishments primarily engaged in—

- Selling time and space to advertisers for media owners as independent representatives—are classified in Industry 541840, Media Representatives; and

- Creating advertising campaigns and placing such advertising in media— are classified in Industry 541810, Advertising Agencies.

54184 Media Representatives

See industry description for 541840 below.

541840 Media Representatives

This industry comprises establishments of independent representatives primarily engaged in selling media time or space for media owners.

Illustrative Examples:

Newspaper advertising representatives (i.e., independent of media owners)
Radio advertising representatives (i.e., independent of media owners)

Publishers' advertising representatives (i.e., independent of media owners)
Television advertising representatives (i.e., independent of media owners)

Cross-References. Establishments primarily engaged in—

- Purchasing advertising time or space from media outlets and reselling it directly to advertising agencies or individual companies—are classified in Industry 541830, Media Buying Agencies; and

- Creating advertising campaigns and placing such advertising in media— are classified in Industry 541810, Advertising Agencies.

54185 Display Advertising

See industry description for 541850 below.

541850 Display Advertising

This industry comprises establishments primarily engaged in creating and designing public display advertising campaign materials, such as printed, painted, or electronic displays; and/or placing such displays on indoor or outdoor billboards and panels, or on or within transit vehicles or facilities, shopping malls, retail (in-store) displays, and other display structures or sites.

US—United States industry only. CAN—United States and Canadian industries are comparable. MEX—United States and Mexican industries are comparable. Blank—Canadian, Mexican, and United States industries are comparable.

Cross-References. Establishments primarily engaged in—

- Providing sign lettering and painting services—are classified in Industry 541890, Other Services Related to Advertising;

- Printing paper on paperboard signs—are classified in Industry 32311, Printing;

- Erecting display boards—are classified in Industry 238990, All Other Specialty Trade Contractors; and

- Manufacturing electrical, mechanical, or plate signs and point-of-sale advertising displays—are classified in Industry 339950, Sign Manufacturing.

54186   Direct Mail Advertising
See industry description for 541860 below.

541860   Direct Mail Advertising

This industry comprises establishments primarily engaged in (1) creating and designing advertising campaigns for the purpose of distributing advertising materials (e.g., coupons, flyers, samples) or specialties (e.g., key chains, magnets, pens with customized messages imprinted) by mail or other direct distribution; and/or (2) preparing advertising materials or specialties for mailing or other direct distribution. These establishments may also compile, maintain, sell, and rent mailing lists.

Cross-References. Establishments primarily engaged in—

- The direct distribution or delivery (e.g., door-to-door, windshield placement) of advertisements or samples—are classified in Industry 541870, Advertising Material Distribution Services;

- Distributing advertising specialties for clients who wish to use such materials for promotional purposes—are classified in Industry 541890, Other Services Related to Advertising;

- Creating advertising campaigns and placing such advertising in media—are classified in Industry 541810, Advertising Agencies;

- Compiling and selling mailing lists without providing direct mail advertising services—are classified in Industry 511140, Directory and Mailing List Publishers; and

- Broadcasting exclusively on the Internet—are classified in Industry 519130, Internet Publishing and Broadcasting and Web Search Portals.

54187   Advertising Material Distribution Services
See industry description for 541870 below.

US—United States industry only. CAN—United States and Canadian industries are comparable. MEX—United States and Mexican industries are comparable. Blank—Canadian, Mexican, and United States industries are comparable.

541870 Advertising Material Distribution Services

This industry comprises establishments primarily engaged in the direct distribution or delivery of advertisements (e.g., circulars, coupons, handbills) or samples. Establishments in this industry use methods, such as delivering advertisements or samples door-to-door, placing flyers or coupons on car windshields in parking lots, or handing out samples in retail stores.

Cross-References. Establishments primarily engaged in—

- Creating and designing advertising campaigns for the purpose of distributing advertising materials or samples through the mail—are classified in Industry 541860, Direct Mail Advertising;

- Publishing newspapers or operating television stations or on-line information services—are classified in Sector 51, Information; and

- Distributing advertising specialties (e.g., key chains, magnets, or pens with customized messages imprinted) to clients who wish to use such materials for promotional purposes—are classified in Industry 541890, Other Services Related to Advertising.

54189 Other Services Related to Advertising
See industry description for 541890 below.

541890 Other Services Related to Advertising^{MEX}

This industry comprises establishments primarily engaged in providing advertising services (except advertising agency services, public relations agency services, media buying agency services, media representative services, display advertising services, direct mail advertising services, advertising material distribution services, and marketing consulting services).

Illustrative Examples:

Advertising specialties (e.g., key chains, magnets, pens) distribution services (except direct mail)
Sign lettering and painting services
Display lettering services
Store window dressing or trimming services

Mannequin decorating services
Welcoming services (i.e., advertising services)
Merchandise demonstration services

Cross-References. Establishments primarily engaged in—

- Creating advertising campaigns and placing such advertising in newspapers, television, or other media—are classified in Industry 541810, Advertising Agencies;

- Designing and implementing public relations campaigns—are classified in Industry 541820, Public Relations Agencies;
- Purchasing advertising time or space from media outlets and reselling it directly to advertising agencies or individual companies—are classified in Industry 541830, Media Buying Agencies;
- Selling media time or space for media owners as independent representatives—are classified in Industry 541840, Media Representatives;
- Providing display advertising services (except aerial)—are classified in Industry 541850, Display Advertising;
- Providing direct distribution or delivery (e.g., door-to-door, windshield placement) of advertisements or samples—are classified in Industry 541870, Advertising Material Distribution Services;
- Providing direct mail advertising services—are classified in Industry 541860, Direct Mail Advertising;
- Publishing newspapers or operating television stations or on-line information services—are classified in Sector 51, Information; and
- Providing marketing consulting services—are classified in U.S. Industry 541613, Marketing Consulting Services.

5419 Other Professional, Scientific, and Technical Services

This industry group comprises establishments engaged in professional, scientific, and technical services (except legal services; accounting, tax preparation, bookkeeping, and related services; architectural, engineering, and related services; specialized design services; computer systems design and related services; management, scientific, and technical consulting services; scientific research and development services; and advertising, public relations and related services).

54191 Marketing Research and Public Opinion Polling
See industry description for 541910 below.

541910 Marketing Research and Public Opinion Polling

This industry comprises establishments primarily engaged in systematically gathering, recording, tabulating, and presenting marketing and public opinion data.

Illustrative Examples:

Broadcast media rating services	Statistical sampling services
Political opinion polling services	Opinion research services
Marketing analysis or research services	

Cross-References. Establishments primarily engaged in—

- Providing research and analysis in economics, sociology, and related fields—are classified in Industry 541720, Research and Development in the Social Sciences and Humanities; and

- Providing advice and counsel on marketing strategies—are classified in U.S. Industry 541613, Marketing Consulting Services.

54192 Photographic Services

This industry comprises establishments primarily engaged in providing still, video, or digital photography services. These establishments may specialize in a particular field of photography, such as commercial and industrial photography, portrait photography, and special events photography. Commercial or portrait photography studios are included in this industry.

Cross-References. Establishments primarily engaged in—

- Producing film and videotape for commercial exhibition or sale—are classified in Industry 51211, Motion Picture and Video Production;

- Developing still photographs—are classified in Industry 81292, Photofinishing;

- Developing motion picture film—are classified in Industry 51219, Postproduction Services and Other Motion Picture and Video Industries;

- Taking, developing, and selling artistic, news, or other types of photographs on a freelance basis, such as photojournalists—are classified in Industry 71151, Independent Artists, Writers, and Performers; and

- Supplying and servicing automatic photography machines in places of business operated by others—are classified in Industry 81299, All Other Personal Services.

541921 Photography Studios, Portrait[US]

This U.S. industry comprises establishments known as portrait studios primarily engaged in providing still, video, or digital portrait photography services.

Illustrative Examples:

Home photography services
School photography services
Passport photography services

Videotaping services for special events (e.g., weddings)

US—United States industry only. CAN—United States and Canadian industries are comparable. MEX—United States and Mexican industries are comparable. Blank—Canadian, Mexican, and United States industries are comparable.

Cross-References. Establishments primarily engaged in—

- Producing film and videotape for commercial exhibition or sale—are classified in Industry 512110, Motion Picture and Video Production;

- Developing still photographs—are classified in Industry 81292, Photofinishing;

- Developing motion picture film—are classified in U.S. Industry 512199, Other Motion Picture and Video Industries;

- Taking, developing, and selling artistic, news, or other types of photographs on a freelance basis, such as photojournalists—are classified in Industry 711510, Independent Artists, Writers, and Performers; and

- Supplying and servicing automatic photography machines in places of business operated by others—are classified in Industry 812990, All Other Personal Services.

541922 Commercial Photography[US]

This U.S. industry comprises establishments primarily engaged in providing commercial photography services, generally for advertising agencies, publishers, and other business and industrial users.

Cross-References. Establishments primarily engaged in—

- Producing film and videotape for commercial exhibition or sale—are classified in Industry 512110, Motion Picture and Video Production;

- Developing still photographs—are classified in Industry 81292, Photofinishing;

- Developing motion picture film—are classified in U.S. Industry 512199, Other Motion Picture and Video Industries;

- Taking, developing, and selling artistic, news, or other types of photographs on a freelance basis, such as photojournalists—are classified in Industry 711510, Independent Artists, Writers, and Performers; and

- Supplying and servicing automatic photography machines in places of business operated by others—are classified in Industry 812990, All Other Personal Services.

54193 Translation and Interpretation Services

See industry description for 541930 below.

US—United States industry only. CAN—United States and Canadian industries are comparable. MEX—United States and Mexican industries are comparable. Blank—Canadian, Mexican, and United States industries are comparable.

541930 Translation and Interpretation Services

This industry comprises establishments primarily engaged in translating written material and interpreting speech from one language to another and establishments primarily engaged in providing sign language services.

Cross-References. Establishments primarily engaged in—

- Providing transcription services—are classified in Industry 561410, Document Preparation Services;

- Providing real-time (i.e., simultaneous) closed captioning services for live television performances, at meetings and conferences—are classified in U.S. Industry 561492, Court Reporting and Stenotype Services;

- Providing film or tape closed captioning services—are classified in U.S. Industry 512191, Teleproduction and Other Postproduction Services; and

- Analyzing handwriting—are classified in Industry 541990, All Other Professional, Scientific, and Technical Services.

54194 Veterinary Services
See industry description for industry 541940 below.

541940 Veterinary Services^{CAN}

This industry comprises establishments of licensed veterinary practitioners primarily engaged in the practice of veterinary medicine, dentistry, or surgery for animals; and establishments primarily engaged in providing testing services for licensed veterinary practitioners.

Illustrative Examples:

Animal hospitals	Veterinarians' offices
Veterinary clinics	Veterinary testing laboratories

Cross-References. Establishments primarily engaged in—

- Providing veterinary research and development services—are classified in Industry 54171, Research and Development in the Physical, Engineering, and Life Sciences;

- Providing nonveterinary pet care services, such as boarding or grooming pets—are classified in Industry 812910, Pet Care (except Veterinary) Services;

- Providing animal breeding services or boarding horses—are classified in Industry 115210, Support Activities for Animal Production; and

---

- Transporting pets—are classified in U.S. Industry 485991, Special Needs Transportation.

54199 All Other Professional, Scientific, and Technical Services
See industry description for 541990 below.

541990 All Other Professional, Scientific, and Technical Services

This industry comprises establishments primarily engaged in the provision of professional, scientific, or technical services (except legal services; accounting, tax preparation, bookkeeping, and related services; architectural, engineering, and related services; specialized design services; computer systems design and related services; management, scientific, and technical consulting services; scientific research and development services; advertising, public relations and related services; market research and public opinion polling; photographic services; translation and interpretation services; and veterinary services).

Illustrative Examples:

Appraisal (except real estate) services
Marine surveyor (i.e., appraiser) services
Arbitration and conciliation services
  (except by lawyer, attorney, or
  paralegal offices)
Patent broker services (i.e., patent
  marketing services)

Commodity inspector services
Pipeline or power line inspection
  (i.e., visual) services
Consumer credit counseling services
Weather forecasting services
Handwriting analysis services

Cross-References. Establishments primarily engaged in—

- Providing legal services—are classified in Industry Group 5411, Legal Services;

- Providing accounting, tax preparation, bookkeeping, and payroll services— are classified in Industry Group 5412, Accounting, Tax Preparation, Bookkeeping, and Payroll Services;

- Providing architectural, engineering, and related services—are classified in Industry Group 5413, Architectural, Engineering, and Related Services;

- Providing specialized design services—are classified in Industry Group 5414, Specialized Design Services;

- Providing computer systems design and related services—are classified in Industry Group 5415, Computer Systems Design and Related Services;

- Providing management, scientific, and technical consulting services—are classified in Industry Group 5416, Management, Scientific, and Technical Consulting Services;

US—United States industry only. CAN—United States and Canadian industries are comparable. MEX—United States and Mexican industries are comparable. Blank—Canadian, Mexican, and United States industries are comparable.

- Providing scientific research and development services—are classified in Industry Group 5417, Scientific Research and Development Services;

- Providing advertising and related services—are classified in Industry Group 5418, Advertising, Public Relations, and Related Services;

- Providing marketing research and public opinion polling—are classified in Industry 541910, Marketing Research and Public Opinion Polling;

- Providing photographic services—are classified in Industry 54192, Photographic Services;

- Providing translation and interpretation services—are classified in Industry 541930, Translation and Interpretation Services;

- Providing veterinary services—are classified in Industry 541940, Veterinary Services; and

- Providing real estate appraisal services—are classified in Industry 531320, Offices of Real Estate Appraisers.

Sector 55—Management of Companies and Enterprises

The Sector as a Whole

The Management of Companies and Enterprises sector comprises (1) establishments that hold the securities of (or other equity interests in) companies and enterprises for the purpose of owning a controlling interest or influencing management decisions or (2) establishments (except government establishments) that administer, oversee, and manage establishments of the company or enterprise and that normally undertake the strategic or organizational planning and decision making role of the company or enterprise. Establishments that administer, oversee, and manage may hold the securities of the company or enterprise.

Establishments in this sector perform essential activities that are often undertaken, in-house, by establishments in many sectors of the economy. By consolidating the performance of these activities of the enterprise at one establishment, economies of scale are achieved.

Government establishments primarily engaged in administering, overseeing, and managing governmental programs are classified in Sector 92, Public Administration. Establishments primarily engaged in providing a range of day-to-day office administrative services, such as financial planning, billing and recordkeeping, personnel, and physical distribution and logistics are classified in Industry 56111, Office Administrative Services.

551 Management of Companies and Enterprises

Industries in the Management of Companies and Enterprises subsector include three main types of establishments: (1) those that hold the securities of (or other equity interests in) companies and enterprises; (2) those (except government establishments) that administer, oversee, and manage other establishments of the company or enterprise but do not hold the securities of these establishments; and (3) those that both administer, oversee, and manage other establishments of the company or enterprise and hold the securities of (or other equity interests in) these establishments. Those establishments that administer, oversee, and manage normally undertake the strategic or organizational planning and decision making role of the company or enterprise.

5511 Management of Companies and Enterprises

55111 Management of Companies and Enterprises

This industry comprises (1) establishments primarily engaged in holding the securities of (or other equity interests in) companies and enterprises for the purpose

---

US—United States industry only. CAN—United States and Canadian industries are comparable. MEX—United States and Mexican industries are comparable. Blank—Canadian, Mexican, and United States industries are comparable.

of owning a controlling interest or influencing the management decisions or (2) establishments (except government establishments) that administer, oversee, and manage other establishments of the company or enterprise and that normally undertake the strategic or organizational planning and decision making role of the company or enterprise. Establishments that administer, oversee, and manage may hold the securities of the company or enterprise.

Cross-References.

- Establishments primarily engaged in holding the securities of companies or enterprises and operating these entities are classified according to the business operated;

- Establishments primarily engaged in holding the securities of depository banks and operating these entities are classified in Industry Group 5221, Depository Credit Intermediation;

- Establishments primarily engaged in providing a single service to other establishments of the company or enterprise, such as trucking, warehousing, research and development, and data processing are classified according to the service provided; and

- Government establishments primarily engaged in administering, overseeing, and managing governmental programs are classified in Sector 92, Public Administration.

551111 Offices of Bank Holding Companies[US]

This U.S. industry comprises legal entities known as bank holding companies primarily engaged in holding the securities of (or other equity interests in) companies and enterprises for the purpose of owning a controlling interest or influencing the management decisions of these firms. The holding companies in this industry do not administer, oversee, and manage other establishments of the company or enterprise whose securities they hold.

Cross-References. Establishments primarily engaged in—

- Holding the securities of (or other equity interests in) a company or enterprise and administering, overseeing, and managing establishments of the company or enterprise whose securities they hold—are classified in U.S. Industry 551114, Corporate, Subsidiary, and Regional Managing Offices; and

- Holding the securities of depository banks and operating these entities— are classified in Industry Group 5221, Depository Credit Intermediation.

551112 Offices of Other Holding Companies[US]

This U.S. industry comprises legal entities known as holding companies (except bank holding) primarily engaged in holding the securities of (or other equity interests in) companies and enterprises for the purpose of owning a controlling interest or influencing the management decisions of these firms. The holding companies in this industry do not administer, oversee, and manage other establishments of the company or enterprise whose securities they hold.

Cross-References. Establishments primarily engaged in—

- Holding the securities of (or other equity interests in) depository banks for the purpose of owning a controlling interest or influencing the management decisions of these firms—are classified in U.S. Industry 551111, Offices of Bank Holding Companies;

- Holding the securities of (or other equity interests in) a company or enterprise and administering, overseeing, and managing establishments of the company or enterprise whose securities they hold—are classified in U.S. Industry 551114, Corporate, Subsidiary, and Regional Managing Offices; and

- Holding the securities of companies or enterprises and operating these entities—are classified according to the business operated.

551114 Corporate, Subsidiary, and Regional Managing Offices[CAN]

This U.S. industry comprises establishments (except government establishments) primarily engaged in administering, overseeing, and managing other establishments of the company or enterprise. These establishments normally undertake the strategic or organizational planning and decision making role of the company or enterprise. Establishments in this industry may hold the securities of the company or enterprise.

Illustrative Examples:

Centralized administrative offices	Holding companies that manage
Head offices	District and regional offices
Corporate offices	Subsidiary management offices

Cross-References.

- Government establishments primarily engaged in administering, overseeing, and managing governmental programs are classified in Sector 92, Public Administration;

- Legal entities known as bank holding companies that do not administer, oversee, and manage other establishments of the companies or enterprises

US—United States industry only. CAN—United States and Canadian industries are comparable. MEX—United States and Mexican industries are comparable. Blank—Canadian, Mexican, and United States industries are comparable.

whose securities they hold are classified in U.S. Industry 551111, Offices of Bank Holding Companies; and

- Legal entities known as holding companies (except bank holding) that do not administer, oversee, and manage other establishments of the companies or enterprises whose securities they hold are classified in U.S. Industry 551112, Offices of Other Holding Companies.

Sector 56—Administrative and Support and Waste Management and Remediation Services

The Sector as a Whole

The Administrative and Support and Waste Management and Remediation Services sector comprises establishments performing routine support activities for the day-to-day operations of other organizations. These essential activities are often undertaken in-house by establishments in many sectors of the economy. The establishments in this sector specialize in one or more of these support activities and provide these services to clients in a variety of industries and, in some cases, to households. Activities performed include: office administration, hiring and placing of personnel, document preparation and similar clerical services, solicitation, collection, security and surveillance services, cleaning, and waste disposal services.

The administrative and management activities performed by establishments in this sector are typically on a contract or fee basis. These activities may also be performed by establishments that are part of the company or enterprise. However, establishments involved in administering, overseeing, and managing other establishments of the company or enterprise, are classified in Sector 55, Management of Companies and Enterprises. Establishments in Sector 55 normally undertake the strategic and organizational planning and decision making role of the company or enterprise. Government establishments engaged in administering, overseeing, and managing governmental programs are classified in Sector 92, Public Administration.

561 Administrative and Support Services

Industries in the Administrative and Support Services subsector group establishments engaged in activities that support the day-to-day operations of other organizations. The processes employed in this sector (e.g., general management, personnel administration, clerical activities, cleaning activities) are often integral parts of the activities of establishments found in all sectors of the economy. The establishments classified in this subsector have specialization in one or more of these activities and can, therefore, provide services to clients in a variety of industries and, in some cases, to households. The individual industries of this subsector are defined on the basis of the particular process that they are engaged in and the particular services they provide.

Many of the activities performed in this subsector are ongoing routine support functions that all businesses and organizations must do and that they have traditionally done for themselves. Recent trends, however, are to contract or purchase such

US—United States industry only. CAN—United States and Canadian industries are comparable. MEX—United States and Mexican industries are comparable. Blank—Canadian, Mexican, and United States industries are comparable.

services from businesses that specialize in such activities and can, therefore, provide the services more efficiently.

The industries in this subsector cannot be viewed as strictly "support." The Travel Arrangement and Reservation Services industry group, includes travel agents, tour operators, and providers of other travel arrangement services, such as hotel and restaurant reservations and arranging the purchase of tickets, serving many types of clients, including individual consumers. This group was placed in this subsector because the services are often of the "support" nature (e.g., travel arrangement) and businesses and other organizations are increasingly the ones purchasing such services.

The administrative and management activities performed by establishments in this sector are typically on a contract or fee basis. These activities may also be performed by establishments that are part of the company or enterprise. However, establishments involved in administering, overseeing, and managing other establishments of the company or enterprise, are classified in Sector 55, Management of Companies and Enterprises. Establishments in Sector 55 normally undertake the strategic and organizational planning and decision making role of the company or enterprise. Government establishments engaged in administering, overseeing, and managing governmental programs are classified in Sector 92, Public Administration.

5611   Office Administrative Services

56111   Office Administrative Services
See industry description for 561110 below.

561110   Office Administrative Services

This industry comprises establishments primarily engaged in providing a range of day-to-day office administrative services, such as financial planning; billing and recordkeeping; personnel; and physical distribution and logistics for others on a contract or fee basis. These establishments do not provide operating staff to carry out the complete operations of a business.

Cross-References. Establishments primarily engaged in—

- Holding the securities or financial assets of companies and enterprises for the purpose of controlling them and influencing their management decisions—are classified in U.S. Industry 551111, Offices of Bank Holding Companies or U.S. Industry 551112, Offices of Other Holding Companies;

- Administering, overseeing, and managing other establishments of the company or enterprise (except government establishments)—are classified in

---

US—United States industry only. CAN- –United States and Canadian industries are comparable. MEX—United States and Mexican industries are comparable. Blank—Canadian, Mexican, and United States industries are comparable.

U.S. Industry 551114, Corporate, Subsidiary, and Regional Managing Offices;

- Providing computer facilities management—are classified in U.S. Industry 541513, Computer Facilities Management Services;

- Providing construction management—are classified in Sector 23, Construction, by type of construction project managed;

- Providing farm management—are classified in U.S. Industry 115116, Farm Management Services;

- Managing real property for others—are classified in Industry 53131, Real Estate Property Managers;

- Providing food services management at institutional, governmental, commercial, or industrial locations—are classified in Industry 722310, Food Service Contractors;

- Providing management advice without day-to-day management—are classified in Industry 54161, Management Consulting Services;

- Providing both management and operating staff for the complete operation of a client's business, such as a hotel, restaurant, mine site, or hospital—are classified according to the industry of the establishment operated; and

- Providing only one of the support services (e.g., accounting services) that establishments in this industry provide—are classified in the appropriate industry according to the service provided.

5612 Facilities Support Services

56121 Facilities Support Services
See industry description for 561210 below.

561210 Facilities Support Services

This industry comprises establishments primarily engaged in providing operating staff to perform a combination of support services within a client's facilities. Establishments in this industry typically provide a combination of services, such as janitorial, maintenance, trash disposal, guard and security, mail routing, reception, laundry, and related services to support operations within facilities. These establishments provide operating staff to carry out these support activities; but are not involved with or responsible for the core business or activities of the client. Establishments providing facilities (except computer and/or data processing) operation support services and establishments providing private jail services or operating correctional facilities (i.e., jails) on a contract or fee basis are included in this industry.

Cross-References.

- Establishments primarily engaged in providing only one of the support services (e.g., janitorial services) that establishments in this industry provide are classified in the appropriate industry according to the service provided;

- Establishments primarily engaged in providing management and operating staff for the complete operation of a client's establishment, such as a hotel, restaurant, mine, or hospital, are classified according to the industry of the establishment operated;

- Establishments primarily engaged in providing on-site management and operation of a client's computer systems and/or data processing facilities are classified in U.S. Industry 541513, Computer Facilities Management Services; and

- Governmental correctional institutions are classified in Industry 922140, Correctional Institutions.

5613 Employment Services

56131 Employment Placement Agencies and Executive Search Services

This industry comprises establishments primarily engaged in one of the following: 1) listing employment vacancies and referring or placing applicants for employment; or 2) providing executive search, recruitment, and placement services.

Illustrative Examples:

Employment agencies   Executive search services
Executive placement services

Cross-References. Establishments primarily engaged in—

- Supplying their own employees for limited periods of time to supplement the working force of a client's business—are classified in Industry 56132, Temporary Help Services;

- Providing human resources and human resource management services to clients—are classified in Industry 56133, Professional Employer Organizations;

- Providing advice and assistance on human resource and personnel policies, practices, and procedures; and employee benefits and compensation sys-

---

tems—are classified in U.S. Industry 54161, Management Consulting Services; and

- Representing models, entertainers, athletes, and other public figures as their agent or manager—are classified in Industry 71141, Agents and Managers for Artists, Athletes, Entertainers, and Other Public Figures.

561311 Employment Placement Agencies[US]

This U.S. industry comprises establishments primarily engaged in listing employment vacancies and in referring or placing applicants for employment. The individuals referred or placed are not employees of the employment agencies.

Illustrative Examples:

Babysitting bureaus (i.e., registries)   Model registries
Employment registries   Employment agencies
Casting agencies or bureaus (i.e., motion
  picture, theatrical, video)

Cross-References. Establishments primarily engaged in—

- Providing executive search, recruitment, and placement services—are classified in U.S. Industry 561312, Executive Search Services;

- Supplying their own employees for limited periods of time to supplement the working force of a client's business—are classified in Industry 561320, Temporary Help Services;

- Providing human resources and human resource management services to clients—are classified in Industry 561330, Professional Employer Organizations; and

- Representing models, entertainers, athletes, and other public figures as their agent or manager—are classified in Industry 711410, Agents and Managers for Artists, Athletes, Entertainers, and Other Public Figures.

561312 Executive Search Services[US]

This U.S. industry comprises establishments primarily engaged in providing executive search, recruitment, and placement services for clients with specific executive and senior management position requirements. The range of services provided by these establishments may include developing a search strategy and position specification based on the culture and needs of the client; researching, identifying, screening, and interviewing candidates; verifying candidate qualifications; and assisting in final offer negotiations and assimilation of the selected candidate. The individuals identified, recruited, or placed are not employees of the executive search services establishments.

Illustrative Examples:

Senior executive search services   Executive search services
Executive placement services

Cross-References. Establishments primarily engaged in—

- Listing employment vacancies and in referring or placing applicants for employment—are classified in U.S. Industry 561311, Employment Placement Agencies;

- Supplying their own employees for limited periods of time to supplement the working force of a client's business—are classified in Industry 561320, Temporary Help Services;

- Providing human resources and human resource management services to clients—are classified in Industry 561330, Professional Employer Organizations;

- Providing advice and assistance on human resource and personnel policies, practices, and procedures; and employee benefits and compensation systems—are classified in U.S. Industry 541612, Human Resources Consulting Services; and

- Representing models, entertainers, athletes, and other public figures as their agent or manager—are classified in Industry 711410, Agents and Managers for Artists, Athletes, Entertainers, and Other Public Figures.

56132 Temporary Help Services
See industry description for 561320 below.

561320 Temporary Help Services

This industry comprises establishments primarily engaged in supplying workers to clients' businesses for limited periods of time to supplement the working force of the client. The individuals provided are employees of the temporary help service establishment. However, these establishments do not provide direct supervision of their employees at the clients' work sites.

Illustrative Examples:

Help supply services   Temporary employment or temporary
Model supply services   staffing services

US—United States industry only. CAN—United States and Canadian industries are comparable. MEX—United States and Mexican industries are comparable. Blank—Canadian, Mexican, and United States industries are comparable.

Labor (except farm) contractors   Manpower pools
(i.e., personnel suppliers)

Cross-References. Establishments primarily engaged in—

- Providing human resources and human resource management services to clients—are classified in Industry 561330, Professional Employer Organizations;

- Supplying farm labor—are classified in U.S. Industry 115115, Farm Labor Contractors and Crew Leaders;

- Providing operating staff to perform a combination of services to support operations within a client's facilities—are classified in Industry 561210, Facilities Support Services;

- Listing employment vacancies and referring or placing applicants for employment—are classified in Industry 561311, Employment Placement Agencies; and

- Representing models, entertainers, athletes, and other public figures as their agent or manager—are classified in Industry 711410, Agents and Managers for Artists, Athletes, Entertainers, and Other Public Figures.

56133 Professional Employer Organizations

See industry description for 561330 below.

561330 Professional Employer Organizations

This industry comprises establishments primarily engaged in providing human resources and human resource management services to client businesses. Establishments in this industry operate in a coemployment relationship with client businesses or organizations and are specialized in performing a wide range of human resource and personnel management duties, such as payroll, payroll tax, benefits administration, workers' compensation, unemployment, and human resource administration. Professional employer organizations (PEOs) are responsible for payroll, including withholding and remitting employment-related taxes, for some or all of the employees of their clients, and also serve as the employer of those employees for benefits and related purposes.

Cross-References. Establishments primarily engaged in—

- Supplying their own employees for limited periods of time to supplement the working force of a client's business—are classified in Industry 561320, Temporary Help Services; and

---

US—United States industry only. CAN—United States and Canadian industries are comparable. MEX—United States and Mexican industries are comparable. Blank—Canadian, Mexican, and United States industries are comparable.

- Listing employment vacancies and in referring or placing applicants for employment—are classified in Industry 561311, Employment Placement Agencies.

5614 Business Support Services

This industry group comprises establishments engaged in performing activities that are ongoing routine business support functions that businesses and organizations traditionally do for themselves.

56141 Document Preparation Services
See industry description for 561410 below.

561410 Document Preparation Services

This industry comprises establishments primarily engaged in one or more of the following: (1) letter or resume writing; (2) document editing or proofreading; (3) typing, word processing, or desktop publishing; and (4) stenography (except court reporting or stenotype recording), transcription, and other secretarial services.

Cross-References. Establishments primarily engaged in—

- Providing verbatim reporting and stenotype recording of live legal proceedings and transcribing subsequent recorded materials—are classified in U.S. Industry 561492, Court Reporting and Stenotype Services;
- Performing prepress and postpress services in support of printing activities—are classified in Industry 32312, Support Activities for Printing;
- Providing document translation services—are classified in Industry 541930, Translation and Interpretation Services;
- Photocopying, duplicating, and other document copying services, with or without a range of other office support services (except printing)—are classified in U.S. Industry 561439, Other Business Service Centers (including Copy Shops); and
- Providing document copying services in combination with printing services, with or without a range of other office support services, and establishments known as quick or digital printers—are classified in Industry 32311, Printing.

56142 Telephone Call Centers

This industry comprises (1) establishments primarily engaged in answering telephone calls and relaying messages to clients and (2) establishments primarily

US—United States industry only. CAN—United States and Canadian industries are comparable. MEX—United States and Mexican industries are comparable. Blank—Canadian, Mexican, and United States industries are comparable.

engaged in providing telemarketing services on a contract or fee basis for others, such as promoting clients' products or services by telephone; taking orders for clients by telephone; and soliciting contributions or providing information for clients by telephone. Telemarketing establishments never own the product or provide the service that they are representing and generally can originate and/or receive calls for others.

Cross-References. Establishments primarily engaged in—

- Providing paging and beeper transmission services—are classified in Industry 51721, Wireless Telecommunications Carriers (except Satellite);
- Organizing and conducting fundraising campaigns on a contract or fee basis, that may include telephone solicitation services—are classified in Industry 56149, Other Business Support Services; and
- Gathering, recording, tabulating, and presenting marketing and public opinion data, that may include telephone canvassing services—are classified in Industry 54191, Marketing Research and Public Opinion Polling.

561421 Telephone Answering Services[US]

This U.S. industry comprises establishments primarily engaged in answering telephone calls and relaying messages to clients.

Cross-References.

Establishments primarily engaged in providing paging or beeper transmission services are classified in Industry 517210, Wireless Telecommunications Carriers (except Satellite).

561422 Telemarketing Bureaus and Other Contact Centers[MEX]

This U.S. industry comprises establishments primarily engaged in operating call centers that initiate or receive communications for others-via telephone, facsimile, email, or other communication modes-for purposes such as: (1) promoting clients' products or services, (2) taking orders for clients, (3) soliciting contributions for a client; and (4) providing information or assistance regarding a client's products or services. These establishments do not own the product or provide the services they are representing on behalf of clients.

Cross-References. Establishments primarily engaged in—

- Answering telephone calls and relaying messages to clients—are classified in U.S. Industry 561421, Telephone Answering Services;

US—United States industry only. CAN—United States and Canadian industries are comparable. MEX—United States and Mexican industries are comparable. Blank—Canadian, Mexican, and United States industries are comparable.

- Organizing and conducting fundraising campaigns on a contract or fee basis, that may include telephone solicitation services—are classified in U.S. Industry 561499, All Other Business Support Services; and

- Gathering, recording, tabulating, and presenting marketing and public opinion data, that may include telephone canvassing services—are classified in Industry 541910, Marketing Research and Public Opinion Polling.

56143 Business Service Centers

This industry comprises (1) establishments primarily engaged in providing mailbox rental and other postal and mailing services (except direct mail advertising); (2) establishments, generally known as copy centers or shops, primarily engaged in providing photocopying, duplicating, blueprinting, and other document copying services without also providing printing services (i.e., offset printing, quick printing, digital printing, prepress services); and (3) establishments that provide a range of office support services (except printing services), such as mailing services, document copying services, facsimile services, word processing services, on-site PC rental services, and office product sales.

Cross-References. Establishments primarily engaged in—

- Operating contract post offices—are classified in Industry 49111, Postal Service;

- Delivering letters and parcels (except under a universal service obligation)— are classified in Subsector 492, Couriers and Messengers;

- Providing voice mailbox services—are classified in Industry 56142, Telephone Call Centers;

- Providing direct mail advertising services—are classified in Industry 54186, Direct Mail Advertising;

- Providing full service office space, whether on a lease or service contract basis—are classified in Industry 53112, Lessors of Nonresidential Buildings (except Miniwarehouses);

- Providing document copying services in combination with printing services, with or without a range of other office support services, and establishments known as quick or digital printers—are classified in Industry 32311, Printing; and

- Providing only one of the support services (e.g., word processing services) that establishments in this industry provide—are classified in the appropriate industry according to the service provided.

US—United States industry only. CAN—United States and Canadian industries are comparable. MEX—United States and Mexican industries are comparable. Blank—Canadian, Mexican, and United States industries are comparable.

http://www.census.gov/naics

561431 Private Mail Centers[US]

This U.S. industry comprises (1) establishments primarily engaged in providing mailbox rental and other postal and mailing (except direct mail advertising) services or (2) establishments engaged in providing these mailing services along with one or more other office support services, such as facsimile services, word processing services, on-site PC rental services, and office product sales.

Cross-References. Establishments primarily engaged in—

- Operating contract post offices—are classified in Industry 491110, Postal Service;
- Delivering letters and parcels (except under a universal service obligation)— are classified in Subsector 492, Couriers and Messengers;
- Providing voice mailbox services—are classified in U.S. Industry 561421, Telephone Answering Services;
- Providing direct mail advertising services—are classified in Industry 541860, Direct Mail Advertising;
- Providing only one of the support services (e.g., word processing services) that establishments in this industry provide—are classified in the appropriate industry according to the service provided; and
- Providing full service office space, whether on a lease or service contract basis—are classified in Industry 531120, Lessors of Nonresidential Buildings (except Miniwarehouses).

561439 Other Business Service Centers (including Copy Shops)[US]

This U.S. industry comprises (1) establishments generally known as copy centers or shops primarily engaged in providing photocopying, duplicating, blueprinting, and other document copying services, without also providing printing services (e.g., offset printing, quick printing, digital printing, prepress services) and (2) establishments (except private mail centers) engaged in providing a range of office support services (except printing services), such as document copying services, facsimile services, word processing services, on-site PC rental services, and office product sales.

Cross-References.

- Establishments engaged in providing document copying services in combination with printing services, with or without a range of other office support services, and establishments known as quick or digital printers are classified in Industry 32311, Printing;

- Establishments engaged in providing mailbox rental and other postal and mailing services with or without one or more other office support services (except printing) are classified in U.S. Industry 561431, Private Mail Centers;

- Establishments exclusively engaged in providing a single office support service (except document copying) to clients, but not the range of office support services that establishments in this industry may provide, are classified according to the service provided; and

- Establishments engaged in providing full service office space, whether on a lease or service contract basis, are classified in Industry 531120, Lessors of Nonresidential Buildings (except Miniwarehouses).

56144   Collection Agencies
See industry description for 561440 below.

561440   Collection Agencies

This industry comprises establishments primarily engaged in collecting payments for claims and remitting payments collected to their clients.

Illustrative Examples:

Account or delinquent account collection services	Bill or debt collection services
Tax collection services on a contract or fee basis	

Cross-References. Establishments primarily engaged in—

- Repossessing tangible assets—are classified in U.S. Industry 561491, Repossession Services; and

- Providing financing to others by factoring accounts receivables (i.e., assuming the risk of collection and credit losses)—are classified in U.S. Industry 522298, All Other Nondepository Credit Intermediation.

56145   Credit Bureaus
See industry description for 561450 below.

561450   Credit Bureaus

This industry comprises establishments primarily engaged in compiling information, such as credit and employment histories on individuals and credit histories

---

on businesses, and providing the information to financial institutions, retailers, and others who have a need to evaluate the creditworthiness of these persons and businesses.

Illustrative Examples:

Credit agencies   Credit investigation services
Credit rating services   Credit reporting bureaus

56149 Other Business Support Services

This industry comprises establishments primarily engaged in providing business support services (except secretarial and other document preparation services; telephone answering or telemarketing services; private mail services or document copying services conducted as separate activities or in conjunction with other office support services; monetary debt collection services; and credit reporting services).

Illustrative Examples:

Address bar coding services   Court reporting services
Mail presorting services   Repossession services
Bar code imprinting services   Fundraising organization services on a
Real-time (i.e., simultaneous) closed   contract or fee basis
  captioning of live television
  performances, meetings, conferences

Cross-References. Establishments primarily engaged in—

- Providing secretarial and other document preparation services—are classified in Industry 56141, Document Preparation Services;

- Providing telephone answering or telemarketing services—are classified in Industry 56142, Telephone Call Centers;

- Providing private mail services; document copying services (except printing services); and/or a range of office support services (except printing)—are classified in Industry 56143, Business Service Centers;

- Providing document copying services in combination with printing services, with or without a range of other office support services, and establishments known as quick or digital printers—are classified in Industry 32311, Printing;

- Providing monetary debt collection services—are classified in Industry 56144, Collection Agencies;

- Providing credit reporting services—are classified in Industry 56145, Credit Bureaus; and

---

- Providing film or tape captioning or subtitling services—are classified in Industry 51219, Postproduction Services and Other Motion Picture and Video Industries.

561491 Repossession Services[US]

This U.S. industry comprises establishments primarily engaged in repossessing tangible assets (e.g., automobiles, boats, equipment, planes, furniture, appliances) for the creditor as a result of delinquent debts.

Cross-References.

Establishments primarily engaged in providing monetary debt collection services are classified in Industry 561440, Collection Agencies.

561492 Court Reporting and Stenotype Services[US]

This U.S. industry comprises establishments primarily engaged in providing verbatim reporting and stenotype recording of live legal proceedings and transcribing subsequent recorded materials.

Illustrative Examples:

Court reporting or stenotype recording services

Real-time (i.e., simultaneous) closed captioning of live television performances, meetings, conferences

Public stenography services

Cross-References. Establishments primarily engaged in—

- Providing stenotype recording of correspondence, reports, and other documents or in providing document transcription services—are classified in Industry 561410, Document Preparation Services; and

- Providing film or tape captioning or subtitling services—are classified in U.S. Industry 512191, Teleproduction and Other Postproduction Services.

561499 All Other Business Support Services[US]

This U.S. industry comprises establishments primarily engaged in providing business support services (except secretarial and other document preparation services; telephone answering and telemarketing services; private mail services or document copying services conducted as separate activities or in conjunction with other office support services; monetary debt collection services; credit reporting services; repossession services; and court reporting and stenotype recording services).

Illustrative Examples:

Address bar coding services	Bar code imprinting services
Fundraising organization services on a contract or fee basis	Mail presorting services

Cross-References. Establishments primarily engaged in—

- Providing secretarial and other document preparation services—are classified in Industry 561410, Document Preparation Services;

- Providing telephone answering or telemarketing services—are classified in Industry 56142, Telephone Call Centers;

- Providing private mail services, document copying services without printing services and/or a range of office support services—are classified in Industry 56143, Business Service Centers;

- Providing document copying services in combination with printing services (with or without one or more other office support services) and establishments known as quick or digital printers—are classified in Industry 32311, Printing;

- Providing monetary debt collection services—are classified in Industry 561440, Collection Agencies;

- Providing credit reporting services—are classified in Industry 561450, Credit Bureaus;

- Providing repossession services—are classified in U.S. Industry 561491, Repossession Services; and

- Providing court reporting and stenotype services—are classified in U.S. Industry 561492, Court Reporting and Stenotype Services.

5615 Travel Arrangement and Reservation Services

56151 Travel Agencies
See industry description for 561510 below.

561510 Travel Agencies

This industry comprises establishments primarily engaged in acting as agents in selling travel, tour, and accommodation services to the general public and commercial clients.

US—United States industry only. CAN—United States and Canadian industries are comparable. MEX—United States and Mexican industries are comparable. Blank—Canadian, Mexican, and United States industries are comparable.

Cross-References. Establishments primarily engaged in—

- Arranging and assembling tours that they generally sell through travel agencies or on their own account—are classified in Industry 561520, Tour Operators;

- Providing guide services, such as archeological, museum, tourist, hunting, or fishing—are classified in Industry 713990, All Other Amusement and Recreation Industries; and

- Providing reservation services (e.g., accommodations, entertainment events, travel)—are classified in U.S. Industry 561599, All Other Travel Arrangement and Reservation Services.

56152 Tour Operators

See industry description for 561520 below.

561520 Tour Operators

This industry comprises establishments primarily engaged in arranging and assembling tours. The tours are sold through travel agencies or tour operators. Travel or wholesale tour operators are included in this industry.

Cross-References. Establishments primarily engaged in—

- Acting as agents in selling travel, tour, and accommodation services to the general public and commercial clients—are classified in Industry 561510, Travel Agencies;

- Conducting scenic and sightseeing tours—are classified in Subsector 487, Scenic and Sightseeing Transportation; and

- Providing guide services, such as archeological, museum, tourist, hunting, or fishing—are classified in Industry 713990, All Other Amusement and Recreation Industries.

56159 Other Travel Arrangement and Reservation Services

This industry comprises establishments (except travel agencies and tour operators) primarily engaged in providing travel arrangement and reservation services.

Illustrative Examples:

Condominium time-share exchange services	Reservation (e.g., airline, car rental, hotel, restaurant) services
Road and travel services automobile clubs	Ticket (e.g., amusement, sports, theatrical) agencies
Convention or visitors bureaus	
Ticket (e.g., airline, bus, cruise ship, sports, theatrical) offices	

Cross-References.

- Establishments primarily engaged in arranging the rental of vacation properties are classified in Industry 53121, Offices of Real Estate Agents and Brokers;

- Travel agencies are classified in Industry 56151, Travel Agencies;

- Tour operators are classified in Industry 56152, Tour Operators;

- Automobile clubs (i.e., enthusiasts' clubs) (except road and travel services) are classified in Industry 81341, Civic and Social Organizations; and

- Establishments primarily engaged in organizing, promoting, and/or managing events, such as business and trade shows, conventions, conferences, and meetings (whether or not they manage and provide the staff to operate the facilities in which these events take place), are classified in Industry 56192, Convention and Trade Show Organizers.

561591 Convention and Visitors Bureaus[US]

This U.S. industry comprises establishments primarily engaged in marketing and promoting communities and facilities to businesses and leisure travelers through a range of activities, such as assisting organizations in locating meeting and convention sites; providing travel information on area attractions, lodging accommodations, restaurants; providing maps; and organizing group tours of local historical, recreational, and cultural attractions.

Cross-References.

Establishments primarily engaged in organizing, promoting, and/or managing events, such as business and trade shows, conventions, conferences, and meetings (whether or not they manage and provide the staff to operate the facilities in which these events take place) are classified in Industry 561920, Convention and Trade Show Organizers.

561599 All Other Travel Arrangement and Reservation Services[US]

This U.S. industry comprises establishments (except travel agencies, tour operators, and convention and visitors bureaus) primarily engaged in providing travel arrangement and reservation services.

Illustrative Examples:

Condominium time-share exchange services	Ticket (e.g., amusement, sports, theatrical) agencies

---

US—United States industry only. CAN—United States and Canadian industries are comparable. MEX—United States and Mexican industries are comparable. Blank—Canadian, Mexican, and United States industries are comparable.

Ticket (e.g., airline, bus, cruise ship, sports, theatrical) offices
Reservation (e.g., airline, car rental, hotel, restaurant) services

Road and travel services automobile clubs

Cross-References.

- Establishments primarily engaged in arranging the rental of vacation properties are classified in Industry 531210, Offices of Real Estate Agents and Brokers;

- Travel agencies are classified in Industry 561510, Travel Agencies;

- Tour operators are classified in Industry 561520, Tour Operators;

- Convention and visitors bureaus are classified in U.S. Industry 561591, Convention and Visitors Bureaus;

- Establishments primarily engaged in organizing, promoting, and/or managing events, such as business and trade shows, conventions, conferences, and meetings (whether or not they manage and provide the staff to operate the facilities in which these events take place) are classified in Industry 561920, Convention and Trade Show Organizers; and

- Automobile clubs (i.e., enthusiasts' clubs) (except road and travel services) are classified in Industry 813410, Civic and Social Organizations.

5616 Investigation and Security Services

56161 Investigation, Guard, and Armored Car Services

This industry comprises establishments primarily engaged in providing one or more of the following: (1) investigation and detective services; (2) guard and patrol services; and (3) picking up and delivering money, receipts, or other valuable items with personnel and equipment to protect such properties while in transit.

Illustrative Examples:

Armored car services
Private detective services
Bodyguard services

Security guard services
Polygraph services

Cross-References. Establishments primarily engaged in—

- Providing credit checks—are classified in Industry 56145, Credit Bureaus; and

- Selling, installing, monitoring, and maintaining security systems and devices (e.g., burglar and fire alarm systems)—are classified in Industry 56162, Security Systems Services.

561611 Investigation Services^{CAN}

This U.S. industry comprises establishments primarily engaged in providing investigation and detective services.

Illustrative Examples:

Fingerprinting services	Polygraph services
Private detective services	Private investigative services

Cross-References.

Establishments primarily engaged in providing credit checks are classified in Industry 561450, Credit Bureaus.

561612 Security Guards and Patrol Services^{CAN}

This U.S. industry comprises establishments primarily engaged in providing guard and patrol services, such as bodyguard, guard dog, and parking security services.

Cross-References.

Establishments primarily engaged in selling, installing, monitoring, and maintaining security systems and devices, such as burglar and fire alarms and locking devices, are classified in Industry 56162, Security Systems Services.

561613 Armored Car Services^{CAN}

This U.S. industry comprises establishments primarily engaged in picking up and delivering money, receipts, or other valuable items. These establishments maintain personnel and equipment to protect such properties while in transit.

56162 Security Systems Services

This industry comprises establishments engaged in (1) selling security systems, such as burglar and fire alarms and locking devices, along with installation, repair, or monitoring services or (2) remote monitoring of electronic security alarm systems.

Cross-References. Establishments primarily engaged in—

- Selling security systems for buildings without installation, repair, or monitoring services—are classified in Sector 42, Wholesale Trade or Sector 44-45, Retail Trade;

US—United States industry only. CAN—United States and Canadian industries are comparable. MEX—United States and Mexican industries are comparable. Blank—Canadian, Mexican, and United States industries are comparable.

- Retailing motor vehicle security systems with or without installation or repair services—are classified in Industry 44131, Automotive Parts and Accessories Stores; and

- Providing key duplication services—are classified in Industry 81149, Other Personal and Household Goods Repair and Maintenance.

561621 Security Systems Services (except Locksmiths)^{CAN}

This U.S. industry comprises establishments primarily engaged in (1) selling security alarm systems, such as burglar and fire alarms, along with installation, repair, or monitoring services or (2) remote monitoring of electronic security alarm systems.

Cross-References. Establishments primarily engaged in—

- Selling security alarm systems for buildings, without installation, repair, or monitoring services—are classified in Sector 42, Wholesale Trade or Sector 44-45, Retail Trade; and

- Retailing motor vehicle security systems with or without installation or repair services—are classified in Industry 441310, Automotive Parts and Accessories Stores.

561622 Locksmiths^{CAN}

This U.S. industry comprises establishments primarily engaged in (1) selling mechanical or electronic locking devices, safes, and security vaults, along with installation, repair, rebuilding, or adjusting services or (2) installing, repairing, rebuilding, and adjusting mechanical or electronic locking devices, safes, and security vaults.

Cross-References. Establishments primarily engaged in—

- Selling security systems, such as locking devices, safes, and vaults, without installation or maintenance services—are classified in Sector 42, Wholesale Trade or Sector 44-45, Retail Trade; and

- Providing key duplication services—are classified in Industry 811490, Other Personal and Household Goods Repair and Maintenance.

5617 Services to Buildings and Dwellings

56171 Exterminating and Pest Control Services
See industry description for 561710 below.

561710 Exterminating and Pest Control Services

This industry comprises establishments primarily engaged in exterminating and controlling birds, mosquitoes, rodents, termites, and other insects and pests (except for crop production and forestry production). Establishments providing fumigation services are included in this industry.

Cross-References.

Establishments primarily engaged in providing pest control for crop or forestry production are classified in Subsector 115, Support Activities for Agriculture and Forestry.

56172 Janitorial Services
See industry description for 561720 below.

561720 Janitorial Services^{MEX}

This industry comprises establishments primarily engaged in cleaning building interiors, interiors of transportation equipment (e.g., aircraft, rail cars, ships), and/or windows.

Illustrative Examples:

Custodial services	Housekeeping (i.e., cleaning) services
Service station cleaning and degreasing services	Washroom sanitation services
	Maid (i.e., cleaning) services

Cross-References. Establishments primarily engaged in—

- Cleaning building exteriors (except sandblasting and window cleaning) or chimneys—are classified in Industry 561790, Other Services to Buildings and Dwellings; and

- Sandblasting building exteriors—are classified in Industry 238990, All Other Specialty Trade Contractors.

56173 Landscaping Services
See industry description for 561730 below.

561730 Landscaping Services

This industry comprises (1) establishments primarily engaged in providing landscape care and maintenance services and/or installing trees, shrubs, plants, lawns,

---

US—United States industry only. CAN—United States and Canadian industries are comparable. MEX—United States and Mexican industries are comparable. Blank—Canadian, Mexican, and United States industries are comparable.

or gardens and (2) establishments primarily engaged in providing these services along with the design of landscape plans and/or the construction (i.e., installation) of walkways, retaining walls, decks, fences, ponds, and similar structures.

Cross-References. Establishments primarily engaged in—

- Installing artificial turf or in constructing (i.e., installing) walkways, retaining walls, decks, fences, ponds, or similar structures—are classified in Sector 23, Construction;

- Planning and designing the development of land areas for projects, such as parks and other recreational areas; airports; highways; hospitals; schools; land subdivisions; and commercial, industrial, and residential areas (without also installing trees, shrubs, plants, lawns/gardens, walkways, retaining walls, decks, and similar items or structures)—are classified in Industry 541320, Landscape Architectural Services; and

- Retailing landscaping materials and providing the installation and maintenance of these materials—are classified in Industry 444220, Nursery, Garden Center, and Farm Supply Stores.

56174 Carpet and Upholstery Cleaning Services
See industry description for 561740 below.

561740 Carpet and Upholstery Cleaning Services

This industry comprises establishments primarily engaged in cleaning and dyeing used rugs, carpets, and upholstery.

Cross-References. Establishments primarily engaged in—

- Rug repair not associated with rug cleaning—are classified in Industry 811490, Other Personal and Household Goods Repair and Maintenance; and

- Reupholstering and repairing furniture—are classified in Industry 811420, Reupholstery and Furniture Repair.

56179 Other Services to Buildings and Dwellings
See industry description for 561790 below.

561790 Other Services to Buildings and Dwellings^MEX

This industry comprises establishments primarily engaged in providing services to buildings and dwellings (except exterminating and pest control; janitorial; landscaping care and maintenance; and carpet and upholstery cleaning).

US—United States industry only. CAN— United States and Canadian industries are comparable. MEX—United States and Mexican industries are comparable. Blank—Canadian, Mexican, and United States industries are comparable.

Illustrative Examples:

Building exterior cleaning services
(except sandblasting and window
cleaning)
Swimming pool cleaning and
maintenance services

Chimney cleaning services
Ventilation duct cleaning services
Drain or gutter cleaning services

Cross-References. Establishments primarily engaged in—

- Providing exterminating and pest control services—are classified in Industry 561710, Exterminating and Pest Control Services;

- Providing janitorial services—are classified in Industry 561720, Janitorial Services;

- Providing landscaping care and maintenance—are classified in Industry 561730, Landscaping Services;

- Providing carpet and upholstery cleaning services—are classified in Industry 561740, Carpet and Upholstery Cleaning Services; and

- Sandblasting building exteriors—are classified in Industry 238990, All Other Specialty Trade Contractors.

5619 Other Support Services

This industry group comprises establishments primarily engaged in providing day-to-day business and other organizational support services (except office administrative services; facilities support services; employment services; business support services; travel arrangement and reservation services; security and investigation services; and services to buildings and dwellings).

56191 Packaging and Labeling Services

See industry description for 561910 below.

561910 Packaging and Labeling Services

This industry comprises establishments primarily engaged in packaging client-owned materials. The services may include labeling and/or imprinting the package.

Illustrative Examples:

Apparel and textile folding and
packaging services
Kit assembling and packaging services

Blister packaging services
Shrink-wrapping services
Gift wrapping services

Cross-References. Establishments primarily engaged in—

- Processing client-owned materials into a different product, such as mixing water and concentrate to produce soft drinks—are classified in Sector 31-33, Manufacturing;
- Providing aerosol packaging services—are classified in U.S. Industry 325998, All Other Miscellaneous Chemical Product and Preparation Manufacturing;
- Providing packing and crating services incidental to transportation—are classified in U.S. Industry 488991, Packing and Crating;
- Providing warehousing services, as well as packaging or other logistics services—are classified in Industry Group 4931, Warehousing and Storage; and
- Providing packing and crating services for agricultural products—are classified in U.S. Industry 115114, Postharvest Crop Activities (except Cotton Ginning).

56192   Convention and Trade Show Organizers

See industry description for 561920 below.

561920   Convention and Trade Show Organizers

This industry comprises establishments primarily engaged in organizing, promoting, and/or managing events, such as business and trade shows, conventions, conferences, and meetings (whether or not they manage and provide the staff to operate the facilities in which these events take place).

Cross-References.

Establishments primarily engaged in organizing, promoting, and/or managing live performing arts productions, sports events, and similar events, such as festivals (whether or not they manage and provide the staff to operate the facilities in which these events take place), are classified in Industry Group 7113, Promoters of Performing Arts, Sports, and Similar Events.

56199   All Other Support Services

See industry description for 561990 below.

561990   All Other Support Services

This industry comprises establishments primarily engaged in providing day-to-day business and other organizational support services (except office administrative

---

services, facilities support services, employment services, business support services, travel arrangement and reservation services, security and investigation services, services to buildings and other structures, packaging and labeling services, and convention and trade show organizing services).

Illustrative Examples:

Bartering services	Inventory taking services
Flagging (i.e., traffic control) services	Contract meter reading services
Bottle exchanges	Lumber grading services
Float decorating services	Diving services on a contract or fee
Cloth cutting, bolting, or winding for the trade	basis

Cross-References. Establishments primarily engaged in—

- Providing office administrative services—are classified in Industry 561110, Office Administrative Services;

- Providing facilities support services—are classified in Industry 561210, Facilities Support Services;

- Providing employment services—are classified in Industry Group 5613, Employment Services;

- Providing business support services—are classified in Industry Group 5614, Business Support Services;

- Providing travel arrangement and reservation services—are classified in Industry Group 5615, Travel Arrangement and Reservation Services;

- Providing security and investigation services—are classified in Industry Group 5616, Investigation and Security Services;

- Providing services to buildings and other structures—are classified in Industry Group 5617, Services to Buildings and Dwellings;

- Providing packaging and labeling services—are classified in Industry 561910, Packaging and Labeling Services; and

- Organizing, promoting, and/or managing conferences, conventions, and trade shows (whether or not they manage and provide the staff to operate the facilities in which these events take place)—are classified in Industry 561920, Convention and Trade Show Organizers.

562 Waste Management and Remediation Services

Industries in the Waste Management and Remediation Services subsector group establishments engaged in the collection, treatment, and disposal of waste materials.

US—United States industry only. CAN—United States and Canadian industries are comparable. MEX—United States and Mexican industries are comparable. Blank—Canadian, Mexican, and United States industries are comparable.

This includes establishments engaged in local hauling of waste materials; operating materials recovery facilities (i.e., those that sort recyclable materials from the trash stream); providing remediation services (i.e., those that provide for the cleanup of contaminated buildings, mine sites, soil, or ground water); and providing septic pumping and other miscellaneous waste management services. There are three industry groups within the subsector that separate these activities into waste collection, waste treatment and disposal, and remediation and other waste management.

Excluded from this subsector are establishments primarily engaged in collecting, treating, and disposing waste through sewer systems or sewage treatment facilities that are classified in Industry 22132, Sewage Treatment Facilities and establishments primarily engaged in long-distance hauling of waste materials that are classified in Industry 48423, Specialized Freight (except Used Goods) Trucking, Long-Distance. Also, there are some activities that appear to be related to waste management, but that are not included in this subsector. For example, establishments primarily engaged in providing waste management consulting services are classified in Industry 54162, Environmental Consulting Services.

5621 Waste Collection^{CAN}

56211 Waste Collection^{CAN}

This industry comprises establishments primarily engaged in (1) collecting and/or hauling hazardous waste, nonhazardous waste, and/or recyclable materials within a local area and/or (2) operating hazardous or nonhazardous waste transfer stations. Hazardous waste collection establishments may be responsible for the identification, treatment, packaging, and labeling of waste for the purposes of transport.

Cross-References. Establishments primarily engaged in—

- Long-distance trucking of waste—are classified in Industry 48423, Specialized Freight (except Used Goods) Trucking, Long-Distance;
- Operating facilities for separating and sorting recyclable materials from nonhazardous waste streams (i.e., garbage) and/or for sorting commingled recyclable materials, such as paper, plastics, and metal cans, into distinct categories—are classified in Industry 56292, Materials Recovery Facilities; and
- Collecting and/or hauling in combination with disposal of waste materials—are classified in Industry 56221, Waste Treatment and Disposal.

562111 Solid Waste Collection^{US}

This U.S. industry comprises establishments primarily engaged in one or more of the following: (1) collecting and/or hauling nonhazardous solid waste (i.e.,

---

US—United States industry only. CAN—United States and Canadian industries are comparable. MEX—United States and Mexican industries are comparable. Blank—Canadian, Mexican, and United States industries are comparable.

garbage) within a local area; (2) operating nonhazardous solid waste transfer stations; and (3) collecting and/or hauling mixed recyclable materials within a local area.

Cross-References. Establishments primarily engaged in—

- Long-distance trucking of waste—are classified in Industry 484230, Specialized Freight (except Used Goods) Trucking, Long-Distance;

- Collecting and/or hauling in combination with disposal of nonhazardous waste materials—are classified in Industry 56221, Waste Treatment and Disposal;

- Collecting and/or hauling hazardous waste within a local area and/or operating hazardous waste transfer stations—are classified in U.S. Industry 562112, Hazardous Waste Collection;

- Collecting and removing debris, such as brush or rubble, within a local area—are classified in U.S. Industry 562119, Other Waste Collection; and

- Operating facilities for separating and sorting recyclable materials from nonhazardous waste streams (i.e., garbage) and/or for sorting commingled recyclable materials, such as paper, plastics, and metal cans, into distinct categories—are classified in Industry 562920, Materials Recovery Facilities.

562112 Hazardous Waste Collection[US]

This U.S. industry comprises establishments primarily engaged in collecting and/or hauling hazardous waste within a local area and/or operating hazardous waste transfer stations. Hazardous waste collection establishments may be responsible for the identification, treatment, packaging, and labeling of waste for the purposes of transport.

Cross-References. Establishments primarily engaged in—

- Long-distance trucking of waste—are classified in Industry 484230, Specialized Freight (except Used Goods) Trucking, Long-Distance;

- Collecting and/or hauling in combination with disposal of hazardous waste materials—are classified in U.S. Industry 562211, Hazardous Waste Treatment and Disposal;

- Collecting and/or hauling nonhazardous solid waste (i.e., garbage) and/or recyclable materials within a local area and/or operating nonhazardous solid waste transfer stations—are classified in U.S. Industry 562111, Solid Waste Collection; and

- Collecting and removing debris, such as brush or rubble, within a local area—are classified in U.S. Industry 562119, Other Waste Collection.

US—United States industry only. CAN—United States and Canadian industries are comparable. MEX—United States and Mexican industries are comparable. Blank—Canadian, Mexican, and United States industries are comparable.

562119 Other Waste Collection^{US}

This U.S. industry comprises establishments primarily engaged in collecting and/or hauling waste (except nonhazardous solid waste and hazardous waste) within a local area. Establishments engaged in brush or rubble removal services are included in this industry.

Cross-References. Establishments primarily engaged in—

- Long-distance trucking of waste—are classified in Industry 484230, Specialized Freight (except Used Goods) Trucking, Long-Distance;

- Collecting and/or hauling in combination with disposal of waste materials— are classified in Industry Group 5622, Waste Treatment and Disposal;

- Collecting and/or hauling nonhazardous solid waste (i.e., garbage) or mixed recyclable materials within a local area or operating nonhazardous solid waste transfer stations—are classified in U.S. Industry 562111, Solid Waste Collection;

- Collecting and/or hauling hazardous waste within a local area or operating hazardous waste transfer stations—are classified in U.S. Industry 562112, Hazardous Waste Collection; and

- Operating facilities for separating and sorting recyclable materials from nonhazardous waste streams (i.e., garbage) and/or for sorting commingled recyclable materials, such as paper, plastics, and metal cans, into distinct categories—are classified in Industry 562920, Materials Recovery Facilities.

5622 Waste Treatment and Disposal^{CAN}

56221 Waste Treatment and Disposal^{CAN}

This industry comprises establishments primarily engaged in (1) operating waste treatment or disposal facilities (except sewer systems or sewage treatment facilities) or (2) the combined activity of collecting and/or hauling of waste materials within a local area and operating waste treatment or disposal facilities. Waste combustors or incinerators (including those that may produce byproducts, such as electricity), solid waste landfills, and compost dumps are included in this industry.

Cross-References. Establishments primarily engaged in—

- Collecting, treating, and disposing waste through sewer systems or sewage treatment facilities—are classified in Industry 22132, Sewage Treatment Facilities; and

---

US—United States industry only. CAN—United States and Canadian industries are comparable. MEX—United States and Mexican industries are comparable. Blank—Canadian, Mexican, and United States industries are comparable.

- Manufacturing compost—are classified in Industry 32531, Fertilizer Manufacturing.

562211 Hazardous Waste Treatment and Disposal[US]

This U.S. industry comprises establishments primarily engaged in (1) operating treatment and/or disposal facilities for hazardous waste or (2) the combined activity of collecting and/or hauling of hazardous waste materials within a local area and operating treatment or disposal facilities for hazardous waste.

Cross-References. Establishments primarily engaged in—

- Operating landfills for the disposal of nonhazardous solid waste—are classified in U.S. Industry 562212, Solid Waste Landfill;
- Operating combustors and incinerators for the disposal of nonhazardous solid waste—are classified in U.S. Industry 562213, Solid Waste Combustors and Incinerators;
- Collecting, treating, and disposing waste through sewer systems or sewage treatment facilities—are classified in Industry 221320, Sewage Treatment Facilities; and
- Operating nonhazardous waste treatment and disposal facilities (except landfills, combustors, incinerators, and sewer systems or sewage treatment facilities)—are classified in U.S. Industry 562219, Other Nonhazardous Waste Treatment and Disposal.

562212 Solid Waste Landfill[US]

This U.S. industry comprises establishments primarily engaged in (1) operating landfills for the disposal of nonhazardous solid waste or (2) the combined activity of collecting and/or hauling nonhazardous waste materials within a local area and operating landfills for the disposal of nonhazardous solid waste.

Cross-References. Establishments primarily engaged in—

- Operating treatment and/or disposal facilities for hazardous waste—are classified in U.S. Industry 562211, Hazardous Waste Treatment and Disposal;
- Operating combustors and incinerators for the disposal of nonhazardous solid waste—are classified in U.S. Industry 562213, Solid Waste Combustors and Incinerators;
- Collecting, treating, and disposing waste through sewer systems or sewage treatment facilities—are classified in Industry 221320, Sewage Treatment Facilities;

US—United States industry only. CAN—United States and Canadian industries are comparable. MEX—United States and Mexican industries are comparable. Blank—Canadian, Mexican, and United States industries are comparable.

- Operating nonhazardous waste treatment and disposal facilities (except landfills, combustors, incinerators, and sewer systems or sewage treatment facilities)—are classified in U.S. Industry 562219, Other Nonhazardous Waste Treatment and Disposal; and

- Manufacturing compost—are classified in U.S. Industry 325314, Fertilizer (Mixing Only) Manufacturing.

562213 Solid Waste Combustors and Incinerators[US]

This U.S. industry comprises establishments primarily engaged in operating combustors and incinerators for the disposal of nonhazardous solid waste. These establishments may produce byproducts, such as electricity and steam.

Cross-References. Establishments primarily engaged in—

- Operating treatment and/or disposal facilities for hazardous waste—are classified in U.S. Industry 562211, Hazardous Waste Treatment and Disposal;

- Operating landfills for the disposal of nonhazardous solid waste—are classified in U.S. Industry 562212, Solid Waste Landfill;

- Collecting, treating, and disposing waste through sewer systems or sewage treatment facilities—are classified in Industry 221320, Sewage Treatment Facilities; and

- Operating nonhazardous waste treatment and disposal facilities (except landfills, combustors, incinerators, and sewer systems or sewage treatment facilities)—are classified in U.S. Industry 562219, Other Nonhazardous Waste Treatment and Disposal.

562219 Other Nonhazardous Waste Treatment and Disposal[US]

This U.S. industry comprises establishments primarily engaged in (1) operating nonhazardous waste treatment and disposal facilities (except landfills, combustors, incinerators and sewer systems or sewage treatment facilities) or (2) the combined activity of collecting and/or hauling of nonhazardous waste materials within a local area and operating waste treatment or disposal facilities (except landfills, combustors, incinerators and sewer systems, or sewage treatment facilities). Compost dumps are included in this industry.

Cross-References. Establishments primarily engaged in—

- Operating landfills for the disposal of nonhazardous solid waste—are classified in U.S. Industry 562212, Solid Waste Landfill;

- Operating combustors and incinerators for the disposal of nonhazardous solid waste—are classified in U.S. Industry 562213, Solid Waste Combustors and Incinerators;

- Collecting, treating, and disposing waste through sewer systems or sewage treatment facilities—are classified in Industry 221320, Sewage Treatment Facilities; and

- Manufacturing compost—are classified in U.S. Industry 325314, Fertilizer (Mixing Only) Manufacturing.

5629 Remediation and Other Waste Management Services[CAN]

This industry group comprises establishments primarily engaged in remediation and other waste management services (except waste collection, waste treatment and disposal, and waste management consulting services).

56291 Remediation Services[CAN]

See industry description for 562910 below.

562910 Remediation Services[CAN]

This industry comprises establishments primarily engaged in one or more of the following: (1) remediation and cleanup of contaminated buildings, mine sites, soil, or ground water; (2) integrated mine reclamation activities, including demolition, soil remediation, waste water treatment, hazardous material removal, contouring land, and revegetation; and (3) asbestos, lead paint, and other toxic material abatement.

Cross-References. Establishments primarily engaged in—

- Developing remedial action plans—are classified in Industry 541620, Environmental Consulting Services;

- Excavating soil—are classified in Industry 238910, Site Preparation Contractors;

- Individual activities as part of a reclamation or remediation project—are classified according to the primary activity;

- Building modifications to alleviate radon gas—are classified in Industry 238990, All Other Specialty Trade Contractors; and

- Collecting, treating, and disposing waste water through sewer systems or sewage treatment facilities—are classified in Industry 221320, Sewage Treatment Facilities.

US—United States industry only. CAN—United States and Canadian industries are comparable. MEX—United States and Mexican industries are comparable. Blank—Canadian, Mexican, and United States industries are comparable.

56292 Materials Recovery Facilities^{CAN}

See industry description for 562920 below.

562920 Materials Recovery Facilities^{CAN}

This industry comprises establishments primarily engaged in (1) operating facilities for separating and sorting recyclable materials from nonhazardous waste streams (i.e., garbage) and/or (2) operating facilities where commingled recyclable materials, such as paper, plastics, used beverage cans, and metals, are sorted into distinct categories.

Cross-References.

Establishments primarily engaged in merchant wholesaling automotive, industrial, and other recyclable materials are classified in Industry 423930, Recyclable Material Merchant Wholesalers.

56299 All Other Waste Management Services^{CAN}

This industry comprises establishments primarily engaged in waste management services (except waste collection, waste treatment and disposal, remediation, operation of materials recovery facilities, and waste management consulting services).

Illustrative Examples:

Beach cleaning and maintenance services
Pumping (i.e., cleaning) cesspools,
   portable toilets, or septic tanks
Cesspool cleaning services

Sewer cleaning and rodding services
Portable toilet renting and/or servicing
Sewer or storm basin cleanout services

Cross-References. Establishments primarily engaged in—

* Collecting and/or hauling waste within a local area—are classified in Industry 56211, Waste Collection;

* Long-distance trucking of waste—are classified in Industry 48423, Specialized Freight (except Used Goods) Trucking, Long-Distance;

* Operating treatment or disposal facilities (except sewer systems or sewage treatment facilities) for waste—are classified in Industry 56221, Waste Treatment and Disposal;

* Collecting, treating, and disposing waste through sewer systems or sewage treatment facilities—are classified in Industry 22132, Sewage Treatment Facilities;

- Remediation and cleanup of contaminated buildings, mine sites, soil, or ground water—are classified in Industry 56291, Remediation Services;

- Operating facilities for separating and sorting recyclable materials from nonhazardous waste streams (i.e., garbage) or where commingled recyclable materials, such as paper, plastics, and metal cans are sorted into distinct categories—are classified in Industry 56292, Materials Recovery Facilities;

- Installing septic tanks—are classified in Industry 23891, Site Preparation Contractors; and

- Providing waste management consulting services, such as developing remedial action plans—are classified in Industry 54162, Environmental Consulting Services.

562991 Septic Tank and Related Services[US]

This U.S. industry comprises establishments primarily engaged in (1) pumping (i.e., cleaning) septic tanks and cesspools and/or (2) renting and/or servicing portable toilets.

Cross-References. Establishments primarily engaged in—

- Installing septic tanks—are classified in Industry 238910, Site Preparation Contractors; and

- Cleaning and rodding sewers and catch basins—are classified in U.S. Industry 562998, All Other Miscellaneous Waste Management Services.

562998 All Other Miscellaneous Waste Management Services[US]

This U.S. industry comprises establishments primarily engaged in providing waste management services (except waste collection, waste treatment and disposal, remediation, operation of materials recovery facilities, septic tank pumping and related services, and waste management consulting services).

Illustrative Examples:

Beach cleaning and maintenance services	Tank cleaning and disposal services,
Sewer or storm basin cleanout services	commercial or industrial
Catch basin cleaning services	Sewer cleaning and rodding services

Cross-References. Establishments primarily engaged in—

- Collecting and/or hauling waste within a local area—are classified in Industry 56211, Waste Collection;

US—United States industry only. CAN—-United States and Canadian industries are comparable. MEX—United States and Mexican industries are comparable. Blank—Canadian, Mexican, and United States industries are comparable.

- Long-distance trucking of waste—are classified in Industry 484230, Specialized Freight (except Used Goods) Trucking, Long-Distance;

- Operating treatment or disposal facilities (except sewer systems or sewage treatment facilities) for waste—are classified in Industry 56221, Waste Treatment and Disposal;

- Collecting, treating, and disposing waste through sewer systems or sewage treatment facilities—are classified in Industry 221320, Sewage Treatment Facilities;

- The remediation and cleanup of contaminated buildings, mine sites, soil, or ground water—are classified in Industry 562910, Remediation Services;

- Operating facilities for separating and sorting recyclable materials from nonhazardous waste streams (i.e., garbage) or for sorting commingled recyclable materials, such as paper, plastics, and metal cans, into distinct categories—are classified in Industry 562920, Materials Recovery Facilities;

- Pumping (i.e., cleaning) cesspools, portable toilets, and septic tanks or renting portable toilets—are classified in U.S. Industry 562991, Septic Tank and Related Services; and

- Providing waste management consulting services, such as developing remedial action plans—are classified in Industry 541620, Environmental Consulting Services.

Sector 61—Educational Services

The Sector as a Whole

The Educational Services sector comprises establishments that provide instruction and training in a wide variety of subjects. This instruction and training is provided by specialized establishments, such as schools, colleges, universities, and training centers. These establishments may be privately owned and operated for profit or not for profit, or they may be publicly owned and operated. They may also offer food and/or accommodation services to their students.

Educational services are usually delivered by teachers or instructors that explain, tell, demonstrate, supervise, and direct learning. Instruction is imparted in diverse settings, such as educational institutions, the workplace, or the home, and through diverse means, such as correspondence, television, the Internet, or other electronic and distance-learning methods. The training provided by these establishments may include the use of simulators and simulation methods. It can be adapted to the particular needs of the students, for example sign language can replace verbal language for teaching students with hearing impairments. All industries in the sector share this commonality of process, namely, labor inputs of instructors with the requisite subject matter expertise and teaching ability.

611 Educational Services

Industries in the Educational Services subsector provide instruction and training in a wide variety of subjects. The instruction and training is provided by specialized establishments, such as schools, colleges, universities, and training centers.

The subsector is structured according to level and type of educational services. Elementary and secondary schools, junior colleges and colleges, universities, and professional schools correspond to a recognized series of formal levels of education designated by diplomas, associate degrees (including equivalent certificates), and degrees. The remaining industry groups are based more on the type of instruction or training offered and the levels are not always as formally defined. The establishments are often highly specialized, many offering instruction in a very limited subject matter, for example ski lessons or one specific computer software package. Within the sector, the level and types of training that are required of the instructors and teachers vary depending on the industry.

Establishments that manage schools and other educational establishments on a contractual basis are classified in this subsector if they both manage the operation and provide the operating staff. Such establishments are classified in the educational services subsector based on the type of facility managed and operated.

US—United States industry only. CAN—United States and Canadian industries are comparable. MEX—United States and Mexican industries are comparable. Blank—Canadian, Mexican, and United States industries are comparable.

6111 Elementary and Secondary Schools

61111 Elementary and Secondary Schools^{CAN}
See industry description for 611110 below.

611110 Elementary and Secondary Schools^{CAN}

This industry comprises establishments primarily engaged in furnishing academic courses and associated course work that comprise a basic preparatory education. A basic preparatory education ordinarily constitutes kindergarten through 12th grade. This industry includes school boards and school districts.

Illustrative Examples:

Elementary schools	Kindergartens
Parochial schools, elementary or secondary	Schools for the physically disabled, elementary or secondary
High schools	Military academies, elementary or secondary
Primary schools	

Cross-References.

- Establishments primarily engaged in providing preschool or prekindergarten education are classified in Industry 624410, Child Day Care Services; and

- Military academies, college level are classified in Industry 611310, Colleges, Universities, and Professional Schools.

6112 Junior Colleges

61121 Junior Colleges
See industry description for 611210 below.

611210 Junior Colleges^{CAN}

This industry comprises establishments primarily engaged in furnishing academic, or academic and technical, courses and granting associate degrees, certificates, or diplomas below the baccalaureate level. The requirement for admission to an associate or equivalent degree program is at least a high school diploma or equivalent general academic training. Instruction may be provided in diverse settings, such as the establishment's or client's training facilities, educational institutions, the workplace, or the home, and through diverse means, such as correspondence, television, the Internet, or other electronic and distance-learning methods.

US—United States industry only. CAN—United States and Canadian industries are comparable. MEX—United States and Mexican industries are comparable. Blank—Canadian, Mexican, and United States industries are comparable.

The training provided by these establishments may include the use of simulators and simulation methods.

6113 Colleges, Universities, and Professional Schools

61131 Colleges, Universities, and Professional Schools
See industry description for 611310 below.

611310 Colleges, Universities, and Professional Schools[CAN]

This industry comprises establishments primarily engaged in furnishing academic courses and granting degrees at baccalaureate or graduate levels. The requirement for admission is at least a high school diploma or equivalent general academic training. Instruction may be provided in diverse settings, such as the establishment's or client's training facilities, educational institutions, the workplace, or the home, and through diverse means, such as correspondence, television, the Internet, or other electronic and distance-learning methods. The training provided by these establishments may include the use of simulators and simulation methods.

Illustrative Examples:

Colleges (except junior colleges)
Theological seminaries offering
  baccalaureate or graduate degrees
Military academies, college level

Universities
Professional schools (e.g., business
  administration, dental, law, medical)

Cross-References.

Establishments primarily engaged in furnishing academic, or academic and technical, courses and granting associate degrees, certificates, or diplomas below the baccalaureate level are classified in Industry 611210, Junior Colleges.

6114 Business Schools and Computer and Management Training

61141 Business and Secretarial Schools
See industry description for 611410 below.

611410 Business and Secretarial Schools[CAN]

This industry comprises establishments primarily engaged in offering courses in office procedures and secretarial and stenographic skills and may offer courses in basic office skills, such as word processing. In addition, these establishments may offer such classes as office machine operation, reception, communications, and other skills designed for individuals pursuing a clerical or secretarial career. Instruction may be provided in diverse settings, such as the establishment's or client's training facilities, educational institutions, the workplace, or the home, and through diverse means, such as correspondence, television, the Internet, or other electronic and distance-learning methods. The training provided by these establishments may include the use of simulators and simulation methods.

Cross-References. Establishments primarily engaged in—

- Offering computer training (except computer repair)—are classified in Industry 611420, Computer Training;
- Offering academic degrees (e.g., baccalaureate, graduate level) in business education—are classified in Industry 611310, Colleges, Universities, and Professional Schools; and
- Offering training in the maintenance and repair of computers—are classified in U.S. Industry 611519, Other Technical and Trade Schools.

61142 Computer Training
See industry description for 611420 below.

611420 Computer Training[CAN]

This industry comprises establishments primarily engaged in conducting computer training (except computer repair), such as computer programming, software packages, computerized business systems, computer electronics technology, computer operations, and local area network management. Instruction may be provided in diverse settings, such as the establishment's or client's training facilities, educational institutions, the workplace, or the home, and through diverse means, such as correspondence, television, the Internet, or other electronic and distance-learning methods. The training provided by these establishments may include the use of simulators and simulation methods.

Cross-References. Establishments primarily engaged in—

- Offering training in the maintenance and repair of computers—are classified in U.S. Industry 611519, Other Technical and Trade Schools; and
- Computer retailing, wholesaling, or computer system designing that may also provide computer training—are classified in their appropriate industries.

61143 Professional and Management Development Training
See industry description for 611430 below.

US—United States industry only. CAN—United States and Canadian industries are comparable. MEX—United States and Mexican industries are comparable. Blank—Canadian, Mexican, and United States industries are comparable.

611430 Professional and Management Development Training[CAN]

This industry comprises establishments primarily engaged in offering an array of short duration courses and seminars for management and professional development. Training for career development may be provided directly to individuals or through employers' training programs; and courses may be customized or modified to meet the special needs of customers. Instruction may be provided in diverse settings, such as the establishment's or client's training facilities, educational institutions, the workplace, or the home, and through diverse means, such as correspondence, television, the Internet, or other electronic and distance-learning methods. The training provided by these establishments may include the use of simulators and simulation methods.

Cross-References.

- Advising clients on human resource and training issues without providing the training—are classified in U.S. Industry 541612, Human Resources Consulting Services; and

- Offering academic degrees (e.g., baccalaureate, graduate level)—are classified in Industry 611310, Colleges, Universities, and Professional Schools.

6115 Technical and Trade Schools

61151 Technical and Trade Schools

This industry comprises establishments primarily engaged in offering vocational and technical training in a variety of technical subjects and trades. The training often leads to job-specific certification. Instruction may be provided in diverse settings, such as the establishment's or client's training facilities, educational institutions, the workplace, or the home, and through diverse means, such as correspondence, television, the Internet, or other electronic and distance-learning methods. The training provided by these establishments may include the use of simulators and simulation methods.

Illustrative Examples:

Apprenticeship training programs
Graphic arts schools
Aviation and flight training instruction
  schools
Modeling schools
Computer repair training

Nursing schools (except academic)
Cosmetology schools
Real estate schools
Electronic equipment repair training
Truck driving schools

US—United States industry only. CAN—United States and Canadian industries are comparable. MEX—United States and Mexican industries are comparable. Blank—Canadian, Mexican, and United States industries are comparable.

Cross-References. Establishments primarily engaged in—

- Offering courses in office procedures and secretarial and stenographic skills—are classified in Industry 61141, Business and Secretarial Schools;

- Offering computer training (except computer repair)—are classified in Industry 61142, Computer Training;

- Offering professional and management development training—are classified in Industry 61143, Professional and Management Development Training;

- Offering academic courses that may also offer technical and trade courses— are classified according to the type of school;

- Specialty air transportation services which may also provide flight training— are classified in Industry 48121, Nonscheduled Air Transportation; and

- Offering registered nursing training—are classified in Industry 61121, Junior Colleges or Industry 61131, Colleges, Universities, and Professional Schools.

611511 Cosmetology and Barber Schools[US]

This U.S. industry comprises establishments primarily engaged in offering training in barbering, hair styling, or the cosmetic arts, such as makeup or skin care. These schools provide job-specific certification.

611512 Flight Training[US]

This U.S. industry comprises establishments primarily engaged in offering aviation and flight training. These establishments may offer vocational training, recreational training, or both.

Cross-References.

Establishments primarily engaged in specialty air transportation services that may also provide flight training are classified in U.S. Industry 481219, Other Nonscheduled Air Transportation.

611513 Apprenticeship Training[US]

This U.S. industry comprises establishments primarily engaged in offering apprenticeship training programs. These programs involve applied training as well as course work.

US—United States industry only. CAN—United States and Canadian industries are comparable. MEX—United States and Mexican industries are comparable. Blank—Canadian, Mexican, and United States industries are comparable.

611519 Other Technical and Trade Schools[US]

This U.S. industry comprises establishments primarily engaged in offering job or career vocational or technical courses (except cosmetology and barber training, aviation and flight training, and apprenticeship training). The curriculums offered by these schools are highly structured and specialized and lead to job-specific certification.

Illustrative Examples:

Bartending schools ,
Modeling schools
Broadcasting schools
Real estate schools

Computer repair training
Truck driving schools
Graphic arts schools

Cross-References. Establishments primarily engaged in—

- Offering courses in office procedures and secretarial and stenographic skills—are classified in Industry 611410, Business and Secretarial Schools;

- Offering computer training (except computer repair)—are classified in Industry 611420, Computer Training;

- Offering professional and management development training—are classified in Industry 611430, Professional and Management Development Training;

- Offering registered nursing training with academic degrees (e.g., associate baccalaureate)—are classified in Industry 611210, Junior Colleges or in Industry 611310, College, Universities, and Professional Schools;

- Offering aviation and flight training—are classified in U.S. Industry 611512, Flight Training;

- Offering cosmetology and barber training—are classified in U.S. Industry 611511, Cosmetology and Barber Schools;

- Offering academic courses that may also offer technical and trade courses—are classified according to the type of school; and

- Offering apprenticeship training programs—are classified in U.S. Industry 611513, Apprenticeship Training.

6116 Other Schools and Instruction

This industry group comprises establishments primarily engaged in offering or providing instruction (except academic schools, colleges, and universities; and business, computer, management, technical, or trade instruction). Instruction may be provided in diverse settings, such as the establishment's or client's training facilities, educational institutions, the workplace, or the home, and through diverse means, such as correspondence, television, the Internet, or other electronic and distance-learning methods. The training provided by these establishments may include the use of simulators and simulation methods.

61161 Fine Arts Schools
See industry description for 611610 below.

611610 Fine Arts Schools^{CAN}

This industry comprises establishments primarily engaged in offering instruction in the arts, including dance, art, drama, and music.

Illustrative Examples:

Art (except commercial and graphic) instruction

Music instruction (e.g., piano, guitar)

Dance instruction

Music schools (except academic)

Dance studios

Performing arts schools (except academic)

Drama schools (except academic)

Photography schools (except commercial photography)

Fine arts schools (except academic)

Cross-References.

- Establishments offering high school diplomas or academic degrees (i.e., even if they specialize in fine arts) are classified elsewhere in this subsector according to the type of school; and

- Establishments primarily engaged in offering courses in commercial and graphic arts and commercial photography are classified in U.S. Industry 611519, Other Technical and Trade Schools.

61162 Sports and Recreation Instruction
See industry description for 611620 below.

611620 Sports and Recreation Instruction^{CAN}

This industry comprises establishments, such as camps and schools, primarily engaged in offering instruction in athletic activities to groups of individuals. Overnight and day sports instruction camps are included in this industry.

Illustrative Examples:

Camps, sports instruction

Professional sports instructors (i.e., not participating in sporting events)

Gymnastics instruction

Sports (e.g., baseball, basketball, football, golf) instruction

---

US—United States industry only. CAN—United States and Canadian industries are comparable. MEX—United States and Mexican industries are comparable. Blank—Canadian, Mexican, and United States industries are comparable.

Cheerleading instruction
Riding instruction academies or schools

Martial arts instruction, camps or schools
Swimming instruction

Cross-References.

- Establishments primarily engaged in operating overnight recreational camps that may offer some athletic instruction in addition to other activities are classified in U.S. Industry 721214, Recreational and Vacation Camps (except Campgrounds);

- Establishments primarily engaged in operating sports and recreation establishments that also offer athletic instruction are classified in Sector 71, Arts, Entertainment, and Recreation;

- Independent (i.e., freelance) athletes engaged in providing sports instruction and participating in spectator sporting events are classified in U.S. Industry 711219, Other Spectator Sports; and

- Establishments primarily engaged in offering academic courses that may also offer athletic instruction are classified according to the type of school.

61163 Language Schools

See industry description for 611630 below.

611630 Language Schools[CAN]

This industry comprises establishments primarily engaged in offering foreign language instruction (including sign language). These establishments are designed to offer language instruction ranging from conversational skills for personal enrichment to intensive training courses for career or educational opportunities.

Cross-References. Establishments primarily engaged in—

- Offering academic courses that may also offer language instruction—are classified according to type of school; and

- Providing translation and interpretation services—are classified in Industry 541930, Translation and Interpretation Services.

61169 All Other Schools and Instruction

This industry comprises establishments primarily engaged in offering instruction (except business, computer, management, technical, trade, fine arts, athletic, and language instruction). Also excluded from this industry are academic schools, colleges, and universities.

US—United States industry only. CAN—United States and Canadian industries are comparable. MEX—United States and Mexican industries are comparable. Blank—Canadian, Mexican, and United States industries are comparable.

Illustrative Examples:

Academic tutoring services
Public speaking training
Automobile driving schools

Speed reading instruction
Exam preparation services

Cross-References. Establishments primarily engaged in—

- Offering elementary and secondary school instruction—are classified in Industry 61111, Elementary and Secondary Schools;

- Offering junior college instruction—are classified in Industry 61121, Junior Colleges;

- Offering college, university, and professional school instruction with academic degrees (e.g., baccalaureate, graduate)—are classified in Industry 61131, Colleges, Universities, and Professional Schools;

- Offering business, computer (except computer repair), and management training—are classified in Industry Group 6114, Business Schools and Computer and Management Training;

- Offering technical and trade school instruction (e.g., computer repair and maintenance)—are classified in Industry 61151, Technical and Trade Schools;

- Offering fine arts instruction—are classified in Industry 61161, Fine Arts Schools;

- Offering sports and recreation instruction—are classified in Industry 61162, Sports and Recreation Instruction; and

- Offering language instruction—are classified in Industry 61163, Language Schools.

611691 Exam Preparation and Tutoring[US]

This U.S. industry comprises establishments primarily engaged in offering preparation for standardized examinations and/or academic tutoring services.

Illustrative Examples:

Academic tutoring services
Learning centers offering remedial
  courses

College board preparation centers
Professional examination review
  instruction

611692 Automobile Driving Schools[US]

This U.S. industry comprises establishments primarily engaged in offering automobile driving instruction.

US—United States industry only. CAN—United States and Canadian industries are comparable. MEX—United States and Mexican industries are comparable. Blank—Canadian, Mexican, and United States industries are comparable.

Cross-References.

Establishments primarily engaged in offering truck and bus driving instruction are classified in U.S. Industry 611519, Other Technical and Trade Schools.

611699 All Other Miscellaneous Schools and Instruction[US]

This U.S. industry comprises establishments primarily engaged in offering instruction (except business, computer, management, technical, trade, fine arts, athletic, language instruction, tutoring, and automobile driving instruction). Also excluded from this industry are academic schools, colleges, and universities.

Illustrative Examples:

Public speaking training   Speed reading instruction
Survival training

Cross-References. Establishments primarily engaged in—

- Offering elementary and secondary school instruction—are classified in Industry 611110, Elementary and Secondary Schools;

- Offering junior college instruction—are classified in Industry 611210, Junior Colleges;

- Offering college, university, and professional school instruction with academic degrees (e.g., baccalaureate, graduate)—are classified in Industry 611310, Colleges, Universities, and Professional Schools;

- Offering business, computer (except computer repair), and management training—are classified in Industry Group 6114, Business Schools and Computer and Management Training;

- Offering technical and trade school instruction (e.g., computer repair and maintenance)—are classified in Industry 61151, Technical and Trade Schools;

- Offering fine arts instruction—are classified in Industry 611610, Fine Arts Schools;

- Offering sports and recreation instruction—are classified in Industry 611620, Sports and Recreation Instruction;

- Offering language instruction—are classified in Industry 611630, Language Schools;

- Offering exam preparation and tutoring services—are classified in U.S. Industry 611691, Exam Preparation and Tutoring; and

- Offering automobile driving instruction—are classified in U.S. Industry 611692, Automobile Driving Schools.

6117   Educational Support Services

61171   Educational Support Services
See industry description for 611710 below.

611710   Educational Support Services

This industry comprises establishments primarily engaged in providing noninstructional services that support educational processes or systems.

Illustrative Examples:

Educational consultants	Student exchange programs
Educational testing services	Educational testing evaluation services
Educational guidance counseling services	

Cross-References. Establishments primarily engaged in—

- Providing job training for the unemployed, underemployed, physically disabled, and persons who have a job market disadvantage because of lack of education or job skills—are classified in Industry 624310, Vocational Rehabilitation Services; and

- Conducting research and analyses in cognitive development—are classified in Industry 541720, Research and Development in the Social Sciences and Humanities.

US—United States industry only. CAN—United States and Canadian industries are comparable. MEX—United States and Mexican industries are comparable. Blank—Canadian, Mexican, and United States industries are comparable.

http://www.census.gov/naics

Sector 62—Health Care and Social Assistance

The Sector as a Whole

The Health Care and Social Assistance sector comprises establishments providing health care and social assistance for individuals. The sector includes both health care and social assistance because it is sometimes difficult to distinguish between the boundaries of these two activities. The industries in this sector are arranged on a continuum starting with those establishments providing medical care exclusively, continuing with those providing health care and social assistance, and finally finishing with those providing only social assistance. The services provided by establishments in this sector are delivered by trained professionals. All industries in the sector share this commonality of process, namely, labor inputs of health practitioners or social workers with the requisite expertise. Many of the industries in the sector are defined based on the educational degree held by the practitioners included in the industry.

Excluded from this sector are aerobic classes in Subsector 713, Amusement, Gambling and Recreation Industries and nonmedical diet and weight reducing centers in Subsector 812, Personal and Laundry Services. Although these can be viewed as health services, these services are not typically delivered by health practitioners.

621 Ambulatory Health Care Services

Industries in the Ambulatory Health Care Services subsector provide health care services directly or indirectly to ambulatory patients and do not usually provide inpatient services. Health practitioners in this subsector provide outpatient services, with the facilities and equipment not usually being the most significant part of the production process.

6211 Offices of Physicians

62111 Offices of Physicians

This industry comprises establishments of health practitioners having the degree of M.D. (Doctor of Medicine) or D.O. (Doctor of Osteopathy) primarily engaged in the independent practice of general or specialized medicine (e.g., anesthesiology, oncology, ophthalmology, psychiatry) or surgery. These practitioners operate private or group practices in their own offices (e.g., centers, clinics) or in the facilities of others, such as hospitals or HMO medical centers.

US—United States industry only. CAN—United States and Canadian industries are comparable. MEX—United States and Mexican industries are comparable. Blank—Canadian, Mexican, and United States industries are comparable.

Cross-References.

- Medical centers primarily engaged in providing emergency medical care for accident or trauma victims and ambulatory surgical centers primarily engaged in providing surgery on an outpatient basis are classified in Industry 62149, Other Outpatient Care Centers;

- Establishments of oral pathologists are classified in Industry 62121, Offices of Dentists; and

- Establishments of speech or voice pathologists are classified in Industry 62134, Offices of Physical, Occupational and Speech Therapists, and Audiologists.

621111   Offices of Physicians (except Mental Health Specialists)[US]

This U.S. industry comprises establishments of health practitioners having the degree of M.D. (Doctor of Medicine) or D.O. (Doctor of Osteopathy) primarily engaged in the independent practice of general or specialized medicine (except psychiatry or psychoanalysis) or surgery. These practitioners operate private or group practices in their own offices (e.g., centers, clinics) or in the facilities of others, such as hospitals or HMO medical centers.

Cross-References.

- Establishments of physicians primarily engaged in the independent practice of psychiatry or psychoanalysis are classified in U.S. Industry 621112, Offices of Physicians, Mental Health Specialists;

- Freestanding medical centers primarily engaged in providing emergency medical care for accident or catastrophe victims and freestanding ambulatory surgical centers primarily engaged in providing surgery on an outpatient basis are classified in U.S. Industry 621493, Freestanding Ambulatory Surgical and Emergency Centers;

- Establishments of oral pathologists are classified in Industry 621210, Offices of Dentists; and

- Establishments of speech or voice pathologists are classified in Industry 621340, Offices of Physical, Occupational and Speech Therapists, and Audiologists.

621112   Offices of Physicians, Mental Health Specialists[US]

This U.S. industry comprises establishments of health practitioners having the degree of M.D. (Doctor of Medicine) or D.O. (Doctor of Osteopathy) primarily engaged in the independent practice of psychiatry or psychoanalysis. These practitioners operate private or group practices in their own offices (e.g., centers, clinics) or in the facilities of others, such as hospitals or HMO medical centers.

6212 Offices of Dentists

62121 Offices of Dentists
See industry description for 621210 below.

621210 Offices of Dentists^{CAN}

This industry comprises establishments of health practitioners having the degree of D.M.D. (Doctor of Dental Medicine), D.D.S. (Doctor of Dental Surgery), or D.D.Sc. (Doctor of Dental Science) primarily engaged in the independent practice of general or specialized dentistry or dental surgery. These practitioners operate private or group practices in their own offices (e.g., centers, clinics) or in the facilities of others, such as hospitals or HMO medical centers. They can provide either comprehensive preventive, cosmetic, or emergency care, or specialize in a single field of dentistry.

Cross-References.
- Establishments known as dental laboratories primarily engaged in making dentures, artificial teeth, and orthodontic appliances to order for dentists are classified in U.S. Industry 339116, Dental Laboratories; and
- Establishments of dental hygienists primarily engaged in cleaning teeth and gums or establishments of denturists primarily engaged in taking impressions for and fitting dentures are classified in U.S. Industry 621399, Offices of All Other Miscellaneous Health Practitioners.

6213 Offices of Other Health Practitioners

This industry group comprises establishments of independent health practitioners (except physicians and dentists).

62131 Offices of Chiropractors
See industry description for 621310 below.

621310 Offices of Chiropractors^{CAN}

This industry comprises establishments of health practitioners having the degree of D.C. (Doctor of Chiropractic) primarily engaged in the independent practice of chiropractic. These practitioners provide diagnostic and therapeutic treatment of neuromusculoskeletal and related disorders through the manipulation and adjustment of the spinal column and extremities, and operate private or group practices in their own offices (e.g., centers, clinics) or in the facilities of others, such as hospitals or HMO medical centers.

62132 Offices of Optometrists
See industry description for 621320 below.

621320 Offices of Optometrists

This industry comprises establishments of health practitioners having the degree of O.D. (Doctor of Optometry) primarily engaged in the independent practice of optometry. These practitioners examine, diagnose, treat, and manage diseases and disorders of the visual system, the eye and associated structures as well as diagnose related systemic conditions. Offices of optometrists prescribe and/or provide eyeglasses, contact lenses, low vision aids, and vision therapy. They operate private or group practices in their own offices (e.g., centers, clinics) or in the facilities of others, such as hospitals or HMO medical centers, and may also provide the same services as opticians, such as selling and fitting prescription eyeglasses and contact lenses.

Cross-References.

- Offices of opticians primarily engaged in selling and fitting prescription eyeglasses and contact lenses are classified in Industry 446130, Optical Goods Stores; and

- Offices of physicians primarily engaged in the independent practice of ophthalmology are classified in U.S. Industry 621111, Offices of Physicians (except Mental Health Specialists).

62133 Offices of Mental Health Practitioners (except Physicians)
See industry description for 621330 below.

621330 Offices of Mental Health Practitioners (except Physicians)CAN

This industry comprises establishments of independent mental health practitioners (except physicians) primarily engaged in (1) the diagnosis and treatment of mental, emotional, and behavioral disorders and/or (2) the diagnosis and treatment of individual or group social dysfunction brought about by such causes as mental illness, alcohol and substance abuse, physical and emotional trauma, or stress. These practitioners operate private or group practices in their own offices (e.g., centers, clinics) or in the facilities of others, such as hospitals or HMO medical centers.

Cross-References.

Establishments of psychiatrists, psychoanalysts, and psychotherapists having the degree of M.D. (Doctor of Medicine) or D.O. (Doctor of Osteopathy) are classified in U.S. Industry 621112, Offices of Physicians, Mental Health Specialists.

62134 Offices of Physical, Occupational and Speech Therapists, and Audiologists

See industry description for 621340 below.

621340 Offices of Physical, Occupational and Speech Therapists, and Audiologists[CAN]

This industry comprises establishments of independent health practitioners primarily engaged in one of the following: (1) providing physical therapy services to patients who have impairments, functional limitations, disabilities, or changes in physical functions and health status resulting from injury, disease or other causes, or who require prevention, wellness or fitness services; (2) planning and administering educational, recreational, and social activities designed to help patients or individuals with disabilities, regain physical or mental functioning or to adapt to their disabilities; and (3) diagnosing and treating speech, language, or hearing problems. These practitioners operate private or group practices in their own offices (e.g., centers, clinics) or in the facilities of others, such as hospitals or HMO medical centers.

Illustrative Examples:

Audiologists' offices
Recreational (e.g., art, dance, music)
  therapists' offices
Industrial therapists' offices

Speech pathologists' offices
Occupational therapists' offices
Physical therapists' offices

62139 Offices of All Other Health Practitioners

This industry comprises establishments of independent health practitioners (except physicians; dentists; chiropractors; optometrists; mental health specialists; physical, occupational, and speech therapists; and audiologists). These practitioners operate private or group practices in their own offices (e.g., centers, clinics) or in the facilities of others, such as hospitals or HMO medical centers.

US—United States industry only. CAN—United States and Canadian industries are comparable. MEX—United States and Mexican industries are comparable. Blank—Canadian, Mexican, and United States industries are comparable.

Illustrative Examples:

Acupuncturists' (except MDs or DOs) offices

Inhalation or respiratory therapists' offices

Dental hygienists' offices

Midwives' offices

Denturists' offices

Naturopaths' offices

Dietitians' offices

Podiatrists' offices

Homeopaths' offices

Registered or licensed practical nurses' offices

Cross-References. Establishments primarily engaged in—

- The independent practice of medicine (i.e., physicians)—are classified in Industry 62111, Offices of Physicians;

- The independent practice of dentistry—are classified in Industry 62121, Offices of Dentists;

- The independent practice of chiropractic—are classified in Industry 62131, Offices of Chiropractors;

- The independent practice of optometry—are classified in Industry 62132, Offices of Optometrists;

- The independent practice of mental health (except physicians)—are classified in Industry 62133, Offices of Mental Health Practitioners (except Physicians); and

- The independent practice of physical, occupational, and speech therapy and audiology—are classified in Industry 62134, Offices of Physical, Occupational and Speech Therapists, and Audiologists.

621391   Offices of Podiatrists[US]

This U.S. industry comprises establishments of health practitioners having the degree of D.P.M. (Doctor of Podiatric Medicine) primarily engaged in the independent practice of podiatry. These practitioners diagnose and treat diseases and deformities of the foot and operate private or group practices in their own offices (e.g., centers, clinics) or in the facilities of others, such as hospitals or HMO medical centers.

621399   Offices of All Other Miscellaneous Health Practitioners[US]

This U.S. industry comprises establishments of independent health practitioners (except physicians; dentists; chiropractors; optometrists; mental health specialists; physical, occupational, and speech therapists; audiologists; and podiatrists). These practitioners operate private or group practices in their own offices (e.g., centers, clinics) or in the facilities of others, such as hospitals or HMO medical centers.

US—United States industry only. CAN—United States and Canadian industries are comparable. MEX—United States and Mexican industries are comparable. Blank—Canadian, Mexican, and United States industries are comparable.

Illustrative Examples:

Acupuncturists' (except MDs or DOs) offices

Hypnotherapists' offices

Dental hygienists' offices

Inhalation or respiratory therapists' offices

Denturists' offices

Midwives' offices

Dietitians' offices

Naturopaths' offices

Homeopaths' offices

Registered or licensed practical nurses' offices

Cross-References. Establishments primarily engaged in—

- The independent practice of medicine (i.e., physicians)—are classified in Industry 62111, Offices of Physicians;

- The independent practice of dentistry—are classified in Industry 621210, Offices of Dentists;

- The independent practice of chiropractic—are classified in Industry 621310, Offices of Chiropractors;

- The independent practice of optometry—are classified in Industry 621320, Offices of Optometrists;

- The independent practice of mental health (except physicians)—are classified in Industry 621330, Offices of Mental Health Practitioners (except Physicians);

- The independent practice of physical, occupational, and speech therapy, and audiology—are classified in Industry 621340, Offices of Physical, Occupational and Speech Therapists, and Audiologists; and

- The independent practice of podiatry—are classified in U.S. Industry 621391, Offices of Podiatrists.

6214 Outpatient Care Centers

62141 Family Planning Centers

See industry description for 621410 below.

621410 Family Planning Centers^{CAN}

This industry comprises establishments with medical staff primarily engaged in providing a range of family planning services on an outpatient basis, such as contraceptive services, genetic and prenatal counseling, voluntary sterilization, and therapeutic and medically induced termination of pregnancy.

Illustrative Examples:

Birth control clinics	Childbirth preparation classes
Fertility clinics	Pregnancy counseling centers

62142 Outpatient Mental Health and Substance Abuse Centers

See industry description for 621420 below.

621420 Outpatient Mental Health and Substance Abuse Centers[CAN]

This industry comprises establishments with medical staff primarily engaged in providing outpatient services related to the diagnosis and treatment of mental health disorders and alcohol and other substance abuse. These establishments generally treat patients who do not require inpatient treatment. They may provide a counseling staff and information regarding a wide range of mental health and substance abuse issues and/or refer patients to more extensive treatment programs, if necessary.

Illustrative Examples:

Outpatient alcoholism treatment centers and clinics (except hospitals)	Outpatient substance abuse treatment centers and clinics (except hospitals)
Outpatient mental health centers and clinics (except hospitals)	Outpatient drug addiction treatment centers and clinics (except hospitals)
Outpatient detoxification centers and clinics (except hospitals)	

Cross-References.

- Establishments known and licensed as hospitals primarily engaged in the inpatient treatment of mental health and substance abuse illnesses with an emphasis on medical treatment and monitoring are classified in Industry 622210, Psychiatric and Substance Abuse Hospitals; and

- Establishments primarily engaged in the inpatient treatment of mental health and substance abuse illness with an emphasis on residential care and counseling rather than medical treatment are classified in Industry 623220, Residential Mental Health and Substance Abuse Facilities.

62149 Other Outpatient Care Centers

This industry comprises establishments with medical staff primarily engaged in providing general or specialized outpatient care (except family planning centers and outpatient mental health and substance abuse centers). Centers or clinics of health practitioners with different degrees from more than one industry practicing within the same establishment (i.e., Doctor of Medicine and Doctor of Dental Medicine) are included in this industry.

Illustrative Examples:

Dialysis centers and clinics
Outpatient biofeedback centers and clinics
Freestanding ambulatory surgical centers and clinics
Outpatient community health centers and clinics

Freestanding emergency medical centers and clinics
Outpatient sleep disorder centers and clinics
Health maintenance organization (HMO) medical centers and clinics

Cross-References.

- Physician walk-in centers are classified in Industry 62111, Offices of Physicians;

- Centers and clinics of health practitioners from the same industry primarily engaged in the independent practice of their profession are classified in Industry 62111, Offices of Physicians; Industry 62121, Offices of Dentists; and Industry Group 6213, Offices of Other Health Practitioners;

- Family planning centers are classified in Industry 62141, Family Planning Centers;

- Outpatient mental health and substance abuse centers are classified in Industry 62142, Outpatient Mental Health and Substance Abuse Centers;

- HMO establishments (except those providing health care services) primarily engaged in underwriting health and medical insurance policies are classified in Industry 52411, Direct Life, Health, and Medical Insurance Carriers; and

- Establishments known and licensed as hospitals that also perform ambulatory surgery and emergency room services are classified in Subsector 622, Hospitals.

621491 HMO Medical Centers[US]

This U.S. industry comprises establishments with physicians and other medical staff primarily engaged in providing a range of outpatient medical services to the health maintenance organization (HMO) subscribers with a focus generally on primary health care. These establishments are owned by the HMO. Included in this industry are HMO establishments that both provide health care services and underwrite health and medical insurance policies.

Cross-References.

- Health practitioners or health practitioner groups contracting to provide their services to subscribers of prepaid health plans are classified in Industry

---

US—United States industry only. CAN—United States and Canadian industries are comparable. MEX—United States and Mexican industries are comparable. Blank—Canadian, Mexican, and United States industries are comparable.

62111, Offices of Physicians; Industry 621210, Offices of Dentists; and Industry Group 6213, Offices of Other Health Practitioners; and

- HMO establishments (except those providing health care services) primarily engaged in underwriting and administering health and medical insurance policies are classified in U.S. Industry 524114, Direct Health and Medical Insurance Carriers.

621492 Kidney Dialysis Centers[US]

This U.S. industry comprises establishments with medical staff primarily engaged in providing outpatient kidney or renal dialysis services.

621493 Freestanding Ambulatory Surgical and Emergency Centers[US]

This U.S. industry comprises establishments with physicians and other medical staff primarily engaged in (1) providing surgical services (e.g., orthoscopic and cataract surgery) on an outpatient basis or (2) providing emergency care services (e.g., setting broken bones, treating lacerations, or tending to patients suffering injuries as a result of accidents, trauma, or medical conditions necessitating immediate medical care) on an outpatient basis. Outpatient surgical establishments have specialized facilities, such as operating and recovery rooms, and specialized equipment, such as anesthetic or X-ray equipment.

Illustrative Examples:

Freestanding ambulatory surgical centers and clinics	Freestanding emergency medical centers and clinics
Freestanding trauma centers (except hospitals)	Urgent medical care centers and clinics (except hospitals)

Cross-References.

- Physician walk-in centers are classified in U.S. Industry 621111, Offices of Physicians (except Mental Health Specialists); and

- Establishments known and licensed as hospitals that also perform ambulatory surgery and emergency room services are classified in Subsector 622, Hospitals.

621498 All Other Outpatient Care Centers[US]

This U.S. industry comprises establishments with medical staff primarily engaged in providing general or specialized outpatient care (except family planning

---

centers, outpatient mental health and substance abuse centers, HMO medical centers, kidney dialysis centers, and freestanding ambulatory surgical and emergency centers). Centers or clinics of health practitioners with different degrees from more than one industry practicing within the same establishment (i.e., Doctor of Medicine and Doctor of Dental Medicine) are included in this industry.

Illustrative Examples:

Outpatient biofeedback centers and clinics

Outpatient pain therapy centers and clinics

Outpatient community health centers and clinics

Outpatient sleep disorder centers and clinics

Cross-References.

- Physician walk-in centers are classified in U.S. Industry 621111, Offices of Physicians (except Mental Health Specialists);

- Centers and clinics of health practitioners from the same industry primarily engaged in the independent practice of their profession are classified in Industry 62111, Offices of Physicians; Industry 621210, Offices of Dentists; and Industry Group 6213, Offices of Other Health Practitioners;

- Family planning centers are classified in Industry 621410, Family Planning Centers;

- Outpatient mental health and substance abuse centers are classified in Industry 621420, Outpatient Mental Health and Substance Abuse Centers;

- HMO medical centers are classified in U.S. Industry 621491, HMO Medical Centers;

- Dialysis centers are classified in U.S. Industry 621492, Kidney Dialysis Centers; and

- Freestanding ambulatory surgical and emergency centers are classified in U.S. Industry 621493, Freestanding Ambulatory Surgical and Emergency Centers.

6215 Medical and Diagnostic Laboratories

62151 Medical and Diagnostic Laboratories

This industry comprises establishments known as medical and diagnostic laboratories primarily engaged in providing analytic or diagnostic services, including body fluid analysis and diagnostic imaging, generally to the medical profession or to the patient on referral from a health practitioner.

US—United States industry only. CAN—United States and Canadian industries are comparable. MEX—United States and Mexican industries are comparable. Blank—Canadian, Mexican, and United States industries are comparable.

Illustrative Examples:

Dental or medical X-ray laboratories

Medical pathology laboratories

Diagnostic imaging centers

Medical testing laboratories

Medical forensic laboratories

Cross-References.

Establishments, such as dental, optical, and orthopedic laboratories, primarily engaged in providing the following activities to the medical profession, respectively: making dentures, artificial teeth, and orthodontic appliances to prescription; grinding of lenses to prescription; and making orthopedic or prosthetic appliances to prescription are classified in Industry 33911, Medical Equipment and Supplies Manufacturing.

621511 Medical Laboratories^{US}

This U.S. industry comprises establishments known as medical laboratories primarily engaged in providing analytic or diagnostic services, including body fluid analysis, generally to the medical profession or to the patient on referral from a health practitioner.

Illustrative Examples:

Blood analysis laboratories

Medical pathology laboratories

Medical bacteriological laboratories

Medical testing laboratories

Medical forensic laboratories

Cross-References.

- Establishments known as dental laboratories primarily engaged in making dentures, artificial teeth, and orthodontic appliances to prescription are classified in U.S. Industry 339116, Dental Laboratories;

- Establishments known as optical laboratories primarily engaged in grinding of lenses to prescription are classified in U.S. Industry 339115, Ophthalmic Goods Manufacturing; and

- Establishments known as orthopedic laboratories primarily engaged in making orthopedic or prosthetic appliances to prescription are classified in U.S. Industry 339113, Surgical Appliance and Supplies Manufacturing.

621512 Diagnostic Imaging Centers^{US}

This U.S. industry comprises establishments known as diagnostic imaging centers primarily engaged in producing images of the patient generally on referral from a health practitioner.

US—United States industry only. CAN—United States and Canadian industries are comparable. MEX—United States and Mexican industries are comparable. Blank—Canadian, Mexican, and United States industries are comparable.

Illustrative Examples:

Computer tomography (CT-scan) centers

Medical radiological laboratories

Dental or medical X-ray laboratories

Ultrasound imaging centers

Magnetic resonance imaging (MRI) centers

6216 Home Health Care Services

62161 Home Health Care Services
See industry description for 621610 below.

621610 Home Health Care Services

This industry comprises establishments primarily engaged in providing skilled nursing services in the home, along with a range of the following: personal care services; homemaker and companion services; physical therapy; medical social services; medications; medical equipment and supplies; counseling; 24-hour home care; occupation and vocational therapy; dietary and nutritional services; speech therapy; audiology; and high-tech care, such as intravenous therapy.

Illustrative Examples:

Home health care agencies

Visiting nurse associations

In-home hospice care services

Cross-References.

- In-home health services provided by establishments of health practitioners and others primarily engaged in the independent practice of their profession are classified in Industry 62111, Offices of Physicians; Industry 621210, Offices of Dentists; Industry Group 6213, Offices of Other Health Practitioners; and U.S. Industry 621999, All Other Miscellaneous Ambulatory Health Care Services; and

- Establishments primarily engaged in renting or leasing products for home health care are classified in U.S. Industry 532291, Home Health Equipment Rental.

6219 Other Ambulatory Health Care Services

This industry group comprises establishments primarily engaged in providing ambulatory health care services (except offices of physicians, dentists, and other health practitioners; outpatient care centers; medical laboratories and diagnostic imaging centers; and home health care providers).

62191   Ambulance Services

See industry description for 621910 below.

621910   Ambulance Services^{MEX}

This industry comprises establishments primarily engaged in providing transportation of patients by ground or air, along with medical care. These services are often provided during a medical emergency but are not restricted to emergencies. The vehicles are equipped with lifesaving equipment operated by medically trained personnel.

Cross-References.

Establishments primarily engaged in providing transportation of the disabled or elderly (without medical care) are classified in U.S. Industry 485991, Special Needs Transportation.

62199   All Other Ambulatory Health Care Services

This industry comprises establishments primarily engaged in providing ambulatory health care services (except office physicians, dentists, and other health practitioners; outpatient care centers; medical and diagnostic laboratories; home health care providers; and ambulances).

Illustrative Examples:

Blood donor stations
Pacemaker monitoring services
Blood or body organ banks
Physical fitness evaluation services
(except by offices of health
practitioners)

Health screening services (except by
offices of health practitioners)
Smoking cessation programs
Hearing testing services (except by
offices of audiologists)

Cross-References.

- Establishments primarily engaged in the independent practice of medicine are classified in Industry 62111, Offices of Physicians;

- Establishments primarily engaged in the independent practice of dentistry are classified in Industry 62121, Offices of Dentists;

- Establishments primarily engaged in the independent practice of health care (except offices of physicians and dentists) are classified in Industry Group 6213, Offices of Other Health Practitioners;

US—United States industry only. CAN—United States and Canadian industries are comparable. MEX—United States and Mexican industries are comparable. Blank—Canadian, Mexican, and United States industries are comparable.

- Establishments primarily engaged in providing general or specialized outpatient care services are classified in Industry Group 6214, Outpatient Care Centers;

- Establishments primarily engaged in providing home health care services are classified in Industry 62161, Home Health Care Services;

- Establishments primarily engaged in transportation of patients by ground or air, along with medical care are classified in Industry 62191, Ambulance Services; and

- Establishments known as medical and diagnostic laboratories primarily engaged in providing analytic or diagnostic services are classified in Industry 62151, Medical and Diagnostic Laboratories.

621991 Blood and Organ Banks[US]

This U.S. industry comprises establishments primarily engaged in collecting, storing, and distributing blood and blood products and storing and distributing body organs.

621999 All Other Miscellaneous Ambulatory Health Care Services[US]

This U.S. industry comprises establishments primarily engaged in providing ambulatory health care services (except offices of physicians, dentists, and other health practitioners; outpatient care centers; medical and diagnostic laboratories; home health care providers; ambulances; and blood and organ banks).

Illustrative Examples:

Health screening services (except by offices of health practitioners)

Physical fitness evaluation services (except by offices of health practitioners)

Hearing testing services (except by offices of audiologists)

Smoking cessation programs

Pacemaker monitoring services

Cross-References.

- Establishments primarily engaged in the independent practice of medicine are classified in Industry 62111, Offices of Physicians;

- Establishments primarily engaged in the independent practice of dentistry are classified in Industry 621210, Offices of Dentists;

- Establishments primarily engaged in the independent practice of health care (except offices of physicians and dentists) are classified in Industry Group 6213, Offices of Other Health Practitioners;

- Establishments primarily engaged in providing general or specialized outpatient care services are classified in Industry Group 6214, Outpatient Care Centers;

- Establishments primarily engaged in providing home health care services are classified in Industry 621610, Home Health Care Services;

- Establishments primarily engaged in the transportation of patients by ground or air, along with medical care are classified in Industry 621910, Ambulance Services;

- Establishments known as medical and diagnostic laboratories primarily engaged in providing analytic or diagnostic services are classified in Industry 62151, Medical and Diagnostic Laboratories; and

- Blood and organ banks are classified in U.S. Industry 621991, Blood and Organ Banks.

622 Hospitals

Industries in the Hospitals subsector provide medical, diagnostic, and treatment services that include physician, nursing, and other health services to inpatients and the specialized accommodation services required by inpatients. Hospitals may also provide outpatient services as a secondary activity. Establishments in the Hospitals subsector provide inpatient health services, many of which can only be provided using the specialized facilities and equipment that form a significant and integral part of the production process.

6221 General Medical and Surgical Hospitals

62211 General Medical and Surgical Hospitals
See industry description for 622110 below.

622110 General Medical and Surgical Hospitals[US]

This industry comprises establishments known and licensed as general medical and surgical hospitals primarily engaged in providing diagnostic and medical treatment (both surgical and nonsurgical) to inpatients with any of a wide variety of medical conditions. These establishments maintain inpatient beds and provide patients with food services that meet their nutritional requirements. These hospitals have an organized staff of physicians and other medical staff to provide patient care services. These establishments usually provide other services, such as outpatient services, anatomical pathology services, diagnostic X-ray services, clinical labora-

---

US—United States industry only. CAN—United States and Canadian industries are comparable. MEX—United States and Mexican industries are comparable. Blank—Canadian, Mexican, and United States industries are comparable.

tory services, operating room services for a variety of procedures, and pharmacy services.

6222 Psychiatric and Substance Abuse Hospitals

62221 Psychiatric and Substance Abuse Hospitals
See industry description for 622210 below.

622210 Psychiatric and Substance Abuse Hospitals[CAN]

This industry comprises establishments known and licensed as psychiatric and substance abuse hospitals primarily engaged in providing diagnostic, medical treatment, and monitoring services for inpatients who suffer from mental illness or substance abuse disorders. The treatment often requires an extended stay in the hospital. These establishments maintain inpatient beds and provide patients with food services that meet their nutritional requirements. They have an organized staff of physicians and other medical staff to provide patient care services. Psychiatric, psychological, and social work services are available at the facility. These hospitals usually provide other services, such as outpatient services, clinical laboratory services, diagnostic X-ray services, and electroencephalograph services.

Cross-References.

- Establishments primarily engaged in providing treatment of mental health and substance abuse illnesses on an exclusively outpatient basis are classified in Industry 621420, Outpatient Mental Health and Substance Abuse Centers;

- Establishments referred to as hospitals but are primarily engaged in providing inpatient treatment of mental health and substance abuse illness with the emphasis on counseling rather than medical treatment are classified in Industry 623220, Residential Mental Health and Substance Abuse Facilities; and

- Establishments referred to as hospitals but are primarily engaged in providing residential care for persons diagnosed with mental retardation are classified in Industry 623210, Residential Mental Retardation Facilities.

6223 Specialty (except Psychiatric and Substance Abuse) Hospitals

62231 Specialty (except Psychiatric and Substance Abuse) Hospitals
See industry description for 622310 below.

US—United States industry only. CAN—United States and Canadian industries are comparable. MEX—United States and Mexican industries are comparable. Blank—Canadian, Mexican, and United States industries are comparable.

622310 Specialty (except Psychiatric and Substance Abuse) Hospitals[CAN]

This industry consists of establishments known and licensed as specialty hospitals primarily engaged in providing diagnostic and medical treatment to inpatients with a specific type of disease or medical condition (except psychiatric or substance abuse). Hospitals providing long-term care for the chronically ill and hospitals providing rehabilitation, restorative, and adjustive services to physically challenged or disabled people are included in this industry. These establishments maintain inpatient beds and provide patients with food services that meet their nutritional requirements. They have an organized staff of physicians and other medical staff to provide patient care services. These hospitals may provide other services, such as outpatient services, diagnostic X-ray services, clinical laboratory services, operating room services, physical therapy services, educational and vocational services, and psychological and social work services.

Cross-References.

- Establishments known and licensed as hospitals primarily engaged in providing diagnostic and therapeutic inpatient services for a variety of medical conditions, both surgical and nonsurgical, are classified in Industry 622110, General Medical and Surgical Hospitals;

- Establishments known and licensed as hospitals primarily engaged in providing diagnostic and treatment services for inpatients with psychiatric or substance abuse illnesses are classified in Industry 622210, Psychiatric and Substance Abuse Hospitals;

- Establishments referred to as hospitals but are primarily engaged in providing inpatient nursing and rehabilitative services to persons requiring convalescence are classified in Industry 623110, Nursing Care Facilities;

- Establishments referred to as hospitals but are primarily engaged in providing residential care of persons diagnosed with mental retardation are classified in Industry 623210, Residential Mental Retardation Facilities; and

- Establishments referred to as hospitals but are primarily engaged in providing inpatient treatment for mental health and substance abuse illnesses with the emphasis on counseling rather than medical treatment are classified in Industry 623220, Residential Mental Health and Substance Abuse Facilities.

623 Nursing and Residential Care Facilities

Industries in the Nursing and Residential Care Facilities subsector provide residential care combined with either nursing, supervisory, or other types of care as

US—United States industry only. CAN—United States and Canadian industries are comparable. MEX—United States and Mexican industries are comparable. Blank—Canadian, Mexican, and United States industries are comparable.

required by the residents. In this subsector, the facilities are a significant part of the production process and the care provided is a mix of health and social services with the health services being largely some level of nursing services.

6231 Nursing Care Facilities

62311 Nursing Care Facilities
See industry description for 623110 below.

623110 Nursing Care Facilities[CAN]

This industry comprises establishments primarily engaged in providing inpatient nursing and rehabilitative services. The care is generally provided for an extended period of time to individuals requiring nursing care. These establishments have a permanent core staff of registered or licensed practical nurses who, along with other staff, provide nursing and continuous personal care services.

Illustrative Examples:

Convalescent homes or convalescent
  hospitals (except psychiatric)
Nursing homes

Homes for the elderly with nursing care
Rest homes with nursing care
Inpatient care hospices

Cross-References.
- Assisted-living facilities with on-site nursing care facilities are classified in U.S. Industry 623311, Continuing Care Retirement Communities; and
- Psychiatric convalescent homes are classified in Industry 623220, Residential Mental Health and Substance Abuse Facilities.

6232 Residential Mental Retardation, Mental Health and Substance Abuse Facilities

This industry group comprises establishments primarily engaged in providing residential care (but not licensed hospital care) to people with mental retardation, mental illness, or substance abuse problems.

62321 Residential Mental Retardation Facilities
See industry description for 623210 below.

623210 Residential Mental Retardation Facilities[CAN]

This industry comprises establishments (e.g., group homes, hospitals, intermediate care facilities) primarily engaged in providing residential care services for

---

US—United States industry only. CAN—United States and Canadian industries are comparable. MEX—United States and Mexican industries are comparable. Blank—Canadian, Mexican, and United States industries are comparable.

persons diagnosed with mental retardation. These facilities may provide some health care, though the focus is room, board, protective supervision, and counseling.

Cross-References.

- Establishments primarily engaged in providing inpatient treatment of mental health and substance abuse illnesses with an emphasis on counseling rather than medical treatment are classified in Industry 623220, Residential Mental Health and Substance Abuse Facilities;

- Establishments primarily engaged in providing treatment of mental health and substance abuse illnesses on an exclusively outpatient basis are classified in Industry 621420, Outpatient Mental Health and Substance Abuse Centers; and

- Establishments known and licensed as hospitals primarily engaged in providing inpatient treatment of mental health and substance abuse illnesses with an emphasis on medical treatment and monitoring are classified in Industry 622210, Psychiatric and Substance Abuse Hospitals.

62322 Residential Mental Health and Substance Abuse Facilities
See industry description for 623220 below.

623220 Residential Mental Health and Substance Abuse Facilities^{US}

This industry comprises establishments primarily engaged in providing residential care and treatment for patients with mental health and substance abuse illnesses. These establishments provide room, board, supervision, and counseling services. Although medical services may be available at these establishments, they are incidental to the counseling, mental rehabilitation, and support services offered. These establishments generally provide a wide range of social services in addition to counseling.

Illustrative Examples:

Alcoholism or drug addiction rehabilitation facilities (except licensed hospitals)
Psychiatric convalescent homes or hospitals

Mental health halfway houses
Residential group homes for the emotionally disturbed

Cross-References.

- Establishments primarily engaged in providing treatment of mental health and substance abuse illnesses on an exclusively outpatient basis are classified in Industry 621420, Outpatient Mental Health and Substance Abuse Centers;

- Establishments primarily engaged in providing residential care for persons diagnosed with mental retardation are classified in Industry 623210, Residential Mental Retardation Facilities; and

- Establishments known and licensed as hospitals primarily engaged in providing inpatient treatment of mental health and substance abuse illnesses with an emphasis on medical treatment and monitoring are classified in Industry 622210, Psychiatric and Substance Abuse Hospitals.

6233 Community Care Facilities for the Elderly

62331 Community Care Facilities for the Elderly

This industry comprises establishments primarily engaged in providing residential and personal care services for (1) the elderly and other persons who are unable to fully care for themselves and/or (2) the elderly and other persons who do not desire to live independently. The care typically includes room, board, supervision, and assistance in daily living, such as housekeeping services. In some instances these establishments provide skilled nursing care for residents in separate on-site facilities.

Illustrative Examples:

Assisted-living facilities
Homes for the elderly without nursing care

Continuing care retirement communities
Rest homes without nursing care

Cross-References.

- Establishments primarily engaged in providing inpatient nursing and rehabilitative services are classified in Industry 62311, Nursing Care Facilities; and

- Apartment or condominium complexes where people live independently in rented housing units are classified in Industry 53111, Lessors of Residential Buildings and Dwellings.

623311 Continuing Care Retirement Communities[US]

This U.S. industry comprises establishments primarily engaged in providing a range of residential and personal care services with on-site nursing care facilities for (1) the elderly and other persons who are unable to fully care for themselves and/or (2) the elderly and other persons who do not desire to live independently. Individuals live in a variety of residential settings with meals, housekeeping, social, leisure, and other services available to assist residents in daily living. Assisted-living facilities with on-site nursing care facilities are included in this industry.

US—United States industry only. CAN—United States and Canadian industries are comparable. MEX—United States and Mexican industries are comparable. Blank—Canadian, Mexican, and United States industries are comparable.

Cross-References.

- Establishments primarily engaged in providing inpatient nursing and rehabilitative services are classified in Industry 623110, Nursing Care Facilities;

- Assisted-living facilities without on-site nursing care facilities are classified in U.S. Industry 623312, Homes for the Elderly; and

- Apartment or condominium complexes where people live independently in rented housing units are classified in Industry 531110, Lessors of Residential Buildings and Dwellings.

623312 Homes for the Elderly[US]

This U.S. industry comprises establishments primarily engaged in providing residential and personal care services (i.e., without on-site nursing care facilities) for (1) the elderly or other persons who are unable to fully care for themselves and/or (2) the elderly or other persons who do not desire to live independently. The care typically includes room, board, supervision, and assistance in daily living, such as housekeeping services.

Illustrative Examples:

Assisted-living facilities without on-site nursing care facilities

Rest homes without nursing care

Homes for the elderly without nursing care

Cross-References.

- Assisted-living facilities with on-site nursing care facilities are classified in U.S. Industry 623311, Continuing Care Retirement Communities;

- Homes for the elderly with nursing care or rest homes with nursing care are classified in Industry 623110, Nursing Care Facilities; and

- Apartment or condominium complexes where people live independently in rented or owned housing units are classified in Industry 53111, Lessors of Residential Buildings and Dwellings.

6239 Other Residential Care Facilities

This industry group comprises establishments of residential care facilities (except residential mental retardation, mental health, and substance abuse facilities and community care facilities for the elderly).

62399 Other Residential Care Facilities

See industry description for 623990 below.

US—United States industry only. CAN—United States and Canadian industries are comparable. MEX—United States and Mexican industries are comparable. Blank—Canadian, Mexican, and United States industries are comparable.

623990 Other Residential Care Facilities[US]

This industry comprises establishments primarily engaged in providing residential care (except residential mental retardation facilities, residential health and substance abuse facilities, continuing care retirement communities, and homes for the elderly). These establishments also provide supervision and personal care services.

Illustrative Examples:

Boot or disciplinary camps (except correctional) for delinquent youth
Group homes for the hearing or visually impaired
Child group foster homes
Halfway group homes for delinquents or ex-offenders

Delinquent youth halfway group homes
Homes for unwed mothers
Group homes for the disabled without nursing care
Orphanages

Cross-References.

- Residential mental retardation facilities are classified in Industry 623210, Residential Mental Retardation Facilities;

- Continuing care retirement communities are classified in U.S. Industry 623311, Continuing Care Retirement Communities;

- Residential mental health and substance abuse facilities are classified in 623220, Residential Mental Health and Substance Abuse Facilities;

- Homes for the elderly without nursing care are classified in U.S. Industry 623312, Homes for the Elderly;

- Establishments primarily engaged in providing inpatient nursing and rehabilitative services are classified in Industry 623110, Nursing Care Facilities;

- Establishments primarily engaged in providing temporary shelter are classified in U.S. Industry 624221, Temporary Shelters; and

- Correctional camps are classified in Industry 922140, Correctional Institutions.

624 Social Assistance

Industries in the Social Assistance subsector provide a wide variety of social assistance services directly to their clients. These services do not include residential or accommodation services, except on a short stay basis.

6241 Individual and Family Services

62411 Child and Youth Services
See industry description for 624110 below.

624110 Child and Youth Services^{CAN}

This industry comprises establishments primarily engaged in providing nonresidential social assistance services for children and youth. These establishments provide for the welfare of children in such areas as adoption and foster care. drug prevention, life skills training, and positive social development.

Illustrative Examples:

Adoption agencies
Youth centers (except recreational only)
Child guidance organizations

Youth self-help organizations
Foster care placement services

Cross-References.

- Youth recreational centers are classified in Industry 713940, Fitness and Recreational Sports Centers;

- Youth recreational sports teams and leagues are classified in Industry 713990, All Other Amusement and Recreation Industries;

- Scouting organizations are classified in Industry 813410, Civic and Social Organizations; and

- Establishments primarily engaged in providing day care services for children are classified in Industry 624410, Child Day Care Services.

62412 Services for the Elderly and Persons with Disabilities
See industry description for 624120 below.

624120 Services for the Elderly and Persons with Disabilities^{CAN}

This industry comprises establishments primarily engaged in providing nonresidential social assistance services to improve the quality of life for the elderly, persons diagnosed with mental retardation, or persons with disabilities. These establishments provide for the welfare of these individuals in such areas as day care, nonmedical home care or homemaker services, social activities, group support, and companionship.

Cross-References. Establishments primarily engaged in—

- Providing job training for persons diagnosed with mental retardation or persons with disabilities—are classified in Industry 624310, Vocational Rehabilitation Services;

- Providing residential care for the elderly, persons diagnosed with mental retardation, or persons with disabilities—are classified in Subsector 623, Nursing and Residential Care Facilities; and

- Providing in-home health care services—are classified in Subsector 621, Ambulatory Health Care Services.

62419 Other Individual and Family Services
See industry description for 624190 below.

624190 Other Individual and Family Services[CAN]

This industry comprises establishments primarily engaged in providing nonresidential individual and family social assistance services (except those specifically directed toward children, the elderly, persons diagnosed with mental retardation, or persons with disabilities).

Illustrative Examples:

Community action services agencies
Marriage counseling services (except by
 offices of mental health practitioners)
Crisis intervention centers
Multipurpose social services
 centers
Family social services agencies

Self-help organizations (except for
 disabled persons, the elderly, persons
 diagnosed with mental retardation)
Family welfare services
Suicide crisis centers
Hotline centers
Telephone counseling services

Cross-References. Establishments primarily engaged in—

- Providing clinical psychological and psychiatric social counseling services—are classified in Industry 621330, Offices of Mental Health Practitioners (except Physicians);

- Providing child and youth social assistance services (except day care)—are classified in Industry 624110, Child and Youth Services;

- Providing child day care services—are classified in Industry 624410, Child Day Care Services;

- Providing social assistance services for the elderly, persons diagnosed with mental retardation, and persons with disabilities—are classified in Industry 624120, Services for the Elderly and Persons with Disabilities;

- Community action advocacy—are classified in U.S. Industry 813319, Other Social Advocacy Organizations; and

- Providing in-home health care services—are classified in Subsector 621, Ambulatory Health Care Services.

6242 Community Food and Housing, and Emergency and Other Relief Services

62421 Community Food Services

See industry description for 624210 below.

624210 Community Food Services[CAN]

This industry comprises establishments primarily engaged in the collection, preparation, and delivery of food for the needy. Establishments in this industry may also distribute clothing and blankets to the poor. These establishments may prepare and deliver meals to persons who by reason of age, disability, or illness are unable to prepare meals for themselves; collect and distribute salvageable or donated food; or prepare and provide meals at fixed or mobile locations. Food banks, meal delivery programs, and soup kitchens are included in this industry.

62422 Community Housing Services

This industry comprises establishments primarily engaged in providing one or more of the following community housing services: (1) short term emergency shelter for victims of domestic violence, sexual assault, or child abuse; (2) temporary residential shelter for the homeless, runaway youths, and patients and families caught in medical crises; (3) transitional housing for low-income individuals and families; (4) volunteer construction or repair of low cost housing, in partnership with the homeowner who may assist in construction or repair work; and (5) repair of homes for elderly or disabled homeowners. These establishments may operate their own shelter; or may subsidize housing using existing homes, apartments, hotels, or motels; or may require a low-cost mortgage or work (sweat) equity.

Cross-References.

Central offices of government housing programs are classified in Industry 92511, Administration of Housing Programs.

US—United States industry only. CAN—United States and Canadian industries are comparable. MEX—United States and Mexican industries are comparable. Blank—Canadian, Mexican, and United States industries are comparable.

624221 Temporary Shelters[US]

This U.S. industry comprises establishments primarily engaged in providing (1) short term emergency shelter for victims of domestic violence, sexual assault, or child abuse and/or (2) temporary residential shelter for homeless individuals or families, runaway youth, and patients and families caught in medical crises. These establishments may operate their own shelters or may subsidize housing using existing homes, apartments, hotels, or motels.

Cross-References.

Establishments primarily engaged in providing emergency shelter for victims of domestic or international disasters or conflicts are classified in Industry 624230, Emergency and Other Relief Services.

624229 Other Community Housing Services[US]

This U.S. industry comprises establishments primarily engaged in providing one or more of the following community housing services: (1) transitional housing to low-income individuals and families; (2) volunteer construction or repair of low-cost housing, in partnership with the homeowner who may assist in the construction or repair work; and (3) the repair of homes for elderly or disabled homeowners. These establishments may subsidize housing using existing homes, apartments, hotels, or motels or may require a low-cost mortgage or sweat equity. These establishments may also provide low-income families with furniture and household supplies.

Cross-References.

Central offices of government housing programs are classified in Industry 925110, Administration of Housing Programs.

62423 Emergency and Other Relief Services
See industry description for 624230 below.

624230 Emergency and Other Relief Services[CAN]

This industry comprises establishments primarily engaged in providing food, shelter, clothing, medical relief, resettlement, and counseling to victims of domestic or international disasters or conflicts (e.g., wars).

US—United States industry only. CAN—United States and Canadian industries are comparable. MEX—United States and Mexican industries are comparable. Blank—Canadian, Mexican, and United States industries are comparable.

6243 Vocational Rehabilitation Services

62431 Vocational Rehabilitation Services
See industry description for 624310 below.

624310 Vocational Rehabilitation Services^{CAN}

This industry comprises (1) establishments primarily engaged in providing vocational rehabilitation or habilitation services, such as job counseling, job training, and work experience, to unemployed and underemployed persons, persons with disabilities, and persons who have a job market disadvantage because of lack of education, job skill, or experience and (2) establishments primarily engaged in providing training and employment to persons with disabilities. Vocational rehabilitation job training facilities (except schools) and sheltered workshops (i.e., work experience centers) are included in this industry.

Cross-References.

- Schools (except high schools) primarily engaged in providing vocational training are classified in Industry 61151, Technical and Trade Schools;

- Vocational high schools are classified in Industry 611110, Elementary and Secondary Schools; and

- Establishments primarily engaged in providing career and vocational counseling (except rehabilitative) are classified in Industry 611710, Educational Support Services.

6244 Child Day Care Services

62441 Child Day Care Services
See industry description for 624410 below.

624410 Child Day Care Services^{CAN}

This industry comprises establishments primarily engaged in providing day care of infants or children. These establishments generally care for preschool children, but may care for older children when they are not in school and may also offer pre-kindergarten educational programs.

Illustrative Examples:

Child day care babysitting services

Child or infant day care centers

Nursery schools

Preschool centers

Cross-References.

Establishments primarily engaged in offering kindergarten educational programs are classified in Industry 611110, Elementary and Secondary Schools.

Sector 71—Arts, Entertainment, and Recreation

The Sector as a Whole

The Arts, Entertainment, and Recreation sector includes a wide range of establishments that operate facilities or provide services to meet varied cultural, entertainment, and recreational interests of their patrons. This sector comprises (1) establishments that are involved in producing, promoting, or participating in live performances, events, or exhibits intended for public viewing; (2) establishments that preserve and exhibit objects and sites of historical, cultural, or educational interest; and (3) establishments that operate facilities or provide services that enable patrons to participate in recreational activities or pursue amusement, hobby, and leisure-time interests.

Some establishments that provide cultural, entertainment, or recreational facilities and services are classified in other sectors. Excluded from this sector are: (1) establishments that provide both accommodations and recreational facilities, such as hunting and fishing camps and resort and casino hotels are classified in Subsector 721, Accommodation; (2) restaurants and night clubs that provide live entertainment in addition to the sale of food and beverages are classified in Subsector 722, Food Services and Drinking Places; (3) motion picture theaters, libraries and archives, and publishers of newspapers, magazines, books, periodicals, and computer software are classified in Sector 51, Information; and (4) establishments using transportation equipment to provide recreational and entertainment services, such as those operating sightseeing buses, dinner cruises, or helicopter rides, are classified in Subsector 487, Scenic and Sightseeing Transportation.

711 Performing Arts, Spectator Sports, and Related Industries

Industries in the Performing Arts, Spectator Sports, and Related Industries subsector group establishments that produce or organize and promote live presentations involving the performances of actors and actresses, singers, dancers, musical groups and artists, athletes, and other entertainers, including independent (i.e., freelance) entertainers and the establishments that manage their careers. The classification recognizes four basic processes: (1) producing (i.e., presenting) events; (2) organizing, managing, and/or promoting events; (3) managing and representing entertainers; and (4) providing the artistic, creative and technical skills necessary to the production of these live events. Also, this subsector contains four industries for performing arts companies. Each is defined on the basis of the particular skills of the entertainers involved in the presentations.

The industry structure for this subsector makes a clear distinction between performing arts companies and performing artists (i.e., independent or freelance).

US—United States industry only. CAN—United States and Canadian industries are comparable. MEX—United States and Mexican industries are comparable. Blank—Canadian, Mexican, and United States industries are comparable.

Although not unique to arts and entertainment, freelancing is a particularly important phenomenon in this Performing Arts, Spectator Sports, and Related Industries subsector. Distinguishing this activity from the production activity is a meaningful process differentiation. This approach, however, is difficult to implement in the case of musical groups (i.e., companies) and artists, especially pop groups. These establishments tend to be more loosely organized and it can be difficult to distinguish companies from freelancers. For this reason, NAICS includes one industry that covers both musical groups and musical artists.

This subsector contains two industries for Industry Group 7113, Promoters of Performing Arts, Sports, and Similar Events, one for those that operate facilities and another for those that do not. This is because there are significant differences in cost structures between those promoters that manage and provide the staff to operate facilities and those that do not. In addition to promoters without facilities, other industries in this subsector include establishments that may operate without permanent facilities. These types of establishments include: performing arts companies; musical groups and artists; spectator sports; and independent (i.e., freelance) artists, writers, and performers.

Excluded from this subsector are nightclubs. Some nightclubs promote live entertainment on a regular basis and it can be argued that they could be classified in Industry Group 7113, Promoters of Performing Arts, Sports, and Similar Events. However, since most of these establishments function as any other drinking place when they do not promote entertainment and because most of their revenue is derived from sale of food and beverages, they are classified in Subsector 722, Food Services and Drinking Places.

7111 Performing Arts Companies

This industry group comprises establishments primarily engaged in producing live presentations involving the performances of actors and actresses, singers, dancers, musical groups and artists, and other performing artists.

71111 Theater Companies and Dinner Theaters
See industry description for 711110 below.

711110 Theater Companies and Dinner Theaters[US]

This industry comprises (1) companies, groups, or theaters primarily engaged in producing the following live theatrical presentations: musicals; operas; plays; and comedy, improvisational, mime, and puppet shows and (2) establishments, commonly known as dinner theaters, engaged in producing live theatrical productions and in providing food and beverages for consumption on the premises. Theater

US—United States industry only. CAN—United States and Canadian industries are comparable. MEX—United States and Mexican industries are comparable. Blank—Canadian, Mexican, and United States industries are comparable.

http://www.census.gov/naics

groups or companies may or may not operate their own theater or other facility for staging their shows.

Illustrative Examples:

Comedy troupes
Opera companies
Live theatrical productions (except dance)

Theatrical stock or repertory companies
Musical theater companies

Cross-References.

- Establishments, such as nightclubs, primarily engaged in providing food and beverages for consumption on the premises and that also present live nontheatrical entertainment, are classified in Subsector 722, Food Services and Drinking Places;

- Establishments primarily engaged in organizing, managing, and/or promoting performing arts productions without producing their own shows are classified in Industry Group 7113, Promoters of Performing Arts, Sports, and Similar Events;

- Companies, groups, or theaters primarily engaged in producing all types of live theatrical dance presentations are classified in Industry 711120, Dance Companies;

- Freelance producers and performing artists (except musicians and vocalists) primarily engaged in theatrical activities independent of a company or group are classified in Industry 711510, Independent Artists, Writers, and Performers; and

- Musicians and vocalists are classified in Industry 711130, Musical Groups and Artists.

71112 Dance Companies

See industry description for 711120 below.

711120 Dance Companies^{CAN}

This industry comprises companies, groups, or theaters primarily engaged in producing all types of live theatrical dance (e.g., ballet, contemporary dance, folk dance) presentations. Dance companies or groups may or may not operate their own theater or other facility for staging their shows.

Cross-References.

- Establishments, such as exotic dance clubs, primarily engaged in providing food and beverages for consumption on the premises and that also present

---

US—United States industry only. CAN—United States and Canadian industries are comparable. MEX—United States and Mexican industries are comparable. Blank—Canadian, Mexican, and United States industries are comparable.

live dance entertainment, are classified in Subsector 722, Food Services and Drinking Places;

- Establishments primarily engaged in organizing, promoting, and/or managing dance productions without producing their own shows are classified in Industry Group 7113, Promoters of Performing Arts, Sports, and Similar Events; and

- Freelance producers and dancers primarily engaged in theatrical activities independent of a company or group are classified in Industry 711510, Independent Artists, Writers, and Performers.

71113 Musical Groups and Artists

See industry description for 711130 below.

711130 Musical Groups and Artists[CAN]

This industry comprises (1) groups primarily engaged in producing live musical entertainment (except theatrical musical or opera productions), and (2) independent (i.e., freelance) artists primarily engaged in providing live musical entertainment. Musical groups and artists may perform in front of a live audience or in a studio, and may or may not operate their own facilities for staging their shows.

Illustrative Examples:

Bands
Musical groups (except theatrical
  musical groups)

Drum and bugle corps (i.e., drill teams)
Orchestras
Independent musicians or vocalists

Cross-References.

- Establishments primarily engaged in organizing, promoting, and/or managing concerts and other musical performances without producing their own shows are classified in Industry Group 7113, Promoters of Performing Arts, Sports, and Similar Events;

- Companies, groups, or theaters primarily engaged in producing theatrical musicals and opera productions are classified in Industry 711110, Theater Companies and Dinner Theaters; and

- Freelance producers (except musical groups and artists) primarily engaged in musical activities independent of a company or group are classified in Industry 711510, Independent Artists, Writers, and Performers.

71119 Other Performing Arts Companies

See industry description for 711190 below.

US—United States industry only. CAN—United States and Canadian industries are comparable. MEX—United States and Mexican industries are comparable. Blank—Canadian, Mexican, and United States industries are comparable.

711190 Other Performing Arts Companies[CAN]

This industry comprises companies or groups (except theater companies, dance companies, musical groups, and artists) primarily engaged in producing live theatrical presentations.

Illustrative Examples:

Carnival traveling shows	Circuses
Ice skating companies	Magic shows

Cross-References.

- Establishments, such as comedy clubs or nightclubs, primarily engaged in providing food and beverages for consumption on the premises and that also present live nontheatrical entertainment are classified in Subsector 722, Food Services and Drinking Places;

- Establishments primarily engaged in organizing, promoting, and/or managing ice skating shows, circuses, and other live performing arts presentations without producing their own shows are classified in Industry Group 7113, Promoters of Performing Arts, Sports, and Similar Events;

- Theater companies and groups (except dance) or dinner theaters engaged in producing musicals; plays; operas; and comedy, improvisational, mime, and puppet shows are classified in Industry 711110, Theater Companies and Dinner Theaters;

- Dance companies or groups are classified in Industry 711120, Dance Companies;

- Freelance producers and performing artists (except musicians and vocalists) are classified in Industry 711510, Independent Artists, Writers, and Performers; and

- Musical groups and independent musicians and vocalists are classified in Industry 711130, Musical Groups and Artists.

7112 Spectator Sports

71121 Spectator Sports

This industry comprises (1) sports teams or clubs primarily participating in live sporting events before a paying audience; (2) establishments primarily engaged in operating racetracks; (3) independent athletes engaged in participating in live sporting or racing events before a paying audience; (4) owners of racing participants,

---

such as cars, dogs, and horses, primarily engaged in entering them in racing events or other spectator sports events; and (5) establishments, such as sports trainers, primarily engaged in providing specialized services to support participants in sports events or competitions. The sports teams and clubs included in this industry may or may not operate their own arena, stadium, or other facility for presenting their games or other spectator sports events.

Cross-References.

- Establishments primarily engaged in promoting sporting events without participating in sporting events are classified in Industry Group 7113, Promoters of Performing Arts, Sports, and Similar Events;

- Establishments, such as youth league baseball teams, primarily engaged in participating in sporting events for recreational purposes without playing before a paying audience are classified in Industry 71399, All Other Amusement and Recreation Industries;

- Amateur, semiprofessional, or professional athletic associations or leagues are classified in Industry 81399, Other Similar Organizations (except Business, Professional, Labor, and Political Organizations);

- Establishments primarily engaged in representing or managing the careers of sports figures are classified in Industry 71141, Agents and Managers for Artists, Athletes, Entertainers, and Other Public Figures;

- Independent athletes engaged in providing sports instruction without participating in sporting events before a paying audience are classified in Industry 61162, Sports and Recreation Instruction;

- Independent athletes exclusively engaged in endorsing products or making speeches are classified in Industry 71151, Independent Artists, Writers, and Performers; and

- Establishments primarily engaged in raising horses, mules, donkeys, and other equines are classified in Industry 11292, Horses and Other Equine Production.

711211 Sports Teams and Clubs[CAN]

This U.S. industry comprises professional or semiprofessional sports teams or clubs primarily engaged in participating in live sporting events, such as baseball, basketball, football, hockey, soccer, and jai alai games, before a paying audience. These establishments may or may not operate their own arena, stadium, or other facility for presenting these events.

US—United States industry only. CAN—United States and Canadian industries are comparable. MEX—United States and Mexican industries are comparable. Blank—Canadian, Mexican, and United States industries are comparable.

Cross-References.

- Establishments primarily engaged in promoting sporting events without participating in sporting events are classified in Industry Group 7113, Promoters of Performing Arts, Sports, and Similar Events;

- Establishments, such as youth league baseball teams, primarily engaged in participating in sporting events for recreational purposes without playing before a paying audience are classified in Industry 713990, All Other Amusement and Recreation Industries; and

- Amateur, semiprofessional, or professional athletic associations or leagues are classified in Industry 813990, Other Similar Organizations (except Business, Professional, Labor, and Political Organizations).

711212 Racetracks[US]

This U.S. industry comprises establishments primarily engaged in operating racetracks. These establishments may also present and/or promote the events, such as auto, dog, and horse races, held in these facilities.

Cross-References.

Owners of racing participants, such as cars, dogs, and horses, primarily engaged in entering them in racing events; trainers of racing participants; and independent athletes, such as jockeys and race car drivers, primarily engaged in participating in racing events are classified in U.S. Industry 711219, Other Spectator Sports.

711219 Other Spectator Sports[US]

This U.S. industry comprises (1) independent athletes, such as professional or semiprofessional golfers, boxers, and race car drivers, primarily engaged in participating in live sporting or racing events before a paying audience; (2) owners of racing participants, such as cars, dogs, and horses, primarily engaged in entering them in racing events or other spectator events; and (3) establishments, such as sports trainers, primarily engaged in providing specialized services required to support participants in sports events or competitions.

Cross-References.

- Establishments primarily engaged in operating racctracks are classified in U.S. Industry 711212, Racetracks;

- Establishments primarily engaged in representing or managing the careers of sports figures are classified in Industry 711410, Agents and Managers for Artists, Athletes, Entertainers, and Other Public Figures;

US—United States industry only. CAN—United States and Canadian industries are comparable. MEX—United States and Mexican industries are comparable. Blank—Canadian, Mexican, and United States industries are comparable.

- Independent athletes engaged in providing sports instruction without participating in sporting events before a paying audience are classified in Industry 611620, Sports and Recreation Instruction;

- Independent athletes exclusively engaged in endorsing products or making speeches are classified in Industry 711510, Independent Artists, Writers, and Performers; and

- Establishments primarily engaged in raising horses, mules, donkeys, and other equines are classified in Industry 112920, Horses and Other Equine Production.

7113 Promoters of Performing Arts, Sports, and Similar Events

71131 Promoters of Performing Arts, Sports, and Similar Events with Facilities
See industry description for 711310 below.

711310 Promoters of Performing Arts, Sports, and Similar Events with Facilities[US]

This industry comprises establishments primarily engaged in (1) organizing, promoting, and/or managing live performing arts productions, sports events, and similar events, such as state fairs, county fairs, agricultural fairs, concerts, and festivals, held in facilities that they manage and operate and/or (2) managing and providing the staff to operate arenas, stadiums, theaters, or other related facilities for rent to other promoters.

Cross-References. Establishments primarily engaged in—

- Producing live performances (but may also promote the performances and/or operate the facilities where the performances take place)—are classified in Industry Group 7111, Performing Arts Companies;

- Operating racetracks (but may also promote the events held in these facilities)—are classified in U.S. Industry 711212, Racetracks;

- Presenting sporting events (but may also promote these sporting events and/or operate the stadiums or arenas where the sporting events take place)—are classified in U.S. Industry 711211, Sports Teams and Clubs;

- Organizing, promoting, and/or managing conventions, conferences, and trade shows (but may also operate the facilities where these events take place)—are classified in Industry 561920, Convention and Trade Show Organizers;

US—United States industry only. CAN—United States and Canadian industries are comparable. MEX—United States and Mexican industries are comparable. Blank—Canadian, Mexican, and United States industries are comparable.

- Organizing, promoting, and/or managing performing arts productions, sports events, and similar events in facilities managed and operated by others— are classified in Industry 711320, Promoters of Performing Arts, Sports, and Similar Events without Facilities; and

- Leasing stadiums, arenas, theaters, and other related facilities to others without operating the facilities—are classified in Industry 531120, Lessors of Nonresidential Buildings (except Miniwarehouses).

71132 Promoters of Performing Arts, Sports, and Similar Events without Facilities

See industry description for 711320 below.

711320 Promoters of Performing Arts, Sports, and Similar Events without Facilities[MEX]

This industry comprises promoters primarily engaged in organizing, promoting, and/or managing live performing arts productions, sports events, and similar events, such as state fairs, county fairs, agricultural fairs, concerts, and festivals, in facilities that are managed and operated by others. Theatrical (except motion picture) booking agencies are included in this industry.

Cross-References. Establishments primarily engaged in—

- Booking motion pictures or videos—are classified in U.S. Industry 512199, Other Motion Picture and Video Industries;

- Producing live performances (but may also promote the performances)— are classified in Industry Group 7111, Performing Arts Companies;

- Operating racetracks (but may also promote the events held in these facilities)—are classified in U.S. Industry 711212, Racetracks;

- Presenting sporting events (but may also promote these events)—are classified in U.S. Industry 711211, Sports Teams and Clubs;

- Organizing, promoting, and/or managing conventions, conferences, and trade shows (but may also operate the facilities where these events take place)—are classified in Industry 561920, Convention and Trade Show Organizers;

- Organizing, promoting, and/or managing performing arts, sports, and similar events in facilities they manage or operate—are classified in Industry 711310, Promoters of Performing Arts, Sports, and Similar Events with Facilities; and

- Operating amateur, semiprofessional, or professional athletic associations or leagues—are classified in Industry 813990, Other Similar Organizations (except Business, Professional, Labor, and Political Organizations).

7114 Agents and Managers for Artists, Athletes, Entertainers, and Other Public Figures

71141 Agents and Managers for Artists, Athletes, Entertainers, and Other Public Figures
See industry description for 711410 below.

711410 Agents and Managers for Artists, Athletes, Entertainers, and Other Public Figures

This industry comprises establishments of agents and managers primarily engaged in representing and/or managing creative and performing artists, sports figures, entertainers, and other public figures. The representation and management includes activities, such as representing clients in contract negotiations; managing or organizing client's financial affairs; and generally promoting the careers of their clients.

Illustrative Examples:

Celebrity agents or managers
Sports figure agents or managers
Literary agents

Talent agents
Modeling agents

Cross-References.

- Establishments primarily engaged in supplying models to clients are classified in Industry 561320, Temporary Help Services; and
- Establishments known as model registries primarily engaged in recruiting and placing models for clients are classified in U.S. Industry 561311, Employment Placement Agencies.

7115 Independent Artists, Writers, and Performers

71151 Independent Artists, Writers, and Performers
See industry description for 711510 below.

711510 Independent Artists, Writers, and Performers

This industry comprises independent (i.e., freelance) individuals primarily engaged in performing in artistic productions, in creating artistic and cultural works or productions, or in providing technical expertise necessary for these productions. This industry also includes athletes and other celebrities exclusively engaged in endorsing products and making speeches or public appearances for which they receive a fee.

Illustrative Examples:

Independent actors or actresses	Independent cartoonists
Independent producers	Independent theatrical costume designers
Independent art restorers	Independent dancers
Independent recording technicians	Independent theatrical lighting
Independent artists (except musical,	technicians
commercial, or medical)	Independent journalists
Independent speakers	

Cross-References.

- Freelance musicians and vocalists are classified in Industry 711130, Musical Groups and Artists;

- Independent commercial artists and graphic designers are classified in Industry 541430, Graphic Design Services; and

- Artisans and craftspersons are classified in Sector 31-33, Manufacturing.

712 Museums, Historical Sites, and Similar Institutions

Industries in the Museums, Historical Sites, and Similar Institutions subsector engage in the preservation and exhibition of objects, sites, and natural wonders of historical, cultural, and/or educational value.

7121 Museums, Historical Sites, and Similar Institutions

71211 Museums

See industry description for 712110 below.

712110 Museums^{US}

This industry comprises establishments primarily engaged in the preservation and exhibition of objects of historical, cultural, and/or educational value.

Illustrative Examples:

Art galleries (except retail)	Science or technology museums
Planetariums	Halls of fame
Art museums	Wax museums

US—United States industry only. CAN—United States and Canadian industries are comparable. MEX—United States and Mexican industries are comparable. Blank—Canadian, Mexican, and United States industries are comparable.

Cross-References.

Commercial art galleries primarily engaged in selling art objects are classified in Industry 453920, Art Dealers.

71212 Historical Sites

See industry description for 712120 below.

712120 Historical Sites

This industry comprises establishments primarily engaged in the preservation and exhibition of sites, buildings, forts, or communities that describe events or persons of particular historical interest. Archeological sites, battlefields, historical ships, and pioneer villages are included in this industry.

71213 Zoos and Botanical Gardens

See industry description for 712130 below.

712130 Zoos and Botanical Gardens^CAN

This industry comprises establishments primarily engaged in the preservation and exhibition of live plant and animal life displays.

Illustrative Examples:

Aquariums   Zoological gardens
Wild animal parks   Aviaries
Arboreta

71219 Nature Parks and Other Similar Institutions

See industry description for 712190 below.

712190 Nature Parks and Other Similar Institutions

This industry comprises establishments primarily engaged in the preservation and exhibition of natural areas or settings.

Illustrative Examples:

Bird or wildlife sanctuaries   Conservation areas
Natural wonder (e.g., cavern, waterfall)   Nature centers or preserves
    tourist attractions   National parks

US—United States industry only. CAN—United States and Canadian industries are comparable. MEX—United States and Mexican industries are comparable. Blank—Canadian, Mexican, and United States industries are comparable.

Cross-References.

Establishments primarily engaged in operating commercial hunting or fishing preserves (e.g., game farms) are classified in Industry 114210, Hunting and Trapping.

713 Amusement, Gambling, and Recreation Industries

Industries in the Amusement, Gambling, and Recreation Industries subsector (1) operate facilities where patrons can primarily engage in sports, recreation, amusement, or gambling activities and/or (2) provide other amusement and recreation services, such as supplying and servicing amusement devices in places of business operated by others; operating sports teams, clubs, or leagues engaged in playing games for recreational purposes; and guiding tours without using transportation equipment.

This subsector does not cover all establishments providing recreational services. Other sectors of NAICS also provide recreational services. Providers of recreational services are often engaged in processes classified in other sectors of NAICS. For example, operators of resorts and hunting and fishing camps provide both accommodation and recreational facilities and services. These establishments are classified in Subsector 721, Accommodation, partly to reflect the significant costs associated with the provision of accommodation services and partly to ensure consistency with international standards. Likewise, establishments using transportation equipment to provide recreational and entertainment services, such as those operating sightseeing buses, dinner cruises, or helicopter rides, are classified in Subsector 48-49, Transportation and Warehousing.

The industry groups in this subsector highlight particular types of activities: amusement parks and arcades, gambling industries, and other amusement and recreation industries. The groups, however, are not all inclusive of the activity. The Gambling Industries industry group does not provide for full coverage of gambling activities. For example, casino hotels are classified in Subsector 721, Accommodation; and horse and dog racing tracks are classified in Industry Group 7112, Spectator Sports.

7131 Amusement Parks and Arcades

This industry group comprises establishments primarily engaged in operating amusement parks and amusement arcades and parlors.

71311 Amusement and Theme Parks
See industry description for 713110 below.

713110 Amusement and Theme Parks^{CAN}

This industry comprises establishments, known as amusement or theme parks, primarily engaged in operating a variety of attractions, such as mechanical rides, water rides, games, shows, theme exhibits, refreshment stands, and picnic grounds. These establishments may lease space to others on a concession basis.

Cross-References. Establishments primarily engaged in—

- Operating mechanical or water rides on a concession basis in amusement parks, fairs, and carnivals or in operating a single attraction, such as a waterslide—are classified in Industry 713990, All Other Amusement and Recreation Industries;

- Operating refreshment stands on a concession basis—are classified in Industry Group 7222, Limited-Service Eating Places;

- Supplying and servicing coin-operated amusement (except gambling) devices in other's facilities—are classified in Industry 713990, All Other Amusement and Recreation Industries;

- Supplying and servicing coin-operated gambling devices (e.g., slot machines) in places of business operated by others—are classified in Industry 713290, Other Gambling Industries; and

- Organizing, promoting, and/or managing events, such as carnivals and fairs, with or without facilities—are classified in Industry Group 7113, Promoters of Performing Arts, Sports, and Similar Events.

71312 Amusement Arcades
See industry description for 713120 below.

713120 Amusement Arcades

This industry comprises establishments primarily engaged in operating amusement (except gambling, billiard, or pool) arcades and parlors.

Cross-References. Establishments primarily engaged in—

- Supplying and servicing coin-operated amusement (except gambling) devices in places of business operated by others or in operating billiard or pool parlors—are classified in Industry 713990, All Other Amusement and Recreation Industries;

- Operating bingo, off-track betting, or slot machine parlors or in supplying and servicing coin-operated gambling devices (e.g., slot machines or video

---

US—United States industry only. CAN—United States and Canadian industries are comparable. MEX—United States and Mexican industries are comparable. Blank—Canadian, Mexican, and United States industries are comparable.

gambling terminals) in places of business operated by others—are classified in Industry 713290, Other Gambling Industries;

- Operating casinos (except casino hotels)—are classified in Industry 713210, Casinos (except Casino Hotels); and

- Operating casino hotels—are classified in Industry 721120, Casino Hotels.

7132 Gambling Industries

This industry group comprises establishments (except casino hotels) primarily engaged in operating gambling facilities, such as casinos, bingo halls, and video gaming terminals, or in the provision of gambling services, such as lotteries and off-track betting. Casino hotels are classified in Industry 72112, Casino Hotels.

71321 Casinos (except Casino Hotels)
See industry description for 713210 below.

713210 Casinos (except Casino Hotels)

This industry comprises establishments primarily engaged in operating gambling facilities that offer table wagering games along with other gambling activities, such as slot machines and sports betting. These establishments often provide food and beverage services. Included in this industry are floating casinos (i.e., gambling cruises, riverboat casinos).

Cross-References. Establishments primarily engaged in—

- Operating bingo, off-track betting, or slot machine parlors or in supplying and servicing coin-operated gambling devices, such as slot machines and video gaming terminals in places of business operated by others—are classified in Industry 713290, Other Gambling Industries; and

- Operating casino hotels—are classified in Industry 721120, Casino Hotels.

71329 Other Gambling Industries
See industry description for 713290 below.

713290 Other Gambling Industries[US]

This industry comprises establishments primarily engaged in operating gambling facilities (except casinos or casino hotels) or providing gambling services.

US—United States industry only. CAN—United States and Canadian industries are comparable. MEX—United States and Mexican industries are comparable. Blank—Canadian, Mexican, and United States industries are comparable.

Illustrative Examples:

Bingo, off-track betting, or slot machine parlors	Bookmakers
Coin-operated gambling device	Lottery ticket sales agents (except retail stores)
concession operators (i.e., supplying and servicing in others' facilities)	Card rooms (e.g., poker rooms)

Cross-References. Establishments primarily engaged in—

- Operating casinos—are classified in Industry 713210, Casinos (except Casino Hotels);

- Operating casino hotels—are classified in Industry 721120, Casino Hotels;

- Operating facilities with coin-operated nongambling amusement devices— are classified in Industry 713120, Amusement Arcades;

- Supplying and servicing coin-operated nongambling amusement devices in places of business operated by others—are classified in Industry 713990, All Other Amusement and Recreation Industries; and

- Operating racetracks or presenting live racing or sporting events—are classified in Industry 71121, Spectator Sports.

7139 Other Amusement and Recreation Industries

71391 Golf Courses and Country Clubs
See industry description for 713910 below.

713910 Golf Courses and Country Clubs

This industry comprises (1) establishments primarily engaged in operating golf courses (except miniature) and (2) establishments primarily engaged in operating golf courses, along with dining facilities and other recreational facilities that are known as country clubs. These establishments often provide food and beverage services, equipment rental services, and golf instruction services.

Cross-References. Establishments primarily engaged in—

- Operating driving ranges and miniature golf courses—are classified in Industry 713990, All Other Amusement and Recreation Industries; and

- Operating resorts where golf facilities are combined with accommodations—are classified in Industry Group 7211, Traveler Accommodation.

US—United States industry only. CAN—United States and Canadian industries are comparable. MEX—United States and Mexican industries are comparable. Blank—Canadian, Mexican, and United States industries are comparable.

71392 Skiing Facilities

See industry description for 713920 below.

713920 Skiing Facilities

This industry comprises establishments engaged in (1) operating downhill, cross-country, or related skiing areas and/or (2) operating equipment, such as ski lifts and tows. These establishments often provide food and beverage services, equipment rental services, and ski instruction services. Four-season resorts without accommodations are included in this industry.

Cross-References.

Establishments primarily engaged in operating resorts where skiing facilities are combined with accommodations are classified in Industry Group 7211, Traveler Accommodation.

71393 Marinas

See industry description for 713930 below.

713930 Marinas

This industry comprises establishments, commonly known as marinas, engaged in operating docking and/or storage facilities for pleasure craft owners, with or without one or more related activities, such as retailing fuel and marine supplies; and repairing, maintaining, or renting pleasure boats.

Cross-References. Establishments primarily engaged in—

- Renting pleasure boats—are classified in U.S. Industry 532292, Recreational Goods Rental;

- Repairing pleasure boats—are classified in Industry 811490, Other Personal and Household Goods Repair and Maintenance;

- Retailing marine supplies—are classified in U.S. Industry 441222, Boat Dealers; and

- Retailing fuel for boats—are classified in Industry 447190, Other Gasoline Stations.

71394 Fitness and Recreational Sports Centers

See industry description for 713940 below.

US—United States industry only. CAN—United States and Canadian industries are comparable. MEX—United States and Mexican industries are comparable. Blank—Canadian, Mexican, and United States industries are comparable.

713940 Fitness and Recreational Sports Centers[CAN]

This industry comprises establishments primarily engaged in operating fitness and recreational sports facilities featuring exercise and other active physical fitness conditioning or recreational sports activities, such as swimming, skating, or racquet sports.

Illustrative Examples:

Aerobic dance or exercise centers
Ice or roller skating rinks
Gymnasiums
Physical fitness centers

Handball, racquetball, or tennis club
  facilities
Swimming or wave pools

Cross-References.

- Establishments primarily engaged in providing nonmedical services to assist clients in attaining or maintaining a desired weight are classified in U.S. Industry 812191, Diet and Weight Reducing Centers;

- Establishments primarily engaged in operating health resorts and spas where recreational facilities are combined with accommodations are classified in Industry 721110, Hotels (except Casino Hotels) and Motels; and

- Recreational sports clubs (i.e., sports teams) not operating sports facilities are classified in Industry 713990, All Other Amusement and Recreation Industries.

71395 Bowling Centers
See industry description for 713950 below.

713950 Bowling Centers

This industry comprises establishments engaged in operating bowling centers. These establishments often provide food and beverage services.

71399 All Other Amusement and Recreation Industries
See industry description for 713990 below.

713990 All Other Amusement and Recreation Industries[CAN]

This industry comprises establishments (except amusement parks and arcades; gambling industries; golf courses and country clubs; skiing facilities; marinas;

US—United States industry only. CAN—United States and Canadian industries are comparable. MEX—United States and Mexican industries are comparable. Blank—Canadian, Mexican, and United States industries are comparable.

fitness and recreational sports centers; and bowling centers) primarily engaged in providing recreational and amusement services.

Illustrative Examples:

Amusement ride or coin-operated nongambling amusement device concession operators (i.e., supplying or servicing in others' facilities)
Miniature golf courses
Archery or shooting ranges
Recreational day camps (except instructional)

Billiard or pool parlors
Recreational or youth sports teams and leagues
Boating clubs (without marinas)
Recreational sports clubs (i.e., sports teams) not operating facilities
Dance halls
Riding stables

Cross-References.

- Establishments primarily engaged in operating amusement parks and arcades are classified in Industry Group 7131, Amusement Parks and Arcades;

- Establishments primarily engaged in operating gambling facilities (except casino hotels) or providing gambling services are classified in Industry Group 7132, Gambling Industries;

- Establishments primarily engaged in operating casino hotels are classified in Industry 721120, Casino Hotels;

- Establishments primarily engaged in operating golf courses (except miniature) and country clubs are classified in Industry 713910, Golf Courses and Country Clubs;

- Establishments primarily engaged in operating skiing facilities without hotel accommodation are classified in Industry 713920, Skiing Facilities;

- Establishments primarily engaged in operating resorts where recreational facilities are combined with lodging are classified in Industry Group 7211, Traveler Accommodation;

- Establishments primarily engaged in operating marinas are classified in Industry 713930, Marinas;

- Establishments primarily engaged in operating fitness and recreational sports centers are classified in Industry 713940, Fitness and Recreational Sports Centers;

- Establishments primarily engaged in operating bowling centers are classified in Industry 713950, Bowling Centers;

- Establishments primarily engaged in operating instructional camps, such as sports camps, fine arts camps, and computer camps, are classified in Sector 61, Educational Services based on the nature of instruction;

US—United States industry only. CAN—United States and Canadian industries are comparable. MEX—United States and Mexican industries are comparable. Blank—Canadian, Mexican, and United States industries are comparable.

- Independent athletes engaged in participating in sporting events before a paying audience are classified in U.S. Industry 711219, Other Spectator Sports;

- Independent athletes engaged in providing sports instruction without participating in sporting events before a paying audience are classified in Industry 611620, Sports and Recreation Instruction;

- Independent athletes exclusively engaged in endorsing products or making speeches are classified in Industry 711510, Independent Artists, Writers, and Performers;

- Establishments primarily engaged in providing scenic and sightseeing transportation are classified in Subsector 487, Scenic and Sightseeing Transportation;

- Aviation clubs primarily engaged in providing specialty air and flying services are classified in U.S. Industry 481219, Other Nonscheduled Air Transportation;

- Aviation clubs primarily engaged in advocating social and political causes are classified in U.S. Industry 813319, Other Social Advocacy Organizations; and

- Amateur, semiprofessional, or professional athletic associations or leagues are classified in Industry 813990, Other Similar Organizations (except Business, Professional, Labor, and Political Organizations).

US—United States industry only. CAN—United States and Canadian industries are comparable. MEX—United States and Mexican industries are comparable. Blank—Canadian, Mexican, and United States industries are comparable.

http://www.census.gov/naics

Sector 72—Accommodation and Food Services

The Sector as a Whole

The Accommodation and Food Services sector comprises establishments providing customers with lodging and/or preparing meals, snacks, and beverages for immediate consumption. The sector includes both accommodation and food services establishments because the two activities are often combined at the same establishment.

Excluded from this sector are civic and social organizations; amusement and recreation parks; theaters; and other recreation or entertainment facilities providing food and beverage services.

721 Accommodation

Industries in the Accommodation subsector provide lodging or short-term accommodations for travelers, vacationers, and others. There is a wide range of establishments in these industries. Some provide lodging only; while others provide meals, laundry services, and recreational facilities, as well as lodging. Lodging establishments are classified in this subsector even if the provision of complementary services generates more revenue. The types of complementary services provided vary from establishment to establishment.

The subsector is organized into three industry groups: (1) traveler accommodation, (2) recreational accommodation, and (3) rooming and boarding houses. The Traveler Accommodation industry group includes establishments that primarily provide traditional types of lodging services. This group includes hotels, motels, and bed and breakfast inns. In addition to lodging, these establishments may provide a range of other services to their guests. The RV (Recreational Vehicle) Parks and Recreational Camps industry group includes establishments that operate lodging facilities primarily designed to accommodate outdoor enthusiasts. Included are travel trailer campsites, recreational vehicle parks, and outdoor adventure retreats. The Rooming and Boarding Houses industry group includes establishments providing temporary or longer-term accommodations, which for the period of occupancy, may serve as a principal residence. Board (i.e., meals) may be provided but is not essential.

Establishments that manage short-stay accommodation establishments (e.g., hotels and motels) on a contractual basis are classified in this subsector if they both manage the operation and provide the operating staff. Such establishments are classified based on the type of facility managed and operated.

US—United States industry only. CAN—United States and Canadian industries are comparable. MEX—United States and Mexican industries are comparable. Blank—Canadian, Mexican, and United States industries are comparable.

7211 Traveler Accommodation

72111 Hotels (except Casino Hotels) and Motels
See industry description for 721110 below.

721110 Hotels (except Casino Hotels) and Motels[US]

This industry comprises establishments primarily engaged in providing short-term lodging in facilities known as hotels, motor hotels, resort hotels, and motels. The establishments in this industry may offer food and beverage services, recreational services, conference rooms and convention services, laundry services, parking, and other services.

Cross-References. Establishments primarily engaged in—

- Providing short-term lodging with a casino on the premises—are classified in Industry 721120, Casino Hotels; and

- Providing short-term lodging in facilities known as bed-and-breakfast inns, youth hostels, housekeeping cabins and cottages, and tourist homes—are classified in Industry 72119, Other Traveler Accommodation.

72112 Casino Hotels
See industry description for 721120 below.

721120 Casino Hotels

This industry comprises establishments primarily engaged in providing short-term lodging in hotel facilities with a casino on the premises. The casino on premises includes table wagering games and may include other gambling activities, such as slot machines and sports betting. These establishments generally offer a range of services and amenities, such as food and beverage services, entertainment, valet parking, swimming pools, and conference and convention facilities.

Cross-References. Establishments primarily engaged in—

- Providing short-term lodging in facilities known as hotels and motels that provide limited gambling activities, such as slot machines, without a casino on the premises—are classified in Industry 721110, Hotels (except Casino Hotels) and Motels; and

- Operating as stand-alone casinos—are classified in Industry 713210, Casinos (except Casino Hotels).

US—United States industry only. CAN—United States and Canadian industries are comparable. MEX—United States and Mexican industries are comparable. Blank—Canadian, Mexican, and United States industries are comparable.

72119 Other Traveler Accommodation

This industry comprises establishments primarily engaged in providing short-term lodging (except hotels, motels, and casino hotels).

Illustrative Examples:

Bed-and-breakfast inns   Youth hostels
Tourist homes   Housekeeping cabins and cottages
Guest houses

Cross-References. Establishments primarily engaged in—

- Providing short-term lodging in facilities known as hotels without a casino on the premises—are classified in Industry 72111, Hotels (except Casino Hotels) and Motels; and
- Providing short-term lodging in facilities known as hotels with a casino on the premises—are classified in Industry 72112, Casino Hotels.

721191 Bed-and-Breakfast Inns[CAN]

This U.S. industry comprises establishments primarily engaged in providing short-term lodging in facilities known as bed-and-breakfast inns. These establishments provide short-term lodging in private homes or small buildings converted for this purpose. Bed-and-breakfast inns are characterized by a highly personalized service and inclusion of a full breakfast in the room rate.

721199 All Other Traveler Accommodation[US]

This U.S. industry comprises establishments primarily engaged in providing short-term lodging (except hotels, motels, casino hotels, and bed-and-breakfast inns).

Illustrative Examples:

Guest houses   Housekeeping cabins and cottages
Tourist homes   Youth hostels

Cross-References. Establishments primarily engaged in—

- Providing short-term lodging in facilities known as hotels without a casino on the premises—are classified in Industry 721110, Hotels (except Casino Hotels) and Motels;
- Providing short-term lodging in facilities known as hotels with a casino on the premises—are classified in Industry 721120, Casino Hotels; and

---

US—United States industry only. CAN—United States and Canadian industries are comparable. MEX—United States and Mexican industries are comparable. Blank—Canadian, Mexican, and United States industries are comparable.

- Providing short-term lodging in establishments known as bed-and-breakfast inns—are classified in U.S. Industry 721191, Bed-and-Breakfast Inns.

7212 RV (Recreational Vehicle) Parks and Recreational Camps

72121 RV (Recreational Vehicle) Parks and Recreational Camps

This industry comprises establishments primarily engaged in operating recreational vehicle parks and campgrounds and recreational and vacation camps. These establishments cater to outdoor enthusiasts and are characterized by the type of accommodation and by the nature and the range of recreational facilities and activities provided to their clients.

Illustrative Examples:

Fishing and hunting camps
Travel trailer campsites
Outdoor adventure retreats

Vacation camps (except instructional, day)
Recreational vehicle parks

Cross-References. Establishments primarily engaged in—

- Operating recreational facilities without accommodations—are classified in Subsector 713, Amusement, Gambling, and Recreation Industries;
- Operating instructional camps, such as sports camps, fine arts camps, and computer camps—are classified in Sector 61, Educational Services, based on the nature of instruction;
- Operating children's day camps (except instructional)—are classified in Industry 71399, All Other Amusement and Recreation Industries; and
- Acting as lessors of residential mobile home sites (i.e., trailer parks)—are classified in Industry 53119, Lessors of Other Real Estate Property.

721211 RV (Recreational Vehicle) Parks and Campgrounds[CAN]

This U.S. industry comprises establishments primarily engaged in operating sites to accommodate campers and their equipment, including tents, tent trailers, travel trailers, and RVs (recreational vehicles). These establishments may provide access to facilities, such as washrooms, laundry rooms, recreation halls and playgrounds, stores, and snack bars.

Cross-References. Establishments primarily engaged in—

- Operating recreational facilities without accommodations—are classified in Subsector 713, Amusement, Gambling, and Recreation Industries; and

---

· US—United States industry only. CAN—United States and Canadian industries are comparable. MEX—United States and Mexican industries are comparable. Blank—Canadian. Mexican. and United States industries are comparable.

- Acting as lessors of residential mobile home sites (i.e., trailer parks)—are classified in Industry 531190, Lessors of Other Real Estate Property.

721214 Recreational and Vacation Camps (except Campgrounds)[US]

This U.S. industry comprises establishments primarily engaged in operating overnight recreational camps, such as children's camps, family vacation camps, hunting and fishing camps, and outdoor adventure retreats that offer trail riding, white-water rafting, hiking, and similar activities. These establishments provide accommodation facilities, such as cabins and fixed campsites, and other amenities, such as food services, recreational facilities and equipment, and organized recreational activities.

Illustrative Examples:

Fishing camps	Hunting camps
Vacation camps (except instructional, day)	Wilderness camps
	Outdoor adventure retreats

Cross-References. Establishments primarily engaged in—

- Operating instructional camps, such as sports camps, fine arts camps, and computer camps—are classified in Sector 61, Educational Services, based on the nature of instruction; and
- Operating children's day camps (except instructional)—are classified in Industry 713990, All Other Amusement and Recreation Industries.

7213 Rooming and Boarding Houses

72131 Rooming and Boarding Houses
See industry description for 721310 below.

721310 Rooming and Boarding Houses[CAN]

This industry comprises establishments primarily engaged in operating rooming and boarding houses and similar facilities, such as fraternity houses, sorority houses, off-campus dormitories, residential clubs, and workers' camps. These establishments provide temporary or longer-term accommodations which, for the period of occupancy, may serve as a principal residence. These establishments also may provide complementary services, such as housekeeping, meals, and laundry services.

US—United States industry only. CAN—United States and Canadian industries are comparable. MEX—United States and Mexican industries are comparable. Blank—Canadian, Mexican, and United States industries are comparable.

Illustrative Examples:

Dormitories (off campus)
Sorority houses
Fraternity houses

Workers' camps
Rooming houses

722 Food Services and Drinking Places

Industries in the Food Services and Drinking Places subsector prepare meals, snacks, and beverages to customer order for immediate on-premises and off-premises consumption. There is a wide range of establishments in these industries. Some provide food and drink only; while others provide various combinations of seating space, waiter/waitress services and incidental amenities, such as limited entertainment. The industries in the subsector are grouped based on the type and level of services provided. The industry groups are full-service restaurants; limited-service eating places; special food services, such as food service contractors, caterers, and mobile food services; and drinking places.

Food and beverage services at hotels and motels; amusement parks, theaters, casinos, country clubs, and similar recreational facilities; and civic and social organizations are included in this subsector only if these services are provided by a separate establishment primarily engaged in providing food and beverage services.

Excluded from this subsector are establishments operating dinner cruises. These establishments are classified in Subsector 487, Scenic and Sightseeing Transportation because those establishments utilize transportation equipment to provide scenic recreational entertainment.

7221 Full-Service Restaurants

This industry group comprises establishments primarily engaged in providing food services to patrons who order and are served while seated (i.e., waiter/waitress service) and pay after eating. Establishments that provide these types of food services to patrons with any combination of other services, such as takeout services, are classified in this industry.

72211 Full-Service Restaurants

See industry description for 722110 below.

722110 Full-Service Restaurants[CAN]

This industry comprises establishments primarily engaged in providing food services to patrons who order and are served while seated (i.e., waiter/waitress service) and pay after eating. These establishments may provide this type of food

---

US—United States industry only. CAN—United States and Canadian industries are comparable. MEX—United States and Mexican industries are comparable. Blank—Canadian, Mexican, and United States industries are comparable.

service to patrons in combination with selling alcoholic beverages, providing carry out services, or presenting live nontheatrical entertainment.

Cross-References. Establishments primarily engaged in—

- Providing food services where patrons generally order or select items and pay before eating—are classified in U.S. Industry 722211, Limited-Service Restaurants;
- Selling a specialty snack or nonalcoholic beverage for consumption on or near the premises—are classified in U.S. Industry 722213, Snack and Nonalcoholic Beverage Bars;
- Preparing and serving alcoholic beverages and known as bars, taverns, or nightclubs—are classified in Industry 722410, Drinking Places (Alcoholic Beverages); and
- Presenting live theatrical productions and providing food and beverages for consumption on the premises—are classified in Industry 711110, Theater Companies and Dinner Theaters.

7222 Limited-Service Eating Places

This industry group comprises establishments primarily engaged in providing food services where patrons generally order or select items and pay before eating. Most establishments do not have waiter/waitress service, but some provide limited service, such as cooking to order (i.e., per special request), bringing food to seated customers, or providing off-site delivery.

72221 Limited-Service Eating Places

This industry comprises establishments primarily engaged in (1) providing food services where patrons generally order or select items and pay before eating or (2) selling a specialty snack or nonalcoholic beverage for consumption on or near the premises. Food and drink may be consumed on the premises, taken out, or delivered to the customer's location. Some establishments (except snack and nonalcoholic beverage bars) in this industry may provide these food services in combination with selling alcoholic beverages.

Illustrative Examples:

Cafeterias
Pizza delivery shops
Fast-food restaurants
Snack bars (e.g., cookies, pretzels, popcorn)

Nonalcoholic beverage bars
Takeout eating places

US—United States industry only. CAN—United States and Canadian industries are comparable. MEX—United States and Mexican industries are comparable. Blank—Canadian, Mexican, and United States industries are comparable.

Cross-References. Establishments primarily engaged in—

- Providing food services to patrons who order and are served while seated and pay after eating in combination with providing takeout service—are classified in Industry 72211, Full-Service Restaurants;
- Retailing confectionery goods and nuts not packaged for immediate consumption—are classified in Industry 44529, Other Specialty Food Stores;
- Retailing baked goods (e.g., pretzels, doughnuts, cookies, and bagels) not baked on the premises and not for immediate consumption—are classified in Industry 44529, Other Specialty Food Stores;
- Retailing baked goods (e.g., doughnuts and bagels) and providing food services to patrons who order and are served while seated and pay after eating—are classified in Industry 72211, Full-Service Restaurants;
- Selling snacks and nonalcoholic beverages from mobile vehicles—are classified in Industry 72233, Mobile Food Services; and
- Preparing and serving alcoholic beverages and known as bars, taverns, or nightclubs—are classified in Industry 72241, Drinking Places (Alcoholic Beverages).

722211 Limited-Service Restaurants[US]

This U.S. industry comprises establishments primarily engaged in providing food services (except snack and nonalcoholic beverage bars) where patrons generally order or select items and pay before eating. Food and drink may be consumed on premises, taken out, or delivered to the customer's location. Some establishments in this industry may provide these food services in combination with selling alcoholic beverages.

Illustrative Examples:

Delicatessen restaurants
Pizza delivery shops
Family restaurants, limited service
Takeout eating places

Fast-food restaurants
Takeout sandwich shops
Limited-service pizza parlors

Cross-References. Establishments primarily engaged in—

- Preparing and serving meals for immediate consumption using cafeteria-style serving equipment, known as cafeterias—are classified in U.S. Industry 722212, Cafeterias, Grill Buffets, and Buffets;
- Providing food services to patrons who order and are served while seated and pay after eating—are classified in Industry 722110, Full-Service Restaurants;

US—United States industry only. CAN—United States and Canadian industries are comparable. MEX—United States and Mexican industries are comparable. Blank—Canadian, Mexican, and United States industries are comparable.

- Selling a specialty snack (e.g., ice cream, frozen yogurt, candy, cookies) or nonalcoholic beverages, for consumption on or near the premises—are classified in U.S. Industry 722213, Snack and Nonalcoholic Beverage Bars;

- Retailing confectionery goods and nuts not packaged for immediate consumption—are classified in U.S. Industry 445292, Confectionery and Nut Stores;

- Retailing baked goods (e.g., pretzels, doughnuts, cookies, and bagels) not baked on the premises and not for immediate consumption—are classified in U.S. Industry 445291, Baked Goods Stores;

- Preparing and serving alcoholic beverages, known as bars, taverns, or nightclubs—are classified in Industry 722410, Drinking Places (Alcoholic Beverages); and

- Selling baked goods (e.g., doughnuts and bagels) and providing food services to patrons who order and are served while seated and pay after eating—are classified in Industry 722110, Full-Service Restaurants.

722212 Cafeterias, Grill Buffets, and Buffets[US]

This industry comprises establishments, known as cafeterias, buffets, or grill buffets, primarily engaged in preparing and serving meals for immediate consumption using cafeteria-style or buffet serving equipment, such as steam tables, refrigerated areas, display grills, and self-service nonalcoholic beverage dispensing equipment. Patrons select from food and drink items on display in a continuous cafeteria line or from buffet stations.

Cross-References. Establishments primarily engaged in—

- Providing food services to patrons who order and are served while seated and pay after eating—are classified in Industry 722110, Full-Service Restaurants; and

- Providing food services where patrons generally order or select items and pay before eating, other than cafeterias, buffets, grill buffets, and snack and nonalcoholic beverage bars—are classified in U.S. Industry 722211, Limited-Service Restaurants.

722213 Snack and Nonalcoholic Beverage Bars[US]

This U.S. industry comprises establishments primarily engaged in (1) preparing and/or serving a specialty snack, such as ice cream, frozen yogurt, cookies, or popcorn or (2) serving nonalcoholic beverages, such as coffee, juices, or sodas for consumption on or near the premises. These establishments may carry and sell a combination of snack, nonalcoholic beverage, and other related products (e.g., coffee beans, mugs, coffee makers) but generally promote and sell a unique snack or nonalcoholic beverage.

Illustrative Examples:

Beverage bars
Carryout service doughnut shops with on-premises baking
Carryout service bagel shops with on-premises baking

Carryout service pretzel shops with on-premises baking
Carryout service cookie shops with on-premises banking
Ice cream parlors

Cross-References. Establishments primarily engaged in—

- Selling one or more of the following food specialties: hamburgers, hot dogs, pizza, chicken, specialty cuisines—are classified in U.S. Industry 722211, Limited-Service Restaurants or Industry 722110, Full-Service Restaurants, based on type of food services provided to patrons;
- Preparing and serving snacks and nonalcoholic beverages from mobile vehicles—are classified in Industry 722330, Mobile Food Services;
- Retailing confectionery goods and nuts not packaged for immediate consumption—are classified in U.S. Industry 445292, Confectionery and Nut Stores;
- Retailing baked goods (e.g., pretzels, doughnuts, cookies, and bagels) not baked on the premises and not for immediate consumption—are classified in U.S. Industry 445291, Baked Goods Stores; and
- Retailing baked goods (e.g., doughnuts and bagels) and providing food services to patrons who order and are served while seated and pay after eating—are classified in Industry 722110, Full-Service Restaurants.

7223 Special Food Services

This industry group comprises establishments primarily engaged in providing food services at one or more of the following locations: (1) the customer's location; (2) a location designated by the customer; or (3) from motorized vehicles or nonmotorized carts.

72231 Food Service Contractors
See industry description for 722310 below.

722310 Food Service Contractors

This industry comprises establishments primarily engaged in providing food services at institutional, governmental, commercial, or industrial locations of others

---

US—United States industry only. CAN—United States and Canadian industries are comparable. MEX—United States and Mexican industries are comparable. Blank—Canadian, Mexican, and United States industries are comparable.

based on contractual arrangements with these type of organizations for a specified period of time. The establishments of this industry provide food services for the convenience of the contracting organization or the contracting organization's customers. The contractual arrangement of these establishments with contracting organizations may vary from type of facility operated (e.g., cafeteria, restaurant, fast-food eating place), revenue sharing, cost structure, to providing personnel. Management staff is always provided by the food service contractors.

Illustrative Examples:

Airline food service contractors	Cafeteria food service contractors (e.g.,
Food concession contractors (e.g., at sporting, entertainment, convention facilities)	at schools, hospitals, government offices)

Cross-References. Establishments primarily engaged in—

- Providing food services on a single-event basis—are classified in Industry 722320, Caterers; and

- Supplying and servicing food vending machines—are classified in Industry 454210, Vending Machine Operators.

72232 Caterers
See industry description for 722320 below.

722320 Caterers

This industry comprises establishments primarily engaged in providing single event-based food services. These establishments generally have equipment and vehicles to transport meals and snacks to events and/or prepare food at an off-premise site. Banquet halls with catering staff are included in this industry. Examples of events catered by establishments in this industry are graduation parties, wedding receptions, business or retirement luncheons, and trade shows.

Cross-References. Establishments primarily engaged in—

- Preparing and serving meals and snacks for immediate consumption from motorized vehicles or nonmotorized carts—are classified in Industry 722330, Mobile Food Services;

- Providing food services at institutional, governmental, commercial, or industrial locations of others (e.g., airline contractors, industrial caterers) or providing food services based on contractual arrangements for a specified period of time—are classified in Industry 722310, Food Service Contractors; and

---

US—United States industry only. CAN—United States and Canadian industries are comparable. MEX—United States and Mexican industries are comparable. Blank—Canadian, Mexican, and United States industries are comparable.

- Renting out facilities without providing catering staff—are classified in Industry 531120, Lessors of Nonresidential Buildings (except Miniwarehouses).

72233 Mobile Food Services

See industry description for 722330 below.

722330 Mobile Food Services

This industry comprises establishments primarily engaged in preparing and serving meals and snacks for immediate consumption from motorized vehicles or nonmotorized carts. The establishment is the central location from which the caterer route is serviced, not each vehicle or cart. Included in this industry are establishments primarily engaged in providing food services from vehicles, such as hot dog carts, and ice cream trucks.

Illustrative Examples:

Ice cream truck vendors
Mobile food concession stands
Mobile canteens

Mobile refreshment stands
Mobile food carts
Mobile snack stands

Cross-References. Establishments primarily engaged in—

- Providing food services where patrons generally order or select items and pay before eating—are classified in U.S. Industry 722211, Limited-Service Restaurants;

- Selling unprepared foods, such as vegetables, melons, and nuts or fruit from carts—are classified in Industry 454390, Other Direct Selling Establishments;

- Selling specialty snacks (e.g., ice cream, frozen yogurt, cookies, popcorn) or nonalcoholic beverages in nonmobile facilities for consumption on or near the premises—are classified in U.S. Industry 722213, Snack and Nonalcoholic Beverage Bars;

- Selling food specialties, such as hamburgers, hot dogs, chicken, pizza, or specialty cuisines from nonmobile facilities—are classified in U.S. Industry 722211, Limited-Service Restaurants or Industry 722110, Full-Service Restaurants, based on type of food services provided to patrons; and

- Operating as street vendors (except food)—are classified in Industry 454390, Other Direct Selling Establishments.

7224 Drinking Places (Alcoholic Beverages)

This industry group comprises establishments primarily engaged in preparing and serving alcoholic beverages for immediate consumption.

72241 Drinking Places (Alcoholic Beverages)
See industry description for 722410 below.

722410 Drinking Places (Alcoholic Beverages)[CAN]

This industry comprises establishments known as bars, taverns, nightclubs, or drinking places primarily engaged in preparing and serving alcoholic beverages for immediate consumption. These establishments may also provide limited food services.

Cross-References. Establishments primarily engaged in—

- Preparing and serving alcoholic beverages (i.e., not known as bars or taverns) and providing food services to patrons who order and are served while seated and pay after eating—are classified in Industry 722110, Full-Service Restaurants;

- Preparing and serving alcoholic beverages (i.e., not known as bars or taverns) and providing food services to patrons who generally order or select items and pay before eating—are classified in Industry 72221, Limited-Service Eating Places;

- Operating a civic or social association with a bar for the association members—are classified in Industry 81341, Civic and Social Organizations;

- Retailing packaged alcoholic beverages not for immediate consumption on the premises—are classified in Industry 445310, Beer, Wine, and Liquor Stores; and

- Operating discotheques or dance clubs without selling alcoholic beverages—are classified in Industry 713990, All Other Amusement and Recreation Industries.

US—United States industry only. CAN—United States and Canadian industries are comparable. MEX—United States and Mexican industries are comparable. Blank—Canadian, Mexican, and United States industries are comparable.

Sector 81—Other Services
(except Public Administration)

The Sector as a Whole

The Other Services (except Public Administration) sector comprises establishments engaged in providing services not specifically provided for elsewhere in the classification system. Establishments in this sector are primarily engaged in activities, such as equipment and machinery repairing, promoting or administering religious activities, grantmaking, advocacy, and providing drycleaning and laundry services, personal care services, death care services, pet care services, photofinishing services, temporary parking services, and dating services.

Private households that engage in employing workers on or about the premises in activities primarily concerned with the operation of the household are included in this sector.

Excluded from this sector are establishments primarily engaged in retailing new equipment and also performing repairs and general maintenance on equipment. These establishments are classified in Sector 44-45, Retail Trade.

811 Repair and Maintenance

Industries in the Repair and Maintenance subsector restore machinery, equipment, and other products to working order. These establishments also typically provide general or routine maintenance (i.e., servicing) on such products to ensure they work efficiently and to prevent breakdown and unnecessary repairs.

The NAICS structure for this subsector brings together most types of repair and maintenance establishments and categorizes them based on production processes (i.e., on the type of repair and maintenance activity performed, and the necessary skills, expertise, and processes that are found in different repair and maintenance establishments). This NAICS classification does not delineate between repair services provided to businesses versus those that serve households. Although some industries primarily serve either businesses or households, separation by class of customer is limited by the fact that many establishments serve both. Establishments repairing computers and consumer electronics products are two examples of such overlap.

The Repair and Maintenance subsector does not include all establishments that do repair and maintenance. For example, a substantial amount of repair is done by establishments that also manufacture machinery, equipment, and other goods. These establishments are included in the Manufacturing sector in NAICS. In addition, repair of transportation equipment is often provided by or based at transportation facilities, such as airports, seaports, and these activities are included in the Transportation and Warehousing sector. A particularly unique situation exists with repair of buildings. Plumbing, electrical installation and repair, painting and decorating, and other construction-related establishments are often involved in performing installation or other work on new construction as well as providing repair services on existing structures. While some specialize in repair, it is difficult to distinguish between the two types and all have been included in the Construction sector.

Excluded from this subsector are establishments primarily engaged in rebuilding or remanufacturing machinery and equipment. These are classified in Sector 31-33, Manufacturing. Also excluded are retail establishments that provide after-sale services and repair. These are classified in Sector 44-45, Retail Trade.

8111 Automotive Repair and Maintenance

This industry group comprises establishments involved in providing repair and maintenance services for automotive vehicles, such as passenger cars, trucks, and vans, and all trailers. Establishments in this industry group employ mechanics with specialized technical skills to diagnose and repair the mechanical and electrical systems for automotive vehicles, repair automotive interiors, and paint or repair automotive exteriors.

81111 Automotive Mechanical and Electrical Repair and Maintenance

This industry comprises establishments primarily engaged in providing mechanical or electrical repair and maintenance services for automotive vehicles, such as passenger cars, trucks and vans, and all trailers. These establishments may specialize in a single service or may provide a wide range of these services.

Cross-References. Establishments primarily engaged in—

- Retailing automotive vehicles and automotive parts and accessories and also providing automotive repair services—are classified in Subsector 441, Motor Vehicle and Parts Dealers;

- Retailing motor fuels and also providing automotive vehicle repair services—are classified in Industry Group 4471, Gasoline Stations;

- Changing motor oil and lubricating the chassis of automotive vehicles— are classified in Industry 81119, Other Automotive Repair and Maintenance;

- Providing automotive vehicle air-conditioning repair—are classified in Industry 81119, Other Automotive Repair and Maintenance; and

- Motorcycle repair and maintenance services—are classified in Industry 81149, Other Personal and Household Goods Repair and Maintenance.

US—United States industry only. CAN—United States and Canadian industries are comparable. MEX—United States and Mexican industries are comparable. Blank—Canadian, Mexican, and United States industries are comparable.

811111 General Automotive Repair[CAN]

This U.S. industry comprises establishments primarily engaged in providing (1) a wide range of mechanical and electrical repair and maintenance services for automotive vehicles, such as passenger cars, trucks, and vans, and all trailers or (2) engine repair and replacement.

Illustrative Examples:

Automobile repair garages (except gasoline service stations)

General automotive repair shops

Automotive engine repair and replacement shops

Cross-References. Establishments primarily engaged in—

- Retailing new automotive parts and accessories and also providing automotive repair services—are classified in Industry 441310, Automotive Parts and Accessories Stores;

- Changing motor oil and lubricating the chassis of automotive vehicles—are classified in U.S. Industry 811191, Automotive Oil Change and Lubrication Shops;

- Replacing and repairing automotive vehicle exhaust systems—are classified in U.S. Industry 811112, Automotive Exhaust System Repair;

- Replacing and repairing automotive vehicle transmissions—are classified in U.S. Industry 811113, Automotive Transmission Repair;

- Retailing motor fuels and also providing automotive vehicle repair services—are classified in Industry Group 4471, Gasoline Stations;

- Retailing automobiles and light trucks for highway use and also providing automotive repair services—are classified in Industry Group 4411, Automobile Dealers; and

- Motorcycle repair and maintenance services—are classified in Industry 811490, Other Personal and Household Goods Repair and Maintenance.

811112 Automotive Exhaust System Repair[CAN]

This U.S. industry comprises establishments primarily engaged in replacing or repairing exhaust systems of automotive vehicles, such as passenger cars, trucks, and vans.

Illustrative Examples:

Automotive exhaust system replacement and repair shops

Automotive muffler replacement and repair shops

US—United States industry only. CAN—United States and Canadian industries are comparable. MEX—United States and Mexican industries are comparable. Blank—Canadian, Mexican, and United States industries are comparable.

Cross-References.

Establishments primarily engaged in motorcycle repair and maintenance services are classified in Industry 811490, Other Personal and Household Goods Repair and Maintenance.

811113 Automotive Transmission Repair[US]

This U.S. industry comprises establishments primarily engaged in replacing or repairing transmissions of automotive vehicles, such as passenger cars, trucks, and vans.

Cross-References.

Establishments primarily engaged in motorcycle repair and maintenance services are classified in Industry 811490, Other Personal and Household Goods Repair and Maintenance.

811118 Other Automotive Mechanical and Electrical Repair and Maintenance[US]

This U.S. industry comprises establishments primarily engaged in providing specialized mechanical or electrical repair and maintenance services (except engine repair and replacement, exhaust systems repair, and transmission repair) for automotive vehicles, such as passenger cars, trucks, and vans, and all trailers.

Illustrative Examples:

Automotive brake repair shops
Automotive radiator repair shops

Automotive electrical repair shops
Automotive tune-up shops

Cross-References. Establishments primarily engaged in—

- Providing a wide range of mechanical and electrical automotive vehicle repair or specializing in engine repair or replacement—are classified in U.S. Industry 811111, General Automotive Repair;
- Replacing and repairing automotive vehicle exhaust systems—are classified in U.S. Industry 811112, Automotive Exhaust System Repair;
- Replacing and repairing automotive vehicle transmissions—are classified in U.S. Industry 811113, Automotive Transmission Repair;
- Providing automotive vehicle air-conditioning repair—are classified in U.S. Industry 811198, All Other Automotive Repair and Maintenance; and
- Motorcycle repair and maintenance services—are classified in Industry 811490, Other Personal and Household Goods Repair and Maintenance.

US—United States industry only. CAN—United States and Canadian industries are comparable. MEX—United States and Mexican industries are comparable. Blank—Canadian, Mexican, and United States industries are comparable.

81112 Automotive Body, Paint, Interior, and Glass Repair

This industry comprises establishments primarily engaged in providing one or more of the following: (1) repairing or customizing automotive vehicles, such as passenger cars, trucks, and vans, and all trailer bodies and interiors; (2) painting automotive vehicle and trailer bodies; (3) replacing, repairing, and/or tinting automotive vehicle glass; and (4) customizing automobile, truck, and van interiors for the physically disabled or other customers with special requirements.

Illustrative Examples:

Automotive body shops   Automotive glass shops
Automotive paint shops

Cross-References. Establishments primarily engaged in—

- Manufacturing automotive vehicles and trailers or customizing these vehicles on an assembly-line basis—are classified in Subsector 336, Transportation Equipment Manufacturing; and

- Motorcycle repair and maintenance services—are classified in Industry 81149, Other Personal and Household Goods Repair and Maintenance.

811121 Automotive Body, Paint, and Interior Repair and Maintenance[CAN]

This U.S. industry comprises establishments primarily engaged in repairing or customizing automotive vehicles, such as passenger cars, trucks, and vans, and all trailer bodies and interiors; and/or painting automotive vehicles and trailer bodies.

Illustrative Examples:

Automotive body shops   Automotive paint shops
Automotive upholstery shops

Cross-References. Establishments primarily engaged in—

- Automotive glass replacement, repair and/or tinting—are classified in U.S. Industry 811122, Automotive Glass Replacement Shops;

- Manufacturing automotive vehicles and trailers or customizing these vehicles on an assembly-line basis—are classified in Subsector 336, Transportation Equipment Manufacturing; and

- Motorcycle repair and maintenance services—are classified in Industry 811490, Other Personal and Household Goods Repair and Maintenance.

US—United States industry only. CAN—United States and Canadian industries are comparable. MEX—United States and Mexican industries are comparable. Blank—Canadian, Mexican, and United States industries are comparable.

811122 Automotive Glass Replacement Shops^{CAN}

This U.S. industry comprises establishments primarily engaged in replacing, repairing, and/or tinting automotive vehicle, such as passenger car, truck, and van, glass.

Cross-References.

Establishments primarily engaged in motorcycle repair and maintenance service are classified in Industry 811490, Other Personal and Household Goods Repair and Maintenance.

81119 Other Automotive Repair and Maintenance

This industry comprises establishments primarily engaged in providing automotive repair and maintenance services (except mechanical and electrical repair and maintenance; transmission repair; and body, paint, interior, and glass repair) for automotive vehicles, such as passenger cars, trucks, and vans, and all trailers.

Illustrative Examples:

Automotive air-conditioning repair shops
Automotive tire repair shops
Automotive oil change and lubrication shops

Car washes
Automotive rustproofing and undercoating shops

Cross-References. Establishments primarily engaged in—

- Tire retreading or recapping—are classified in Industry 32621, Tire Manufacturing;
- Automotive vehicle mechanical and electrical repair and maintenance—are classified in Industry 81111, Automotive Mechanical and Electrical Repair and Maintenance;
- Automotive body, paint, interior, and glass repair—are classified in Industry 81112, Automotive Body, Paint, Interior, and Glass Repair; and
- Motorcycle repair and maintenance services—are classified in Industry 81149, Other Personal and Household Goods Repair and Maintenance.

811191 Automotive Oil Change and Lubrication Shops^{US}

This U.S. industry comprises establishments primarily engaged in changing motor oil and lubricating the chassis of automotive vehicles, such as passenger cars, trucks, and vans.

US—United States industry only. CAN—United States and Canadian industries are comparable. MEX—United States and Mexican industries are comparable. Blank—Canadian, Mexican, and United States industries are comparable.

Cross-References.

Establishments primarily engaged in motorcycle repair and maintenance services are classified in Industry 811490, Other Personal and Household Goods, Repair and Maintenance.

811192 Car Washes[CAN]

This U.S. industry comprises establishments primarily engaged in cleaning, washing, and/or waxing automotive vehicles, such as passenger cars, trucks, and vans, and trailers.

Illustrative Examples:

Automotive detail shops   Car washes
Mobile car and truck washes

811198 All Other Automotive Repair and Maintenance[US]

This U.S. industry comprises establishments primarily engaged in providing automotive repair and maintenance services (except mechanical and electrical repair and maintenance; body, paint, interior, and glass repair; motor oil change and lubrication; and car washing) for automotive vehicles, such as passenger cars, trucks, and vans, and all trailers.

Illustrative Examples:

Automotive air-conditioning repair shops   Automotive rustproofing and
Automotive tire repair (except   undercoating shops
  retreading) shops

Cross-References. Establishments primarily engaged in—

- • Tire retreading or recapping—are classified in U.S. Industry 326212, Tire Retreading;

- • Providing a range of mechanical and electrical automotive vehicle repair or specializing in engine repair or replacement—are classified in U.S. Industry 811111, General Automotive Repair;

- • Replacing and repairing automotive vehicle exhaust systems—are classified in U.S. Industry 811112, Automotive Exhaust System Repair;

- • Replacing and repairing automotive vehicle transmissions—are classified in U.S. Industry 811113, Automotive Transmission Repair;

- Repairing or customizing automotive vehicle bodies and interiors—are classified in U.S. Industry 811121, Automotive Body, Paint, and Interior Repair and Maintenance;

- Replacing, repairing, and/or tinting automotive glass—are classified in U.S. Industry 811122, Automotive Glass Replacement Shops;

- Changing motor oil and lubricating the chassis of automotive vehicles—are classified in U.S. Industry 811191, Automotive Oil Change and Lubrication Shops;

- Cleaning, washing, and/or waxing automotive vehicles and trailers—are classified in U.S. Industry 811192, Car Washes;

- Motorcycle repair and maintenance services—are classified in Industry 811490, Other Personal and Household Goods Repair and Maintenance; and

- Retailing and installing audio equipment—are classified in Industry 441310, Automotive Parts and Accessories Stores.

8112 Electronic and Precision Equipment Repair and Maintenance

This industry group comprises establishments primarily engaged in repairing electronic equipment, such as computers and communications equipment, and highly specialized precision instruments. Establishments in this industry group typically have staff skilled in repairing items having complex, electronic components.

81121 Electronic and Precision Equipment Repair and Maintenance

This industry comprises establishments primarily engaged in repairing and maintaining one or more of the following: (1) consumer electronic equipment; (2) computers; (3) office machines; (4) communication equipment; and (5) other electronic and precision equipment and instruments, without retailing these products as new. Establishments in this industry repair items, such as microscopes, radar and sonar equipment, televisions, stereos, video recorders, computers, fax machines, photocopying machines, two-way radios and other communications equipment, scientific instruments, and medical equipment.

Cross-References. Establishments primarily engaged in—

- Installing and monitoring home security systems—are classified in Industry 56162, Security Systems Services;

- Retailing new radios, televisions, and other consumer electronics and also providing repair services—are classified in Industry 44311, Appliance, Television, and Other Electronics Stores;

US—United States industry only. CAN—United States and Canadian industries are comparable. MEX—United States and Mexican industries are comparable. Blank—Canadian, Mexican, and United States industries are comparable.

http://www.census.gov/naics

- Retailing new computers and computer peripherals and also providing repair services—are classified in Industry 44312, Computer and Software Stores; and

- Rewinding armatures and rebuilding electric motors on a factory basis—are classified in Industry 33531, Electrical Equipment Manufacturing.

811211 Consumer Electronics Repair and Maintenance[MEX]

This U.S. industry comprises establishments primarily engaged in repairing and maintaining consumer electronics, such as televisions, stereos, speakers, video recorders, CD players, radios, and cameras, without retailing new consumer electronics.

Cross-References. Establishments primarily engaged in—

- Repairing computers and peripheral equipment—are classified in U.S. Industry 811212, Computer and Office Machine Repair and Maintenance;

- Installing and monitoring home security systems—are classified in U.S. Industry 561621, Security Systems Services (except Locksmiths);

- Retailing new radios, televisions, and other consumer electronics and also providing repair services—are classified in U.S. Industry 443112, Radio, Television, and Other Electronics Stores; and

- Repairing two-way radios—are classified in U.S. Industry 811213, Communication Equipment Repair and Maintenance.

811212 Computer and Office Machine Repair and Maintenance[US]

This U.S. industry comprises establishments primarily engaged in repairing and maintaining computers and office machines without retailing new computers and office machines, such as photocopying machines; computer terminals, storage devices, and printers; and CD-ROM drives.

Cross-References. Establishments primarily engaged in—

- Retailing new computers and computer peripherals and also providing repair services—are classified in Industry 443120, Computer and Software Stores; and

- Repairing and servicing fax machines—are classified in Industry 811213, Communication Equipment Repair and Maintenance.

811213 Communication Equipment Repair and Maintenance[US]

This U.S. industry comprises establishments primarily engaged in repairing and maintaining communications equipment without retailing new communication equipment, such as telephones, fax machines, communications transmission equipment, and two-way radios.

Cross-References. Establishments primarily engaged in—

- Retailing new telephones and also providing repair services—are classified in U.S. Industry 443112, Radio, Television, and Other Electronics Stores; and

- Repairing stereo and other consumer electronic equipment—are classified in U.S. Industry 811211, Consumer Electronics Repair and Maintenance.

811219 Other Electronic and Precision Equipment Repair and Maintenance[US]

This U.S. industry comprises establishments primarily engaged in repairing and maintaining (without retailing) electronic and precision equipment (except consumer electronics, computers and office machines, and communications equipment). Establishments in this industry repair and maintain equipment, such as medical diagnostic imaging equipment, measuring and surveying instruments, laboratory instruments, and radar and sonar equipment.

Cross-References. Establishments primarily engaged in—

- Rewinding armatures and rebuilding electric motors on a factory basis— are classified in U.S. Industry 335312, Motor and Generator Manufacturing;

- Repairing stereo and other consumer electronic equipment—are classified in U.S. Industry 811211, Consumer Electronics Repair and Maintenance;

- Repairing computers and office machines—are classified in U.S. Industry 811212, Computer and Office Machine Repair and Maintenance; and

- Repairing communications equipment—are classified in U.S. Industry 811213, Communication Equipment Repair and Maintenance.

8113 Commercial and Industrial Machinery and Equipment (except Automotive and Electronic) Repair and Maintenance

81131 Commercial and Industrial Machinery and Equipment (except Automotive and Electronic) Repair and Maintenance
See industry description for 811310 below.

811310 Commercial and Industrial Machinery and Equipment (except Automotive and Electronic) Repair and Maintenance[CAN]

This industry comprises establishments primarily engaged in the repair and maintenance of commercial and industrial machinery and equipment. Establishments in this industry either sharpen/install commercial and industrial machinery blades and saws or provide welding (e.g., automotive, general) repair services; or repair agricultural and other heavy and industrial machinery and equipment (e.g., forklifts and other materials handling equipment, machine tools, commercial refrigeration equipment, construction equipment, and mining machinery).

Cross-References. Establishments primarily engaged in—

* Automotive repair (except welding) and maintenance are—classified in Industry Group 8111, Automotive Repair and Maintenance;

* Repairing and maintaining electronic and precision equipment—are classified in Industry 81121, Electronic and Precision Equipment Repair and Maintenance;

* Repairing and servicing aircraft—are classified in Industry 488190, Other Support Activities for Air Transportation;

* Converting, rebuilding, and overhauling aircraft—are classified in Industry 33641, Aerospace Product and Parts Manufacturing;

* Repairing and servicing railroad cars and engines—are classified in Industry 488210, Support Activities for Rail Transportation;

* Rebuilding or remanufacturing railroad engines and cars—are classified in Industry 336510, Railroad Rolling Stock Manufacturing;

* Repairing and overhauling ships at floating dry docks—are classified in Industry 488390, Other Support Activities for Water Transportation;

* Repairing and overhauling ships at shipyards—are classified in U.S. Industry 336611, Ship Building and Repairing;

* Rewinding armatures or rebuilding electric motors on a factory basis—are classified in U.S. Industry 335312, Motor and Generator Manufacturing; and

* Repairing and maintaining home and garden equipment (e.g., sharpening or installing blades and saws)—are classified in Industry 811411, Home and Garden Equipment Repair and Maintenance.

US—United States industry only. CAN—United States and Canadian industries are comparable. MEX—United States and Mexican industries are comparable. Blank—Canadian, Mexican, and United States industries are comparable.

8114 Personal and Household Goods Repair and Maintenance

81141 Home and Garden Equipment and Appliance Repair and Maintenance

This industry comprises establishments primarily engaged in repairing and servicing home and garden equipment and/or household-type appliances without retailing new equipment or appliances. Establishments in this industry repair and maintain items, such as lawnmowers, edgers, snow- and leaf-blowers, washing machines, clothes dryers, and refrigerators.

Cross-References. Establishments primarily engaged in—

- Retailing outdoor power equipment and also providing repair services— are classified in Industry 44421, Outdoor Power Equipment Stores;

- Retailing an array of new appliances and also providing repair services— are classified in Industry 44311, Appliance, Television, and Other Electronics Stores;

- Repairing, servicing, or installing central heating and air-conditioning equipment—are classified in Industry 23822, Plumbing, Heating, and Air-Conditioning Contractors; and

- Repairing commercial refrigeration equipment—are classified in Industry 81131, Commercial and Industrial Machinery and Equipment (except Automotive and Electronic) Repair and Maintenance.

811411 Home and Garden Equipment Repair and Maintenance[CAN]

This U.S. industry comprises establishments primarily engaged in repairing and servicing home and garden equipment without retailing new home and garden equipment, such as lawnmowers, handheld power tools, edgers, snow- and leaf-blowers, and trimmers.

Cross-References.

Establishments primarily engaged in retailing new outdoor power equipment and also providing repair services are classified in Industry 444210, Outdoor Power Equipment Stores.

811412 Appliance Repair and Maintenance[CAN]

This U.S. industry comprises establishments primarily engaged in repairing and servicing household appliances without retailing new appliances, such as refrigerators, stoves, washing machines, clothes dryers, and room air-conditioners.

US—United States industry only. CAN—United States and Canadian industries are comparable. MEX—United States and Mexican industries are comparable. Blank—Canadian, Mexican, and United States industries are comparable.

Cross-References. Establishments primarily engaged in—

- Installing central heating and air-conditioning equipment—are classified in Industry 238220, Plumbing, Heating, and Air-Conditioning Contractors;

- Repairing commercial refrigeration equipment—are classified in Industry 811310, Commercial and Industrial Machinery and Equipment (except Automotive and Electronic) Repair and Maintenance; and

- Retailing an array of new appliances and also providing repair services— are classified in U.S. Industry 443111, Household Appliance Stores.

81142 Reupholstery and Furniture Repair
See industry description for 811420 below.

811420 Reupholstery and Furniture Repair

This industry comprises establishments primarily engaged in one or more of the following: (1) reupholstering furniture; (2) refinishing furniture; (3) repairing furniture; and (4) repairing and restoring furniture.

Cross-References. Establishments primarily engaged in—

- Automotive vehicle and trailer upholstery repair—are classified in U.S. Industry 811121, Automotive Body, Paint, and Interior Repair and Maintenance; and

- The restoration of museum pieces—are classified in Industry 711510, Independent Artists, Writers, and Performers.

81143 Footwear and Leather Goods Repair
See industry description for 811430 below.

811430 Footwear and Leather Goods Repair

This industry comprises establishments primarily engaged in repairing footwear and/or repairing other leather or leather-like goods without retailing new footwear and leather or leather-like goods, such as handbags and briefcases.

Cross-References. Establishments primarily engaged in—

- Retailing new luggage and leather goods and also providing repair services—are classified in Industry 448320, Luggage and Leather Goods Stores;

- Shining shoes—are classified in Industry 812990, All Other Personal Services; and

- Repairing leather clothing—are classified in Industry 811490, Other Personal and Household Goods Repair and Maintenance.

81149 Other Personal and Household Goods Repair and Maintenance

See industry description for 811490 below.

811490 Other Personal and Household Goods Repair and Maintenance[CAN]

This industry comprises establishments primarily engaged in repairing and servicing personal or household-type goods without retailing new personal or household-type goods (except home and garden equipment, appliances, furniture, and footwear and leather goods). Establishments in this industry repair items, such as garments; watches; jewelry; musical instruments; bicycles and motorcycles; motorboats, canoes, sailboats, and other recreational boats.

Cross-References. Establishments primarily engaged in—

- Repairing home and garden equipment—are classified in U.S. Industry 811411, Home and Garden Equipment Repair and Maintenance;

- Repairing appliances—are classified in U.S. Industry 811412, Appliance Repair and Maintenance;

- Reupholstering and repairing furniture—are classified in Industry 811420, Reupholstery and Furniture Repair;

- Repairing footwear and leather goods—are classified in Industry 811430, Footwear and Leather Goods Repair;

- Operating marinas and providing a range of other services including boat cleaning and repair—are classified in Industry 713930, Marinas; and

- Drycleaning garments—are classified in Industry Group 8123, Drycleaning and Laundry Services.

812 Personal and Laundry Services

Industries in the Personal and Laundry Services subsector group establishments that provide personal and laundry services to individuals, households, and businesses. Services performed include: personal care services; death care services; laundry and drycleaning services; and a wide range of other personal services,

---

such as pet care (except veterinary) services, photofinishing services, temporary parking services, and dating services.

The Personal and Laundry Services subsector is by no means all-inclusive of the services that could be termed personal services (i.e., those provided to individuals rather than businesses). There are many other subsectors, as well as sectors, that provide services to persons. Establishments providing legal, accounting, tax preparation, architectural, portrait photography, and similar professional services are classified in Sector 54; Professional, Scientific, and Technical Services; those providing job placement, travel arrangement, home security, interior and exterior house cleaning, exterminating, lawn and garden care, and similar support services are classified in Sector 56, Administrative and Support, Waste Management and Remediation Services; those providing health and social services are classified in Sector 62, Health Care and Social Assistance; those providing amusement and recreation services are classified in Sector 71, Arts, Entertainment and Recreation; those providing educational instruction are classified in Sector 61, Educational Services; those providing repair services are classified in Subsector 811, Repair and Maintenance; and those providing spiritual, civic, and advocacy services are classified in Subsector 813, Religious, Grantmaking, Civic, Professional, and Similar Organizations.

8121 Personal Care Services[CAN]

This industry group comprises establishments, such as barber and beauty shops, that provide appearance care services to individual consumers.

81211 Hair, Nail, and Skin Care Services[CAN]

This industry comprises establishments primarily engaged in one or more of the following: (1) providing hair care services; (2) providing nail care services; and (3) providing facials or applying makeup (except permanent makeup).

Illustrative Examples:

Barber shops	Nail salons
Hair stylist shops	Cosmetology salons
Beauty salons	

Cross-References. Establishments primarily engaged in—

- Offering training in barbering, hair styling, or the cosmetic arts—are classified in Industry 61151, Technical and Trade Schools;

- Providing massage, electrolysis (i.e., hair removal), permanent makeup, or tanning services—are classified in Industry 81219, Other Personal Care Services; and

---

US—United States industry only. CAN—United States and Canadian industries are comparable. MEX—United States and Mexican industries are comparable. Blank—Canadian, Mexican, and United States industries are comparable.

- Providing medical skin care services (e.g., cosmetic surgery, dermatology)—are classified in Sector 62, Health Care and Social Assistance.

812111 Barber Shops^{US}

This U.S. industry comprises establishments known as barber shops or men's hair stylist shops primarily engaged in cutting, trimming, and styling men's and boys' hair; and/or shaving and trimming men's beards.

Cross-References. Establishments primarily engaged in—

- Offering training in barbering—are classified in U.S. Industry 611511, Cosmetology and Barber Schools; and

- Providing hair care services (except establishments known as barber shops or men's hair stylists)—are classified in U.S. Industry 812112, Beauty Salons.

812112 Beauty Salons^{US}

This U.S. industry comprises establishments (except those known as barber shops or men's hair stylist shops) primarily engaged in one or more of the following: (1) cutting, trimming, shampooing, coloring, waving, or styling hair; (2) providing facials; and (3) applying makeup (except permanent makeup).

Illustrative Examples:

Beauty parlors or shops	Hairdressing salons or shops
Facial salons or shops	Cosmetology salons or shops
Combined beauty and barber shops	Unisex or women's hair stylist shops

Cross-References. Establishments primarily engaged in—

- Cutting, trimming, and styling men's and boys' hair (known as barber shops or men's hair stylist shops)—are classified in U.S. Industry 812111, Barber Shops;

- Offering training in hair styling or the cosmetic arts—are classified in U.S. Industry 611511, Cosmetology and Barber Schools;

- Providing nail care services—are classified in U.S. Industry 812113, Nail Salons;

- Providing massage, electrolysis (i.e., hair removal), permanent makeup, or tanning services—are classified in U.S. Industry 812199, Other Personal Care Services; and

- Providing medical skin care services (e.g., cosmetic surgery, dermatology)—are classified in Sector 62, Health Care and Social Assistance.

US— United States industry only. CAN— United States and Canadian industries are comparable. MEX—United States and Mexican industries are comparable. Blank—Canadian, Mexican, and United States industries are comparable.

812113 Nail Salons[US]

This U.S. industry comprises establishments primarily engaged in providing nail care services, such as manicures, pedicures, and nail extensions.

81219 Other Personal Care Services[CAN]

This industry comprises establishments primarily engaged in providing personal care services (except hair, nail, facial, or nonpermanent makeup services).

Illustrative Examples:

Depilatory or electrolysis (i.e., hair removal) salons
Permanent makeup salons
Ear piercing services
Steam or turkish baths
Hair replacement (except by offices of physicians) or weaving services
Tanning salons
Massage parlors
Tattoo parlors
Nonmedical diet and weight reducing centers

Cross-References. Establishments primarily engaged in—

- Providing hair, nail, facial, or nonpermanent makeup services—are classified in Industry 81211, Hair, Nail, and Skin Care Services;
- Operating physical fitness facilities—are classified in Industry 71394, Fitness and Recreational Sports Centers;
- Operating health resorts and spas that provide lodging—are classified in Industry 72111, Hotels (except Casino Hotels) and Motels; and
- Providing medical or surgical hair replacement or weight reduction—are classified in Sector 62, Health Care and Social Assistance.

812191 Diet and Weight Reducing Centers[US]

This U.S. industry comprises establishments primarily engaged in providing nonmedical services to assist clients in attaining or maintaining a desired weight. The sale of weight reduction products, such as food supplements, may be an integral component of the program. These services typically include individual or group counseling, menu and exercise planning, and weight and body measurement monitoring.

Cross-References. Establishments primarily engaged in—

- Operating physical fitness facilities—are classified in Industry 713940, Fitness and Recreational Sports Centers;

- Operating health resorts and spas that provide lodging—are classified in Industry 721110, Hotels (except Casino Hotels) and Motels; and

- Providing medical or surgical weight reduction—are classified in Sector 62, Health Care and Social Assistance.

812199 Other Personal Care Services[US]

This U.S. industry comprises establishments primarily engaged in providing personal care services (except hair, nail, facial, nonpermanent makeup, or nonmedical diet and weight reducing services).

Illustrative Examples:

Depilatory or electrolysis (i.e., hair removal) salons
Saunas
Ear piercing services
Steam or turkish baths
Hair replacement (except by offices of physicians) or weaving services

Tanning salons
Massage parlors
Tattoo parlors
Permanent makeup salons

Cross-References. Establishments primarily engaged in—

- Cutting, trimming, and styling men's and boys' hair (known as barber shops or men's hair stylist shops)—are classified in U.S. Industry 812111, Barber Shops;

- Providing hair, facial, or nonpermanent makeup services (except establishments known as barber shops or men's hair stylist shops)—are classified in U.S. Industry 812112, Beauty Salons;

- Nail care services—are classified in U.S. Industry 812113, Nail Salons;

- Providing nonmedical diet and weight reducing services—are classified in U.S. Industry 812191, Diet and Weight Reducing Centers; and

- Providing medical or surgical hair replacement or weight reduction services—are classified in Sector 62, Health Care and Social Assistance.

8122 Death Care Services[CAN]

81221 Funeral Homes and Funeral Services[CAN]

See industry description for 812210 below.

US—United States industry only. CAN—United States and Canadian industries are comparable. MEX—United States and Mexican industries are comparable. Blank—Canadian, Mexican, and United States industries are comparable.

812210 Funeral Homes and Funeral Services^{CAN}

This industry comprises establishments primarily engaged in preparing the dead for burial or interment and conducting funerals (i.e., providing facilities for wakes, arranging transportation for the dead, selling caskets and related merchandise). Funeral homes combined with crematories are included in this industry.

Cross-References.

Establishments (except funeral homes) primarily engaged in cremating the dead are classified in Industry 812220, Cemeteries and Crematories.

81222 Cemeteries and Crematories^{CAN}
See industry description for 812220 below.

812220 Cemeteries and Crematories^{CAN}

This industry comprises establishments primarily engaged in operating sites or structures reserved for the interment of human or animal remains and/or cremating the dead.

Illustrative Examples:

Cemetery associations (i.e., operators of   Pet cemeteries
  cemeteries)   Mausoleums
Memorial gardens (i.e., burial places)
Crematories (except combined with
  funeral homes)

Cross-References.

Crematories combined with funeral homes are classified in Industry 812210, Funeral Homes and Funeral Services.

8123 Drycleaning and Laundry Services^{CAN}

81231 Coin-Operated Laundries and Drycleaners^{CAN}
See industry description for 812310 below.

812310 Coin-Operated Laundries and Drycleaners^{CAN}

This industry comprises establishments primarily engaged in (1) operating facilities with coin-operated or similar self-service laundry and drycleaning equipment

---

for customer use on the premises and/or (2) supplying and servicing coin-operated or similar self-service laundry and drycleaning equipment for customer use in places of business operated by others, such as apartments and dormitories.

81232 Drycleaning and Laundry Services (except Coin-Operated)[CAN]
See industry description for 812320 below.

812320 Drycleaning and Laundry Services (except Coin-Operated)[CAN]

This industry comprises establishments primarily engaged in one or more of the following: (1) providing drycleaning services (except coin-operated); (2) providing laundering services (except linen and uniform supply or coin-operated); (3) providing dropoff and pickup sites for laundries and/or drycleaners; and (4) providing specialty cleaning services for specific types of garments and other textile items (except carpets and upholstery), such as fur, leather, or suede garments; wedding gowns; hats; draperies; and pillows. These establishments may provide all, a combination of, or none of the cleaning services on the premises.

Cross-References. Establishments primarily engaged in—

- Supplying laundered linens and uniforms on a rental or contract basis— are classified in Industry 81233, Linen and Uniform Supply;

- Operating coin-operated or similar self-service laundry or drycleaning facilities—are classified in Industry 812310, Coin-Operated Laundries and Drycleaners; and

- Cleaning used carpets and upholstery—are classified in Industry 561740, Carpet and Upholstery Cleaning Services.

81233 Linen and Uniform Supply[CAN]

This industry comprises establishments primarily engaged in supplying, on a rental or contract basis, laundered items, such as uniforms, gowns and coats, table linens, bed linens, towels, clean room apparel, and treated mops or shop towels.

812331 Linen Supply[US]

This U.S. industry comprises establishments primarily engaged in supplying, on a rental or contract basis, laundered items, such as table and bed linens; towels; diapers; and uniforms, gowns, or coats of the type used by doctors, nurses, barbers, beauticians, and waitresses.

US—United States industry only. CAN—United States and Canadian industries are comparable. MEX—United States and Mexican industries are comparable. Blank—Canadian, Mexican, and United States industries are comparable.

Cross-References.

Establishments primarily engaged in supplying, on a rental or contract basis, laundered industrial work uniforms and related work clothing are classified in U.S. Industry 812332, Industrial Launderers.

812332 Industrial Launderers[US]

This U.S. industry comprises establishments primarily engaged in supplying, on a rental or contract basis, laundered industrial work uniforms and related work clothing, such as protective apparel (flame and heat resistant) and clean room apparel; dust control items, such as treated mops, rugs, mats, dust tool covers, cloths, and shop or wiping towels.

Cross-References.

Establishments primarily engaged in supplying, on a rental or contract basis, laundered uniforms, gowns or coats of the type used by doctors, nurses, barbers, beauticians, and waitresses are classified in U.S. Industry 812331, Linen Supply.

8129 Other Personal Services[CAN]

This industry group comprises establishments primarily engaged in providing personal services (except personal care services, death care services, or drycleaning and laundry services).

81291 Pet Care (except Veterinary) Services[CAN]
See industry description for 812910 below.

812910 Pet Care (except Veterinary) Services[CAN]

This industry comprises establishments primarily engaged in providing pet care services (except veterinary), such as boarding, grooming, sitting, and training pets.

Cross-References. Establishments primarily engaged in—

- Practicing veterinary medicine—are classified in Industry 541940, Veterinary Services;

- Boarding horses—are classified in Industry 115210, Support Activities for Animal Production; and

- Transporting pets—are classified in U.S. Industry 485991, Special Needs Transportation.

81292 Photofinishing^{CAN}

This industry comprises establishments primarily engaged in developing film and/or making photographic slides, prints, and enlargements.

Cross-References.

Establishments primarily engaged in processing motion picture film for the motion picture and television industries are classified in Industry 51219, Postproduction Services and Other Motion Picture and Video Industries.

812921 Photofinishing Laboratories (except One-Hour)^{CAN}

This U.S. industry comprises establishments (except those known as "one-hour" photofinishing labs) primarily engaged in developing film and/or making photographic slides, prints, and enlargements.

Cross-References.

- Establishments primarily engaged in processing motion picture film for the motion picture and television industries are classified in U.S. Industry 512199, Other Motion Picture and Video Industries; and
- Establishments known as "one-hour" photofinishing labs are classified in U.S. Industry 812922, One-Hour Photofinishing.

812922 One-Hour Photofinishing^{CAN}

This U.S. industry comprises establishments known as "one-hour" photofinishing labs primarily engaged in developing film and/or making photographic slides, prints, and enlargements on a short turnaround or while-you-wait basis.

Cross-References.

Photofinishing laboratories (except those known as "one-hour" photofinishing labs) are classified in U.S. Industry 812921, Photofinishing Laboratories (except One-Hour).

81293 Parking Lots and Garages^{CAN}
See industry description for 812930 below.

812930 Parking Lots and Garages^{CAN}

This industry comprises establishments primarily engaged in providing parking space for motor vehicles, usually on an hourly, daily, or monthly basis and/or valet parking services.

US—United States industry only. CAN—United States and Canadian industries are comparable. MEX—United States and Mexican industries are comparable. Blank—Canadian, Mexican, and United States industries are comparable.

http://www.census.gov/naics

Cross-References.

Establishments primarily engaged in providing extended or dead storage of motor vehicles are classified in Industry 493190, Other Warehousing and Storage.

81299 All Other Personal Services[CAN]

See industry description for 812990 below.

812990 All Other Personal Services[CAN]

This industry comprises establishments primarily engaged in providing personal services (except personal care services, death care services, drycleaning and laundry services, pet care services, photofinishing services, or parking space and/or valet parking services).

Illustrative Examples:

Bail bonding or bondsperson services
Shoeshine services
Coin-operated personal services machine
(e.g., blood pressure, locker,
photographic, scale, shoeshine)
concession operators

Social escort services
Consumer buying services
Wedding planning services
Dating services

Cross-References. Establishments primarily engaged in—

- Providing personal care services—are classified in Industry Group 8121, Personal Care Services;

- Providing death care services—are classified in Industry Group 8122, Death Care Services;

- Providing drycleaning and laundry services—are classified in Industry Group 8123, Drycleaning and Laundry Services;

- Providing pet care (except veterinary) services—are classified in Industry 812910, Pet Care (except Veterinary) Services;

- Practicing veterinary medicine—are classified in Industry 541940, Veterinary Services;

- Providing photofinishing services—are classified in Industry 81292, Photofinishing; and

- Providing parking space for motor vehicles and/or valet parking services—are classified in Industry 812930, Parking Lots and Garages.

US—United States industry only. CAN—United States and Canadian industries are comparable. MEX—United States and Mexican industries are comparable. Blank—Canadian, Mexican, and United States industries are comparable.

813 Religious, Grantmaking, Civic, Professional, and Similar Organizations

Industries in the Religious, Grantmaking, Civic, Professional, and Similar Organizations subsector group establishments that organize and promote religious activities; support various causes through grantmaking; advocate various social and political causes; and promote and defend the interests of their members.

The industry groups within the subsector are defined in terms of their activities, such as establishments that provide funding for specific causes or for a variety of charitable causes; establishments that advocate and actively promote causes and beliefs for the public good; and establishments that have an active membership structure to promote causes and represent the interests of their members. Establishments in this subsector may publish newsletters, books, and periodicals, for distribution to their membership.

8131 Religious Organizations[CAN]

81311 Religious Organizations[CAN]

See industry description for 813110 below.

813110 Religious Organizations[CAN]

This industry comprises (1) establishments primarily engaged in operating religious organizations, such as churches, religious temples, and monasteries, and/or (2) establishments primarily engaged in administering an organized religion or promoting religious activities.

Illustrative Examples:

Churches	Synagogues
Shrines, religious	Mosques, religious
Monasteries (except schools)	Temples, religious

Cross-References.

- Schools, colleges, or universities operated by religious organizations are classified in Sector 61, Educational Services;

- Radio and television stations operated by religious organizations are classified in Subsector 515, Broadcasting (except Internet);

- Publishing houses operated by religious organizations are classified in Subsector 511, Publishing Industries (except Internet);

US—United States industry only. CAN—United States and Canadian industries are comparable. MEX—United States and Mexican industries are comparable. Blank—Canadian, Mexican, and United States industries are comparable.

http://www.census.gov/naics

- Establishments operated by religious organizations primarily engaged in health and social assistance for individuals are classified in Sector 62, Health Care and Social Assistance; and

- Used merchandise stores operated by religious organizations are classified in Industry 453310, Used Merchandise Stores.

8132 Grantmaking and Giving Services[CAN]

81321 Grantmaking and Giving Services[CAN]

This industry comprises (1) establishments known as grantmaking foundations or charitable trusts and (2) establishments primarily engaged in raising funds for a wide range of social welfare activities, such as health, educational, scientific, and cultural activities.

Cross-References. Establishments primarily engaged in—

- Providing trust management services for others—are classified in Industry 52392, Portfolio Management;

- Organizing and conducting fundraising campaigns on a contract or fee basis—are classified in Industry 56149, Other Business Support Services;

- Providing telemarketing services for others—are classified in Industry 56142, Telephone Call Centers;

- Raising funds for political purposes—are classified in Industry 81394, Political Organizations;

- Advocating social causes or issues—are classified in Industry 81331, Social Advocacy Organizations; and

- Conducting health research—are classified in Industry 54171, Research and Development in the Physical, Engineering, and Life Sciences.

813211 Grantmaking Foundations[US]

This U.S. industry comprises establishments known as grantmaking foundations or charitable trusts. Establishments in this industry award grants from trust funds based on a competitive selection process or the preferences of the foundation managers and grantors; or fund a single entity, such as a museum or university.

Illustrative Examples:

Community foundations	Scholarship trusts
Philanthropic trusts	Grantmaking foundations
Corporate foundations, awarding grants	

US—United States industry only. CAN—United States and Canadian industries are comparable. MEX—United States and Mexican industries are comparable. Blank—Canadian, Mexican, and United States industries are comparable.

Cross-References.

Establishments primarily engaged in providing trust management services for others are classified in Industry 523920, Portfolio Management.

813212 Voluntary Health Organizations[US]

This U.S. industry comprises establishments primarily engaged in raising funds for health related research, such as disease (e.g., heart, cancer, diabetes) prevention, health education, and patient services.

Illustrative Examples:

Disease awareness fundraising
organizations
Health research fundraising organizations

Disease research (e.g., heart, cancer)
fundraising organizations
Voluntary health organizations

Cross-References.

- Establishments primarily engaged in raising funds for a wide range of social welfare activities, such as educational, scientific, cultural, or health, are classified in U.S. Industry 813219, Other Grantmaking and Giving Services;

- Establishments primarily engaged in organizing and conducting fundraising campaigns on a contract or fee basis are classified in U.S. Industry 561499, All Other Business Support Services;

- Establishments primarily engaged in providing telemarketing services for others are classified in U.S. Industry 561422, Telemarketing Bureaus and Other Contact Centers;

- Establishments known as grantmaking foundations or charitable trusts are classified in U.S. Industry 813211, Grantmaking Foundations;

- Establishments primarily engaged in conducting biotechnology research and development in health sciences are classified in 541711, Research and Development in Biotechnology; and

- Establishments primarily engaged in conducting health research (except biotechnology research and development) are classified in Industry 541712, Research and Development in the Physical, Engineering, and Life Sciences (except Biotechnology).

813219 Other Grantmaking and Giving Services[US]

This U.S. industry comprises establishments (except voluntary health organizations) primarily engaged in raising funds for a wide range of social welfare activities, such as educational, scientific, cultural, and health.

US—United States industry only. CAN—United States and Canadian industries are comparable. MEX—United States and Mexican industries are comparable. Blank—Canadian, Mexican, and United States industries are comparable.

http://www.census.gov/naics

Illustrative Examples:

Community chests   Federated charities
United fund councils   United funds for colleges

Cross-References.

- Establishments primarily engaged in raising funds for health related research are classified in U.S. Industry 813212, Voluntary Health Organizations;

- Establishments known as grantmaking foundations or charitable trusts are classified in U.S. Industry 813211, Grantmaking Foundations;

- Establishments primarily engaged in organizing and conducting fundraising campaigns on a contract or fee basis are classified in U.S. Industry 561499, All Other Business Support Services;

- Establishments primarily engaged in providing telemarketing services for others are classified in U.S. Industry 561422, Telemarketing Bureaus and Other Contact Centers;

- Establishments primarily engaged in raising funds for political purposes are classified in Industry 813940, Political Organizations; and

- Establishments primarily engaged in advocating social causes or issues are classified in Industry 81331, Social Advocacy Organizations.

8133 Social Advocacy Organizations^CAN

81331 Social Advocacy Organizations^CAN

This industry comprises establishments primarily engaged in promoting a particular cause or working for the realization of a specific social or political goal to benefit a broad or specific constituency. These organizations may solicit contributions and offer memberships to support these goals.

Illustrative Examples:

Community action advocacy   Human rights advocacy organizations
organizations   Environmental advocacy organizations
Firearms advocacy organizations   Wildlife preservation organizations
Conservation advocacy organizations

Cross-References. Establishments primarily engaged in—

- Promoting the civic and social interests of their members—are classified in Industry 81341, Civic and Social Organizations;

- Promoting the interests of organized labor and union employees—are classified in Industry 81393, Labor Unions and Similar Labor Organizations; and

---

US—United States industry only. CAN—United States and Canadian industries are comparable. MEX—United States and Mexican industries are comparable. Blank—Canadian, Mexican, and United States industries are comparable.

- Providing legal services for social advocacy organizations—are classified in Industry Group 5411, Legal Services.

813311 Human Rights Organizations[US]

This U.S. industry comprises establishments primarily engaged in promoting causes associated with human rights either for a broad or specific constituency. Establishments in this industry address issues, such as protecting and promoting the broad constitutional rights and civil liberties of individuals and those suffering from neglect, abuse, or exploitation; promoting the interests of specific groups, such as children, women, senior citizens, or persons with disabilities; improving relations between racial, ethnic, and cultural groups; and promoting voter education and registration. These organizations may solicit contributions and offer memberships to support these causes.

Illustrative Examples:

Civil liberties organizations
Senior citizens' advocacy organizations

Human rights advocacy organizations
Veterans' rights organizations

Cross-References. Establishments primarily engaged in—

- Promoting the interests of organized labor and union employees—are classified in Industry 813930, Labor Unions and Similar Labor Organizations; and
- Providing legal services for human rights organizations—are classified in Industry Group 5411, Legal Services.

813312 Environment, Conservation and Wildlife Organizations[US]

This U.S. industry comprises establishments primarily engaged in promoting the preservation and protection of the environment and wildlife. Establishments in this industry address issues, such as clean air and water; global warming; conserving and developing natural resources, including land, plant, water, and energy resources; and protecting and preserving wildlife and endangered species. These organizations may solicit contributions and offer memberships to support these causes.

Illustrative Examples:

Animal rights organizations
Natural resource preservation organizations

Conservation advocacy organizations
Wildlife preservation organizations
Humane societies

Cross-References.

Establishments primarily engaged in providing legal services for environment, conservation, and wildlife organizations are classified in Industry Group 5411, Legal Services.

813319 Other Social Advocacy Organizations[US]

This U.S. industry comprises establishments primarily engaged in social advocacy (except human rights and environmental protection, conservation, and wildlife preservation). Establishments in this industry address issues, such as peace and international understanding; community action (excluding civic organizations); or advancing social causes, such as firearms safety, drunk driving prevention, or drug abuse awareness. These organizations may solicit contributions and offer memberships to support these causes.

Illustrative Examples:

Community action advocacy
organizations
Substance abuse prevention advocacy
organizations

Firearms advocacy organizations
Taxpayers' advocacy organizations
Peace advocacy organizations

Cross-References. Establishments primarily engaged in—

* Advocating human rights issues—are classified in U.S. Industry 813311, Human Rights Organizations;

* Promoting the preservation and protection of the environment and wildlife— are classified in U.S. Industry 813312, Environment, Conservation and Wildlife Organizations;

* Promoting the civic and social interests of their members—are classified in Industry 813410, Civic and Social Organizations;

* Providing legal services for social advocacy organizations—are classified in Industry Group 5411, Legal Services; and

* Providing community action services, such as community action services agencies—are classified in Industry 624190, Other Individual and Family Services.

8134 Civic and Social Organizations[CAN]

81341 Civic and Social Organizations[CAN]
See industry description for 813410 below.

813410 Civic and Social Organizations[CAN]

This industry comprises establishments primarily engaged in promoting the civic and social interests of their members. Establishments in this industry may operate bars and restaurants for their members.

US—United States industry only. CAN—United States and Canadian industries are comparable. MEX—United States and Mexican industries are comparable. Blank—Canadian, Mexican, and United States industries are comparable.

Illustrative Examples:

Alumni associations
Granges
Automobile clubs (except travel)
Parent-teacher associations
Booster clubs

Scouting organizations
Ethnic associations
Social clubs
Fraternal lodges
Veterans' membership organizations

Cross-References.

- Establishments of insurance offices operated by fraternal benefit organizations are classified in Subsector 524, Insurance Carriers and Related Activities;

- Establishments primarily engaged in operating residential fraternity and sorority houses are classified in Industry 721310, Rooming and Boarding Houses; and

- Establishments primarily engaged in providing travel arrangements and reservation services, such as automobile travel clubs or motor travel clubs are classified in U.S. Industry 561599, All Other Travel Arrangement and Reservation Services.

8139 Business, Professional, Labor, Political, and Similar Organizations^{CAN}

This industry group comprises establishments primarily engaged in promoting the interests of their members (except religious organizations, social advocacy organizations, and civic and social organizations). Examples of establishments in this industry are business associations, professional organizations, labor unions, and political organizations.

81391 Business Associations^{CAN}

See industry description for 813910 below.

813910 Business Associations^{CAN}

This industry comprises establishments primarily engaged in promoting the business interests of their members. These establishments may conduct research on new products and services; develop market statistics; sponsor quality and certification standards; lobby public officials; or publish newsletters, books, or periodicals for distribution to their members.

Illustrative Examples:

Agricultural organizations (except youth
  farming organizations, farm granges)
Real estate boards

Chambers of commerce
Trade associations
Manufacturers' associations

Cross-References.

- Establishments owned by their members but organized to perform a specific business function, such as common marketing of crops, joint advertising, or buying cooperatives, are classified according to their primary activity;

- Establishments primarily engaged in promoting the professional interests of their members and the profession as a whole are classified in Industry 813920, Professional Organizations;

- Establishments primarily engaged in promoting the interests of organized labor and union employees, such as trade unions, are classified in Industry 813930, Labor Unions and Similar Labor Organizations; and

- Establishments primarily engaged in lobbying public officials (i.e., lobbyists) are classified in Industry 541820, Public Relations Agencies.

81392 Professional Organizations^{CAN}

See industry description for 813920 below.

813920 Professional Organizations^{CAN}

This industry comprises establishments primarily engaged in promoting the professional interests of their members and the profession as a whole. These establishments may conduct research; develop statistics; sponsor quality and certification standards; lobby public officials; or publish newsletters, books, or periodicals, for distribution to their members.

Illustrative Examples:

Bar associations	Engineers' associations
Learned societies	Professional standards review boards
Dentists' associations	Health professionals' associations
Peer review boards	Scientists' associations

Cross-References. Establishments primarily engaged in—

- Promoting the business interests of their members—are classified in Industry 813910, Business Associations; and

- Lobbying public officials (i.e., lobbyists)—are classified in Industry 541820, Public Relations Agencies.

81393 Labor Unions and Similar Labor Organizations^{CAN}

See industry description for 813930 below.

813930 Labor Unions and Similar Labor Organizations[CAN]

This industry comprises establishments primarily engaged in promoting the interests of organized labor and union employees.

81394 Political Organizations[CAN]

See industry description for 813940 below.

813940 Political Organizations[CAN]

This industry comprises establishments primarily engaged in promoting the interests of national, state, or local political parties or candidates. Included are political groups organized to raise funds for a political party or individual candidates.

Illustrative Examples:

Campaign organizations, political
Political organizations or clubs
Political action committees (PACs)

Political parties
Political campaign organizations

Cross-References. Establishments primarily engaged in—

- Organizing and conducting fundraising campaigns on a contract or fee basis—are classified in U.S. Industry 561499, All Other Business Support Services; and

- Providing telemarketing services for others—are classified in U.S. Industry 561422, Telemarketing Bureaus and Other Contact Centers.

81399 Other Similar Organizations (except Business, Professional, Labor, and Political Organizations)[CAN]

See industry description for 813990 below.

813990 Other Similar Organizations (except Business, Professional, Labor, and Political Organizations)[CAN]

This industry comprises establishments (except religious organizations, social advocacy organizations, civic and social organizations, business associations, professional organizations, labor unions, and political organizations) primarily engaged in promoting the interests of their members.

US—United States industry only. CAN—United States and Canadian industries are comparable. MEX—United States and Mexican industries are comparable. Blank—Canadian, Mexican, and United States industries are comparable.

Illustrative Examples:

Athletic associations, regulatory or administrative
Property owners' associations
Condominium and homeowners' associations

Tenant associations (except advocacy)
Cooperative owners' associations

Cross-References. Establishments primarily engaged in—

* Operating religious organizations, such as churches, religious temples, and monasteries—are classified in Industry 813110, Religious Organizations;

* Raising funds for a wide range of social welfare activities and establishments known as grantmaking foundations or charitable trusts—are classified in Industry 81321, Grantmaking and Giving Services;

* Advocating social causes or issues—are classified in Industry 81331, Social Advocacy Organizations;

* Promoting the civic and social interests of their members—are classified in Industry 813410, Civic and Social Organizations;

* Promoting the business interests of their members—are classified in Industry 813910, Business Associations;

* Promoting the professional interests of their members and the profession as a whole—are classified in Industry 813920, Professional Organizations;

* Promoting the interests of organized labor and union employees—are classified in Industry 813930, Labor Unions and Similar Labor Organizations;

* Promoting the interests of national, state, or local political parties or candidates—are classified in Industry 813940, Political Organizations; and

* Providing recreational and amusement services, such as recreational or youth sports teams and leagues—are classified in Industry 713990, All Other Amusement and Recreation Industries.

814 Private Households

Industries in the Private Households subsector include private households that engage in employing workers on or about the premises in activities primarily concerned with the operation of the household. These private households may employ individuals, such as cooks, maids, butlers, and outside workers, such as gardeners, caretakers, and other maintenance workers.

8141 Private Households

81411 Private Households
See industry description for 814110 below.

US—United States industry only. CAN—United States and Canadian industries are comparable. MEX—United States and Mexican industries are comparable. Blank—Canadian, Mexican, and United States industries are comparable.

814110 Private Households

This industry comprises private households primarily engaged in employing workers on or about the premises in activities primarily concerned with the operation of the household. These private households may employ individuals, such as cooks, maids, nannies, butlers, and outside workers, such as gardeners, caretakers, and other maintenance workers.

US—United States industry only. CAN—United States and Canadian industries are comparable. MEX—United States and Mexican industries are comparable. Blank—Canadian, Mexican, and United States industries are comparable.

http://www.census.gov/naics

Sector 92—Public Administration

The Sector as a Whole

The Public Administration sector consists of establishments of federal, state, and local government agencies that administer, oversee, and manage public programs and have executive, legislative, or judicial authority over other institutions within a given area. These agencies also set policy, create laws, adjudicate civil and criminal legal cases, provide for public safety and for national defense. In general, government establishments in the Public Administration sector oversee governmental programs and activities that are not performed by private establishments. Establishments in this sector typically are engaged in the organization and financing of the production of public goods and services, most of which are provided for free or at prices that are not economically significant.

Government establishments also engage in a wide range of productive activities covering not only public goods and services but also individual goods and services similar to those produced in sectors typically identified with private-sector establishments. In general, ownership is not a criterion for classification in NAICS. Therefore, government establishments engaged in the production of private-sector-like goods and services should be classified in the same industry as private-sector establishments engaged in similar activities.

As a practical matter, it is difficult to identify separate establishment detail for many government agencies. To the extent that separate establishment records are available, the administration of governmental programs is classified in Sector 92, Public Administration, while the operation of that same governmental program is classified elsewhere in NAICS based on the activities performed. For example, the governmental administrative authority for an airport is classified in Industry 92612, Regulation and Administration of Transportation Programs, while operating the airport is classified in Industry 48811, Airport Operations. When separate records for multi-establishment companies are not available to distinguish between the administration of a governmental program and the operation of it, the establishment is classified in Sector 92, Public Administration.

Examples of government-provided goods and services that are classified in sectors other than Public Administration include: schools, classified in Sector 61, Educational Services; hospitals, classified in Subsector 622, Hospitals; establishments operating transportation facilities, classified in Sector 48-49, Transportation and Warehousing; the operation of utilities, classified in Sector 22, Utilities; and the Government Printing Office, classified in Subsector 323, Printing and Related Support Activities.

US—United States industry only. CAN—United States and Canadian industries are comparable. MEX—United States and Mexican industries are comparable. Blank—Canadian, Mexican, and United States industries are comparable.

921 Executive, Legislative, and Other General Government Support^{US}

The Executive, Legislative, and Other General Government Support subsector groups offices of government executives, legislative bodies, public finance and general government support.

9211 Executive, Legislative, and Other General Government Support^{US}

92111 Executive Offices^{US}
See industry description for 921110 below.

921110 Executive Offices^{US}

This industry comprises government establishments serving as offices of chief executives and their advisory committees and commissions. This industry includes offices of the president, governors, and mayors, in addition to executive advisory commissions.

92112 Legislative Bodies^{US}
See industry description for 921120 below.

921120 Legislative Bodies^{US}

This industry comprises government establishments serving as legislative bodies and their advisory committees and commissions. Included in this industry are legislative bodies, such as Congress, state legislatures, and advisory and study legislative commissions.

92113 Public Finance Activities^{US}
See industry description for 921130 below.

921130 Public Finance Activities^{US}

This industry comprises government establishments primarily engaged in public finance, taxation and monetary policy. Included are financial administration activities, such as monetary policy; tax administration and collection; custody and disbursement of funds; debt and investment administration; auditing activities; and government employee retirement trust fund administration.

US—United States industry only. CAN—United States and Canadian industries are comparable. MEX—United States and Mexican industries are comparable. Blank—Canadian, Mexican, and United States industries are comparable.

Cross-References. Establishments primarily engaged in—

- Administering income maintenance programs—are classified in Industry 923130, Administration of Human Resource Programs (except Education, Public Health, and Veterans' Affairs Programs);

- Regulating insurance and banking institutions—are classified in Industry 926150, Regulation, Licensing, and Inspection of Miscellaneous Commercial Sectors; and

- Performing central banking functions, such as issuing currency and acting as the fiscal agent for the central government—are classified in Industry 521110, Monetary Authorities-Central Bank.

92114 Executive and Legislative Offices, Combined^{US}

See industry description for 921140 below.

921140 Executive and Legislative Offices, Combined^{US}

This industry comprises government establishments serving as councils and boards of commissioners or supervisors and such bodies where the chief executive (e.g., county executive or city mayor) is a member of the legislative body (e.g., county or city council) itself.

Cross-References. Establishments primarily engaged in—

- Serving as offices of chief executives—are classified in Industry 921110, Executive Offices; and

- Serving as legislative bodies—are classified in Industry 921120, Legislative Bodies.

92115 American Indian and Alaska Native Tribal Governments^{US}

See industry description for 921150 below.

921150 American Indian and Alaska Native Tribal Governments^{US}

This industry comprises American Indian and Alaska Native governing bodies. Establishments in this industry perform legislative, judicial, and administrative functions for their American Indian and Alaska Native lands. Included in this industry are American Indian and Alaska Native councils, courts, and law enforcement bodies.

Cross-References.

- Establishments primarily engaged in providing funding for American Indian and Alaska Native tribal programs through commercial activities, such as gaming, are classified in the industry of the commercial activity; and

- Government establishments providing public administration of American Indian and Alaska Native affairs are classified in Industry 921190, Other General Government Support.

92119 Other General Government Support[US]
See industry description for 921190 below.

921190 Other General Government Support[US]

This industry comprises government establishments primarily engaged in providing general support for government. Such support services include personnel services, election boards, and other general government support establishments that are not classified elsewhere in public administration.

Illustrative Examples:

Civil rights commissions	Supply agencies, government
Personnel offices, government	General services departments,
Civil service commissions	government

Cross-References.

- Government establishments primarily engaged in serving as offices of chief executives and their advisory committees and commissions are classified in Industry 921110, Executive Offices;

- Government establishments primarily engaged in serving as legislative bodies and their advisory committees and commissions are classified in Industry 921120, Legislative Bodies;

- Government establishments primarily engaged in providing administration of public finance, tax collection, and monetary policy programs are classified in Industry 921130, Public Finance Activities;

- Government establishments primarily engaged in serving as combined executive and legislative offices are classified in Industry 921140, Executive and Legislative Offices, Combined; and

- Establishments primarily engaged in serving as American Indian or Alaska Native tribal leadership are classified in Industry 921150, American Indian and Alaska Native Tribal Governments.

US—United States industry only. CAN—United States and Canadian industries are comparable. MEX—United States and Mexican industries are comparable. Blank—Canadian, Mexican, and United States industries are comparable.

922 Justice, Public Order, and Safety Activities[US]

The Justice, Public Order, and Safety Activities subsector groups government establishments engaged in the administration of justice, public order, and safety programs.

9221 Justice, Public Order, and Safety Activities[US]

92211 Courts[US]
See industry description for 922110 below.

922110 Courts[US]

This industry comprises civilian courts of law (except Indian tribal and Alaska Native courts). Included in this industry are civilian courts, courts of law, and sheriffs' offices conducting court functions only.

Cross-References.

- Government establishments primarily engaged in operating military courts are classified in Industry 928110, National Security; and
- Establishments primarily engaged in operating Indian tribal or Alaska Native courts are classified in Industry 921150, American Indian and Alaska Native Tribal Governments.

92212 Police Protection[US]
See industry description for 922120 below.

922120 Police Protection[US]

This industry comprises government establishments primarily engaged in criminal and civil law enforcement, police, traffic safety, and other activities related to the enforcement of the law and preservation of order. Combined police and fire departments are included in this industry.

Cross-References.

- Government establishments primarily engaged in prosecution are classified in Industry 922130, Legal Counsel and Prosecution;
- Government establishments primarily engaged in collection of law enforcement statistics are classified in Industry 922190, Other Justice, Public Order, and Safety Activities;

US—United States industry only. CAN—United States and Canadian industries are comparable. MEX—United States and Mexican industries are comparable. Blank—Canadian, Mexican, and United States industries are comparable.

- Government establishments primarily engaged in providing police service for the military or National Guard are classified in Industry 928110, National Security;
- Government establishments primarily engaged in providing police service for tribal governments are classified in Industry 921150, American Indian and Alaska Native Tribal Governments;
- Government establishments primarily engaged in enforcing immigration laws are classified in Industry 928120, International Affairs;
- Sheriffs' offices conducting court functions only are classified in Industry 922110, Courts; and
- Private establishments primarily engaged in providing security and investigation services are classified in Industry 56161, Investigation, Guard, and Armored Car Services.

92213 Legal Counsel and Prosecution[US]

See industry description for 922130 below.

922130 Legal Counsel and Prosecution[US]

This industry comprises government establishments primarily engaged in providing legal counsel or prosecution services for the government.

Illustrative Examples:

Attorney generals' offices
Public defenders' offices

District attorneys' offices
Public prosecutors' offices

Cross-References.

Government establishments primarily engaged in collecting criminal justice statistics are classified in Industry 922190, Other Justice, Public Order, and Safety Activities.

92214 Correctional Institutions[US]

See industry description for 922140 below.

922140 Correctional Institutions[US]

This industry comprises government establishments primarily engaged in managing and operating correctional institutions. The facility is generally designed for the confinement, correction, and rehabilitation of adult and/or juvenile offenders sentenced by a court.

US—United States industry only. CAN—United States and Canadian industries are comparable. MEX—United States and Mexican industries are comparable. Blank—Canadian, Mexican, and United States industries are comparable.

Illustrative Examples:

Correctional institutions, public administration	Detention centers, public administration
Penitentiaries, public administration	Prisons, public administration
	Jails, public administration

Cross-References.

- Government establishments primarily engaged in operating half-way houses for ex-criminal offenders and delinquent youths are classified in Industry 623990, Other Residential Care Facilities; and

- Establishments primarily engaged in managing or operating correctional facilities owned by others are classified in Industry 561210, Facilities Support Services.

92215 Parole Offices and Probation Offices[US]
See industry description for 922150 below.

922150 Parole Offices and Probation Offices[US]

This industry comprises government establishments primarily engaged in judicially administering probation offices, parole offices and boards, and pardon boards.

Cross-References.

- Private establishments primarily engaged in providing parole or probation services are classified in Industry 624190, Other Individual and Family Services; and

- Government establishments primarily engaged in providing probation, parole, and pardon activities as an integral part of a central administrative corrections' office are classified in Industry 922140, Correctional Institutions.

92216 Fire Protection[US]
See industry description for 922160 below.

922160 Fire Protection[US]

This industry comprises government establishments primarily engaged in fire fighting and other related fire protection activities. Government establishments providing combined fire protection and ambulance or rescue services are classified in this industry.

US—United States industry only. CAN—United States and Canadian industries are comparable. MEX—United States and Mexican industries are comparable. Blank—Canadian, Mexican, and United States industries are comparable.

Cross-References. Establishments primarily engaged in—

- Forest fire fighting—are classified in Industry 115310, Support Activities for Forestry;

- Providing combined police and fire protection services—are classified in Industry 922120, Police Protection;

- Providing fire fighting services as a commercial activity—are classified in Industry 561990, All Other Support Services; and

- Providing ambulance services without fire protection service—are classified in Industry 621910, Ambulance Services.

92219   Other Justice, Public Order, and Safety Activities[US]
See industry description for 922190 below.

922190   Other Justice, Public Order, and Safety Activities[US]

This industry comprises government establishments primarily engaged in public order and safety (except courts, police protection, legal counsel and prosecution, correctional institutions, parole offices, probation offices, pardon boards, and fire protection). These establishments include the general administration of public order and safety programs. Government establishments responsible for the collection of statistics on public safety are included in this industry.

Illustrative Examples:

Consumer product safety commissions, public administration	Disaster preparedness and management offices, government
Emergency planning and management offices, government	Public safety bureaus and statistics centers, government

Cross-References. Government establishments primarily engaged in—

- Serving as civilian courts of law (except Indian tribal and Alaska Native)— are classified in Industry 922110, Courts;

- Criminal and civil law enforcement, police, traffic safety and similar activities related to the enforcement of law—are classified in Industry 922120, Police Protection;

- Providing legal counsel to or prosecution services for their governments— are classified in Industry 922130, Legal Counsel and Prosecution;

- The confinement, correction, and rehabilitation of adult and juvenile offenders sentenced by a court—are classified in Industry 922140, Correctional Institutions;

- Judicially administering probation offices, parole offices and boards, and pardon boards—are classified in Industry 922150, Parole Offices and Probation Offices; and

- Fire fighting and other related fire protection activities—are classified in Industry 922160, Fire Protection.

923 Administration of Human Resource Programs^{US}

The Administration of Human Resource Programs subsector groups government establishments primarily engaged in the administration of human resource programs.

9231 Administration of Human Resource Programs^{US}

92311 Administration of Education Programs^{US}
See industry description for 923110 below.

923110 Administration of Education Programs^{US}

This industry comprises government establishments primarily engaged in the central coordination, planning, supervision and administration of funds, policies, intergovernmental activities, statistical reports and data collection, and centralized programs for educational administration. Government scholarship programs are included in this industry.

Illustrative Examples:

Education offices, nonoperating, public administration
State education departments

Education statistics centers, government
University regents or boards, government

Cross-References.

Schools and local school boards are classified in Subsector 611, Educational Services.

92312 Administration of Public Health Programs^{US}
See industry description for 923120 below.

923120 Administration of Public Health Programs^{US}

This industry comprises government establishments primarily engaged in the planning, administration, and coordination of public health programs and services,

US—United States industry only. CAN—United States and Canadian industries are comparable. MEX—United States and Mexican industries are comparable. Blank—Canadian, Mexican, and United States industries are comparable.

including environmental health activities, mental health, categorical health programs, health statistics, and immunization services. Government establishments primarily engaged in conducting public health-related inspections are included in this industry.

Illustrative Examples:

Communicable disease program administration, public administration

Mental health program administration, public administration

Coroners' offices, public administration

Public health program administration, nonoperating, public administration

Health program administration, public administration

Cross-References. Government establishments primarily engaged in—

- Operating hospitals (i.e., government or military)—are classified in Subsector 622, Hospitals;

- Providing health care in a clinical setting (i.e., military or government clinics)—are classified in Subsector 621, Ambulatory Health Care Services; and

- Inspecting food, plants, animals, and other agriculture products—are classified in Industry 926140, Regulation of Agricultural Marketing and Commodities.

92313 Administration of Human Resource Programs (except Education, Public Health, and Veterans' Affairs Programs)[US]
See industry description for 923130 below.

923130 Administration of Human Resource Programs (except Education, Public Health, and Veterans' Affairs Programs)[US]

This industry comprises government establishments primarily engaged in the planning, administration, and coordination of programs for public assistance, social work, and welfare activities. The administration of Social Security, disability insurance, Medicare, unemployment insurance, and workers' compensation programs are included in this industry.

Cross-References. Government establishments primarily engaged in—

- Administering veterans' programs—are classified in Industry 923140, Administration of Veterans' Affairs;

- Operating state employment job service offices—are classified in U.S. Industry 561311, Employment Placement Agencies; and

---

- Operating programs for public assistance, social work, and welfare—are classified in Subsector 624, Social Assistance.

92314 Administration of Veterans' Affairs^{US}

See industry description for 923140 below.

923140 Administration of Veterans' Affairs^{US}

This industry comprises government establishments primarily engaged in the administration of programs of assistance, training, counseling, and other services to veterans and their dependents, heirs or survivors. Included in this industry are Veterans' Affairs offices that maintain liaison and coordinate activities with other service organizations and governmental agencies.

Cross-References.

- Government establishments operating veterans' hospitals are classified in Subsector 622, Hospitals;
- Establishments providing veterans' insurance are classified in Subsector 524, Insurance Carriers and Related Activities; and
- Establishments operating civic and social organizations for veterans are classified in Industry 813410, Civic and Social Organizations.

924 Administration of Environmental Quality Programs^{US}

The Administration of Environmental Quality Programs subsector groups government establishments primarily engaged in the administration of environmental quality.

9241 Administration of Environmental Quality Programs^{US}

92411 Administration of Air and Water Resource and Solid Waste Management Programs^{US}

See industry description for 924110 below.

924110 Administration of Air and Water Resource and Solid Waste Management Programs^{US}

This industry comprises government establishments primarily engaged in one or more of the following: (1) the administration, regulation, and enforcement of air and water resource programs; (2) the administration and regulation of solid waste management programs; (3) the administration and regulation of water and air pollution control and prevention programs; (4) the administration and regulation of flood control programs; (5) the administration and regulation of drainage development and water resource consumption programs; (6) the administration and regulation of toxic waste removal and cleanup programs; and (7) coordination of these activities at intergovernmental levels.

Illustrative Examples:

Environmental protection program administration, public administration

Waste management program (except sanitation districts), administration, public administration

Pollution control program administration, public administration

Water control and quality program administration, public administration

Cross-References. Government establishments primarily engaged in—

- Operating water and irrigation systems—are classified in Industry 221310, Water Supply and Irrigation Systems;

- Administering sanitation districts—are classified in Industry 926130, Regulation and Administration of Communications, Electric, Gas, and Other Utilities;

- Operating sewage treatment facilities—are classified in Industry 221320, Sewage Treatment Facilities; and

- Providing waste collection, treatment, disposal, and/or remediation—are classified in Subsector 562, Waste Management and Remediation Services.

92412   Administration of Conservation Programs^{US}

See industry description for 924120 below.

924120   Administration of Conservation Programs^{US}

This industry comprises government establishments primarily engaged in the administration, regulation, supervision and control of land use, including recreational areas; conservation and preservation of natural resources; erosion control; geological survey program administration; weather forecasting program administration; and the administration and protection of publicly and privately owned forest lands. Government establishments responsible for planning, management, regulation and conservation of game, fish, and wildlife populations, including wildlife management areas and field stations; and other administrative matters relating to the protection of fish, game, and wildlife are included in this industry.

US—United States industry only. CAN—United States and Canadian industries are comparable. MEX—United States and Mexican industries are comparable. Blank—Canadian, Mexican, and United States industries are comparable.

Cross-References. Government establishments primarily engaged in—

- Operating parks—are classified in Industry 712190, Nature Parks and Other Similar Institutions;

- Operating forest property—are classified in Subsector 113, Forestry and Logging;

- Geophysical surveying and/or mapping—are classified in Industry 541360, Geophysical Surveying and Mapping Services;

- Surveying and/or mapping (except geophysical)—are classified in Industry 541370, Surveying and Mapping (except Geophysical) Services;

- Weather forecasting—are classified in Industry 541990, All Other Professional, Scientific, and Technical Services;

- Operating fish and game preserves—are classified in Industry 712130, Zoos and Botanical Gardens; and

- Serving as urban planning commissions—are classified in Industry 925120, Administration of Urban Planning and Community and Rural Development.

925 Administration of Housing Programs, Urban Planning, and Community Development[US]

The Administration of Housing Programs, Urban Planning, and Community Development subsector groups government establishments primarily engaged in the administration of housing, urban planning, and community development.

9251 Administration of Housing Programs, Urban Planning, and Community Development[US]

92511 Administration of Housing Programs[US]
See industry description for 925110 below.

925110 Administration of Housing Programs[US]

This industry comprises government establishments primarily engaged in the administration and planning of housing programs.

Cross-References. Government establishments primarily engaged in—

- Operating government rental housing—are classified in Subsector 531, Real Estate;

- Conducting building inspections and enforcing building codes and standards—are classified in Industry 926150, Regulation, Licensing, and Inspection of Miscellaneous Commercial Sectors; and

- Buying, pooling, and repackaging mortgages or home loans for sale to others on the secondary market—are classified in U.S. Industry 522294, Secondary Market Financing.

92512 Administration of Urban Planning and Community and Rural Development[US]
See industry description for 925120 below.

925120 Administration of Urban Planning and Community and Rural Development[US]

This industry comprises government establishments primarily engaged in the administration and planning of the development of urban and rural areas. Included in this industry are government zoning boards and commissions.

Illustrative Examples:

Land redevelopment agencies, government

Urban planning commissions, government

Regional planning and development program administration, public administration

Zoning boards and commissions, public administration

926 Administration of Economic Programs[US]

This subsector comprises government establishments primarily engaged in the administration of economic programs.

9261 Administration of Economic Program[US]

92611 Administration of General Economic Programs[US]
See industry description for 926110 below.

926110 Administration of General Economic Programs[US]

This industry comprises government establishments primarily engaged in the administration, promotion and development of economic resources, including business, industry, and tourism. Included in this industry are government establishments responsible for the development of general statistical data and analyses and promotion of the general economic well-being of the governed area.

Illustrative Examples:

Consumer protection offices, public administration

Small business development agencies, public administration

Economic development agencies, government

Trade commissions, government

General economics statistical agencies, public administration

92612 Regulation and Administration of Transportation Programs[US]

See industry description for 926120 below.

926120 Regulation and Administration of Transportation Programs[US]

This industry comprises government establishments primarily engaged in the administration, regulation, licensing, planning, inspection, and investigation of transportation services and facilities. Included in this industry are government establishments responsible for motor vehicle and operator licensing, the Coast Guard (except the Coast Guard Academy), and parking authorities.

Cross-References. Government establishments primarily engaged in—

- Operating airports, railroads, depots, ports, toll roads and bridges, and other transportation facilities—are classified in Sector 48-49, Transportation and Warehousing;

- Operating parking lots and parking garages—are classified in Industry 812930, Parking Lots and Garages;

- Operating automobile safety inspection and emission testing facilities—are classified in Industry Group 8111, Automotive Repair and Maintenance;

- Building and/or maintaining roads and highways—are classified in Industry 237310, Highway, Street, and Bridge Construction;

- Providing air traffic control services—are classified in U.S. Industry 488111, Air Traffic Control; and

- Operating weigh stations—are classified in Industry 488490, Other Support Activities for Road Transportation.

92613 Regulation and Administration of Communications, Electric, Gas, and Other Utilities[US]
See industry description for 926130 below.

926130 Regulation and Administration of Communications, Electric, Gas, and Other Utilities[US]

This industry comprises government establishments primarily engaged in the administration, regulation, licensing and inspection of utilities, such as communications, electric power (including fossil, nuclear, solar, water, and wind), gas and water supply, and sewerage.

Cross-References.

Government establishments primarily engaged in operating utilities are classified in Subsector 221, Utilities.

92614 Regulation of Agricultural Marketing and Commodities[US]
See industry description for 926140 below.

926140 Regulation of Agricultural Marketing and Commodities[US]

This industry comprises government establishments primarily engaged in the planning, administration, and coordination of agricultural programs for production, marketing, and utilization, including educational and promotional activities. Included in this industry are government establishments responsible for regulating and controlling the grading and inspection of food, plants, animals, and other agricultural products.

Cross-References. Government establishments primarily engaged in—

- Administering programs for developing economic data about agricultural and trade in agricultural products—are classified in Industry 926110, Administration of General Economic Programs;
- Administering programs for the conservation of natural resources—are classified in Industry Group 9241, Administration of Environmental Quality Programs; and
- Administering food stamp programs—are classified in Industry 923130, Administration of Human Resource Programs (except Education, Public Health, and Veterans' Affairs Programs).

92615 Regulation, Licensing, and Inspection of Miscellaneous Commercial Sectors[US]
See industry description for 926150 below.

US—United States industry only. CAN—United States and Canadian industries are comparable. MEX—United States and Mexican industries are comparable. Blank—Canadian, Mexican, and United States industries are comparable.

926150 Regulation, Licensing, and Inspection of Miscellaneous Commercial Sectors[US]

This industry comprises government establishments primarily engaged in the regulation, licensing, and inspection of commercial sectors, such as retail trade, professional occupations, manufacturing, mining, construction, and services. Included in this industry are government establishments maintaining physical standards, regulating hazardous conditions not elsewhere classified, and enforcing alcoholic beverage control regulations.

Illustrative Examples:

Alcoholic beverage control boards, public administration
Labor management negotiations boards, government
Banking regulatory agencies, public administration
Licensing and permit issuance for business operations, government
Building inspections, government
Licensing and permit issuance for professional occupations, government
Insurance commissions, government
Securities regulation commissions, public administration

Cross-References. Government establishments primarily engaged in—

- Regulating, administering, and inspecting transportation services and facilities—are classified in Industry 926120, Regulation and Administration of Transportation Programs; and

- Regulating, administering, and inspecting communications, electric, gas, and other utilities—are classified in Industry 926130, Regulation and Administration of Communications, Electric, Gas, and Other Utilities.

927 Space Research and Technology[US]

This subsector group comprises government establishments that conduct space research.

9271 Space Research and Technology[US]

92711 Space Research and Technology[US]
See industry description for 927110 below.

927110 Space Research and Technology[US]

This industry comprises government establishments primarily engaged in the administration and operations of space flights, space research, and space explora-

---

tion. Included in this industry are government establishments operating space flight centers.

Cross-References.

- Private establishments primarily engaged in providing space freight transportation are classified in U.S. Industry 481212, Nonscheduled Chartered Freight Air Transportation;

- Government establishments primarily engaged in manufacturing aerospace vehicles and parts are classified in Industry 33641, Aerospace Product and Parts Manufacturing; and

- Government establishments primarily engaged in manufacturing space satellites are classified in Industry 334220, Radio and Television Broadcasting and Wireless Communications Equipment Manufacturing.

928 National Security and International Affairs^{US}

This subsector comprises government establishments primarily engaged in national security and international affairs.

9281 National Security and International Affairs^{US}

92811 National Security^{US}
See industry description for 928110 below.

928110 National Security^{US}

This industry comprises government establishments of the Armed Forces, including the National Guard, primarily engaged in national security and related activities.

Illustrative Examples:

Air Force	Marine Corps
Military police	National Guard
Army	Military courts
Military training schools (except military service academies)	Navy

Cross-References. Government establishments primarily engaged in—

- Operating military service academies—are classified in Industry 611310, Colleges, Universities, and Professional Schools; and

- Regulating and administering water transportation, such as the U.S. Coast Guard and the Merchant Marine—are classified in Industry 926120, Regulation and Administration of Transportation Programs.

92812 International Affairs[US]

See industry description for 928120 below.

928120 International Affairs[US]

This industry comprises establishments of U.S. and foreign governments primarily engaged in international affairs and programs relating to other nations and peoples.

Cross-References.

- Private sector trade associations and councils are classified in Industry 813910, Business Associations; and

- Government establishments administering international trade, such as trade commissions and councils are classified in Industry 926110, Administration of General Economic Programs.

Part II

List of Short Titles

List of Short Titles

Standard Short Titles for 2007 NAICS United States are shown below. They have been created for the use of those who find that space limitations preclude the use of the full title for the dissemination of data classified to NAICS. The adoption of these titles is recommended in all cases when the full title cannot be used.

The standard short titles are limited to 45 spaces. If the official full title falls within 45 spaces, it remains unchanged.

Note: For definitions of abbreviations and acronyms see page 974.

Code	Short title	Code	Short title
11	**AGRICULTURE, FORESTRY, FISHING AND HUNTING**	1114	Greenhouse and nursery production
		11141	Food crops grown under cover
111	**Crop production**	111411	Mushroom production
1111	Oilseed and grain farming	111419	Other food crops grown under cover
11111	Soybean farming	11142	Nursery and floriculture production
111110	Soybean farming	111421	Nursery and tree production
11112	Oilseed, except soybean, farming	111422	Floriculture production
111120	Oilseed, except soybean, farming	1119	Other crop farming
11113	Dry pea and bean farming	11191	Tobacco farming
111130	Dry pea and bean farming	111910	Tobacco farming
11114	Wheat farming	11192	Cotton farming
111140	Wheat farming	111920	Cotton farming
11115	Corn farming	11193	Sugarcane farming
111150	Corn farming	111930	Sugarcane farming
11116	Rice farming	11194	Hay farming
111160	Rice farming	111940	Hay farming
11119	Other grain farming	11199	All other crop farming
111191	Oilseed and grain combination farming	111991	Sugar beet farming
		111992	Peanut farming
111199	All other grain farming	111998	All other miscellaneous crop farming
1112	Vegetable and melon farming		
11121	Vegetable and melon farming	**112**	**Animal production**
111211	Potato farming	1121	Cattle ranching and farming
111219	Other vegetable and melon farming	11211	Beef cattle ranching, farming, and feedlots
1113	Fruit and tree nut farming	112111	Beef cattle ranching and farming
11131	Orange groves		
111310	Orange groves	112112	Cattle feedlots
11132	Citrus, except orange, groves	11212	Dairy cattle and milk production
111320	Citrus, except orange, groves	112120	Dairy cattle and milk production
11133	Noncitrus fruit and tree nut farming	11213	Dual-purpose cattle ranching and farming
111331	Apple orchards	112130	Dual-purpose cattle ranching and farming
111332	Grape vineyards		
111333	Strawberry farming	1122	Hog and pig farming
111334	Berry, except strawberry, farming	11221	Hog and pig farming
111335	Tree nut farming	112210	Hog and pig farming
111336	Fruit and tree nut combination farming	1123	Poultry and egg production
111339	Other noncitrus fruit farming	11231	Chicken egg production

Note: For definitions of abbreviations and acronyms see page 974.

Code	Short title
112310	Chicken egg production
11232	Broilers and meat type chicken production
112320	Broilers and meat type chicken production
11233	Turkey production
112330	Turkey production
11234	Poultry hatcheries
112340	Poultry hatcheries
11239	Other poultry production
112390	Other poultry production
1124	Sheep and goat farming
11241	Sheep farming
112410	Sheep farming
11242	Goat farming
112420	Goat farming
1125	Aquaculture
11251	Aquaculture
112511	Finfish farming and fish hatcheries
112512	Shellfish farming
112519	Other aquaculture
1129	Other animal production
11291	Apiculture
112910	Apiculture
11292	Horses and other equine production
112920	Horses and other equine production
11293	Fur-bearing animal and rabbit production
112930	Fur-bearing animal and rabbit production
11299	All other animal production
112990	All other animal production

113 Forestry and logging

Code	Short title
1131	Timber tract operations
11311	Timber tract operations
113110	Timber tract operations
1132	Forest nursery and gathering forest products
11321	Forest nursery and gathering forest products

Code	Short title
113210	Forest nursery and gathering forest products
1133	Logging
11331	Logging
113310	Logging

114 Fishing, hunting and trapping

Code	Short title
1141	Fishing
11411	Fishing
114111	Finfish fishing
114112	Shellfish fishing
114119	Other marine fishing
1142	Hunting and trapping
11421	Hunting and trapping
114210	Hunting and trapping

115 Agriculture and forestry support activities

Code	Short title
1151	Support activities for crop production
11511	Support activities for crop production
115111	Cotton ginning
115112	Soil preparation, planting, and cultivating
115113	Crop harvesting, primarily by machine
115114	Other postharvest crop activities
115115	Farm labor contractors and crew leaders
115116	Farm management services
1152	Support activities for animal production
11521	Support activities for animal production
115210	Support activities for animal production
1153	Support activities for forestry
11531	Support activities for forestry
115310	Support activities for forestry

Note: For definitions of abbreviations and acronyms see page 974.

Code	Short title	Code	Short title
21	**MINING, QUARRYING, AND OIL AND GAS EXTRACTION**	21232	Sand, gravel, clay, and refractory mining
		212321	Construction sand and gravel mining
211	**Oil and gas extraction**	212322	Industrial sand mining
2111	Oil and gas extraction	212324	Kaolin and ball clay mining
21111	Oil and gas extraction	212325	Clay, ceramic, and refractory minerals mining
211111	Crude petroleum and natural gas extraction	21239	Other nonmetallic mineral mining
211112	Natural gas liquid extraction	212391	Potash, soda, and borate mineral mining
212	Mining, except oil and gas	212392	Phosphate rock mining
2121	Coal mining	212393	Other chemical and fertilizer mineral mining
21211	Coal mining	212399	All other nonmetallic mineral mining
212111	Bituminous coal and lignite surface mining		
212112	Bituminous coal underground mining	**213**	**Support activities for mining**
212113	Anthracite mining	2131	Support activities for mining
2122	Metal ore mining	21311	Support activities for mining
21221	Iron ore mining	213111	Drilling oil and gas wells
212210	Iron ore mining	213112	Support activities for oil and gas operations
21222	Gold ore and silver ore mining	213113	Support activities for coal mining
212221	Gold ore mining		
212222	Silver ore mining	213114	Support activities for metal mining
21223	Copper, nickel, lead, and zinc mining	213115	Support activities for nonmetallic minerals
212231	Lead ore and zinc ore mining		
212234	Copper ore and nickel ore mining	**22**	**UTILITIES**
21229	Other metal ore mining	**221**	**Utilities**
212291	Uranium-radium-vanadium ore mining	2211	Power generation and supply
212299	All other metal ore mining	22111	Electric power generation
2123	Nonmetallic mineral mining and quarrying	221111	Hydroelectric power generation
21231	Stone mining and quarrying	221112	Fossil fuel electric power generation
212311	Dimension stone mining and quarrying	221113	Nuclear electric power generation
212312	Crushed and broken limestone mining	221119	Other electric power generation
212313	Crushed and broken granite mining	22112	Electric power transmission and distribution
212319	Other crushed and broken stone mining	221121	Electric bulk power transmission and control

Note: For definitions of abbreviations and acronyms see page 974.

Code	Short title	Code	Short title
221122	Electric power distribution	23712	Oil and gas pipeline construction
2212	Natural gas distribution	237120	Oil and gas pipeline construction
22121	Natural gas distribution		
221210	Natural gas distribution	23713	Power and communication system construction
2213	Water, sewage and other systems		
22131	Water supply and irrigation systems	237130	Power and communication system construction
221310	Water supply and irrigation systems	2372	Land subdivision
		23721	Land subdivision
22132	Sewage treatment facilities	237210	Land subdivision
221320	Sewage treatment facilities	2373	Highway, street, and bridge construction
22133	Steam and air-conditioning supply	23731	Highway, street, and bridge construction
221330	Steam and air-conditioning supply	237310	Highway, street, and bridge construction

23   CONSTRUCTION

236   Construction of buildings

		2379	Other heavy construction
2361	Residential building construction	23799	Other heavy construction
23611	Residential building construction	237990	Other heavy construction

238   Specialty trade contractors

Code	Short title	Code	Short title
236115	New single-family general contractors	2381	Building foundation and exterior contractors
236116	New multifamily general contractors	23811	Poured concrete structure contractors
236117	New housing operative builders	238110	Poured concrete structure contractors
236118	Residential remodelers		
2362	Nonresidential building construction	23812	Steel and precast concrete contractors
23621	Industrial building construction	238120	Steel and precast concrete contractors
236210	Industrial building construction		
23622	Commercial building construction	23813	Framing contractors
		238130	Framing contractors
236220	Commercial building construction	23814	Masonry contractors
		238140	Masonry contractors
		23815	Glass and glazing contractors

237   Heavy and civil engineering construction

		238150	Glass and glazing contractors
2371	Utility system construction	23816	Roofing contractors
23711	Water and sewer system construction	238160	Roofing contractors
		23817	Siding contractors
		238170	Siding contractors
237110	Water and sewer system construction	23819	Other building exterior contractors

Note: For definitions of abbreviations and acronyms see page 974.

Code	Short title	Code	Short title
238190	Other building exterior contractors	311119	Other animal food manufacturing
2382	Building equipment contractors	3112	Grain and oilseed milling
23821	Electrical and wiring contractors	31121	Flour milling and malt manufacturing
238210	Electrical and wiring contractors	311211	Flour milling
23822	Plumbing and HVAC contractors	311212	Rice milling
		311213	Malt manufacturing
238220	Plumbing and HVAC contractors	31122	Starch and vegetable oil manufacturing
23829	Other building equipment contractors	311221	Wet corn milling
238290	Other building equipment contractors	311222	Soybean processing
		311223	Other oilseed processing
2383	Building finishing contractors	311225	Fats and oils refining and blending
23831	Drywall and insulation contractors	31123	Breakfast cereal manufacturing
238310	Drywall and insulation contractors	311230	Breakfast cereal manufacturing
23832	Painting and wall covering contractors	3113	Sugar and confectionery product manufacturing
238320	Painting and wall covering contractors	31131	Sugar manufacturing
		311311	Sugarcane mills
23833	Flooring contractors	311312	Cane sugar refining
238330	Flooring contractors	311313	Beet sugar manufacturing
23834	Tile and terrazzo contractors	31132	Confectionery manufacturing from cacao beans
238340	Tile and terrazzo contractors	311320	Confectionery manufacturing from cacao beans
23835	Finish carpentry contractors	31133	Confectionery mfg. from purchased chocolate
238350	Finish carpentry contractors	311330	Confectionery mfg. from purchased chocolate
23839	Other building finishing contractors	31134	Nonchocolate confectionery manufacturing
238390	Other building finishing contractors	311340	Nonchocolate confectionery manufacturing
2389	Other specialty trade contractors	3114	Fruit and vegetable preserving and specialty
23891	Site preparation contractors	31141	Frozen food manufacturing
238910	Site preparation contractors	311411	Frozen fruit and vegetable manufacturing
23899	All other specialty trade contractors	311412	Frozen specialty food manufacturing
238990	All other specialty trade contractors	31142	Fruit and vegetable canning and drying
31-33	**MANUFACTURING**	311421	Fruit and vegetable canning
311	**Food manufacturing**		
3111	Animal food manufacturing		
31111	Animal food manufacturing		
311111	Dog and cat food manufacturing		

Note: For definitions of abbreviations and acronyms see page 974.

Code	Short title
311422	Specialty canning
311423	Dried and dehydrated food manufacturing
3115	Dairy product manufacturing
31151	Dairy product, except frozen, manufacturing
311511	Fluid milk manufacturing
311512	Creamery butter manufacturing
311513	Cheese manufacturing
311514	Dry, condensed, and evaporated dairy products
31152	Ice cream and frozen dessert manufacturing
311520	Ice cream and frozen dessert manufacturing
3116	Animal slaughtering and processing
31161	Animal slaughtering and processing
311611	Animal, except poultry, slaughtering
311612	Meat processed from carcasses
311613	Rendering and meat byproduct processing
311615	Poultry processing
3117	Seafood product preparation and packaging
31171	Seafood product preparation and packaging
311711	Seafood canning
311712	Fresh and frozen seafood processing
3118	Bakeries and tortilla manufacturing
31181	Bread and bakery product manufacturing
311811	Retail bakeries
311812	Commercial bakeries
311813	Frozen cakes and other pastries manufacturing
31182	Cookie, cracker, and pasta manufacturing
311821	Cookie and cracker manufacturing
311822	Mixes and dough made from purchased flour

Code	Short title
311823	Dry pasta manufacturing
31183	Tortilla manufacturing
311830	Tortilla manufacturing
3119	Other food manufacturing
31191	Snack food manufacturing
311911	Roasted nuts and peanut butter manufacturing
311919	Other snack food manufacturing
31192	Coffee and tea manufacturing
311920	Coffee and tea manufacturing
31193	Flavoring syrup and concentrate manufacturing
311930	Flavoring syrup and concentrate manufacturing
31194	Seasoning and dressing manufacturing
311941	Mayonnaise, dressing, and sauce manufacturing
311942	Spice and extract manufacturing
31199	All other food manufacturing
311991	Perishable prepared food manufacturing
311999	All other miscellaneous food manufacturing
312	**Beverage and tobacco product manufacturing**
3121	Beverage manufacturing
31211	Soft drink and ice manufacturing
312111	Soft drink manufacturing
312112	Bottled water manufacturing
312113	Ice manufacturing
31212	Breweries
312120	Breweries
31213	Wineries
312130	Wineries
31214	Distilleries
312140	Distilleries
3122	Tobacco manufacturing
31221	Tobacco stemming and redrying
312210	Tobacco stemming and redrying
31222	Tobacco product manufacturing
312221	Cigarette manufacturing

Note: For definitions of abbreviations and acronyms see page 974.

Code	Short title
312229	Other tobacco product manufacturing
313	**Textile mills**
3131	Fiber, yarn, and thread mills
31311	Fiber, yarn, and thread mills
313111	Yarn spinning mills
313112	Yarn texturizing and twisting mills
313113	Thread mills
3132	Fabric mills
31321	Broadwoven fabric mills
313210	Broadwoven fabric mills
31322	Narrow fabric mills and schiffli embroidery
313221	Narrow fabric mills
313222	Schiffli machine embroidery
31323	Nonwoven fabric mills
313230	Nonwoven fabric mills
31324	Knit fabric mills
313241	Weft knit fabric mills
313249	Other knit fabric and lace mills
3133	Textile and fabric finishing mills
31331	Textile and fabric finishing mills
313311	Broadwoven fabric finishing mills
313312	Other textile and fabric finishing mills
31332	Fabric coating mills
313320	Fabric coating mills
314	**Textile product mills**
3141	Textile furnishings mills
31411	Carpet and rug mills
314110	Carpet and rug mills
31412	Curtain and linen mills
314121	Curtain and drapery mills
314129	Other household textile product mills
3149	Other textile product mills
31491	Textile bag and canvas mills
314911	Textile bag mills

Code	Short title
314912	Canvas and related product mills
31499	All other textile product mills
314991	Rope, cordage, and twine mills
314992	Tire cord and tire fabric mills
314999	All other miscellaneous textile product mills
315	**Apparel manufacturing**
3151	Apparel knitting mills
31511	Hosiery and sock mills
315111	Sheer hosiery mills
315119	Other hosiery and sock mills
31519	Other apparel knitting mills
315191	Outerwear knitting mills
315192	Underwear and nightwear knitting mills
3152	Cut and sew apparel manufacturing
31521	Cut and sew apparel contractors
315211	Men's and boys' apparel contractors
315212	Women's, girls', infants' apparel contractors
31522	Men's and boys' cut and sew apparel mfg
315221	Men's and boys' underwear and nightwear mfg
315222	Men's and boys' suit, coat, and overcoat mfg
315223	Men's and boys' shirt, except work shirt, mfg
315224	Men's and boys' pants, except work pants, mfg
315225	Men's and boys' work clothing manufacturing
315228	Other men's and boys' outerwear manufacturing
31523	Women's and girls' cut and sew apparel mfg
315231	Women's and girls' lingerie and nightwear mfg
315232	Women's and girls' blouse and shirt mfg
315233	Women's and girls' dress manufacturing

Note: For definitions of abbreviations and acronyms see page 974.

Code	Short title
315234	Women's and girls' suit, coat, and skirt mfg
315239	Other women's and girls' outerwear mfg
31529	Other cut and sew apparel manufacturing
315291	Infants' cut and sew apparel manufacturing
315292	Fur and leather apparel manufacturing
315299	All other cut and sew apparel manufacturing
3159	Accessories and other apparel manufacturing
31599	Accessories and other apparel manufacturing
315991	Hat, cap, and millinery manufacturing
315992	Glove and mitten manufacturing
315993	Men's and boys' neckwear manufacturing
315999	All other accessory and apparel manufacturing
316	**Leather and allied product manufacturing**
3161	Leather and hide tanning and finishing
31611	Leather and hide tanning and finishing
316110	Leather and hide tanning and finishing
3162	Footwear manufacturing
31621	Footwear manufacturing
316211	Rubber and plastics footwear manufacturing
316212	House slipper manufacturing
316213	Men's nonathletic footwear manufacturing
316214	Women's nonathletic footwear manufacturing
316219	Other footwear manufacturing
3169	Other leather product manufacturing
31699	Other leather product manufacturing

Code	Short title
316991	Luggage manufacturing
316992	Women's handbag and purse manufacturing
316993	Other personal leather good manufacturing
316999	All other leather and allied good mfg.
321	**Wood product manufacturing**
3211	Sawmills and wood preservation
32111	Sawmills and wood preservation
321113	Sawmills
321114	Wood preservation
3212	Plywood and engineered wood product mfg.
32121	Plywood and engineered wood product mfg.
321211	Hardwood veneer and plywood manufacturing
321212	Softwood veneer and plywood manufacturing
321213	Engineered wood member manufacturing
321214	Truss manufacturing
321219	Reconstituted wood product manufacturing
3219	Other wood product manufacturing
32191	Millwork
321911	Wood window and door manufacturing
321912	Cut stock, resawing lumber, and planing
321918	Other millwork, including flooring
32192	Wood container and pallet manufacturing
321920	Wood container and pallet manufacturing
32199	All other wood product manufacturing
321991	Manufactured home, mobile home, manufacturing
321992	Prefabricated wood building manufacturing

Note: For definitions of abbreviations and acronyms see page 974.

Code	Short title
321999	Miscellaneous wood product manufacturing

322   Paper manufacturing

Code	Short title
3221	Pulp, paper, and paperboard mills
32211	Pulp mills
322110	Pulp mills
32212	Paper mills
322121	Paper, except newsprint, mills
322122	Newsprint mills
32213	Paperboard mills
322130	Paperboard mills
3222	Converted paper product manufacturing
32221	Paperboard container manufacturing
322211	Corrugated and solid fiber box manufacturing
322212	Folding paperboard box manufacturing
322213	Setup paperboard box manufacturing
322214	Fiber can, tube, and drum manufacturing
322215	Nonfolding sanitary food container mfg.
32222	Paper bag and coated and treated paper mfg.
322221	Coated and laminated packaging paper mfg.
322222	Coated and laminated paper manufacturing
322223	Coated paper bag and pouch manufacturing
322224	Uncoated paper and multiwall bag mfg.
322225	Flexible packaging foil manufacturing
322226	Surface-coated paperboard manufacturing
32223	Stationery product manufacturing
322231	Die-cut paper office supplies manufacturing

Code	Short title
322232	Envelope manufacturing
322233	Stationery and related product manufacturing
32229	Other converted paper product manufacturing
322291	Sanitary paper product manufacturing
322299	All other converted paper product mfg.

323   Printing and related support activities

Code	Short title
3231	Printing and related support activities
32311	Printing
323110	Commercial lithographic printing
323111	Commercial gravure printing
323112	Commercial flexographic printing
323113	Commercial screen printing
323114	Quick printing
323115	Digital printing
323116	Manifold business forms printing
323117	Books printing
323118	Blankbook and looseleaf binder manufacturing
323119	Other commercial printing
32312	Support activities for printing
323121	Tradebinding and related work
323122	Prepress services

324   Petroleum and coal products manufacturing

Code	Short title
3241	Petroleum and coal products manufacturing
32411	Petroleum refineries
324110	Petroleum refineries
32412	Asphalt paving and roofing materials mfg.
324121	Asphalt paving mixture and block mfg.
324122	Asphalt shingle and coating materials mfg.

Note: For definitions of abbreviations and acronyms see page 974.

Code	Short title	Code	Short title
32419	Other petroleum and coal products mfg.	325222	Noncellulosic organic fiber manufacturing
324191	Petroleum lubricating oil and grease mfg.	3253	Agricultural chemical manufacturing
324199	All other petroleum and coal products mfg.	32531	Fertilizer manufacturing
		325311	Nitrogenous fertilizer manufacturing
325	**Chemical manufacturing**	325312	Phosphatic fertilizer manufacturing
3251	Basic chemical manufacturing	325314	Fertilizer, mixing only, manufacturing
32511	Petrochemical manufacturing		
325110	Petrochemical manufacturing	32532	Pesticide and other ag. chemical mfg.
32512	Industrial gas manufacturing	325320	Pesticide and other ag. chemical mfg.
325120	Industrial gas manufacturing		
32513	Synthetic dye and pigment manufacturing	3254	Pharmaceutical and medicine manufacturing
325131	Inorganic dye and pigment manufacturing	32541	Pharmaceutical and medicine manufacturing
325132	Synthetic organic dye and pigment mfg.	325411	Medicinal and botanical manufacturing
32518	Other basic inorganic chemical manufacturing	325412	Pharmaceutical preparation manufacturing
325181	Alkalies and chlorine manufacturing	325413	In-vitro diagnostic substance manufacturing
325182	Carbon black manufacturing	325414	Other biological product manufacturing
325188	All other basic inorganic chemical mfg.	3255	Paint, coating, and adhesive manufacturing
32519	Other basic organic chemical manufacturing	32551	Paint and coating manufacturing
325191	Gum and wood chemical manufacturing	325510	Paint and coating manufacturing
325192	Cyclic crude and intermediate manufacturing	32552	Adhesive manufacturing
325193	Ethyl alcohol manufacturing	325520	Adhesive manufacturing
325199	All other basic organic chemical mfg.	3256	Soap, cleaning compound, and toiletry mfg.
3252	Resin, rubber, and artificial fibers mfg.	32561	Soap and cleaning compound manufacturing
32521	Resin and synthetic rubber manufacturing	325611	Soap and other detergent manufacturing
325211	Plastics material and resin manufacturing	325612	Polish and other sanitation good mfg.
325212	Synthetic rubber manufacturing	325613	Surface active agent manufacturing
32522	Artificial fibers and filaments manufacturing	32562	Toilet preparation manufacturing
325221	Cellulosic organic fiber manufacturing		

Note: For definitions of abbreviations and acronyms see page 974.

Code	Short title	Code	Short title
325620	Toilet preparation manufacturing	32616	Plastics bottle manufacturing
3259	Other chemical product and preparation mfg.	326160	Plastics bottle manufacturing
		32619	Other plastics product manufacturing
32591	Printing ink manufacturing	326191	Plastics plumbing fixture manufacturing
325910	Printing ink manufacturing		
32592	Explosives manufacturing	326192	Resilient floor covering manufacturing
325920	Explosives manufacturing		
32599	All other chemical preparation manufacturing	326199	All other plastics product manufacturing
325991	Custom compounding of purchased resins	3262	Rubber product manufacturing
		32621	Tire manufacturing
325992	Photographic film and chemical manufacturing	326211	Tire manufacturing, except retreading
325998	Other miscellaneous chemical product mfg.	326212	Tire retreading
		32622	Rubber and plastics hose and belting mfg.
326	**Plastics and rubber products manufacturing**	326220	Rubber and plastics hose and belting mfg.
3261	Plastics product manufacturing	32629	Other rubber product manufacturing
32611	Plastics packaging materials, film and sheet	326291	Rubber product mfg. for mechanical use
326111	Plastics bag and pouch manufacturing	326299	All other rubber product manufacturing
326112	Plastics packaging film and sheet mfg.		
326113	Nonpackaging plastics film and sheet mfg.	**327**	**Nonmetallic mineral product manufacturing**
32612	Plastics pipe, fittings, and profile shapes	3271	Clay product and refractory manufacturing
326121	Unlaminated plastics profile shape mfg.	32711	Pottery, ceramics, and plumbing fixture mfg.
326122	Plastics pipe and pipe fitting manufacturing	327111	Vitreous china plumbing fixture manufacturing
32613	Laminated plastics plate, sheet, and shapes	327112	Vitreous china and earthenware articles mfg.
326130	Laminated plastics plate, sheet, and shapes	327113	Porcelain electrical supply manufacturing
32614	Polystyrene foam product manufacturing	32712	Clay building material and refractories mfg.
326140	Polystyrene foam product manufacturing	327121	Brick and structural clay tile manufacturing
32615	Urethane and other foam product manufacturing	327122	Ceramic wall and floor tile manufacturing
326150	Urethane and other foam product manufacturing	327123	Other structural clay product manufacturing

Note: For definitions of abbreviations and acronyms see page 974.

Code	Short title
327124	Clay refractory manufacturing
327125	Nonclay refractory manufacturing
3272	Glass and glass product manufacturing
32721	Glass and glass product manufacturing
327211	Flat glass manufacturing
327212	Other pressed and blown glass and glassware
327213	Glass container manufacturing
327215	Glass product mfg. made of purchased glass
3273	Cement and concrete product manufacturing
32731	Cement manufacturing
327310	Cement manufacturing
32732	Ready-mix concrete manufacturing
327320	Ready-mix concrete manufacturing
32733	Concrete pipe, brick, and block manufacturing
327331	Concrete block and brick manufacturing
327332	Concrete pipe manufacturing
32739	Other concrete product manufacturing
327390	Other concrete product manufacturing
3274	Lime and gypsum product manufacturing
32741	Lime manufacturing
327410	Lime manufacturing
32742	Gypsum product manufacturing
327420	Gypsum product manufacturing
3279	Other nonmetallic mineral products
32791	Abrasive product manufacturing
327910	Abrasive product manufacturing
32799	All other nonmetallic mineral products mfg.
327991	Cut stone and stone product manufacturing
327992	Ground or treated minerals and earths mfg.

Code	Short title
327993	Mineral wool manufacturing
327999	Miscellaneous nonmetallic mineral products
331	**Primary metal manufacturing**
3311	Iron and steel mills and ferroalloy mfg.
33111	Iron and steel mills and ferroalloy mfg.
331111	Iron and steel mills
331112	Ferroalloy and related product manufacturing
3312	Steel product mfg. from purchased steel
33121	Iron, steel pipe and tube from purchase steel
331210	Iron, steel pipe and tube from purchase steel
33122	Rolling and drawing of purchased steel
331221	Rolled steel shape manufacturing
331222	Steel wire drawing
3313	Alumina and aluminum production
33131	Alumina and aluminum production
331311	Alumina refining
331312	Primary aluminum production
331314	Secondary smelting and alloying of aluminum
331315	Aluminum sheet, plate, and foil manufacturing
331316	Aluminum extruded product manufacturing
331319	Other aluminum rolling and drawing
3314	Other nonferrous metal production
33141	Other nonferrous metal production
331411	Primary smelting and refining of copper
331419	Primary nonferrous metal, except Cu and Al

Note: For definitions of abbreviations and acronyms see page 974.

Code	Short title
33142	Rolled, drawn, extruded, and alloyed copper
331421	Copper rolling, drawing, and extruding
331422	Copper wire, except mechanical, drawing
331423	Secondary processing of copper
33149	Nonferrous metal, except Cu and Al, shaping
331491	Nonferrous metal, except Cu and Al, shaping
331492	Secondary processing of other nonferrous
3315	Foundries
33151	Ferrous metal foundries
331511	Iron foundries
331512	Steel investment foundries
331513	Steel foundries, except investment
33152	Nonferrous metal foundries
331521	Aluminum die-casting foundries
331522	Nonferrous, except Al, die-casting foundries
331524	Aluminum foundries, except die-casting
331525	Copper foundries, except die-casting
331528	Other nonferrous foundries, exc. die-casting
332	**Fabricated metal product manufacturing**
3321	Forging and stamping
33211	Forging and stamping
332111	Iron and steel forging
332112	Nonferrous forging
332114	Custom roll forming
332115	Crown and closure manufacturing
332116	Metal stamping
332117	Powder metallurgy part manufacturing
3322	Cutlery and handtool manufacturing
33221	Cutlery and handtool manufacturing

Code	Short title
332211	Cutlery and flatware, except precious, mfg.
332212	Hand and edge tool manufacturing
332213	Saw blade and handsaw manufacturing
332214	Kitchen utensil, pot, and pan manufacturing
3323	Architectural and structural metals mfg.
33231	Plate work and fabricated structural products
332311	Prefabricated metal buildings and components
332312	Fabricated structural metal manufacturing
332313	Plate work manufacturing
33232	Ornamental and architectural metal products
332321	Metal window and door manufacturing
332322	Sheet metal work manufacturing
332323	Ornamental and architectural metal work mfg.
3324	Boiler, tank, and shipping container mfg.
33241	Power boiler and heat exchanger manufacturing
332410	Power boiler and heat exchanger manufacturing
33242	Metal tank, heavy gauge, manufacturing
332420	Metal tank, heavy gauge, manufacturing
33243	Metal can, box, and other container mfg.
332431	Metal can manufacturing
332439	Other metal container manufacturing
3325	Hardware manufacturing
33251	Hardware manufacturing
332510	Hardware manufacturing
3326	Spring and wire product manufacturing
33261	Spring and wire product manufacturing

Note: For definitions of abbreviations and acronyms see page 974.

Code	Short title	Code	Short title
332611	Spring, heavy gauge, manufacturing	332996	Fabricated pipe and pipe fitting mfg.
332612	Spring, light gauge, manufacturing	332997	Industrial pattern manufacturing
332618	Other fabricated wire product manufacturing	332998	Enameled iron and metal sanitary ware mfg.
3327	Machine shops and threaded product mfg.	332999	Miscellaneous fabricated metal product mfg.
33271	Machine shops	**333**	**Machinery manufacturing**
332710	Machine shops	3331	Ag., construction, and mining machinery mfg.
33272	Turned product and screw, nut, and bolt mfg.	33311	Agricultural implement manufacturing
332721	Precision turned product manufacturing	333111	Farm machinery and equipment manufacturing
332722	Bolt, nut, screw, rivet, and washer mfg.	333112	Lawn and garden equipment manufacturing
3328	Coating, engraving, and heat treating metals	33312	Construction machinery manufacturing
33281	Coating, engraving, and heat treating metals	333120	Construction machinery manufacturing
332811	Metal heat treating	33313	Mining and oil and gas field machinery mfg.
332812	Metal coating and nonprecious engraving	333131	Mining machinery and equipment manufacturing
332813	Electroplating, anodizing, and coloring metal	333132	Oil and gas field machinery and equipment
3329	Other fabricated metal product manufacturing	3332	Industrial machinery manufacturing
33291	Metal valve manufacturing	33321	Sawmill and woodworking machinery
332911	Industrial valve manufacturing	333210	Sawmill and woodworking machinery
332912	Fluid power valve and hose fitting mfg.	33322	Plastics and rubber industry machinery
332913	Plumbing fixture fitting and trim mfg.	333220	Plastics and rubber industry machinery
332919	Other metal valve and pipe fitting mfg.	33329	Other industrial machinery manufacturing
33299	All other fabricated metal product mfg.	333291	Paper industry machinery manufacturing
332991	Ball and roller bearing manufacturing	333292	Textile machinery manufacturing
332992	Small arms ammunition manufacturing	333293	Printing machinery and equipment mfg.
332993	Ammunition, except small arms, manufacturing		
332994	Small arms manufacturing		
332995	Other ordnance and accessories manufacturing		

Note: For definitions of abbreviations and acronyms see page 974.

Code	Short title	Code	Short title
333294	Food product machinery manufacturing	333516	Rolling mill machinery and equipment mfg.
333295	Semiconductor machinery manufacturing	333518	Other metalworking machinery manufacturing
333298	All other industrial machinery manufacturing	3336	Turbine and power transmission equipment mfg.
3333	Commercial and service industry machinery	33361	Turbine and power transmission equipment mfg.
33331	Commercial and service industry machinery	333611	Turbine and turbine generator set units mfg.
333311	Automatic vending machine manufacturing	333612	Speed changer, drive, and gear manufacturing
333312	Commercial laundry and drycleaning machinery	333613	Mechanical power transmission equipment mfg.
333313	Office machinery manufacturing	333618	Other engine equipment manufacturing
333314	Optical instrument and lens manufacturing	3339	Other general purpose machinery manufacturing
333315	Photographic and photocopying equipment mfg.	33391	Pump and compressor manufacturing
333319	Other commercial and service machinery mfg.	333911	Pump and pumping equipment manufacturing
3334	HVAC and commercial refrigeration equipment	333912	Air and gas compressor manufacturing
33341	HVAC and commercial refrigeration equipment	333913	Measuring and dispensing pump manufacturing
333411	Air purification equipment manufacturing	33392	Material handling equipment manufacturing
333412	Industrial and commercial fan and blower mfg.	333921	Elevator and moving stairway manufacturing
333414	Heating equipment, except warm air furnaces	333922	Conveyor and conveying equipment mfg.
333415	AC, refrigeration, and forced air heating	333923	Overhead cranes, hoists, and monorail systems
3335	Metalworking machinery manufacturing	333924	Industrial truck, trailer, and stacker mfg.
33351	Metalworking machinery manufacturing	33399	All other general purpose machinery mfg.
333511	Industrial mold manufacturing	333991	Power-driven handtool manufacturing
333512	Metal cutting machine tool manufacturing	333992	Welding and soldering equipment manufacturing
333513	Metal forming machine tool manufacturing	333993	Packaging machinery manufacturing
333514	Special tool, die, jig, and fixture mfg.	333994	Industrial process furnace and oven mfg.
333515	Cutting tool and machine tool accessory mfg.		

Note: For definitions of abbreviations and acronyms see page 974.

Code	Short title	Code	Short title
333995	Fluid power cylinder and actuator mfg.	33441	Semiconductor and electronic component mfg.
333996	Fluid power pump and motor manufacturing	334411	Electron tube manufacturing
333997	Scale and balance manufacturing	334412	Bare printed circuit board manufacturing
333999	Miscellaneous general purpose machinery mfg.	334413	Semiconductors and related device mfg.
334	**Computer and electronic product manufacturing**	334414	Electronic capacitor manufacturing
		334415	Electronic resistor manufacturing
3341	Computer and peripheral equipment mfg.	334416	Electronic coils, transformers, and inductors
33411	Computer and peripheral equipment mfg.	334417	Electronic connector manufacturing
334111	Electronic computer manufacturing	334418	Printed circuit assembly manufacturing
334112	Computer storage device manufacturing	334419	Other electronic component manufacturing
334113	Computer terminal manufacturing	3345	Electronic instrument manufacturing
334119	Other computer peripheral equipment mfg.	33451	Electronic instrument manufacturing
3342	Communications equipment manufacturing	334510	Electromedical apparatus manufacturing
33421	Telephone apparatus manufacturing	334511	Search, detection, and navigation instruments
334210	Telephone apparatus manufacturing	334512	Automatic environmental control manufacturing
33422	Broadcast and wireless communications equip.	334513	Industrial process variable instruments
334220	Broadcast and wireless communications equip.	334514	Totalizing fluid meters and counting devices
33429	Other communications equipment manufacturing	334515	Electricity and signal testing instruments
334290	Other communications equipment manufacturing	334516	Analytical laboratory instrument mfg.
3343	Audio and video equipment manufacturing	334517	Irradiation apparatus manufacturing
33431	Audio and video equipment manufacturing	334518	Watch, clock, and part manufacturing
334310	Audio and video equipment manufacturing	334519	Other measuring and controlling device mfg.
3344	Semiconductor and electronic component mfg.	3346	Magnetic media manufacturing and reproducing

Note: For definitions of abbreviations and acronyms see page 974.

Code	Short title
33461	Magnetic media manufacturing and reproducing
334611	Software reproducing
334612	Audio and video media reproduction
334613	Magnetic and optical recording media mfg.
335	**Electrical equipment and appliance mfg.**
3351	Electric lighting equipment manufacturing
33511	Electric lamp bulb and part manufacturing
335110	Electric lamp bulb and part manufacturing
33512	Lighting fixture manufacturing
335121	Residential electric lighting fixture mfg.
335122	Nonresidential electric lighting fixture mfg.
335129	Other lighting equipment manufacturing
3352	Household appliance manufacturing
33521	Small electrical appliance manufacturing
335211	Electric housewares and household fan mfg.
335212	Household vacuum cleaner manufacturing
33522	Major appliance manufacturing
335221	Household cooking appliance manufacturing
335222	Household refrigerator and home freezer mfg.
335224	Household laundry equipment manufacturing
335228	Other major household appliance manufacturing
3353	Electrical equipment manufacturing
33531	Electrical equipment manufacturing
335311	Electric power and specialty transformer mfg.

Code	Short title
335312	Motor and generator manufacturing
335313	Switchgear and switchboard apparatus mfg.
335314	Relay and industrial control manufacturing
3359	Other electrical equipment and component mfg.
33591	Battery manufacturing
335911	Storage battery manufacturing
335912	Primary battery manufacturing
33592	Communication and energy wire and cable mfg.
335921	Fiber optic cable manufacturing
335929	Other communication and energy wire mfg.
33593	Wiring device manufacturing
335931	Current-carrying wiring device manufacturing
335932	Noncurrent-carrying wiring device mfg.
33599	Other electrical equipment and component mfg.
335991	Carbon and graphite product manufacturing
335999	Miscellaneous electrical equipment mfg.
336	**Transportation equipment manufacturing**
3361	Motor vehicle manufacturing
33611	Automobile and light truck manufacturing
336111	Automobile manufacturing
336112	Light truck and utility vehicle manufacturing
33612	Heavy duty truck manufacturing
336120	Heavy duty truck manufacturing
3362	Motor vehicle body and trailer manufacturing
33621	Motor vehicle body and trailer manufacturing
336211	Motor vehicle body manufacturing
336212	Truck trailer manufacturing

Note: For definitions of abbreviations and acronyms see page 974.

Code	Short title	Code	Short title
336213	Motor home manufacturing	336411	Aircraft manufacturing
336214	Travel trailer and camper manufacturing	336412	Aircraft engine and engine parts mfg.
3363	Motor vehicle parts manufacturing	336413	Other aircraft parts and equipment
33631	Motor vehicle gasoline engine and parts mfg.	336414	Guided missile and space vehicle mfg.
336311	Carburetor, piston, ring, and valve mfg.	336415	Space vehicle propulsion units and parts mfg.
336312	Gasoline engine and engine parts mfg.	336419	Other guided missile and space vehicle parts
33632	Motor vehicle electric equipment	3365	Railroad rolling stock manufacturing
336321	Vehicular lighting equipment manufacturing	33651	Railroad rolling stock manufacturing
336322	Other motor vehicle electric equipment mfg.	336510	Railroad rolling stock manufacturing
33633	Motor vehicle steering and suspension parts	3366	Ship and boat building
		33661	Ship and boat building
336330	Motor vehicle steering and suspension parts	336611	Ship building and repairing
		336612	Boat building
33634	Motor vehicle brake system manufacturing	3369	Other transportation equipment manufacturing
336340	Motor vehicle brake system manufacturing	33699	Other transportation equipment manufacturing
33635	Motor vehicle power train components mfg.	336991	Motorcycle, bicycle, and parts manufacturing
336350	Motor vehicle power train components mfg.	336992	Military armored vehicles and tank parts mfg.
33636	Motor vehicle seating and interior trim mfg.	336999	All other transportation equipment mfg.
336360	Motor vehicle seating and interior trim mfg.	**337**	**Furniture and related product manufacturing**
33637	Motor vehicle metal stamping	3371	Household and institutional furniture mfg.
336370	Motor vehicle metal stamping		
33639	Other motor vehicle parts manufacturing	33711	Wood kitchen cabinet and countertop mfg.
336391	Motor vehicle air-conditioning manufacturing	337110	Wood kitchen cabinet and countertop mfg.
336399	All other motor vehicle parts manufacturing	33712	Other household and institutional furniture
3364	Aerospace product and parts manufacturing	337121	Upholstered household furniture manufacturing
33641	Aerospace product and parts manufacturing	337122	Nonupholstered wood household furniture mfg.

Note: For definitions of abbreviations and acronyms see page 974.

Code	Short title
337124	Metal household furniture manufacturing
337125	Household furniture, exc. wood or metal, mfg.
337127	Institutional furniture manufacturing
337129	Wood TV, radio, and sewing machine housings
3372	Office furniture and fixtures manufacturing
33721.	Office furniture and fixtures manufacturing
337211	Wood office furniture manufacturing
337212	Custom architectural woodwork and millwork
337214	Office furniture, except wood, manufacturing
337215	Showcases, partitions, shelving, and lockers
3379	Other furniture related product manufacturing
33791	Mattress manufacturing
337910	Mattress manufacturing
33792	Blind and shade manufacturing
337920	Blind and shade manufacturing
339	**Miscellaneous manufacturing**
3391	Medical equipment and supplies manufacturing
33911	Medical equipment and supplies manufacturing
339112	Surgical and medical instrument manufacturing
339113	Surgical appliance and supplies manufacturing
339114	Dental equipment and supplies manufacturing
339115	Ophthalmic goods manufacturing
339116	Dental laboratories
3399	Other miscellaneous manufacturing
33991	Jewelry and silverware manufacturing

Code	Short title
339911	Jewelry, except costume, manufacturing
339912	Silverware and hollowware manufacturing
339913	Jewelers' material and lapidary work mfg.
339914	Costume jewelry and novelty manufacturing
33992	Sporting and athletic goods manufacturing
339920	Sporting and athletic goods manufacturing
33993	Doll, toy, and game manufacturing
339931	Doll and stuffed toy manufacturing
339932	Game, toy, and children's vehicle mfg.
33994	Office supplies, except paper, manufacturing
339941	Pen and mechanical pencil manufacturing
339942	Lead pencil and art good manufacturing
339943	Marking device manufacturing
339944	Carbon paper and inked ribbon manufacturing
33995	Sign manufacturing
339950	Sign manufacturing
33999	All other miscellaneous manufacturing
339991	Gasket, packing, and sealing device mfg.
339992	Musical instrument manufacturing
339993	Fastener, button, needle, and pin mfg.
339994	Broom, brush, and mop manufacturing
339995	Burial casket manufacturing
339999	All other miscellaneous manufacturing

Note: For definitions of abbreviations and acronyms see page 974.

Code	Short title	Code	Short title
42	**WHOLESALE TRADE**	423390	Other const. material merchant wholesalers
423	**Merchant wholesalers, durable goods**	4234	Commercial equip. merchant wholesalers
4231	Motor vehicle and parts merchant wholesalers	42341	Photographic equip. merchant wholesalers
42311	Motor vehicle merchant wholesalers	423410	Photographic equip. merchant wholesalers
423110	Motor vehicle merchant wholesalers	42342	Office equipment merchant wholesalers
42312	New motor vehicle parts merchant wholesalers	423420	Office equipment merchant wholesalers
423120	New motor vehicle parts merchant wholesalers	42343	Computer and software merchant wholesalers
42313	Tire and tube merchant wholesalers	423430	Computer and software merchant wholesalers
423130	Tire and tube merchant wholesalers	42344	Other commercial equip. merchant wholesalers
42314	Used motor vehicle parts merchant wholesalers	423440	Other commercial equip. merchant wholesalers
423140	Used motor vehicle parts merchant wholesalers	42345	Medical equipment merchant wholesalers
4232	Furniture and furnishing merchant wholesalers	423450	Medical equipment merchant wholesalers
42321	Furniture merchant wholesalers	42346	Ophthalmic goods merchant wholesalers
423210	Furniture merchant wholesalers	423460	Ophthalmic goods merchant wholesalers
42322	Home furnishing merchant wholesalers	42349	Other professional equip. merchant wholesaler
423220	Home furnishing merchant wholesalers	423490	Other professional equip. merchant wholesaler
4233	Lumber and const. supply merchant wholesalers	4235	Metal and mineral merchant wholesalers
42331	Lumber and wood merchant wholesalers	42351	Metal merchant wholesalers
423310	Lumber and wood merchant wholesalers	423510	Metal merchant wholesalers
42332	Masonry material merchant wholesalers	42352	Coal and other mineral merchant wholesalers
423320	Masonry material merchant wholesalers	423520	Coal and other mineral merchant wholesalers
42333	Roofing and siding merchant wholesalers	4236	Electric goods merchant wholesalers
423330	Roofing and siding merchant wholesalers	42361	Elec. equip. and wiring merchant wholesalers
42339	Other const. material merchant wholesalers	423610	Elec. equip. and wiring merchant wholesalers

Note: For definitions of abbreviations and acronyms see page 974.

Code	Short title
42362	Electric appliance merchant wholesalers
423620	Electric appliance merchant wholesalers
42369	Other electronic parts merchant wholesalers
423690	Other electronic parts merchant wholesalers
4237	Hardware and plumbing merchant wholesalers
42371	Hardware merchant wholesalers
423710	Hardware merchant wholesalers
42372	Plumbing equip. merchant wholesalers
423720	Plumbing equip. merchant wholesalers
42373	HVAC equip. merchant wholesalers
423730	HVAC equip. merchant wholesalers
42374	Refrigeration equip. merchant wholesalers
423740	Refrigeration equip. merchant wholesalers
4238	Machinery and supply merchant wholesalers
42381	Construction equipment merchant wholesalers
423810	Construction equipment merchant wholesalers
42382	Farm and garden equip. merchant wholesalers
423820	Farm and garden equip. merchant wholesalers
42383	Industrial machinery merchant wholesalers
423830	Industrial machinery merchant wholesalers
42384	Industrial supplies merchant wholesalers
423840	Industrial supplies merchant wholesalers
42385	Service estab. equip. merchant wholesalers
423850	Service estab. equip. merchant wholesalers

Code	Short title
42386	Other transport. goods merchant wholesalers
423860	Other transport. goods merchant wholesalers
4239	Misc. durable goods merchant wholesalers
42391	Sporting goods merchant wholesalers
423910	Sporting goods merchant wholesalers
42392	Toy and hobby goods merchant wholesalers
423920	Toy and hobby goods merchant wholesalers
42393	Recyclable material merchant wholesalers
423930	Recyclable material merchant wholesalers
42394	Jewelry merchant wholesalers
423940	Jewelry merchant wholesalers
42399	All other durable goods merchant wholesalers
423990	All other durable goods merchant wholesalers
424	**Merchant wholesalers, nondurable goods**
4241	Paper and paper product merchant wholesalers
42411	Printing and writing paper merch. whls.
424110	Printing and writing paper merch. whls.
42412	Office supplies merchant wholesalers
424120	Office supplies merchant wholesalers
42413	Industrial paper merchant wholesalers
424130	Industrial paper merchant wholesalers
4242	Druggists' goods merchant wholesalers
42421	Druggists' goods merchant wholesalers

Note: For definitions of abbreviations and acronyms see page 974.

Code	Short title	Code	Short title
424210	Druggists' goods merchant wholesalers	424470	Meat and meat product merchant wholesalers
4243	Apparel and piece goods merchant wholesalers	42448	Fruit and vegetable merchant wholesalers
42431	Piece goods merchant wholesalers	424480	Fruit and vegetable merchant wholesalers
424310	Piece goods merchant wholesalers	42449	Other grocery product merchant wholesalers
42432	Men's and boys' clothing merchant wholesalers	424490	Other grocery product merchant wholesalers
424320	Men's and boys' clothing merchant wholesalers	4245	Farm product raw material merch. whls.
42433	Women's and children's clothing merch. whls.	42451	Grain and field bean merchant wholesalers
424330	Women's and children's clothing merch. whls.	424510	Grain and field bean merchant wholesalers
42434	Footwear merchant wholesalers	42452	Livestock merchant wholesalers
424340	Footwear merchant wholesalers	424520	Livestock merchant wholesalers
4244	Grocery and related product wholesalers	42459	Other farm product raw material merch. whls.
42441	General line grocery merchant wholesalers	424590	Other farm product raw material merch. whls.
424410	General line grocery merchant wholesalers	4246	Chemical merchant wholesalers
42442	Packaged frozen food merchant wholesalers	42461	Plastics materials merchant wholesalers
424420	Packaged frozen food merchant wholesalers	424610	Plastics materials merchant wholesalers
42443	Dairy product merchant wholesalers	42469	Other chemicals merchant wholesalers
424430	Dairy product merchant wholesalers	424690	Other chemicals merchant wholesalers
42444	Poultry product merchant wholesalers	4247	Petroleum merchant wholesalers
424440	Poultry product merchant wholesalers	42471	Petroleum bulk stations and terminals
42445	Confectionery merchant wholesalers	424710	Petroleum bulk stations and terminals
424450	Confectionery merchant wholesalers	42472	Other petroleum merchant wholesalers
42446	Fish and seafood merchant wholesalers	424720	Other petroleum merchant wholesalers
424460	Fish and seafood merchant wholesalers	4248	Alcoholic beverage merchant wholesalers
42447	Meat and meat product merchant wholesalers	42481	Beer and ale merchant wholesalers
		424810	Beer and ale merchant wholesalers

Note: For definitions of abbreviations and acronyms see page 974.

Code	Short title
42482	Wine and spirit merchant wholesalers
424820	Wine and spirit merchant wholesalers
4249	Misc. nondurable goods merchant wholesalers
42491	Farm supplies merchant wholesalers
424910	Farm supplies merchant wholesalers
42492	Book and periodical merchant wholesalers
424920	Book and periodical merchant wholesalers
42493	Nursery and florist merchant wholesalers
424930	Nursery and florist merchant wholesalers
42494	Tobacco and tobacco product merch. whls.
424940	Tobacco and tobacco product merch. whls.
42495	Paint and supplies merchant wholesalers
424950	Paint and supplies merchant wholesalers
42499	Other nondurable goods merchant wholesalers
424990	Other nondurable goods merchant wholesalers
425	**Electronic markets and agents and brokers**
4251	Electronic markets and agents and brokers
42511	Business to business electronic markets
425110	Business to business electronic markets
42512	Wholesale trade agents and brokers
425120	Wholesale trade agents and brokers

Code	Short title
44-45	**RETAIL TRADE**
441	**Motor vehicle and parts dealers**
4411	Automobile dealers
44111	New car dealers
441110	New car dealers
44112	Used car dealers
441120	Used car dealers
4412	Other motor vehicle dealers
44121	Recreational vehicle dealers
441210	Recreational vehicle dealers
44122	Motorcycle, boat, and other vehicle dealers
441221	Motorcycle, ATV, personal watercraft dealers
441222	Boat dealers
441229	All other motor vehicle dealers
4413	Auto parts, accessories, and tire stores
44131	Automotive parts and accessories stores
441310	Automotive parts and accessories stores
44132	Tire dealers
441320	Tire dealers
442	**Furniture and home furnishings stores**
4421	Furniture stores
44211	Furniture stores
442110	Furniture stores
4422	Home furnishings stores
44221	Floor covering stores
442210	Floor covering stores
44229	Other home furnishings stores
442291	Window treatment stores
442299	All other home furnishings stores
443	**Electronics and appliance stores**
4431	Electronics and appliance stores
44311	Appliance, TV, and other electronics stores

Note: For definitions of abbreviations and acronyms see page 974.

Code	Short title
443111	Household appliance stores
443112	Radio, TV, and other electronics stores
44312	Computer and software stores
443120	Computer and software stores
44313	Camera and photographic supplies stores
443130	Camera and photographic supplies stores
444	**Building material and garden supply stores**
4441	Building material and supplies dealers
44411	Home centers
444110	Home centers
44412	Paint and wallpaper stores
444120	Paint and wallpaper stores
44413	Hardware stores
444130	Hardware stores
44419	Other building material dealers
444190	Other building material dealers
4442	Lawn and garden equipment and supplies stores
44421	Outdoor power equipment stores
444210	Outdoor power equipment stores
44422	Nursery, garden, and farm supply stores
444220	Nursery, garden, and farm supply stores
445	**Food and beverage stores**
4451	Grocery stores
44511	Supermarkets and other grocery stores
445110	Supermarkets and other grocery stores
44512	Convenience stores
445120	Convenience stores
4452	Specialty food stores
44521	Meat markets
445210	Meat markets
44522	Fish and seafood markets

Code	Short title
445220	Fish and seafood markets
44523	Fruit and vegetable markets
445230	Fruit and vegetable markets
44529	Other specialty food stores
445291	Baked goods stores
445292	Confectionery and nut stores
445299	All other specialty food stores
4453	Beer, wine, and liquor stores
44531	Beer, wine, and liquor stores
445310	Beer, wine, and liquor stores
446	**Health and personal care stores**
4461	Health and personal care stores
44611	Pharmacies and drug stores
446110	Pharmacies and drug stores
44612	Cosmetic and beauty supply stores
446120	Cosmetic and beauty supply stores
44613	Optical goods stores
446130	Optical goods stores
44619	Other health and personal care stores
446191	Food, health, supplement stores
446199	All other health and personal care stores
447	**Gasoline stations**
4471	Gasoline stations
44711	Gasoline stations with convenience stores
447110	Gasoline stations with convenience stores
44719	Other gasoline stations
447190	Other gasoline stations
448	**Clothing and clothing accessories stores**
4481	Clothing stores
44811	Men's clothing stores
448110	Men's clothing stores
44812	Women's clothing stores
448120	Women's clothing stores

Note: For definitions of abbreviations and acronyms see page 974.

Code	Short title
44813	Children's and infants' clothing stores
448130	Children's and infants' clothing stores
44814	Family clothing stores
448140	Family clothing stores
44815	Clothing accessories stores
448150	Clothing accessories stores
44819	Other clothing stores
448190	Other clothing stores
4482	Shoe stores
44821	Shoe stores
448210	Shoe stores
4483	Jewelry, luggage, and leather goods stores
44831	Jewelry stores
448310	Jewelry stores
44832	Luggage and leather goods stores
448320	Luggage and leather goods stores
451	**Sporting goods, hobby, book and music stores**
4511	Sporting goods and musical instrument stores
45111	Sporting goods stores
451110	Sporting goods stores
45112	Hobby, toy, and game stores
451120	Hobby, toy, and game stores
45113	Sewing, needlework, and piece goods stores
451130	Sewing, needlework, and piece goods stores
45114	Musical instrument and supplies stores
451140	Musical instrument and supplies stores
4512	Book, periodical, and music stores
45121	Book stores and news dealers
451211	Book stores
451212	News dealers and newsstands
45122	Precorded tape, CD, and record stores

Code	Short title
451220	Precorded tape, CD, and record stores
452	**General merchandise stores**
4521	Department stores
45211	Department stores
452111	Department stores, except discount
452112	Discount department stores
4529	Other general merchandise stores
45291	Warehouse clubs and supercenters
452910	Warehouse clubs and supercenters
45299	All other general merchandise stores
452990	All other general merchandise stores
453	**Miscellaneous store retailers**
4531	Florists
45311	Florists
453110	Florists
4532	Office supplies, stationery, and gift stores
45321	Office supplies and stationery stores
453210	Office supplies and stationery stores
45322	Gift, novelty, and souvenir stores
453220	Gift, novelty, and souvenir stores
4533	Used merchandise stores
45331	Used merchandise stores
453310	Used merchandise stores
4539	Other miscellaneous store retailers
45391	Pet and pet supplies stores
453910	Pet and pet supplies stores
45392	Art dealers
453920	Art dealers
45393	Manufactured, mobile, home dealers

Note: For definitions of abbreviations and acronyms see page 974.

Code	Short title
453930	Manufactured, mobile, home dealers
45399	All other miscellaneous store retailers
453991	Tobacco stores
453998	Store retailers not specified elsewhere
454	**Nonstore retailers**
4541	Electronic shopping and mail-order houses
45411	Electronic shopping and mail-order houses
454111	Electronic shopping
454112	Electronic auctions
454113	Mail-order houses
4542	Vending machine operators
45421	Vending machine operators
454210	Vending machine operators
4543	Direct selling establishments
45431	Fuel dealers
454311	Heating oil dealers
454312	Liquefied petroleum gas, bottled gas, dealers
454319	Other fuel dealers
45439	Other direct selling establishments
454390	Other direct selling establishments
48-49	**TRANSPORTATION AND WAREHOUSING**
481	**Air transportation**
4811	Scheduled air transportation
48111	Scheduled air transportation
481111	Scheduled passenger air transportation
481112	Scheduled freight air transportation
4812	Nonscheduled air transportation
48121	Nonscheduled air transportation
481211	Nonscheduled air passenger chartering
481212	Nonscheduled air freight chartering

Code	Short title
481219	Other nonscheduled air transportation
482	**Rail transportation**
4821	Rail transportation
48211	Rail transportation
482111	Line-haul railroads
482112	Short line railroads
483	**Water transportation**
4831	Sea, coastal, and Great Lakes transportation
48311	Sea, coastal, and Great Lakes transportation
483111	Deep sea freight transportation
483112	Deep sea passenger transportation
483113	Coastal and Great Lakes freight transport.
483114	Coastal and Great Lakes passenger transport.
4832	Inland water transportation
48321	Inland water transportation
483211	Inland water freight transportation
483212	Inland water passenger transportation
484	**Truck transportation**
4841	General freight trucking
48411	General freight trucking, local
484110	General freight trucking, local
48412	General freight trucking, long-distance
484121	General freight trucking, long-distance TL
484122	General freight trucking, long-distance LTL
4842	Specialized freight trucking
48421	Used household and office goods moving
484210	Used household and office goods moving
48422	Other specialized trucking, local
484220	Other specialized trucking, local

Note: For definitions of abbreviations and acronyms see page 974.

Code	Short title
48423	Other specialized trucking, long-distance
484230	Other specialized trucking, long-distance

485   Transit and ground passenger transportation

Code	Short title
4851	Urban transit systems
48511	Urban transit systems
485111	Mixed mode transit systems
485112	Commuter rail systems
485113	Bus and other motor vehicle transit systems
485119	Other urban transit systems
4852	Interurban and rural bus transportation
48521	Interurban and rural bus transportation
485210	Interurban and rural bus transportation
4853	Taxi and limousine service
48531	Taxi service
485310	Taxi service
48532	Limousine service
485320	Limousine service
4854	School and employee bus transportation
48541	School and employee bus transportation
485410	School and employee bus transportation
4855	Charter bus industry
48551	Charter bus industry
485510	Charter bus industry
4859	Other ground passenger transportation
48599	Other ground passenger transportation
485991	Special needs transportation
485999	All other ground passenger transportation

486   Pipeline transportation

Code	Short title
4861	Pipeline transportation of crude oil

Code	Short title
48611	Pipeline transportation of crude oil
486110	Pipeline transportation of crude oil
4862	Pipeline transportation of natural gas
48621	Pipeline transportation of natural gas
486210	Pipeline transportation of natural gas
4869	Other pipeline transportation
48691	Refined petroleum product pipeline transport.
486910	Refined petroleum product pipeline transport.
48699	All other pipeline transportation
486990	All other pipeline transportation

487   Scenic and sightseeing transportation

Code	Short title
4871	Scenic and sightseeing transportation, land
48711	Scenic and sightseeing transportation, land
487110	Scenic and sightseeing transportation, land
4872	Scenic and sightseeing transportation, water
48721	Scenic and sightseeing transportation, water
487210	Scenic and sightseeing transportation, water
4879	Scenic and sightseeing transportation, other
48799	Scenic and sightseeing transportation, other
487990	Scenic and sightseeing transportation, other

488   Support activities for transportation

Code	Short title
4881	Support activities for air transportation
48811	Airport operations
488111	Air traffic control

Note: For definitions of abbreviations and acronyms see page 974.

Code	Short title	Code	Short title
488119	Other airport operations	**491**	**Postal service**
48819	Other support activities for air transport.	4911	Postal service
		49111	Postal service
488190	Other support activities for air transport.	491110	Postal service
4882	Support activities for rail transportation	**492**	**Couriers and messengers**
48821	Support activities for rail transportation	4921	Couriers and express delivery services
488210	Support activities for rail transportation	49211	Couriers and express delivery services
4883	Support activities for water transportation	492110	Couriers and express delivery services
48831	Port and harbor operations	4922	Local messengers and local delivery
488310	Port and harbor operations		
48832	Marine cargo handling	49221	Local messengers and local delivery
488320	Marine cargo handling		
48833	Navigational services to shipping	492210	Local messengers and local delivery
488330	Navigational services to shipping	**493**	**Warehousing and storage**
48839	Other support activities for water transport.	4931	Warehousing and storage
		49311	General warehousing and storage
488390	Other support activities for water transport.	493110	General warehousing and storage
4884	Support activities for road transportation	49312	Refrigerated warehousing and storage
48841	Motor vehicle towing		
488410	Motor vehicle towing	493120	Refrigerated warehousing and storage
48849	Other support activities for road transport.	49313	Farm product warehousing and storage
488490	Other support activities for road transport.	493130	Farm product warehousing and storage
4885	Freight transportation arrangement	49319	Other warehousing and storage
48851	Freight transportation arrangement	493190	Other warehousing and storage
488510	Freight transportation arrangement	**51**	**INFORMATION**
4889	Other support activities for transportation	**511**	**Publishing industries, except Internet**
48899	Other support activities for transportation	5111	Newspaper, book, and directory publishers
488991	Packing and crating	51111	Newspaper publishers
488999	All other support activities for transport.	511110	Newspaper publishers
		51112	Periodical publishers

Note: For definitions of abbreviations and acronyms see page 974.

Code	Short title
511120	Periodical publishers
51113	Book publishers
511130	Book publishers
51114	Directory and mailing list publishers
511140	Directory and mailing list publishers
51119	Other publishers
511191	Greeting card publishers
511199	All other publishers
5112	Software publishers
51121	Software publishers
511210	Software publishers

512   Motion picture and sound recording industries

Code	Short title
5121	Motion picture and video industries
51211	Motion picture and video production
512110	Motion picture and video production
51212	Motion picture and video distribution
512120	Motion picture and video distribution
51213	Motion picture and video exhibition
512131	Motion picture theaters, except drive-ins
512132	Drive-in motion picture theaters
51219	Postproduction and other related industries
512191	Teleproduction and postproduction services
512199	Other motion picture and video industries
5122	Sound recording industries
51221	Record production
512210	Record production
51222	Integrated record production and distribution
512220	Integrated record production and distribution

Code	Short title
51223	Music publishers
512230	Music publishers
51224	Sound recording studios
512240	Sound recording studios
51229	Other sound recording industries
512290	Other sound recording industries

515   Broadcasting, except Internet

Code	Short title
5151	Radio and television broadcasting
51511	Radio broadcasting
515111	Radio networks
515112	Radio stations
51512	Television broadcasting
515120	Television broadcasting
5152	Cable and other subscription programming
51521	Cable and other subscription programming
515210	Cable and other subscription programming

517   Telecommunications

Code	Short title
5171	Wired telecommunications carriers
51711	Wired telecommunications carriers
517110	Wired telecommunications carriers
5172	Wireless telecommunications carriers
51721	Wireless telecommunications carriers
517210	Wireless telecommunications carriers
5174	Satellite telecommunications
51741	Satellite telecommunications
517410	Satellite telecommunications
5179	Other telecommunications
51791	Other telecommunications
517911	Telecommunications resellers
517919	All other telecommunications

Note: For definitions of abbreviations and acronyms see page 974.

Code	Short title	Code	Short title
518	**Data processing, hosting and related services**	5222	Nondepository credit intermediation
5182	Data processing, hosting and related services	52221	Credit card issuing
		522210	Credit card issuing
51821	Data processing, hosting and related services	52222	Sales financing
		522220	Sales financing
518210	Data processing, hosting and related services	52229	Other nondepository credit intermediation
		522291	Consumer lending
519	**Other information services**	522292	Real estate credit
5191	Other information services	522293	International trade financing
51911	News syndicates	522294	Secondary market financing
519110	News syndicates	522298	All other nondepository credit intermediation
51912	Libraries and archives		
519120	Libraries and archives	5223	Activities related to credit intermediation
51913	Internet publishing and web search portals	52231	Mortgage and nonmortgage loan brokers
519130	Internet publishing and web search portals	522310	Mortgage and nonmortgage loan brokers
51919	All other information services	52232	Financial transaction processing and clearing
519190	All other information services	522320	Financial transaction processing and clearing
52	**FINANCE AND INSURANCE**	52239	Other credit intermediation activities
521	**Monetary authorities—central bank**	522390	Other credit intermediation activities
5211	Monetary authorities—central bank	**523**	**Securities, commodity contracts, investments**
52111	Monetary authorities—central bank	5231	Securities and commodity contracts brokerage
521110	Monetary authorities—central bank	52311	Investment banking and securities dealing
522	**Credit intermediation and related activities**	523110	Investment banking and securities dealing
5221	Depository credit intermediation	52312	Securities brokerage
52211	Commercial banking	523120	Securities brokerage
522110	Commercial banking	52313	Commodity contracts dealing
52212	Savings institutions	523130	Commodity contracts dealing
522120	Savings institutions	52314	Commodity contracts brokerage
52213	Credit unions	523140	Commodity contracts brokerage
522130	Credit unions	5232	Securities and commodity exchanges
52219	Other depository credit intermediation		
522190	Other depository credit intermediation		

Note: For definitions of abbreviations and acronyms see page 974.

Code	Short title	Code	Short title
52321	Securities and commodity exchanges	524298	All other insurance related activities
523210	Securities and commodity exchanges	**525**	**Funds, trusts, and other financial vehicles**
5239	Other financial investment activities	5251	Insurance and employee benefit funds
52391	Miscellaneous intermediation	52511	Pension funds
523910	Miscellaneous intermediation	525110	Pension funds
52392	Portfolio management	52512	Health and welfare funds
523920	Portfolio management	525120	Health and welfare funds
52393	Investment advice	52519	Other insurance funds
523930	Investment advice	525190	Other insurance funds
52399	All other financial investment activities	5259	Other investment pools and funds
523991	Trust, fiduciary, and custody activities	52591	Open-end investment funds
523999	Miscellaneous financial investment activities	525910	Open-end investment funds
		52592	Trusts, estates, and agency accounts
524	**Insurance carriers and related activities**	525920	Trusts, estates, and agency accounts
5241	Insurance carriers	52599	Other financial vehicles
52411	Direct life and health insurance carriers	525990	Other financial vehicles
524113	Direct life insurance carriers	**53**	**REAL ESTATE AND RENTAL AND LEASING**
524114	Direct health and medical insurance carriers	**531**	**Real estate**
52412	Direct insurers, except life and health	5311	Lessors of real estate
524126	Direct property and casualty insurers	53111	Lessors of residential buildings
524127	Direct title insurance carriers	531110	Lessors of residential buildings
524128	Other direct insurance carriers	53112	Lessors of nonresidential buildings
52413	Reinsurance carriers	531120	Lessors of nonresidential buildings
524130	Reinsurance carriers	53113	Miniwarehouse and self-storage unit operators
5242	Insurance agencies and brokerages	531130	Miniwarehouse and self-storage unit operators
52421	Insurance agencies and brokerages	53119	Lessors of other real estate property
524210	Insurance agencies and brokerages	531190	Lessors of other real estate property
52429	Other insurance related activities	5312	Offices of real estate agents and brokers
524291	Claims adjusting		
524292	Third party administration of insurance funds		

Note: For definitions of abbreviations and acronyms see page 974.

Code	Short title	Code	Short title
53121	Offices of real estate agents and brokers	53241	Heavy machinery rental and leasing
531210	Offices of real estate agents and brokers	532411	Transportation equipment rental and leasing
5313	Activities related to real estate	532412	Other heavy machinery rental and leasing
53131	Real estate property managers	53242	Office equipment rental and leasing
531311	Residential property managers		
531312	Nonresidential property managers	532420	Office equipment rental and leasing
53132	Offices of real estate appraisers	53249	Other machinery rental and leasing
531320	Offices of real estate appraisers		
53139	Other activities related to real estate	532490	Other machinery rental and leasing
531390	Other activities related to real estate	**533**	**Lessors of nonfinancial intangible assets**
532	**Rental and leasing services**	5331	Lessors of nonfinancial intangible assets
5321	Automotive equipment rental and leasing	53311	Lessors of nonfinancial intangible assets
53211	Passenger car rental and leasing	533110	Lessors of nonfinancial intangible assets
532111	Passenger car rental		
532112	Passenger car leasing	**54**	**PROFESSIONAL AND TECHNICAL SERVICES**
53212	Truck, trailer, and RV rental and leasing		
532120	Truck, trailer, and RV rental and leasing	**541**	**Professional and technical services**
5322	Consumer goods rental	5411	Legal services
53221	Consumer electronics and appliances rental	54111	Offices of lawyers
		541110	Offices of lawyers
532210	Consumer electronics and appliances rental	54112	Offices of notaries
		541120	Offices of notaries
53222	Formal wear and costume rental	54119	Other legal services
532220	Formal wear and costume rental	541191	Title abstract and settlement offices
53223	Video tape and disc rental	541199	All other legal services
532230	Video tape and disc rental	5412	Accounting and bookkeeping services
53229	Other consumer goods rental		
532291	Home health equipment rental	54121	Accounting and bookkeeping services
532292	Recreational goods rental		
532299	All other consumer goods rental	541211	Offices of certified public accountants
5323	General rental centers		
53231	General rental centers	541213	Tax preparation services
532310	General rental centers	541214	Payroll services
5324	Machinery and equipment rental and leasing		

Note: For definitions of abbreviations and acronyms see page 974.

Code	Short title	Code	Short title
541219	Other accounting services	5416	Management and technical consulting services
5413	Architectural and engineering services	54161	Management consulting services
54131	Architectural services	541611	Administrative management consulting services
541310	Architectural services	541612	Human resources consulting services
54132	Landscape architectural services		
541320	Landscape architectural services	541613	Marketing consulting services
54133	Engineering services	541614	Process and logistics consulting services
541330	Engineering services		
54134	Drafting services	541618	Other management consulting services
541340	Drafting services		
54135	Building inspection services	54162	Environmental consulting services
541350	Building inspection services		
54136	Geophysical surveying and mapping services	541620	Environmental consulting services
541360	Geophysical surveying and mapping services	54169	Other technical consulting services
54137	Other surveying and mapping services	541690	Other technical consulting services
541370	Other surveying and mapping services	5417	Scientific research and development services
54138	Testing laboratories	54171	Physical, engineering and biological research
541380	Testing laboratories		
5414	Specialized design services	541711	Research and development in biotechnology
54141	Interior design services		
541410	Interior design services	541712	Other physical and biological research
54142	Industrial design services		
541420	Industrial design services	54172	Social science and humanities research
54143	Graphic design services		
541430	Graphic design services	541720	Social science and humanities research
54149	Other specialized design services	5418	Advertising, PR, and related services
541490	Other specialized design services		
5415	Computer systems design and related services	54181	Advertising agencies
		541810	Advertising agencies
54151	Computer systems design and related services	54182	Public relations agencies
		541820	Public relations agencies
541511	Custom computer programming services	54183	Media buying agencies
		541830	Media buying agencies
541512	Computer systems design services	54184	Media representatives
		541840	Media representatives
541513	Computer facilities management services	54185	Display advertising
		541850	Display advertising
541519	Other computer related services	54186	Direct mail advertising

Note: For definitions of abbreviations and acronyms see page 974.

Code	Short title	Code	Short title
541860	Direct mail advertising	56	**ADMINISTRATIVE AND WASTE SERVICES**
54187	Advertising material distribution services		
541870	Advertising material distribution services	561	**Administrative and support services**
54189	Other services related to advertising	5611	Office administrative services
541890	Other services related to advertising	56111	Office administrative services
5419	Other professional and technical services	561110	Office administrative services
		5612	Facilities support services
54191	Marketing research and public opinion polling	56121	Facilities support services
		561210	Facilities support services
541910	Marketing research and public opinion polling	5613	Employment services
		56131	Employment placement and executive search
54192	Photographic services	561311	Employment placement agencies
541921	Photography studios, portrait	561312	Executive search services
541922	Commercial photography	56132	Temporary help services
54193	Translation and interpretation services	561320	Temporary help services
		56133	Professional employer organizations
541930	Translation and interpretation services	561330	Professional employer organizations
54194	Veterinary services	5614	Business support services
541940	Veterinary services	56141	Document preparation services
54199	All other professional and technical services	561410	Document preparation services
		56142	Telephone call centers
541990	All other professional and technical services	561421	Telephone answering services
		561422	Telemarketing and other contact centers
55	**MANAGEMENT OF COMPANIES AND ENTERPRISES**	56143	Business service centers
		561431	Private mail centers
		561439	Other business service centers
551	**Management of companies and enterprises**	56144	Collection agencies
		561440	Collection agencies
		56145	Credit bureaus
5511	Management of companies and enterprises	561450	Credit bureaus
		56149	Other business support services
55111	Management of companies and enterprises	561491	Repossession services
		561492	Court reporting and stenotype services
551111	Offices of bank holding companies	561499	All other business support services
551112	Offices of other holding companies		
551114	Managing offices	5615	Travel arrangement and reservation services

Note: For definitions of abbreviations and acronyms see page 974.

Code	Short title
56151	Travel agencies
561510	Travel agencies
56152	Tour operators
561520	Tour operators
56159	Other travel arrangement services
561591	Convention and visitors bureaus
561599	All other travel arrangement services
5616	Investigation and security services
56161	Security and armored car services
561611	Investigation services
561612	Security guards and patrol services
561613	Armored car services
56162	Security systems services
561621	Security systems services, except locksmiths
561622	Locksmiths
5617	Services to buildings and dwellings
56171	Exterminating and pest control services
561710	Exterminating and pest control services
56172	Janitorial services
561720	Janitorial services
56173	Landscaping services
561730	Landscaping services
56174	Carpet and upholstery cleaning services
561740	Carpet and upholstery cleaning services
56179	Other services to buildings and dwellings
561790	Other services to buildings and dwellings
5619	Other support services
56191	Packaging and labeling services
561910	Packaging and labeling services
56192	Convention and trade show organizers

Code	Short title
561920	Convention and trade show organizers
56199	All other support services
561990	All other support services
562	**Waste management and remediation services**
5621	Waste collection
56211	Waste collection
562111	Solid waste collection
562112	Hazardous waste collection
562119	Other waste collection
5622	Waste treatment and disposal
56221	Waste treatment and disposal
562211	Hazardous waste treatment and disposal
562212	Solid waste landfill
562213	Solid waste combustors and incinerators
562219	Other nonhazardous waste disposal
5629	Remediation and other waste services
56291	Remediation services
562910	Remediation services
56292	Materials recovery facilities
562920	Materials recovery facilities
56299	All other waste management services
562991	Septic tank and related services
562998	Miscellaneous waste management services
61	**EDUCATIONAL SERVICES**
611	**Educational services**
6111	Elementary and secondary schools
61111	Elementary and secondary schools
611110	Elementary and secondary schools
6112	Junior colleges
61121	Junior colleges
611210	Junior colleges
6113	Colleges and universities

Note: For definitions of abbreviations and acronyms see page 974.

Code	Short title	Code	Short title
61131	Colleges and universities	62121	Offices of dentists
611310	Colleges and universities	621210	Offices of dentists
6114	Business, computer and management training	6213	Offices of other health practitioners
61141	Business and secretarial schools	62131	Offices of chiropractors
611410	Business and secretarial schools	621310	Offices of chiropractors
61142	Computer training	62132	Offices of optometrists
611420	Computer training	621320	Offices of optometrists
61143	Management training	62133	Offices of mental health practitioners
611430	Management training		
6115	Technical and trade schools	621330	Offices of mental health practitioners
61151	Technical and trade schools		
611511	Cosmetology and barber schools	62134	Offices of specialty therapists
611512	Flight training	621340	Offices of specialty therapists
611513	Apprenticeship training	62139	Offices of all other health practitioners
611519	Other technical and trade schools		
		621391	Offices of podiatrists
6116	Other schools and instruction	621399	Offices of miscellaneous health practitioners
61161	Fine arts schools		
611610	Fine arts schools	6214	Outpatient care centers
61162	Sports and recreation instruction	62141	Family planning centers
611620	Sports and recreation instruction	621410	Family planning centers
61163	Language schools	62142	Outpatient mental health centers
611630	Language schools	621420	Outpatient mental health centers
61169	All other schools and instruction	62149	Other outpatient care centers
		621491	HMO medical centers
611691	Exam preparation and tutoring	621492	Kidney dialysis centers
611692	Automobile driving schools	621493	Freestanding emergency medical centers
611699	Miscellaneous schools and instruction		
		621498	All other outpatient care centers
6117	Educational support services	6215	Medical and diagnostic laboratories
61171	Educational support services		
611710	Educational support services	62151	Medical and diagnostic laboratories
62	**HEALTH CARE AND SOCIAL ASSISTANCE**		
		621511	Medical laboratories
		621512	Diagnostic imaging centers
621	**Ambulatory health care services**	6216	Home health care services
		62161	Home health care services
6211	Offices of physicians	621610	Home health care services
62111	Offices of physicians	6219	Other ambulatory health care services
621111	Offices of physicians, except mental health		
		62191	Ambulance services
621112	Offices of mental health physicians	621910	Ambulance services
		62199	All other ambulatory health care services
6212	Offices of dentists		

Note: For definitions of abbreviations and acronyms see page 974.

Code	Short title	Code	Short title
621991	Blood and organ banks	624	**Social assistance**
621999	Miscellaneous ambulatory health care services	6241	Individual and family services
		62411	Child and youth services
622	**Hospitals**	624110	Child and youth services
6221	General medical and surgical hospitals	62412	Services for the elderly and disabled
62211	General medical and surgical hospitals	624120	Services for the elderly and disabled
622110	General medical and surgical hospitals	62419	Other individual and family services
6222	Psychiatric and substance abuse hospitals	624190	Other individual and family services
62221	Psychiatric and substance abuse hospitals	6242	Emergency and other relief services
622210	Psychiatric and substance abuse hospitals	62421	Community food services
		624210	Community food services
6223	Other hospitals	62422	Community housing services
62231	Other hospitals	624221	Temporary shelters
622310	Other hospitals	624229	Other community housing services
623	**Nursing and residential care facilities**	62423	Emergency and other relief services
6231	Nursing care facilities	624230	Emergency and other relief services
62311	Nursing care facilities	6243	Vocational rehabilitation services
623110	Nursing care facilities	62431	Vocational rehabilitation services
6232	Residential mental health facilities	624310	Vocational rehabilitation services
62321	Residential mental retardation facilities	6244	Child day care services
623210	Residential mental retardation facilities	62441	Child day care services
62322	Residential mental and substance abuse care	624410	Child day care services
623220	Residential mental and substance abuse care	**71**	**ARTS, ENTERTAINMENT, AND RECREATION**
6233	Community care facilities for the elderly	**711**	**Performing arts and spectator sports**
62331	Community care facilities for the elderly		
623311	Continuing care retirement communities	7111	Performing arts companies
623312	Homes for the elderly	71111	Theater companies and dinner theaters
6239	Other residential care facilities	711110	Theater companies and dinner theaters
62399	Other residential care facilities		
623990	Other residential care facilities	71112	Dance companies

Note: For definitions of abbreviations and acronyms see page 974.

Code	Short title	Code	Short title
711120	Dance companies	**713**	**Amusements, gambling, and recreation**
71113	Musical groups and artists		
711130	Musical groups and artists	7131	Amusement parks and arcades
71119	Other performing arts companies	71311	Amusement and theme parks
711190	Other performing arts companies	713110	Amusement and theme parks
		71312	Amusement arcades
7112	Spectator sports	713120	Amusement arcades
71121	Spectator sports	7132	Gambling industries
711211	Sports teams and clubs	71321	Casinos, except casino hotels
711212	Racetracks	713210	Casinos, except casino hotels
711219	Other spectator sports	71329	Other gambling industries
7113	Promoters of performing arts and sports	713290	Other gambling industries
		7139	Other amusement and recreation industries
71131	Promoters with facilities		
711310	Promoters with facilities	71391	Golf courses and country clubs
71132	Promoters without facilities	713910	Golf courses and country clubs
711320	Promoters without facilities	71392	Skiing facilities
7114	Agents and managers for public figures	713920	Skiing facilities
		71393	Marinas
71141	Agents and managers for public figures	713930	Marinas
		71394	Fitness and recreational sports centers
711410	Agents and managers for public figures		
		713940	Fitness and recreational sports centers
7115	Independent artists, writers, and performers		
		71395	Bowling centers
71151	Independent artists, writers, and performers	713950	Bowling centers
		71399	All other amusement and recreation industries
711510	Independent artists, writers, and performers		
		713990	All other amusement and recreation industries
712	**Museums, historical sites, zoos, and parks**		
		72	**ACCOMMODATION AND FOOD SERVICES**
7121	Museums, historical sites, zoos, and parks		
		721	**Accommodation**
71211	Museums		
712110	Museums	7211	Traveler accommodation
71212	Historical sites	72111	Hotels and motels, except casino hotels
712120	Historical sites		
71213	Zoos and botanical gardens	721110	Hotels and motels, except casino hotels
712130	Zoos and botanical gardens		
71219	Nature parks and other similar institutions	72112	Casino hotels
		721120	Casino hotels
712190	Nature parks and other similar institutions	72119	Other traveler accommodation
		721191	Bed-and-breakfast inns

Note: For definitions of abbreviations and acronyms see page 974.

Code	Short title
721199	All other traveler accommodation
7212	RV parks and recreational camps
72121	RV parks and recreational camps
721211	RV parks and campgrounds
721214	Recreational and vacation camps
7213	Rooming and boarding houses
72131	Rooming and boarding houses
721310	Rooming and boarding houses
722	**Food services and drinking places**
7221	Full-service restaurants
72211	Full-service restaurants
722110	Full-service restaurants
7222	Limited-service eating places
72221	Limited-service eating places
722211	Limited-service restaurants
722212	Cafeterias, grill buffets, and buffets
722213	Snack and nonalcoholic beverage bars
7223	Special food services
72231	Food service contractors
722310	Food service contractors
72232	Caterers
722320	Caterers
72233	Mobile food services
722330	Mobile food services
7224	Drinking places, alcoholic beverages
72241	Drinking places, alcoholic beverages
722410	Drinking places, alcoholic beverages
81	**OTHER SERVICES, EXCEPT PUBLIC ADMINISTRATION**
811	**Repair and maintenance**
8111	Automotive repair and maintenance

Code	Short title
81111	Automotive mechanical and electrical repair
811111	General automotive repair
811112	Automotive exhaust system repair
811113	Automotive transmission repair
811118	Other automotive mechanical and elec. repair
81112	Automotive body, interior, and glass repair
811121	Automotive body and interior repair
811122	Automotive glass replacement shops
81119	Other automotive repair and maintenance
811191	Automotive oil change and lubrication shops
811192	Car washes
811198	All other automotive repair and maintenance
8112	Electronic equipment repair and maintenance
81121	Electronic equipment repair and maintenance
811211	Consumer electronics repair and maintenance
811212	Computer and office machine repair
811213	Communication equipment repair
811219	Other electronic equipment repair
8113	Commercial machinery repair and maintenance
81131	Commercial machinery repair and maintenance
811310	Commercial machinery repair and maintenance
8114	Household goods repair and maintenance
81141	Home and garden equip. and appliance repair
811411	Home and garden equipment repair

Note: For definitions of abbreviations and acronyms see page 974.

Code	Short title
811412	Appliance repair and maintenance
81142	Reupholstery and furniture repair
811420	Reupholstery and furniture repair
81143	Footwear and leather goods repair
811430	Footwear and leather goods repair
81149	Other household goods repair and maintenance
811490	Other household goods repair and maintenance
812	**Personal and laundry services**
8121	Personal care services
81211	Hair, nail, and skin care services
812111	Barber shops
812112	Beauty salons
812113	Nail salons
81219	Other personal care services
812191	Diet and weight reducing centers
812199	Other personal care services
8122	Death care services
81221	Funeral homes and funeral services
812210	Funeral homes and funeral services
81222	Cemeteries and crematories
812220	Cemeteries and crematories
8123	Drycleaning and laundry services
81231	Coin-operated laundries and drycleaners
812310	Coin-operated laundries and drycleaners
81232	Drycleaning and laundry services
812320	Drycleaning and laundry services
81233	Linen and uniform supply
812331	Linen supply

Code	Short title
812332	Industrial launderers
8129	Other personal services
81291	Pet care, except veterinary, services
812910	Pet care, except veterinary, services
81292	Photofinishing
812921	Photofinishing laboratories, except one-hour
812922	One-hour photofinishing
81293	Parking lots and garages
812930	Parking lots and garages
81299	All other personal services
812990	All other personal services
813	**Membership associations and organizations**
8131	Religious organizations
81311	Religious organizations
813110	Religious organizations
8132	Grantmaking and giving services
81321	Grantmaking and giving services
813211	Grantmaking foundations
813212	Voluntary health organizations
813219	Other grantmaking and giving services
8133	Social advocacy organizations
81331	Social advocacy organizations
813311	Human rights organizations
813312	Environment and conservation organizations
813319	Other social advocacy organizations
8134	Civic and social organizations
81341	Civic and social organizations
813410	Civic and social organizations
8139	Professional and similar organizations
81391	Business associations
813910	Business associations
81392	Professional organizations
813920	Professional organizations

Note: For definitions of abbreviations and acronyms see page 974.

Code	Short title
81393	Labor unions and similar labor organizations
813930	Labor unions and similar labor organizations
81394	Political organizations
813940	Political organizations
81399	Other similar organizations
813990	Other similar organizations
814	**Private households**
8141	Private households
81411	Private households
814110	Private households
92	**PUBLIC ADMINISTRATION**
921	**Executive, legislative and general government**
9211	Executive, legislative and general government
92111	Executive offices
921110	Executive offices
92112	Legislative bodies
921120	Legislative bodies
92113	Public finance activities
921130	Public finance activities
92114	Executive and legislative offices, combined
921140	Executive and legislative offices, combined
92115	Tribal governments
921150	Tribal governments
92119	Other general government support
921190	Other general government support
922	**Justice, public order, and safety activities**
9221	Justice, public order, and safety activities
92211	Courts
922110	Courts
92212	Police protection
922120	Police protection
92213	Legal counsel and prosecution

Code	Short title
922130	Legal counsel and prosecution
92214	Correctional institutions
922140	Correctional institutions
92215	Parole offices and probation offices
922150	Parole offices and probation offices
92216	Fire protection
922160	Fire protection
92219	Other justice and safety activities
922190	Other justice and safety activities
923	**Administration of human resource programs**
9231	Administration of human resource programs
92311	Administration of education programs
923110	Administration of education programs
92312	Administration of public health programs
923120	Administration of public health programs
92313	Other human resource programs administration
923130	Other human resource programs administration
92314	Administration of veterans' affairs
923140	Administration of veterans' affairs
924	**Administration of environmental programs**
9241	Administration of environmental programs
92411	Air, water, and waste program administration
924110	Air, water, and waste program administration
92412	Administration of conservation programs

Note: For definitions of abbreviations and acronyms see page 974.

Code	Short title	Code	Short title
924120	Administration of conservation programs	92613	Utility regulation and administration
925	**Community and housing program administration**	926130	Utility regulation and administration
9251	Community and housing program administration	92614	Agricultural market and commodity regulation
92511	Administration of housing programs	926140	Agricultural market and commodity regulation
925110	Administration of housing programs	92615	Licensing and regulating commercial sectors
92512	Urban and rural development administration	926150	Licensing and regulating commercial sectors
925120	Urban and rural development administration	**927**	**Space research and technology**
926	**Administration of economic programs**	9271	Space research and technology
9261	Administration of economic programs	92711	Space research and technology
92611	Administration of general economic programs	927110	Space research and technology
926110	Administration of general economic programs	**928**	**National security and international affairs**
92612	Transportation program administration	9281	National security and international affairs
926120	Transportation program administration	92811	National security
		928110	National security
		92812	International affairs
		928120	International affairs

Note: For definitions of abbreviations and acronyms see page 974.

Abbreviations and Acronyms Used in Short Titles

Abbreviation/Acronym	Word
AC	air conditioning
ag.	agriculture
Al	aluminum
CD	compact disc
const.	construction
Cu	copper
elec.	electrical
equip.	equipment
estab.	establishment
exc.	except
HVAC	heating, ventilation, and air-conditioning
LTL	less than truckload
merch.	merchant
mfg. or mfg	manufacturing
misc.	miscellaneous
PR	public relations
RV	recreational vehicle
TL	truckload
transport.	transportation
TV	television
whls.	wholesalers

Part III

Appendixes

Appendixes A and B map the changes for 2007 NAICS to the 2002 NAICS in 2007 NAICS sequence (Appendix A) and 2002 NAICS sequence (Appendix B). The tables do not provide a comprehensive guide to all economic activities, but rather provide a map for the largest and most important changes from 2002 to 2007.

A full concordance for 2002 NAICS to 2007 NAICS is available on the Census Bureau's Website at www.census.gov/naics.

Appendix A
2007 NAICS U.S. Matched to
2002 NAICS U.S.

2007 NAICS Code	2007 NAICS U.S. Description	2002 NAICS Code	2002 NAICS U.S. Description
CAN 111211	Potato Farming	111211	Potato Farming
		*111219	Other Vegetable (except Potato) and Melon Farming—*sweet potato and yam farming*
CAN 111219	Other Vegetable (except Potato) and Melon Farming	*111219	Other Vegetable (except Potato) and Melon Farming—*except sweet potato and yam farming*
US 111998	All Other Miscellaneous Crop Farming	*111998	All Other Miscellaneous Crop Farming—*except algae, seaweed, and other plant aquaculture*
US 112519	Other Aquaculture	112519	Other Animal Aquaculture
		*111998	All Other Miscellaneous Crop Farming—*algae, seaweed, and other plant aquaculture*
US 314999	All Other Miscellaneous Textile Product Mills	314999	All Other Miscellaneous Textile Product Mills
		*315211	Men's and Boys' Cut and Sew Apparel Contractors—*embroidery contractors*
		*315212	Women's, Girls' and Infants' Cut and Sew Apparel Contractors—*embroidery contractors*
US 315211	Men's and Boys' Cut and Sew Apparel Contractors	*315211	Men's and Boys' Cut and Sew Apparel Contractors—*except embroidery contractors*
US 315212	Women's, Girls' and Infants' Cut and Sew Apparel Contractors	*315212	Women's, Girls' and Infants' Cut and Sew Apparel Contractors—*except embroidery contractors*
US 326199	All Other Plastics Product Manufacturing	*326199	All Other Plastics Product Manufacturing—*except inflatable plastics boats*

US—United States industry only. CAN—United States and Canadian industries are comparable. MEX—United States and Mexican industries are comparable. Blank—Canadian, Mexican, and United States industries are comparable. *—Part of 2002 NAICS United States industry.

2007 NAICS Code	2007 NAICS U.S. Description	2002 NAICS Code	2002 NAICS U.S. Description
US 326291	Rubber Product Manufacturing for Mechanical Use	*326291	Rubber Product Manufacturing for Mechanical Use—*except rubber tubing for mechanical use*
US 326299	All Other Rubber Product Manufacturing	*326299	All Other Rubber Product Manufacturing—*except inflatable rubber boats*
		*326291	Rubber Product Manufacturing for Mechanical Use—*rubber tubing for mechanical use*
US 333298	All Other Industrial Machinery Manufacturing	333298	All Other Industrial Machinery Manufacturing
		*339111	Laboratory Apparatus and Furniture Manufacturing—*laboratory distilling equipment*
US 333415	Air-Conditioning and Warm Air Heating Equipment and Commercial and Industrial Refrigeration Equipment Manufacturing	333415	Air-Conditioning and Warm Air Heating Equipment and Commercial and Industrial Refrigeration Equipment Manufacturing
		*339111	Laboratory Apparatus and Furniture Manufacturing—*laboratory freezers*
US 333994	Industrial Process Furnace and Oven Manufacturing	333994	Industrial Process Furnace and Oven Manufacturing
		*339111	Laboratory Apparatus and Furniture Manufacturing—*laboratory furnaces and ovens*
US 333997	Scale and Balance Manufacturing	333997	Scale and Balance (except Laboratory) Manufacturing
		*339111	Laboratory Apparatus and Furniture Manufacturing—*laboratory scales and balances*
US 333999	All Other Miscellaneous General Purpose Machinery Manufacturing	333999	All Other Miscellaneous General Purpose Machinery Manufacturing
		*339111	Laboratory Apparatus and Furniture Manufacturing—*laboratory centrifuges*
334220	Radio and Television Broadcasting and Wireless Communications Equipment Manufacturing	*334220	Radio and Television Broadcasting and Wireless Communications Equipment Manufacturing—*except communications signal testing and evaluation equipment*

US—United States industry only. CAN—United States and Canadian industries are comparable. MEX—United States and Mexican industries are comparable. Blank—Canadian, Mexican, and United States industries are comparable. *—Part of 2002 NAICS United States industry.

2007 NAICS Code	2007 NAICS U.S. Description	2002 NAICS Code	2002 NAICS U.S. Description
US 334515	Instrument Manufacturing for Measuring and Testing Electricity and Electrical Signals	334515	Instrument Manufacturing for Measuring and Testing Electricity and Electrical Signals
		*334220	Radio and Television Broadcasting and Wireless Communications Equipment Manufacturing— *communications signal testing and evaluation equipment*
CAN 336612	Boat Building	336612	Boat Building
		*326199	All Other Plastics Product Manufacturing—*inflatable plastics boats*
		*326299	All Other Rubber Product Manufacturing—*inflatable rubber boats*
CAN 337127	Institutional Furniture Manufacturing	337127	Institutional Furniture Manufacturing
		*339111	Laboratory Apparatus and Furniture Manufacturing— *laboratory furniture (e.g., stools, tables, benches)*
US 339113	Surgical Appliance and Supplies Manufacturing	339113	Surgical Appliance and Supplies Manufacturing
		*339111	Laboratory Apparatus and Furniture Manufacturing— *except laboratory furniture, scales, balances, furnaces, ovens, centrifuges, distilling equipment, and freezers*
517	Telecommunications		
5171	Wired Telecommunications Carriers		
51711	Wired Telecommunications Carriers		
US 517110	Wired Telecommunications Carriers	517110	Wired Telecommunications Carriers
		517510	Cable and Other Program Distribution
		*518111	Internet Service Providers— *broadband Internet service providers (e.g., cable, DSL)*

US—United States industry only. CAN—United States and Canadian industries are comparable. MEX—United States and Mexican industries are comparable. Blank—Canadian, Mexican, and United States industries are comparable. *—Part of 2002 NAICS United States industry.

2007 NAICS Code	2007 NAICS U.S. Description	2002 NAICS Code	2002 NAICS U.S. Description
5172	Wireless Telecommunications Carriers (except Satellite)		
51721	Wireless Telecommunications Carriers (except Satellite)		
517210	Wireless Telecommunications Carriers (except Satellite)	517211	Paging
		517212	Cellular and Other Wireless Telecommunications
5174	Satellite Telecommunications		
51741	Satellite Telecommunications		
517410	Satellite Telecommunications	517410	Satellite Telecommunications
5179	Other Telecommunications		
51791	Other Telecommunications		
US 517911	Telecommunications Resellers	517310	Telecommunications Resellers
US 517919	All Other Telecommunications	517910	Other Telecommunications
		*518111	Internet Service Providers— *ISPs providing services via client-supplied telecommunications connections*
518	Data Processing, Hosting, and Related Services		
5182	Data Processing, Hosting, and Related Services		
51821	Data Processing, Hosting, and Related Services		
518210	Data Processing, Hosting, and Related Services	518210	Data Processing, Hosting, and Related Services
519	Other Information Services		
5191	Other Information Services		
51911	News Syndicates		
519110	News Syndicates	519110	News Syndicates
51912	Libraries and Archives		
US 519120	Libraries and Archives	519120	Libraries and Archives
51913	Internet Publishing and Broadcasting and Web Search Portals		
519130	Internet Publishing and Broadcasting and Web Search Portals	516110	Internet Publishing and Broadcasting
		518112	Web Search Portals

US—United States industry only. CAN—United States and Canadian industries are comparable. MEX—United States and Mexican industries are comparable. Blank—Canadian, Mexican, and United States industries are comparable. *—Part of 2002 NAICS United States industry.

2007 NAICS Code	2007 NAICS U.S. Description	2002 NAICS Code	2002 NAICS U.S. Description
51919	All Other Information Services		
519190	All Other Information Services	519190	All Other Information Services
US 525990	Other Financial Vehicles	525990	Other Financial Vehicles
		*525930	Real Estate Investment Trusts—*hybrid or mortgage REITs primarily in underwriting or investing in mortgages*
US 531110	Lessors of Residential Buildings and Dwellings	531110	Lessors of Residential Buildings and Dwellings
		*525930	Real Estate Investment Trusts—*hybrid or equity REITs primarily leasing residential Buildings and Dwellings*
CAN 531120	Lessors of Nonresidential Buildings (except Miniwarehouses)	531120	Lessors of Nonresidential Buildings (except Miniwarehouses)
		*525930	Real Estate Investment Trusts—*hybrid or equity REITs primarily leasing nonresidential buildings*
CAN 531130	Lessors of Miniwarehouses and Self-Storage Units	531130	Lessors of Miniwarehouses and Self-Storage Units
		*525930	Real Estate Investment Trusts—*hybrid or equity REITs primarily leasing miniwarehouses and self-storage units*
CAN 531190	Lessors of Other Real Estate Property	531190	Lessors of Other Real Estate Property
		*525930	Real Estate Investment Trusts—*hybrid or equity REITs primarily leasing other real estate property*
CAN 541612	Human Resources Consulting Services	*541612	Human Resources and Executive Search Consulting Services—*except executive search consulting services*
US 541711	Research and Development in Biotechnology	*541710	Research and Development in the Physical, Engineering, and Life Sciences—*biotechnology research and development*

US—United States industry only. CAN—United States and Canadian industries are comparable. MEX—United States and Mexican industries are comparable. Blank—Canadian, Mexican, and United States industries are comparable. *—Part of 2002 NAICS United States industry.

2007 NAICS Code	2007 NAICS U.S. Description	2002 NAICS Code	2002 NAICS U.S. Description
US 541712	Research and Development in the Physical, Engineering, and Life Sciences (except Biotechnology)	*541710	Research and Development in the Physical, Engineering, and Life Sciences—*except biotechnology research and development*
US 561311	Employment Placement Agencies	561310	Employment Placement Agencies
US 561312	Executive Search Services	*541612	Human Resources and Executive Search Consulting Services—*executive search consulting services*

Appendix B
2002 NAICS U.S. Matched to
2007 NAICS U.S.

2002 NAICS Code	2002 NAICS U.S. Description	2007 NAICS Code	2007 NAICS U.S. Description
111219	Other Vegetable (except Potato) and Melon Farming		
	sweet potato and yam farming	111211	Potato Farming (pt)
	except sweet potato and yam farming	111219	Other Vegetable (except Potato) and Melon Farming
111998	All Other Miscellaneous Crop Farming		
	except algae, seaweed, and other plant aquaculture	111998	All Other Miscellaneous Crop Farming
	algae, seaweed, and other plant aquaculture	112519	Other Aquaculture (pt)
315211	Men's and Boys' Cut and Sew Apparel Contractors		
	embroidery contractors	314999	All Other Miscellaneous Textile Product Mills (pt)
	except embroidery contractors	315211	Men's and Boys' Cut and Sew Apparel Contractors
315212	Women's, Girls', and Infants' Cut and Sew Apparel Contractors		
	embroidery contractors	314999	All Other Miscellaneous Textile Product Mills (pt)
	except embroidery contractors	315212	Women's, Girls', and Infants' Cut and Sew Apparel Contractors
326199	All Other Plastics Product Manufacturing		
	except inflatable plastics boats	326199	All Other Plastics Product Manufacturing
	inflatable plastics boats	336612	Boat Building (pt)
326291	Rubber Product Manufacturing for Mechanical Use		
	except rubber tubing for mechanical use	326291	Rubber Product Manufacturing for Mechanical Use
	rubber tubing for mechanical use	326299	All Other Rubber Product Manufacturing (pt)

(pt)—Part of 2007 NAICS United States industry.

2002 NAICS Code	2002 NAICS U.S. Description	2007 NAICS Code	2007 NAICS U.S. Description
326299	All Other Rubber Product Manufacturing		
	except inflatable rubber boats	326299	All Other Rubber Product Manufacturing (pt)
	inflatable rubber boats	336612	Boat Building (pt)
334220	Radio and Television Broadcasting and Wireless Communications Equipment Manufacturing		
	except communications signal testing and evaluation equipment	334220	Radio and Television Broadcasting and Wireless Communications Equipment Manufacturing
	communications signal testing and evaluation equipment	334515	Instrument Manufacturing for Measuring and Testing Electricity and Electrical Signals (pt)
339111	Laboratory Apparatus and Furniture Manufacturing		
	laboratory distilling equipment	333298	All Other Industrial Machinery Manufacturing (pt)
	laboratory freezers	333415	Air-Conditioning and Warm Air Heating Equipment and Commercial and Industrial Refrigeration Equipment Manufacturing (pt)
	laboratory furnaces and ovens	333994	Industrial Process Furnace and Oven Manufacturing (pt)
	laboratory scales and balances	333997	Scale and Balance Manufacturing (pt)
	laboratory centrifuges	333999	All Other Miscellaneous General Purpose Machinery Manufacturing (pt)
	laboratory furniture (e.g., stools, tables, benches)	337127	Institutional Furniture Manufacturing (pt)
	except laboratory distilling equipment, freezers, furnaces, ovens, scales, balances, centrifuges, and furniture	339113	Surgical Appliance and Supplies Manufacturing (pt)
516110	Internet Publishing and Broadcasting	519130	Internet Publishing and Broadcasting and Web Search Portals (pt)
517110	Wired Telecommunications Carriers	517110	Wired Telecommunications Carriers (pt)

(pt)—Part of 2007 NAICS United States industry.

2002 NAICS Code	2002 NAICS U.S. Description	2007 NAICS Code	2007 NAICS U.S. Description
517211	Paging	517210	Wireless Telecommunications Carriers (except Satellite) (pt)
517212	Cellular and Other Wireless Telecommunications	517210	Wireless Telecommunications Carriers (except Satellite) (pt)
517310	Telecommunications Resellers	517911	Telecommunications Resellers
517510	Cable and Other Program Distribution	517110	Wired Telecommunications Carriers (pt)
517910	Other Telecommunications	517919	All Other Telecommunications (pt)
518111	Internet Service Providers		
	broadband Internet service providers (e.g., cable, DSL)	517110	Wired Telecommunications Carriers (pt)
	Internet service providers providing services via client-supplied telecommunications connection	517919	All Other Telecommunications (pt)
518112	Web Search Portals	519130	Internet Publishing and Broadcasting and Web Search Portals (pt)
525930	Real Estate Investment Trusts		
	hybrid or equity REITs primarily leasing residential buildings and dwellings	531110	Lessors of Residential Buildings and Dwellings (pt)
	hybrid or equity REITS primarily leasing nonresidential buildings	531120	Lessors of Nonresidential Buildings (except Miniwarehouses) (pt)
	hybrid or equity REITs primarily leasing miniwarehouses or self-storage units	531130	Lessors of Miniwarehouses and Self-Storage Units (pt)
	hybrid or equity REITS primarily leasing other real estate property	531190	Lessors of Other Real Estate Property (pt)
	hybrid or mortgage REITs primarily underwriting or investing in mortgages	525990	Other Financial Vehicles (pt)
541612	Human Resources and Executive Search Consulting Services		
	except executive search consulting services	541612	Human Resources Consulting Services
	executive search consulting services	561312	Executive Search Services

(pt)—Part of 2007 NAICS United States industry.

2002 NAICS Code	2002 NAICS U.S. Description	2007 NAICS Code	2007 NAICS U.S. Description
541710	Research and Development in the Physical, Engineering, and Life Sciences		
	biotechnology research and development	541711	Research and Development in Biotechnology
	except biotechnology research and development	541712	Research and Development in the Physical, Engineering, and Life Sciences (except Biotechnology)

(pt)—Part of 2007 NAICS United States industry.

Part IV

Alphabetic Index

Alphabetic Index

325191	Acetone, natural, manufacturing
325199	Acetone, synthetic, manufacturing
332420	Acetylene cylinders, heavy gauge metal, manufacturing
325120	Acetylene manufacturing
325411	Acetylsalicylic acid manufacturing
325132	Acid dyes, synthetic organic, manufacturing
325199	Acid esters, not specified elsewhere by process, manufacturing
324110	Acid oils made in petroleum refineries
236210	Acid plant construction
562211	Acid waste disposal facilities
562211	Acid waste treatment facilities
334513	Acidity (i.e., pH) instruments, industrial process type, manufacturing
334516	Acidity (i.e., pH) measuring equipment, laboratory analysis-type, manufacturing
213112	Acidizing oil and gas field wells on a contract basis
311511	Acidophilus milk manufacturing
424690	Acids merchant wholesalers
325199	Acids, organic, not specified elsewhere by process, manufacturing
111219	Acorn squash farming, field, bedding plant and seed production
238310	Acoustical ceiling tile and panel installation
541330	Acoustical engineering consulting services
238310	Acoustical foam (i.e., sound barrier) installation
332323	Acoustical suspension systems, metal, manufacturing
541330	Acoustical system engineering design services
541380	Acoustics testing laboratories or services
325199	Acrolein manufacturing
325212	Acrylate rubber manufacturing
325212	Acrylate-butadiene rubber manufacturing
313112	Acrylic and modacrylic filament yarn throwing, twisting, texturizing, or winding purchased yarn
325222	Acrylic fibers and filaments manufacturing
326113	Acrylic film and unlaminated sheet (except packaging) manufacturing
325211	Acrylic resins manufacturing
325212	Acrylic rubber manufacturing
313111	Acrylic spun yarns made from purchased fiber
325222	Acrylonitrile fibers and filaments manufacturing
325199	Acrylonitrile manufacturing
325211	Acrylonitrile-butadiene-styrene (ABS) resins manufacturing
334519	Actinometers, meteorological, manufacturing
339931	Action figures manufacturing
325998	Activated carbon or charcoal manufacturing
624120	Activity centers for disabled persons, the elderly, and persons diagnosed with mental retardation
711510	Actors, independent
711510	Actresses, independent
541612	Actuarial consulting services (except insurance actuarial services)
524298	Actuarial services, insurance
333995	Actuators, fluid power, manufacturing
621399	Acupuncturists' (except MDs or DOs) offices (e.g., centers, clinics)
621111	Acupuncturists' (MDs or DOs) offices (e.g., centers, clinics)
325110	Acyclic hydrocarbons (e.g., butene, ethylene, propene) (except acetylene) made from refined petroleum or liquid hydrocarbons
332993	Adapters, bombcluster, manufacturing
333313	Adding machines manufacturing

236118 Addition, alteration and renovation (i.e., construction), multifamily building

236118 Addition, alteration and renovation (i.e., construction), residential building

236220 Addition, alteration and renovation general contractors, commercial and institutional building

236220 Addition, alteration and renovation general contractors, commercial warehouse

236220 Addition, alteration and renovation general contractors, hotel and motel

236220 Addition, alteration and renovation general contractors, industrial warehouse

236118 Addition, alteration and renovation of single-family dwellings

236220 Addition, alteration and renovation operative builders, commercial and institutional building

236220 Addition, alteration and renovation operative builders, commercial warehouse

236220 Addition, alteration and renovation operative builders, hotel and motel

236210 Addition, alteration and renovation operative builders, industrial building (except warehouses)

236220 Addition, alteration and renovation operative builders, industrial warehouse

236220 Addition, alteration and renovation, commercial and institutional building

236220 Addition, alteration and renovation, commercial warehouse

236210 Addition, alteration and renovation, general contractors, industrial building (except warehouses)

236220 Addition, alteration and renovation, hotel and motel

236210 Addition, alteration and renovation, industrial building (except warehouses)

236220 Addition, alteration and renovation, industrial warehouse

236118 Addition, alteration and renovation, multifamily building, general contractors

236118 Addition, alteration and renovation, multifamily building, operative builders

236118 Addition, alteration and renovation, residential building, general contractors

236118 Addition, alteration and renovation, residential building, operative builders

236118 Addition, alteration and renovation, single-family housing, general contractors

236118 Addition, alteration and renovation, single-family housing, operative builders

325998 Additive preparations for gasoline (e.g., antiknock preparations, detergents, gum inhibitors) manufacturing

561499 Address bar coding services

511140 Address list publishers (except exlusive Internet publishing)

511140 Address list publishers and printing combined

323112 Address lists flexographic printing without publishing

323111 Address lists gravure printing without publishing

323110 Address lists lithographic (offset) printing without publishing

323119 Address lists printing (except flexographic, gravure, lithographic, quick, screen) without publishing

323113 Address lists screen printing without publishing

423420 Addressing machines merchant wholesalers

322222   Adhesive tape (except medical) made from purchased materials

339113   Adhesive tape, medical, manufacturing

325520   Adhesives (except asphalt, dental, gypsum base) manufacturing

424690   Adhesives and sealants merchant wholesalers

325199   Adipic acid esters or amines manufacturing

325199   Adipic acid manufacturing

325199   Adiponitrile manufacturing

236220   Administration building construction

922110   Administrative courts

541611   Administrative management consulting services

561110   Administrative management services

523991   Administrators of private estates

327123   Adobe bricks manufacturing

624110   Adoption agencies

624110   Adoption services, child

325411   Adrenal derivatives, uncompounded, manufacturing

325412   Adrenal medicinal preparations manufacturing

611691   Adult literacy instruction

541810   Advertising agencies

541810   Advertising agency consulting services

541870   Advertising material (e.g., coupons, flyers, samples) direct distribution services

541860   Advertising material preparation services for mailing or other direct distribution

323110   Advertising materials (e.g., coupons, flyers) lithographic (offset) printing without publishing

541840   Advertising media representatives (i.e., independent of media owners)

511120   Advertising periodical publishers (except exclusive Internet publishing)

511120   Advertising periodical publishers and printing combined

519130   Advertising periodical publishers, exclusively on Internet

541850   Advertising services, indoor or outdoor display

541890   Advertising specialty (e.g., keychain, magnet, pen) distribution services

541850   Advertising, aerial

921110   Advisory commissions, executive government

921120   Advisory commissions, legislative

487990   Aerial cable car, scenic and sightseeing, operation

333315   Aerial cameras manufacturing

115112   Aerial dusting or spraying (i.e., using specialized or dedicated aircraft)

541360   Aerial geophysical surveying services

238910   Aerial or picker truck, construction, rental with operator

541370   Aerial surveying (except geophysical) services

487990   Aerial tramway, scenic and sightseeing, operation

333923   Aerial work platforms manufacturing

713940   Aerobic dance and exercise centers

423860   Aeronautical equipment and supplies merchant wholesalers

334511   Aeronautical systems and instruments manufacturing

325998   Aerosol can filling on a job order or contract basis

332431   Aerosol cans, light gauge metal, manufacturing

325998   Aerosol packaging services

332919   Aerosol valves manufacturing

332410   Aftercoolers (i.e., heat exchangers) manufacturing

325620   After-shave preparations manufacturing

323119	Agricultural magazines and periodicals printing (except flexographic, gravure, lithographic, quick, screen) without publishing
323113	Agricultural magazines and periodicals screen printing without publishing
926140	Agricultural marketing services government
813910	Agricultural organizations (except youth farming organizations, farm granges)
926140	Agricultural pest and weed regulation, government
484220	Agricultural products trucking, local
531190	Agricultural property rental leasing
926140	Agriculture fair boards administration
115115	Agriculture production or harvesting crews
541712	Agriculture research and development laboratories or services (except biotechnology research and development)
541690	Agrology consulting services
541690	Agronomy consulting services
624110	Aid to families with dependent children (AFDC)
621910	Air ambulance services
336399	Air bag assemblies manufacturing
336612	Air boat building
336340	Air brake systems and parts, automotive, truck, and bus, manufacturing
481212	Air cargo carriers (except air couriers), nonscheduled
481112	Air cargo carriers (except air couriers), scheduled
332439	Air cargo containers, light gauge metal, manufacturing
335313	Air circuit breakers manufacturing
481111	Air commuter carriers, scheduled
333912	Air compressors manufacturing

492110	Air courier services (except establishments operating under a universal service obligation)
332322	Air cowls, sheet metal (except stampings), manufacturing
336399	Air filters, automotive, truck, and bus, manufacturing
334512	Air flow controllers (except valves), air-conditioning and refrigeration, manufacturing
928110	Air Force
313230	Air laid nonwoven fabrics manufacturing
481211	Air passenger carriers, nonscheduled
481111	Air passenger carriers, scheduled
423730	Air pollution control equipment and supplies merchant wholesalers
335211	Air purification equipment, portable, manufacturing
333411	Air purification equipment, stationary, manufacturing
332420	Air receiver tanks, heavy gauge metal, manufacturing
333411	Air scrubbing systems manufacturing
711310	Air show managers with facilities
711320	Air show managers without facilities
711310	Air show organizers with facilities
711320	Air show organizers without facilities
711310	Air show promoters with facilities
711320	Air show promoters without facilities
238220	Air system balancing and testing
481211	Air taxi services
334511	Air traffic control radar systems and equipment manufacturing
611519	Air traffic control schools
488111	Air traffic control services (except military)
928110	Air traffic control, military
238220	Air vent installation

488190	Aircraft maintenance and repair services (except factory conversion, factory overhaul, factory rebuilding)
336411	Aircraft manufacturing
423860	Aircraft merchant wholesalers
336411	Aircraft overhauling
488119	Aircraft parking service
336413	Aircraft propellers and parts manufacturing
336411	Aircraft rebuilding (i.e., restoration to original design specifications)
532411	Aircraft rental and leasing
336360	Aircraft seats manufacturing
488190	Aircraft testing services
314999	Aircraft tie down strap assemblies (except leather) manufacturing
326211	Aircraft tire manufacturing
336412	Aircraft turbines manufacturing
811420	Aircraft upholstery repair
333412	Aircurtains manufacturing
336413	Airframe assemblies (except for guided missiles) manufacturing
336419	Airframe assemblies for guided missiles manufacturing
334511	Airframe equipment instruments manufacturing
325612	Airfreshners manufacturing
722310	Airline food services contractors
561599	Airline reservation services
561599	Airline ticket offices
332313	Airlocks, fabricated metal plate work, manufacturing
481112	Airmail carriers, scheduled
532411	Airplane rental or leasing
488119	Airport baggage handling services
236220	Airport building construction
488119	Airport cargo handling services
531190	Airport leasing, not operating airport, rental or leasing
335311	Airport lighting transformers manufacturing
485999	Airport limousine services (i.e., shuttle)
488119	Airport operators (e.g., civil, international, national)
237310	Airport runway construction
238210	Airport runway lighting contractors
237310	Airport runway line painting (e.g., striping)
488119	Airport runway maintenance services
485999	Airport shuttle services
236220	Airport terminal construction
488119	Airports, civil, operation and maintenance
334511	Airspeed instruments (aeronautical) manufacturing
212399	Alabaster mining and/or beneficiating
423610	Alarm apparatus, electric, merchant wholesalers
334518	Alarm clocks manufacturing
238210	Alarm system (e.g., fire, burglar), electric, installation only
334290	Alarm system central monitoring equipment manufacturing
561621	Alarm system monitoring services
334290	Alarm systems and equipment manufacturing
561621	Alarm systems sales combined with installation, repair, or monitoring services
323118	Albums (e.g., photo, scrap) and refills manufacturing
424120	Albums, photo, merchant wholesalers
424690	Alcohol, industrial, merchant wholesalers
922120	Alcohol, tobacco, and firearms control
926150	Alcoholic beverage control boards
492210	Alcoholic beverage delivery service
722410	Alcoholic beverage drinking places
312140	Alcoholic beverages (except brandy) distilling
424810	Alcoholic beverages (except distilled spirits, wine) merchant wholesalers

312130 Alcoholic beverages, brandy, distilling

424820 Alcoholic beverages, wine and distilled spirits merchant wholesalers

624190 Alcoholism and drug addiction self-help organizations

624190 Alcoholism counseling (except medical treatment), nonresidential

623220 Alcoholism rehabilitation facilities (except licensed hospitals), residential

622210 Alcoholism rehabilitation hospitals

624190 Alcoholism self-help organizations

621420 Alcoholism treatment centers and clinics (except hospitals), outpatient

325199 Aldehydes manufacturing

312120 Ale brewing

424810 Ale merchant wholesalers

111940 Alfalfa hay farming

311119 Alfalfa meal, dehydrated, manufacturing

424910 Alfalfa merchant wholesalers

311119 Alfalfa prepared as feed for animals

111998 Alfalfa seed farming

111419 Alfalfa sprout farming, grown under cover

311119 Alfalfa, cubed, manufacturing

112519 Algae farming

325199 Alginates (e.g., calcium, potassium, sodium) manufacturing

325199 Alginic acid manufacturing

334519 Alidades, surveying, manufacturing

333319 Alignment equipment, motor vehicle, manufacturing

325110 Aliphatic (e.g., hydrocarbons) (except acetylene) made from refined petroleum or liquid hydrocarbons

324110 Aliphatic chemicals (i.e., acyclic) made in petroleum refineries

325181 Alkalies manufacturing

424690 Alkalies merchant wholesalers

335912 Alkaline cell primary batteries manufacturing

335911 Alkaline cell storage batteries (i.e., nickel-cadmium, nickel-iron, silver oxide-zinc) manufacturing

335912 Alkaline manganese primary batteries manufacturing

325211 Alkyd resins manufacturing

324110 Alkylates made in petroleum refineries

325414 Allergenic extracts (except diagnostic substances) manufacturing

325414 Allergens manufacturing

621111 Allergists' offices (e.g., centers, clinics)

112519 Alligator production, farm raising

331513 Alloy steel castings (except investment), unfinished, manufacturing

331314 Alloying purchased aluminum metals

331423 Alloying purchased copper

331423 Alloying purchased copper metals

331492 Alloying purchased nonferrous metals (except aluminum, copper)

441221 All-terrain vehicle (ATV) dealers

423110 All-terrain vehicles (ATVs) merchant wholesalers

336999 All-terrain vehicles (ATVs), wheeled or tracked, manufacturing

325211 Allyl resins manufacturing

323121 Almanac binding without printing

511130 Almanac publishers (except exclusive Internet publishing)

511130 Almanac publishers and printing combined

519130 Almanac publishers, exclusively on Internet

323117 Almanacs printing and binding without publishing

323117   Almanacs printing without publishing
111335   Almond farming
115114   Almond hulling and shelling
311999   Almond pastes manufacturing
111998   Aloe farming
112990   Alpaca production
721110   Alpine skiing facilities with accommodations (i.e., ski resort)
713920   Alpine skiing facilities without accommodations
237130   Alternative energy (e.g., geothermal, ocean wave, solar, wind) structure construction
334515   Alternator and generator testers manufacturing
336322   Alternators and generators for internal combustion engines manufacturing
334511   Altimeters, aeronautical, manufacturing
212391   Alum, natural, mining and/or beneficiating
327125   Alumina fused refractories manufacturing
327113   Alumina porcelain insulators manufacturing
331311   Alumina refining
327125   Aluminous refractory cement manufacturing
331312   Aluminum alloys made from bauxite or alumina producing primary aluminum and manufacturing
331314   Aluminum alloys made from scrap or dross
331316   Aluminum bar made by extruding purchased aluminum
331316   Aluminum bar made in integrated secondary smelting and extruding mills
331314   Aluminum billet made from purchased aluminum
331314   Aluminum billet made in integrated secondary smelting and rolling mills
332431   Aluminum cans, light gauge metal, manufacturing

331524   Aluminum castings (except die-castings), unfinished, manufacturing
325188   Aluminum chloride manufacturing
332812   Aluminum coating of metal products for the trade
325188   Aluminum compounds, not specified elsewhere by process, manufacturing
331521   Aluminum die-casting foundries
331521   Aluminum die-castings, unfinished, manufacturing
238350   Aluminum door and window, residential-type, installation
331314   Aluminum extrusion ingot (i.e., billet), secondary
331314   Aluminum flakes made from purchased aluminum
331315   Aluminum foil made by flat rolling purchased aluminum
331315   Aluminum foil made in integrated secondary smelting and flat rolling mills
332112   Aluminum forgings made from purchased metals, unfinished
331524   Aluminum foundries (except die-casting)
332999   Aluminum freezer foil not made in rolling mills
325188   Aluminum hydroxide (i.e., alumina trihydrate) manufacturing
331312   Aluminum ingot and other primary aluminum production shapes made from bauxite or alumina
331314   Aluminum ingot made from purchased aluminum
331314   Aluminum ingot, secondary smelting of aluminum and manufacturing
331314   Aluminum ingot, secondary, manufacturing
332999   Aluminum ladders manufacturing
327910   Aluminum oxide (fused) abrasives manufacturing
331311   Aluminum oxide refining

331316 Aluminum pipe made by extruding purchased aluminum

331316 Aluminum pipe made in integrated secondary smelting and extruding mills

236210 Aluminum plant construction

331315 Aluminum plate made by continuous casting purchased aluminum

331315 Aluminum plate made by flat rolling purchased aluminum

331315 Aluminum plate made in integrated secondary smelting and continuous casting mills

331315 Aluminum plate made in integrated secondary smelting and flat rolling mills

331312 Aluminum producing from alumina

331314 Aluminum recovering from scrap and making ingot and billet (except by rolling)

331316 Aluminum rod made by extruding purchased aluminum

331316 Aluminum rod made in integrated secondary smelting and extruding mills

331312 Aluminum shapes (e.g., bar, ingot, rod, sheet) made by producing primary aluminum and manufacturing

331315 Aluminum sheet made by flat rolling purchased aluminum

331315 Aluminum sheet made in integrated secondary smelting and flat rolling mills

238170 Aluminum siding installation

331314 Aluminum smelting, secondary, and making ingot and billet (except by rolling)

325188 Aluminum sulfate manufacturing

331316 Aluminum tube blooms made by extruding purchased aluminum

331316 Aluminum tube blooms made in integrated secondary smelting and extruding mills

331316 Aluminum tube made by drawing or extruding purchased aluminum

331316 Aluminum tube made in integrated secondary smelting and drawing plants

331316 Aluminum tube made in integrated secondary smelting and extruding mills

331315 Aluminum welded tube made by flat rolling purchased aluminum

331315 Aluminum welded tube made in integrated secondary smelting and flat rolling mills

813410 Alumni associations

813410 Alumni clubs

325188 Alums (e.g., aluminum ammonium sulfate, aluminum potassium sulfate) manufacturing

212393 Alunite mining and/or beneficiating

515112 AM radio stations

333131 Amalgamators (i.e., metallurgical and mining machinery) manufacturing

339114 Amalgams, dental, manufacturing

111998 Amaranth farming

713990 Amateur sports teams, recreational

325920 Amatols manufacturing

212393 Amblygonite mining and/or beneficiating

922160 Ambulance and fire service combined

336211 Ambulance bodies manufacturing

423110 Ambulance merchant wholesalers

621910 Ambulance services, air or ground

336211 Ambulances assembling on purchased chassis

621493 Ambulatory surgical centers and clinics, freestanding

921150 American Indian or Alaska Native tribal councils

921150 American Indian or Alaska Native tribal courts

921150 American Indian or Alaska Native, tribal chief's or chairman's office

212399 Amethyst mining and/or beneficiating

334516 Amino acid analyzers, laboratory-type, manufacturing

325211 Amino resins manufacturing

325211 Amino-aldehyde resins manufacturing

325192 Aminoanthraquinone manufacturing

325192 Aminoazobenzene manufacturing

325192 Aminoazotoluene manufacturing

325192 Aminophenol manufacturing

424690 Ammonia (except fertilizer material) merchant wholesalers

325311 Ammonia, anhydrous and aqueous, manufacturing

424910 Ammonia, fertilizer material, merchant wholesalers

325612 Ammonia, household-type, manufacturing

325188 Ammonium chloride manufacturing

325188 Ammonium compounds, not specified elsewhere by process, manufacturing

325188 Ammonium hydroxide manufacturing

325188 Ammonium molybdate manufacturing

325311 Ammonium nitrate manufacturing

325188 Ammonium perchlorate manufacturing

325312 Ammonium phosphates manufacturing

236210 Ammonium plant construction

325311 Ammonium sulfate manufacturing

325188 Ammonium thiosulfate manufacturing

423990 Ammunition (except sporting) merchant wholesalers

332993 Ammunition (i.e., more than 30 mm., more than 1.18 inch) manufacturing

321920 Ammunition boxes, wood, manufacturing

332439 Ammunition boxes, light gauge metal, manufacturing

332994 Ammunition carts (i.e., 30 mm or less, 1.18 inch or less) manufacturing

332995 Ammunition carts (i.e., more than 30 mm., more than 1.18 inch) manufacturing

332993 Ammunition loading and assembling plants

332992 Ammunition, small arms (i.e., 30 mm. or less, 1.18 inch or less), manufacturing

423910 Ammunition, sporting, merchant wholesalers

334515 Ampere-hour meters manufacturing

325411 Amphetamines, uncompounded, manufacturing

334310 Amplifiers (e.g., auto, home, musical instrument, public address) manufacturing

334220 Amplifiers, (e.g., RF power and IF), broadcast and studio equipment, manufacturing

335999 Amplifiers, magnetic, pulse, and maser, manufacturing

713120 Amusement arcades

713990 Amusement device (except gambling) concession operators (i.e., supplying and servicing in others' facilities)

713120 Amusement device (except gambling) parlors, coin-operated

713120 Amusement devices (except gambling) operated in own facilities

236220 Amusement facility construction

339999 Amusement machines, coin-operated, manufacturing

423850 Amusement park equipment merchant wholesalers

713110 Amusement parks (e.g., theme, water)

713990	Amusement ride concession operators (i.e., supplying and servicing in others' facilities)
325199	Amyl acetate manufacturing
325412	Analgesic preparations manufacturing
334111	Analog computers manufacturing
423490	Analytical instruments (e.g., chromatographic, photometers, spectrographs) merchant wholesalers
334515	Analyzers for testing electrical characteristics manufacturing
334513	Analyzers, industrial process control type, manufacturing
237990	Anchored earth retention contractors
114111	Anchovy fishing
212325	Andalusite mining and/or beneficiating
332999	Andirons manufacturing
339112	Anesthesia apparatus manufacturing
621111	Anesthesiologists' offices (e.g., centers, clinics)
325412	Ancsthctic prcparations manufacturing
325411	Anesthetics, uncompounded, manufacturing
325412	Angiourographic diagnostic preparations manufacturing
332999	Angle irons, metal, manufacturing
333515	Angle rings (i.e., a machine tool accessory) manufacturing
332911	Angle valves, industrial-typc, manufacturing
334511	Angle-of-attack instrumentation manufacturing
334511	Angle-of-yaw instrumentation manufacturing
112420	Angora goat farming
325311	Anhydrous ammonia manufacturing
311512	Anhydrous butterfat manufacturing
325222	Anidex fibers and filaments manufacturing
325192	Aniline manufacturing

112519	Animal aquaculture (except finfish, shellfish)
325182	Animal black manufacturing
813910	Animal breeders' associations
812220	Animal cemeteries
712130	Animal exhibits, live
311611	Animal fats (except poultry and small game) produced in slaughtering plants
311613	Animal fats rendering
311119	Animal feed mills (except dog and cat) manufacturing
311111	Animal feed mills, dog and cat, manufacturing
424910	Animal feeds (except pet food) merchant wholesalers
311119	Animal feeds, prepared (except dog and cat), manufacturing
311111	Animal feeds, prepared, dog and cat, manufacturing
313112	Animal fiber yarn twisting or winding of purchased yarn
812910	Animal grooming services
424590	Animal hair merchant wholesalers
541940	Animal hospitals
311613	Animal oil rendering
926140	Animal quarantine service, government
813312	Animal rights organizations
712130	Animal safari parks
115210	Animal semen banks
236220	Animal shelter and clinic construction
812910	Animal shelters
114210	Animal trapping, commercial
332999	Animal traps, metal (except wire), manufacturing
813312	Animal welfare associations or leagues
336999	Animal-drawn vehicles and parts manufacturing
711510	Animated cartoon artists, independent
512120	Animated cartoon distribution
512110	Animated cartoon production
512110	Animated cartoon production and distribution
325998	Anise oil manufacturing

315119	Anklets, sheer hosiery or socks, knitting or knitting and finishing
325191	Annato extract manufacturing
332811	Annealing metals and metal products for the trade
332420	Annealing vats, heavy gauge metal, manufacturing
711510	Announcers, independent radio and television
524113	Annuities underwriting
332991	Annular ball bearings manufacturing
334513	Annunciators, relay and solid-state types, industrial display, manufacturing
333298	Anodizing equipment manufacturing
332813	Anodizing metals and metal products for the trade
423620	Answering machines, telephone, merchant wholesalers
561421	Answering services, telephone
325320	Ant poisons manufacturing
325412	Antacid preparations manufacturing
238290	Antenna, household-type, installation
423690	Antennas merchant wholesalers
334220	Antennas, satellite, manufacturing
334220	Antennas, transmitting and receiving, manufacturing
325412	Anthelmintic preparations manufacturing
325192	Anthracene manufacturing
212113	Anthracite beneficiating (e.g., crushing, screening, washing, cleaning, sizing)
213113	Anthracite mine tunneling on a contract basis
212113	Anthracite mining and/or beneficiating
213113	Anthracite mining services (except site preparation and related construction contractor activities) on a contract basis
325132	Anthraquinone dyes manufacturing
332995	Antiaircraft artillery manufacturing
325412	Antibacterial preparations manufacturing
325412	Antibiotic preparations manufacturing
424210	Antibiotics merchant wholesalers
325411	Antibiotics, uncompounded, manufacturing
325411	Anticholinergics, uncompounded, manufacturing
325411	Anticonvulsants, uncompounded, manufacturing
325412	Antidepressant preparations manufacturing
325411	Antidepressants, uncompounded, manufacturing
424690	Antifreeze merchant wholesalers
325998	Antifreeze preparations manufacturing
325414	Antigens manufacturing
325412	Antihistamine preparations manufacturing
325131	Antimony based pigments manufacturing
212299	Antimony concentrates mining and/or beneficiating
212299	Antimony ores mining and/or beneficiating
325188	Antimony oxide (except pigments) manufacturing
331419	Antimony refining, primary
325412	Antineoplastic preparations manufacturing
325620	Antiperspirants, personal, manufacturing
813319	Antipoverty advocacy organizations
325412	Antipyretic preparations manufacturing
811121	Antique and classic automotive restoration
441120	Antique auto dealers
424920	Antique book merchant wholesalers
453310	Antique dealers (except motor vehicles)
423210	Antique furniture merchant wholesalers

811420	Antique furniture repair and restoration shops
423220	Antique homefurnishing merchant wholesalers
423220	Antique houseware merchant wholesalers
423940	Antique jewelry merchant wholesalers
453310	Antique shops
332913	Antiscald bath and shower valves, plumbing, manufacturing
325998	Antiscaling compounds manufacturing
325412	Antiseptic preparations manufacturing
424210	Antiseptics merchant wholesalers
325414	Antiserums manufacturing
325412	Antispasmodic preparations manufacturing
332995	Antisubmarine projectors manufacturing
332995	Antitank rocket launchers manufacturing
325414	Antitoxins manufacturing
325414	Antivenoms manufacturing
236116	Apartment building construction general contractors
236117	Apartment building operative builders
531110	Apartment building rental or leasing
531110	Apartment hotel rental or leasing
531311	Apartment managers' offices
531110	Apartment rental or leasing
212392	Apatite mining and/or beneficiating
212325	Aplite mining and/or beneficiating
446110	Apothecaries
331491	Apparatus wire and cord (except aluminum, copper) made from purchased nonferrous metals (except aluminum, copper) in wire drawing plants
331422	Apparatus wire or cord made from purchased copper in wire drawing plants
331319	Apparatus wire or cord made in aluminum wire drawing plants
448150	Apparel accessory stores
314999	Apparel fillings (e.g., cotton mill waste, kapok) manufacturing
315999	Apparel findings and trimmings cut and sewn from purchased fabric (except apparel contractors)
561910	Apparel folding and packaging services
812320	Apparel pressing services
448130	Apparel stores, children's and infants' clothing
448110	Apparel stores, men's and boys' clothing
453310	Apparel stores, used clothing
448120	Apparel stores, women's and girls' clothing
315211	Apparel trimmings and findings, men's and boys', cut and sew apparel contractors
315212	Apparel trimmings and findings, women's, girls', and infants', cut and sew apparel contractors
424310	Apparel trimmings merchant wholesalers
313221	Apparel webbings manufacturing
315292	Apparel, fur (except apparel contractors), manufacturing
315211	Apparel, fur, men's and boys', cut and sew apparel contractors
315212	Apparel, fur, women's, girls', and infants', cut and sew apparel contractors
315211	Apparel, men's and boys', cut and sew apparel contractors
315212	Apparel, women's, girls', and infants', cut and sew contractors
111331	Apple orchards
312130	Applejack distilling

334512	Appliance controls manufacturing
335999	Appliance cords made from purchased insulated wire
332510	Appliance hardware, metal, manufacturing
334512	Appliance regulators (except switches) manufacturing
532210	Appliance rental
443111	Appliance stores, household-type
453310	Appliance stores, household-type, used
334518	Appliance timers manufacturing
811412	Appliance, household-type, repair and maintenance services without retailing new appliances
423720	Appliances, gas (except dryers, freezers, refrigerators), merchant wholesalers
423620	Appliances, household-type (except gas ranges, gas water heaters), merchant wholesalers
423450	Appliances, surgical, merchant wholesalers
518210	Application hosting
518210	Application service providers (ASPs)
541511	Applications software programming services, custom computer
511210	Applications software, computer, packaged
321999	Applicators, wood, manufacturing
315211	Appliqueing on men's and boys' apparel
314999	Appliqueing on textile products (except apparel)
315212	Appliqueing on women's, girls', and infants' apparel
323118	Appointment books and refills manufacturing
541990	Appraisal (except real estate) services
531320	Appraisal services, real estate
531320	Appraisers' offices, real estate
611513	Apprenticeship training programs

111339	Apricot farming
812331	Apron supply services
316999	Aprons for textile machinery, leather, manufacturing
316999	Aprons, leather (e.g., blacksmith's, welder's), manufacturing
315999	Aprons, waterproof (e.g., plastics, rubberized fabric), rubberizing fabric and manufacturing aprons
315212	Aprons, waterproof (including plastics, rubberized fabric), women's, girls', and infants', cut and sew apparel contractors
315999	Aprons, waterproof (including rubberized fabric, plastics), cut and sewn from purchased fabric (except apparel contractors)
315211	Aprons, waterproof (including rubberized fabric, plastics), men's and boys', cut and sew apparel contractors
315211	Aprons, work (except leather), men's and boys, cut and sew apparel contractors
315212	Aprons, work (except leather), women's, girls', and infants', cut and sew apparel contractors
315225	Aprons, work (except leather, waterproof), men's and boys', cut and sewn from purchased fabric (except apparel contractors)
315239	Aprons, work (except waterproof, leather), women's, misses', and girls', cut and sewn from purchased fabric (except apparel contractors)
332999	Aquarium accessories, metal, manufacturing
712130	Aquariums
327215	Aquariums made from purchased glass
237110	Aqueduct construction

541990 Arbitration and conciliation services (except by attorney, paralegal)
333513 Arbor presses, metalworking, manufacturing
712130 Arboreta
712130 Arboretums
561730 Arborist services
333515 Arbors (i.e., a machine tool accessory) manufacturing
334510 Arc lamp units, electrotherapeutic (except infrared, ultraviolet), manufacturing
335129 Arc lighting fixtures (except electrotherapeutic), electric, manufacturing
333992 Arc welding equipment manufacturing
713120 Arcades, amusement
339113 Arch supports, orthopedic, manufacturing
541720 Archeological research and development services
712120 Archeological sites (i.e., public display)
339920 Archery equipment manufacturing
423910 Archery equipment merchant wholesalers
713990 Archery ranges
321213 Arches, glue laminated or pre-engineered wood, manufacturing
541310 Architects' (except landscape) offices
541310 Architects' (except landscape) private practices
813920 Architects' associations
423490 Architect's equipment and supplies merchant wholesalers
541320 Architects' offices, landscape
541320 Architects' private practices, landscape
541310 Architectural (except landscape) consultants' offices
541310 Architectural (except landscape) design services
541310 Architectural (except landscape) services

327331 Architectural block, concrete (e.g., fluted, ground face, screen, slump, split), manufacturing
325510 Architectural coatings (i.e., paint) manufacturing
332323 Architectural metalwork manufacturing
423390 Architectural metalwork merchant wholesalers
327112 Architectural sculptures, clay, manufacturing
327991 Architectural sculptures, stone, manufacturing
541320 Architectural services, landscape
327123 Architectural terra cotta manufacturing
327390 Architectural wall panels, precast concrete, manufacturing
337212 Architectural woodwork and fixtures (i.e., custom designed interiors) manufacturing
519120 Archives
316211 Arctics, plastics or plastics soled fabric upper, manufacturing
316211 Arctics, rubber or rubber soled fabric, manufacturing
335311 Arc-welding transformers, separate solid-state, manufacturing
335129 Area and sports luminaries (e.g., stadium lighting fixtures), electric, manufacturing
236220 Arena construction
711310 Arena operators
531120 Arena, no promotion of events, rental or leasing
212311 Argillite mining or quarrying
325120 Argon manufacturing
315999 Arm bands, elastic, cut and sewn from purchased fabric (except apparel contractors)
315211 Arm bands, elastic, men's and boys', cut and sew apparel contractors

315212	Arm bands, elastic, women's, girls', and infants', cut and sew apparel contractors
335314	Armature relays manufacturing
335312	Armature rewinding on a factory basis
811310	Armature rewinding services (except on an assembly line or factory basis)
335312	Armatures, industrial, manufacturing
928110	Armed forces
332993	Arming and fusing devices, missile, manufacturing
331111	Armor plate made in iron and steel mills
331422	Armored cable made from purchased copper in wire drawing plants
331422	Armored cable, copper, made in integrated secondary smelting and drawing plants
561613	Armored car services
336992	Armored military vehicles (except tanks) and parts manufacturing
236220	Armory construction
928110	Army
424690	Aromatic chemicals merchant wholesalers
113210	Aromatic wood gathering
488999	Arrangement of car pools and vanpools
335931	Arrestors and coils, lighting, manufacturing
325320	Arsenate insecticides manufacturing
325188	Arsenates (except insecticides) manufacturing
325131	Arsenic based pigments manufacturing
325188	Arsenic compounds, not specified elsewhere by process, manufacturing
212393	Arsenic mineral mining and/or beneficiating
325320	Arsenite insecticides manufacturing
325188	Arsenites manufacturing

611610	Art (except commercial or graphic) instruction
453920	Art auctions
453920	Art dealers
712110	Art galleries (except retail)
453920	Art galleries retailing art
327420	Art goods (e.g., gypsum, plaster of paris) manufacturing
424990	Art goods merchant wholesalers
712110	Art museums
314999	Art needlework contractors on apparel
314999	Art needlework on clothing for the trade
511199	Art print (except exclusive Internet publishing) publishers
323111	Art print gravure printing without publishing
511199	Art print publishers and printing combined
323112	Art prints flexographic printing without publishing
323110	Art prints lithographic (offset) printing without publishing
323119	Art prints printing (except flexographic, digital, gravure, lithographic, quick, screen) without publishing
323113	Art prints screen printing without publishing
511199	Art publishers (except exclusive Internet publishing)
519130	Art publishers, exclusively on Internet
711510	Art restorers, independent
611610	Art schools (except academic), fine
611519	Art schools, commercial or graphic
541430	Art services, commercial
541430	Art services, graphic
541430	Art studios, commercial
453998	Art supply stores
621340	Art therapists' offices (e.g., centers, clinics)
237110	Artesian well construction
111219	Artichoke farming, field, bedding plant and seed production

311421 Artichokes, canned, manufacturing

424990 Artificial Christmas trees merchant wholesalers

339999 Artificial flower arrangements assembled from purchased components

424930 Artificial flowers merchant wholesalers

334511 Artificial horizon instrumentation manufacturing

115210 Artificial insemination services for livestock

115210 Artificial insemination services for pets

339113 Artificial limbs manufacturing

238990 Artificial turf installation

312111 Artificially carbonated waters manufacturing

332993 Artillery ammunition (i.e., more than 30 mm., more than 1.18 inch) manufacturing

711510 Artists (except commercial, musical), independent

711510 Artists (i.e., painters), independent

711410 Artists' agents or managers

339942 Artist's paint manufacturing

339942 Artist's supplies (except paper) manufacturing

424990 Artists' supplies merchant wholesalers

541430 Artists, independent commercial

541430 Artists, independent graphic

541430 Artists, independent medical

926110 Arts and cultural program administration, government

711310 Arts event managers with facilities

711320 Arts event managers without facilities

711310 Arts event organizers with facilities

711320 Arts event organizers without facilities

711310 Arts event promoters with facilities

711320 Arts event promoters without facilities

711310 Arts festival managers with facilities

711320 Arts festival managers without facilities

711310 Arts festival organizers with facilities

711320 Arts festival organizers without facilities

711310 Arts festival promoters with facilities

711320 Arts festival promoters without facilities

562910 Asbestos abatement services

212399 Asbestos mining and/or beneficiating

327999 Asbestos products (except brake shoes and clutches) manufacutring

562910 Asbestos removal contractors

325411 Ascorbic acid (i.e., vitamin C), uncompounded, manufacturing

315211 Ascots, men's and boys', cut and sew apparel contractors

315993 Ascots, men's and boys', cut and sewn from purchased fabric (except apparel contractors)

562111 Ash collection services

562111 Ash hauling, local

212399 Ash, volcanic, mining and/or beneficiating

327215 Ashtrays made from purchased glass

327212 Ashtrays, glass, made in glass making plants

327112 Ashtrays, pottery, manufacturing

111219 Asparagus farming, field, bedding plant and seed production

324110 Asphalt and asphaltic materials made in petroleum refineries

423320 Asphalt and concrete mixtures merchant wholesalers

238990 Asphalt coating and sealing, residential and commercial parking lot and driveway

238330 Asphalt flooring, installation only

322121	Asphalt paper made in paper mills
237310	Asphalt paving (i.e., highway, road, street, public sidewalk)
324121	Asphalt paving blocks made from purchased asphaltic materials
324121	Asphalt paving mixtures made from purchased asphaltic materials
324110	Asphalt paving mixtures made in petroleum refineries
324121	Asphalt road compounds made from purchased asphaltic materials
212399	Asphalt rock mining and/or beneficiating
238160	Asphalt roof shingle installation
324122	Asphalt roofing cements made from purchased asphaltic materials
324122	Asphalt roofing coatings made from purchased asphaltic materials
333120	Asphalt roofing construction machinery manufacturing
423330	Asphalt roofing shingles merchant wholesalers
324122	Asphalt saturated boards made from purchased asphaltic materials
324122	Asphalt saturated mats and felts made from purchased asphaltic materials and paper
324122	Asphalt shingles made from purchased asphaltic materials
212399	Asphalt, native, mining and/or beneficiating
238990	Asphalting, residential and commercial driveway and parking area
518210	ASPs (Application Service Providers)
541380	Assaying services
336213	Assembly line conversions of purchased vans and mini-vans
336312	Assembly line rebuilding of automotive and truck gasoline engines

336350	Assembly line rebuilding of automotive, truck, and bus transmissions
333518	Assembly machines manufacturing
236210	Assembly plant construction
336120	Assembly plants, heavy trucks, and buses on chassis of own manufacture
336112	Assembly plants, light trucks on chassis of own manufacture
336112	Assembly plants, mini-vans on chassis of own manufacture
336111	Assembly plants, passenger car, on chassis of own manufacture
336112	Assembly plants, sport utility vehicles on chassis of own manufacture
921130	Assessor's offices, tax
325613	Assistants, textile and leather finishing, manufacturing
623311	Assisted-living facilities with on-site nursing facilities
623312	Assisted-living facilities without on-site nursing care facilities
813311	Associations for retired persons, advocacy
522120	Associations, savings and loan
325412	Astringent preparations manufacturing
812990	Astrology services
711219	Athletes, amateur, independent
711219	Athletes, independent (i.e., participating in live sports events)
813990	Athletic associations, regulatory
315228	Athletic clothing (except team athletic uniforms), men's, boys' and unisex (i.e., sized without regard to gender), cut and sewn from purchased fabric (except apparel contractors)
315239	Athletic clothing (except team athletic uniforms), women's, misses', and girls', cut and sewn from purchased fabric (except apparel contractors)

315191	Athletic clothing made in apparel knitting mills
315211	Athletic clothing, men's and boys', cut and sew apparel contractors
315212	Athletic clothing, women's, girls', and infants', cut and sew apparel contractors
713940	Athletic club facilities, physical fitness
713990	Athletic clubs (i.e., sports teams) not operating sports facilities, recreational
236220	Athletic court, indoor, construction
451110	Athletic equipment and supply stores (including uniforms)
237990	Athletic field (except stadium) construction
424340	Athletic footwear merchant wholesalers
339920	Athletic goods (except ammunition, clothing, footwear, small arms) manufacturing
423910	Athletic goods (except apparel, footwear, nonspecialty) merchant wholesalers
813990	Athletic leagues (i.e., regulating bodies)
448210	Athletic shoe (except bowling, golf, spiked) stores
316219	Athletic shoes (except rubber or plastics soled with fabric upper) manufacturing
316211	Athletic shoes, plastics or plastics soled, fabric upper (except cleated), manufacturing
316211	Athletic shoes, rubber or rubber soled, fabric uppers (except cleated), manufacturing
315119	Athletic socks, knitting or knitting and finishing
423910	Athletic uniforms merchant wholesalers
315299	Athletic uniforms, team, cut and sewn from purchased fabric (except apparel contractors)
315211	Athletic uniforms, team, men's and boys', cut and sew apparel contractors
315212	Athletic uniforms, team, women's, girls', and infants, cut and sew apparel contractors
511130	Atlas publishers (except exclusive Internet publishing)
511130	Atlas publishers and printing combined
519130	Atlas publishers, exclusively on Internet
323112	Atlases flexographic printing without publishing
323111	Atlases gravure printing without publishing
323110	Atlases lithographic (offset) printing without publishing
323119	Atlases printing (except flexographic, digital, gravure, lithographic, quick, screen) without publishing
323113	Atlases screen printing without publishing
238290	ATMs (automatic teller machines) installation
334119	ATMs (automatic teller machines) manufacturing
335999	Atom smashers (i.e., particle accelerators) manufacturing
339999	Atomizers (e.g., perfumes) manufacturing
325411	Atropine and derivatives manufacturing
316991	Attache cases, all materials, manufacturing
333112	Attachments, powered lawn and garden equipment, manufacturing
333412	Attic fans manufacturing
238310	Attic space insulating
922130	Attorney generals' offices
541110	Attorneys' offices
541110	Attorneys' private practices
453998	Auction houses (general merchandise)
424590	Auction markets, tobacco, horses, mules
561990	Auctioneers, independent

454112	Auctions, Internet retail
423990	Audio and video tapes and disks, prerecorded, merchant wholesalers
337129	Audio cabinets (i.e., housings), wood, manufacturing
238210	Audio equipment installation (except automotive) contractors
443112	Audio equipment stores (except automotive)
423620	Audio equipment, household-type, merchant wholesalers
512290	Audio recording of meetings or conferences
512240	Audio recording post-production services
532490	Audio visual equipment rental or leasing
334515	Audiofrequency oscillators manufacturing
334510	Audiological equipment, electromedical, manufacturing
621340	Audiologists' offices (e.g., centers, clinics)
334515	Audiometers (except medical) manufacturing
334613	Audiotape, blank, manufacturing
423690	Audiotapes, blank, merchant wholesalers
541211	Auditing accountants' (i.e., CPAs) offices
541211	Auditing accountants' (i.e., CPAs) private practices
541211	Auditing services (i.e., CPA services), accounts
236220	Auditorium construction
531120	Auditorium rental or leasing
541211	Auditors' (i.e., CPAs) offices, accounts
541211	Auditors' (i.e., CPAs) private practices, accounts
921190	Auditor's offices, government
213113	Auger coal mining services (except site preparation and related construction contractor activities) on a contract basis
333120	Augers (except mining-type) manufacturing
333131	Augers, mining-type, manufacturing
332212	Augers, nonpowered, manufacturing
711410	Authors' agents or managers
711510	Authors, independent
423120	Auto body shop supplies, merchant wholesalers
721110	Auto courts, lodging
441310	Auto supply stores
339114	Autoclaves, dental, manufacturing
332420	Autoclaves, industrial-type, heavy gauge metal, manufacturing
339113	Autoclaves, laboratory-type (except dental), manufacturing
336411	Autogiros manufacturing
238290	Automated and revolving door installation
334510	Automated blood and body fluid analyzers (except laboratory) manufacturing
522320	Automated clearinghouses, bank or check (except central bank)
518210	Automated data processing services
332911	Automatic (i.e., controlling-type, regulating) valves, industrial-type, manufacturing
334516	Automatic chemical analyzers, laboratory-type, manufacturing
238290	Automatic gate (e.g., garage, parking lot) installation
812310	Automatic laundries, coin-operated
454210	Automatic merchandising machine operators
333512	Automatic screw machines, metal cutting type, manufacturing
334119	Automatic teller machines (ATM) manufacturing
423420	Automatic teller machines (ATM) merchant wholesalers
336350	Automatic transmissions, automotive, truck, and bus, manufacturing

423120 Automobile accessories (except tires, tubes) merchant wholesalers

334220 Automobile antennas manufacturing

425120 Automobile auctions, wholesale

336211 Automobile bodies, passenger car, manufacturing

484220 Automobile carrier trucking, local

484230 Automobile carrier trucking, long-distance

813410 Automobile clubs (except road and travel services)

561599 Automobile clubs, road and travel services

721110 Automobile courts, lodging

493190 Automobile dead storage

441110 Automobile dealers, new only or new and used

441120 Automobile dealers, used only

611692 Automobile driving schools

522220 Automobile finance leasing companies

522220 Automobile financing

423120 Automobile glass merchant wholesalers

332510 Automobile hardware, metal, manufacturing

541420 Automobile industrial design services

524126 Automobile insurance carriers, direct

532112 Automobile leasing

333921 Automobile lifts (i.e., garage-type, service station) manufacturing

423110 Automobile merchant wholesalers

812930 Automobile parking garages or lots

441310 Automobile parts dealers

325612 Automobile polishes and cleaners manufacturing

541380 Automobile proving and testing grounds

711212 Automobile racetracks

611620 Automobile racing schools

711219 Automobile racing teams

334310 Automobile radio receivers manufacturing

532111 Automobile rental

485320 Automobile rental with driver (except shuttle service, taxis)

561491 Automobile repossession services

336360 Automobile seat covers manufacturing

336360 Automobile seat frames, metal, manufacturing

423120 Automobile service station equipment merchant wholesalers

561920 Automobile show managers

561920 Automobile show organizers

561920 Automobile show promoters

332618 Automobile skid chains made from purchased wire

335911 Automobile storage batteries manufacturing

332611 Automobile suspension springs, heavy gauge metal, manufacturing

336212 Automobile transporter trailers, multi-car, manufacturing

336214 Automobile transporter trailers, single car, manufacturing

336360 Automobile trimmings, textile, manufacturing

333923 Automobile wrecker (i.e., tow truck) hoists manufacturing

336211 Automobile wrecker truck bodies manufacturing

336211 Automobile wreckers assembling on purchased chassis

336111 Automobiles assembling on chassis of own manufacture

339932 Automobiles, children's, manufacturing

423730 Automotive air-conditioners merchant wholesalers

811198 Automotive air-conditioning repair shops

441310 Automotive audio equipment stores

811121 Automotive body shops

811118 Automotive brake repair shops

424690	Automotive chemicals (except lubricating greases, lubrication oils) merchant wholesalers
811192	Automotive detailing services (i.e., cleaning, polishing)
334515	Automotive electrical engine diagnostic equipment manufacturing
811118	Automotive electrical repair shops
335931	Automotive electrical switches manufacturing
334519	Automotive emissions testing equipment manufacturing
811198	Automotive emissions testing services
811111	Automotive engine repair and replacement shops
811112	Automotive exhaust system repair and replacement shops
811118	Automotive front end alignment shops
811122	Automotive glass shops
336322	Automotive harness and ignition sets manufacturing
335110	Automotive light bulbs manufacturing
336321	Automotive lighting fixtures manufacturing
336399	Automotive mirrors, framed, manufacturing
811191	Automotive oil change and lubrication shops
331319	Automotive or aircraft wire and cable made in aluminum wire drawing plants
811121	Automotive paint shops
441310	Automotive parts and supply stores
441310	Automotive parts dealers, used
423120	Automotive parts, new, merchant wholesalers
811118	Automotive radiator repair shops
423620	Automotive radios merchant wholesalers
811111	Automotive repair and replacement shops, general
811198	Automotive rustproofing and undercoating shops
811198	Automotive safety inspection services
334290	Automotive theft alarm systems manufacturing
441320	Automotive tire dealers
811198	Automotive tire repair (except retreading) shops
811113	Automotive transmission repair shops
811118	Automotive tune-up shops
811121	Automotive upholstery shops
811192	Automotive washing and polishing
336330	Automotive, truck and bus steering assemblies and parts manufacturing
336330	Automotive, truck and bus suspension assemblies and parts (except springs) manufacturing
339992	Autophones (organs with perforated music rolls) manufacturing
335311	Autotransformers for switchboards (except telephone switchboards) manufacturing
335311	Autotransformers manufacturing
237990	Avalanche, rockslide, or mudslide protection construction
712130	Aviaries
112990	Aviaries (i.e., raising birds for sale)
813319	Aviation advocacy organizations
481219	Aviation clubs providing a variety of air transportation activities to the general public
488119	Aviation clubs, primarily providing flying field services to the general public
713990	Aviation clubs, recreational
324110	Aviation fuels manufacturing
611512	Aviation schools
111339	Avocado farming
332212	Awls manufacturing
238190	Awning installation
423390	Awnings (except canvas) merchant wholesalers

314912 Awnings and canopies, outdoor, made from purchased fabrics

424990 Awnings, canvas, merchant wholesalers

326199 Awnings, rigid plastics or fiberglass, manufacturing

332322 Awnings, sheet metal (except stampings), manufacturing

332212 Axes manufacturing

336350 Axle bearings, automotive, truck, and bus, manufacturing

331111 Axles, rolled or forged, made in iron and steel mills

111421 Azalea farming

325920 Azides explosive materials manufacturing

325132 Azine dyes manufacturing

325132 Azo dyes manufacturing

325192 Azobenzene manufacturing

424330 Baby clothing merchant wholesalers

448130 Baby clothing shops

311422 Baby foods (including meats) canning

424490 Baby foods, canned, merchant wholesalers

311514 Baby formula, fresh, processed, and bottled, manufacturing

423210 Baby furniture merchant wholesalers

325620 Baby powder and baby oil manufacturing

333997 Baby scales manufacturing

812990 Baby shoe bronzing services

561311 Babysitting bureaus (i.e., registries)

624410 Babysitting services in provider's own home, child day care

624410 Babysitting services, child day care

238910 Backfilling, construction

332913 Backflow preventors, plumbing, manufacturing

112111 Backgrounding, cattle

238910 Backhoe rental with operator

333120 Backhoes manufacturing

311612 Bacon, slab and sliced, made from purchased carcasses

311611 Bacon, slab and sliced, produced in slaughtering plants

325414 Bacterial vaccines manufacturing

325414 Bacterins (i.e., bacterial vaccines) manufacturing

621511 Bacteriological laboratories, diagnostic

621511 Bacteriological laboratories, medical

541712 Bacteriological research and development laboratories or services (except biotechnology research and development)

314999 Badges, fabric, manufacturing

332999 Badges, metal, manufacturing

326199 Badges, plastics, manufacturing

339920 Badminton equipment manufacturing

332313 Baffles, fabricated metal plate work, manufacturing

316110 Bag leather manufacturing

332993 Bag loading plants, ammunition, manufacturing

333993 Bag opening, filling, and closing machines manufacturing

722110 Bagel shops, full service

722213 Bagel shops, on premise baking and carryout service

311812 Bagels made in commercial bakeries

322223 Bags (except plastics only) made by laminating or coating combinations of purchased plastics, foil and paper

316991 Bags (i.e., luggage), all materials, manufacturing

313249 Bags and bagging fabric made in warp knitting mills

313241 Bags and bagging fabrics made in weft knitting mills

316991 Bags, athletic, manufacturing

322223 Bags, coated paper, made from purchased paper

322223 Bags, foil, made from purchased foil

339920 Bags, golf, manufacturing

313111 Bags, hemp, made from purchased fiber
322224 Bags, multiwall, made from purchased uncoated paper
424130 Bags, paper and disposable plastics, merchant wholesalers
322224 Bags, paper, uncoated, made from purchased paper
326111 Bags, plastics film, single wall or multiwall, manufacturing
314911 Bags, plastics, made from purchased woven plastics
339920 Bags, punching, manufacturing
314911 Bags, rubberized fabric, manufacturing
314999 Bags, sleeping, manufacturing
314911 Bags, textile, made from purchased woven or knitted materials
424990 Bags, textile, merchant wholesalers
322224 Bags, uncoated paper, made from purchased paper
812990 Bail bonding services
339920 Bait, artificial, fishing, manufacturing
423910 Bait, artificial, merchant wholesalers
424990 Bait, live, merchant wholesalers
112511 Baitfish production, farm raising
311422 Baked beans canning
311813 Baked goods (except bread, bread-type rolls), frozen, manufacturing
445291 Baked goods stores, retailing only (except immediate consumption)
445210 Baked ham stores
311811 Bakeries with baking from flour on the premises, retailing not for immediate consumption
315211 Bakers' service apparel, washable, men's and boys', cut and sew apparel contractors
315225 Bakers' service apparel, washable, men's and boys', cut and sewn from purchased fabric (except apparel contractors)

315212 Bakers' service apparel, washable, women's, cut and sew apparel contractors
315239 Bakers' service apparel, washable, women's, misses', and girls', cut and sewn from purchased fabric (except apparel contractors)
333294 Bakery machinery and equipment manufacturing
423830 Bakery machinery and equipment merchant wholesalers
333294 Bakery ovens manufacturing
424490 Bakery products (except frozen) merchant wholesalers
311821 Bakery products, dry (e.g., biscuits, cookies, crackers), manufacturing
311812 Bakery products, fresh (i.e., bread, cakes, doughnuts, pastries), made in commercial bakeries
424420 Bakery products, frozen, merchant wholesalers
311320 Baking chocolate made from cacao beans
311330 Baking chocolate made from purchased chocolate
311999 Baking powder manufacturing
423440 Balances and scales (except laboratory) merchant wholesalers
423490 Balances and scales, laboratory (except dental, medical), merchant wholesalers
333997 Balances, including laboratory-type, manufacturing
333319 Balancing equipment, motor vehicle, manufacturing
332323 Balcony railings, metal, manufacturing
238190 Balcony, metal, installation
238120 Balcony, precast concrete, installation
333111 Bale throwers manufacturing
332618 Bale ties made from purchased wire
333111 Balers, farm-type (e.g., cotton, hay, straw), manufacturing

333999	Baling machinery (e.g., paper, scrap metal) manufacturing
332991	Ball bearings manufacturing
212324	Ball clay mining and/or beneficiating
333613	Ball joints (except aircraft, motor vehicle) manufacturing
339941	Ball point pens manufacturing
332911	Ball valves, industrial-type, manufacturing
335311	Ballasts (i.e., transformers) manufacturing
711120	Ballet companies
711510	Ballet dancers, independent
711120	Ballet productions, live theatrical
611610	Ballet schools (except academic)
316219	Ballet slippers manufacturing
453220	Balloon shops
812990	Balloon-o-gram services
326199	Balloons, plastics, manufacturing
326299	Balloons, rubber, manufacturing
713990	Ballrooms
339920	Balls, baseball, basketball, football, golf, tennis, pool, and bowling, manufacturing
339932	Balls, rubber (except athletic equipment), manufacturing
331111	Balls, steel, made in iron and steel mills
113210	Balsam needles gathering
111339	Banana farming
115114	Banana ripening
315299	Band uniforms cut and sewn from purchased fabric (except apparel contractors)
315211	Band uniforms, men's and boys', cut and sew apparel contractors
315212	Band uniforms, women's, girls', and infants', cut and sew apparel contractors
339113	Bandages and dressings, surgical and orthopedic, manufacturing
424210	Bandages merchant wholesalers
315212	Bandeaux, women's and girls', cut and sew apparel contractors
315231	Bandeaux, women's, misses', and girls', cut and sewn from purchased fabric (except apparel contractors)
711130	Bands
711130	Bands, dance
711130	Bands, musical
333210	Bandsaws, woodworking-type, manufacturing
339992	Banjos and parts manufacturing
334511	Bank and turn indicators and components (aeronautical instruments) manufacturing
236220	Bank building construction
531120	Bank building rental or leasing
332999	Bank chests, metal, manufacturing
522320	Bank clearinghouse associations
524128	Bank deposit insurance carriers, direct
332323	Bank fixtures, ornamental metal, manufacturing
551111	Bank holding companies (except managing)
523991	Bank trust offices
813910	Bankers' associations
926150	Banking regulatory agencies
611519	Banking schools (training in banking)
521110	Banking, central
523110	Banking, investment
525920	Bankruptcy estates
522110	Banks, commercial
522210	Banks, credit card
521110	Banks, Federal Reserve
522190	Banks, industrial (i.e., known as), depository
522298	Banks, industrial (i.e., known as), nondepository
522190	Banks, private (i.e., unincorporated)
522120	Banks, savings
522293	Banks, trade (i.e., international trade financing)
314999	Banners made from purchased fabrics

332323	Bannisters, metal, manufacturing
531120	Banquet hall rental or leasing
722320	Banquet halls with catering staff
327991	Baptismal fonts, cut stone, manufacturing
813920	Bar associations
561499	Bar code imprinting services
331316	Bar made by extruding purchased aluminum
331319	Bar made by rolling purchased aluminum
333516	Bar mill machinery, metalworking, manufacturing
325611	Bar soaps manufacturing
331316	Bar, aluminum, made in integrated secondary smelting and extruding mills
331319	Bar, aluminum, made in integrated secondary smelting and rolling mills
331421	Bar, copper and copper alloy, made from purchased copper or in integrated secondary smelting and rolling, drawing or extruding plants
331491	Bar, nonferrous metals (except aluminum, copper), made from purchased metals in wire drawing plants or in integrated secondary smelting and rolling, drawing, or extruding plants
311421	Barbecue sauce manufacturing
335221	Barbecues, grills, and braziers manufacturing
331222	Barbed and twisted wire made in wire drawing plants
332618	Barbed wire made from purchased wire
611511	Barber colleges
236220	Barber shop construction
423850	Barber shop equipment and supplies merchant wholesalers
812111	Barber shops
332211	Barber's scissors, manufacturing
315211	Barbers' service apparel, washable, men's and boys', cut and sew apparel contractors

315225	Barbers' service apparel, washable, men's and boys', cut and sewn from purchased fabric (except apparel contractors)
325412	Barbiturate preparations manufacturing
325411	Barbiturates, uncompounded, manufacturing
325411	Barbituric acid manufacturing
336611	Barge building
532411	Barge rental or leasing
332312	Barge sections, prefabricated metal, manufacturing
483211	Barge transportation, canal (freight)
483113	Barge transportation, coastal or Great Lakes (including St. Lawrence Seaway)
212393	Barite mining and/or beneficiating
327992	Barite processing beyond beneficiation
325188	Barium compounds, not specified elsewhere by process, manufacturing
325188	Barium hydroxide manufacturing
325412	Barium in-vivo diagnostic substances manufacturing
212393	Barium ores mining and/or beneficiating
327992	Barium processing beyond beneficiation
113210	Bark gathering
111199	Barley farming, field and seed production
311119	Barley feed, chopped, crushed or ground, manufacturing
311211	Barley flour manufacturing
311213	Barley, malt, manufacturing
332323	Barn stanchions and standards manufacturing
334519	Barographs manufacturing
334519	Barometers manufacturing
332410	Barometric condensers manufacturing
236220	Barrack construction
321920	Barrel heading and staves manufacturing

332994 Barrels, gun (i.e., 30 mm. or less, 1.18 inch or less), manufacturing

332995 Barrels, gun (i.e., more than 30 mm., more than 1.18 inch), manufacturing

332439 Barrels, light gauge metal, manufacturing

423840 Barrels, new and reconditioned, merchant wholesalers

321920 Barrels, wood, coopered, manufacturing

332999 Barricades, metal, manufacturing

541110 Barristers' offices

541110 Barristers' private practices

722410 Bars (i.e., drinking places), alcoholic beverage

331411 Bars made in primary copper smelting and refining mills

331111 Bars, concrete reinforcing (rebar) made in steel mills

331221 Bars, concrete reinforcing (rebar), made from purchased steel in steel rolling mills

332312 Bars, concrete reinforcing, manufacturing

331111 Bars, iron, made in iron and steel mills

423510 Bars, metal (except precious), merchant wholesalers

331221 Bars, steel, made in cold rolling mills made from purchased steel

331111 Bars, steel, made in iron and steel mills

611519 Bartending schools

561990 Bartering services

325131 Barytes based pigments manufacturing

212393 Barytes mining and/or beneficiating

212319 Basalt crushed and broken stone mining and/or beneficiating

212311 Basalt mining or quarrying

561210 Base facilities operation support services

315211 Baseball caps (except plastics), men's and boys', cut and sew apparel contractors

315212 Baseball caps (except plastics), women's, girls', and infants', cut and sew apparel contractors

315991 Baseball caps cut and sewn from purchased fabric (except apparel contractors)

711211 Baseball clubs, professional or semiprofessional

713990 Baseball clubs, recreational

339920 Baseball equipment and supplies (except footwear, uniforms) manufacturing

423910 Baseball equipment and supplies merchant wholesalers

611620 Baseball instruction, camps, or schools

711211 Baseball teams, professional or semiprofessional

315299 Baseball uniforms cut and sewn from purchased fabric (except apparel contractors)

315211 Baseball uniforms, men's and boys', cut and sew apparel contractors

315212 Baseball uniforms, women's and girls', cut and sew apparel contractors

423730 Baseboard heaters, electric, non-portable, merchant wholesalers

333414 Baseboard heating equipment manufacturing

321918 Baseboards, floor, wood, manufacturing

332321 Baseboards, metal, manufacturing

711211 Basketball clubs, professional or semiprofessional

713990 Basketball clubs, recreational

339920 Basketball equipment and supplies (except footwear, uniforms) manufacturing

611620 Basketball instruction, camps, or schools

711211 Basketball teams, professional or semiprofessional

315299 Basketball uniforms cut and sewn from purchased fabric (except apparel contractors)

315211 Basketball uniforms, men's and boys', cut and sew apparel contractors

315212 Basketball uniforms, women's and girls', cut and sew apparel contractors

424990 Baskets merchant wholesalers

331222 Baskets, iron or steel, made in wire drawing plants

332618 Baskets, metal, made from purchased wire

321920 Baskets, wood (e.g., round stave, veneer), manufacturing

337125 Bassinets, reed and rattan, manufacturing

339992 Bassoons manufacturing

212299 Bastnaesite mining and/or beneficiating

335211 Bath fans with integral lighting fixture, residential, manufacturing

335211 Bath fans, residential, manufacturing

314110 Bath mats and bath sets made in carpet mills

326299 Bath mats, rubber, manufacturing

325620 Bath salts manufacturing

442299 Bath shops

238390 Bath tub refinishing on site

713990 Bathing beaches

315999 Bathing caps, rubber, manufacturing

315191 Bathing suits made in apparel knitting mills

315291 Bathing suits, infants', cut and sewn from purchased fabric (except apparel contractors)

315211 Bathing suits, men's and boys', cut and sew apparel contractors

315228 Bathing suits, men's and boys', cut and sewn from purchased fabric (except apparel contractors)

315212 Bathing suits, women's, girls', and infants', cut and sew apparel contractors

315239 Bathing suits, women's, misses', and girls', cut and sewn from purchased fabric (except apparel contractors)

315192 Bathrobes made in apparel knitting mills

315291 Bathrobes, infants', cut and sewn from purchased fabric (except apparel contractors)

315211 Bathrobes, men's and boys', cut and sew apparel contractors

315221 Bathrobes, men's and boys', cut and sewn from purchased fabric (except apparel contractors)

315212 Bathrobes, women's, girls', and infants', cut and sew apparel contractors

315231 Bathrobes, women's, misses', and girls', cut and sewn from purchased fabric (except apparel contractors)

423220 Bathroom accessories merchant wholesalers

327111 Bathroom accessories, vitreous china and earthenware, manufacturing

326199 Bathroom and toilet accessories, plastics, manufacturing

332998 Bathroom fixtures, metal, manufacturing

238220 Bathroom plumbing fixture and sanitary ware installation

333997 Bathroom scales manufacturing

337110 Bathroom vanities (except freestanding), stock or custom wood, manufacturing

812199 Baths, steam or turkish

332998 Bathtubs, metal, manufacturing

326191 Bathtubs, plastics, manufacturing

611620 Baton instruction

624221 Battered women's shelters

423610 Batteries (except automotive) merchant wholesalers

423120 Batteries, automotive, merchant wholesalers

335912 Batteries, primary, dry or wet, manufacturing

335911 Batteries, rechargeable, manufacturing

335911 Batteries, storage, manufacturing

311822 Batters, prepared, made from purchased flour

311211 Batters, prepared, made in flour mills

335999 Battery chargers, solid-state, manufacturing

334515 Battery testers, electrical, manufacturing

712120 Battlefields

314999 Batts and batting (except nonwoven fabrics) manufacturing

327125 Bauxite brick manufacturing

212299 Bauxite mining and/or beneficiating

325998 Bay oil manufacturing

454390 Bazaars (i.e., temporary stands)

332994 BB guns manufacturing

332992 BB shot manufacturing

532292 Beach chair rental

713990 Beach clubs, recreational

562998 Beach maintenance and cleaning services

316211 Beach sandals, plastics or plastics soled fabric upper, manufacturing

316211 Beach sandals, rubber or ruber soled fabric upper, manufacturing

532292 Beach umbrella rental

339999 Beach umbrellas manufacturing

713990 Beaches, bathing

315191 Beachwear made in apparel knitting mills

315291 Beachwear, infants', cut and sewn from purchased fabric (except apparel contractors)

315211 Beachwear, men's and boys', cut and sew apparel contractors

315228 Beachwear, men's and boys', cut and sewn from purchased fabric (except apparel contractors)

315212 Beachwear, women's, girls', and infants', cut and sew apparel contractors

315239 Beachwear, women's, misses', and girls', cut and sewn from purchased fabric (except apparel contractors)

333513 Beader machines, metalworking, manufacturing

314999 Beading on textile products (except apparel) for the trade

333292 Beaming machinery for yarn manufacturing

313112 Beaming yarn

321113 Beams, wood, made from logs or bolts

111219 Bean (except dry) farming, field and seed production

115114 Bean cleaning

111130 Bean farming, dry, field and seed production

111419 Bean sprout farming, grown under cover

311422 Beans, baked, canning

424510 Beans, dry, merchant wholesalers

332212 Bearing pullers, handtools, manufacturing

336312 Bearings (e.g., camshaft, crankshaft, connecting rod), automotive and truck gasoline engine, manufacturing

423840 Bearings merchant wholesalers

332991 Bearings, ball and roller, manufacturing

333613 Bearings, plain (except internal combustion engine), manufacturing

812112 Beautician services

611511 Beauty schools

812112 Beauty and barber shops, combined

711310 Beauty pageant managers with facilities

711320 Beauty pageant managers without facilities

711310 Beauty pageant organizers with facilities

711320 Beauty pageant organizers without facilities

711310	Beauty pageant promoters with facilities
711320	Beauty pageant promoters without facilities
423850	Beauty parlor equipment and supplies merchant wholesalers
812112	Beauty parlors
424210	Beauty preparations merchant wholesalers
236220	Beauty salon construction
812112	Beauty salons
812112	Beauty shops
424210	Beauty supplies merchant wholesalers
446120	Beauty supply stores
721191	Bed and breakfast inns
337122	Bed frames, wood household-type, manufacturing
812331	Bed linen supply services
442110	Bed stores, retail
335211	Bedcoverings, electric, manufacturing
111422	Bedding plant growing (except vegetable and melon bedding plants)
315212	Bedjackets, women's, girls' and infants', cut and sew apparel contractors
315231	Bedjackets, women's, misses' juniors', and girls', cut and sewn from purchased fabric (except apparel contractors)
337122	Bedroom furniture (except upholstered), wood household-type, manufacturing
337122	Beds (except hospital), wood household-type, manufacturing
337124	Beds (including cabinet and folding), metal household-type (except hospital), manufacturing
339113	Beds, hospital, manufacturing
423450	Beds, hospital, merchant wholesalers
337910	Beds, sleep-system ensembles (i.e., flotation, adjustable), manufacturing
337122	Beds, wood dormitory-type, manufacturing
337122	Beds, wood hotel-type, manufacturing
314129	Bedspreads and bed sets made from purchased fabrics
313249	Bedspreads and bed sets made in lace mills
313249	Bedspreads and bed sets made in warp knitting mills
313241	Bedspreads and bed sets made in weft knitting mills
112910	Bee production (i.e., apiculture)
311611	Beef carcasses, half carcasses, primal and sub-primal cuts, produced in slaughtering plants
112112	Beef cattle feedlots (except stockyards for transportation)
112111	Beef cattle ranching or farming
311611	Beef produced in slaughtering plants
311612	Beef stew made from purchased carcasses
311612	Beef, primal and sub-primal cuts, made from purchased carcasses
424910	Beekeeping supplies merchant wholesalers
517210	Beeper (i.e., radio pager) communication carriers
327213	Beer bottles, glass, manufacturing
312120	Beer brewing
332431	Beer cans, light gauge metal, manufacturing
333415	Beer cooling and dispensing equipment manufacturing
332439	Beer kegs, light gauge metal, manufacturing
424810	Beer merchant wholesalers
445310	Beer stores, packaged
325612	Beeswax polishes and waxes manufacturing
112910	Beeswax production
111219	Beet farming (except sugar beets), field, bedding plant and seed production
311313	Beet pulp, dried, manufacturing
311313	Beet sugar refining
541720	Behavioral research and development services

333111   Berry harvesting machines manufacturing

212299   Beryl mining and/or beneficiating

327113   Beryllia porcelain insulators manufacturing

331528   Beryllium castings (except die-castings), unfinished manufacturing

212299   Beryllium concentrates beneficiating

331522   Beryllium die-castings, unfinished, manufacturing

212299   Beryllium ores mining and/or beneficiating

325188   Beryllium oxide manufacturing

331419   Beryllium refining, primary

334517   Beta-ray irradiation equipment manufacturing

335999   Betatrons manufacturing

813910   Better business bureaus

722213   Beverage (e.g., coffee, juice, soft drink) bars, nonalcoholic, fixed location

311930   Beverage bases manufacturing

424490   Beverage bases merchant wholesalers

423830   Beverage bottling machinery merchant wholesalers

424490   Beverage concentrates merchant wholesalers

327213   Beverage containers, glass, manufacturing

423740   Beverage coolers, mechanical, merchant wholesalers

311930   Beverage flavorings (except coffee based) manufacturing

722330   Beverage stands, nonalcoholic, mobile

311930   Beverage syrups (except coffee based) manufacturing

424810   Beverages, alcoholic (except distilled spirits, wine), merchant wholesalers

312120   Beverages, beer, ale, and malt liquors, manufacturing

311514   Beverages, dietary, dairy and nondairy based

312111   Beverages, fruit and vegetable drinks, cocktails, and ades, manufacturing

311421   Beverages, fruit and vegetable juice, manufacturing

312140   Beverages, liquors (except brandies), manufacturing

311511   Beverages, milk based (except dietary), manufacturing

312112   Beverages, naturally carbonated bottled water, manufacturing

312111   Beverages, soft drink (including artificially carbonated waters), manufacturing

424820   Beverages, wine and distilled spirits, merchant wholesalers

312130   Beverages, wines and brandies, manufacturing

314999   Bias bindings made from purchased fabrics

313221   Bias bindings, woven, manufacturing

611699   Bible schools (except degree granting)

813110   Bible societies

315999   Bibs and aprons, waterproof (e.g., plastics, rubber, similar materials), cut and sewn from purchased fabric (except apparel contractors)

315211   Bibs and aprons, waterproof (e.g., plastics, rubber, similar materials), men's and boys', cut and sew apparel contractors

315999   Bibs and aprons, waterproof (e.g., plastics, rubber, similar materials), rubberizing fabric and manufacturing bibs and aprons

315212   Bibs and aprons, waterproof (e.g., plastics, rubber, similar materials), women's, girls', and infants', cut and sew apparel contractors

315212   Bibs, waterproof, cut and sew apparel contractors

451110   Bicycle (except motorized) shops

453310 Bicycle (except motorized) shops, used
492210 Bicycle courier
333912 Bicycle pumps manufacturing
532292 Bicycle rental
811490 Bicycle repair and maintenance shops without retailing new bicycles
441221 Bicycle shops, motorized
423110 Bicycle, motorized, merchant wholesalers
423910 Bicycles (except motorized) merchant wholesalers
336991 Bicycles and parts manufacturing
327111 Bidets, vitreous china, manufacturing
561440 Bill collection services
541850 Billboard display advertising services
238990 Billboard erection
339950 Billboards manufacturing
333516 Billet mill machinery, metalworking, manufacturing
331111 Billets, steel, made in iron and steel mills
316993 Billfolds, all materials, manufacturing
339920 Billiard equipment and supplies manufacturing
423910 Billiard equipment and supplies merchant wholesalers
713990 Billiard parlors
713990 Billiard rooms
541219 Billing services
322130 Binder's board manufacturing
424120 Binders, looseleaf, merchant wholesalers
333293 Bindery machinery manufacturing
314999 Binding carpets and rugs for the trade
333313 Binding equipment (i.e., plastics or tape binding), office-type, manufacturing
424310 Binding, textile, merchant wholesalers
314999 Bindings, bias, made from purchased fabrics

313221 Bindings, narrow woven, manufacturing
713290 Bingo halls
713290 Bingo parlors
316991 Binocular cases manufacturing
333314 Binoculars manufacturing
423460 Binoculars merchant wholesalers
332313 Bins, fabricated metal plate work, manufacturing
332439 Bins, light gauge metal, manufacturing
423390 Bins, storage, merchant wholesalers
621498 Biofeedback centers and clinics, outpatient
339113 Biohazard protective clothing and accessories manufacturing
541380 Biological (except medical, veterinary) testing laboratories or services
541690 Biological consulting services
621511 Biological laboratories, diagnostic
424210 Biologicals and allied products merchant wholesalers
541712 Biology research and development laboratories or services (except biotechnology research and development)
334119 Biometrics system input device (e.g., retinal scan, iris pattern recognition, hand geometry) manufacturing
541711 Biotechnology research and development laboratories or service in botany
541711 Biotechnology research and development laboratories or services
541711 Biotechnology research and development laboratories or services in agriculture
541711 Biotechnology research and development laboratories or services in bacteriology
541711 Biotechnology research and development laboratories or services in biology

541711 Biotechnology research and development laboratories or services in chemical sciences

541711 Biotechnology research and development laboratories or services in entomology

541711 Biotechnology research and development laboratories or services in environmental science

541711 Biotechnology research and development laboratories or services in food science

541711 Biotechnology research and development laboratories or services in genetics

541711 Biotechnology research and development laboratories or services in health sciences

541711 Biotechnology research and development laboratories or services in industrial research

541711 Biotechnology research and development laboratories or services in the medical sciences

541711 Biotechnology research and development laboratories or services in the physical sciences

541711 Biotechnology research and development laboratories or services in the veterinary sciences

311119 Bird feed, prepared, manufacturing

112990 Bird production (e.g., canaries, love birds, parakeets, parrots)

561710 Bird proofing services

712190 Bird sanctuaries

621410 Birth control clinics

326299 Birth control devices (i.e., diaphragms, prophylactics) manufacturing

325412 Birth control pills manufacturing

311812 Biscuits, bread-type, made in commercial bakeries

331419 Bismuth refining, primary

112990 Bison production

333515 Bits and knives for metalworking lathes, planers, and shapers manufacturing

333515 Bits, drill, metalworking, manufacturing

332212 Bits, edge tool, woodworking, manufacturing

333120 Bits, rock drill, construction and surface mining-type, manufacturing

333132 Bits, rock drill, oil and gas field-type, manufacturing

333131 Bits, rock drill, underground mining-type, manufacturing

212111 Bituminous coal and lignite surface mine site development for own account

212111 Bituminous coal cleaning plants

212111 Bituminous coal crushing

213113 Bituminous coal mining services (except site preparation and related construction contractor activities) on a contract basis

212111 Bituminous coal or lignite beneficiating (e.g., cleaning, crushing, screening, washing)

213113 Bituminous coal or lignite surface mine site development (except site preparation and related construction contractor activities) on a contract basis

212111 Bituminous coal screening plants

212111 Bituminous coal stripping (except on a contract, fee, or other basis)

213113 Bituminous coal stripping service on a contract basis

212111 Bituminous coal surface mining and/or beneficiating

212112 Bituminous coal underground mine site development for own account

212112 Bituminous coal underground mining or mining and beneficiating

212111 Bituminous coal washeries

212319 Bituminous limestone mining and/or beneficiating

213113 Bituminous or lignite auger mining service on a contract basis

212319 Bituminous sandstone mining and/or beneficiating

325131 Black pigments (except carbon black, bone black, lamp black) manufacturing

423510 Black plate merchant wholesalers

111334 Blackberry farming

423490 Blackboards merchant wholesalers

339942 Blackboards, framed, manufacturing

327991 Blackboards, unframed, slate, manufacturing

331111 Blackplate made in iron and steel mills

316999 Blacksmith's aprons, leather, manufacturing

311312 Blackstrap invert made from purchased raw cane sugar

311311 Blackstrap molasses made in sugarcane mill

238990 Blacktop work, residential and commercial driveway and parking area

811310 Blade sharpening, commercial and industrial machinery and equipment

423710 Blades (e.g., knife, saw) merchant wholesalers

333120 Blades for graders, scrapers, bulldozers, and snowplows manufacturing

332211 Blades, knife and razor, manufacturing

424210 Blades, razor, merchant wholesalers

332213 Blades, saw, all types, manufacturing

325131 Blanc fixe (i.e., barium sulfate, precipitated) manufacturing

332992 Blank cartridges (i.e., 30 mm. or less, 1.18 inch or less) manufacturing

423690 Blank CDs and DVDs, merchant wholesalers

423690 Blank diskette merchant wholesalers

334613 Blank tapes, audio and video, manufacturing

423690 Blank tapes, audio and video, merchant wholesalers

323118 Blankbooks and refills manufacturing

424120 Blankbooks merchant wholesalers

314911 Blanket bags manufacturing

314129 Blankets (except electric) made from purchased fabrics or felts

423220 Blankets (except electric) merchant wholesalers

313210 Blankets and bedspreads made in broadwoven fabric mills

335211 Blankets, electric, manufacturing

423620 Blankets, electric, merchant wholesalers

313230 Blankets, nonwoven fabric, manufacturing

327212 Blanks for electric light bulbs, glass, made in glass making plants

333515 Blanks, cutting tool, manufacturing

327215 Blanks, ophthalmic lens and optical glass, made from purchased glass

327212 Blanks, ophthalmic lens and optical glass, made in glass making plants

321912 Blanks, wood (e.g., bowling pins, handles, textile machinery accessories), manufacturing

311411 Blast freezing on a contract basis

236210 Blast furnace construction

327992 Blast furnace slag processing

331111 Blast furnaces

238910 Blast hole drilling (except mining)

212322 Blast sand quarrying and/or beneficiating

325920 Blasting accessories (e.g., caps, fuses, ignitors, squibbs) manufacturing

325920	Blasting powders manufacturing
213113	Blasting services, coal mining, on a contract basis
213114	Blasting services, metal mining, on a contract basis
213115	Blasting services, nonmetallic minerals mining (except fuels) on a contract basis
238910	Blasting, building demolition
238910	Blasting, construction site
238390	Bleacher installation
337127	Bleacher seating manufacturing
424690	Bleaches merchant wholesalers
325612	Bleaches, formulated for household use, manufacturing
325188	Bleaching agents, inorganic, manufacturing
325199	Bleaching agents, organic, manufacturing
313311	Bleaching broadwoven fabrics
212325	Bleaching clay mining and/or beneficiating
333292	Bleaching machinery for textiles manufacturing
313312	Bleaching textile products, apparel, and fabrics (except broadwoven)
212231	Blende (zinc) mining and/or beneficiating
311211	Blended flour made in flour mills
335211	Blenders, household-type electric, manufacturing
325620	Blending and compounding perfume bases
311119	Blending animal feed
312130	Blending brandy
312140	Blending distilled beverages (except brandy)
312130	Blending wines
336411	Blimps (i.e., aircraft) manufacturing
337920	Blinds (e.g., mini, venetian, vertical), all materials, manufacturing
423220	Blinds and shades, window, merchant wholesalers
331411	Blister copper manufacturing
561910	Blister packaging services
333923	Block and tackle manufacturing
312113	Block ice manufacturing
324121	Blocks, asphalt paving, made from purchased asphaltic materials
327331	Blocks, concrete and cinder, manufacturing
327124	Blocks, fire clay, manufacturing
327212	Blocks, glass, made in glass making plants
321999	Blocks, tackle, wood, manufacturing
321999	Blocks, tailors' pressing wood, manufacturing
621511	Blood analysis laboratories
334516	Blood bank process equipment manufacturing
621991	Blood banks
325413	Blood derivative in-vitro diagnostic substances manufacturing
325414	Blood derivatives manufacturing
424210	Blood derivatives merchant wholesalers
621991	Blood donor stations
325414	Blood fractions manufacturing
325413	Blood glucose test kits manufacturing
424210	Blood plasma merchant wholesalers
339112	Blood pressure apparatus manufacturing
621999	Blood pressure screening facilities
621999	Blood pressure screening services
812990	Blood pressure testing machine concession operators, coin-operated
339113	Blood testing apparatus, laboratory-type, manufacturing
339112	Blood transfusion equipment manufacturing
333516	Blooming and slabbing mill machinery, metalworking, manufacturing
331111	Blooms, steel, made in iron and steel mills
315191	Blouses made in apparel knitting mills
315291	Blouses, infants', manufacturing

315212 Blouses, women's, girls', and infants', cut and sew apparel contractors

315232 Blouses, women's, misses', and girls', cut and sewn from purchased fabric (except apparel contractors)

335211 Blow dryers, household-type electric, manufacturing

333220 Blow molding machinery for plastics manufacturing

332212 Blow torches manufacturing

333412 Blower filter units manufacturing

238220 Blower or fan, cooling and dry heating, installation

333111 Blowers, forage, manufacturing

423830 Blowers, industrial, merchant wholesalers

333112 Blowers, leaf, manufacturing

238310 Blown-in insulation (e.g., cellulose, vermiculite) installation

221210 Blue gas, carbureted, production and distribution

111334 Blueberry farming

114111 Bluefish fishing

111998 Bluegrass-Kentucky seed farming

541340 Blueprint drafting services

333315 Blueprint equipment manufacturing

423420 Blueprinting equipment merchant wholesalers

561439 Blueprinting services

212311 Bluestone mining or quarrying

325620 Blushes, face, manufacturing

921130 Board of Governors, Federal Reserve

321219 Board, bagasse, manufacturing

327420 Board, gypsum, manufacturing

321219 Board, particle, manufacturing

115210 Boarding horses (except racehorses)

721310 Boarding houses

611110 Boarding schools, elementary or secondary

812910 Boarding services, pet

921120 Boards of supervisors, county and local

813910 Boards of trade

324122 Boards, asphalt saturated, made from purchased asphaltic materials

321999 Boards, bulletin, wood and cork, manufacturing

321999 Boards, wood (e.g., clip, ironing, meat, pastry), manufacturing

321113 Boards, wood, made from logs or bolts

321912 Boards, wood, resawing purchased lumber

336321 Boat and ship lighting fixtures manufacturing

441222 Boat dealers, new and used

541330 Boat engineering design services

484220 Boat hauling, truck, local

484230 Boat hauling, truck, long-distance

238990 Boat lift installation

333923 Boat lifts manufacturing

532411 Boat rental (except pleasure)

532411 Boat rental or leasing, commercial

532292 Boat rental, pleasure

332312 Boat sections, prefabricated metal, manufacturing

441222 Boat trailer dealers

336212 Boat transporter trailers, multi-unit, manufacturing

336214 Boat transporter trailers, single-unit, manufacturing

336612 Boat yards (i.e., boat manufacturing facilities)

487210 Boat, fishing charter, operation

811490 Boat, pleasure, repair and maintenance services without retailing new boats

713930 Boating clubs with marinas

713990 Boating clubs without marinas

423860 Boats (except pleasure) merchant wholesalers

336612 Boats (i.e., suitable or intended for personal use) manufacturing

336612 Boats, inflatable plastics (except toy-type), manufacturing

423910 Boats, pleasure (e.g., canoes, motorboats, sailboats), merchant wholesalers

321912 Bobbin blocks and blanks, wood, manufacturing

322214 Bobbins, fiber, made from purchased paperboard

333292 Bobbins, textile machinery, manufacturing

339920 Bobsleds manufacturing

812320 Bobtailers, laundry and drycleaning

713990 Boccie ball courts

423110 Bodies, motor vehicle, merchant wholesalers

713940 Body building studios, physical fitness

561612 Body guard services

811121 Body shops, automotive

315191 Body stockings made in apparel knitting mills

315212 Body stockings, women's, girls', and infants', cut and sew apparel contractors

315239 Body stockings, women's, misses', and girls', cut and sewn from purchased fabric (except apparel contractors)

332995 Bofors guns manufacturing

238290 Boiler and pipe insulation installation

332410 Boiler casings manufacturing

238220 Boiler chipping, cleaning and scaling

334513 Boiler controls, industrial, power, and marine-type, manufacturing

332919 Boiler couplings and drains, plumbing and heating-type, manufacturing

238290 Boiler covering installation

332911 Boiler gauge cocks, industrial-type, manufacturing

331210 Boiler tubes, wrought, made from purchased iron

238220 Boiler, heating, installation

423720 Boilers (e.g., heating, hot water, power, steam) merchant wholesalers

333414 Boilers, heating, manufacturing

332410 Boilers, power, manufacturing

311612 Bologna made from purchased carcasses

332722 Bolts, metal, manufacturing

326199 Bolts, nuts, and rivets, plastics, manufacturing

333924 Bomb lifts manufacturing

332993 Bomb loading and assembling plants

332993 Bombcluster adapters manufacturing

332993 Bombs manufacturing

523120 Bond brokerages

523110 Bond dealing (i.e., acting as a principal in dealing securities to investors)

322233 Bond paper made from purchased paper

322121 Bond paper made in paper mills

493190 Bonded warehousing (except farm products, general merchandise, refrigerated)

493130 Bonded warehousing, farm products (except refrigerated)

493110 Bonded warehousing, general merchandise

493120 Bonded warehousing, refrigerated

313230 Bonded-fiber fabrics manufacturing

332812 Bonderizing metal and metal products for the trade

524126 Bonding, fidelity or surety insurance, direct

812990 Bondsperson services

325182 Bone black manufacturing

327112 Bone china manufacturing

339112 Bone drills manufacturing

311119 Bone meal prepared as feed for animals and fowls

339999 Bone novelties manufacturing

339112 Bone plates and screws manufacturing

339112 Bone rongeurs manufacturing

311613 Bones, fat, rendering

511130 Book (e.g., hardback, paperback, tape) publishers (except exclusive Internet publishing)

323121 Book binding shops

323121 Book binding without printing
454113 Book clubs, not publishing, mail-order
813410 Book discussion clubs
332999 Book ends, metal, manufacturing
322222 Book paper made by coating purchased paper
322222 Book paper, coated, made from purchased paper
322121 Book paper, coated, made in paper mills
511130 Book publishers and printing combined
519130 Book publishers, exclusively on Internet
511130 Book publishers, university press (except exclusive Internet publishing)
451211 Book stores
453310 Book stores, used
316110 Bookbinder's leather manufacturing
333293 Bookbinding machines manufacturing
323121 Bookbinding without printing
337125 Bookcases (except wood and metal), household-type, manufacturing
337214 Bookcases (except wood), office-type, manufacturing
337124 Bookcases, metal household-type, manufacturing
337122 Bookcases, wood household-type, manufacturing
337211 Bookcases, wood office-type, manufacturing
713290 Bookies
512199 Booking agencies, motion picture
512199 Booking agencies, motion picture or video productions
711320 Booking agencies, theatrical (except motion picture)
541219 Bookkeepers' offices
541219 Bookkeepers' private practices
423420 Bookkeeping machines merchant wholesalers
541219 Bookkeeping services
713290 Bookmakers

519120 Bookmobiles
424920 Books merchant wholesalers
323117 Books printing and binding without publishing
323117 Books printing without publishing
424120 Books, sales or receipt, merchant wholesalers
323116 Books, sales, manifold, printing
339920 Boomerangs manufacturing
813410 Booster clubs
486990 Booster pumping station (except natural gas, petroleum)
486110 Booster pumping station, crude oil transportation
486210 Booster pumping station, natural gas transportation
486910 Booster pumping station, refined petroleum products transportation
332993 Boosters and bursters, artillery, manufacturing
335311 Boosters, feeder voltage (i.e., electrical transformers), manufacturing
423850 Boot and shoe cut stock and findings merchant wholesalers
316999 Boot and shoe cut stock and findings, leather, manufacturing
321999 Boot and shoe lasts, all materials, manufacturing
623990 Boot camps for delinquent youth
333298 Boot making and repairing machinery manufacturing
811430 Boot repair shops without retailing new boots
812990 Bootblack parlors
424340 Boots (e.g., hiking, western, work) merchant wholesalers
316219 Boots, dress and casual (except plastics, rubber), children's and infants', manufacturing
316213 Boots, dress and casual (except plastics, rubber), men's, manufacturing
316214 Boots, dress and casual (except plastics, rubber), women's, manufacturing

316219	Boots, hiking (except rubber, plastics), children's and infants', manufacturing
316213	Boots, hiking (except rubber, plastics), men's, manufacturing
316214	Boots, hiking (except rubber, plastics), women's, manufacturing
316211	Boots, plastics or plastics soled fabric upper, manufacturing
316211	Boots, rubber or rubber soled fabric upper, manufacturing
212391	Borate, natural, mining and/or beneficiating
325188	Borax (i.e., sodium borate) manufacturing
212391	Borax, crude, ground or pulverized, mining and/or beneficiating
325320	Bordeaux mixture insecticides manufacturing
325188	Boric acid manufacturing
333512	Boring machines, metalworking, manufacturing
213114	Boring test holes for metal mining on a contract basis
213115	Boring test holes for nonmetallic minerals mining (except fuels) on a contract basis
333512	Boring, drilling, and milling machine combinations, metalworking, manufacturing
238910	Boring, for building construction
212391	Boron compounds prepared at beneficiating plants
325188	Boron compounds, not specified elsewhere by process, manufacturing
212391	Boron mineral mining and/or beneficiating
325188	Borosilicate manufacturing
424210	Botanical drugs and herbs merchant wholesalers
325412	Botanical extract preparations (except in-vitro diagnostics) manufacturing
712130	Botanical gardens

325320	Botanical insecticides manufacturing
424210	Botanicals merchant wholesalers
541712	Botany research and development laboratories or services (except biotechnology research and development)
326199	Bottle caps and lids, plastics, manufacturing
332115	Bottle caps and tops, metal, stamping
321999	Bottle corks manufacturing
321999	Bottle covers, willow, rattan, and reed, manufacturing
561990	Bottle exchanges
335211	Bottle warmers, household-type electric, manufacturing
333993	Bottle washers, packaging machinery, manufacturing
454312	Bottled gas dealers, direct selling
424490	Bottled water (except water treating) merchant wholesalers
454390	Bottled water providers, direct selling
423840	Bottles (except waste) merchant wholesalers
327213	Bottles (i.e., bottling, canning, packaging), glass, manufacturing
326160	Bottles, plastics, manufacturing
332439	Bottles, vacuum, light gauge metal, manufacturing
423930	Bottles, waste, merchant wholesalers
333993	Bottling machinery (e.g., capping, filling, labeling, sterilizing, washing) manufacturing
423830	Bottling machinery and equipment merchant wholesalers
335121	Boudoir lamp fixtures manufacturing
311422	Bouillon canning
311423	Bouillon made in dehydration plants
212319	Boulder crushed and broken mining and/or beneficiating

324199 Boulets (i.e., fuel bricks) made from refined petroleum

424590 Bovine semen merchant wholesalers

315211 Bow ties, men's and boys', cut and sew apparel contractors

315993 Bow ties, men's and boys', cut and sewn from purchased fabric (except apparel contractors)

238290 Bowling alley equipment installation

713950 Bowling alleys

337127 Bowling center furniture manufacturing

713950 Bowling centers

423910 Bowling equipment and supplies merchant wholesalers

451110 Bowling equipment and supply stores

611620 Bowling instruction

713990 Bowling leagues or teams, recreational

321912 Bowling pin blanks manufacturing

339920 Bowling pin machines, automatic, manufacturing

326199 Bowls and bowl covers, plastics, manufacturing

321999 Bowls, wood, turned and shaped, manufacturing

314999 Bows made from purchased fabrics

339920 Bows, archery, manufacturing

316999 Bows, shoe, leather, manufacturing

321920 Box cleats, wood, manufacturing

311991 Box lunches (for sale off premises) manufacturing

321920 Box shook manufacturing

337910 Box springs, assembled, made from purchased spring

316999 Box toes (i.e., shoe cut stock), leather, manufacturing

311612 Boxed beef made from purchased carcasses

311611 Boxed beef produced in slaughtering plants

311612 Boxed meat produced from purchased carcasses

311611 Boxed meats produced in slaughtering plants

711219 Boxers, independent professional

423840 Boxes and crates, industrial (except disposable plastics, paperboard, waste), merchant wholesalers

321920 Boxes, cigar, wood or part wood, manufacturing

322211 Boxes, corrugated and solid fiber, made from purchased paper or paperboard

335932 Boxes, electrical wiring (e.g., junction, outlet, switch), manufacturing

322212 Boxes, folding (except corrugated), made from purchased paperboard

316991 Boxes, hat (except paper or paperboard), manufacturing

321920 Boxes, jewelry, wood or part wood, manufacturing

316999 Boxes, leather, manufacturing

332439 Boxes, light gauge metal, manufacturing

424130 Boxes, paperboard and disposable plastics, merchant wholesalers

322215 Boxes, sanitary food (except folding), made from purchased paper or paperboard

322213 Boxes, setup (i.e., not shipped flat), made from purchased paperboard

322211 Boxes, shipping, laminated paper and paperboard, made from purchased paperboard

336211 Boxes, truck (e.g., cargo, dump, utility, van), assembled on purchased chassis

423930 Boxes, waste, merchant wholesalers

321920 Boxes, wood, manufacturing

321920 Boxes, wood, plain or fabric covered, nailed or lock corner, manufacturing

711211	Boxing clubs, professional or semiprofessional
713990	Boxing clubs, recreational
339920	Boxing equipment manufacturing
711310	Boxing event managers with facilities
711320	Boxing event managers without facilities
711310	Boxing event organizers with facilities
711320	Boxing event organizers without facilities
711310	Boxing event promoters with facilities
711320	Boxing event promoters without facilities
337215	Boxspring frames manufacturing
813410	Boy guiding organizations
623990	Boys' and girls' residential facilities (e.g., homes, ranches, villages)
721214	Boys' camps (except day, instructional)
611620	Boys' camps, sports instruction
611620	Boys' camps, sports instructor
713990	Boys' day camps (except instructional)
315119	Boys' socks manufacturing
111334	Boysenberry farming
339911	Bracelets, precious metal, manufacturing
115112	Bracing of orchard trees and vines
332510	Brackets (i.e., builder's hardware-type), metal, manufacturing
332618	Brackets made from purchased wire
321918	Brackets, wood, manufacturing
423710	Brads merchant wholesalers
331222	Brads, iron or steel, wire or cut, made in wire drawing plants
332618	Brads, metal, made from purchased wire
333292	Braiding machinery for textiles manufacturing
313221	Braiding narrow fabrics

336340	Brake and brake parts, automotive, truck, and bus, manufacturing
336340	Brake caliper assemblies, automotive, truck, and bus, manufacturing
336340	Brake cylinders, master and wheel, automotive, truck, and bus, manufacturing
336340	Brake discs (rotor), automotive, truck, and bus, manufacturing
336340	Brake drums, automotive, truck, and bus, manufacturing
325998	Brake fluid, synthetic, manufacturing
324191	Brake fluids, petroleum, made from refined petroleum
336340	Brake hose assemblies manufacturing
336340	Brake pads and shoes, automotive, truck, and bus, manufacturing
811118	Brake repair shops, automotive
333319	Brake service equipment (except mechanic's hand tools), motor vehicle, manufacturing
336340	Brake shoes and pads, asbestos, manufacturing
335314	Brakes and clutches, electromagnetic, manufacturing
336510	Brakes and parts for railroad rolling stock manufacturing
335314	Brakes, electromagnetic, manufacturing
333513	Brakes, press, metalworking, manufacturing
311212	Bran and other residues of milling rice
522110	Branches of foreign banks
521110	Branches, Federal Reserve Bank
533110	Brand name licensing
115210	Branding
339943	Branding irons (i.e., marking irons) manufacturing
424820	Brandy and brandy spirits merchant wholesalers
312130	Brandy distilling

315212	Bra-slips, women's and girls', cut and sew apparel contractors
315231	Bra-slips, women's, misses', and juniors', cut and sewn from purchased fabric (except apparel contractors)
331522	Brass die-castings, unfinished, manufacturing
331525	Brass foundries (except die-casting)
423720	Brass goods, plumbers', merchant wholesalers
325612	Brass polishes manufacturing
331421	Brass products, rolling, drawing, or extruding, made from purchased copper or in integrated secondary smelting and rolling, drawing or extruding plants
315212	Brassieres cut and sew apparel contractors
315231	Brassieres cut and sewn from purchased fabric (except apparel contractors)
332323	Brasswork, ornamental, manufacturing
335221	Braziers, barbecue, manufacturing
111335	Brazil nut farming
325191	Brazilwood extract manufacturing
332811	Brazing (i.e., hardening) metals and metal products for the trade
311822	Bread and bread-type roll mixes made from purchased flour
311812	Bread and bread-type rolls made in commercial bakeries
311999	Bread crumbs not made in bakeries
335211	Bread machines, household-type electric, manufacturing
333294	Bread slicing machinery manufacturing
333993	Bread wrapping machines manufacturing
212113	Breakers, anthracite mining and/or beneficiating
333131	Breakers, coal, manufacturing

332919	Breakers, vacuum, plumbing, manufacturing
311340	Breakfast bars, nonchocolate covered, manufacturing
311230	Breakfast cereals manufacturing
424490	Breakfast cereals merchant wholesalers
237990	Breakwater construction
332313	Breechings, fabricated metal plate work, manufacturing
112990	Breeding of pets (e.g., birds, cats, dogs)
115210	Breeding, animal, services
312120	Breweries
311211	Brewers' and distillers' flakes and grits, corn, manufacturing
311213	Brewers' malt manufacturing
325191	Brewers' pitch made by distillation of wood
311212	Brewers' rice manufacturing
424490	Brewers' yeast merchant wholesalers
333294	Brewery machinery manufacturing
238990	Brick driveway contractors
238990	Brick paver (e.g., driveways, patios, sidewalks) installation
238140	Brick veneer, installation
238140	Bricklaying contractors
423320	Bricks (except refractory) merchant wholesalers
327121	Bricks (i.e., common, face, glazed, hollow, vitrified), clay, manufacturing
327123	Bricks, adobe, manufacturing
327124	Bricks, clay refractory, manufacturing
327331	Bricks, concrete, manufacturing
327215	Bricks, glass, made from purchased glass
327212	Bricks, glass, made in glass making plants
327125	Bricks, nonclay refractory, manufacturing
315233	Bridal dresses or gowns, custom made
315233	Bridal dresses or gowns, women's, misses', and girls', cut and sewn from purchased fabric (except apparel contractors)

315212	Bridal dresses or gowns, women's, misses', and juniors', apparel contractors
448190	Bridal gown shops (except custom)
532220	Bridal wear rental
333999	Bridge and gate lifting machinery manufacturing
611699	Bridge and other card game instruction
321114	Bridge and trestle parts, wood, treating
237310	Bridge approach construction
713990	Bridge clubs, recreational
237310	Bridge construction
237310	Bridge decking construction
238320	Bridge painting
332312	Bridge sections, prefabricated metal, manufacturing
488490	Bridge, tunnel, and highway operations
339116	Bridges, custom made in dental laboratories
334515	Bridges, electrical (e.g., Kelvin, megohm, vacuum tube, Wheatstone), manufacturing
316110	Bridle leather manufacturing
237990	Bridle path construction
316991	Briefcases, all materials, manufacturing
315291	Briefs, infants', cut and sewn from purchased fabric (except apparel contractors)
315192	Briefs, underwear, made in apparel knitting mills
315211	Briefs, underwear, men's and boys', cut and sew apparel contractors
315221	Briefs, underwear, men's and boys', cut and sewn from purchased fabric (except apparel contractors)
315231	Briefs, underwear, women's, misses', and girls', cut and sewn from purchased fabric (except apparel contractors)
315212	Briefs, women's, girls', and infants', cut and sew apparel contractors

212393	Brimstone mining and/or beneficiating
311421	Brining of fruits and vegetables
212210	Briquets, iron, mining and/or beneficiating
324199	Briquettes, petroleum, made from refined petroleum
424590	Bristles merchant wholesalers
322130	Bristols board stock manufacturing
322121	Bristols paper stock manufacturing
333515	Broaches (i.e., a machine tool accessory) manufacturing
333512	Broaching machines, metalworking, manufacturing
334220	Broadcast equipment (including studio), for radio and television, manufacturing
541910	Broadcast media rating services
423690	Broadcasting equipment merchant wholesalers
519130	Broadcasting exclusively on Internet, audio
519130	Broadcasting exclusively on Internet, video
515111	Broadcasting networks, radio
515120	Broadcasting networks, television
611519	Broadcasting schools
236220	Broadcasting station construction
515112	Broadcasting stations (except exclusively on Internet), radio
515120	Broadcasting stations, television
515112	Broadcasting studio, radio station
711110	Broadway theaters
313210	Broadwoven fabrics (except rugs, tire fabrics) weaving
313311	Broadwoven fabrics finishing
313210	Brocades weaving
111219	Broccoli farming, field, bedding plant and seed production
112320	Broiler chicken production
523140	Brokerages, commodity contracts
524210	Brokerages, insurance
522310	Brokerages, loan
522310	Brokerages, mortgage

531210 Brokerages, real estate
523120 Brokerages, securities
524210 Brokers' offices, insurance
522310 Brokers' offices, loan
522310 Brokers' offices, mortgage
531210 Brokers' offices, real estate
325188 Bromine manufacturing
325199 Bromochloromethane manufacturing
339112 Bronchoscopes (except electromedical) manufacturing
334510 Bronchoscopes, electromedical, manufacturing
331522 Bronze die-castings, unfinished, manufacturing
331525 Bronze foundries (except die-casting)
325910 Bronze printing inks manufacturing
331421 Bronze products, rolling, drawing, or extruding, made from purchased copper or in integrated secondary smelting and rolling, drawing or extruding plants
111199 Broomcorn farming
424590 Broomcorn merchant wholesalers
423220 Brooms and brushes, household-type, merchant wholesalers
339994 Brooms, hand and machine, manufacturing
311422 Broth (except seafood) canning
311313 Brown beet sugar refining
212111 Brown coal mining and/or beneficiating
212210 Brown ore mining and/or beneficiating
311313 Brown sugar made from beet sugar
311312 Brown sugar made from purchased raw cane sugar
311311 Brown sugar made in sugarcane mill
325411 Brucine manufacturing
212325 Brucite mining and/or beneficiating
335991 Brush blocks, carbon or molded graphite, manufacturing

321912 Brush blocks, wood, turned and shaped
562119 Brush collection services
562119 Brush hauling, local
562119 Brush removal services
335991 Brushes and brush stock contacts, electric, carbon and graphite, manufacturing
339942 Brushes, artists', manufacturing
339994 Brushes, household-type and industrial, manufacturing
339994 Brushes, paint (except artists'), manufacturing
326299 Brushes, rubber, manufacturing
333512 Brushing machines, metalworking, manufacturing
335991 Brushplates, carbon or graphite, manufacturing
111219 Brussel sprout farming, field, bedding plant and seed production
325620 Bubble bath preparations manufacturing
326199 Bubble packaging materials, plastics, manufacturing
333120 Bucket and scarifier teeth manufacturing
333922 Buckets, elevator or conveyor, manufacturing
333120 Buckets, excavating (e.g., clamshell, concrete, drag scraper, dragline, shovel), manufacturing
321920 Buckets, wood, coopered, manufacturing
339993 Buckles and buckle parts (including shoe) manufacturing
111199 Buckwheat farming
311211 Buckwheat flour manufacturing
921130 Budget agencies, government
112990 Buffalo production
722212 Buffet eating places
337122 Buffets (furniture), wood, manufacturing
333512 Buffing and polishing machines, metalworking, manufacturing
327910 Buffing and polishing wheels, abrasive and nonabrasive, manufacturing

325612 Buffing compounds manufacturing

333991 Buffing machines, handheld power-driven, manufacturing

332813 Buffing metals and metal products for the trade

316110 Buffings, russet, manufacturing

332510 Builder's hardware, metal, manufacturing

541310 Building architectural design services

238210 Building automation system installation contractors

423320 Building blocks (e.g., cinder, concrete) merchant wholesalers

423310 Building board (e.g., fiber, flake, particle) merchant wholesalers

561720 Building cleaning services, interior

561720 Building cleaning services, janitorial

238910 Building demolition

561790 Building exterior cleaning services (except sand blasting, window cleaning)

238390 Building fixture and fitting (except mechanical equipment) installation

238130 Building framing (except structural steel)

541350 Building inspection bureaus

541350 Building inspection services

926150 Building inspections, government

238310 Building insulation contractors

237210 Building lot subdividing

326199 Building materials (e.g., fascia, panels, siding, soffit), plastics, manufacturing

444190 Building materials supply dealers

423390 Building materials, fiberglass (except insulation, roofing, siding), merchant wholesalers

213112 Building oil and gas well foundations on a contract basis

326199 Building panels, corrugated and flat, plastics, manufacturing

423390 Building paper merchant wholesalers

322121 Building paper stock manufacturing

334512 Building services monitoring controls, automatic, manufacturing

925110 Building standards agencies, government

423320 Building stone merchant wholesalers

327121 Building tile, clay, manufacturing

531110 Building, apartment, rental or leasing

213112 Building, erecting, repairing, and dismantling oil and gas field rigs and derricks on a contract basis

531120 Building, nonresidential (except miniwarehouse), rental or leasing

236118 Building, residential, addition, alteration and renovation

531110 Building, residential, rental or leasing

321991 Buildings, mobile, commercial use, manufacturing

332311 Buildings, prefabricated metal, manufacturing

423390 Buildings, prefabricated nonwood, merchant wholesalers

423310 Buildings, prefabricated wood, merchant wholesalers

321992 Buildings, prefabricated, wood, manufacturing

238350 Built-in wood cabinets constructed on site

327999 Built-up mica manufacturing

335110 Bulbs, electric light, complete, manufacturing

311211 Bulgur (flour) manufacturing

424710 Bulk gasoline stations

484220 Bulk liquids trucking, local

484230 Bulk liquids trucking, long-distance

484110 Bulk mail truck transportation, contract, local
484121 Bulk mail truck transportation, contract, long-distance (TL)
493190 Bulk petroleum storage
424710 Bulk stations, petroleum
332420 Bulk storage tanks, heavy gauge metal, manufacturing
237990 Bulkhead wall or embarkment construction
115210 Bull testing stations
532412 Bulldozer rental or leasing without operator
238910 Bulldozer rental with operator
333120 Bulldozers manufacturing
332992 Bullet jackets and cores (i.e., 30 mm. or less, 1.18 inch or less) manufacturing
321999 Bulletin boards, wood and cork, manufacturing
339113 Bulletproof vests manufacturing
212221 Bullion, gold, produced at the mine
212222 Bullion, silver, produced at the mine
336399 Bumpers and bumperettes assembled, automotive, truck, and bus, manufacturing
333313 Bundling machinery (e.g., box strapping, mail, newspaper) manufacturing
321999 Bungs, wood, manufacturing
236220 Bunkhouse construction
339113 Bunsen burners manufacturing
315212 Buntings, infants', cut and sew apparel contractors
315291 Buntings, infants', cut and sewn from purchased fabric (except apparel contractors)
334513 Buoyancy instruments, industrial process-type, manufacturing
321999 Buoys, cork, manufacturing
332313 Buoys, fabricated plate work metal, manufacturing
561621 Burglar alarm monitoring services
561621 Burglar alarm sales combined with installation, repair, or monitoring services

238210 Burglar alarm system, electric, installation only
334290 Burglar alarm systems and equipment manufacturing
524126 Burglary and theft insurance carriers, direct
339995 Burial caskets and cases manufacturing
423850 Burial caskets merchant wholesalers
315299 Burial garments cut and sewn from purchased fabric (except apparel contractors)
315211 Burial garments, men's and boys', cut and sew apparel contractors
315212 Burial garments, women's, girls' and infants', cut and sew apparel contractors
524128 Burial insurance carriers, direct
339995 Burial vaults (except concrete, stone) manufacturing
327390 Burial vaults, concrete and precast terrazzo, manufacturing
327991 Burial vaults, stone, manufacturing
424990 Burlap merchant wholesalers
711110 Burlesque companies
212325 Burley mining and/or beneficiating
313311 Burling and mending broadwoven fabrics
313312 Burling and mending fabrics (except broadwoven)
335311 Burner ignition transformers manufacturing
423720 Burners, fuel oil and distillate oil, merchant wholesalers
333414 Burners, heating, manufacturing
332811 Burning metals and metal products for the trade
333512 Burnishing machines, metalworking, manufacturing
321999 Burnt wood articles manufacturing
314999 Burnt-out laces manufacturing
112920 Burro production
212399 Burrstones, natural, mining and/or beneficiating

335313	Bus bar structures, switchgear-type, manufacturing
335931	Bus bars, electrical conductors (except switchgear-type), manufacturing
336211	Bus bodies assembling on purchased chassis
336211	Bus bodies manufacturing
541850	Bus card advertising services
485510	Bus charter services (except scenic, sightseeing)
541850	Bus display advertising services
611519	Bus driver training
485210	Bus line operation, intercity
485113	Bus line, local (except mixed mode)
423110	Bus merchant wholesalers
485410	Bus operation, school and employee
532120	Bus rental or leasing
485113	Bus services, urban and suburban (except mixed mode)
236220	Bus shelter construction
236220	Bus terminal construction
488490	Bus terminal operation, independent
561599	Bus ticket offices
485113	Bus transit systems (except mixed mode)
336120	Buses (except trackless trolley) assembling on chassis of own manufacture
487110	Buses, scenic and sightseeing operation
336510	Buses, trackless trolley, manufacturing
333613	Bushings, plain (except internal combustion engine), manufacturing
326199	Bushings, plastics, manufacturing
321999	Bushings, wood, manufacturing
813910	Business associations
541990	Business brokers (except real estate brokers)
611410	Business colleges or schools not offering academic degrees
611310	Business colleges or schools offering baccalaureate or graduate degrees

323112	Business directories flexographic printing without publishing
323111	Business directories gravure printing without publishing
323110	Business directories lithographic (offset) printing without publishing
323119	Business directories printing (except flexographic, gravure, lithographic, quick, screen) without publishing
323113	Business directories screen printing without publishing
511140	Business directory publishers (except exclusive Internet publishing)
511140	Business directory publishers and printing combined
519130	Business directory publishers, exclusively on Internet
323112	Business forms (except manifold) flexographic printing without publishing
323111	Business forms (except manifold) gravure printing without publishing
323110	Business forms (except manifold) lithographic printing
323119	Business forms (except manifold) printing (except flexographic, gravure, lithographic, quick, screen) without publishing
323113	Business forms (except manifold) screen printing without publishing
323116	Business forms, manifold, printing
423420	Business machines and equipment (except computers) merchant wholesalers
541611	Business management consulting services
561110	Business management services
541720	Business research and development services
611410	Business schools not offering academic degrees

561439 Business service centers (except private mail centers)
561439 Business service centers (except private mail centers) providing range of office support services (except printing)
541611 Business start-up consulting services
425110 Business to business electronic markets, durable goods, wholesale trade
425110 Business to business electronic markets, nondurable goods, wholesale trade
454111 Business to Consumer retail sales Internet sites
325211 Butadiene copolymers containing less than 50 percent butadiene manufacturing
325212 Butadiene copolymers containing more than 50 percent butadiene manufacturing
325199 Butadiene made from alcohol
325110 Butadiene made from refined petroleum or liquid hydrocarbons
325212 Butadiene rubber (i.e., polybutadiene) manufacturing
325110 Butane made from refined petroleum or liquid hydrocarbons
211112 Butane, natural, mining
445210 Butcher shops
332211 Butcher's knives manufacturing
311512 Butter manufacturing
424430 Butter merchant wholesalers
333294 Butter processing machinery manufacturing
311512 Butter, creamery and whey, manufacturing
332911 Butterfly valves, industrial-type, manufacturing
311511 Buttermilk manufacturing
111219 Butternut squash farming, field, bedding plant and seed production
335912 Button cells, primary batteries, manufacturing

333298 Buttonhole and eyelet machinery manufacturing
315211 Buttonhole making apparel contractors, men's and boys'
315212 Buttonhole making apparel contractors, women's, misses', girls', and infants' (except fur)
315212 Buttonhole making, fur goods, women's, girls', and infants', cut and sew apparel contractors
315211 Buttonholing and button covering apparel contractors, men's and boys'
315212 Buttonholing and button covering apparel contractors, women's, misses', and girls'
339993 Buttons (except precious metal, precious stones, semiprecious stones) manufacturing
339911 Buttons, precious metal, precious stones, semiprecious stones, manufacturing
325199 Butyl acetate manufacturing
325212 Butyl rubber manufacturing
324110 Butylene (i.e., butene) made in petroleum refineries
325110 Butylene made from refined petroleum or liquid hydrocarbons
531210 Buyers' agents, real estate, offices
531210 Buying agencies, real estate
531210 Buying real estate for others (i.e., agents, brokers)
485310 Cab (i.e., taxi) services
336112 Cab and chassis, light trucks and vans, manufacturing
111219 Cabbage farming, field, bedding plant and seed production
236115 Cabin construction general contractors
336612 Cabin cruiser
334511 Cabin environment indicators, transmitters, and sensors manufacturing
236117 Cabin operative builders
332510 Cabinet hardware, metal, manufacturing

444190 Cabinet stores, kitchen (except custom), to be installed
238350 Cabinet work performed at the construction site
238350 Cabinetry work performed at the construction site
337214 Cabinets (except wood), office-type, freestanding, manufacturing
337129 Cabinets (i.e., housings), wood (e.g., sewing machines, stereo, television), manufacturing
337110 Cabinets, kitchen (except freestanding), stock or custom wood, manufacturing
423310 Cabinets, kitchen, built in, merchant wholesalers
423210 Cabinets, kitchen, free standing, merchant wholesalers
337124 Cabinets, metal (i.e., bathroom, kitchen) (except freestanding), manufacturing
337124 Cabinets, metal household-type, freestanding, manufacturing
337124 Cabinets, metal, radio and television, manufacturing
238350 Cabinets, wood built-in, constructed on site
337122 Cabinets, wood household-type, freestanding, manufacturing
337211 Cabinets, wood office-type, freestanding, manufacturing
721199 Cabins, housekeeping
515210 Cable broadcasting networks
485119 Cable car systems (except mixed mode), commuter
487110 Cable car, land, scenic and sightseeing operation
334220 Cable decoders manufacturing
237130 Cable laying (e.g., cable television, electricity, marine, telephone), including underground
517110 Cable program distribution operators
238990 Cable splicing (except electrical or fiber optic)
238210 Cable splicing, electrical or fiber optic

517110 Cable television distribution services
238210 Cable television hookup contractors
515210 Cable television networks
334220 Cable television transmission and receiving equipment manufacturing
517110 Cable TV providers (except networks)
331422 Cable, copper (e.g., armored, bare, insulated), made from purchased copper in wire drawing plants
331422 Cable, copper (e.g., armored, bare, insulated), made in integrated secondary smelting and wire drawing plants
331222 Cable, iron or steel, insulated or armored, made in wire drawing plants
335929 Cable, nonferrous, insulated, or armored, made from purchased nonferrous wire
332618 Cable, noninsulated wire, made from purchased wire
423510 Cable, wire (except insulated), merchant wholesalers
333111 Cabs for agricultural machinery manufacturing
333120 Cabs for construction machinery manufacturing
333924 Cabs for industrial trucks manufacturing
111339 Cactus fruit farming
541512 CAD (computer-aided design) systems integration design services
541370 Cadastral surveying services
339920 Caddy carts manufacturing
331419 Cadmium refining, primary
541512 CAE (computer-aided engineering) systems integration design services
337215 Cafeteria fixtures manufacturing
722310 Cafeteria food services contractors (e.g., government office cafeterias, hospital cafeterias, school cafeterias)

337127 Cafeteria furniture manufacturing
337127 Cafeteria tables and benches manufacturing
722212 Cafeterias
325411 Caffeine and derivatives (i.e., basic chemicals) manufacturing
315291 Caftans, infants', cut and sewn from purchased fabric (except apparel contractors)
315211 Caftans, men's and boys', cut and sew apparel contractors
315223 Caftans, men's and boys', cut and sewn from purchased fabric (except apparel contractors)
315212 Caftans, women's, girls', and infants', cut and sew apparel contractors
315231 Caftans, women's, misses' and girls', cut and sewn from purchased fabric (except apparel contractors)
332618 Cages made from purchased wire
238910 Caisson (i.e., drilled building foundations) construction
237990 Caisson (i.e., marine or pneumatic structures) construction
332420 Caissons, underwater work, heavy gauge metal, manufacturing
311999 Cake frosting manufacturing
311822 Cake mixes made from purchased flour
311340 Cake ornaments, confectionery, manufacturing
311813 Cake, frozen, manufacturing
311812 Cakes, baking (except frozen), made in commercial bakeries
212231 Calamine mining and/or beneficiating
212221 Calaverite mining and/or beneficiating
212312 Calcareous tufa crushed and broken stone mining and/or beneficiating

212311 Calcareous tufa mining or quarrying
325510 Calcimines manufacturing
424950 Calcimines, merchant wholesalers
212392 Calcined phosphate rock mining and/or beneficiating
324199 Calcining petroleum coke from refined petroleum
212399 Calcite mining and/or beneficiating
325188 Calcium carbide, chloride, and hypochlorite manufacturing
325199 Calcium citrate manufacturing
327410 Calcium hydroxide (i.e., hydrated lime) manufacturing
325188 Calcium hypochlorite manufacturing
325188 Calcium inorganic compounds, not specified elsewhere by process, manufacturing
325199 Calcium organic compounds, not specified elsewhere by process, manufacturing
325199 Calcium oxalate manufacturing
327410 Calcium oxide (i.e., quicklime) manufacturing
423420 Calculators and calculating machines merchant wholesalers
333313 Calculators manufacturing
511199 Calendar publishers (except exclusive Internet publishing)
511199 Calendar publishers and printing combined
519130 Calendar publishers, exclusively on Internet
453998 Calendar shops
323112 Calendars flexographic printing without publishing
323111 Calendars gravure printing without publishing
323110 Calendars lithographic (offset) printing without publishing
323119 Calendars printing (except flexographic, digital, lithographic, gravure, quick, screen) without publishing
323113 Calendars screen printing without publishing

313311	Calendering broadwoven fabrics
333220	Calendering machinery for plastics manufacturing
333292	Calendering machinery for textiles manufacturing
313312	Calendering textile products, apparel, and fabrics (except broadwoven)
112111	Calf (e.g., feeder, stocker, veal) production
315119	Calf high sheer hosiery knitting or knitting and finishing
541380	Calibration and certification testing laboratories or services
332212	Calipers and dividers, machinists' precision tools, manufacturing
336340	Calipers, brake, automotive, truck, and bus, manufacturing
339992	Calliopes (steam organs) manufacturing
541512	CAM (computer-aided manufacturing) systems integration design services
532210	Camcorder rental
334310	Camcorders manufacturing
326211	Camelback (i.e., retreading material) manufacturing
333220	Camelback (i.e., retreading materials) machinery manufacturing
316991	Camera carrying bags, all materials, manufacturing
423410	Camera equipment and supplies, photographic, merchant wholesalers
333314	Camera lenses manufacturing
811211	Camera repair shops without retailing new cameras
443130	Camera shops, photographic
423410	Camera, television, merchant wholesalers
423410	Camera, video (except household-type) merchant wholesalers
711510	Cameramen, independent (freelance)
333315	Cameras (except digital, television, video) manufacturing

334220	Cameras, television, manufacturing
315212	Camisoles, women's and girls', cut and sew apparel contractors
315231	Camisoles, women's, misses' and girls', cut and sewn from purchased fabric (except apparel contractors)
337124	Camp furniture, metal, manufacturing
337125	Camp furniture, reed and rattan, manufacturing
337122	Camp furniture, wood, manufacturing
813940	Campaign organizations, political
441210	Camper dealers, recreational
532120	Camper rental
336214	Camper units, slide-in, for pick-up trucks, manufacturing
721211	Campgrounds
325191	Camphor, natural, manufacturing
325199	Camphor, synthetic, manufacturing
423910	Camping equipment and supplies merchant wholesalers
423110	Camping trailer merchant wholesalers
336214	Camping trailers and chassis manufacturing
721214	Camps (except day, instructional)
713990	Camps (except instructional), day
623990	Camps, boot or disciplinary (except correctional), for delinquent youth
611620	Camps, sports instruction
333515	Cams (i.e., a machine tool accessory) manufacturing
333513	Can forming machines, metalworking, manufacturing
332618	Can keys made from purchased wire
332431	Can lids and ends, light gauge metal, manufacturing
332212	Can openers (except electric) manufacturing

335211 Can openers, household-type electric, manufacturing
483211 Canal barge transportation (freight)
237990 Canal construction
488310 Canal maintenance services (except dredging)
488310 Canal operation
483212 Canal passenger transportation
221310 Canal, irrigation
333313 Canceling machinery, postal office-type, manufacturing
923120 Cancer detection program administration
622310 Cancer hospitals
311340 Candied fruits and fruit peel manufacturing
713950 Candle pin bowling alleys
713950 Candle pin bowling centers
453998 Candle shops
339999 Candles manufacturing
424990 Candles merchant wholesalers
311320 Candy bars, chocolate (including chocolate covered), made from cacao beans
311340 Candy bars, nonchocolate, manufacturing
424450 Candy merchant wholesalers
311330 Candy stores, chocolate, candy made on premises not for immediate consumption
311340 Candy stores, nonchocolate, candy made on premises, not for immediate consumption
445292 Candy stores, packaged, retailing only
311320 Candy, chocolate, made from cacao beans
111930 Cane farming, sugar, field production
311312 Cane sugar made from purchased raw cane sugar
311311 Cane sugar made in sugarcane mill
424490 Cane sugar, refined, merchant wholesalers
311312 Cane syrup made from purchased raw cane sugar
311311 Cane syrup made in sugarcane mill

339999 Canes (except orthopedic) manufacturing
332993 Canisters, ammunition, manufacturing
424490 Canned foods (e.g., fish, meat, seafood, soups) merchant wholesalers
311611 Canned meats (except poultry) produced in slaughtering plants
311911 Canned nuts manufacturing
236210 Cannery construction
311711 Cannery, fish
311711 Cannery, shellfish
311421 Canning fruits and vegetables
311421 Canning jams and jellies
333993 Canning machinery manufacturing
311615 Canning poultry (except baby and pet food)
311422 Canning soups (except seafood)
423840 Canning supplies merchant wholesalers
311711 Canning, fish, crustacea, and molluscs
332995 Cannons manufacturing
339112 Cannulae manufacturing
532292 Canoe rental
713990 Canoeing, recreational
311225 Canola (rapeseed) oil, cake and meal, made from purchased oils
311223 Canola (rapeseed) oil, cake and meal, made in crushing mills
111120 Canola farming, field and seed production
332322 Canopies, sheet metal (except stampings), manufacturing
332431 Cans, aluminum, light gauge metal, manufacturing
332431 Cans, light guage metal, manufacturing
332431 Cans, steel, light gauge metal, manufacturing
111219 Cantaloupe farming, field, bedding plant and seed production
722213 Canteens, fixed location
722330 Canteens, mobile

321912	Cants, resawed (lumber), manufacturing
314911	Canvas bags manufacturing
339942	Canvas board, artist's, manufacturing
314912	Canvas products (except bags) made from purchased canvas or canvas substitutes
424990	Canvas products merchant wholesalers
316211	Canvas shoes, plastics soled fabric upper, manufacturing
316211	Canvas shoes, rubber soled fabric upper, manufacturing
339942	Canvas, artist's, prepared on frames, manufacturing
313210	Canvases weaving
454390	Canvassers (door-to-door), headquarters for retail sale of merchandise, direct selling
335999	Capacitors (except electronic), fixed and variable, manufacturing
334414	Capacitors, electronic, fixed and variable, manufacturing
423690	Capacitors, electronic, merchant wholesalers
315212	Capes (except fur), women's, girls' and infants', cut and sew apparel contractors
315234	Capes (except fur, waterproof), women's, misses', and girls', cut and sewn from purchased fabric (except apparel contractors)
315292	Capes, fur (except apparel contractors), manufacturing
315212	Capes, fur, women's, girls', and infants', cut and sew apparel contractors
315299	Capes, waterproof (e.g., plastics, rubber, similar materials), cut and sewn from purchased fabric (except apparel contractors)
237110	Capping of water wells
333993	Capping, sealing, and lidding packaging machinery manufacturing
325199	Caprolactam manufacturing

315991	Caps (except fur, leather) cut and sewn from purchased fabric (except apparel contractors)
315991	Caps (i.e., apparel accessory) cut and sewn from purchased fabric (except fur, leather, apparel contractors)
315211	Caps (i.e., apparel accessory), men's and boys', cut and sew apparel contractors
315212	Caps (i.e., apparel accessory), women's, girls', and infants', cut and sew apparel contractors
315299	Caps and gowns, academic, cut and sewn from purchased fabric (except apparel contractors)
315211	Caps and gowns, academic, men's and boys', cut and sew apparel contractors
315212	Caps and gowns, academic, women's and girls', cut and sew apparel contractors
335931	Caps and plugs, attachment, electric, manufacturing
332115	Caps and tops, bottle, metal, stamping
336214	Caps for pick-up trucks manufacturing
325998	Caps for toy pistols manufacturing
315191	Caps made in apparel knitting mills
325920	Caps, blasting and detonating, manufacturing
332993	Caps, bomb, manufacturing
315292	Caps, fur (except apparel contractors), manufacturing
316999	Caps, heel and toe, leather, manufacturing
315292	Caps, leather (except apparel contractors), manufacturing
315991	Caps, textiles, straw, fur-felt, and wool-felt, cut and sewn from purchased fabric (except apparel contractors)

315211 Caps, textiles, straw, fur-felt, and wool-felt, men's and boys', cut and sew apparel contractors

315212 Caps, textiles, straw, fur-felt, and wool-felt, women's, girls', and infants', cut and sew apparel contractors

325998 Capsules, gelatin, empty, manufacturing

334290 Car alarm manufacturing

336211 Car bodies, kit, manufacturing

811192 Car detailers

532112 Car leasing

483212 Car lighters (i.e., ferries), inland waters (except on Great Lakes system)

485999 Car pool operation

488999 Car pools, arrangement of

532111 Car rental

532111 Car rental agencies

561599 Car rental reservation services

811111 Car repair shops, general

332999 Car seals, metal, manufacturing

337125 Car seats, infant (except metal), manufacturing

334310 Car stereos manufacturing

423850 Car wash equipment and supplies merchant wholesalers

811192 Car washes

331111 Car wheels, rolled steel, made in iron and steel mills

325188 Carbides (e.g., boron, calcium, silicon, tungsten) manufacturing

332994 Carbines manufacturing

325199 Carbinol manufacturing

325211 Carbohydrate plastics manufacturing

334510 Carbon arc lamp units, electrotherapeutic (except infrared and ultraviolet), manufacturing

325182 Carbon black manufacturing

424690 Carbon black merchant wholesalers

327125 Carbon brick manufacturing

325120 Carbon dioxide manufacturing

325188 Carbon disulfide manufacturing

335991 Carbon electrodes and contacts, electric, manufacturing

325188 Carbon inorganic compounds manufacturing

334290 Carbon monoxide detectors manufacturing

423690 Carbon monoxide detectors, electronic, merchant wholesalers

325199 Carbon organic compounds, not specified elsewhere by process, manufacturing

339944 Carbon paper manufacturing

335991 Carbon specialties for aerospace use (except gaskets) manufacturing

335991 Carbon specialties for electrical use manufacturing

335991 Carbon specialties for mechanical use (except gaskets) manufacturing

325199 Carbon tetrachloride manufacturing

325998 Carbon, activated, manufacturing

312111 Carbonated soda manufacturing

312111 Carbonated soft drinks manufacturing

325188 Carbonic acid manufacturing

333292 Carbonizing equipment for processing wool manufacturing

313312 Carbonizing textile fibers

335991 Carbons, electric, manufacturing

335991 Carbons, lighting, manufacturing

325998 Carburetor cleaners manufacturing

336311 Carburetors, all types, manufacturing

316993 Card cases (except metal) manufacturing

339911 Card cases, precious metal, manufacturing

713290 Card rooms (e.g., poker rooms)

453220 Card shops, greeting

337122 Card table sets (furniture), wood, manufacturing

337124 Card table sets, metal, manufacturing

424130 Cardboard products merchant wholesalers

322130 Cardboard stock manufacturing

322226 Cardboard, laminated or surface coated, made from purchased paperboard

313230 Carded nonwoven fabrics manufacturing

313111 Carded yarn manufacturing

325412 Cardiac preparations manufacturing

333292 Carding machinery for textiles manufacturing

313312 Carding textile fibers

334510 Cardiodynameter manufacturing

334510 Cardiographs manufacturing

621111 Cardiologists' offices (e.g., centers, clinics)

334510 Cardiophone, electric, manufacturing

334510 Cardioscope manufacturing

334510 Cardiotachometer manufacturing

323119 Cards (e.g., business, greeting, playing, postcards, trading) engraving printing without publishing

323112 Cards (e.g., business, greeting, playing, postcards, trading) flexographic printing without publishing

323111 Cards (e.g., business, greeting, playing, postcards, trading) gravure printing without publishing

323119 Cards (e.g., business, greeting, playing, postcards, trading) letterpress printing without publishing

323110 Cards (e.g., business, greeting, playing, postcards, trading) lithographic (offset) printing without publishing

323119 Cards (e.g., business, greeting, playing, postcards, trading) printing (except flexographic, gravure, lithographic, quick, screen) without publishing

323113 Cards (e.g., business, greeting, playing, postcards, trading) screen printing without publishing

322299 Cards, die-cut (except office supply) made from purchased paper or paperboard

322231 Cards, die-cut office supply (e.g., index, library, time recording), made from purchased paper or paperboard

424120 Cards, greeting, merchant wholesalers

****** Cards, publishing—see specific product

481112 Cargo carriers, air, scheduled

488390 Cargo checkers, marine

488330 Cargo salvaging, marine

336611 Cargo ship building

488390 Cargo surveyors, marine

488490 Cargo surveyors, truck transportation

333319 Carnival and amusement park rides manufacturing

333319 Carnival and amusement park shooting gallery machinery manufacturing

423850 Carnival equipment merchant wholesalers

713990 Carnival ride concession operators (i.e., supplying and servicing in others' facilities)

711190 Carnival traveling shows

212291 Carnotite mining and/or beneficiating

333922 Carousel conveyors (e.g., luggage) manufacturing

333319 Carousels (i.e., merry-go-rounds) manufacturing

238350 Carpenters (except framing)

611513 Carpenters' apprenticeship training

332212 Carpenter's handtools, nonelectric (except saws), manufacturing

532490 Carpentry equipment rental or leasing

238350 Carpentry work (except framing)

238130 Carpentry, framing

333319 Carpet and floor cleaning equipment, electric commercial-type, manufacturing

335212 Carpet and floor cleaning equipment, household-type electric, manufacturing

532490 Carpet and rug cleaning equipment rental or leasing

313111 Carpet and rug yarn spinning

532299 Carpet and rug, residential, rental

561740 Carpet cleaning on customers' premises

561740 Carpet cleaning plants

561740 Carpet cleaning services

314999 Carpet cutting and binding

313210 Carpet linings (except felt) weaving

423220 Carpet merchant wholesalers

313230 Carpet paddings, nonwoven, manufacturing

442210 Carpet stores

333319 Carpet sweepers, mechanical, manufacturing

238330 Carpet, installation only

314110 Carpets and rugs made from textile materials

321999 Carpets, cork, manufacturing

332311 Carports, prefabricated metal, manufacturing

487110 Carriage, horse-drawn, operation

339932 Carriages, baby, manufacturing

339932 Carriages, doll, manufacturing

334210 Carrier equipment (i.e., analog, digital), telephone, manufacturing

111219 Carrot farming, field, bedding plant and seed production

311991 Carrots, cut, peeled or sliced fresh, manufacturing

722211 Carryout restaurants

336111 Cars, electric, for highway use, assembling on chassis of own manufacture

333131 Cars, mining, manufacturing

541370 Cartographic surveying services

333993 Carton filling machinery manufacturing

322299 Cartons, egg, molded pulp manufacturing

322212 Cartons, folding (except milk), made from purchased paperboard

322215 Cartons, milk, made from purchased paper or paperboard

424130 Cartons, paper and paperboard, merchant wholesalers

711510 Cartoonists, independent

333991 Cartridge (i.e., powder) handheld power-driven tools manufacturing

332992 Cartridge cases for ammunition (i.e., 30 mm. or less, 1.18 inch or less) manufacturing

331421 Cartridge cups, discs, and sheets, copper and copper alloy, made from purchased copper or in integrated secondary smelting and rolling, drawing or extruding plants

424120 Cartridge toner merchant wholesalers

332992 Cartridges (i.e., 30 mm. or less, 1.18 inch or less) manufacturing

339920 Carts, caddy, manufacturing

423860 Carts, golf, motorized passenger merchant wholesalers

333924 Carts, grocery, made from purchased wire

333112 Carts, lawn and garden-type, manufacturing

332211 Carving sets manufacturing

333319 Carwashing machinery manufacturing

111219 Casaba melon farming, field, bedding plant and seed production

316110 Case leather manufacturing

325222 Casein fibers and filaments manufacturing

325211 Casein plastics manufacturing

311514 Casein, dry and wet, manufacturing

332321 Casements, metal, manufacturing

316993 Cases, jewelry (except metal), manufacturing

339914   Cases, jewelry, metal (except precious), manufacturing

339911   Cases, jewelry, precious metal, manufacturing

316991   Cases, luggage, manufacturing

316991   Cases, musical instrument, manufacturing

321920   Cases, shipping, wood, wirebound, manufacturing

321920   Cases, wood packing, nailed or lock corner, manufacturing

321920   Cases, wood shipping, nailed or lock corner, manufacturing

332439   Cash boxes, light gauge metal, manufacturing

532420   Cash register rental or leasing

333313   Cash registers (except point of sales terminals) manufacturing

423420   Cash registers merchant wholesalers

111335   Cashew farming

211112   Casing-head butane and propane production

326121   Casings, sausage, nonrigid plastics, manufacturing

332313   Casings, scroll, fabricated metal plate work, manufacturing

332322   Casings, sheet metal (except stampings), manufacturing

236220   Casino construction

721120   Casino hotels

713210   Casinos (except casino hotels)

332510   Casket hardware, metal, manufacturing

339995   Caskets, burial, manufacturing

423850   Caskets, burial, merchant wholesalers

321920   Casks, wood, coopered, manufacturing

111219   Cassava farming, field and seed casava production

335211   Casseroles, household-type electric, manufacturing

334612   Cassette tapes, pre-recorded audio, mass reproducing

532230   Cassette, prerecorded video, rental

423990   Cassettes, prerecorded audio and video, merchant wholesalers

331511   Cast iron brake shoes, railroad, manufacturing

331511   Cast iron pipe and pipe fittings manufacturing

423510   Cast iron pipe merchant wholesalers

331511   Cast iron railroad car wheels manufacturing

331513   Cast steel railroad car wheels, unfinished, manufacturing

327390   Cast stone, concrete (except structural), manufacturing

327124   Castable refractories, clay, manufacturing

327125   Castable refractories, nonclay, manufacturing

332510   Casters, furniture, metal manufacturing

332510   Casters, industrial, metal, manufacturing

561311   Casting agencies (i.e., motion picture, theatrical, video)

561311   Casting agencies, motion picture or video

561311   Casting agencies, theatrical

561311   Casting bureaus (e.g., motion picture, theatrical, video)

561311   Casting bureaus, motion picture or video

561311   Casting bureaus, theatrical

331528   Castings (except die-castings), nonferrous metals (except aluminum, copper), unfinished manufacturing

331524   Castings (except die-castings), unfinished, aluminum, manufacturing

331525   Castings (except die-castings), unfinished, copper, manufacturing

331511   Castings, compacted graphite iron, unfinished, manufacturing

331511   Castings, malleable iron, unfinished, manufacturing

331513   Castings, steel (except investment), unfinished, manufacturing

331511 Castings, unfinished iron (e.g., ductile, gray, malleable, semisteel), manufacturing

311223 Castor oil and pomace made in crushing mills

316213 Casual shoes (except athletic, plastics, rubber), men's, manufacturing

316214 Casual shoes (except athletic, rubber, plastics), women's, manufacturing

316219 Casual shoes (except rubber, plastics), children's and infants', manufacturing

524126 Casualty insurance carriers, direct

621512 CAT (computerized axial tomography) scanner centers

311111 Cat food manufacturing

325998 Cat litter manufacturing

112990 Cat production

511199 Catalog (i.e., mail order, store merchandise) publishers (except exclusive Internet publishing)

511199 Catalog (i.e., mail order, store merchandise) publishers and printing combined

454113 Catalog (i.e., order taking) offices of mail-order houses

511140 Catalog of collections publishers (except exclusive Internet publishing)

511140 Catalog of collections publishers and printing combined

519130 Catalog of collections publishers, exclusively on Internet

452990 Catalog showrooms, general merchandise (except catalog mail-order)

323112 Catalogs flexographic printing without publishing

323111 Catalogs gravure printing without publishing

323110 Catalogs lithographic (offset) printing without publishing

323112 Catalogs of collections flexographic printing without publishing

323111 Catalogs of collections gravure printing without publishing

323110 Catalogs of collections lithographic (offset) printing without publishing

323119 Catalogs of collections printing (except flexographic, gravure, lithographic, quick, screen) without publishing

323113 Catalogs of collections screen printing without publishing

323119 Catalogs printing (except flexographic, gravure, lithographic, quick, screen) without publishing

323113 Catalogs screen printing without publishing

336399 Catalytic converters, engine exhaust, automotive, truck, and bus, manufacturing

332995 Catapult guns manufacturing

562998 Catch basin cleaning services

722320 Caterers

722320 Catering services, social

112511 Catfish production, farm raising

325412 Cathartic preparations manufacturing

339112 Catheters manufacturing

334411 Cathode ray tubes (CRT) manufacturing

335999 Cathodic protection equipment manufacturing

238190 Cathodic protection, installation

212399 Catlinite mining and/or beneficiating

424990 Cats merchant wholesalers

311421 Catsup manufacturing

112111 Cattle conditioning operations

112111 Cattle farming or ranching

333111 Cattle feeding and watering equipment manufacturing

112112 Cattle feedlots (except stockyards for transportation)

311119 Cattle feeds, supplements, concentrates, and premixes, manufacturing

424520 Cattle merchant wholesalers

115210	Cattle spraying
111219	Cauliflower farming, field, bedding plant and seed production
238390	Caulking (i.e., waterproofing) contractors
325520	Caulking compounds (except gypsum base) manufacturing
332212	Caulking guns, nonpowered, manufacturing
424690	Caulking materials merchant wholesalers
524291	Cause-of-loss investigators, insurance
237310	Causeway construction
325181	Caustic potash manufacturing
325181	Caustic soda (i.e., sodium hydroxide) manufacturing
424690	Caustic soda merchant wholesalers
712190	Caverns (i.e., natural wonder tourist attractions)
334220	CB (citizens band) radios manufacturing
332212	C-clamps manufacturing
334112	CD-ROM drives manufacturing
334611	CD-ROM, software, mass reproducing
337122	Cedar chests manufacturing
325998	Cedar oil manufacturing
238130	Ceiling beam, wood, installation
444190	Ceiling fan stores
335211	Ceiling fans with integral lighting fixture, residential, manufacturing
335211	Ceiling fans, residential, manufacturing
335122	Ceiling lighting fixtures, commercial, industrial, and institutional, manufacturing
335121	Ceiling lighting fixtures, residential, manufacturing
321912	Ceiling lumber, dressed, resawing purchased lumber
321113	Ceiling lumber, made from logs or bolts
238310	Ceiling tile installation
238390	Ceiling, metal, installation
334519	Ceilometers manufacturing
711410	Celebrities' agents or managers

711510	Celebrity spokespersons, independent
111219	Celery farming, field, bedding plant and seed production
212393	Celestite mining and/or beneficiating
325221	Cellophane film or sheet manufacturing
424120	Cellophane tape merchant wholesalers
339992	Cellos and parts manufacturing
237130	Cellular phone tower construction
517210	Cellular telephone communication carriers
517210	Cellular telephone services
443112	Cellular telephone stores
334220	Cellular telephones manufacturing
423690	Cellular telephones merchant wholesalers
325199	Cellulose acetate (except resins) manufacturing
325211	Cellulose acetate resins manufacturing
325211	Cellulose nitrate resins manufacturing
325211	Cellulose propionate resins manufacturing
325211	Cellulose resins manufacturing
325211	Cellulose xanthate (viscose) manufacturing
238310	Cellulosic fiber insulation installation
325221	Cellulosic fibers and filaments manufacturing
325221	Cellulosic filament yarn manufacturing
326113	Cellulosic plastics film and unlaminated sheet (except packaging) manufacturing
325221	Cellulosic staple fibers manufacturing
327310	Cement (e.g., hydraulic, masonry, portland, pozzolana) manufacturing
238140	Cement block laying
327310	Cement clinker manufacturing
333298	Cement kilns manufacturing
423320	Cement merchant wholesalers

236210 Cement plant construction

212312 Cement rock crushed and broken stone mining and/or beneficiating

327124 Cement, clay refractory, manufacturing

327420 Cement, Keene's (i.e., tiling plaster), manufacturing

325520 Cement, rubber, manufacturing

213112 Cementing oil and gas well casings on a contract basis

423830 Cement-making machinery merchant wholesalers

324122 Cements, asphalt roofing, made from purchased asphaltic materials

339114 Cements, dental, manufacturing

812220 Cemeteries

812220 Cemetery associations (i.e., operators)

812220 Cemetery management services

453998 Cemetery memorial dealers (e.g., headstones, markers, vaults)

561730 Cemetery plot care services

333512 Centering machines, metalworking, manufacturing

519120 Centers for documentation (i.e., archives)

624120 Centers, senior citizens'

238220 Central air-conditioning equipment installation

521110 Central bank, monetary authorities

238220 Central cooling equipment and piping installation

238220 Central heating equipment and piping installation

423730 Central heating equipment, warm-air, merchant wholesalers

325412 Central nervous system stimulant preparations manufacturing

334210 Central office and switching equipment, telephone, manufacturing

333319 Central vacuuming systems, commercial-type, manufacturing

335212 Central vacuuming systems, household-type, manufacturing

551114 Centralized administrative offices

327320 Central-mixed concrete manufacturing

333911 Centrifugal pumps manufacturing

333999 Centrifuges, industrial and laboratory-type, manufacturing

325411 Cephalosporin, uncompounded, manufacturing

325131 Ceramic colors manufacturing

423320 Ceramic construction materials (except refractory) merchant wholesalers

327999 Ceramic fiber manufacturing

333994 Ceramic kilns and furnaces manufacturing

238340 Ceramic tile installation

444190 Ceramic tile stores

327122 Ceramic tiles, floor and wall, manufacturing

611610 Ceramics instruction

311211 Cereal grain flour manufacturing

311211 Cereal grain germ manufacturing

424490 Cereal products merchant wholesalers

212299 Cerium concentrates mining and/or beneficiating

212299 Cerium ores mining and/or beneficiating

325188 Cerium salts manufacturing

523120 Certificate of deposit (CD) brokers' offices

923110 Certification of schools and teachers

541211 Certified accountants' offices

523930 Certified financial planners, customized, fees paid by client

541211 Certified public accountants' (CPAs) offices

212231 Cerussite mining and/or beneficiating

339113 Cervical collars manufacturing

325188	Cesium and cesium compounds, not specified elsewhere by process, manufacturing
562991	Cesspool cleaning services
238910	Cesspool construction
325199	Cetyl alcohol manufacturing
335211	Chafing dishes, household-type electric, manufacturing
332999	Chain fittings manufacturing
333923	Chain hoists manufacturing
332323	Chain ladders, metal, manufacturing
238990	Chain link fence installation
332618	Chain link fencing and fence gates made from purchased wire
331222	Chain link fencing, iron or steel, made in wire drawing plants
332618	Chain made from purchased wire
332213	Chain saw blades manufacturing
333991	Chain saws, handheld power-driven, manufacturing
332618	Chain, welded, made from purchased wire
339911	Chains or necklace, precious metal, manufacturing
333613	Chains, power transmission, manufacturing
334519	Chains, surveyor's, manufacturing
423830	Chainsaws merchant wholesalers
337121	Chair and couch springs, assembled, manufacturing
337215	Chair glides manufacturing
337215	Chair seats for furniture manufacturing
337122	Chairs (except upholstered), wood household-type, manufacturing
337214	Chairs (except wood), office-type, manufacturing
337127	Chairs, barber and beauty (i.e., hydraulic), manufacturing
337127	Chairs, barber, beauty shop (i.e., hydraulic), manufacturing
337125	Chairs, cane, wood household-type, manufacturing

339114	Chairs, dentist's, manufacturing
337124	Chairs, metal household-type (except upholstered), manufacturing
337127	Chairs, portable folding, auditorium-type, manufacturing
337127	Chairs, stacking, auditorium-type, manufacturing
337121	Chairs, upholstered household-type (except dining room, kitchen), manufacturing
337211	Chairs, wood office-type, manufacturing
212234	Chalcocite mining and/or beneficiating
212234	Chalcopyrite mining and/or beneficiating
339942	Chalk (e.g., artist's, blackboard, carpenter's, marking, tailor's), manufacturing
212312	Chalk crushed and broken stone mining and/or beneficiating
212312	Chalk, ground or otherwise treated, mining and/or beneficiating
339942	Chalkboards, framed, manufacturing
711130	Chamber musical groups
711130	Chamber orchestras
813910	Chambers of commerce
313210	Chambrays weaving
333512	Chamfering machines, metalworking, manufacturing
316110	Chamois leather manufacturing
424990	Chamois, leather, merchant wholesalers
312130	Champagne method sparkling wine, manufacturing
335122	Chandeliers, commercial, industrial, and institutional electric, manufacturing
335121	Chandeliers, residential, manufacturing
333311	Change making machines manufacturing
325182	Channel black manufacturing
237990	Channel construction
332323	Channels, furring metal, manufacturing

325191 Charcoal (except activated) manufacturing
325191 Charcoal briquettes, wood, manufacturing
424990 Charcoal merchant wholesalers
325998 Charcoal, activated, manufacturing
522210 Charge card issuing
813211 Charitable trusts, awarding grants
611699 Charm schools
481212 Charter air freight services
481211 Charter air passenger services
485510 Charter bus services (except scenic, sightseeing)
487210 Charter fishing boat operation
333515 Chasers (i.e., a machine tool accessory) manufacturing
212399 Chasers mining and/or beneficiating
332812 Chasing metals and metal products for the trade
336111 Chassis, automobile, manufacturing
336120 Chassis, heavy truck, with or without cabs, manufacturing
336112 Chassis, light truck and utility, manufacturing
423110 Chassis, motor vehicle, merchant wholesalers
561311 Chauffeur registries
611519 Chauffeur training
315991 Chauffeurs' hats and caps cut and sewn from purchased fabric (except apparel contractors)
315211 Chauffeurs' hats and caps, men's, cut and sew apparel contractors
315212 Chauffeurs' hats and caps, women's, cut and sew apparel contractors
522390 Check cashing services
521110 Check clearing activities of the central bank
522320 Check clearing services (except central banks)
522320 Check clearinghouse services (except central banks)

423420 Check handling machines merchant wholesalers
812990 Check room services
522320 Check validation services
332911 Check valves, industrial-type, manufacturing
333313 Check writing machines manufacturing
316993 Checkbook covers, (except metal), manufacturing
339911 Checkbook covers, precious metal, manufacturing
323116 Checkbooks and refills printing
339932 Checkers and checkerboards manufacturing
611620 Cheerleading instruction, camps, or schools
311513 Cheese (except cottage cheese) manufacturing
311513 Cheese analogs manufacturing
311941 Cheese based salad dressing manufacturing
424450 Cheese confections (e.g., curls, puffs) merchant wholesalers
311919 Cheese curls and puffs manufacturing
424430 Cheese merchant wholesalers
333294 Cheese processing machinery manufacturing
311513 Cheese products, imitation or substitute, manufacturing
311513 Cheese spreads manufacturing
311511 Cheese, cottage, manufacturing
311513 Cheese, imitation or substitute, manufacturing
311513 Cheese, natural (except cottage cheese), manufacturing
313210 Cheesecloths weaving
236210 Chemical (except petrochemical process type) plant construction
424690 Chemical additives (e.g., concrete, food, fuel, oil) merchant wholesalers
541690 Chemical consulting services
541330 Chemical engineering services
313311 Chemical finishing (e.g., fire, mildew, water resistance) broadwoven fabrics

313312 Chemical finishing (e.g., fire, mildew, water resistance) fabrics (except broadwoven and textile products)

424690 Chemical gases merchant wholesalers

423830 Chemical industries machinery and equipment merchant wholesalers

333298 Chemical kilns manufacturing

332710 Chemical milling job shops

333512 Chemical milling machines, metalworking, manufacturing

333298 Chemical processing machinery and equipment manufacturing

541712 Chemical research and development laboratories or services (except biotechnology research and development)

327112 Chemical stoneware (i.e., pottery products) manufacturing

326191 Chemical toilets, plastics, manufacturing

115112 Chemical treatment of soil for crops

213112 Chemically treating oil and gas wells (e.g., acidizing, bailing, swabbing) on a contract basis

424690 Chemicals (except agriculture) (e.g., automotive, household, industrial, photographic) merchant wholesalers

424910 Chemicals, agricultural, merchant wholesalers

315191 Chemises made in apparel knitting mills

315212 Chemises, women's and girls', cut and sew apparel contractors

315231 Chemises, women's, misses' and girls', cut and sewn from purchased fabric (except apparel contractors)

111339 Cherry farming

113210 Cherry gum, gathering

339932 Chessmen and chessboards manufacturing

325191 Chestnut extract manufacturing

113210 Chestnut gum, gathering

321920 Chests for tools, wood, manufacturing

332999 Chests, fire or burglary resistive, metal, manufacturing

332999 Chests, money, metal, manufacturing

332999 Chests, safe deposit, metal, manufacturing

311340 Chewing gum base manufacturing

333294 Chewing gum machinery manufacturing

311340 Chewing gum manufacturing

424450 Chewing gum merchant wholesalers

312229 Chewing tobacco manufacturing

424940 Chewing tobacco merchant wholesalers

424440 Chicken and chicken products (except canned and packaged frozen) merchant wholesalers

333111 Chicken brooders manufacturing

321920 Chicken coops (i.e., crates), wood, wirebound for shipping poultry, manufacturing

321992 Chicken coops, prefabricated, wood, manufacturing

112310 Chicken egg production

112310 Chicken eggs (table, hatching) production

333111 Chicken feeders manufacturing

311119 Chicken feeds, prepared, manufacturing

112340 Chicken hatcheries

332618 Chicken netting made from purchased wire

112320 Chicken production (except egg laying)

311615 Chickens, processing, fresh, frozen, canned, or cooked (except baby and pet food)

311615 Chickens, slaughtering and dressing

424590 Chicks merchant wholesalers

111998 Chicory farming

624410 Child day care centers

624410 Child day care services

624410 Child day care services in provider's own home

624410 Child day care, before or after school, separate from schools
623990 Child group foster homes
624110 Child guidance agencies
624110 Child welfare services
621410 Childbirth preparation classes
721214 Children's camps (except day, instructional)
424330 Children's clothing merchant wholesalers
511199 Children's coloring book publishers (except exclusive Internet publishing)
519130 Children's coloring book publishers, exclusively on Internet
622110 Children's hospitals, general
622210 Children's hospitals, psychiatric or substance abuse
622310 Children's hospitals, specialty (except psychiatric, substance abuse)
316219 Children's shoes (except orthopedic extension, plastics, rubber) manufacturing
315119 Children's socks manufacturing
423920 Children's vehicles (except bicycles) merchant wholesalers
623990 Children's villages
311422 Chili con carne canning
311942 Chili pepper or powder manufacturing
311421 Chili sauce manufacturing
238220 Chilled water system installation
339992 Chimes and parts (musical instruments) manufacturing
335999 Chimes, electric, manufacturing
327390 Chimney caps, concrete, manufacturing
561790 Chimney cleaning services
238220 Chimney liner installation
561790 Chimney sweep (i.e., cleaning) services
238140 Chimney, brick, block or stone, contractors
238110 Chimney, concrete, construction
212324 China clay mining and/or beneficiating

337122 China closets, wood, manufacturing
327112 China cooking ware manufacturing
811490 China repair services
327112 China tableware, vitreous, manufacturing
442299 Chinaware stores
423440 Chinaware, commercial, merchant wholesalers
423220 Chinaware, household-type, merchant wholesalers
112930 Chinchilla production
311422 Chinese foods canning
311999 Chinese noodles, fried, manufacturing
111219 Chinese pea farming, bedding plant and seed production
313210 Chintzes weaving
333298 Chip placement machinery manufacturing
322130 Chipboard (i.e., paperboard) stock manufacturing
321219 Chipboard (I.e., particle core, wood chip face), manufacturing
322226 Chipboard, laminated or surface coated, made from purchased paperboard
321113 Chipper mills (except portable)
333112 Chippers (i.e., shredders), lawn and garden-type, manufacturing
333120 Chippers, portable, commercial (e.g., brush, limb, log), manufacturing
333291 Chippers, stationary (e.g., log), manufacturing
424450 Chips (e.g., corn, potato) merchant wholesalers
621310 Chiropractors' offices (e.g., centers, clinics)
332212 Chisels manufacturing
333991 Chissels, handheld power-driven, manufacturing
111219 Chive farming, field, bedding plant and seed production
325199 Chloral manufacturing
325320 Chlordane insecticides manufacturing

325188	Chloride of lime manufacturing
325212	Chlorinated rubber, synthetic, manufacturing
325188	Chlorine compounds, not specified elsewhere by process, manufacturing
325188	Chlorine dioxide manufacturing
325181	Chlorine manufacturing
325199	Chloroacetic acid manufacturing
325192	Chlorobenzene manufacturing
325120	Chlorodifluoromethane manufacturing
325120	Chlorofluorocarbon gases manufacturing
325199	Chloroform manufacturing
325192	Chloronaphthalene manufacturing
325192	Chlorophenol manufacturing
325199	Chloropicrin manufacturing
325212	Chloroprene rubber manufacturing
325212	Chlorosulfonated polyethylenes manufacturing
325188	Chlorosulfonic acid manufacturing
325192	Chlorotoluene manufacturing
311330	Chocolate (coating, instant, liquor, syrups) made from purchased chocolate
311320	Chocolate (e.g., coatings, instant, liquor, syrups) made from cacao beans
424490	Chocolate (except candy) merchant wholesalers
311320	Chocolate bars made from cocoa beans
424450	Chocolate candy merchant wholesalers
311330	Chocolate coatings and syrups made from purchased chocolate
311330	Chocolate covered candy bars made from purchased chocolate
311330	Chocolate covered granola bars made from purchased chocolate
311511	Chocolate drink (milk based) manufacturing
311511	Chocolate milk manufacturing
333294	Chocolate processing machinery manufacturing
311320	Chocolate, confectionery, made from cacao beans
711130	Choirs
334416	Chokes for electronic circuitry manufacturing
325414	Cholera serums manufacturing
325320	Cholinesterse inhibitors used as insecticides manufacturing
311412	Chop suey, frozen, manufacturing
115113	Chopping and silo filling
711510	Choreographers, independent
311412	Chow mein, frozen, manufacturing
311711	Chowders, fish and seafood, canning
311712	Chowders, frozen fish and seafood, manufacturing
621399	Christian Science practitioners' offices (e.g., centers, clinics)
424990	Christmas ornaments merchant wholesalers
453220	Christmas stores
333132	Christmas tree assemblies, oil and gas field-type, manufacturing
111421	Christmas tree growing
335129	Christmas tree lighting sets, electric, manufacturing
339999	Christmas tree ornaments (except electric, glass) manufacturing
327215	Christmas tree ornaments made from purchased glass
327212	Christmas tree ornaments, glass, made in glass making plants
424990	Christmas trees (e.g., artificial, cut) merchant wholesalers
339999	Christmas trees, artificial, manufacturing
454390	Christmas trees, cut, direct selling
334516	Chromatographic instruments, laboratory-type, manufacturing
334513	Chromatographs, industrial process-type, manufacturing

325131 Chrome pigments (e.g., chrome green, chrome orange, chrome yellow) manufacturing
332813 Chrome plating metals and metal products for the trade
325188 Chromic acid manufacturing
212299 Chromite mining and/or beneficiating
325188 Chromium compounds, not specified elsewhere by process, manufacturing
212299 Chromium concentrates beneficiating
212299 Chromium ore mining and/or beneficiating
325188 Chromium oxide manufacturing
331419 Chromium refining, primary
325188 Chromium salts manufacturing
622310 Chronic disease hospitals
334518 Chronographs manufacturing
334518 Chronometers manufacturing
334516 Chronoscopes manufacturing
333512 Chucking machines, automatic, metalworking, manufacturing
333515 Chucks (i.e., a machine tool accessory) manufacturing
238290 Church bell and tower clock installation
337127 Church furniture (except concrete, stone) manufacturing
423490 Church supplies (except plated ware, silverware) merchant wholesalers
813110 Churches
332313 Chutes, fabricated metal plate work, manufacturing
333294 Cider presses manufacturing
311941 Cider vinegar manufacturing
312130 Cider, alcoholic, manufacturing
311941 Cider, nonalcoholic, manufacturing
326199 Cigar and cigarette holders, plastics, manufacturing
321920 Cigar boxes, wood and part wood, manufacturing
316993 Cigar cases (except metal) manufacturing
339911 Cigar cases, precious metal, manufacturing
312229 Cigar manufacturing

453991 Cigar stores
316993 Cigarette cases (except metal) manufacturing
339911 Cigarette cases, precious metal, manufacturing
339999 Cigarette holders manufacturing
339999 Cigarette lighter flints manufacturing
339999 Cigarette lighters (except precious metal) manufacturing
424990 Cigarette lighters merchant wholesalers
333298 Cigarette making machinery manufacturing
322299 Cigarette paper made from purchased paper
322121 Cigarette paper made in paper mills
322299 Cigarette paper, book, made from purchased paper
453991 Cigarette stands, permanent
454390 Cigarette stands, temporary
325221 Cigarette tow, cellulosic fiber, manufacturing
333311 Cigarette vending machines manufacturing
312221 Cigarettes manufacturing
424940 Cigarettes merchant wholesalers
424940 Cigars merchant wholesalers
325411 Cinchona and derivatives (i.e., basic chemicals) manufacturing
327331 Cinder (clinker) block, concrete, manufacturing
238140 Cinder block installation
236220 Cinema construction
512131 Cinemas
711510 Cinematographers, independent
212299 Cinnabar mining and/or beneficiating
333298 Circuit board making machinery manufacturing
423690 Circuit boards merchant wholesalers
334412 Circuit boards, printed, bare, manufacturing
423610 Circuit breakers merchant wholesalers
335313 Circuit breakers, air, manufacturing

335313	Circuit breakers, power, manufacturing
922110	Circuit courts
334515	Circuit testers manufacturing
423690	Circuits, integrated, merchant wholesalers
313241	Circular (i.e., weft) fabrics knitting
541870	Circular direct distribution services
333292	Circular knitting machinery manufacturing
333991	Circular saws, handheld power-driven, manufacturing
333210	Circular saws, woodworking-type, stationary, manufacturing
519120	Circulating libraries
711190	Circus companies
711190	Circuses
334220	Citizens band (CB) radios manufacturing
325199	Citral manufacturing
325199	Citrates, not specified elsewhere by process, manufacturing
325199	Citric acid manufacturing
325998	Citronella oil manufacturing
325199	Citronellal manufacturing
115112	Citrus grove cultivation services
111320	Citrus groves (except orange)
311119	Citrus pulp, cattle feed, manufacturing
311411	Citrus pulp, frozen, manufacturing
921120	City and town councils
921110	City and town managers' offices
485113	City bus services (except mixed mode)
922110	City or county courts
541320	City planning services
813410	Civic associations
236220	Civic center construction
541330	Civil engineering services
813311	Civil liberties organizations
921190	Civil rights commissions
921190	Civil service commissions
524291	Claims adjusting, insurance
524292	Claims processing services, insurance, third-party
114112	Clam digging
112512	Clam production, farm raising
333515	Clamps (i.e., a machine tool accessory) manufacturing
339112	Clamps, surgical, manufacturing
339992	Clarinets and parts manufacturing
316999	Clasps, shoe (leather), manufacturing
813410	Classic car clubs
711120	Classical dance companies
711130	Classical musical artists, independent
711130	Classical musical groups
212325	Clay (except kaolin, ball) mining and/or beneficiating
327112	Clay and ceramic statuary manufacturing
212325	Clay bleaching
423320	Clay construction materials (except refractory) merchant wholesalers
327124	Clay refractories (e.g., mortar, brick, tile, block) manufacturing
212324	Clay, ball, mining and/or beneficiating
212325	Clay, ceramic and refractory minerals, mining and/or beneficiating
212325	Clay, fire, mining and/or beneficiating
339942	Clay, modeling, manufacturing
212324	Clay, natural, mining and/or beneficiating
333298	Clayworking and tempering machinery manufacturing
812332	Clean room apparel supply services
236210	Clean room construction
339113	Clean room suits and accessories manufacturing
812320	Cleaners, drycleaning and laundry service (except coin-operated)
335212	Cleaners, household-type electric vacuum, manufacturing
561790	Cleaning (e.g., power sweeping, washing) driveways and parking lots

332813	Cleaning and descaling metals and metal products for the trade
812320	Cleaning and dyeing plants (except rug cleaning plants)
311212	Cleaning and polishing rice
561790	Cleaning building exteriors (except sand blasting, window cleaning)
238990	Cleaning building interiors during and immediately after construction
561740	Cleaning carpets
424690	Cleaning compounds and preparations merchant wholesalers
335999	Cleaning equipment, ultrasonic (except dental, medical), manufacturing
561720	Cleaning homes
333131	Cleaning machinery, mining-type, manufacturing
238990	Cleaning new building interiors immediately after construction
561720	Cleaning offices
213112	Cleaning oil and gas field lease tanks on a contract basis
213112	Cleaning out (e.g., bailing out, steam cleaning, swabbing) wells on a contract basis
212113	Cleaning plants, anthracite coal
212111	Cleaning plants, bituminous coal
561740	Cleaning plants, carpet and rug
115210	Cleaning poultry houses
561740	Cleaning rugs
561740	Cleaning services, carpet and rug
561720	Cleaning shopping centers
561790	Cleaning swimming pools
213112	Cleaning wells on a contract basis
213112	Cleaning, repairing, and dismantling oil and gas field lease tanks on a contract basis
321918	Clear and finger joint wood moldings manufacturing
522320	Clearinghouses, bank or check
523999	Clearinghouses, commodity exchange or securities exchange
316219	Cleated athletic shoes manufacturing
332211	Cleavers manufacturing
315299	Clerical vestments cut and sewn from purchased fabric (except apparel contractors)
315191	Clerical vestments made in apparel knitting mills
315211	Clerical vestments, men's and boys, cut and sew apparel contractors
315212	Clerical vestments, women's and girls', cut and sew apparel contractors
316211	Climbing shoes, plastics or plastics soled fabric upper, manufacturing
316211	Climbing shoes, rubber or rubber soled fabric upper, manufacturing
236220	Clinic construction
621111	Clinical pathologists' offices (e.g., centers, clinics)
621330	Clinical psychologists' offices (e.g., centers, clinics)
******	Clinics, medical—see type
621498	Clinics/centers of health practitioners from more than one industry practicing within the same establishment
621498	Clinics/centers of health practitioners with multi-industry degrees
321999	Clipboards, wood, manufacturing
332212	Clippers for animal use, nonelectric, manufacturing
332211	Clippers, fingernail and toenail, manufacturing
519190	Clipping services, news
332994	Clips, gun (i.e., 30 mm. or less, 1.18 inch or less), manufacturing
332995	Clips, gun (i.e., more than 30 mm., more than 1.18 inch), manufacturing

334518 Clock materials and parts (except crystals) manufacturing

334518 Clock or watch springs, precision, made from purchased wire

334310 Clock radios manufacturing

811490 Clock repair shops without retailing new clocks

448310 Clock shops

334518 Clocks assembling

334518 Clocks assembling from purchased components

423940 Clocks merchant wholesalers

541711 Cloning research and experimental development laboratories

561492 Closed captioning services, real-time (i.e., simultaneous)

512191 Closed captioning services, taped material

517110 Closed circuit television (CCTV)

517110 Closed circuit television (CCTV) services

334220 Closed circuit television equipment manufacturing

525990 Closed-end investment funds

453998 Closet organizer stores

238390 Closet organizer system installation

332115 Closures, metal, stamping

424130 Closures, paper and disposable plastics, merchant wholesalers

327910 Cloth (e.g., aluminum oxide, garnet, emery, silicon carbide) coated manufacturing

561990 Cloth cutting, bolting, or winding for the trade

333292 Cloth spreading machinery manufacturing

321999 Cloth winding reels, wood

332618 Cloth, woven wire, made from purchased wire

334512 Clothes dryer controls, including dryness controls, manufacturing

423620 Clothes dryer, gas and electric, merchant wholesalers

811412 Clothes dryer, household-type, repair and maintenance services without retailing new clothes dryers

321999 Clothes dryers (clothes horses), wood manufacturing

424990 Clothes hangers merchant wholesalers

326199 Clothes hangers, plastics, manufacturing

321999 Clothes poles, wood, manufacturing

326199 Clothespins, plastics, manufacturing

321999 Clothespins, wood, manufacturing

448150 Clothing accessories stores

424330 Clothing accessories, women's, children's, and infants', merchant wholesalers

541490 Clothing design services

532220 Clothing rental (except industrial launderer, linen supply)

811490 Clothing repair shops, alterations only

448130 Clothing stores, children's and infants'

448140 Clothing stores, family

448110 Clothing stores, men's and boys'

453310 Clothing stores, used

448120 Clothing stores, women's and girls'

339931 Clothing, doll, manufacturing

315292 Clothing, fur (except apparel contractors), manufacturing

315211 Clothing, fur, men's and boys', cut and sew apparel contractors

315212 Clothing, fur, women's, girls', and infants', cut and sew apparel contractors

315292 Clothing, leather or sheep-lined (except apparel contractors), manufacturing

315211 Clothing, leather or sheep-lined, men's and boys', cut and sew apparel contractors

315212 Clothing, leather or sheep-lined, women's, girls', and infants', cut and sew apparel contractors

424320 Clothing, men's and boys', merchant wholesalers

315291 Clothing, water resistant, infants', cut and sewn from purchased fabric (except apparel contractors)

315211 Clothing, water resistant, men's and boys', cut and sew apparel contractors

315228 Clothing, water resistant, not specified elsewhere, men's and boys', cut and sewn from purchased fabric (except apparel contractors)

315239 Clothing, water resistant, not specified elsewhere, women's, misses', and girls', cut and sewn from purchased fabric (except apparel contractors)

315212 Clothing, water resistant, women's, girls' and infants', cut and sew apparel contractors

315299 Clothing, waterproof, cut and sewn from purchased fabric (except apparel contractors)

315211 Clothing, waterproof, men's and boys', cut and sew apparel contractors

315212 Clothing, waterproof, women's, girls', and infants', cut and sew apparel contractors

315291 Clothing, water-repellent, infants', cut and sewn from purchased fabric (except apparel contractors)

315211 Clothing, water-repellent, men's and boys', cut and sew apparel contractors

315228 Clothing, water-repellent, not specified elsewhere, men's and boys', cut and sewn from purchased fabric (except apparel contractors)

315239 Clothing, water-repellent, not specified elsewhere, women's, misses', and girls', cut and sewn from purchased fabric (except apparel contractors)

315212 Clothing, water-repellent, women's, girls', and infants', cut and sew apparel contractors

424330 Clothing, women's, children's, and infants', merchant wholesalers

339994 Cloths (except chemically treated), dusting and polishing, manufacturing

325612 Cloths, dusting and polishing, chemically treated, manufacturing

325998 Clove oil manufacturing

111940 Clover hay farming

111998 Clover seed farming

721310 Clubs, residential

339920 Clubs, sporting goods (e.g., golf, Indian), manufacturing

336350 Clutches and clutch discs, asbestos, manufacturing

525990 CMOs (collateralized mortgage obligations)

325413 Coagulation in-vitro diagnostic substances manufacturing

325412 Coagulation in-vivo diagnostic substances manufacturing

333922 Coal and ore conveyors manufacturing

212113 Coal beneficiating plants, anthracite

212111 Coal beneficiating plants, bituminous or lignite (surface or underground)

333131 Coal breakers, cutters, and pulverizers manufacturing

332322 Coal chutes, sheet metal (except stampings), manufacturing

454319 Coal dealers, direct selling

211111 Coal gasification at mine site

484220 Coal hauling, truck, local

211111 Coal liquefaction at mine site

423520 Coal merchant wholesalers

213113 Coal mining services (except site preparation and related construction contractor activities)

213113 Coal mining support services (tunneling, blasting, training, overburden removal)(except site preparation and related construction contractor activities)

486990 Coal pipeline transportation

211111 Coal pyrolysis

325192 Coal tar distillates manufacturing

324121 Coal tar paving materials made from purchased coal tar

424690 Coal tar products, primary and intermediate, merchant wholesalers

325211 Coal tar resins manufacturing

212113 Coal, anthracite, mining and/or beneficiating

212111 Coal, bituminous, beneficiating

212112 Coal, bituminous, underground mining or mining and beneficiating

212111 Coal, brown, mining and/or beneficiating

926120 Coast Guard (except academy)

483113 Coastal freight transportation to and from domestic ports

483114 Coastal passenger transportation to and from domestic ports

483113 Coastal shipping of freight to and from domestic ports

812331 Coat (e.g., barber's, beautician's, doctor's, nurse's) supply services

332618 Coat hangers made from purchased wire

315292 Coat linings, fur (except apparel contractors), manufacturing

315211 Coat linings, fur, men's and boys', cut and sew apparel contractors

315212 Coat linings, fur, women's, girls', and infants', cut and sew apparel contractors

448190 Coat stores

315999 Coat trimmings fabric cut and sewn from purchased fabric (except apparel contractors)

315211 Coat trimmings, fabric, men's and boys', cut and sew apparel contractors

315212 Coat trimmings, fabric, women's, girls', and infants', cut and sew apparel contractors

322226 Coated board made from purchased paperboard

322130 Coated board made in paperboard mills

324122 Coating compounds, tar, made from purchased asphaltic materials

238390 Coating concrete structures with plastics

332812 Coating metals and metal products for the trade

332812 Coating of metal and metal products with plastics for the trade

335110 Coating purchased light bulbs

322222 Coating purchased papers for nonpackaging applications (except photosensitive paper)

322221 Coating purchased papers for packaging applications

311320 Coatings, chocolate, made from cacao beans

315239 Coats (except fur, leather, tailored, waterproof), women's, misses', and girls', cut and sewn from purchased fabric (except apparel contractors)

315228 Coats (except fur, leather, tailored, waterproof, work), men's and boys', cut and sewn from purchased fabric (except apparel contractors)

315292 Coats (including tailored), leather or sheep-lined (except apparel contractors), manufacturing

315212 Coats (including tailored, leather, or sheep-lined), women's, girls', and infants', cut and sew apparel contractors

315292 Coats, artificial leather, cut and sewn from purchased fabric (except apparel contractors)

315211 Coats, artificial leather, men's and boys', cut and sew apparel contractors

315212 Coats, artificial leather, women's, girls', and infants', cut and sew apparel contractors

315292 Coats, fur (except apparel contractors), manufacturing

315211 Coats, fur, men's and boys', cut and sew apparel contractors

315212 Coats, fur, women's, girls', and infants', cut and sew apparel contractors

315291 Coats, infants' (except waterproof), cut and sewn from purchased fabric (except apparel contractors)

315292 Coats, leather, (except apparel contractors)

315211 Coats, leather, men's and boys', cut and sew apparel contractors

315212 Coats, leather, women's, girls', and infants', cut and sew apparel contractors

315211 Coats, men's and boys', cut and sew apparel contractors

315211 Coats, nontailored service apparel (e.g., laboratory, mechanics', medical), men's and boys', cut and sew apparel contractors

315225 Coats, nontailored service apparel (e.g., laboratory, mechanics', medical), men's and boys', cut and sewn from purchased fabric (except apparel contractors)

315212 Coats, nontailored service apparel (e.g., laboratory, medical, mechanics'), women's and girls', cut and sew apparel contractors

315239 Coats, nontailored service apparel (e.g., laboratory, medical, mechanics'), women's, misses', and girls', cut and sewn from purchased fabric (except apparel contractors)

315222 Coats, tailored (except fur, leather), men's and boys', cut and sewn from purchased fabric (except apparel contractors)

315234 Coats, tailored (except fur, leather), women's, misses', and girls', cut and sewn from purchased fabric

315299 Coats, waterproof (e.g., plastics, rubberized fabric, similar materials) rubberizing fabric and manufacturing coats

315211 Coats, waterproof (i.e., plastic, rubberized fabric, similar materials), men's and boys', cut and sew apparel contractors

315212 Coats, waterproof (i.e., plastics, rubberized fabric, similar materials), women's, girls', and infants', cut and sew apparel contractors

315299 Coats, waterproof, (e.g., plastics, rubberized fabric, similar materials) cut and sewn from purchased fabric (except apparel contractors)

315212 Coats, women's, girls', and infants', cut and sew apparel contractors

331319 Coaxial cable made in aluminum wire drawing plants

423610 Coaxial cable merchant wholesalers

331422 Coaxial cable, copper, made from purchased copper in wire drawing plants

331491	Coaxial cable, nonferrous metals (except aluminum, copper), made from purchased nonferrous metals (except aluminum, copper) in wire drawing plants
335929	Coaxial cable, nonferrous, made from purchased nonferrous wire
334417	Coaxial connectors manufacturing
339991	Coaxial mechanical face seals manufacturing
325188	Cobalt 60 (i.e., radioactive cobalt) manufacturing
325188	Cobalt chloride manufacturing
325188	Cobalt compounds, not specified elsewhere by process, manufacturing
212299	Cobalt concentrates beneficiating
212299	Cobalt ores mining and/or beneficiating
331419	Cobalt refining, primary
325188	Cobalt sulfate manufacturing
325411	Cocaine and derivatives (i.e., basic chemicals) manufacturing
332913	Cocks, drain, plumbing, manufacturing
722410	Cocktail lounges
311999	Cocktail mixes, dry, manufacturing
424820	Cocktails, alcoholic, premixed, merchant wholesalers
311320	Cocoa (e.g., instant, mix, mixed with other ingredients, powder drink, powdered) made from cacao beans
424590	Cocoa beans merchant wholesalers
311320	Cocoa butter made from cocoa beans
311330	Cocoa, powdered drink, prepared, made from purchased chocolate
311330	Cocoa, powdered, made from purchased chocolate

311330	Cocoa, powdered, mixed with other ingredients, made from purchased chocolate
311225	Coconut oil made from purchased oils
311223	Coconut oil made in crushing mills
111339	Coconut tree farming
311999	Coconut, desiccated and shredded, manufacturing
114111	Cod catching
114111	Cod fishing
311711	Cod liver oil extraction, crude, produced in a cannery
311712	Cod liver oil extraction, crude, produced in a fresh and frozen seafood plant
325411	Cod liver oil, medicinal, uncompounded, manufacturing
325411	Codeine and derivatives (i.e., basic chemicals) manufacturing
333993	Coding, dating, and imprinting packaging machinery manufacturing
445299	Coffee and tea (i.e., packaged) stores
722330	Coffee carts, mobile
311920	Coffee concentrates (i.e., instant coffee) manufacturing
311920	Coffee extracts manufacturing
111339	Coffee farming
322299	Coffee filters made from purchased paper
311920	Coffee flavoring and syrups (i.e., made from coffee) manufacturing
333319	Coffee makers and urns, commercial-type, manufacturing
335211	Coffee makers, household-type electric, manufacturing
424490	Coffee merchant wholesalers
311920	Coffee roasting
333294	Coffee roasting and grinding machinery (i.e., food manufacturing-type) manufacturing
722213	Coffee shops, on premise brewing

311920 Coffee substitute manufacturing
337122 Coffee tables, wood, manufacturing
311920 Coffee, blended, manufacturing
312111 Coffee, iced, manufacturing
311920 Coffee, instant and freeze dried, manufacturing
454390 Coffee-break service providers, direct selling
237990 Cofferdam construction
487110 Cog railway, scenic and sightseeing, operation
237130 Co-generation plant construction
541720 Cognitive research and development services
811310 Coil rewinding (except on an assembly line or factory basis)
333518 Coil winding and cutting machinery, metalworking, manufacturing
332612 Coiled springs (except clock, watch), light gauge, made from purchased wire or strip, manufacturing
332611 Coiled springs, heavy gauge metal, manufacturing
335312 Coils for motors and generators manufacturing
336322 Coils, ignition, internal combustion engines, manufacturing
332996 Coils, pipe, made from purchased metal pipe
333313 Coin counting machinery manufacturing
561990 Coin pick-up services, parking meter
316993 Coin purses (except metal) manufacturing
339911 Coin purses, precious metal, manufacturing
423420 Coin sorting machines merchant wholesalers
333313 Coin wrapping machines manufacturing
339999 Coin-operated amusement machines (except jukebox) manufacturing
812310 Coin-operated drycleaners and laundries

713290 Coin-operated gambling device concession operators (i.e., supplying and servicing in others' facilities)
339999 Coin-operated gambling devices manufacturing
423990 Coin-operated game machines merchant wholesalers
334310 Coin-operated jukebox manufacturing
812310 Coin-operated laundry and drycleaning routes (i.e., concession operators)
423440 Coin-operated merchandising machine merchant wholesalers
713990 Coin-operated nongambling amusement device concession operators (i.e., supplying and servicing in others' facilities)
812990 Coin-operated personal service machine (e.g., blood pressure, locker, photographic, scale, shoeshine) concession operators
423440 Coin-operated phonographs and vending machines merchant wholesalers
333311 Coin-operated vending machines manufacturing
423940 Coins merchant wholesalers
423520 Coke merchant wholesalers
221210 Coke oven gas, production and distribution
324199 Coke oven products (e.g., coke, gases, tars) made in coke oven establishments
331111 Coke oven products made in iron and steel mills
324110 Coke, petroleum, made in petroleum refineries
335110 Cold cathode fluorescent lamp tubes manufacturing
332111 Cold forgings made from purchased iron or steel, unfinished
332112 Cold forgings made from purchased nonferrous metals, unfinished
325412 Cold remedies manufacturing

333516 Cold rolling mill machinery, metalworking, manufacturing
331221 Cold rolling steel shapes (e.g., bar, plate, rod, sheet, strip) made from purchased steel
493120 Cold storage locker services
423740 Cold storage machinery merchant wholesalers
236220 Cold storage plant construction
493120 Cold storage warehousing
311991 Cole slaw, fresh, manufacturing
212391 Colemanite mining and/or beneficiating
311612 Collagen sausage casings made from purchased hides
332439 Collapsible tubes (e.g., toothpaste, glue), light gauge metal, manufacturing
315191 Collar and cuff sets made in apparel knitting mills
315212 Collar and cuff sets, women's, girls' and infants', cut and sew apparel contractors
315239 Collar and cuff sets, women's, misses' and girls', cut and sewn from purchased fabric (except apparel contractors)
316110 Collar leather, manufacturing
111219 Collard farming, field, bedding plant and seed production
333515 Collars (i.e., a machine tool accessory) manufacturing
316999 Collars and collar pads (i.e., harness) manufacturing
316999 Collars, dog, manufacturing
333613 Collars, shaft for power transmission equipment, manufacturing
525990 Collateralized mortgage obligations (CMOs)
333293 Collating machinery for printing and bookbinding manufacturing
333313 Collating machinery, office-type, manufacturing
453220 Collectible gift shops (e.g., crystal, pewter, porcelain)
812320 Collecting and distributing agents, laundry and drycleaning

561440 Collection agencies
561440 Collection agencies, accounts
221320 Collection, treatment, and disposal of waste through a sewer system
335312 Collector rings for motors and generators manufacturing
453998 Collector's items shops (e.g., autograph, card, coin, stamp)
454113 Collector's items, mail-order houses
611691 College board preparation centers
611691 College entrance exam preparation instruction
611710 College selection services
611310 Colleges (except junior colleges)
611511 Colleges, barber and beauty
611210 Colleges, community
611210 Colleges, junior
611310 Colleges, universities, and professional schools
333515 Collets (i.e., a machine tool accessory) manufacturing
325620 Colognes manufacturing
424210 Colognes merchant wholesalers
334510 Colonscopes, electromedical, manufacturing
812199 Color consulting services (i.e., personal care services)
325131 Color pigments, inorganic (except bone black, carbon black, lamp black), manufacturing
325132 Color pigments, organic (except animal black, bone black), manufacturing
323122 Color separation services, for the printing trade
334516 Colorimeters, laboratory-type, manufacturing
423920 Coloring books merchant wholesalers
316110 Coloring leather
332813 Coloring metals and metal products (except coating) for the trade
339113 Colostomy appliances manufacturing

812220	Columbariums
212299	Columbite mining and/or beneficiating
212299	Columbium ores mining and/or beneficiating
327420	Columns, architectural or ornamental plaster work, manufacturing
332420	Columns, fractionating, heavy gauge metal, manufacturing
321918	Columns, porch, wood, manufacturing
316993	Comb cases (except metal) manufacturing
339911	Comb cases, precious metal, manufacturing
334512	Combination limit and fan controls manufacturing
112990	Combination livestock farming (except dairy, poultry)
334512	Combination oil and hydronic controls manufacturing
333111	Combines (i.e., harvester-threshers) manufacturing
313312	Combing and converting top
333292	Combing machinery for textiles manufacturing
313312	Combing textile fibers
115113	Combining, agricultural
332999	Combs, metal, manufacturing
326199	Combs, plastics, manufacturing
326299	Combs, rubber, manufacturing
334513	Combustion control instruments (except commercial, household furnace-type) manufacturing
541330	Combustion engineering consulting services
562211	Combustors, hazardous waste
562213	Combustors, nonhazardous solid waste
711510	Comedians, independent
711110	Comedy troupes
812990	Comfort station operation
314129	Comforters made from purchased fabrics
511120	Comic book publishers (except exclusive Internet publishing)
511120	Comic book publishers and printing combined (except exclusive Internet publishing)
519130	Comic book publishers, exclusively on Internet
323112	Comic books flexographic printing without publishing
323111	Comic books gravure printing without publishing
323110	Comic books lithographic (offset) printing without publishing
323119	Comic books printing (except flexographic, gravure, lithographic, screen) without publishing
323113	Comic books screen printing without publishing
811310	Commercial and industrial machinery repair and maintenance services
541430	Commercial art services
541430	Commercial artists, independent
311812	Commercial bakeries
522110	Commercial banking
522110	Commercial banks
236220	Commercial building construction
236220	Commercial building construction general contractors
236220	Commercial building construction operative builders
531120	Commercial building rental or leasing
561450	Commercial credit reporting bureaus
323115	Commercial digital printing
323119	Commercial engraving printing
323112	Commercial flexographic printing
238220	Commercial freezer installation
323111	Commercial gravure printing
541430	Commercial illustration services
541430	Commercial illustrators, independent
238290	Commercial kitchen food preparation equipment (e.g., mixers, ovens, stoves) installation

323119 Commercial letterpress printing
335122 Commercial lighting fixtures, electric, manufacturing
323110 Commercial lithographic (offset) printing
523120 Commercial note brokers' offices
523110 Commercial paper dealing (i.e., acting as a principal in dealing securities to investors)
541922 Commercial photography services
323119 Commercial printing (except flexographic, digital, gravure, lithographic, quick, screen)
531312 · Commercial property managing
323114 Commercial quick printing
531210 Commercial real estate agencies
531210 Commercial real estate agents' offices
531312 Commercial real estate property managers' offices
811310 Commercial refrigeration equipment repair and maintenance services
238220 Commercial refrigeration system installation
323113 Commercial screen printing
424120 Commercial stationery suppliers merchant wholesalers
334518 Commercial timing mechanisms manufacturing
512110 Commercials, television, production
238290 Commercial-type door installation
445110 Commissaries, primarily groceries
523130 Commodity contract trading companies
523140 Commodity contracts brokerages
523140 Commodity contracts brokers' offices
523130 Commodity contracts dealing (i.e., acting as a principal in dealing commodities to investors)
523210 Commodity contracts exchanges

523140 Commodity contracts floor brokers
523130 Commodity contracts floor traders (i.e., acting as a principal in dealing commodities to investors)
523130 Commodity contracts floor trading (i.e., acting as a principal in dealing commodities to investors)
523140 Commodity contracts options brokerages
523130 Commodity contracts options dealing (i.e., acting as a principal in dealing commodities to investors)
523130 Commodity contracts traders (i.e., acting as a principal in dealing commodities to investors)
522298 Commodity Credit Corporation
523140 Commodity futures brokerages
541990 Commodity inspection services
212325 Common clay mining and/or beneficiating
212321 Common sand quarrying and/or beneficiating
212325 Common shale mining and/or beneficiating
923120 Communicable disease program administration
237130 Communication antenna construction
541430 Communication design services, visual
238210 Communication equipment installation
811213 Communication equipment repair and maintenance services
237130 Communication tower construction
926130 Communications commissions
423690 Communications equipment merchant wholesalers
334220 Communications equipment, mobile and microwave, manufacturing
334210 Communications headgear, telephone, manufacturing

926130 Communications licensing commissions and agencies

334515 Communications signal testing equipment

335929 Communications wire and cable, nonferrous, made from purchased nonferrous wire

331319 Communications wire or cable made in aluminum wire drawing plants

331422 Communications wire or cable, copper, made from purchased copper in wire drawing plants

331491 Communications wire or cable, nonferrous metals (except aluminum, copper), made from purchased nonferrous metals (except aluminum, copper) in wire drawing plants

311812 Communion wafer manufacturing

813319 Community action advocacy organizations

624190 Community action service agencies

624120 Community centers (except recreational only), adult

624110 Community centers (except recreational only), youth

813219 Community chests

611210 Community colleges

611210 Community colleges offering a wide variety of academic and technical training

925120 Community development agencies, government

813211 Community foundations

621498 Community health centers and clinics, outpatient

923120 Community health programs administration

624210 Community meals, social services

712110 Community museums

924120 Community recreation programs, government

923130 Community social service program administration

711110 Community theaters

335312 Commutators, electric motor, manufacturing

481111 Commuter air carriers, scheduled

485113 Commuter bus operation (except mixed mode)

485112 Commuter rail systems (except mixed mode)

485111 Commuter transit systems, mixed mode (e.g., bus, commuter rail, subway combination)

334310 Compact disc players (e.g., automotive, household-type) manufacturing

423990 Compact discs (CDs), prerecorded, merchant wholesalers

334611 Compact discs (i.e., CD-ROM), software, mass reproducing

334612 Compact discs, prerecorded audio, mass reproducing

334613 Compact discs, recordable or rewritable, blank, manufacturing

335110 Compact fluorescent light bulbs manufacturing

339911 Compacts, precious metal, manufacturing

316993 Compacts, solid leather, manufacturing

112990 Companion animals production (e.g., cats, dogs, parakeets, parrots)

624120 Companion services for disabled persons, the elderly, and persons diagnosed with mental retardation

333314 Comparators, optical, manufacturing

334511 Compasses, gyroscopic and magnetic (except portable), manufacturing

334519 Compasses, portable magnetic-type, manufacturing

541612 Compensation consulting services

541612 Compensation planning services

525190 Compensation, workers, insurance funds

311119   Complete feed, livestock, manufacturing

711510   Composers, independent

322214   Composite cans (i.e., foil-fiber and other combinations) manufacturing

562219   Compost dumps

325314   Compost manufacturing

325120   Compressed and liquefied industrial gas manufacturing

332911   Compressed gas cylinder valves manufacturing

424690   Compressed gases (except LP gas) merchant wholesalers

321219   Compression modified wood manufacturing

333220   Compression molding machinery for plastics manufacturing

339991   Compression packings manufacturing

532490   Compressor, air and gas, rental or leasing

237120   Compressor, metering and pumping station, gas and oil pipeline, construction

423830   Compressors (except air-conditioning, refrigeration) merchant wholesalers

333912   Compressors, air and gas, general purpose-type, manufacturing

423730   Compressors, air-conditioning, merchant wholesalers

336391   Compressors, motor vehicle air-conditioning, manufacturing

423740   Compressors, refrigeration, merchant wholesalers

238210   Computer and network cable installation

541712   Computer and related hardware research and development laboratories or services

423430   Computer boards, loaded, merchant wholesalers

423690   Computer boards, unloaded, merchant wholesalers

334419   Computer cable sets (e.g., monitor, printer) manufacturing

423690   Computer chips merchant wholesalers

518210   Computer data storage services

541519   Computer disaster recovery services

813410   Computer enthusiasts clubs

811212   Computer equipment repair and maintenance services without retailing new computers

443120   Computer equipment stores

238330   Computer flooring installation

323116   Computer forms (manifold or continuous) printing

337124   Computer furniture, metal household-type, manufacturing

337122   Computer furniture, wood household-type, manufacturing

541512   Computer hardware consulting services or consultants

518210   Computer input preparation services

334119   Computer input/output equipment (except terminals) manufacturing

611420   Computer operator training

424120   Computer paper supplies merchant wholesalers

322231   Computer paper, single layered continuous, die-cut, made from purchased paper

423430   Computer peripheral equipment merchant wholesalers

532420   Computer peripheral equipment rental or leasing

811212   Computer peripheral equipment repair and maintenance, without retailing new computer peripheral equipment

325992   Computer printer toner cartridges manufacturing

423430   Computer printers merchant wholesalers

541511   Computer program or software development, custom

611420   Computer programming schools

541511   Computer programming services, custom

532420   Computer rental or leasing

811212	Computer repair and maintenance services, without retailing new computers
611519	Computer repair training
334111	Computer servers manufacturing
541511	Computer software analysis and design services, custom
541512	Computer software consulting services or consultants
541511	Computer software programming services, custom
511210	Computer software publishers, packaged
511210	Computer software publishing and reproduction
541511	Computer software support services, custom
334613	Computer software tapes and disks, blank, rigid and floppy, manufacturing
611420	Computer software training
454113	Computer software, mail-order houses
423430	Computer software, packaged, merchant wholesalers
443120	Computer stores
541513	Computer systems facilities (i.e., clients' facilities) management and operation services
541512	Computer systems integration analysis and design services
541512	Computer systems integration design consulting services
541512	Computer systems integrator services
334113	Computer terminals manufacturing
518210	Computer time leasing
518210	Computer time rental
518210	Computer time sharing services
621512	Computer tomography (CT-SCAN) centers
611420	Computer training (except repair)
532230	Computer video game rental
541512	Computer-aided design (CAD) systems integration design services

541512	Computer-aided engineering (CAE) systems integration design services
541512	Computer-aided manufacturing (CAM) systems integration design services
334517	Computerized axial tomography (CT/CAT) scanners manufacturing
334512	Computerized environmental control systems for buildings manufacturing
334111	Computers manufacturing
423430	Computers merchant wholesalers
325411	Concentrated medicinal chemicals, uncompounded, manufacturing
311930	Concentrates, drink (except frozen fruit juice), manufacturing
311930	Concentrates, flavoring (except coffee based), manufacturing
311411	Concentrates, frozen fruit juice, manufacturing
423520	Concentrates, metallic, merchant wholesalers
333131	Concentration machinery, mining-type, manufacturing
711130	Concert artists, independent
711320	Concert booking agencies
711310	Concert hall operators
531120	Concert hall, no promotion of events, rental or leasing
711310	Concert managers with facilities
711320	Concert managers without facilities
711310	Concert organizers with facilities
711320	Concert organizers without facilities
711310	Concert promoters with facilities
711320	Concert promoters without facilities
713990	Concession operators, amusement device (except gambling) and ride
812990	Concierge services

926150 Conciliation and mediation services, government

325998 Concrete additive preparations (e.g., curing, hardening) manufacturing

424690 Concrete additives merchant wholesalers

327320 Concrete batch plants (including temporary)

238140 Concrete block laying

238910 Concrete breaking and cutting for demolition

423320 Concrete building products merchant wholesalers

238390 Concrete coating, glazing or sealing

238110 Concrete finishing

333120 Concrete finishing machinery manufacturing

238110 Concrete floor surfacing

238190 Concrete form contractors

332322 Concrete forms, sheet metal (except stampings), manufacturing

327390 Concrete furniture (e.g., benches, tables) manufacturing

333120 Concrete gunning equipment manufacturing

333120 Concrete mixing machinery, portable, manufacturing

238990 Concrete patio construction

237310 Concrete paving (i.e., highway, road, street, public sidewalk)

238990 Concrete paving, residential and commercial driveway and parking area

238110 Concrete pouring

423810 Concrete processing equipment merchant wholesalers

238120 Concrete product (e.g., structural precast, structural prestressed) installation

333298 Concrete products forming machinery manufacturing

327390 Concrete products, precast (except block, brick and pipe), manufacturing

238110 Concrete pumping (i.e., placement)

238120 Concrete reinforcement placement

332312 Concrete reinforcing bar (rebar) assemblies, fabrication

331111 Concrete reinforcing bar (rebar) made in iron and steel mills

331221 Concrete reinforcing bar (rebar), made from purchased steel in cold rolling mills

331221 Concrete reinforcing bar (rebar), made from purchased steel in steel rolling mills

423510 Concrete reinforcing bars merchant wholesalers

332618 Concrete reinforcing mesh made from purchased wire

238110 Concrete repair

238110 Concrete resurfacing

238990 Concrete sawing and drilling (except demolition)

327390 Concrete tanks manufacturing

327999 Concrete, dry mixture, manufacturing

211112 Condensate, cycle, natural gas production

333294 Condensed and evaporated milk machinery manufacturing

311514 Condensed milk manufacturing

311514 Condensed, evaporated or powdered whey, manufacturing

332410 Condenser boxes, metal, manufacturing

335999 Condensers (except electronic), fixed and variable, manufacturing

334414 Condensers, electronic, manufacturing

423690 Condensers, electronic, merchant wholesalers

332410 Condensers, steam, manufacturing

335312 Condensers, synchronous, electric, manufacturing

423830 Condensing units (except air-conditioning, refrigeration) merchant wholesalers

423730 Condensing units, air-conditioning, merchant wholesalers

423740 Condensing units, refrigeration, merchant wholesalers
326299 Condom manufacturing
813990 Condominium corporations
531312 Condominium managers' offices, commercial
531311 Condominium managers' offices, residential
236117 Condominium operative builders
813990 Condominium owners' associations
561599 Condominium time share exchange services
236116 Condominium, multifamily, construction general contractors
236115 Condominium, single-family, construction general contractors
335931 Conductor connectors, solderless connectors, sleeves, or soldering lugs, manufacturing
327123 Conduit, vitrified clay, manufacturing
331210 Conduit, welded and lock joint, made from purchased iron or steel
335932 Conduits and fittings, electrical, manufacturing
327332 Conduits, concrete, manufacturing
322214 Cones (e.g., winding yarn, string, ribbon, cloth), fiber, made from purchased paperboard
311821 Cones, ice cream, manufacturing
327112 Cones, pyrometric, earthenware, manufacturing
311313 Confectioner's beet sugar manufacturing
311312 Confectioner's powdered sugar made from purchased raw cane sugar
311320 Confectionery chocolate made from cacao beans
333294 Confectionery machinery manufacturing

424450 Confectionery merchant wholesalers
722213 Confectionery snack shops, made on premises with carryout services
445292 Confectionery stores, packaged, retailing only
311340 Confectionery, nonchocolate, manufacturing
531120 Conference center, no promotion of events, rental or leasing
322299 Confetti made from purchased paper
921120 Congress of the United States
336312 Connecting rods, automotive and truck gasoline engine, manufacturing
335931 Connectors and terminals for electrical devices manufacturing
335931 Connectors, electric cord, manufacturing
334417 Connectors, electronic (e.g., coaxial, cylindrical, printed circuit, rack and panel), manufacturing
423690 Connectors, electronic, merchant wholesalers
335313 Connectors, power, manufacturing
335931 Connectors, solderless (wiring devices), manufacturing
335931 Connectors, twist on wire (i.e., nuts), manufacturing
813312 Conscrvation advocacy organizations
924120 Conservation and reclamation agencies
712190 Conservation areas
611310 Conservatories of music (colleges or universities)
712130 Conservatories, botanical
711510 Conservators (i.e., art, artifact restorers), independent
611610 Conservatory of music (except academic)
453310 Consignment shops, used merchandise

336350 Constant velocity joints, automotive, truck, and bus, manufacturing

813940 Constituencies' associations, political party

325520 Construction adhesives (except asphalt, gypsum base) manufacturing

813910 Construction associations

238990 Construction elevator (i.e., temporary use during construction) erection and dismantling

541330 Construction engineering services

238910 Construction equipment (except crane) rental with operator

532412 Construction form rental

522292 Construction lending

423810 Construction machinery and equipment merchant wholesalers

532412 Construction machinery and equipment rental or leasing without operator

811310 Construction machinery and equipment repair and maintenance services

333120 Construction machinery manufacturing

236220 Construction management, commercial and institutional building

237990 Construction management, dam

237310 Construction management, highway, road, street and bridge

236210 Construction management, industrial building (except warehouses)

237990 Construction management, marine structure

237990 Construction management, mass transit

236116 Construction management, multifamily building

237120 Construction management, oil and gas pipeline

237120 Construction management, oil refinery and petrochemical complex

237990 Construction management, outdoor recreation facility

237130 Construction management, power and communication transmission line

236118 Construction management, residential remodeling

236115 Construction management, single-family building

237990 Construction management, tunnel

237110 Construction management, water and sewage treatment plant

237110 Construction management, water and sewer line

423610 Construction materials, electrical, merchant wholesalers

322233 Construction paper, school and art, made from purchased paper

322121 Construction paper, school and art, made in paper mills

212321 Construction sand and gravel beneficiating (e.g., grinding, screening, washing)

212321 Construction sand or gravel dredging

333120 Construction-type tractors and attachments manufacturing

928120 Consulates

****** Consultants—see specific activity

813920 Consultants' associations

531390 Consultants', real estate (except appraisers), offices

541330 Consulting engineers' offices

541330 Consulting engineers' private practices

812990 Consumer buying services

541990 Consumer credit counseling services

561450 Consumer credit reporting bureaus

423620 Consumer electronics merchant wholesalers

334514	Controls, revolution and timing instruments, manufacturing
623110	Convalescent homes or convalescent hospitals (except psychiatric)
623220	Convalescent homes or hospitals for psychiatric patients
446199	Convalescent supply stores
335221	Convection ovens (including portable), household-type, manufacturing
445120	Convenience food stores
447110	Convenience food with gasoline stations
335931	Convenience outlets, electric, manufacturing
561591	Convention and visitors bureaus
561591	Convention bureaus
531120	Convention center, no promotion of events, rental or leasing
561920	Convention managers
561920	Convention organizers
561920	Convention promoters
561920	Convention services
813110	Convents (except schools)
424130	Converted paper (except stationery and office supplies) merchant wholesalers
313311	Converters, broadwoven piece goods
335312	Converters, phase and rotary, electrical equipment, manufacturing
337121	Convertible sofas (except futons) manufacturing
336399	Convertible tops for automotive, truck, and bus, manufacturing
313311	Converting textiles, broadwoven
313312	Converting textiles, narrow woven
316110	Convertors, leather
313312	Convertors, narrow woven piece goods
423830	Conveying equipment (except farm) merchant wholesalers
423820	Conveying equipment, farm, merchant wholesalers
326220	Conveyor belts, rubber, manufacturing
238290	Conveyor system installation
333922	Conveyors, farm-type, manufacturing
311612	Cooked meats made from purchased carcasses
311822	Cookie dough made from purchased flour
722213	Cookie shops, on premise baking and carryout service
311821	Cookies manufacturing
424490	Cookies merchant wholesalers
311821	Cookies, filled, manufacturing
335211	Cooking appliances (except convection, microwave ovens), household-type electric portable, manufacturing
311320	Cooking chocolate made from cacao beans
333319	Cooking equipment (i.e., fryers, microwave ovens, ovens, ranges), commercial-type, manufacturing
423440	Cooking equipment, commercial, merchant wholesalers
423620	Cooking equipment, electric household-type, merchant wholesalers
423720	Cooking equipment, gas, household-type, merchant wholesalers
424490	Cooking oils merchant wholesalers
611519	Cooking schools
331511	Cooking utensils, cast iron, manufacturing
332214	Cooking utensils, fabricated metal, manufacturing
327212	Cooking utensils, glass and glass ceramic, made in glass making plants
423220	Cooking utensils, household-type, merchant wholesalers
327112	Cooking ware (e.g., stoneware, coarse earthenware, pottery), manufacturing
327215	Cooking ware made from purchased glass

327212 Cooking ware made in glass making plants

327112 Cooking ware, china, manufacturing

327112 Cooking ware, fine earthenware, manufacturing

221330 Cooled air distribution

326199 Coolers or ice chests, plastics (except foam), manufacturing

326140 Coolers or ice chests, polystyrene foam, manufacturing

333415 Coolers, refrigeration, manufacturing

333415 Coolers, water, manufacturing

238220 Cooling tower installation

333415 Cooling towers manufacturing

321920 Cooperage manufacturing

321920 Cooperage stock (e.g., heading, hoops, staves) manufacturing

423840 Cooperage stock merchant wholesalers

321920 Cooperage stock mills

531311 Cooperative apartment managers' offices

236117 Cooperative apartment operative builders

236116 Cooperative apartment, construction general contractors

812331 Cooperative hospital laundries (i.e., linen supply services)

524113 Cooperative life insurance organizations

813990 Cooperative owners' associations

321920 Coopered tubs manufacturing

332212 Coordinate and contour measuring machines, machinists' precision tools, manufacturing

532420 Copier rental or leasing

327123 Coping, wall, clay, manufacturing

327390 Copings, concrete, manufacturing

331525 Copper alloy castings (except die-castings), unfinished, manufacturing

331423 Copper alloys (e.g., brass, bronze) made from purchased metal or scrap

331411 Copper alloys made in primary copper smelting and refining mills

331423 Copper and copper-based shapes (e.g., cake, ingot, slag, wire bar) made from purchased metal or scrap

325131 Copper base pigments manufacturing

212234 Copper beneficiating plants

325188 Copper chloride manufacturing

325612 Copper cleaners manufacturing

325188 Copper compounds, not specified elsewhere by process, manufacturing

331411 Copper concentrate refining

331522 Copper die-casting foundries

331522 Copper die-castings, unfinished, manufacturing

331421 Copper foil made from purchased metal or scrap

332999 Copper foil not made in rolling mills

332112 Copper forgings made from purchased metals, unfinished

331525 Copper foundries (except die-casting)

325188 Copper iodide manufacturing

212234 Copper ore concentrates recovery

212234 Copper ore mine site development for own account

212234 Copper ores mining and/or beneficiating

331423 Copper powder, flakes, and paste made from purchased copper

331421 Copper products (except communication wire, energy wire) made by drawing purchased copper

331421 Copper products (except communication wire, energy wire) made by rolling, drawing, or extruding purchased copper

331421　Copper products (except communication wire, energy wire) made in integrated secondary smelting and extruding mills

331421　Copper products (except communication wire, energy wire) made in integrated secondary smelting mills and drawing plants

238160　Copper roofing installation

331423　Copper secondary smelting and alloying

331423　Copper secondary smelting and refining from purchased metal or scrap

331411　Copper shapes (e.g., bar, billet, ingot, plate, sheet) made in primary copper smelting and refining mills

331411　Copper smelting and refining, primary

325188　Copper sulfate manufacturing

212234　Copper-water precipitates

561439　Copy centers (except combined with printing services)

561439　Copy shops (except combined with printing services)

423420　Copying machines merchant wholesalers

314991　Cord (except tire, wire) manufacturing

335931　Cord connectors, electric, manufacturing

314992　Cord for reinforcing rubber tires, industrial belting, and fuel cells manufacturing

331422　Cord sets, flexible, made from purchased copper in wire drawing plants

331319　Cord sets, flexible, made in aluminum wire drawing plants

331491　Cord sets, flexible, nonferrous metals (except aluminum, copper), made from purchased nonferrous metals (except aluminum, copper) in wire drawing plants

314991　Cordage (except wire) manufacturing

333292　Cordage and rope (except wire) making machines manufacturing

423840　Cordage merchant wholesalers

325920　Cordite explosive materials manufacturing

334210　Cordless telephones (except cellular) manufacturing

313221　Cords and braids, narrow woven, manufacturing

313210　Corduroys weaving

333994　Core baking and mold drying ovens manufacturing

213112　Core cutting in oil and gas wells, on a contract basis

238910　Core drilling and test boring for construction

213112　Core drilling, exploration services, oil and gas field

333131　Core drills, underground mining-type, manufacturing

322214　Cores (i.e., all-fiber, nonfiber ends of any material), fiber, made from purchased paperboard

332992　Cores, bullet (i.e., 30 mm. or less, 1.18 inch or less), manufacturing

332997　Cores, sand foundry, manufacturing

423840　Cork merchant wholesalers

321999　Cork products (except gaskets) manufacturing

321999　Corks, bottle, manufacturing

111421　Corms farming

311230　Corn breakfast foods manufacturing

311919　Corn chips and related corn snacks manufacturing

424450　Corn chips and related corn snacks merchant wholesalers

311340　Corn confections manufacturing

321992　Corn cribs, prefabricated, wood, manufacturing

311221　Corn dextrin manufacturing

115114　Corn drying

111150　Corn farming (except sweet corn), field and seed production

311211　Corn flour manufacturing

311221	Corn gluten feed manufacturing
311221	Corn gluten meal manufacturing
333111	Corn heads for combines manufacturing
311211	Corn meal made in flour mills
311221	Corn oil cake and meal manufacturing
311225	Corn oil made from purchased oils
311221	Corn oil mills
311221	Corn oil, crude and refined, made by wet milling corn
333111	Corn pickers and shellers manufacturing
335211	Corn poppers, household-type electric, manufacturing
333294	Corn popping machinery (i.e., food manufacturing-type) manufacturing
333319	Corn popping machines, commercial-type, manufacturing
339113	Corn remover and bunion pad manufacturing
115114	Corn shelling
311221	Corn starch manufacturing
311221	Corn sweeteners (e.g., dextrose, fructose, glucose) made by wet milling corn
311999	Corn syrups made from purchased sweeteners
311213	Corn, malt, manufacturing
339112	Corneal microscopes manufacturing
311612	Corned meats made from purchases carcasses
316999	Corners, luggage, leather, manufacturing
339992	Cornets and parts manufacturing
332322	Cornices, sheet metal (except stampings), manufacturing
321918	Cornices, wood, manufacturing
112320	Cornish hen production
424490	Cornmeal, edible, merchant wholesalers
212325	Cornwall stone mining and/or beneficiating
923120	Coroners' offices
522130	Corporate credit unions
813211	Corporate foundations, awarding grants
541430	Corporate identification (i.e., logo) design services
541110	Corporate law offices
551114	Corporate offices
115210	Corralling, drovers
332323	Corrals, metal, manufacturing
325998	Correction fluids (i.e., typewriter) manufacturing
922140	Correctional boot camps
561210	Correctional facility operation on a contract or fee basis
922140	Correctional institutions
237120	Corrosion protection, underground pipeline and oil storage tank
322211	Corrugated and solid fiber boxes made from purchased paper or paperboard
322211	Corrugated and solid fiberboard pads made from purchased paper or paperboard
238160	Corrugated metal roofing installation
322211	Corrugated paper made from purchased paper or paperboard
331221	Corrugating iron or steel in cold rolling mills made from purchased iron or steel
315212	Corselets cut and sew apparel contractors
315231	Corselets, women's, misses', and girls', cut and sewn from purchased fabric (except apparel contractors)
315212	Corsets and allied garments (except surgical), women's, cut and sew apparel contractors
315231	Corsets and allied garments (except surgical), women's, misses', and girls', cut and sewn from purchased fabric (except apparel contractors)
339113	Corsets, surgical, manufacturing
325411	Cortisone, uncompounded, manufacturing
212399	Corundum mining and/or beneficiating

316993   Cosmetic bags (except metal) manufacturing
339911   Cosmetic bags, precious metal, manufacturing
325620   Cosmetic creams, lotions, and oils manufacturing
561910   Cosmetic kit assembling and packaging services
424210   Cosmetics merchant wholesalers
446120   Cosmetics stores
812112   Cosmetology salons or shops
611511   Cosmetology schools
541490   Costume design services (except independent theatrical costume designers)
711510   Costume designers, independent theatrical
339914   Costume jewelry manufacturing
423940   Costume jewelry merchant wholesalers
448150   Costume jewelry stores
532220   Costume rental
448190   Costume stores (including theatrical)
315299   Costumes (e.g., lodge, masquerade, theatrical) cut and sewn from purchased fabric (except apparel contractors)
315212   Costumes (e.g., lodge, masquerade, theatrical) women's, girls' and infants', cut and sew apparel contractors
315211   Costumes (e.g., lodge, masquerade, theatrical), men's and boys', cut and sew apparel contractors
337121   Cot springs, assembled, manufacturing
337124   Cots, metal household-type, manufacturing
337122   Cots, wood household-type, manufacturing
311511   Cottage cheese manufacturing
236115   Cottage construction general contractors
236117   Cottage operative builders
531110   Cottage rental or leasing
721199   Cottages, housekeeping

332722   Cotter pins, metal, manufacturing
424990   Cotton (except raw) merchant wholesalers
339113   Cotton and cotton balls, absorbent, manufacturing
333111   Cotton balers and presses manufacturing
314999   Cotton battings (except nonwoven batting) manufacturing
313111   Cotton cordage spun yarns made from purchased fiber
313210   Cotton fabrics, broadwoven, weaving
313221   Cotton fabrics, narrow woven weaving
111920   Cotton farming, field and seed production
322121   Cotton fiber paper stock manufacturing
115111   Cotton ginning
333111   Cotton ginning machinery manufacturing
333111   Cotton picker and stripper harvesting machinery manufacturing
313111   Cotton spun yarns made from purchased fiber
313113   Cotton thread manufacturing
339113   Cotton tipped applicators manufacturing
115113   Cotton, machine harvesting
424590   Cotton, raw, merchant wholesalers
111920   Cottonseed farming
311225   Cottonseed oil made from purchased oils
311223   Cottonseed oil, cake and meal, made in crushing mills
337121   Couch springs, assembled, manufacturing
337121   Couches, upholstered, manufacturing
311340   Cough drops (except medicated) manufacturing
325412   Cough drops, medicated, manufacturing
325412   Cough medicines manufacturing

334513 Coulometric analyzers, industrial process-type, manufacturing
334516 Coulometric analyzers, laboratory-type, manufacturing
325199 Coumarin manufacturing
325211 Coumarone-indene resins manufacturing
926110 Councils of Economic Advisers
624190 Counseling services
621410 Counseling services, family planning
541110 Counselors' at law offices
541110 Counselors' at law private practices
334519 Count rate meters, nuclear radiation, manufacturing
238350 Counter top, residential-type, installation
334514 Counter type registers manufacturing
337215 Counter units (except refrigerated) manufacturing
333515 Counterbores (i.e., a machine tool accessory), metalworking, manufacturing
332212 Counterbores and countersinking bits, woodworking, manufacturing
334511 Countermeasure sets (e.g., active countermeasures, jamming equipment) manufacturing
334514 Counters (e.g., electrical, electronic, mechanical), totalizing, manufacturing
316999 Counters (i.e., shoe cut stock), leather, manufacturing
333415 Counters and display cases, refrigerated, manufacturing
334514 Counters, revolution, manufacturing
333515 Countersinks (i.e., a machine tool accessory) manufacturing
238390 Countertop and cabinet, metal (except residential-type), installation
337215 Countertops (except kitchen and bathroom), wood or plastics laminated on wood, manufacturing

337110 Countertops (i.e., kitchen, bathroom), wood or plastics laminated on wood, manufacturing
326199 Countertops, plastics, manufacturing
327991 Countertops, stone, manufacturing
337110 Countertops, wood, manufacturing
334514 Counting devices manufacturing
713910 Country clubs
711130 Country musical artists, independent
711130 Country musical groups
921120 County commissioners
925120 County development agencies
921110 County supervisors' and executives' offices
923110 County supervisors of education (except school boards)
332919 Couplings, hose, metal (except fluid power), manufacturing
333613 Couplings, mechanical power transmission, manufacturing
332996 Couplings, pipe, made from purchased metal pipe
541870 Coupon direct distribution services
561990 Coupon processing services
561990 Coupon redemption services (i.e., clearinghouse)
492110 Courier services (i.e., intercity network) (except establishments operating under a universal service obligation)
611410 Court reporting schools
561492 Court reporting services
922110 Courts of law, civilian (except American Indian or Alaska Native)
921150 Courts, American Indian or Alaska Native
922110 Courts, civilian (except American Indian or Alaska Native)
928110 Courts, military
922110 Courts, small claims

315211 Coveralls, work, men's and boys', cut and sew apparel contractors

315225 Coveralls, work, men's and boys', cut and sewn from purchased fabric (except apparel contractors)

315212 Coveralls, work, women's, girls', and infants', cut and sew apparel contractors

315239 Coveralls, work, women's, misses', and girls', cut and sewn from purchased fabric (except apparel contractors)

314912 Covers (e.g., boat, swimming pool, truck) made from purchased fabrics

332313 Covers, annealing, fabricated metal plate work, manufacturing

321999 Covers, bottle and demijohn, willow, rattan, and reed, manufacturing

332313 Covers, floating, fabricated metal plate work, manufacturing

332322 Cowls, sheet metal (except stampings), manufacturing

111219 Cowpea (except dry) farming, field and seed production

111130 Cowpea farming, dry, field and seed production

541211 CPAs' (certified public accountants) offices

611699 CPR (cardiac pulmonary resusitation) training and certification

332618 Crab traps made from purchased wire

114112 Crabbing

333294 Cracker making machinery manufacturing

311821 Crackers (e.g., graham, soda) manufacturing

333518 Cradle assembly machinery (i.e., wire making equipment) manufacturing

337122 Cradles, wood, manufacturing

453220 Craft (except craft supply) stores

339932 Craft and hobby kits and sets manufacturing

561920 Craft fair managers

561920 Craft fair organizers

561920 Craft fair promoters

423920 Craft kits merchant wholesalers

451120 Craft supply stores (except needlecraft)

611513 Craft union apprenticeship training programs

111334 Cranberry farming

335314 Crane and hoist controls, including metal mill, manufacturing

532412 Crane rental or leasing without operator

238990 Crane rental with operator

423810 Cranes (except industrial) merchant wholesalers

333120 Cranes, construction-type, manufacturing

333924 Cranes, industrial truck, manufacturing

423830 Cranes, industrial, merchant wholesalers

423810 Cranes, mining, merchant wholesalers

333923 Cranes, overhead traveling, manufacturing

325998 Crankcase additive preparations manufacturing

336312 Crankshaft assemblies, automotive and truck gasoline engine, manufacturing

333512 Crankshaft grinding machines metal cutting type, manufacturing

321920 Crates (e.g., berry, butter, fruit, vegetable) made of wood, wirebound, manufacturing

488991 Crating goods for shipping

112512 Crawfish production, farm raising

238910 Crawler tractor rental with operator

114112 Crayfish fishing

339942 Crayons manufacturing

311511 Cream manufacturing

424430 Cream merchant wholesalers

325199 Cream of tartar manufacturing

333111 Cream separators, farm-type, manufacturing
333294 Cream separators, industrial, manufacturing
424430 Cream stations merchant wholesalers
311514 Cream, dried and powdered, manufacturing
311512 Creamery butter manufacturing
424430 Creamery products (except canned) merchant wholesalers
424490 Creamery products, canned, merchant wholesalers
313311 Crease resistant finishing of broadwoven fabric
313312 Crease resistant finishing of fabrics (except broadwoven)
561450 Credit agencies
323119 Credit and identification card imprinting and embossing
326199 Credit and identification card stock, plastics, manufacturing
524126 Credit and other financial responsibility insurance carriers, direct
561450 Credit bureaus
522210 Credit card banks
522210 Credit card issuing
812990 Credit card notification services (i.e., lost or stolen card reporting)
522320 Credit card processing services
561450 Credit investigation services
524113 Credit life insurance carriers, direct
561450 Credit rating services
541990 Credit repair (i.e., counseling) services, consumer
561450 Credit reporting bureaus
522130 Credit unions
333999 Cremating ovens manufacturing
812220 Crematories (except combined with funeral homes)
111219 Crenshaw melon farming, field, bedding plant and seed production
325192 Creosote made by distillation of coal tar
325191 Creosote made by distillation of wood tar

321114 Creosoting of wood
322299 Crepe paper made from purchased paper
325211 Cresol resins manufacturing
325211 Cresol-furfural resins manufacturing
325192 Cresols made by distillation of coal tar
325192 Cresylic acids made from refined petroleum or natural gas
115115 Crew leaders, farm labor
315119 Crew socks knitting or knitting and finishing
237990 Cribbing (i.e., shore protection), construction
337124 Cribs (i.e., baby beds), metal, manufacturing
337122 Cribs (i.e., baby beds), wood, manufacturing
112990 Cricket production
922120 Criminal investigation offices, government
922190 Criminal justice statistics centers, government
541110 Criminal law offices
111998 Crimson cloves seed farming
624190 Crisis intervention centers
114111 Croaker fishing
313111 Crochet spun yarns (e.g., cotton, manmade fiber, silk, wool) made from purchased fiber
314999 Crochet ware made from purchased materials
335211 Crock pots, household-type electric, manufacturing
327112 Crockery manufacturing
311812 Croissants, baking, made in commercial bakeries
115114 Crop cleaning
333111 Crop driers manufacturing
115112 Crop dusting
524126 Crop insurance carrier, direct
423820 Crop preparation machinery (e.g., cleaning, conditioning, drying) merchant wholesalers
115112 Crop spraying
316999 Crops, riding, manufacturing
339920 Croquet sets manufacturing

713920	Cross country skiing facilities without accommodations
332911	Cross valves, industrial-type, manufacturing
321114	Crossties, treating
311812	Croutons and bread crumbs made in commercial bakeries
423840	Crowns and closures, metal, merchant wholesalers
332115	Crowns, metal (e.g., bottle, can), stamping
334411	CRT (cathode ray tube) manufacturing
327124	Crucibles, fire clay, manufacturing
327125	Crucibles, graphite, magnesite, chrome, silica, or other nonclay materials, manufacturing
311221	Crude corn oil manufacturing
424720	Crude oil merchant wholesalers (except bulk stations, terminals)
486110	Crude oil pipeline transportation
324110	Crude oil refining
424710	Crude oil terminals
211111	Crude petroleum from oil sand
211111	Crude petroleum from oil shale
211111	Crude petroleum production
324110	Crude petroleum refineries
424990	Crude rubber merchant wholesalers
336322	Cruise control mechanisms, electronic, automotive, truck, and bus, manufacturing
483114	Cruise lines (i.e., deep sea passenger transportation to and from domestic ports, including Puerto Rico)
483112	Cruise lines (i.e., deep sea passenger transportation to or from foreign ports)
561599	Cruise ship ticket offices
713210	Cruises, gambling
115310	Cruising timber
311812	Crullers (except frozen) made in commercial bakeries
311813	Crullers, frozen, made in a commercial bakery

423320	Crushed stone merchant wholesalers
333120	Crushing machinery, portable, manufacturing
333131	Crushing machinery, stationary, manufacturing
212111	Crushing plants, bituminous coal
333120	Crushing, pulverizing, and screening machinery, portable, manufacturing
112512	Crustacean production, farm raising
339113	Crutches and walkers manufacturing
423450	Crutches merchant wholesalers
532291	Crutches, invalid, rental
332420	Cryogenic tanks, heavy gauge metal, manufacturing
212399	Cryolite mining and/or beneficiating
311340	Crystallized fruits and fruit peel manufacturing
334419	Crystals and crystal assemblies, electronic, manufacturing
334517	CT/CAT (computerized axial tomography) scanners manufacturing
621512	CT-SCAN (computer tomography) centers
335313	Cubicles (i.e., electric switchboard equipment) manufacturing
111219	Cucumber farming (except under cover), field, bedding plant and seed production
111419	Cucumber farming, grown under cover
339993	Cuff links (except precious) manufacturing
339911	Cuff links, precious metal, manufacturing
332999	Cuffs, leg, iron, manufacturing
611519	Culinary arts schools
112310	Cull hen production
212113	Culm bank recovery, anthracite (except on a contract basis)
213113	Culm bank recovery, anthracite, on a contract basis

333313 Currency counting machinery manufacturing
423420 Currency handling machines merchant wholesalers
335311 Current limiting reactors, electrical, manufacturing
334515 Current measuring equipment manufacturing
335931 Current taps, attachment plug and screw shell types, manufacturing
423610 Current-carrying wiring devices merchant wholesalers
316110 Currying furs
316110 Currying leather
442291 Curtain and drapery stores, packaged
812320 Curtain cleaning services
337920 Curtain or drapery fixtures (e.g., poles, rods, rollers) manufacturing
337920 Curtain rods and fittings manufacturing
321999 Curtain stretchers, wood, manufacturing
238150 Curtain wall, glass, installation
238190 Curtain wall, metal, installation
332323 Curtain wall, metal, manufacturing
238120 Curtain wall, precast concrete, installation
313210 Curtains and draperies made in broadwoven fabric mills
314121 Curtains and draperies, window, made from purchased fabrics
313249 Curtains made in lace mills
313249 Curtains made in warp knitting mills
313241 Curtains made in weft knitting mills
423220 Curtains merchant wholesalers
337121 Cushion springs, assembled, manufacturing
314129 Cushions (except carpet, springs) made from purchased fabrics
326150 Cushions, carpet and rug, urethane and other foam plastics (except polystrene), manufacturing

311520 Custard, frozen, manufacturing
561720 Custodial services
337212 Custom architectural millwork and fixtures, manufacturing on a job shop basis
236116 Custom builders (except operative), multifamily buildings
236115 Custom builders (except operative), single-family home
236117 Custom builders, operative builders, multifamily buildings
236117 Custom builders, operative builders, single-family home
325991 Custom compounding (i.e., blending and mixing) of purchased plastics resins
337212 Custom design interiors (i.e., coordinated furniture, architectural woodwork, fixtures), manufacturing
311119 Custom milling of animal feed
442299 Custom picture frame shops
333513 Custom roll forming machines, metalworking, manufacturing
332114 Custom roll forming metal products
321113 Custom sawmills
311611 Custom slaughtering
315223 Custom tailors, men's and boys' dress shirts, cut and sewn from purchased fabric
315222 Custom tailors, men's and boys' suits, cut and sewn from purchased fabric
315233 Custom tailors, women's, misses' and girls' dresses cut and sewn from purchased fabric (except apparel contractors)
541613 Customer service management consulting services
488510 Customs brokers
921130 Customs bureaus
541614 Customs consulting services
327215 Cut and engraved glassware made from purchased glass
315211 Cut and sew apparel contractors, men's and boys'

315212 Cut and sew apparel contractors, women's, girls', and infants'
111422 Cut flower growing
111422 Cut rose growing
316999 Cut stock for boots and shoes manufacturing
321912 Cut stock manufacturing
327991 Cut stone bases (e.g., desk sets pedestals, lamps, plaques and similar small particles) manufacturing
327991 Cut stone products (e.g., blocks, statuary) manufacturing
811490 Cutlery (e.g., knives, scissors) sharpening, household-type
423710 Cutlery merchant wholesalers
332211 Cutlery, nonprecious and precious plated metal, manufacturing
339912 Cutlery, precious metal (except precious plated), manufacturing
333512 Cut-off machines, metalworking, manufacturing
335931 Cutouts, switch and fuse, manufacturing
333131 Cutters, coal, manufacturing
332212 Cutters, glass, manufacturing
333515 Cutters, metal milling, manufacturing
113310 Cutting and transporting timber
213112 Cutting cores in oil and gas wells on a contract basis
332212 Cutting dies (e.g., paper, leather, textile) manufacturing
332212 Cutting dies (except metal cutting) manufacturing
333514 Cutting dies, metalworking, manufacturing
315211 Cutting fabric owned by others for men's and boys' apparel
315212 Cutting fabric owned by others for women's, girls', and infants' apparel
339114 Cutting instruments, dental, manufacturing
333512 Cutting machines, metalworking, manufacturing
238910 Cutting new rights of way

316110 Cutting of leather
424470 Cutting of purchased carcasses (except boxed meat cut on an assembly-line basis) merchant wholesalers
324191 Cutting oils made from refined petroleum
325998 Cutting oils, synthetic, manufacturing
113310 Cutting timber
327215 Cutting, engraving, etching, painting or polishing purchased glass
111422 Cuttings farming
325188 Cyanides manufacturing
212325 Cyanite mining and/or beneficiating
211112 Cycle condensate production
325110 Cyclic aromatic hydrocarbons made from refined petroleum or liquid hydrocarbons
324110 Cyclic aromatic hydrocarbons made in petroleum refineries
424690 Cyclic crudes and intermediates merchant wholesalers
325192 Cyclic crudes made by distillation of coal tar
325212 Cyclo rubber, synthetic, manufacturing
325192 Cyclohexane manufacturing
332313 Cyclones, industrial, fabricated metal plate work, manufacturing
325192 Cyclopentane made from refined petroleum or natural gas
325192 Cyclopropane made from refined petroleum or natural gas
325412 Cyclopropane medicinal preparations manufacturing
325191 Cycloterpenes manufacturing
335999 Cyclotrons manufacturing
333512 Cylinder boring machines metal cutting type, manufacturing
336312 Cylinder heads, automotive and truck gasoline engine, manufacturing
327332 Cylinder pipe, prestressed concrete, manufacturing

332618 Cylinder wire cloth made from purchased wire
332994 Cylinders and clips, gun (i.e., 30 mm. or less, 1.18 inch or less), manufacturing
332995 Cylinders and clips, gun (i.e., more than 30 mm., more than 1.18 inch), manufacturing
333995 Cylinders, fluid power, manufacturing
336340 Cylinders, master brake (new and rebuilt), manufacturing
332420 Cylinders, pressure, heavy gauge metal, manufacturing
334417 Cylindrical connectors, electronic, manufacturing
332991 Cylindrical roller bearings manufacturing
339992 Cymbals and parts manufacturing
339112 Cystoscopes (except electromedical) manufacturing
334510 Cystoscopes, electromedical, manufacturing
325413 Cytology and histology in-vitro diagnostic substances manufacturing
621511 Cytology health laboratories
112120 Dairy cattle farming
311119 Dairy cattle feeds supplements, concentrates, and premixes, manufacturing
424430 Dairy depots merchant wholesalers
311514 Dairy food canning
112420 Dairy goat farming
112111 Dairy heifer replacement production
541690 Dairy herd consulting services
115210 Dairy herd improvement associations
445299 Dairy product stores
424430 Dairy products (except canned, dried) merchant wholesalers
424490 Dairy products, dried or canned, merchant wholesalers
424430 Dairy products, frozen, merchant wholesalers
112410 Dairy sheep farming
237990 Dam construction

332312 Dam gates, metal plate, manufacturing
334512 Damper operators (e.g., electric, pneumatic, thermostatic) manufacturing
332322 Dampers, sheet metal (except stampings), manufacturing
238390 Dampproofing contractors
711130 Dance bands
713940 Dance centers, aerobic
711120 Dance companies
711310 Dance festival managers with facilities
711320 Dance festival managers without facilities
711310 Dance festival organizers with facilities
711320 Dance festival organizers without facilities
711310 Dance festival promoters with facilities
711320 Dance festival promoters without facilities
531120 Dance hall rental or leasing
713990 Dance halls
611610 Dance instruction
711120 Dance productions, live theatrical
611610 Dance schools
611610 Dance studios
711120 Dance theaters
621340 Dance therapists' offices (e.g., centers, clinics)
711120 Dance troupes
711510 Dancers, independent
313113 Darning thread (e.g., cotton, manmade fibers, silk, wool) manufacturing
332994 Dart guns manufacturing
339932 Darts and dart games manufacturing
518210 Data capture imaging services
334210 Data communications equipment (e.g., bridges, gateways, routers) manufacturing
518210 Data entry services
334513 Data loggers, industrial process-type, manufacturing

518210 Data processing computer services

541513 Data processing facilities (i.e., clients' facilities) management and operation services

423430 Data processing machines, computer, merchant wholesalers

518210 Data processing services (except payroll services, financial transaction processing services)

323112 Databases flexographic printing without publishing

323111 Databases gravure printing without publishing

323110 Databases lithographic (offset) printing without publishing

323119 Databases printing (except flexographic, gravure, lithographic, quick, screen) without publishing

323113 Databases screen printing without publishing

111339 Date farming

339943 Date stamps, hand operated, manufacturing

311423 Dates, dried, made in dehydration plant

311340 Dates, sugared and stuffed, manufacturing

334518 Dating devices and machines (except rubber stamps) manufacturing

812990 Dating services

333923 Davits manufacturing

****** Day camps, instructional—see type of instruction

624120 Day care centers for disabled persons, the elderly, and persons diagnosed with mental retardation

624120 Day care centers, adult

624410 Day care centers, child or infant

624410 Day care services, child or infant

812199 Day spas

621310 DCs' (doctors of chiropractic) offices (e.g., centers, clinics)

621210 DDSs' (doctors of dental surgery) offices (e.g., centers, clinics)

325320 DDT (dichlorodiphenyltrichloroethane) insecticides manufacturing

922120 DEA (Drug Enforcement Administration)

332510 Dead bolts, metal, manufacturing

****** Dealers—see type

561440 Debt collection services

333512 Deburring machines, metalworking, manufacturing

334515 Decade boxes (i.e., capacitance, inductance, resistance) manufacturing

325199 Decahydronaphthalene manufacturing

327112 Decalcomania on china and glass for the trade

339999 Decalcomania work (except on china, glass)

238190 Deck and grate (except roof), metal, installation

238350 Deck construction, residential-type

327215 Decorated glassware made from purchased glass

327112 Decorating china (e.g., encrusting gold, silver, other metal on china) for the trade

541410 Decorating consulting services, interior

335129 Decorative area lighting fixtures (except residential) manufacturing

335121 Decorative area lighting fixtures, residential, manufacturing

712110 Decorative art museums

238150 Decorative glass and mirror installation

327212 Decorative glassware made in glass making plants

335110 Decorative lamp bulbs manufacturing

238190 Decorative steel and wrought iron work installation

314999 Decorative stitching contractors on apparel

314999 Decorative stitching on textile articles and apparel

321918 Decorative wood moldings (e.g., base, chair rail, crown, shoe) manufacturing

115114 Decorticating flax

483113 Deep sea freight transportation to or from domestic ports (including Puerto Rico)

483111 Deep sea freight transportation to or from foreign ports

483114 Deep sea passenger transportation to and from domestic ports (including Puerto Rico)

483112 Deep sea passenger transportation to or from foreign ports

333319 Deep-fat fryers, commercial-type, manufacturing

335211 Deep-fat fryers, household-type electric, manufacturing

112990 Deer production

334510 Defibrilators manufacturing

325312 Defluorinated phosphates manufacturing

325998 Defoamers and antifoaming agents manufacturing

325320 Defoliants manufacturing

325998 Degreasing preparations for machinery parts manufacturing

325612 Degreasing preparations, household-type, manufacturing

333415 Dehumidifiers (except portable electric) manufacturing

335211 Dehumidifiers, portable electric, manufacturing

311514 Dehydrated milk manufacturing

311423 Dehydrating fruits and vegetables

311423 Dehydrating potato products (e.g., flakes, granules)

325998 Deicing preparations manufacturing

322110 Deinking plants

322110 Deinking recovered paper

722211 Delicatessen restaurants

333997 Delicatessen scales manufacturing

445210 Delicatessens (except grocery store, restaurants)

445110 Delicatessens primarily retailing a range of grocery items and meats

561440 Delinquent account collection services

623990 Delinquent youth halfway group homes

115114 Delinting cottonseed

332618 Delivery cases made from purchased wire

492210 Delivery service (except as part of intercity carrier network, U.S. Postal Service)

334515 Demand meters, electric, manufacturing

541720 Demographic research and development services

238910 Demolition contractor

238910 Demolition, building and structure

541890 Demonstration services, merchandise

336212 Demountable cargo containers manufacturing

325193 Denatured alcohol manufacturing

313210 Denims weaving

321219 Densified wood manufacturing

333315 Densitometers (except laboratory analytical) manufacturing

334516 Densitometers, laboratory analytical, manufacturing

334513 Density and specific gravity instruments, industrial process-type, manufacturing

339114 Dental alloys for amalgams manufacturing

339114 Dental chairs manufacturing

423450 Dental chairs merchant wholesalers

339114 Dental equipment and instruments manufacturing

423450 Dental equipment and supplies merchant wholesalers

811219 Dental equipment repair and maintenance services
325620 Dental floss manufacturing
339114 Dental glues and cements manufacturing
339114 Dental hand instruments (e.g., forceps) manufacturing
611519 Dental hygienist schools
621399 Dental hygienists' offices (e.g., centers, clinics)
339114 Dental impression materials manufacturing
339114 Dental instrument delivery systems manufacturing
524114 Dental insurance carriers, direct
339116 Dental laboratories
339114 Dental laboratory equipment manufacturing
541712 Dental research and development laboratories or services
611310 Dental schools
621210 Dental surgeons' offices (e.g., centers, clinics)
611519 Dental technician schools
339114 Dental wax manufacturing
621512 Dental X-ray laboratories
325611 Dentifrices manufacturing
424210 Dentifrices merchant wholesalers
813920 Dentists' associations
621210 Dentists' offices (e.g., centers, clinics)
423450 Dentists' professional supplies merchant wholesalers
325620 Denture adhesives manufacturing
325620 Denture cleaners, effervescent, manufacturing
339114 Denture materials manufacturing
339116 Dentures, custom made in dental laboratories
621399 Denturists' offices (e.g., centers, clinics)
561720 Deodorant servicing of rest rooms
325612 Deodorants (except personal) manufacturing

424690 Deodorants (except personal) merchant wholesalers
325620 Deodorants, personal, manufacturing
424210 Deodorants, personal, merchant wholesalers
238290 Deodorization (i.e., air filtration) system installation
561720 Deodorizing services
452111 Department stores (except discount department stores)
452112 Department stores, discount
812199 Depilatory (i.e., hair removal) salons
325620 Depilatory preparations manufacturing
332813 Depolishing metals and metal products for the trade
523999 Deposit brokers
524128 Deposit or share insurance carriers, direct
522110 Depository trust companies
339113 Depressors, tongue, manufacturing
332995 Depth charge projectors manufacturing
332993 Depth charges manufacturing
325412 Dermatological preparations manufacturing
621111 Dermatologists' offices (e.g., centers, clinics)
213112 Derrick building, repairing, and dismantling at oil and gas fields on a contract basis
333132 Derricks, oil and gas field-type, manufacturing
325998 Desalination kits manufacturing
327992 Desiccants, activated clay, manufacturing
335211 Desk fans, electric, manufacturing
335122 Desk lamps, commercial, electric, manufacturing
335121 Desk lamps, residential, electric, manufacturing
316999 Desk sets, leather, manufacturing
337214 Desks (except wood), office-type, manufacturing

337122	Desks, wood household-type, manufacturing
337211	Desks, wood office-type, manufacturing
561410	Desktop publishing services (I.e. document preparation service)
424430	Desserts, dairy, merchant wholesalers
311520	Desserts, frozen (except bakery), manufacturing
311813	Desserts, frozen bakery, manufacturing
811192	Detailing services (i.e., cleaning and polishing), automotive
115112	Detasseling corn
561611	Detective agencies
334519	Detectors, scintillation, manufacturing
922140	Detention centers
325611	Detergents (e.g., dishwashing, industrial, laundry) manufacturing
424690	Detergents merchant wholesalers
331492	Detinning scrap (e.g., cans)
325920	Detonating caps, cord, fuses, and primers manufacturing
325920	Detonators (except ammunition) manufacturing
332993	Detonators, ammunition (i.e., more than 30 mm., more than 1.18 inch), manufacturing
621420	Detoxification centers and clinics (except hospitals), outpatient
622210	Detoxification hospitals
325188	Deuterium oxide (i.e., heavy water) manufacturing
325992	Developers, prepared photographic, manufacturing
336411	Developing and producing prototypes for aircraft
336412	Developing and producing prototypes for aircraft engines and engine parts
336413	Developing and producing prototypes for aircraft parts (except engines) and auxiliary equipment

336414	Developing and producing prototypes for complete guided missiles and space vehicles
336419	Developing and producing prototypes for guided missile and space vehicle components
336415	Developing and producing prototypes for guided missile and space vehicle engines
333315	Developing equipment, film, manufacturing
926110	Development assistance program administration
813311	Developmentally disabled advocacy organizations
238910	Dewatering contractors
111334	Dewberry farming
325520	Dextrin glues manufacturing
311221	Dextrin made by wet milling corn
212319	Diabase crushed and broken stone mining and/or beneficiating
212311	Diabase mining or quarrying
325412	Diagnostic biological preparations (except in-vitro) manufacturing
811198	Diagnostic centers without repair, automotive
334510	Diagnostic equipment, electromedical, manufacturing
423450	Diagnostic equipment, medical, merchant wholesalers
334510	Diagnostic equipment, MRI (magnetic resonance imaging), manufacturing
621512	Diagnostic imaging centers (medical)
811219	Diagnostic imaging equipment repair and maintenance services
424210	Diagnostic reagents merchant wholesalers
325413	Diagnostic substances, in-vitro, manufacturing
424210	Diagnostics, in-vitro and in-vivo, merchant wholesalers
332212	Dial indicators, machinists' precision tools, manufacturing

517919 Dial-up Internet service providers, using client-supplied telecommunications connections

621492 Dialysis centers and clinics

334510 Dialysis equipment, electromedical, manufacturing

325312 Diammonium phosphates manufacturing

332618 Diamond cloths made from purchased wire

339913 Diamond cutting and polishing

333514 Diamond dies, metalworking, manufacturing

327910 Diamond dressing wheels manufacturing

423940 Diamonds (except industrial) merchant wholesalers

423840 Diamonds, industrial, merchant wholesalers

212399 Diamonds, industrial, mining and/or beneficiating

315212 Diaper covers, water resistant and waterproof, cut and sew apparel contractors

315291 Diaper covers, waterproof, infants', cut and sewn from purchased fabric (except apparel contractors)

812331 Diaper supply services

314999 Diapers (except disposable) made from purchased fabrics

424330 Diapers (except paper) merchant wholesalers

322291 Diapers, disposable, made from purchased paper or textile fiber

322121 Diapers, disposable, made in paper mills

424130 Diapers, paper, merchant wholesalers

326299 Diaphragms (i.e., birth control device), rubber, manufacturing

323118 Diaries manufacturing

511199 Diary and time scheduler publishers (except exclusive Internet publishing)

519130 Diary and time scheduler publishers, exclusively on Internet

212325 Diaspore mining and/or beneficiating

334510 Diathermy apparatus, electromedical, manufacturing

334510 Diathermy units manufacturing

212399 Diatomaceous earth mining and/or beneficitating

327992 Diatomaceous earth processing beyond beneficiation

212399 Diatomite mining and/or beneficiating

325992 Diazo (i.e., whiteprint) paper and cloth, sensitized, manufacturing

325120 Dichlorodifluoromethane manufacturing

325188 Dichromates manufacturing

315212 Dickeys, women's, girls', and infants', cut and sew apparel contractors

315239 Dickeys, women's, misses' and girls', cut and sewn from purchased fabric (except apparel contractors)

333313 Dictating machines manufacturing

423420 Dictating machines merchant wholesalers

561410 Dictation services

611699 Diction schools

323117 Dictionaries printing and binding without publishing

323117 Dictionaries printing without publishing

323121 Dictionary binding without printing

511130 Dictionary publishers (except exclusive Internet publishing)

511130 Dictionary publishers and printing combined

519130 Dictionary publishers, exclusively on Internet

325211 Dicyandiamine resins manufacturing

333514 Die sets for metal stamping presses manufacturing

333512 Die sinking machines, metalworking, manufacturing

333511 Die-casting dies manufacturing

333513   Die-casting machines, metalworking, manufacturing

331521   Die-castings, aluminum, unfinished, manufacturing

331522   Die-castings, nonferrous metals (except aluminum), unfinished, manufacturing

322299   Die-cut paper products (except for office use) made from purchased paper or paperboard

322231   Die-cut paper products for office use made from purchased paper or paperboard

333994   Dielectric industrial heating equipment manufacturing

333514   Dies and die holders for metal cutting and forming (except threading) manufacturing

333515   Dies and taps (i.e., a machine tool accessory) manufacturing

332212   Dies, cutting (except metal cutting), manufacturing

333514   Dies, metalworking (except threading), manufacturing

333514   Dies, plastics forming, manufacturing

332212   Dies, steel rule (except metal cutting), manufacturing

333514   Dies, steel rule, metal cutting, manufacturing

333618   Diesel and semidiesel engines manufacturing

324110   Diesel fuels made in petroleum refineries

812191   Diet centers, non-medical

812191   Diet workshops

311514   Dietary drinks, dairy and nondairy based, manufacturing

325192   Diethylcyclohexane manufacturing

325199   Diethylene glycol manufacturing

813920   Dietitians' associations

621399   Dietitians' offices (e.g., centers, clinics)

336350   Differential and rear axle assemblies, automotive, truck, and bus, manufacturing

334513   Differential pressure instruments, industrial process-type, manufacturing

334516   Differential thermal analysis instruments, laboratory-type, manufacturing

332420   Digesters, industrial-type, heavy gauge metal, manufacturing

325412   Digestive system preparations manufacturing

238910   Digging foundations

334119   Digital cameras manufacturing

334111   Digital computers manufacturing

334513   Digital displays of process variables manufacturing

334515   Digital panel meters, electricity measuring, manufacturing

323115   Digital printing (e.g., billboards, other large format graphic materials)

323115   Digital printing (e.g., graphics, high resolution)

333293   Digital printing presses manufacturing

334515   Digital test equipment (e.g., electronic and electrical circuits and equipment testing) manufacturing

334310   Digital video disc players manufacturing

423990   Digital video discs (DVDs), prerecorded, merchant wholesalers

325412   Digitalis medicinal preparations manufacturing

325411   Digitoxin, uncompounded, manufacturing

325211   Diisocyanate resins manufacturing

237990   Dike and other flood control structure construction

111219   Dill farming, field and seed production

321113   Dimension lumber, hardwood, made from logs or bolts

321912   Dimension lumber, hardwood, resawing purchased lumber

321113   Dimension lumber, made from logs or bolts

321912 Dimension lumber, resawing purchased lumber

321113 Dimension lumber, softwood, made from logs or bolts

321912 Dimension lumber, softwood, resawing purchased lumber

321912 Dimension stock, hardwood, manufacturing

321912 Dimension stock, softwood, manufacturing

321912 Dimension stock, wood, manufacturing

327991 Dimension stone dressing and manufacturing

327991 Dimension stone for buildings manufacturing

212311 Dimension stone mining or quarrying

325199 Dimethyl divinyl acetylene (di-isopropenyl acetylene) manufacturing

325199 Dimethylhydrazine manufacturing

335931 Dimmer switches, outlet box mounting-type, manufacturing

722110 Diners, full service

337124 Dinette sets, metal household-type, manufacturing

337124 Dining room chairs (including upholstered), metal, manufacturing

337125 Dining room chairs (including upholstered), plastics manufacturing

337122 Dining room chairs (including upholstered), wood, manufacturing

337124 Dining room furniture, metal household-type, manufacturing

337122 Dining room furniture, wood household-type, manufacturing

487210 Dinner cruises

711110 Dinner theaters

311412 Dinners, frozen (except seafood-based), manufacturing

311712 Dinners, frozen seafood, manufacturing

424420 Dinners, frozen, merchant wholesalers

326199 Dinnerware, plastics (except polystyrene foam), manufacturing

326140 Dinnerware, polystyrene foam, manufacturing

334515 Diode and transistor testers manufacturing

423690 Diodes merchant wholesalers

334413 Diodes, solid-state (e.g., germanium, silicon), manufacturing

212313 Diorite crushed and broken stone mining and/or beneficiating

212311 Diorite mining or quarrying

325192 Diphenylamine manufacturing

928120 Diplomatic services

311941 Dips (except cheese and sour cream based) manufacturing

325320 Dips (i.e., pesticides), cattle and sheep, manufacturing

311513 Dips, cheese based, manufacturing

311511 Dips, sour cream based, manufacturing

334112 Direct access storage devices manufacturing

517110 Direct broadcast satellite (DBS) services

325132 Direct dyes manufacturing

541860 Direct mail advertising services

541860 Direct mail or other direct distribution advertising campaign services

454113 Direct mailers (i.e., selling own merchandise)

331111 Direct reduction of iron ore

454390 Direct selling of merchandise (door-to-door)

213111 Directional drilling of oil and gas wells on a contract basis

812210 Director services, funeral

323112 Directories flexographic printing without publishing

323111 Directories gravure printing without publishing

323110 Directories lithographic (offset) printing without publishing

323119   Directories printing (except flexographic, gravure, lithographic, quick, screen) without publishing

323113   Directories screen printing without publishing

711510   Directors (i.e., film, motion picture, music, theatrical), independent

711510   Directors, independent motion picture

711510   Directors, independent music

511140   Directory and mailing list publishers (except exclusive Internet publishing)

511140   Directory and mailing list publishers and printing combined

511140   Directory publishers (except exclusive Internet publishing)

511140   Directory publishers and printing combined

519130   Directory publishers, exclusively on Internet

541870   Directory, telephone, distribution on a contract basis

517110   Direct-to-home satellite system (DTH) services

238910   Dirt moving for construction

524113   Disability insurance carriers, direct

524113   Disability insurance underwriting, direct

624120   Disability support groups

623990   Disabled group homes without nursing care

922190   Disaster preparedness and management offices, government

624230   Disaster relief services

711510   Disc jockeys, independent

623990   Disciplinary camps for delinquent youth

713990   Discotheques (except those serving alcoholic beverages)

812990   Discount buying services

511199   Discount coupon book publishers (except exclusive Internet publishing)

511199   Discount coupon book publishers and printing combined

519130   Discount coupon book publishers, exclusively on Internet

323112   Discount coupon books flexographic printing without publishing

323111   Discount coupon books gravure printing without publishing

323110   Discount coupon books lithographic (offset) printing without publishing

323119   Discount coupon books printing (except flexographic, gravure, lithographic, quick, screen) without publishing

323113   Discount coupon books screen printing without publishing

452112   Discount department stores

813212   Disease awareness fundraising organizations

115112   Disease control for crops

813212   Disease research (e.g., cancer, heart) fundraising organizations

541940   Disease testing services, veterinary

313249   Dishcloths made in warp knitting mills

313241   Dishcloths made in weft knitting mills

423220   Dishes, household-type (except disposable plastics, paper), merchant wholesalers

424130   Dishes, paper and disposable plastics, merchant wholesalers

327112   Dishes, pottery, manufacturing

339932   Dishes, toy, manufacturing

321999   Dishes, wood, manufacturing

325611   Dishwasher detergents manufacturing

335228   Dishwashers, household-type, manufacturing

423620   Dishwashers, household-type, merchant wholesalers

423440   Dishwashing equipment, commercial-type, merchant wholesalers

333319	Dishwashing machines, commercial-type, manufacturing
335228	Dishwashing machines, household-type, manufacturing
325612	Disinfectants, household-type and industrial, manufacturing
518210	Disk and diskette conversion services
518210	Disk and diskette recertification services
332611	Disk and ring springs, heavy gauge metal, manufacturing
334112	Disk drives, computer, manufacturing
423430	Disk drives, computer, merchant wholesalers
334613	Diskettes, blank, manufacturing
423690	Diskettes, blank, merchant wholesalers
238910	Dismantling engineering structures (e.g., oil storage tank)
238290	Dismantling large-scale machinery and equipment
213112	Dismantling of oil well rigs on a contract basis
333913	Dispensing and measuring pumps (e.g., gasoline, lubricants) manufacturing
325132	Disperse dyes manufacturing
325510	Dispersions, pigment, manufacturing
541850	Display advertising services
423440	Display cases (except refrigerated) merchant wholesalers
337215	Display cases and fixtures (except refrigerated) manufacturing
333415	Display cases, refrigerated, manufacturing
423740	Display cases, refrigerated, merchant wholesalers
334513	Display instruments, industrial process control-type, manufacturing
541890	Display lettering services

339950	Displays (e.g., counter, floor, point-of-purchase) manufacturing
335912	Disposable flashlight batteries manufacturing
424130	Disposable plastics products (e.g., boxes, cups, cutlery, dishes, sanitary food containers) merchant wholesalers
334511	Distance measuring equipment (DME), aeronautical, manufacturing
325191	Distillates, wood, manufacturing
333994	Distillation ovens, charcoal and coke, manufacturing
424820	Distilled alcoholic beverages merchant wholesalers
325998	Distilled water manufacturing
312140	Distilleries
311213	Distiller's malt manufacturing
423830	Distillery machinery merchant wholesalers
312140	Distilling alcoholic beverages (except brandy)
312130	Distilling brandy
333298	Distilling equipment (except beverage), including laboratory-type, **manufacturing**
333294	Distilling equipment, beverage, manufacturing
312140	Distilling potable liquor (except brandy)
334515	Distortion meters and analyzers manufacturing
335313	Distribution boards, electric, manufacturing
335313	Distribution cutouts manufacturing
423610	Distribution equipment, electrical, merchant wholesalers
237120	Distribution line, gas and oil, construction
237110	Distribution line, sewer and water, construction
221330	Distribution of cooled air
221122	Distribution of electric power
221330	Distribution of heated air

221210	Distribution of manufactured gas
221210	Distribution of natural gas
221330	Distribution of steam heat
335311	Distribution transformers, electric, manufacturing
336322	Distributor cap and rotor for internal combustion engines manufacturing
813910	Distributors' associations
336322	Distributors for internal combustion engines manufacturing
551114	District and regional offices
922130	District attorneys' offices
333120	Ditchers and trenchers, self-propelled, manufacturing
325412	Diuretic preparations manufacturing
332212	Dividers, machinists' precision tools, manufacturing
451110	Diving equipment stores
561990	Diving services on a contract or fee basis
621210	DMDs' (doctors of dental medicine) offices (e.g., centers, clinics)
541711	DNA technologies (e.g., microarrays) research and experimental development laboratories
621511	DNA testing laboratories
531120	Dock and associated building rental or leasing
237990	Dock construction
488330	Docking and undocking marine vessel services
488310	Docking facility operations
621310	Doctors of chiropractic (DCs) offices (e.g., centers, clinics)
621210	Doctors of dental medicine (DMDs) offices (e.g., centers, clinics)
621210	Doctors of dental surgery (DDSs) offices (e.g., centers, clinics)
621320	Doctors of optometry (ODs) offices (e.g., centers, clinics)
621112	Doctors of osteopathy (DOs), mental health, offices (e.g., centers, clinics)
621111	Doctors of osteopathy (DOs, except mental health) offices (e.g., centers, clinics)
621391	Doctors of podiatry (DPs) offices (e.g., centers, clinics)
621330	Doctors of psychology offices (e.g., centers, clinics)
561439	Document copying services (except combined with printing services)
561439	Document duplicating services (except combined with printing services)
561410	Document preparation services
561990	Document shredding services
493190	Document storage and warehousing
561410	Document transcription services
325110	Dodecene made from refined petroleum or liquid hydrocarbons
311111	Dog and cat food (e.g., canned, dry, frozen, semimoist), manufacturing
311111	Dog food manufacturing
316999	Dog furnishings (e.g., collars, harnesses, leashes, muzzles), manufacturing
711219	Dog owners, race (i.e., racing dogs)
812910	Dog pounds
112990	Dog production
711212	Dog racetracks
711219	Dog racing kennels
424990	Dogs merchant wholesalers
322299	Doilies, paper, made from purchased paper
339932	Doll carriages and carts manufacturing
339931	Doll clothing manufacturing
452990	Dollar stores
333924	Dollies manufacturing
423920	Dolls merchant wholesalers
339931	Dolls, doll parts, and doll clothing (except wigs) manufacturing

212312 Dolomite crushed and broken stone mining and/or beneficiating

212311 Dolomite mining or quarrying

327410 Dolomite, dead-burned, manufacturing

327410 Dolomitic lime manufacturing

212319 Dolomitic marble crushed and broken stone mining and/or beneficiating

212311 Dolomitic marble mining or quarrying

114111 Dolphin fishing

112920 Donkey production

332321 Door and jamb assemblies, metal, manufacturing

238350 Door and window frame construction

238350 Door and window, prefabricated, installation

332321 Door frames and sash, metal, manufacturing

321911 Door frames and sash, wood and covered wood, manufacturing

332322 Door hoods, sheet metal (except stampings), manufacturing

321911 Door jambs, wood, manufacturing

332510 Door locks, metal, manufacturing

332510 Door opening and closing devices (except electrical), metal, manufacturing

335999 Door opening and closing devices, electrical, manufacturing

321918 Door shutters, wood, manufacturing

444190 Door stores

321918 Door trim, wood molding, manufacturing

321911 Door units, prehung, wood and covered wood, manufacturing

238290 Door, commercial- or industrial-type, installation

238350 Door, folding, installation

314110 Doormats, all materials (except entirely of rubber or plastics), manufacturing

326199 Doormats, plastics, manufacturing

326299 Doormats, rubber, manufacturing

423310 Doors and door frames merchant wholesalers

326199 Doors and door frames, plastics, manufacturing

321911 Doors, combination screen-storm, wood, manufacturing

332321 Doors, metal, manufacturing

332999 Doors, safe and vault, metal, manufacturing

327215 Doors, unframed glass, made from purchased glass

321911 Doors, wood and covered wood, manufacturing

541870 Door-to-door distribution of advertising materials (e.g., coupons, flyers, samples)

454390 Door-to-door retailing of merchandise, direct selling

325510 Dopes, paint, and laquer, manufacturing

336612 Dories building

721310 Dormitories, off campus

236220 Dormitory construction

621112 DOs' (doctors of osteopathy), mental health, offices (e.g., centers, clinics)

621111 DOs' (doctors of osteopathy, except mental health) offices (e.g., centers, clinics)

334519 Dosimetry devices manufacturing

333294 Dough mixing machinery (i.e., food manufacturing-type) manufacturing

722110 Doughnut shops, full service

722213 Doughnut shops, on premise baking and carryout service

311812 Doughnuts (except frozen) made in commercial bakeries

311813 Doughnuts, frozen, manufacturing

424420 Doughs, frozen, merchant wholesalers

311211 Doughs, prepared, made in flour mills

311822 Doughs, refrigerated or frozen, made from purchased flour

333210 Dovetailing machines, woodworking-type, manufacturing

332722 Dowel pins, metal, manufacturing

321999 Dowels, wood, manufacturing

315291 Down-filled clothing, infants', cut and sewn from purchased fabric (except apparel contractors)

315211 Down-filled clothing, men's and boys', cut and sew apparel contractors

315228 Down-filled clothing, men's and boys', cut and sewn from purchased fabric (except apparel contractors)

315212 Down-filled clothing, women's, girls' and infants' cut and sew apparel contractors

315239 Down-filled clothing, women's, misses', and girls', cut and sewn from purchased fabric (except apparel contractors)

713920 Downhill skiing facilities without accommodations

238170 Downspout, gutter, and gutter guard installation

332322 Downspouts, sheet metal (except stampings), manufacturing

621391 DPs' (doctors of podiatry) offices (e.g., centers, clinics)

334513 Draft gauges, industrial process-type, manufacturing

334519 Drafting instruments manufacturing

423490 Drafting instruments merchant wholesalers

339942 Drafting materials (except instruments and tables) manufacturing

541340 Drafting services

337127 Drafting tables and boards manufacturing

423490 Drafting tables merchant wholesalers

541340 Draftsmen's offices

711212 Drag strips

333120 Draglines, crawler, manufacturing

325191 Dragon's blood manufacturing

333111 Drags, farm-type equipment, manufacturing

333120 Drags, road construction and road maintenance equipment, manufacturing

212399 Dragstones mining and/or beneficiating

561790 Drain cleaning services

332913 Drain cocks, plumbing, manufacturing

325612 Drain pipe cleaners manufacturing

332999 Drain plugs, magnetic, metal, manufacturing

327123 Drain tile, clay, manufacturing

238220 Drain, waste and vent system installation

237990 Drainage canal and ditch construction

237990 Drainage project construction

238910 Drainage system (e.g., cesspool, septic tank) installation

337110 Drainboards, wood or plastics laminated on wood, manufacturing

213113 Draining or pumping coal mines on a contract basis

213114 Draining or pumping of metal mines on a contract basis

213115 Draining or pumping of nonmetallic mineral mines (except fuels) on a contract basis

611610 Drama schools (except academic)

314121 Draperies made from purchased fabrics or sheet goods

423220 Draperies merchant wholesalers

812320 Drapery cleaning services

238390 Drapery fixture (e.g., hardware, rods, tracks) installation

339113 Drapes, surgical, disposable, manufacturing

333518 Draw bench machines manufacturing

315192 Drawers, apparel, made in apparel knitting mills

315211 Drawers, men's and boys', cut and sew apparel contractors

315221 Drawers, men's and boys', cut and sewn from purchased fabric (except apparel contractors)

315212 Drawers, women's, girls', and infants', cut and sew apparel contractors

315231 Drawers, women's, misses', and girls', cut and sewn from purchased fabric (except apparel contractors)

325998 Drawing inks manufacturing

331222 Drawing iron or steel wire from purchased iron or steel

331222 Drawing iron or steel wire from purchased iron or steel and fabricating wire products

333292 Drawing machinery for textiles manufacturing

337127 Drawing tables and boards, artist's, manufacturing

332212 Drawknives manufacturing

336611 Dredge building

237990 Dredging (e.g., canal, channel, ditch, waterway)

333120 Dredging machinery manufacturing

315992 Dress and semidress gloves cut and sewn from purchased fabric (except apparel contractors)

315191 Dress and semidress gloves made in apparel knitting mills

315211 Dress and semidress gloves, men's and boys', cut and sew apparel contractors

315212 Dress and semidress gloves, women's, girls', and infants', cut and sew apparel contractors

316219 Dress shoes, children's and infants', manufacturing

316213 Dress shoes, men's, manufacturing

316214 Dress shoes, women's, manufacturing

448190 Dress shops

532220 Dress suit rental

315999 Dress trimmings cut and sewn from purchased fabric (except apparel contractors)

315212 Dress trimmings, women's, girls', and infants', cut and sew apparel contractors

424990 Dressed furs and skins merchant wholesalers

337124 Dressers, metal, manufacturing

337122 Dressers, wood, manufacturing

315191 Dresses made in apparel knitting mills

424330 Dresses merchant wholesalers

315191 Dresses, hand-knit, manufacturing

315291 Dresses, infants', cut and sewn from purchased fabric (except apparel contractors)

315233 Dresses, women's, misses', and girls', cut and sewn from purchased fabric (except apparel contractors)

315212 Dresses, women's, misses', girls', and infants', cut and sew apparel contractors

316110 Dressing (i.e., bleaching, blending, currying, scraping, tanning) furs

315212 Dressing gowns, women's, girls', and infants', cut and sew apparel contractors

315231 Dressing gowns, women's, misses', and girls', cut and sewn from purchased fabric (except apparel contractors)

316110 Dressing hides

311615 Dressing small game

337124 Dressing tables, metal, manufacturing

337122 Dressing tables, wood, manufacturing

423450 Dressings, medical, merchant wholesalers

339113 Dressings, surgical, manufacturing

424490 Dried foods (e.g., fruits, milk, vegetables) merchant wholesalers

311612   Dried meats made from purchased carcasses

212392   Dried phosphate rock mining and/or beneficiating

325510   Driers, paint and varnish, manufacturing

325992   Driers, photographic chemical, manufacturing

333315   Driers, photographic, manufacturing

334511   Driftmeters, aeronautical, manufacturing

333515   Drill bits, metalworking, manufacturing

332212   Drill bits, woodworking, manufacturing

333512   Drill presses, metalworking, manufacturing

333210   Drill presses, woodworking-type, manufacturing

332999   Drill stands, metal, manufacturing

238910   Drilled pier (i.e., for building foundations) contractors

238910   Drilled shaft (i.e., drilled building foundations) construction

339913   Drilling pearls

336611   Drilling and production platforms, floating, oil and gas, building

213111   Drilling directional oil and gas field wells on a contract basis

333132   Drilling equipment, oil and gas field-type, manufacturing

333131   Drilling equipment, underground mining-type, manufacturing

213111   Drilling for gas on a contract basis

213111   Drilling for oil on a contract basis

213111   Drilling gas and oil field wells on a contract basis

333512   Drilling machines, metalworking, manufacturing

325998   Drilling mud compounds, conditioners, and additives (except bentonites) manufacturing

424690   Drilling muds merchant wholesalers

213111   Drilling oil and gas field service wells on a contract basis

213112   Drilling rat holes and mouse holes at oil and gas fields on a contract basis

333132   Drilling rigs, oil and gas field-type, manufacturing

213113   Drilling services for coal mining on a contract basis

213114   Drilling services for metal mining on a contract basis

213115   Drilling services for nonmetallic mineral (except fuels) mining on a contract basis

213112   Drilling shot holes at oil and gas fields on a contract basis

213112   Drilling site preparation at oil and gas fields on a contract basis

213111   Drilling water intake wells, oil and gas field on a contract basis

237110   Drilling water wells (except water intake wells in oil and gas fields)

313210   Drills weaving

333131   Drills, core, underground mining-type, manufacturing

339114   Drills, dental, manufacturing

332212   Drills, hand held, nonelectric, manufacturing

333991   Drills, handheld power-driven (except heavy construction and mining type), manufacturing

333131   Drills, rock, underground mining-type, manufacturing

213112   Drill-stem testing in oil, gas, dry, and service well drilling on a contract basis

311999   Drink powder mixes (except chocolate, coffee, milk based, tea) manufacturing

311320   Drink powdered mixes, cocoa, made from cacao

311330   Drink powdered mixes, cocoa, made from purchased cocoa

311511 Drink, chocolate milk, manufacturing
238220 Drinking fountain installation
332998 Drinking fountains (except mechanically refrigerated), metal, manufacturing
326191 Drinking fountains (except mechanically refrigerated), plastics, manufacturing
333415 Drinking fountains, refrigerated, manufacturing
327111 Drinking fountains, vitreous china, non-refrigerated, manufacturing
722410 Drinking places (i.e., bars, lounges, taverns), alcoholic
312111 Drinks, fruit (except juice), manufacturing
333613 Drive chains, bicycle and motorcycle, manufacturing
336350 Drive shafts and half shafts, automotive, truck, and bus, manufacturing
512132 Drive-in motion picture theaters
237990 Drive-in movie facility construction
722211 Drive-in restaurants
611692 Driver education
611692 Driver training schools (except bus, heavy equipment, truck)
711219 Drivers, harness or race car
333612 Drives, high-speed industrial (except hydrostatic), manufacturing
561790 Driveway cleaning (e.g., power sweeping, washing) services
238990 Driveway paving or sealing
713990 Driving ranges, golf
488490 Driving services (e.g., automobile, truck delivery)
238310 Drop ceiling installation
332111 Drop forgings made from purchased iron or steel, unfinished
333513 Drop hammers, metal forging and shaping, manufacturing
812320 Drop-off and pick-up sites for laundries and drycleaners
813319 Drug abuse prevention advocacy organizations

623220 Drug addiction rehabilitation facilities (except licensed hospitals), residential
622210 Drug addiction rehabilitation hospitals
624190 Drug addiction self-help organizations
621420 Drug addiction treatment centers and clinics (except hospitals), outpatient
922120 Drug enforcement agencies and offices
424210 Drug proprietaries merchant wholesalers
446110 Drug stores
424210 Druggists' sundries merchant wholesalers
424210 Drugs merchant wholesalers
711130 Drum and bugle corps (i.e., drill teams)
333924 Drum cradles manufacturing
339992 Drums (musical instruments), parts, and accessories manufacturing
332439 Drums, light gauge metal, manufacturing
423840 Drums, new and reconditioned, merchant wholesalers
326199 Drums, plastics (i.e., containers), manufacturing
321920 Drums, plywood, manufacturing
321920 Drums, shipping, wood, wirebound, manufacturing
813319 Drunk driving prevention advocacy organizations
311422 Dry beans canning
424510 Dry beans merchant wholesalers
484230 Dry bulk carrier, truck, long-distance
484220 Dry bulk trucking (except garbage collection, garbage hauling), local
335912 Dry cell primary batteries, single and multiple cell, manufacturing
335912 Dry cells, primary (e.g., AAA, AA, C, D, 9V), manufacturing
236220 Dry cleaning plant construction
238220 Dry heating equipment installation

325120 Dry ice (i.e., solid carbon dioxide) manufacturing
424690 Dry ice merchant wholesalers
311514 Dry milk manufacturing
333294 Dry milk processing machinery manufacturing
311514 Dry milk products and mixture manufacturing
311514 Dry milk products for animal feed manufacturing
327999 Dry mix concrete manufacturing
311822 Dry mixes made from purchased flour
311823 Dry pasta manufacturing
311823 Dry pasta packaged with other ingredients made in dry pasta plants
335211 Dry shavers (i.e., electric razors) manufacturing
238910 Dry well construction
812320 Drycleaner drop-off and pick-up sites
812320 Drycleaners (except coin-operated)
335224 Drycleaning and laundry machines, household-type, manufacturing
333312 Drycleaning equipment and machinery manufacturing
423850 Drycleaning equipment and supplies merchant wholesalers
812310 Drycleaning machine routes (i.e., concession operators), coin-operated or similar self-service
812320 Drycleaning plants (except rug cleaning plants)
325612 Drycleaning preparations manufacturing
812320 Drycleaning services (except coin-operated)
812310 Drycleaning services, coin-operated or similar self-service
336611 Drydock, floating, building
488390 Drydocks, floating (i.e., routine repair and maintenance of ships)
423620 Dryer, clothes, gas and electric, merchant wholesalers
532210 Dryer, clothes, rental

335224 Dryers, clothes, household-type, gas and electric, manufacturing
423620 Dryers, hair, merchant wholesalers
335224 Dryers, household-type laundry, manufacturing
339113 Dryers, laboratory-type, manufacturing
333312 Dryers, laundry (except household-type), manufacturing
311711 Drying fish and seafood
333298 Drying kilns, lumber, manufacturing
333292 Drying machinery for textiles manufacturing
238310 Drywall contractors
238310 Drywall finishing (e.g., sanding, spackling, stippling, taping, texturing)
238310 Drywall hanging
238310 Drywall installation
423320 Drywall supplies merchant wholesalers
713950 Duck pin bowling alleys
713950 Duck pin bowling centers
112390 Duck production
313210 Ducks weaving
311615 Ducks, processing, fresh, frozen, canned, or cooked
311615 Ducks, slaughtering and dressing
561790 Duct cleaning services
238290 Duct insulation installation
322222 Duct tape made from purchased materials
238220 Duct work (e.g., cooling, dust collection, exhaust, heating, ventilation) installation
331511 Ductile iron castings, unfinished, manufacturing
331511 Ductile iron foundries
332313 Ducting, fabricated metal plate work, manufacturing
335313 Ducts for electrical switchboard apparatus manufacturing
332322 Ducts, sheet metal, manufacturing
721214 Dude ranches

339920 Dumbbells manufacturing
238290 Dumbwaiter installation
333921 Dumbwaiters manufacturing
212325 Dumortierite mining and/or beneficiating
336212 Dump trailer manufacturing
484220 Dump trucking (e.g., gravel, sand, top soil)
562119 Dump trucking of rubble or brush with collection or disposal
333131 Dumpers, mining car, manufacturing
562219 Dumps, compost
562212 Dumps, nonhazardous solid waste (e.g., trash)
336211 Dump-truck lifting mechanisms manufacturing
315291 Dungarees, infants', cut and sewn from purchased fabric (except apparel contractors)
315211 Dungarees, men's and boys', cut and sew apparel contractors
315224 Dungarees, men's and boys', cut and sewn from purchased fabric (except apparel contractors)
315212 Dungarees, women's girls' and infants', cut and sew apparel contractors
315239 Dungarees, women's, misses', and girls', cut and sewn from pruchased fabric (except apparel contractors)
236116 Duplex (i.e., one unit above the other), construction general contractors
236115 Duplex (i.e., side-by-side) construction general contractors
531110 Duplex houses (i.e., single family) rental or leasing
236117 Duplex operative builders
335931 Duplex receptacles, electrical, manufacturing
325910 Duplicating inks manufacturing
532420 Duplicating machine (e.g., copier) rental or leasing

333512 Duplicating machines (e.g., key cutting), metalworking, manufacturing
425120 Durable goods agents and brokers, wholesale trade
425110 Durable goods business to business electronic markets, wholesale trade
311211 Durum flour manufacturing
333411 Dust and fume collecting equipment manufacturing
314999 Dust cloths made from purchased fabrics
238220 Dust collecting and bag house equipment installation
423730 Dust collection equipment merchant wholesalers
812332 Dust control textile item (e.g., cloths, mats, mops, rugs, shop towels) supply services
315212 Dusters (i.e., apparel), women's and girls', cut and sew apparel contractors
315231 Dusters (i.e., apparel), women's, misses', and girls', cut and sewn from purchased fabric (except apparel contractors)
333111 Dusters, farm-type, manufacturing
115112 Dusting crops
445310 Duty free liquor shops
334112 DVD (digital video disc) drives, computer peripheral equipment, manufacturing
334310 DVD (digital video disc) players manufacturing
531110 Dwelling rental or leasing
332311 Dwellings, prefabricated metal, manufacturing
325998 Dye preparations, clothing, household-type, manufacturing
313311 Dyeing broadwoven fabrics
316110 Dyeing furs
313312 Dyeing gloves, woven or knit, for the trade
316110 Dyeing leather
333292 Dyeing machinery for textiles manufacturing

313312 Dyeing textile products and fabrics (except broadwoven fabrics)
424690 Dyes, industrial, merchant wholesalers
325131 Dyes, inorganic, manufacturing
325191 Dyes, natural, manufacturing
325132 Dyes, synthetic organic, manufacturing
424690 Dyestuffs merchant wholesalers
325920 Dynamite manufacturing
334519 Dynamometers manufacturing
335312 Dynamos, electric (except automotive), manufacturing
335312 Dynamotors manufacturing
812199 Ear piercing services
532412 Earth moving equipment rental or leasing without operator
237990 Earth retention system construction
334220 Earth station communications equipment manufacturing
517919 Earth stations (except satellite telecommunication carriers)
517410 Earth stations for satellite communication carriers
212399 Earth, diatomaceous, mining and/or beneficiating
212325 Earth, fuller's (e.g., all natural bleaching clays), mining and/ or beneficiating
327112 Earthenware table and kitchen articles, coarse, manufacturing
327112 Earthenware, commercial and household, semivitreous, manufacturing
237990 Earth-filled dam construction
311119 Earthworm food and bedding manufacturing
112990 Earthworm hatcheries
339942 Easels, artists', manufacturing
424130 Eating utensils, disposable plastics, merchant wholesalers
332322 Eaves, sheet metal (except stampings), manufacturing
238170 Eavestrough installation
327112 Ecclesiastical statuary, clay, manufacturing
327420 Ecclesiastical statuary, gypsum, manufacturing

327999 Ecclesiastical statuary, paper mache, manufacturing
327991 Ecclesiastical statuary, stone, manufacturing
332999 Ecclesiastical ware, precious plated metal, manufacturing
541690 Economic consulting services
926110 Economic development agencies, government
928120 Economic development assistance (i.e., international), government
541720 Economic research and development services
332410 Economizers (i.e., power boiler accessory) manufacturing
522298 Edge Act corporations (except international trade financing)
522293 Edge Act corporations (i.e., international trade financing)
332212 Edge tools, woodworking (e.g., augers, bits, countersinks), manufacturing
333315 Editing equipment, motion picture (e.g., rewinders, splicers, titlers, viewers), manufacturing
561410 Editing services
923110 Education offices, nonoperating
923110 Education program administration
923110 Education statistics centers, government
236220 Educational building construction
611710 Educational consultants
611710 Educational guidance counseling services
611710 Educational support services
611710 Educational testing evaluation services
611710 Educational testing services
813211 Educational trusts, awarding grants
813920 Educators' associations
114111 Eel fishing
325412 Effervescent salts manufacturing
541614 Efficiency management (i.e., efficiency expert) consulting services

321920 Egg cases, wood, manufacturing
335211 Egg cookers, household-type electric, manufacturing
112340 Egg hatcheries, poultry
311823 Egg noodles, dry, manufacturing
311991 Egg noodles, fresh, manufacturing
112310 Egg production, chicken
112330 Egg production, turkey
311999 Egg substitutes manufacturing
312140 Eggnog, alcoholic, manufacturing
311514 Eggnog, canned, nonalcoholic, manufacturing
311511 Eggnog, fresh, nonalcoholic, manufacturing
311511 Eggnog, nonalcoholic (except canned), manufacturing
111219 Eggplant farming (except under cover), field, bedding plant and seed production
111419 Eggplant farming, grown under cover
424440 Eggs merchant wholesalers
112310 Eggs, chicken (table, hatching) production
311999 Eggs, processed, manufacturing
334515 Elapsed time meters, electronic, manufacturing
313210 Elastic fabrics, more than 12 inches in width, weaving
313221 Elastic fabrics, narrow woven, manufacturing
339113 Elastic hosiery, orthopedic, manufacturing
325222 Elastomeric fibers and filaments manufacturing
325211 Elastomers (except synthetic rubber) manufacturing
325212 Elastomers, synthetic rubber, manufacturing
332322 Elbows for conductor pipe, hot air ducts, and stovepipe, sheet metal (except stampings), manufacturing
332919 Elbows, pipe, metal (except made from purchased pipe), manufacturing
921190 Election boards

334512 Electric air cleaner controls, automatic, manufacturing
334513 Electric and electronic controllers, industrial process-type, manufacturing
336111 Electric automobiles for highway use manufacturing
335999 Electric bells manufacturing
335211 Electric blankets manufacturing
423620 Electric blankets merchant wholesalers
335211 Electric comfort heating equipment, portable, manufacturing
238210 Electric contracting
335999 Electric fence chargers manufacturing
335311 Electric furnace transformers manufacturing
334512 Electric heat proportioning controls, modulating controls, manufacturing
335110 Electric lamp bulb parts (except glass blanks) manufacturing
335110 Electric lamps (i.e., light bulbs) manufacturing
237130 Electric light and power plant (except hydroelectric) construction
335110 Electric light bulbs, complete, manufacturing
423610 Electric light fixtures merchant wholesalers
811310 Electric motor repair and maintenance services, commercial or industrial
423610 Electric motors, wiring supplies, and lighting fixtures merchant wholesalers
339992 Electric musical instruments manufacturing
333618 Electric outboard motors manufacturing
221122 Electric power brokers
221121 Electric power control
238210 Electric power control panel and outlet installation
221122 Electric power distribution systems

221119	Electric power generation, (except fossil fuel, hydroelectric, nuclear)
221112	Electric power generation, fossil fuel (e.g., coal, oil, gas)
221111	Electric power generation, hydroelectric
221113	Electric power generation, nuclear
221119	Electric power generation, solar
221119	Electric power generation, tidal
221119	Electric power generation, wind
237130	Electric power transmission line and tower construction
221121	Electric power transmission systems
334512	Electric space heater controls, automatic, manufacturing
335211	Electric space heaters, portable, manufacturing
333415	Electric warm air (i.e., forced air) furnaces manufacturing
238210	Electrical contractors
541330	Electrical engineering services
238210	Electrical equipment and appliance installation
811310	Electrical generating and transmission equipment repair and maintenance services
541360	Electrical geophysical surveying services
336322	Electrical ignition cable sets for internal combustion engines manufacturing
811219	Electrical measuring instrument repair and maintenance services
335932	Electrical metallic tube (EMTs) manufacturing
561990	Electrical meter reading services, contract
334515	Electrical network analyzers manufacturing
334515	Electrical power measuring equipment manufacturing
811118	Electrical repair shops, automotive
339950	Electrical signs manufacturing
423440	Electrical signs merchant wholesalers

444190	Electrical supply stores
541380	Electrical testing laboratories or services
238210	Electrical wiring contractors
238210	Electrical work
238210	Electrical, electrical wiring, and low voltage electrical work
335211	Electrically heated bed coverings manufacturing
238210	Electrician
611513	Electricians' apprenticeship training
334515	Electricity and electrical signal measuring instruments manufacturing
334515	Electricity and electrical signal testing equipment manufacturing
237130	Electricity generating plant (except hydroelectric) construction
237990	Electricity generating plant, hydroelectric, construction
334510	Electrocardiographs manufacturing
335999	Electrochemical generators (i.e., fuel cells) manufacturing
333512	Electrochemical milling machines, metalworking, manufacturing
333512	Electrode discharge metal cutting machines manufacturing
333992	Electrode holders, welding, manufacturing
335991	Electrodes for thermal and electrolytic uses, carbon and graphite, manufacturing
334513	Electrodes used in industrial process measurement manufacturing
335110	Electrodes, cold cathode fluorescent lamp, manufacturing
333992	Electrodes, welding, manufacturing
334510	Electroencephalographs manufacturing
334510	Electrogastrograph manufacturing

332912	Electrohydraulic servo valves, fluid power, manufacturing
812199	Electrolysis (i.e., hair removal) salons
325412	Electrolyte in-vivo diagnostic substances manufacturing
334513	Electrolytic conductivity instruments, industrial process-type, manufacturing
334516	Electrolytic conductivity instruments, laboratory-type, manufacturing
333512	Electrolytic metal cutting machines manufacturing
334513	Electromagnetic flowmeters manufacturing
541360	Electromagnetic geophysical surveying services
334514	Electromechanical counters manufacturing
334510	Electromedical diagnostic equipment manufacturing
334510	Electromedical equipment manufacturing
423450	Electromedical equipment merchant wholesalers
334510	Electromedical therapy equipment manufacturing
331112	Electrometallurgical ferroalloy manufacturing
331111	Electrometallurgical steel manufacturing
334510	Electromyographs manufacturing
333992	Electron beam welding equipment manufacturing
335999	Electron linear accelerators manufacturing
334516	Electron microprobes, laboratory-type, manufacturing
334516	Electron microscopes manufacturing
334516	Electron paramagnetic spin-type apparatus manufacturing
333298	Electron tube machinery manufacturing
334411	Electron tube parts (e.g., bases, getters, guns) (except glass blanks) manufacturing
327215	Electron tube parts, glass blanks, made from purchased glass
327212	Electron tube parts, glass blanks, made in glass making plants
334515	Electron tube test equipment manufacturing
334411	Electron tubes manufacturing
333512	Electron-discharge metal cutting machines manufacturing
454112	Electronic auctions, retail
238210	Electronic containment fencing for pets, installation
238210	Electronic control installation and service
238210	Electronic control system installation
518210	Electronic data processing services
511140	Electronic directory publishers (except exclusive Internet publishing)
519130	Electronic directory publishers, exclusively on Internet
611519	Electronic equipment repair training
522320	Electronic financial payment services
522320	Electronic funds transfer services
713120	Electronic game arcades
423920	Electronic games merchant wholesalers
334511	Electronic guidance systems and equipment manufacturing
425110	Electronic markets, durable goods, business to business, wholesale trade
425110	Electronic markets, nondurable goods, business to business, wholesale trade
443112	Electronic part and component stores
423690	Electronic parts (e.g., condensers, connectors, switches) merchant wholesalers
323122	Electronic prepress services for the printing trade

541712   Electronic research and development laboratories or services

334515   Electronic test equipment for testing electrical characteristics manufacturing

541380   Electronic testing laboratories or services

334514   Electronic totalizing counters manufacturing

339932   Electronic toys and games manufacturing

423690   Electronic tubes (e.g., industrial, receiving, transmitting) merchant wholesalers

334516   Electrophoresis instruments manufacturing

333298   Electroplating machinery and equipment manufacturing

332813   Electroplating metals and formed products for the trade

238320   Electrostatic painting, on site, contractors

335999   Electrostatic particle accelerators manufacturing

333411   Electrostatic precipitation equipment manufacturing

334510   Electrotherapeutic apparatus manufacturing

335110   Electrotherapeutic lamp bulbs for ultraviolet and infrared radiation manufacturing

334510   Electrotherapy units manufacturing

323122   Electrotype plate preparation services

333293   Electrotyping machinery manufacturing

334516   Elemental analyzers manufacturing

611110   Elementary and secondary schools

611110   Elementary schools

237310   Elevated highway construction

332323   Elevator guide rails, metal, manufacturing

238290   Elevator installation

423830   Elevators merchant wholesalers

333921   Elevators, passenger and freight, manufacturing

112990   Elk production

325998   Embalming fluids manufacturing

812210   Embalming services

237990   Embankment construction

928120   Embassies

313311   Embossing broadwoven fabrics

316110   Embossing leather

323122   Embossing plate preparation services

339943   Embossing stamps manufacturing

313312   Embossing textile products and fabrics (except broadwoven)

313222   Embroideries, Schiffli machine, manufacturing

314999   Embroidering contractors on apparel

314999   Embroidering on textile products for the trade

339932   Embroidery kits manufacturing

333292   Embroidery machinery manufacturing

424310   Embroidery products merchant wholesalers

313111   Embroidery spun yarns (e.g., cotton, manmade fiber, silk, wool) made from purchased fiber

313113   Embroidery thread (e.g., cotton, manmade fibers, silk, wool) manufacturing

335122   Emergency lighting (i.e., battery backup) manufacturing

621493   Emergency medical centers and clinics, freestanding

621910   Emergency medical transportation services, air or ground

922190   Emergency planning and management offices, government

453998   Emergency preparedness supply stores

624230   Emergency relief services

488410   Emergency road services (i.e., tow service)

624221 Emergency shelters (except for victims of domestic or international disasters or conflicts)
624230 Emergency shelters for victims of domestic or international disasters or conflicts
212399 Emery mining and/or beneficiating
811198 Emissions testing without repair, automotive
541612 Employee assessment consulting services
541612 Employee benefit consulting services
525110 Employee benefit pension plans
525120 Employee benefit plans (except pension)
524292 Employee benefit plans, third-party administrative processing services
485410 Employee bus services
541612 Employee compensation consulting services
561330 Employee leasing services
813930 Employees' associations for improvement of wages and working conditions
561311 Employment agencies
561311 Employment agencies, motion picture or video
561311 Employment agencies, radio or television
561311 Employment agencies, theatrical
561311 Employment placement agencies or services
561311 Employment referral agencies or services
561311 Employment registries
335932 EMTs (electrical metallic tube) manufacturing
112390 Emu production
325613 Emulsifiers (i.e., surface-active agents) manufacturing
325510 Enamel paints manufacturing
212322 Enamel sand quarrying and/or beneficiating
332214 Enameled metal cutting utensils
332812 Enameling metals and metal products for the trade

333994 Enameling ovens manufacturing
424950 Enamels merchant wholesalers
339114 Enamels, dental, manufacturing
323121 Encyclopedia binding without printing
511130 Encyclopedia publishers (except exclusive Internet publishing)
511130 Encyclopedia publishers and printing combined
519130 Encyclopedia publishers, exclusively on Internet
323117 Encyclopedias printing and binding without publishing
323117 Encyclopedias printing without publishing
337124 End tables, metal, manufacturing
337122 End tables, wood, manufacturing
111219 Endive farming (except under cover), field, bedding plant and seed production
111419 Endive farming, grown under cover
325411 Endocrine products, uncompounded, manufacturing
424210 Endocrine substances merchant wholesalers
621210 Endodontists' offices (e.g., centers, clinics)
334510 Endoscopic equipment, electromedical (e.g., bronchoscopes, colonoscopes, cystoscopes), manufacturing
325320 Endrin insecticides manufacturing
624229 Energy assistance programs
541690 Energy consulting services
334512 Energy cutoff controls, residential and commercial types, manufacturing
926110 Energy development and conservation agencies, nonoperating
926130 Energy development and conservation programs, government
334515 Energy measuring equipment, electrical, manufacturing
926110 Energy program administration

331319 Energy wire or cable made in aluminum wire drawing plants

331422 Energy wire or cable, copper, made from purchased copper in wire drawing plants

331491 Energy wire or cable, nonferrous metals (except aluminum, copper), made from purchased nonferrous metals (except aluminum, copper) in wire drawing plants

924110 Enforcement of environmental and pollution control regulations

336312 Engine block assemblies, automotive and truck gasoline, manufacturing

325998 Engine degreasers manufacturing

336311 Engine intake and exhaust valves manufacturing

811310 Engine repair (except automotive, small engine)

811111 Engine repair and replacement shops, automotive

811411 Engine repair, small engine

325998 Engine starting fluids manufacturing

423120 Engine testing equipment, motor vehicle, merchant wholesalers

541330 Engineering consulting services

541330 Engineering design services

541712 Engineering research and development laboratories or services

541330 Engineering services

238320 Engineering structure (e.g., oil storage tank, water tower) painting

813920 Engineers' associations

423490 Engineers' equipment and supplies merchant wholesalers

541330 Engineers' offices

541330 Engineers' private practices

336412 Engines and engine parts, aircraft (except carburetors, pistons, piston rings, valves), manufacturing

336312 Engines (except diesel), automotive and truck, manufacturing

423860 Engines and parts, aircraft, merchant wholesalers

423120 Engines and parts, automotive, new, merchant wholesalers

423860 Engines and turbines, marine, merchant wholesalers

333618 Engines, diesel and semidiesel, manufacturing

333618 Engines, diesel locomotive, manufacturing

423830 Engines, internal combustion (except aircraft, automotive), merchant wholesalers

333618 Engines, internal combustion (except aircraft, nondiesel automotive), manufacturing

333618 Engines, natural gas, manufacturing

111219 English pea farming (except under cover), field, bedding plant and seed production

111419 English pea farming, grown under cover

332212 Engraver's handtools, nonpowered, manufacturing

339911 Engraving and etching precious metal (except precious plated) jewelry

339912 Engraving and etching precious metal flatware

339914 Engraving and/or etching costume jewelry

423830 Engraving machinery merchant wholesalers

332812 Engraving metals and metal products (except printing plates) for the trade

323122 Engraving printing plate, for the printing trade

333315 Enlargers, photographic, manufacturing

315191 Ensemble dresses made in apparel knitting mills

315212 Ensemble dresses, women's, girls', and infants', cut and sew apparel contractors

315233 Ensemble dresses, women's, misses', and girls', cut and sewn from purchased fabric (except apparel contractors)

711130 Ensembles, musical

926110 Enterprise development program administration

711410 Entertainers' agents or managers

711510 Entertainers, independent

519130 Entertainment sites, Internet

541712 Entomological research and development laboratories or services (except biotechnology research and development)

115112 Entomological service, agricultural

541690 Entomology consulting services

333291 Envelope making machinery manufacturing

424110 Envelope paper, bulk, merchant wholesalers

333313 Envelope stuffing, scaling, and addressing machinery manufacturing

322232 Envelopes (i.e., mailing, stationery) made from any material

424120 Envelopes merchant wholesalers

813312 Environmental advocacy organizations

541620 Environmental consulting services

238210 Environmental control system installation

541330 Environmental engineering services

923120 Environmental health program administration

924110 Environmental protection program administration

562910 Environmental remediation services

541712 Environmental research and development laboratories or services (except biotechnology research and development)

541380 Environmental testing laboratories or services

325413 Enzyme and isoenzyme in-vitro diagnostic substances manufacturing

325199 Enzyme proteins (i.e., basic synthetic chemicals) (except pharmaceutical use) manufacturing

325411 Enzyme proteins (i.e., basic synthetic chemicals), pharmaceutical use, manufacturing

325132 Eosin dyes manufacturing

325411 Ephedrine and derivatives (i.e., basic chemicals) manufacturing

325211 Epichlorohydrin bisphenol manufacturing

325211 Epichlorohydrin diphenol manufacturing

325212 Epichlorohydrin elastomers manufacturing

325520 Epoxy adhesives manufacturing

238190 Epoxy application contractors

325510 Epoxy coatings made from purchased resins

325211 Epoxy resins manufacturing

923130 Equal employment opportunity offices

115210 Equine boarding

522220 Equipment finance leasing

238910 Equipment rental (except crane), construction, with operator

531130 Equity real estate investment trusts (REITs), primarily leasing miniwarehouses and self-storage units

531120 Equity real estate investment trusts (REITs), primarily leasing nonresidential buildings (except miniwarehouses)

531190 Equity real estate investment trusts (REITs), primarily leasing real estate (except residential buildings and dwellings, nonresidential buildings, miniwarehouses, and self-storage units)

531110   Equity real estate investment trusts (REITs), primarily leasing residential buildings and dwellings

326299   Erasers, rubber or rubber and abrasive combined, manufacturing

238120   Erecting structural steel

238190   Erection and dismantling, poured concrete form

325411   Ergot alkaloids (i.e., basic chemicals) manufacturing

541330   Erosion control engineering services

238290   Escalator installation

333921   Escalators manufacturing

423830   Escalators merchant wholesalers

111219   Escarole farming (except under cover), field, bedding plant and seed production

111419   Escarole farming, grown under cover

812990   Escort services, social

523991   Escrow agencies (except real estate)

531390   Escrow agencies, real estate

325998   Essential oils manufacturing

424690   Essential oils merchant wholesalers

325199   Essential oils, synthetic, manufacturing

541990   Estate assessment (i.e., appraisal) services

541110   Estate law offices

325211   Ester gum manufacturing

325199   Esters, not specified elsewhere by process, manufacturing

812112   Esthetician (i.e., skin care) services

115310   Estimating timber

454111   E-tailers

333295   Etching equipment, semiconductor, manufacturing

332812   Etching metals and metal products (except printing plates) for the trade

325110   Ethane made from refined petroleum or liquid hydrocarbons

211112   Ethane recovered from oil and gas field gases

325193   Ethanol, nonpotable, manufacturing

813410   Ethnic associations

711510   Ethnic dancers, independent

711320   Ethnic festival managers without facilities

711320   Ethnic festival organizers without facilities

711310   Ethnic festival promoters with facilities

711320   Ethnic festival promoters without facilities

325191   Ethyl acetate, natural, manufacturing

325199   Ethyl acetate, synthetic, manufacturing

424820   Ethyl alcohol merchant wholesalers

325193   Ethyl alcohol, nonpotable, manufacturing

312140   Ethyl alcohol, potable, manufacturing

325199   Ethyl butyrate manufacturing

325199   Ethyl cellulose (except resins) manufacturing

325199   Ethyl chloride manufacturing

325199   Ethyl ether manufacturing

325199   Ethyl formate manufacturing

325199   Ethyl nitrite manufacturing

325199   Ethyl perhydrophenanthrene manufacturing

325110   Ethylbenzene made from refined petroleum or liquid hydrocarbons

325211   Ethylcellulose plastics manufacturing

325199   Ethylene glycol ether manufacturing

325199   Ethylene glycol manufacturing

325110   Ethylene made from refined petroleum or liquid hydrocarbons

324110   Ethylene made in petroleum refineries

325199   Ethylene oxide manufacturing

325212   Ethylene-propylene rubber manufacturing

325212 Ethylene-propylene-nonconjugated diene (EPDM) rubber manufacturing

325211 Ethylene-vinyl acetate resins manufacturing

325998 Eucalyptus oil manufacturing

311514 Evaporated milk manufacturing

334519 Evaporation meters manufacturing

333415 Evaporative condensers (i.e., heat transfer equipment) manufacturing

611691 Exam preparation services

423810 Excavating machinery and equipment merchant wholesalers

213112 Excavating mud pits, slush pits, and cellars at oil and gas fields on a contract basis

238910 Excavating, earthmoving or land clearing, mining (except overburden removal at open pit mine sites or quarries)

238910 Excavating, earthmoving, or land clearing contractors

238910 Excavation contractors

333120 Excavators (e.g., power shovels) manufacturing

321999 Excelsior (e.g., pads, wrappers) manufacturing

523999 Exchange clearinghouses, commodities or securities

332410 Exchangers, heat, manufacturing

523210 Exchanges, commodity contracts

523210 Exchanges, securities

335312 Exciter assemblies, motor and generator, manufacturing

531210 Exclusive buyers' agencies

531210 Exclusive buyers' agents, offices of

487210 Excursion boat operation

921140 Executive and legislative office combinations

561110 Executive management services

921110 Executive offices, federal, state, and local (e.g., governor, mayor, president)

561312 Executive placement services

561312 Executive search services

531120 Executive suites (i.e., full service office space provision)

713940 Exercise centers

532292 Exercise equipment rental

451110 Exercise equipment stores

339920 Exercise machines manufacturing

621340 Exercise physiologists' offices (e.g., centers, clinics)

336399 Exhaust and tail pipes, automotive, truck, and bus, manufacturing

333412 Exhaust fans, industrial and commercial-type, manufacturing

238220 Exhaust system (e.g., kitchens, industrial work areas) installation

811112 Exhaust system repair and replacement shops, automotive

336399 Exhaust systems and parts, automotive, truck, and bus, manufacturing

531120 Exhibition hall, no promotion of events, rental or leasing

624190 Exoffender rehabilitation agencies

624190 Exoffender self-help organizations

316110 Exotic leathers manufacturing

332312 Expansion joints, metal, manufacturing

541712 Experimental farms

213113 Exploration services for coal (except geophysical surveying and mapping) on a contract basis

213114 Exploration services for metal (except geophysical surveying and mapping) on a contract basis

213115 Exploration services for nonmetallic minerals (except geophysical surveying and mapping) on a contract basis

213112 Exploration services for oil and gas (except geophysical surveying and mapping) on a contract basis

424690 Explosives (except ammunition, fireworks) merchant wholesalers

325920 Explosives manufacturing

522293 Export trading companies (i.e., international trade financing)

522293 Export-Import banks

333315 Exposure meters, photographic, manufacturing

492110 Express delivery services (except establishments operating under a universal service obligation)

622310 Extended care hospitals (except mental, substance abuse)

335999 Extension cords made from purchased insulated wire

321999 Extension ladders, wood, manufacturing

321999 Extension planks, wood, manufacturing

238310 Exterior insulation finish system installation

321918 Exterior wood shutters manufacturing

325320 Exterminating chemical products (e.g., fungicides, insecticides, pesticides) manufacturing

561710 Exterminating services

423990 Extinguishers, fire, merchant wholesalers

333120 Extractors, piling, manufacturing

311920 Extracts, essences and preparations, coffee, manufacturing

311920 Extracts, essences and preparations, tea, manufacturing

311942 Extracts, food (except coffee, meat), manufacturing

311942 Extracts, malt, manufacturing

325191 Extracts, natural dyeing and tanning, manufacturing

326291 Extruded, molded or lathe-cut rubber goods manufacturing

333220 Extruding machinery for plastics and rubber manufacturing

333292 Extruding machinery for yarn manufacturing

333513 Extruding machines, metalworking, manufacturing

331319 Extrusion billet made by rolling purchased aluminum

331319 Extrusion billet, aluminum, made in integrated secondary smelting and rolling mills

333514 Extrusion dies for use with all materials manufacturing

331319 Extrusion ingot made by rolling purchased aluminum

331319 Extrusion ingot, aluminum, made in integrated secondary smelting and rolling mills

331312 Extrusion ingot, primary aluminum, manufacturing

325412 Eye and ear preparations manufacturing

621991 Eye banks

339112 Eye examining instruments and apparatus manufacturing

325620 Eye make-up (e.g., eye shadow, eyebrow pencil, mascara) manufacturing

622310 Eye, ear, nose, and throat hospitals

316993 Eyeglass cases, all materials, manufacturing

339115 Eyeglass frames (i.e., fronts and temples), ophthalmic, manufacturing

423460 Eyeglasses merchant wholesalers

315211 Eyelet making contractors on men's and boys' apparel

315212 Eyelet making contractors on women's, misses', girls', and infants' apparel

339993 Eyelets, metal, manufacturing

339115 Eyes, glass and plastics, manufacturing

313312 Fabric (except broadwoven) finishing

451130 Fabric shops

325612 Fabric softeners manufacturing

238310 Fabric wall system, noise insulating, installation

624190	Family welfare services
326220	Fan belts, rubber or plastics, manufacturing
334512	Fan controls, temperature responsive, manufacturing
316110	Fancy leathers manufacturing
335211	Fans (except attic), household-type electric, manufacturing
336322	Fans, electric cooling, automotive, truck, and bus, manufacturing
335211	Fans, household-type kitchen, manufacturing
423620	Fans, household-type, merchant wholesalers
333412	Fans, industrial and commercial-type, manufacturing
423830	Fans, industrial, merchant wholesalers
334514	Fare collection equipment manufacturing
311211	Farina (except breakfast food) made in flour mills
311230	Farina, breakfast cereal, manufacturing
236220	Farm building construction
332311	Farm buildings, prefabricated metal, manufacturing
321992	Farm buildings, prefabricated wood, manufacturing
237990	Farm drainage tile installation
532490	Farm equipment rental or leasing
813410	Farm granges
115115	Farm labor contractors
423820	Farm machinery and equipment merchant wholesalers
811310	Farm machinery and equipment repair and maintenance services
115116	Farm management services
522292	Farm mortgage lending
493130	Farm product warehousing and storage (except refrigerated)
493120	Farm product warehousing and storage, refrigerated
484220	Farm products hauling, local
484230	Farm products trucking, long-distance

332420	Farm storage tanks, heavy gauge metal, manufacturing
424910	Farm supplies merchant wholesalers
444220	Farm supply stores
532490	Farm tractor rental or leasing
333111	Farm tractors and attachments manufacturing
333111	Farm wagons manufacturing
813910	Farmers' associations
813910	Farmers' unions
******	Farming—see type
531190	Farmland rental or leasing
333922	Farm-type conveyors manufacturing
115210	Farriers
112210	Farrow-to-finish operations
238170	Fascia and soffit installation
541490	Fashion design services
541490	Fashion designer services
423710	Fasteners (e.g., bolts, nuts, rivets, screws) merchant wholesalers
339993	Fasteners (e.g., glove, hook-and-eye, slide, snap) manufacturing
722211	Fast-food restaurants
334511	Fathometers manufacturing
334519	Fatigue testing machines, industrial, mechanical, manufacturing
311611	Fats, animal (except poultry, small game), produced in slaughtering plants
311613	Fats, animal, rendering
112112	Fattening cattle
325199	Fatty acid esters and amines manufacturing
325199	Fatty acids (e.g., margaric, oleic, stearic) manufacturing
325199	Fatty alcohols manufacturing
327111	Faucet handles, vitreous china and earthenware, manufacturing
332913	Faucets, plumbing, manufacturing
532420	Fax machine rental or leasing
811213	Fax machine repair and maintenance services
339999	Feather dusters manufacturing

315291 Feather-filled clothing, infants', cut and sewn from purchased fabric (except apparel contractors)

315239 Feather-filled clothing, jackets, and vests, women's, misses', and juniors', cut and sewn from purchased fabric (except apparel contractors)

315211 Feather-filled clothing, men's and boys', cut and sew apparel contractors

315228 Feather-filled clothing, men's and boys', cut and sewn from purchased fabric (except apparel contractors)

315212 Feather-filled clothing, women's, girls', and infants', cut and sew apparel contractors

424590 Feathers merchant wholesalers

339999 Feathers, preparing (i.e., for use in apparel and textile products)

519110 Feature syndicates (i.e., advice columns, comic, news)

522294 Federal Agricultural Mortgage Corporation

926120 Federal Aviation Administration (except air traffic control)

922120 Federal Bureau of Investigation (FBI)

926130 Federal Communications Commission (FCC)

522130 Federal credit unions

522298 Federal Home Loan Banks (FHLB)

522294 Federal Home Loan Mortgage Corporation (FHLMC)

522294 Federal Intermediate Credit Bank

522292 Federal Land Banks

522294 Federal National Mortgage Association (FNMA)

922120 Federal police services

521110 Federal Reserve Banks or Branches

921130 Federal Reserve Board of Governors

522120 Federal savings and loan associations (S&L)

522120 Federal savings banks

813219 Federated charities

813930 Federation of workers, labor organizations

813930 Federations of labor

424910 Feed additives merchant wholesalers

316999 Feed bags for horses manufacturing

314911 Feed bags made from purchased woven or knitted materials

311119 Feed concentrates, animal, manufacturing

311514 Feed grade dry milk products manufacturing

311119 Feed premixes, animal, manufacturing

333111 Feed processing equipment, farm-type, manufacturing

444220 Feed stores (except pet)

453910 Feed stores, pet

311119 Feed supplements, animal (except cat, dog), manufacturing

311111 Feed supplements, dog and cat, manufacturing

112112 Feed yards (except stockyards for transportation), cattle

112111 Feeder calf production

112210 Feeder pig farming

335311 Feeder voltage regulators and boosters (i.e., electrical transformers) manufacturing

423820 Feeders, animal, merchant wholesalers

333131 Feeders, mineral beneficiating-type, manufacturing

112112 Feedlots (except stockyards for transportation), cattle

112210 Feedlots (except stockyards for transportation), hog

112410 Feedlots (except stockyards for transportation), lamb

424910 Feeds (except pet) merchant wholesalers

311111 Feeds, prepared for dog and cat, manufacturing

311119　Feeds, prepared, for animals (except cat, dog) manufacturing
311119　Feeds, specialty (e.g., guinea pig, mice, mink), manufacturing
212325　Feldspar mining and/or beneficiating
327992　Feldspar processing beyond beneficiation
424990　Felt merchant wholesalers
339941　Felt tip markers manufacturing
322121　Felts, asphalt, made in paper mills
313210　Felts, broadwoven, weaving
313230　Felts, nonwoven, manufacturing
331222　Fence gates, posts, and fittings, iron or steel, made in wire drawing plants
238990　Fence installation (except electronic containment fencing for pets)
331111　Fence posts, iron or steel, made in iron and steel mills
332323　Fences and gates (except wire), metal, manufacturing
423390　Fencing (except wood) merchant wholesalers
332618　Fencing and fence gates made from purchased wire
423390　Fencing and fencing accessories, wire, merchant wholesalers
238990　Fencing contractors (except electronic containment fencing for pets)
444190　Fencing dealers
339920　Fencing equipment (sporting goods) manufacturing
321999　Fencing, prefabricated sections, wood, manufacturing
321999　Fencing, wood (except rough pickets, poles, and rails), manufacturing
423310　Fencing, wood, merchant wholesalers
212299　Ferberite ores and concentrates mining and/or beneficiating
333298　Fermentation equipment, chemical, manufacturing

424810　Fermented malt beverages merchant wholesalers
332420　Fermention tanks, heavy gauge metal tanks, manufacturing
325188　Ferric chloride manufacturing
325188　Ferric oxide manufacturing
325131　Ferric oxide pigments manufacturing
333319　Ferris wheels manufacturing
212299　Ferroalloy ores (except vanadium) (e.g., chromium, columbium, molybdenum, tungsten) mining and/or beneficiating
331112　Ferroalloys manufacturing
423510　Ferroalloys merchant wholesalers
331112　Ferrochromium manufacturing
325188　Ferrocyanides manufacturing
331112　Ferromanganese manufacturing
331112　Ferromolybdenum manufacturing
331112　Ferrophosphorus manufacturing
331112　Ferrosilicon manufacturing
331112　Ferrotitanium manufacturing
331112　Ferrotungsten manufacturing
332111　Ferrous forgings made from purchased iron or steel, unfinished
423510　Ferrous metals merchant wholesalers
331112　Ferrovanadium manufacturing
483114　Ferry passenger transportation, Great Lakes (including St. Lawrence Seaway)
336611　Ferryboat building
621410　Fertility clinics
424910　Fertilizer and fertilizer materials merchant wholesalers
115112　Fertilizer application for crops
212393　Fertilizer minerals, natural, mining and/or beneficiating
325314　Fertilizers, mixed, made in plants not manufacturing fertilizer materials
325311　Fertilizers, mixed, made in plants producing nitrogenous fertilizer materials

325312 Fertilizers, mixed, made in plants producing phosphatic fertilizer materials

325311 Fertilizers, natural organic (except compost), manufacturing

325311 Fertilizers, of animal waste origin, manufacturing

325311 Fertilizers, of sewage origin, manufacturing

561730 Fertilizing lawns

333111 Fertilizing machinery, farm-type, manufacturing

111998 Fescue seed farming

711310 Festival managers with facilities

711320 Festival managers without facilities

711310 Festival of arts managers with facilities

711320 Festival of arts managers without facilities

711310 Festival of arts organizers with facilities

711320 Festival of arts organizers without facilities

711310 Festival of arts promoters with facilities

711320 Festival of arts promoters without facilities

711310 Festival organizers with facilities

711320 Festival organizers without facilities

711310 Festival promoters with facilities

711320 Festival promoters without facilities

325412 Fever remedy preparations manufacturing

522294 FHLMC (Federal Home Loan Mortgage Corporation)

322214 Fiber cans and drums (i.e., all-fiber, nonfiber ends of any material) made from purchased paperboard

424130 Fiber cans and drums merchant wholesalers

322214 Fiber drums made from purchased paperboard

337125 Fiber furniture (except upholstered), household-type, manufacturing

238210 Fiber optic cable (except transmission lines) installation

335921 Fiber optic cable made from purchased fiber optic strand

237130 Fiber optic cable transmission line construction

334417 Fiber optic connectors manufacturing

322214 Fiber spools, reels, blocks made from purchased paperboard

322214 Fiber tubes made from purchased paperboard

314999 Fiber, textile recovery from textile mill waste and rags

321219 Fiberboard manufacturing

423310 Fiberboard merchant wholesalers

423390 Fiberglass building materials (except insulation, roofing, siding) merchant wholesalers

424310 Fiberglass fabrics merchant wholesalers

313210 Fiberglass fabrics weaving

327993 Fiberglass insulation products manufacturing

313221 Fiberglasses, narrow woven, weaving

325221 Fibers and filaments, cellulosic, manufacturing and texturizing

325222 Fibers and filaments, noncellulosic, manufacturing and texturizing

335991 Fibers, carbon and graphite, manufacturing

327212 Fibers, glass, textile, made in glass making plants

424690 Fibers, manmade, merchant wholesalers

424590 Fibers, vegetable, merchant wholesalers

323121 Fiction book binding without printing

511130 Fiction book publishers (except exclusive Internet publishing)

511130 Fiction book publishers and printing combined

519130	Fiction book publishers, exclusively on Internet
323117	Fiction books printing and binding without publishing
323117	Fiction books printing without publishing
524126	Fidelity insurance carriers, direct
531390	Fiduciaries', real estate, offices
523991	Fiduciary agencies (except real estate)
332995	Field artillery manufacturing
315211	Field jackets, military, cut and sew apparel contractors
315228	Field jackets, military, men's and boys', cut and sewn from purchased fabric (except apparel contractors)
111421	Field nurseries (i.e., growing of flowers and shrubbery)
238140	Field stone (i.e., masonry) installation
334515	Field strength and intensity measuring equipment, electrical, manufacturing
336211	Fifth wheel assemblies manufacturing
111339	Fig farming
711219	Figure skaters, independent
335110	Filaments for electric lamp bulbs manufacturing
111335	Filbert farming
115114	Filbert hulling and shelling
424120	File cards and folders merchant wholesalers
322231	File folders (e.g., accordion, expanding, hanging, manila) made from purchased paper and paperboard
333515	Files (i.e., a machine tool accessory) manufacturing
332212	Files, handheld, manufacturing
337214	Filing cabinets (except wood), office-type, manufacturing
337211	Filing cabinets, wood, office type, manufacturing
333512	Filing machines, metalworking, manufacturing
212399	Fill dirt pits mining and/or beneficiating

325510	Fillers, wood (e.g., dry, liquid, paste), manufacturing
314999	Filling (except nonwoven textile), upholstery, manufacturing
311999	Fillings, cake or pie (except fruits, meat, vegetables), manufacturing
711510	Film actors, independent
519120	Film archives
541380	Film badge testing (i.e., radiation testing) laboratories or services
812921	Film developing and printing (except motion picture, one-hour)
812922	Film developing and printing, one hour
333315	Film developing equipment manufacturing
423410	Film developing equipment merchant wholesalers
512120	Film distribution agencies
512120	Film distribution, motion picture and video
512131	Film festivals exhibitors
512120	Film libraries, commercial distribution
512199	Film libraries, motion picture or video, stock footage
512191	Film or tape closed captioning
512191	Film or video transfer services
512199	Film processing laboratories, motion picture
711510	Film producers, independent
512110	Film studios producing films
423410	Film, photographic, merchant wholesalers
326113	Film, plastics (except packaging), manufacturing
326112	Film, plastics, packaging, manufacturing
325992	Film, sensitized (e.g., camera, motion picture, X-ray), manufacturing
512110	Films, motion picture production
512110	Films, motion picture production and distribution

424130	Filter papers merchant wholesalers
327112	Filtering media, pottery, manufacturing
336399	Filters (e.g., air, engine oil, fuel) automotive, truck, and bus, manufacturing
333411	Filters, air-conditioner, manufacturing
334419	Filters, electronic component-type, manufacturing
333411	Filters, furnace, manufacturing
333999	Filters, industrial and general line (except internal combustion engine, warm air furnace), manufacturing
322299	Filters, paper, made from purchased paper
221310	Filtration plant, water
212322	Filtration sand quarrying and/or beneficiating
332993	Fin assemblies, mortar, manufacturing
332993	Fin assemblies, torpedo and bomb, manufacturing
522291	Finance companies (i.e., unsecured cash loans)
523140	Financial futures brokerages
551112	Financial holding companies
523930	Financial investment advice services, customized, fees paid by client
511120	Financial magazine and periodical publishers (except exclusive Internet publishing)
511120	Financial magazine and periodical publishers and printing combined
519130	Financial magazine and periodical publishers, exclusively on Internet
323112	Financial magazines and periodicals flexographic printing without publishing
323111	Financial magazines and periodicals gravure printing without publishing
323110	Financial magazines and periodicals lithographic (offset) printing without publishing
323119	Financial magazines and periodicals printing (except flexographic, gravure, lithographic, quick, screen) without publishing
323113	Financial magazines and periodicals screen printing without publishing
541611	Financial management consulting (except investment advice) services
523930	Financial planning services, customized, fees paid by client
522320	Financial transactions processing (except central bank)
521110	Financial transactions processing of the central bank
522220	Financing, sales
522294	Financing, secondary market
316999	Findings, boot and shoe, manufacturing
339913	Findings, jeweler's, manufacturing
315212	Findings, suit and coat (e.g., coat fronts, pockets), women's, girls', and infants', cut and sew apparel contractors
315999	Findings, suit and coat (e.g., coat fronts, pockets), cut and sewn from purchased fabric (except apparel contractors)
315211	Findings, suit and coat (e.g., coat fronts, pockets), men's and boys', cut and sew apparel contractors
712110	Fine arts museums
611610	Fine arts schools (except academic)
722110	Fine dining restaurants, full service
424110	Fine paper, bulk, merchant wholesalers
114111	Finfish fishing (e.g., flounder, salmon, trout)
112511	Finfish production, farm raising
112511	Finfish, hatcheries

321213	Finger joint lumber manufacturing
561611	Fingerprint services
238350	Finish carpentry
314110	Finishing (e.g., dyeing) rugs and carpets
325613	Finishing agents, textile and leather, manufacturing
238310	Finishing drywall contractors
316110	Finishing hides and skins on a contract basis
316110	Finishing leather
333292	Finishing machinery for textile manufacturing
313311	Finishing plants, broadwoven fabric
611110	Finishing schools, secondary
561621	Fire alarm monitoring services
561621	Fire alarm sales combined with installation, repair, or monitoring services
238210	Fire alarm system, electric, installation only
236220	Fire and flood restoration of commercial and institutional buildings
236118	Fire and flood restoration, multifamily building, general contractors
236118	Fire and flood restoration, single-family housing, general contractors
922160	Fire and rescue service
212325	Fire clay mining and/or beneficiating
922160	Fire departments (e.g., government, volunteer (except private))
334290	Fire detection and alarm systems manufacturing
334519	Fire detector systems, nonelectric, manufacturing
332321	Fire doors, metal, manufacturing
238190	Fire escape installation
332323	Fire escapes, metal, manufacturing
325998	Fire extinguisher chemical preparations manufacturing
424690	Fire extinguisher preparations merchant wholesalers
423990	Fire extinguisher sales combined with rental and/or service, merchant wholesalers
423990	Fire extinguishers merchant wholesalers
339999	Fire extinguishers, portable, manufacturing
611519	Fire fighter training schools
561990	Fire fighting services as a commercial activity
314999	Fire hose, textile, made from purchased materials
237110	Fire hydrant installation
332911	Fire hydrant valves manufacturing
332911	Fire hydrants, complete, manufacturing
524126	Fire insurance carriers, direct
541380	Fire insurance underwriters' laboratories
524291	Fire investigators
922160	Fire marshals' offices
922160	Fire prevention offices, government
115310	Fire prevention, forest
325998	Fire retardant chemical preparations manufacturing
238220	Fire sprinkler system installation
236220	Fire station construction
423990	Firearms (except sporting) merchant wholesalers
813319	Firearms advocacy organizations
332994	Firearms, small, manufacturing
423910	Firearms, sporting, merchant wholesalers
336611	Fireboat building
327124	Firebrick, clay refractories, manufacturing
315211	Firefighters' dress uniforms, men's, cut and sew apparel contractors
315222	Firefighters' dress uniforms, men's, cut and sewn from purchased fabric (except apparel contractors)

114111   Fisheries, finfish
114112   Fisheries, shellfish
487210   Fishing boat charter operation
336611   Fishing boat, commercial, building
721214   Fishing camps with accommodation facilities
713990   Fishing clubs, recreational
423910   Fishing equipment and supplies (except commercial) merchant wholesalers
213112   Fishing for tools at oil and gas fields on a contract basis
713990   Fishing guide services
332211   Fishing knives manufacturing
314999   Fishing nets made from purchased materials
713990   Fishing piers
114210   Fishing preserves
451110   Fishing supply stores (e.g., bait)
339920   Fishing tackle and equipment (except lines, nets, seines) manufacturing
713940   Fitness centers
423910   Fitness equipment and supplies merchant wholesalers
713940   Fitness salons
713940   Fitness spas without accommodations
326122   Fittings and unions, rigid plastics pipe, manufacturing
423720   Fittings and valves, plumbers', merchant wholesalers
326122   Fittings, rigid plastics pipe, manufacturing
331511   Fittings, soil and pressure pipe, cast iron, manufacturing
713950   Five pin bowling centers
488119   Fixed base operators
722213   Fixed location refreshment stands
325992   Fixers, prepared photographic, manufacturing
337920   Fixtures (e.g., poles, rods, rollers), curtain and drapery, manufacturing
423610   Fixtures, electric lighting, merchant wholesalers

423440   Fixtures, store (except refrigerated), merchant wholesalers
337215   Fixtures, store display, manufacturing
453998   Flag and banner shops
561990   Flagging (i.e., traffic control) services
238990   Flagpole installation
332323   Flagpoles, metal, manufacturing
321999   Flagpoles, wood, manufacturing
314999   Flags, textile (e.g., banners, bunting, emblems, pennants), made from purchased fabrics
212311   Flagstone mining or quarrying
327991   Flagstones cutting
321219   Flakeboard manufacturing
331221   Flakes made from purchased iron or steel
331314   Flakes, aluminum, made from purchased aluminum
331111   Flakes, iron or steel, made in iron and steel mills
334516   Flame photometers manufacturing
812332   Flame resistant clothing supply services
334512   Flame safety controls for furnaces and boilers manufacturing
332995   Flame throwers manufacturing
333512   Flange facing machines, metalworking, manufacturing
332991   Flange units, ball or roller bearing, manufacturing
332919   Flanges and flange unions, pipe, metal, manufacturing
315223   Flannel shirts (except work shirts), men's and boys', cut and sewn from purchased fabric (except apparel contractors)
315291   Flannel shirts, infants', cut and sewn from purchased fabric (except apparel contractors)
315211   Flannel shirts, men's and boys', cut and sew apparel contractors

315212	Flannel shirts, women's, girls', and infants', cut and sew apparel contractors
315232	Flannel shirts, women's, misses', and girls', cut and sewn from purchased fabric (except apparel contrctors)
315225	Flannel shirts, work, men's and boys', cut and sewn from purchased fabric (except apparel contractors)
313210	Flannels, broadwoven, weaving
325998	Flares manufacturing
333315	Flash apparatus, photographic, manufacturing
335110	Flash bulbs, photographic, manufacturing
238170	Flashing contractors
335912	Flashlight batteries, disposable, manufacturing
335110	Flashlight bulb manufacturing
335129	Flashlights manufacturing
423610	Flashlights merchant wholesalers
313249	Flat (i.e., warp) fabrics knitting
331221	Flat bright steel strip made in cold rolling mills made from purchased steel
327211	Flat glass (e.g., float, plate) manufacturing
423390	Flat glass merchant wholesalers
334119	Flat panel displays (i.e., complete units), computer peripheral equipment, manufacturing
332612	Flat springs (except clock, watch), light gauge, made from purchased wire or strip, manufacturing
332611	Flat springs, heavy gauge metal, manufacturing
336212	Flatbed trailers, commercial, manufacturing
484220	Flatbed trucking, local
484230	Flatbed trucking, long-distance
331111	Flats, iron or steel, made in iron and steel mills
321920	Flats, wood, greenhouse, manufacturing

423220	Flatware (except plated, precious) merchant wholesalers
332211	Flatware, nonprecious and precious plated metal, manufacturing
423940	Flatware, precious and plated, merchant wholesalers
311942	Flavor extracts (except coffee) manufacturing
311511	Flavored milk drinks manufacturing
312111	Flavored water manufacturing
311930	Flavoring concentrates (except coffee based) manufacturing
424490	Flavoring extracts (except for fountain use) merchant wholesalers
325199	Flavoring materials (i.e., basic synthetic chemicals such as coumarin) manufacturing
311930	Flavoring pastes, powders, and syrups for soft drink manufacturing
313111	Flax spun yarns made from purchased fiber
111120	Flaxseed farming, field and seed production
311225	Flaxseed oil made from purchased oils
311223	Flaxseed oil made in crushing mills
531190	Flea market space (except under roof) rental or leasing
531120	Flea market space, under roof, rental or leasing
454390	Flea markets, temporary location, direct selling
453310	Flea markets, used merchandise, permanent
325320	Flea powders or sprays manufacturing
532112	Fleet leasing, passenger vehicle
316110	Fleshers, leather (i.e., flesh side of split leather), manufacturing
334112	Flexible (i.e., floppy) magnetic disk drives manufacturing
332999	Flexible metal hose and tubing manufacturing

322221	Flexible packaging sheet materials (except foil-paper laminates) made by coating or laminating purchased paper
322225	Flexible packaging sheet materials made by laminating purchased foil
326112	Flexible packaging, plastics film, manufacturing
334412	Flexible wiring boards, bare, manufacturing
325910	Flexographic inks manufacturing
323122	Flexographic plate preparation services
323112	Flexographic printing (except books, manifold business forms, printing grey goods)
333293	Flexographic printing presses manufacturing
339920	Flies, artificial fishing, manufacturing
334511	Flight and navigation sensors, transmitters, and displays manufacturing
611519	Flight attendant schools
334511	Flight recorders (i.e., black boxes) manufacturing
333319	Flight simulation machinery manufacturing
611512	Flight training schools
212325	Flint clay mining and/or beneficiating
327992	Flint processing beyond beneficiation
339999	Flints, lighter, manufacturing
321113	Flitches (i.e., veneer stock) made in sawmills
334512	Float controls, residential and commercial types, manufacturing
561990	Float decorating services
541490	Float design services
327124	Floaters, glasshouse, clay, manufacturing
713210	Floating casinos (i.e., gambling cruises, riverboat casinos)
332313	Floating covers, fabricated metal plate work, manufacturing

332812	Flocking metals and metal products for the trade
237990	Flood control project construction
332312	Flood gates, metal plate, manufacturing
335129	Floodlights (i.e., lighting fixtures) manufacturing
237990	Floodway canal and ditch construction
321918	Floor baseboards, wood, manufacturing
442210	Floor covering stores (except wood or ceramic tile only)
444190	Floor covering stores, wood or ceramic tile only
423220	Floor coverings merchant wholesalers
326192	Floor coverings, linoleum, manufacturing
326192	Floor coverings, resilient, manufacturing
326192	Floor coverings, rubber, manufacturing
326192	Floor coverings, vinyl, manufacturing
332312	Floor jacks, metal, manufacturing
335121	Floor lamps (i.e., lighting fixtures), residential, manufacturing
238330	Floor laying, scraping, finishing and refinishing
423850	Floor maintenance equipment merchant wholesalers
326299	Floor mats (e.g., bath, door), rubber, manufacturing
325612	Floor polishes and waxes manufacturing
332312	Floor posts, adjustable metal, manufacturing
532490	Floor sanding machine rental or leasing
333319	Floor sanding, washing, and polishing machines, commercial-type, manufacturing
335212	Floor scrubbing and shampooing machines, household-type electric, manufacturing

335211 Floor standing fans, household-type electric, manufacturing
238330 Floor tile and sheets, installation only
327122 Floor tile, ceramic, manufacturing
321214 Floor trusses, wood, manufacturing
335212 Floor waxers and polishers, household-type electric, manufacturing
532490 Floor waxing equipment rental or leasing
332323 Flooring, open steel (i.e., grating), manufacturing
332322 Flooring, sheet metal (except stampings), manufacturing
321114 Flooring, wood block, treating
321918 Flooring, wood, manufacturing
423310 Flooring, wood, merchant wholesalers
334112 Floppy disk drives manufacturing
561422 Floral wire services (i.e., telemarketing services)
453110 Florists
327112 Florists' articles, red earthenware, manufacturing
424930 Florist's supplies merchant wholesalers
333131 Flotation machinery, mining-type, manufacturing
114111 Flounder fishing
314911 Flour bags made from purchased woven or knitted materials
424490 Flour merchant wholesalers
333294 Flour milling machinery manufacturing
311230 Flour mills, breakfast cereal, manufacturing
311211 Flour mills, cereals grains (except breakfast cereals, rice)
311211 Flour mixes made in flour mills
311822 Flour, blended or self-rising, made from purchased flour
311211 Flour, blended, prepared, or self-rising (except rice), made in flour mills
311213 Flour, malt, manufacturing

311212 Flour, rice, manufacturing
321999 Flour, wood, manufacturing
335314 Flow actuated electrical switches manufacturing
334513 Flow instruments, industrial process-type, manufacturing
327420 Flower boxes, plaster of paris, manufacturing
111421 Flower bulb growing
424910 Flower bulbs merchant wholesalers
111422 Flower growing
327112 Flower pots, red earthenware, manufacturing
111422 Flower seed production
453998 Flower shops, artificial or dried
453110 Flower shops, fresh
561920 Flower show managers
561920 Flower show organizers
561920 Flower show promoters
424930 Flowers merchant wholesalers
339999 Flowers, artificial (except glass, plastics), manufacturing
327123 Flue lining, clay, manufacturing
423320 Flue pipe and linings merchant wholesalers
332322 Flues, stove and furnace, sheet metal (except stampings), manufacturing
332439 Fluid milk shipping containers, light gauge metal, manufacturing
311511 Fluid milk substitutes processing
333995 Fluid power actuators manufacturing
332912 Fluid power aircraft subassemblies manufacturing
333995 Fluid power cylinders manufacturing
332912 Fluid power hose assemblies manufacturing
333996 Fluid power motors manufacturing
333996 Fluid power pumps manufacturing
332912 Fluid power valves and hose fittings manufacturing

334513 Fluidic devices, circuits, and systems for process control, manufacturing

423830 Fluid-power transmission equipment merchant wholesalers

332313 Flumes, fabricated metal plate work, manufacturing

332322 Flumes, sheet metal (except stampings), manufacturing

325188 Fluoboric acid manufacturing

335311 Fluorescent ballasts (i.e., transformers) manufacturing

325132 Fluorescent dyes manufacturing

335110 Fluorescent lamp tubes, electric, manufacturing

335122 Fluorescent lighting fixtures, commercial, institutional, and industrial electric, manufacturing

335121 Fluorescent lighting fixtures, residential, manufacturing

335311 Fluorescent lighting transformers manufacturing

325120 Fluorinated hydrocarbon gases manufacturing

325188 Fluorine manufacturing

212393 Fluorite mining and/or beneficiating

325212 Fluoro rubbers manufacturing

325212 Fluorocarbon derivative rubbers manufacturing

325222 Fluorocarbon fibers and filaments manufacturing

325120 Fluorocarbon gases manufacturing

325211 Fluorohydrocarbon resins manufacturing

325211 Fluoro-polymer resins manufacturing

334517 Fluoroscopes manufacturing

334517 Fluoroscopic X-ray apparatus and tubes manufacturing

212393 Fluorspar mining and/or beneficiating

335110 Fluroescent lamp electrodes, cold cathode, manufacturing

332998 Flush tanks, metal, manufacturing

332913 Flush valves, plumbing, manufacturing

339992 Flutes and parts manufacturing

325998 Fluxes (e.g., brazing, galvanizing, soldering, welding) manufacturing

325320 Fly sprays manufacturing

339999 Fly swatters manufacturing

541870 Flyer direct distribution (except direct mail) services

713990 Flying clubs, recreational

488119 Flying field operators

611512 Flying instruction

335129 Flytraps, electrical, manufacturing

336312 Flywheels and ring gears, automotive and truck gasoline engine, manufacturing

515112 FM radio stations

522294 FNMA (Federal National Mortgage Association)

238310 Foam insulation installation

326150 Foam plastics products (except polystrene) manufacturing

326140 Foam polystyrene products manufacturing

424990 Foam rubber merchant wholesalers

424610 Foam, plastics, resins and shapes, merchant wholesalers

322223 Foil bags made from purchased foil

332999 Foil containers (except bags) manufacturing

332999 Foil not made in rolling mills

322225 Foil sheet, laminating purchased foil sheets for packaging applications

331315 Foil, aluminum, made by flat rolling purchased aluminum

331315 Foil, aluminum, made in integrated secondary smelting and flat rolling mills

331421 Foil, copper, made from purchased metal or scrap

331491 Foil, gold, made by rolling purchased metals or scrap

331491 Foil, nickel, made by rolling purchased metals or scrap

331491   Foil, silver, made by rolling
         purchased metals or scrap
424120   Folders, file, merchant
         wholesalers
561910   Folding and packaging services,
         textile and apparel
322130   Folding boxboard stock
         manufacturing
322212   Folding boxes (except
         corrugated) made from
         purchased paperboard
322212   Folding paper and paperboard
         containers (except corrugated)
         made from purchased
         paperboard
111422   Foliage growing
711120   Folk dance companies
711510   Folk dancers, independent
445110   Food (i.e., groceries) stores
446191   Food (i.e., health) supplement
         stores
336999   Food (vendor) carts on wheels
         manufacturing
624210   Food banks
722330   Food carts, mobile
333294   Food choppers, grinders,
         mixers, and slicers (i.e., food
         manufacturing-type)
         manufacturing
311942   Food coloring, natural,
         manufacturing
325132   Food coloring, synthetic,
         manufacturing
722310   Food concession contractors
         (e.g., convention facilities,
         entertainment facilities,
         sporting facilities)
722330   Food concession stands, mobile
322299   Food containers made from
         molded pulp
326140   Food containers, polystyrene
         foam, manufacturing
322215   Food containers, sanitary
         (except folding), made from
         purchased paper or paperboard
322212   Food containers, sanitary,
         folding, made from purchased
         paperboard

333294   Food dehydrating equipment
         (except household-type)
         manufacturing
923130   Food distribution program
         administration, government
311942   Food extracts (except coffee,
         meat) manufacturing
926140   Food inspection agencies
811310   Food machinery repair and
         maintenance services
335211   Food mixers, household-type
         electric, manufacturing
333993   Food packaging machinery
         manufacturing
327213   Food packaging, glass,
         manufacturing
236210   Food processing plant
         construction
541712   Food research and development
         laboratories or services
         (except biotechnology research
         and development)
722310   Food service contractors, airline
722310   Food service contractors,
         cafeteria
722310   Food service contractors,
         concession operator (e.g.,
         convention facilities,
         entertainment facilities,
         sporting facilities)
423440   Food service equipment (except
         refrigerated), commercial,
         merchant wholesalers
923120   Food service health inspections
326111   Food storage bags, plastics film,
         single wall or multiwall,
         manufacturing
541380   Food testing laboratories or
         services
322299   Food trays, molded pulp,
         manufacturing
333319   Food warming equipment,
         commercial-type,
         manufacturing
335228   Food waste disposal units,
         household-type, manufacturing
311991   Food, prepared, perishable,
         packaged for individual resale

423830 Food-processing machinery and equipment merchant wholesalers

339113 Foot appliances, orthopedic, manufacturing

621391 Foot specialists' (podiatry) offices (e.g., centers, clinics)

711211 Football clubs, professional or semiprofessional

713990 Football clubs, recreational

339920 Football equipment and supplies (except footwear, uniforms) manufacturing

423910 Football equipment and supplies merchant wholesalers

611620 Football instruction, camps, or schools

711211 Football teams, professional or semiprofessional

316211 Footholds, plastics or plastics soled fabric upper, manufacturing

316211 Footholds, rubber or rubber soled fabric upper, manufacturing

315119 Footies, sheer, knitting or knitting and finishing

238110 Footing and foundation concrete contractors

451110 Footwear (e.g., bowling, golf, spiked), specialty sports, stores

316211 Footwear (except house slippers), plastics or plastics soled fabric uppers, manufacturing

333298 Footwear making or repairing machinery manufacturing

424340 Footwear merchant wholesalers

326199 Footwear parts (e.g., heels, soles), plastics, manufacturing

326299 Footwear parts (e.g., heels, soles, soling strips), rubber, manufacturing

316219 Footwear, athletic (except rubber or plastics soled with fabric upper), manufacturing

316219 Footwear, children's (except house slippers, orthopedic extension, plastics, rubber), manufacturing

316219 Footwear, children's, leather or vinyl upper with rubber or plastics soles, manufacturing

316213 Footwear, men's (except house slippers, athletic, orthopedic extension, plastics, rubber), manufacturing

316213 Footwear, men's leather or vinyl upper with rubber or plastics soles, manufacturing

316214 Footwear, women's (except house slippers, athletic, orthopedic extension, plastics, rubber) manufacturing

316214 Footwear, women's leather or vinyl upper with rubber or plastics soles, manufacturing

339112 Forceps, surgical, manufacturing

523130 Foreign currency exchange dealing (i.e., acting as a principal in dealing commodities to investors)

523130 Foreign currency exchange services (i.e., selling to the public)

928120 Foreign economic and social development services, government

928120 Foreign government service

611630 Foreign language schools

928120 Foreign missions

541380 Forensic (except medical) laboratories or services

621511 Forensic laboratories, medical

621111 Forensic pathologists' offices

531190 Forest land rental or leasing

115310 Forest management plans preparation

113210 Forest nurseries for reforestation, growing trees

423990 Forest products (except lumber) merchant wholesalers

484230 Forest products trucking, long-distance

423810 Forestry machinery and equipment merchant wholesalers

532412 Forestry machinery and equipment rental or leasing

811310 Forestry machinery and equipment repair and maintenance services

541712 Forestry research and development laboratories or services

115310 Forestry services

333513 Forging machinery and hammers manufacturing

332111 Forgings made from purchased iron or steel, unfinished

331111 Forgings, iron or steel, made in iron and steel mills

811310 Forklift repair and maintenance services

423830 Forklift trucks (except log) merchant wholesalers

333924 Forklifts manufacturing

332212 Forks, handtools (e.g., garden, hay, manure), manufacturing

332211 Forks, table, nonprecious and precious plated metal, manufacturing

331222 Form ties made in wire drawing plants

315211 Formal jackets, men's and boys', cut and sew apparel contractors

315222 Formal jackets, men's and boys', cut and sewn from purchased fabric (except apparel contractors)

532220 Formal wear rental

325199 Formaldehyde manufacturing

325199 Formalin manufacturing

325199 Formic acid manufacturing

238190 Forming contractor

333513 Forming machines (except drawing), metalworking, manufacturing

327112 Forms for dipped rubber products, pottery, manufacturing

238190 Forms for poured concrete, erecting and dismantling

423420 Forms handling machines merchant wholesalers

332322 Forms, concrete, sheet metal (except stampings), manufacturing

321999 Forms, display, boot and shoe, all materials, manufacturing

424120 Forms, paper (e.g., business, office, sales), merchant wholesalers

312130 Fortified wines manufacturing

812990 Fortune-telling services

624110 Foster care placement agencies

624110 Foster home placement services

238140 Foundation (e.g., brick, block, stone), building, contractors

238390 Foundation dampproofing (including installing rigid foam insulation)

238910 Foundation digging (i.e., excavation)

238910 Foundation drilling contractors

315212 Foundation garments, women's and girls', cut and sew apparel contractors

315231 Foundation garments, women's, misses', and girls', cut and sewn from purchased fabric (except apparel contractors)

238110 Foundation, building, poured concrete, contractors

238130 Foundation, building, wood, contractors

325620 Foundations (i.e., make-up) manufacturing

331528 Foundries (except die-casting), nonferrous metals (except aluminum, copper)

331524 Foundries, aluminum (except die-casting)

331525 Foundries, brass, bronze, and copper (except die-casting) manufacturing

331525 Foundries, copper (except die-casting)

331521 Foundries, die-casting, aluminum

331522 Foundries, die-casting, nonferrous metals (except aluminum)

331511 Foundries, iron (i.e., ductile, gray, malleable, semisteel)

331513 Foundries, steel (except investment)

331512 Foundries, steel investment

333511	Foundry casting molds manufacturing
236210	Foundry construction
325998	Foundry core oil, wash, and wax manufacturing
332997	Foundry cores manufacturing
423830	Foundry machinery and equipment merchant wholesalers
811310	Foundry machinery and equipment repair and maintenance services
332997	Foundry pattern making
423510	Foundry products merchant wholesalers
212322	Foundry sand quarrying and/or beneficiating
424450	Fountain fruits and syrups merchant wholesalers
335129	Fountain lighting fixtures manufacturing
339941	Fountain pens manufacturing
332999	Fountains (except drinking), metal, manufacturing
332998	Fountains, drinking (except mechanically refrigerated), metal, manufacturing
423720	Fountains, drinking (except refrigerated), merchant wholesalers
423740	Fountains, drinking, refrigerated, merchant wholesalers
327420	Fountains, plaster of paris, manufacturing
333415	Fountains, refrigerated drinking, manufacturing
713920	Four season ski resorts without accommodations
333291	Fourdrinier machinery manufacturing
332618	Fourdrinier wire cloth made from purchased wire
112930	Fox production
335312	Fractional horsepower electric motors manufacturing
333298	Fractionating equipment, chemical, manufacturing
211112	Fractionating natural gas liquids

333319	Frame and body alignment equipment, motor vehicle, manufacturing
332999	Frames and handles, handbag and luggage, metal, manufacturing
423220	Frames and pictures merchant wholesalers
339942	Frames for artist's canvases (i.e., stretchers) manufacturing
333292	Frames for textile making machinery manufacturing
332321	Frames, door and window, metal, manufacturing
321911	Frames, door and window, wood, manufacturing
332999	Frames, metal, lamp shade, manufacturing
332999	Frames, metal, umbrella and parasol, manufacturing
339999	Frames, mirror and picture, all materials, manufacturing
423460	Frames, ophthalmic, merchant wholesalers
238130	Framework, house, contractors
238130	Framing contractors
533110	Franchise agreements, leasing, selling or licensing, without providing other services
813410	Fraternal associations or lodges, social or civic
524113	Fraternal life insurance organizations
813410	Fraternal lodges
813410	Fraternal organizations
813410	Fraternities (except residential)
721310	Fraternity houses
621493	Freestanding ambulatory surgical centers and clinics
621493	Freestanding emergency medical centers and clinics
311423	Freeze-dried, food processing, fruits and vegetables
811310	Freezer, commercial, repair and maintenance services
335222	Freezers, chest and upright household-type, manufacturing
423620	Freezers, household-type, merchant wholesalers

333415 Freezing equipment, industrial and commercial-type, manufacturing

311712 Freezing fish (e.g., blocks, fillets, ready-to-serve products)

488210 Freight car cleaning services

481112 Freight carriers (except air couriers), air, scheduled

481212 Freight charter services, air

488510 Freight forwarding

482111 Freight railways, line-haul

482112 Freight railways, short-line or beltline

541614 Freight rate auditor services

541614 Freight rate consulting services

483113 Freight shipping on the Great Lakes system (including St. Lawrence Seaway)

541614 Freight traffic consulting services

481212 Freight transportation, air, charter services

481212 Freight transportation, air, nonscheduled

483113 Freight transportation, deep sea, to and from domestic ports

483111 Freight transportation, deep sea, to or from foreign ports

483211 Freight transportation, inland waters (except on Great Lakes system)

311411 French fries, frozen, pre-cooked, manufacturing

311412 French toast, frozen, manufacturing

335312 Frequency converters (i.e., electric generators) manufacturing

334515 Frequency meters (e.g., electrical, electronic, mechanical) manufacturing

334515 Frequency synthesizers manufacturing

238310 Fresco (i.e., decorative plaster finishing) contractors

424460 Fresh fish merchant wholesalers

424480 Fresh fruits, vegetables and berries merchant wholesalers

424470 Fresh meats merchant wholesalers

424440 Fresh poultry merchant wholesalers

424460 Fresh seafood merchant wholesalers

339992 Fretted instruments and parts manufacturing

313221 Fringes weaving

325510 Frit manufacturing

114119 Frog fishing

112519 Frog production, farm raising

331111 Frogs, iron or steel, made in iron and steel mills

811118 Front end alignment shops, automotive

423820 Frost protection machinery merchant wholesalers

311999 Frosting, prepared, manufacturing

311411 Frozen ades, drinks and cocktail mixes, manufacturing

311812 Frozen bread and bread-type rolls, made in commercial bakeries

311813 Frozen cake manufacturing

311411 Frozen citrus pulp manufacturing

311520 Frozen custard manufacturing

722213 Frozen custard stands, fixed location

311520 Frozen desserts (except bakery) manufacturing

311412 Frozen dinners (except seafood-based) manufacturing

311822 Frozen doughs made from purchased flour

424460 Frozen fish (except packaged) merchant wholesalers

454390 Frozen food and freezer plan providers, direct selling

326111 Frozen food bags, plastics film, single wall or multiwall, manufacturing

311412 Frozen food entrees (except seafood based), packaged, manufacturing

424420 Frozen foods, packaged (except dairy products), merchant wholesalers

311411	Frozen fruit and vegetable processing		311421	Fruit juices, fresh, manufacturing
311411	Frozen fruits, fruit juices, and vegetables, manufacturing		445230	Fruit markets
311612	Frozen meat pies (i.e., tourtires) made from purchased carcasses		311340	Fruit peel products (e.g., candied, crystallized, glace, glazed) manufacturing
445210	Frozen meat stores		311421	Fruit pickling
424470	Frozen meats (except packaged) merchant wholesalers		311421	Fruit pie fillings, canning
311412	Frozen pizza manufacturing		311520	Fruit pops, frozen, manufacturing
311412	Frozen pot pies manufacturing		115114	Fruit precooling
424440	Frozen poultry (except packaged) merchant wholesalers		115114	Fruit sorting, grading, and packing
311412	Frozen rice dishes manufacturing		445230	Fruit stands, permanent
			454390	Fruit stands, temporary
424460	Frozen seafood (except packaged) merchant wholesalers		111421	Fruit stock (e.g., plants, seedlings, trees) growing
311412	Frozen side dishes manufacturing		311930	Fruit syrups, flavoring, manufacturing
			115113	Fruit, machine harvesting
311412	Frozen soups (except seafood) manufacturing		115114	Fruit, sun drying
			115114	Fruit, vacuum cooling
311412	Frozen waffles manufacturing		311340	Fruits (e.g., candied, crystallized, glazed) manufacturing
111336	Fruit and tree nut combination farming		326199	Fruits and vegetables, artificial, plastics, manufacturing
445230	Fruit and vegetable stands, permanent		311423	Fruits dehydrating (except sun drying)
311423	Fruit and vegetables, dehydrating, manufacturing		311421	Fruits pickling
321920	Fruit baskets, veneer and splint, manufacturing		339999	Fruits, artificial (except glass, plastics), manufacturing
311421	Fruit brining		327215	Fruits, artificial, made from purchased glass
311421	Fruit butters manufacturing			
321920	Fruit crates, wood, wirebound, manufacturing		327212	Fruits, artificial, made in glass making plants
312111	Fruit drinks (except juice), manufacturing		311421	Fruits, canned, manufacturing
			424490	Fruits, canned, merchant wholesalers
311942	Fruit extracts manufacturing		424480	Fruits, fresh, merchant wholesalers
111419	Fruit farming, grown under cover		311411	Fruits, frozen, manufacturing
311211	Fruit flour, meal, and powders, manufacturing		424420	Fruits, frozen, merchant wholesalers
333111	Fruit harvesting machines manufacturing		112320	Fryer chicken production
			335211	Fryers, household-type electric, manufacturing
311421	Fruit juice canning			
311411	Fruit juice concentrates, frozen, manufacturing		311320	Fudge, chocolate, made from cacao beans

311330 Fudge, chocolate, made from purchased chocolate

311340 Fudge, nonchocolate, manufacturing

326299 Fuel bladders, rubber, manufacturing

324199 Fuel briquettes or boulets made from refined petroleum

335999 Fuel cells, electrochemical generators, manufacturing

334413 Fuel cells, solid-state, manufacturing

334519 Fuel densitometers, aircraft engine, manufacturing

336312 Fuel injection systems and parts, automotive and truck gasoline engine, manufacturing

334519 Fuel mixture indicators, aircraft engine, manufacturing

454311 Fuel oil (i.e., heating) dealers, direct selling

424710 Fuel oil bulk stations and terminals

238220 Fuel oil burner installation

424720 Fuel oil merchant wholesalers (except bulk stations, terminals)

424720 Fuel oil truck jobbers

324110 Fuel oils manufacturing

325188 Fuel propellants, solid inorganic, not specified elsewhere by process, manufacturing

325199 Fuel propellants, solid organic, not specified elsewhere by process, manufacturing

336322 Fuel pumps, electric, automotive, truck, and bus, manufacturing

336312 Fuel pumps, mechanical, automotive and truck gasoline engine, manufacturing

334519 Fuel system instruments, aircraft, manufacturing

334519 Fuel totalizers, aircraft engine, manufacturing

423520 Fuel, coal and coke, merchant wholesalers

424720 Fueling aircraft (except on contract basis)

488190 Fueling aircraft on a contract or fee basis

324110 Fuels, jet, manufacturing

531120 Full service office space provision

722110 Full service restaurants

212325 Fuller's earth mining and/or beneficiating

327992 Fuller's earth processing beyond beneficiating

332313 Fumigating chambers, fabricated metal plate work, manufacturing

115114 Fumigating grain

561710 Fumigating services (except crop fumigating)

334515 Function generators manufacturing

561499 Fundraising campaign organization services on a contract or fee basis

334119 Funds transfer devices manufacturing

525110 Funds, employee benefit pension

525120 Funds, health and welfare

525990 Funds, mutual, closed-end

525910 Funds, mutual, open-ended

525110 Funds, pension

525190 Funds, self-insurance (except employee benefit funds)

812210 Funeral director services

812210 Funeral homes

812210 Funeral homes combined with crematories

524128 Funeral insurance carriers, direct

812210 Funeral parlors

325320 Fungicides manufacturing

315292 Fur accessories and trimings (except apparel contractors) manufacturing

315211 Fur accessories and trimings, men's and boys', cut and sew apparel contractors

315212 Fur accessories and trimings, women's, girls', and infants', cut and sew apparel contractors

315292 Fur apparel (e.g., capes, coats, hats, jackets, neckpieces) (except apparel contractors) manufacturing

315211 Fur apparel (e.g., capes, coats, hats, jackets, neckpieces), men's and boys', cut and sew apparel contractors

315212 Fur apparel (e.g., capes, coats, hats, jackets, neckpieces), women's, girls', and infants', cut and sew apparel contractors

448190 Fur apparel stores

112930 Fur bearing animal production

315292 Fur clothing (except apparel contractors) manufacturing

424330 Fur clothing merchant wholesalers

315211 Fur clothing, men's and boys', cut and sew apparel contractors

315212 Fur clothing, women's, girls', and infants', cut and sew apparel contractors

423930 Fur cuttings and scraps merchant wholesalers

541490 Fur design services

315211 Fur finishers, liners, and buttonhole makers, men's and boys', cut and sew apparel contractors

315212 Fur finishers, liners, and buttonhole makers, women's, girls', and infants', cut and sew apparel contractors

812320 Fur garment cleaning services

811490 Fur garment repair shops without retailing new fur garments

315292 Fur plates and trimmings (except apparel contractors) manufacturing

315211 Fur plates and trimmings, men's and boys', cut and sew apparel contractors

315212 Fur plates and trimmings, women's, girls', and infants', cut and sew apparel contractors

532220 Fur rental

493120 Fur storage warehousing for the trade

316110 Fur stripping

236210 Furnace (i.e., industrial plant structure) construction

325182 Furnace black manufacturing

332322 Furnace casings, sheet metal (except stampings), manufacturing

238220 Furnace conversion (i.e., from one fuel to another)

333411 Furnace filters manufacturing

332322 Furnace flues, sheet metal (except stampings), manufacturing

238220 Furnace humidifier installation

238220 Furnace installation

238220 Furnace, forced air, installation

333414 Furnaces (except forced air), heating, manufacturing

333994 Furnaces and ovens for drying and redrying, industrial process-type, manufacturing

333994 Furnaces and ovens, semiconductor wafer, manufacturing

423720 Furnaces, (except forced air), heating, merchant wholesalers

339114 Furnaces, dental laboratory, manufacturing

333414 Furnaces, floor and wall, manufacturing

333994 Furnaces, industrial and laboratory-type (except dental), manufacturing

423830 Furnaces, industrial process, merchant wholesalers

333415 Furnaces, warm air (i.e., forced air), manufacturing

423730 Furnaces, warm air (i.e., forced air), merchant wholesalers

424320 Furnishings (except shoes), men's and boys', merchant wholesalers

424330 Furnishings (except shoes), women's, girls' and infants', merchant wholesalers

448150 Furnishings stores, men's and boys'

448150 Furnishings stores, women's and girls'

423210 Furniture (except drafting tables, hospital beds, medical furniture) merchant wholesalers

337124 Furniture (except upholstered), metal household-type, manufacturing

337214 Furniture (except wood), office-type, padded, upholstered, or plain, manufacturing

337125 Furniture (except wood, metal, upholstered) indoor and outdoor household-type, manufacturing

532299 Furniture (i.e., residential) rental centers

442110 Furniture and appliance stores (i.e., primarily retailing furniture)

561740 Furniture cleaning on customers' premises

561740 Furniture cleaning services

541420 Furniture design services

321912 Furniture dimension stock, hardwood, unfinished, manufacturing

321912 Furniture dimension stock, softwood, unfinished, manufacturing

321912 Furniture dimension stock, unfinished wood, manufacturing

337215 Furniture frames and parts, metal, manufacturing

337215 Furniture frames, wood, manufacturing

332510 Furniture hardware, metal, manufacturing

321999 Furniture inlays manufacturing

484210 Furniture moving, used

423210 Furniture parts merchant wholesalers

337215 Furniture parts, finished metal, manufacturing

337215 Furniture parts, finished plastics, manufacturing

337215 Furniture parts, finished wood, manufacturing

325612 Furniture polishes and waxes manufacturing

811420 Furniture refinishing shops

811420 Furniture repair shops

811420 Furniture reupholstering shops

332612 Furniture springs, light gauge, unassembled, made from purchased wire or strip

321912 Furniture squares, unfinished hardwood, manufacturing

442110 Furniture stores (e.g., household, office, outdoor)

453310 Furniture stores, used

327215 Furniture tops, glass (e.g., beveled, cut, polished), made from purchased glass

314999 Furniture trimmings made from purchased fabrics

327991 Furniture, cut stone (i.e., benches, tables, church), manufacturing

337127 Furniture, factory-type (e.g., cabinets, stools, tool stands, work benches), manufacturing

532291 Furniture, home health, rental

339113 Furniture, hospital, specialized (e.g., hospital beds, operating room furniture), manufacturing

337121 Furniture, household-type, upholstered on frames of any material, manufacturing

532490 Furniture, institutional (i.e. public building), rental or leasing

337127 Furniture, institutional, manufacturing

337127 Furniture, laboratory-type (e.g., benches, cabinets, stools, tables), manufacturing

532420 Furniture, office, rental or leasing

337211 Furniture, office-type, padded, upholstered, or plain wood, manufacturing

337124 Furniture, outdoor metal household-type (e.g., beach, garden, lawn, porch), manufacturing

337122 Furniture, outdoor wood household-type (e.g., beach, garden, lawn, porch), manufacturing

337127 Furniture, public building (e.g., church, library, school, theater), manufacturing

532299 Furniture, residential, rental or leasing

337127 Furniture, restaurant-type, manufacturing

337122 Furniture, unassembled or knock-down wood household-type, manufacturing

337122 Furniture, unfinished wood household-type, manufacturing

337122 Furniture, wood household-type, not upholstered (except TV and radio housings, and sewing machine cabinets), manufacturing

448190 Furriers

332323 Furring channels, sheet metal, manufacturing

316110 Furs, dressed (e.g., bleached, curried, dyed, scraped, tanned), manufacturing

424990 Furs, dressed, merchant wholesalers

424590 Furs, raw, merchant wholesalers

335313 Fuse clips and blocks, electric, manufacturing

335931 Fuse cutouts manufacturing

335313 Fuse mountings, electric power, manufacturing

332993 Fuses ammunition (i.e., more than 30 mm., more than 1.18 inch) manufacturing

423610 Fuses, electric, merchant wholesalers

335313 Fuses, electrical, manufacturing

325191 Fustic wood extract manufacturing

337122 Futon frames manufacturing

523140 Futures commodity contracts brokerages

523140 Futures commodity contracts brokers' offices

523130 Futures commodity contracts dealing (i.e., acting as a principal in dealing commodities to investors)

523210 Futures commodity contracts exchanges

212319 Gabbro crushed and broken stone mining and/or beneficiating

212311 Gabbro mining or quarrying

237990 Gabion construction

316211 Gaiters, plastics or plastics soled fabric upper, manufacturing

316211 Gaiters, rubber or rubber soled fabric upper, manufacturing

212231 Galena mining and/or beneficiating

712110 Galleries, art (except retail)

453920 Galleries, art, retail

713990 Galleries, shooting

316211 Galoshes, plastics or plastics soled fabric upper, manufacturing

316211 Galoshes, rubber, or rubber soled fabric upper, manufacturing

238160 Galvanized iron roofing installation

333516 Galvanizing machinery manufacturing

331111 Galvanizing metals and metal formed products made in iron and steel mills

332812 Galvanizing metals and metal products for the trade

334515 Galvanometers (except geophysical) manufacturing

334519 Galvanometers, geophysical, manufacturing

325191 Gambier extract manufacturing

921130 Gambling control boards, nonoperating

713290 Gambling control boards, operating gambling activities

713210 Gambling cruises
713290 Gambling device arcades or parlors, coin-operated
713290 Gambling device concession operators (i.e., supplying and servicing in others' facilities), coin-operated
924120 Game and inland fish agencies
334611 Game cartridge software, mass reproducing
114210 Game preserves, commercial
114210 Game propagation
114210 Game retreats
519130 Game sites, Internet
423430 Game software merchant wholesalers
451120 Game stores (including electronic)
924120 Game wardens
423920 Games (except coin-operated) merchant wholesalers
339932 Games (except-coin operated), children's and adult, manufacturing
339999 Games, coin-operated, manufacturing
423990 Games, coin-operated, merchant wholesalers
334611 Games, computer software, mass reproducing
511210 Games, computer software, publishing
334517 Gamma ray irradiation equipment manufacturing
212319 Ganister crushed and broken stone mining and/or beneficiating
236220 Garage and service station, commercial, construction
444190 Garage door dealers
335999 Garage door openers manufacturing
238290 Garage door, commercial- or industrial-type, installation
238350 Garage door, residential-type, installation
332321 Garage doors, metal, manufacturing
321911 Garage doors, wood, manufacturing

812930 Garages, automobile parking
811198 Garages, do-it-yourself automotive repair
811111 Garages, general automotive repair (except gasoline service stations)
332311 Garages, prefabricated metal, manufacturing
321992 Garages, prefabricated wood, manufacturing
332439 Garbage cans, light gauge metal, manufacturing
562111 Garbage collection services
562213 Garbage disposal combustors or incinerators
562212 Garbage disposal landfills
236210 Garbage disposal plant construction
333319 Garbage disposal units, commercial-type, manufacturing
423440 Garbage disposal units, commercial-type, merchant wholesalers
335228 Garbage disposal units, household-type, manufacturing
423620 Garbage disposal units, household-type, merchant wholesalers
562212 Garbage dumps
562111 Garbage hauling, local
333994 Garbage incinerators (except precast concrete) manufacturing
327390 Garbage incinerators, precast concrete, manufacturing
562111 Garbage pick-up services
336211 Garbage truck bodies manufacturing
336120 Garbage trucks assembling on chassis of own manufacture
336211 Garbage trucks assembling on purchased chassis
111130 Garbanzo farming, dry, field and seed production
236116 Garden apartment construction general contractors
236117 Garden apartment operative builders
444220 Garden centers

813410   Garden clubs
811411   Garden equipment repair and
         maintenance services without
         retailing new garden
         equipment
327390   Garden furniture, precast
         concrete, manufacturing
327991   Garden furniture, stone,
         manufacturing
337122   Garden furniture, wood,
         manufacturing
326220   Garden hose, rubber or plastics,
         manufacturing
423820   Garden machinery and
         equipment merchant
         wholesalers
333112   Garden machinery and
         equipment, powered,
         manufacturing
561730   Garden maintenance services
541320   Garden planning services
327112   Garden pottery manufacturing
444210   Garden power equipment stores
424910   Garden supplies (e.g., fertilizers,
         pesticides) merchant
         wholesalers
811411   Garden tool sharpening and
         repair services
532490   Garden tractor rental or leasing
339999   Garden umbrellas
         manufacturing
712130   Gardens, zoological or botanical
111219   Garlic farming (except under
         cover), field, bedding plant
         and seed production
111419   Garlic farming, grown under
         cover
811490   Garment alteration and/or repair
         shops without retailing new
         garments
812320   Garment cleaning (e.g., fur,
         leather, suede) services
321999   Garment hangers, wood,
         manufacturing
316110   Garment leather manufacturing
314911   Garment storage bags
         manufacturing
315292   Garments, leather or sheep-lined
         (except apparel contractors),
         manufacturing

315211   Garments, leather or sheep-
         lined, men's and boys', cut
         and sew apparel contractors
315212   Garments, leather or sheep-
         lined, women's, girls', and
         infants', cut and sew apparel
         contractors
313320   Garments, oiling (i.e.,
         waterproofing)
212399   Garnet mining and/or
         beneficiating
333292   Garnetting machinery for
         textiles manufacturing
314999   Garnetting of textile waste and
         rags
315212   Garter belts cut and sew apparel
         contractors
315231   Garter belts cut and sewn from
         purchased fabric (except
         apparel contractors)
315212   Garters, women's, cut and sew
         apparel contractors
315231   Garters, women's, misses', and
         girls', cut and sewn from
         purchased fabric (except
         apparel contractors)
334513   Gas analyzers, industrial
         process-type, manufacturing
334516   Gas analyzers, laboratory-type,
         manufacturing
334513   Gas and liquid analysis
         instruments, industrial
         process-type, manufacturing
334512   Gas burner automatic controls
         (except valves) manufacturing
333414   Gas burners, heating,
         manufacturing
334513   Gas chromatographic
         instruments, industrial
         process-type, manufacturing
334516   Gas chromatographic
         instruments, laboratory-type,
         manufacturing
333414   Gas fireplaces manufacturing
423720   Gas fireplaces merchant
         wholesalers
238220   Gas fitting contractor
334513   Gas flow instrumentation,
         industrial process-type,
         manufacturing

333999 Gas generating machinery, general purpose-type, manufacturing

423720 Gas hot water heaters merchant wholesalers

334519 Gas leak detectors manufacturing

523999 Gas lease brokers' offices

335129 Gas lighting fixtures manufacturing

423990 Gas lighting fixtures merchant wholesalers

238220 Gas line installation, individual hookup, contractors

333298 Gas liquefying machinery manufacturing

237120 Gas main construction

339113 Gas masks manufacturing

561990 Gas meter reading services, contract

423720 Gas ranges merchant wholesalers

333319 Gas ranges, commercial-type, manufacturing

335221 Gas ranges, household-type, manufacturing

333999 Gas separating machinery manufacturing

333414 Gas space heaters manufacturing

332420 Gas storage tanks, heavy gauge metal, manufacturing

336399 Gas tanks assembled, automotive, truck, and bus, manufacturing

333611 Gas turbine generator set units manufacturing

333611 Gas turbines (except aircraft) manufacturing

336412 Gas turbines, aircraft, manufacturing

332911 Gas valves, industrial-type, manufacturing

333992 Gas welding equipment manufacturing

333992 Gas welding rods, coated or cored, manufacturing

213111 Gas well drilling on a contract basis

333132 Gas well machinery and equipment manufacturing

213112 Gas well rig building, repairing, and dismantling on a contract basis

213112 Gas, compressing natural, in the field on a contract basis

221210 Gas, manufactured, production and distribution

221210 Gas, mixed natural and manufactured, production and distribution

211112 Gas, natural liquefied petroleum, extraction

221210 Gas, natural, distribution

211111 Gas, natural, extraction

211112 Gas, natural, liquids, extraction

486210 Gas, natural, pipeline operation

211112 Gas, residue, extraction

424690 Gases, compressed and liquefied (except liquefied petroleum gas), merchant wholesalers

325120 Gases, industrial (i.e., compressed, liquefied, solid), manufacturing

211112 Gases, petroleum, liquefied, extraction

339991 Gasket, packing, and sealing devices manufacturing

339991 Gaskets manufacturing

423840 Gaskets merchant wholesalers

334514 Gasmeters, consumption registering, manufacturing

334514 Gasmeters, large capacity, domestic and industrial, manufacturing

333414 Gas-oil burners, combination, manufacturing

424710 Gasoline bulk stations and terminals

334514 Gasoline dispensing meters (except pumps) manufacturing

336412 Gasoline engine parts (except carburetors, pistons, piston rings, valves), aircraft, manufacturing

336312 Gasoline engine parts, mechanical (except carburetors, pistons, piston rings, valves), automotive and truck, manufacturing

333618 Gasoline engines (except aircraft, automotive, truck) manufacturing

336412 Gasoline engines, aircraft, manufacturing

336312 Gasoline engines, automotive and truck, manufacturing

324110 Gasoline made in petroleum refineries

423120 Gasoline marketing equipment merchant wholesalers

333913 Gasoline measuring and dispensing pumps manufacturing

424720 Gasoline merchant wholesalers (except bulk stations, terminals)

486910 Gasoline pipeline transportation

238290 Gasoline pump, service station, installation

423120 Gasoline service station equipment merchant wholesalers

447110 Gasoline stations with convenience stores

447190 Gasoline stations without convenience stores

447110 Gasoline with convenience stores

211112 Gasoline, natural, production

313312 Gassing yarn (i.e., singeing)

621111 Gastroenterologists' offices (e.g., centers, clinics)

339112 Gastroscopes (except electromedical) manufacturing

334510 Gastroscopes, electromedical, manufacturing

333999 Gate and bridge lifting machinery manufacturing

332911 Gate valves, industrial-type, manufacturing

332323 Gates, holding, sheet metal, manufacturing

332323 Gates, metal (except wire), manufacturing

237120 Gathering line, gas and oil field, construction

113210 Gathering of forest products (e.g., barks, gums, needles, seeds)

113210 Gathering, extracting, and selling tree seeds

332212 Gauge blocks, machinists' precision tools, manufacturing

334514 Gauges (e.g., oil pressure, water temperature, speedometer, tachometer), motor vehicle, manufacturing

334513 Gauges (i.e., analog, digital), industrial process-type, manufacturing

334514 Gauges for computing pressure-temperature corrections manufacturing

333314 Gauges, machinist's precision tool, optical, manufacturing

332212 Gauges, machinists' precision tools (except optical), manufacturing

424210 Gauze merchant wholesalers

339113 Gauze, surgical, made from purchased fabric

313210 Gauzes, surgical, made in broadwoven fabric mills

321999 Gavels, wood, manufacturing

333512 Gear cutting and finishing machines, metalworking, manufacturing

332212 Gear pullers, handtools, manufacturing

333513 Gear rolling machines, metalworking, manufacturing

333612 Gearmotors (i.e., power transmission equipment) manufacturing

336350 Gears (e.g., crown, pinion, spider), automotive, truck, and bus, manufacturing

333612 Gears, power transmission (except aircraft, motor vehicle), manufacturing

112390 Geese production

311615 Geese, processing, fresh, frozen, canned, or cooked

311615 Geese, slaughtering and dressing

334519 Geiger counters manufacturing

325998 Gelatin (except dessert preparations) manufacturing

335312 Generators for storage battery chargers (except internal combustion engine and aircraft) manufacturing
423610 Generators, electrical (except motor vehicle), merchant wholesalers
423120 Generators, motor vehicle electrical, new, merchant wholesalers
423140 Generators, motor vehicle electrical, used, merchant wholesalers
332995 Generators, smoke, manufacturing
334517 Generators, X-ray, manufacturing
621511 Genetic testing laboratories
541712 Genetics research and development laboratories or services (except biotechnology research and development)
541690 Geochemical consulting services
321992 Geodesic domes, prefabricated, wood, manufacturing
541370 Geodetic surveying services
541370 Geographic information system (GIS) base mapping services
541330 Geological engineering services
213112 Geological exploration (except surveying) for oil and gas on a contract basis
541712 Geological research and development laboratories or services
924120 Geological research program administration
541360 Geological surveying services
541330 Geophysical engineering services
213112 Geophysical exploration (except surveying) for oil and gas on a contract basis
334519 Geophysical instruments manufacturing
541360 Geophysical mapping services
541360 Geophysical surveying services
541370 Geospatial mapping services
541380 Geotechnical testing laboratories or services

237110 Geothermal drilling
221330 Geothermal steam production
325199 Geraniol manufacturing
331492 Germanium recovering from scrap and/or alloying purchased metals
331419 Germanium refining, primary
335931 GFCI (ground fault circuit interrupters) manufacturing
711510 Ghost writers, independent
453220 Gift shops
453220 Gift stands, permanent location
322222 Gift wrap made from purchased materials
424120 Gift wrapping paper merchant wholesalers
561910 Gift wrapping services
212399 Gilsonite mining and/or beneficiating
111219 Gingerroot farming (except under cover), field, bedding plant and seed production
111419 Gingerroot farming, grown under cover
115111 Ginning cotton
111219 Ginseng farming (except under cover), field, bedding plant and seed production
111419 Ginseng farming, grown under cover
113210 Ginseng gathering
327390 Girders and beams, prestressed concrete, manufacturing
327390 Girders, prestressed concrete, manufacturing
315192 Girdles and other foundation garments made in apparel knitting mills
315212 Girdles, women's, cut and sew apparel contractors
315231 Girdles, women's, misses', and girls', cut and sewn from purchased fabric (except apparel contractors)
813410 Girl guiding organizations
721214 Girls' camps (except day, instructional)
611620 Girls' camps, sports instruction
713990 Girls' day camps (except instructional)

315111 Girls' hosiery, sheer, full length or knee length, knitting and finishing

315119 Girls' socks manufacturing

325411 Glandular derivatives, uncompounded, manufacturing

325412 Glandular medicinal preparations manufacturing

325612 Glass and tile cleaning preparations manufacturing

327215 Glass blanks for electric light bulbs made from purchased glass

327212 Glass blanks for electric light bulbs made in glass making plants

238140 Glass block laying

334290 Glass breakage detection and signaling devices

313210 Glass broadwoven fabrics weaving

238150 Glass cladding (i.e., curtain wall), installation

238150 Glass coating and tinting (except automotive) contractors

313221 Glass fabrics, narrow woven weaving

238310 Glass fiber insulation installation

327212 Glass fiber, optical, made in glass making plants

327212 Glass fiber, textile type, made in glass making plants

238150 Glass installation (except automotive) contractors

811122 Glass installation, automotive repair

327212 Glass making and blowing by hand

333298 Glass making machinery (e.g., blowing, forming, molding) manufacturing

327213 Glass packaging containers manufacturing

238150 Glass partitions, installation

327215 Glass products (except packaging containers) made from purchased glass

327212 Glass products (except packaging containers) made in a glass making plants

212322 Glass sand quarrying and/or beneficiating

423930 Glass scrap merchant wholesalers

811122 Glass shops, automotive

444190 Glass stores

811122 Glass tinting, automotive

238140 Glass unit (i.e., glass block) masonry

811122 Glass work, automotive

327215 Glass, automotive, made from purchased glass

423120 Glass, automotive, merchant wholesalers

327211 Glass, plate, made in glass making plants

423390 Glass, plate, merchant wholesalers

333314 Glasses, field or opera, manufacturing

327124 Glasshouse refractories manufacturing

322299 Glassine wrapping paper made from purchased paper

322121 Glassine wrapping paper made in paper mills

327215 Glassware for industrial, scientific, and technical use made from purchased glass

327212 Glassware for industrial, scientific, and technical use made in glass making plants

327215 Glassware for lighting fixtures made from purchased glass

327212 Glassware for lighting fixtures made in glass making plants

442299 Glassware stores

327215 Glassware, art decorative and novelty, made from purchased glass

327212 Glassware, art, decorative, and novelty made in glass making plants

327215 Glassware, cutting and engraving, made from purchased glass

423220   Glassware, household-type, merchant wholesalers
423450   Glassware, medical, merchant wholesalers
325188   Glauber's salt manufacturing
212391   Glauber's salt mining and/or beneficiating
325510   Glaziers' putty manufacturing
238150   Glazing contractors
315292   Glazing furs
332812   Glazing metals and metal products for the trade
334511   Glide slope instrumentation manufacturing
487990   Glider excursions
336411   Gliders (i.e., aircraft) manufacturing
334220   Global positioning system (GPS) equipment manufacturing
511130   Globe cover publishers
511130   Globe cover publishers and printing combined
323112   Globe covers and maps flexographic printing without publishing
323111   Globe covers and maps gravure printing without publishing
323110   Globe covers and maps lithographic (offset) printing without publishing
323119   Globe covers and maps printing (except flexographic, digital, gravure, lithographic, quick, screen) without publishing
323113   Globe covers and maps screen printing without publishing
332911   Globe valves, industrial-type, manufacturing
339999   Globes, geographical, manufacturing
316110   Glove leather manufacturing
315992   Glove linings (except fur) manufacturing
315292   Glove linings, fur (except apparel contractors), manufacturing
315211   Glove linings, fur, men's and boys', cut and sew apparel contractors

315212   Glove linings, fur, women's, girls', and infants', cut and sew apparel contractors
315992   Gloves and mittens (except athletic), leather, fabric, fur, or combinations, cut and sewn from purchased fabric (except apparel contractors)
315211   Gloves and mittens (except athletic), leather, fabric, fur, or combinations, men's and boys', cut and sew apparel contractors
315212   Gloves and mittens (except athletic), leather, fabric, fur, or combinations, women's, girls', and infants', cut and sew apparel contractors
315992   Gloves and mittens, woven or knit, cut and sewn from purchased fabric (except apparel contractors), manufacturing
315212   Gloves and mittens, woven or knit, women's, girls', and infants', cut and sew apparel contractors
315191   Gloves, knit, made in apparel knitting mills
315211   Gloves, leather (except athletic), men's and boys', cut and sew apparel contractors
315212   Gloves, leather (except athletic), women's, girls', and infants', cut and sew apparel contractors
315992   Gloves, leather (except athletic, cut and sewn apparel contractors), manufacturing
424320   Gloves, men's and boys', merchant wholesalers
326199   Gloves, plastics, manufacturing
339113   Gloves, rubber (e.g., electrician's, examination, household-type, surgeon's), manufacturing
339920   Gloves, sport and athletic (e.g., baseball, boxing, racketball, handball), manufacturing

424330 Gloves, women's, children's, and infants', merchant wholesalers
335110 Glow lamp bulbs manufacturing
339114 Glue, dental, manufacturing
325520 Glues (except dental) manufacturing
424690 Glues merchant wholesalers
311221 Gluten feed, flour, and meal, made by wet milling corn
311221 Gluten manufacturing
325611 Glycerin (i.e., glycerol), natural, manufacturing
325199 Glycerin (i.e., glycerol), synthetic, manufacturing
325411 Glycosides, uncompounded, manufacturing
212313 Gneiss crushed and broken stone mining and/or beneficiating
212311 Gneiss mining or quarrying
522294 GNMA (Government National Mortgage Association)
112420 Goat farming (e.g., meat, milk, mohair production)
424520 Goats merchant wholesalers
713990 Gocart raceways (i.e., amusement rides)
713990 Gocart tracks (i.e., amusement rides)
336999 Gocarts (except children's) manufacturing
423910 Gocarts merchant wholesalers
339932 Go-carts, children's, manufacturing
339115 Goggles (e.g., industrial, safety, sun, underwater) manufacturing
331491 Gold and gold alloy bar, sheet, strip, and tubing made from purchased metals or scrap
332813 Gold and silver plating metals and metal products for the trade
332999 Gold beating (i.e., foil, leaf)
331419 Gold bullion or dore bar produced at primary metal refineries
332999 Gold foil and leaf not made in rolling mills

331491 Gold foil made by rolling purchased metals or scrap
212221 Gold lode mining and/or beneficiating
212221 Gold ore mine site development for own account
212221 Gold ore mining and/or beneficiating plants
212221 Gold ores, concentrates, bullion, and/or precipitates mining and/or beneficiating
212221 Gold placer mining and/or beneficiating
325910 Gold printing inks manufacturing
331492 Gold recovering from scrap and/or alloying purchased metals
331419 Gold refining, primary
331491 Gold rolling and drawing purchased metals or scrap
323121 Gold stamping books for the trade
813410 Golden age clubs
112511 Goldfish production, farm raising
713910 Golf and country clubs
441229 Golf cart dealers, powered
532292 Golf cart rental
423910 Golf carts (except motorized passenger) merchant wholesalers
336999 Golf carts and similar motorized passenger carriers manufacturing
423860 Golf carts, motorized passenger, merchant wholesalers
336999 Golf carts, powered, manufacturing
237990 Golf course construction
541320 Golf course design services
713910 Golf courses (except miniature, pitch-n-putt)
713990 Golf courses, miniature
713990 Golf courses, pitch-n-putt
713990 Golf driving ranges
423910 Golf equipment and supplies merchant wholesalers
611620 Golf instruction, camps, or schools

713990   Golf practice ranges

451110   Golf pro shops

316219   Golf shoes, men's cleated, manufacturing

316219   Golf shoes, women's cleated, manufacturing

711219   Golfers, independent professional (i.e., participating in sports events)

339920   Golfing equipment (e.g., bags, balls, caddy carts, clubs, tees) manufacturing

335999   Gongs, electric, manufacturing

111334   Gooseberry farming

332212   Gouges, woodworking, manufacturing

445299   Gourmet food stores

561210   Government base facilities operation support services

522294   Government National Mortgage Association (GNMA)

522294   Government-sponsored enterprises providing secondary market financing

336312   Governors for automotive gasoline engines manufacturing

921110   Governors' offices

333618   Governors, diesel engine, manufacturing

333618   Governors, gasoline engine (except automotive), manufacturing

333611   Governors, steam, manufacturing

812331   Gown (e.g., doctors, nurses, hospital, beauticians) supply services

532220   Gown rental

315299   Gowns (e.g., academic, choir, clerical) cut and sewn from purchased fabric (except apparel contractors)

315211   Gowns (e.g., academic, choir, clerical), men's and boys', cut and sew apparel contractors

315212   Gowns (e.g., academic, choir, clerical), women's, and girls', cut and sew apparel contractors

315212   Gowns, formal, women's and girls', cut and sew apparel contractors

315233   Gowns, formal, women's, misses', and girls', cut and sewn from purchased fabric (except apparel contractors)

315299   Gowns, hospital, surgical and patient, cut and sewn from purchased fabric (except apparel contractors)

315211   Gowns, hospital, surgical and patient, men's and boys', cut and sew apparel contractors

315212   Gowns, hospital, surgical and patient, women's, girls', and infants', cut and sew apparel contractors

315212   Gowns, wedding, women's, cut and sew apparel contractors

315233   Gowns, wedding, women's, misses', and girls', cut and sewn from purchased fabric (except apparel contractors)

334220   GPS (global positioning system) equipment manufacturing

333120   Grader attachments manufacturing

333120   Graders, road, manufacturing

238910   Grading construction sites

333294   Grading, cleaning, and sorting machinery (i.e., food manufacturing-type) manufacturing

333111   Grading, cleaning, and sorting machinery, farm-type, manufacturing

237310   Grading, highway, road, street and airport runway

334512   Gradual switches, pneumatic, manufacturing

532220   Graduation cap and gown rental

315299   Graduation caps and gowns cut and sewn from purchased fabric (except apparel contractors)

315211   Graduation caps and gowns, men's and boys', cut and sew apparel contractors

315212 Graduation caps and gowns, women's and girls', cut and sew apparel contractors
311211 Graham flour manufacturing
311821 Graham wafers manufacturing
212399 Grahamite mining and/or beneficiating
312140 Grain alcohol, beverage, manufacturing
325193 Grain alcohol, nonpotable, manufacturing
115114 Grain cleaning
333111 Grain drills manufacturing
115114 Grain drying
236220 Grain elevator construction
424510 Grain elevators merchant wholesalers grain
493130 Grain elevators, storage only
115114 Grain fumigation
115114 Grain grinding (except custom grinding for animal feed)
311119 Grain grinding, custom, for animal feed
484220 Grain hauling, local
484230 Grain hauling, long-distance
488210 Grain leveling and trimming in railroad cars
321999 Grain measures, wood, turned and shaped, manufacturing
424510 Grain merchant wholesalers
333294 Grain milling machinery manufacturing
311211 Grain mills (except animal feed, breakfast cereal, rice)
311119 Grain mills, animal feed
311230 Grain mills, breakfast cereal
311212 Grain mills, rice
333111 Grain stackers manufacturing
311230 Grain, breakfast cereal, manufacturing
312120 Grain, brewers' spent, manufacturing
115113 Grain, machine harvesting
327910 Grains, abrasive, natural and artificial, manufacturing
813410 Granges
212313 Granite beneficiating plants (e.g., grinding or pulverizing)

212313 Granite crushed and broken stone mining and/or beneficiating
212311 Granite mining or quarrying
238140 Granite, exterior, contractors
238340 Granite, interior, installation
311320 Granola bars and clusters, chocolate, made from cacao beans
311330 Granola bars and clusters, chocolate, made from purchased chocolate
311340 Granola bars and clusters, nonchocolate, manufacturing
311230 Granola, cereal (except bars and clusters), manufacturing
813211 Grantmaking foundations
311313 Granulated beet sugar manufacturing
311312 Granulated cane sugar made from purchased raw cane sugar
311311 Granulated cane sugar made from sugar cane
333220 Granulator and pelletizer machinery for plastics manufacturing
212319 Granules, slate, mining and/or beneficiating
312130 Grape farming and making wine
111332 Grape farming without making wine
111320 Grapefruit groves
325998 Grapefruit oil manufacturing
311423 Grapes, artificially drying
541430 Graphic art and related design services
541430 Graphic artists, independent
325992 Graphic arts plates, sensitized, manufacturing
611519 Graphic arts schools
541430 Graphic design services
334515 Graphic recording meters, electric, manufacturing
335991 Graphite electrodes and contacts, electric, manufacturing
212399 Graphite mining and/or beneficiating

335991 Graphite specialties for aerospace use (except gaskets) manufacturing

335991 Graphite specialties for electrical use manufacturing

335991 Graphite specialties for mechanical use (except gaskets) manufacturing

327992 Graphite, natural (e.g., ground, pulverized, refined, blended), manufacturing

111940 Grass hay farming

333111 Grass mowing equipment (except lawn and garden) manufacturing

332212 Grass mowing equipment, nonpowered lawn and garden, manufacturing

333112 Grass mowing equipment, powered lawn and garden, manufacturing

111998 Grass seed farming

332323 Gratings (i.e., open steel flooring) manufacturing

333314 Gratings, diffraction, manufacturing

238910 Grave excavation contractors

484220 Gravel hauling, local

484230 Gravel hauling, long-distance

212321 Gravel quarrying and/or beneficiating

423320 Gravel, construction, merchant wholesalers

541360 Gravity geophysical surveying services

325910 Gravure inks manufacturing

323122 Gravure plate and cylinder preparation services

323111 Gravure printing (except books, manifold business forms, printing grey goods)

333293 Gravure printing presses manufacturing

311422 Gravy canning

311942 Gravy mixes, dry, manufacturing

331511 Gray iron foundries

531190 Grazing land rental or leasing

311613 Grease rendering

339991 Grease seals manufacturing

562998 Grease trap cleaning

311225 Grease, inedible, animal and vegetable, refining and blending purchased oils

424990 Greases, inedible animal and vegetable, merchant wholesalers

324191 Greases, petroleum lubricating, made from refined petroleum

325998 Greases, synthetic lubricating, manufacturing

483113 Great Lakes freight transportation (including St. Lawrence Seaway)

483114 Great Lakes passenger transportation (including St. Lawrence Seaway)

111219 Green bean farming, field and seed production

111219 Green cowpea farming, field and seed production

111219 Green lima bean farming, field and seed production

111219 Green pea farming, field and seed production

332311 Greenhouses, prefabricated metal, manufacturing

212399 Greensand mining and/or beneficiating

212311 Greenstone mining or quarrying

511191 Greeting card publishers (except exclusive Internet publishing)

511191 Greeting card publishers and printing combined

519130 Greeting card publishers, exclusively on Internet

453220 Greeting card shops

323112 Greeting cards (e.g., birthday, holiday, sympathy) flexographic printing without publishing

323111 Greeting cards (e.g., birthday, holiday, sympathy) gravure printing without publishing

323110 Greeting cards (e.g., birthday, holiday, sympathy) lithographic (offset) printing without publishing

323119 Greeting cards (e.g., birthday, holiday, sympathy) printing (except flexographic, gravure, lithographic, quick, screen) without publishing

323113 Greeting cards (e.g., birthday, holiday, sympathy) screen printing without publishing

323119 Greeting cards engraving printing without publishing

323119 Greeting cards letterpress printing without publishing

424120 Greeting cards merchant wholesalers

332994 Grenade launchers manufacturing

332993 Grenades, hand or projectile, manufacturing

711212 Greyhound dog racetracks

335211 Griddles and grills, household-type portable electric, manufacturing

332618 Grilles and grillwork made from purchased wire

332323 Grills and grillwork, sheet metal, manufacturing

332323 Grillwork, ornamental metal, manufacturing

333991 Grinders, handheld power-driven, manufacturing

325411 Grinding and milling botanicals (i.e., for medicinal use)

327910 Grinding balls, ceramic, manufacturing

333512 Grinding machines, metalworking, manufacturing

332813 Grinding metal castings for the trade

324191 Grinding oils, petroleum, made from refined petroleum

212399 Grinding pebbles mining and/or beneficiating

212322 Grinding sand quarrying and/or beneficiating

311942 Grinding spices

327910 Grinding wheels manufacturing

212399 Grindstones mining and/or beneficiating

326299 Grips and handles, rubber, manufacturing

311211 Grits and flakes, corn brewer's, manufacturing

212319 Grits crushed and broken stone mining and/or beneficiating

424410 Groceries, general-line, merchant wholesalers

322224 Grocers' bags and sacks made from purchased uncoated paper

326111 Grocery bags, plastics film, single wall or multiwall, manufacturing

333924 Grocery carts made from purchased wire

492210 Grocery delivery services (i.e., independent service from grocery store)

445110 Grocery stores

423840 Grommets merchant wholesalers

326299 Grommets, rubber, manufacturing

812910 Grooming services, animal

335931 Ground clamps (i.e., electric wiring devices) manufacturing

335931 Ground fault circuit interrupters (GFCI) manufacturing

238910 Ground thawing for construction site digging

322122 Groundwood paper products (e.g., publication and printing paper, tablet stock, wallpaper base) made in newsprint mills

424110 Groundwood paper, bulk, merchant wholesalers

322121 Groundwood paper, coated, laminated, or treated in paper mills

322222 Groundwood paper, coated, made from purchased paper

322121 Groundwood paper, coated, made in paper mills

322122 Groundwood paper, newsprint, made in paper mills

322110 Groundwood pulp manufacturing

624410 Group day care centers, child or infant

623990 Group foster homes for children

623110 Group homes for the disabled with nursing care

623990	Group homes for the disabled without nursing care
623990	Group homes for the hearing impaired
623990	Group homes for the visually impaired
623210	Group homes, mental retardation
621491	Group hospitalization plans providing health care services
524114	Group hospitalization plans without providing health care services
114111	Grouper fishing
238110	Grouting (i.e., reinforcing with concrete)
335122	Grow light fixtures (except residential) manufacturing
335121	Grow light fixtures, residential, electric, manufacturing
813910	Growers' associations
212393	Guano mining and/or beneficiating
111998	Guar farming
524127	Guaranteeing titles
561612	Guard dog services
812910	Guard dog training services
561612	Guard services
237310	Guardrail construction
332322	Guardrails, highway, sheet metal (except stampings), manufacturing
332323	Guards, bannisters, and railings, sheet metal, manufacturing
332618	Guards, wire, made from purchased wire
111339	Guavas farming
721199	Guest houses
721214	Guest ranches with accommodation facilities
812910	Guide dog training services
713990	Guide services (i.e., fishing, hunting, tourist)
713990	Guide services, fishing
713990	Guide services, hunting
713990	Guide services, tourist
511130	Guide, street map, publishers (except exclusive Internet publishing)
511130	Guide, street map, publishers and printing combined
519130	Guide, street map, publishers, exclusively on Internet
336415	Guided missile and space vehicle engine manufacturing
541712	Guided missile and space vehicle engine research and development
336414	Guided missile and space vehicle manufacturing
336419	Guided missile and space vehicle parts (except engines) manufacturing
541712	Guided missile and space vehicle parts (except engines) research and development
423860	Guided missiles and space vehicles merchant wholesalers
336414	Guided missiles, complete, assembling
323112	Guides, street map, flexographic printing without publishing
323111	Guides, street map, gravure printing without publishing
323110	Guides, street map, lithographic (offset) printing without publishing
323119	Guides, street map, printing (except flexographic, digital, gravure, lithographic, quick, screen) without publishing
323113	Guides, street map, screen printing without publishing
339992	Guitars and parts, electric and nonelectric, manufacturing
113210	Gum (i.e., forest product) gathering
325191	Gum and wood chemicals manufacturing
424690	Gum and wood chemicals merchant wholesalers
311340	Gum, chewing, manufacturing
424450	Gum, chewing, merchant wholesalers
322222	Gummed paper products (e.g., labels, sheets, tapes) made from purchased paper

424130 Gummed tapes (except cellophane) merchant wholesalers
424120 Gummed tapes, cellophane, merchant wholesalers
332994 Gun barrels (i.e., 30 mm. or less, 1.18 inch or less) manufacturing
332995 Gun barrels (i.e., more than 30 mm., more than 1.18 inch) manufacturing
713990 Gun clubs, recreational
813319 Gun control organizations
332111 Gun forgings made from purchased iron or steel, unfinished
331111 Gun forgings made in iron and steel mills
332994 Gun magazines (i.e., 30 mm. or less, 1.18 inch or less) manufacturing
332995 Gun magazines (i.e., more than 30 mm., more than 1.18 inch) manufacturing
811490 Gun repair and maintenance shops without retailing new guns
451110 Gun shops
333314 Gun sighting and fire control equipment and instruments, optical, manufacturing
333314 Gun sights, optical, manufacturing
332612 Gun springs, light gauge, made from purchased wire or strip, manufacturing
321912 Gun stock blanks manufacturing
332510 Gun trigger locks, metal, manufacturing
332995 Gun turrets (i.e., more than 30 mm., more than 1.18 inch) manufacturing
238110 Gunite contractors
334413 Gunn effect devices manufacturing
238110 Gunning shotcrete
325920 Gunpowder manufacturing
423990 Guns (except sporting) merchant wholesalers

332994 Guns (i.e., 30 mm. or less, 1.18 inch or less) manufacturing
332995 Guns (i.e., more than 30 mm., more than 1.18 inch) manufacturing
332994 Guns, BB and pellet, manufacturing
332212 Guns, caulking, nonpowered, manufacturing
423910 Guns, sporting equipment, merchant wholesalers
811490 Gunsmith shops without retailing new guns
238170 Gutter and downspout contractors
561790 Gutter cleaning services
423330 Gutters and down spouts (except wood) merchant wholesalers
332114 Gutters and down spouts sheet metal, custom roll formed, manufacturing
326199 Gutters and down spouts, plastics, manufacturing
238170 Gutters, seamless roof, formed and installed on site
332322 Gutters, sheet metal (except custom roll formed), manufacturing
339920 Gymnasium and playground equipment, manufacturing
713940 Gymnasiums
611620 Gymnastics instruction, camps, or schools
339113 Gynecological supplies and appliances manufacturing
621111 Gynecologists' offices (e.g., centers, clinics)
212399 Gypsite mining and/or beneficiating
238310 Gypsum board installation
327420 Gypsum building products manufacturing
423390 Gypsum building products merchant wholesalers
212399 Gypsum mining and/or beneficiating
327420 Gypsum products (e.g., block, board, plaster, lath, rock, tile) manufacturing

334511	Gyrocompasses manufacturing
334511	Gyrogimbals manufacturing
334511	Gyroscopes manufacturing
624310	Habilitation job counseling and training, vocational
114111	Haddock fishing
212299	Hafnium mining and/or beneficiating
424310	Hair accessories merchant wholesalers
326299	Hair care products (e.g., combs, curlers), rubber, manufacturing
333111	Hair clippers for animal use, electric, manufacturing
332212	Hair clippers for animal use, nonelectric, manufacturing
335211	Hair clippers for human use, electric, manufacturing
332211	Hair clippers for human use, nonelectric, manufacturing
325620	Hair coloring preparations manufacturing
335211	Hair curlers, household-type electric, manufacturing
332999	Hair curlers, metal, manufacturing
335211	Hair driers, electric (except equipment designed for beauty parlor use), manufacturing
423620	Hair dryers merchant wholesalers
333319	Hair dryers, beauty parlor-type, manufacturing
339999	Hair nets made from purchased netting
325620	Hair preparations (e.g., conditioners, dyes, rinses, shampoos) manufacturing
424210	Hair preparations (except professional) merchant wholesalers
423850	Hair preparations, professional, merchant wholesalers
812199	Hair removal (i.e., dipilatory, electrolysis) services
812199	Hair replacement services (except by offices of physicians)
325620	Hair sprays manufacturing
812112	Hair stylist salons or shops, unisex or women's
812111	Hair stylist services, men's
812112	Hair stylist services, unisex or women's
812111	Hair stylist shops, men's
812199	Hair weaving services
339994	Hairbrushes manufacturing
424990	Hairbrushes merchant wholesalers
812112	Hairdresser services
812112	Hairdressing salons or shops, unisex or women's
339999	Hairpieces (e.g., toupees, wigs, wiglets) manufacturing
424990	Hairpieces (e.g., toupees, wigs, wiglets) merchant wholesalers
339993	Hairpins (except rubber) manufacturing
326299	Hairpins, rubber, manufacturing
332612	Hairsprings (except clock, watch), light gauge, made from purchased wire or strip, manufacturing
114111	Hake fishing
623990	Halfway group homes for delinquents and ex-offenders
623220	Halfway houses for patients with mental health illnesses
623220	Halfway houses, substance abuse (e.g., alcoholism, drug addiction)
114111	Halibut fishing
531120	Hall and banquet room, nonresidential, rental or leasing
334413	Hall effect devices manufacturing
531120	Hall, nonresidential, rental or leasing
712110	Halls of fame
335110	Halogen light bulbs manufacturing
325192	Halogenated aromatic hydrocarbon derivatives manufacturing
325199	Halogenated hydrocarbon derivatives (except aromatic) manufacturing
311340	Halvah manufacturing

332111 Hammer forgings made from purchased iron or steel, unfinished
332112 Hammer forgings made from purchased nonferrous metals, unfinished
333120 Hammer mill machinery (i.e., rock and ore crushing machines), portable, manufacturing
333131 Hammer mill machinery (i.e., rock and ore crushing machines), stationary, manufacturing
332212 Hammers, handtools, manufacturing
339992 Hammers, piano, manufacturing
321999 Hammers, wood, meat, manufacturing
314999 Hammocks, fabric, manufacturing
337124 Hammocks, metal framed, manufacturing
337122 Hammocks, wood framed, manufacturing
326199 Hampers, laundry, plastics, manufacturing
337125 Hampers, laundry, reed, wicker, rattan, manufacturing
332322 Hampers, laundry, sheet metal (except stampings), manufacturing
311611 Hams (except poultry) produced in slaughtering plants
311612 Hams, canned, made from purchased carcasses
311615 Hams, poultry, manufacturing
311612 Hams, preserved (except poultry), made from purchased carcasses
327215 Hand blowing purchased glass
334111 Hand held computers (e.g., PDAs) manufacturing
313249 Hand knitting lace or warp fabric products
812320 Hand laundries
325620 Hand lotions manufacturing
339943 Hand operated stamps (e.g., canceling, postmark, shoe, textile marking) manufacturing

325611 Hand soaps (e.g., hard, liquid, soft) manufacturing
334518 Hand stamps (e.g., date, time), timing mechanism operated, manufacturing
333924 Hand trucks manufacturing
313221 Hand weaving fabric, 12 inches or less (30cm)
313210 Hand weaving fabrics, more than 12 inches (30 cm) in width
316110 Handbag leather manufacturing
448150 Handbag stores
316993 Handbags (except metal), men's, manufacturing
424330 Handbags merchant wholesalers
339911 Handbags, precious metal, manufacturing
316992 Handbags, women's, all materials (except precious metal), manufacturing
713940 Handball club facilities
541870 Handbill direct distribution services
332999 Handcuffs manufacturing
332212 Handheld edge tools (except saws, scissors-type), nonelectric, manufacturing
485991 Handicapped passenger transportation services
611110 Handicapped, schools for, elementary or secondary
611610 Handicrafts instruction
315999 Handkerchiefs (except paper) cut and sewn from purchased fabric
315211 Handkerchiefs (except paper), men's and boys', cut and sew apparel contractors
315212 Handkerchiefs (except paper), women's, girls', and infants', cut and sew apparel contractors
322291 Handkerchiefs, paper, made from purchased paper
321912 Handle blanks, wood, manufacturing
321912 Handle stock, sawed or planed, manufacturing

321999   Handles (e.g., broom, mop, handtool), wood, manufacturing
424990   Handles (e.g., broom, mop, paint) merchant wholesalers
326199   Handles (e.g., brush, tool, umbrella), plastics, manufacturing
316999   Handles (e.g., luggage, whip), leather, manufacturing
332999   Handles (e.g., parasol, umbrella), metal, manufacturing
327111   Handles, faucet, vitreous china and earthenware, manufacturing
541420   Handtool industrial design services
332212   Handtool metal blades (e.g., putty knives, scrapers, screw drivers) manufacturing
423710   Handtools (except motor vehicle mechanics', machinists' precision) merchant wholesalers
332212   Handtools, machinists' precision, manufacturing
423830   Handtools, machinists' precision, merchant wholesalers
332212   Handtools, motor vehicle mechanics', manufacturing
423120   Handtools, motor vehicle mechanics', merchant wholesalers
333991   Handtools, power-driven, manufacturing
444130   Handtools, power-driven, repair and maintenance services retailing new power-driven handtools
811411   Handtools, power-driven, repair and maintenance services without retailing new power-driven handtools
541990   Handwriting analysis services
541990   Handwriting expert services
236220   Handyman construction service, commercial and institutional building

236118   Handyman construction service, residential building
336411   Hang gliders manufacturing
236220   Hangar construction
332321   Hangar doors, metal, manufacturing
488119   Hangar rental, aircraft
321999   Hangers, wooden, garment, manufacturing
111422   Hanging basket plant growing
237990   Harbor construction
488310   Harbor maintenance services (except dredging)
488310   Harbor operation
487210   Harbor sightseeing tours
488330   Harbor tugboat services
213112   Hard banding oil and gas field service on a contract basis
311340   Hard candies manufacturing
212113   Hard coal (i.e., anthracite) surface mining
212113   Hard coal (i.e., anthracite) underground mining
334112   Hard disk drives manufacturing
334613   Hard drive media manufacturing
313210   Hard fiber fabrics, broadwoven, weaving
313111   Hard fiber spun yarns made from purchased fiber
313113   Hard fiber thread manufacturing
313221   Hard fiber, narrow woven, weaving
339113   Hard hats manufacturing
321219   Hardboard manufacturing
332811   Hardening (i.e., heat treating) metals and metal products for the trade
334519   Hardness testing equipment manufacturing
423710   Hardware (except motor vehicle) merchant wholesalers
332618   Hardware cloth, woven wire, made from purchased wire
444130   Hardware stores
423120   Hardware, motor vehicle, merchant wholesalers
326199   Hardware, plastics, manufacturing
335932   Hardware, transmission pole and line, manufacturing

423610 Hardware, transmission pole and line, merchant wholesalers
321912 Hardwood dimension lumber and stock, resawing purchased lumber
325191 Hardwood distillates manufacturing
444190 Hardwood flooring dealers
238330 Hardwood flooring, installation only
321211 Hardwood plywood composites manufacturing
321211 Hardwood veneer or plywood manufacturing
339992 Harmonicas manufacturing
334419 Harness assemblies for electronic use manufacturing
711219 Harness drivers
424910 Harness equipment merchant wholesalers
316110 Harness leather manufacturing
332999 Harness parts, metal, manufacturing
711212 Harness racetracks
316999 Harnesses and harness parts, leather, manufacturing
316999 Harnesses, dog, manufacturing
339992 Harps and parts manufacturing
339992 Harpsichords manufacturing
333111 Harrows (e.g., disc, spring, tine) manufacturing
315991 Harvest hats, straw, manufacturing
113210 Harvesting berries or nuts from native and non-cultivated plants
333111 Harvesting machinery and equipment, agriculture, manufacturing
423820 Harvesting machinery and equipment, agriculture, merchant wholesalers
335211 Hassock fans, electric, manufacturing
448150 Hat and cap stores
339999 Hat blocks manufacturing
315991 Hat bodies (e.g., fur-felt, straw, wool-felt) cut and sewn from purchased fabric (except apparel contractors)

315211 Hat bodies (e.g., fur-felt, straw, wool-felt), men's and boys', cut and sew apparel contractors
315212 Hat bodies (e.g., fur-felt, straw, wool-felt), women's, girls', and infants', cut and sew apparel contractors
812320 Hat cleaning services
315999 Hat findings cut and sewn from purchased fabric (except apparel contractors)
315211 Hat findings, men's and boys', cut and sew apparel contractors
315212 Hat findings, women's, girls', and infants', cut and sew apparel contractors
315999 Hat linings and trimmings cut and sewn from purchased fabric (except apparel contractors)
315211 Hat linings and trimmings, men's and boys', cut and sew apparel contractors
315212 Hat linings and trimmings, women's, girls', and infants', cut and sew apparel contractors
112511 Hatcheries, finfish
112340 Hatcheries, poultry
112512 Hatcheries, shellfish
236220 Hatchery construction
332212 Hatchets manufacturing
315991 Hats (except fur, knitting mill products, leather) cut and sewn from purchased fabric (except apparel contractors)
424320 Hats and caps, men's and boys', merchant wholesalers
424330 Hats and caps, women's, girls' and infants', merchant wholesalers
322299 Hats made from purchased paper
315191 Hats made in apparel knitting mills
315991 Hats, cloth, cut and sewn from purchased fabric (except apparel contractors)

315211	Hats, cloth, men's and boys', cut and sew apparel contractors
315212	Hats, cloth, women's, girls', and infants', cut and sew apparel contractors
315292	Hats, fur (except apparel contractors), manufacturing
315211	Hats, fur, men's and boys', cut and sew apparel contractors
315212	Hats, fur, women's, girls', and infants', cut and sew apparel contractors
315991	Hats, fur-felt, straw, and wool-felt, cut and sewn from purchased fabric (except apparel contractors)
315211	Hats, fur-felt, straw, and wool-felt, men's and boys', cut and sew apparel contractors
315212	Hats, fur-felt, straw, and wool-felt, women's, girls', and infants', cut and sew apparel contractors
315292	Hats, leather (except apparel contractors), manufacturing
315211	Hats, leather, men's and boys', cut and sew apparel contractors
315212	Hats, leather, women's, girls', and infants', cut and sew apparel contractors
315211	Hats, men's and boys', cut and sew apparel contractors
315991	Hats, trimmed, cut and sewn from purchased fabric (except apparel contractors)
315211	Hats, trimmed, men's and boys', cut and sew apparel contractors
315212	Hats, trimmed, women's, girls', and infants', cut and sew apparel contractors
315212	Hats, women's, girls', and infants', cut and sew apparel contractors
333111	Hay balers and presses manufacturing
111940	Hay farming (e.g., alfalfa hay, clover hay, grass hay)
424910	Hay merchant wholesalers
115113	Hay mowing, raking, baling, and chopping
111998	Hay seed farming
311119	Hay, cubed, manufacturing
333111	Haying machines manufacturing
423820	Haying machines merchant wholesalers
562112	Hazardous waste collection services
562211	Hazardous waste disposal facilities
562211	Hazardous waste disposal facilities combined with collection and/or local hauling of hazardous waste
562211	Hazardous waste material disposal facilities
562211	Hazardous waste material treatment facilities
562211	Hazardous waste treatment facilities
562211	Hazardous waste treatment facilities combined with collection and/or local hauling of hazardous waste
111335	Hazelnut farming
334613	Head cleaners for magnetic tape equipment, manufacturing
551114	Head offices
311212	Head rice manufacturing
624410	Head start programs, separate from schools
315999	Headbands, women's and girls', cut and sewn from purchased fabric (except apparel contractors)
315212	Headbands, women's, girls', and infants', cut and sew apparel contractors
337122	Headboards, wood, manufacturing
321920	Heading, barrel (i.e., cooperage stock), wood, manufacturing
334419	Heads (e.g., recording, read/write) manufacturing
334511	Heads-up display (HUD) systems, aeronautical, manufacturing

236220	Health and athletic club construction
525120	Health and welfare funds
713940	Health club facilities, physical fitness
424490	Health foods (except fresh fruits, vegetables) merchant wholesalers
424480	Health foods, fresh fruits and vegetables, merchant wholesalers
524114	Health insurance carriers, direct
335110	Health lamp bulbs, infrared and ultraviolet radiation, manufacturing
621491	Health maintenance organization (HMO) medical centers and clinics
923120	Health planning and development agencies, government
813920	Health professionals' associations
926150	Health professions licensure agencies
923120	Health program administration
541712	Health research and development laboratories or services (except biotechnology research and development)
813212	Health research fundraising organizations
621999	Health screening services (except by offices of health practitioners)
621111	Health screening services in physicians' offices
721110	Health spas (i.e., physical fitness facilities) with accommodations
713940	Health spas without accommodations, physical fitness
923120	Health statistics centers, government
713940	Health studios, physical fitness
446199	Hearing aid stores
423450	Hearing aids merchant wholesalers

334510	Hearing aids, electronic, manufacturing
621999	Hearing testing services (except by offices of audiologists)
621340	Hearing testing services by offices of audiologists
336211	Hearse bodies manufacturing
532111	Hearse rental
485320	Hearse rental with driver
336111	Hearses assembling on chassis of own manufacture
336211	Hearses assembling on purchased chassis
334510	Heart-lung machine, manufacturing
332410	Heat exchangers manufacturing
238220	Heat pump installation
333415	Heat pumps manufacturing
423730	Heat pumps merchant wholesalers
325992	Heat sensitized (i.e., thermal) paper made from purchased paper
335991	Heat shields, carbon or graphite, manufacturing
332811	Heat treating metals and metal products for the trade
333994	Heat treating ovens, industrial process-type, manufacturing
221330	Heat, steam, distribution
221330	Heated air distribution
335211	Heaters, portable electric space, manufacturing
423620	Heaters, portable electric, merchant wholesalers
333414	Heaters, space (except portable electric), manufacturing
333414	Heaters, swimming pool, manufacturing
335211	Heaters, tape, manufacturing
333415	Heating and air conditioning combination units manufacturing
238220	Heating and cooling duct work installation
334512	Heating and cooling system controls, residential and commercial, manufacturing

238220 Heating and ventilation system component (e.g., air registers, diffusers, filters, grilles, sound attenuators) installation

238220 Heating boiler installation

423720 Heating boilers, steam and hot water, merchant wholesalers

238220 Heating contractors

541330 Heating engineering consulting services

238220 Heating equipment installation

333414 Heating equipment, hot water (except hot water heaters), manufacturing

423720 Heating equipment, hot water, merchant wholesalers

423730 Heating equipment, warm air (i.e. forced air), merchant wholesalers

333415 Heating equipment, warm air (i.e., forced air), manufacturing

454311 Heating oil dealers, direct selling

324110 Heating oils made in petroleum refineries

335211 Heating pads, electric, manufacturing

334512 Heating regulators manufacturing

221330 Heating steam (suppliers of heat) providers

335211 Heating units for electric appliances manufacturing

333414 Heating units, baseboard, manufacturing

238220 Heating, ventilation and air-conditioning (HVAC) contractors

532412 Heavy construction equipment rental without operator

611519 Heavy equipment operation schools

611519 Heavy equipment repair training

811310 Heavy machinery and equipment repair and maintenance services

336120 Heavy trucks assembling on chassis of own manufacture

336211 Heavy trucks assembling on purchased chassis

325188 Heavy water (i.e., deuterium oxide) manufacturing

332212 Hedge shears and trimmers, nonelectric, manufacturing

333112 Hedge trimmers, powered, manufacturing

316999 Heel caps, leather or metal, manufacturing

316999 Heel lifts, leather, manufacturing

321999 Heels, boot and shoe, finished wood, manufacturing

316999 Heels, boot and shoe, leather, manufacturing

332611 Helical springs, hot wound heavy gauge metal, manufacturing

332612 Helical springs, light gauge, made from purchased wire or strip, manufacturing

481212 Helicopter carriers, freight, nonscheduled

481112 Helicopter freight carriers, scheduled

481211 Helicopter passenger carriers (except scenic, sightseeing), nonscheduled

481111 Helicopter passenger carriers, scheduled

487990 Helicopter ride, scenic and sightseeing, operation

336411 Helicopters manufacturing

325120 Helium manufacturing

325120 Helium recovery from natural gas

339113 Helmets (except athletic), safety (e.g., motorized vehicle crash helmets, space helmets), manufacturing

339920 Helmets, athletic (except motorized vehicle crash helmets), manufacturing

561320 Help supply services

212210 Hematite mining and/or beneficiating

334516 Hematology instruments manufacturing

325413 Hematology in-vitro diagnostic substances manufacturing
325412 Hematology in-vivo diagnostic substances manufacturing
325414 Hematology products (except diagnostic substances) manufacturing
325191 Hemlock extract manufacturing
113210 Hemlock gum gathering
621492 Hemodialysis centers and clinics
313111 Hemp bags made from purchased fiber
313111 Hemp ropes made from purchased fiber
313111 Hemp spun yarns made from purchased fiber
315211 Hemstitching apparel contractors on men's and boys' apparel
315212 Hemstitching apparel contractors on women's, girls', and infants' apparel
325110 Heptanes made from refined petroleum or liquid hydrocarbons
325110 Heptenes made from refined petroleum or liquid hydrocarbons
111419 Herb farming, grown under cover
111998 Herb farming, open field
111421 Herbaceous perennial growing
621399 Herbalists' offices (e.g., centers, clinics)
712110 Herbariums
325320 Herbicides manufacturing
711310 Heritage festival managers with facilities
711320 Heritage festival managers without facilities
711310 Heritage festival organizers with facilities
711320 Heritage festival organizers without facilities
711310 Heritage festival promoters with facilities
711320 Heritage festival promoters without facilities
712120 Heritage villages

238150 Hermetically sealed window unit, commercial type, installation
238350 Hermetically sealed window unit, residential-type, installation
114111 Herring fishing
325199 Heterocyclic chemicals, not specified elsewhere by process, manufacturing
325199 Hexadecanol manufacturing
325199 Hexamethylenediamine manufacturing
325199 Hexamethylenetetramine manufacturing
325199 Hexanol manufacturing
311221 HFCS (high fructose corn syrup) manufacturing
311611 Hides and skins produced in slaughtering plants
316110 Hides and skins, finishing on a contract basis
424590 Hides merchant wholesalers
316110 Hides, tanning, currying, dressing, and finishing
337122 High chairs, wood, children's, manufacturing
311221 High fructose corn syrup (HFCS) manufacturing
335110 High intensity lamp bulbs manufacturing
331112 High percentage nonferrous alloying elements (i.e., ferroalloys) manufacturing
611110 High schools
611110 High schools offering both academic and technical courses
611110 High schools offering both academic and vocational courses
236116 High-rise apartment construction general contractors
236117 High-rise apartment operative builders
332312 Highway bridge sections, prefabricated metal, manufacturing
237310 Highway construction

332322	Highway guardrails, sheet metal (except stampings), manufacturing
333120	Highway line marking machinery manufacturing
237310	Highway line painting
922120	Highway patrols, police
336120	Highway tractors assembled on chassis of own manufacture
336211	Highway tractors assembling on purchased chassis
238210	Highway, street and bridge lighting and electrical signal installation
332510	Hinges, metal, manufacturing
813410	Historical clubs
712120	Historical forts
712110	Historical museums
712120	Historical ships
712120	Historical sites
336399	Hitches, trailer, automotive, truck, and bus, manufacturing
325413	HIV test kits manufacturing
621491	HMO (health maintenance organization) medical centers and clinics
451120	Hobby shops
339932	Hobbyhorses manufacturing
423920	Hobbyists' supplies merchant wholesalers
333515	Hobs (i.e., metal gear cutting tool) manufacturing
711211	Hockey clubs, professional or semiprofessional
713990	Hockey clubs, recreational
339920	Hockey equipment (except apparel) manufacturing
423910	Hockey equipment and supplies merchant wholesalers
611620	Hockey instruction, camps, or schools
339920	Hockey skates manufacturing
711211	Hockey teams, professional or semiprofessional
713990	Hockey teams, recreational
115112	Hoeing
332212	Hoes, garden and mason's handtools, manufacturing
112210	Hog and pig (including breeding, farrowing, nursery, and finishing activities) farming
333111	Hog feeding and watering equipment manufacturing
112210	Hog feedlots (except stockyards for transportation)
424520	Hogs merchant wholesalers
321920	Hogsheads, coopered wood, manufacturing
238290	Hoisting and placement of large-scale apparatus
333923	Hoists (except aircraft loading) manufacturing
423830	Hoists (except automotive) merchant wholesalers
333924	Hoists, aircraft loading, manufacturing
423120	Hoists, automotive, merchant wholesalers
551112	Holding companies (except bank, managing)
551114	Holding companies that manage
551111	Holding companies, bank (except managing)
333313	Holepunchers (except hand operated), office-type, manufacturing
339942	Holepunchers, hand operated, manufacturing
339912	Hollowware, precious metal, manufacturing
332999	Hollowware, precious plated metal, manufacturing
316999	Holsters, leather, manufacturing
452990	Home and auto supply stores
532310	Home and garden equipment rental centers
238210	Home automation system installation
236116	Home builders (except operative), multifamily
236115	Home builders (except operative), single-family
236117	Home builders, operative
332115	Home canning lids and rings, metal stamping
621610	Home care of elderly, medical

624120 Home care of elderly, non-medical

444110 Home centers, building materials

624229 Home construction organizations, work (sweat) equity

454390 Home delivery newspaper routes, direct selling

337124 Home entertainment centers, metal, manufacturing

337122 Home entertainment centers, wood, manufacturing

522292 Home equity credit lending

621610 Home health agencies

611519 Home health aid schools

621610 Home health care agencies

532291 Home health furniture and equipment rental

236118 Home improvement (e.g., adding on, remodeling, renovating)

236118 Home improvement (e.g., adding on, remodeling, renovating), multifamily building, general contractors

236118 Home improvement (e.g., adding on, remodeling, renovating), multifamily building, operative builders

236118 Home improvement (e.g., adding on, remodeling, renovating), single-family housing, general contractors

236118 Home improvement (e.g., adding on, remodeling, renovating), single-family housing, operative builders

444110 Home improvement centers

541350 Home inspection services

621610 Home nursing services (except private practices)

621399 Home nursing services, private practice

236118 Home renovation

453998 Home security equipment stores

561920 Home show managers

561920 Home show organizers

561920 Home show promoters

334310 Home stereo systems manufacturing

334310 Home tape recorders and players (e.g., cartridge, cassette, reel) manufacturing

334310 Home theater audio and video equipment manufacturing

238210 Home theater installation

333512 Home workshop metal cutting machine tools (except handtools, welding equipment) manufacturing

423220 Homefurnishings merchant wholesalers

442299 Homefurnishings stores

624221 Homeless shelters

624120 Homemaker's service for elderly or disabled persons, non-medical

621399 Homeopaths' offices (e.g., centers, clinics)

813990 Homeowners' associations

813990 Homeowners' associations, condominium

524126 Homeowners' insurance carriers, direct

524128 Homeowners' warranty insurance carriers, direct

623990 Homes for children with health care incidental

623220 Homes for emotionally disturbed adults or children

623110 Homes for the aged with nursing care

623312 Homes for the aged without nursing care

623110 Homes for the elderly with nursing care

623312 Homes for the elderly without nursing care

623990 Homes for unwed mothers

623210 Homes with or without health care, mental retardation

623220 Homes, psychiatric convalescent

311211 Hominy grits (except breakfast food), manufacturing

311230 Hominy grits, prepared as cereal breakfast food, manufacturing

311421 Hominy, canned, manufacturing

333294	Homogenizing machinery, food, manufacturing
311511	Homogenizing milk
212399	Hones mining and/or beneficiating
112910	Honey bee production
424490	Honey merchant wholesalers
311999	Honey processing
111219	Honeydew melon farming, field, bedding plant and seed production
333512	Honing and lapping machines, metal cutting type, manufacturing
333515	Honing heads (i.e., a machine tool accessory) manufacturing
922140	Honor camps, correctional
332313	Hoods, industrial, fabricated metal plate work, manufacturing
332322	Hoods, range (except household-type), sheet metal (except stampings), manufacturing
335211	Hoods, range, household-type, manufacturing
115210	Hoof trimming
339993	Hook and eye fasteners (i.e., sewing accessories) manufacturing
332722	Hook and eye latches, metal, manufacturing
313221	Hook and loop fastener fabric manufacturing
332722	Hooks (i.e., general purpose fasteners), metal, manufacturing
339920	Hooks, fishing, manufacturing
332212	Hooks, handtools (e.g., baling, bush, grass, husking), manufacturing
332722	Hooks, metal screw, manufacturing
331111	Hoops made in iron and steel mills
331111	Hoops, galvanized, made in iron and steel mills
332999	Hoops, metal (except wire), fabricated from purchased metal

321920	Hoops, sawed or split wood for tight or slack cooperage, manufacturing
311942	Hop extract manufacturing
424490	Hop extract merchant wholesalers
111998	Hop farming
333515	Hopper feed devices (i.e., a machine tool accessory) manufacturing
332313	Hoppers, fabricated metal plate work, manufacturing
332439	Hoppers, light gauge metal, manufacturing
424590	Hops merchant wholesalers
334511	Horizon situation instrumentation manufacturing
237990	Horizontal drilling (e.g., underground cable, pipeline, sewer installation)
325413	Hormone in-vitro diagnostic substances manufacturing
325412	Hormone preparations (except in-vitro diagnostics) manufacturing
325411	Hormones and derivatives, uncompounded, manufacturing
112920	Horse (including thoroughbreds) production
332999	Horse bits manufacturing
316999	Horse boots and muzzles manufacturing
711212	Horse racetracks
711219	Horse racing stables
713990	Horse rental services, recreational saddle
711310	Horse show managers with facilities
711320	Horse show managers without facilities
711310	Horse show organizers with facilities
711320	Horse show organizers without facilities
711310	Horse show promoters with facilities
711320	Horse show promoters without facilities
336214	Horse trailers (except fifth-wheel-type) manufacturing

336212 Horse trailers, fifth-wheel-type, manufacturing
713990 Horseback riding, recreational
487110 Horse-drawn carriage operation
311611 Horsemeat produced in slaughtering plants
311111 Horsemeat, processing, for dog and cat food
311421 Horseradish (except sauce) canning
311941 Horseradish, prepared sauce, manufacturing
115210 Horses (except racehorses), boarding
424590 Horses merchant wholesalers
115210 Horses, training (except racehorses)
331222 Horseshoe nails, iron or steel, made in wire drawing plants
115210 Horseshoeing
332111 Horseshoes, ferrous forged, made from purchased iron or steel
541690 Horticultural consulting services
332912 Hose assemblies for fluid power systems manufacturing
332722 Hose clamps, metal, manufacturing
332912 Hose couplings and fittings, fluid power, manufacturing
332919 Hose couplings, metal (except fluid power), manufacturing
313221 Hose fabrics, tubular, weaving
332999 Hose, flexible metal, manufacturing
423840 Hose, industrial, merchant wholesalers
326220 Hoses, reinforced, rubber or plastics, manufacturing
326220 Hoses, rubberized fabric, manufacturing
315119 Hosiery (except sheer), women's, girls' and infants', manufacturing
333292 Hosiery machines manufacturing
448190 Hosiery stores
424320 Hosiery, men's and boys', merchant wholesalers

339113 Hosiery, orthopedic support, manufacturing
315111 Hosiery, sheer, women's, misses', and girls' full-length and knee-length, knitting or knitting and finishing
424330 Hosiery, women's and girls', merchant wholesalers
424330 Hosiery, women's, children's, and infants', merchant wholesalers
621610 Hospice care services, in home
623110 Hospices, inpatient care
813920 Hospital administrators' associations
524114 Hospital and medical service plans, direct, without providing health care services
813910 Hospital associations
532291 Hospital bed rental and leasing (i.e. home use)
339113 Hospital beds manufacturing
423450 Hospital beds merchant wholesalers
236220 Hospital construction
423450 Hospital equipment and supplies merchant wholesalers
532291 Hospital equipment rental (i.e. home use)
532291 Hospital furniture and equipment rental (i.e. home use)
423450 Hospital furniture merchant wholesalers
339113 Hospital furniture, specialized (e.g., hospital beds, operating room furniture)
926150 Hospital licensure agencies
611519 Hospital management schools (except academic)
611310 Hospital management schools offering baccalaureate or graduate degrees
315211 Hospital service apparel, washable, men's and boys', cut and sew apparel contractors

315225 Hospital service apparel, washable, men's and boys', cut and sewn from purchased fabric (except apparel contractors)

315212 Hospital service apparel, washable, women's and girls', cut and sew apparel contractors

315239 Hospital service apparel, washable, women's, misses', and girls', cut and sewn from purchased fabric (except apparel contractors)

611519 Hospitality management schools (except academic)

611310 Hospitality management schools offering baccalaureate or graduate degrees

524114 Hospitalization insurance carriers, direct, without providing health care services

****** Hospitals—see type

622210 Hospitals for alcoholics

622210 Hospitals, addiction

541940 Hospitals, animal

622110 Hospitals, general medical and surgical

622110 Hospitals, general pediatric

622210 Hospitals, mental (except mental retardation)

623210 Hospitals, mental retardation

622210 Hospitals, psychiatric (except convalescent)

623220 Hospitals, psychiatric convalescent

622210 Hospitals, psychiatric pediatric

622310 Hospitals, specialty (except psychiatric, substance abuse)

622210 Hospitals, substance abuse

721199 Hostels

487990 Hot air balloon ride, scenic and sightseeing, operation

333311 Hot beverage vending machines manufacturing

332812 Hot dip galvanizing metals and metal products for the trade

311612 Hot dogs (except poultry) made from purchased carcasses

311611 Hot dogs (except poultry) produced in slaughtering plants

311615 Hot dogs, poultry, manufacturing

332111 Hot forgings made from purchased iron or steel, unfinished

332112 Hot forgings made from purchased nonferrous metals, unfinished

213112 Hot oil treating of oil field tanks on a contract basis

213112 Hot shot service on a contract basis

333516 Hot strip mill machinery, metalworking, manufacturing

453998 Hot tub stores

423910 Hot tubs merchant wholesalers

321920 Hot tubs, coopered, manufacturing

326191 Hot tubs, plastics or fiberglass, manufacturing

326299 Hot water bottles, rubber, manufacturing

335228 Hot water heaters (including nonelectric), household-type, manufacturing

238220 Hot water heating system installation

238220 Hot water tank installation

531120 Hotel building rental or leasing, not operating hotel

236220 Hotel construction

423440 Hotel equipment and supplies (except furniture) merchant wholesalers

423210 Hotel furniture merchant wholesalers

561110 Hotel management services (except complete operation of client's business)

721110 Hotel management services (i.e., providing management and operating staff to run hotel)

561599 Hotel reservation services

327112 Hotel tableware and kitchen articles, vitreous china, manufacturing

531110   Houses rental or leasing
332311   Houses, prefabricated metal, manufacturing
321991   Houses, prefabricated mobile homes, manufacturing
321992   Houses, prefabricated, wood (except mobile homes), manufacturing
454390   House-to-house direct selling
423220   Housewares (except electric) merchant wholesalers
442299   Housewares stores
423620   Housewares, electric, merchant wholesalers
624229   Housing assistance agencies
531110   Housing authorities operating residential buildings
925110   Housing authorities, nonoperating
236117   Housing construction, merchant builder
236117   Housing construction, operative builder
922120   Housing police, government
925110   Housing programs, planning and development, government
624229   Housing repair organizations, volunteer
236116   Housing, multifamily, construction general contractors
236115   Housing, single-family, construction general contractors
336612   Hovercraft building
487210   Hovercraft sightseeing operation
332995   Howitzers manufacturing
321999   Hubs, wood, manufacturing
111334   Huckleberry farming
113210   Huckleberry greens, gathering of
334511   HUD (heads-up display) systems, aeronautical, manufacturing
212299   Huebnerite mining and/or beneficiating
115114   Hulling and shelling of nuts
333111   Hulling machinery, farm-type, manufacturing
712110   Human history museums

541612   Human resource consulting services
813311   Human rights advocacy organizations
921190   Human rights commissions, government
813312   Humane societies
541720   Humanities research and development services
423730   Humidifiers and dehumidifiers (except portable) merchant wholesalers
423620   Humidifiers and dehumidifiers, portable, merchant wholesalers
335211   Humidifiers, portable electric, manufacturing
333415   Humidifying equipment (except portable) manufacturing
334512   Humidistats (e.g., duct, skeleton, wall) manufacturing
238210   Humidity control system installation
334512   Humidity controls, air-conditioning-type, manufacturing
334519   Humidity instruments (except industrial process and air-conditioning type) manufacturing
334513   Humidity instruments, industrial process-type, manufacturing
212399   Humus, peat, mining and/or beneficiating
721214   Hunting camps with accommodation facilities
713990   Hunting clubs, recreational
315211   Hunting coats and vests, men's and boys', cut and sew apparel contractors
315228   Hunting coats and vests, men's and boys', cut and sewn from purchased fabric (except apparel contractors)
423910   Hunting equipment and supplies merchant wholesalers
713990   Hunting guide services
332211   Hunting knives manufacturing
114210   Hunting preserves
238220   HVAC (heating, ventilation and air-conditioning) contractors

334111 Hybrid computers manufacturing
334413 Hybrid integrated circuits manufacturing
112511 Hybrid striped bass production
327410 Hydrated lime (i.e., calcium hydroxide) manufacturing
332912 Hydraulic aircraft subassemblies manufacturing
333995 Hydraulic cylinders, fluid power, manufacturing
811310 Hydraulic equipment repair and maintenance services
324110 Hydraulic fluids made in petroleum refineries
324191 Hydraulic fluids, petroleum, made from refined petroleum
325998 Hydraulic fluids, synthetic, manufacturing
213112 Hydraulic fracturing wells on a contract basis
332912 Hydraulic hose fittings, fluid power, manufacturing
326220 Hydraulic hoses (without fitting), rubber or plastics, manufacturing
423830 Hydraulic power transmission equipment merchant wholesalers
423830 Hydraulic pumps and parts merchant wholesalers
333996 Hydraulic pumps, fluid power, manufacturing
336340 Hydraulic slave cylinders, automotive, truck, and bus clutch, manufacturing
333611 Hydraulic turbine generator set units manufacturing
333611 Hydraulic turbines manufacturing
332912 Hydraulic valves, fluid power, manufacturing
325188 Hydrazine manufacturing
325188 Hydrochloric acid manufacturing
325188 Hydrocyanic acid manufacturing
238910 Hydrodemolition (i.e., demolition with pressurized water) contractors

237990 Hydroelectric generating facility construction
221111 Hydroelectric power generation
325188 Hydrofluoric acid manufacturing
325188 Hydrofluosilicic acid manufacturing
336611 Hydrofoil vessel building and repairing in shipyard
325120 Hydrogen manufacturing
325188 Hydrogen peroxide manufacturing
325188 Hydrogen sulfide manufacturing
311225 Hydrogenating purchased oil
541370 Hydrographic mapping services
541370 Hydrographic surveying services
541690 Hydrology consulting services
334519 Hydrometers (except industrial process-type) manufacturing
334513 Hydrometers, industrial process-type, manufacturing
334512 Hydronic circulator control, automatic, manufacturing
423720 Hydronic heating equipment and supplies merchant wholesalers
333414 Hydronic heating equipment manufacturing
238220 Hydronic heating system installation
334512 Hydronic limit control manufacturing
334512 Hydronic limit, pressure, and temperature controls, manufacturing
334511 Hydrophones manufacturing
111419 Hydroponic crop farming
325192 Hydroquinone manufacturing
561730 Hydroseeding services (e.g., decorative, erosion control purposes)
333996 Hydrostatic drives manufacturing
541380 Hydrostatic testing laboratories or services
333996 Hydrostatic transmissions manufacturing
325188 Hydrosulfites manufacturing
339113 Hydrotherapy equipment manufacturing

334519	Hygrometers (except industrial process-type) manufacturing
334513	Hygrometers, industrial process-type, manufacturing
334519	Hygrothermographs manufacturing
621399	Hypnotherapists' offices (e.g., centers, clinics)
325411	Hypnotic drugs, uncompounded, manufacturing
325188	Hypochlorites manufacturing
339112	Hypodermic needles and syringes manufacturing
325188	Hypophosphites manufacturing
312113	Ice (except dry ice) manufacturing
424990	Ice (except dry ice) merchant wholesalers
238170	Ice apron, roof, installation
334512	Ice bank controls manufacturing
335222	Ice boxes, household-type, manufacturing
326199	Ice buckets, plastics (except foam), manufacturing
326140	Ice buckets, polystyrene foam, manufacturing
326150	Ice buckets, urethane or other plastics foam (except polystyrene), manufacturing
332439	Ice chests or coolers, light gauge metal, manufacturing
326150	Ice chests or coolers, urethane or other plastics foam (except polystyrene) manufacturing
445299	Ice cream (i.e., packaged) stores
424430	Ice cream and ices merchant wholesalers
311821	Ice cream cones manufacturing
424490	Ice cream cones merchant wholesalers
333294	Ice cream making machinery manufacturing
311520	Ice cream manufacturing
424430	Ice cream merchant wholesalers
311514	Ice cream mix manufacturing
722213	Ice cream parlors
311520	Ice cream specialties manufacturing
722330	Ice cream truck vendors
333311	Ice cream vending machines manufacturing
335211	Ice crushers, household-type electric, manufacturing
333999	Ice crushers, industrial and commercial-type, manufacturing
711211	Ice hockey clubs, professional or semiprofessional
713990	Ice hockey clubs, recreational
334512	Ice maker controls manufacturing
333415	Ice making machinery manufacturing
423740	Ice making machines merchant wholesalers
311520	Ice milk manufacturing
311514	Ice milk mix manufacturing
311520	Ice milk specialties manufacturing
237990	Ice rink (except indoor) construction
236220	Ice rink, indoor, construction
339920	Ice skates manufacturing
711190	Ice skating companies
713940	Ice skating rinks
711190	Ice skating shows
312130	Ice wine
325120	Ice, dry, manufacturing
424690	Ice, dry, merchant wholesalers
312111	Iced coffee manufacturing
312111	Iced tea manufacturing
212399	Iceland spar (i.e., optical grade calcite), mining and/or beneficiating
311520	Ices, flavored sherbets, manufacturing
332999	Identification plates, metal, manufacturing
423410	Identity recorders merchant wholesalers
332993	Igniters, ammunition tracer (i.e., more than 30 mm., more than 1.18 inch), manufacturing
334512	Ignition controls for gas appliances and furnaces, automatic, manufacturing
336322	Ignition points and condensers for internal combustion engines manufacturing

334515 Ignition testing instruments manufacturing

336322 Ignition wiring harness for internal combustion engines manufacturing

321213 I-joists, wood, fabricating

335122 Illuminated indoor lighting fixtures (e.g., directional, exit) manufacturing

541430 Illustrators, independent commercial

212299 Ilmenite ores mining and/or beneficiating

327420 Images, small gypsum, manufacturing

327999 Images, small papier-mache, manufacturing

323122 Imagesetting services, prepress

312221 Imitation tobacco cigarettes, manufacturing

335211 Immersion heaters, household-type electric, manufacturing

624230 Immigrant resettlement services

928120 Immigration services

923120 Immunization program administration

621111 Immunologists' offices (e.g., centers, clinics)

334516 Immunology instruments, laboratory, manufacturing

333991 Impact wrenches, handheld power-driven, manufacturing

334515 Impedance measuring equipment manufacturing

334514 Impeller and counter driven flow meters manufacturing

339113 Implants, surgical, manufacturing

213112 Impounding and storing salt water in connection with petroleum production

221310 Impounding reservoirs, irrigation

339114 Impression material, dental, manufacturing

711110 Improvisational theaters

334512 In-built thermostats, filled system and bimetal types, manufacturing

335110 Incandescent filament lamp bulbs, complete, manufacturing

325998 Incense manufacturing

334512 Incinerator control systems, residential and commercial-type, manufacturing

236210 Incinerator, mass-burn type, construction

236210 Incinerator, municipal waste disposal, construction

333994 Incinerators (except precast concrete) manufacturing

238290 Incinerators, building equipment type, installation

562211 Incinerators, hazardous waste, operating

562213 Incinerators, nonhazardous solid waste

327390 Incinerators, precast concrete, manufacturing

541213 Income tax compilation services

541213 Income tax return preparation services

333313 Incoming mail handling equipment (e.g., opening, scanning, sorting) manufacturing

339113 Incubators, infant, manufacturing

339113 Incubators, laboratory-type, manufacturing

333111 Incubators, poultry, manufacturing

325998 Indelible inks manufacturing

488190 Independent pilot, air (except owner-operators)

488490 Independent truck driver (except owner-operators)

333515 Indexing, rotary tables (i.e., a machine tool accessory) manufacturing

325998 India inks manufacturing

921190 Indian affairs programs, government

334515 Indicating instruments, electric, manufacturing

334519 Indicator testers, turntable, manufacturing

334513	Indicators, industrial process control-type, manufacturing
325188	Indium chloride manufacturing
624190	Individual and family social services, multi-purpose
523910	Individuals investing in financial contracts on own account
541850	Indoor display advertising services
713120	Indoor play areas
236220	Indoor swimming pool construction
333994	Induction heating equipment, industrial process-type, manufacturing
334416	Inductors, electronic component-type (e.g., chokes, coils, transformers), manufacturing
813910	Industrial associations
522190	Industrial banks (i.e., known as), depository
522298	Industrial banks (i.e., known as), nondepository
314992	Industrial belting reinforcement, cord and fabric, manufacturing
236210	Industrial building (except warehouses) construction
236210	Industrial building (except warehouses) construction, general contractors
236210	Industrial building (except warehouses) construction, operative builders
531120	Industrial building rental or leasing
722310	Industrial caterers (i.e., providing food services on a contractural arrangement (except single-event basis))
424690	Industrial chemicals merchant wholesalers
423840	Industrial containers merchant wholesalers
335314	Industrial controls (e.g., push button, selector, and pilot switches, manufacturing
423610	Industrial controls, electrical, merchant wholesalers

541420	Industrial design consulting services
533110	Industrial design licensing
541420	Industrial design services
926110	Industrial development program administration
423840	Industrial diamonds merchant wholesalers
541330	Industrial engineering services
811310	Industrial equipment and machinery repair and maintenance services
315211	Industrial garments, men's and boys', cut and sew apparel contractors
315225	Industrial garments, men's and boys', cut and sewn from purchased fabric (except apparel contractors)
315212	Industrial garments, women's and girls', cut and sew apparel contractors
315239	Industrial garments, women's, misses', and girls', cut and sewn from purchased fabric (except apparel contractors)
325120	Industrial gases manufacturing
424690	Industrial gases merchant wholesalers
327212	Industrial glassware and glass products, pressed or blown, made in glass making plants
327215	Industrial glassware made from purchased glass
813930	Industrial labor unions
541320	Industrial land use planning services
812332	Industrial launderers
335122	Industrial lighting fixtures, electric, manufacturing
522298	Industrial loan companies, nondepository
336510	Industrial locomotives and parts manufacturing
423830	Industrial machinery and equipment (except electrical) merchant wholesalers
335122	Industrial mercury lighting fixtures, electric, manufacturing

333511 Industrial molds (except steel ingot) manufacturing
331511 Industrial molds, steel ingot, manufacturing
332997 Industrial pattern manufacturing
334513 Industrial process control instruments manufacturing
238220 Industrial process piping installation
325510 Industrial product finishes and coatings (i.e., paint) manufacturing
541712 Industrial research and development laboratories or services (except biotechnology research and development)
423450 Industrial safety devices (e.g., eye shields, face shields, first-aid kits) merchant wholesalers
325998 Industrial salt manufacturing
424690 Industrial salts merchant wholesalers
212322 Industrial sand beneficiating (e.g., screening, washing)
212322 Industrial sand sandpits and dredging
333997 Industrial scales manufacturing
423840 Industrial supplies (except disposable plastics, paper) merchant wholesalers
424130 Industrial supplies, disposable plastics, paper, merchant wholesalers
541380 Industrial testing laboratories or services
621340 Industrial therapists' offices (e.g., centers, clinics)
811310 Industrial truck (e.g., forklifts) repair and maintenance services
532490 Industrial truck rental or leasing
333924 Industrial trucks and tractors manufacturing
423830 Industrial trucks, tractors, or trailers merchant wholesalers
812332 Industrial uniform supply services
423930 Industrial wastes to be reclaimed merchant wholesalers

311611 Inedible products (e.g., hides, skins, pulled wool, wool grease) produced in slaughtering plants
334511 Inertial navigation systems, aeronautical, manufacturing
311422 Infant and junior food canning
311230 Infant cereals, dry, manufacturing
624410 Infant day care centers
624410 Infant day care services
339113 Infant incubators manufacturing
315291 Infants' apparel cut and sewn from purchased fabric (except apparel contractors)
424330 Infants' clothing merchant wholesalers
315212 Infants' cut and sew apparel contractors
311514 Infant's formulas manufacturing
316219 Infant's shoes (except plastics, rubber), manufacturing
315291 Infants water resistant outerwear cut and sewn from purchased fabric (except apparel contractors)
336612 Inflatable plastic boats, heavy-duty, manufacturing
336612 Inflatable rubber boats, heavy-duty, manufacturing
541512 Information management computer systems integration design services
334516 Infrared analytical instruments, laboratory-type, manufacturing
334511 Infrared homing systems, aeronautical, manufacturing
334513 Infrared instruments, industrial process-type, manufacturing
335110 Infrared lamp bulbs manufacturing
335129 Infrared lamp fixtures manufacturing
333994 Infrared ovens, industrial, manufacturing
334413 Infrared sensors, solid-state, manufacturing
621498 Infusion therapy centers and clinics, outpatient

331319	Ingot made by rolling purchased aluminum
331111	Ingot made in iron and steel mills
331319	Ingot, aluminum, made in integrated secondary smelting and rolling mills
331492	Ingot, nonferrous metals (except aluminum, copper), secondary smelting and refining
331312	Ingot, primary aluminum, manufacturing
331419	Ingot, primary, nonferrous metals (except aluminum, copper), manufacturing
423510	Ingots (except precious) merchant wholesalers
423940	Ingots, precious, merchant wholesalers
621399	Inhalation therapists' offices (e.g., centers, clinics)
339112	Inhalation therapy equipment manufacturing
339112	Inhalators, surgical and medical, manufacturing
325998	Inhibitors (e.g., corrosion, oxidation, polymerization) manufacturing
454390	In-home sales of merchandise, direct selling
333220	Injection molding machinery for plastics manufacturing
325612	Ink eradicators manufacturing
424120	Ink, writing, merchant wholesalers
339944	Inked ribbons manufacturing
424120	Inked ribbons merchant wholesalers
325910	Inkjet cartridges manufacturing
325910	Inkjet inks manufacturing
325910	Inks, printing, manufacturing
423840	Inks, printing, merchant wholesalers
325998	Inks, writing, manufacturing
316999	Inner soles, leather, manufacturing
326211	Inner tubes manufacturing
337910	Innerspring cushions manufacturing
721191	Inns, bed and breakfast

424690	Inorganic chemicals merchant wholesalers
325131	Inorganic pigments (except bone black, carbon black, lamp black) manufacturing
334119	Input/output equipment, computer (except terminals), manufacturing
115112	Insect control for crops
335129	Insect lamps, electric, manufacturing
332618	Insect screening made from purchased wire
325320	Insecticides manufacturing
333515	Inserts, cutting tool, manufacturing
541350	Inspection bureaus, building
926150	Inspection for labor standards
488490	Inspection or weighing services, truck transportation
488190	Inspection services, aircraft
541350	Inspection services, building or home
213112	Installing production equipment at the oil or gas field on a contract basis
522220	Installment sales financing
311920	Instant coffee manufacturing
311230	Instant hot cereals manufacturing
323114	Instant printing (i.e., quick printing)
311920	Instant tea manufacturing
236220	Institutional building construction
236220	Institutional building construction general contractors
236220	Institutional building construction operative builders
337127	Institutional furniture manufacturing
335122	Institutional lighting fixtures, electric, manufacturing
522120	Institutions, savings
******	Instruction—see type of training
512110	Instructional video production

336322 Instrument control panels (i.e., assembling purchased gauges), automotive, truck, and bus, manufacturing

334511 Instrument landing system instrumentation, airborne or airport, manufacturing

333314 Instrument lenses manufacturing

334514 Instrument panels, assembling gauges made in the same establishment

334515 Instrument shunts manufacturing

332612 Instrument springs, precision (except clock, watch), light gauge, made from purchased wire or strip, manufacturing

335311 Instrument transformers (except complete instruments) for metering or protective relaying use manufacturing

334519 Instrumentation for reactor controls, auxiliary, manufacturing

423830 Instruments (except electrical) (e.g., controlling, indicating, recording) merchant wholesalers

334513 Instruments for industrial process control manufacturing

334515 Instruments for measuring electrical quantities manufacturing

334511 Instruments, aeronautical, manufacturing

334515 Instruments, electric (i.e., testing electrical characteristics), manufacturing

339112 Instruments, mechanical microsurgical, manufacturing

339992 Instruments, musical, manufacturing

423990 Instruments, musical, merchant wholesalers

423490 Instruments, professional and scientific, merchant wholesalers

331422 Insulated wire or cable made from purchased copper in wire drawing plants

331319 Insulated wire or cable made in aluminum wire drawing plants

423610 Insulated wire or cable merchant wholesalers

331422 Insulated wire or cable, copper, made in integrated secondary smelting and wire drawing plants

322299 Insulating batts, fills, or blankets made from purchased paper

327993 Insulating batts, fills, or blankets, fiberglass, manufacturing

327124 Insulating firebrick and shapes, clay, manufacturing

327215 Insulating glass, sealed units, made from purchased glass

327211 Insulating glass, sealed units, made in glass making plants

321999 Insulating materials, cork, manufacturing

325998 Insulating oils manufacturing

335929 Insulating purchased nonferrous wire

326150 Insulation and cushioning, foam plastics (except polystrene), manufacturing

326140 Insulation and cushioning, polystyrene foam plastics, manufacturing

321219 Insulation board, cellular fiber, manufacturing

238310 Insulation contractors

423330 Insulation materials (except wood) merchant wholesalers

238290 Insulation, boiler, duct and pipe, installation

335932 Insulators, electrical (except glass, porcelain), manufacturing

327113 Insulators, electrical porcelain, manufacturing

327215 Insulators, electrical, glass, made from purchased glass

327212 Insulators, electrical, glass, made in glass making plants

423610 Insulators, electrical, merchant wholesalers.

325412	Insulin preparations manufacturing
325411	Insulin, uncompounded, manufacturing
524298	Insurance actuarial services
524298	Insurance advisory services
524210	Insurance agencies
524210	Insurance brokerages
531120	Insurance building rental or leasing
524113	Insurance carriers, disability, direct
524126	Insurance carriers, fidelity, direct
524114	Insurance carriers, health, direct
524113	Insurance carriers, life, direct
524126	Insurance carriers, property and casualty, direct
524126	Insurance carriers, surety, direct
524127	Insurance carriers, title, direct
524291	Insurance claims adjusting
524291	Insurance claims investigation services
524292	Insurance claims processing services, third party
926150	Insurance commissions, government
524298	Insurance coverage consulting services
524298	Insurance exchanges
524292	Insurance fund, third party administrative services (except claims adjusting only)
551112	Insurance holding companies
524298	Insurance investigation services (except claims investigation)
524298	Insurance loss prevention services
524292	Insurance plan administrative services (except claims adjusting only), third-party
524298	Insurance processing, contract or fee basis
524298	Insurance rate making services
524298	Insurance reporting services
524291	Insurance settlement offices
524298	Insurance underwriters laboratories and standards services

524113	Insurance underwriting, disability, direct
524114	Insurance underwriting, health and medical, direct
524113	Insurance underwriting, life, direct
524126	Insurance underwriting, property and casualty, direct
524127	Insurance underwriting, title, direct
813910	Insurers' associations
323111	Intaglio printing
335312	Integral horsepower electric motors manufacturing
423690	Integrated circuits merchant wholesalers
334413	Integrated microcircuits manufacturing
512220	Integrated record companies (i.e., releasing, promoting, distributing)
512220	Integrated record production and distribution
334515	Integrated-circuit testers manufacturing
334515	Integrating electricity meters manufacturing
334514	Integrating meters, nonelectric, manufacturing
712110	Interactive museums
485210	Intercity bus line operation
483113	Intercoastal freight transportation to and from domestic ports
483114	Intercoastal transportation of passengers to and from domestic ports
334290	Intercom systems and equipment manufacturing
238210	Intercommunication (intercom) system installation
332410	Intercooler shells manufacturing
333314	Interferometers manufacturing
541410	Interior decorating consultant services
541410	Interior decorating consulting services
541410	Interior design consulting services
541410	Interior design services

331525   Investment castings, copper (except die-castings), unfinished, manufacturing
331528   Investment castings, nonferrous metal (except aluminum, copper), unfinished, manufacturing
331512   Investment castings, steel, unfinished, manufacturing
523910   Investment clubs
525990   Investment funds, closed-end
525910   Investment funds, open-ended
523920   Investment management
325413   In-vitro diagnostic substances manufacturing
325412   In-vivo diagnostic substances manufacturing
325188   Iodides manufacturing
325412   Iodinated in-vivo diagnostic substances manufacturing
325188   Iodine, crude or resublimed, manufacturing
334519   Ion chambers manufacturing
325211   Ion exchange resins manufacturing
325211   Ionomer resins manufacturing
325199   Ionone manufacturing
331491   Iridium bar, rod, sheet, strip and tubing made from purchased metals or scrap
212299   Iridium mining and/or beneficiating
331492   Iridium recovering from scrap and/or alloying purchased metals
331419   Iridium refining, primary
423390   Iron and steel architectural shapes merchant wholesalers
325131   Iron based pigments manufacturing
331511   Iron castings, unfinished, manufacturing
325188   Iron compounds, not specified elsewhere by process, manufacturing
332111   Iron forgings made from purchased iron, unfinished
331511   Iron foundries
339113   Iron lungs manufacturing

212210   Iron ore (e.g., hematite, magnetite, siderite, taconite) mining and/or beneficiating
212210   Iron ore agglomerates mining and/or beneficiating
212210   Iron ore beneficiating plants (e.g., agglomeration, sintering)
212210   Iron ore mine site development for own account
331111   Iron ore recovery from open hearth slag
212210   Iron ore, blocked, mining and/or beneficiating
331111   Iron sinter made in iron and steel mills
325188   Iron sulphate manufacturing
238120   Iron work, structural, contractors
331111   Iron, pig, manufacturing
335224   Ironers and mangles, household-type (except portable irons), manufacturing
332999   Ironing boards, metal, manufacturing
321999   Ironing boards, wood, manufacturing
335211   Irons, household-type electric, manufacturing
334517   Irradiation apparatus and tubes (e.g., industrial, medical diagnostic, medical therapeutic, research, scientific), manufacturing
334517   Irradiation equipment manufacturing
115114   Irradiation of fruits and vegetables
926130   Irrigation districts, nonoperating
423820   Irrigation equipment merchant wholesalers
333111   Irrigation equipment, agriculture, manufacturing
327332   Irrigation pipe, concrete, manufacturing
332322   Irrigation pipe, sheet metal (except stampings), manufacturing
237110   Irrigation project construction (except lawn)
221310   Irrigation system operation

325110 Isobutane made from refined petroleum or liquid hydrocarbons

211112 Isobutane recovered from oil and gas field gases

325110 Isobutene made from refined petroleum or liquid hydrocarbons

325211 Isobutylene polymer resins manufacturing

325212 Isobutylene-isoprene rubber manufacturing

325212 Isocyanate rubber manufacturing

325192 Isocyanates manufacturing

335311 Isolation transformers manufacturing

211112 Isopentane recovered from oil and gas field gases

325110 Isoprene made from refined petroleum or liquid hydrocarbons

325199 Isopropyl alcohol manufacturing

522210 Issuing, credit card

311422 Italian foods canning

339112 IV apparatus manufacturing

333120 Jack hammers manufacturing

315191 Jackets made in apparel knitting mills

332992 Jackets, bullet (i.e., 30 mm. or less, 1.18 inch or less), manufacturing

315292 Jackets, fur (except apparel contractors), manufacturing

315211 Jackets, fur, men's and boys', cut and sew apparel contractors

315212 Jackets, fur, women's, girls', and infants', cut and sew apparel contractors

332313 Jackets, industrial, fabricated metal plate work, manufacturing

315291 Jackets, infants', cut and sewn from purchased fabric (except apparel contractors)

315292 Jackets, leather (except welders') or sheep-lined (except apparel contractors), manufacturing

315211 Jackets, leather (except welders') or sheep-lined, men's and boys', cut and sew apparel contractors

315212 Jackets, leather (except welders') or sheep-lined, women's, girls', and infants', cut and sew apparel contractors

315211 Jackets, men's and boys', cut and sew apparel contractors

315225 Jackets, nontailored work, men's and boys', cut and sewn from purchased fabric (except apparel contractors)

315239 Jackets, nontailored work, women's, misses', and girls', cut and sewn from purchased fabric (except apparel contractors)

315239 Jackets, nontailored, women's, misses', and girls', cut and sewn from purchased fabric (except apparel contractors)

315228 Jackets, not tailored (except work), men's and boys', cut and sewn from purchased fabric (except apparel contractors)

315211 Jackets, service apparel (e.g., laboratory, medical), men's and boys', cut and sew apparel contractors

315225 Jackets, service apparel (e.g., laboratory, medical), men's and boys', cut and sewn from purchased fabric (except apparel contractors)

315212 Jackets, service apparel (e.g., laboratory, medical), women's and girls', cut and sew apparel contractors

315239 Jackets, service apparel (e.g., laboratory, medical), women's, misses', and girls', cut and sewn from purchased fabric (except apparel contractors)

315291 Jackets, ski, infants', cut and sewn from purchased fabric (except apparel contractors)

315211 Jackets, ski, men's and boys', cut and sew apparel contractors

315228 Jackets, ski, men's and boys', cut and sewn from purchased fabric (except apparel contractors)

315212 Jackets, ski, women's, girls', and infants', cut and sew apparel contractors

315239 Jackets, ski, women's, misses', and girls', cut and sewn from purchased fabric (except apparel contractors)

315222 Jackets, tailored (except fur, leather, sheep-lined), men's and boys', cut and sewn from purchased fabric (except apparel contractors)

315234 Jackets, tailored (except fur, sheep-lined), women's, misses', and girls', cut and sewn from purchased fabric (except apparel contractors)

315211 Jackets, tailored, men's and boys', cut and sew apparel contractors

315212 Jackets, tailored, women's, girls', and infants', cut and sew apparel contractors

316999 Jackets, welder's, leather, manufacturing

315212 Jackets, women's, girls', and infants', cut and sew apparel contractors

332212 Jacks (except hydraulic, pneumatic) manufacturing

333999 Jacks, hydraulic and pneumatic, manufacturing

333292 Jacquard card cutting machinery manufacturing

313210 Jacquard woven fabrics weaving

212399 Jade mining and/or beneficiating

611620 Jai alai instruction, camps, or schools

711211 Jai alai teams, professional or semiprofessional

236220 Jail construction

561210 Jail operation on a contract or fee basis

922140 Jails (except private operation of)

561210 Jails, privately operated

332321 Jalousies, metal, manufacturing

424690 Janitorial chemicals merchant wholesalers

423850 Janitorial equipment and supplies merchant wholesalers

453998 Janitorial equipment and supplies stores

561720 Janitorial services

561720 Janitorial services, aircraft

332812 Japanning metals and metal products for the trade

316110 Japanning of leather

333994 Japanning ovens manufacturing

327213 Jars for packaging, bottling, and canning, glass, manufacturing

326199 Jars, plastics, manufacturing

711120 Jazz dance companies

711510 Jazz dancers, independent

711130 Jazz musical artists, independent

711130 Jazz musical groups

315211 Jean-cut casual slacks, men's and boys', cut and sew apparel contractors

315224 Jean-cut casual slacks, men's and boys', cut and sewn from purchased fabric (except apparel contractors)

315212 Jean-cut casual slacks, women's, girls, and infants', cut and sew apparel contractors

315239 Jean-cut casual slacks, women's, misses', and girls', cut and sewn from purchased fabric (except apparel contractors)

315291 Jeans, infants', cut and sewn from purchased fabric (except apparel contractors)

315211 Jeans, men's and boys', cut and sew apparel contractors

315239 Jeans, women's, misses', and girls', cut and sewn from purchased fabric (except apparel contractors)

315212 Jeans, women's, misses', girls', and infants', cut and sew apparel contractors

311421 Jellies and jams manufacturing

424490 Jellies and jams merchant wholesalers

311340 Jelly candies manufacturing

315191 Jerseys made in apparel knitting mills

315211 Jerseys, men's and boys', cut and sew apparel contractors

315223 Jerseys, men's and boys', cut and sewn from purchased fabric (except apparel contractors)

315212 Jerseys, women's, girls', and infants', cut and sew apparel contractors

315232 Jerseys, women's, misses', and girls', cut and sewn from purchased fabric (except apparel contractors)

324110 Jet fuels manufacturing

336412 Jet propulsion and internal combustion engines and parts, aircraft, manufacturing

332993 Jet propulsion projectiles (except guided missiles) manufacturing

237990 Jetty construction

339911 Jewel settings and mountings, precious metal, manufacturing

339913 Jeweler's findings and materials manufacturing

423940 Jewelers' findings merchant wholesalers

332212 Jeweler's handtools, nonelectric, manufacturing

424990 Jewelry boxes merchant wholesalers

541490 Jewelry design services

423940 Jewelry merchant wholesalers

811490 Jewelry repair shops without retailing new jewelry

448150 Jewelry stores, costume

448310 Jewelry stores, precious

339914 Jewelry, costume, manufacturing

339911 Jewelry, natural or cultured pearls, manufacturing

339911 Jewelry, precious metal, manufacturing

333514 Jigs (e.g., checking, gauging, inspection) manufacturing

333514 Jigs and fixtures for use with machine tools manufacturing

333991 Jigsaws, handheld power-driven, manufacturing

333210 Jigsaws, woodworking-type, stationary, manufacturing

624310 Job counseling, vocational rehabilitation or habilitation

323119 Job printing (except flexographic, digital, gravure, lithographic, quick, screen)

323119 Job printing, engraving

323112 Job printing, flexographic

323111 Job printing, gravure

323119 Job printing, letterpress

323110 Job printing, lithographic

323110 Job printing, offset

323113 Job printing, screen

336370 Job stampings, automotive, metal, manufacturing

624310 Job training, vocational rehabilitation or habilitation

711219 Jockeys, horse racing

339920 Jogging machines, manufacturing

315191 Jogging suits made in apparel knitting mills

315291 Jogging suits, infants', cut and sewn from purchased fabric (except apparel contractors)

315211 Jogging suits, men's and boys', cut and sew apparel contractors

315228 Jogging suits, men's and boys', cut and sewn from purchased fabric (except apparel contractors)

315212 Jogging suits, women's, girls', and infants', cut and sew apparel contractors

315239 Jogging suits, women's, misses', and girls', cut and sewn from purchased fabric (except apparel contractors)

325520 Joint compounds (except gypsum base) manufacturing

327420 Joint compounds, gypsum based, manufacturing

333210 Jointers, woodworking-type, manufacturing

333613 Joints, swivel (except aircraft, motor vehicle), manufacturing

333613 Joints, universal (except aircraft, motor vehicle), manufacturing

336413 Joints, universal, aircraft, manufacturing

336350 Joints, universal, automotive, truck, and bus, manufacturing

332312 Joists, fabricated bar, manufacturing

332322 Joists, sheet metal (except stampings), manufacturing

111998 Jojoba farming

711510 Journalists, independent (freelance)

334119 Joystick devices manufacturing

611620 Judo instruction, camps, or schools

326150 Jugs, vacuum, foam plastics (except polystyrene), manufacturing

332439 Jugs, vacuum, light gauge metal, manufacturing

326140 Jugs, vacuum, polystyrene foam plastics, manufacturing

333294 Juice extractors (i.e., food manufacturing-type) manufacturing

335211 Juice extractors, household-type electric, manufacturing

311520 Juice pops, frozen, manufacturing

424490 Juices, canned or fresh, merchant wholesalers

424420 Juices, frozen, merchant wholesalers

311411 Juices, fruit or vegetable concentrates, frozen, manufacturing

311421 Juices, fruit or vegetable, canned manufacturing

311421 Juices, fruit or vegetable, fresh, manufacturing

311411 Juices, fruit or vegetable, frozen, manufacturing

713990 Jukebox concession operators (i.e., supplying and servicing in others' facilities)

334310 Jukeboxes manufacturing

315212 Jumpsuits, women's, girls', and infants', cut and sew apparel contractors

315234 Jumpsuits, women's, misses', and girls', cut and sewn from purchased fabric (except apparel contractors)

335932 Junction boxes, electrical wiring, manufacturing

813910 Junior chambers of commerce

611210 Junior colleges

611210 Junior colleges offering a wide variety of academic and technical training

611110 Junior high schools

313210 Jute bags made in broadwoven mills

424310 Jute piece goods (except burlap) merchant wholesalers

337124 Juvenile furniture (except upholstered), metal manufacturing

337122 Juvenile furniture (except upholstered), wood, manufacturing

337125 Juvenile furniture, rattan and reed, manufacturing

337121 Juvenile furniture, upholstered, manufacturing

623990 Juvenile halfway group homes

511120 Juvenile magazine and periodical publishers (except exclusive Internet publishing)

511120 Juvenile magazine and periodical publishers and printing combined

519130 Juvenile magazine and periodical publishers, exclusively on Internet

323112 Juvenile magazines and periodicals flexographic printing without publishing

323111 Juvenile magazines and periodicals gravure printing without publishing

323110 Juvenile magazines and periodicals lithographic (offset) printing without publishing

323119 Juvenile magazines and periodicals printing (except flexographic, gravure, lithographic, quick, screen) without publishing

323113 Juvenile magazines and periodicals screen printing without publishing

111219 Kale farming, field, bedding plant and seed production

212324 Kaolin mining and/or beneficiating

327992 Kaolin, processing beyond beneficiation

611620 Karate instruction, camps or schools

713990 Kayaking, recreational

327420 Keene's cement manufacturing

321920 Kegs, wood, coopered, manufacturing

311119 Kelp meal and pellets, animal feed manufacturing

334515 Kelvin bridges (i.e., electrical measuring instruments) manufacturing

111998 Kenaf farming

112990 Kennels, breeding and raising stock for sale

711219 Kennels, dog racing

812910 Kennels, pet boarding

212391 Kernite mining and/or beneficiating

211111 Kerogen processing

324110 Kerosene manufacturing

333414 Kerosene space heaters manufacturing

311421 Ketchup manufacturing

325199 Ketone compounds, not specified elsewhere by process, manufacturing

332420 Kettles, heavy gauge metal, manufacturing

332510 Key blanks, metal, manufacturing

316993 Key cases (except metal) manufacturing

339911 Key cases, precious metal, manufacturing

333512 Key cutting machines, metal cutting type, manufacturing

811490 Key duplicating shops

332618 Key rings made from purchased wire

334119 Keyboards, computer peripheral equipment, manufacturing

339992 Keyboards, piano or organ, manufacturing

336322 Keyless entry systems, automotive, truck, and bus, manufacturing

423710 Keys and locks merchant wholesalers

334210 Keysets, telephone, manufacturing

621492 Kidney dialysis centers and clinics

236210 Kiln construction

321999 Kiln drying lumber

327124 Kiln furniture, clay, manufacturing

333994 Kilns (except cement, chemical, wood) manufacturing

333298 Kilns (i.e., cement, chemical, wood) manufacturing

423830 Kilns, industrial, merchant wholesalers

611110 Kindergartens

334519 Kinematic test and measuring equipment manufacturing

561910 Kit assembling and packaging services

336211 Kit car bodies manufacturing

423620 Kitchen appliances, household-type, electric, merchant wholesalers

327112 Kitchen articles, coarse earthenware, manufacturing

444190 Kitchen cabinet (except custom) stores

337110   Kitchen cabinets (except freestanding), stock or custom wood, manufacturing
238350   Kitchen cabinets and counters, constructed on site
423310   Kitchen cabinets, built in, merchant wholesalers
337122   Kitchen chairs (e.g., upholstered), wood, manufacturing
337124   Kitchen chairs (including upholstered), metal, manufacturing
337125   Kitchen chairs (including upholstered), plastics manufacturing
332211   Kitchen cutlery, nonprecious and precious plated metal, manufacturing
325612   Kitchen degreasing and cleaning preparations manufacturing
337124   Kitchen furniture, household-type, metal, manufacturing
337124   Kitchen furniture, metal household-type, manufacturing
337122   Kitchen furniture, wood household-type, manufacturing
238220   Kitchen sink and hardware installation
423440   Kitchen utensils, commercial, merchant wholesalers
332214   Kitchen utensils, fabricated metal (e.g., colanders, garlic presses, ice cream scoops, spatulas), manufacturing
423220   Kitchen utensils, household-type, merchant wholesalers
326199   Kitchen utensils, plastics, manufacturing
442299   Kitchenware stores
327112   Kitchenware, commercial and household-type, vitreous china, manufacturing
327112   Kitchenware, semivitreous earthenware, manufacturing
321999   Kitchenware, wood, manufacturing
339932   Kites manufacturing
111339   Kiwi fruit farming
334411   Klystron tubes manufacturing

314911   Knapsacks (e.g., backpacks, book bags) manufacturing
314911   Knapsacks, made from purchased woven or knitted materials
315211   Knickers, dress, men's and boys', cut and sew apparel contractors
315291   Knickers, infants', cut and sewn from purchased fabric (except apparel contractors)
315228   Knickers, men's and boys', cut and sewn from purchased fabric (except apparel contractors)
315212   Knickers, women's, girls', and infants', cut and sew apparel contractors
315239   Knickers, women's, misses', and girls', cut and sewn from purchased fabric (except apparel contractors)
337122   Knickknack shelves, wood, manufacturing
332211   Knife blades manufacturing
332211   Knife blanks manufacturing
335313   Knife switches, electric power switchgear-type, manufacturing
311812   Knishes (except frozen) made in commercial bakeries
311813   Knishes, frozen, manufacturing
315992   Knit gloves cut and sewn from purchased fabric (except apparel contractors)
315191   Knit gloves made in apparel knitting mills
315211   Knit gloves, men's and boys', cut and sew apparel contractors
315212   Knit gloves, women's, girls', and infants', cut and sew apparel contractors
313113   Knitting and crocheting thread manufacturing
313249   Knitting and finishing lace
313249   Knitting and finishing warp fabric
313241   Knitting and finishing weft fabric

313249 Knitting lace
333292 Knitting machinery
    manufacturing
313111 Knitting spun yarns (e.g.,
    cotton, manmade fiber, silk,
    wool) made from purchased
    fiber
313249 Knitting warp fabric
313241 Knitting weft fabric
332211 Knives (e.g., hunting, pocket,
    table nonprecious, table
    precious plated) manufacturing
423710 Knives (except disposable
    plastics) merchant wholesalers
333515 Knives and bits for
    metalworking lathes, planers,
    and shapers manufacturing
332212 Knives and bits for
    woodworking lathes, planers,
    and shapers manufacturing
424130 Knives, disposable plastics,
    merchant wholesalers
335211 Knives, household-type electric
    carving, manufacturing
339112 Knives, surgical, manufacturing
339992 Knobs, organ, manufacturing
321999 Knobs, wood, manufacturing
333292 Knot tying machinery for
    textiles manufacturing
333513 Knurling machines,
    metalworking, manufacturing
322130 Kraft liner board manufacturing
322121 Kraft paper stock manufacturing
212325 Kyanite mining and/or
    beneficiating
339942 Label making equipment,
    handheld, manufacturing
333993 Labeling (i.e., packaging)
    machinery manufacturing
561910 Labeling services
313221 Labels weaving
323110 Labels, lithographic (offset)
    printing, on a job-order basis
424310 Labels, textile, merchant
    wholesalers
561320 Labor (except farm) contractors
    (i.e., personnel suppliers)
561320 Labor (except farm) pools
115115 Labor contractors, farm
813930 Labor federations

561330 Labor leasing services
926150 Labor management negotiations
    boards, government
541612 Labor relations consulting
    services
926110 Labor statistics agencies
813930 Labor unions (except
    apprenticeship programs)
****** Laboratories (see specific type)
621512 Laboratories, dental X-ray
621511 Laboratories, medical (except
    radiological, X-ray)
621512 Laboratories, medical
    radiological or X-ray
334516 Laboratory analytical
    instruments (except optical)
    manufacturing
333314 Laboratory analytical optical
    instruments (e.g.,
    microscopes) manufacturing
311119 Laboratory animal feed
    manufacturing
112990 Laboratory animal production
    (e.g., guinea pigs, mice, rats)
315211 Laboratory coats, men's and
    boys', cut and sew apparel
    contractors
315225 Laboratory coats, men's and
    boys', cut and sewn from
    purchased fabric (except
    apparel contractors)
315212 Laboratory coats, women's, cut
    and sew apparel contractors
315239 Laboratory coats, women's,
    misses', and girls', cut and
    sewn from purchased fabric
    (except apparel contractors)
236220 Laboratory construction
423490 Laboratory equipment (except
    dental, medical, ophthalmic)
    merchant wholesalers
423450 Laboratory equipment, dental
    and medical, merchant
    wholesalers
238390 Laboratory furniture and
    equipment installation
327215 Laboratory glassware (e.g.,
    beakers, test tubes, vials)
    made from purchased glass

327212 Laboratory glassware (e.g., beakers, test tubes, vials) made in glass making plants

811219 Laboratory instrument repair and maintenance services

512199 Laboratory services, motion picture

334515 Laboratory standards testing instruments (e.g., capacitance, electrical resistance, inductance) manufacturing

541380 Laboratory testing (except medical, veterinary) services

621511 Laboratory testing services, medical (except radiological, X-ray)

621512 Laboratory testing services, medical radiological or X-ray

541940 Laboratory testing services, veterinary

339113 Laboratory-type evaporation apparatus manufacturing

333415 Laboratory-type freezers manufacturing

339113 Laboratory-type sample preparation apparatus manufacturing

333292 Lace and net making machinery manufacturing

316110 Lace leather manufacturing

313249 Lace manufacturing

313249 Lace products (except apparel) made in lace mills

314999 Lace, burnt-out, manufacturing

313221 Laces (e.g. shoe), textile, manufacturing

316999 Laces (e.g., shoe), leather, manufacturing

332812 Lacquering metals and metal products for the trade

333994 Lacquering ovens manufacturing

325510 Lacquers manufacturing

424950 Lacquers merchant wholesalers

325199 Lactic acid manufacturing

311514 Lactose manufacturing

332999 Ladder jacks, metal, manufacturing

321999 Ladder jacks, wood, manufacturing

321912 Ladder rounds or rungs, hardwood, manufacturing

423830 Ladders merchant wholesalers

321999 Ladders, extension, wood, manufacturing

326199 Ladders, fiberglass, manufacturing

332323 Ladders, metal chain, manufacturing

332323 Ladders, permanently installed, metal, manufacturing

332999 Ladders, portable metal, manufacturing

332313 Ladle bails, fabricated metal plate work, manufacturing

332313 Ladles, fabricated metal plate work, manufacturing

312120 Lager brewing

237110 Lagoon, sewage treatment construction

483211 Lake freight transportation (except on Great Lakes system)

483113 Lake freight transportation, Great Lakes (including St. Lawrence Seaway)

483212 Lake passenger transportation (except on Great Lakes system)

483114 Lake passenger transportation, Great Lakes (including St. Lawrence Seaway)

325132 Lakes (i.e., organic pigments) manufacturing

311611 Lamb carcasses, half carcasses, primal and sub-primal cuts, produced in slaughtering plants

112410 Lamb feedlots (except stockyards for transportation)

311612 Lamb, primal and sub-primal cuts, made from purchased carcasses

327215 Laminated glass made from purchased glass

327211 Laminated glass made in glass making plants

326130 Laminated plastics plate, rod, and sheet, manufacturing

321213 Laminated structural wood members (except trusses) manufacturing

321213 Laminated veneer lumber (LVL) manufacturing

322225 Laminating foil for flexible packaging applications

332813 Laminating metals and metal formed products without fabricating

322222 Laminating purchased foil sheets for nonpackaging applications

322226 Laminating purchased paperboard

322222 Laminating purchased papers for nonpackaging applications

322221 Laminating purchased papers for packaging applications

313320 Laminating purchased textiles

335311 Lamp ballasts manufacturing

327112 Lamp bases, pottery, manufacturing

325182 Lamp black manufacturing

335110 Lamp bulb parts (except glass blanks), electric, manufacturing

335110 Lamp bulbs and tubes, electric (i.e., fluorescent, incandescent filament, vapor), manufacturing

335110 Lamp bulbs and tubes, health, infrared and ultraviolet radiation, manufacturing

332618 Lamp frames, wire, made from purchased wire

335931 Lamp holders manufacturing

332999 Lamp shade frames, metal, manufacturing

335121 Lamp shades (except glass, plastics), residential, manufacturing

327215 Lamp shades made from purchased glass

327212 Lamp shades made in glass making plants

326199 Lamp shades, plastics, manufacturing

442299 Lamp shops, electric

335931 Lamp sockets and receptacles (i.e., electric wiring devices) manufacturing

423220 Lamps (i.e., lighting fixtures) merchant wholesalers

335122 Lamps (i.e., lighting fixtures), commercial, industrial, and institutional, manufacturing

335121 Lamps (i.e., lighting fixtures), residential, electric, manufacturing

335129 Lamps, insect, electric fixture, manufacturing

334517 Lamps, X-ray, manufacturing

237210 Land (except cemeteries) subdividers

237210 Land acquisition, assembling and subdividing

238910 Land clearing

237990 Land drainage contractors

238910 Land leveling contractors

924120 Land management program administration

423820 Land preparation machinery, agricultural, merchant wholesalers

333120 Land preparation machinery, construction, manufacturing

423810 Land preparation machinery, construction, merchant wholesalers

925120 Land redevelopment agencies, government

531190 Land rental or leasing

237210 Land subdividing and utility installation (e.g., electric, sewer and water)

541370 Land surveying services

335312 Land transportation motors and generators manufacturing

541320 Land use design services

541320 Land use planning services

562212 Landfills

332312 Landing mats, aircraft, metal, manufacturing

541320 Landscape architects' offices

541320 Landscape architects' private practices

541320 Landscape architectural services

561730 Landscape care and maintenance services
541320 Landscape consulting services
561730 Landscape contractors (except construction)
541320 Landscape design services
561730 Landscape installation services
541320 Landscape planning services
561730 Landscaping services (except planning)
541930 Language interpretation services
541720 Language research and development services
611630 Language schools
541930 Language services (e.g., interpretation, sign, translation)
541930 Language translation services
335129 Lanterns (e.g., carbide, electric, gas, gasoline, kerosene) manufacturing
339913 Lapidary work manufacturing
334111 Laptop computers manufacturing
311613 Lard made from purchased fat
424470 Lard merchant wholesalers
311611 Lard produced in slaughtering plants
333512 Laser boring, drilling, and cutting machines, metalworking, manufacturing
334413 Laser diodes manufacturing
532230 Laser disc, video, rental
334612 Laser disks, prerecorded video, mass reproducing
334510 Laser equipment, electromedical, manufacturing
621493 Laser surgery centers, freestanding
334510 Laser systems and equipment, medical, manufacturing
333992 Laser welding equipment manufacturing
316999 Lashes (i.e., whips) manufacturing
321999 Last sole patterns, all materials, manufacturing
212325 Laterite mining and/or beneficiating

326299 Latex foam rubber manufacturing
326299 Latex foam rubber products manufacturing
325510 Latex paint (i.e., water based) manufacturing
325212 Latex rubber, synthetic, manufacturing
332323 Lath, expanded metal, manufacturing
321219 Lath, fiber, manufacturing
327420 Lath, gypsum, manufacturing
321912 Lath, wood, manufacturing
333512 Lathes, metalworking, manufacturing
333210 Lathes, woodworking-type, manufacturing
238310 Lathing contractors
321912 Lathmills, wood
316110 Latigo leather manufacturing
812332 Laundered mat and rug supply services
812332 Launderers, industrial
812310 Launderettes
812320 Laundries (except coin-operated, linen supply, uniform supply)
812310 Laundries, coin-operated or similar self-service
812331 Laundries, linen and uniform supply
812310 Laundromats
812320 Laundry and drycleaning agents
314911 Laundry bags made from purchased woven or knitted materials
812320 Laundry drop-off and pick-up sites
335224 Laundry equipment (e.g., dryers, washers), household-type, manufacturing
333312 Laundry extractors manufacturing
332439 Laundry hampers, light gauge metal, manufacturing
337125 Laundry hampers, rattan, reed, wicker or willow, manufacturing

812310 Laundry machine routes (i.e., concession operators), coin-operated or similar self-service

333312 Laundry machinery and equipment (except household-type) manufacturing

423620 Laundry machinery and equipment, household-type (e.g., dryers, washers), merchant wholesalers

423850 Laundry machinery, equipment, and supplies, commercial, merchant wholesalers

314999 Laundry nets made from purchased materials

333312 Laundry pressing machines (except household-type) manufacturing

812320 Laundry services (except coin-operated, linen supply, uniform supply)

812310 Laundry services, coin-operated or similar self-service

812332 Laundry services, industrial

812331 Laundry services, linen supply

325611 Laundry soap, chips, and powder manufacturing

424690 Laundry soap, chips, and powder, merchant wholesalers

332998 Laundry tubs, metal, manufacturing

326191 Laundry tubs, plastics, manufacturing

325199 Lauric acid esters and amines manufacturing

332998 Lavatories, metal, manufacturing

327111 Lavatories, vitreous china, manufacturing

922190 Law enforcement statistics centers, government

541110 Law firms

541110 Law offices

541110 Law practices

611310 Law schools

333112 Lawn and garden equipment manufacturing

811411 Lawn and garden equipment repair and maintenance services without retailing new lawn and garden equipment

713990 Lawn bowling clubs

561730 Lawn care services (e.g., fertilizing, mowing, seeding, spraying)

424910 Lawn care supplies (e.g., chemicals, fertilizers, pesticides) merchant wholesalers

332212 Lawn edgers, nonpowered, manufacturing

333112 Lawn edgers, powered, manufacturing

561730 Lawn fertilizing services

337125 Lawn furniture (except concrete, metal, stone, wood) manufacturing

337124 Lawn furniture, metal, manufacturing

337122 Lawn furniture, wood, manufacturing

332919 Lawn hose nozzles and lawn sprinklers manufacturing

423820 Lawn maintenance machinery and equipment merchant wholesalers

561730 Lawn maintenance services

811411 Lawn mower repair and maintenance shops without retailing new lawn mowers

423820 Lawn mowers merchant wholesalers

561730 Lawn mowing services

444210 Lawn power equipment stores

561730 Lawn seeding services

561730 Lawn spraying services

238220 Lawn sprinkler system installation

444220 Lawn supply stores

532490 Lawnmower rental or leasing

333112 Lawnmowers (except agricultural-type), powered, manufacturing

333111 Lawnmowers, agricultural-type, powered, manufacturing

332212 Lawnmowers, nonpowered, manufacturing

541110 Lawyers' offices

541110 Lawyers' private practices

325412 Laxative preparations manufacturing

112310	Layer-type chicken production
334419	LCD (liquid crystal display) unit screens manufacturing
212291	Leaching of uranium, radium, or vanadium ores
335911	Lead acid storage batteries manufacturing
331491	Lead and lead alloy bar, pipe, plate, rod, sheet, strip, and tubing made from purchased metals or scrap
325131	Lead based pigments manufacturing
331528	Lead castings (except die-castings), unfinished, manufacturing
331522	Lead die-castings, unfinished, manufacturing
332999	Lead foil not made in rolling mills
238390	Lead lining walls for x-ray room contractors
212231	Lead ore mine site development for own account
212231	Lead ore mining and/or beneficiating
325188	Lead oxides (except pigments) manufacturing
562910	Lead paint abatement services
562910	Lead paint removal contractors
325131	Lead pigments manufacturing
331492	Lead recovering from scrap and/or alloying purchased metals
331491	Lead rolling, drawing, or extruding purchased metals or scrap
325188	Lead silicate manufacturing
331419	Lead smelting and refining, primary
327992	Lead, black (i.e., natural graphite), ground, refined, or blended, manufacturing
335110	Lead-in wires, electric lamp, made from purchased wire
212231	Lead-zinc ore mining and/or beneficiating
333112	Leaf blowers manufacturing
332212	Leaf skimmers and rakes, nonpowered swimming pool, manufacturing
332611	Leaf springs, heavy gauge metal, manufacturing
424590	Leaf tobacco merchant wholesalers
332999	Leaf, metal, manufacturing
334519	Leak detectors, water, manufacturing
813920	Learned societies
611691	Learning centers offering remedial courses
541720	Learning disabilities research and development services
211111	Lease condensate production
213112	Lease tank cleaning and repairing on a contract basis
316999	Leashes, dog, manufacturing
******	Leasing—see type of property or article being leased
522220	Leasing in combination with sales financing
315292	Leather apparel (e.g., capes, coats, hats, jackets) (except apparel contractors) manufacturing
315211	Leather apparel (e.g., capes, coats, hats, jackets), men's and boys', cut and sew apparel contractors
315212	Leather apparel (e.g., capes, coats, hats, jackets), women's, girls', and infants', cut and sew apparel contractors
316999	Leather belting manufacturing
315292	Leather clothing (except apparel contractors) manufacturing
315212	Leather clothing manufacturing, women's, girls', and infants', cut and sew apparel contractors
315211	Leather clothing, men's and boys', cut and sew apparel contractors
448190	Leather coat stores
316110	Leather coloring, cutting, embossing, and japanning
316110	Leather converters

424990 Leather cut stock (except boot, shoe) merchant wholesalers

316999 Leather cut stock for shoe and boot manufacturing

424340 Leather cut stock for shoe and boot merchant wholesalers

316219 Leather footwear (except house slippers, men's, women's) manufacturing

316213 Leather footwear, men's (except athletic, slippers), manufacturing

316212 Leather footwear, slippers, manufacturing

316214 Leather footwear, women's (except athletic, slippers), manufacturing

812320 Leather garment cleaning services

315211 Leather gloves or mittens (except athletic), men's and boys', cut and sew apparel contractors

315212 Leather gloves or mittens (except athletic), women's, girls', and infants', cut and sew apparel contractors

315992 Leather gloves or mittens (except athletic, cut and sewn apparel contractors) manufacturing

339920 Leather gloves, athletic, manufacturing

424990 Leather goods (except belting, footwear, handbags, gloves, luggage) merchant wholesalers

811430 Leather goods repair shops without retailing new leather goods

448320 Leather goods stores

316993 Leather goods, small personal (e.g., coin purses, eyeglass cases, key cases), manufacturing

316992 Leather handbags and purses manufacturing

316212 Leather house slippers manufacturing

316991 Leather luggage manufacturing

316110 Leather tanning, currying, and finishing

316219 Leather upper athletic footwear manufacturing

316999 Leather welting manufacturing

333298 Leather working machinery manufacturing

313320 Leather, artificial, made from purchased fabric

322226 Leatherboard (i.e., paperboard based) made from purchased paperboard

322130 Leatherboard (i.e., paperboard based) made in paperboard mills

311225 Lecithin made from purchased oils

311223 Lecithin, cottonseed, made in crushing mills

311222 Lecithin, soybean, made in crushing mills

334413 LED (light emitting diode) manufacturing

111219 Leek farming, field, bedding plant and seed production

541110 Legal aid services

922130 Legal counsel offices, government

315119 Leggings knitting or knitting and finishing

315291 Leggings, infants', cut and sewn from purchased fabric (except apparel contractors)

316999 Leggings, welder's, leather, manufacturing

315212 Leggings, women's, girls', and infants', cut and sew apparel contractors

315239 Leggings, women's, misses' and girls', cut and sewn from purchased fabric (except apparel contractors)

315239 Leggings, women's, misses', and girls', cut and sewn from purchased fabric (except apparel contractors)

921140 Legislative and executive office combinations.

921120 Legislative assemblies

921120	Legislative bodies (e.g., federal, local, and state)
921120	Legislative commissions
111320	Lemon groves
325998	Lemon oil manufacturing
519120	Lending libraries
423460	Lens blanks, ophthalmic, merchant wholesalers
327215	Lens blanks, optical and ophthalmic, made from purchased glass
327212	Lens blanks, optical and ophthalmic, made in glass making plants
326199	Lens blanks, plastics ophthalmic or optical, manufacturing
333314	Lens coating (except ophthalmic)
339115	Lens coating, ophthalmic
333314	Lens grinding (except ophthalmic)
339115	Lens grinding, ophthalmic (except in retail stores)
446130	Lens grinding, ophthalmic, in retail stores
333315	Lens hoods, camera, manufacturing
333314	Lens mounting (except ophthalmic)
339115	Lens mounts, ophthalmic, manufacturing
333314	Lens polishing (except ophthalmic)
339115	Lens polishing, ophthalmic
333314	Lenses (except ophthalmic) manufacturing
339115	Lenses, ophthalmic, manufacturing
111130	Lentil farming, dry, field and seed production
315191	Leotards made in apparel knitting mills
315212	Leotards, women's, girls', and infants', cut and sew apparel contractors
315239	Leotards, women's, misses', and girls', cut and sewn from purchased fabric (except apparel contractors)

212393	Lepidolite mining and/or beneficiating
622310	Leprosy hospitals
******	Lessors—see specific type of asset or property being rented or leased
531130	Lessors of miniwarehouses
531120	Lessors of nonresidential buildings (except miniwarehouses)
531110	Lessors of residential buildings and dwellings
531130	Lessors of self storage units
333313	Letter folding, stuffing, and sealing machinery manufacturing
333515	Letter pins (e.g., gauging, measuring) manufacturing
561410	Letter writing services
325910	Letterpress inks manufacturing
323122	Letterpress plate preparation services
333293	Letterpress printing presses manufacturing
339950	Letters for signs manufacturing
322231	Letters, die-cut, made from purchased cardboard
111219	Lettuce farming, field, bedding plant and seed production
237990	Levee construction
334513	Level and bulk measuring instruments, industrial process-type, manufacturing
334519	Level gauges, radiation-type, manufacturing
334519	Levels and tapes, surveying, manufacturing
332212	Levels, carpenter's, manufacturing
524126	Liability insurance carriers, direct
519120	Libraries (except motion picture stock footage, motion picture commercial distribution)
512199	Libraries, motion picture stock footage film
512199	Libraries, videotape, stock footage
236220	Library construction

561990 License issuing services (except government), motor vehicle

621399 Licensed practical nurses' (LPNs) offices (e.g., centers, clinics)

926130 Licensing and inspecting of utilities

926150 Licensing and permit issuance for business operations, government

926150 Licensing and permit issuance for professional occupations, government

926120 Licensing of transportation equipment, facilities, and services

311340 Licorice candy manufacturing

332431 Lids and ends, can, light gauge metal, manufacturing

332115 Lids, jar, metal, stamping

561611 Lie detection services

334519 Lie detectors manufacturing

611699 Life guard training

524210 Life insurance agencies

524113 Life insurance carriers, direct

339113 Life preservers manufacturing

524130 Life reinsurance carriers

541712 Life sciences research and development laboratories or services (except biotechnology research and development)

423830 Lift trucks, industrial, merchant wholesalers

316999 Lifts, heel, leather, manufacturing

333298 Light bulb and tube (i.e., electric lamp) machinery manufacturing

335110 Light bulbs manufacturing

423610 Light bulbs merchant wholesalers

335110 Light bulbs, sealed beam automotive, manufacturing

334413 Light emitting diodes (LED) manufacturing

333315 Light meters, photographic, manufacturing

336510 Light rail cars and equipment manufacturing

237990 Light rail system construction

485119 Light rail systems (except mixed mode), commuter

334511 Light reconnaissance and surveillance systems and equipment manufacturing

334512 Light responsive appliance controls manufacturing

441110 Light utility truck dealers, new only or new and used

441120 Light utility truck dealers, used only

336112 Light utility trucks assembling on chassis of own manufacture

325998 Lighter fluids (e.g., charcoal, cigarette) manufacturing

483211 Lighterage (i.e., freight transportation except vessel supply services)

339999 Lighters, cigar and cigarette (except motor vehicle, precious metal), manufacturing

339911 Lighters, cigar and cigarette, clad with precious metal, manufacturing

424990 Lighters, cigar and cigarette, merchant wholesalers

488310 Lighthouse operation

335991 Lighting carbons manufacturing

541490 Lighting design services

423990 Lighting equipment, gas, merchant wholesalers

444190 Lighting fixture stores

335129 Lighting fixtures, airport (e.g., approach, ramp, runway, taxi), manufacturing

335122 Lighting fixtures, commercial electric, manufacturing

423610 Lighting fixtures, electric, merchant wholesalers

335122 Lighting fixtures, industrial electric, manufacturing

335122 Lighting fixtures, institutional electric, manufacturing

335129 Lighting fixtures, nonelectric (e.g., propane, kerosene, carbide), manufacturing

335121 Lighting fixtures, residential electric, manufacturing

561790	Lighting maintenance services (e.g., bulb and fuse replacement and cleaning)
238210	Lighting system installation
711510	Lighting technicians, theatrical, independent
335311	Lighting transformers manufacturing
335311	Lighting transformers, street and airport, manufacturing
335931	Lightning arrestors and coils manufacturing
238290	Lightning protection equipment (e.g., lightning rod) installation
335931	Lightning protection equipment manufacturing
238290	Lightning rod and conductor installation
325211	Lignin plastics manufacturing
213113	Lignite mining services (except site preparation and related construction contractor activities) on a contract basis
212111	Lignite surface mining and/or beneficiating
111130	Lima bean farming, dry, field and seed production
339113	Limbs, artificial, manufacturing
423320	Lime (except agricultural) merchant wholesalers
111320	Lime groves
325998	Lime oil manufacturing
327410	Lime production
212312	Lime rock, ground, mining and/or beneficiating
424910	Lime, agricultural, merchant wholesalers
212312	Limestone (except bituminous) crushed and broken stone mining and/or beneficiating
212312	Limestone beneficiating plants (e.g., grinding or pulverizing)
212311	Limestone mining or quarrying
212319	Limestone, bituminous, mining and/or beneficiating
325320	Lime-sulfur fungicides manufacturing

334512	Limit controls (e.g., air-conditioning, appliance, heating) manufacturing
511199	Limited editions art print publishers (except exclusive Internet publishing)
452990	Limited price variety stores
212210	Limonite mining and/or beneficiating
532111	Limousine rental without driver
485320	Limousine services (except shuttle services)
485320	Limousines for hire with driver (except taxis)
325320	Lindane pesticides manufacturing
334512	Line or limit control for electric heat manufacturing
561730	Line slash (i.e., rights of way) maintenance services
238910	Line slashing or cutting (except maintenance)
335311	Line voltage regulators (i.e., electric transformers) manufacturing
335999	Linear accelerators manufacturing
332991	Linear ball bearings manufacturing
334514	Linear counters manufacturing
325222	Linear esters fibers and filaments manufacturing
332991	Linear roller bearings manufacturing
442299	Linen stores
812331	Linen supply services
423220	Linens (e.g., bath, bed, table) merchant wholesalers
314129	Linens made from purchased materials
327123	Liner brick and plates, vitrified clay, manufacturing
332313	Liners, industrial, fabricated metal plate work, manufacturing
114111	Lingcod fishing
424330	Lingerie merchant wholesalers
448190	Lingerie stores
315212	Lingerie, women's, cut and sew apparel contractors

315231 Lingerie, women's, misses', and girls', cut and sewn from purchased fabric (except apparel contractors)
316110 Lining leather manufacturing
316999 Linings, boot and shoe, leather, manufacturing
314999 Linings, casket, manufacturing
315211 Linings, hat, men's, cut and sew apparel contractors
315999 Linings, hat, men's, cut and sewn from purchased fabric (except apparel contractors)
314999 Linings, luggage, manufacturing
332999 Linings, metal safe and vault, manufacturing
332994 Links, ammunition (i.e., 30 mm. or less, 1.18 inch or less), manufacturing
332995 Links, ammunition (i.e., more than 30 mm., more than 1.18 inch), manufacturing
325199 Linoleic acid esters and amines manufacturing
326192 Linoleum floor coverings manufacturing
238330 Linoleum, installation only
333293 Linotype machines manufacturing
311225 Linseed oil made from purchased oils
311223 Linseed oil, cake and meal, made in crushing mills
327390 Lintels, concrete, manufacturing
325412 Lip balms manufacturing
325620 Lipsticks manufacturing
424690 Liquefied gases (except LP) merchant wholesalers
424710 Liquefied petroleum gas (LPG) bulk stations and terminals
332420 Liquefied petroleum gas (LPG) cylinders manufacturing
454312 Liquefied petroleum gas (LPG) dealers, direct selling
221210 Liquefied petroleum gas (LPG) distribution through mains
324110 Liquefied petroleum gas (LPG) made in refineries

424720 Liquefied petroleum gas (LPG) merchant wholesalers (except bulk stations, terminals)
211112 Liquefied petroleum gases (LPG), natural
325120 Liquid air manufacturing
334513 Liquid analysis instruments, industrial process-type, manufacturing
311313 Liquid beet syrup manufacturing
334516 Liquid chromatographic instruments, laboratory-type, manufacturing
334513 Liquid concentration instruments, industrial process-type, manufacturing
334514 Liquid flow meters manufacturing
211112 Liquid hydrocarbons recovered from oil and gas field gases
334512 Liquid level controls, residential and commercial heating-type, manufacturing
334513 Liquid level instruments, industrial process-type, manufacturing
332420 Liquid oxygen tanks manufacturing
311313 Liquid sugar made from beet sugar
311312 Liquid sugar made from purchased raw cane sugar
311311 Liquid sugar made in sugarcane mill
211112 Liquids, natural gas (e.g., ethane, isobutane, natural gasoline, propane) recovered from oil and gas field gases
445310 Liquor stores, package
311320 Liquor, chocolate, made from cacao beans
311330 Liquor, chocolate, made from purchased chocolate
424820 Liquors merchant wholesalers
312130 Liquors, brandy, distilling and blending
424820 Liquors, distilled, merchant wholesalers

312140 Liquors, distilling and blending (except brandy)
339942 List finders and roledex address files manufacturing
531390 Listing services, real estate
711410 Literary agents
325131 Litharge manufacturing
335912 Lithium batteries, primary, manufacturing
325188 Lithium compounds, not specified elsewhere by process, manufacturing
212393 Lithium mineral mining and/or beneficiating
325910 Lithographic inks manufacturing
323122 Lithographic plate preparation services
323110 Lithographic printing (except books, manifold business forms, printing grey goods, quick printing)
333293 Lithographic printing presses manufacturing
325131 Lithopone manufacturing
334510 Lithotripters manufacturing
711310 Live arts center operators
424990 Live bait merchant wholesalers
711310 Live theater operators
332995 Livens projectors (i.e., ordnance) manufacturing
541690 Livestock breeding consulting services
115210 Livestock breeding services (except consulting)
424910 Livestock feeds merchant wholesalers
311119 Livestock feeds, supplements, concentrates and premixes, manufacturing
541940 Livestock inspecting and testing services, veterinary
115210 Livestock spraying
484220 Livestock trucking, local
484230 Livestock trucking, long-distance
541940 Livestock veterinary services
337124 Living room furniture (except upholstered), metal, manufacturing

337122 Living room furniture (except upholstered), wood, manufacturing
337121 Living room furniture, upholstered, manufacturing
112990 Llama production
334418 Loaded computer boards manufacturing
423430 Loaded computer boards merchant wholesalers
333120 Loaders, shovel, manufacturing
332993 Loading and assembling bombs
488490 Loading and unloading at truck terminals
488320 Loading and unloading services at ports and harbors
488210 Loading and unloading services at rail terminals
333131 Loading machines, underground mining, manufacturing
334418 Loading printed circuit boards
522310 Loan brokerages
522310 Loan brokers' or agents' offices (i.e., independent)
522291 Loan companies (i.e., consumer, personal, small, student)
522292 Loan correspondents (i.e., lending funds with real estate as collateral)
522390 Loan servicing
541820 Lobbying services
541820 Lobbyists' offices
114112 Lobster fishing
334210 Local area network (LAN) communications equipment (e.g., bridges, gateways, routers) manufacturing
541512 Local area network (LAN) computer systems integration design services
611420 Local area network (LAN) management training
485113 Local bus services (except mixed mode)
492210 Local letter and parcel delivery services (except as part of intercity carrier network, U.S. Postal Service)

517410 Long-distance telephone satellite communication carriers
488320 Longshoremen services
333292 Loom bobbins manufacturing
333292 Loom reeds manufacturing
333292 Looms for textiles manufacturing
333292 Loopers for textiles manufacturing
323118 Looseleaf binders and devices manufacturing
424120 Looseleaf binders merchant wholesalers
322233 Looseleaf fillers and paper made from purchased paper
322121 Looseleaf fillers and paper made in paper mills
524291 Loss control consultants
325620 Lotions (e.g., body, face, hand) manufacturing
713290 Lottery control boards (i.e., operating lotteries)
921130 Lottery control boards, nonoperating
713290 Lottery corporations
713290 Lottery ticket sales agents (except retail stores)
334119 Lottery ticket sales terminal manufacturing
713290 Lottery ticket vendors (except retail stores)
334310 Loudspeakers manufacturing
722410 Lounges, cocktail
315192 Lounging robes and dressing gowns made in apparel knitting mills
315291 Lounging robes and dressing gowns, infants', cut and sewn from purchased fabric (except apparel contractors)
315211 Lounging robes and dressing gowns, men's and boys', cut and sew apparel contractors
315221 Lounging robes and dressing gowns, men's and boys', cut and sewn from purchased fabric (except apparel contractors)

315212 Lounging robes and dressing gowns, women's, girls', and infants', cut and sew apparel contractors
315231 Lounging robes and dressing gowns, women's, misses', and girls', cut and sewn from purchased fabric (except apparel contractors)
333314 Loupes (e.g., jewelers) manufacturing
321911 Louver windows and doors, made from purchased glass with wood frame
332321 Louver windows, metal, manufacturing
332322 Louvers, sheet metal (except stampings), manufacturing
236117 Low income housing construction operative builders
236116 Low income housing, multifamily, construction general contractors
236115 Low income housing, single-family, construction general contractors
238160 Low slope roofing installation
238210 Low voltage electrical work
335121 Low voltage lighting equipment, residential, electric, manufacturing
236116 Low-rise apartment construction general contractors
236117 Low-rise apartment operative builders
311340 Lozenges, nonmedicated, candy, manufacturing
621399 LPNs' (licensed practical nurses) offices (e.g., centers, clinics)
484122 LTL (less-than-truckload) long-distance freight trucking
424710 Lubricating oils and greases bulk stations and terminals
324110 Lubricating oils and greases made in petroleum refineries
424720 Lubricating oils and greases merchant wholesalers (except bulk stations, terminals)

324191 Lubricating oils and greases, petroleum, made from refined petroleum
325998 Lubricating oils and greases, synthetic, manufacturing
811191 Lubrication shops, automotive
336510 Lubrication systems, locomotive (except pumps), manufacturing
332510 Luggage hardware, metal, manufacturing
314999 Luggage linings manufacturing
423990 Luggage merchant wholesalers
336399 Luggage racks, car top, automotive, truck, and bus, manufacturing
811430 Luggage repair shops without retailing new luggage
448320 Luggage stores
316991 Luggage, all materials, manufacturing
335931 Lugs and connectors, electrical, manufacturing
423610 Lugs and connectors, electrical, merchant wholesalers
423310 Lumber (e.g., dressed, finished, rough) merchant wholesalers
321113 Lumber (i.e., rough, dressed) made from logs or bolts
561990 Lumber grading services
444190 Lumber retailing yards
493190 Lumber storage terminals
321113 Lumber, hardwood dimension, made from logs or bolts
321912 Lumber, hardwood dimension, resawing purchased lumber
321999 Lumber, kiln drying
321213 Lumber, parallel strand, manufacturing
321113 Lumber, softwood dimension, made from logs or bolts
321912 Lumber, softwood dimension, resawing purchased lumber
335122 Luminous panel ceilings, electric, manufacturing
335311 Luminous tube transformers manufacturing
332439 Lunch boxes, light gauge metal, manufacturing
722330 Lunch wagons

311612 Luncheon meat (except poultry) made from purchased carcasses
311611 Luncheon meat (except poultry) produced in slaughtering plants
311615 Luncheon meat, poultry, manufacturing
532111 Luxury automobile rental
485320 Luxury automobiles for hire with driver (except taxis)
321213 LVL (laminated veneer lumber) manufacturing
325612 Lye, household-type, manufacturing
111335 Macadamia farming
424490 Macaroni merchant wholesalers
311823 Macaroni, dry, manufacturing
311991 Macaroni, fresh, manufacturing
311412 Macaroni, frozen, manufacturing
332212 Machetes manufacturing
332999 Machine bases, metal, manufacturing
332322 Machine guards, sheet metal (except stampings), manufacturing
332994 Machine gun belts (i.e., 30 mm. or less, 1.18 inch or less) manufacturing
332995 Machine gun belts (i.e., more than 30 mm., more than 1.18 inch) manufacturing
332994 Machine guns (i.e., 30 mm. or less, 1.18 inch or less) manufacturing
332995 Machine guns (i.e., more than 30 mm., more than 1.18 inch) manufacturing
332722 Machine keys, metal, manufacturing
332212 Machine knives (except metal cutting) manufacturing
333515 Machine knives, metal cutting, manufacturing
238290 Machine rigging
332710 Machine shops
333515 Machine tool attachments and accessories manufacturing

335311	Machine tool transformers manufacturing
423830	Machine tools and accessories merchant wholesalers
811310	Machine tools repair and maintenance services
333512	Machine tools, metal cutting, manufacturing
333513	Machine tools, metal forming, manufacturing
238290	Machinery and equipment, large-scale, installation
522220	Machinery finance leasing
238910	Machinery, construction (except cranes), rental with operator
423420	Machines, office, merchant wholesalers
332212	Machinists' precision measuring tools (except optical) manufacturing
423830	Machinists' precision measuring tools merchant wholesalers
334511	Machmeters manufacturing
114111	Mackerel fishing
315291	Mackinaws, infants', cut and sewn from purchased fabric (except apparel contractors)
315211	Mackinaws, men's and boys', cut and sew apparel contractors
315228	Mackinaws, men's and boys', cut and sewn from purchased fabric (except apparel contractors)
315212	Mackinaws, women's, girls', and infants', cut and sew apparel contractors
315239	Mackinaws, women's, misses', and girls', cut and sewn from purchased fabric (except apparel contractors)
541840	Magazine advertising representatives (i.e., independent of media owners)
511120	Magazine publishers (except exclusive Internet publishing)
511120	Magazine publishers and printing combined
519130	Magazine publishers, exclusively on Internet
337122	Magazine racks, wood, manufacturing
451212	Magazine stands (i.e., permanent)
323112	Magazines and periodicals flexographic printing without publishing
323111	Magazines and periodicals gravure printing without publishing
323110	Magazines and periodicals lithographic (offset) printing without publishing
323119	Magazines and periodicals printing (except flexographic, gravure, lithographic, quick, screen) without publishing
323113	Magazines and periodicals screen printing without publishing
424920	Magazines merchant wholesalers
711190	Magic shows
451120	Magic supply stores
711510	Magicians, independent
327125	Magnesia refractory cement manufacturing
325411	Magnesia, medicinal, uncompounded, manufacturing
212325	Magnesite mining and/or beneficiating
327992	Magnesite, crude (e.g., calcined, dead-burned, ground), manufacturing
331491	Magnesium and magnesium alloy bar, rod, shape, sheet, strip, and tubing made from purchased metals or scrap
325188	Magnesium carbonate manufacturing
331528	Magnesium castings (except die-castings), unfinished, manufacturing
325188	Magnesium chloride manufacturing
325188	Magnesium compounds, not specified elsewhere by process, manufacturing
331522	Magnesium die-castings, unfinished, manufacturing

331491 Magnesium foil made by rolling purchased metals or scrap

332999 Magnesium foil not made in rolling mills

331492 Magnesium recovering from scrap and/or alloying purchased metals

331419 Magnesium refining, primary

331491 Magnesium rolling, drawing, or extruding purchased metals or scrap

331422 Magnet wire, insulated, made from purchased copper in wire drawing plants

331319 Magnet wire, insulated, made in aluminum wire drawing plants

331491 Magnet wire, nonferrous metals (except aluminum, copper), made from purchased nonferrous metals (except aluminum, copper) in wire drawing plants

334613 Magnetic and optical media, blank, manufacturing

334514 Magnetic counters manufacturing

334513 Magnetic flow meters, industrial process-type, manufacturing

333513 Magnetic forming machines, metalworking, manufacturing

541360 Magnetic geophysical surveying services

334119 Magnetic ink recognition devices, computer peripheral equipment, manufacturing

334613 Magnetic recording media for tapes, cassettes, and disks, manufacturing

621512 Magnetic resonance imaging (MRI) centers

334510 Magnetic resonance imaging (MRI) medical diagnostic equipment manufacturing

334516 Magnetic resonance imaging (MRI) type apparatus (except medical diagnostic) manufacturing

334613 Magnetic tapes, cassettes and disks, blank, manufacturing

423690 Magnetic tapes, cassettes, and disks, blank, merchant wholesalers

334112 Magnetic/optical combination storage units for computers manufacturing

334519 Magnetometers manufacturing

334411 Magnetron tubes manufacturing

327113 Magnets, permanent, ceramic or ferrite, manufacturing

332999 Magnets, permanent, metallic, manufacturing

339115 Magnifiers, corrective vision-type, manufacturing

333314 Magnifying glasses (except corrective vision-type) manufacturing

333314 Magnifying instruments, optical, manufacturing

114111 Mahimahi fishing

561311 Maid registries

561720 Maid services (i.e., cleaning services)

238990 Mail box units, outdoor, multiple box-type, erection

337215 Mail carrier cases and tables, wood, manufacturing

332322 Mail chutes, sheet metal (except stampings), manufacturing

561499 Mail consolidation services

333313 Mail handling machinery, post office-type, manufacturing

561499 Mail presorting services

561431 Mailbox rental centers, private

561431 Mailbox rental services combined with one or more other office support services, private

332439 Mailboxes, light gauge metal, manufacturing

322214 Mailing cases and tubes, paper fiber (i.e., all-fiber, nonfiber ends of any material), made from purchased paperboard

532420 Mailing equipment rental or leasing

511140 Mailing list publishers (except exclusive Internet publishing)

423420 Mailing machines merchant wholesalers

454113	Mail-order houses
334111	Mainframe computers manufacturing
488190	Maintenance and repair services, aircraft (except factory conversion, factory overhaul, factory rebuilding)
561730	Maintenance of plants and shrubs in buildings
488210	Maintenance of rights-of-way and structures, railway
488119	Maintenance services, runway
488310	Maintenance services, waterfront terminal (except dredging)
711211	Major league baseball clubs
812112	Make-up (except permanent) salons
325620	Make-up (i.e., cosmetics) manufacturing
812199	Make-up salons, permanent
523110	Making markets for securities
337125	Malacca furniture (except upholstered), household-type, manufacturing
325320	Malathion insecticides manufacturing
325192	Maleic anhydride manufacturing
531120	Mall property operation (i.e., not operating contained businesses) rental or leasing
331511	Malleable iron foundries
332212	Mallets (e.g., rubber, wood) manufacturing
321999	Mallets, wood, manufacturing
325199	Malonic dinitrile manufacturing
524126	Malpractice insurance carriers, direct
311942	Malt extract and syrups manufacturing
424490	Malt extract merchant wholesalers
311213	Malt flour manufacturing
312120	Malt liquor brewing
311213	Malt manufacturing
424490	Malt merchant wholesalers
333294	Malt milling machinery manufacturing
311213	Malt sprouts manufacturing
311514	Malted milk manufacturing

311213	Malting (germinating and drying grains)
311221	Maltodextrins manufacturing
621512	Mammogram (i.e., breast imaging) centers
711410	Management agencies for artists, entertainers, and other public figures
611430	Management development training
561110	Management services (except complete operation of client's business)
115116	Management services, farm
711310	Managers of agricultural fairs with facilities
711320	Managers of agricultural fairs without facilities
711310	Managers of arts events with facilities
711320	Managers of arts events without facilities
711310	Managers of festivals with facilities
711320	Managers of festivals without facilities
711310	Managers of live performing arts productions (e.g., concerts) with facilities
711320	Managers of live performing arts productions (e.g., concerts) without facilities
711310	Managers of sports events with facilities
711320	Managers of sports events without facilities
531312	Managers' offices, commercial condominium
531312	Managers' offices, commercial real estate
531312	Managers' offices, nonresidential real estate
531311	Managers' offices, residential condominium
531311	Managers' offices, residential real estate
711410	Managers, authors'
711410	Managers, celebrities'
561920	Managers, convention
711410	Managers, entertainers'

711410 Managers, public figures'
711410 Managers, sports figures'
561920 Managers, trade fair or show
531312 Managing commercial condominiums
531312 Managing commercial real estate
531311 Managing cooperative apartments
523920 Managing investment funds
523920 Managing mutual funds
561110 Managing offices of dentists
561110 Managing offices of physicians and surgeons
561110 Managing offices of professionals (e.g., dentists, physicians, surgeons)
523920 Managing personal investment trusts
531311 Managing residential condominiums
531311 Managing residential real estate
523920 Managing trusts
111320 Mandarin groves
339992 Mandolins manufacturing
333515 Mandrels (i.e., a machine tool accessory) manufacturing
212299 Manganese concentrates beneficiating
325188 Manganese dioxide manufacturing
331112 Manganese metal ferroalloys manufacturing
212299 Manganese ores mining and/or beneficiating
212210 Manganiferous ores valued for iron content, mining and/or beneficiating
212299 Manganiferousares ores (not valued for iron content) mining and/or beneficiating
212299 Manganite mining and/or beneficiating
111339 Mango farming
325191 Mangrove extract manufacturing
331511 Manhole covers, cast iron, manufacturing
812113 Manicure and pedicure salons
611511 Manicure and pedicure schools

325620 Manicure preparations manufacturing
812113 Manicurist services
323116 Manifold business forms printing
336312 Manifolds (i.e., intake and exhaust), automotive and truck gasoline engine, manufacturing
332996 Manifolds, pipe, made from purchased metal pipe
322231 Manila folders, die-cut, made from purchased paper or paperboard
325221 Manmade cellulosic fibers manufacturing
313221 Manmade fabric, narrow woven, weaving
313210 Manmade fabrics, broadwoven, weaving
313113 Manmade fiber thread manufacturing
424690 Man-made fibers merchant wholesalers
325222 Manmade noncellulosic fibers and filaments manufacturing
313111 Manmade staple spun yarns made from purchased fiber
541890 Mannequin decorating services
339999 Mannequins manufacturing
423440 Mannequins merchant wholesalers
325920 Mannitol hexanitrate explosive materials manufacturing
334513 Manometers, industrial process-type, manufacturing
561320 Manpower pools
238340 Mantel, marble or stone, installation
621399 Manual-arts therapists' offices (e.g., centers, clinics)
423390 Manufactured (i.e., mobile) homes merchant wholesalers
321991 Manufactured (mobile) buildings for commercial use (e.g., banks, offices) manufacturing
321991 Manufactured (mobile) classrooms manufacturing

453930 Manufactured (mobile) home dealers
531190 Manufactured (mobile) home parks
453930 Manufactured (mobile) home parts and accessory dealers
238990 Manufactured (mobile) home set up and tie down
531190 Manufactured (mobile) home sites rental or leasing
321991 Manufactured (mobile) homes manufacturing
221210 Manufactured gas production and distribution
813910 Manufacturers' associations
236210 Manufacturing building construction
531120 Manufacturing building rental or leasing
532490 Manufacturing machinery and equipment rental or leasing
541614 Manufacturing management consulting services
541614 Manufacturing operations improvement consulting services
511130 Map publishers (except exclusive Internet publishing)
511130 Map publishers and printing combined
519130 Map publishers, exclusively on Internet
111998 Maple sap concentrating (i.e., producing pure maple syrup in the field)
111998 Maple sap gathering
111998 Maple syrup (i.e., maple sap reducing)
311999 Maple syrup mixing into other products
541370 Mapping (except geophysical) services
541360 Mapping services, geophysical
424920 Maps (except globe, school, wall) merchant wholesalers
323112 Maps flexographic printing without publishing
323111 Maps gravure printing without publishing

323110 Maps lithographic (offset) printing without publishing
323119 Maps printing (except flexographic, digital, gravure, lithographic, quick, screen) without publishing
323113 Maps screen printing without publishing
212319 Marble crushed and broken stone mining and/or beneficiating
212311 Marble mining or quarrying
238140 Marble, granite and slate, exterior, contractors
238340 Marble, granite and slate, interior, contractors
339932 Marbles manufacturing
212393 Marcasite mining and/or beneficiating
325199 Margaric acid manufacturing
311221 Margarine and other corn oils made by wet milling corn
424490 Margarine merchant wholesalers
311225 Margarine-butter blend made from purchased fats and oils
311225 Margarines (including imitation) made from purchased fats and oils
713930 Marinas
335314 Marine and navy auxiliary controls, manufacturing
713930 Marine basins, operation of
488390 Marine cargo checkers and surveyors
488320 Marine cargo handling services
237990 Marine construction
928110 Marine Corps
541330 Marine engineering services
333618 Marine engines manufacturing
332510 Marine hardware, metal, manufacturing
332999 Marine horns, compressed air or steam, metal, manufacturing
524126 Marine insurance carriers, direct
712110 Marine museums
611519 Marine navigational schools
325510 Marine paints manufacturing
332410 Marine power boilers manufacturing

334220 Marine radio communications equipment manufacturing
524130 Marine reinsurance carriers
488330 Marine salvaging services
447190 Marine service stations
488510 Marine shipping agency
335911 Marine storage batteries manufacturing
423860 Marine supplies (except pleasure) merchant wholesalers
423910 Marine supplies, pleasure, merchant wholesalers
441222 Marine supply dealers
541990 Marine surveyor (i.e., ship appraiser) services
488330 Marine vessel traffic reporting services
339999 Marionettes (i.e., puppets) manufacturing
339942 Marker boards (i.e., whiteboards) manufacturing
523110 Market making for securities
541910 Marketing analysis services
541613 Marketing consulting services
541613 Marketing management consulting services
541910 Marketing research services
339943 Marking devices manufacturing
424120 Marking devices merchant wholesalers
333518 Marking machines, metal, manufacturing
212312 Marl crushed and broken stone mining and/or beneficiating
311421 Marmalade manufacturing
321999 Marquetry, wood, manufacturing
624190 Marriage counseling services (except by offices of mental health practitioners)
922120 Marshals' offices
311340 Marshmallow creme manufacturing
311340 Marshmallows manufacturing
611620 Martial arts instruction, camps, or schools
311340 Marzipan (i.e., candy) manufacturing

335999 Maser (i.e., microwave amplification by stimulated emission of radiation) amplifiers manufacturing
321999 Mashers, potato, wood, manufacturing
322222 Masking tape made from purchased paper
444190 Masonry (e.g., block, brick, stone) dealers
238140 Masonry contractors
238140 Masonry pointing, cleaning or caulking
332212 Mason's handtools manufacturing
423320 Mason's materials merchant wholesalers
334516 Mass spectrometers manufacturing
334516 Mass spectroscopy instrumentation manufacturing
335211 Massage machines, electric (except designed for beauty and barber shop use), manufacturing
812199 Massage parlors
611519 Massage therapist instruction
621399 Massage therapists' offices
512210 Master recording leasing and licensing
424690 Mastics (except construction) merchant wholesalers
321999 Masts, wood, manufacturing
812332 Mat and rug supply services
325998 Matches and match books manufacturing
424990 Matches and match books merchant wholesalers
238290 Materials handling equipment installation
811310 Materials handling equipment repair and maintenance services
423830 Materials handling machinery and equipment merchant wholesalers
532490 Materials handling machinery and equipment rental or leasing

541614	Materials management consulting services
562920	Materials recovery facilities (MRF)
236210	Materials recovery facility construction
923120	Maternity and child health program administration
315212	Maternity bras and corsets, women's, cut and sew apparel contractors
315231	Maternity bras and corsets, women's, misses', and girls', cut and sewn from purchased fabric (except apparel contractors)
622310	Maternity hospitals
448120	Maternity shops
541712	Mathematics research and development laboratories or services
332618	Mats and matting made from purchased wire
332212	Mattocks (i.e., handtools) manufacturing
326299	Mattress protectors, rubber, manufacturing
332612	Mattress springs and spring units, light gauge, made from purchased wire or strip
442110	Mattress stores (including waterbeds)
337910	Mattresses (i.e., box spring, innerspring, noninnerspring) manufacturing
337910	Mattresses made from felt, foam rubber, urethane and similar materials
423210	Mattresses merchant wholesalers
326199	Mattresses, air, plastics, manufacturing
326299	Mattresses, air, rubber, manufacturing
311812	Matzo baking made in commercial bakeries
332212	Mauls, metal, manufacturing
321999	Mauls, wood, manufacturing
236220	Mausoleum (i.e., building) construction

812220	Mausoleums
311941	Mayonnaise manufacturing
921110	Mayor's offices
321219	MDF (medium density fiberboard) manufacturing
621112	MDs' (medical doctors), mental health, offices (e.g., centers, clinics)
621111	MDs' (medical doctors, except mental health) offices (e.g., centers, clinics)
624210	Meal delivery programs
311119	Meal, alfalfa, manufacturing
311119	Meal, bone, prepared as feed for animals and fowls, manufacturing
311211	Meal, corn, for human consumption made in flour mills
423830	Measuring and testing equipment (except automotive) merchant wholesalers
333515	Measuring attachments (e.g., sine bars) for machine tool manufacturing
334515	Measuring equipment for electronic and electrical circuits and equipment manufacturing
811219	Measuring instrument repair and maintenance services
334515	Measuring instruments and meters, electric, manufacturing
334513	Measuring instruments, industrial process control-type, manufacturing
332212	Measuring tools, machinist's (except optical), manufacturing
334514	Measuring wheels manufacturing
311613	Meat and bone meal and tankage, produced in rendering plant
311612	Meat canning (except baby, pet food, poultry), made from purchased carcasses
311611	Meat canning (except poultry) produced in slaughtering plants

311422 Meat canning, baby food, manufacturing

311111 Meat canning, dog and cat, pet food, made from purchased carcasses

311615 Meat canning, poultry (except baby and pet food), manufacturing

311612 Meat extracts made from purchased carcasses

333294 Meat grinders, food-type, manufacturing

445210 Meat markets

311615 Meat products (e.g., hot dogs, luncheon meats, sausages) made from a combination of poultry and other meats

311612 Meat products canning (except baby, pet food, poultry) made from purchased carcasses

311111 Meat products, dog and cat, pet food, canning, made from purchased carcasses

311612 Meats (except poultry), cured or smoked, made from purchased carcasses

424470 Meats and meat products (except canned, packaged frozen) merchant wholesalers

311611 Meats fresh, chilled or frozen (except poultry and small game), produced in slaughtering plants

424490 Meats, canned, merchant wholesalers

424470 Meats, cured or smoked, merchant wholesalers

311611 Meats, cured or smoked, produced in slaughtering plants

311612 Meats, fresh or chilled (except poultry and small game), frozen, made from purchased carcasses

424470 Meats, fresh, merchant wholesalers

424470 Meats, frozen (except packaged), merchant wholesalers

424420 Meats, packaged frozen, merchant wholesalers

238220 Mechanical contractors

541330 Mechanical engineering services

238290 Mechanical equipment insulation

313311 Mechanical finishing of broadwoven fabrics

316110 Mechanical leather manufacturing

334513 Mechanical measuring instruments, industrial process-type, manufacturing

339942 Mechanical pencil refills manufacturing

339941 Mechanical pencils manufacturing

811310 Mechanical power transmission equipment repair and maintenance services

423840 Mechanical power transmission supplies (e.g., gears, pulleys, sprockets) merchant wholesalers

326291 Mechanical rubber goods (i.e., extruded, lathe-cut, molded) manufacturing

423840 Mechanical rubber goods merchant wholesalers

541380 Mechanical testing laboratories or services

611513 Mechanic's apprenticeship training

333924 Mechanic's creepers manufacturing

325611 Mechanic's hand soaps and pastes manufacturing

332212 Mechanic's handtools, nonpowered, manufacturing

611519 Mechanic's schools (except apprenticeship)

423120 Mechanic's tools merchant wholesalers

333311 Mechanisms for coin-operated machines manufacturing

334518 Mechanisms, clockwork operated device, manufacturing

541840 Media advertising representatives (i.e., independent of media owners)
541830 Media buying agencies
541830 Media buying services
541840 Media representatives (i.e., independent of media owners)
518210 Media streaming services
926150 Mediation and conciliation services, government
541990 Mediation product services (except by lawyer, attorney, paralegal offices, family and social services)
624190 Mediation, social service, family, agencies
811219 Medical and surgical equipment repair and maintenance services
541430 Medical art services
541430 Medical artists, independent
923130 Medical assistance programs administration, government
813920 Medical associations
531120 Medical building rental or leasing
334510 Medical cleaning equipment, ultrasonic, manufacturing
524298 Medical cost evaluation services
621112 Medical doctors' (MDs), mental health, offices (e.g. centers, clinics)
621111 Medical doctors' (MDs, except mental health) offices (e.g., centers, clinics)
423450 Medical dressings merchant wholesalers
532490 Medical equipment (except home health furniture and equipment) rental or leasing
446199 Medical equipment and supplies stores
423450 Medical equipment merchant wholesalers
423450 Medical furniture merchant wholesalers
327215 Medical glassware made from purchased glass
327212 Medical glassware made in glass making plants

423450 Medical glassware merchant wholesalers
541430 Medical illustration services
541430 Medical illustrators, independent
423450 Medical instruments merchant wholesalers
524114 Medical insurance carriers, direct
511120 Medical journal and periodical publishers (except exclusive Internet publishing)
511120 Medical journal and periodical publishers and printing combined
519130 Medical journal and periodical publishers, exclusively on Internet "
621511 Medical laboratories (except radiological, X-ray)
621512 Medical laboratories, radiological or X-ray
541611 Medical office management consulting services or consultants
561110 Medical office management services
621511 Medical pathology laboratories
541922 Medical photography services
334517 Medical radiation therapy equipment manufacturing
621512 Medical radiological laboratories
524130 Medical reinsurance carriers
541712 Medical research and development laboratories or services (except biotechnology research and development)
611310 Medical schools
315211 Medical service apparel, men's and boys', cut and sew apparel contractors
315225 Medical service apparel, men's and boys', cut and sewn from purchased fabric (except apparel contractors)
315212 Medical service apparel, women's, cut and sew apparel contractors

315239 Medical service apparel, women's, misses', and girls', cut and sewn from purchased fabric (except apparel contractors)
524114 Medical service plans without providing health care services
424210 Medical sundries, rubber, merchant wholesalers
423450 Medical supplies merchant wholesalers
611519 Medical technician schools
339112 Medical thermometers manufacturing
334510 Medical ultrasound equipment manufacturing
621512 Medical X-ray laboratories
923130 Medicare and Medicaid administration
325411 Medicinal chemicals, uncompounded, manufacturing
337110 Medicine cabinets (except freestanding), wood household-type, manufacturing
337124 Medicine cabinets, metal household-type, manufacturing
321219 Medium density fiberboard (MDF) manufacturing
212399 Meerschaum mining and/or beneficiating
531120 Meeting hall and room rental or leasing
325211 Melamine resins manufacturing
111219 Melon farming (e.g., cantaloupe, casaba, honeydew, watermelon), field, bedding plant and seed production
111419 Melon farming, grown under cover
313230 Melt blown nonwoven fabrics manufacturing
315291 Melton jackets, infants', cut and sewn from purchased fabric (except apparel contractors)
315211 Melton jackets, men's and boys', cut and sew apparel contractors
315228 Melton jackets, men's and boys', cut and sewn from purchased fabric (except apparel contractors)

315212 Melton jackets, women's, girls', and infants', cut and sew apparel contractors
315239 Melton jackets, women's, misses', and girls', cut and sewn from purchased fabric (except apparel contractors)
813410 Membership associations, civic or social
721110 Membership hotels
812220 Memorial gardens (i.e., burial places)
334418 Memory boards manufacturing
712130 Menageries
114111 Menhaden fishing
424320 Men's and boys' clothing merchant wholesalers
424320 Men's and boys' furnishings (except shoes) merchant wholesalers
315119 Men's socks knitting or knitting and finishing
623210 Mental retardation intermediate care facilities
622210 Mental (except mental retardation) hospitals
621420 Mental health centers and clinics (except hospitals), outpatient
623220 Mental health facilities, residential
623220 Mental health halfway houses
622210 Mental health hospitals
621112 Mental health physicians' offices (e.g., centers, clinics)
923120 Mental health program administration
623210 Mental retardation facilities (e.g., homes, hospitals, intermediate care facilities), residential
623210 Mental retardation homes
623210 Mental retardation hospitals
813311 Mentally retarded advocacy groups
561450 Mercantile credit reporting bureaus
313311 Mercerizing broadwoven fabrics
333292 Mercerizing machinery manufacturing

313312 Mercerizing narrow woven textile products and fabrics (except broadwoven)

326111 Merchandise bags, plastics film, single wall or multiwall, manufacturing

423440 Merchandising machines, coin-operated, merchant wholesalers

236117 Merchant builders (i.e., building on own land, for sale), residential

926120 Merchant Marine (except academy)

813910 Merchants' associations

335912 Mercuric oxide batteries manufacturing

212299 Mercury (quicksilver) mining and/or beneficiating

335999 Mercury arc rectifiers (i.e., electrical apparatus) manufacturing

325188 Mercury chloride manufacturing

325188 Mercury compounds, not specified elsewhere by process, manufacturing

325920 Mercury fulminate explosive materials manufacturing

335110 Mercury halide lamp bulbs manufacturing

212299 Mercury ores mining and/or beneficiating

325188 Mercury oxide manufacturing

332618 Mesh made from purchased wire

331422 Mesh, wire, made from purchased copper in wire drawing plants

331319 Mesh, wire, made in aluminum wire drawing plants

331111 Mesh, wire, made in iron and steel mills

331222 Mesh, wire, made in wire drawing mills

331491 Mesh, wire, nonferrous metals (except aluminum, copper), made from purchased nonferrous metals (except aluminum, copper) in wire drawing plants

561421 Message services, telephone answering

492210 Messenger service

325412 Metabolite in-vivo diagnostic substances manufacturing

332431 Metal cans, light gauge metal, manufacturing

333298 Metal casting machinery and equipment manufacturing

333512 Metal cutting machine tools manufacturing

332213 Metal cutting saw blades manufacturing

424690 Metal cyanides merchant wholesalers

333513 Metal deposit forming machines manufacturing

334519 Metal detectors manufacturing

339113 Metal fabric and mesh safety gloves manufacturing

332999 Metal foil containers (except bags) manufacturing

333513 Metal forming machine tools manufacturing

337121 Metal framed furniture, household-type, upholstered, manufacturing

238190 Metal furring contractors

339943 Metal hand stamps manufacturing

333994 Metal melting furnaces, industrial, manufacturing

213114 Metal mining support services (shaft sinking, tunneling, blasting) (except site preparation and related construction contractor activities)

336370 Metal motor vehicle body parts stamping

423520 Metal ores merchant wholesalers

334413 Metal oxide silicon (MOS) devices manufacturing

423510 Metal pipe merchant wholesalers

325612 Metal polishes (i.e., tarnish removers) manufacturing

331314 Metal powder and flake made from purchased aluminum

331423 Metal powder and flake made from purchased copper
331221 Metal powder and flake made from purchased iron or steel
331492 Metal powder and flake nonferrous (except aluminum, copper) made from purchased metal
236210 Metal processing plant construction
423510 Metal products (e.g., bars, ingots, plates, rods, shapes, sheets) merchant wholesalers
423930 Metal scrap and waste merchant wholesalers
238170 Metal siding installation
332116 Metal stampings (except automotive, cans, cooking, closures, crowns), unfinished, manufacturing
335991 Metal-graphite product manufacturing
423520 Metallic concentrates merchant wholesalers
325131 Metallic pigments, inorganic, manufacturing
325199 Metallic soap manufacturing
313320 Metallizing purchased textiles
541380 Metallurgical testing laboratories or services
423510 Metals sales offices
423510 Metals service centers
423510 Metals, ferrous and nonferrous, merchant wholesalers
423940 Metals, precious, merchant wholesalers
333512 Metalworking lathes manufacturing
423830 Metalworking machinery and equipment merchant wholesalers
532490 Metalworking machinery and equipment rental or leasing
334519 Meteorologic tracking systems manufacturing
811219 Meteorological instrument repair and maintenance services
334519 Meteorological instruments manufacturing

541990 Meteorological services
561990 Meter reading services, contract
334514 Metering devices (except electrical and industrial process control) manufacturing
335313 Metering panels, electric, manufacturing
334514 Meters (except electrical and industrial process control) manufacturing
423830 Meters (except electrical, parking) merchant wholesalers
334515 Meters, electrical (i.e., graphic recording, panelboard, pocket, portable), manufacturing
423610 Meters, electrical, merchant wholesalers
334513 Meters, industrial process control-type, manufacturing
334514 Meters, parking, manufacturing
423850 Meters, parking, merchant wholesalers
334515 Meters, power factor and phase angle, manufacturing
325320 Methoxychlor insecticides manufacturing
325191 Methyl acetone manufacturing
325211 Methyl acrylate resins manufacturing
325199 Methyl alcohol (i.e., methanol), synthetic, manufacturing
325191 Methyl alcohol (methanol), natural, manufacturing
325211 Methyl cellulose resins manufacturing
325199 Methyl chloride manufacturing
325211 Methyl methacrylate resins manufacturing
325199 Methyl perhydrofluorine manufacturing
325199 Methyl salicylate manufacturing
325132 Methyl violet toners manufacturing
325199 Methylamine manufacturing
325199 Methylene chloride manufacturing
311422 Mexican foods canning
311412 Mexican foods, frozen, manufacturing

212399   Mica mining and/or beneficiating
327992   Mica processing beyond beneficiation
327999   Mica products manufacturing
212319   Mica schist crushed and broken stone mining and/or beneficiating
212311   Mica schist mining or quarrying
311119   Micro and macro premixes, livestock, manufacturing
334516   Microbiology instruments manufacturing
325413   Microbiology, virology, and serology in-vitro diagnostic substances manufacturing
334111   Microcomputers manufacturing
334413   Microcontroller chip manufacturing
333315   Microfiche equipment (e.g., cameras, projectors, readers) manufacturing
518210   Microfiche recording and imaging services
333315   Microfilm equipment (e.g., cameras, projectors, readers) manufacturing
423420   Microfilm equipment and supplies merchant wholesalers
518210   Microfilm recording and imaging services
212299   Microlite mining and/or beneficiating
333295   Micro-lithography equipment, semiconductor, manufacturing
332212   Micrometers, machinist's precision tools, manufacturing
334310   Microphones manufacturing
334516   Microprobes (e.g., electron, ion, laser, X-ray) manufacturing
334413   Microprocessor chip manufacturing
333314   Microscopes (except electron, proton) manufacturing
334516   Microscopes, electron and proton, manufacturing
237990   Microtunneling contractors
334220   Microwave communications equipment manufacturing

334419   Microwave components manufacturing
811412   Microwave oven, household-type, repair and maintenance services, without retailing new microwave ovens
335221   Microwave ovens (including portable), household-type, manufacturing
333319   Microwave ovens, commercial-type, manufacturing
237130   Microwave relay tower construction
517911   Microwave telecommunication resellers
334515   Microwave test equipment manufacturing
326199   Microwaveware, plastics, manufacturing
315291   Middies, infants', cut and sewn from purchased fabric (except apparel contractors)
315212   Middies, women's, girls' and infants', cut and sew apparel contractors
315232   Middies, women's, misses', and girls', cut and sewn from purchased fabric (except apparel contractors)
611110   Middle schools
621399   Midwives' offices (e.g., centers, clinics)
721310   Migrant workers' camps
611310   Military academies, college level
611110   Military academies, elementary or secondary
928110   Military bases and camps
315211   Military dress uniforms, men's and boys', cut and sew apparel contractors
315222   Military dress uniforms, men's and boys', cut and sewn from purchased fabric (except apparel contractors)
315234   Military dress uniforms, tailored, women's, misses' and girls', cut and sewn from purchased fabric (except apparel contractors)

315212	Military dress uniforms, women's, cut and sew apparel contractors
332999	Military insignia, metal, manufacturing
314999	Military insignia, textile, manufacturing
712110	Military museums
928110	Military police
928110	Military reserve armories and bases
611310	Military service academies (college)
928110	Military training schools (except academies)
423860	Military vehicles (except trucks) merchant wholesalers
311511	Milk based drinks (except dietary) manufacturing
311514	Milk based drinks, dietary, manufacturing
322130	Milk carton board made in paperboard mills
322226	Milk carton board stock made from purchased paperboard
311511	Milk drink, chocolate, manufacturing
484220	Milk hauling, local
311511	Milk pasteurizing
311511	Milk processing (e.g., bottling, homogenizing, pasteurizing, vitaminizing) manufacturing
333294	Milk processing (except farm-type) machinery manufacturing
112120	Milk production, dairy cattle
311511	Milk substitutes manufacturing
115210	Milk testing for butterfat and milk solids
311511	Milk, acidophilus, manufacturing
424490	Milk, canned or dried, merchant wholesalers
311514	Milk, concentrated, condensed, dried, evaporated, and powdered, manufacturing
311511	Milk, fluid (except canned), manufacturing
424430	Milk, fluid (except canned), merchant wholesalers
311514	Milk, malted, manufacturing
311514	Milk, powdered, manufacturing
311514	Milk, ultra-high temperature, manufacturing
112120	Milking dairy cattle
112420	Milking dairy goat
112410	Milking dairy sheep
423820	Milking machinery and equipment merchant wholesalers
333111	Milking machines manufacturing
311514	Milkshake mixes manufacturing
314999	Mill menders, contract, woven fabrics
316999	Mill strapping for textile mills, leather, manufacturing
423840	Mill supplies merchant wholesalers
315991	Millinery cut and sewn from purchased fabric (except apparel contractors)
424330	Millinery merchant wholesalers
424310	Millinery supplies merchant wholesalers
315999	Millinery trimmings cut and sewn from purchased fabric (except apparel contractors)
315211	Millinery trimmings, men's and boys', cut and sew apparel contractors
315212	Millinery trimmings, women's, girls', and infants', cut and sew apparel contractors
315211	Millinery, men's and boys', cut and sew apparel contractors
315212	Millinery, women's, girls', and infants', cut and sew apparel contractors
333512	Milling machines, metalworking, manufacturing
311212	Milling rice
212399	Millstones mining and/or beneficiating
238350	Millwork installation
423310	Millwork merchant wholesalers
337212	Millwork, custom architectural, manufacturing
321114	Millwork, treating
238290	Millwrights

111199 Milo farming, field and seed production
711110 Mime theaters
333922 Mine conveyors manufacturing
213114 Mine development (except site preparation and related construction contractor activities) for metal mining on a contract basis
213115 Mine development for nonmetallic minerals mining (except fuels) on a contract basis
236210 Mine loading and discharging station construction
321114 Mine props, treating
562910 Mine reclamation services, integrated (e.g., demolition, hazardous material removal, soil remediation)
213113 Mine shaft sinking services for coal mining on a contract basis
213114 Mine shaft sinking services for metal mining on a contract basis
213115 Mine shaft sinking services for nonmetallic minerals (except fuels) on a contract basis
238910 Mine site preparation and related construction activities, construction contractors
321114 Mine ties, wood, treated, manufacturing
213113 Mine tunneling services for coal mining on a contract basis
213114 Mine tunneling services for metal mining on a contract basis
213115 Mine tunneling services for nonmetallic minerals (except fuels) on a contract basis
325131 Mineral colors and pigments manufacturing
311119 Mineral feed supplements (except cat, dog) manufacturing
212393 Mineral pigments, natural, mining and/or beneficiating

333131 Mineral processing and beneficiating machinery manufacturing
523910 Mineral royalties or leases dealing (i.e., acting as a principal in dealing royalties or leases to investors)
311119 Mineral supplements, animal (except cat, dog), manufacturing
424910 Mineral supplements, animal, merchant wholesalers
238310 Mineral wool insulation installation
327993 Mineral wool insulation materials manufacturing
327993 Mineral wool products (e.g., board, insulation, tile) manufacturing
423520 Minerals (except construction materials, petroleum) merchant wholesalers
335129 Miner's lamps manufacturing
332993 Mines, ammunition, manufacturing
713990 Miniature golf courses
337920 Miniblinds manufacturing
334111 Minicomputers manufacturing
331111 Mini-mills, steel
926150 Minimum wage program administration
****** Mining—see type
813910 Mining associations
333131 Mining cars manufacturing
423810 Mining cranes merchant wholesalers
541330 Mining engineering services
336510 Mining locomotives and parts manufacturing
423810 Mining machinery and equipment (except petroleum) merchant wholesalers
532412 Mining machinery and equipment rental or leasing
811310 Mining machinery and equipment repair and maintenance services
423830 Mining machinery and equipment, petroleum, merchant wholesalers

531190 Mining property leasing

336112 Minivans assembling on chassis of own manufacture

531130 Miniwarehouse rental or leasing

112930 Mink production

112511 Minnow production, farm raising

711211 Minor league baseball clubs

111998 Mint farming

238150 Mirror installation

423220 Mirrors (except automotive) merchant wholesalers

423120 Mirrors, automotive, merchant wholesalers

327215 Mirrors, framed (except automotive) or unframed, made from purchased glass

333314 Mirrors, optical, manufacturing

237990 Missile facility construction

332993 Missile warheads manufacturing

561611 Missing person tracing services

813110 Missions, religious organization

332212 Miter boxes manufacturing

315992 Mittens cut and sewn from purchased fabric (except apparel contractors)

315191 Mittens, knit, made in apparel knitting mills

315992 Mittens, leather (except apparel contractors), manufacturing

315211 Mittens, leather, men's and boys', cut and sew apparel contractors

315212 Mittens, leather, women's, girls', and infants', cut and sew apparel contractors

315211 Mittens, men's and boys', cut and sew apparel contractors

315212 Mittens, women's, girls', and infants', cut and sew apparel contractors

315992 Mittens, woven or knit, cut and sewn from purchased fabric (except apparel contractors)

315211 Mittens, woven or knit, men's and boys', cut and sew apparel contractors

315212 Mittens, woven or knit, women's, girls', and infants', cut and sew apparel contractors

311230 Mix grain breakfast manufacturing

311514 Mix, ice cream, manufacturing

312140 Mixed drinks, alcoholic, manufacturing

111940 Mixed hay farming

485111 Mixed mode transit systems (e.g., bus, commuter rail, subway combinations)

333120 Mixers, concrete, portable, manufacturing

424490 Mixes (e.g., cake, dessert, pie) merchant wholesalers

311211 Mixes, flour (e.g., biscuit, cake, doughnut, pancake) made in flour mills

311822 Mixes, flour (e.g., biscuit, cake, doughnut, pancake), made from purchased flour

325314 Mixing purchased fertilizer materials

531190 Mobile (manufactured) home parks

531190 Mobile (manufactured) home site rental or leasing

531110 Mobile (manufactured) home, on site, rental or leasing

621512 Mobile breast imaging centers

811192 Mobile car and truck washes

334220 Mobile communications equipment manufacturing

311119 Mobile feed mill

722330 Mobile food stands

453930 Mobile home dealers, manufactured

321991 Mobile home manufacturing

532120 Mobile home rental (except on site)

484220 Mobile home towing services, local

484230 Mobile home towing services, long-distance

712110 Mobile museums

624210 Mobile soup kitchens

333924 Mobile straddle carriers manufacturing

517210	Mobile telephone communication carriers, except satellite
621512	Mobile X-ray facilities (medical)
316219	Moccasins manufacturing
325222	Modacrylic fibers and filaments manufacturing
313111	Modacrylic spun yarns made from purchased fiber
339932	Model kits manufacturing
423920	Model kits merchant wholesalers
339932	Model railroad manufacturing
561311	Model registries
561320	Model supply services
711410	Modeling agents
339942	Modeling clay manufacturing
611519	Modeling schools
711410	Models' agents or managers
339999	Models, anatomical, manufacturing
711510	Models, independent
339932	Models, toy and hobby (e.g., airplane, boat, ship), manufacturing
423690	Modems merchant wholesalers
334210	Modems, carrier equipment, manufacturing
711120	Modern dance companies
238390	Modular furniture system attachment and installation
337214	Modular furniture systems (except wood frame), office-type, manufacturing
337211	Modular furniture systems, wood frame office-type, manufacturing
236115	Modular house assembly on site by general contractors
236117	Modular housing, residential, assembled on site by operative builders
334518	Modules for clocks and watches manufacturing
112420	Mohair farming
313112	Mohair yarn twisting or winding of purchased yarn
424590	Mohair, raw, merchant wholesalers
334516	Moisture analyzers, laboratory-type, manufacturing
334513	Moisture meters, industrial process-type, manufacturing
311312	Molasses made from purchased raw cane sugar
311313	Molasses made from sugar beets
311311	Molasses made in sugarcane mill
424490	Molasses merchant wholesalers
311312	Molasses, blackstrap, made from purchased raw cane sugar
311311	Molasses, blackstrap, made in sugarcane mill
339991	Molded packings and seals manufacturing
322299	Molded pulp products (e.g., egg cartons, food containers, food trays) manufacturing
423310	Molding (e.g., sheet metal, wood) merchant wholesalers
332321	Molding and trim (except motor vehicle), metal, manufacturing
238350	Molding or trim, wood or plastic, installation
212322	Molding sand quarrying and/or beneficiating
336370	Moldings and trim, motor vehicle, stamping
321918	Moldings, clear and finger joint wood, manufacturing
321918	Moldings, wood and covered wood, manufacturing
333511	Molds (except steel ingot), industrial, manufacturing
331511	Molds for casting steel ingots manufacturing
333511	Molds for forming materials (e.g., glass, plastics, rubber) manufacturing
333511	Molds for metal casting (except steel ingot) manufacturing
333511	Molds for plastics and rubber working machinery manufacturing
331511	Molds, steel ingot, industrial, manufacturing

112512 Mollusk production, farm raising
212299 Molybdenite mining and/or beneficiating
331491 Molybdenum and molybdenum alloy bar, plate, pipe, rod, sheet, tubing, and wire made from purchased metals or scrap
212299 Molybdenum ores mining and/or beneficiating
331491 Molybdenum rolling, drawing, or extruding purchased metals or scrap
331112 Molybdenum silicon ferroalloys manufacturing
212299 Molybdite mining and/or beneficiating
813110 Monasteries (except schools)
212299 Monazite mining and/or beneficiating
521110 Monetary authorities, central bank
332999 Money chests, metal, manufacturing
525990 Money market mutual funds, closed-end
525910 Money market mutual funds, open-ended
522390 Money order issuance services
522390 Money transmission services
334119 Monitors, computer peripheral equipment, manufacturing
325120 Monochlorodifluoromethane manufacturing
334516 Monochrometers, laboratory-type, manufacturing
334413 Monolithic integrated circuits (solid state) manufacturing
325199 Monomethylparaminophenol sulfate manufacturing
237990 Monorail construction
333923 Monorail systems (except passenger-type) manufacturing
485119 Monorail transit systems (except mixed mode), commuter
487110 Monorail, scenic and sightseeing, operation
325199 Monosodium glutamate manufacturing

611110 Montessori schools, elementary or secondary
236220 Monument (i.e., building) construction
453998 Monument (i.e., burial marker) dealers
423990 Monuments and grave markers merchant wholesalers
327991 Monuments and tombstone, cut stone (except finishing or lettering to order only), manufacturing
333319 Mop wringers manufacturing
441221 Moped dealers
423110 Moped merchant wholesalers
532292 Moped rental
336991 Mopeds and parts manufacturing
339994 Mops, floor and dust, manufacturing
325132 Mordant dyes manufacturing
325613 Mordants manufacturing
325411 Morphine and derivatives (i.e., basic chemicals) manufacturing
522190 Morris Plans (i.e., known as), depository
522298 Morris Plans (i.e., known as), nondepository
333120 Mortar mixers, portable, manufacturing
332993 Mortar shells manufacturing
327125 Mortar, nonclay refractory, manufacturing
332995 Mortars manufacturing
327124 Mortars, clay refractory, manufacturing
522292 Mortgage banking (i.e., nondepository mortgage lending)
522310 Mortgage brokerages
522310 Mortgage brokers' or agents' offices (i.e., independent)
522292 Mortgage companies
524126 Mortgage guaranty insurance carriers, direct
525990 Mortgage real estate investment trusts (REITs)
812210 Mortician services

333210	Mortisers, woodworking-type, manufacturing
812210	Mortuaries
334413	MOS (metal oxide silicon) devices manufacturing
327122	Mosaic tile, ceramic, manufacturing
238340	Mosaic work
813110	Mosques, religious
926130	Mosquito eradication districts
561710	Mosquito eradication services
113210	Moss gathering
531120	Motel building, not operating motel, rental or leasing
236220	Motel construction
561110	Motel management services (except complete operation of client's business)
721110	Motels
325320	Moth repellants manufacturing
423430	Mother boards merchant wholesalers
334290	Motion alarms (e.g., swimming pool, perimeter) manufacturing
334290	Motion detectors, security system, manufacturing
512110	Motion picture and video production
512110	Motion picture and video production and distribution
512191	Motion picture animation, post-production
512199	Motion picture booking agencies
333315	Motion picture cameras manufacturing
423410	Motion picture cameras, equipment, and supplies merchant wholesalers
541690	Motion picture consulting services
711510	Motion picture directors, independent
512120	Motion picture distribution exclusive of production
532490	Motion picture equipment rental or leasing
512131	Motion picture exhibition

512131	Motion picture exhibitors for airlines
512131	Motion picture exhibitors, itinerant
512120	Motion picture film distributors
512199	Motion picture film laboratories
512120	Motion picture film libraries
519120	Motion picture film libraries, archives
512199	Motion picture film libraries, stock footage
325992	Motion picture film manufacturing
512199	Motion picture film reproduction for theatrical distribution
512199	Motion picture laboratories
512191	Motion picture or video editing services
512191	Motion picture or video post-production services
512191	Motion picture or video titling
711510	Motion picture producers, independent
512110	Motion picture production
512110	Motion picture production and distribution
512191	Motion picture production special effects, post-production
333315	Motion picture projectors manufacturing
512110	Motion picture studios, producing motion pictures
512132	Motion picture theaters, drive-in
512131	Motion picture theaters, indoor
532220	Motion picture wardrobe and costume rental
711510	Motivational speakers, independent
926120	Motor carrier licensing and inspection offices
485210	Motor coach operation, interurban and rural
335314	Motor control accessories (including overload relays) manufacturing
335314	Motor control centers, manufacturing

335314 Motor controls, electric, manufacturing

423610 Motor controls, electric, merchant wholesalers

721110 Motor courts

484110 Motor freight carrier, general, local

484122 Motor freight carrier, general, long-distance, less-than-truckload (LTL)

484121 Motor freight carrier, general, long-distance, truckload (TL)

484210 Motor freight carrier, used household goods

335312 Motor generator sets (except automotive, turbine generator sets) manufacturing

333611 Motor generator sets, turbo generators, manufacturing

441210 Motor home dealers

423110 Motor home merchant wholesalers

532120 Motor home rental

336213 Motor homes, self-contained, assembling on purchased chassis

336120 Motor homes, self-contained, mounted on heavy truck chassis of own manufacture

336112 Motor homes, self-contained, mounted on light duty truck chassis of own manufacture

721110 Motor hotels without casinos

721110 Motor inns

721110 Motor lodges

324191 Motor oils, petroleum, made from refined petroleum

325998 Motor oils, synthetic, manufacturing

811310 Motor repair and maintenance services, commercial or industrial

441221 Motor scooters dealers

336991 Motor scooters manufacturing

335314 Motor starters, contractors, and controllers, industrial, manufacturing

561599 Motor travel clubs

333997 Motor truck scales manufacturing

236210 Motor vehicle assembly plant construction

326220 Motor vehicle belts, rubber or plastics, manufacturing

238290 Motor vehicle garage and service station mechanical equipment (e.g., gasoline pumps, hoists) installation

332510 Motor vehicle hardware, metal, manufacturing

326220 Motor vehicle hoses, rubber or plastics, manufacturing

334514 Motor vehicle instruments (e.g., fuel level gauges, oil pressure, speedometers, tachometers, water temperature) manufacturing

423120 Motor vehicle instruments, electric, merchant wholesalers

336360 Motor vehicle interior systems (e.g., headliners, panels, seats, trims) manufacturing

561990 Motor vehicle license issuing services, private franchise

926120 Motor vehicle licensing offices, government

423110 Motor vehicle merchant wholesalers

336370 Motor vehicle metal bumper stampings

336370 Motor vehicle metal parts stamping

336370 Motor vehicle metal stampings (e.g., body parts, fenders, hub caps, tops, trim) manufacturing

326199 Motor vehicle moldings and extrusions, plastics, manufacturing

325510 Motor vehicle paints manufacturing

423120 Motor vehicle parts and accessories, new, merchant wholesalers

423140 Motor vehicle parts, used, merchant wholesalers

336360 Motor vehicle seats manufacturing

336360 Motor vehicle seats, metal framed, manufacturing

423130	Motor vehicle tire and tube merchant wholesalers
326211	Motor vehicle tires manufacturing
488410	Motor vehicle towing services
336360	Motor vehicle trimmings manufacturing
441221	Motorbike dealers
811490	Motorboat (i.e., inboard and outboard) repair and maintenance services
336612	Motorboat, inboard or outboard, building
441221	Motorcycle dealers
423110	Motorcycle merchant wholesalers
441221	Motorcycle parts and accessories dealers
423120	Motorcycle parts, new, merchant wholesalers
711212	Motorcycle racetracks
711219	Motorcycle racing teams
532292	Motorcycle rental
811490	Motorcycle repair shops without retailing new motorcycles
336991	Motorcycles and parts manufacturing
423860	Motorized passenger golf carts merchant wholesalers
335312	Motors, electric (except engine starting motors, gearmotors, outboard), manufacturing
423610	Motors, electric, merchant wholesalers
333996	Motors, fluid power, manufacturing
333612	Motors, gear, manufacturing
333618	Motors, outboard, manufacturing
423910	Motors, outboard, merchant wholesalers
336322	Motors, starter, for internal combustion engines, manufacturing
713990	Mountain hiking, recreational
561910	Mounting merchandise on cards
334119	Mouse devices, computer peripheral equipment, manufacturing

213112	Mouse hole and rat hole drilling at oil and gas fields on a contract basis
339992	Mouthpieces for musical instruments manufacturing
325620	Mouthwashes (except medicinal) manufacturing
325412	Mouthwashes, medicated, manufacturing
334518	Movements, watch or clock, manufacturing
512110	Movie production and distribution
512131	Movie theaters (except drive-in)
512132	Movie theaters, drive-in
238290	Moving sidewalk installation
561730	Mowing services (e.g., highway, lawn, road strip)
562920	MRF (materials recovery facilities)
621512	MRI (magnetic resonance imaging) centers
334510	MRI (magnetic resonance imaging) medical diagnostic equipment manufacturing
325520	Mucilage adhesives manufacturing
213112	Mud service for oil field drilling on a contract basis
238110	Mud-jacking contractors
811112	Muffler repair and replacement shops
336399	Mufflers and resonators, automotive, truck, and buses manufacturing
315191	Mufflers made in apparel knitting mills
423120	Mufflers, exhaust, merchant wholesalers
315211	Mufflers, men's and boys', cut and sew apparel contractors
315993	Mufflers, men's and boys', cut and sewn from purchased fabric (except apparel contractors)
315999	Mufflers, women's and girls', cut and sewn from purchased fabric (except apparel contractors)

315212	Mufflers, women's, girls', and infants', cut and sew apparel contractors
424910	Mulch merchant wholesalers
333112	Mulchers, lawn and garden-type, manufacturing
112920	Mule production
424590	Mules merchant wholesalers
114111	Mullet fishing
517110	Multichannel multipoint distribution services (MMDS)
712110	Multidisciplinary museums
236116	Multifamily building construction general contractors
236117	Multifamily building operative builders
334515	Multimeters manufacturing
334210	Multiplex equipment, telephone, manufacturing
624190	Multiservice centers, neighborhood
212391	Muriate of potash, mining
325412	Muscle relaxant preparations manufacturing
212399	Muscovite mining and/or beneficiating
236220	Museum construction
712110	Museums
111411	Mushroom farming
111411	Mushroom spawn farming
311421	Mushrooms canning
519120	Music archives
711510	Music arrangers, independent
512230	Music book (i.e., bound sheet music) publishers
512230	Music book (i.e., bound sheet music) publishers and printing combined
323117	Music books printing or printing and binding without publishing
339999	Music boxes manufacturing
512230	Music copyright authorizing use
512230	Music copyright buying and licensing
711510	Music directors, independent
711310	Music festival managers with facilities
711320	Music festival managers without facilities
711310	Music festival organizers with facilities
711320	Music festival organizers without facilities
711310	Music festival promoters with facilities
711320	Music festival promoters without facilities
611610	Music instruction (e.g., guitar, piano)
515112	Music program distribution (except exclusively on Internet), radio
517110	Music program distribution, cable or satellite
512290	Music program distribution, pre-recorded
512230	Music publishers
339992	Music rolls, perforated, manufacturing
611610	Music schools (except academic)
451220	Music stores (e.g., cassette, compact disc, record, tape)
453310	Music stores (e.g., cassette, instrument, record, tape), used
451140	Music stores (i.e., instrument)
621340	Music therapists' offices (e.g., centers, clinics)
512110	Music video production
512110	Music video production and distribution
323112	Music, sheet, flexographic printing without publishing
323111	Music, sheet, gravure printing without publishing
323110	Music, sheet, lithographic (offset) printing without publishing
424990	Music, sheet, merchant wholesalers
323119	Music, sheet, printing (except flexographic, gravure, lithographic, quick, screen) without publishing
512230	Music, sheet, publishers and printing combined

323113	Music, sheet, screen printing without publishing
711130	Musical artists, independent
711130	Musical groups (except musical theater groups)
339992	Musical instrument accessories (e.g., mouthpieces, reeds, stands, traps) manufacturing
423990	Musical instrument accessories and supplies merchant wholesalers
316991	Musical instrument cases, all materials, manufacturing
532299	Musical instrument rental
811490	Musical instrument repair shops without retailing new musical instruments
451140	Musical instrument stores
339992	Musical instruments (except toy) manufacturing
423990	Musical instruments merchant wholesalers
339932	Musical instruments, toy, manufacturing
711130	Musical productions (except musical theater productions), live
512220	Musical recording, releasing, promoting, and distributing
423990	Musical recordings (e.g., compact discs, records, tapes) merchant wholesalers
711110	Musical theater companies or groups
711110	Musical theater productions, live
711130	Musicians, independent
111219	Muskmelon farming, field, bedding plant and seed production
114112	Mussel fishing
112512	Mussel production, farm raising
111120	Mustard seed farming, field and seed production
311941	Mustard, prepared, manufacturing
523120	Mutual fund agencies (i.e., brokerages)
523120	Mutual fund agents' (i.e., brokers') offices

523920	Mutual fund managing
525990	Mutual funds, closed-end
525910	Mutual funds, open-ended
522120	Mutual savings banks
621511	Mycology health laboratories
325191	Myrobalans extract manufacturing
333991	Nail guns, handheld power-driven, manufacturing
333513	Nail heading machines manufacturing
325620	Nail polish remover manufacturing
325620	Nail polishes manufacturing
812113	Nail salons
333991	Nailers and staplers, handheld power-driven, manufacturing
423510	Nails merchant wholesalers
331319	Nails, aluminum, made in wire drawing plants
332618	Nails, brads, and staples made from purchased wire
331222	Nails, iron or steel, made in wire drawing plants
331491	Nails, nonferrous metals (except aluminum, copper), made from purchased nonferrous metals (except aluminum, copper) in wire drawing plants
332999	Name plate blanks, metal, manufacturing
541711	Nanobiotechnologies research and experimental development laboratories
325998	Napalm manufacturing
325192	Naphtha made by distillation of coal tar
324110	Naphtha made in petroleum refineries
325192	Naphtha, solvent, made by distillation of coal tar
325192	Naphthalene made from refined petroleum or natural gas
325192	Naphthalenesulfonic acid manufacturing
325199	Naphthenic acid soaps manufacturing
325192	Naphthenic acids made from refined petroleum or natural gas

324110	Naphthenic acids made in petroleum refineries
325192	Naphthol, alpha and beta, manufacturing
325192	Naphtholsulfonic acids manufacturing
423220	Napkins (except paper) merchant wholesalers
314129	Napkins made from purchased fabrics
424130	Napkins, paper, merchant wholesalers
322291	Napkins, table, made from purchased paper
322121	Napkins, table, made in paper mills
313311	Napping broadwoven fabrics
333292	Napping machinery for textiles manufacturing
313312	Napping textile products and fabrics (except broadwoven fabrics)
313221	Narrow fabrics weaving
927110	National Aeronautics and Space Administration
522110	National commercial banks
522298	National Credit Union Administration (NCUA)
928110	National Guard
712190	National parks
926120	National Transportation Safety Board
311422	Nationality specialty foods canning
311412	Nationality specialty foods, frozen, manufacturing
212399	Native asphalt mining and/or beneficiating
327310	Natural (i.e., calcined earth) cement manufacturing
212399	Natural abrasives (e.g., emery, grindstones, hones, pumice) (except sand) mining and/or beneficiating
313113	Natural fiber (i.e., hemp, linen, ramie) thread manufacturing
313210	Natural fiber fabrics (i.e., jute, linen, hemp, ramie), broadwoven, weaving
313221	Natural fiber fabrics (i.e., jute, linen, hemp, ramie), narrow woven, weaving
313111	Natural fiber spun yarns (i.e., hemp, jute, ramie, flax) made from purchased fiber
221210	Natural gas brokers
221210	Natural gas distribution systems
333618	Natural gas engines manufacturing
211112	Natural gas liquids (e.g., ethane, isobutane, natural gasoline, propane) recovered from oil and gas field gases
486910	Natural gas liquids pipeline transportation
221210	Natural gas marketers
237120	Natural gas pipeline construction
486210	Natural gas pipeline transportation
238220	Natural gas piping installation
237120	Natural gas processing plant construction
211111	Natural gas production
486210	Natural gas transmission (i.e., processing plants to local distribution systems)
211111	Natural gas, offshore production
211112	Natural gasoline recovered from oil and gas field gases
712110	Natural history museums
325199	Natural nonfood coloring, manufacturing
813312	Natural resource preservation organizations
712110	Natural science museums
712190	Natural wonder tourist attractions (e.g., caverns, waterfalls)
312112	Naturally carbonated water, purifying and bottling
712190	Nature centers
712190	Nature parks
712190	Nature preserves
712190	Nature reserves
621399	Naturopaths' offices (e.g., centers, clinics)
334511	Nautical systems and instruments manufacturing

332995   Naval artillery manufacturing
336611   Naval ship building
325191   Naval stores, gum or wood, manufacturing
811219   Navigational instruments (e.g., radar, sonar) repair and maintenance services
423860   Navigational instruments (except electronic) merchant wholesalers
334511   Navigational instruments manufacturing
423690   Navigational instruments, electronic (e.g., radar, sonar), merchant wholesalers
928110   Navy
312120   Near beer brewing
311613   Neatsfoot oil rendering
315292   Neckpieces, fur (except apparel contractors), manufacturing
315211   Neckpieces, fur, men's and boys', cut and sew apparel contractors
315212   Neckpieces, fur, women's, girls', and infants', cut and sew apparel contractors
315191   Neckties made in apparel knitting mills
315211   Neckties, men's and boys', cut and sew apparel contractors
315993   Neckties, men's and boys', cut and sewn from purchased fabric (except apparel contractors)
424320   Neckties, men's and boys', merchant wholesalers
315999   Neckties, women's and girls', cut and sewn from purchased fabric (except apparel contractors)
315212   Neckties, women's, girls', and infants', cut and sew apparel contractors
315191   Neckwear made in a apparel knitting mills
448150   Neckwear stores
315993   Neckwear, men's and boys', cut and sewn from purchased fabric (except apparel contractors)

315211   Neckwear, men's and boys', cut and sew apparel contractors
315212   Neckwear, women's, girls' and infants', cut and sew apparel contractors
111339   Nectarine farming
332991   Needle roller bearings manufacturing
451130   Needlecraft sewing supply stores
339993   Needles (except hypodermic, phonograph, styli) manufacturing
333292   Needles for knitting machinery manufacturing
339112   Needles, hypodermic and suture, manufacturing
334419   Needles, phonograph and styli, manufacturing
424310   Needles, sewing, merchant wholesalers
314999   Needlework art contractors on apparel
315192   Negligees made in apparel knitting mills
315212   Negligees, women's, cut and sew apparel contractors
315231   Negligees, women's, misses', and girls', cut and sewn from purchased fabric (except apparel contractors)
813319   Neighborhood development advocacy organizations
325120   Neon manufacturing
339950   Neon signs manufacturing
325212   Neoprene manufacturing
212325   Nepheline syenite mining and/or beneficiating
334516   Nephelometers (except meteorological) manufacturing
334519   Nephoscopes manufacturing
333292   Net and lace making machinery manufacturing
424310   Net goods merchant wholesalers
313210   Nets and nettings, more than 12 inches in width, weaving
313249   Netting made in warp knitting mills
313241   Netting made in weft knitting mills

313249	Netting made on a lace or net machine
326199	Netting, plastics, manufacturing
332618	Netting, woven, made from purchased wire
515111	Network broadcasting service, radio
515111	Network radio broadcasting
541512	Network systems integration design services, computer
515120	Network television broadcasting
515210	Networks, cable television
622310	Neurological hospitals
621111	Neurologists' offices (e.g., centers, clinics)
621111	Neuropathologists' offices (e.g., centers, clinics)
312140	Neutral spirit, beverages (except fruit), manufacturing
424820	Neutral spirits merchant wholesalers
334516	Neutron activation analysis instruments manufacturing
441110	New car dealers
541613	New product development consulting services
321918	Newel posts, wood, manufacturing
519190	News clipping services
451212	News dealers
519110	News picture gathering and distributing services
519110	News reporting services
519110	News service syndicates
519110	News ticker services
511120	Newsletter publishers (except exclusive Internet publishing)
511120	Newsletter publishers and printing combined (except Internet)
519130	Newsletter publishers, exclusively on Internet
323112	Newsletters flexographic printing without publishing
323111	Newsletters gravure printing without publishing
323110	Newsletters lithographic (offset) printing without publishing

323119	Newsletters printing (except flexographic, gravure, lithographic, quick, screen) without publishing
323113	Newsletters screen printing without publishing
541840	Newspaper advertising representatives (i.e., independent of media owners)
424920	Newspaper agencies merchant wholesalers
511110	Newspaper branch offices
711510	Newspaper columnists, independent (freelance)
519110	Newspaper feature syndicates
333293	Newspaper inserting equipment manufacturing
511110	Newspaper publishers (except exclusive Internet publishing)
511110	Newspaper publishers and printing combined
519130	Newspaper publishing, exclusively on Internet
323112	Newspapers flexographic printing without publishing
323111	Newspapers gravure printing without publishing
323110	Newspapers lithographic (offset) printing without publishing
424920	Newspapers merchant wholesalers
323119	Newspapers printing (except flexographic, gravure, lithographic, quick, screen) without publishing
323113	Newspapers screen printing without publishing
424110	Newsprint merchant wholesalers
322122	Newsprint mills
322122	Newsprint paper, manufacturing
451212	Newsstands (i.e., permanent)
339941	Nibs (i.e., pen points) manufacturing
331522	Nickel alloy die-castings, unfinished, manufacturing
325188	Nickel ammonium sulfate manufacturing

331491 Nickel and nickel alloy pipe, plate, sheet, strip, and tubing made from purchased metals or scrap

335911 Nickel cadmium storage batteries manufacturing

325188 Nickel carbonate manufacturing

331528 Nickel castings (except die-castings), unfinished, manufacturing

325188 Nickel compounds, not specified elsewhere by process, manufacturing

212234 Nickel concentrates recovery

331522 Nickel die-castings, unfinished, manufacturing

332999 Nickel foil not made in rolling mills

212234 Nickel ore beneficiating plants

212234 Nickel ore mine site development for own account

212234 Nickel ores mining and/or beneficiating

331492 Nickel recovering from scrap and/or alloying purchased metals

331419 Nickel refining, primary

331491 Nickel rolling, drawing, or extruding purchased metals or scrap

325188 Nickel sulfate manufacturing

325411 Nicotine and derivatives (i.e., basic chemicals) manufacturing

325320 Nicotine insecticides manufacturing

337122 Night stands, wood, manufacturing

333314 Night vision optical device manufacturing

713990 Nightclubs without alcoholic beverages

722410 Nightclubs, alcoholic beverage

315192 Nightgowns made in apparel knitting mills

315291 Nightgowns, infants', cut and sewn from purchased fabric (except apparel contractors)

315211 Nightgowns, men's and boys', cut and sew apparel contractors

315221 Nightgowns, men's and boys', cut and sewn from purchased fabric (except apparel contractors)

315212 Nightgowns, women's, girls', and infants', cut and sew apparel contractors

315231 Nightgowns, women's, misses', and girls', cut and sewn from purchased fabric (except apparel contractors)

315192 Nightshirts made in apparel knitting mills

315291 Nightshirts, infants', cut and sewn from purchased fabric (except apparel contractors)

315211 Nightshirts, men's and boys', cut and sew apparel contractors

315221 Nightshirts, men's and boys', cut and sewn from purchased fabric (except apparel contractors)

315212 Nightshirts, women's, girls', and infants', cut and sew apparel contractors

315231 Nightshirts, women's, misses', and girls', cut and sewn from purchased fabric (except contractors)

315192 Nightwear made in apparel knitting mills

315291 Nightwear, infants', cut and sewn from purchased fabric (except apparel contractors)

315211 Nightwear, men's and boys', cut and sew apparel contractors

315221 Nightwear, men's and boys', cut and sewn from purchased fabric (except apparel contractors)

424320 Nightwear, men's and boys', merchant wholesalers

315212 Nightwear, women's, girls', and infants', cut and sew apparel contractors

315231	Nightwear, women's, misses', and girls', cut and sewn from purchased fabric (except apparel contractors)
331419	Niobium refining, primary
326299	Nipples and teething rings, rubber, manufacturing
332996	Nipples, metal, made from purchased pipe
325192	Nitrated hydrocarbon derivatives manufacturing
325311	Nitric acid manufacturing
325212	Nitrile rubber manufacturing
325212	Nitrile-butadiene rubber manufacturing
325212	Nitrile-chloroprene rubbers manufacturing
325192	Nitroaniline manufacturing
325192	Nitrobenzene manufacturing
325211	Nitrocellulose (i.e., pyroxylin) resins manufacturing
325920	Nitrocellulose explosive materials manufacturing
325221	Nitrocellulose fibers manufacturing
325120	Nitrogen manufacturing
325311	Nitrogenous fertilizer materials manufacturing
325314	Nitrogenous fertilizers made by mixing purchased materials
325920	Nitroglycerin explosive materials manufacturing
325192	Nitrophenol manufacturing
325192	Nitrosated hydrocarbon derivatives manufacturing
325132	Nitroso dyes manufacturing
325920	Nitrostarch explosive materials manufacturing
325199	Nitrous ether manufacturing
325120	Nitrous oxide manufacturing
325411	N-methylpiperazine manufacturing
924110	NOAA (National Oceanic and Atmospheric Administration)
339113	Noise protectors, personal, manufacturing
312120	Nonalcoholic beer brewing
312130	Nonalcoholic wines manufacturing
551112	Nonbank holding companies (except managing)
325222	Noncellulosic fibers and filaments manufacturing
325222	Noncellulosic filament yarn manufacturing
325222	Noncellulosic staple fibers and filaments manufacturing
111339	Noncitrus fruit farming
327125	Nonclay refractories (e.g., block, brick, mortar, tile) manufacturing
311514	Nondairy creamers, dry, manufacturing
311511	Nondairy creamers, liquid, manufacturing
541380	Non-destructive testing laboratories or services
425120	Nondurable goods agents and brokers, wholesale trade
425110	Nondurable goods business to business electronic markets, wholesale trade
325110	Nonene made from refined petroleum or liquid hydrocarbons
311514	Nonfat dry milk manufacturing
331522	Nonferrous (except aluminum) die-casting foundries
331492	Nonferrous alloys (except aluminum, copper) made from purchased nonferrous metals
331492	Nonferrous alloys (except aluminum, copper) made in integrated secondary smelting and alloying plants
331419	Nonferrous metal (except aluminum, copper) shapes made in primary nonferrous metal smelting and refining mills
331491	Nonferrous metal shapes (except aluminum, copper) made by rolling, drawing, or extruding purchased nonferrous metal
331491	Nonferrous metal shapes (except aluminum, copper) made in integrated secondary smelting and extruding mills

331491 Nonferrous metal shapes (except aluminum, copper) made in integrated secondary smelting and rolling mills

331491 Nonferrous metal shapes (except aluminum, copper) made in integrated secondary smelting mills and wire drawing plants

331528 Nonferrous metals (except aluminum, copper) foundries (except die-casting)

331419 Nonferrous metals (except aluminum, copper) made in primary nonferrous metal smelting and refining mills

331492 Nonferrous metals (except aluminum, copper) secondary smelting and refining

331419 Nonferrous metals (except aluminum, copper) smelting and refining, primary

331528 Nonferrous metals (except aluminum, copper) unfinished castings (except die-castings) manufacturing

423510 Nonferrous metals (except precious) merchant wholesalers

331491 Nonferrous wire (except aluminum, copper) made from purchased nonferrous metals (except aluminum, copper) in wire drawing plants

331491 Nonferrous wire (except aluminum, copper) made in integrated secondary smelting mills and wire drawing plants

323121 Nonfiction book binding without printing

511130 Nonfiction book publishers (except exclusive Internet publshing)

511130 Nonfiction book publishers and printing combined

519130 Nonfiction book publishers, exclusively on Internet

323117 Nonfiction books printing and binding without publishing

323117 Nonfiction books printing without publishing

562219 Nonhazardous waste treatment and disposal facilities (except combustors, incinerators, landfills, sewer systems, sewage treatment facilities)

423510 Noninsulated wire merchant wholesalers

423520 Nonmetallic minerals (except precious and semiprecious stones and minerals used in construction, such as sand and gravel)

213115 Nonmetallic minerals mining support services (e.g., blasting, shaft sinking, tunneling) (except site preparation and related construction contractor activities)on a contract basis

325412 Nonprescription drug preparations manufacturing

424210 Nonprescription drugs merchant wholesalers

531312 Nonresidential property managing

531120 Nonresidential building (except miniwarehouse) rental or leasing

481212 Nonscheduled air freight transportation

481211 Nonscheduled air passenger transportation

332214 Nonstick metal cooking utensils

337122 Nonupholstered, household-type, custom wood furniture, manufacturing

313230 Nonwoven fabric tapes manufacturing

313230 Nonwoven fabrics manufacturing

313230 Nonwoven felts manufacturing

311999 Noodle mixes made from purchased dry ingredients

311423 Noodle mixes made in dehydration plants

311823 Noodle mixes made in dry pasta plants

311823 Noodles, dry, manufacturing

311991 Noodles, fresh, manufacturing

311999	Noodles, fried, manufacturing
339113	Nose and ear plugs manufacturing
541199	Notary public services
541199	Notary publics' private practices
334111	Notebook computers manufacturing
322233	Notebooks (including mechanically bound by wire, or plastics) made from purchased paper
424120	Notebooks merchant wholesalers
332999	Novelties and specialties, nonprecious metal and precious plated, manufacturing
424990	Novelties merchant wholesalers
316999	Novelties, leather (e.g., cigarette lighter covers, key fobs), manufacturing
339999	Novelties, not specified elsewhere, manufacturing
339911	Novelties, precious metal (except precious plated), manufacturing
321999	Novelties, wood fiber, manufacturing
453220	Novelty shops
314999	Novelty stitching contractors on apparel
326199	Nozzles, aerosol spray, plastics, manufacturing
332919	Nozzles, fire fighting, manufacturing
332919	Nozzles, lawn hose, manufacturing
325212	N-type rubber manufacturing
332911	Nuclear application valves manufacturing
541690	Nuclear energy consulting services
926130	Nuclear energy inspection and regulation offices
325188	Nuclear fuel scrap reprocessing
325188	Nuclear fuels, inorganic, manufacturing
334519	Nuclear instrument modules manufacturing
334517	Nuclear irradiation equipment manufacturing

325412	Nuclear medicine (e.g., radioactive isotopes) preparations manufacturing
237130	Nuclear power plant construction
332410	Nuclear reactor steam supply systems manufacturing
332410	Nuclear reactors control rod drive mechanisms manufacturing
332410	Nuclear reactors manufacturing
332313	Nuclear shielding, fabricated metal plate work, manufacturing
332420	Nuclear waste casks, heavy gauge metal, manufacturing
237990	Nuclear waste disposal site construction
541711	Nucleic acid chemistry research and experimental development laboratories
721214	Nudist camps with accommodation facilities
713990	Nudist camps without accommodations
335314	Numerical controls, manufacturing
333512	Numerically controlled metal cutting machine tools manufacturing
812990	Numerology services
621610	Nurse associations, visiting
561311	Nurse registries
113210	Nurseries for reforestation growing trees
444220	Nursery and garden centers without tree production
337122	Nursery furniture (except upholstered), wood, manufacturing
337124	Nursery furniture, metal, manufacturing
624410	Nursery schools
424930	Nursery stock (except plant bulbs, seeds) merchant wholesalers
111421	Nursery stock growing
111421	Nursery with tree production (except for reforestation)
611519	Nurse's aides schools

813920	Nurses' associations		313112	Nylon yarn twisting or winding of purchased yarn
621399	Nurses', licensed practical or registered, offices (e.g., centers, clinics)		315111	Nylons, sheer, women's, misses', and girls' full-length and knee-length, knitting or knitting and finishing
621610	Nursing agencies, primarily providing home nursing services		325191	Oak extract manufacturing
623110	Nursing care facilities		321999	Oars, wood, manufacturing
623110	Nursing homes		111199	Oat farming, field and seed production
611519	Nursing schools (except academic)		311211	Oat flour manufacturing
445292	Nut (i.e., packaged) stores		311230	Oatmeal (i.e., cereal breakfast food) manufacturing
115114	Nut hulling and shelling			
331221	Nut rods, iron or steel, made in cold rolling mills		311230	Oats, breakfast cereal, manufacturing
331111	Nut rods, iron or steel, made in iron and steel mills		311230	Oats, rolled (i.e., cereal breakfast food), manufacturing
333111	Nut shellers, farm-type, manufacturing		812910	Obedience training services, pet
446191	Nutrition (i.e., food supplement) stores		339992	Oboes manufacturing
			713990	Observation towers
621399	Nutritionists' offices (e.g., centers, clinics)		712110	Observatories (except research institutions)
424450	Nuts (e.g., canned, roasted, salted) merchant wholesalers		541712	Observatories, research institutions
311320	Nuts, chocolate covered, made from cacao beans		622310	Obstetrical hospital
			621111	Obstetricians' offices (e.g., centers, clinics)
311330	Nuts, chocolate covered, made from purchased chocolate		339992	Ocarinas manufacturing
311340	Nuts, covered (except chocolate covered), manufacturing		926150	Occupational safety and health administration
311911	Nuts, kernels and seeds, roasting and processing		926150	Occupational safety and health standards agencies
115113	Nuts, machine harvesting		813920	Occupational therapists' associations
332722	Nuts, metal, manufacturing			
311911	Nuts, salted, roasted, cooked, canned, manufacturing		621340	Occupational therapists' offices (e.g., centers, clinics)
424590	Nuts, unprocessed or shelled only, merchant wholesalers		541712	Oceanographic research and development laboratories or services
325222	Nylon fibers and filaments manufacturing		212393	Ocher mining and/or beneficiating
315111	Nylon hosiery, sheer, women's, misses', and girls' full-length and knee-length, knitting or knitting and finishing		325131	Ocher pigments manufacturing
			339992	Octophones manufacturing
			114112	Octopus fishing
325211	Nylon resins manufacturing		621320	ODs' (doctors of optometry) offices (e.g., centers, clinics)
313111	Nylon spun yarns made from purchased fiber		332995	Oerlikon guns manufacturing
			721310	Off campus dormitories
313113	Nylon thread manufacturing		624190	Offender self-help organizations

336999	Off-highway tracked vehicles (except construction, armored military) manufacturing
333120	Off-highway trucks manufacturing
561110	Office administration services
541512	Office automation computer systems integration design services
236220	Office building construction
531120	Office building rental or leasing
561720	Office cleaning services
423420	Office equipment merchant wholesalers
337214	Office furniture (except wood), padded, upholstered, or plain (except wood), manufacturing
423210	Office furniture merchant wholesalers
532420	Office furniture rental or leasing
442110	Office furniture stores
238390	Office furniture, modular system, installation
337211	Office furniture, padded, upholstered, or plain wood, manufacturing
561320	Office help supply services
811212	Office machine repair and maintenance services (except communication equipment)
532420	Office machinery and equipment rental or leasing
423420	Office machines merchant wholesalers
561110	Office management services
322121	Office paper (e.g., computer printer, photocopy, plain paper) made in paper mills
322233	Office paper (e.g., computer printer, photocopy, plain paper), cut sheet, made from purchased paper
424120	Office supplies (except furniture, machines) merchant wholesalers
322231	Office supplies, die-cut paper, made from purchased paper or paperboard
561320	Office supply pools
453210	Office supply stores

336999	Off-road all-terrain vehicles (ATVs), wheeled or tracked, manufacturing
441221	Off-road all-terrain vehicles (ATVs), wheeled or tracked, dealers
325910	Offset inks manufacturing
323122	Offset plate preparation services
323110	Offset printing (except books, manifold business forms, printing grey goods)
333293	Offset printing presses manufacturing
211111	Offshore crude petroleum production
211111	Offshore natural gas production
713290	Off-track betting parlors
334515	Ohmmeters manufacturing
324110	Oil (i.e., petroleum) refineries
325998	Oil additive preparations manufacturing
324110	Oil additives made in petroleum refineries
424690	Oil additives merchant wholesalers
211111	Oil and gas field development for own account
237120	Oil and gas field distribution line construction
211111	Oil and gas field exploration for own account
213112	Oil and gas field services (except contract drilling, site preparation and related construction contractor activities) on a contract basis
333132	Oil and gas field-type drilling machinery and equipment (except offshore floating platforms) manufacturing
336611	Oil and gas offshore floating platforms manufacturing
213111	Oil and gas well drilling services (redrilling, spudding, tailing) on a contract basis
238220	Oil burner installation
333414	Oil burners, heating, manufacturing
423720	Oil burners, heating, merchant wholesalers

811191 Oil change and lubrication shops, automotive

424690 Oil drilling muds merchant wholesalers

213112 Oil field exploration (except surveying) on a contract basis

532412 Oil field machinery and equipment rental or leasing

237310 Oil field road construction

423120 Oil filters, automotive, merchant wholesalers

336399 Oil filters, automotive, truck, and bus, manufacturing

424590 Oil kernels merchant wholesalers

523999 Oil lease brokers' offices

211112 Oil line drip, natural gas liquid

333913 Oil measuring and dispensing pumps manufacturing

424590 Oil nuts merchant wholesalers

237120 Oil pipeline construction

237120 Oil refinery construction

533110 Oil royalty companies

523910 Oil royalty dealing (i.e., acting as a principal in dealing royalties to investors)

533110 Oil royalty leasing

213112 Oil sampling services on a contract basis

339991 Oil seals manufacturing

211111 Oil shale mining and/or beneficiating

562910 Oil spill cleanup services

332420 Oil storage tanks, heavy gauge metal, manufacturing

333319 Oil water separators manufacturing

532412 Oil well drilling machinery and equipment rental or leasing

213111 Oil well drilling on a contract basis

213112 Oil well logging on a contract basis

423830 Oil well machinery and equipment merchant wholesalers

213112 Oil well rig building, repairing, and dismantling, on a contract basis

423830 Oil well supply houses merchant wholesalers

311613 Oil, animal, rendering

311221 Oil, corn crude and refined, made by wet milling corn

311225 Oil, olive, made from purchased oils

424710 Oil, petroleum, bulk stations and terminals

424720 Oil, petroleum, merchant wholesalers (except bulk stations, terminals)

311225 Oil, vegetable stearin, made from purchased oils

423930 Oil, waste, merchant wholesalers

324199 Oil-based additives made from refined petroleum

313320 Oilcloth manufacturing

313320 Oiling of purchased textiles and apparel

325998 Oils (e.g., cutting, lubricating), synthetic, manufacturing

325192 Oils made by distillation of coal tar

424490 Oils, cooking and salad, merchant wholesalers

324110 Oils, fuel, manufacturing

424990 Oils, inedible, animal or vegetable, merchant wholesalers

324191 Oils, lubricating petroleum, made from refined petroleum

325998 Oils, lubricating, synthetic, manufacturing

324191 Oils, petroleum lubricating, re-refining used

325613 Oils, soluble (i.e., textile finishing assistants), manufacturing

325411 Oils, vegetable and animal, medicinal, uncompounded, manufacturing

325191 Oils, wood, made by distillation of wood

111191 Oilseed and grain combination farming, field and seed production

424990 Oilseed cake and meal merchant wholesalers

333294	Oilseed crushing and extracting machinery manufacturing
111120	Oilseed farming (except soybean), field and seed production
424590	Oilseeds merchant wholesalers
212399	Oilstones mining and/or beneficiating
333911	Oil-well and oil-field pumps manufacturing
111219	Okra farming, field, bedding plant and seed production
623312	Old age homes without nursing care
923130	Old age survivors and disability programs
623312	Old soldiers' homes without nursing care
325222	Olefin fibers and filaments manufacturing
325110	Olefins made from refined petroleum or liquid hydrocarbons
325199	Oleic acid (i.e., red oil) manufacturing
325199	Oleic acid esters manufacturing
325188	Oleum (i.e., fuming sulfuric acid) manufacturing
111339	Olive farming
311225	Olive oil made from purchased oils
311223	Olive oil made in crushing mills
311421	Olives brined
311423	Olives, dried, made in dehydration plant
212325	Olivine, non-gem, mining and/or beneficiating
334511	Omnibearing instrumentation manufacturing
621111	Oncologists' offices (e.g., centers, clinics)
812922	One-hour photofinishing services
111219	Onion farming, field, bedding plant and seed production
311421	Onions pickled
517919	On-line access service providers, using client-supplied telecommunications (e.g., dial-up ISPs)
517110	On-line access service providers, using own operated wired telecommunications infrastructure
212319	Onyx marble crushed and broken stone mining and/or beneficiating
212311	Onyx marble mining or quarrying
512132	Open air motion picture theaters
711110	Opera companies
315991	Opera hats cut and sewn from purchased fabric (except apparel contractors)
315211	Opera hats, men's and boys', cut and sew apparel contractors
315212	Opera hats, women's, girls', and infants', cut and sew apparel contractors
711130	Opera singers, independent
927110	Operating and launching government satellites
339113	Operating room tables manufacturing
511210	Operating systems software, computer, packaged
541614	Operations research consulting services
236220	Operative builders (i.e., building on own land, for sale), commercial and institutional building
236210	Operative builders (i.e., building on own land, for sale), industrial building (except warehouses)
236117	Operative builders (i.e., building on own land, for sale), residential
236117	Operative builders (i.e., building on own land, for sale), single-family housing
325411	Ophthalmic agents, uncompounded, manufacturing
423460	Ophthalmic goods (except cameras) merchant wholesalers
339112	Ophthalmic instruments and apparatus (except laser surgical) manufacturing
621111	Ophthalmologists' offices (e.g., centers, clinics)

339112	Ophthalmometers and ophthalmoscopes manufacturing
541910	Opinion research services
325411	Opium and opium derivatives (i.e., basic chemicals) manufacturing
333314	Optical alignment and display instruments (except photographic) manufacturing
334112	Optical disk drives manufacturing
423460	Optical goods (except cameras) merchant wholesalers
446130	Optical goods stores (except offices of optometrists)
212399	Optical grade calcite mining and/or beneficiating
333314	Optical gun sighting and fire control equipment and instruments manufacturing
811219	Optical instrument repair and maintenance services (e.g. microscopes, telescopes)
333298	Optical lens making and grinding machinery manufacturing
334119	Optical readers and scanners manufacturing
518210	Optical scanning services
333314	Optical test and inspection equipment manufacturing
334413	Optoelectronic devices manufacturing
339112	Optometers manufacturing
423460	Optometric equipment and supplies merchant wholesalers
813920	Optometrists' associations
621320	Optometrists' offices (e.g., centers, clinics)
621210	Oral and maxillofacial surgeons' offices (e.g., centers, clinics)
325412	Oral contraceptive preparations manufacturing
621210	Oral pathologists' offices (e.g., centers, clinics)
111310	Orange groves
325998	Orange oil manufacturing

115112	Orchard cultivation services (e.g., bracing, planting, pruning, removal, spraying, surgery)
111998	Orchard grass seed farming
711510	Orchestra conductors, independent
711130	Orchestras
454113	Order taking offices of mail-order houses
561422	Order-taking for clients over the internet
423990	Ordnance and accessories merchant wholesalers
236210	Ore and metal refinery construction
423520	Ore concentrates merchant wholesalers
333131	Ore crushing, washing, screening, and loading machinery manufacturing
423520	Ores (e.g., gold, iron, lead, silver, zinc) merchant wholesalers
621991	Organ banks, body
621991	Organ donor centers, body
424690	Organic chemicals merchant wholesalers
325222	Organic noncellulosic fibers and filaments manufacturing
325132	Organic pigments, dyes, lakes, and toners manufacturing
541612	Organization development consulting services
928120	Organization for Economic Cooperation and Development
928120	Organization of American States
326199	Organizers for closets, drawers, and shelves, plastics, manufacturing
711310	Organizers of agricultural fairs with facilities
711320	Organizers of agricultural fairs without facilities
711310	Organizers of arts events with facilities
711320	Organizers of arts events without facilities

711310 Organizers of festivals with facilities

711320 Organizers of festivals without facilities

711310 Organizers of live performing arts productions (e.g., concerts) with facilities

711320 Organizers of live performing arts productions (e.g., concerts) without facilities

711310 Organizers of sports events with facilities

711320 Organizers of sports events without facilities

325199 Organo-inorganic compound manufacturing

325320 Organo-phosphate based insecticides manufacturing

321219 Oriented strandboard (OSB) manufacturing

327420 Ornamental and architectural plaster work (e.g., columns, mantels, molding) manufacturing

112511 Ornamental fish production, farm raising

423390 Ornamental ironwork merchant wholesalers

238190 Ornamental metal work installation

332323 Ornamental metalwork manufacturing

111422 Ornamental plant growing

561730 Ornamental tree and shrub services

321918 Ornamental woodwork (e.g., cornices, mantels) manufacturing

339999 Ornaments, Christmas tree (except electric, glass), manufacturing

335129 Ornaments, Christmas tree, electric, manufacturing

327212 Ornaments, Christmas tree, glass, made in glass making plants

327215 Ornaments, Christmas tree, made from purchased glass

623990 Orphanages

325998 Orris oil manufacturing

325192 Orthodichlorobenzene manufacturing

339116 Orthodontic appliance, custom made in dental laboratories

339114 Orthodontic appliances manufacturing

621210 Orthodontists' offices (e.g., centers, clinics)

339113 Orthopedic canes manufacturing

339113 Orthopedic device manufacturing and sale in retail environment

339113 Orthopedic devices manufacturing

423450 Orthopedic equipment and supplies merchant wholesalers

339113 Orthopedic extension shoes manufacturing

339113 Orthopedic hosiery, elastic, manufacturing

622310 Orthopedic hospitals

621111 Orthopedic physicians' offices (e.g., centers, clinics)

327420 Orthopedic plaster, gypsum, manufacturing

316219 Orthopedic shoes (except extension shoes), children's, manufacturing

316213 Orthopedic shoes (except extension shoes), men's, manufacturing

316214 Orthopedic shoes (except extension shoes), women's, manufacturing

448210 Orthopedic shoes stores

621111 Orthopedic surgeons' offices (e.g., centers, clinics)

321219 OSB (oriented strandboard) manufacturing

334515 Oscillators (e.g., instrument type audiofrequency and radiofrequency) manufacturing

334515 Oscilloscopes manufacturing

212299 Osmium mining and/or beneficiating

334516 Osmometers manufacturing

325998 Ossein manufacturing

622110 Osteopathic hospitals

621111	Osteopathic physicians' (except mental health) offices (e.g., centers, clinics)
112390	Ostrich production
621111	Otolaryngologists' offices (e.g., centers, clinics)
334510	Otoscopes, electromedical, manufacturing
337121	Ottomans, upholstered, manufacturing
441222	Outboard motor dealers
811490	Outboard motor repair shops
333618	Outboard motors manufacturing
423910	Outboard motors merchant wholesalers
713990	Outdoor adventure operations (e.g., white water rafting) without accommodations
721214	Outdoor adventure retreats with accommodation facilities
541850	Outdoor display advertising services
423210	Outdoor furniture merchant wholesalers
237990	Outdoor recreation facility construction
451110	Outdoor sporting equipment stores
315191	Outerwear handknitted for the trade
424320	Outerwear, men's and boys', merchant wholesalers
424330	Outerwear, women's, children's, and infants', merchant wholesalers
335932	Outlet boxes, electrical wiring, manufacturing
335931	Outlets (i.e., receptacles), electrical, manufacturing
335931	Outlets, convenience, electrical, manufacturing
541850	Out-of-home media (i.e., display) advertising services
621420	Outpatient mental health centers and clinics (except hospitals)
621420	Outpatient treatment centers and clinics (except hospitals) for substance abuse (i.e., alcoholism, drug addiction)
621420	Outpatient treatment centers and clinics for alcoholism
621420	Outpatient treatment centers and clinics for drug addiction
325612	Oven cleaners manufacturing
334512	Oven temperature controls, nonindustrial, manufacturing
811412	Oven, household-type, repair and maintenance services without retailing new ovens
236210	Oven, industrial plant, construction
423720	Ovens (except electric), household-type, merchant wholesalers
333294	Ovens, bakery, manufacturing
333319	Ovens, commercial-type, manufacturing
423440	Ovens, commercial-type, merchant wholesalers
423620	Ovens, electric household-type, merchant wholesalers
335221	Ovens, freestanding household-type, manufacturing
333994	Ovens, industrial process and laboratory-type, manufacturing
423830	Ovens, industrial, merchant wholesalers
335211	Ovens, portable household-type (except microwave and convection ovens), manufacturing
335221	Ovens, portable household-type convention and microwave, manufacturing
327215	Ovenware made from purchased glass
327212	Ovenware, glass, made in glass making plants
315211	Overall jackets, work, men's and boys', cut and sew apparel contractors
315225	Overall jackets, work, men's and boys', cut and sewn from purchased fabric (except apparel contractors)
315211	Overalls, work, men's and boys', cut and sew apparel contractors

315225 Overalls, work, men's and boys', cut and sewn from purchased fabric (except apparel contractors)
213113 Overburden removal for coal mining on a contract basis
213114 Overburden removal for metal mining on a contract basis
213115 Overburden removal for nonmetallic minerals mining (except fuels) on a contract basis
315211 Overcoats, men's and boys', cut and sew apparel contractors
315222 Overcoats, men's and boys', cut and sewn from purchased fabric (except apparel contractors)
315212 Overcoats, women's, girls', and infants', cut and sew apparel contractors
315234 Overcoats, women's, misses', and girls', cut and sewn from purchased fabric (except apparel contractors)
333922 Overhead conveyors manufacturing
238290 Overhead door, commercial- or industrial-type, installation
238350 Overhead door, residential-type, installation
333315 Overhead projectors (except computer peripheral) manufacturing
334119 Overhead projectors, computer peripheral-type, manufacturing
333923 Overhead traveling cranes manufacturing
237310 Overpass construction
316211 Overshoes, plastics or plastics soled fabric upper, manufacturing
316211 Overshoes, rubber, or rubber soled fabric, manufacturing
325199 Oxalates (e.g., ammonium oxalate, ethyl oxalate, sodium oxalate) manufacturing
325199 Oxalic acid manufacturing
532291 Oxygen equipment rental (i.e. home use)

325120 Oxygen manufacturing
339112 Oxygen tents manufacturing
114112 Oyster dredging
112512 Oyster production, farm raising
212399 Ozokerite mining and/or beneficiating
333319 Ozone machines for water purification manufacturing
621999 Pacemaker monitoring services
334510 Pacemakers manufacturing
326299 Pacifiers, rubber, manufacturing
713990 Pack trains (i.e., trail riding), recreational
445310 Package stores (i.e., liquor)
511210 Packaged computer software publishers
326112 Packaging film, plastics, single-web or multiweb, manufacturing
115114 Packaging fresh or farm-dried fruits and vegetables
541420 Packaging industrial design services
333993 Packaging machinery manufacturing
423840 Packaging material merchant wholesalers
561910 Packaging services (except packing and crating for transportation)
326150 Packaging, foam plastics (except polystyrene), manufacturing
326199 Packaging, plastics (e.g., blister, bubble), manufacturing
325998 Packer's fluids manufacturing
488991 Packing and preparing goods for shipping
321920 Packing cases, wood, nailed or lock corner, manufacturing
321920 Packing crates, wood, manufacturing
115114 Packing fruits and vegetables
423830 Packing machinery and equipment merchant wholesalers
423840 Packing materials merchant wholesalers
813940 PACs (Political Action Committees)

316211	Pacs, plastics or plastics soled fabric upper, manufacturing
316211	Pacs, rubber or rubber soled fabric upper, manufacturing
322232	Padded envelopes manufacturing
314999	Padding and wadding (except nonwoven fabric) manufacturing
424310	Paddings, apparel, merchant wholesalers
321999	Paddles, wood, manufacturing
332510	Padlocks, metal, manufacturing
314129	Pads and protectors (e.g., ironing board, mattress, table), textile, made from purchased fabrics or felts
313230	Pads and wadding, nonwoven, manufacturing
322211	Pads, corrugated and solid fiberboard, made from purchased paper or paperboard
322233	Pads, desk, made from purchased paper
321999	Pads, excelsior, wood, manufacturing
322291	Pads, incontinent and bed, manufacturing
332999	Pads, soap impregnated scouring, manufacturing
321999	Pads, table, rattan, reed, and willow, manufacturing
443112	Pager and mobile phone stores
334220	Pagers manufacturing
517210	Paging services, except satellite
321920	Pails, coopered wood, manufacturing
326199	Pails, plastics, manufacturing
321920	Pails, plywood, manufacturing
321920	Pails, wood, manufacturing
621498	Pain therapy centers and clinics, outpatient
325510	Paint and varnish removers manufacturing
238320	Paint and wallpaper stripping
333994	Paint baking and drying ovens manufacturing
339994	Paint rollers manufacturing
424950	Paint rollers merchant wholesalers

811121	Paint shops,
333991	Paint spray guns, and pneumatic, manufacturing
333912	Paint sprayers (i.e., compressor and spray gun unit) manufacturing
332999	Paint sticks, metal, manufacturing
326199	Paint sticks, plastics, manufacturing
321999	Paint sticks, wood, manufacturing
444120	Paint stores
325510	Paint thinner and reducer preparations manufacturing
325510	Paintbrush cleaners manufacturing
339994	Paintbrushes manufacturing
424950	Paintbrushes merchant wholesalers
711510	Painters (i.e., artists), independent
424950	Painter's supplies (except artists', turpentine) merchant wholesalers
238320	Painting (except roof) contractors
238320	Painting and wallpapering
237310	Painting lines on highways, streets and bridges
332812	Painting metals and metal products for the trade
711510	Painting restorers, independent
237310	Painting traffic lanes or parking lots
238160	Painting, spraying, or coating, roof
325510	Paints (except artist's) manufacturing
424950	Paints (except artists') merchant wholesalers
339942	Paints, artist's, manufacturing
424990	Paints, artist's, merchant wholesalers
325510	Paints, emulsion (i.e., latex paint), manufacturing
325510	Paints, oil and alkyd vehicle, manufacturing
315192	Pajamas made in apparel knitting mills

315291 Pajamas, infants', cut and sewn from purchased fabric (except apparel contractors)

315211 Pajamas, men's and boys', cut and sew apparel contractors

315221 Pajamas, men's and boys', cut and sewn from purchased fabric (except apparel contractors)

315231 Pajamas, women's and girls', cut and sewn from purchased fabric (except apparel contractors)

315212 Pajamas, women's, girls', and infants', cut and sew apparel contractors

339942 Palettes, artist's, manufacturing

212299 Palladium mining and/or beneficiating

321920 Pallet containers, wood or wood and metal combination, manufacturing

333924 Pallet movers manufacturing

333924 Pallet or skid jacks manufacturing

332999 Pallet parts, metal, manufacturing

321920 Pallet parts, wood, manufacturing

532490 Pallet rental or leasing

423830 Pallets and skids merchant wholesalers

322211 Pallets, corrugated and solid fiber, made from purchased paper or paperboard

332999 Pallets, metal, manufacturing

321920 Pallets, wood or wood and metal combination, manufacturing

812990 Palm reading services

325199 Palmitic acid esters and amines manufacturing

311225 Palm-kernel oil made from purchased oils

311223 Palm-kernel oil, cake, and meal made in crushing mills

323121 Pamphlet binding without printing

511130 Pamphlet publishers (except exclusive Internet publishing)

511130 Pamphlet publishers and printing combined

519130 Pamphlet publishers, exclusively on Internet

424920 Pamphlets merchant wholesalers

323117 Pamphlets printing and binding without publishing

323117 Pamphlets printing without publishing

315991 Panama hats cut and sewn from purchased fabric (except apparel contractors)

315211 Panama hats, men's and boys', cut and sew apparel contractors

315212 Panama hats, women's, girls', and infants', cut and sew apparel contractors

311822 Pancake mixes made from purchased flour

311999 Pancake syrups (except pure maple) manufacturing

311412 Pancakes, frozen, manufacturing

238310 Panel or rigid board insulation installation

321918 Panel work, wood millwork, manufacturing

238390 Panel, metal, installation

334513 Panelboard indicators, recorders, and controllers, receiver industrial process-type, manufacturing

335313 Panelboards, electric power distribution, manufacturing

423610 Panelboards, electric power distribution, merchant wholesalers

238350 Paneling installation

423310 Paneling merchant wholesalers

236117 Panelized housing, residential, assembled on site by operative builders

236116 Panelized multifamily housing assembled on site by general contractors

236117 Panelized multifamily housing assembled on site by operative builders

236115   Panelized single-family house assembly on site by general contractors

335313   Panels, generator control and metering, manufacturing

321211   Panels, hardwood plywood, manufacturing

332311   Panels, prefabricated metal building, manufacturing

321992   Panels, prefabricated wood building, manufacturing

321212   Panels, softwood plywood, manufacturing

315192   Panties made in apparel knitting mills

315291   Panties, infants', cut and sewn from purchased fabric (except apparel contractors)

315212   Panties, women's and girls', cut and sew apparel contractors

315231   Panties, women's, misses', and girls', cut and sewn from purchased fabric (except apparel contractors)

315239   Pants outfits (except pantsuits), women's, misses', and girls', cut and sewn from purchased fabric (except apparel contractors)

315212   Pants outfits, women's, girls', and infants', cut and sew apparel contractors

315211   Pants, althletic, men's and boys', cut and sew apparel contractors

315291   Pants, athletic, infants', cut and sewn from purchased fabric (except apparel contractors)

315191   Pants, athletic, made in apparel knitting mills

315228   Pants, athletic, men's and boys' (e.g., gymnastic, ski), cut and sewn from purchased fabric (except apparel contractors)

315212   Pants, athletic, women's, girls', and infants', cut and sew apparel contractors

315239   Pants, athletic, women's, misses', and girls', cut and sewn from purchased fabric (except apparel contractors)

315211   Pants, dress, men's and boys', cut and sew apparel contractors

315224   Pants, dress, men's and boys', cut and sewn from purchased fabric (except apparel contractors)

315291   Pants, infants' waterproof, cut and sewn from purchased fabric (except apparel contractors)

315212   Pants, infants', cut and sew apparel contractors

315291   Pants, infants', cut and sewn from purchased fabric (except apparel contractors)

315292   Pants, leather (except apparel contractors), manufacturing

315211   Pants, leather, men's and boys', cut and sew apparel contractors

315211   Pants, men's and boys', cut and sew apparel contractors

315191   Pants, outerwear, made in apparel knitting mills

315299   Pants, rubber and rubberized fabric, made in the same establishment as the basic material

315291   Pants, sweat, infant's, cut and sewn from purchased fabric (except apparel contractors)

315228   Pants, sweat, men's and boys', cut and sewn from purchased fabric (except apparel contractors)

315212   Pants, sweat, women's, girls', and infants', cut and sew apparel contractors

315239   Pants, sweat, women's, misses', and girls', cut and sewn from purchased fabric (except apparel contractors)

315211   Pants, unisex sweat, cut and sew apparel contractors

315228   Pants, unisex sweat, cut and sewn from purchased fabric (except apparel contractors)

315299   Pants, vulcanized rubber, manufacturing

315299 Pants, waterproof outerwear (except infants'), cut and sewn from purchased fabric (except apparel contractors)

315211 Pants, waterproof outerwear, men's and boys', cut and sew apparel contractors

315212 Pants, waterproof outerwear, women's, girls', and infants', cut and sew apparel contractors

315212 Pants, women's, girls', and infants', cut and sew apparel contractors

315239 Pants, women's, misses', and girls', cut and sewn from purchased fabric (except apparel contractors)

315211 Pants, work (except dungarees, jeans), men's and boys', cut and sew apparel contractors

315225 Pants, work (except dungarees, jeans), men's and boys', cut and sewn from purchased fabric (except apparel contractors)

315291 Pantsuits, infants', cut and sewn from purchased fabric (except apparel contractors)

315212 Pantsuits, women's, girls', and infants', cut and sew apparel contractors

315234 Pantsuits, women's, misses', and girls', cut and sewn from purchased fabric (except apparel contractors)

315212 Panty girdles cut and sew apparel contractors

315231 Panty girdles, women's, misses', and girls', cut and sewn from purchased fabric (except apparel contractors)

315111 Panty hose, women's and girls', knitting or knitting and finishing

111339 Papaya farming

327910 Paper (e.g., aluminum oxide, emery, garnet, silicon carbide), abrasive coated, made from purchased paper

424110 Paper (e.g., fine, printing, writing), bulk, merchant wholesalers

322121 Paper (except newsprint, uncoated groundwood) manufacturing

322121 Paper (except newsprint, uncoated groundwood) products made in paper mills

322121 Paper (except newsprint, uncoated groundwood), coated, laminated or treated, made in paper mills

424130 Paper (except office supplies, printing paper, stationery, writing paper) merchant wholesalers

333291 Paper and paperboard coating and finishing machinery manufacturing

333291 Paper and paperboard converting machinery manufacturing

333291 Paper and paperboard corrugating machinery manufacturing

333291 Paper and paperboard cutting and folding machinery manufacturing

333291 Paper and paperboard die-cutting and stamping machinery manufacturing

423830 Paper and pulp industries manufacturing machinery merchant wholesalers

333291 Paper bag making machinery manufacturing

424130 Paper bags merchant wholesalers

322223 Paper bags, coated, made from purchased paper

322224 Paper bags, uncoated, made from purchased paper

212324 Paper clay mining and/or beneficiating

332618 Paper clips made from purchased wire

331222 Paper clips, iron or steel, made in wire drawing plants

322215	Paper cups made from purchased paper or paperboard
339942	Paper cutters, office-type, manufacturing
322299	Paper dishes (e.g., cups, plates) made from molded pulp
322215	Paper dishes (e.g., cups, plates) made from purchased paper or paperboard
315212	Paper dresses, women's, girls', and infants', cut and sew apparel contractors
315233	Paper dresses, women's, misses, and girls', cut and sewn from purchased fabric (except apparel contractors)
313221	Paper fabric, narrow woven, weaving
313210	Paper fabrics, broadwoven, weaving
332618	Paper machine wire cloth made from purchased wire
333291	Paper making machinery manufacturing
811310	Paper making machinery repair and maintenance services
322121	Paper mills (except newsprint, uncoated groundwood paper mills)
322122	Paper mills, newsprint
322122	Paper mills, uncoated groundwood
322291	Paper napkins and tablecloths made from purchased paper
322299	Paper novelties made from purchased paper
236210	Paper or pulp mill construction
322215	Paper plates made from purchased paper or paperboard
322299	Paper products (except office supply), die-cut, made from purchased paper or paperboard
322231	Paper products, die-cut office supply, made from purchased paper or paperboard
332992	Paper shells (i.e., 30 mm. or less, 1.18 inch or less) manufacturing
322121	Paper stock for conversion into paper products (e.g., bag and sack stock, envelope stock, tissue stock, wallpaper stock) manufacturing
322291	Paper towels made from purchased paper
322121	Paper towels made in paper mills
313111	Paper yarn manufacturing
322121	Paper, asphalt, made in paper mills
423390	Paper, building, merchant wholesalers
339944	Paper, carbon, manufacturing
322211	Paper, corrugated, made from purchased paper or paperboard
523110	Paper, dealing of commercial (i.e., acting as principal in dealing securities to investors)
322122	Paper, newsprint and uncoated groundwood, manufacturing
424120	Paper, office (e.g., carbon, computer, copier, typewriter), merchant wholesalers
325992	Paper, photographic sensitized, manufacturing
423930	Paper, scrap, merchant wholesalers
339944	Paper, stencil, manufacturing
322130	Paperboard (e.g., can/drum stock, container board, corrugating medium, folding carton stock, linerboard, tube) manufacturing
424130	Paperboard and paperboard products (except office supplies) merchant wholesalers
333291	Paperboard box making machinery manufacturing
322130	Paperboard coating, laminating, or treating in paperboard mills
333291	Paperboard making machinery manufacturing
322130	Paperboard mills
322130	Paperboard products (e.g., containers) made in paperboard mills

322226 Paperboard, pasted, lined, laminated, or surface coated, made from purchased paperboard
238320 Paperhanging and removal contractors
238320 Paperhanging or removal contractors
327999 Papier-mache statuary and related art goods (e.g., urns, vases) manufacturing
713990 Para sailing, recreational
314999 Parachutes manufacturing
213112 Paraffin services, oil and gas field, on a contract basis
324110 Paraffin waxes made in petroleum refineries
325110 Paraffins made from refined petroleum or liquid hydrocarbons
541199 Paralegal services
321213 Parallel strand lumber manufacturing
621399 Paramedics' offices (e.g., centers, clinics)
325132 Pararosaniline dyes manufacturing
621511 Parasitology health laboratories
339999 Parasols manufacturing
325320 Parathion insecticides manufacturing
485991 Paratransit transportation services
561431 Parcel mailing services combined with one or more other office support services, private
561431 Parcel mailing services, private
333997 Parcel post scales manufacturing
316110 Parchment leather manufacturing
922150 Pardon boards and offices
624190 Parenting support services
813410 Parent-teachers' associations
325320 Paris green insecticides manufacturing
237990 Park and recreational open space improvement construction

922120 Park police
332812 Parkerizing metals and metal products for the trade
236220 Parking garage construction
812930 Parking garages, automobile
561790 Parking lot cleaning (e.g., power sweeping, washing) services
237310 Parking lot marking and line painting
238990 Parking lot paving and sealing
812930 Parking lots, automobile
334514 Parking meters manufacturing
561612 Parking security services
488119 Parking services, aircraft
812930 Parking services, valet
713110 Parks (e.g., theme, water), amusement
924120 Parks and recreation commission, government
712190 Parks, national
712190 Parks, nature
712130 Parks, wild animal
237310 Parkway construction
611310 Parochial schools, college level
611110 Parochial schools, elementary or secondary
624190 Parole offices, privately operated
922150 Parole offices, publicly administered
238330 Parquet flooring installation
321918 Parquet flooring, hardwood, manufacturing
321918 Parquetry, hardwood, manufacturing
111219 Parsley farming, field, bedding plant and seed production
111219 Parsnip farming, field, bedding plant and seed production
335999 Particle accelerators, high voltage, manufacturing
334516 Particle beam excitation instruments, laboratory-type, manufacturing
334516 Particle size analyzers manufacturing
321219 Particleboard manufacturing
423310 Particleboard merchant wholesalers

238390	Partition (e.g., office, washroom), metal, installation
238390	Partition, moveable and/or demountable, installation
337215	Partitions for floor attachment, prefabricated, manufacturing
423440	Partitions merchant wholesalers
322211	Partitions, corrugated and solid fiber, made from purchased paper or paperboard
337215	Partitions, freestanding, prefabricated, manufacturing
332323	Partitions, ornamental metal, manufacturing
441310	Parts and accessories dealers, automotive
423120	Parts, new, motor vehicle, merchant wholesalers
423140	Parts, used, motor vehicle, merchant wholesalers
532299	Party (i.e., banquet) equipment rental
453220	Party goods (e.g., paper supplies, decorations, novelties) stores
454390	Party plan merchandisers, direct selling
812990	Party planning services
532299	Party rental supply centers
481211	Passenger air transportation, nonscheduled
481111	Passenger air transportation, scheduled
333922	Passenger baggage belt loaders (except industrial truck) manufacturing
532112	Passenger car leasing
532111	Passenger car rental
481211	Passenger carriers, air, nonscheduled
481111	Passenger carriers, air, scheduled
485320	Passenger limousine rental with driver (except shuttle service, taxi)
482111	Passenger railways, line-haul
336611	Passenger ship building
483114	Passenger transportation, coastal or Great Lakes (including St. Lawrence Seaway)
483114	Passenger transportation, deep sea, to and from domestic ports (including Puerto Rico)
483112	Passenger transportation, deep sea, to or from foreign ports
483212	Passenger transportation, inland waters (except on Great Lakes system)
532112	Passenger van leasing
532111	Passenger van rental
532111	Passenger van rental agencies
485320	Passenger van rental with driver (except shuttle service, taxi)
532112	Passenger vehicle fleet leasing
111339	Passion fruit farming
928120	Passport issuing services
541921	Passport photography services
311422	Pasta based products canning
333294	Pasta making machinery (i.e., food manufacturing-type) manufacturing
311999	Pasta mixes made from purchased dry ingredients
311823	Pasta, dry, manufacturing
311991	Pasta, fresh, manufacturing
331314	Paste made from purchased aluminum
331423	Paste made from purchased copper
331221	Paste made from purchased iron or steel
331111	Paste, iron or steel, made in iron and steel mills
331492	Paste, nonferrous metals (except aluminum, copper), made from purchased metal
325520	Pastes, adhesive, manufacturing
311421	Pastes, fruit and vegetable, canning
333294	Pasteurizing equipment, food, manufacturing
311511	Pasteurizing milk
311612	Pastrami made from purchased carcasses
311812	Pastries (e.g., Danish, French), fresh, made in commercial bakeries
311813	Pastries (e.g., Danish, French), frozen, manufacturing

311822 Pastries, uncooked, manufacturing

321999 Pastry boards, wood, manufacturing

541199 Patent agent services (i.e., patent filing and searching services)

541110 Patent attorneys' offices

541110 Patent attorneys' private practices

541990 Patent broker services (i.e., patent marketing services)

533110 Patent buying and licensing

533110 Patent leasing

316110 Patent leather manufacturing

325412 Patent medicine preparations manufacturing

621511 Pathological analysis laboratories

621111 Pathologists' (except oral, speech, voice) offices (e.g., centers, clinics)

621111 Pathologists', forensic, offices (e.g., centers, clinics)

621111 Pathologists', neuropathological, offices (e.g., centers, clinics)

621210 Pathologists', oral, offices (e.g., centers, clinics)

621340 Pathologists', speech or voice, offices (e.g., centers, clinics)

621111 Pathologists', surgical, offices (e.g., centers, clinics)

621511 Pathology laboratories, medical

334510 Patient monitoring equipment (e.g., intensive care, coronary care unit) manufacturing

423450 Patient monitoring equipment merchant wholesalers

327331 Patio block, concrete, manufacturing

238990 Patio construction

336611 Patrol boat building

561612 Patrol services, security

541990 Patrolling (i.e., visual inspection) of electric transmission or gas lines

511199 Pattern and plan (e.g., clothing patterns) publishers (except exclusive Internet publishing)

511199 Pattern and plan (e.g., clothing patterns) publishers and printing combined

519130 Pattern and plan (e.g., clothing patterns) publishers, exclusively on Internet

332997 Patterns (except shoe), industrial, manufacturing

423830 Patterns (except shoe), industrial, merchant wholesalers

323112 Patterns and plans (e.g., clothing patterns) flexographic printing without publishing

323111 Patterns and plans (e.g., clothing patterns) gravure printing without publishing

323110 Patterns and plans (e.g., clothing patterns) lithographic (offset) printing without publishing

323119 Patterns and plans (e.g., clothing patterns) printing (except flexographic, gravure, lithographic, blueprinting, quick, screen) without publishing

323113 Patterns and plans (e.g., clothing patterns) screen printing without publishing

339999 Patterns, shoe, manufacturing

423850 Patterns, shoe, merchant wholesalers

237310 Pavement, highway, road, street, bridge or airport runway, construction

238990 Paver, brick (e.g., driveway, patio, sidewalk), installation

212399 Pavers mining and/or beneficiating

324121 Paving blocks and mixtures made from purchased asphaltic materials

327331 Paving blocks, concrete, manufacturing

327121 Paving brick, clay, manufacturing

333120 Paving machinery manufacturing

238990	Paving, residential and commercial driveway and parking lot
522298	Pawnshops
812990	Pay telephone equipment concession operators
515210	Pay television networks
515210	Pay-per-view cable programming
541214	Payroll processing services
334210	PBX (private branch exchange) equipment manufacturing
111219	Pea (except dry) farming, field and seed production
111130	Pea farming, dry, field and seed production
813319	Peace advocacy organizations
928120	Peace Corps
111339	Peach farming
325132	Peacock blue lake manufacturing
311911	Peanut butter blended with jelly manufacturing
311911	Peanut butter manufacturing
311223	Peanut cake, meal, and oil made in crushing mills
333111	Peanut combines (i.e., diggers, packers, threshers) manufacturing
111992	Peanut farming
311225	Peanut oil made from purchased oils
333294	Peanut roasting machines (i.e., food manufacturing-type) manufacturing
115114	Peanut shelling
115113	Peanut, machine harvesting
111339	Pear farming
339913	Pearl drilling, peeling, or sawing
325131	Pearl essence pigment, synthetic, manufacturing
331511	Pearlitic castings, malleable iron, unfinished, manufacturing
423940	Pearls merchant wholesalers
339914	Pearls, costume, manufacturing
212399	Peat grinding
212399	Peat humus mining and/or beneficiating
212399	Peat mining and/or beneficiating
327999	Peat pots, molded pulp, manufacturing
212321	Pebbles (except grinding) mining and/or beneficiating
212399	Pebbles grinding
111335	Pecan farming
115114	Pecan hulling and shelling
311942	Pectin manufacturing
621111	Pediatricians' (except mental health) offices (e.g., centers, clinics)
621112	Pediatricians', mental health, offices (e.g., centers, clinics)
812113	Pedicure and manicure salons
812113	Pedicurist services
115210	Pedigree (i.e., livestock, pets, poultry) record services
334514	Pedometers manufacturing
813920	Peer review boards
212325	Pegmatite, feldspar, mining and/or beneficiating
316999	Pegs, leather shoe, manufacturing
332994	Pellet guns manufacturing
333131	Pellet mills machinery, mining-type, manufacturing
332992	Pellets, air rifle and pistol, manufacturing
316110	Pelts bleaching, currying, dyeing, scraping, and tanning
424590	Pelts, raw, merchant wholesalers
339112	Pelvimeters manufacturing
339941	Pen refills and cartridges manufacturing
339942	Pencil leads manufacturing
339942	Pencil sharpeners manufacturing
321999	Pencil slats, wood, manufacturing
339942	Pencils (except mechanical) manufacturing
424120	Pencils merchant wholesalers
339941	Pencils, mechanical, manufacturing
335122	Pendant lamps (except residential), electric, manufacturing

335121 Pendant lamps fixtures, residential electric, manufacturing
325613 Penetrants manufacturing
325998 Penetrating fluids, synthetic, manufacturing
325412 Penicillin preparations manufacturing
325411 Penicillin, uncompounded, manufacturing
922140 Penitentiaries
236220 Penitentiary construction
212113 Pennsylvania anthracite mining and/or beneficiating
339941 Pens manufacturing
424120 Pens, writing, merchant wholesalers
523920 Pension fund managing
524292 Pension fund, third party administrative services
525110 Pension funds
525110 Pension plans (e.g., employee benefit, retirement)
332313 Penstocks, fabricated metal plate, manufacturing
325192 Pentachlorophenol manufacturing
325199 Pentaerythritol manufacturing
325110 Pentanes made from refined petroleum or liquid hydrocarbons
325110 Pentenes made from refined petroleum or liquid hydrocarbons
325920 Pentolite explosive materials manufacturing
561330 PEO (professional employer organizations)
111219 Pepper (e.g., bell, chili, green, hot, red, sweet) farming
311942 Pepper (i.e., spice) manufacturing
325998 Peppermint oil manufacturing
313210 Percales weaving
114111 Perch fishing
325188 Perchloric acid manufacturing
325199 Perchloroethylene manufacturing
335211 Percolators, household-type electric, manufacturing

332992 Percussion caps (i.e., 30 mm. or less, 1.18 inch or less), ammunition, manufacturing
339992 Percussion musical instruments manufacturing
213112 Perforating oil and gas well casings on a contract basis
711510 Performers (i.e., entertainers), independent
711510 Performing artists, independent
711310 Performing arts center operators
611610 Performing arts schools (except academic)
325199 Perfume materials (i.e., basic synthetic chemicals, such as terpineol) manufacturing
446120 Perfume stores
325620 Perfumes manufacturing
424210 Perfumes merchant wholesalers
511120 Periodical publishers (except exclusive Internet publishing)
511120 Periodical publishers and printing combined
519130 Periodical publishers, exclusively on Internet
323112 Periodicals flexographic printing without publishing
323111 Periodicals gravure printing without publishing
323110 Periodicals lithographic (offset) printing without publishing
424920 Periodicals merchant wholesalers
323119 Periodicals printing (except flexographic, gravure, lithographic, quick, screen) without publishing
323113 Periodicals screen printing without publishing
621210 Periodontists' offices (e.g., centers, clinics)
334418 Peripheral controller boards manufacturing
423430 Peripheral equipment, computer, merchant wholesalers
333314 Periscopes manufacturing
327992 Perlite aggregates manufacturing
212399 Perlite mining and/or beneficiating

327992	Perlite, expanded, manufacturing
331524	Permanent mold castings, aluminum, unfinished, manufacturing
331525	Permanent mold castings, copper, unfinished, manufacturing
331528	Permanent mold castings, nonferrous metal (except alumninum, copper), unfinished, manufacturing
325620	Permanent wave preparations manufacturing
238130	Permanent wood foundation installation
325188	Peroxides, inorganic, manufacturing
325199	Peroxides, organic, manufacturing
325132	Persian orange lake manufacturing
111339	Persimmon farming
334418	Personal computer modems manufacturing
334111	Personal computers manufacturing
522291	Personal credit institutions (i.e., unsecured cash loans)
525920	Personal estates (i.e., managing assets)
522291	Personal finance companies (i.e., unsecured cash loans)
812990	Personal fitness trainer
339914	Personal goods, metal (except precious), manufacturing
551112	Personal holding companies
525920	Personal investment trusts
523991	Personal investments trust administration
523920	Personal investments trusts, managing
316993	Personal leather goods (e.g., coin purses, eyeglass cases, key cases), small, manufacturing
561612	Personal protection services (except security systems services)

339113	Personal safety devices, not specified elsewhere, manufacturing
424130	Personal sanitary paper products merchant wholesalers
812990	Personal shopping services
525920	Personal trusts
441221	Personal watercraft dealers
336999	Personal watercraft manufacturing
532292	Personal watercraft rental
561320	Personnel (e.g., industrial, office) suppliers
813920	Personnel management associations
541612	Personnel management consulting services
921190	Personnel offices, government
325320	Pest (e.g., ant, rat, roach, rodent) control poison manufacturing
561710	Pest control (except agricultural, forestry) services
926140	Pest control programs, agriculture, government
115112	Pest control services, agricultural
115310	Pest control services, forestry
424690	Pesticides (except agricultural) merchant wholesalers
325320	Pesticides manufacturing
424910	Pesticides, agricultural, merchant wholesalers
334510	PET (positron emission tomography) scanners manufacturing
812910	Pet boarding services
812220	Pet cemeteries
311119	Pet food (except cat, dog) manufacturing
424490	Pet food merchant wholesalers
311111	Pet food, dog and cat, manufacturing
812910	Pet grooming services
524128	Pet health insurance carriers, direct
541940	Pet hospitals
926150	Pet licensing
453910	Pet shops
812910	Pet sitting services

424990	Pet supplies (except pet food) merchant wholesalers
453910	Pet supply stores
812910	Pet training services
324110	Petrochemical feedstocks made in petroleum refineries
237120	Petrochemical plant construction
324110	Petrochemicals made in petroleum refineries
424710	Petroleum and petroleum products bulk stations and terminals
424720	Petroleum and petroleum products merchant wholesalers (except bulk stations, terminals)
425120	Petroleum brokers
324110	Petroleum coke made in petroleum refineries
324110	Petroleum cracking and reforming
324110	Petroleum distillation
541330	Petroleum engineering services
211112	Petroleum gases, liquefied, recovering from oil and gas field gases
324199	Petroleum jelly made from refined petroleum
324110	Petroleum jelly made in petroleum refineries
324191	Petroleum lubricating oils made from refined petroleum
324110	Petroleum lubricating oils made in petroleum refineries
486110	Petroleum pipelines, crude
486910	Petroleum pipelines, refined
325211	Petroleum polymer resins manufacturing
324110	Petroleum refineries
237120	Petroleum refinery construction
333298	Petroleum refining machinery manufacturing
332420	Petroleum storage tanks, heavy gauge metal, manufacturing
324199	Petroleum waxes made from refined petroleum
211111	Petroleum, crude, production (i.e., extraction)
424990	Pets merchant wholesalers
712130	Petting zoos

337127	Pews, church, manufacturing
339912	Pewter ware manufacturing
236210	Pharmaceutical manufacturing plant construction
325412	Pharmaceutical preparations (e.g., capsules, liniments, ointments, tablets) manufacturing
424210	Pharmaceuticals merchant wholesalers
446110	Pharmacies
813920	Pharmacists' associations
334515	Phase angle meters manufacturing
335312	Phase converters (i.e., electrical equipment) manufacturing
112390	Pheasant production
325192	Phenol manufacturing
325211	Phenol-formaldehyde resins manufacturing
325211	Phenol-furfural resins manufacturing
325211	Phenolic resins manufacturing
325211	Phenoxy resins manufacturing
813211	Philanthropic trusts, awarding grants
212399	Phlogopite mining and/or beneficiating
334510	Phonocardiographs manufacturing
334612	Phonograph records manufacturing
423990	Phonograph records merchant wholesalers
423440	Phonographs, coin-operated, merchant wholesalers
325199	Phosgene manufacturing
212392	Phosphate rock mining and/or beneficiating
325312	Phosphatic fertilizer materials manufacturing
325314	Phosphatic fertilizers made by mixing purchased materials
325132	Phosphomolybdic acid lakes and toners manufacturing
325199	Phosphoric acid esters manufacturing
325312	Phosphoric acid manufacturing

325188   Phosphorus compounds, not specified elsewhere by process, manufacturing

325188   Phosphorus oxychloride manufacturing

325132   Phosphotungstic acid lakes and toners manufacturing

323118   Photo albums and refills manufacturing

424120   Photo albums merchant wholesalers

323122   Photocomposition services, for the printing trade

424120   Photocopy supplies merchant wholesalers

811212   Photocopying machine repair and maintenance services without retailing new photocopying machines

333315   Photocopying machines manufacturing

561439   Photocopying services (except combined with printing services)

325992   Photocopying toner cartridges manufacturing

334413   Photoelectric cells, solid-state (e.g., electronic eye), manufacturing

333293   Photoengraving machinery manufacturing

323122   Photoengraving plate preparation services

423410   Photofinishing equipment merchant wholesalers

812921   Photofinishing labs (except one-hour)

812922   Photofinishing labs, one-hour

812921   Photofinishing services (except one-hour)

812922   Photofinishing services, one-hour

335110   Photoflash and photoflood lamp bulbs and tubes manufacturing

333315   Photoflash equipment manufacturing

541370   Photogrammetric mapping services

322299   Photograph folders, mats, and mounts manufacturing

541922   Photographers specializing in aerial photography

711510   Photographers, independent artistic

325992   Photographic chemicals manufacturing

333315   Photographic equipment (except lenses) manufacturing

423410   Photographic equipment and supplies merchant wholesalers

532210   Photographic equipment rental

811211   Photographic equipment repair shops without retailing new photographic equipment

423410   Photographic film merchant wholesalers

325992   Photographic film, cloth, paper, and plate, sensitized, manufacturing

333314   Photographic lenses manufacturing

812990   Photographic machine concession operators, coin-operated

443130   Photographic supply stores

326113   Photographic, micrographic, and X-ray plastics, sheet, and film (except sensitized), manufacturing

611610   Photography schools, art

611519   Photography schools, commercial

541922   Photography services, commercial

541921   Photography services, portrait (e.g., still, video)

541922   Photography studios, commercial

541921   Photography studios, portrait

711510   Photojournalists, independent (freelance)

327212   Photomask blanks, glass, made in glass making plants

325992   Photomasks manufacturing

334516   Photometers (except photographic exposure meters) manufacturing

334516   Photonexcitation analyzers manufacturing

334413 Photonic integrated circuits manufacturing

325992 Photosensitized paper manufacturing

323122 Phototypesetting services

334413 Photovoltaic devices, solid-state, manufacturing

812990 Phrenology services

325199 Phthalate acid manufacturing

325211 Phthalic alkyd resins manufacturing

325192 Phthalic anhydride manufacturing

325211 Phthalic anhydride resins manufacturing

325132 Phthalocyanine pigments manufacturing

541614 Physical distribution consulting services

621340 Physical equestrian therapist offices (e.g., centers, clinics)

713940 Physical fitness centers

621999 Physical fitness evaluation services (except by offices of health practitioners)

713940 Physical fitness facilities

713940 Physical fitness studios

334519 Physical properties testing and inspection equipment manufacturing

622310 Physical rehabilitation hospitals

541712 Physical science research and development laboratories or services (except biotechnology research and development)

621340 Physical therapists' offices (e.g., centers, clinics)

621340 Physical therapy offices (e.g., centers, clinics)

621340 Physical-integration practitioners' offices (e.g., centers, clinics)

621111 Physicians' (except mental health) offices (e.g., centers, clinics)

621399 Physicians' assistants' offices (e.g., centers, clinics)

621112 Physicians', mental health, offices (e.g., centers, clinics)

541690 Physics consulting services

541712 Physics research and development laboratories or services

621340 Physiotherapists' offices (e.g., centers, clinics)

339112 Physiotherapy equipment (except electrotherapeutic) manufacturing

325411 Physostigmine and derivatives (i.e., basic chemicals) manufacturing

332510 Piano hardware, metal, manufacturing

339992 Piano parts and materials (except piano hardware) manufacturing

532299 Piano rental

451140 Piano stores

339992 Piccolos and parts manufacturing

333292 Picker machinery for textiles manufacturing

333292 Picker sticks for looms manufacturing

311712 Picking crab meat

333516 Picklers and pickling machinery, metalworking, manufacturing

311421 Pickles manufacturing

311421 Pickling fruits and vegetables

332813 Pickling metals and metal products for the trade

332212 Picks (i.e., handtools) manufacturing

812320 Pickup and drop-off sites for drycleaners and laundries

336214 Pickup canopies, caps, or covers manufacturing

336112 Pick-up trucks, light duty, assembling on chassis of own manufacture

713990 Picnic grounds

326199 Picnic jugs, plastics (except foam), manufacturing

325920 Picric acid explosive materials manufacturing

334511 Pictorial situation instrumentation manufacturing

442299 Picture frame shops, custom

311822	Pie crust shells, uncooked, made from purchased flour
424310	Piece goods (except burlap, felt) merchant wholesalers
451130	Piece goods stores
424990	Piece goods, burlap and felt, merchant wholesalers
237990	Pier construction
531120	Piers and associated building rental or leasing
713110	Piers, amusement
424420	Pies (e.g., fruit, meat, poultry), frozen, merchant wholesalers
311812	Pies, fresh, made in commercial bakeries
311813	Pies, frozen, manufacturing
334419	Piezoelectric crystals manufacturing
334419	Piezoelectric devices manufacturing
112210	Pig farming
331111	Pig iron manufacturing
423510	Pig iron merchant wholesalers
325132	Pigment, scarlet lake, manufacturing
325132	Pigments (except animal black, bone black), organic, manufacturing
325131	Pigments (except bone black, carbon black, lamp black), inorganic, manufacturing
212393	Pigments, natural, mineral, mining and/or beneficiating
424950	Pigments, paint, merchant wholesalers
311612	Pig's feet, cooked and pickled, made from purchased carcasses
114111	Pilchard fishing
238910	Pile driving, building foundation
237990	Pile driving, marine
313249	Pile fabrics made in warp knitting mills
313241	Pile fabrics made in weft knitting mills
332313	Pile shells, fabricated metal plate, manufacturing
332322	Pile shells, sheet metal (except stampings), manufacturing
333120	Pile-driving equipment manufacturing
238910	Piling (i.e., bored, cast-in-place, drilled), building foundation, contractors
321114	Pilings, foundation and marine construction, treating
331111	Pilings, iron or steel plain sheet, made in iron and steel mills
321114	Pilings, round wood, cutting and treating
321114	Pilings, wood, treating
332991	Pillow blocks with ball or roller bearings manufacturing
812320	Pillow cleaning services
314129	Pillowcases, bed, made from purchased fabrics
314129	Pillows, bed, made from purchased materials
488490	Pilot car services (i.e., wide load warning services)
488330	Piloting services, water transportation
713120	Pinball arcades
713990	Pinball machine concession operators (i.e., supplying and servicing in others' facilities)
339999	Pinball machines, coin-operated, manufacturing
113210	Pine gum extracting
325191	Pine oil manufacturing
111339	Pineapple farming
325191	Pinene manufacturing
713990	Ping pong parlors
212325	Pinite mining and/or beneficiating
339993	Pins (except precious) manufacturing
339911	Pins and brooches, precious metal, manufacturing
712120	Pioneer villages
331210	Pipe (e.g., heavy riveted, lock joint, seamless, welded) made from purchased iron or steel
332996	Pipe and pipe fittings made from purchased metal pipe
331511	Pipe and pipe fittings, cast iron, manufacturing

333516 Pipe and tube rolling mill machinery, metalworking, manufacturing

332323 Pipe bannisters, metal, manufacturing

326299 Pipe bits and stems, tobacco, hard rubber, manufacturing

339999 Pipe cleaners manufacturing

332996 Pipe couplings made from purchased metal pipe

331511 Pipe couplings, cast iron, manufacturing

238290 Pipe covering

333512 Pipe cutting and threading machines, metalworking, manufacturing

332996 Pipe fabricating (i.e., bending, cutting, threading) made from purchased metal pipe

238220 Pipe fitting contractors

326122 Pipe fittings, rigid plastics, manufacturing

332323 Pipe guards, metal, manufacturing

332999 Pipe hangers and supports, metal, manufacturing

332996 Pipe headers made from purchased metal pipe

237120 Pipe lining (except thermal insulating) contractors

331316 Pipe made by extruding purchased aluminum

332323 Pipe railings, metal, manufacturing

325520 Pipe sealing compounds manufacturing

213112 Pipe testing services, oil and gas field, on a contract basis

424940 Pipe tobacco merchant wholesalers

312229 Pipe tobacco, prepared, manufacturing

331316 Pipe, aluminum, made in integrated secondary smelting and extruding mills

327332 Pipe, concrete, manufacturing

238290 Pipe, duct and boiler insulation

331421 Pipe, extruded and drawn, brass, bronze, and copper, made from purchased copper or in integrated secondary smelting and rolling, drawing or extruding plants

332313 Pipe, fabricated metal plate, manufacturing

331111 Pipe, iron or steel, made in iron and steel mills

423510 Pipe, metal, merchant wholesalers

331491 Pipe, nonferrous metals (except aluminum, copper), made from purchased metals or scrap

326122 Pipe, rigid plastics, manufacturing

332322 Pipe, sheet metal (except stampings), manufacturing

515112 Piped-in music services, radio transmitted

237990 Pipe-jacking contractors

237120 Pipeline construction on oil and gas field gathering lines to point of distribution on a contract basis

541990 Pipeline inspection (i.e., visual) services

423830 Pipeline machinery and equipment merchant wholesalers

237120 Pipeline rehabilitation contractors

488999 Pipeline terminal facilities, independently operated

486990 Pipeline transportation (except crude oil, natural gas, refined petroleum products)

486110 Pipeline transportation, crude oil

486910 Pipeline transportation, gasoline and other refined petroleum products

486210 Pipeline transportation, natural gas

237120 Pipeline wrapping contractors

237120 Pipeline, gas and oil, construction

339992 Pipes, organ, manufacturing

339999	Pipes, smoker's, manufacturing
212399	Pipestones mining and/or beneficiating
111335	Pistachio farming
332994	Pistols manufacturing
336311	Pistons and piston rings manufacturing
423830	Pistons, hydraulic and pneumatic, merchant wholesalers
325192	Pitch made by distillation of coal tar
324122	Pitch, roofing, made from purchased asphaltic materials
325191	Pitch, wood, manufacturing
212291	Pitchblende mining and/or beneficiating
334519	Pitometers manufacturing
325411	Pituitary gland derivatives, uncompounded, manufacturing
325412	Pituitary gland preparations manufacturing
722211	Pizza delivery shops
311822	Pizza doughs made from purchased flour
722110	Pizza parlors, full service
722211	Pizza parlors, limited-service
424490	Pizzas (except frozen) merchant wholesalers
311991	Pizzas, fresh, manufacturing
311412	Pizzas, frozen, manufacturing
424420	Pizzas, frozen, merchant wholesalers
722110	Pizzerias, full service
722211	Pizzerias, limited-service (e.g., take-out)
314129	Placemats, all materials, made from purchased materials
561311	Placement agencies or services, employment
621991	Placenta banks
212221	Placer gold mining and/or beneficiating
212222	Placer silver mining and/or beneficiating
813110	Places of worship
238120	Placing and tying reinforcing rod at a construction site
334417	Planar cable connectors manufacturing

333210	Planers woodworking-type, stationary, manufacturing
333120	Planers, bituminous, manufacturing
333991	Planers, handheld power-driven, manufacturing
333512	Planers, metalworking, manufacturing
332212	Planes, handheld, nonpowered, manufacturing
712110	Planetariums
321912	Planing mills (except millwork)
321918	Planing mills, millwork
321912	Planing purchased lumber
525120	Plans, health and welfare related employee benefit
522190	Plans, Morris (i.e., known as), depository
522298	Plans, Morris (i.e., known as), nondepository
525110	Plans, pension
561730	Plant and shrub maintenance in buildings
112519	Plant aquaculture
424990	Plant food merchant wholesalers
325311	Plant foods, mixed, made in plants producing nitrogenous fertilizer materials
325312	Plant foods, mixed, made in plants producing phosphatic fertilizer materials
325320	Plant growth regulants manufacturing
561730	Plant maintenance services
111422	Plant, ornamental, growing
111422	Plant, potted flower and foliage, growing
111339	Plantain farming
115112	Planting crops
423820	Planting machinery and equipment, farm-type, merchant wholesalers
333111	Planting machines, farm-type, manufacturing
333513	Plasma jet spray metal forming machines manufacturing
333512	Plasma process metal cutting machines (except welding equipment) manufacturing

333992	Plasma welding equipment manufacturing
621991	Plasmapheresis centers
325414	Plasmas manufacturing
424210	Plasmas, blood, merchant wholesalers
327420	Plaster and plasterboard, gypsum, manufacturing
423320	Plaster merchant wholesalers
327420	Plaster of paris manufacturing
327420	Plaster of paris products (e.g., columns, statuary, urns) manufacturing
327420	Plaster, gypsum, manufacturing
238310	Plastering (i.e., ornamental, plain) contractors
212325	Plastic fire clay mining and/or beneficiating
621111	Plastic surgeons' offices (e.g., centers, clinics)
325510	Plastic wood fillers manufacturing
325199	Plasticizers (i.e., basic synthetic chemicals) manufacturing
424610	Plasticizers merchant wholesalers
337125	Plastics (including fiberglass) furniture (except upholstered), household-type, manufacturing
326220	Plastics and rubber belts and hoses (without fittings) manufacturing
325211	Plastics and synthetic resins regenerating, precipitating, and coagulating
424130	Plastics bags merchant wholesalers
424610	Plastics basic shapes (e.g., film, rod, sheet, sheeting, tubing) merchant wholesalers
313320	Plastics coating of textiles and apparel
326113	Plastics film and unlaminated sheet (except packaging) manufacturing
424610	Plastics foam merchant wholesalers
423840	Plastics foam packing and packaging materials merchant wholesalers

424990	Plastics foam products (except disposable) merchant wholesalers
424130	Plastics foam products, disposable (except packaging, packing), merchant wholesalers
315299	Plastics gowns (except infants') cut and sewn from purchased fabric (except apparel contractors)
315291	Plastics gowns, infants', cut and sewn from purchased fabric (except apparel contractors)
315211	Plastics gowns, men's and boys', cut and sew apparel contractors
315212	Plastics gowns, women's, girls', and infants, cut and sew apparel contractors
423830	Plastics industries machinery, equipment, and supplies merchant wholesalers
337110	Plastics laminated over particleboard (e.g., fixture tops) manufacturing
424610	Plastics materials merchant wholesalers
315299	Plastics rainwear cut and sewn from purchased fabric (except apparel contractors)
315211	Plastics rainwear, men's and boys', cut and sewn apparel contractors
315212	Plastics rainwear, women's, girls', and infants', cut and sew apparel contractors
325991	Plastics resins compounding from recycled materials
424610	Plastics resins merchant wholesalers
325991	Plastics resins, custom compounding of purchased
423930	Plastics scrap merchant wholesalers
333220	Plastics working machinery manufacturing
325510	Plastisol coating compounds manufacturing

524126 Plate glass insurance carriers, direct

423390 Plate glass merchant wholesalers

333516 Plate rolling mill machinery, metalworking, manufacturing

332313 Plate work (e.g., bending, cutting, punching, shaping, welding), fabricated metal, manufacturing

331315 Plate, aluminum, made by continuous casting purchased aluminum

331315 Plate, aluminum, made by flat rolling purchased aluminum

331315 Plate, aluminum, made in integrated secondary smelting and continuous casting mills

331315 Plate, aluminum, made in integrated secondary smelting and flat rolling mills

331421 Plate, copper and copper alloy, made from purchased copper or in integrated secondary smelting and rolling, drawing or extruding plants

331111 Plate, iron or steel, made in iron and steel mills

326130 Plate, laminated plastics, manufacturing

331491 Plate, nonferrous metals (except aluminum, copper), made from purchased metals or scrap

332211 Plated metal cutlery manufacturing

423940 Plated metal cutlery or flatware merchant wholesalers

332211 Plated metal flatware manufacturing

332999 Plated ware (e.g., ecclesiastical ware, hollowware, toilet ware) manufacturing

335932 Plates (i.e., outlet or switch covers), face, manufacturing

322299 Plates, molded pulp, manufacturing

326140 Plates, polystyrene foam, manufacturing

332813 Plating metals and metal products for the trade

331491 Platinum and platinum alloy rolling, drawing, or extruding from purchased metals or scrap

331491 Platinum and platinum alloy sheet and tubing made from purchased metals or scrap

332999 Platinum foil and leaf not made in rolling mills

212299 Platinum mining and/or beneficiating

331492 Platinum recovering from scrap and/or alloying purchased metals

331419 Platinum refining, primary

237990 Play ground construction

423910 Playground equipment and supplies merchant wholesalers

238990 Playground equipment installation

423920 Playing cards merchant wholesalers

337124 Playpens, children's metal, manufacturing

337122 Playpens, children's wood, manufacturing

315291 Playsuits, infants', cut and sewn from purchased fabric (except apparel contractors)

315212 Playsuits, women's, girls', and infants', cut and sew apparel contractors

315239 Playsuits, women's, misses', and girls', cut and sewn from purchased fabric (except apparel contractors)

711510 Playwrights, independent

532292 Pleasure boat rental

336612 Pleasure boats manufacturing

423910 Pleasure boats merchant wholesalers

315211 Pleating contractors on men's and boys' apparel

315212 Pleating contractors on women's, girls', and infants' apparel

332212 Pliers, handtools, manufacturing

327331 Plinth blocks, precast terrazzo, manufacturing

334119 Plotters, computer, manufacturing

115112 Plowing

333120 Plows, construction (e.g., excavating, grading), manufacturing

423820 Plows, farm, merchant wholesalers

333111 Plows, farm-type, manufacturing

111422 Plug (i.e., floriculture products) growing

332911 Plug valves, industrial-type, manufacturing

213112 Plugging and abandoning wells on a contract basis

335931 Plugs, electric cord, manufacturing

332999 Plugs, magnetic metal drain, manufacturing

321999 Plugs, wood, manufacturing

111339 Plum farming

238220 Plumbers

611513 Plumbers' apprenticeship training

423720 Plumbers' brass goods merchant wholesalers

332212 Plumbers' handtools, nonpowered, manufacturing

325520 Plumbers' putty manufacturing

238220 Plumbing and heating contractors

332919 Plumbing and heating inline valves (e.g., check, cutoffs, stop) manufacturing

423720 Plumbing and heating valves merchant wholesalers

238220 Plumbing contractors

423720 Plumbing equipment merchant wholesalers

532490 Plumbing equipment rental or leasing

332913 Plumbing fittings and couplings (e.g., compression fittings, metal elbows, metal unions) manufacturing

332913 Plumbing fixture fittings and trim, all materials, manufacturing

238220 Plumbing fixture installation

326191 Plumbing fixtures (e.g., shower stalls, toilets, urinals), plastics or fiberglass, manufacturing

423720 Plumbing fixtures merchant wholesalers

332998 Plumbing fixtures, metal, manufacturing

327111 Plumbing fixtures, vitreous china, manufacturing

423720 Plumbing supplies merchant wholesalers

444190 Plumbing supply stores

423310 Plywood merchant wholesalers

321211 Plywood, faced with nonwood materials, hardwood, manufacturing

321212 Plywood, faced with nonwood materials, softwood, manufacturing

321211 Plywood, hardwood faced, manufacturing

321211 Plywood, hardwood, manufacturing

321212 Plywood, softwood faced, manufacturing

321212 Plywood, softwood, manufacturing

332912 Pneumatic aircraft subassemblies manufacturing

334513 Pneumatic controllers, industrial process type, manufacturing

333995 Pneumatic cylinders, fluid power, manufacturing

326220 Pneumatic hose (without fittings), rubber or plastics, manufacturing

332912 Pneumatic hose fittings, fluid power, manufacturing

423830 Pneumatic pumps and parts merchant wholesalers

333996 Pneumatic pumps, fluid power, manufacturing

334512 Pneumatic relays, air-conditioning-type, manufacturing

238290	Pneumatic tube conveyor system installation
333922	Pneumatic tube conveyors manufacturing
332912	Pneumatic valves, fluid power, manufacturing
322231	Pocket folders made from purchased paper or paperboard
332211	Pocket knives manufacturing
339911	Pocketbooks, precious metal, men's or women's, manufacturing
315211	Pockets (e.g., coat, suit), men's and boys', cut and sew apparel contractors
315212	Pockets (e.g., coat, suit), women's, girls', and infants', cut and sew apparel contractors
621391	Podiatrists' offices (e.g., centers, clinics)
813410	Poetry clubs
711510	Poets, independent
334119	Point of sale terminals manufacturing
423420	Point of sale terminals merchant wholesalers
334119	Pointing devices, computer peripheral equipment, manufacturing
315292	Pointing furs
339114	Points, abrasive dental, manufacturing
334516	Polariscopes manufacturing
334516	Polarizers manufacturing
334516	Polarographic equipment manufacturing
238990	Pole (e.g., telephone) removal
237130	Pole line construction
423610	Pole line hardware merchant wholesalers
327390	Poles, concrete, manufacturing
423510	Poles, metal, merchant wholesalers
321114	Poles, round wood, cutting and treating
321113	Poles, wood, made from from log or bolts
321114	Poles, wood, treating
922120	Police academies
922120	Police and fire departments, combined
315991	Police caps and hats (except protective head gear) cut and sewn from purchased fabric (except apparel contractors)
315211	Police caps and hats (except protective head gear), men's, cut and sew apparel contractors
315212	Police caps and hats (except protective head gear), women's, cut and sew apparel contractors
922120	Police departments (except American Indian or Alaska Native)
315222	Police dress uniforms, men's, cut and sewn from purchased fabric (except apparel contractors)
315234	Police dress uniforms, women's, cut and sewn from purchased fabric (except apparel contractors)
453998	Police supply stores
611519	Police training schools
315211	Police uniforms, men's, cut and sew apparel contractors
315212	Police uniforms, women's, cut and sew apparel contractors
921150	Police, American Indian or Alaska Native tribal
311212	Polished rice manufacturing
333991	Polishers, handheld power-driven, manufacturing
325612	Polishes (e.g., automobile, furniture, metal, shoe) manufacturing
424690	Polishes (e.g., automobile, furniture, metal, shoe, stove) merchant wholesalers
333512	Polishing and buffing machines, metalworking, manufacturing
332813	Polishing metals and metal products for the trade
325612	Polishing preparations manufacturing
327910	Polishing wheels manufacturing

813940 Political action committees (PACs)

813940 Political campaign organizations

711510 Political cartoonists, independent

541820 Political consulting services

541910 Political opinion polling services

813940 Political organizations or clubs

813940 Political parties

115112 Pollinating

114111 Pollock fishing

423830 Pollution control equipment (except air) merchant wholesalers

423730 Pollution control equipment, air, merchant wholesalers

924110 Pollution control program administration

541380 Pollution testing (except automotive emissions testing) services

315191 Polo shirts made in apparel knitting mills

315211 Polo shirts, men's and boys', cut and sew apparel contractors

315223 Polo shirts, men's and boys', cut and sewn from purchased fabric (except apparel contractors)

315212 Polo shirts, women's, girls', and infants', cut and sew apparel contractors

315232 Polo shirts, women's, misses', and girls', cut and sewn from purchased fabric (except apparel contractors)

325211 Polyacrylonitrile resins manufacturing

325211 Polyamide resins manufacturing

325211 Polycarbonate resins manufacturing

325222 Polyester fibers and filaments manufacturing

313112 Polyester filament yarn throwing, twisting, texturizing, or winding of purchased yarn

326113 Polyester film and unlaminated sheet (except packaging) manufacturing

325211 Polyester resins manufacturing

313111 Polyester spun yarns made from purchased fiber

313113 Polyester thread manufacturing

326113 Polyethylene film and unlaminated sheet (except packaging) manufacturing

325211 Polyethylene resins manufacturing

325212 Polyethylene rubber manufacturing

325211 Polyethylene terephathalate (PET) resins manufacturing

325222 Polyethylene terephthalate (PET) fibers and filaments manufacturing

334519 Polygraph machines manufacturing

561611 Polygraph services

325211 Polyhexamethylenediamine adipamide resins manufacturing

325199 Polyhydric alcohol esters and amines manufacturing

325199 Polyhydric alcohols manufacturing

325211 Polyisobutylene resins manufacturing

325212 Polyisobutylene rubber manufacturing

325212 Polyisobutylene-isoprene rubber manufacturing

325211 Polymethacrylate resins manufacturing

325212 Polymethylene rubber manufacturing

325222 Polyolefin fibers and filaments manufacturing

313112 Polypropylene filament yarn throwing, twisting, texturizing, or winding of puchased yarn

326113 Polypropylene film and unlaminated sheet (except packaging) manufacturing

325211 Polypropylene resins manufacturing

313111 Polypropylene spun yarns made from purchased fiber

238310 Polystyrene board insulation installation

326140 Polystyrene foam packaging manufacturing

325211 Polystyrene resins manufacturing

325212 Polysulfide rubber manufacturing

325211 Polytetrafluoroethylene resins manufacturing

325510 Polyurethane coatings manufacturing

326150 Polyurethane foam products manufacturing

325211 Polyurethane resins manufacturing

325211 Polyvinyl alcohol resins manufacturing

325211 Polyvinyl chloride (PVC) resins manufacturing

325222 Polyvinyl ester fibers and filaments manufacturing

326113 Polyvinyl film and unlaminated sheet (except packaging) manufacturing

325211 Polyvinyl halide resins manufacturing

325211 Polyvinyl resins manufacturing

325222 Polyvinylidene chloride (i.e., saran) fibers and filaments manufacturing

111339 Pomegranate farming

315299 Ponchos and similar waterproof raincoats (except infants') cut and sewn from purchased fabric (except apparel contractors)

315291 Ponchos and similar waterproof raincoats, infants', cut and sewn from purchased fabric (except apparel contractors)

315211 Ponchos and similar waterproof raincoats, men's and boys', cut and sew apparel contractors

315212 Ponchos and similar waterproof raincoats, women's, girls', and infants', cut and sew apparel contractors

112920 Pony production

423910 Pool (billiards) supplies merchant wholesalers

423910 Pool (swimming) and equipment merchant wholesalers

713990 Pool halls

713990 Pool parlors

713990 Pool rooms

312111 Pop, soda, manufacturing

311919 Popcorn (except candy covered), popped, manufacturing

311999 Popcorn (except popped) manufacturing

311340 Popcorn balls manufacturing

111150 Popcorn farming, field and seed production

424450 Popcorn merchant wholesalers

335211 Popcorn poppers, household-type electric, manufacturing

311340 Popcorn, candy covered popped, manufacturing

313210 Poplins weaving

621391 Popopediatricians' offices (e.g., centers, clinics)

711130 Popular musical artists, independent

711130 Popular musical groups

532120 Popup camper rental

327113 Porcelain parts, electrical and electronic device, molded, manufacturing

327112 Porcelain, chemical, manufacturing

236118 Porch construction, residential-type

337122 Porch furniture (except upholstered), wood, manufacturing

337920 Porch shades, wood slat, manufacturing

337124 Porch swings, metal, manufacturing

321918 Porch work (e.g., columns, newels, rails, trellises), wood, manufacturing

114111 Porgy fishing

311422 Pork and beans canning

311611 Pork carcasses, half carcasses, and primal and sub-primal cuts produced in slaughtering plants

311919 Pork rinds manufacturing

311612 Pork, primal and sub-primal cuts, made from purchased carcasses

926120 Port authorities and districts, nonoperating

237990 Port facility construction

488310 Port facility operation

332311 Portable buildings, prefabricated metal, manufacturing

332998 Portable chemical toilets, metal, manufacturing

334111 Portable computers manufacturing

335211 Portable cooking appliances (except convection, microwave ovens), household-type electric, manufacturing

335211 Portable electric space heaters manufacturing

335211 Portable hair dryers, electric, manufacturing

335211 Portable humidifiers and dehumidifiers manufacturing

334290 Portable intrusion detection and signaling devices manufacturing

334310 Portable stereo systems manufacturing

334515 Portable test meters manufacturing

562991 Portable toilet pumping (i.e., cleaning) services

562991 Portable toilet renting and/or servicing

326191 Portable toilets, plastics, manufacturing

519130 Portals, web search

312120 Porter brewing

424810 Porter merchant wholesalers

812990 Porter services

523920 Portfolio fund managing

541921 Portrait photography services

541921 Portrait photography studios

334511 Position indicators (e.g., for landing gear, stabilizers), airframe equipment, manufacturing

336312 Positive crankcase ventilation (PCV) valves, engine, manufacturing

334514 Positive displacement meters manufacturing

621512 Positron emission tomography (PET) scanner centers

334510 Positron emission tomography (PET) scanners manufacturing

238130 Post framing contractors

332212 Post hole diggers, nonpowered, manufacturing

333120 Post hole diggers, powered, manufacturing

236220 Post office construction

333997 Post office-type scales manufacturing

333313 Postage meters manufacturing

423420 Postage meters merchant wholesalers

333311 Postage stamp vending machines manufacturing

491110 Postal delivery services, local, operated by U.S. Postal Service

491110 Postal delivery services, local, operated on a contract basis

337215 Postal service lock boxes manufacturing

491110 Postal services operated by U.S. Postal Service

491110 Postal stations operated by U.S. Postal Service

491110 Postal stations operated on a contract basis

511199 Postcard publishers (except exclusive Internet publishing)

511199 Postcard publishers and printing combined

519130 Postcard publishers, exclusively on Internet

323112 Postcards flexographic printing without publishing

323111 Postcards gravure printing without publishing

323110	Postcards lithographic (offset) printing without publishing
424120	Postcards merchant wholesalers
323119	Postcards printing (except flexographic, gravure, lithographic, quick, screen) without publishing
323113	Postcards screen printing without publishing
511199	Poster publishers (except exclusive Internet publishing)
511199	Poster publishers and printing combined
519130	Poster publishers, exclusively on Internet
323112	Posters flexographic printing without publishing
323111	Posters gravure printing without publishing
323110	Posters lithographic (offset) printing without publishing
323119	Posters printing (except flexographic, digital, gravure, lithographic, quick, screen) without publishing
323113	Posters screen printing without publishing
238990	Posthole digging
323121	Postpress services (e.g., beveling, bronzing, folding, gluing, edging, foil stamping, gilding) on printed materials
512191	Post-production facilities, motion picture or video
327390	Posts, concrete, manufacturing
321114	Posts, round wood, cutting and treating
321114	Posts, wood, treating
512191	Post-synchronization sound dubbing
311412	Pot pies, frozen, manufacturing
212391	Potash mining and/or beneficiating
325314	Potassic fertilizers made by mixing purchased materials
325188	Potassium aluminum sulfate manufacturing
325188	Potassium bichromate and chromate manufacturing

325199	Potassium bitartrate manufacturing
325188	Potassium bromide manufacturing
212391	Potassium bromide, natural, mining and/or beneficiating
325181	Potassium carbonate manufacturing
325188	Potassium chlorate manufacturing
325188	Potassium chloride manufacturing
212391	Potassium chloride mining and/ or beneficiating
212391	Potassium compounds prepared at beneficiating plants
212391	Potassium compounds, natural, mining and/or beneficiating
325188	Potassium cyanide manufacturing
325181	Potassium hydroxide (i.e., caustic potash) manufacturing
325188	Potassium hypochlorate manufacturing
325188	Potassium inorganic compounds, not specified elsewhere by process, manufacturing
325188	Potassium iodide manufacturing
325188	Potassium nitrate manufacturing
325199	Potassium organic compounds, not specified elsewhere by process, manufacturing
325188	Potassium permanganate manufacturing
325188	Potassium salts manufacturing
212391	Potassium salts, natural, mining and/or beneficiating
325188	Potassium sulfate manufacturing
424450	Potato chips and related snacks merchant wholesalers
311919	Potato chips manufacturing
115114	Potato curing
333111	Potato diggers, harvesters, and planters manufacturing
111211	Potato farming, field and seed potato production
311211	Potato flour manufacturing
332214	Potato mashers manufacturing

311999 Potato mixes made from purchased dry ingredients
311423 Potato products (e.g., flakes, granules) dehydrating
311221 Potato starches manufacturing
311919 Potato sticks manufacturing
311991 Potatoes, peeled or cut, manufacturing
334515 Potentiometric instruments (except industrial process-type) manufacturing
334513 Potentiometric instruments (except X-Y recorders), industrial process-type, manufacturing
237310 Pothole filling, highway, road, street or bridge
339999 Potpourri manufacturing
332420 Pots (e.g., annealing, melting, smelting), heavy gauge metal, manufacturing
332214 Pots and pans, fabricated metal, manufacturing
327124 Pots, glass-house, clay refractory, manufacturing
311612 Potted meats made from purchased carcasses
327112 Pottery made and sold on site
327112 Pottery products (except plumbing fixtures and porcelain electrical goods) manufacturing
325314 Potting soil manufacturing
311615 Poultry (e.g., canned, cooked, fresh, frozen) manufacturing
311615 Poultry (e.g., canned, cooked, fresh, frozen) processing
424440 Poultry and poultry products (except canned, packaged frozen) merchant wholesalers
333111 Poultry brooders, feeders, and waterers manufacturing
311615 Poultry canning (except baby, pet food)
115210 Poultry catching services
445210 Poultry dealers
423820 Poultry equipment merchant wholesalers
311119 Poultry feeds, supplements, and concentrates manufacturing

112340 Poultry hatcheries
332618 Poultry netting made from purchased wire
311615 Poultry slaughtering, dressing, and packing
424490 Poultry, canned, merchant wholesalers
424440 Poultry, live and dressed, merchant wholesalers
424420 Poultry, packaged frozen, merchant wholesalers
333991 Powder actuated handheld power tools manufacturing
332812 Powder coating metals and metal products for the trade
325510 Powder coatings manufacturing
331221 Powder made from purchased iron or steel
331314 Powder made from purchased aluminum
331423 Powder made from purchased copper
333513 Powder metal forming presses manufacturing
332117 Powder metallurgy products manufactured on a job or order basis
314999 Powder puffs and mitts manufacturing
331111 Powder, iron or steel, made in iron and steel mills
331492 Powder, nonferrous metals (except aluminum, copper), made from purchased metal
311999 Powdered drink mixes (except chocolate, coffee, tea, milk based) manufacturing
311514 Powdered milk manufacturing
325620 Powders (e.g., baby, body, face, talcum, toilet) manufacturing
311999 Powders, baking, manufacturing
333912 Power (i.e., pressure) washer units manufacturing
441222 Power boat dealers
238290 Power boiler, installation only
332410 Power boilers manufacturing
335313 Power circuit breakers manufacturing
335313 Power connectors manufacturing

335999 Power converter units (i.e., AC to DC), static, manufacturing

444210 Power equipment stores, outdoor

334515 Power factor meters manufacturing

335313 Power fuses (i.e., 600 volts and over) manufacturing

238290 Power generating equipment installation

221119 Power generation, electric (except fossil fuel, hydroelectric, nonhazardous solid waste, nuclear)

221112 Power generation, fossil fuel (e.g., coal, gas, oil), electric

221111 Power generation, hydroelectric

562213 Power generation, nonhazardous solid waste combustor or incinerator electric

221113 Power generation, nuclear electric

221119 Power generation, solar electric

221119 Power generation, tidal electric

221119 Power generation, wind electric

335312 Power generators manufacturing

423710 Power handtools (e.g., drills, sanders, saws) merchant wholesalers

812320 Power laundries, family

541990 Power line inspection (i.e., visual) services

237130 Power line stringing

334515 Power measuring equipment, electrical, manufacturing

237130 Power plant (except hydroelectric) construction

237990 Power plant, hydroelectric, construction

238910 Power shovel, construction, rental with operator

336330 Power steering hose assemblies manufacturing

336330 Power steering pumps manufacturing

335999 Power supplies, regulated and unregulated, manufacturing

335313 Power switchboards manufacturing

335313 Power switching equipment manufacturing

335311 Power transformers, electric, manufacturing

423610 Power transmission equipment, electrical, merchant wholesalers

423840 Power transmission supplies (e.g., gears, pulleys, sprockets), mechanical, merchant wholesalers

333319 Power washer cleaning equipment manufacturing

532490 Power washer rental or leasing

561790 Power washing building exteriors

336322 Power window and door lock systems, automotive, truck, and bus, manufacturing

238910 Power, communication and pipe line right of way clearance (except maintenance)

333991 Power-driven handtools manufacturing

212399 Pozzolana mining and/or beneficiating

621399 Practical nurses' offices (e.g., centers, clinics), licensed

315299 Prayer shawls cut and sewn from purchased fabric (except apparel contractors)

315191 Prayer shawls made in apparel knitting mills

315211 Prayer shawls, men's and boys', cut and sew apparel contractors

315212 Prayer shawls, women's, girls', and infants', cut and sew apparel contractors

327331 Precast concrete block and brick manufacturing

238120 Precast concrete panel, slab, or form installation

327332 Precast concrete pipe manufacturing

327390 Precast concrete products (except brick, block, pipe) manufacturing

423940 Precious and semiprecious stones merchant wholesalers

331491 Precious metal bar, rod, sheet, strip, and tubing made from purchased metals or scrap

423940 Precious metals merchant wholesalers

331492 Precious metals recovering from scrap and/or alloying purchased metals

331419 Precious metals refining, primary

212399 Precious stones mining and/or beneficiating

811219 Precision equipment calibration

332212 Precision tools, machinist's (except optical), manufacturing

332721 Precision turned product manufacturing

236117 Precut housing, residential, assembled on site by operative builders

236116 Precut multifamily housing assembled on site by general contractors

236115 Precut single-family housing assembly on site by general contractors

334514 Predetermined counters manufacturing

444190 Prefabricated building dealers

423390 Prefabricated buildings (except wood) merchant wholesalers

332311 Prefabricated buildings, metal, manufacturing

423310 Prefabricated buildings, wood, merchant wholesalers

236220 Prefabricated commercial building erection

321992 Prefabricated homes (except mobile homes), wood, manufacturing

332311 Prefabricated homes, metal, manufacturing

236210 Prefabricated industrial building (except warehouses) erection

236220 Prefabricated institutional building erection

238350 Prefabricated kitchen and bath cabinet, residential-type, installation

238350 Prefabricated sash and door installation

321992 Prefabricated wood buildings manufacturing

238130 Prefabricated wood frame component (e.g., trusses) installation

321211 Prefinished hardwood plywood manufacturing

321212 Prefinished softwood plywood manufacturing

621410 Pregnancy counseling centers

325413 Pregnancy test kits manufacturing

624410 Pre-kindergarten centers (except part of elementary school system)

236115 Premanufactured housing assembly on site by general contractors

236117 Premanufactured housing assembly on site by operative builders

334611 Prepackaged software, mass reproducing

424990 Pre-paid calling card distribution, merchant wholesalers

517911 Pre-paid calling cards, telecommunications resellers

213112 Preparation of oil and gas field drilling sites (except site preparation and related construction contractor activities) on a contract basis

212113 Preparation plants, anthracite

611110 Preparatory schools, elementary or secondary

311822 Prepared flour mixes made from purchased flour

311211 Prepared flour mixes made in flour mills

424490 Prepared foods (except frozen) merchant wholesalers

424420 Prepared foods, frozen (except dairy products), merchant wholesalers

424430 Prepared foods, frozen dairy, merchant wholesalers

311991   Prepared meals, perishable, packaged for individual resale

311941   Prepared sauces (except gravy, tomato based) manufacturing

237210   Preparing and subdividing land for sale

488991   Preparing goods for transportation (i.e., crating, packing)

323122   Prepress printing services (e.g., color separation, imagesetting, photocomposition, typesetting)

541350   Prepurchase home inspection services

423990   Prerecorded audio and video tapes and discs merchant wholesalers

512220   Prerecorded audio tapes and compact discs integrated manufacture, release, and distribution

334612   Pre-recorded magnetic audio tapes and cassettes mass reproducing

454113   Prerecorded tape, compact disc, and record mail-order houses

624410   Preschool centers

424210   Prescription drugs merchant wholesalers

111421   Preseeded mat farming

311421   Preserves (e.g., imitation) canning

321114   Preserving purchased wood and wood products

313311   Preshrinking broadwoven fabrics

313312   Preshrinking textile products and fabrics (except broadwoven)

921110   President's office, United States

325611   Presoaks manufacturing

333513   Press brakes, metalworking, manufacturing

519190   Press clipping services

332111   Press forgings made from purchased iron or steel, unfinished

332112   Press forgings made from purchased nonferrous metals, unfinished

424130   Pressed and molded pulp goods (e.g., egg cartons, shipping supplies) merchant wholesalers

313230   Pressed felts manufacturing

321999   Pressed logs of sawdust and other wood particles, nonpetroleum binder, manufacturing

333513   Presses (e.g., bending, punching, shearing, stamping), metal forming, manufacturing

333294   Presses (i.e., food manufacturing-type) manufacturing

333210   Presses for making composite woods (e.g., hardboard, medium density fiberboard (MDF), particleboard, plywood) manufacturing

333111   Presses, farm-type, manufacturing

333999   Presses, metal baling, manufacturing

333293   Presses, printing (except textile), manufacturing

321999   Pressing blocks, wood, tailor's, manufacturing

336350   Pressure and clutch plate assemblies, automotive, truck, and bus, manufacturing

334519   Pressure and vacuum indicators, aircraft engine, manufacturing

332911   Pressure control valves (except fluid power), industrial-type, manufacturing

332912   Pressure control valves, fluid power, manufacturing

334512   Pressure controllers, air-conditioning system-type, manufacturing

332214   Pressure cookers, household-type, manufacturing

334513   Pressure gauges (e.g., dial, digital), industrial process-type, manufacturing

334513   Pressure instruments, industrial process-type, manufacturing

327332   Pressure pipe, reinforced concrete, manufacturing

322222 Pressure sensitive paper and tape (except medical) made from purchased materials
334519 Pressure transducers manufacturing
321113 Pressure treated lumber made from logs or bolts and treated
321114 Pressure treated lumber made from purchased lumber
561790 Pressure washing (e.g., buildings, decks, fences)
334512 Pressurestats manufacturing
238120 Prestressed concrete beam, slab or other component installation
327331 Prestressed concrete blocks or bricks manufacturing
327332 Prestressed concrete pipes manufacturing
327390 Prestressed concrete products (except blocks, bricks, pipes) manufacturing
722213 Pretzel shops, on premise baking and carryout service
424490 Pretzels (except frozen) merchant wholesalers
311919 Pretzels (except soft) manufacturing
424420 Pretzels, frozen, merchant wholesalers
311812 Pretzels, soft, manufacturing
335129 Prewired poles, brackets, and accessories for electric lighting, manufacturing
926150 Price control agencies
111339 Prickly pear farming
331312 Primary aluminum production and manufacturing aluminum alloys
331312 Primary aluminum production and manufacturing aluminum shapes (e.g., bar, ingot, rod, sheet)
335912 Primary batteries manufacturing
334513 Primary elements for process flow measurement (i.e., orifice plates) manufacturing
334512 Primary oil burner controls (e.g., cadmium cells, stack controls) manufacturing

334513 Primary process temperature sensors manufacturing
331312 Primary refining of aluminum
331411 Primary refining of copper
331419 Primary refining of nonferrous metals (except aluminum, copper)
611110 Primary schools
331312 Primary smelting of aluminum
331411 Primary smelting of copper
331419 Primary smelting of nonferrous metals (except aluminum, copper)
335312 Prime mover generator sets (except turbine generator sets) manufacturing
332993 Primers (i.e., more than 30 mm., more than 1.18 inch), ammunition, manufacturing
325510 Primers, paint, manufacturing
323115 Print shops, digital
323119 Print shops, engraving
323112 Print shops, flexographic
323111 Print shops, gravure
323119 Print shops, letterpress
323110 Print shops, lithographic (offset) (except grey goods, manifold business forms, printing books, quick printing)
323114 Print shops, quick
323113 Print shops, screen
334418 Printed circuit assemblies manufacturing
334418 Printed circuit boards loading
423690 Printed circuit boards merchant wholesalers
334412 Printed circuit boards, bare, manufacturing
334419 Printed circuit laminates manufacturing
334119 Printers, computer, manufacturing
423430 Printers, computer, merchant wholesalers
323117 Printing and binding books without publishing
323117 Printing books without publishing
313311 Printing broadwoven fabrics grey goods

561990	Printing brokers
313312	Printing fabric grey goods (except broadwoven)
325910	Printing inks manufacturing
423840	Printing inks merchant wholesalers
333292	Printing machinery for textiles manufacturing
323116	Printing manifold business forms
424120	Printing paper (except bulk) merchant wholesalers
424110	Printing paper, bulk, merchant wholesalers
236210	Printing plant construction
333293	Printing plate engraving machinery manufacturing
323122	Printing plate preparation services
333293	Printing plates, blank (except photosentive), manufacturing
323121	Printing postpress services (e.g., beveling, bronzing, folding, gluing, edging, foil stamping) to printed products (e.g., books, cards, paper)
323122	Printing prepress services (e.g., color separation, imagesetting, photocomposition, typesetting)
333293	Printing press rollers manufacturing
333293	Printing presses (except textile) manufacturing
313312	Printing textile products (except apparel)
811310	Printing trade machinery repair and maintenance services
423830	Printing trade machinery, equipment, and supplies merchant wholesalers
323115	Printing, digital (e.g., billboards, other large format graphical materials)
323115	Printing, digital (e.g., graphics, high resolution)
323119	Printing, engraving, on paper products
323112	Printing, flexographic (except books, grey goods, manifold business forms)
323111	Printing, gravure (except books, grey goods, manifold business forms)
323119	Printing, letterpress (except books, grey goods, manifold business forms)
323110	Printing, lithographic (except books, grey goods, manifold business forms, quick printing)
323110	Printing, photo-offset (except books, grey goods, manifold business forms, printing books)
323114	Printing, quick
323113	Printing, screen (except books, manifold business forms, grey goods)
333314	Prisms, optical, manufacturing
337127	Prison bed manufacturing
236220	Prison construction
922140	Prison farms
922140	Prisons
522190	Private banks (i.e., unincorporated)
334210	Private branch exchange (PBX) equipment manufacturing
611310	Private colleges (except community or junior college)
561611	Private detective services
238210	Private driveway or parking area lighting contractors
525920	Private estates (i.e., administering on behalf of beneficiaries)
814110	Private households employing domestic personnel
814110	Private households with employees
561611	Private investigation services (except credit)
561431	Private mail centers
561431	Private mailbox rental centers
611110	Private schools, elementary or secondary
561990	Private volunteer fire fighting
493190	Private warehousing and storage (except farm products, general merchandise, refrigerated)

493130 Private warehousing and storage, farm products (except refrigerated)
493110 Private warehousing and storage, general merchandise
493120 Private warehousing and storage, refrigerated
451110 Pro shops (e.g., golf, skiing, tennis)
624190 Probation offices, privately operated
922150 Probation offices, publicly administered
212391 Probertite mining and/or quarrying
334510 Probes, electric medical, manufacturing
339112 Probes, surgical, manufacturing
325411 Procaine and derivatives (i.e., basic chemicals) manufacturing
334513 Process control instruments, industrial, manufacturing
238220 Process piping installation
541199 Process server services
541199 Process serving services
311513 Processed cheeses manufacturing
424470 Processed meats (e.g., luncheon, sausage) merchant wholesalers
311612 Processed meats manufacturing
424440 Processed poultry (e.g., luncheon) merchant wholesalers
311615 Processed poultry manufacturing
522320 Processing financial transactions
314999 Processing of textile mill waste and recovering fibers
621111 Proctologists' offices (e.g., centers, clinics)
424910 Produce containers merchant wholesalers
445230 Produce markets
445230 Produce stands, permanent
454390 Produce stands, temporary
424480 Produce, fresh, merchant wholesalers
813910 Producers' associations
711510 Producers, independent

561910 Product sterilization and packaging services
541380 Product testing laboratories or services
524128 Product warranty insurance carriers, direct
334514 Production counters manufacturing
541614 Production planning and control consulting services
541614 Productivity improvement consulting services
813920 Professional associations
711219 Professional athletes, independent (i.e., participating in sports events)
711211 Professional baseball clubs
323121 Professional book binding without printing
511130 Professional book publishers (except exclusive Internet publishing)
511130 Professional book publishers and printing combined
519130 Professional book publishers, exclusively on Internet
323117 Professional books printing and binding without publishing
323117 Professional books printing without publishing
611430 Professional development training
561330 Professional employer organizations (PEO)
423490 Professional equipment and supplies (except dental, medical, ophthalmic) merchant wholesalers
611691 Professional examination review instructions
711211 Professional football clubs
423490 Professional instruments merchant wholesalers
511120 Professional magazine and periodical publishers (except exclusive Internet publishing)
511120 Professional magazine and periodical publishers and printing combined

519130 Professional magazine and periodical publishers, exclusively on Internet

323112 Professional magazines and periodicals flexographic printing without publishing

323111 Professional magazines and periodicals gravure printing without publishing

323110 Professional magazines and periodicals lithographic (offset) printing without publishing

323119 Professional magazines and periodicals printing (except flexographic, gravure, lithographic, quick, screen) without publishing

323113 Professional magazines and periodicals screen printing without publishing

813920 Professional membership associations

531120 Professional office building rental or leasing

611310 Professional schools (e.g., business administration, dental, law, medical)

315211 Professional service apparel, washable, men's and boys', cut and sew apparel contractors

315225 Professional service apparel, washable, men's and boys', cut and sewn from purchased fabric (except apparel contractors)

315212 Professional service apparel, washable, women's, cut and sew apparel contractors

315239 Professional service apparel, washable, women's, misses', and girls', cut and sewn from purchased fabric (except apparel contractors)

611620 Professional sports (e.g., golf, skiing, swimming, tennis) instructors (i.e., not participating in sporting events)

711211 Professional sports clubs

711310 Professional sports promoters with facilities

711320 Professional sports promoters without facilities

813920 Professional standards review boards

326130 Profile shapes (e.g., plate, rod, sheet), laminated plastics, manufacturing

326121 Profile shapes (e.g., rod, tube), nonrigid plastics, manufacturing

525990 Profit-sharing funds

512110 Program producing, television

334513 Programmers, process-type, manufacturing

511210 Programming language and compiler software publishers, packaged

541511 Programming services, custom computer

332993 Projectiles (except guided missile), jet propulsion, manufacturing

333315 Projection equipment (e.g., motion picture, slide), photographic, manufacturing

423410 Projection equipment (e.g., motion picture, slide), photographic, merchant wholesalers

333314 Projection lenses manufacturing

333315 Projection screens (i.e., motion picture, overhead, slide) manufacturing

334310 Projection television manufacturing

332995 Projectors (e.g., antisub, depth charge release, grenade, livens, rocket), ordnance, manufacturing

711310 Promoters of agricultural fairs with facilities

711320 Promoters of agricultural fairs without facilities

711310 Promoters of arts events with facilities

711320 Promoters of arts events without facilities

561920	Promoters of conventions with or without facilities
711310	Promoters of festivals with facilities
711320	Promoters of festivals without facilities
711310	Promoters of live performing arts productions (e.g., concerts) with facilities
711320	Promoters of live performing arts productions (e.g., concerts) without facilities
711310	Promoters of sports events with facilities
711320	Promoters of sports events without facilities
561920	Promoters of trade fairs or shows with or without facilities
561410	Proofreading services
111421	Propagation material farming
424710	Propane bulk stations and terminals
324110	Propane gases made in petroleum refineries
211112	Propane recovered from oil and gas field gases
333518	Propeller straightening presses manufacturing
334514	Propeller type meters with registers manufacturing
332999	Propellers, ship and boat, made from purchased metal
524126	Property and casualty insurance carriers, direct
524130	Property and casualty reinsurance carriers
524126	Property damage insurance carriers, direct
531312	Property managers' offices, commercial real estate
531312	Property managers' offices, nonresidential real estate
531311	Property managers' offices, residential real estate
531312	Property managing, commercial real estate
531312	Property managing, nonresidential real estate
531311	Property managing, residential real estate
813990	Property owners' associations
561612	Property protection services (except armored car, security systems)
921130	Property tax assessors' offices
326299	Prophylactics manufacturing
112910	Propolis production, bees
336415	Propulsion units and parts, guided missile and space vehicle, manufacturing
325199	Propylcarbinol manufacturing
324110	Propylene (i.e., propene) made in petroleum refineries
325199	Propylene glycol manufacturing
325110	Propylene made from refined petroleum or liquid hydrocarbons
325211	Propylene resins manufacturing
213113	Prospect and test drilling services for coal mining on contract basis
213114	Prospect and test drilling services for metal mining on contract basis
213115	Prospect and test drilling services for nonmetallic mineral mining (except fuels) on a contract basis
339113	Prosthetic appliances and supplies manufacturing
423450	Prosthetic appliances and supplies merchant wholesalers
446199	Prosthetic stores
621210	Prosthodontists' offices (e.g., centers, clinics)
561612	Protection services (except armored car, security systems), personal or property
812332	Protective apparel supply services
523999	Protective committees, security holders
316211	Protective footwear, plastics or plastics-soled fabric upper, manufacturing
316211	Protective footwear, rubber or rubber-soled fabric upper, manufacturing

561612   Protective guard services
339920   Protectors, sports (e.g., baseball, basketball, hockey), manufacturing
334516   Protein analyzers, laboratory-type, manufacturing
541711   Protein engineering research and experimental development laboratories
325222   Protein fibers and filaments manufacturing
325211   Protein plastics manufacturing
712190   Provincial parks
334511   Proximity warning (i.e., collision avoidance) equipment manufacturing
111339   Prune farming
332212   Pruners manufacturing
311423   Prunes, dried, made in dehydration plants
115112   Pruning of orchard trees and vines
561730   Pruning services, ornamental tree and shrub
325131   Prussian blue pigments manufacturing
332212   Pry (i.e., crow) bars manufacturing
212299   Psilomelane mining and/or beneficiating
621420   Psychiatric centers and clinics (except hospitals), outpatient
623220   Psychiatric convalescent homes or hospitals
622210   Psychiatric hospitals (except convalescent)
621112   Psychiatrists' offices (e.g., centers, clinics)
812990   Psychic services
621330   Psychoanalysts' (except MDs or DOs) offices (e.g., centers, clinics)
621112   Psychoanalysts' (MDs or DOs) offices (e.g., centers, clinics)
813920   Psychologists' associations
621330   Psychologists' offices (e.g., centers, clinics), clinical
541720   Psychology research and development services

621330   Psychotherapists' (except MDs or DOs) offices (e.g., centers, clinics)
621112   Psychotherapists' (MDs or DOs) offices (e.g., centers, clinics)
541211   Public accountants' (CPAs) offices, certified
541211   Public accountants' (CPAs) private practices, certified
541219   Public accountants' (except CPAs) offices
541219   Public accountants' (except CPAs) private practices
238210   Public address system installation
532490   Public address system rental or leasing
811213   Public address system repair and maintenance services
334310   Public address systems and equipment manufacturing
423690   Public address systems and equipment merchant wholesalers
423210   Public building furniture merchant wholesalers
922130   Public defenders' offices
711410   Public figures' agents or managers
923120   Public health program administration, nonoperating
541910   Public opinion polling services
541910   Public opinion research services
922150   Public parole offices
922150   Public probation offices
921190   Public property management services, government
922130   Public prosecutors' offices
541820   Public relations agencies
541820   Public relations consulting services
541820   Public relations services
813319   Public safety advocacy organizations
922190   Public safety bureaus and statistics centers, government
922190   Public safety statistics centers, government

926130 Public service (except transportation) commissions, nonoperating
813410 Public speaking improvement clubs
611699 Public speaking training
561492 Public stenography services
926120 Public transportation commissions, nonoperating
926130 Public utility (except transportation) commissions, nonoperating
813910 Public utility associations
551112 Public utility holding companies
236220 Public warehouse construction
493190 Public warehousing and storage (except farm products, general merchandise, refrigerated, self storage)
493110 Public warehousing and storage (except self storage), general merchandise
493130 Public warehousing and storage, farm products (except refrigerated)
493120 Public warehousing and storage, refrigerated
****** Publishers—see specific type
511130 Publishers (except exclusive Internet publishing), book
511140 Publishers (except exclusive Internet publishing), directory
511191 Publishers (except exclusive Internet publishing), greeting card
511120 Publishers (except exclusive Internet publishing), magazine
511130 Publishers (except exclusive Internet publishing), map
511120 Publishers (except exclusive Internet publishing), periodical
511199 Publishers (except exclusive Internet publishing), racing form
541840 Publishers' advertising representatives (i.e., independent of media owners)
****** Publishers and printing combined—see specific type of publisher

****** Publishers or publishing—see specific type
511130 Publishers, book, combined with printing
511191 Publishers, greeting card, combined with printing
519130 Publishers, Internet greeting card
519130 Publishers, Internet map
519130 Publishers, Internet racing form
511120 Publishers, magazine, combined with printing
512230 Publishers, music
511110 Publishers, newspaper (except exclusive Internet publishing)
511110 Publishers, newspaper, combined with printing
511210 Publishers, packaged computer software
511120 Publishers, periodical, combined with printing
311520 Pudding pops, frozen, manufacturing
311999 Puddings, canned dessert, manufacturing
311999 Puddings, dessert, manufacturing
333923 Pulleys (except power transmission), metal, manufacturing
333613 Pulleys, power transmission, manufacturing
321999 Pulleys, wood, manufacturing
213112 Pulling oil and gas field casings, tubes, or rods on a contract basis
621111 Pulmonary specialists' offices (e.g., centers, clinics)
322122 Pulp and newsprint combined manufacturing
322121 Pulp and paper (except groundwood, newsprint) combined manufacturing
322130 Pulp and paperboard combined manufacturing
333291 Pulp making machinery manufacturing

322110 Pulp manufacturing (i.e., chemical, mechanical, or semichemical processes) without making paper

322110 Pulp manufacturing (made from bagasse, linters, rags, straw, wastepaper, or wood) without making paper

322122 Pulp mills and groundwood paper, uncoated and untreated, manufacturing

322110 Pulp mills not making paper or paperboard

322122 Pulp mills producing newsprint paper

322121 Pulp mills producing paper (except groundwood, newsprint)

322130 Pulp mills producing paperboard

322299 Pulp products, molded, manufacturing

333291 Pulp, paper, and paperboard molding machinery manufacturing

212399 Pulpstones, natural, mining and/or beneficiating

113310 Pulpwood logging camps

423990 Pulpwood merchant wholesalers

334515 Pulse (i.e., signal) generators manufacturing

334519 Pulse analyzers, nuclear monitoring, manufacturing

327992 Pumice (except abrasives) processing beyond beneficiation

327910 Pumice and pumicite abrasives manufacturing

212399 Pumice mining and/or beneficiating

212399 Pumicite mining and/or beneficiating

562991 Pumping (i.e., cleaning) cesspools and septic tanks

562991 Pumping (i.e., cleaning) portable toilets

213112 Pumping oil and gas wells on a contract basis

213113 Pumping or draining coal mines on a contract basis

213114 Pumping or draining metal mines on a contract basis

213115 Pumping or draining nonmetallic mineral mines (except fuel) on a contract basis

237120 Pumping station, gas and oil transmission, construction

237110 Pumping station, water and sewage system, construction

238220 Pumping system, water, installation

111219 Pumpkin farming, field and seed production

423120 Pumps (e.g., fuel, oil, power steering, water), automotive, merchant wholesalers

336312 Pumps (e.g., fuel, oil, water), mechanical, automotive and truck gasoline engine (except power steering), manufacturing

333911 Pumps (except fluid power), general purpose, manufacturing

316214 Pumps (i.e., dress shoes) manufacturing

423830 Pumps and pumping equipment, industrial-type, merchant wholesalers

333911 Pumps for railroad equipment lubrication systems manufacturing

333996 Pumps, fluid power, manufacturing

333911 Pumps, industrial and commercial-type, general purpose, manufacturing

333913 Pumps, measuring and dispensing (e.g., gasoline), manufacturing

333911 Pumps, oil field or well, manufacturing

333911 Pumps, sump or water, residential-type, manufacturing

313230 Punched felts manufacturing

332212 Punches (except paper), nonpowered handtool, manufacturing

333514	Punches for use with machine tools manufacturing
333513	Punching machines, metalworking, manufacturing
711110	Puppet theaters
339999	Puppets manufacturing
921190	Purchasing and supply agencies, government
522298	Purchasing of accounts receivable
332323	Purlins, metal, manufacturing
316993	Purses (except precious metal), men's, manufacturing
316992	Purses (except precious metal), women's, manufacturing
339911	Purses, precious metal or clad with precious metal, manufacturing
333515	Pushers (i.e., a machine tool accessory) manufacturing
332212	Putty knives manufacturing
423920	Puzzles merchant wholesalers
326122	PVC pipe manufacturing
325320	Pyrethrin insecticides manufacturing
334519	Pyrheliometers manufacturing
212393	Pyrite concentrates mining and/ or beneficiating
212393	Pyrite mining and/or beneficiating
325191	Pyroligneous acids manufacturing
212299	Pyrolusite mining and/or beneficiating
327112	Pyrometer tubes manufacturing
334513	Pyrometers, industrial process-type, manufacturing
327112	Pyrometric cones, earthenware, manufacturing
212399	Pyrophyllite mining and/or beneficiating
327992	Pyrophyllite processing beyond beneficiation
332994	Pyrotechnic pistols and projectors manufacturing
325998	Pyrotechnics (e.g., flares, flashlight bombs, signals) manufacturing
325211	Pyroxylin (i.e., nitrocellulose) resins manufacturing
212393	Pyrrhotite mining and/or beneficiating
112390	Quail production
611430	Quality assurance training
541990	Quantity surveyor services
327122	Quarry tiles, clay, manufacturing
333131	Quarrying machinery and equipment manufacturing
423810	Quarrying machinery and equipment merchant wholesalers
316999	Quarters (i.e., shoe cut stock), leather, manufacturing
212399	Quartz crystal, pure, mining and/or beneficiating
334419	Quartz crystals, electronic application, manufacturing
212319	Quartzite crushed and broken stone mining and/or beneficiating
212311	Quartzite dimension stone mining or quarrying
325191	Quebracho extracts manufacturing
112910	Queen bee production
325191	Quercitron extracts manufacturing
323114	Quick printing
327410	Quicklime (i.e., calcium oxide) manufacturing
811191	Quick-lube shops
212299	Quicksilver ores and metal mining and/or beneficiating
314999	Quilting of textiles
314129	Quilts made from purchased materials
111339	Quince farming
325411	Quinine and derivatives (i.e., basic chemicals) manufacturing
523999	Quotation services, securities
523999	Quotation services, stock
311119	Rabbit food manufacturing
112930	Rabbit production
311615	Rabbits processing (i.e., canned, cooked, fresh, frozen)
311615	Rabbits slaughtering and dressing
711219	Race car drivers

711219   Race car owners (i.e., racing cars)
336999   Race cars manufacturing
711219   Race dog owners (i.e., racing dogs)
711219   Racehorse owners (i.e., racing horses)
711219   Racehorse trainers
711219   Racehorse training
332991   Races, ball or roller bearings, manufacturing
511199   Racetrack program publishers (except Internet)
511199   Racetrack program publishers and printing combined
519130   Racetrack program publishers, exclusively on Internet
323112   Racetrack programs flexographic printing without publishing
323111   Racetrack programs gravure printing without publishing
323110   Racetrack programs lithographic (offset) printing without publishing
323119   Racetrack programs printing (except flexographic, gravure, lithographic, quick, screen) without publishing
323113   Racetrack programs screen printing without publishing
711212   Racetracks (e.g., automobile, dog, horse)
713990   Racetracks, slot car (i.e., amusement devices)
335932   Raceways manufacturing
713990   Raceways, gocart (i.e., amusement rides)
511199   Racing form publishers (except exclusive Internet publishing)
511199   Racing form publishers and printing combined
519130   Racing form publishers, exclusively on Internet
323112   Racing forms flexographic printing without publishing
323111   Racing forms gravure printing without publishing

323110   Racing forms lithographic (offset) printing without publishing
323119   Racing forms printing (except flexographic, gravure, lithographic, quick, screen) without publishing
323113   Racing forms screen printing without publishing
711219   Racing stables, horse
711219   Racing teams (e.g., automobile, motorcycle, snowmobile)
334417   Rack and panel connectors manufacturing
336330   Rack and pinion steering assemblies manufacturing
336399   Racks (e.g., bicycle, luggage, ski, tire), automotive, truck, and buses manufacturing
332313   Racks (e.g., trash), fabricated metal plate, manufacturing
332618   Racks, household-type, made from purchased wire
713940   Racquetball club facilities
811219   Radar and sonar equipement repair and maintenance services
334511   Radar detectors manufacturing
423690   Radar equipment merchant wholesalers
517919   Radar station operations
334511   Radar systems and equipment manufacturing
334515   Radar testing instruments, electric, manufacturing
334519   RADIAC (radioactivity detection, identification, and computation) equipment manufacturing
238220   Radiant floor heating equipment installation
334519   Radiation detection and monitoring instruments manufacturing
541380   Radiation dosimetry (i.e., radiation testing) laboratories or services
812332   Radiation protection garment supply services

339113 Radiation shielding aprons, gloves, and sheeting manufacturing
541380 Radiation testing laboratories or services
325998 Radiator additive preparations manufacturing
326220 Radiator and heater hoses, rubber or plastics, manufacturing
811118 Radiator repair shops, automotive
332322 Radiator shields and enclosures, sheet metal (except stampings), manufacturing
333414 Radiators (except motor vehicle, portable electric) manufacturing
336399 Radiators and cores manufacturing
423120 Radiators, motor vehicle, merchant wholesalers
335211 Radiators, portable electric, manufacturing
541840 Radio advertising representatives (i.e., independent of media owners)
236220 Radio and television broadcast studio construction
443112 Radio and television stores
332312 Radio and television tower sections, fabricated structural metal, manufacturing
488330 Radio beacon (i.e., ship navigation) services
515112 Radio broadcasting (except exclusively on Internet) stations (e.g., AM, FM, shortwave)
515111 Radio broadcasting network services
515111 Radio broadcasting networks
515111 Radio broadcasting syndicates
711510 Radio commentators, independent
541690 Radio consulting services
511120 Radio guide publishers (except exclusive Internet publishing)
511120 Radio guide publishers and printing combined

519130 Radio guide publishers, exclusively on Internet
323112 Radio guides flexographic printing without publishing
323111 Radio guides gravure printing without publishing
323110 Radio guides lithographic (offset) printing without publishing
323119 Radio guides printing (except flexographic, gravure, lithographic, quick, screen) without publishing
323113 Radio guides screen printing without publishing
334310 Radio headphones manufacturing
326199 Radio housings, plastics, manufacturing
334511 Radio magnetic instrumentation (RMI) manufacturing
517210 Radio paging services communications carriers
423690 Radio parts and accessories (e.g., transitors, tubes) merchant wholesalers
512290 Radio program tape production (except independent producers)
334310 Radio receiving sets manufacturing
811211 Radio repair and maintenance services without retailing new radios
811211 Radio repair, automotive, without retailing new
323111 Radio schedule gravure printing without publishing
511120 Radio schedule publishers (except exclusive Internet publishing)
511120 Radio schedule publishers and printing combined
519130 Radio schedule publishers, exclusively on Internet
323112 Radio schedules flexographic printing without publishing
323110 Radio schedules lithographic (offset) printing without publishing

323119 Radio schedules printing (except flexographic, gravure, lithographic, quick, screen) without publishing

323113 Radio schedules screen printing without publishing

236220 Radio station construction

515112 Radio stations (except exclusively on Internet)

561410 Radio transcription services

334220 Radio transmitting antennas and ground equipment manufacturing

237130 Radio transmitting tower construction

325188 Radioactive elements manufacturing

541360 Radioactive geophysical surveying services

325412 Radioactive in-vivo diagnostic substances manufacturing

325188 Radioactive isotopes manufacturing

424210 Radioactive pharmaceutical isotopes merchant wholesalers

562112 Radioactive waste collecting and/or local hauling

562211 Radioactive waste collecting and/or local hauling in combination with disposal and/or treatment facilities

562211 Radioactive waste disposal facilities

484230 Radioactive waste hauling, long-distance

562211 Radioactive waste treatment facilities

334519 Radioactivity detection, identification, and computation (RADIAC) equipment manufacturing

334515 Radiofrequency measuring equipment manufacturing

334515 Radiofrequency oscillators manufacturing

541380 Radiographic testing laboratories or services

541380 Radiographing welded joints on pipes and fittings

541380 Radiography inspection services

621512 Radiological laboratories, medical

621512 Radiological laboratory services, medical

621111 Radiologists' offices (e.g., centers, clinics)

423690 Radios (except household-type) merchant wholesalers

423620 Radios, household-type, merchant wholesalers

111219 Radish farming, field and seed production

325188 Radium chloride manufacturing

334517 Radium equipment manufacturing

325188 Radium luminous compounds manufacturing

212291 Radium ores mining and/or beneficiating

238990 Radon gas alleviation contractors

541380 Radon testing laboratories or services

326299 Rafts, swimming pool-type, rubber inflatable, manufacturing

423930 Rags merchant wholesalers

335931 Rail bonds, propulsion and signal circuit electric, manufacturing

331111 Rail joints and fastenings made in iron and steel mills

336510 Rail laying and tamping equipment manufacturing

485112 Rail transportation (except mixed mode), commuter

332323 Railings, metal, manufacturing

321918 Railings, wood stair, manufacturing

926120 Railroad and warehouse commissions, nonoperating

333613 Railroad car journal bearings, plain, manufacturing

532411 Railroad car rental and leasing

336510 Railroad cars and car equipment manufacturing

423860 Railroad cars merchant wholesalers

336510 Railroad cars, self-propelled, manufacturing

237990 Railroad construction
331111 Railroad crossings, iron or steel, made in iron and steel mills
423860 Railroad equipment and supplies merchant wholesalers
336510 Railroad locomotives and parts (except diesel engines) manufacturing
339932 Railroad models, hobby and toy, manufacturing
923130 Railroad Retirement Board
531190 Railroad right of way leasing
336510 Railroad rolling stock manufacturing
336360 Railroad seating manufacturing
334290 Railroad signaling equipment manufacturing
238210 Railroad signalling equipment installation
488210 Railroad switching services
488210 Railroad terminals, independent operation
561599 Railroad ticket offices
321114 Railroad ties (i.e., bridge, cross, switch) treating
423990 Railroad ties, wood, merchant wholesalers
333997 Railroad track scales manufacturing
482111 Railroad transportation, line-haul
487110 Railroad transportation, scenic and sightseeing
482112 Railroad transportation, short-line or beltline
487110 Railroad, scenic and sightseeing, operation
482111 Railroads, line-haul
482112 Railroads, short-line or beltline
321999 Rails (except rough), wood fence, manufacturing
423510 Rails and accessories, metal, merchant wholesalers
331319 Rails made by rolling or drawing purchased aluminum
331111 Rails rerolled or renewed in iron and steel mills
331319 Rails, aluminum, made in integrated secondary smelting and drawing plants

331319 Rails, aluminum, made in integrated secondary smelting and rolling mills
331111 Rails, iron or steel, made in iron and steel mills
113310 Rails, rough wood, manufacturing
332312 Railway bridge sections, prefabricated metal, manufacturing
237990 Railway construction (e.g., interlocker, roadbed, signal, track)
335312 Railway motors and control equipment, electric, manufacturing
237990 Railway roadbed construction
236220 Railway station construction
485112 Railway systems (except mixed mode), commuter
488210 Railway terminals, independent operation
482111 Railway transportation, line-haul
487110 Railway transportation, scenic and sightseeing
482112 Railway transportation, short-line or beltline
334519 Rain gauges manufacturing
315211 Raincoats water resistant, men's and boys', cut and sew apparel contractors
313320 Raincoats waterproofing (i.e., oiling)
315299 Raincoats, rubber or rubberized fabric, manufacturing
315291 Raincoats, water resistant, infants', cut and sewn from purchased fabric (except apparel contractors)
315228 Raincoats, water resistant, nontailored, men's and boys', cut and sewn from purchased fabric (except apparel contractors)
315239 Raincoats, water resistant, nontailored, women's, misses', and girls', cut and sewn from purchased fabric (except apparel contractors)

315222 Raincoats, water resistant, tailored, men's and boys', cut and sewn from purchased fabric (except apparel contractors)

315234 Raincoats, water resistant, tailored, women's, misses', and girls', cut and sewn from purchased fabric (except apparel contractors)

315212 Raincoats, water resistant, women's, girls', and infants', cut and sew apparel contractors

315299 Raincoats, waterproof (except infants'), cut and sewn from purchased fabric (except apparel contractors)

315291 Raincoats, waterproof, infants', cut and sewn from purchased fabric (except apparel contractors)

315211 Raincoats, waterproof, men's and boys', cut and sew apparel contractors

315212 Raincoats, waterproof, women's, girls', and infants', cut and sew apparel contractors

315291 Raincoats, water-repellent, infants', cut and sewn from purchased fabric (except apparel contractors)

315211 Raincoats, water-repellent, men's and boys', cut and sew apparel contractors

315228 Raincoats, water-repellent, nontailored, men's and boys', cut and sewn from purchased fabric (except apparel contractors)

315239 Raincoats, water-repellent, nontailored, women's, misses', and girls', cut and sewn from purchased fabric (except apparel contractors)

315222 Raincoats, water-repellent, tailored, men's and boys', cut and sewn from purchased fabric (except apparel contractors)

315234 Raincoats, water-repellent, tailored, women's, misses', and girls', cut and sewn from purchased fabric (except apparel contractors)

315212 Raincoats, water-repellent, women's, girls', and infants', cut and sew apparel contractors

111332 Raisin farming

112990 Raising swans, peacocks, flamingos, or other adornment birds

311423 Raisins made in dehydration plants

333111 Rakes, hay, manufacturing

332212 Rakes, nonpowered handtool, manufacturing

313111 Ramie spun yarns made from purchased fiber

316999 Rands (i.e., shoe cut stock), leather, manufacturing

333315 Range finders, photographic, manufacturing

335211 Range hoods with integral lighting fixtures, household-type, manufacturing

335211 Range hoods, household-type, manufacturing

333319 Ranges, commercial-type, manufacturing

335221 Ranges, household-type cooking, manufacturing

624190 Rape crisis centers

311225 Rapeseed (i.e., canola) oil made from purchased oils

311223 Rapeseed (i.e., canola) oil made in crushing mills

111120 Rapeseed farming, field and seed production

336510 Rapid transit cars and equipment manufacturing

325188 Rare earth compounds, not specified elsewhere by process, manufacturing

531110 Real estate rental or leasing of residential building

611519 Real estate schools

524127 Real estate title insurance carriers, direct

237210 Real property (except cemeteries) subdivision

561492 Real-time (i.e., simultaneous) closed captioning of live television performances, meetings, conferences, and so forth

333515 Reamers (i.e., a machine tool accessory) manufacturing

333512 Reaming machines, metalworking, manufacturing

238120 Rebar contractors

323121 Rebinding books, magazines, or pamphlets

515112 Rebroadcast radio stations (except exclusively on Internet)

336312 Rebuilding automotive and truck gasoline engines

326212 Rebuilding tires

326212 Recapping tires

424120 Receipt books merchant wholesalers

334220 Receiver-transmitter units (i.e., transceivers) manufacturing

335931 Receptacles (i.e., outlets), electrical, manufacturing

423610 Receptacles, electrical, merchant wholesalers

531120 Reception hall rental or leasing

335122 Recessed lighting housings and trim (except residential), electric, manufacturing

335121 Recessed lighting housings and trim, residential electric, manufacturing

335911 Rechargeable battery packs made from purchased battery cells and housings

335911 Rechargeable nickel cadmium (NICAD) batteries manufacturing

314999 Reclaimed wool processing

326299 Reclaiming rubber from waste or scrap

337121 Recliners, upholstered, manufacturing

332994 Recoil mechanisms (i.e., 30 mm. or less, 1.18 inch or less), gun, manufacturing

332995 Recoil mechanisms (i.e., more than 30 mm., more than 1.18 inch), gun, manufacturing

332995 Recoilless rifles manufacturing

541711 Recombinant DNA research and experimental development laboratories

423840 Reconditioned barrels and drums merchant wholesalers

213111 Reconditioning oil and gas field wells on a contract basis

811310 Reconditioning shipping barrels and drums

321219 Reconstituted wood panels manufacturing

321219 Reconstituted wood sheets and boards manufacturing

312229 Reconstituting tobacco

512210 Record producers (except independent)

711510 Record producers, independent

512210 Record production (except independent record producers) without duplication or distribution

512220 Record releasing, promoting, and distributing combined with mass duplication

451220 Record stores, new

453310 Record stores, used

423620 Recorders (e.g., tape, video), household-type, merchant wholesalers

334513 Recorders, industrial process control-type, manufacturing

334515 Recorders, oscillographic, manufacturing

512290 Recording books on tape or disc (except publishers)

512290 Recording seminars and conferences, audio

512240 Recording studios, sound, operating on a contract or fee basis

326199	Reels, plastics, manufacturing
321999	Reels, plywood, manufacturing
321999	Reels, wood, manufacturing
711219	Referees and umpires
519120	Reference libraries
561311	Referral agencies or services, employment
624190	Referral services for personal and social problems
486910	Refined petroleum products pipeline transportation
324110	Refineries, petroleum
324110	Refinery gases made in petroleum refineries
423830	Refinery machinery and equipment merchant wholesalers
237120	Refinery, petroleum, construction
331312	Refining aluminum, primary
331314	Refining aluminum, secondary
331411	Refining copper, primary
331423	Refining copper, secondary
331419	Refining nonferrous metals and alloys (except aluminum, copper), primary
331492	Refining nonferrous metals and alloys (except aluminum, copper), secondary
335129	Reflectors for lighting equipment, metal, manufacturing
333314	Reflectors, optical, manufacturing
326199	Reflectors, plastics, manufacturing
115310	Reforestation
922140	Reformatories
325991	Reformulating plastics resins from recycled plastics products
334513	Refractometers, industrial process-type, manufacturing
334516	Refractometers, laboratory-type, manufacturing
327124	Refractories (e.g., block, brick, mortar, tile), clay, manufacturing
327125	Refractories (e.g., block, brick, mortar, tile), nonclay, manufacturing
238140	Refractory brick contractors
327125	Refractory cement, nonclay, manufacturing
423840	Refractory materials (e.g., block, brick, mortar, tile) merchant wholesalers
212325	Refractory minerals mining and/ or beneficiating
722330	Refreshment stands, mobile
423740	Refrigerated display cases merchant wholesalers
311822	Refrigerated doughs made from purchased flour
333415	Refrigerated lockers manufacturing
484220	Refrigerated products trucking, local
484230	Refrigerated products trucking, long-distance
493120	Refrigerated warehousing
333415	Refrigeration compressors manufacturing
334512	Refrigeration controls, residential and commercial-type, manufacturing
423740	Refrigeration equipment and supplies, commercial-type, merchant wholesalers
811310	Refrigeration equipment repair and maintenance services, industrial and commercial-type
333415	Refrigeration equipment, industrial and commercial-type, manufacturing
238220	Refrigeration system (e.g., commercial, industrial, scientific) installation
334512	Refrigeration thermostats manufacturing
423740	Refrigeration units, motor vehicle, merchant wholesalers
333415	Refrigeration units, truck-type, manufacturing
334512	Refrigeration/air-conditioning defrost controls manufacturing
532210	Refrigerator rental

811412 Refrigerator, household-type, repair and maintenance services without retailing new refrigerators

335222 Refrigerator/freezer combinations, household-type, manufacturing

335222 Refrigerators (e.g., absorption, mechanical), household-type, manufacturing

423740 Refrigerators (e.g., reach-in, walk-in), commercial-type, merchant wholesalers

423620 Refrigerators, household-type, merchant wholesalers

624230 Refugee settlement services

562212 Refuse collecting and operating solid waste landfills

562111 Refuse collection services

562213 Refuse disposal combustors or incinerators

562212 Refuse disposal landfills

236210 Refuse disposal plant construction

562111 Refuse hauling, local

484230 Refuse hauling, long-distance

325221 Regenerated cellulosic fibers manufacturing

925120 Regional planning and development program administration

621399 Registered nurses' (RNs) offices (e.g., centers, clinics)

334514 Registers, linear tallying, manufacturing

332323 Registers, metal air, manufacturing

561311 Registries, employment

561311 Registries, teacher

335311 Regulating transformers, power system-type, manufacturing

926140 Regulation and inspection of agricultural products

926130 Regulation of utilities

335311 Regulators (i.e., electric transformers), feeder voltage, manufacturing

336322 Regulators, motor vehicle voltage for internal combustion engines manufacturing

335313 Regulators, power, manufacturing

423610 Regulators, voltage (except motor vehicle), merchant wholesalers

624190 Rehabilitation agencies for offenders

622310 Rehabilitation hospitals (except alcoholism, drug addiction)

622210 Rehabilitation hospitals, alcoholism and drug addiction

624310 Rehabilitation job counseling and training, vocational

922150 Rehabilitation services, correctional, government

332618 Reinforcing mesh, concrete, made from purchased wire

238120 Reinforcing rod, bar, mesh and cage installation

238120 Reinforcing steel contractors

524130 Reinsurance carriers

334515 Relays (except electrical, electronic), instrument, manufacturing

423610 Relays merchant wholesalers

335314 Relays, electrical and electronic, manufacturing

624230 Relief services, disaster

624230 Relief services, emergency

323121 Religious book binding without printing

511130 Religious book publishers (except exclusive Internet publishing)

511130 Religious book publishers and printing combined

519130 Religious book publishers, exclusively on Internet

451211 Religious book stores

323117 Religious books printing and binding without publishing

323117 Religious books printing without publishing

236220 Religious building (e.g., church, synagogue, mosque, temple) construction

337127	Religious furniture manufacturing
423210	Religious furniture merchant wholesalers
453998	Religious goods (except books) stores
511120	Religious magazine and periodical publishers (except exclusive Internet publishing)
511120	Religious magazine and periodical publishers and printing combined
519130	Religious magazine and periodical publishers, exclusively on Internet
323112	Religious magazines and periodicals flexographic printing without publishing
323111	Religious magazines and periodicals gravure printing without publishing
323110	Religious magazines and periodicals lithographic (offset) printing without publishing
323119	Religious magazines and periodicals printing (except flexographic, gravure, lithographic, quick, screen) without publishing
323113	Religious magazines and periodicals screen printing without publishing
813110	Religious organizations
423490	Religious supplies merchant wholesalers
311421	Relishes canning
562910	Remediation and clean up of contaminated buildings, mine sites, soil, or ground water
562910	Remediation services, environmental
525990	REMICs (real estate mortgage investment conduits)
522294	REMICs (real estate mortgage investment conduits) issuing, private
424310	Remnants, piece goods, merchant wholesalers

236118	Remodeling and renovating general contractors, multifamily building
236118	Remodeling and renovating general contractors, residential
236118	Remodeling and renovating general contractors, single-family housing
236118	Remodeling and renovating operative builders
236118	Remodeling and renovating single-family housing
236118	Remodeling and renovating, residential building
334290	Remote control units (e.g., garage door, television) manufacturing
541360	Remote sensing geophysical surveying services
213112	Removal of condensate gasoline from field gathering lines on a contract basis
213113	Removal of overburden for coal mining on a contract basis
213114	Removal of overburden for metal mining on a contract basis
213115	Removal of overburden for nonmetallic minerals mining (except fuels) on a contract basis
562920	Removal of recyclable materials from a waste stream
621492	Renal dialysis centers and clinics
311613	Rendering animals (carrion) for feed
311613	Rendering fats
311613	Rendering plants
424990	Rennets merchant wholesalers
926150	Rent control agencies
******	Rental—see type of article or property being rented
532310	Rent-all centers
532490	Renting coin-operated amusement devices (except concession operators)
531210	Renting real estate for others (i.e., agents, brokers)

541611	Reorganizational consulting services
522294	Repackaging loans for sale to others (i.e., private conduits)
******	Repair—see type of article being repaired
237310	Repair, highway, road, street, bridge or airport runway
323121	Repairing books
334210	Repeater and transceiver equipment, carrier line, manufacturing
711110	Repertory companies, theatrical
322231	Report covers made from purchased paper or paperboard
711510	Reporters, independent (freelance)
561491	Repossession services
512199	Reproduction of motion picture films for theatrical distribution
115210	Reproductive flushing services for animals
621410	Reproductive health services centers
561439	Reprographic services
712130	Reptile exhibits, live
324191	Re-refining used petroleum lubricating oils
321912	Resawing purchased lumber
621910	Rescue services, air
621910	Rescue services, medical
517410	Resellers, satellite telecommunication
517911	Resellers, telecommunication (except satellite)
325411	Reserpines (i.e., basic chemicals) manufacturing
561599	Reservation (e.g., airline, car rental, hotel, restaurant) services
522320	Reserve and liquidity services (except central bank)
237110	Reservoir construction
721310	Residence clubs, organizational
531110	Residential building rental or leasing
561720	Residential cleaning services
721310	Residential clubs

236116	Residential construction, multifamily, general contractors
236115	Residential construction, single-family, general contractors
623220	Residential group homes for the emotionally disturbed
531110	Residential hotel rental or leasing
236117	Residential operative builders
531311	Residential property managing
531210	Residential real estate agencies
531210	Residential real estate agents' offices
531210	Residential real estate brokerages
531210	Residential real estate brokers' offices
531311	Residential real estate property managers' offices
531190	Residential trailer parks
211112	Residue gas production
326192	Resilient floor coverings (e.g., sheet, tile) manufacturing
238330	Resilient floor tile or sheet (e.g., linoleum, rubber, vinyl), installation only
325211	Resins, plastics (except custom compounding purchased resins), manufacturing
424610	Resins, plastics, merchant wholesalers
424690	Resins, synthetic rubber, merchant wholesalers
334515	Resistance measuring equipment manufacturing
334513	Resistance thermometers and bulbs, industrial process-type, manufacturing
333992	Resistance welding equipment manufacturing
334415	Resistors, electronic, manufacturing
423690	Resistors, electronic, merchant wholesalers
335312	Resolvers manufacturing
334516	Resonance instruments (i.e., laboratory-type) manufacturing
334419	Resonant reed devices, electronic, manufacturing

325192	Resorcinol manufacturing
721120	Resort hotels with casinos
721110	Resort hotels without casinos
334510	Respiratory analysis equipment, electromedical, manufacturing
339113	Respiratory protection mask manufacturing
621399	Respiratory therapists' offices (e.g., centers, clinics)
623110	Rest homes with nursing care
623312	Rest homes without nursing care
561720	Rest room cleaning services
812990	Rest room operation
813910	Restaurant associations
236220	Restaurant construction
423440	Restaurant equipment (except furniture) merchant wholesalers
337127	Restaurant furniture (e.g., carts, chairs, foodwagons, tables) manufacturing
423210	Restaurant furniture merchant wholesalers
561720	Restaurant kitchen cleaning services
611519	Restaurant management schools (except academic)
492210	Restaurant meals delivery services (i.e., independent delivery services)
722211	Restaurants, carryout
722211	Restaurants, fast food
722110	Restaurants, full service
811420	Restoration and repair of antique furniture
811121	Restoration shops, antique and classic automotive
339113	Restraints, patient, manufacturing
561410	Resume writing services
238330	Resurfacing hardwood flooring
237310	Resurfacing, highway, road, street, bridge or airport runway
******	Retail—see type of dealer, shop, or store
333997	Retail scales (e.g., butcher, delicatessen, produce) manufacturing

813910	Retailers' associations
238110	Retaining wall (except anchored earth), poured concrete, construction
238140	Retaining wall, masonry (i.e., block, brick, stone), construction
237990	Retaining walls, anchored (e.g., with piles, soil nails, tieback anchors), construction
325998	Retarders (e.g., flameproofing agents, mildewproofing agents) manufacturing
339112	Retinoscopes (except electromedical) manufacturing
334510	Retinoscopes, electromedical, manufacturing
813410	Retirement associations, social
623311	Retirement communities, continuing care
623110	Retirement homes with nursing care
623312	Retirement homes without nursing care
531110	Retirement hotel rental or leasing
525110	Retirement pension plans
332420	Retorts, heavy gauge metal, manufacturing
339112	Retractors, medical, manufacturing
326211	Retreading materials, tire, manufacturing
326212	Retreading tires
813110	Retreat houses, religious
115114	Retting flax
811420	Reupholstery shops, furniture
522292	Reverse mortgage lending
237990	Revetment construction
332994	Revolvers manufacturing
238290	Revolving door installation
811310	Rewinding armatures (except on an assembly line or factory basis)
213111	Reworking oil and gas wells on a contract basis
331419	Rhenium refining, primary
335931	Rheostats (i.e., dimmer switches), current carrying wiring device, manufacturing

334419 Rheostats, electronic, manufacturing

335314 Rheostats, industrial control, manufacturing

212299 Rhodium mining and/or beneficiating

212299 Rhodochrosite mining and/or beneficiating

111219 Rhubarb farming, field and seed production

111419 Rhubarb, grown under cover

339944 Ribbons (e.g., cash register, printer, typewriter), inked, manufacturing

314999 Ribbons made from purchased fabrics

313221 Ribbons made in narrow woven fabric mills

313230 Ribbons made in nonwoven fabric mills

339944 Ribbons, inked, manufacturing

424120 Ribbons, inked, merchant wholesalers

424310 Ribbons, textile, merchant wholesalers

111160 Rice (except wild rice) farming, field and seed production

311212 Rice bran, flour, and meals, manufacturing

311230 Rice breakfast foods manufacturing

311212 Rice cleaning and polishing

115114 Rice drying

311212 Rice flour manufacturing

311213 Rice malt manufacturing

311212 Rice meal manufacturing

311212 Rice milling

311999 Rice mixes (i.e., uncooked and packaged with other ingredients) made from purchased rice and dry ingredients

311423 Rice mixes (i.e., uncooked and packaged with other ingredients) made in dehydration plants

311212 Rice mixes (i.e., uncooked and packaged with other ingredients) made in rice mills

311221 Rice starches manufacturing

311212 Rice, brewer's, manufacturing

311212 Rice, brown, manufacturing

424490 Rice, polished, merchant wholesalers

424510 Rice, unpolished, merchant wholesalers

315211 Riding clothes, men's and boys', cut and sew apparel contractors

315228 Riding clothes, men's and boys', cut and sewn from purchased fabric (except apparel contractors)

315212 Riding clothes, women's and girls', cut and sew apparel contractors

315239 Riding clothes, women's, misses', and girls', cut and sewn from purchased fabric (except apparel contractors)

713990 Riding clubs, recreational

316999 Riding crops manufacturing

611620 Riding instruction academies or schools

713990 Riding stables

713990 Rifle clubs, recreational

332994 Rifles (except recoilless, toy) manufacturing

332994 Rifles, BB and pellet, manufacturing

332994 Rifles, pneumatic, manufacturing

332995 Rifles, recoilless, manufacturing

339932 Rifles, toy, manufacturing

333512 Rifling machines, metalworking, manufacturing

213112 Rig skidding, oil and gas field, on a contract basis

238290 Rigging large-scale equipment

238910 Right of way cutting (except maintenance)

336612 Rigid inflatable boats (RIBs) manufacturing

336399 Rims, automotive, truck, and bus wheel, manufacturing

336311 Rings, piston, manufacturing

713940 Rinks, ice or roller skating

212319 Riprap (except granite, limestone) preparation plants

212319	Riprap (except limestone and granite) mining or quarrying
237990	Riprap installation
212313	Riprap, granite, mining or quarrying
212313	Riprap, granite, preparation plants
212312	Riprap, limestone, mining or quarrying
212312	Riprap, limestone, preparation plants
483211	River freight transportation
483212	River passenger transportation
713990	River rafting, recreational
713210	Riverboat casinos
333991	Riveting guns, handheld power-driven, manufacturing
333513	Riveting machines, metalworking, manufacturing
332722	Rivets, metal, manufacturing
621399	RNs' (registered nurses) offices (e.g., centers, clinics)
325320	Roach poisons manufacturing
711110	Road companies, theatrical
237310	Road construction
423810	Road construction and maintenance machinery merchant wholesalers
324199	Road oils made from refined petroleum
324110	Road oils made in petroleum refineries
311911	Roasted nuts and seeds manufacturing
112320	Roaster chicken production
335211	Roasters (i.e., cooking appliances), household-type electric, manufacturing
311920	Roasting coffee
333294	Roasting machinery manufacturing
315291	Robes, lounging, infants', cut and sewn from purchased fabric (except apparel contractors)
315192	Robes, lounging, made in apparel knitting mills
315211	Robes, lounging, men's and boys', cut and sew apparel contractors

315221	Robes, lounging, men's and boys', cut and sewn from purchased fabric (except apparel contractors)
315212	Robes, lounging, women's, girls', and infants', cut and sew apparel contractors
315231	Robes, lounging, women's, misses', and girls', cut and sewn from purchased fabric (except apparel contractors)
333120	Rock crushing machinery, portable, manufacturing
333131	Rock crushing machinery, stationary, manufacturing
333132	Rock drill bits, oil and gas field-type, manufacturing
333120	Rock drills, construction and surface mining-type, manufacturing
333131	Rock drills, underground mining-type, manufacturing
711130	Rock musical artists, independent
711130	Rock musical groups
237990	Rock removal, underwater
212393	Rock salt mining and/or beneficiating
336312	Rocker arms and parts, automotive and truck gasoline engine, manufacturing
337122	Rockers (except upholstered), wood, manufacturing
337121	Rockers, upholstered, manufacturing
332313	Rocket casings, fabricated metal work, manufacturing
336412	Rocket engines, aircraft, manufacturing
336415	Rocket engines, guided missile, manufacturing
332995	Rocket launchers manufacturing
336414	Rockets (guided missiles), space and military, complete, manufacturing
332993	Rockets, ammunition (except guided missiles, pyrotechnic), manufacturing
114111	Rockfish fishing
339932	Rocking horses manufacturing

324122	Roofing cements, asphalt, made from purchased asphaltic materials
324122	Roofing coatings made from purchased asphaltic materials
238160	Roofing contractors
324122	Roofing felts made from purchased asphaltic materials
444190	Roofing material dealers
423330	Roofing materials (except wood) merchant wholesalers
423310	Roofing materials, wood, merchant wholesalers
327123	Roofing tile, clay, manufacturing
327390	Roofing tile, concrete, manufacturing
238160	Roofing, built-up tar and gravel, installation
332322	Roofing, sheet metal (except stampings), manufacturing
333415	Room air-conditioners manufacturing
423620	Room air-conditioners merchant wholesalers
337122	Room dividers, wood household-type, manufacturing
333414	Room heaters (except portable electric) manufacturing
335211	Room heaters, portable electric, manufacturing
334512	Room thermostats manufacturing
721310	Rooming and boarding houses
325320	Root removing chemicals manufacturing
311221	Root starches manufacturing
332999	Rope fittings manufacturing
332618	Rope, wire, made from purchased wire
314991	Ropes (except wire rope) manufacturing
423840	Ropes (except wire rope) merchant wholesalers
313111	Ropes, hemp, made from purchased fiber
423510	Ropes, wire (except insulated), merchant wholesalers

339911	Rosaries and other small religious articles, precious metal, manufacturing
212291	Roscoelite (vanadium hydromica) mining and/or beneficiating
111421	Rose bush growing
325211	Rosins (i.e., modified resins) manufacturing
325191	Rosins made by distillation of pine gum or pine wood
424690	Rosins merchant wholesalers
333111	Rotary hoes manufacturing
333111	Rotary tillers, farm-type, manufacturing
334514	Rotary type meters, consumption registering, manufacturing
325320	Rotenone insecticides manufacturing
323111	Rotogravure printing
323122	Rotogravure printing plates and cylinders preparation services
335312	Rotor retainers and housings manufacturing
335312	Rotors (i.e., for motors) manufacturing
325620	Rouge, cosmetic, manufacturing
321920	Round stave baskets (e.g., fruit, vegetable) manufacturing
321912	Rounds or rungs, furniture, hardwood, manufacturing
331111	Rounds, tube, steel, made in iron and steel mills
423990	Roundwood merchant wholesalers
213112	Roustabout mining services, on a contract basis
333991	Routers, handheld power-driven, manufacturing
333292	Roving machinery for textiles manufacturing
236115	Row house (i.e., single-family type) construction general contractors
236117	Row house construction operative builders
532292	Rowboat rental
336612	Rowboats manufacturing
713990	Rowing clubs, recreational

112910 Royal jelly production, bees
326220 Rubber and plastics belts and hoses (without fittings) manufacturing
326299 Rubber bands manufacturing
325520 Rubber cements manufacturing
212324 Rubber clay mining and/or beneficiating
238290 Rubber door installation
326192 Rubber floor coverings manufacturing
326291 Rubber goods, mechanical (i.e., extruded, lathe-cut, molded), manufacturing
423840 Rubber goods, mechanical (i.e., extruded, lathe-cut, molded), merchant wholesalers
424210 Rubber goods, medical, merchant wholesalers
325998 Rubber processing preparations (e.g., accelerators, stabilizers) manufacturing
423930 Rubber scrap and scrap tires merchant wholesalers
339943 Rubber stamps manufacturing
424120 Rubber stamps, merchant wholesalers
313221 Rubber thread and yarns, fabric covered, manufacturing
326299 Rubber tubing manufacturing
333220 Rubber working machinery manufacturing
424990 Rubber, crude, merchant wholesalers
325212 Rubber, synthetic, manufacturing
313320 Rubberizing purchased capes
313320 Rubberizing purchased cloaks
313320 Rubberizing purchased clothing
313320 Rubberizing purchased coats
313320 Rubberizing purchased textiles and apparel
212399 Rubbing stones mining and/or beneficiating
562111 Rubbish (i.e., nonhazardous solid waste) hauling, local
562111 Rubbish collection services
562213 Rubbish disposal combustors or incinerators
562212 Rubbish disposal landfills

484220 Rubbish hauling without collection or disposal, truck, local
484230 Rubbish hauling without collection or disposal, truck, long-distance
562119 Rubble hauling, local
562119 Rubble removal services
212399 Ruby mining and/or beneficiating
532299 Rug and carpet rental
561740 Rug cleaning plants
325612 Rug cleaning preparations manufacturing
561740 Rug cleaning services
442210 Rug stores
314110 Rugs and carpets made from textile materials
423220 Rugs merchant wholesalers
321999 Rulers and rules (except slide), wood, manufacturing
332212 Rulers, metal, manufacturing
326199 Rulers, plastics, manufacturing
334519 Rules, slide, manufacturing
624221 Runaway youth shelters
488119 Runway maintenance services
237310 Runway, airport, line painting (e.g., striping)
485210 Rural bus services
324191 Rust arresting petroleum compounds made from refined petroleum
325998 Rust preventive preparations manufacturing
325612 Rust removers manufacturing
238320 Rustproofing (except automotive)
332812 Rustproofing metals and metal products for the trade
811198 Rustproofing shops, automotive
111219 Rutabaga farming, field and seed production
212299 Ruthenium ore mining and/or beneficiating
212299 Rutile mining and/or beneficiating
721211 RV (recreational vehicle) parks
532120 RV (recreational vehicle) rental or leasing
441210 RV dealers

111199	Rye farming, field and seed production
311211	Rye flour manufacturing
311213	Rye malt manufacturing
111998	Ryegrass seed farming
114111	Sablefish fishing
325199	Saccharin manufacturing
325620	Sachet, scented, manufacturing
322224	Sacks, multiwall, made from purchased uncoated paper
424130	Sacks, paper, merchant wholesalers
713990	Saddle horse rental services, recreational
325612	Saddle soaps manufacturing
321999	Saddle trees, wood, manufacturing
316110	Saddlery leather manufacturing
424910	Saddlery merchant wholesalers
332999	Saddlery parts, metal, manufacturing
811430	Saddlery repair shops without retailing new saddlery
451110	Saddlery stores
316999	Saddles and parts, leather, manufacturing
332999	Safe deposit boxes and chests, metal, manufacturing
332999	Safe doors and linings, metal, manufacturing
332999	Safes, metal, manufacturing
423420	Safes, security, merchant wholesalers
332911	Safety (i.e., pop-off) valves, industrial-type, manufacturing
316999	Safety belts, leather, manufacturing
541690	Safety consulting services
325920	Safety fuses, blasting, manufacturing
327215	Safety glass (including motor vehicle) made from purchased glass
238990	Safety net system, erecting and dismantling at construction site
339993	Safety pins manufacturing
332211	Safety razor blades manufacturing
332211	Safety razors manufacturing

111120	Safflower farming, field and seed production
311225	Safflower oil made from purchased oils
311223	Safflower oil made in crushing mills
441222	Sail boat dealers
339920	Sailboards manufacturing
336612	Sailboat building, not done in shipyards
532292	Sailboat rental
713930	Sailing clubs with marinas
713990	Sailing clubs without marinas
336611	Sailing ships, commercial, manufacturing
314912	Sails made from purchased fabrics
325181	Sal soda (i.e., washing soda) manufacturing
311423	Salad dressing mixes, dry, made in a dehydration plant
311942	Salad dressing mixes, dry, manufacturing
311941	Salad dressings manufacturing
424490	Salad dressings merchant wholesalers
424490	Salad oils merchant wholesalers
311991	Salads, fresh or refrigerated, manufacturing
424120	Sales books merchant wholesalers
323116	Sales books, manifold, printing
522220	Sales financing
541613	Sales management consulting services
325199	Salicylic acid (except medicinal) manufacturing
325411	Salicylic acid, medicinal, uncompounded, manufacturing
212391	Salines (except common salt) mining and/or beneficiating
114111	Salmon fishing
236220	Salon construction
311421	Salsa canning
325998	Salt (except table) manufacturing
311942	Salt substitute manufacturing
213112	Salt water disposal systems, oil and gas field, on a contract basis

212393 Salt, common, mining and/or beneficiating
212393 Salt, rock, mining and/or beneficiating
311942 Salt, table, manufacturing
424490 Salt, table, merchant wholesalers
311612 Salted meats made from purchased carcasses
311821 Saltines manufacturing
424210 Salts, bath, merchant wholesalers
424690 Salts, industrial, merchant wholesalers
334516 Sample analysis instruments (except medical) manufacturing
316991 Sample cases, all materials, manufacturing
334519 Sample changers, nuclear radiation, manufacturing
541870 Sample direct distribution services
323121 Samples mounting
541910 Sampling services, statistical
423320 Sand (except industrial) merchant wholesalers
212321 Sand and gravel quarrying (i.e., construction grade) and/or beneficiating
213112 Sand blasting pipelines on lease, oil and gas field on a contract basis
331524 Sand castings, aluminum, unfinished, manufacturing
331525 Sand castings, copper and copper-base alloy, unfinished, manufacturing
331528 Sand castings, nonferrous metals (except aluminum, copper), unfinished, manufacturing
484220 Sand hauling, local
484230 Sand hauling, long-distance
333120 Sand mixers manufacturing
212322 Sand, blast, quarrying and/or beneficiating
212321 Sand, construction grade, quarrying and/or beneficiating

212322 Sand, industrial (e.g., engine, filtration, glass grinding), quarrying and/or beneficiating
423840 Sand, industrial, merchant wholesalers
316219 Sandals, children's (except rubber, plastics), manufacturing
316213 Sandals, men's footwear (except rubber, plastics), manufacturing
316211 Sandals, plastics or plastics soled fabric upper, manufacturing
316211 Sandals, rubber or rubber soled fabric upper, manufacturing
316214 Sandals, women's footwear (except rubber, plastics), manufacturing
332813 Sandblasting metals and metal products for the trade
238990 Sandblasting, building exterior
333991 Sanders, handheld power-driven, manufacturing
333319 Sanding machines, floor, manufacturing
333210 Sanding machines, woodworking-type, stationary, manufacturing
333291 Sandpaper making machines manufacturing
327910 Sandpaper manufacturing
212319 Sandstone crushed and broken stone mining
212311 Sandstone mining or quarrying
212399 Sandstone, bituminous, mining and/or beneficiating
722211 Sandwich shops, limited-service
311612 Sandwich spreads, meat, made from purchased carcasses
311941 Sandwich spreads, salad dressing based, manufacturing
335211 Sandwich toasters and grills, household-type electric, manufacturing
424490 Sandwiches merchant wholesalers
311991 Sandwiches, fresh (i.e., assembled and packaged for wholesale market), manufacturing

322212	Sanitary food container, folding, made from purchased paperboard
424130	Sanitary food containers (e.g., disposable plastics, paper, paperboard) merchant wholesalers
322215	Sanitary food containers (except folding) made from purchased paper or paperboard
562212	Sanitary landfills
322291	Sanitary napkins and tampons made from purchased paper or textile fiber
322121	Sanitary napkins and tampons made in paper mills
322121	Sanitary paper products (except newsprint, uncoated groundwood) made in paper mills
424130	Sanitary paper products merchant wholesalers
322121	Sanitary paper stock manufacturing
322291	Sanitary products made from purchased sanitary paper stock
322121	Sanitary products made in paper mills
237110	Sanitary sewer construction
332998	Sanitary ware (e.g., bathtubs, lavatories, sinks), metal, manufacturing
238220	Sanitary ware installation
423720	Sanitary ware, china or enameled iron, merchant wholesalers
541620	Sanitation consulting services
926130	Sanitation districts, nonoperating
924110	Sanitation engineering agencies, government
212399	Sapphire mining and/or beneficiating
325222	Saran (i.e., polyvinylidene chloride) fibers and filaments manufacturing
332612	Sash balance springs, light gauge, made from purchased wire or strip

332321	Sash, door and window, metal, manufacturing
321911	Sash, door and window, wood and covered wood, manufacturing
316991	Satchels, all materials, manufacturing
334220	Satellite antennas manufacturing
334220	Satellite communications equipment manufacturing
238290	Satellite dish, household-type, installation
517110	Satellite master antenna television service (SMATV)
515111	Satellite radio networks
237130	Satellite receiving station construction
517410	Satellite telecommunication carriers
517410	Satellite telecommunication resellers
517919	Satellite telemetry operations on a contract or fee basis
517110	Satellite television distribution systems
515210	Satellite television networks
517919	Satellite tracking stations
325131	Satin white pigments manufacturing
335311	Saturable transformers manufacturing
324122	Saturated felts made from purchased paper
322121	Saturated felts made in paper mills
311423	Sauce mixes, dry, made in dehydration plants
311942	Sauce mixes, dry, manufacturing
311941	Sauces (except tomato based) manufacturing
311941	Sauces for meat (except tomato based) manufacturing
311941	Sauces for seafood (except tomato based) manufacturing
311941	Sauces for vegetable (except tomato based) manufacturing
311421	Sauces, tomato-based, canning
311421	Sauerkraut manufacturing

335211 Sauna heaters, electric, manufacturing

321992 Sauna rooms, prefabricated, wood, manufacturing

812199 Saunas

311612 Sausage and similar cased products made from purchased carcasses

424490 Sausage casings merchant wholesalers

311612 Sausage casings, collagen, made from purchased hides

311611 Sausage casings, natural, produced in slaughtering plant

326121 Sausage casings, plastics, manufacturing

522120 Savings and loan associations (S&L)

524113 Savings bank life insurance carriers, direct

522120 Savings banks

522120 Savings institutions

332213 Saw blades, all types, manufacturing

811411 Saw repair and maintenance (except sawmills) without retailing new saws

321113 Sawdust and shavings (i.e., sawmill byproducts) manufacturing

424990 Sawdust merchant wholesalers

321999 Sawdust, regrinding

321113 Sawed lumber made in sawmills

321912 Sawed lumber, resawing purchased lumber

333512 Sawing machines, metalworking, manufacturing

333210 Sawmill equipment manufacturing

532490 Sawmill machinery rental or leasing

423830 Sawmill machinery, equipment, and supplies merchant wholesalers

321113 Sawmills

333210 Saws, bench and table, power-driven, woodworking-type, manufacturing

332213 Saws, hand, nonpowered, manufacturing

333991 Saws, handheld power-driven, manufacturing

339112 Saws, surgical, manufacturing

339992 Saxophones and parts manufacturing

238990 Scaffold erecting and dismantling

423810 Scaffolding merchant wholesalers

532490 Scaffolding rental or leasing

332323 Scaffolds, metal, manufacturing

334519 Scalers, nuclear radiation, manufacturing

333997 Scales, including laboratory-type, manufacturing

114112 Scallop fishing

812199 Scalp treating services

518210 Scanning services, optical

333210 Scarfing machines, woodworking-type, manufacturing

333516 Scarfing units, rolling mill machinery, metalworking, manufacturing

333120 Scarifiers, road, manufacturing

325132 Scarlet 2 R lake manufacturing

315191 Scarves made in apparel knitting mills

315211 Scarves, men's and boys', cut and sew apparel contractors

315993 Scarves, men's and boys', cut and sewn from purchased fabric (except apparel contractors)

315212 Scarves, women's, girls', and infants', cut and sew apparel contractors

315999 Scarves, women's, misses', and girls', cut and sewn from purchased fabric (except apparel contractors)

336350 Scattershield, engine, manufacturing

711510 Scenery designers, independent theatrical

532490 Scenery, theatrical, rental or leasing

487990	Scenic and sightseeing excursions, aerial
487110	Scenic and sightseeing excursions, land
487210	Scenic and sightseeing excursions, water
481112	Scheduled air freight carriers
481112	Scheduled air freight transportation
481111	Scheduled air passenger carriers
481111	Scheduled air passenger transportation
212299	Scheelite mining and/or beneficiating
313222	Schiffli machine embroideries manufacturing
333292	Schiffli machinery manufacturing
212319	Schist, mica, crushed and broken stone, mining and/or beneficiating
212311	Schist, mica, mining or quarrying
511120	Scholarly journal publishers (except exclusive Internet publishing)
511120	Scholarly journal publishers and printing combined
519130	Scholarly journal publishers, exclusively on Internet
323112	Scholarly journals flexographic printing without publishing
323111	Scholarly journals gravure printing without publishing
323110	Scholarly journals lithographic (offset) printing without publishing
323119	Scholarly journals printing (except flexographic, gravure, lithographic, quick, screen) without publishing
323113	Scholarly journals screen printing without publishing
813211	Scholarship trusts (i.e., grantmaking, charitable trust foundations)
511120	Scholastic magazine and periodical publishers (except exclusive Internet publishing)
511120	Scholastic magazine and periodical publishers and printing combined
519130	Scholastic magazine and periodical publishers, exclusively on Internet
323112	Scholastic magazines and periodicals flexographic printing without publishing
323111	Scholastic magazines and periodicals gravure printing without publishing
323110	Scholastic magazines and periodicals lithographic (offset) printing without publishing
323119	Scholastic magazines and periodicals printing (except flexographic, gravure, lithographic, quick, screen) without publishing
323113	Scholastic magazines and periodicals screen printing without publishing
611110	School boards, elementary and secondary
511130	School book publishers (except exclusive Internet publishing)
511130	School book publishers and printing combined
519130	School book publishers, exclusively on Internet
323117	School books printing and binding without publishing
323117	School books printing without publishing
236220	School building construction
611710	School bus attendant services
423110	School bus merchant wholesalers
532120	School bus rental or leasing
485410	School bus services
336211	School buses assembling on purchased chassis
611110	School districts, elementary or secondary
423490	School equipment and supplies (except books, furniture) merchant wholesalers
337127	School furniture manufacturing

423210	School furniture merchant wholesalers
541921	School photography (i.e., portrait photography) services
453210	School supply stores
511130	School textbook publishers (except exclusive Internet publishing)
511130	School textbook publishers and printing combined
519130	School textbook publishers, exclusively on Internet
323121	School textbooks binding without printing
448190	School uniform stores
611110	Schools for the handicapped, elementary or secondary
611110	Schools for the mentally retarded (except preschool, job training, vocational rehabilitation)
611110	Schools for the physically disabled, elementary or secondary
611512	Schools, aviation
611511	Schools, barber
611511	Schools, beauty
611410	Schools, business, not offering academic degrees
611310	Schools, correspondence, college level
611511	Schools, cosmetology
611610	Schools, drama (except academic)
611110	Schools, elementary
611210	Schools, junior college
611210	Schools, junior college vocational
611630	Schools, language
611310	Schools, medical
611610	Schools, music (except academic)
611310	Schools, professional (colleges or universities)
611110	Schools, secondary
611620	Schools, sports instruction
712110	Science and technology museums
339932	Science kits (e.g., chemistry sets, microscopes, natural science sets) manufacturing
327215	Scientific apparatus glassware made from purchased glass
813920	Scientific associations
327215	Scientific glassware made from purchased glass
327212	Scientific glassware, pressed or blown, made in glass making plants
423490	Scientific instruments merchant wholesalers
511120	Scientific journal and periodical publishers (except exclusive Internet publishing)
511120	Scientific journal and periodical publishers and printing combined
519130	Scientific journal and periodical publishers, exclusively on Internet
423490	Scientific laboratory equipment merchant wholesalers
334519	Scintillation detectors manufacturing
335211	Scissors, electric, manufacturing
332211	Scissors, nonelectric, manufacturing
332212	Scoops, metal (except kitchen-type), manufacturing
321999	Scoops, wood, manufacturing
339932	Scooters, children's, manufacturing
339950	Scoreboards manufacturing
212399	Scoria mining and/or beneficiating
313312	Scouring and combing textile fibers
325611	Scouring cleansers (e.g., pastes, powders) manufacturing
332999	Scouring pads, soap impregnated, manufacturing
813410	Scouting organizations
423930	Scrap materials (e.g., automotive, industrial) merchant wholesalers
323118	Scrapbooks and refills manufacturing

424120	Scrapbooks merchant wholesalers
333131	Scraper loaders, underground mining-type, manufacturing
333120	Scrapers, construction-type, manufacturing
332321	Screen doors, metal frame, manufacturing
323122	Screen for printing, preparation services
323113	Screen printing (except books, manifold business forms, grey goods)
323113	Screen printing apparel and textile products (e.g. caps, napkins, placemats, T-shirts, towels) (except grey goods)
313311	Screen printing broadwoven fabric grey goods
325910	Screen process inks manufacturing
333999	Screening and sifting machinery for general industrial use manufacturing
333120	Screening machinery, portable, manufacturing
333131	Screening machinery, stationary, manufacturing
212399	Screening peat
212113	Screening plants, anthracite
212111	Screening plants, bituminous coal or lignite
326199	Screening, window, plastics, manufacturing
711510	Screenplay writers, independent
313312	Screenprinting fabric grey goods (except broadwoven) and textile products (except apparel)
334419	Screens for liquid crystal display (LCD) manufacturing
332321	Screens, door and window, metal frame, manufacturing
321911	Screens, door and window, wood framed, manufacturing
333315	Screens, projection (i.e., motion picture, overhead, slide), manufacturing
423310	Screens, window and door, merchant wholesalers

333512	Screw and nut slotting machines, metalworking, manufacturing
333922	Screw conveyors manufacturing
332212	Screw drivers, nonelectric, manufacturing
332722	Screw eyes, metal, manufacturing
333518	Screwdowns and boxes machinery, metal, manufacturing
333991	Screwdrivers and nut drivers, handheld power-driven, manufacturing
333518	Screwdriving machines manufacturing
332212	Screwjacks manufacturing
332722	Screws, metal, manufacturing
711510	Script writers, independent
238220	Scrubber, air purification, installation
339920	Scuba diving equipment manufacturing
611620	Scuba instruction, camps, or schools
711510	Sculptors, independent
611610	Sculpture instruction
327420	Sculptures (e.g., gypsum, plaster of paris) manufacturing
327112	Sculptures, architectural, clay, manufacturing
332212	Scythes manufacturing
212399	Scythestones mining and/or beneficiating
114111	Sea bass fishing
114111	Sea herring fishing
713990	Sea kayaking, recreational
112519	Sea plant agriculture
114111	Sea trout fishing
114112	Sea urchin fishing
424460	Seafood (except canned, packaged frozen) merchant wholesalers
311711	Seafood and seafood products canning
311711	Seafood and seafood products curing
311712	Seafood dinners, frozen, manufacturing
445220	Seafood markets

311712 Seafood products, fresh prepared, manufacturing
311712 Seafood products, frozen, manufacturing
424490 Seafood, canned, merchant wholesalers
311712 Seafood, fresh prepared, manufacturing
311712 Seafood, frozen, manufacturing
424420 Seafoods, packaged frozen, merchant wholesalers
339943 Seal presses (e.g., notary), hand operated, manufacturing
424690 Sealants merchant wholesalers
335110 Sealed beam automotive light bulbs manufacturing
325520 Sealing compounds for pipe threads and joints manufacturing
423840 Seals merchant wholesalers
339991 Seals, grease or oil, manufacturing
333992 Seam welding equipment manufacturing
334511 Search and detection systems and instruments manufacturing
519130 Search portals, Internet
335129 Searchlights, electric and nonelectric, manufacturing
453220 Seasonal and holiday decoration stores
721110 Seasonal hotels without casinos
561730 Seasonal property maintenance services (i.e., snow plowing in winter, landscaping during other seasons)
311942 Seasoning salt manufacturing
336360 Seat belts, motor vehicle and aircraft, manufacturing
423120 Seat covers, automotive, merchant wholesalers
321999 Seat covers, rattan, manufacturing
326150 Seat cushions, foam plastics (except polystyrene), manufacturing
316999 Seatbelts, leather, manufacturing
336360 Seats for public conveyances, manufacturing
336360 Seats, railroad, manufacturing

321999 Seats, toilet, wood, manufacturing
237990 Seawall, wave protection, construction
488310 Seaway operation
112519 Seaweed farming
114119 Seaweed gathering
311711 Seaweed processing (e.g., dulse)
325199 Sebacic acid esters manufacturing
325199 Sebacic acid manufacturing
611630 Second language instruction
522294 Secondary market financing (i.e., buying, pooling, repackaging loans for sale to others)
331492 Secondary refining of nonferrous metals (except aluminum, copper)
611110 Secondary schools offering both academic and technical courses
331492 Secondary smelting of nonferrous metals (except aluminum, copper)
453310 Second-hand merchandise stores
611410 Secretarial schools
561410 Secretarial services
332311 Sections for prefabricated metal buildings manufacturing
321992 Sections, prefabricated wood building, manufacturing
523120 Securities brokerages
523120 Securities brokers' offices
523991 Securities custodians
523110 Securities dealers (i.e., acting as a principal in dealing securities to investors)
523110 Securities dealing (i.e., acting as a principal in dealing securities to investors)
523110 Securities distributing (i.e., acting as a principal in dealing securities to investors)
523210 Securities exchanges
523120 Securities floor brokers
523110 Securities floor traders (i.e., acting as a principal in dealing securities to investors)
523110 Securities flotation companies

523999	Securities holders' protective services
523110	Securities originating (i.e., acting as a principal in dealing securities to investors)
926150	Securities regulation commissions
523110	Securities trading (i.e., acting as a principal in dealing securities to investors)
523999	Securities transfer agencies
523110	Securities underwriting
561621	Security alarm systems sales combined with installation, repair, or monitoring services
238210	Security and fire system, installation only
541690	Security consulting services
561612	Security guard services
611519	Security guard training
561612	Security patrol services
423420	Security safes merchant wholesalers
561621	Security system monitoring services
423610	Security systems merchant wholesalers
325412	Sedative preparations manufacturing
212399	Sedge peat mining and/or beneficiating
237990	Sediment control system construction
333131	Sedimentary mineral machinery manufacturing
314911	Seed bags made from purchased woven or knitted materials
115112	Seed bed preparing
115114	Seed cleaning
322232	Seed packets made from purchased paper
115114	Seed processing, post-harvest for propagation
541380	Seed testing laboratories or services
325320	Seed treatment preparations manufacturing
333111	Seeders, farm-type, manufacturing

333112	Seeders, lawn and garden-type, manufacturing
115112	Seeding crops
561730	Seeding lawns
424450	Seeds (e.g., canned, roasted, salted) merchant wholesalers
424910	Seeds (e.g., field, flower, garden) merchant wholesalers
311911	Seeds, snack (e.g., canned, cooked, roasted, salted) manufacturing
541360	Seismic geophysical surveying services
213112	Seismograph exploration (except surveying) for oil and gas on a contract basis
334519	Seismographs manufacturing
334519	Seismometers manufacturing
334519	Seismoscopes manufacturing
212399	Selenite mining and/or beneficiating
331491	Selenium bar, rod, sheet, strip, and tubing made from purchased metals or scrap
325188	Selenium compounds, not specified elsewhere by process, manufacturing
325188	Selenium dioxide manufacturing
331492	Selenium recovering from scrap and/or alloying purchased metals
331419	Selenium refining, primary
611699	Self defense (except martial arts) instruction
624190	Self-help organizations (except for disabled persons, the elderly, persons diagnosed with mental retardation)
624120	Self-help organizations for disabled persons, the elderly, and persons diagnosed with mental retardation
624110	Self-help organizations, youth
525190	Self-insurance funds (except employee benefit funds)
811192	Self-service carwash
812310	Self-service drycleaners and laundries
531130	Self-storage unit rental or leasing

531130 Self-storage warehousing
531210 Selling real estate for others (i.e., agents, brokers)
115210 Semen collection
424590 Semen, bovine, merchant wholesalers
212111 Semianthracite surface mining and/or beneficiating
212112 Semianthracite underground mining or mining and beneficiating
212111 Semibituminous coal surface mining and/or beneficiating
212112 Semibituminous coal underground mining or mining and beneficiating
333295 Semiconductor assembly and packaging machinery manufacturing
335999 Semiconductor battery chargers manufacturing
334413 Semiconductor circuit networks (i.e., solid-state integrated circuits) manufacturing
334413 Semiconductor devices manufacturing
423690 Semiconductor devices merchant wholesalers
334413 Semiconductor dice and wafers manufacturing
335999 Semiconductor high-voltage power supplies manufacturing
333295 Semiconductor making machinery manufacturing
334413 Semiconductor memory chips manufacturing
334515 Semiconductor test equipment manufacturing
333618 Semidiesel engines manufacturing
423510 Semi-finished metal products merchant wholesalers
611110 Seminaries, below university grade
611310 Seminaries, theological, offering baccalaureate or graduate degrees
212399 Semiprecious stones mining and/or beneficiating
711211 Semiprofessional baseball clubs
711211 Semiprofessional football clubs
711211 Semiprofessional sports clubs
331511 Semisteel foundries
336212 Semi-trailer manufacturing
532120 Semi-trailer rental or leasing
311211 Semolina flour manufacturing
624120 Senior citizens activity centers
813311 Senior citizens advocacy organizations
813410 Senior citizens' associations, social
624120 Senior citizens centers
623312 Senior citizens' homes without nursing care
485991 Senior citizens transportation services
561312 Senior executive search services
325992 Sensitized cloth or paper (e.g., blueprint, photographic) manufacturing
333315 Sensitometers, photographic, manufacturing
334510 Sentinel, cardiac, manufacturing
238910 Septic system contractors
238910 Septic tank and weeping tile installation
562991 Septic tank cleaning services
562991 Septic tank pumping (i.e., cleaning) services
423390 Septic tanks (except concrete) merchant wholesalers
423320 Septic tanks, concrete, merchant wholesalers
332420 Septic tanks, heavy gauge metal, manufacturing
326199 Septic tanks, plastics or fiberglass, manufacturing
334512 Sequencing controls for electric heating equipment manufacturing
335999 Series capacitors (except electronic) manufacturing
212319 Serpentine crushed and broken stone mining and/or beneficiating
212311 Serpentine mining or quarrying
325414 Serums (except diagnostic substances) manufacturing

315211	Service apparel, washable, men's and boys', cut and sew apparel contractors
315225	Service apparel, washable, men's and boys', cut and sewn from purchased fabric (except apparel contractors)
315212	Service apparel, washable, women's, cut and sew apparel contractors
315239	Service apparel, washable, women's, misses' and girls', cut and sewn from purchased fabric (except apparel contractors)
423850	Service establishment equipment and supplies merchant wholesalers
813910	Service industries associations
237120	Service line, gas and oil, construction
811310	Service machinery and equipment repair and maintenance services
561720	Service station cleaning and degreasing services
236220	Service station construction
447190	Service stations, gasoline
213111	Service well drilling on a contract basis
213112	Servicing oil and gas wells on a contract basis
337124	Serving carts, metal household-type, manufacturing
337122	Serving carts, wood household-type, manufacturing
335312	Servomotors manufacturing
111120	Sesame farming, field and seed production
711510	Set designers, independent theatrical
541191	Settlement offices, real estate
322213	Setup (i.e., not shipped flat) boxes made from purchased paperboard
322130	Setup boxboard stock manufacturing
237110	Sewage collection and disposal line construction

237110	Sewage disposal plant construction
221320	Sewage disposal plants
333319	Sewage treatment equipment manufacturing
237110	Sewage treatment plant construction
221320	Sewage treatment plants or facilities
562998	Sewer cleaning and rodding services
562998	Sewer cleanout services
237110	Sewer construction
238220	Sewer hook-up and connection, building
237110	Sewer main, pipe and connection, construction
327123	Sewer pipe and fittings, clay, manufacturing
331511	Sewer pipe, cast iron, manufacturing
327332	Sewer pipe, concrete, manufacturing
221320	Sewer systems
424310	Sewing accessories merchant wholesalers
339999	Sewing and mending kits assembling
316993	Sewing cases (except metal) manufacturing
339911	Sewing cases, precious metal, manufacturing
315211	Sewing fabric owned by others for men's and boys' apparel
315212	Sewing fabric owned by others for women's, girls' and infants' apparel
337129	Sewing machine cabinets, wood, manufacturing
443111	Sewing machine stores, household-type
811412	Sewing machine, household-type, repair shops without retailing new sewing machines
333298	Sewing machines (including household-type) manufacturing
423620	Sewing machines, household-type, merchant wholesalers
423830	Sewing machines, industrial, merchant wholesalers

451130 Sewing supply stores

313113 Sewing threads manufacturing

334511 Sextants (except surveying) manufacturing

334519 Sextants, surveying, manufacturing

337920 Shade pulls, window, manufacturing

335121 Shades, lamp (except glass, plastics), residential-type, manufacturing

337920 Shades, window (except outdoor canvas awnings), manufacturing

213113 Shaft sinking for coal mines on a contract basis

213114 Shaft sinking for metal mines on a contract basis

238160 Shake and shingle, roof, installation

321113 Shakes (i.e., hand split shingles) manufacturing

212325 Shale (except oil shale) mining and/or beneficiating

327992 Shale, expanded, manufacturing

211111 Shale, oil, mining and/or beneficiating

111219 Shallot farming, field and seed production

325620 Shampoos and conditioners, hair, manufacturing

316999 Shanks, shoe, leather, manufacturing

333210 Shapers, woodworking-type, manufacturing

114111 Shark fishing

339994 Shaving brushes manufacturing

333512 Shaving machines, metalworking, manufacturing

325620 Shaving preparations (e.g., creams, gels, lotions, powders) manufacturing

424210 Shaving preparations merchant wholesalers

333513 Shearing machines, metal forming, manufacturing

316110 Shearling (i.e., prepared sheepskin) manufacturing

333991 Shears and nibblers, handheld power-driven, manufacturing

332211 Shears, nonelectric, household-type (e.g., kitchen, barber, tailor) manufacturing

332212 Shears, nonelectric, tool-type (e.g., garden, pruners, tinsnip), manufacturing

333111 Shears, powered, for use on animals, manufacturing

322121 Sheathing paper (except newsprint, uncoated groundwood) made in paper mills

324122 Sheathing, asphalt saturated, made from refined petroleum

238130 Sheathing, wood, installation

333613 Sheaves, mechanical power transmission, manufacturing

332311 Sheds, (e.g., garden, storage, utility) prefabricated metal, manufacturing

321992 Sheds, (e.g., garden, storage, utility) prefabricated wood, manufacturing

115210 Sheep dipping and shearing

112410 Sheep farming (e.g., meat, milk, wool production)

424520 Sheep merchant wholesalers

333111 Sheep shears, powered, manufacturing

326140 Sheet (i.e., board), polystyrene foam insulation, manufacturing

238220 Sheet metal duct work installation

333513 Sheet metal forming machines manufacturing

238160 Sheet metal roofing installation

423330 Sheet metal roofing materials merchant wholesalers

332322 Sheet metal work (except stampings) manufacturing

611513 Sheet metal workers' apprenticeship training

323112 Sheet music flexographic printing without publishing

323111 Sheet music gravure printing without publishing

323110 Sheet music lithographic (offset) printing without publishing

424990 Sheet music merchant wholesalers
323119 Sheet music printing (except flexographic, gravure, lithographic, qiuck, screen) without publishing
512230 Sheet music publishers
512230 Sheet music publishers and printing combined
323113 Sheet music screen printing without publishing
451140 Sheet music stores
331111 Sheet pilings, plain, iron or steel, made in iron and steel mills
331315 Sheet, aluminum, made by flat rolling purchased aluminum
331315 Sheet, aluminum, made in integrated secondary smelting and flat rolling mills
331421 Sheet, copper and copper alloy, made from purchased copper or in integrated secondary smelting and rolling, drawing or extruding plants
326130 Sheet, laminated plastics (except flexible packaging), manufacturing
326113 Sheet, plastics, unlaminated (except packaging), manufacturing
326299 Sheeting, rubber, manufacturing
314129 Sheets and pillowcases made from purchased fabrics
313210 Sheets and pillowcases made in broadwoven fabric mills
331111 Sheets, steel, made in iron and steel mills
311119 Shell crushing and grinding for animal feed
311119 Shell crushing for feed
332993 Shell loading and assembly plants
212399 Shell mining and/or beneficiating
339999 Shell novelties
331111 Shell slugs, steel, made in iron and steel mills
325510 Shellac manufacturing
424950 Shellac merchant wholesalers

311711 Shellfish and shellfish products canning
311711 Shellfish curing
114112 Shellfish fishing (e.g., clam, crab, oyster, shrimp)
112512 Shellfish hatcheries
311712 Shellfish products, fresh prepared, manufacturing
311712 Shellfish products, frozen, manufacturing
311712 Shellfish, fresh prepared, manufacturing
311712 Shellfish, frozen, manufacturing
332993 Shells, artillery, manufacturing
332992 Shells, small arms (i.e., 30 mm. or less, 1.18 inch or less), manufacturing
624310 Sheltered workshops (i.e., work experience centers)
624221 Shelters (except for victims of domestic or international disasters or conflicts), emergency
624230 Shelters for victims of domestic or international disasters or conflicts, emergency
624221 Shelters, battered women's
624221 Shelters, homeless
624221 Shelters, runaway youth
624221 Shelters, temporary (e.g., battered women's, homeless, runaway youth)
337215 Shelving (except wire) manufacturing
423440 Shelving, commercial, merchant wholesalers
238390 Shelving, metal, constructed on site
332618 Shelving, wire, made from purchased wire
238350 Shelving, wood, constructed on site
332812 Sherardizing of metals and metal products for the trade
311520 Sherbets manufacturing
922120 Sheriffs' offices (except court functions only)
922110 Sheriffs' offices, court functions only
332999 Shims, metal, manufacturing

321113	Shingle mills, wood
423330	Shingles (except wood) merchant wholesalers
324122	Shingles made from purchased asphaltic materials
423310	Shingles, wood, merchant wholesalers
321113	Shingles, wood, sawed or hand split, manufacturing
331525	Ship and boat propellers, cast brass, bronze and copper (except die-casting), unfinished, manufacturing
424990	Ship chandler merchant wholesalers
483113	Ship chartering with crew, coastal or Great Lakes freight transportation (including St. Lawrence Seaway)
483114	Ship chartering with crew, coastal or Great Lakes passenger transportation (including St. Lawrence Seaway)
483111	Ship chartering with crew, deep sea freight transportation to or from foreign ports
483112	Ship chartering with crew, deep sea passenger transportation to or from foreign ports
483211	Ship chartering with crew, freight transportation, inland waters (except on Great Lakes system)
483212	Ship chartering with crew, passenger transportation, inland waters (except on Great Lakes system)
333923	Ship cranes and derricks manufacturing
561311	Ship crew employment agencies
561311	Ship crew registries
423930	Ship dismantling (except at floating drydocks and shipyards) merchant wholesalers
488390	Ship dismantling at floating drydock
336611	Ship dismantling at shipyards
337127	Ship furniture manufacturing
488320	Ship hold cleaning services
238350	Ship joinery contractors
238320	Ship painting contractors
532411	Ship rental or leasing without operators
336611	Ship repair done in a shipyard
336611	Ship scaling services done at a shipyard
488390	Ship scaling services not done at a shipyard
332312	Ship sections, prefabricated metal, manufacturing
331422	Shipboard cable made from purchased copper in wire drawing plants
331319	Shipboard cable made in aluminum wire drawing plants
488510	Shipping agents (freight forwarding)
314911	Shipping bags made from purchased woven or knitted materials
332439	Shipping barrels, drums, kegs, and pails, light gauge metal, manufacturing
321920	Shipping cases and drums, wood, wirebound, manufacturing
321920	Shipping cases, wood, nailed or lock corner, manufacturing
813910	Shipping companies' associations
423840	Shipping containers (except disposable plastics, paper) merchant wholesalers
322211	Shipping containers made from purchased paperboard
322211	Shipping containers, corrugated, made from purchased paper or paperboard
321920	Shipping crates, wood, manufacturing
483113	Shipping freight to and from domestic ports (i.e., coastal, deep sea (including Puerto Rico), Great Lakes system (including St. Lawrence Seaway))
483111	Shipping freight to or from foreign ports, deep sea

483211	Shipping freight, inland waters (except on Great Lakes system)
326150	Shipping pads and shaped cushioning, foam plastics (except polystyrene), manufacturing
326140	Shipping pads and shaped cushioning, polystyrene foam, manufacturing
423840	Shipping pails, metal, merchant wholesalers
323112	Shipping registers flexographic printing without publishing
323111	Shipping registers gravure printing without publishing
323110	Shipping registers lithographic (offset) printing without publishing
323113	Shipping registers screen printing without publishing
424130	Shipping supplies, paper and disposable plastics, merchant wholesalers
336611	Ships (i.e., not suitable or intended for personal use) manufacturing
423860	Ships merchant wholesalers
517210	Ship-to-shore broadcasting communication carriers, except satellite
336611	Shipyard (i.e., facility capable of building ships)
315223	Shirts, outerwear (except work shirts), men's and boys', cut and sewn from purchased fabric (except apparel contractors)
315225	Shirts, outerwear work, men's and boys', cut and sewn from purchased fabric (except apparel contractors)
315291	Shirts, outerwear, infants', cut and sewn from purchased fabric (except apparel contractors)
315191	Shirts, outerwear, made in apparel knitting mills

315211	Shirts, outerwear, men's and boys', cut and sew apparel contractors
315223	Shirts, outerwear, unisex (i.e., sized without regard to gender), cut and sewn from purchased fabric (except apparel contractors)
315212	Shirts, outerwear, women's, girls', and infants', cut and sew apparel contractors
315232	Shirts, outerwear, women's, misses', and girls', cut and sewn from purchased fabric (except apparel contractors)
315291	Shirts, underwear, infants', cut and sewn from purchased fabric (except apparel contractors).
315192	Shirts, underwear, made in apparel knitting mills
315211	Shirts, underwear, men's and boys', cut and sew apparel contractors
315221	Shirts, underwear, men's and boys', cut and sewn from purchased fabric (except apparel contractors)
315212	Shirts, underwear, women's, girls', and infants', cut and sew apparel contractors
315231	Shirts, underwear, women's, misses', and girls', cut and sewn from purchased fabric (except apparel contractors)
111411	Shitake mushroom farming
336330	Shock absorbers, automotive, truck, and bus, manufacturing
448210	Shoe (except bowling, golf, spiked) stores
326299	Shoe and boot parts (e.g., heels, soles, soling strips), rubber, manufacturing
322212	Shoe boxes, folding, made from purchased paperboard
322213	Shoe boxes, setup, made from purchased paperboard
541490	Shoe design services
321999	Shoe display forms, all materials, manufacturing

316991 Shoe kits (i.e., cases), all materials, manufacturing
333298 Shoe making and repairing machinery manufacturing
423830 Shoe manufacturing and repairing machinery merchant wholesalers
326199 Shoe parts (e.g., heels, soles), plastics, manufacturing
335211 Shoe polishers, household-type electric, manufacturing
325612 Shoe polishes and cleaners manufacturing
423850 Shoe repair materials merchant wholesalers
811430 Shoe repair shops without retailing new shoes
316999 Shoe soles, leather, manufacturing
448210 Shoe stores, orthopedic
451110 Shoe stores, specialty sports footwear (e.g., bowling, golf, spiked)
321999 Shoe stretchers manufacturing
321999 Shoe trees manufacturing
424340 Shoes merchant wholesalers
316219 Shoes, athletic (except rubber or plastics soled with fabric upper), manufacturing
316219 Shoes, ballet, manufacturing
316219 Shoes, children's and infant's (except house slippers, orthopedic extension, plastics, rubber), manufacturing
316219 Shoes, cleated or spiked, all materials, manufacturing
316213 Shoes, men's (except house slippers, athletic, rubber, orthopedic extension), manufacturing
339113 Shoes, orthopedic extension, manufacturing
316211 Shoes, plastics or plastics soled fabric upper (except cleated athletic), manufacturing
316211 Shoes, rubber or rubber soled fabric upper (except cleated athletic), manufacturing
316219 Shoes, theatrical, manufacturing

316214 Shoes, women's (except house slippers, athletic, orthopedic extension, plastic, rubber), manufacturing
316219 Shoes, wooden, manufacturing
812990 Shoeshine parlors
812990 Shoeshine services
321920 Shook, box, manufacturing
713990 Shooting clubs, recreational
713990 Shooting galleries
713990 Shooting ranges
423120 Shop equipment, service station, merchant wholesalers
424130 Shopping bags, paper and plastics, merchant wholesalers
531120 Shopping center (i.e., not operating contained businesses) rental or leasing
236220 Shopping center construction
236220 Shopping mall construction
812990 Shopping services, personal
****** Shops—see type
238990 Shoring, construction
111421 Short rotation woody tree growing (i.e., growing and harvesting cycle ten years or less)
311223 Shortening (except soybean) made in crushing mills
311225 Shortening made from purchased fats and oils
311222 Shortening, soybean, made in crushing mills
424490 Shortening, vegetable, merchant wholesalers
482112 Short-line railroads
315291 Shorts, outerwear, infants', cut and sewn from purchased fabric (except apparel contractors)
315191 Shorts, outerwear, made in apparel knitting mills
315211 Shorts, outerwear, men's and boys', cut and sew apparel contractors
315228 Shorts, outerwear, men's and boys', cut and sewn from purchased fabric (except apparel contractors)

315212   Shorts, outerwear, women's, girls', and infants', cut and sew apparel contractors

315239   Shorts, outerwear, women's, misses', and girls', cut and sewn from purchased fabric (except apparel contractors)

315192   Shorts, underwear, made in apparel knitting mills

315211   Shorts, underwear, men's and boys', cut and sew apparel contractors

315221   Shorts, underwear, men's and boys', cut and sewn from purchased fabric (except apparel contractors)

522298   Short-term inventory credit lending

213112   Shot hole drilling, oil and gas field, on a contract basis

332811   Shot peening metal and metal products for the trade

332992   Shot, BB, manufacturing

332992   Shot, lead, manufacturing

332992   Shot, pellet, manufacturing

332992   Shot, steel, manufacturing

238110   Shotcrete contractors

332992   Shotgun shells manufacturing

332994   Shotguns manufacturing

333120   Shovel loaders manufacturing

332212   Shovels, handheld, manufacturing

333120   Shovels, power, manufacturing

337215   Showcases (except refrigerated) manufacturing

423440   Showcases (except refrigerated) merchant wholesalers

333415   Showcases, refrigerated, manufacturing

314129   Shower and bath curtains, all materials, made from purchased fabric or sheet goods

332913   Shower heads, plumbing, manufacturing

332998   Shower receptors, metal, manufacturing

332999   Shower rods, metal, manufacturing

316211   Shower sandals or slippers, rubber, manufacturing

332998   Shower stalls, metal, manufacturing

326191   Shower stalls, plastics or fiberglass, manufacturing

115210   Showing of cattle, hogs, sheep, goats, and poultry

333111   Shredders, farm-type, manufacturing

212399   Shredding peat mining and/or beneficiating

114112   Shrimp fishing

112512   Shrimp production, farm raising

813110   Shrines, religious

561910   Shrink wrapping services

313311   Shrinking broadwoven fabrics

313312   Shrinking textile products and fabrics (except broadwoven)

561730   Shrub services (e.g., bracing, planting, pruning, removal, spraying, surgery, trimming)

111421   Shrubbery farming

311712   Shucking and packing fresh shellfish

488490   Shunting of trailers in truck terminals

488210   Shunting trailers in rail terminals

334515   Shunts, instrument, manufacturing

238190   Shutter installation

332321   Shutters, door and window, metal, manufacturing

321918   Shutters, door and window, wood and covered wood, manufacturing

326199   Shutters, plastics, manufacturing

321918   Shutters, wood, manufacturing

485999   Shuttle services (except employee bus)

333292   Shuttles for textile weaving machinery manufacturing

446199   Sick room supply stores

332212   Sickles manufacturing

212210   Siderite mining and/or beneficiating

238990   Sidewalk construction, residential and commercial

237310   Sidewalk, public, construction

238170	Siding (e.g., vinyl, wood, aluminum) installation
423330	Siding (except wood) merchant wholesalers
238170	Siding contractors
444190	Siding dealers
324122	Siding made from purchased asphaltic materials
321113	Siding mills, wood
321113	Siding, dressed lumber, manufacturing
326199	Siding, plastics, manufacturing
332322	Siding, sheet metal (except stampings), manufacturing
423310	Siding, wood, merchant wholesalers
212393	Sienna mining and/or beneficiating
325131	Sienna pigment manufacturing
333294	Sieves and screening equipment (i.e., food manufacturing-type) manufacturing
333298	Sieves and screening equipment, chemical preparation-type, manufacturing
333999	Sieves and screening equipment, general purpose-type, manufacturing
333131	Sieves and screening equipment, mineral beneficiating, manufacturing
332618	Sieves, made from purchased wire, manufacturing
333294	Sifting machine (i.e., food manufacturing-type) manufacturing
333314	Sights, telescopic, manufacturing
487210	Sightseeing boat operation
487110	Sightseeing bus operation
487110	Sightseeing operation, human-drawn vehicle
238990	Sign (except on highways, streets, bridges and tunnels) erection
237310	Sign erection, highway, roads street or bridge
611630	Sign language instruction
611630	Sign language schools
541930	Sign language services
541890	Sign lettering and painting services
238990	Sign, building, erection
331422	Signal and control cable made from purchased copper in wire drawing plants
331319	Signal and control cable made in aluminum wire drawing plants
334515	Signal generators and averagers manufacturing
423610	Signal systems and devices merchant wholesalers
335311	Signaling transformers, electric, manufacturing
334290	Signals (e.g., highway, pedestrian, railway, traffic) manufacturing
423990	Signs (except electrical) merchant wholesalers
339950	Signs and signboards (except paper, paperboard) manufacturing
423440	Signs, electrical, merchant wholesalers
325188	Silica gel manufacturing
212322	Silica mining and/or beneficiating
212322	Silica sand quarrying and/or beneficiating
325188	Silica, amorphous, manufacturing
325188	Silicofluorides manufacturing
331112	Silicomanganese ferroalloys manufacturing
327910	Silicon carbide abrasives manufacturing
334413	Silicon wafers, chemically doped, manufacturing
334413	Silicon wave guides manufacturing
327992	Silicon, ultra high purity, manufacturing
325199	Silicone (except resins) manufacturing
325211	Silicone resins manufacturing
325212	Silicone rubber manufacturing
313210	Silk fabrics, broadwoven, weaving

541430	Silk screen design services
333292	Silk screens for textile fabrics manufacturing
313111	Silk spun yarns made from purchased fiber
313113	Silk thread manufacturing
313112	Silk throwing, spooling, twisting, or winding of puchased yarn
424590	Silk, raw, merchant wholesalers
212325	Sillimanite mining and/or beneficiating
327390	Sills, concrete, manufacturing
236220	Silo construction
327390	Silos, prefabricated concrete, manufacturing
332311	Silos, prefabricated metal, manufacturing
331491	Silver and silver alloy bar, rod, sheet, strip, and tubing made from purchased metals or scrap
332999	Silver beating (i.e., foil, leaf)
325188	Silver bromide manufacturing
331419	Silver bullion or dore bar produced at primary metal refineries
325188	Silver chloride manufacturing
325188	Silver compounds, not specified elsewhere by process, manufacturing
332999	Silver foil and leaf not made in rolling mills
331491	Silver foil made by rolling purchased metals or scrap
325188	Silver nitrate manufacturing
212222	Silver ores mining and/or beneficiating
325612	Silver polishes manufacturing
331492	Silver recovering from scrap and/or alloying purchased metals
331492	Silver recovering from used photographic film or X-ray plates
331419	Silver refining, primary
331491	Silver rolling, drawing, or extruding purchased metals or scrap
532299	Silverware rental
423940	Silverware, precious and plated, merchant wholesalers
333515	Sine bars (i.e., a machine tool accessory) manufacturing
711130	Singers, independent
813410	Singing societies
812990	Singing telegram services
531110	Single family house rental or leasing
621512	Single photon emission computerized tomography (SPECT) centers
236115	Single-family attached housing construction general contractors
236115	Single-family detached housing construction general contractors
236115	Single-family homes built on land owned by others, general contractors of
236115	Single-family house construction by general contractors
236117	Single-family housing built on own land for sale (i.e., operative builders)
236117	Single-family housing construction operative builders
213113	Sinking shafts for coal mining on a contract basis
213114	Sinking shafts for metal mining on a contract basis
332998	Sinks, metal, manufacturing
326191	Sinks, plastics, manufacturing
327111	Sinks, vitreous china, manufacturing
212210	Sintered iron ore produced at the mine
212392	Sintered phosphate rock mining and/or beneficiating
334290	Sirens (e.g., air raid, industrial, marine, vehicle) manufacturing
541611	Site location consulting services
541620	Site remediation consulting services
562910	Site remediation services
541611	Site selection consulting services

812990	Sitting services, house
812910	Sitting services, pet
313311	Sizing of broadwoven fabrics
313312	Sizing of fabric (except broadwoven)
339920	Skateboards manufacturing
339920	Skates and parts, ice and roller, manufacturing
713990	Skeet shooting facilities
331111	Skelp, iron or steel, made in iron and steel mills
711510	Sketch artists, independent
321999	Skewers, wood, manufacturing
541320	Ski area design services
541320	Ski area planning services
532292	Ski equipment rental
713920	Ski lift and tow operators
721110	Ski lodges and resorts with accommodations
315191	Ski pants made in apparel knitting mills
315291	Ski pants, infants', cut and sewn from purchased fabric (except apparel contractors)
315211	Ski pants, men's and boys', cut and sew apparel contractors
315228	Ski pants, men's and boys', cut and sewn from purchased fabric (except apparel contractors)
315212	Ski pants, women's, girls', and infants', cut and sew apparel contractors
315239	Ski pants, women's, misses', and girls', cut and sewn from purchased fabric (except apparel contractors)
713920	Ski resorts without accommodations
315191	Ski suits made in apparel knitting mills
315291	Ski suits, infants', cut and sewn from purchased fabric (except apparel contractors)
315211	Ski suits, men's and boys', cut and sew apparel contractors
315228	Ski suits, men's and boys', cut and sewn from purchased fabric (except apparel contractors)
315212	Ski suits, women's, girls', and infants', cut and sew apparel contractors
315239	Ski suits, women's, misses', and girls', cut and sewn from purchased fabric (except apparel contractors)
237990	Ski tow construction
532490	Skid rental or leasing
213112	Skidding of rigs, oil and gas field, on a contract basis
321920	Skids and pallets, wood or wood and metal combination, manufacturing
332999	Skids, metal, manufacturing
711219	Skiers, independent (i.e., participating in sports events)
423910	Skiing equipment and supplies merchant wholesalers
713920	Skiing facilities, cross country, without accommodations
713920	Skiing facilities, downhill, without accommodations
611620	Skiing instruction, camps, or schools
623110	Skilled nursing facilities
561910	Skin blister packaging services
611620	Skin diving instruction, camps, or schools
339112	Skin grafting equipment manufacturing
424990	Skins, dressed, merchant wholesalers
424590	Skins, raw, merchant wholesalers
316110	Skins, tanning, currying and finishing
561611	Skip tracing services
316110	Skirting leather manufacturing
315234	Skirts (except tennis skirts), women's, misses', and girls', cut and sewn from purchased fabric (except apparel contractors)
315191	Skirts made in apparel knitting mills
315291	Skirts, infants', cut and sewn from purchased fabric (except apparel contractors)

315239	Skirts, tennis, women's, misses', and girls', cut and sewn from purchased fabric (except apparel contractors)
315212	Skirts, women's, misses', girls', and infants', cut and sew apparel contractors
339920	Skis and skiing equipment (except apparel) manufacturing
316110	Skivers, leather, manufacturing
611620	Sky diving instruction, camps, or schools
238160	Skylight installation
332321	Skylights, metal, manufacturing
331419	Slab, nonferrous metals (except aluminum, copper), primary
331312	Slab, primary aluminum, manufacturing
331111	Slab, steel, made in iron and steel mills
315191	Slacks made in apparel knitting mills
315291	Slacks, infants', cut and sewn from purchased fabric (except apparel contractors)
315291	Slacks, jean-cut casual, infants', cut and sewn from purchased fabric (except apparel contractors)
315191	Slacks, jean-cut casual, made in apparel knitting mills
315211	Slacks, jean-cut casual, men's and boys', cut and sew apparel contractors
315224	Slacks, jean-cut casual, men's and boys', cut and sewn from purchased fabric (except apparel contractors)
315212	Slacks, jean-cut casual, women's, girls', and infants', cut and sew apparel contractors
315239	Slacks, jean-cut casual, women's, misses', and girls', cut and sewn from purchased fabric (except apparel contractors)
315211	Slacks, men's and boys', cut and sew apparel contractors
315224	Slacks, men's and boys', cut and sewn from purchased fabric (except apparel contractors)
315212	Slacks, women's, girls', and infants', cut and sew apparel contractors
315239	Slacks, women's, misses', and girls', cut and sewn from purchased fabric (except apparel contractors)
333120	Slag mixers, portable, manufacturing
238140	Slate (i.e., masonry) contractors
212319	Slate crushed and broken stone mining and/or beneficiating
212311	Slate mining or quarrying
327991	Slate products manufacturing
238340	Slate, interior, installation
311611	Slaughtering, custom
311991	Slaw, cole, fresh, manufacturing
332212	Sledgehammers manufacturing
339932	Sleds, children's, manufacturing
621498	Sleep disorder centers and clinics, outpatient
337215	Sleeper mechanisms, convertible bed, manufacturing
314999	Sleeping bags manufacturing
316999	Sleeves, welder's, leather, manufacturing
333294	Slicing machinery (i.e., food manufacturing-type) manufacturing
339993	Slide fasteners (i.e., zippers) manufacturing
332618	Slings, lifting, made from purchased wire
212324	Slip clay mining and/or beneficiating
335312	Slip rings for motors and generators manufacturing
423220	Slipcovers merchant wholesalers
314129	Slipcovers, all materials, made from purchased materials
316212	Slipper socks made from purchased socks
315119	Slipper socks made in sock mills
424340	Slippers merchant wholesalers

316219 Slippers, ballet, manufacturing
316212 Slippers, house, manufacturing
315192 Slips made in apparel knitting mills
315212 Slips, women's and girls', cut and sew apparel contractors
315231 Slips, women's, misses', and girls', cut and sewn from purchased fabric (except apparel contractors)
522294 SLMA (Student Loan Marketing Association)
713990 Slot car racetracks (i.e., amusement devices)
713290 Slot machine concession operators (i.e., supplying and servicing in others' facilities)
713290 Slot machine parlors
339999 Slot machines manufacturing
333512 Slotting machines, metalworking, manufacturing
562212 Sludge disposal sites
333999 Sludge tables manufacturing
327331 Slumped brick manufacturing
486990 Slurry pipeline transportation
213112 Slush pits and cellars, excavation of, on a contract basis
541940 Small animal veterinary services
332992 Small arms ammunition (i.e., 30 mm. or less, 1.18 inch or less) manufacturing
926110 Small business development agencies
811411 Small engine repair and maintenance shops
311615 Small game, processing, fresh, frozen, canned or cooked
311615 Small game, slaughtering, dressing and packing
522291 Small loan companies (i.e., unsecured cash loans)
236210 Smelter construction
331492 Smelting and refining of nonferrous metals (except aluminum, copper), secondary
423830 Smelting machinery and equipment merchant wholesalers

331492 Smelting nonferrous metals (except aluminum, copper), secondary
331419 Smelting of nonferrous metals (except aluminum, copper), primary
333994 Smelting ovens manufacturing
332420 Smelting pots and retorts manufacturing
212231 Smithsonite mining and/or beneficiating
238210 Smoke detection system, installation only
334290 Smoke detectors manufacturing
423620 Smoke detectors, household-type, merchant wholesalers
332995 Smoke generators manufacturing
311612 Smoked meats made from purchased carcasses
424990 Smokers' supplies merchant wholesalers
453991 Smokers' supply stores
332313 Smokestacks, fabricated metal boiler plate, manufacturing
621999 Smoking cessation programs
312229 Smoking tobacco (e.g., cigarette, pipe) manufacturing
333311 Snack and confection vending machines manufacturing
722213 Snack bars (e.g., cookies, popcorn, pretzels), fixed location
722330 Snack stands, mobile
111219 Snap bean farming (i.e., bush and pole), field and seed production
335931 Snap switches (i.e., electric wiring devices) manufacturing
114111 Snapper fishing
488490 Snow clearing, highways and bridges, road transportation
321912 Snow fence lath manufacturing
321999 Snow fence, sections or rolls, manufacturing
333415 Snow making machinery manufacturing
238210 Snow melting cable, electric, installation

238220 Snow melting system (e.g., hot water, glycol) installation

111219 Snow pea farming, field and seed production

333120 Snow plow attachments (except lawn, garden-type) manufacturing

333112 Snow plow attachments, lawn and garden-type, manufacturing

561790 Snow plowing driveways and parking lots (i.e., not combined with any other service)

561730 Snow plowing services combined with landscaping services (i.e., seasonal property maintenance services)

423810 Snow plows merchant wholesalers

488490 Snow removal, highway

532292 Snow ski equipment rental

423810 Snowblowers (except household-type) merchant wholesalers

333112 Snowblowers and throwers, residential-type, manufacturing

423820 Snowblowers, household-type, merchant wholesalers

441229 Snowmobile dealers

423110 Snowmobile merchant wholesalers

711212 Snowmobile racetracks

711219 Snowmobile racing teams

336999 Snowmobiles and parts manufacturing

713990 Snowmobiling, recreational

339920 Snowshoes manufacturing

315191 Snowsuits made in apparel knitting mills

315291 Snowsuits, infants', cut and sewn from purchased fabric (except apparel contractors)

315211 Snowsuits, men's and boys', cut and sew apparel contractors

315228 Snowsuits, men's and boys', cut and sewn from purchased fabric (except apparel contractors)

315212 Snowsuits, women's, girls', and infants', cut and sew apparel contractors

315239 Snowsuits, women's, misses', and girls', cut and sewn from purchased fabric (except apparel contractors)

312229 Snuff manufacturing

424940 Snuff merchant wholesalers

327111 Soap dishes, vitreous china and earthenware, manufacturing

332999 Soap dispensers, metal, manufacturing

325611 Soaps (e.g., bar, chip, powder) manufacturing

212399 Soapstone mining and/or beneficiating

711211 Soccer clubs, professional or semiprofessional

713990 Soccer clubs, recreational

611620 Soccer instruction, camps, or schools

711211 Soccer teams, professional or semiprofessional

923130 Social assistance cost-sharing, government

813319 Social change advocacy organizations

813410 Social clubs

812990 Social escort services

813410 Social organizations, civic and fraternal

541720 Social science research and development services

923130 Social Security Administration (SSA), federal

813319 Social service advocacy organizations

624190 Social service agencies, family

624190 Social service centers, multipurpose

424120 Social stationery merchant wholesalers

621330 Social workers', mental health, offices (e.g., centers, clinics)

813920 Social workers' associations

541720 Sociological research and development services

541720 Sociology research and development services

332212 Sockets and socket sets manufacturing
335931 Sockets, electric, manufacturing
315119 Socks knitting or knitting and finishing
315119 Socks, men's and boy's, manufacturing
316212 Socks, slipper, made from purchased socks
315119 Socks, slipper, made in sock mills
111421 Sod farming
333111 Sod harvesting machines manufacturing
561730 Sod laying services
325181 Soda ash manufacturing
212391 Soda ash mining and/or beneficiating
212391 Soda ash, natural, mining and/ or beneficiating
327213 Soda bottles, glass, manufacturing
312111 Soda carbonated, manufacturing
311821 Soda crackers manufacturing
333415 Soda fountain cooling and dispensing equipment manufacturing
423440 Soda fountain fixtures (except refrigerated) merchant wholesalers
311930 Soda fountain syrups manufacturing
312111 Soda pop manufacturing
325199 Sodium acetate manufacturing
325199 Sodium alginate manufacturing
325188 Sodium aluminate manufacturing
325188 Sodium aluminum sulfate manufacturing
325188 Sodium antimoniate manufacturing
325188 Sodium arsenite (except insecticides) manufacturing
325320 Sodium arsenite insecticides manufacturing
325199 Sodium benzoate manufacturing
325181 Sodium bicarbonate manufacturing
325188 Sodium bichromate and chromate manufacturing

325188 Sodium borate manufacturing
212391 Sodium borates, natural, mining and/or beneficiating
325188 Sodium borohydride manufacturing
325188 Sodium bromide manufacturing
325181 Sodium carbonate (i.e., soda ash) manufacturing
212391 Sodium carbonates, natural, mining and/or beneficiating
325188 Sodium chlorate manufacturing
325412 Sodium chloride pharmaceutical preparations manufacturing
212393 Sodium chloride, rock salt, mining and/or beneficiating
212391 Sodium compounds prepared at beneficiating plants
212391 Sodium compounds, natural (except common salt), mining and/or beneficiating
325188 Sodium cyanide manufacturing
325199 Sodium glutamate manufacturing
325188 Sodium hydrosulfite manufacturing
325181 Sodium hydroxide (i.e., caustic soda) manufacturing
325188 Sodium hypochlorite manufacturing
325188 Sodium inorganic compounds, not specified elsewhere by process, manufacturing
325188 Sodium molybdate manufacturing
325199 Sodium organic compounds, not specified elsewhere by process, manufacturing
325199 Sodium pentachlorophenate manufacturing
325188 Sodium perborate manufacturing
325188 Sodium peroxide manufacturing
325188 Sodium phosphate manufacturing
325188 Sodium polyphosphate manufacturing
325412 Sodium salicylate preparations manufacturing
325188 Sodium silicate (i.e., water glass) manufacturing

325188	Sodium silicofluoride manufacturing
325188	Sodium stannate manufacturing
325188	Sodium sulfate manufacturing
212391	Sodium sulfate, natural, mining and/or beneficiating
325199	Sodium sulfoxalate formaldehyde manufacturing
325188	Sodium tetraborate manufacturing
325188	Sodium thiosulfate manufacturing
325188	Sodium tungstate manufacturing
325188	Sodium uranate manufacturing
335110	Sodium vapor lamp bulbs manufacturing
337121	Sofa beds and chair beds, upholstered, manufacturing
337121	Sofas, convertible (except futons), manufacturing
337121	Sofas, upholstered, manufacturing
722213	Soft drink beverage bars, nonalcoholic, fixed location
332431	Soft drink cans manufacturing
311930	Soft drink concentrates (i.e., syrup) manufacturing
445299	Soft drink stores, bottled
333311	Soft drink vending machines manufacturing
312111	Soft drinks manufacturing
424490	Soft drinks merchant wholesalers
311812	Soft pretzels made in a commercial bakery
325613	Softeners, leather or textile, manufacturing
541511	Software analysis and design services, custom computer
611420	Software application training
511210	Software computer, packaged, publishers
541519	Software installation services, computer
541511	Software programming services, custom computer
511210	Software publishers
511210	Software publishers, packaged
443120	Software stores, computer
423430	Software, computer, packaged, merchant wholesalers
334611	Software, packaged, mass reproducing
321912	Softwood dimension lumber and stock, resawing purchased lumber
325191	Softwood distillates manufacturing
321212	Softwood plywood composites manufacturing
321212	Softwood veneer or plywood manufacturing
238910	Soil compacting
924120	Soil conservation services, government
331511	Soil pipe, cast iron, manufacturing
562910	Soil remediation services
238910	Soil test drilling
325998	Soil testing kits manufacturing
541380	Soil testing laboratories or services
334413	Solar cells manufacturing
423690	Solar cells merchant wholesalers
926130	Solar energy regulation
333414	Solar energy heating equipment manufacturing
238220	Solar heating equipment installation
423720	Solar heating panels and equipment merchant wholesalers
333414	Solar heating systems manufacturing
335122	Solar lighting fixtures (except residential), electric, manufacturing
335121	Solar lighting fixtures, residential, electric, manufacturing
237130	Solar power structure construction
238160	Solar reflecting coating, roof, application
423330	Solar reflective film merchant wholesalers
334519	Solarimeters manufacturing

331491 Solder wire, nonferrous metals (except aluminum, copper), made from purchased metals or scrap

333992 Soldering equipment (except hand held) manufacturing

332212 Soldering guns and irons, handheld (including electric), manufacturing

332212 Soldering iron tips and tiplets manufacturing

335931 Solderless connectors (electric wiring devices) manufacturing

316110 Sole leather manufacturing

335314 Solenoid switches, industrial, manufacturing

332911 Solenoid valves (except fluid power), industrial-type, manufacturing

332912 Solenoid valves, fluid power, manufacturing

334419 Solenoids for electronic applications manufacturing

316999 Soles, boot and shoe, leather, manufacturing

922130 Solicitors' offices, government

541110 Solicitors' offices, private

541110 Solicitors' private practices

325188 Solid fuel propellants, inorganic, not specified elsewhere by process, manufacturing

562213 Solid waste combustors or incinerators, nonhazardous

562212 Solid waste landfills combined with collection and/or local hauling of nonhazardous waste materials

562212 Solid waste landfills, nonhazardous

711130 Soloists, independent musical

325132 Solvent dyes manufacturing

324110 Solvents made in petroleum refineries

334511 Sonabuoys manufacturing

423690 Sonar equipment merchant wholesalers

334511 Sonar fish finders manufacturing

334511 Sonar systems and equipment manufacturing

512230 Song publishers

512230 Song publishers and printing combined

711510 Song writers, independent

325612 Soot removing chemicals manufacturing

325199 Sorbitol manufacturing

111199 Sorghum farming, field and seed production

311211 Sorghum flour manufacturing

111998 Sorghum sudan seed farming

311999 Sorghum syrup manufacturing

813410 Sororities (except residential)

721310 Sorority houses

115114 Sorting, grading, cleaning, and packing of fruits and vegetables

532490 Sound and lighting equipment rental or leasing

512191 Sound dubbing services, motion picture

238210 Sound equipment installation

423330 Sound insulation merchant wholesalers

512240 Sound recording studios (except integrated record companies)

512220 Sound recording, integrated production, reproduction, release, and distribution

512220 Sound recording, releasing, promoting, and distributing

238310 Soundproofing contractors

332431 Soup cans, light gauge metal, manufacturing

624210 Soup kitchens

311423 Soup mixes made in a dehydration plant

311999 Soup mixes, dry, made from purchased dry ingredients

424490 Soups (except frozen) merchant wholesalers

311422 Soups (except seafood) canning

311711 Soups, fish and seafood, canning

311412 Soups, frozen (except seafood), manufacturing

311712 Soups, frozen fish and shellfish, manufacturing

424420 Soups, frozen, merchant wholesalers

311511	Sour cream manufacturing
311511	Sour cream substitutes manufacturing
453220	Souvenir shops
311941	Soy sauce manufacturing
311222	Soybean cakes and meal manufacturing
311225	Soybean cooking oil made from purchased oils
111110	Soybean farming, field and seed production
325222	Soybean fibers and filaments manufacturing
311222	Soybean flour and grits manufacturing
311222	Soybean millfeed made in oil mills
311222	Soybean oil mills
311222	Soybean oil, cake, and meal, made in crushing mills
311222	Soybean oil, crude, manufacturing
311222	Soybean oil, deodorized, made in oil mills
311222	Soybean oil, refined, made in crushing mills
325211	Soybean plastics manufacturing
311222	Soybean protein concentrates made in crushing mills
311222	Soybean protein isolates made in crushing mills
424510	Soybeans merchant wholesalers
336419	Space capsules manufacturing
927110	Space flight operations, government
333414	Space heaters (except portable electric) manufacturing
334220	Space satellites, communications, manufacturing
332313	Space simulation chambers, fabricated metal plate work, manufacturing
339113	Space suits manufacturing
481212	Space transportation, freight, nonscheduled
334511	Space vehicle guidance systems and equipment manufacturing
336414	Space vehicles, complete, manufacturing

332212	Spades and shovels, handheld, manufacturing
311422	Spaghetti canning
424490	Spaghetti merchant wholesalers
311421	Spaghetti sauce canning
111219	Spaghetti squash farming, field, bedding plant and seed production
311823	Spaghetti, dry, manufacturing
313210	Spandex broadwoven fabrics
325222	Spandex fiber, filaments, and yarn manufacturing
113210	Spanish moss gathering
212399	Spar, iceland, mining and/or beneficiating
327113	Spark plug insulators, porcelain, manufacturing
334515	Spark plug testing instruments, electric, manufacturing
336322	Spark plugs for internal combustion engines manufacturing
312130	Sparkling wines manufacturing
321999	Spars, wood, manufacturing
713940	Spas without accommodations, fitness
316999	Spats, leather, manufacturing
326299	Spatulas, rubber, manufacturing
337129	Speaker cabinets (i.e., housings), wood, manufacturing
334310	Speaker systems manufacturing
711410	Speakers' bureaus
813410	Speakers' clubs
711510	Speakers, independent
325998	Spearmint oil manufacturing
711510	Special effect technicians, independent
512191	Special effects for motion picture production, post-production
519130	Special interest portals (e.g., parents sharing information about child rearing, etc.), internet
485991	Special needs passenger transportation services
525990	Special purpose financial vehicles

336211	Special purpose highway vehicle (e.g., firefighting vehicles) assembling on purchased chassis
336211	Special purpose highway vehicle (e.g., firefighting vehicles) bodies manufacturing
336120	Special purpose highway vehicles (e.g., firefighting vehicles) assembling on heavy chassis of own manufacture
423830	Special purpose industrial machinery and equipment merchant wholesalers
445299	Specialty food stores
316110	Specialty leathers manufacturing
515210	Specialty television (e.g., music, sports, news) cable networks
335311	Specialty transformers, electric, manufacturing
424210	Specialty-line pharmaceuticals merchant wholesalers
334516	Specific ion measuring instruments, laboratory-type, manufacturing
238390	Spectator seating installation
334516	Spectrofluorometers manufacturing
334516	Spectrographs manufacturing
334516	Spectrometers (e.g., electron diffraction, mass, NMR, Raman) manufacturing
334519	Spectrometers (e.g., liquid scintillation, nuclear) manufacturing
334516	Spectrophotometers (e.g., atomic absorption, atomic emission, flame, fluorescence, infrared, Raman, visible) manufacturing
334515	Spectrum analyzers manufacturing
236220	Speculative builders (i.e., building on own land, for sale), commercial and institutional building
236210	Speculative builders (i.e., building on own land, for sale), industrial building (except warehouses)
236117	Speculative builders (i.e., building on own land, for sale), multifamily housing
236117	Speculative builders (i.e., building on own land, for sale), residential
236117	Speculative builders (i.e., building on own land, for sale), single-family housing
339112	Speculums manufacturing
541930	Speech (i.e., language) interpretation services
621340	Speech clinicians' offices (e.g., centers, clinics)
621340	Speech defect clinics
621340	Speech pathologists' offices (e.g., centers, clinics)
621340	Speech therapists' offices (e.g., centers, clinics)
333612	Speed changers (i.e., power transmission equipment) manufacturing
611699	Speed reading instruction
333612	Speed reducers (i.e., power transmission equipment) manufacturing
441310	Speed shops
334511	Speed, pitch, and roll navigational instruments and systems manufacturing
711212	Speedways
621991	Sperm banks, human
113210	Sphagnum moss gathering
212231	Sphalerite mining and/or beneficiating
339112	Sphygmomanometers manufacturing
111998	Spice farming
111419	Spice farming, grown under cover
311942	Spice grinding and blending
311942	Spice mixtures manufacturing
445299	Spice stores
311942	Spices and spice mix manufacturing
424490	Spices merchant wholesalers
331112	Spiegeleisen ferroalloys manufacturing
332913	Spigots, plumbing fixture fitting, manufacturing

321999 Spigots, wood, manufacturing
331111 Spike rods made in iron and steel mills
332618 Spikes made from purchased wire
331222 Spikes, iron or steel, made in wire drawing plants
423510 Spikes, metal, merchant wholesalers
237990 Spillway, floodwater, construction
111219 Spinach farming, field, bedding plant and seed production
333292 Spindles for textile machinery manufacturing
313111 Spinning carpet and rug yarn from purchased fiber
333292 Spinning machinery for textiles manufacturing
333513 Spinning machines, metalworking, manufacturing
332116 Spinning unfinished metal products
313111 Spinning yarn from purchased fiber
332618 Spiral cloth made from purchased wire
312140 Spirits, distilled (except brandy), manufacturing
424820 Spirits, distilled, merchant wholesalers
333513 Spline rolling machines, metalworking, manufacturing
321920 Splint baskets for fruits and vegetables, manufacturing
339113 Splints manufacturing
316110 Splits, leather, manufacturing
212393 Spodumene mining and/or beneficiating
321999 Spokes, wood, manufacturing
114119 Sponge gathering
331111 Sponge iron
424990 Sponges merchant wholesalers
332999 Sponges, metal scouring, manufacturing
326199 Sponges, plastics, manufacturing
326299 Sponges, rubber, manufacturing
313311 Sponging broadwoven fabrics

313312 Sponging textile products and fabrics (except broadwoven)
313112 Spooling of yarn
313112 Spooling of yarns for the trade
321999 Spools (except for textile machinery), wood, manufacturing
333292 Spools for textile machinery manufacturing
332211 Spoons, table, nonprecious and precious plated metal, manufacturing
315222 Sport coats (except fur, leather), men's and boys', cut and sewn from purchased fabric (except apparel contractors)
315292 Sport coats, fur (except apparel contractors), manufacturing
315211 Sport coats, fur, men's and boys', cut and sew apparel contractors
315292 Sport coats, leather (including artificial and tailored) (except apparel contractors), manufacturing
315211 Sport coats, leather (including artificial and tailored), men's and boys', cut and sew apparel contractors
315211 Sport coats, men's and boys', cut and sew apparel contractors
315211 Sport shirts, men's and boys', cut and sew apparel contractors
315223 Sport shirts, men's and boys', cut and sewn from purchased fabric (except apparel contractors)
532112 Sport utility vehicle leasing
423110 Sport utility vehicle merchant wholesalers
532111 Sport utility vehicle rental
336112 Sport utility vehicles assembling on chassis of own manufacture
811490 Sporting equipment repair and maintenance without retailing new sports equipment

423910	Sporting firearms and ammunition merchant wholesalers
339920	Sporting goods (except ammunition, clothing, footwear, small arms) manufacturing
423910	Sporting goods and supplies merchant wholesalers
532292	Sporting goods rental
451110	Sporting goods stores
453310	Sporting goods stores, used
711510	Sports announcers, independent
711310	Sports arena operators
611620	Sports camps (e.g., baseball, basketball, football), instructional
315228	Sports clothing (except team uniforms), men's and boys', cut and sewn from purchased fabric (except apparel contractors)
315239	Sports clothing (except team uniforms), women's, misses', and girls', cut and sewn from purchased fabric (except apparel contractors)
315191	Sports clothing made in apparel knitting mills
315211	Sports clothing, men's and boys', cut and sew apparel contractors
315299	Sports clothing, team uniforms, cut and sewn from purchased fabric (except apparel contractors)
315212	Sports clothing, women's and girls', cut and sew apparel contractors
713940	Sports club facilities, physical fitness
713990	Sports clubs (i.e., sports teams) not operating sports facilities, recreational
711211	Sports clubs, professional or semiprofessional
423910	Sports equipment and supplies merchant wholesalers
532292	Sports equipment rental

711310	Sports event managers with facilities
711320	Sports event managers without facilities
711310	Sports event organizers with facilities
711320	Sports event organizers without facilities
711310	Sports event promoters with facilities
711320	Sports event promoters without facilities
237990	Sports field construction
711410	Sports figures' agents or managers
451110	Sports gear stores (e.g., outdoors, scuba, skiing)
813990	Sports governing bodies
712110	Sports halls of fame
611620	Sports instruction, camps, or schools
611620	Sports instructors, independent (i.e., not participating in sporting events)
813990	Sports leagues (i.e., regulating bodies)
621340	Sports physical therapists' offices (e.g., centers, clinics)
711219	Sports professionals, independent (i.e., participating in sports events)
315191	Sports shirts made in apparel knitting mills
711310	Sports stadium operators
713990	Sports teams and leagues, recreational or youth
711211	Sports teams, professional or semiprofessional
561599	Sports ticket offices
711219	Sports trainers, independent
424320	Sportswear, men's and boys', merchant wholesalers
325612	Spot removers (except laundry presoaks) manufacturing
333992	Spot welding equipment manufacturing
335129	Spotlights (except vehicular) manufacturing
336321	Spotlights, vehicular, manufacturing

332322 Spouts, sheet metal (except stampings), manufacturing

424950 Spray painting equipment (except industrial-type) merchant wholesalers

423830 Spray painting equipment, industrial-type, merchant wholesalers

333111 Sprayers and dusters, farm-type, manufacturing

423820 Sprayers, farm-type, merchant wholesalers

333912 Sprayers, manual pump, general purpose-type, manufacturing

115112 Spraying crops

561730 Spraying lawns

811198 Spray-on bedliner installation for trucks

333111 Spreaders, farm-type, manufacturing

423820 Spreaders, fertilizer, merchant wholesalers

333112 Spreaders, lawn and garden-type, manufacturing

115112 Spreading lime for crops

311513 Spreads, cheese, manufacturing

332722 Spring pins, metal, manufacturing

332722 Spring washers, metal, manufacturing

312112 Spring waters, purifying and bottling

333513 Spring winding and forming machines, metalworking, manufacturing

332612 Springs and spring units for seats, light gauge, made from purchased wire or strip

337910 Springs, assembled bed and box, made from purchased springs

334518 Springs, clock and watch, made from purchased wire

332611 Springs, heavy gauge metal, manufacturing

332612 Springs, light gauge (except clock, watch), made from purchased wire or strip

332612 Springs, precision (except clock, watch), light gauge, made from purchased wire or strip

423510 Springs, steel, merchant wholesalers

238220 Sprinkler system, building, installation

333999 Sprinkler systems, automatic fire, manufacturing

423850 Sprinkler systems, fire, merchant wholesalers

423820 Sprinklers, agricultural, merchant wholesalers

332919 Sprinklers, lawn, manufacturing

333613 Sprockets, power transmission equipment, manufacturing

113210 Spruce gum gathering

213111 Spudding in oil and gas wells on a contract basis

313230 Spunbonded fabrics manufacturing

332212 Squares, carpenters', metal, manufacturing

713940 Squash club facilities

339920 Squash equipment (except apparel) manufacturing

111219 Squash farming, field, bedding plant and seed production

114112 Squid fishing

332999 Stabilizing bars, cargo, metal, manufacturing

711219 Stables, horse racing

713990 Stables, riding

423830 Stackers, industrial, merchant wholesalers

333924 Stackers, industrial, truck-type, manufacturing

333924 Stackers, portable (except farm), manufacturing

236220 Stadium and arena construction

711310 Stadium operators

531120 Stadium rental or leasing without promotion of events

337127 Stadium seating manufacturing

561330 Staff leasing services

335129 Stage lighting equipment manufacturing

711510 Stage set (e.g., concert, motion picture, television) erecting and dismantling, independent

327211 Stained glass and stained glass products made in glass making plants
238150 Stained glass installation
327215 Stained glass products made from purchased glass
331513 Stainless steel castings (except investment), unfinished, manufacturing
331111 Stainless steel made in iron and steel mills
325510 Stains (except biological) manufacturing
424950 Stains merchant wholesalers
325132 Stains, biological, manufacturing
332323 Stair railings, metal, manufacturing
321918 Stair railings, wood, manufacturing
332323 Stair treads, metal, manufacturing
326299 Stair treads, rubber, manufacturing
332323 Staircases, metal, manufacturing
332323 Stairs, metal, manufacturing
238190 Stairway, metal, installation
238120 Stairway, precast concrete, installation
238350 Stairway, wood, installation
333921 Stairways, moving, manufacturing
321918 Stairwork (e.g., newel posts, railings, staircases, stairs), wood, manufacturing
321999 Stakes, surveyor's, wood, manufacturing
333111 Stalk choppers (i.e., shredders) manufacturing
332323 Stalls, metal, manufacturing
325998 Stamp pad ink manufacturing
339943 Stamp pads manufacturing
339943 Stamping devices, hand operated, manufacturing
333513 Stamping machines, metalworking, manufacturing
336370 Stamping metal motor vehicle body parts
336370 Stamping metal motor vehicle moldings and trims

332116 Stampings (except automotive, cans, cooking, closures, crowns), metal, unfinished, manufacturing
713210 Stand alone casinos (except slot machine parlors)
334515 Standards and calibration equipment for electrical measuring manufacturing
813920 Standards review committees, professional
926150 Standards, setting and management, agencies, government
334515 Standing wave ratio measuring equipment manufacturing
337215 Stands (except wire), merchandise display, manufacturing
711510 Standup comedians, independent
325188 Stannic and stannous chloride manufacturing
339942 Staple removers manufacturing
333991 Staplers and nailers, handheld power-driven, manufacturing
339942 Staplers manufacturing
332618 Staples made from purchased wire
423710 Staples merchant wholesalers
331222 Staples, iron or steel, made in wire drawing plants
325520 Starch glues manufacturing
311221 Starches (except laundry) manufacturing
325612 Starches, laundry, manufacturing
112310 Started pullet production
336322 Starter and starter parts for internal combustion engines manufacturing
522110 State commercial banks
522130 State credit unions
928120 State Department
923110 State education departments
561311 State operated employment job services offices
922120 State police
522120 State savings and loan associations

522120	State savings banks
921130	State tax commissions
334413	Static converters, integrated circuits, manufacturing
334512	Static pressure regulators manufacturing
332410	Stationary power boilers manufacturing
327112	Stationery articles, pottery, manufacturing
322233	Stationery made from purchased paper
453210	Stationery stores
424120	Stationery supplies merchant wholesalers
323112	Stationery, flexographic printing, on a job-order basis
323111	Stationery, gravure printing, on a job-order basis
323110	Stationery, lithographic (offset) printing, on a job-order basis
323114	Stationery, quick printing, on a job-order basis
323113	Stationery, screen printing, on a job-order basis
335312	Stators for motors manufacturing
327420	Statuary (e.g., gypsum, plaster of paris) manufacturing
424990	Statuary goods (except religious) merchant wholesalers
327112	Statuary, clay and ceramic, manufacturing
327991	Statuary, marble, manufacturing
327999	Statuary, vases, and urns, papier-mache, manufacturing
238990	Statue erection
212399	Staurolite mining and/or beneficiating
321920	Staves, barrel, sawed or split, manufacturing
316999	Stays, shoe, leather, manufacturing
722110	Steak houses, full service
722211	Steak houses, limited-service
812199	Steam baths
561790	Steam cleaning building exteriors

213112	Steam cleaning oil and gas wells on a contract basis
332410	Steam condensers manufacturing
333319	Steam cookers, commercial-type, manufacturing
335211	Steam cookers, household-type, manufacturing
611513	Steam fitters' apprenticeship training
238220	Steam fitting contractors
332919	Steam fittings, metal, manufacturing
221330	Steam heat distribution
333414	Steam heating equipment manufacturing
221330	Steam heating systems (i.e., suppliers of heat)
334512	Steam pressure controls, residential and commercial heating-type, manufacturing
221330	Steam production and distribution
333999	Steam separating machinery manufacturing
221330	Steam supply systems, including geothermal
333319	Steam tables manufacturing
487110	Steam train excursions
332911	Steam traps, industrial-type, manufacturing
333611	Steam turbine generator set units manufacturing
333611	Steam turbines manufacturing
532411	Steamship rental or leasing without operators
325199	Stearic acid esters manufacturing
325199	Stearic acid manufacturing
325199	Stearic acid salts manufacturing
311613	Stearin, animal, rendering
212399	Steatite mining and/or beneficiating
327113	Steatite porcelain insulators manufacturing
331111	Steel balls made in iron and steel mills
332431	Steel cans, light gauge metal, manufacturing

331513	Steel castings (except investment), unfinished, manufacturing
332111	Steel forgings made from purchased steel, unfinished
331513	Steel foundries (except investment)
238130	Steel framing contractors
331512	Steel investment castings, unfinished, manufacturing
331512	Steel investment foundries
332312	Steel joists manufacturing
331111	Steel manufacturing
423510	Steel merchant wholesalers
236210	Steel mill construction
331111	Steel mill products (e.g., bar, plate, rod, sheet, structural shapes) manufacturing
331111	Steel mills
332312	Steel railroad car racks manufacturing
238120	Steel reinforcing contractors
327910	Steel shot abrasives manufacturing
332999	Steel wool manufacturing
423510	Steel wool merchant wholesalers
331111	Steel, from pig iron, manufacturing
238160	Steep slope roofing installation
238990	Steeplejack work
311221	Steepwater concentrate manufacturing
336330	Steering boxes, manual and power assist, manufacturing
336330	Steering columns, automotive, truck, and bus, manufacturing
336330	Steering wheels, automotive, truck, and bus, manufacturing
327215	Stemware made from purchased glass
327212	Stemware, glass, made in glass making plants
325910	Stencil inks manufacturing
339944	Stencil paper manufacturing
339943	Stencils for painting and marking (e.g., cardboard, metal) manufacturing
561410	Stenographic services (except court or stenographic reporting)
333313	Stenography machinery manufacturing
561492	Stenography services, public
561492	Stenotype recording services
332999	Stepladders, metal, manufacturing
321999	Stepladders, wood, manufacturing
337129	Stereo cabinets (i.e., housings), wood, manufacturing
423620	Stereo equipment merchant wholesalers
532210	Stereo equipment rental
811211	Stereo equipment repair shops without retailing new stereo equipment
325212	Stereo rubber manufacturing
443112	Stereo stores (except automotive)
441310	Stereo stores, automotive
339114	Sterilizers, dental, manufacturing
339113	Sterilizers, hospital and surgical, manufacturing
339113	Sterilizers, laboratory-type (except dental), manufacturing
332313	Sterilizing chambers, fabricated metal plate work, manufacturing
325411	Steriods, uncompounded, manufacturing
339112	Stethoscopes manufacturing
488320	Stevedoring services
339920	Sticks, sports (e.g., hockey, lacrosse), manufacturing
325132	Stilbene dyes manufacturing
324110	Still gases made in petroleum refineries
332420	Stills, heavy gauge metal, manufacturing
333293	Stitchers and trimmers book binding equipment manufacturing
314999	Stitching, decorative and novelty, contractors on apparel

314999	Stitching, decorative and novelty, on textile articles and apparel		333298	Stone working machinery manufacturing
523120	Stock brokerages		423320	Stone, building or crushed, merchant wholesalers
523120	Stock brokers' offices		212319	Stone, crushed and broken (except granite or limestone), mining and/or beneficiating
711212	Stock car racetracks			
711219	Stock car racing teams			
711110	Stock companies, theatrical		212311	Stone, dimension, mining or quarrying
523210	Stock exchanges			
512199	Stock footage film libraries		332212	Stonecutters' handtools, nonpowered, manufacturing
512290	Stock music and other audio services		212399	Stones, abrasive (e.g., emery, grindstones, hones, pumice), mining and/or beneficiating
523120	Stock options brokerages			
523110	Stock options dealing (i.e., acting as a principal in dealing securities to investors)		423940	Stones, precious and semiprecious, merchant wholesalers
523210	Stock or commodity options exchanges		327999	Stones, synthetic, for gem stones and industrial use, manufacturing
519190	Stock photo agencies			
523999	Stock quotation services		327112	Stoneware (i.e., pottery products) manufacturing
512290	Stock sound library (e.g., general background sounds, stock music)		212325	Stoneware clay mining and/or beneficiating
523999	Stock transfer agencies		238140	Stonework (i.e., masonry) contractors
321912	Stock, chair, unfinished hardwood, manufacturing		337124	Stools, metal household-type (except upholstered), manufacturing
112111	Stocker calf production			
315111	Stockings (except socks), sheer, manufacturing		337122	Stools, wood household-type (except upholstered), manufacturing
315111	Stockings, sheer, women's, misses', and girls', full-length and knee-length, knitting or knitting and finishing		621999	Stop smoking clinics
			332911	Stop valves, industrial-type, manufacturing
488999	Stockyards (i.e., not for fattening or selling livestock), transportation		332913	Stopcock drains, plumbing, manufacturing
			321999	Stoppers, cork, manufacturing
			326299	Stoppers, rubber, manufacturing
212319	Stone (except limestone and granite) beneficiating plants (e.g., grinding)		423610	Storage batteries (except automotive) merchant wholesalers
333131	Stone beneficiating machinery manufacturing		335911	Storage batteries manufacturing
332213	Stone cutting saw blades manufacturing		335312	Storage battery chargers (except internal combustion engine-type) manufacturing
238340	Stone flooring installation			
313311	Stone washing broadwoven fabrics		423390	Storage bins merchant wholesalers
313312	Stone washing textile products, apparel, and fabrics (except broadwoven)		334112	Storage devices, computer, manufacturing

236220 Storage elevator construction
486210 Storage of natural gas
237120 Storage tank, natural gas or oil, tank farm or field, construction
332420 Storage tanks, heavy gauge metal, manufacturing
423510 Storage tanks, metal, merchant wholesalers
236220 Store construction
541850 Store display advertising services
337215 Store display fixtures manufacturing
423440 Store equipment (except furniture) merchant wholesalers
423440 Store fixtures (except refrigerated) merchant wholesalers
238190 Store front, metal or metal frame, installation
423210 Store furniture merchant wholesalers
****** Stores—see type
562998 Storm basin cleanout services
332321 Storm doors and windows, metal, manufacturing
321911 Storm doors and windows, wood framed, manufacturing
237110 Storm sewer construction
711510 Storytellers, independent
312120 Stout brewing
332322 Stove boards, sheet metal (except stampings), manufacturing
327123 Stove lining, clay, manufacturing
332322 Stove pipes and flues, sheet metal (except stampings), manufacturing
811412 Stove, household-type, repair and maintenance services without retailing new stoves
335221 Stoves, ceramic disk element, household-type, manufacturing
333319 Stoves, commercial-type, manufacturing

423720 Stoves, cooking and heating (except electric), household-type, merchant wholesalers
335221 Stoves, household-type cooking, manufacturing
333924 Straddle carriers, mobile, manufacturing
332211 Straight razors manufacturing
332911 Straightway (i.e., Y-type) valves, industrial-type, manufacturing
333999 Strainers, pipeline, manufacturing
321219 Strandboard, oriented, manufacturing
332618 Stranded wire, uninsulated, made from purchased wire
316110 Strap leather manufacturing
332999 Strappings, metal, manufacturing
316999 Straps (except watch), leather, manufacturing
316993 Straps, watch (except metal), manufacturing
339911 Straps, watch, precious metal, manufacturing
541611 Strategic planning consulting services
213112 Stratigraphic drilling, oil and gas field exploration on a contract basis
321999 Straw baskets manufacturing
315991 Straw hats manufacturing
424910 Straw merchant wholesalers
111333 Strawberry farming
488490 Street cleaning service
237310 Street construction
335129 Street lighting fixtures (except traffic signals) manufacturing
519130 Street map and guide publishers, exclusively on Internet
511130 Street map guide publishers (except exclusive Internet publishing)
485119 Street railway systems (except mixed mode), commuter
423810 Street sweeping and cleaning equipment merchant wholesalers

454390 Street vendors (except food)

722330 Street vendors, food

238990 Street, interlocking brick (i.e., not mortared), installation

237990 Streetcar line construction

336510 Streetcars and car equipment, urban transit, manufacturing

713940 Strength development centers

336211 Stretch limousines assembling on purchased chassis

321999 Stretchers, curtain, wood, manufacturing

339113 Stretchers, medical, manufacturing

333513 Stretching machines, metalworking, manufacturing

111219 String bean farming, field and seed production

314991 Strings (except musical instrument) manufacturing

339992 Strings, musical instrument, manufacturing

212113 Strip mining, anthracite, on own account

212111 Strip mining, bituminous coal or lignite, on own account

212111 Strip mining, lignite, on own account

331421 Strip, copper and copper alloy, made from purchased copper or in integrated secondary smelting and rolling, drawing or extruding plants

331111 Strip, galvanized iron or steel, made in iron and steel mills

331111 Strip, iron or steel, made in iron and steel mills

331491 Strip, nonferrous metals (except aluminum, copper), made from purchased metals or scrap

211111 Stripper well production

213113 Stripping overburden services for coal mining on a contract basis

213114 Stripping overburden services for metal mining on a contract basis

213115 Stripping overburden services for nonmetallic minerals mining (except fuels) on a contract basis

334515 Stroboscopes manufacturing

335110 Strobotrons manufacturing

339932 Strollers, baby, manufacturing

212393 Strontianite mining and/or beneficiating

325188 Strontium carbonate manufacturing

325188 Strontium compounds, not specified elsewhere by process, manufacturing

212393 Strontium mineral mining and/or beneficiating

325188 Strontium nitrate manufacturing

423510 Structural assemblies, metal, merchant wholesalers

423390 Structural assemblies, prefabricated (except wood), merchant wholesalers

423310 Structural assemblies, prefabricated wood, merchant wholesalers

423320 Structural clay tile (except refractory) merchant wholesalers

327121 Structural clay tile manufacturing

321114 Structural lumber and timber, treating

321213 Structural members, glue laminated or pre-engineered wood, manufacturing

333516 Structural rolling mill machinery, metalworking, manufacturing

331319 Structural shapes made by rolling purchased aluminum

331319 Structural shapes, aluminum, made in integrated secondary smelting and rolling mills

331111 Structural shapes, iron or steel, made in iron and steel mills

238120 Structural steel erecting or iron work contractors

332312 Structural steel, fabricated, manufacturing

541850	Subway card display advertising services
336510	Subway cars manufacturing
423860	Subway cars merchant wholesalers
237990	Subway construction
485119	Subway systems (except mixed mode), commuter
339112	Suction therapy apparatus manufacturing
812320	Suede garment cleaning services
313311	Sueding broadwoven fabrics
313312	Sueding textile products and fabrics (except broadwoven)
111991	Sugar beet farming
115113	Sugar beets, machine harvesting
311221	Sugar made by wet milling corn
333294	Sugar refining machinery manufacturing
325998	Sugar substitutes (i.e., synthetic sweeteners blended with other ingredients) made from purchased synthetic sweeteners
325199	Sugar substitutes (i.e., synthetic sweeteners blended with other ingredients) made in synthetic sweetener establishments
311312	Sugar, cane, made from purchased raw cane sugar
311311	Sugar, clarified, granulated, and raw, made in sugarcane mill
311312	Sugar, confectionery, made from purchased raw cane sugar
311313	Sugar, confectionery, made from sugar beets
311311	Sugar, confectionery, made in sugarcane mill
311312	Sugar, granulated, made from purchased raw cane sugar
311313	Sugar, granulated, made from sugar beets
311311	Sugar, granulated, made in sugarcane mill
311312	Sugar, invert, made from purchased raw cane sugar
311313	Sugar, invert, made from sugar beets

311311	Sugar, invert, made in sugarcane mill
311313	Sugar, liquid, made from sugar beets
311311	Sugar, raw, made in sugarcane mill
424590	Sugar, raw, merchant wholesalers
311312	Sugar, refined, made from purchased raw cane sugar
424490	Sugar, refined, merchant wholesalers
111930	Sugarcane farming, field production
311311	Sugarcane mills
311311	Sugarcane refining
115113	Sugarcane, machine harvesting
624190	Suicide crisis centers
532220	Suit rental
315999	Suit trimmings cut and sewn from purchased fabric (except apparel contractors)
315211	Suit trimmings, men's and boys', cut and sew apparel contractors
332510	Suitcase hardware, metal, manufacturing
316991	Suitcases, all materials, manufacturing
315211	Suits (i.e., nontailored, tailored, work), men's and boys', cut and sew apparel contractors
315212	Suits (i.e., nontailored, tailored, work), women's, misses', girls', and infants', cut and sew apparel contractors
315191	Suits made in apparel knitting mills
339113	Suits, firefighting, manufacturing
315291	Suits, infants' (e.g., warm-up, jogging, snowsuits), cut and sewn from purchased fabric (except apparel contractors)
424320	Suits, men's and boys', merchant wholesalers
315228	Suits, nontailored (e.g., jogging, snow, ski, warm-up), men's and boys', cut and sewn from purchased fabric (except apparel contractors)

315239 Suits, nontailored (e.g., jogging, snowsuit, warm-up), women's, misses', and girls', cut and sewn from purchased fabric (except apparel contractors)
339113 Suits, space, manufacturing
315222 Suits, tailored, men's and boys', cut and sewn from purchased fabric (except apparel contractors)
315234 Suits, tailored, women's, misses', and girls', cut and sewn from purchased fabric (except apparel contractors)
325411 Sulfa drugs, uncompounded, manufacturing
212391 Sulfate, sodium, mining and/or beneficiating
325188 Sulfides and sulfites manufacturing
325188 Sulfocyanides manufacturing
325411 Sulfonamides, uncompounded, manufacturing
325188 Sulfur and sulfur compounds, not specified elsewhere by process, manufacturing
325188 Sulfur chloride manufacturing
325188 Sulfur dioxide manufacturing
325188 Sulfur hexafluoride gas manufacturing
325320 Sulfur insecticides manufacturing
212393 Sulfur mining and/or beneficiating
211112 Sulfur recovered from natural gas
325188 Sulfur recovering or refining (except from sour natural gas)
212393 Sulfur, native, mining and/or beneficiating
325188 Sulfuric acid manufacturing
424690 Sulfuric acid merchant wholesalers
325192 Sulphonated derivatives manufacturing
311423 Sulphured fruits and vegetables manufacturing
325191 Sumac extract manufacturing
721214 Summer camps (except day, instructional)

713990 Summer day camps (except instructional)
721110 Summer resort hotels without casinos
711110 Summer theaters
238220 Sump pump installation
333911 Sump pumps, residential-type, manufacturing
115114 Sun drying of dates, prunes, raisins, and olives
115114 Sun drying of fruits and vegetables
115114 Sun drying of tomatoes
812199 Sun tanning salons
111120 Sunflower farming, field and seed production
311223 Sunflower seed oil, cake and meal, made in crushing mills
446130 Sunglass stores
339115 Sunglasses and goggles manufacturing
423460 Sunglasses merchant wholesalers
336399 Sunroofs and parts, automotive, truck, and bus, manufacturing
236118 Sun-room additions, residential
325620 Sunscreen lotions and oils manufacturing
315291 Sunsuits, infants', cut and sewn from purchased fabric (except apparel contractors)
325620 Suntan lotions and oils manufacturing
331111 Superalloys, iron or steel, manufacturing
331492 Superalloys, nonferrous based, made from purchased metals or scrap
445110 Supermarkets
325312 Superphosphates manufacturing
452910 Superstores (i.e., food and general merchandise)
921190 Supply agencies, government
332913 Supply line assemblies, plumbing (i.e., flexible hose with fittings), manufacturing
624190 Support group services
339113 Supports, orthopedic (e.g., abdominal, ankle, arch, kneecap), manufacturing

325412   Suppositories manufacturing
524126   Surety insurance carriers, direct
325613   Surface active agents manufacturing
424690   Surface active agents merchant wholesalers
334516   Surface area analyzers manufacturing
334512   Surface burner controls, temperature, manufacturing
322226   Surface coating purchased paperboard
333120   Surface mining machinery (except drilling) manufacturing
333295   Surface mount machinery for making printed circuit boards manufacturing
237310   Surfacing, highway, road, street, bridge or airport runway
532292   Surfboard rental
339920   Surfboards manufacturing
335999   Surge suppressors manufacturing
621111   Surgeons' (except dental) offices (e.g., centers, clinics)
541940   Surgeons' offices, veterinary
621210   Surgeons', dental, offices (e.g., centers, clinics)
115112   Surgery on trees and vines
541940   Surgery services, veterinary
423450   Surgical appliances merchant wholesalers
339112   Surgical clamps manufacturing
339113   Surgical dressings manufacturing
339113   Surgical implants manufacturing
811219   Surgical instrument repair and maintenance services
423450   Surgical instruments and apparatus merchant wholesalers
339112   Surgical knife blades and handles manufacturing
621111   Surgical pathologists' offices (e.g., centers, clinics)
339112   Surgical stapling devices manufacturing

339113   Surgical supplies (except medical instruments) manufacturing
423450   Surgical supplies merchant wholesalers
334510   Surgical support systems (e.g., heart-lung machines) (except iron lungs) manufacturing
423450   Surgical towels merchant wholesalers
311711   Surimi canning
311712   Surimi, fresh and frozen, manufacturing
238210   Surveillance system, installation only
213112   Surveying (except seismographic) oil or gas wells on a contract basis
541370   Surveying and mapping services (except geophysical)
423490   Surveying equipment and supplies merchant wholesalers
811219   Surveying instrument repair and maintenance services
334519   Surveying instruments manufacturing
541360   Surveying services, geophysical
321999   Surveyor's stakes, wood, manufacturing
611699   Survival training instruction
238310   Suspended ceiling installation
315999   Suspenders cut and sewn from purchased fabric (except apparel contractors)
315211   Suspenders, men's and boys', cut and sew apparel contractors
315212   Suspenders, women's, girls', and infants', cut and sew apparel contractors
811118   Suspension repair shops, automotive
339113   Sutures, surgical, manufacturing
213112   Swabbing oil or gas wells on a contract basis
333513   Swaging machines, metalworking, manufacturing
487210   Swamp buggy operation
323121   Swatches and samples, mounting for the trade

332999 Swatters, fly, metal, manufacturing
315299 Sweat bands cut and sewn from purchased fabric (except apparel contractors)
315191 Sweat bands made in apparel knitting mills
315211 Sweat bands, men's and boys', cut and sew apparel contractors
315212 Sweat bands, women's, girls', and infants', cut and sew apparel contractors
315191 Sweat pants made in apparel knitting mills
315291 Sweat pants, infants', cut and sewn from purchased fabric (except apparel contractors)
315228 Sweat pants, men's, boys', and unisex (i.e., sized without regard to gender), cut and sewn from purchased fabric (except apparel contractors)
315211 Sweat pants, men's, boys', and unisex, cut and sew apparel contractors
315212 Sweat pants, women's, girls', and infants', cut and sew apparel contractors
315239 Sweat pants, women's, misses', and girls', cut and sewn from purchased fabric (except apparel contractors)
315191 Sweat suits made in apparel knitting mills
315291 Sweat suits, infants', cut and sewn from purchased fabric (except apparel contractors)
315211 Sweat suits, men's and boys', cut and sew apparel contractors
315228 Sweat suits, men's and boys', cut and sewn from purchased fabric (except apparel contractors)
315212 Sweat suits, women's, girls', and infants', cut and sew apparel contractors

315239 Sweat suits, women's, misses', and girls', cut and sewn from purchased fabric (except apparel contractors)
316110 Sweatband leather manufacturing
315191 Sweater jackets made in apparel knitting mills
315291 Sweater jackets, infants', cut and sewn from purchased fabric (except apparel contractors)
315211 Sweater jackets, men's and boys', cut and sew apparel contractors
315228 Sweater jackets, men's and boys', cut and sewn from purchased fabric (except apparel contractors)
315212 Sweater jackets, women's, girls', and infants', cut and sew apparel contractors
315239 Sweater jackets, women's, misses', and girls', cut and sewn from purchased fabric (except apparel contractors)
315191 Sweater vests made in apparel knitting mills
315291 Sweater vests, infants', cut and sewn from purchased fabric (except apparel contractors)
315211 Sweater vests, men's and boys', cut and sew apparel contractors
315228 Sweater vests, men's and boys', cut and sewn from purchased fabric (except apparel contractors)
315212 Sweater vests, women's, girls', and infants', cut and sew apparel contractors
315239 Sweater vests, women's, misses', and girls', cut and sewn from purchased fabric (except apparel contractors)
315191 Sweaters made in apparel knitting mills
315291 Sweaters, infants', cut and sewn from purchased fabric (except apparel contractors)

315211	Sweaters, men's and boys', cut and sew apparel contractors
315228	Sweaters, men's and boys', cut and sewn from purchased fabric (except apparel contractors)
315212	Sweaters, women's, and girls', and infants', cut and sew apparel contractors
315239	Sweaters, women's, misses', and girls', cut and sewn from purchased fabric (except apparel contractors)
315191	Sweatshirts made in apparel knitting mills
315291	Sweatshirts, infants', cut and sewn from purchased fabric (except apparel contractors)
315211	Sweatshirts, men's and boys', cut and sew apparel contractors
315223	Sweatshirts, men's and boys', cut and sewn from purchased fabric (except apparel contractors)
315223	Sweatshirts, outerwear, unisex (sized without regard to gender), cut and sewn from purchased fabric (except apparel contractors)
315212	Sweatshirts, women's, girls', and infants', cut and sew apparel contractors
315232	Sweatshirts, women's, misses', and girls', cut and sewn from purchased fabric (except apparel contractors)
334515	Sweep generators manufacturing
334515	Sweep oscillators manufacturing
335212	Sweepers, household-type electric vacuum, manufacturing
325612	Sweeping compounds, absorbent, manufacturing
111219	Sweet corn farming, field and seed production
111219	Sweet pepper farming, field, bedding plant and seed production
115114	Sweet potato curing

111211	Sweet potato farming, field and seed potato production
311812	Sweet yeast goods (except frozen) manufacturing
311813	Sweet yeast goods, frozen, manufacturing
311999	Sweetening syrups (except pure maple) manufacturing
236220	Swimming facility, indoor, construction
611620	Swimming instruction
325998	Swimming pool chemical preparations manufacturing
561790	Swimming pool cleaning and maintenance services
326199	Swimming pool covers and liners, plastics, manufacturing
333319	Swimming pool filter systems manufacturing
333414	Swimming pool heaters manufacturing
335129	Swimming pool lighting fixtures manufacturing
238990	Swimming pool screen enclosure construction
453998	Swimming pool supply stores
238990	Swimming pool, outdoor, construction
713940	Swimming pools
423910	Swimming pools and equipment merchant wholesalers
339920	Swimming pools, above ground, manufacturing
326199	Swimming pools, fiberglass, manufacturing
315191	Swimsuits made in apparel knitting mills
315291	Swimsuits, infants', cut and sewn from purchased fabric (except apparel contractors)
315211	Swimsuits, men's and boys', cut and sew apparel contractors
315228	Swimsuits, men's and boys', cut and sewn from purchased fabric (except apparel contractors)
315212	Swimsuits, women's, girls', and infants', cut and sew apparel contractors

315239 Swimsuits, women's, misses', and girls', cut and sewn from purchased fabric (except apparel contractors)
448190 Swimwear stores
424320 Swimwear, men's and boys', merchant wholesalers
424330 Swimwear, women's, children's, and infants', merchant wholesalers
311119 Swine feed, complete, manufacturing
311119 Swine feed, supplements, concentrates, and premixes, manufacturing
424520 Swine merchant wholesalers
335932 Switch boxes, electrical wiring, manufacturing
335931 Switch cutouts manufacturing
335313 Switchboards and parts, power, manufacturing
423610 Switchboards, electrical distribution, merchant wholesalers
335931 Switches for electrical wiring (e.g., pressure, pushbutton, snap, tumbler) manufacturing
334419 Switches for electronic applications manufacturing
335313 Switches, electric power (except pushbotton, snap, solenoid, tumbler), manufacturing
423610 Switches, electrical, merchant wholesalers
423690 Switches, electronic, merchant wholesalers
335931 Switches, outlet box mounting type, manufacturing
334512 Switches, pneumatic positioning remote, manufacturing
334512 Switches, thermostatic, manufacturing
335313 Switchgear and switchgear accessories manufacturing
335313 Switching equipment, power, manufacturing
334210 Switching equipment, telephone, manufacturing
488210 Switching services, railroad
114111 Swordfish fishing

332211 Swords, nonprecious and precious plated metal, manufacturing
212313 Syenite (except nepheline) crushed and broken stone mining and/or beneficiating
212311 Syenite (except nepheline) mining or quarrying
212325 Syenite, nepheline, mining and/or beneficiating
212221 Sylvanite mining and/or beneficiating
711130 Symphony orchestras
813110 Synagogues
335312 Synchronous condensers and timing motors, electric, manufacturing
335312 Synchronous motors manufacturing
334515 Synchroscopes manufacturing
519110 Syndicates, news
339992 Synthesizers, music, manufacturing
311340 Synthetic chocolate manufacturing
325212 Synthetic rubber (i.e., vulcanizable elastomers) manufacturing
424690 Synthetic rubber merchant wholesalers
327999 Synthetic stones, for gem stones and industrial use, manufacturing
325199 Synthetic sweeteners (i.e., sweetening agents) manufacturing
339112 Syringes, hypodermic, manufacturing
424490 Syrup (except fountain) merchant wholesalers
311313 Syrup made from sugar beets
311930 Syrup, beverage, manufacturing
311312 Syrup, cane, made from purchased raw cane sugar
311311 Syrup, cane, made in sugarcane mill
311320 Syrup, chocolate, made from cacao beans
311330 Syrup, chocolate, made from purchased chocolate

311999 Syrup, corn (except wet milled), manufacturing
311221 Syrup, corn, made by wet milling
311930 Syrup, flavoring (except coffee based), manufacturing
311920 Syrup, flavoring, coffee based, manufacturing
424450 Syrup, fountain, merchant wholesalers
111998 Syrup, pure maple (i.e., maple syrup reducing)
311999 Syrup, sweetening (except pure maple), manufacturing
311999 Syrup, table, artificially flavored, manufacturing
541512 Systems integration design consulting services, computer
541512 Systems integration design services, computer
532299 Table and banquet accessory rental
327112 Table articles, coarse earthenware, manufacturing
327112 Table articles, earthenware, manufacturing
327112 Table articles, fine earthenware (i.e., whiteware), manufacturing
327112 Table articles, vitreous china, manufacturing
332211 Table cutlery, nonprecious and precious plated metal, manufacturing
339912 Table cutlery, precious metal, manufacturing
335121 Table lamps (i.e., lighting fixtures) manufacturing
812331 Table linen supply services
311225 Table oil made from purchased oils
311221 Table oil, corn, made by wet milling
311942 Table salt manufacturing
327991 Table tops, marble, manufacturing
314129 Tablecloths (except paper) made from purchased materials
313210 Tablecloths made in broadwoven fabric mills

313249 Tablecloths made in lace mills
313249 Tablecloths made in warp knitting mills
313241 Tablecloths made in weft knitting mills
322291 Tablecloths, paper, made from purchased paper
337214 Tables (except wood), office-type, manufacturing
337124 Tables, metal household-type, manufacturing
337122 Tables, wood household-type, manufacturing
337211 Tables, wood, office-type, manufacturing
322233 Tablets (e.g., memo, note, writing) made from purchased paper
322121 Tablets (e.g., memo, note, writing) made in paper mills
332999 Tablets, metal, manufacturing
423220 Tableware (except disposable, plated, precious) merchant wholesalers
327215 Tableware made from purchased glass
327212 Tableware made in glass making plants
532299 Tableware rental
424130 Tableware, disposable, merchant wholesalers
423940 Tableware, precious and plated, merchant wholesalers
327112 Tableware, vitreous china, manufacturing
334515 Tachometer generators manufacturing
451110 Tack shops
321999 Tackle blocks, wood, manufacturing
451110 Tackle shops (i.e., fishing)
339920 Tackle, fishing (except line, nets, seines), manufacturing
423710 Tacks merchant wholesalers
331222 Tacks, iron or steel, made in wire drawing plants
332618 Tacks, metal, made from purchased wire
212210 Taconite concentrates or agglomerates beneficiating

212210	Taconite ores mining and/or beneficiating
334511	Taffrail logs manufacturing
213111	Tailing in oil and gas field wells on a contract basis
811490	Tailor shops, alterations only
315211	Tailored dress and sport coats, men's and boys', cut and sew apparel contractors
315222	Tailored dress and sport coats, men's and boys', cut and sewn from purchased fabric (except apparel contractors)
332211	Tailors' scissors, nonelectric, manufacturing
423850	Tailors' supplies merchant wholesalers
******	Tailors—see specific apparel manufacturing
722211	Take out eating places
212399	Talc mining and/or beneficiating
327992	Talc processing beyond beneficiation
325620	Talcum powders manufacturing
711410	Talent agencies
711410	Talent agents
541214	Talent payment services
325191	Tall oil (except skimmings) manufacturing
311611	Tallow produced in a slaughtering plant
311613	Tallow produced in rendering plant
334514	Tally counters manufacturing
334514	Tallying meters (except clocks, electricity meters, watches) manufacturing
333120	Tampers, powered, manufacturing
332995	Tampion guns manufacturing
111320	Tangelo groves
111320	Tangerine groves
332995	Tank artillery manufacturing
336211	Tank bodies for trucks manufacturing
562998	Tank cleaning and disposal services, commercial or industrial
562991	Tank cleaning services, septic
238990	Tank lining contractors
315291	Tank tops, infants', cut and sewn from purchased fabric (except apparel contractors)
315211	Tank tops, men's and boys', cut and sew apparel contractors
315191	Tank tops, outerwear, made in apparel knitting mills
315223	Tank tops, outerwear, men's and boys', cut and sewn from purchased fabric (except apparel contractors)
315232	Tank tops, outerwear, women's, misses', and girls', cut and sewn from purchased fabric (except apparel contractors)
315192	Tank tops, underwear, made in apparel knitting mills
315221	Tank tops, underwear, men's and boys', cut and sewn from purchased fabric (except apparel contractors)
315231	Tank tops, underwear, women's, misses', and girls', cut and sewn from purchased fabric (except apparel contractors)
315212	Tank tops, women's, girls', and infants', cut and sew apparel contractors
336212	Tank trailer, liquid and dry bulk, manufacturing
334514	Tank truck meters manufacturing
336211	Tank trucks (e.g., fuel oil, milk, water) assembling on purchased chassis
532411	Tanker rental or leasing
484220	Tanker trucking (e.g., chemical, juice, milk, petroleum), local
484230	Tanker trucking (e.g., chemical, juice, milk, petroleum), long-distance
327390	Tanks, concrete, manufacturing
327111	Tanks, flush, vitreous china, manufacturing
332420	Tanks, heavy gauge metal, manufacturing
336992	Tanks, military (including factory rebuilding), manufacturing

333315	Tanks, photographic developing, fixing, and washing, manufacturing
423510	Tanks, storage metal, merchant wholesalers
326199	Tanks, storage, plastics or fiberglass, manufacturing
321920	Tanks, wood, coopered, manufacturing
316110	Tannery leather manufacturing
333298	Tannery machinery manufacturing
325191	Tannic acid (i.e., tannins) manufacturing
325188	Tanning agents, inorganic, manufacturing
325199	Tanning agents, synthetic organic, manufacturing
316110	Tanning and currying furs
325191	Tanning extracts and materials, natural, manufacturing
812199	Tanning salons
212299	Tantalite mining and/or beneficiating
212299	Tantalum ores mining and/or beneficiating
331419	Tantalum refining, primary
711120	Tap dance companies
339942	Tape dispensers manufacturing
512120	Tape distribution for television
332212	Tape measures, metal, manufacturing
334310	Tape players and recorders, household-type, manufacturing
423620	Tape players and recorders, household-type, merchant wholesalers
532210	Tape recorder rental
561990	Tape slitting (e.g., cutting plastic or leather into widths) for the trade
334112	Tape storage units (e.g., drive backups), computer peripheral equipment, manufacturing
512191	Tape transfer service
332991	Tapered roller bearings manufacturing
322231	Tapes (e.g., adding machine, calculator, cash register) made from purchased paper

313221	Tapes weaving
423690	Tapes, blank, audio and video, merchant wholesalers
424120	Tapes, cellophane, merchant wholesalers
334613	Tapes, magnetic recording (i.e., audio, data, video), blank, manufacturing
339113	Tapes, medical adhesive, manufacturing
423450	Tapes, medical and surgical, merchant wholesalers
313230	Tapes, nonwoven fabric, manufacturing
423990	Tapes, prerecorded, audio or video, merchant wholesalers
322222	Tapes, pressure sensitive (e.g., cellophane, masking), gummed, made from purchased paper or other materials
334519	Tapes, surveyor's, manufacturing
424310	Tapes, textile, merchant wholesalers
313320	Tapes, varnished and coated (except magnetic), made from purchased fabric
238310	Taping and finishing drywall
311221	Tapioca manufacturing
333512	Tapping machines, metalworking, manufacturing
333515	Taps and dies (i.e., a machine tool accessory) manufacturing
335931	Taps, current, attachment plug and screw shell types, manufacturing
316999	Taps, shoe, leather, manufacturing
325211	Tar acid resins manufacturing
324121	Tar and asphalt paving mixtures made from purchased asphaltic materials
325191	Tar and tar oils made by distillation of wood
325192	Tar made by distillation of coal tar
324110	Tar made in petroleum refineries

324122 Tar paper made from purchased asphaltic materials and paper
324122 Tar paper, building and roofing, made from purchased paper
322121 Tar paper, building and roofing, made in paper mills
324122 Tar roofing cements and coatings made from purchased asphaltic materials
211111 Tar sands mining
336411 Target drones, aircraft, manufacturing
336413 Targets, trailer type, aircraft, manufacturing
541614 Tariff rate consulting services
541614 Tariff rate information services
111219 Taro farming, field and seed production
314912 Tarpaulins made from purchased fabrics
423330 Tarred felts merchant wholesalers
237310 Tarring roads
311941 Tartar sauce manufacturing
325199 Tartaric acid manufacturing
325199 Tartrates, not specified elsewhere by process, manufacturing
812199 Tattoo parlors
722410 Taverns (i.e., drinking places)
561440 Tax collection services on a contract or fee basis
541110 Tax law attorneys' offices
541110 Tax law attorneys' private practices
523910 Tax liens dealing (i.e., acting as a principal in dealing tax liens to investors)
541213 Tax return preparation services
921130 Taxation departments
541850 Taxicab card advertising services
485310 Taxicab dispatch services
485310 Taxicab fleet operators
423110 Taxicab merchant wholesalers
485310 Taxicab organizations
485310 Taxicab owner-operators
485310 Taxicab services
711510 Taxidermists, independent

423850 Taxidermy supplies merchant wholesalers
334514 Taximeters manufacturing
813319 Taxpayers' advocacy organizations
311920 Tea (except herbal) manufacturing
445299 Tea and coffee (i.e., packaged) stores
311920 Tea blending
111998 Tea farming
424490 Tea merchant wholesalers
311920 Tea, herbal, manufacturing
312111 Tea, iced, manufacturing
311920 Tea, instant, manufacturing
113210 Teaberries gathering
923110 Teacher certification bureaus
561311 Teacher registries
333319 Teaching machines (e.g., flight simulators) manufacturing
423490 Teaching machines (except computers), electronic, merchant wholesalers
332214 Teakettles and coffee pots, fabricated metal (except electric, glass), manufacturing
335211 Teakettles, electric, manufacturing
327212 Teakettles, glass and glass ceramic, made in glass making plants
315299 Team athletic uniforms cut and sewn from purchased fabric (except apparel contractors)
315211 Team athletic uniforms, men's and boys', cut and sew apparel contractors
315212 Team athletic uniforms, women's and girls', cut and sew apparel contractors
325199 Tear gas manufacturing
313311 Teaseling broadwoven fabrics
313312 Teaseling fabrics (except broadwoven)
325412 Technetium medicinal preparations manufacturing
327212 Technical glassware and glass products, pressed or blown, made in glass making plants

327215   Technical glassware made from purchased glass

511120   Technical magazine and periodical publishers (except exclusive Internet publishing)

511120   Technical magazine and periodical publishers and printing combined

519130   Technical magazine and periodical publishers, exclusively on Internet

323112   Technical magazines and periodicals flexographic printing without publishing

323111   Technical magazines and periodicals gravure printing without publishing

323110   Technical magazines and periodicals lithographic (offset) printing without publishing

323119   Technical magazines and periodicals printing (except flexographic, gravure, lithographic, quick, screen) without publishing

323113   Technical magazines and periodicals screen printing without publishing

511130   Technical manual and paperback book publishers (except exclusive Internet publishing)

511130   Technical manual and paperback book publishers and printing combined

323121   Technical manual paper (books) binding without printing

511130   Technical manual publishers (except exclusive Internet publishing)

519130   Technical manual publishers, exclusively on Internet

323117   Technical manuals and papers (books) printing and binding without publishing

323117   Technical manuals and papers (books) printing without publishing

711510   Technical writers, independent

315212   Teddies, women's, cut and sew apparel contractors

315231   Teddies, women's, misses', and girls', cut and sewn from purchased fabric (except apparel contractors)

624110   Teen outreach services

339114   Teeth (except customized) manufacturing

339116   Teeth, custom made in dental laboratories

423450   Teeth, dental, merchant wholesalers

517210   Telecommunications carriers, cellular telephone

517110   Telecommunications carriers, wired

238210   Telecommunications equipment and wiring (except transmission line) installation contractors

532490   Telecommunications equipment rental or leasing

541618   Telecommunications management consulting services

517911   Telecommunications resellers

561499   Teleconferencing services

812990   Telegram services, singing

423690   Telegraph equipment merchant wholesalers

561422   Telemarketing bureaus

561422   Telemarketing services on a contract or fee basis

334513   Telemetering instruments, industrial process-type, manufacturing

517919   Telemetry and tracking system operations on a contract or fee basis

334416   Telephone and telegraph transformers, electronic component-type, manufacturing

334210   Telephone answering machines manufacturing

423620   Telephone answering machines merchant wholesalers

561421   Telephone answering services

337215	Telephone booths manufacturing
561422	Telephone call centers
334210	Telephone carrier line equipment manufacturing
334210	Telephone carrier switching equipment manufacturing
517410	Telephone communications carriers, satellite
517210	Telephone communications carriers, wireless (except satellite)
517911	Telephone communications resellers (except satellite)
624190	Telephone counseling services
323112	Telephone directories flexographic printing without publishing
323111	Telephone directories gravure printing without publishing
323110	Telephone directories lithographic (offset) printing without publishing
323119	Telephone directories printing (except flexographic, gravure, lithographic, quick, screen) without publishing
323113	Telephone directories screen printing without publishing
541870	Telephone directory distribution services, door-to-door
511140	Telephone directory publishers (except exclusive Internet publishing)
511140	Telephone directory publishers and printing combined
519130	Telephone directory publishers, exclusively on Internet
238210	Telephone equipment and building wiring installation
423690	Telephone equipment merchant wholesalers
811213	Telephone equipment repair and maintenance services without retailing new telephone equipment
238210	Telephone installation contractors
237130	Telephone line construction
237130	Telephone line stringing

561422	Telephone solicitation services on a contract or fee basis
443112	Telephone stores (including cellular)
519190	Telephone-based recorded information services
334210	Telephones (except cellular telephone) manufacturing
423690	Telephones merchant wholesalers
334220	Telephones, cellular, manufacturing
334210	Telephones, coin-operated, manufacturing
334113	Teleprinters (i.e., computer terminals) manufacturing
512191	Teleproduction services
333314	Telescopes manufacturing
334310	Television (TV) sets manufacturing
541840	Television advertising representatives (i.e., independent of media owners)
443112	Television and radio stores
515120	Television broadcasting networks
515120	Television broadcasting stations
337129	Television cabinets (i.e., housings), wood, manufacturing
423410	Television cameras merchant wholesalers
512110	Television commercial production
561311	Television employment agencies
511120	Television guide publishers (except exclusive Internet publishing)
511120	Television guide publishers and printing combined
519130	Television guide publishers, exclusively on Internet
323112	Television guides flexographic printing without publishing
323111	Television guides gravure printing without publishing
323110	Television guides lithographic (offset) printing without publishing

323119	Television guides printing (except flexographic, gravure, lithographic, quick, screen) without publishing
323113	Television guides screen printing without publishing
326199	Television housings, plastics, manufacturing
517110	Television operations, closed circuit
454113	Television order, home shopping
334411	Television picture tubes manufacturing
711510	Television producers, independent
532210	Television rental
811211	Television repair services without retailing new televisions
423620	Television sets merchant wholesalers
512110	Television show production
512120	Television show syndicators
236220	Television station construction
515210	Television subscription services
332312	Television tower sections, fabricated structural metal, manufacturing
334220	Television transmitting antennas and ground equipment manufacturing
237130	Television transmitting tower construction
334220	Television, closed-circuit equipment, manufacturing
212221	Telluride (gold) mining and/or beneficiating
331419	Tellurium refining, primary
813319	Temperance organizations
238210	Temperature control system installation
334512	Temperature controls, automatic, residential and commercial-types, manufacturing
334513	Temperature instruments, industrial process-type (except glass and bimetal thermometers), manufacturing
334512	Temperature sensors for motor windings manufacturing
327215	Tempered glass made from purchased glass
332811	Tempering metals and metal products for the trade
331111	Template, made in iron and steel mills, manufacturing
334519	Templates, drafting, manufacturing
339115	Temples and fronts (i.e., eyeglass frames), ophthalmic, manufacturing
813110	Temples, religious
561320	Temporary employment services
561320	Temporary help services
624221	Temporary housing for families of medical patients
624221	Temporary shelters (e.g., battered women's, homeless, runaway youth)
561320	Temporary staffing services
713950	Ten pin bowling alleys
713950	Ten pin bowling centers
813319	Tenants' advocacy associations
813990	Tenants' associations (except advocacy)
813319	Tenants' associations, advocacy
713940	Tennis club facilities
236220	Tennis court, indoor, construction
713940	Tennis courts
237990	Tennis courts, outdoor, construction
423910	Tennis equipment and supplies merchant wholesalers
339920	Tennis goods (e.g., balls, frames, rackets) manufacturing
611620	Tennis instruction, camps, or schools
711219	Tennis professionals, independent (i.e., participating in sports events)
315191	Tennis shirts made in apparel knitting mills
315291	Tennis shirts, infants', cut and sewn from purchased fabric (except apparel contractors)

315211 Tennis shirts, men's and boys', cut and sew apparel contractors

315223 Tennis shirts, men's and boys', cut and sewn from purchased fabric (except apparel contractors)

315212 Tennis shirts, women's, girls', and infants', cut and sew apparel contractors

315239 Tennis shirts, women's, misses', and girls', cut and sewn from purchased fabric (except apparel contractors)

315191 Tennis skirts made in apparel knitting mills

315212 Tennis skirts, women's and girls', cut and sew apparel contractors

315239 Tennis skirts, women's, misses', and girls', cut and sewn from purchased fabric (except apparel contractors)

334510 TENS (transcutaneous electrical nerve stimulator) manufacturing

334519 Tensile strength testing equipment manufacturing

321999 Tent poles, wood, manufacturing

336214 Tent trailers (hard top and soft top) manufacturing

532292 Tent, camping, rental

532299 Tent, party, rental

314912 Tents made from purchased fabrics

335931 Terminals and connectors for electrical devices manufacturing

334113 Terminals, computer, manufacturing

424710 Terminals, petroleum

561710 Termite control services

325320 Termite poisons manufacturing

331111 Terneplate made in iron and steel mills

423510 Terneplate merchant wholesalers

331111 Ternes, iron or steel, long or short, made in iron and steel mills

325199 Terpineol manufacturing

114119 Terrapin fishing

238340 Terrazzo and tile refinishing

238340 Terrazzo contractors

327390 Terrazzo products, precast (except brick, block and pipe), manufacturing

313210 Terry broadwoven fabrics weaving

325199 Tert-butylated bis (p-phenoxyphenyl) ether fluid manufacturing

238910 Test boring for construction

611710 Test development and evaluation services, educational

213114 Test drilling for metal mining on a contract basis

213115 Test drilling for nonmetallic minerals mining (except fuel) on a contract basis

334515 Test equipment for electronic and electrical circuits and equipment manufacturing

334515 Test sets, ignition harness, manufacturing

525920 Testamentary trusts

334519 Testers for checking hydraulic controls on aircraft manufacturing

423830 Testing and measuring equipment, electrical (except automotive), merchant wholesalers

334519 Testing equipment (e.g., abrasion, shearing strength, tensile strength, torsion) manufacturing

541380 Testing laboratories (except medical, veterinary)

621511 Testing laboratories, medical

541940 Testing laboratories, veterinary

541940 Testing services for veterinarians

488190 Testing services, aircraft

611710 Testing services, educational

333993	Testing, weighing, inspecting, packaging machinery manufacturing
325199	Tetrachloroethylene manufacturing
325411	Tetracycline, uncompounded, manufacturing
325199	Tetraethyl lead manufacturing
325920	Tetryl explosive materials manufacturing
323117	Textbooks printing and binding without publishing
323117	Textbooks printing without publishing
314911	Textile bags made from purchased woven or knitted materials
424990	Textile bags merchant wholesalers
313210	Textile broadwoven fabrics mills
561990	Textile cutting services
541490	Textile design services
325613	Textile finishing assistants manufacturing
333292	Textile finishing machinery (e.g., bleaching, dyeing, mercerizing, printing) manufacturing
314999	Textile fire hose made from purchased material
561910	Textile folding and packaging services
327212	Textile glass fibers made in glass making plants
327112	Textile guides, porcelain, manufacturing
316999	Textile leathers (e.g., apron picker leather, mill strapping) manufacturing
423830	Textile machinery and equipment merchant wholesalers
532490	Textile machinery rental or leasing
811310	Textile machinery repair and maintenance services
333292	Textile making machinery (except sewing machines) manufacturing

236210	Textile mill construction
313210	Textile mills, broadwoven fabrics
313221	Textile mills, narrow woven fabric
313221	Textile narrow woven fabric mills
325910	Textile printing inks manufacturing
333292	Textile printing machinery manufacturing
313210	Textile products (except apparel) made in broadwoven fabric mills
313249	Textile products (except apparel) made in lace mills
313221	Textile products (except apparel) made in narrow woven fabric mills
313249	Textile products (except apparel) made in warp knitting mills
313241	Textile products (except apparel) made in weft knitting mills
313312	Textile products finishing
325613	Textile scouring agents manufacturing
423930	Textile waste merchant wholesalers
313320	Textile waterproofing
424310	Textiles (except burlap, felt) merchant wholesalers
325221	Texturizing cellulosic yarn made in the same establishment
333292	Texturizing machinery for textiles manufacturing
325222	Texturizing noncellulosic yarn made in the same establishment
313112	Texturizing purchased yarn
212299	Thallium mining and/or beneficiating
711110	Theater companies (except dance)
711110	Theater companies (except dance), amateur
711120	Theater companies, dance
236220	Theater construction

423410 Theater equipment (except seats) merchant wholesalers
711310 Theater festival managers with facilities
711320 Theater festival managers without facilities
711310 Theater festival organizers with facilities
711320 Theater festival organizers without facilities
711310 Theater festival promoters with facilities
711320 Theater festival promoters without facilities
711310 Theater operators
611610 Theater schools
337127 Theater seating manufacturing
423210 Theater seats merchant wholesalers
531120 Theater, property operation, rental or leasing
711120 Theaters, dance
711110 Theaters, dinner
711110 Theaters, live theatrical production (except dance)
512131 Theaters, motion picture (except drive-in)
512132 Theaters, motion picture, drive-in
512131 Theaters, motion picture, indoor
711110 Theaters, musical
512132 Theaters, outdoor motion picture
711320 Theatrical booking agencies (except motion picture)
315299 Theatrical costumes cut and sewn from purchased fabric (except apparel contractors)
315211 Theatrical costumes, men's and boys', cut and sew apparel contractors
315212 Theatrical costumes, women's, girls', and infants', cut and sew apparel contractors
711120 Theatrical dance productions, live
561311 Theatrical employment agencies
532490 Theatrical equipment (except costumes) rental or leasing

711310 Theatrical production managers with facilities
711320 Theatrical production managers without facilities
711310 Theatrical production organizers with facilities
711320 Theatrical production organizers without facilities
711310 Theatrical production promoters with facilities
711320 Theatrical production promoters without facilities
711110 Theatrical repertory companies
711110 Theatrical road companies
339999 Theatrical scenery manufacturing
711110 Theatrical stock companies
711410 Theatrical talent agents
561599 Theatrical ticket offices
532220 Theatrical wardrobe and costume rental
334290 Theft prevention signaling devices (e.g., door entrance annunciation, holdup signaling devices, personal duress signaling devices), manufacturing
713110 Theme parks, amusement
325411 Theobromine and derivatives (i.e., basic chemicals) manufacturing
333314 Theodolites manufacturing
334519 Theodolites, surveying, manufacturing
611310 Theological seminaries offering baccalaureate or graduate degrees
334517 Therapeutic X-ray apparatus and tubes (e.g., medical, industrial, research) manufacturing
****** Therapists' offices—see type
423450 Therapy equipment merchant wholesalers
334516 Thermal analysis instruments, laboratory-type, manufacturing
334516 Thermal conductivity instruments and sensors manufacturing

334513 Thermal conductivity instruments, industrial process-type, manufacturing

326140 Thermal insulation, polystyrene foam, manufacturing

237130 Thermal power plant construction

541380 Thermal testing laboratories or services

334415 Thermistors manufacturing

334513 Thermistors, industrial process-type, manufacturing

334519 Thermocouples (except industrial process, aircraft type, glass vacuum) manufacturing

334512 Thermocouples, glass vacuum, manufacturing

334513 Thermocouples, industrial process-type, manufacturing

335999 Thermoelectric generators manufacturing

333993 Thermoform, blister, and skin packaging machinery manufacturing

333220 Thermoforming machinery for plastics manufacturing

334516 Thermogravimetric analyzers manufacturing

334519 Thermometer, liquid-in-glass and bimetal types (except medical), manufacturing

423450 Thermometers merchant wholesalers

334513 Thermometers, filled system industrial process-type, manufacturing

339112 Thermometers, medical, manufacturing

325211 Thermoplastic resins and plastics materials manufacturing

325211 Thermosetting plastics resins manufacturing

325212 Thermosetting vulcanizable elastomers manufacturing

332911 Thermostatic traps, industrial-type, manufacturing

334512 Thermostats (e.g., air-conditioning, appliance, comfort heating, refrigeration) manufacturing

334519 Thickness gauging instruments, ultrasonic, manufacturing

332999 Thimbles for wire rope manufacturing

334413 Thin film integrated circuits manufacturing

333295 Thin layer deposition equipment, semiconductor, manufacturing

115112 Thinning of crops, mechanical and chemical

325188 Thiocyanate manufacturing

325199 Thioglycolic acid manufacturing

325212 Thiol rubber manufacturing

212299 Thorite mining and/or beneficiating

212299 Thorium ores mining and/or beneficiating

711212 Thoroughbred racetracks

424310 Thread (except industrial) merchant wholesalers

333515 Thread cutting dies (i.e., a machine tool accessory) manufacturing

313312 Thread finishing

333292 Thread making machinery manufacturing

313113 Thread mills

333513 Thread rolling machines, metalworking, manufacturing

313113 Thread, all fibers, manufacturing

423840 Thread, industrial, merchant wholesalers

326299 Thread, rubber (except fabric covered), manufacturing

333512 Threading machines, metalworking, manufacturing

115113 Threshing service

453310 Thrift shops, used merchandise

333298 Through-hole machinery, printed circuit board loading, manufacturing

325221 Throwing cellulosic yarn made in the same establishment

334513	Time cycle and program controllers, industrial process-type, manufacturing
334518	Time locks manufacturing
323118	Time planners/organizers and refills manufacturing
334512	Time program controls, air-conditioning systems, manufacturing
423420	Time recording machines merchant wholesalers
561599	Time share exchange services, condominium
334518	Time stamps containing clock mechanisms manufacturing
335313	Time switches, electrical switchgear apparatus, manufacturing
334518	Timers for industrial use, clockwork mechanism, manufacturing
236115	Time-share condominium construction general contractors
236117	Time-share condominium construction operative builders
326220	Timing belt, rubber or plastics, manufacturing
335314	Timing devices, mechanical and solid-state (except clockwork), manufacturing
336312	Timing gears and chains, automotive and truck gasoline engine, manufacturing
334518	Timing mechanisms, clockwork, manufacturing
335312	Timing motors, synchronous, electric, manufacturing
331491	Tin and tin alloy bar, pipe, rod, sheet, strip, and tubing made from purchased metals or scrap
331419	Tin base alloys made in primary tin smelting and refining mills
325188	Tin chloride manufacturing
325188	Tin compounds, not specified elsewhere by process, manufacturing
212299	Tin metal concentrates beneficiating

212299	Tin metal ores mining and/or beneficiating
325188	Tin oxide manufacturing
332431	Tin plate cans, light gauge metal, manufacturing
423510	Tin plate merchant wholesalers
331492	Tin recovering from scrap and/or alloying purchased metals
331419	Tin refining, primary
331491	Tin rolling, drawing, or extruding purchased metals or scrap
325188	Tin salts manufacturing
325412	Tincture of iodine preparations manufacturing
332999	Tinfoil not made in rolling mills
331111	Tin-free steel made in iron and steel mills
332212	Tinners' snips manufacturing
331111	Tinplate made in iron and steel mills
339999	Tinsel manufacturing
325998	Tint and dye preparations, household-type (except hair), manufacturing
325620	Tints, dyes, and rinses, hair, manufacturing
212111	Tipple operation, bituminous coal mining and/or beneficiating
236210	Tipple, mining, construction
316999	Tips, shoe, leather, manufacturing
423130	Tire and tube repair materials merchant wholesalers
332618	Tire chains made from purchased wire
314992	Tire cord and fabric, all materials, manufacturing
336360	Tire covers made from purchased fabric
441320	Tire dealers, automotive
325998	Tire inflators, aerosol, manufacturing
333220	Tire making machinery manufacturing
333319	Tire mounting machines, motor vehicle, manufacturing
333220	Tire recapping machinery manufacturing

423830 Tire recapping machinery merchant wholesalers

326211 Tire repair materials manufacturing

811198 Tire repair shops (except retreading), automotive

326212 Tire retreading, recapping or rebuilding

333220 Tire shredding machinery manufacturing

423130 Tire tubes, motor vehicle, merchant wholesalers

326211 Tires (e.g., pneumatic, semi-pneumatic, solid rubber) manufacturing

423130 Tires, new, motor vehicle, merchant wholesalers

326199 Tires, plastics, manufacturing

423930 Tires, scrap, merchant wholesalers

423130 Tires, used (except scrap), merchant wholesalers

111421 Tissue culture farming

322121 Tissue paper stock manufacturing

424130 Tissue paper, toilet and facial, merchant wholesalers

327113 Titania porcelain insulators manufacturing

212299 Titaniferous-magnetite ores, valued chiefly for titanium content, mining and/or beneficiating

331491 Titanium and titanium alloy bar, billet, rod, sheet, strip, and tubing made from purchased metals or scrap

325131 Titanium based pigments manufacturing

331528 Titanium castings (except die-castings), unfinished, manufacturing

212299 Titanium concentrates beneficiating

331522 Titanium die-castings, unfinished, manufacturing

325188 Titanium dioxide manufacturing

332112 Titanium forgings made from purchased metals, unfinished

212299 Titanium ores mining and/or beneficiating

331419 Titanium refining, primary

331491 Titanium rolling, drawing, or extruding purchased metals or scrap

541191 Title abstract companies, real estate

541191 Title companies, real estate

524127 Title insurance carriers, real estate, direct

541191 Title search companies, real estate

519190 Title search services (except real estate)

512191 Titling of motion picture film or video

334516 Titrimeters manufacturing

325920 TNT (trinitrotoluene) manufacturing

335211 Toaster ovens, household-type electric, manufacturing

423620 Toasters, electric, merchant wholesalers

335211 Toasters, household-type electric, manufacturing

424940 Tobacco (except leaf) merchant wholesalers

111910 Tobacco farming, field and seed production

115114 Tobacco grading

333111 Tobacco harvester machines manufacturing

321920 Tobacco hogshead stock, manufacturing

321920 Tobacco hogsheads, manufacturing

312210 Tobacco leaf processing and aging

339999 Tobacco pipes manufacturing

316993 Tobacco pouches (except metal) manufacturing

339911 Tobacco pouches, precious metal, manufacturing

333298 Tobacco processing machinery (except farm-type) manufacturing

312229 Tobacco products (e.g., chewing, smoking, snuff) manufacturing

424940	Tobacco products merchant wholesalers
312229	Tobacco products, imitation (except cigarettes) manufacturing
312229	Tobacco sheeting services
312210	Tobacco stemming and redrying
453991	Tobacco stores
424590	Tobacco, leaf, merchant wholesalers
339920	Toboggans manufacturing
316999	Toe caps, leather, manufacturing
311340	Toffee manufacturing
311991	Tofu (i.e., bean curd) (except frozen desserts) manufacturing
311520	Tofu frozen desserts manufacturing
332722	Toggle bolts, metal, manufacturing
325612	Toilet bowl cleaners manufacturing
332998	Toilet fixtures, metal, manufacturing
326191	Toilet fixtures, plastics, manufacturing
327111	Toilet fixtures, vitreous china, manufacturing
316993	Toilet kits and cases (except metal) manufacturing
339911	Toilet kits and cases, precious metal, manufacturing
322291	Toilet paper made from purchased paper
322121	Toilet paper made in paper mills
325620	Toilet preparations (e.g., cosmetics, deodorants, perfumes) manufacturing
424210	Toilet preparations merchant wholesalers
562991	Toilet renting and/or servicing, portable
321999	Toilet seats, wood, manufacturing
325611	Toilet soaps manufacturing
424210	Toilet soaps merchant wholesalers
424130	Toilet tissue merchant wholesalers

332999	Toilet ware, precious plated metal, manufacturing
325620	Toilet water manufacturing
424210	Toiletries merchant wholesalers
334210	Toll switching equipment, telephone, manufacturing
325110	Toluene made from refined petroleum or liquid hydrocarbons
324110	Toluene made in petroleum refineries
325192	Toluidines manufacturing
111219	Tomato farming (except under cover), field, bedding plant and seed production
111419	Tomato farming, grown under cover
333111	Tomato harvesting machines manufacturing
325992	Toner cartridges manufacturing
424120	Toner cartridges merchant wholesalers
325992	Toner cartridges rebuilding
325132	Toners (except electrostatic, photographic) manufacturing
325992	Toners, electrostatic and photographic, manufacturing
339113	Tongue depressors manufacturing
316999	Tongues, boot and shoe, leather, manufacturing
339112	Tonometers, medical, manufacturing
332439	Tool boxes, light gauge metal, manufacturing
321920	Tool chests, wood, manufacturing
321999	Tool handles, wood, turned and shaped, manufacturing
541420	Tool industrial design services
337127	Tool stands, factory, manufacturing
331111	Tool steel made in iron and steel mills
444130	Tool stores, power and hand (except outdoor)
333515	Toolholders (i.e., a machine tool accessory) manufacturing
333515	Tools and accessories for machine tools manufacturing

313241 Towels and washcloths made in weft knitting mills
423220 Towels and washcloths merchant wholesalers
314129 Towels or washcloths made from purchased fabrics
423840 Towels, industrial, merchant wholesalers
322291 Towels, paper, made from purchased paper
322121 Towels, paper, made in paper mills
423450 Towels, surgical, merchant wholesalers
237130 Tower, power distribution and communication, construction
336399 Towing bars and systems manufacturing
483211 Towing service, inland waters (except on Great Lakes system)
488410 Towing services, motor vehicle
236115 Town house (i.e., single-family type) construction by general contractors
236117 Town house construction operative builders
531110 Town house rental or leasing
541320 Town planners' offices
541320 Town planning services
562910 Toxic material abatement services
562910 Toxic material removal contractors
621511 Toxicology health laboratories
325414 Toxoids (e.g., diphtheria, tetanus) manufacturing
339932 Toy furniture and household-type equipment manufacturing
451120 Toy stores
339932 Toys (except dolls, stuffed toys) manufacturing
423920 Toys (including electronic) merchant wholesalers
339931 Toys, doll, manufacturing
339931 Toys, stuffed, manufacturing
333515 Tracer and tapering machine tool attachments manufacturing

332993 Tracer igniters, ammunition (i.e., more than 30 mm., more than 1.18 inch), manufacturing
339920 Track and field athletic equipment (except apparel, footwear) manufacturing
335121 Track lighting fixtures and equipment, residential, electric, manufacturing
484220 Tracked vehicle freight transportation, local
484230 Tracked vehicle freight transportation, long-distance
487110 Tracked vehicle sightseeing operation
339113 Traction apparatus manufacturing
811310 Tractor, farm or construction equipment repair and maintenance services
532490 Tractor, farm, rental or leasing
532490 Tractor, garden, rental or leasing
333120 Tractors and attachments, construction-type, manufacturing
333111 Tractors and attachments, farm-type, manufacturing
333112 Tractors and attachments, lawn and garden-type, manufacturing
333120 Tractors, crawler, manufacturing
423820 Tractors, farm and garden, merchant wholesalers
423110 Tractors, highway, merchant wholesalers
333924 Tractors, industrial, manufacturing
423830 Tractors, industrial, merchant wholesalers
811411 Tractors, lawn and garden repair and maintenance services without retailing new lawn and garden tractors
336120 Tractors, truck for highway use, assembled on chassis of own manufacture
813910 Trade associations
522293 Trade banks (i.e., international trade financing)

323121	Trade binding services
926110	Trade commissions, government
926110	Trade development program administration
561920	Trade fair managers
561920	Trade fair organizers
561920	Trade fair promoters
522293	Trade financing, international
511120	Trade journal publishers (except exclusive Internet publishing)
511120	Trade journal publishers and printing combined
519130	Trade journal publishers, exclusively on Internet
323112	Trade journals flexographic printing without publishing
323111	Trade journals gravure printing without publishing
323110	Trade journals lithographic (offset) printing without publishing
323119	Trade journals printing (except flexographic, gravure, lithographic, quick, screen) without publishing
323113	Trade journals screen printing without publishing
511120	Trade magazine and periodical publishers (except exclusive Internet publishing)
511120	Trade magazine and periodical publishers and printing combined
519130	Trade magazine and periodical publishers, exclusively on Internet
323112	Trade magazines and periodicals flexographic printing without publishing
323111	Trade magazines and periodicals gravure printing without publishing
323110	Trade magazines and periodicals lithographic (offset) printing without publishing
323119	Trade magazines and periodicals printing (except flexographic, gravure, lithographic, quick, screen) without publishing
323113	Trade magazines and periodicals screen printing without publishing
238390	Trade show exhibit installation and dismantling contractors
561920	Trade show managers
561920	Trade show organizers
561920	Trade show promoters
611513	Trade union apprenticeship training programs
813930	Trade unions (except apprenticeship programs)
813930	Trade unions, local
533110	Trademark licensing
523130	Trading companies, commodity contracts
452990	Trading posts, general merchandise
523110	Trading securities (i.e., acting as a principal in dealing securities to investors)
561990	Trading stamp promotion and sale to stores
561990	Trading stamp redemption services
334290	Traffic advisory and signalling systems manufacturing
922110	Traffic courts
541330	Traffic engineering consulting services
237310	Traffic lane painting
519110	Traffic reporting services
238210	Traffic signal installation
334290	Traffic signals manufacturing
237990	Trail construction
721214	Trail riding camps with accommodation facilities
713990	Trail riding, recreational
336399	Trailer hitches, motor vehicle, manufacturing
531190	Trailer park or court, residential
423120	Trailer parts, new, merchant wholesalers
532120	Trailer rental or leasing
336214	Trailers for transporting horses (except fifth-wheel-type) manufacturing
336214	Trailers, camping, manufacturing

336212	Trailers, fifth-wheel type, for transporting horses, manufacturing
423830	Trailers, industrial, merchant wholesalers
423110	Trailers, motor vehicle, merchant wholesalers
115210	Training horses (except racehorses)
315212	Training pants (i.e., underwear), infants', cut and sew apparel contractors
315291	Training pants (i.e., underwear), infants', cut and sewn from purchased fabric (except apparel contractors)
711219	Training race dogs
711219	Training racehorses
339932	Trains and equipment, toy, electric or mechanical, manufacturing
713990	Trampoline facilities, recreational
485119	Tramway systems (except mixed mode), commuter
487990	Tramway, aerial, scenic and sightseeing operation
332994	Tranquilizer guns, manufacturing
325412	Tranquilizer preparations manufacturing
336350	Transaxles, automotive, truck, and bus, manufacturing
334220	Transceivers (i.e., transmitter-receiver units) manufacturing
561410	Transcription services
334510	Transcutaneous electrical nerve stimulators (TENS) manufacturing
334419	Transducers (except pressure) manufacturing
334519	Transducers, pressure, manufacturing
325199	Transestrification of vegetable oils to produce fuels or fuel additives
484110	Transfer (trucking) services, general freight, local
523999	Transfer agencies, securities
237130	Transformer station and substation, electric power, construction
423610	Transformers (except electronic) merchant wholesalers
335311	Transformers, electric power, manufacturing
334416	Transformers, electronic component-types, manufacturing
423690	Transformers, electronic, merchant wholesalers
335311	Transformers, ignition, for use on domestic fuel burners, manufacturing
335311	Transformers, reactor, manufacturing
335311	Transformers, separate solid-state arc-welding, manufacturing
335912	Transistor radio batteries manufacturing
334413	Transistors manufacturing
423690	Transistors merchant wholesalers
541850	Transit advertising services
922120	Transit police
926120	Transit systems and authorities, nonoperating
485111	Transit systems, mixed mode (e.g., bus, commuter rail, subway combinations)
624229	Transitional housing agencies
327320	Transit-mixed concrete manufacturing
334519	Transits, surveying, manufacturing
541930	Translation services, language
237130	Transmission and distribution line construction
335311	Transmission and distribution voltage regulators manufacturing
316999	Transmission belting, leather, manufacturing
326220	Transmission belts, rubber, manufacturing
336399	Transmission coolers manufacturing

423610	Transmission equipment, electrical, merchant wholesalers
324191	Transmission fluids, petroleum, made from refined petroleum
325998	Transmission fluids, synthetic, manufacturing
221121	Transmission of electric power
486210	Transmission of natural gas via pipeline (i.e., processing plants to local distribution systems)
335932	Transmission pole and line hardware manufacturing
811113	Transmission repair shops, automotive
332312	Transmission tower sections, fabricated structural metal, manufacturing
336350	Transmissions and parts, automotive, truck, and bus, manufacturing
423690	Transmitters merchant wholesalers
334513	Transmitters, industrial process control-type, manufacturing
333111	Transplanters, farm-type, manufacturing
115112	Transplanting services
******	Transportation—see mode
481212	Transportation by spacecraft, freight
926120	Transportation departments, nonoperating
423860	Transportation equipment and supplies (except marine pleasure craft, motor vehicles) merchant wholesalers
336360	Transportation equipment seating manufacturing
541614	Transportation management consulting services
926120	Transportation regulatory agencies
926120	Transportation safety programs, government
483111	Transporting freight to or from foreign ports, deep sea
483112	Transporting passengers to or from foreign ports, deep sea

212319	Trap rock crushed and broken stone mining and/or beneficiating
212311	Trap rock mining or quarrying
332618	Traps, animal and fish, made from purchased wire
332919	Traps, water, manufacturing
423910	Trapshooting equipment and supplies merchant wholesalers
713990	Trapshooting facilities, recreational
333319	Trash and garbage compactors, commercial-type, manufacturing
335228	Trash and garbage compactors, household-type, manufacturing
326111	Trash bags, plastics film, single wall or multiwall, manufacturing
562111	Trash collection services
326199	Trash containers, plastics, manufacturing
562213	Trash disposal combustors or incinerators
562212	Trash disposal landfills
562111	Trash hauling, local
484230	Trash hauling, long-distance
332313	Trash racks, fabricated metal plate work, manufacturing
621493	Trauma centers (except hospitals), freestanding
561510	Travel agencies
511130	Travel guide book publishers (except exclusive Internet publishing)
511130	Travel guide book publishers and printing combined
519130	Travel guide book publishers, exclusively on Internet
323117	Travel guide books printing and binding without publishing
323117	Travel guide books printing without publishing
561520	Travel tour operators
423110	Travel trailer (e.g., tent trailers) merchant wholesalers
721211	Travel trailer campsites
441210	Travel trailer dealers
336214	Travel trailers, recreational, manufacturing

624190	Travelers' aid centers
522390	Travelers' check issuance services
316991	Traveling bags, all materials, manufacturing
712110	Traveling museum exhibits
711190	Traveling shows, carnival
334411	Traveling wave tubes manufacturing
212312	Travertine crushed and broken stone mining and/or beneficiating
212311	Travertine mining or quarrying
337127	Tray trucks, restaurant, manufacturing
321920	Trays, carrier, wood, manufacturing
322299	Trays, food, molded pulp, manufacturing
333315	Trays, photographic printing and processing, manufacturing
332618	Trays, wire, made from purchased wire
321999	Trays, wood, wicker, and bagasse, manufacturing
326211	Tread rubber (i.e., camelback) manufacturing
332323	Treads, metal stair, manufacturing
921130	Treasurers' offices, government
321114	Treating purchased wood and wood products
238160	Treating roofs (by spraying, painting or coating)
321114	Treating wood products with creosote or other preservatives
561730	Tree and brush trimming, overhead utility line
113310	Tree chipping in the field
111421	Tree crop farming (except forestry), short rotation growing and harvesting cycle
111335	Tree nut farming
311225	Tree nut oils (e.g., tung, walnut) made from purchased oils
311223	Tree nut oils (e.g., tung, walnut) made in crushing mill
561730	Tree pruning services
561730	Tree removal services
113210	Tree seed extracting

113210	Tree seed gathering
113210	Tree seed growing for reforestation
561730	Tree services (e.g., bracing, planting, pruning, removal, spraying, surgery, trimming)
333111	Tree shakers (e.g., citrus, nut, soft fruit) manufacturing
561730	Tree surgery services
561730	Tree trimming services
339999	Trees and plants, artificial, manufacturing
424930	Trees merchant wholesalers
321918	Trellises, wood, manufacturing
238910	Trenching (except underwater)
333120	Trenching machines manufacturing
237990	Trenching, underwater
237310	Trestle construction
321114	Trestle parts, wood, treating
325221	Triacetate fibers and yarns manufacturing
921150	Tribal chief's or chairman's office, American Indian or Alaska Native
921150	Tribal councils, American Indian or Alaska Native
921150	Tribal courts, American Indian or Alaska Native
325199	Trichloroethylene manufacturing
325199	Trichlorophenoxyacetic acid manufacturing
325199	Tricresyl phosphate manufacturing
339932	Tricycles (except metal) manufacturing
336991	Tricycles, metal, adult and children's, manufacturing
325199	Tridecyl alcohol manufacturing
238350	Trim and finish carpentry contractors
332321	Trim and molding (except motor vehicle), metal, manufacturing
332321	Trim, metal, manufacturing
321918	Trim, wood and covered wood, manufacturing
333112	Trimmers, hedge, electric, manufacturing

332212	Trimmers, hedge, nonelectric, manufacturing
333112	Trimmers, string, lawn and garden-type, manufacturing
315292	Trimmings, fur (except apparel contractors), manufacturing
315211	Trimmings, fur, men's and boys', cut and sew apparel contractors
315212	Trimmings, fur, women's, girls', and infants', cut and sew apparel contractors
316999	Trimmings, shoe, leather, manufacturing
325920	Trinitrotoluene (TNT) manufacturing
325199	Triphenyl phosphate manufacturing
333315	Tripods, camera and projector, manufacturing
212399	Tripoli mining and/or beneficiating
339112	Trocars manufacturing
485119	Trolley systems (except mixed mode), commuter
487110	Trolley, scenic and sightseeing, operation
339992	Trombones and parts manufacturing
212391	Trona mining and/or beneficiating
423940	Trophies merchant wholesalers
332999	Trophies, nonprecious and precious plated metal, manufacturing
339912	Trophies, precious metal, (except precious plated) manufacturing
453998	Trophy (including awards and plaques) shops
321999	Trophy bases, wood, manufacturing
424990	Tropical fish merchant wholesalers
112511	Tropical fish production, farm raising
561730	Tropical plant maintenance services
335129	Trouble lights manufacturing

332322	Troughs, elevator, sheet meta (except stampings), manufacturing
332313	Troughs, industrial, fabricated metal plate work, manufacturing
335211	Trouser pressers, household-type electric, manufacturing
315191	Trousers made in apparel knitting mills
315211	Trousers, men's and boys', cut and sew apparel contractors
315224	Trousers, men's and boys', cut and sewn from purchased fabric (except apparel contractors)
114111	Trout fishing
112511	Trout production, farm raising
332212	Trowels manufacturing
532120	Truck (except industrial) rental or leasing
811192	Truck and bus washes
336211	Truck bodies and cabs manufacturing
336211	Truck bodies assembling on purchased chassis
336214	Truck campers (i.e., slide-in campers) manufacturing
441310	Truck cap stores
611519	Truck driving schools
111219	Truck farming, field, bedding plant and seed production
522220	Truck finance leasing
423120	Truck parts, new, merchant wholesalers
811310	Truck refrigeration repair and maintenance services
811111	Truck repair shops, general
447190	Truck stops
236220	Truck terminal construction
532120	Truck tractor rental or leasing
336120	Truck tractors for highway use, assembling on chassis of own manufacture
336211	Truck tractors for highway use, assembling on purchased chassis
423110	Truck tractors, road, merchant wholesalers
811121	Truck trailer body shops

336212 Truck trailer manufacturing

423110 Truck trailer merchant wholesalers

811121 Truck trailer paint and body repair

488490 Truck weighing station operation

532490 Truck, industrial, rental or leasing

488490 Trucking terminals, independently operated

484210 Trucking used household, office, or institutional furniture and equipment

484110 Trucking, general freight, local

484122 Trucking, general freight, long-distance, less-than-truckload (LTL)

484121 Trucking, general freight, long-distance, truckload (TL)

484220 Trucking, specialized freight (except used goods), local

484230 Trucking, specialized freight (except used goods), long-distance

327320 Truck-mixed concrete manufacturing

336120 Trucks, heavy, assembling on chassis of own manufacture

333924 Trucks, industrial, manufacturing

423830 Trucks, industrial, merchant wholesalers

336112 Trucks, light duty, assembling on chassis of own manufacture

333120 Trucks, off-highway, manufacturing

423110 Trucks, road, merchant wholesalers

111419 Truffles farming, grown under cover

339992 Trumpets and parts manufacturing

316991 Trunks (i.e., luggage), all materials, manufacturing

332313 Truss plates, metal, manufacturing

321214 Trusses, glue laminated or pre-engineered wood, manufacturing

321214 Trusses, wood roof or floor, manufacturing

321214 Trusses, wood, glue laminated or metal connected, manufacturing

523991 Trust administration, personal investment

523991 Trust companies, nondepository

813211 Trusts, charitable, awarding grants

813211 Trusts, educational, awarding grants

525920 Trusts, estates, and agency accounts

813211 Trusts, religious, awarding grants

448190 T-shirt shops, custom printed

315291 T-shirts, outerwear, infants', cut and sewn from purchased fabric (except apparel contractors)

315191 T-shirts, outerwear, made in apparel knitting mills

315223 T-shirts, outerwear, men's and boys', cut and sewn from purchased fabric (except apparel contractors)

315211 T-shirts, outerwear, men's, boys' and unisex, cut and sew apparel contractors

315223 T-shirts, outerwear, unisex (i.e., sized without regard to gender), cut and sewn from purchased fabric (except apparel contractors)

315212 T-shirts, outerwear, women's, girls', and infants', cut and sew apparel contractors

315232 T-shirts, outerwear, women's, misses', and girls', cut and sewn from purchased fabric (except apparel contractors)

315291 T-shirts, underwear, infants', cut and sewn from purchased fabric (except apparel contractors)

315192   T-shirts, underwear, made in apparel knitting mills

315211   T-shirts, underwear, men's and boys', cut and sew apparel contractors

315221   T-shirts, underwear, men's and boys', cut and sewn from purchased fabric (except apparel contractors)

315231   T-shirts, underwear, women's, misses', and girls', cut and sewn from purchased fabric (except apparel contractors)

315212   T-shirts, underwear, women's, misses', girls', and infants', cut and sew apparel contractors

334519   T-squares (drafting) manufacturing

325612   Tub and tile cleaning preparations manufacturing

331210   Tube (e.g., heavy riveted, lock joint, seamless, welded) made from purchased iron or steel

332912   Tube and hose fittings, fluid power, manufacturing

331316   Tube blooms made by extruding purchased aluminum

331316   Tube blooms, aluminum, made in integrated secondary smelting and extruding mills

331316   Tube made by drawing or extruding purchased aluminum

333516   Tube rolling mill machinery, metalworking, manufacturing

331111   Tube rounds, iron or steel, made in iron and steel mills

331316   Tube, aluminum, made in integrated secondary smelting and drawing plants

331316   Tube, aluminum, made in integrated secondary smelting and extruding mills

331111   Tube, iron or steel, made in iron and steel mills

326121   Tube, nonrigid plastics, manufacturing

331315   Tube, welded, aluminum, made by flat rolling purchased aluminum

331315   Tube, welded, aluminum, made in integrated secondary smelting and flat rolling mills

325414   Tuberculin (i.e., tuberculo-protein derived) manufacturing

622310   Tuberculosis and other respiratory illness hospitals

332996   Tubes made from purchased metal pipe

334411   Tubes, cathode ray, manufacturing

334411   Tubes, electron, manufacturing

423690   Tubes, electronic (e.g., industrial, receiving, transmitting), merchant wholesalers

334411   Tubes, electronic, manufacturing

334411   Tubes, klystron, manufacturing

334517   Tubes, X-ray, manufacturing

331421   Tubing, copper and copper alloy, made from purchased copper or in integrated secondary smelting and rolling, drawing or extruding plants

332999   Tubing, flexible metal, manufacturing

331210   Tubing, mechanical and hypodermic sizes, cold-drawn stainless steel, made from purchased steel

423510   Tubing, metal, merchant wholesalers

331491   Tubing, nonferrous metals (except aluminum, copper), made from purchased metals or scrap

331111   Tubing, seamless steel, made in iron and steel mills

331111   Tubing, wrought iron or steel, made in iron and steel mills

332998   Tubs, laundry and bath, metal, manufacturing

238140   Tuck pointing contractors

212312   Tufa, calcareous, crushed and broken stone, mining and/or beneficiating

212311   Tufa, calcareous, mining or quarrying

333292	Tufting machinery for textiles manufacturing
336611	Tugboat building
532411	Tugboat rental or leasing
488330	Tugboat services, harbor operation
326199	Tumblers, plastics, manufacturing
332813	Tumbling (i.e., cleaning and polishing) metal and metal products for the trade
114111	Tuna fishing
811118	Tune-up shops, automotive
325188	Tungstates (e.g., ammonium tungstate, sodium tungstate) manufacturing
331491	Tungsten bar, rod, sheet, strip, and tubing made by rolling, drawing, or extruding purchased metals or scrap
331492	Tungsten carbide powder made by metallurgical process
325188	Tungsten compounds, not specified elsewhere by process, manufacturing
212299	Tungsten concentrates beneficiating
212299	Tungsten ores mining and/or beneficiating
811490	Tuning and repair of musical instruments
339992	Tuning forks manufacturing
237990	Tunnel construction
238210	Tunnel lighting contractors
332313	Tunnel lining, fabricated metal plate work, manufacturing
213113	Tunneling services for coal mining on a contract basis
332313	Tunnels, wind, fabricated metal plate work, manufacturing
334513	Turbidity instruments, industrial process-type, manufacturing
334516	Turbidometers, laboratory-type, manufacturing
334513	Turbine flow meters, industrial process-type, manufacturing
333611	Turbine generator set units manufacturing
334514	Turbine meters, consumption registering, manufacturing

333611	Turbines (except aircraft) manufacturing
423830	Turbines (except transportation) merchant wholesalers
423860	Turbines, transportation, merchant wholesalers
561730	Turf (except artificial) installation services
238990	Turf, artificial, installation
424440	Turkey and turkey products (except canned and packaged frozen) merchant wholesalers
112330	Turkey egg production
311119	Turkey feeds, prepared, manufacturing
112340	Turkey hatcheries
112330	Turkey production
311615	Turkeys, processing, fresh, frozen, canned, or cooked
311615	Turkeys, slaughtering and dressing
812199	Turkish bathhouses
812199	Turkish baths
332722	Turnbuckles, metal, manufacturing
333512	Turning machines (i.e., lathes), metalworking, manufacturing
321912	Turnings, furniture, unfinished wood, manufacturing
111219	Turnip farming, field, bedding plant and seed production
325191	Turpentine made by distillation of pine gum or pine wood
424690	Turpentine merchant wholesalers
212399	Turquoise mining and/or beneficiating
333512	Turret lathes, metalworking, manufacturing
332995	Turrets, gun, manufacturing
114119	Turtle fishing
112519	Turtle production, farm raising
611691	Tutoring, academic
532220	Tuxedo rental
315222	Tuxedos cut and sewn from purchased fabric (except apparel contractors)
315211	Tuxedos, cut and sew apparel contractors

237310	Underpass construction
238990	Underpinning, construction
812210	Undertaker services
423850	Undertakers' equipment and supplies merchant wholesalers
335129	Underwater lighting fixtures manufacturing
334511	Underwater navigational systems manufacturing
336612	Underwater remotely operated vehicles (ROVs) manufacturing
315192	Underwear made in apparel knitting mills
315192	Underwear shirts made in apparel knitting mills
315291	Underwear shirts, infants', cut and sewn from purchased fabric (except apparel contractors)
315211	Underwear shirts, men's and boys', cut and sew apparel contractors
315221	Underwear shirts, men's and boys', cut and sewn from purchased fabric (except apparel contractors)
315212	Underwear shirts, women's, girls', and infants', cut and sew apparel contractors
315231	Underwear shirts, women's, misses', and girls', cut and sewn from purchased fabric (except apparel contractors)
315192	Underwear shorts made in apparel knitting mills
315291	Underwear shorts, infants', cut and sewn from purchased fabric (except apparel contractors)
315211	Underwear shorts, men's and boys', cut and sew apparel contractors
315221	Underwear shorts, men's and boys', cut and sewn from purchased fabric (except apparel contractors)
315212	Underwear shorts, women's, girls', and infants', cut and sew apparel contractors

315231	Underwear shorts, women's, misses', and girls', cut and sewn from purchased fabric (except apparel contractors)
315291	Underwear, infants', cut and sewn from purchased fabric (except apparel contractors)
315211	Underwear, men's and boys', cut and sew apparel contractors
315221	Underwear, men's and boys', cut and sewn from purchased fabric (except apparel contractors)
424320	Underwear, men's and boys', merchant wholesalers
424330	Underwear, women's, children's, and infants', merchant wholesalers
315231	Underwear, women's, misses', and girls', cut and sewn from purchased fabric (except apparel contractors)
315212	Underwear, women's, misses', girls', and infants', cut and sew apparel contractors
523110	Underwriting securities
923130	Unemployment insurance program administration
812331	Uniform (except industrial) supply services
315991	Uniform hats and caps cut and sewn from purchased fabric (except apparel contractors)
315211	Uniform hats and caps, men's and boys', cut and sew apparel contractors
315212	Uniform hats and caps, women's, and girls', cut and sew apparel contractors
315232	Uniform shirts (except team athletic), women's, misses', and girls', cut and sewn from purchased fabric (except apparel contractors)
315223	Uniform shirts (except team athletic, work), men's and boys', cut and sewn from purchased fabric (except apparel contractors)

315211 Uniform shirts, men's and boys', cut and sew apparel contractors

315299 Uniform shirts, team athletic, cut and sewn from purchased fabric (except apparel contractors)

315212 Uniform shirts, women's and girls', cut and sew apparel contractors

315225 Uniform shirts, work, men's and boys', cut and sewn from purchased fabric (except apparel contractors)

448190 Uniform stores (except athletic)

451110 Uniform stores, athletic

812332 Uniform supply services, industrial

315299 Uniforms, band, cut and sewn from purchased fabric (except apparel contractors)

315211 Uniforms, band, men's and boys', cut and sew apparel contractors

315212 Uniforms, band, women's, girls', and infants', cut and sew apparel contractors

315211 Uniforms, dress (e.g., fire fighter, military, police), men's, cut and sew apparel contractors

315222 Uniforms, dress (e.g., fire fighter, military, police), men's, cut and sewn from purchased fabric (except apparel contractors)

315212 Uniforms, dress (e.g., military, police, fire fighter), women's, cut and sew apparel contractors

315234 Uniforms, dress, tailored (e.g., fire fighter, military, police), women's, misses', and girls', cut and sewn from purchased fabric (except apparel contractors)

315228 Uniforms, nontailored (except work), men's and boys', cut and sewn from purchased fabric (except apparel contractors)

315225 Uniforms, nontailored work, men's, cut and sewn from purchased fabric (except apparel contractors)

315191 Uniforms, nontailored, made in apparel knitting mills

315211 Uniforms, nontailored, men's and boys', cut and sew apparel contractors

315212 Uniforms, nontailored, women's and girls', cut and sew apparel contractors

315239 Uniforms, nontailored, women's, misses', and girls', cut and sewn from purchased fabric (except team athletic, apparel contractors)

315299 Uniforms, team athletic, cut and sewn from purchased fabric (except apparel contractors)

315211 Uniforms, team athletic, men's and boys', cut and sew apparel contractors

315212 Uniforms, team athletic, women's and girls', cut and sew apparel contractors

335999 Uninterruptible power supplies (UPS) manufacturing

525120 Union health and welfare funds

525110 Union pension funds

315192 Union suits made in apparel knitting mills

315291 Union suits, infants', cut and sewn from purchased fabric (except apparel contractors)

315211 Union suits, men's and boys', cut and sew apparel contractors

315221 Union suits, men's and boys', cut and sewn from purchased fabric (except apparel contractors)

315212 Union suits, women's, girls', and infants', cut and sew apparel contractors

315231	Union suits, women's, misses', and girls', cut and sewn from purchased fabric (except apparel contractors)
813930	Unions (except apprenticeship programs), labor
522130	Unions, credit
332919	Unions, pipe, metal (except made from purchased pipe), manufacturing
424330	Unisex clothing merchant wholesalers
448140	Unisex clothing stores
812112	Unisex hair stylist shops
333414	Unit heaters (except portable electric) manufacturing
335211	Unit heaters, portable electric, manufacturing
525990	Unit investment trust funds
323116	Unit set forms (e.g., manifold credit card slips) printing
813219	United fund councils
813219	United funds for colleges
928120	United Nations
333613	Universal joints (except aircraft, motor vehicle) manufacturing
336413	Universal joints, aircraft, manufacturing
336350	Universal joints, automotive, truck, and bus, manufacturing
611310	Universities
813410	University clubs
511130	University press publishers (except exclusive Internet publishing)
519130	University press publishers, exclusively on Internet
923110	University regents or boards, government
311812	Unleavened bread made in commercial bakeries
423690	Unloaded computer board merchant wholesalers
337121	Upholstered furniture, household-type, custom, manufacturing
337121	Upholstered furniture, household-type, on frames of any material, manufacturing

423850	Upholsterers' equipment and supplies (except fabrics) merchant wholesalers
314999	Upholstering filling (except nonwoven fabric) manufacturing
811420	Upholstery (except motor vehicle) repair services
561740	Upholstery cleaning on customers' premises
561740	Upholstery cleaning services
316110	Upholstery leather manufacturing
451130	Upholstery materials stores
811121	Upholstery shops, automotive
332612	Upholstery springs and spring units, light gauge, made from purchased wire or strip
316110	Upper leather manufacturing
316999	Uppers (i.e., shoe cut stock), leather, manufacturing
335999	UPS (uninterruptible power supplies) manufacturing
332111	Upset forgings made from purchased iron or steel, unfinished
332112	Upset forgings made from purchased nonferrous metals, unfinished
333513	Upsetters (i.e., forging machines) manufacturing
212291	Uraninite (pitchblende) mining and/or beneficiating
325188	Uranium compounds, not specified elsewhere by process, manufacturing
212291	Uranium ores mining and/or beneficiating
325188	Uranium oxide manufacturing
331419	Uranium refining, primary
325188	Uranium, enriched, manufacturing
212291	Uranium-radium-vanadium ore mine site development for own account
212291	Uranium-radium-vanadium ores mining and/or beneficiating
485113	Urban bus line services (except mixed mode)

485112 Urban commuter rail systems (except mixed mode)
541320 Urban planners' offices
925120 Urban planning commissions, government
541320 Urban planning services
485111 Urban transit systems, mixed mode (e.g., bus, commuter rail, subway combinations)
325311 Urea manufacturing
325211 Urea resins manufacturing
325211 Urea-formaldehyde resins manufacturing
238310 Urethane foam insulation application
326150 Urethane foam products manufacturing
325212 Urethane rubber manufacturing
621493 Urgent medical care centers and clinics (except hospitals), freestanding
332998 Urinals, metal, manufacturing
326191 Urinals, plastics, manufacturing
327111 Urinals, vitreous china, manufacturing
621511 Urinalysis laboratories
327420 Urns (e.g., gypsum, plaster of paris) manufacturing
335211 Urns, household-type electric, manufacturing
621111 Urologists' offices (e.g., centers, clinics)
441229 Used aircraft dealers
441310 Used automotive parts stores
441320 Used automotive tire dealers
453310 Used bicycle (except motorized) shops
441222 Used boat dealers
441120 Used car dealers
423110 Used car merchant wholesalers
484210 Used household and office goods moving
453930 Used manufactured (mobile) home dealers
453310 Used merchandise dealers (except motor vehicles and parts)
453310 Used merchandise stores
441221 Used motorcycle dealers

423140 Used parts, motor vehicle, merchant wholesalers
441210 Used recreational vehicle (RV) dealers
441320 Used tire dealers
423130 Used tires, motor vehicle, merchant wholesalers
441229 Used utility trailer dealers
541618 Utilities management consulting services
332311 Utility buildings, prefabricated metal, manufacturing
326199 Utility containers (e.g., baskets, bins, boxes, buckets, dishpans, pails), plastics (except foam), manufacturing
237130 Utility line (i.e., communication, electric power), construction
237110 Utility line (i.e., sewer, water), construction
511210 Utility software, computer, packaged
441229 Utility trailer dealers
423110 Utility trailer merchant wholesalers
532120 Utility trailer rental or leasing
336214 Utility trailers manufacturing
531190 Vacant lot rental or leasing
531190 Vacation and recreation land rental or leasing
721214 Vacation camps (except campgrounds, day instructional)
236115 Vacation home, single-family, construction by general contractors
236117 Vacation housing construction operative builders
115210 Vaccinating livestock (except by veterinarians)
541940 Vaccination services, veterinary
325414 Vaccines (i.e., bacterial, virus) manufacturing
424210 Vaccines merchant wholesalers
332439 Vacuum bottles and jugs, light gauge metal, manufacturing
336340 Vacuum brake booster, automotive, truck, and bus, manufacturing

326220   Vacuum cleaner belts, rubber or plastics, manufacturing
443111   Vacuum cleaner stores, household-type
335212   Vacuum cleaners (e.g., canister, handheld, upright) household-type electric, manufacturing
335212   Vacuum cleaners and sweepers, household-type electric, manufacturing
423620   Vacuum cleaners, household-type, merchant wholesalers
333319   Vacuum cleaners, industrial and commercial-type, manufacturing
238290   Vacuum cleaning system, built-in, installation
333912   Vacuum pumps (except laboratory) manufacturing
339113   Vacuum pumps, laboratory-type, manufacturing
335314   Vacuum relays manufacturing
332420   Vacuum tanks, heavy gauge metal, manufacturing
327215   Vacuum tube blanks, glass, made from purchased glass
327212   Vacuum tube blanks, glass, made in glass making plants
334411   Vacuum tubes manufacturing
488119   Vacuuming of airport runways
333112   Vacuums, yard, manufacturing
812930   Valet parking services
316991   Valises, all materials, manufacturing
325191   Valonia extract manufacturing
333512   Valve grinding machines, metalworking, manufacturing
423840   Valves (except hydraulic, plumbing, pneumatic) merchant wholesalers
332911   Valves for nuclear applications manufacturing
332911   Valves for water works and municipal water systems manufacturing
336311   Valves, engine, intake and exhaust, manufacturing
332912   Valves, hydraulic and pneumatic, fluid power, manufacturing

423830   Valves, hydraulic and pneumatic, merchant wholesalers
332911   Valves, industrial-type (e.g., check, gate, globe, relief, safety), manufacturing
332919   Valves, inline plumbing and heating (e.g., cutoffs, stop), manufacturing
423720   Valves, plumbing and heating, merchant wholesalers
316999   Vamps, leather, manufacturing
532120   Van (except passenger) rental or leasing without driver
532112   Van (passenger) leasing
532111   Van (passenger) rental
336213   Van and minivan conversions on purchased chassis
811121   Van conversion shops (except on assembly line or factory basis)
484210   Van lines, moving and storage services
212291   Vanadium ores mining and/or beneficiating
325199   Vanillin, synthetic, manufacturing
337110   Vanities (except freestanding), stock or custom wood, manufacturing
337122   Vanities, freestanding, wood, manufacturing
337124   Vanities, metal household-type, manufacturing
316993   Vanity cases, leather, manufacturing
337110   Vanity tops, wood or plastics laminated on wood, manufacturing
485999   Vanpool operation
488999   Vanpools, arrangement of
336112   Vans, commercial and passenger light duty, assembling on chassis of own manufacture
334512   Vapor heating controls manufacturing
335110   Vapor lamps, electric, manufacturing

333999	Vapor separating machinery manufacturing
335211	Vaporizers, household-type electric, manufacturing
334513	Variable control instruments, industrial process-type, manufacturing
311612	Variety meats, edible organs, made from purchased meats
311611	Variety meats, edible organs, made in slaughtering plants
452990	Variety stores
334415	Varistors manufacturing
325510	Varnishes manufacturing
424950	Varnishes merchant wholesalers
332812	Varnishing metals and metal products for the trade
313320	Varnishing purchased textiles and apparel
327420	Vases (e.g., gypsum, plaster of paris) manufacturing
327215	Vases, glass, made from purchased glass
327212	Vases, glass, made in glass making plants
327112	Vases, pottery (e.g., china, earthenware, stoneware), manufacturing
325132	Vat dyes, synthetic, manufacturing
332420	Vats, heavy gauge metal, manufacturing
332439	Vats, light gauge metal, manufacturing
711110	Vaudeville companies
332999	Vault doors and linings, metal, manufacturing
238290	Vault, safe and banking machine installation
332999	Vaults (except burial), metal, manufacturing
339995	Vaults (except concrete) manufacturing
326220	V-belts, rubber or plastics, manufacturing
334310	VCR (video cassette recorder) manufacturing
112111	Veal calf production

311611	Veal carcasses, half carcasses, primal and sub-primal cuts, produced in slaughtering plants
311612	Veal, primal and sub-primal cuts, made from purchased carcasses
325411	Vegetable alkaloids (i.e., basic chemicals) (e.g., caffeine, codeine, morphine, nicotine), manufacturing
111211	Vegetable and melon farming, potato dominant crop, field and seed production
111219	Vegetable and melon farming, vegetable (except potato) and melon dominant crops, field, bedding plants and seed production
111211	Vegetable and potato farming, potato dominant crop, field and seed potato production
111219	Vegetable and potato farming, vegetable (except potato) dominant crops, field, bedding plants and seed production
321920	Vegetable baskets, veneer and splint, manufacturing
311421	Vegetable brining
424990	Vegetable cake and meal merchant wholesalers
311421	Vegetable canning
321920	Vegetable crates, wood, wirebound, manufacturing
424910	Vegetable dusts and sprays merchant wholesalers
111419	Vegetable farming, grown under cover
311211	Vegetable flour manufacturing
311211	Vegetable flour, meal, and powders, made in flour mills
311411	Vegetable juice concentrates, frozen, manufacturing
311421	Vegetable juices canning
311421	Vegetable juices, fresh, manufacturing
445230	Vegetable markets
333294	Vegetable oil processing machinery manufacturing

311223 Vegetable oils (except soybean) made in crushing mills
311225 Vegetable oils made from purchased oils
115114 Vegetable precooling
115114 Vegetable sorting, grading, and packing
311221 Vegetable starches manufacturing
115114 Vegetable sun drying
115114 Vegetable vacuum cooling
311423 Vegetables dehydrating
311421 Vegetables pickling
424490 Vegetables, canned, merchant wholesalers
311991 Vegetables, cut or peeled, fresh, manufacturing
424480 Vegetables, fresh, merchant wholesalers
311411 Vegetables, frozen, manufacturing
424420 Vegetables, frozen, merchant wholesalers
115113 Vegetables, machine harvesting
238290 Vehicle lift installation
333997 Vehicle scales manufacturing
321912 Vehicle stock, hardwood, manufacturing
336991 Vehicle, children's, metal manufacturing
339932 Vehicles, children's (except bicycles and metal tricycles), manufacturing
423920 Vehicles, children's (except bicycles), merchant wholesalers
423110 Vehicles, recreational, merchant wholesalers
336321 Vehicular lighting fixtures manufacturing
316110 Vellum leather manufacturing
313210 Velvets, manmade fiber and silk, weaving
238290 Vending machine installation
454210 Vending machine merchandisers, sale of products
532490 Vending machine rental
333311 Vending machines manufacturing

423440 Vending machines merchant wholesalers
333210 Veneer and plywood forming machinery manufacturing
321920 Veneer baskets, for fruits and vegetables, manufacturing
321211 Veneer mills, hardwood
321212 Veneer mills, softwood
321999 Veneer work, inlaid, manufacturing
811490 Venetian blind repair and maintenance shops without retailing new venetian blinds
321918 Venetian blind slats, wood, manufacturing
337920 Venetian blinds manufacturing
238390 Ventilated wire shelving (i.e., closet organizing-type) installation
238220 Ventilating contractors
423730 Ventilating equipment and supplies (except household-type fans) merchant wholesalers
333412 Ventilating fans, industrial and commercial-type, manufacturing
335211 Ventilating kitchen fans, household-type electric, manufacturing
335211 Ventilation and exhaust fans (except attic fans), household-type, manufacturing
561790 Ventilation duct cleaning services
332322 Ventilators, sheet metal (except stampings), manufacturing
523910 Venture capital companies
212319 Verde' antique crushed and broken stone mining and/or beneficiating
212311 Verde' antique mining or quarrying
212399 Vermiculite mining and/or beneficiating
327992 Vermiculite, exfoliated, manufacturing
325412 Vermifuge preparations manufacturing

325131	Vermilion pigments manufacturing
312130	Vermouth manufacturing
337920	Vertical blinds manufacturing
332420	Vessels, heavy gauge metal, manufacturing
315299	Vestments, academic and clerical, cut and sewn from purchased fabric (except apparel contractors)
315211	Vestments, academic and clerical, men's and boys', cut and sew apparel contractors
315212	Vestments, academic and clerical, women's and girls', cut and sew apparel contractors
315292	Vests, leather, fur, or sheep-lined (except apparel contractors), manufacturing
315211	Vests, leather, fur, or sheep-lined, men's and boys', cut and sew apparel contractors
315212	Vests, leather, fur, or sheep-lined, women's, girls', and infants', cut and sew apparel contractors
315211	Vests, men's and boys', cut and sew apparel contractors
315228	Vests, nontailored, men's and boys', cut and sewn from purchased fabric (except apparel contractors)
315239	Vests, nontailored, women's, misses', and girls', cut and sewn from purchased fabric (except apparel contractors)
315222	Vests, tailored, men's and boys', cut and sewn from purchased fabric (except apparel contractors)
315234	Vests, tailored, women's, misses', and girls', cut and sewn from purchased fabric
315212	Vests, women's, girls', and infants', cut and sew apparel contractors
813410	Veterans' membership organizations
923140	Veterans' affairs offices

923140	Veterans' benefits program administration, government
813311	Veterans' rights organizations
423490	Veterinarians' equipment and supplies merchant wholesalers
339112	Veterinarians' instruments and apparatus manufacturing
424210	Veterinarians' medicines merchant wholesalers
541940	Veterinarians' offices
541940	Veterinarians' practices
541940	Veterinary clinics
325412	Veterinary medicinal preparations manufacturing
541712	Veterinary research and development laboratories or services (except biotechnology research and development)
541940	Veterinary services
541940	Veterinary services, livestock
541940	Veterinary services, pets and other animal specialties
541940	Veterinary testing laboratories
523910	Viatical settlement companies
339992	Vibraphones manufacturing
238390	Vibration isolation contractors
334519	Vibration meters, analyzers, and calibrators, manufacturing
541380	Vibration testing laboratories or services
333120	Vibrators, concrete, manufacturing
518210	Video and audio streaming services
519130	Video broadcasting, exclusively on Internet
334220	Video camera (except household-type, television broadcast) manufacturing
423410	Video cameras (except household-type) merchant wholesalers
334310	Video cameras, household-type, manufacturing
423620	Video cameras, household-type, merchant wholesalers
811211	Video cassette recorder (VCR) repair services without retailing new video cassette recorders

532210	Video cassette recorder rental
334310	Video cassette recorders (VCR) manufacturing
334613	Video cassettes, blank, manufacturing
334612	Video cassettes, pre-recorded, mass reproducing
512191	Video conversion services (i.e., between formats)
532210	Video disc player rental
532230	Video disc rental for home electronic equipment (e.g., VCR)
713290	Video gambling device concession operators (i.e., supplying and servicing in others' facilities)
713120	Video game arcades (except gambling)
339932	Video game machines (except coin-operated) manufacturing
532230	Video game rental
443120	Video game software stores
713290	Video gaming device concession operators (i.e., supplying and servicing in others' facilities)
541921	Video photography services, portrait
512191	Video post-production services
512110	Video production
512110	Video production and distribution
532210	Video recorder rental
334612	Video tape or disk mass reproducing
532210	Video tape player rental
532230	Video tape rental for home electronic equipment (e.g., VCR)
532230	Video tape rental stores
451220	Video tape stores
334613	Video tapes, blank, manufacturing
423690	Video tapes, blank, merchant wholesalers
423990	Video tapes, prerecorded, merchant wholesalers
541922	Video taping services for legal depositions

541921	Video taping services, special events (e.g., birthdays, weddings)
561499	Videoconferencing services
512199	Videotape libraries, stock footage
311941	Vinegar manufacturing
115112	Vineyard cultivation services
325199	Vinyl acetate (except resins) manufacturing
325211	Vinyl acetate resins manufacturing
326113	Vinyl and vinyl copolymer film and unlaminated sheet (except packaging) manufacturing
325211	Vinyl chloride resins manufacturing
313320	Vinyl coated fabrics manufacturing
325222	Vinyl fibers and filaments manufacturing
326192	Vinyl floor coverings manufacturing
238330	Vinyl flooring contractors
325211	Vinyl resins manufacturing
423330	Vinyl siding merchant wholesalers
238170	Vinyl siding, soffit and fascia, installation
316219	Vinyl upper athletic footwear manufacturing
325222	Vinylidene chloride fiber and filament manufacturing
325211	Vinylidene resins manufacturing
339992	Violas and parts manufacturing
339992	Violins and parts manufacturing
325413	Viral in-vitro diagnostic test substances manufacturing
325414	Virus vaccines manufacturing
325221	Viscose fibers, bands, strips, and yarn manufacturing
334519	Viscosimeters (except industrial process type) manufacturing
334513	Viscosimeters, industrial process-type, manufacturing
332212	Vises (except machine tool attachments) manufacturing
621610	Visiting nurse associations
561591	Visitors bureaus

325412 Vitamin preparations manufacturing
446191 Vitamin stores
424210 Vitamins merchant wholesalers
325411 Vitamins, uncompounded, manufacturing
711130 Vocalists, independent
611513 Vocational apprenticeship training
624310 Vocational habilitation job counseling
624310 Vocational habilitation job training facilities (except schools)
624310 Vocational rehabilitation agencies
624310 Vocational rehabilitation job counseling
624310 Vocational rehabilitation job training facilities (except schools)
624310 Vocational rehabilitation or habilitation services (e.g., job counseling, job training, work experience)
611610 Voice instruction
561421 Voice mailbox services
621340 Voice pathologists' offices (e.g., centers, clinics)
517919 VoIP service providers, using client-supplied telecommunications connections
517110 VoIP service providers, using own operated wired telecommunications infrastructure "
212399 Volcanic ash mining and/or beneficiating
212319 Volcanic rock crushed and broken stone mining and/or beneficiating
212311 Volcanic rock, mining or quarrying
335311 Voltage regulating transformers, electric power, manufacturing
423610 Voltage regulators (except motor vehicle) merchant wholesalers

336322 Voltage regulators for internal combustion engines manufacturing
334413 Voltage regulators, integrated circuits, manufacturing
335311 Voltage regulators, transmission and distribution, manufacturing
334515 Voltmeters manufacturing
813212 Voluntary health organizations
624229 Volunteer housing repair organizations
333313 Voting machines manufacturing
423850 Voting machines merchant wholesalers
322214 Vulcanized fiber products made from purchased paperboard
325212 Vulcanized oils manufacturing
333220 Vulcanizing machinery manufacturing
332992 Wads, ammunition, manufacturing
333295 Wafer processing equipment, semiconductor, manufacturing
321219 Waferboard manufacturing
334413 Wafers (semiconductor devices) manufacturing
335211 Waffle irons, household-type electric, manufacturing
311412 Waffles, frozen, manufacturing
926150 Wage control agencies, government
339932 Wagons, children's (e.g., coaster, express, and play), manufacturing
333111 Wagons, farm-type, manufacturing
333112 Wagons, lawn and garden-type, manufacturing
321918 Wainscots, wood, manufacturing
561421 Wakeup call services
532291 Walker, invalid, rental
339932 Walkers, baby (vehicles), manufacturing
621111 Walk-in physicians' offices (e.g., centers, clinics)
333921 Walkways, moving, manufacturing

238310 Wall cavity and attic space insulation installation

334518 Wall clocks manufacturing

238130 Wall component (i.e., exterior, interior), prefabricated, installation

238320 Wall covering or removal contractors

424950 Wall coverings (e.g., fabric, plastics) merchant wholesalers

335122 Wall lamps (i.e., lighting fixtures), commericial, institutional, and industrial electric, manufacturing

335121 Wall lamps (i.e., lighting fixtures), residential electric, manufacturing

327122 Wall tile, ceramic, manufacturing

423310 Wallboard merchant wholesalers

327420 Wallboard, gypsum, manufacturing

316993 Wallets (except metal) manufacturing

339911 Wallets, precious metal, manufacturing

444120 Wallpaper and wall coverings stores

325612 Wallpaper cleaners manufacturing

238320 Wallpaper hanging and removal contractors

322222 Wallpaper made from purchased papers or other materials

424950 Wallpaper merchant wholesalers

238320 Wallpaper stripping

111335 Walnut farming

115114 Walnut hulling and shelling

712110 War museums

316991 Wardrobe bags (i.e., luggage) manufacturing

532220 Wardrobe rental

337124 Wardrobes, metal household-type, manufacturing

337122 Wardrobes, wood household-type, manufacturing

452910 Warehouse clubs (i.e., food and general merchandise)

236220 Warehouse construction (e.g., commercial, industrial, manufacturing, private)

238220 Warehouse refrigeration system installation

236220 Warehouse, commercial and institutional, construction

236220 Warehouse, industrial, construction

332311 Warehouses, prefabricated metal, manufacturing

493190 Warehousing (except farm products, general merchandise, refrigerated)

493110 Warehousing (including foreign trade zones), general merchandise

493110 Warehousing and storage, general merchandise

813910 Warehousing associations

493130 Warehousing, farm products (except refrigerated)

493120 Warehousing, refrigerated

531130 Warehousing, self storage

334511 Warfare countermeasures equipment manufacturing

423730 Warm air heating equipment merchant wholesalers

238220 Warm air heating system installation

335211 Warming trays, electric, manufacturing

315191 Warmup suits made in apparel knitting mills

315291 Warmup suits, infants', cut and sewn from purchased fabric (except apparel contractors)

315211 Warmup suits, men's and boys', cut and sew apparel contractors

315228 Warmup suits, men's and boys', cut and sewn from purchased fabric (except apparel contractors)

315212 Warmup suits, women's, girls', and infants', cut and sew apparel contractors

315239 Warmup suits, women's, misses', and girls', cut and sewn from purchased fabric (except apparel contractors)

313249 Warp fabrics knitting
333292 Warping machinery manufacturing
524128 Warranty insurance carriers (e.g., appliance, automobile, homeowners, product), direct
333319 Wash water recycling machinery manufacturing
315211 Washable service apparel (e.g., barbers', hospital, professional), men's and boys', cut and sew apparel contractors
315225 Washable service apparel (e.g., barbers', hospital, professional), men's and boys', cut and sewn from purchased fabric (except apparel contractors)
315212 Washable service apparel, women's and girls', cut and sew apparel contractors
315239 Washable service apparel, women's, misses', and girls', cut and sewn from purchased fabric (except apparel contractors)
321999 Washboards, wood and part wood, manufacturing
532210 Washer, clothes, rental
212113 Washeries, anthracite
212111 Washeries, bituminous coal or lignite
333131 Washers, aggregate and sand, stationary, manufacturing
332722 Washers, metal, manufacturing
236210 Washery, mining, construction
811412 Washing machine, household-type, repair and maintenance services without retailing new washing machine
335224 Washing machines, household-type, manufacturing
333312 Washing machines, laundry (except household-type), manufacturing
561720 Washroom sanitation services
562219 Waste (except sewage) treatment facilities, nonhazardous

562119 Waste (except solid and hazardous) collection services
562119 Waste (except solid and hazardous) hauling, local
562112 Waste collection services, hazardous
562111 Waste collection services, nonhazardous solid
221320 Waste collection, treatment, and disposal through a sewer system
562213 Waste disposal combustors or incinerators, nonhazardous solid
562211 Waste disposal facilities, hazardous
562212 Waste disposal landfills, nonhazardous solid
236210 Waste disposal plant (except sewage treatment) construction
484230 Waste hauling, hazardous, long-distance
562112 Waste hauling, local, hazardous
562111 Waste hauling, local, nonhazardous solid
484230 Waste hauling, nonhazardous, long-distance
924110 Waste management program administration
423930 Waste materials merchant wholesalers
562920 Waste recovery facilities
562112 Waste transfer stations, hazardous
562111 Waste transfer stations, nonhazardous solid
562211 Waste treatment facilities, hazardous
562211 Waste treatment plants, hazardous
322214 Wastebaskets, fiber made from purchased paperboard
316993 Watch bands (except metal) manufacturing
339914 Watch bands, metal (except precious), manufacturing
339911 Watch bands, precious metal, manufacturing
335912 Watch batteries manufacturing

327215	Watch crystals made from purchased glass
326199	Watch crystals, plastics, manufacturing
334518	Watch jewels manufacturing
811490	Watch repair shops without retailing new watches
448310	Watch shops
334518	Watchcase manufacturing
334518	Watches and parts (except crystals) manufacturing
423940	Watches and parts merchant wholesalers
333415	Water (i.e., drinking) coolers, mechanical, manufacturing
325412	Water (i.e., drinking) decontamination or purification tablets manufacturing
337124	Water bed frames, metal, manufacturing
337122	Water bed frames, wood, manufacturing
337910	Water bed mattresses manufacturing
327111	Water closet bowls, vitreous china, manufacturing
332998	Water closets, metal, manufacturing
339942	Water colors, artist's, manufacturing
924110	Water control and quality program administration
423740	Water coolers, mechanical, merchant wholesalers
237110	Water desalination plant construction
221310	Water distribution (except irrigation)
221310	Water distribution for irrigation
237110	Water filtration plant construction
221310	Water filtration plant operation
334512	Water heater controls manufacturing
238220	Water heater installation
811412	Water heater repair and maintenance services without retailing new water heaters

333319	Water heaters (except boilers), commercial-type, manufacturing
423720	Water heaters (except electric) merchant wholesalers
335228	Water heaters (including nonelectric), household-type, manufacturing
423620	Water heaters, electric, merchant wholesalers
326220	Water hoses, rubber or plastics, manufacturing
213111	Water intake well drilling, oil and gas field on a contract basis
334519	Water leak detectors manufacturing
237110	Water main and line construction
238220	Water meter installation
713110	Water parks, amusement
238290	Water pipe insulating
331511	Water pipe, cast iron, manufacturing
335211	Water pulsating devices, household-type electric, manufacturing
237110	Water pumping or lift station construction
333319	Water purification equipment manufacturing
334513	Water quality monitoring and control systems manufacturing
325510	Water repellant coatings for wood, concrete and masonry manufacturing
315211	Water resistant apparel, men's and boys', cut and sew apparel contractors
315228	Water resistant jackets and windbreakers, nontailored, men's and boys', cut and sewn from purchased fabric (except apparel contractors)
315239	Water resistant jackets and windbreakers, not tailored, women's, misses' and girls', cut and sewn from purchased fabric (except apparel contractors)

315228 Water resistant outerwear (except overcoats), men's and boys', cut and sewn from purchased fabric (except apparel contractors)

315239 Water resistant outerwear (except overcoats), women's, misses', and girls', cut and sewn from purchased fabric (except apparel contractors)

315291 Water resistant outerwear infants', cut and sewn from purchased fabric (except apparel contractors)

315212 Water resistant outerwear, women's, girls', and infants', cut and sew apparel contractors

315222 Water resistant overcoats, men's and boys', cut and sewn from purchased fabric (except apparel contractors)

315234 Water resistant overcoats, women's, misses', and girls', cut and sewn from purchased fabric (except apparel contractors)

316211 Water shoes, plastics or plastics soled fabric upper, manufacturing

316211 Water shoes, rubber or rubber soled fabric upper, manufacturing

483212 Water shuttle services

532292 Water ski rental

238220 Water softener installation

454390 Water softener service providers, direct selling

423720 Water softening and conditioning equipment merchant wholesalers

424690 Water softening compounds merchant wholesalers

333319 Water softening equipment manufacturing

445299 Water stores, bottled

221310 Water supply systems

238220 Water system balancing and testing contractors

237110 Water system storage tank and tower construction

332420 Water tanks, heavy gauge metal, manufacturing

483212 Water taxi services

332919 Water traps manufacturing

221310 Water treatment and distribution

333319 Water treatment equipment manufacturing

423830 Water treatment equipment, industrial, merchant wholesalers

423850 Water treatment equipment, municipal, merchant wholesalers

237110 Water treatment plant construction

221310 Water treatment plants

333611 Water turbines manufacturing

333132 Water well drilling machinery manufacturing

237110 Water well drilling, digging, boring or sinking (except water intake wells in oil and gas fields)

237110 Water well pump and well piping system installation

312111 Water, artificially carbonated, manufacturing

424490 Water, bottled (except water treating), merchant wholesalers

325998 Water, distilled, manufacturing

312111 Water, flavored, manufacturing

312112 Water, naturally carbonated, purifying and bottling

712190 Waterfalls (i.e., natural wonder tourist attractions)

488310 Waterfront terminal operation (e.g., docks, piers, wharves)

326199 Watering cans, plastics, manufacturing

325611 Waterless hand soaps manufacturing

111219 Watermelon farming, field, bedding plant and seed production

334514 Watermeters, consumption registering, manufacturing

315299   Waterproof outerwear cut and sewn from purchased fabric (except apparel contractors)

315211   Waterproof outerwear, men's and boys', cut and sew apparel contractors

315299   Waterproof outerwear, rubberizing fabric and manufacturing outerwear

315212   Waterproof outerwear, women's, girls', and infants', cut and sew apparel contractors

313320   Waterproofing apparel, fabrics and textile products (e.g., oiling, rubberizing, waxing, varnishing)

238390   Waterproofing contractors

315228   Water-repellent outerwear (except overcoats), men's and boys', cut and sewn from purchased fabric (except apparel contractors)

315239   Water-repellent outerwear (except overcoats), women's, misses', and girls', cut and sewn from purchased fabric (except apparel contractors)

315291   Water-repellent outerwear, infants', cut and sewn from purchased fabric (except apparel contractors)

315211   Water-repellent outerwear, men's and boys', cut and sew apparel contractors

315212   Water-repellent outerwear, women's, girls', and infants', cut and sew apparel contractors

315222   Water-repellent overcoats, men's and boys', cut and sewn from purchased fabric (except apparel contractors)

315234   Water-repellent overcoats, women's, misses', and girls', cut and sewn from purchased fabric (except apparel contractors)

713990   Waterslides (i.e., amusement rides)

332911   Waterworks and municipal water system valves manufacturing

334515   Watt-hour and demand meters, combined, manufacturing

334515   Watt-hour and time switch meters, combined, manufacturing

334515   Watt-hour meters, electric, manufacturing

325191   Wattle extract manufacturing

334515   Wattmeters manufacturing

713940   Wave pools

334515   Waveform measuring and/or analyzing equipment manufacturing

339999   Wax figures (i.e., mannequins) manufacturing

712110   Wax museums

325612   Wax removers manufacturing

322222   Waxed paper for nonpackaging applications made from purchased paper

322221   Waxed paper for packaging applications made from purchased paper

424130   Waxed paper merchant wholesalers

424690   Waxes (except petroleum) merchant wholesalers

324199   Waxes, petroleum, made from refined petroleum

324110   Waxes, petroleum, made in petroleum refineries

325612   Waxes, polishing (e.g., floor, furniture), manufacturing

313320   Waxing purchased textiles and apparel

115114   Waxing, fruits or vegetables

112210   Weaning pig operations

336992   Weapons, self-propelled, manufacturing

541990   Weather forecasting services

924120   Weather research program administration

321918   Weather strip, wood, manufacturing

238390   Weather stripping installation

423330   Weather stripping merchant wholesalers

334519 Weather tracking equipment manufacturing
333999 Weather vanes manufacturing
331422 Weatherproof wire or cable made from purchased copper in wire drawing plants
331319 Weatherproof wire or cable made in aluminum wire drawing plants
238390 Weatherproofing concrete
332321 Weatherstrip, metal, manufacturing
314999 Weatherstripping made from purchased textiles
313221 Weaving and finishing narrow fabrics
313210 Weaving and finishing of broadwoven fabrics (except rugs, tire fabric)
313210 Weaving broadwoven fabrics (except rugs, tire fabrics)
313210 Weaving broadwoven felts
313221 Weaving fabric less than 12 inches (30cm)
313210 Weaving fabrics more than 12 inches (30cm) in width
333292 Weaving machinery manufacturing
313221 Weaving narrow fabrics
314110 Weaving rugs, carpets, and mats
541511 Web (i.e., Internet) page design services, custom
519130 Web broadcasting
519130 Web communities
518210 Web hosting
454111 Web retailers
519130 Web search portals
313221 Webbing weaving
321999 Webbing, cane, reed, and rattan, manufacturing
812990 Wedding chapels (except churches)
315212 Wedding dresses, women's, cut and sew apparel contractors
315233 Wedding dresses, women's, misses', and girls', cut and sewn from purchased fabric (except apparel contractors)
541921 Wedding photography services

812990 Wedding planning services
561730 Weed control and fertilizing services (except crop)
115112 Weed control services for crops
926140 Weed control, agriculture, government
333111 Weeding machines, farm-type, manufacturing
238910 Weeping tile installation
313241 Weft fabrics knitting
811219 Weighing equipment (e.g., balance, scales) repair and maintenance services
812191 Weight loss centers, non-medical
812191 Weight reducing centers, non-medical
713940 Weight training centers
541890 Welcoming services (i.e., advertising services)
331222 Welded iron or steel wire fabric made in wire drawing plants
316999 Welders' aprons, leather, manufacturing
339113 Welder's hoods manufacturing
316999 Welders' jackets, leggings, and sleeves, leather, manufacturing
333992 Welding equipment manufacturing
532412 Welding equipment rental or leasing
424690 Welding gases merchant wholesalers
423830 Welding machinery and equipment merchant wholesalers
333514 Welding positioners (i.e., jigs) manufacturing
811310 Welding repair services (e.g., automotive, general)
331491 Welding rod, uncoated, nonferrous metals (except aluminum, copper), made from purchased metals or scrap
423840 Welding supplies (except welding gases) merchant wholesalers
333992 Welding wire or rods (i.e., coated, cored) manufacturing

238190	Welding, on site, contractors
332313	Weldments manufacturing
923130	Welfare administration, nonoperating
923130	Welfare programs administration
624190	Welfare service centers, multi-program
213112	Well casing running, cutting and pulling, oil and gas field on a contract basis
331210	Well casings (e.g., heavy riveted, lock joint, welded, wrought) made from purchased iron or steel
331111	Well casings, iron or steel, made in iron and steel mills
213111	Well drilling (i.e., oil, gas, water intake wells) on a contract basis
532412	Well drilling machinery and equipment rental or leasing
333132	Well logging equipment manufacturing
213112	Well logging, oil and gas field, on a contract basis
213112	Well plugging, oil and gas field, on a contract basis
213112	Well pumping, oil and gas field, on a contract basis
213112	Well servicing, oil and gas field, on a contract basis
213112	Well surveying, oil and gas field, on a contract basis
332322	Wells, light, sheet metal (except stampings), manufacturing
316110	Welting leather manufacturing
448140	Western wear stores
316110	Wet blues manufacturing
313230	Wet laid nonwoven fabrics manufacturing
322130	Wet machine board mills
311221	Wet milling corn and other vegetables
339920	Wet suits manufacturing
325613	Wetting agents manufacturing
487210	Whale watching excursions
237990	Wharf construction
488310	Wharf operation
311211	Wheat bran manufacturing

311230	Wheat breakfast cereal manufacturing
111140	Wheat farming, field and seed production
311211	Wheat flour manufacturing
311211	Wheat germ manufacturing
311213	Wheat malt manufacturing
334515	Wheatstone bridges (i.e., electrical measuring instruments) manufacturing
811118	Wheel alignment shops, automotive
532291	Wheel chair rental
334511	Wheel position indicators and transmitters, aircraft, manufacturing
332212	Wheel pullers, handtools, manufacturing
333924	Wheelbarrows manufacturing
339113	Wheelchairs manufacturing
423450	Wheelchairs merchant wholesalers
336399	Wheels (i.e., rims), automotive, truck, and bus, manufacturing
327910	Wheels, abrasive, manufacturing
331111	Wheels, car and locomotive, iron or steel, made in iron and steel mills
423120	Wheels, motor vehicle, new, merchant wholesalers
327910	Wheels, polishing and grinding, manufacturing
336330	Wheels, steering, automotive, truck, and bus, manufacturing
327910	Whetstones manufacturing
212399	Whetstones mining and/or beneficiating
311512	Whey butter manufacturing
311514	Whey, condensed, dried, evaporated, and powdered, manufacturing
311513	Whey, raw, liquid, manufacturing
311511	Whipped topping (except dry mix, frozen) manufacturing
311514	Whipped topping, dry mix, manufacturing
311412	Whipped topping, frozen, manufacturing

335211 Whippers, household-type electric, manufacturing
311511 Whipping cream manufacturing
316999 Whips, horse, manufacturing
316999 Whipstocks manufacturing
339113 Whirlpool baths (i.e., hydrotherapy equipment) manufacturing
423450 Whirlpool baths merchant wholesalers
493190 Whiskey warehousing
325131 White extender pigments (e.g., barytes, blanc fixe, whiting) manufacturing
331528 White metal castings (except die-castings), unfinished, manufacturing
713990 White water rafting, recreational
238320 Whitewashing contractors
212312 Whiting crushed and broken stone, mining and/or beneficiating
114111 Whiting fishing
325131 Whiting manufacturing
334519 Whole body counters, nuclear, manufacturing
****** Wholesale—see type of product
561520 Wholesale tour operators
813910 Wholesalers' associations
337125 Wicker furniture (except upholstered), household-type, manufacturing
313221 Wicks manufacturing
334210 Wide area network communications equipment (e.g., bridges, gateways, routers) manufacturing
448150 Wig and hairpiece stores
424990 Wigs merchant wholesalers
339999 Wigs, wiglets, toupees, hair pieces, manufacturing
712130 Wild animal parks
111199 Wild rice farming, field and seed production
721214 Wilderness camps
711510 Wildlife artists, independent
924120 Wildlife conservation agencies
813312 Wildlife preservation organizations
712190 Wildlife sanctuaries

212231 Willemite mining and/or beneficiating
337125 Willow furniture (except upholstered), household-type, manufacturing
321999 Willow ware (except furniture) manufacturing
333923 Winches manufacturing
423830 Winches merchant wholesalers
924120 Wind and water erosion control agencies, government
334519 Wind direction indicators manufacturing
926130 Wind generated electrical power regulation
237130 Wind power structure construction
333611 Wind powered turbine generator sets manufacturing
333611 Wind turbines (i.e., windmill) manufacturing
315291 Windbreakers, infants', cut and sewn from purchased fabric (except apparel contractors)
315211 Windbreakers, men's and boys', cut and sew apparel contractors
315228 Windbreakers, men's and boys', cut and sewn from purchased fabric (except apparel contractors)
315212 Windbreakers, women's, girls', and infants', cut and sew apparel contractors
315239 Windbreakers, women's, misses', and girls', cut and sewn from purchased fabric (except apparel contractors)
333292 Winding machinery for textiles manufacturing
313112 Winding purchased yarn
313112 Winding, spooling, beaming and rewinding of purchased yarn
333611 Windmills, electric power, generation-type, manufacturing
333111 Windmills, farm-type, manufacturing

238350 Window and door (residential-type) of any material, prefabricated, installation

325612 Window cleaning preparations manufacturing

561720 Window cleaning services

541890 Window dressing or trimming services, store

332321 Window frames and sash, metal, manufacturing

321911 Window frames and sash, wood and covered wood, manufacturing

238350 Window installation

238150 Window pane or sheet installation

326199 Window sashes, vinyl, manufacturing

332618 Window screening, woven, made from purchased wire

332321 Window screens, metal frame, manufacturing

321911 Window screens, wood framed, manufacturing

238390 Window shade and blind installation

811490 Window shade repair and maintenance shops

337920 Window shade rollers and fittings manufacturing

337920 Window shades (except awnings) manufacturing

423220 Window shades and blinds merchant wholesalers

444190 Window stores

811122 Window tinting, automotive

442291 Window treatment stores

321918 Window trim, wood and covered wood moldings, manufacturing

321911 Window units, wood and covered wood, manufacturing

238350 Window, metal-frame residential-type, installation

238350 Window, wood, installation

423310 Windows and window frames merchant wholesalers

326199 Windows and window frames, plastics, manufacturing

326199 Windows and window frames, vinyl, manufacturing

321911 Windows, louver, wood, manufacturing

332321 Windows, metal, manufacturing

321911 Windows, wood and covered wood, manufacturing

325612 Windshield washer fluid manufacturing

336322 Windshield washer pumps, automotive, truck, and bus, manufacturing

336399 Windshield wiper blades and refills manufacturing

336322 Windshield wiper systems, automotive, truck, and bus, manufacturing

326199 Windshields, plastics, manufacturing

312130 Wine coolers manufacturing

424820 Wine coolers, alcoholic, merchant wholesalers

445310 Wine shops, packaged

312130 Wineries

312130 Wines manufacturing

424820 Wines merchant wholesalers

312130 Wines, cooking, manufacturing

325998 Wintergreen oil manufacturing

336399 Wipers, windshield, automotive, truck, and bus, manufacturing

313230 Wipes, nonwoven fabric, manufacturing

423840 Wiping cloths merchant wholesalers

423510 Wire (except insulated) merchant wholesalers

423510 Wire and cable (except electrical) merchant wholesalers

333298 Wire and cable insulating machinery manufacturing

331222 Wire cages, iron or steel, made in wire drawing plants

331222 Wire carts (e.g., grocery, household, industrial), iron or steel, made in wire drawing plants

331422 Wire cloth made from purchased copper in wire drawing plants

331319 Wire cloth made in aluminum wire drawing plants

331422 Wire cloth, copper, made in integrated secondary smelting and wire drawing plants

331222 Wire cloth, iron or steel, made in wire drawing plants

331491 Wire cloth, nonferrous metals (except aluminum, copper), made from purchased metals or scrap

423390 Wire fencing and fencing accessories merchant wholesalers

331222 Wire garment hangers, iron or steel, made in wire drawing plants

519110 Wire photo services

331111 Wire products, iron or steel, made in iron and steel mills

331222 Wire products, iron or steel, made in wire drawing plants

423510 Wire rope (except insulated) merchant wholesalers

333923 Wire rope hoists manufacturing

423510 Wire screening merchant wholesalers

331319 Wire screening, aluminum, made in integrated secondary smelting and drawing plants

331491 Wire screening, nonferrous metals (except aluminum, copper), made from purchased nonferrous metals (except aluminum, copper) in wire drawing plants

561422 Wire services (i.e., telemarketing services), floral

519110 Wire services, news

331319 Wire, armored, made in aluminum wire drawing plants

331319 Wire, bare, made in aluminum wire drawing plants

331422 Wire, copper (except mechanical) (e.g., armored, bare, insulated), made from purchased copper in wire drawing plants

331422 Wire, copper (except mechanical) (e.g., armored, bare, insulated), made in integrated secondary smelting and wire drawing plants

331221 Wire, flat, rolled strip, made in cold rolling mills

331319 Wire, insulated, made in aluminum wire drawing plants

423610 Wire, insulated, merchant wholesalers

331222 Wire, iron or steel (e.g., armored, bare, insulated), made in wire drawing plants

331421 Wire, mechanical, copper and copper alloy, made from purchased copper or in integrated secondary smelting and rolling, drawing or extruding plants

331491 Wire, nonferrous metals (except aluminum, copper), made from purchased nonferrous metals (except aluminum, copper) in wire drawing plants

331491 Wire, nonferrous metals (except aluminum, copper), made in integrated secondary smelting mills and wire drawing plants

517911 Wired telecommunication resellers

333518 Wiredrawing and fabricating machinery and equipment (except dies) manufacturing

333514 Wiredrawing and straightening dies manufacturing

517210 Wireless data communication carriers, except satellite

517210 Wireless Internet service providers, except satellite

517911 Wireless telecommunication resellers (except satellite)

517210 Wireless telephone communications carriers (except satellite)

517210 Wireless video services, except satellite

213112 Wireline services, oil and gas field, on a contract basis

336322   Wiring harness and ignition sets for internal combustion engines manufacturing

423610   Wiring supplies merchant wholesalers

325191   Witch hazel extract manufacturing

212299   Wolframite mining and/or beneficiating

212399   Wollastonite mining and/or beneficiating

424330   Women's and children's clothing accessories merchant wholesalers

813410   Women's auxiliaries

923130   Women's bureaus

424330   Women's clothing merchant wholesalers

813410   Women's clubs

624221   Women's shelters, battered

325191   Wood alcohol, natural, manufacturing

325199   Wood alcohol, synthetic, manufacturing

424990   Wood carvings merchant wholesalers

113310   Wood chipping in the field

321113   Wood chips made in sawmills

332213   Wood cutting saw blades manufacturing

325191   Wood distillates manufacturing

321911   Wood door frames and sash manufacturing

333298   Wood drying kilns manufacturing

321114   Wood fence (i.e., pickets, poling, rails), treating

423310   Wood fencing merchant wholesalers

325510   Wood fillers manufacturing

238330   Wood floor finishing (e.g., coating, sanding)

321918   Wood flooring manufacturing

423310   Wood flooring merchant wholesalers

238330   Wood flooring, installation only

321999   Wood flour manufacturing

238130   Wood frame component (e.g., truss) fabrication on site

337121   Wood framed furniture, upholstered, household-type, manufacturing

321999   Wood heel blocks manufacturing

321999   Wood heels, finished, manufacturing

321213   Wood I-joists manufacturing

321918   Wood moldings (e.g., pre-finished, unfinished), clear and finger joint, manufacturing

325191   Wood oils manufacturing

423990   Wood products (e.g., chips, posts, shavings, ties) merchant wholesalers

321114   Wood products, creosoting purchased wood products

322110   Wood pulp manufacturing

424990   Wood pulp merchant wholesalers

423310   Wood shingles merchant wholesalers

321918   Wood shutters manufacturing

423310   Wood siding merchant wholesalers

238170   Wood siding, installation

333414   Wood stoves manufacturing

424690   Wood treating preparations merchant wholesalers

333210   Wood verneer laminating and gluing machines manufacturing

321911   Wood window frames and sash manufacturing

321999   Wood wool (excelsior) manufacturing

442299   Wood-burning stove stores

321999   Woodenware, kitchen and household, manufacturing

532490   Woodworking machinery and equipment rental or leasing

423830   Woodworking machinery merchant wholesalers

333210   Woodworking machines (except handheld) manufacturing

333292   Wool and worsted finishing machinery manufacturing

313210   Wool fabrics, broadwoven, weaving

313221 Wool fabrics, narrow woven, weaving
313111 Wool spun yarn made from purchased fiber
313312 Wool tops and noils manufacturing
424590 Wool tops and noils merchant wholesalers
314999 Wool waste processing
313112 Wool yarn, twisting or winding of purchased yarn
424590 Wool, raw, merchant wholesalers
311941 Worcestershire sauce manufacturing
333313 Word processing equipment, dedicated, manufacturing
561410 Word processing services
624229 Work (sweat) equity home construction organizations
337127 Work benches manufacturing
812332 Work clothing and uniform supply services, industrial
424320 Work clothing, men's and boys', merchant wholesalers
315211 Work coats and jackets, men's and boys', cut and sew apparel contractors
315225 Work coats and jackets, men's and boys', cut and sewn from purchased fabric (except apparel contractors)
624310 Work experience centers (i.e., sheltered workshops)
315191 Work gloves and mittens, knit, made in apparel knitting mills
315992 Work gloves, leather (except apparel contractors), manufacturing
315211 Work gloves, leather, men's and boys', cut and sew apparel contractors
315212 Work gloves, leather, women's and girls', cut and sew apparel contractors
315225 Work pants (except dungarees, jeans), men's and boys', cut and sewn from purchased fabric (except apparel contractors)

315211 Work pants, men's and boys', cut and sew apparel contractors
315211 Work shirts, men's and boys', cut and sew apparel contractors
315225 Work shirts, men's and boys', cut and sewn from purchased fabric (except apparel contractors)
316213 Work shoes, men's (except rubber or plastics protective footwear), manufacturing
721310 Workers' camps
525190 Workers' compensation insurance funds
524126 Workers' compensation insurance underwriting
923130 Workers' compensation program administration
721310 Workers' dormitories
213111 Workover of oil and gas wells on a contract basis
624310 Workshops for persons with disabilities
334111 Workstations, computer, manufacturing
928120 World Bank
813319 World peace and understanding advocacy organizations
112990 Worm production
424990 Worms merchant wholesalers
313210 Worsted fabrics weaving
321999 Wrappers, excelsior, manufacturing
333993 Wrapping (i.e., packaging) machinery manufacturing
424130 Wrapping paper (except giftwrap) merchant wholesalers
339999 Wreaths, artificial, manufacturing
488410 Wrecker services (i.e., towing services), motor vehicle
238910 Wrecking, building or other structure
332212 Wrenches, handtools, nonpowered, manufacturing
333991 Wrenches, impact, handheld power-driven, manufacturing

711219	Wrestlers, independent professional
711310	Wrestling event managers with facilities
711320	Wrestling event managers without facilities
711310	Wrestling event organizers with facilities
711320	Wrestling event organizers without facilities
711310	Wrestling event promoters with facilities
711320	Wrestling event promoters without facilities
711510	Writers of advertising copy, independent
711510	Writers, independent (freelance)
813410	Writing clubs
325998	Writing inks manufacturing
424120	Writing paper (except bulk) merchant wholesalers
322233	Writing paper and envelopes, boxed sets, made from purchased paper
322121	Writing paper made in paper mills
322233	Writing paper, cut sheet, made from purchased paper
337124	Wrought iron furniture (except upholstered), household-type, manufacturing
332996	Wrought iron or steel pipe and tubing made from purchased metal pipe
331111	Wrought iron or steel pipe and tubing made in iron and steel mills
212299	Wulfenite mining and/or beneficiating
212399	Wurtzilite mining and/or beneficiating
325320	Xanthone insecticides manufacturing
335110	X-mas tree light bulbs manufacturing
334517	X-ray apparatus and tubes (e.g., control, industrial, medical, research) manufacturing
325992	X-ray film and plates, sensitized, manufacturing

334517	X-ray generators manufacturing
541380	X-ray inspection services
334517	X-ray irradiation equipment manufacturing
621512	X-ray laboratories, medical or dental
423450	X-ray machines and parts, medical and dental, merchant wholesalers
334517	X-ray tubes manufacturing
334515	X-Y recorders (i.e., plotters (except computer peripheral equipment)) manufacturing
325110	Xylene made from refined petroleum or liquid hydrocarbons
324110	Xylene made in petroleum refineries
339992	Xylophones and parts manufacturing
713930	Yacht basins
336612	Yacht building, not done in shipyards
713930	Yacht clubs with marinas
713990	Yacht clubs without marinas
532292	Yacht rental without crew
336611	Yachts built in shipyards
111211	Yam farming, field and seed production
424310	Yard goods, textile (except burlap, felt), merchant wholesalers
335121	Yard Lights, residential electric, manufacturing
332212	Yardsticks, metal, manufacturing
321999	Yardsticks, wood, manufacturing
313111	Yarn spinning mills
313111	Yarn spun from purchased fiber
333292	Yarn texturizing machines manufacturing
313112	Yarn throwing, twisting, and winding of purchased yarn
313111	Yarn, carpet and rug, spun from purchased fiber
325221	Yarn, cellulosic filament, manufacturing
325221	Yarn, cellulosic filament, manufacturing and texturizing

333298	Zipper making machinery manufacturing
313221	Zipper tape weaving
339993	Zippers (i.e., slide fasteners) manufacturing
424310	Zippers merchant wholesalers
331491	Zirconium and zirconium alloy bar, rod, billet, sheet, strip, and tubing made from purchased metals or scrap
212299	Zirconium concentrates beneficiating
212299	Zirconium ores mining and/or beneficiating
331419	Zirconium refining, primary
331491	Zirconium rolling, drawing, or extruding purchased metals or scrap
339992	Zithers and parts manufacturing
925120	Zoning boards and commissions
712130	Zoological gardens
712130	Zoos
111219	Zucchini farming, field, bedding plant and seed production